**DO NOT REMOVE
CARDS FROM POCKET**

Statistical Forecasts
of the
United States

Statistical Forecasts
of the
United States

Edited by
James E. Person, Jr.

Sean R. Pollock,
Associate Editor

Gale Research Inc. Detroit ∎ Washington, D.C. ∎ London

James E. Person, Jr., *Editor*

Suzanne M. Bourgoin, Tina N. Grant, Marie A. Lazzari,
Sean R. Pollock, Jelena O. Krstović, *Associate Editors*
David Engelman, Meggin M. Condino, Kathryn Horste,
L. Mpho Mabunda, Mark F. Mikula,
Deborah A. Stanley, *Editorial Assistants*

Jeanne A. Gough, *Permissions and Production Manager*
Sandra C. Davis, *Text Permissions Supervisor*
Maria L. Franklin, Michele M. Lonoconus, *Permissions Associate*
Jennifer A. Arnold, Brandy C. Merritt, *Permissions Assistants*

Victoria B. Cariappa, *Research Manager*
Maureen Richards, *Research Supervisor*
Robert S. Lazich, Mary Beth McElmeel, Tamara C. Nott, *Editorial Associates*
Karen Farrelly, Kelly Hill, Julie Leonard, Stefanie Scarlett, *Editorial Assistants*

Mary Beth Trimper, *Production Director*
Mary Kelley, *Production Assistant*
Cynthia Baldwin, *Art Director*
Terrence Glenn, *Cover Design*

Editorial Code and Data, Inc. Staff

Nancy Ratliff, *Data Entry Associate*
Larisa Volchegurskaya, *Assistant Editor*

TABLE OF CONTENTS

CHAPTER 2 - BUSINESS, BANKING, FINANCE, AND ECONOMICS continued:

CHAPTER 5 - EDUCATION continued:

CHAPTER 5 - EDUCATION continued:

CHAPTER 5 - EDUCATION continued:

CHAPTER 6 - ENVIRONMENTAL ISSUES AND NATURAL RESOURCES continued:

CHAPTER 6 - ENVIRONMENTAL ISSUES AND NATURAL RESOURCES continued:

CHAPTER 8 - INCOME, PRICES, AND SPENDING continued:

CHAPTER 9 - LABOR, EMPLOYMENT, OCCUPATIONS, AND EARNINGS continued:

CHAPTER 9 - LABOR, EMPLOYMENT, OCCUPATIONS, AND EARNINGS continued:

CHAPTER 9 - LABOR, EMPLOYMENT, OCCUPATIONS, AND EARNINGS continued:

CHAPTER 14 - TRANSPORTATION continued:

INTRODUCTION

Statistical Forecasts of the United States (*SFUS*) is a compilation of published information forecasting all aspects of American life through the year 2000 and beyond.

The need for *SFUS* was prompted by the lack of a single reference source from which a broad spectrum of statistical projections might be found. Of equal importance, the approach of the twenty-first century — called by some "The Information Century" — emphasized the need for a resource providing statistical forecasts relevant to a wide range of information seekers. *SFUS* is not a guide indicating how best to prepare for the twenty-first century; rather, it is a comprehensive sourcebook from which the reader is free to draw for the purpose of assembling reports, compiling studies, or simply satisfying personal curiosity.

The statistical material presented is drawn from governmental, corporate, and private sources. *SFUS* provides the reader with:

- Over 800 discrete tables, charts, graphs, and short narratives.

- Broad coverage of subject areas pertinent to life in the United States.

- Easy-to-access chapters, organized by topic and subtopic.

- A key to pertinent acronyms.

- A detailed subject index.

- An index of projections by year.

SCOPE

SFUS provides statistical coverage of a wide range of subjects concerning future life and living conditions in the United States. And since the data which follows is largely drawn from current reports, books, and periodicals, *SFUS* reflects contemporary concerns and emphases. (This is especially true in the chapter entitled "Military Affairs," which contains data compiled in the post-Cold War era, a time of declining tension between traditional enemies.) The majority of tables offer data for the late 1990s and the early twenty-first century. For certain topics, retrospective data, tracking trends across past decades and forecasting these trends into the future, have been included as well.

Care has been taken to present as balanced a view as possible of all topics. The editors have not injected their own philosophical preconceptions into the selection, presentation, or interpretation of the data. It is worth noting, however, that for the sake of brevity the prose descriptions that accompanied many tables in their original sources have been excluded. These descriptions present the assumptions or mathematical logic by which statisticians arrived at their forecasts. Interested readers are thus encouraged to revisit the original sources noted beneath each table, in order to gain a greater understanding of the reasoning behind the data.

SOURCES

Data published in *SFUS* was culled from federal and state government publications, corporate sources, private organizations, and other non-governmental material published in books and periodicals. Much of this material, before appearing in this volume, was not otherwise indexed in a manner useful to the reader interested in statistical forecasts. Several thousand articles and reports were examined during the preparation of *SFUS*, and of these some 780 discrete items were edited for inclusion here.

ORGANIZATION

Statistical Forecasts of the United States is divided into fourteen chapters, each of which focus upon specific topics. Within each topic there appear individual tables and other statistical media, organized by subtopic.

Each table title, or headline, is preceded by a table number. (All tables are numbered and may be accessed by headline or number from the Table of Contents. Statistical data may also be accessed via the Subject Index or the Index of Forecasts by Year.) Immediately beneath the headline, the statistical data is displayed as a table, a graph, a chart, or a prose statement. Where data requires explanation, and where such explanations are readily accessible, a brief head note is presented. In some cases, such explanatory notes may not be necessary or accessible and, thus, are not included.

At the bottom of each table, the source of the data presented immediately above is identified. If the source cited has identified another source from which data was derived, that preceding source is also identified. Footnotes or other explanatory notes are placed after the source information. Where possible, abbreviations and acronyms are defined; most definitions also appear in the section titled List of Abbreviations, while others appear within the footnotes.

INDEXES

SFUS features both a Subject Index and an Index of Forecasts by Year. Entries listed in these indexes are followed by table and page numbers.

SUGGESTIONS ARE WELCOME

Readers who wish to suggest new features or subject areas to appear in future editions of *SFUS* are cordially invited to write to the editor.

LIST OF ABBREVIATIONS

A . . . . Acre
AASHTO . . . . . . American Association of State Highway and Transportation Officials
ABS . . . . Anti-Lock Brake System
ADA . . . . Average Daily Attendance
AEO . . . . Annual Energy Outlook
AFDC . . . . Aid to Families with Dependent Children
AFUDC . . . . . . Allowance for Funds Used During Construction
AGA . . . . American Gas Association
AHS . . . . Annual Housing Survey
AIDS . . . . Acquired Immune Deficiency Syndrome
AIP . . . . American Institute of Planners
AMA . . . . American Medical Association
ANL . . . . Argonne National Laboratory
AOOG . . . . Annual Outlook for Oil and Gas
AQCR . . . . Air Quality Control Region
ARP . . . . Acreage Reduction Program
ATC . . . . Air Traffic Control
BA . . . . Budget Authority
Btu . . . . British Thermal Unit
Bu . . . . Bushel
BVAR . . . . Bayesian Vector Autoregression Model
CAA . . . . Clean Air Act
CAD . . . . Computer-Aided Design
CAFE . . . . Corporate Average Fuel Economy
CAI . . . . Computer-Aided Instruction
CAM . . . . Computer-Aided Manufacturing
CBO . . . . Congressional Budget Office
CCC . . . . Commodity Credit Corporation
CEO . . . . Chief Executive Officer

CFCs	Chlorofluorocarbons (CFC-11 and CFC-12)
CH4	Methane
cm	Centimeters
CMSA	Consolidated Metropolitan Statistical Area
CO2	Carbon Dioxide
COPD	Chronic Obstructive Pulmonary Disease
CPI	Consumer Price Index
CPS	Current Population Survey
CRP	Conservation Reserve Program
cwe	Carcass Weight Equivalent
Cwt	Hundredweight
DI	Disability Insurance
DoD	Department of Defense
DOE	Department of Energy
Doz	Dozen
DRI	Data Resources, Inc.
EC	European Community
EEG	Electroencephalogram
EEI	Edison Electrical Institute
EIA	Energy Information Administration
EKG	Electrocardiogram
ELVEC	Electric Vehicle Simulation Program
EMM	Electricity Market Module
ENC	East North Central
EPA	Environmental Protection Agency
ESC	East South Central
ESOP	Employee Stock Ownership Plan
ETV	Electric Test Vehicle
FAA	Federal Aviation Administration
FAPRI	Food and Agricultural Policy Research Institute
FCC	Federal Communications Commission
FHWA	Federal Highway Administration
FMG	Foreign Medical Graduates
FOB	Free on Board
FOR	Farmer-Owned Reserve
FSC	Foreign Sales Corporations
FTE	Full-Time Equivalent
FY	Fiscal Year(s)
GA	General Aviation
GDP	Gross Domestic Product
g/bhp.h	Grams per Brake Horsepower Hour

GNP . . . . Gross National Product
GRI . . . . Gas Research Institute
HCFC-22 . . . . . . Hydrochlorofluorocarbons
HFMA . . . . Healthcare Financial Management Corporation
HI . . . . Hospital Insurance
HIV . . . . Human Immunodeficiency Virus
HU . . . . Heavy Users
ICD-9 . . . . International Classification of Diseases, Ninth Revision
ICE . . . . Internal Combustion Engine
IMF . . . . International Monetary Fund
IPEDS . . . . . . Integrated Postsecondary Education Data System
IRS . . . . Internal Revenue Service
ITA . . . . International Trade Administration
kg . . . . Kilograms
kWh . . . . Kilowatt Hours
kWh/lb . . . . . . Kilowatt Hours per Pound
lb . . . . Pound
LDC . . . . . . Less Developed Country
LF . . . . Labor Force
Li-MS . . . . . . Lithium-Metal Sulfide
MA . . . . Middle-Atlantic
Mi . . . . Miles
Mi2 . . . . Square Miles
mmt . . . . Million Metric Tons
MPG . . . . . . Miles Per Gallon
MSW . . . . . . Municipal Solid Waste
Mt . . . . Mountain
mt, Mt . . . . . . Metric Tons
MVMA . . . . . . Motor Vehicles Manufacturers' Association
Mw . . . . Megawatt
MWe . . . . . . Megawatts of Electric Power
N2O . . . . Nitrous Oxide
NA . . . . Not Available
NA . . . . Not Applicable
NAHB . . . . . . National Association of Home Builders of the United
　　　　　　　　　States
NAPAP . . . . . . National Acid Precipitation Assessment Program
NAS . . . . National Air Space
NB . . . . Narrow-Bodied
NCA . . . . National Coal Association
NCCD . . . . . . National Council on Crime and Delinquency

NCES	National Center for Education Statistics
NCM	National Coal Model
NE	New England
ne	Negligible
NEDS	National Emission Data System
NERC	North American Electric Reliability Council
NES	National Energy Stategy
NFA	Normal Flexible Acreage
Ni-Fe	Nickel-Iron
Ni-Zn	Nickel-Zinc
NOx	Nitrogen Oxides
NPD	New Product Development
NPIAS	National Plan of Integrated Airport Systems
NYSE	New York Stock Exchange
OASDI	Old Age and Survivor Disability Insurance
OASI	Old Age and Survivor Insurance
OBERS	Office of Business Economics Research Service
OCC	Old Corrugated Containers
OECD	Organization for Economic Cooperation and Development
OMG	Old Magazines
ONP	Old Newspapers
OPEC	Organization of Petroleum Exporting Countries
ORNL	Oak Ridge National Laboratory
OTA	Office of Technology Assessment
OWP	Old Wastepaper
Pac	Pacific
PLD	Paid Land Diversion
Pb-acid	Lead-Acid
PC	Personal Computer
Pkg	Packaging
PLD	Paid Land Diversion
PPB	Parts Per Billion
PPM	Parts Per Million
PPT	Parts Per Trillion
R&D	Research and Development
RECAPS	Recharge Capacity Projection System
REPS	Regional Emissions Projection System
RIA	Regulatory Impact Analysis
RPA	Rangeland Renewable Resources Planning Act
RPM	Revenue Passenger Mile
RSPA	Research and Special Programs Administration

SA	South Atlantic
SIP	State Implementation Program
SMPG	Seat Miles Per Gallon
So2	Sulfur Dioxide
SPR	Strategic Petroleum Reserve
T	Ton
T&D	Transmission and Distribution
TEEMS	Transportation Energy and Emissions Modeling System
TMT	Ton-Miles Traveled
USDA	United States Department of Agriculture
USFMG	U.S. Foreign Medical Graduates
USMG	U.S. Medical Graduates
USSR	United Soviet Socialist Republic
VMT	Vehicle Miles Traveled
WB	Wide-Bodied
WEFA	Wharton Econometric Forecasting Associates
Wh/lb	Watt Hours per Pound
WNC	West North Central
WSC	West South Central
Zn-Cl2	Zinc-Chlorine

Statistical Forecasts
of the
United States

Chapter 1

AGRICULTURE

Employment Prospects

★ 1 ★

Agriculture-Related Occupational Outlook, 1990-2005

While the number of self-employed farmers is expected to decline by 224,000 between 1990 and 2005, an increase in some agriculture-related occupations is projected.

[Numbers in percent]

Occupational group	1990 employment distribution		Projected job growth, 1990-2005[1]
	Rural	Urban	
Executive, administrative, and managerial	8.7	13.4	27.4
Professional specialty	10.6	14.2	32.3
Technicians and related support	2.5	3.5	36.9
Marketing and sales	10.3	12.6	24.1
Administrative support occupations, including clerical	12.6	16.7	13.1
Service occupations	14.4	13.2	29.2
Agricultural, forestry, fishing, and related occupations	7.3	1.7	4.5
Precision production, craft, and repair	13.1	11.1	12.6
Operators, fabricators, and laborers	20.5	13.6	4.2
Total	100.0	100.0	20.1

Source: Agricultural Outlook, No. 183, March, 1992, p. 29. Primary sources: Bureau of the Census, *Current Population Survey*; Bureau of Labor Statistics projections from *Monthly Labor Review*, November, 1991. *Note:* 1. Moderate-growth scenario.

Income, Expenses, Prices, and Policies

★ 2 ★

Cash Receipts From Farming, 1993-2001

[Numbers in billions of dollars]

	1993	1994	1995	1996	97-2001 Avg.
Farm Marketings and CCC loans	171.00	174.73	179.24	182.86	194.95
Crops	83.85	85.68	88.65	91.78	96.27
Feed grains	19.54	20.00	20.73	21.38	21.13
Corn	14.25	14.61	15.18	15.72	15.62
Sorghum	1.13	1.13	1.17	1.20	1.21
Barley	0.76	0.78	0.81	0.84	0.86
Oats	0.22	0.23	0.23	0.24	0.24
Hay	3.17	3.26	3.34	3.39	3.20
Food grains	7.65	7.78	8.32	8.96	10.03
Wheat	6.59	6.60	7.10	7.71	8.57
Rice	1.05	1.17	1.20	1.24	1.45
Rye	0.02	0.02	0.02	0.02	0.02
Oilseeds	13.30	13.45	13.97	14.46	14.27
Cotton	5.73	5.76	5.82	5.95	6.16
Other[1]	37.63	38.68	39.82	41.03	44.68
Livestock and products	87.15	89.05	90.59	91.08	98.68
Red meats	49.52	50.17	50.48	50.61	54.85
Cattle, calves	38.98	38.59	37.93	38.64	42.52
Hogs	10.13	11.17	12.14	11.56	11.92
Sheep, lambs	0.41	0.41	0.41	0.41	0.41
Dairy products	18.74	19.12	19.57	19.95	20.87
Poultry, eggs	16.41	17.23	17.96	17.92	20.14
Broilers	9.13	9.63	10.13	10.12	11.54
Turkeys	2.64	2.88	3.05	2.96	3.53
Chicken eggs	4.12	4.17	4.22	4.28	4.43
Other poultry	0.51	0.54	0.56	0.56	0.64
Other livestock[2]	2.48	2.54	2.58	2.60	2.83

[Continued]

★ 2 ★

Cash Receipts From Farming, 1993-2001
[Continued]

	1993	1994	1995	1996	97-2001 Avg.
Government payments	8.66	8.22	7.12	6.46	5.75
Total cash receipts	179.66	182.95	186.36	189.32	200.70

Source: *FAPRI 1992 U.S. Agricultural Outlook,* Food and Agricultural Policy Research Institute, Iowa State University and University of Missouri-Columbia, 1992, p. 93. Figures from 1989 to 1992 are excluded. *Notes:* 1. Includes tobacco, vegetables, and melons, fruits and tree nuts, and other crops. 2. Includes horses, mules, and agriculture.

★ 3 ★

Corn Policy and Market Prices, 1992-2001
[Numbers in dollars per bushel]

	1992-1993	1993-1994	1994-1995	1995-1996	1996-1997	1997-2001
Target price	2.75	2.75	2.75	2.75	2.75	2.75
Loan rate	2.19	2.26	2.30	2.39	2.34	2.26
Market price	1.72	1.72	1.67	1.66	1.68	1.66

Source: *FAPRI 1992 U.S. Agricultural Outlook,* Food and Agricultural Policy Research Institute, Iowa State University and University of Missouri-Columbia, 1992, p. 14. Figures from 1980 to 1991 are excluded. Magnitudes estimated from published chart.

★ 4 ★

Farm Income Statistics, 1993-2001
[Numbers in billions of dollars]

	1992	1993	1994	1995	1996	97-2001 Avg.
Farm receipts	174.50	178.22	182.11	186.85	190.77	203.88
Crops	82.80	83.85	85.68	88.65	91.78	96.27
Livestock	84.61	87.15	89.05	90.59	91.08	98.68
Farm related[1]	7.09	7.22	7.37	7.61	7.91	8.93
Government payments	7.91	8.66	8.22	7.12	6.46	5.75
Gross cash income	182.41	186.88	190.33	193.97	197.22	209.63
Nonmoney income	6.52	6.70	6.84	6.96	6.99	7.55
Value of inventory change	1.48	0.13	1.14	1.13	1.00	0.54
Gross farm income	190.41	193.72	198.31	202.06	205.21	217.73
Cash expenses[2]	127.60	129.85	132.35	135.89	140.27	146.54
Total expenses	147.22	150.09	153.54	158.28	163.70	170.82
Net cash income	54.81	57.03	57.98	58.08	56.95	63.09

[Continued]

★ 4 ★

Farm Income Statistics, 1993-2001
[Continued]

	1992	1993	1994	1995	1996	97-2001 Avg.
Net farm income	43.19	43.63	44.77	43.77	41.51	46.90
Deflated (1982 $)[3]	36.46	35.56	35.01	32.97	29.95	29.47

Source: "Farm Income Statistics," *FAPRI 1992 U.S. Agricultural Outlook*, Food and Agricultural Policy Research Institute, Iowa State University and University of Missouri-Columbia, 1992, p. 95. *Notes*: Figures from 1989 to 1992 are excluded. 1. Income from machine hire, custom work, sales of forest products, and other miscellaneous cash sources. 2. Excludes capital consumption, perquisites to hired labor, and farm household expenses. 3. Deflated by the prices paid index, all items, index: 1982 = 100.

★ 5 ★

Farm Income, 1992-2001

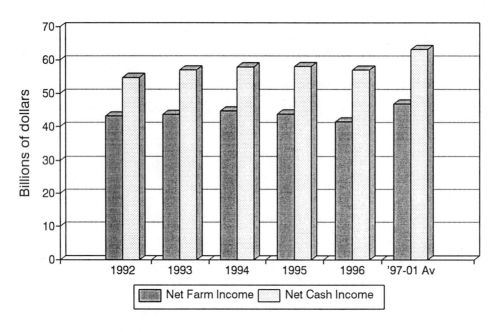

[Numbers in billions of dollars]

	1992	1993	1994	1995	1996	1997-2001
Net cash income	54.81	57.03	57.98	58.08	56.95	63.09
Net farm income	43.19	43.63	44.77	43.77	41.51	46.90

Source: FAPRI 1992 U.S. Agricultural Outlook, Food and Agricultural Policy Research Institute, Iowa State University and University of Missouri-Columbia, 1992, p. 18. Figures from 1980 to 1991 are excluded. Magnitudes estimated from published chart.

★ 6 ★

Farm Production Expenses, 1993-2001
[Numbers in billions of dollars]

	1993	1994	1995	1996	97-2001 Avg.
Farm-origin inputs	40.22	40.60	41.36	42.79	42.80
Feed	22.18	22.47	23.28	24.28	22.67
Purchased livestock	14.01	14.02	13.84	14.10	15.35
Seed	4.03	4.11	4.23	4.41	4.78
Manufactured inputs	22.18	22.72	23.36	24.11	26.62
Fertilizer, lime	7.62	7.73	7.89	8.06	8.66
Petroleum fuel, oils	6.10	6.29	6.48	6.73	7.44
Electricity	2.22	2.26	2.33	2.39	2.63
Pesticides	6.24	6.44	6.67	6.94	7.89
Total interest charges	15.15	15.61	16.31	17.04	16.58
Short-term interest	7.39	7.65	8.04	8.46	8.34
Real estate interest	7.77	7.96	8.27	8.57	8.24
Other operating expenses	40.58	41.40	42.33	43.45	46.86
Repair, operation of capital items	7.76	7.99	8.23	8.52	9.31
Contract, hired labor	14.12	14.32	14.57	14.88	16.00
Machine hire, custom work	2.82	2.87	2.94	3.03	3.37
Marketing, storage, and transportation	4.18	4.34	4.52	4.70	5.27
Miscellaneous	11.70	11.88	12.07	12.32	12.92
Other overhead expenses	31.96	33.21	34.92	36.31	37.96
Capital consumption	17.54	18.50	19.69	20.73	21.58
Property taxes	5.92	6.13	6.35	6.58	7.25
Rent to nonoperators	8.50	8.58	8.89	9.00	9.14
Production expenses	150.09	153.54	158.28	163.70	170.82
Cash[1]	132.05	134.55	138.09	142.47	148.74
Cost of operator dwelling	2.20	2.20	2.20	2.20	2.20
Excluding operator dwelling	129.85	132.35	135.89	140.27	146.54
Noncash[1]	18.04	19.00	20.19	21.23	22.08
Capital consumption	17.54	18.50	19.69	20.73	21.58
Perquisites to hired labor	0.50	0.50	0.50	0.50	0.50

Source: *FAPRI 1992 U.S. Agricultural Outlook*, Food and Agricultural Policy Research Institute, Iowa State University and University of Missouri-Columbia, 1992, p. 94. Figures from 1989 to 1992 are excluded. *Note:* 1. Includes cost of operator dwelling.

★ 7 ★

Farm Program Provisions, 1993-2001

	1993-1994	1994-1995	1995-1996	1996-1997	1997-2001
Target price (Dollars per bushel)					
Corn	2.75	2.75	2.75	2.75	2.75
Sorghum	2.61	2.61	2.61	2.61	2.61
Barley	2.36	2.36	2.36	2.36	2.36
Oats	1.45	1.45	1.45	1.45	1.45
Wheat	4.00	4.00	4.00	4.00	4.00
Rice (dollars/cwt)	10.71	10.71	10.71	10.71	10.71
Cotton (cents/lb.)	0.73	0.73	0.73	0.73	0.73
Loan rates					
Corn	1.72	1.67	1.66	1.68	1.66
Sorghum	1.63	1.59	1.57	1.60	1.57
Barley	1.40	1.36	1.35	1.37	1.35
Oats	0.88	0.86	0.85	0.87	0.85
Soybeans	5.02	5.02	5.02	5.02	5.02
Wheat	2.41	2.29	2.17	2.17	2.26
Rice (dollars/cwt)	6.50	6.50	6.50	6.50	6.63
Cotton (dollars/lb.)	0.53	0.53	0.52	0.52	0.52
Sugarcane (cents/lb.)	18.00	18.00	18.00	18.00	18.00
Acreage Reduction Program (ARP) Rate (Percent)					
Corn	7.5	7.5	5.0	5.0	7.5
Sorghum	7.5	7.5	5.0	5.0	7.5
Barley	7.5	7.5	5.0	5.0	7.5
Oats	0.0	0.0	0.0	0.0	0.0
Wheat	5.0	5.0	5.0	5.0	5.0
Rice	5.0	5.0	5.0	5.0	5.0
Cotton	5.0	5.0	5.0	5.0	5.0
Normal flexed area rate	15.0	15.0	15.0	15.0	15.0
Other idled area (Million acres)					
Conservation reserve	37.1	38.5	40.0	38.0	12.3
0/92-50/92	12.5	13.3	13.6	12.5	17.0
CRP rental rate (Dollars per acre)					
New enrollment	60.00	60.00	60.00	-	-
Average	49.71	50.09	50.44	50.83	55.64
Export Enhancement Program Expenditures (Million dollars, fiscal year)	776.00	844.00	903.00	907.00	997.00

[Continued]

★ 7 ★

Farm Program Provisions, 1993-2001
[Continued]

	1993-1994	1994-1995	1995-1996	1996-1997	1997-2001
(Dollars per hundredweight, calendar year)					
Milk support price	10.10	10.10	10.10	10.10	10.40
Milk assessment	0.11	0.11	0.11	0.00	0.00

Source: FAPRI 1992 U.S. Agricultural Outlook, Food and Agricultural Policy Research Institute, Iowa State University and University of Missouri-Columbia, 1992, p. 23. Figures from 1989 to 1992 are excluded.

★ 8 ★

Government Costs, 1993-2001
[Numbers in billions of dollars per fiscal year]

	1993	1994	1995	1996	97-2001 Avg.
Feed grains	3.79	3.01	1.98	2.26	2.91
Corn	3.41	2.66	1.70	1.97	2.50
Sorghum	0.24	0.22	0.16	0.19	0.26
Barley	0.10	0.09	0.08	0.07	0.12
Oats	0.02	0.02	0.01	0.01	0.02
Wheat	2.11	1.96	1.81	1.53	1.35
Soybeans	0.03	0.09	-0.10	-0.17	0.00
Cotton	0.69	0.83	0.83	0.57	0.76
Rice	0.82	0.53	0.47	0.44	0.28
Dairy	0.42	0.37	0.32	0.41	0.33
Export programs	0.98	1.04	1.10	1.11	1.20
Net interest	0.84	0.78	0.73	0.71	0.76
Disaster payments	0.00	0.00	0.00	0.00	0.00
Other net costs	0.35	0.34	0.33	0.33	0.34
Net CCC outlays	10.02	8.95	7.48	7.17	7.91
Conservation reserve	1.80	1.90	1.99	2.01	0.99
Total government costs	11.82	10.85	9.47	9.18	8.89

Source: FAPRI 1992 U.S. Agricultural Outlook, Food and Agricultural Policy Research Institute, Iowa State University and University of Missouri-Columbia, 1992, p. 91. Figures from 1989 to 1992 are excluded.

★ 9 ★

Livestock Prices, 1992-2001

[Numbers in dollars per hundredweight]

	1992	1993	1994	1995	1996	1997-2001
Omaha Steers	74	73	70	68	69	82
Barrows and Gilts	48	53	53	56	53	56
12-City Broilers	42	45	52	54	51	54

Source: FAPRI 1992 U.S. Agricultural Outlook, Food and Agricultural Policy Research Institute, Iowa State University and University of Missouri-Columbia, 1992, p. 16. Figures from 1980 to 1991 are excluded. Magnitudes estimated from published chart.

★ 10 ★

Net Returns for Wheat, Corn, Sorghum, Barley, Oats, Soybeans, Cotton, and Rice, 1993-2001

	93/94	94/95	95/96	96/97	97/2001 Avg.
Net returns (Dollars per acre)					
Wheat					
Participant	82.87	79.29	80.07	79.98	74.41
Nonparticipant	50.86	50.19	58.02	62.82	58.95
Corn					
Participant	164.32	155.54	160.23	155.77	139.68
Nonparticipant	127.71	130.18	137.73	128.74	109.80
Sorghum					
Participant	84.38	81.63	84.40	81.97	73.63
Nonparticipant	68.38	66.32	70.28	66.06	55.23
Barley					
Participant	69.74	65.96	69.41	66.12	57.99
Nonparticipant	63.35	58.22	63.97	58.57	48.62
Oats					
Participant	55.53	48.62	46.52	45.55	35.22
Nonparticipant	39.72	41.76	40.08	41.97	26.10
Soybeans	121.60	122.69	132.80	133.05	118.82
Cotton					
Participant	190.31	187.39	187.45	184.96	161.03
Nonparticipant	136.78	133.11	140.77	140.25	103.14

[Continued]

★ 10 ★

Net Returns for Wheat, Corn, Sorghum, Barley, Oats, Soybeans, Cotton, and Rice, 1993-2001

[Continued]

	93/94	94/95	95/96	96/97	97/2001 Avg.
Rice					
Participant	203.57	196.43	190.69	188.82	180.13
Nonparticipant	71.57	67.24	63.59	73.28	99.95
Total net returns	31.87	31.14	32.23	31.73	29.65
(Billion dollars)					
Wheat	6.15	6.01	6.14	6.18	6.21
Corn	12.84	12.30	12.68	12.18	11.17
Sorghum	1.03	1.01	1.04	1.01	0.98
Barley	0.70	0.69	0.72	0.69	0.70
Oats	0.40	0.40	0.37	0.38	0.28
Soybeans	7.31	7.40	7.99	8.07	7.44
Cotton	2.68	2.61	2.60	2.54	2.26
Rice	0.76	0.71	0.69	0.67	0.62
Disaster payments	0.00	0.00	0.00	0.00	0.00

Source: *FAPRI 1992 U.S. Agricultural Outlook,* Food and Agricultural Policy Research Institute, Iowa State University and University of Missouri-Columbia, 1992, p. 87. Figures from 1989 to 1992 are excluded.

★ 11 ★

Planted and Idled Land, 1992-2001

[Numbers in millions of acres]

	1992-1993	1993-1994	1994-1995	1995	1996	1997-2001 Av
Planted	265	265	264	264	265	272
Conservation reserve	325	329	330	330	329	320
Annual program idled	275	276	276	275	276	282

Source: *FAPRI 1992 U.S. Agriculture Outlook,* Food and Agriculture Policy Research Institute, Iowa State University and University of Missouri-Columbia, 1992, p. 15. Figures from 1980 to 1991 are excluded. Magnitudes estimated from published chart.

★ 12 ★

Variables Related to the Farm Financial Situation, 1993-2000

Item	Unit	1993	1994	1995	1996	1997	1998	1999	2000
Gross cash income									
Crops	Mil $	87952	89150	92627	97942	104043	111062	117934	123996
Livestock	Mil $	84083	89289	95886	102202	107529	113440	120388	126318
Government payments	Mil $	8763	7815	8262	7928	6090	3603	2183	1795
Farm related	Mil $	7825	8094	8362	8631	8900	9168	9437	9705
Total	Mil $	188624	194348	205137	216703	226562	237273	249941	261814
Cash expenses	Mil $	129011	133209	136655	143263	151814	161957	172388	180889
Net cash income									
Nominal	Mil $	59613	61139	68482	73441	74748	75317	77553	80925
1982-84	Mil $	41184	40810	43914	45170	44095	42610	42046	42052
Price of farm land in the Corn Belt[1]	$/Acre	1329	1322	1307	1315	1327	1355	1401	1454

Source: "Variables Related to the Farm Financial Situation," *National-International Agricultural Outlook to the Year 2000*, Special Report 42, December, 1992, p. 22. Michigan State University Agricultural Experiment Station, East Landing, Michigan. Data from 1990 through 1992 are not included. *Note:* 1. Average for Minnesota, Iowa, Missouri, Illinois, Indiana, and Ohio.

Production and Technology

★ 13 ★

Development of New Food Products, 1990-2000

Year	Total new foods[1]	"Significant" new foods[2]
1990	10,301	1,296
1991	11,888	1,417
1992	13,068	1,568
1993	14,374	1,724
1994	15,811	1,797
1995	17,392	1,987
1996	19,121	2,295
1997	21,033	2,523
1998	23,136	2,776

[Continued]

★ 13 ★

Development of New Food Products, 1990-2000

[Continued]

Year	Total new foods[1]	"Significant" new foods[2]
1999	25,439	3,053
2000	27,983	3,419

Source: "New Products, New Realities," Bill Gorman and *Prepared Foods'* editors, *Interservice: The Journal of the American Logistics Association* 12, No. 1, Winter, 1992, p. 51. *Notes:* 1. Estimated at 10% annual growth. 2. Estimated at 12% annual growth.

★ 14 ★

Production and Technology, 1990-2010

Scenarios are useful for organizing thinking about what the future may hold. They are not predictions, but sketches of certain key features of the future situation based on plausible extensions of existing trends. The following scenarios project the state of U.S. agricultural production and technology and the environmental consequences of this production and technology for the year 2010.

Future U.S. agricultural production will reflect domestic and export demands for food and fiber. Population growth is the main driver of domestic demand. Population projections by the United Nations indicate about a 13 percent increase in the U.S. population between 1990 and 2010. Increases in income can also drive demand for food, but because most Americans now are adequately nourished, these increases will add little to demand.

Exports reflect both the growth of demand in foreign markets and the ability of American farmers to compete in those markets. Foreign demand for food reflects population growth outside the United States and per-capita income growth in the less developed countries (LDCs). According to United Nations projections, 95 percent of global population growth between 1990 and 2010 will be in the LDCs. Because millions of people in these countries are ill-nourished, increases in their incomes would stimulate increases in demand for food.

Studies conducted at Resources for the Future indicate that because of population and income growth in LDCs, these countries will account for 75 percent of the global increase in demand for food between 1990 and 2010. Globally, demand for wheat, feedgrains (corn and sorghum fed to animals), and soybeans, which by weight and use of agricultural resources account for the bulk of U.S. agricultural exports, would increase 26 percent over this period.

[Continued]

★ 14 ★

Production and Technology, 1990-2010
[Continued]

To understand how this demand might affect the quantity of U.S. production of wheat, feedgrains, and soybeans, consider three export scenarios. In the first—the baseline scenario—the United States retains its present shares of world trade in the three crops. In the second—the high export demand scenario—the United States increases its shares. In the third—the low export demand scenario—it loses some of its present shares.

In the 1980s the United States accounted for 39 percent of world trade in wheat, 59 percent of the trade in feedgrains (74 percent of the corn trade), and 53 percent of the trade in soybeans. In the baseline scenario these shares remain constant. U.S. exports of the three crops would increase from an annual average of 114 million metric tons (mmt) in 1987/1991 to 161 mmt in 2010. Total production of the crops, for both domestic consumption and export, would rise from 316 mmt in 1987/1991 to 425 mmt in 2010, an increase of 34 percent. The increase in export demand would contribute 50 percent more than the increase in domestic demand to the total production increase.

In the high export demand scenario, production of grains and soybeans is 520 mmt in 2010, about 65 percent higher than in 1987/1991. World trade in these crops grows faster than in the baseline scenario due to more rapid growth in population and per capita income in the less developed countries. U.S. shares of the trade are higher than those projected in the baseline scenario because of the increased competitive strength of the United States in the trade. This strength might result from unexpectedly rapid breakthroughs by American researchers working on agricultural biotechnologies, and from quick adoption of the new technologies by American farmers. The historical record of diffusion of agricultural technology indicates that in time farmers in other countries would adopt the new practices, eroding the increased competitive edge of the United States. In the interim, however, the U.S. advantage could permit American farmers to increase their shares of international markets.

In the low export demand scenario, world trade in grains and soybeans grows more slowly than in the baseline scenario. This slower growth reflects slower population and income growth in the LDCs and a successful drive by those countries to increase self-sufficiency in food production. It also reflects the weakened competitive position of the United States due to reduced investment in the development of new agricultural technology and cost-increasing constraints on agriculture to achieve increased environmental protection. The combination of these factors is such that in the low export demand scenario production of grains and soybeans in 2010 is 363 mmt, about 15 percent higher than in 1987/1991.

Source: "Scenarios of Future U.S. Agricultural Production and Technology and Their Environmental Costs," Pierre R. Crosson, *Resources*, No. 107, Spring 1992, pp. 6-9. Primary source: A report prepared by Crosson for the U.S. Environmental Protection Agency.

★ 15 ★

Technological Developments in Crops and Machinery, 2001

Thirteen years from now the most immediately noticeable change around the old farmstead may be a tractor that drives around by itself, guided only by radar or satellite. But the most radical changes in farming will not be in the machines but in the crops. By manipulating genes, bioengineers may soon custom-design drought-resistant, high-yielding crops that fight pests without toxic chemicals.

Winston Brill, vice president of research and development at Agracetus in Middleton, Wisconsin, and a pioneer in the genetic engineering of plants, foresees the mixing and matching of genes from different kinds of organisms. "Scientists are already adding bacterial genes to plants, plant genes to bacteria, and animal genes to plants," he says. While this won't make the legendary tomato-cow hybrid a reality, it will lead to better crops by century's end. For example, bacterial genes that are natural pesticides have been added to many plants and could someday be added to corn; and animal genes that regulate amino acid production might also improve corn by upping its protein content.

Within just a few years [Brill] expects to see corn with built-in insect resistance, soybeans with greater protein content, and higher yields for both crops.

Brill also predicts that, despite staunch opposition by environmental activists, genetically engineered micro-organisms will play an important role in agriculture by 2001. One variety of modified bacteria has already proved successful at preventing frost from forming on leaves; another could turn out to produce natural weed-controlling chemicals, thus replacing some of today's toxic herbicides; while a third could improve a plant's ability to absorb fertilizer and further reduce chemical use.

Today chemical fertilizers are usually applied to a field uniformly: soil samples are taken, the nutrients measured, and an analysis made of the types of fertilizer the soil requires. Then a blend is applied throughout the field.

However, the composition of soil in a field can change from acre to acre. The ideal blend of nutrients for one acre may be too potent or too weak for another. Applying a uniform mixture throughout is inefficient and wasteful— and contributes to the problem of groundwater contamination from agricultural chemicals. By 2001, though, almost every square foot of soil in a field will receive a precise dose of custom-designed fertilizer. . . .

What effect will custom-designed crops and high-tech machinery have on production? If projections made two years ago by the U.S. Office of Technology Assessment prove to be accurate, U.S. corn production may rise as high as 9.7 billion bushels in the year 2000, up from 7.7 billion bushels in 1984. Adoption of new technologies will account for much of that increase. And production of other crops is expected to follow a similar pattern.

[Continued]

★ 15 ★

Technological Developments in Crops and Machinery, 2001
[Continued]

But there will be a downside to all this. In 2001 there may be as few as 1.25 million farmers in the United States—900,000 fewer than there are now. All these technological improvements will cost money, and the biggest and wealthiest farmers will be the ones best able to afford them. Not only that: As crops become more plentiful, they'll bring lower and lower prices, driving out less efficient farmers altogether. Farming will be thriving at the turn of the century—but a traditional way of life will be fast disappearing.

Source: "2001 Agriculture: High Tech Hits the Dirt," Alex Kozlov, *Discover* 9, No. 11, November, 1988, pp. 58-9.

★ 16 ★

Timber Harvesting Systems, 2000-2040

Over the next 50 years, the logging industry will increasingly use more efficient and productive harvest and transport systems. These will counter the present systems which are, according to Dennis P. Bradley, socially and economically inefficient, resulting in excessive costs, waste, and frequently jeopardization of future forest productivity.

[Numbers in percent]

	2000	2010	2020	2030	2040
Section and region					
East-flat terrain					
South-Cable skidding	30.0	25.0	20.0	15.0	10.0
Grapple skidding	47.0	51.0	55.0	59.0	63.0
Bobtail trucks and farm tractors	16.0	15.0	14.0	13.0	12.0
Whole-tree chipping	7.0	9.0	11.0	13.0	15.0
Total	100.0	100.0	100.0	100.0	100.0
North-cable skidding	50.0	40.0	31.0	22.0	14.0
Grapple skidding	29.0	33.0	36.0	39.0	41.0
Forwarders	9.0	13.0	17.0	20.0	24.0
Whole-tree chipping	11.0	14.0	16.0	19.0	21.0
Total	100.0	100.0	100.0	100.0	100.0
East-mountainous terrain (systems used in both North and South)					
Cable yarding	16.0	22.0	28.0	34.0	40.0
Skidding and forwarding	84.0	78.0	72.0	66.0	60.0
Total	100.0	100.0	100.0	100.0	100.0
West-Douglas fir subregion					
Highlead	18.0	16.0	14.0	12.0	10.0
Skyline-short	38.0	38.5	39.0	39.5	40.0
Medium	8.0	8.5	9.0	9.5	10.0

[Continued]

★ 16 ★

Timber Harvesting Systems, 2000-2040
[Continued]

	2000	2010	2020	2030	2040
Long	2.6	2.7	2.8	2.9	3.0
Tractors	33.4	34.3	35.2	36.1	37.0
Total	100.0	100.0	100.0	100.0	100.0
West-Ponderosa pine subregion					
Highlead	3.4	3.8	4.2	4.6	5.0
Skyline-short	12.6	13.2	13.8	14.4	15.0
Medium	6.4	6.8	7.2	7.6	8.0
Long	0.4	0.8	1.2	1.6	2.0
Tractors	77.2	75.4	73.6	71.8	70.0
Total	100.0	100.0	100.0	100.0	100.0
West-Pacific Southwest subregion					
Highlead	6.1	5.8	5.6	5.3	5.0
Skyline-short	24.0	24.8	25.4	26.2	27.0
Medium	8.3	9.2	10.2	11.1	12.0
Long	0.2	0.4	0.6	0.8	1.0
Tractors	61.4	59.8	58.2	56.6	55.0
Total	100.0	100.0	100.0	100.0	100.0
Rocky Mountain subregion					
Tractors and jammers	83.9	81.7	79.5	77.2	75.0
Cable yarding	16.1	18.3	20.5	22.8	25.0
Total	100.0	100.0	100.0	100.0	100.0

Source: "Ignorance of Logging Costs Harms Long-Term Forestry," Dennis P. Bradley, *Forest Industries* 118, No. 5, June, 1991, p. 30.

Supply and Utilization

★ 17 ★

Barley, 1993-2001

	1993-1994	1994-1995	1995-1996	1996-1997	1997-2001 Avg
Percent					
Program					
ARP rate	7.5	7.5	5.0	5.0	7.5
PLD rate	0.0	0.0	0.0	0.0	0.0
NFA rate	15.0	15.0	15.0	15.0	15.0
Participation rate	76.2	76.0	77.5	75.8	76.8

[Continued]

★ 17 ★

Barley, 1993-2001
[Continued]

	1993-1994	1994-1995	1995-1996	1996-1997	1997-2001 Avg
Million acres					
Area					
Base area	11.3	11.3	11.2	11.3	13.3
ARP/PLD/0-92	2.2	2.1	2.2	1.9	3.1
CRP idled	2.9	3.0	3.1	3.0	0.9
Net flexed area	-0.7	-0.5	-0.6	-0.5	-0.5
Payment planted	4.8	4.7	4.8	5.0	5.2
Planted area	8.1	8.7	8.5	8.9	9.4
Harvested area	7.4	8.0	7.7	8.1	8.6
Bushels per acre					
Yield					
Actual	57.8	58.0	58.6	58.9	60.1
Program	45.2	45.2	45.2	45.2	45.2
Million bushels					
Supply	584	612	608	629	672
Beginning stocks	136	130	134	131	135
Production	428	462	454	479	517
Imports	20	20	20	20	20
Domestic use	393	397	399	403	419
Feed, residual	204	205	205	206	215
Food, seed, ind.	189	192	194	197	204
Exports	61	81	78	94	117
Total use	455	478	477	497	536
Ending stocks	130	134	131	133	135
FOR, special program	0	0	0	0	0
CCC inventory	0	0	0	0	0
9-month loan	12	12	10	11	15
'Free' stocks	118	123	121	121	121
Dollars					
Prices and returns					
Farm price/bu.	2.14	2.08	2.20	2.15	2.05
Loan rate/bu.	1.40	1.36	1.35	1.37	1.35
Target price/bu.	2.36	2.36	2.36	2.36	2.36
FOB Pacific NW/mt	107.60	104.65	110.75	108.14	103.27
Variable expenses/a.	63.42	65.52	67.96	70.89	77.53
Partic. returns/a.	69.74	65.96	69.41	66.12	57.99
Nonpartic. returns/a.	63.35	58.22	63.97	58.57	48.62

Source: FAPRI 1992 U.S. Agriculture Outlook, Food and Agriculture Policy Research Institute, Iowa State University and University of Missouri-Columbia, 1992, p. 51. Figures from 1989 to 1992 are excluded.

★ 18 ★

Beef, 1993-2001

	1993	1994	1995	1996	1997-2001 Avg
Million pounds					
Supply					
Beginning stocks	333	349	361	375	376
Imports	2,310	2,310	2,310	2,310	2,310
Change (%)	0.0	0.0	0.0	0.0	
Production	24,101	24,634	25,238	25,565	24,514
Change (%)	3.0	2.2	2.5	1.3	
Total	26,745	27,293	27,909	28,251	27,200
Change (%)	2.4	2.1	2.3	1.2	
Disappearance					
Domestic use	25,035	25,345	25,678	25,749	24,599
Change (%)	2.1	1.2	1.3	0.3	
Exports	1,360	1,587	1,855	2,118	2,228
Change (%)	7.4	16.7	16.9	14.2	
Total	26,395	26,932	27,533	27,867	26,827
Change (%)	2.4	2.0	2.2	1.2	
Ending stocks	349	361	375	384	373
Change (%)	4.9	3.4	3.9	2.2	
Pounds					
Per capita consumption	68.15	68.39	68.73	68.38	63.93
Change (%)	1.2	0.3	0.5	-0.5	
Dollars per hundredweight					
Prices					
1,000-1,100 lb. fed steers	72.22	70.94	68.90	69.82	81.78
Change (%)	-1.5	-1.8	-2.9	1.3	
600-700 lb. feeder steers	85.43	83.76	80.68	81.36	93.26
Change (%)	-1.8	-2.0	-3.7	0.8	
Utility cows	50.71	47.32	43.79	44.43	49.82
Change (%)	-1.6	-6.7	-7.5	1.5	
Dollars per pound					
Retail beef	2.82	2.78	2.73	2.76	3.06
Change (%)	-1.2	-1.4	-1.8	1.2	
Dollars per cow					
Net returns					
Cow-calf	58.17	38.99	14.11	10.16	52.18
Dollars per hundredweight					
Feeder-finisher	-5.42	-6.27	-7.18	-7.28	-2.21

Source: FAPRI 1992 U.S. Agriculture Outlook, Food and Agriculture Policy Research Institute, Iowa State University and University of Missouri-Columbia, 1992, p. 71. Figures from 1989 to 1992 are excluded.

★ 19 ★

Broilers, 1993-2001

	1993	1994	1995	1996	1997-2001 Avg
Million pounds					
Supply					
Beginning stocks	52	57	56	56	65
Production	21,231	21,890	22,651	23,234	25,404
Change (%)	3.0	3.1	3.5	2.6	
Total	21,283	21,947	22,707	23,290	25,469
Change (%)	3.1	3.1	3.5	2.6	
Disappearance					
Domestic use	20,114	20,796	21,535	21,943	23,839
Change (%)	3.8	3.4	3.6	1.9	
Exports	1,112	1,095	1,116	1,293	1,561
Change (%)	-9.2	-1.5	1.9	15.9	
Total	21,226	21,891	22,651	23,236	25,400
Change (%)	3.1	3.1	3.5	2.6	
Ending stocks	57	56	56	55	70
Change (%)	8.7	-1.8	0.5	-3.2	
Pounds					
Per capita consumption	77.67	79.59	81.75	82.66	87.83
Change (%)	2.9	2.5	2.7	1.1	
Cents per pound					
Prices					
12-city wholesale	52.60	53.55	54.52	52.95	55.73
Change (%)	7.0	1.8	1.8	-2.9	
Net returns	4.39	4.76	4.97	2.53	5.10

Source: *FAPRI 1992 U.S. Agriculture Outlook*, Food and Agriculture Policy Research Institute, Iowa State University and University of Missouri-Columbia, 1992, p. 75. Figures from 1989 to 1992 are excluded.

★ 20 ★

Corn and Feed-Grain-Related Variables, 1993-2000

Item	Unit	Crop years							
		1993	1994	1995	1996	1997	1998	1999	2000
Feed grain									
Production	Mil Mt	245	249	248	255	265	280	294	304
Fed to livestock	Mil Mt	145	147	149	151	153	155	159	162
Non-feed utilization	Mil Mt	46	49	55	55	57	58	60	61
Exports	Mil Mt	49	52	56	60	64	68	72	76
Ending stocks	Mil Mt	61	63	53	43	34	35	40	45
Ending stocks/utilization	Ratio	0.252	0.255	0.203	0.163	0.125	0.125	0.137	0.150

[Continued]

★ 20 ★

Corn and Feed-Grain-Related Variables, 1993-2000
[Continued]

Item	Unit	Crop years							
		1993	1994	1995	1996	1997	1998	1999	2000
Production of corn	Mil Bu	8460	8667	8657	8932	9294	9902	10428	10864
Production of other feed grain	Mil Mt	30	29	28	28	28	28	29	28
Loan rate	$/Bu	1.72	1.67	1.62	1.62	1.62	1.78	1.79	1.88
Target price	$/Bu	2.75	2.75	2.75	2.75	2.75	2.75	2.75	2.75
Farm price	$/Bu	2.23	2.16	2.25	2.40	2.60	2.87	2.83	2.94
Gross margin over variable costs Participants[1]									
Nominal	$/A	158	157	160	172	178	205	199	212
1982-84$	$/A	109	105	102	106	105	116	108	110
Nonparticipants[1]									
Nominal	$/A	126	117	127	146	171	205	199	212
1982-84$	$/A	87	78	82	90	101	116	108	110

Source: National-International Agricultural Outlook to the Year 2000, Special Report 42, December, 1992, p. 15. Michigan State University Agricultural Experiment Station, East Lansing, Michigan. Data from 1990 through 1992 are excluded. *Note:* 1. Feed Grain Program.

★ 21 ★

Corn, 1993-2001

	1993-1994	1994-1995	1995-1996	1996-1997	1997-2001 Avg
Program (percent)					
ARP rate	7.5	7.5	5.0	5.0	7.5
PLD rate	0.0	0.0	0.0	0.0	0.0
NFA rate	15.0	15.0	15.0	15.0	15.0
Participation rate	79.1	77.8	78.0	75.8	76.3
Area (million acres)					
Base area	82.4	82.1	81.9	82.0	85.1
ARP/PLD/0-92	7.8	7.4	5.9	5.6	8.5
CRP idled	4.4	4.6	4.9	4.8	1.7
Net flexed area	-3.3	-2.9	-2.8	-2.7	-3.2
Payment planted	45.6	44.9	46.4	45.3	44.7
Planted area	74.6	75.0	76.1	76.4	76.1
Harvested area	67.7	68.2	69.5	70.0	70.8
Yield (bushels per acre)					
Actual	121.6	123.0	124.0	125.3	128.6
Program	104.6	104.6	104.6	104.6	104.6

[Continued]

★ 21 ★

Corn, 1993-2001

[Continued]

	1993-1994	1994-1995	1995-1996	1996-1997	1997-2001 Avg
Supply (million bushels)	9,666	9,801	9,994	10,149	10,598
Beginning stocks	1,427	1,405	1,376	1,367	1,482
Production	8,234	8,391	8,613	8,777	9,111
Imports	5	5	5	5	5
Domestic use (million bushels)	6,594	6,734	6,918	6,987	7,147
Feed, residual	5,122	5,207	5,338	5,355	5,367
Alcohol	462	494	523	554	640
Seed	20	20	21	21	21
Food, other	990	1,013	1,037	1,059	1,118
Exports (million bushels)	1,666	1,690	1,709	1,751	1,957
Total use (million bushels)	8,261	8,424	8,627	8,739	9,104
Ending stocks (million bushels)	1,405	1,376	1,367	1,410	1,494
FOR, special program	0	0	0	0	0
CCC inventory	0	0	0	0	0
9-month loan	313	267	237	262	294
'Free' stocks	1,092	1,109	1,130	1,148	1,200
Price and returns (dolllars)					
Farm price/bu.	2.26	2.30	2.39	2.34	2.26
Loan rate/bu.	1.72	1.67	1.66	1.68	1.66
Target price/bu.	2.75	2.75	2.75	2.75	2.75
FOB Gulf price/mt	102.65	104.21	108.01	105.91	102.63
Variable expenses/a.	147.27	152.39	158.13	164.23	181.15
Partic. returns/a.	164.32	155.54	160.23	155.77	139.68
Nonpartic. returns/a.	127.71	130.18	137.73	128.74	109.80

Source: FAPRI 1992 U.S. Agriculture Outlook, Food and Agriculture Policy Research Institute, Iowa State University and University of Missouri-Columbia, 1992, p. 47. Figures from 1989 to 1992 are excluded.

★ 22 ★

Cotton, 1993-2001

	1993-1994	1994-1995	1995-1996	1996-1997	1997-2001 Avg
Percent					
Program					
ARP rate	5.0	5.0	5.0	5.0	5.0
PLD rate	0.0	0.0	0.0	0.0	0.0
NFA rate	15.0	15.0	15.0	15.0	15.0
Participation rate	89.1	89.9	88.3	85.6	80.5

[Continued]

★ 22 ★

Cotton, 1993-2001
[Continued]

	1993-1994	1994-1995	1995-1996	1996-1997	1997-2001 Avg
Million acres					
Area					
Base area	14.76	14.72	14.69	14.74	15.79
ARP/PLD/0-92	1.15	1.21	1.21	1.18	1.47
CRP idled	1.41	1.45	1.48	1.43	0.37
Net flexed area	0.00	-0.03	-0.06	-0.07	-0.19
Payment planted	9.14	9.15	8.93	8.66	8.38
Planted area	13.63	13.36	13.27	13.23	13.82
Harvested area	12.97	12.70	12.60	12.56	13.10
Pounds per acre					
Yield					
Actual	654	659	666	677	698
Program	590	590	590	590	590
Million bales					
Supply	21.89	22.47	22.70	22.88	24.65
Beginning stocks	4.21	5.03	5.19	5.16	5.59
Production	17.67	17.43	17.50	17.71	19.05
Imports	0.01	0.01	0.01	0.01	0.01
Domestic use	99.0	100.6	102.6	104.5	109.2
Mill use	9.58	9.66	9.89	10.03	10.16
Exports	7.38	7.72	7.75	7.87	8.80
Total use	16.96	17.38	17.64	17.90	18.96
Unaccounted	0.10	0.10	0.10	0.10	0.10
Ending stocks	5.03	5.19	5.16	5.07	5.78
CCC inventory	0.00	0.00	0.00	0.00	0.00
'Free' stocks	5.03	5.19	5.16	5.07	5.78
Dollars					
Price and returns					
Farm price/lb	0.604	0.603	0.618	0.623	0.599
Loan rate/lb	0.531	0.534	0.518	0.517	0.516
Target price/lb	0.729	0.729	0.729	0.729	0.729
Export value/mt	1,502	1,507	1,546	1,557	1,497
Variable expenses/a.	304.22	312.08	322.53	334.09	368.03
Partic. returns/a.	190.31	187.39	187.45	184.96	161.03
Nonpartic. returns/a.	136.78	133.11	140.77	140.25	103.14

Source: FAPRI 1992 U.S. Agriculture Outlook, Food and Agriculture Policy Research Institute, Iowa State University and University of Missouri-Columbia, 1992, p. 65. Figures from 1989 to 1992 are excluded.

★ 23 ★

Hay, 1993-2001

	1993-1994	1994-1995	1995-1996	1996-1997	1997-2001 Avg
Million acres					
Area	62.2	62.3	62.4	62.7	64.2
Tons per acre					
Yield	2.50	2.53	2.55	2.58	2.65
Million tons					
Supply	184.2	186.1	188.4	191.2	203.1
Production	155.6	157.3	159.1	161.4	170.5
Beginning stocks	28.6	28.8	29.3	29.7	32.6
Disappearance	155.3	156.8	158.6	160.7	169.6
Ending stocks	28.8	29.3	29.7	30.5	33.5
Dollars per ton					
Prices					
All-hay (crop year)	71.22	72.81	73.97	73.43	63.86
Alfalfa (calendar year)	75.82	77.76	79.18	79.17	69.33

Source: FAPRI 1992 U.S. Agriculture Outlook, Food and Agriculture Policy Research Institute, Iowa State University and University of Missouri-Columbia, 1992, p. 55. Figures from 1989 to 1992 are excluded.

★ 24 ★

High-Fructose Corn Syrup, 1993-2001

	1993	1994	1995	1996	1997-2001 Avg
Supply (000 short tons, raw value)	6,697	6,815	6,923	7,042	7,374
Production	6,557	6,675	6,783	6,902	7,234
Imports	140	140	140	140	140
Utilization	6,697	6,815	6,923	7,042	7,374
Consumption	6,537	6,655	6,763	6,882	7,214
Exports	160	160	160	160	160
Net change in stocks	0	0	0	0	0
Price (cents per pound)					
Chicago wholesale	19.26	19.41	19.59	19.81	20.68

Source: FAPRI 1992 U.S. Agriculture Outlook, Food and Agriculture Policy Research Institute, Iowa State University and University of Missouri-Columbia, 1992, p. 68. Figures from 1989 to 1992 are excluded.

★ 25 ★

Hog and Cattle-Related Variables, 1993-2000

Item	Unit	Calendar years							
		1993	1994	1995	1996	1997	1998	1999	2000
Beef cows on farms, Jan. 1	1000	34099	33592	32931	32284	31824	31712	31923	32332
Cattle on feed, Jan. 1	1000	11379	11209	11061	10944	10850	10748	10677	10645
Beef production[1]	Mil Lbs	23960	24132	24041	23625	23122	22680	22437	22579
Steer prices[2]	$/cwt	72.01	72.12	74.76	80.80	88.08	95.69	102.17	104.97
Feeder cattle prices[3]									
Calves	$/cwt	92.88	92.84	97.74	108.25	120.45	131.51	140.22	144.14
Yearlings	$/cwt	84.59	84.98	89.15	97.90	108.07	117.45	125.01	128.55
Gross margins over cost of feed and feeder[4]									
Nominal	$/cwt	3.77	4.15	6.27	8.81	9.60	9.74	8.72	6.76
1982-84 $	$/cwt	2.61	2.77	4.02	5.42	5.66	5.51	4.73	3.51
Pork production[1]	Mil. lbs	17346	16610	15984	16106	16676	17184	17363	17300
Price of barrows and gilts[5]	$/cwt	39.74	49.34	59.34	62.92	62.12	62.34	66.18	71.53
Gross margins over cost of feed[4]									
Nominal	$/cwt	12.64	21.40	30.78	32.40	29.75	27.91	29.62	34.56
1982-84$	$/cwt	8.73	14.29	19.74	19.93	17.55	15.79	16.06	17.96

Source: National-International Agricultural Outlook to the Year 2000, Special Report 42, December, 1992, p. 19. Michigan State University Agricultural Experiment Station, East Lansing, Michigan. Figures from 1990 through 1992 are excluded. *Notes:* 1. Carcass weight. 2. Omaha. 3. Kansas City. 4. Feed that is purchased or produced on the farm, the latter priced at opportunity cost. 5. Seven major markets.

★ 26 ★

Livestock Consumption and Availability, 1993-2000

Item	Unit	Years							
		1993	1994	1995	1996	1997	1998	1999	2000
Beef[1]	Lb.	64.3	63.7	62.6	60.8	58.8	56.9	55.4	54.9
Pork[1]	Lb.	49.8	47.2	45.0	44.9	46.0	46.9	47.0	46.3
Broilers[2]	Lb.	49.3	51.1	53.2	55.5	57.8	60.1	62.5	64.8
Turkeys[2]	Lb.	15.1	15.6	16.1	16.7	17.3	17.8	18.4	18.9
Fish[3]	Lb.	15.8	16.0	16.3	16.5	16.8	17.1	17.3	17.6
Milk[4]	Lb.	555.2	557.1	558.9	560.6	562.5	564.4	566.3	568.4
Eggs[2]	Doz	22.7	22.2	21.9	21.8	21.8	21.6	21.3	21.1

Source: National-International Agricultural Outlook to the Year 2000, Special Report 42, December, 1992, p. 6. Michigan State University Agricultural Experiment Station, East Lansing, Michigan. Figures from 1990 through 1992 are excluded. *Notes:* 1. Availability per capita. 2. Production per capita. 3. Consumption per capita. 4. Commercial disappearance in milk equivalent per capita.

★ 27 ★

Meat Consumption, 1993-2001

	1993	1994	1995	1996	1997-2001 Avg
Pounds					
Beef	68.15	68.39	68.73	68.38	63.93
Change (%)	1.2	0.3	0.5	-0.5	
Pork	51.65	49.14	48.41	49.38	47.60
Change (%)	-2.6	-4.9	-1.5	2.0	
Broiler	77.67	79.59	81.75	82.66	87.83
Change (%)	2.9	2.5	2.7	1.1	
Turkey	19.44	20.02	20.37	20.88	22.44
Change (%)	2.1	3.0	1.7	2.5	
Total	216.90	217.15	219.26	221.31	221.80
Change (%)	0.9	0.1	1.0	0.9	

Source: FAPRI 1992 U.S. Agricultural Outlook, Food and Agricultural Policy Research Institute, Iowa State University and University of Missouri-Columbia, 1992, p. 77. Figures from 1989 to 1992 are excluded.

★ 28 ★

Meat Expenditures, 1993-2001

	1993	1994	1995	1996	1997-2001 Avg
Dollars					
Beef	191.91	189.98	187.48	188.70	195.41
Change (%)	-0.0	-1.0	-1.3	0.6	
Pork	108.75	111.12	112.17	112.20	118.49
Change (%)	5.0	2.2	0.9	0.0	
Broiler	66.82	72.08	76.99	76.18	89.20
Change (%)	8.5	7.9	6.8	-1.1	
Turkey	19.01	19.90	20.89	20.51	24.35
Change (%)	8.0	4.7	5.0	-1.8	
Total	386.48	393.07	397.53	397.59	427.46
Change (%)	3.1	1.7	1.1	0.0	

Source: FAPRI 1992 U.S. Agricultural Outlook, Food and Agricultural Policy Research Institute, Iowa State University and University of Missouri-Columbia, 1992, p. 77. Figures from 1989 to 1992 are excluded.

★ 29 ★

Milk and Dairy Products, 1993-2001

	1993	1994	1995	1996	1997-2001 Avg
Supply					
Million head					
Milk cows	9.78	9.69	9.59	9.49	9.22
Production per cow					
1,000 pounds					
production per cow	15.47	15.78	16.08	16.39	17.41
Billion pounds milk equivalent					
Total production	151.35	152.87	154.24	155.59	160.47
Consumption					
Fluid consumption	57.67	58.27	58.71	59.21	60.44
Manufacturing milk use	90.52	91.49	92.45	93.32	97.08
Net Gov't removals[1]	5.69	5.25	4.83	4.33	3.45
Butter	3.31	3.23	3.09	2.87	2.50
Cheese	0.63	0.48	0.43	0.43	0.48
Nonfat dry milk	1.69	1.48	1.25	0.96	0.41
Dollars per hundredweight					
Milk prices and returns					
All-milk farm price	12.48	12.61	12.79	12.93	13.10
Support price	10.10	10.10.	10.10	10.10	10.40
Net returns	2.73	2.63	2.60	2.64	2.72
Pounds					
Per capita consumption					
Fluid	222.79	223.11	222.97	223.16	222.86
Butter	4.33	4.27	4.15	4.05	3.90
Nonfat dry milk	2.63	2.66	2.65	2.62	2.59
Cheese	25.58	26.01	26.56	27.12	28.93
Dollars per pound					
Wholesale product prices					
Butter	0.90	0.90	0.91	0.91	0.93
Nonfat dry milk	0.94	0.94	0.94	0.94	0.97
Cheese	1.29	1.31	1.34	1.36	1.40
CCC purchase prices					
Butter	0.87	0.87	0.87	0.87	0.90
Nonfat dry milk	0.91	0.91	0.91	0.91	0.94
Cheese	1.11	1.11	1.11	1.11	1.14

Source: FAPRI 1992 U.S. Agricultural Outlook, Food and Agricultural Policy Research Institute, Iowa State University and University Of Missouri-Columbia, 1992, p. 79. Figures from 1989 to 1992 are excluded. *Note: 1.* Total solids basis.

★ 30 ★

Milk Production-Related Variables, 1993-2000

Item	Unit	Calendar years							
		1993	1994	1995	1996	1997	1998	1999	2000
Milk cows on farms, Jan.1	1000	9792	9745	9649	9504	9423	9437	9447	9460
Milk production	Mil lb	151528	153087	154006	153944	154860	157292	159584	162156
Milk production per cow	1000 lbs	15.475	15.710	15.960	16.198	16.435	16.668	16.893	17.141
Ending stocks of dairy products[1]	Mil lb	16009	15149	13840	11761	9810.2	8840.5	8371.8	8328.9
Farm price	$/Cwt	12.50	12.71	13.08	13.64	14.20	14.57	14.88	15.13
Support price	$/Cwt	10.10	10.10	10.10	10.10	10.10	10.10	10.10	10.10
Gross margin over feed costs[2]									
Nominal	$/Cwt	9.74	9.87	10.23	10.64	11.00	11.13	11.21	11.45
1982-84 $									
Per cwt	$/Cwt	6.73	6.59	6.56	6.54	6.49	6.30	6.08	5.95
Per cow	$/cow	104	104	105	106	107	105	103	102

Source: National - International Agriculture Outlook to the Year 2000, Special Report 42, December, 1992, p. 18. Michigan State University Agricultural Experiment Station, East Lansing, Michigan. Figures from 1990 through 1992 are excluded. *Notes:* 1. Milkfat basis. 2. Feed that is purchased or produced on the farm, the latter priced at opportunity cost.

★ 31 ★

Milk Productivity Increases by Percentage, 1987-2000

Year	A trend increase in productivity				Trend plus 16% additional increases in productivity			
	Northeast	Lake States	Pacific	All other	Northeast	Lake States	Pacific	All other
1987	-117.7	-139.3	-594.5	15.7	-117.7	-139.3	-594.5	15.7
1988	-57.8	-117.8	-387.5	-4.3	-57.8	-117.8	-387.5	-4.3
1989	-94.6	-37.3	-596.2	-12.9	-94.6	-37.3	-596.2	-12.9
1990	-25.9	-65.0	120.8	-46.8	-25.5	-63.2	138.5	-46.9
1991	-41.0	-90.8	-90.0	-45.9	-36.0	-80.8	-223.5	-47.0
1992	-36.8	-85.9	-308.5	-53.1	-23.9	-59.6	-158.0	-54.1
1993	45.7	-38.7	66.7	-60.1	41.3	-20.1	99.1	-66.1
1994	110.3	30.0	603.7	-70.0	21.0	-92.1	-37.6	-58.0
1995	100.6	53.9	1276.9	-71.1	-25.2	-108.8	11.8	-54.9
1996	81.4	102.9	1382.7	-87.3	-53.0	-51.7	63.9	-68.1
1997	42.4	137.7	1194.8	-95.7	-76.8	-5.8	-93.8	-76.0
1998	67.1	153.6	567.4	-110.5	-67.3	0.1	-462.3	-93.0
1999	30.7	158.1	-704.2	-102.6	-102.4	32.8	-1120.3	-95.3
2000	24.5	158.3	-1369.0	-102.2	-132.4	48.0	-1662.7	-100.2

Source: "Regional and Temporal Impacts of Technical Change in the U.S. Dairy Sector," Alfons Weersink and Loren W. Tauer, *American Journal of Agricultural Economics* 72, No. 4, November, 1990, p. 933. Assumes percentage changes in regional dairy net income from 1986 actual values.

★ 32 ★

Milk Productivity Increases by Region, 1990-2000

Year	A trend increase in productivity				Trend plus 16% additional increases in productivity			
	Northeast	Lake States	Pacific	All other	Northeast	Lake States	Pacific	All other
1990	.210	.298	.160	.332	.209	.299	.160	.332
1991	.212	.304	.164	.320	.212	.305	.163	.320
1992	.215	.309	.161	.315	.214	.311	.167	.308
1993	.220	.306	.164	.310	.216	.310	.167	.307
1994	.220	.304	.166	.310	.216	.306	.177	.301
1995	.214	.299	.170	.317	.223	.314	.172	.291
1996	.215	.297	.172	.316	.222	.318	.179	.282
1997	.216	.296	.176	.312	.222	.313	.180	.286
1998	.215	.301	.173	.312	.223	.314	.180	.284
1999	.212	.299	.175	.314	.216	.316	.181	.287
2000	.214	.295	.177	.315	.216	.314	.183	.287

Source: "Regional and Temporal Impacts of Technical Change in the U.S. Dairy Sector," Alfons Weersink and Loren W. Tauer, *American Journal of Agricultural Economics* 72, No. 4, November, 1990, p. 932. Figures for 1988 and 1989 are excluded.

★ 33 ★

Milk Supply and Demand, 1990-2000

Year	Northeast		Lake states		Pacific		All other		National			
	Milk supply (mil lbs)	Milk cows (000's)	Milk supply (mil lbs)	Milk cows (000's)	Milk supply (mil lbs)	Milk cows (000's)	Milk supply (mil lbs)	Milk cows (000's)	Milk demand (bil lbs)	Milk price ($/cwt)	CCC purchases (bil lbs)	Support price ($/cwt)
1990	29,024	2,034	41,385	2,805	22,191	1,293	46,029	3,320	132.8	11.39	5.8	10.10
1991	29,451	2,022	42,255	2,755	22,590	1,285	44,346	3,147	134.3	10.93	4.3	9.60
1992	30,112	1,991	43,609	2,703	23,538	1,276	43,577	3,012	135.7	10.94	5.1	9.60
1993	30,731	1,970	44,101	2,657	23,841	1,270	43,719	2,894	136.9	10.47	5.5	9.10
1994	31,447	1,974	44,567	2,671	25,786	1,266	43,781	2,938	138.5	9.92	7.1	8.60
1995	31,236	1,934	44,047	2,592	24,166	1,239	40,899	2,645	140.1	9.45	0.2	8.10
1996	30,548	1,893	43,860	2,505	24,613	1,227	38,839	2,456	141.6	9.99	-3.7	8.60
1997	31,153	1,869	43,957	2,497	25,366	1,213	40,165	2,506	142.4	10.49	-1.8	9.10
1998	32,804	1,845	46,141	2,380	26,476	1,212	41,731	2,314	142.5	10.87	4.7	9.60
1999	32,477	1,819	47,568	2,250	27,310	1,215	43,132	2,185	143.4	10.85	7.1	9.60
2000	32,672	1,782	47,553	1,905	27,782	1,196	43,455	1,810	144.5	10.40	7.0	9.10

Source: "Regional and Temporal Impacts of Technical Change in the U.S. Dairy Sector," Alfons Weersink and Loren W. Tauer, *American Journal of Agricultural Economics* 72, No. 4, November, 1990, p. 931. Assumes a logistic adoption of 16% additional increase from 1990 through 1996 over a strictly linear trend increase.

★ 34 ★

Milk Supply and Demand, 1994-2000

Year	Northeast Milk supply (mil lbs)	Northeast Milk cows (000's)	Lake states Milk supply (mil lbs)	Lake states Milk cows (000's)	Pacific Milk supply (mil lbs)	Pacific Milk cows (000's)	All other Milk supply (mil lbs)	All other Milk cows (000's)	National Milk demand (bil lbs)	National Milk price ($/cwt)	National CCC pur-chases (bil lbs)	National Support price ($/cwt)
1994	30,141	1,988	41,681	2,729	22,707	1,272	42,402	3,002	138.0	12.41	-1.1	11.10
1995	30,338	1,991	42,226	2,749	24,066	1,263	44,830	3,009	140.1	12.87	1.4	11.60
1996	30,976	1,998	42,777	2,751	24,802	1,258	45,569	2,997	141.1	13.37	3.0	12.10
1997	31,307	1,987	42,957	2,693	25,559	1,243	45,164	2,928	141.9	13.85	3.1	12.60
1998	32,655	1,904	45,754	2,677	26,372	1,267	47,442	2,879	142.0	14.26	10.2	13.10
1999	32,799	1,828	46,142	2,414	27,093	1,292	48,535	2,869	142.9	13.76	11.7	12.60
2000	32,669	1,640	45,065	2,123	27,058	1,289	48,180	2,735	144.0	13.30	8.9	12.10

Source: "Regional and Temporal Impacts of Technical Change in the U.S. Dairy Sector," Alfons Weersink and Loren W. Tauer, *American Journal of Agricultural Economics* 72, No. 4, November, 1990, p. 930. Assumes future productivity increases as a linear trend of historical productivity increases. Figures from 1988 to 1993 are excluded.

★ 35 ★

Oats, 1993-2001

	1993-1994	1994-1995	1995-1996	1996-1997	1997-2001 Avg
Percent					
Program					
ARP rate	0.0	0.0	0.0	0.0	0.0
PLD rate	0.0	0.0	0.0	0.0	0.0
NFA rate	15.0	15.0	15.0	15.0	15.0
Participation rate	24.9	29.5	25.2	24.3	25.4
Million acres					
Area					
Base area	7.2	7.2	7.1	7.2	8.1
ARP/PLD/0-92	0.5	0.5	0.5	0.5	0.8
CRP idled	1.4	1.5	1.5	1.4	0.5
Net flexed area	-0.2	-0.2	-0.2	-0.3	-0.3
Payment planted	0.9	1.1	0.9	0.9	0.8
Planted area	8.9	8.6	8.5	8.3	9.1
Harvested area	5.1	4.8	4.9	4.8	5.3
Bushels per acre					
Yield					
Actual	61.3	61.8	62.3	62.8	64.4
Program	47.0	47.0	47.0	47.0	47.0

[Continued]

★ 35 ★

Oats, 1993-2001

[Continued]

	1993-1994	1994-1995	1995-1996	1996-1997	1997-2001 Avg
Million bushels					
Supply	478	473	481	474	514
Beginning stocks	98	104	101	102	108
Production	310	296	308	299	338
Imports	71	74	72	73	67
Domestic use	373	371	378	374	402
Feed, residual	245	241	246	240	261
Food, seed, ind.	128	130	131	134	141
Exports	1	1	1	1	1
Total use	374	372	379	375	403
Ending stocks	104	101	102	99	111
FOR, special program	0	0	0	0	0
CCC inventory	0	0	0	0	0
9-month loan	0	0	0	0	0
'Free' stocks	104	101	102	99	111
Dollars					
Prices and returns					
Farm price/bu.	1.21	1.28	1.29	1.36	1.22
Loan rate/bu.	0.88	0.86	0.85	0.87	0.85
Target price/bu.	1.45	1.45	1.45	1.45	1.45
Variable expenses/a.	51.86	53.99	56.51	59.34	66.67
Partic. returns/a.	55.53	48.62	46.52	45.55	35.22
Nonpartic. returns/a.	39.72	41.76	40.08	41.97	26.10

Source: FAPRI 1992 U.S. Agriculture Outlook, Food and Agriculture Policy Research Institute, Iowa State University and University of Missouri-Columbia, 1992, p. 53. Figures from 1989 to 1992 are excluded.

★ 36 ★

Planted and Idled Area, 1993-2001

[Numbers in millions of acres]

	93/94	94/95	95/96	96/97	97-2001 Avg
15-crop total area	322.7	323.9	323.7	322.9	313.9
Planted	263.1	261.9	262.1	264.6	274.4
Program	113.1	115.3	115.6	112.0	110.8
Nonprogram	150.0	146.6	146.4	152.7	163.6
Idled	59.6	62.0	61.6	58.3	39.5
ARP/PLD/0-92	22.5	23.4	21.6	20.3	27.2
CRP	37.1	38.5	40.0	38.0	12.3
Wheat total area	93.3	92.7	92.8	92.7	92.4

[Continued]

★ 36 ★

Planted and Idled Area, 1993-2001

[Continued]

	93/94	94/95	95/96	96/97	97-2001 Avg
Planted	74.6	72.1	71.9	73.2	79.2
Program	44.0	46.8	45.8	43.4	43.0
Nonprogram	30.5	25.4	26.1	29.8	36.1
ARP/PLD/0-92	7.7	9.2	9.2	8.4	9.8
CRP	11.0	11.3	11.7	11.1	3.5
Corn total area	86.8	87.0	86.9	86.8	86.3
Planted	74.6	75.0	76.1	76.4	76.1
Program	45.6	44.9	46.4	45.3	44.7
Nonprogram	29.0	30.0	29.6	31.1	31.4
ARP/PLD/0-92	7.8	7.4	5.9	5.6	8.5
CRP	4.4	4.6	4.9	4.8	1.7
Sorghum total area	15.3	15.5	15.4	15.3	14.7
Planted	10.3	10.6	10.6	10.7	10.8
Program	6.0	6.0	6.2	6.2	6.4
Nonprogram	4.2	4.6	4.4	4.5	4.5
ARP/PLD/0-92	2.5	2.3	2.2	2.1	3.2
CRP	2.5	2.6	2.7	2.4	0.7
Barley total area	13.2	13.8	13.7	13.7	13.4
Planted	8.1	8.7	8.5	8.9	9.4
Program	4.8	4.7	4.8	5.0	5.2
Nonprogram	3.3	4.0	3.7	3.9	4.2
ARP/PLD/0-92	2.2	2.1	2.2	1.9	3.1
CRP	2.9	3.0	3.1	3.0	0.9
Oats total area	10.7	10.6	10.5	10.3	10.4
Planted	8.9	8.6	8.5	8.3	9.1
Program	0.9	1.1	0.9	0.9	0.8
Nonprogram	8.0	7.5	7.6	7.5	8.3
ARP/PLD/0-92	0.5	0.5	0.5	0.5	0.8
CRP	1.4	1.5	1.5	1.4	0.5
Soybean total area	64.6	65.1	65.1	65.3	64.2
Planted	60.1	60.3	60.2	60.7	62.6
CRP	4.5	4.7	5.0	4.7	1.7
Cotton total area	16.2	16.0	16.0	15.8	15.7
Planted	13.6	13.4	13.3	13.2	13.8
Program	9.1	9.2	8.9	8.7	8.4
Nonprogram	4.5	4.2	4.3	4.6	5.4
ARP/PLD/50-92	1.1	1.2	1.2	1.2	1.5
CRP	1.4	1.5	1.5	1.4	0.4
Rice total area	3.5	3.4	3.5	3.4	3.5

[Continued]

★ 36 ★

Planted and Idled Area, 1993-2001

[Continued]

	93/94	94/95	95/96	96/97	97-2001 Avg
Planted	2.7	2.9	2.9	2.9	3.0
Program	2.6	2.6	2.5	2.5	2.4
Nonprogram	0.2	0.3	0.3	0.4	0.6
ARP/PLD/50-92	0.7	0.6	0.6	0.6	0.5
CRP	0.0	0.0	0.0	0.0	0.0
Sugar					
Harvested	2.2	2.2	2.2	2.3	2.2
6 other crops[1]					
Planted[2]	8.0	8.0	8.0	8.0	8.1
Other CRP area	9.0	9.3	9.7	9.2	3.0
Hay					
Harvested	62.2	62.3	62.4	62.7	64.2
15 crops + hay	384.9	386.1	386.1	385.5	378.2
Planted	325.3	324.1	324.4	327.3	338.6
Program	113.1	115.3	115.6	112.0	110.8
Nonprogram	212.3	208.9	208.8	215.3	227.8
Idled	59.6	62.0	61.6	58.3	39.5
ARP/PLD-92/50-92	22.5	23.4	21.6	20.3	27.2
CRP	37.1	38.5	40.0	38.0	12.3

Source: FAPRI 1992 U.S. Agricultural Outlook, Food and Agricultural Policy Research Institute, Iowa State University and University of Missouri-Columbia, 1992, pp. 83-4. Figures from 1989 to 1992 are excluded. *Notes:* 1. Sunflowers, peanuts, edible beans, tobacco, rye, and flaxseed. 2. Harvested area for tobacco and rye.

★ 37 ★

Pork, 1993-2001

	1993	1994	1995	1996	1997-2001 Avg
Million pounds					
Supply					
Beginning stocks	384	357	331	329	357
Imports	734	778	857	731	591
Change (%)	-6.5	6.0	10.2	-14.7	
Production	16,804	16,026	15,782	16,525	16,519
Change (%)	-1.1	-4.6	-1.5	4.7	
Total	17,922	17,161	16,970	17,585	17,466
Change (%)	-1.5	-4.2	-1.1	3.6	

[Continued]

★ 37 ★

Pork, 1993-2001
[Continued]

	1993	1994	1995	1996	1997-2001 Avg
Disappearance					
Domestic use	17,224	16,533	16,421	16,881	16,628
Change (%)	-1.7	-4.0	-0.7	2.8	
Exports	340	297	220	343	484
Change (%)	16.8	-12.6	-25.9	55.9	
Total	17,564	16,830	16,641	17,224	17,112
Change (%)	-1.4	-4.2	-1.1	3.5	
Ending stocks	357	331	329	361	354
Change (%)	-6.9	-7.5	-0.5	9.7	
Pounds					
Per capita consumption	51.65	49.14	48.41	49.38	47.60
Change (%)	-2.6	-4.9	-1.5	2.0	
Dollars per hundredweight					
Prices					
Barrows, gilts	44.98	52.04	56.71	51.67	53.88
Change (%)	9.5	15.7	9.0	-8.9	
Sows	42.43	49.13	51.00	45.16	45.73
Change (%)	17.0	15.8	3.8	-11.5	
Dollars per pound					
Retail pork	2.11	2.26	2.32	2.27	2.50
Change (%)	7.8	7.4	2.5	-1.9	
Dollars per hundredweight					
Net returns					
Farrow-finisher	1.36	7.90	11.53	4.76	7.10

Source: FAPRI 1992 U.S. Agriculture Outlook, Food and Agriculture Policy Research Institute, Iowa State University and University of Missouri-Columbia, 1992, p. 73. Figures from 1989 to 1992 are excluded.

★ 38 ★

Poultry-Related Variables, 1993-2000

Item	Unit	Calendar years							
		1993	1994	1995	1996	1997	1998	1999	2000
Broilers									
Production[1]	Mil. Lbs	21911	22982	24162	25449	26779	28127	29501	30923
Price[2]	Cents/Lb	47.8	51.7	56.1	57.7	57.2	57.2	58.7	59.9
Gross margin over feed costs									
Nominal	Cents/Lb	31.4	34.8	38.6	38.8	37.3	36.2	36.5	37.4
1982-84 $	Cents/Lb	21.7	23.3	24.8	23.9	22.0	20.5	19.8	19.4

[Continued]

★ 38 ★

Poultry-Related Variables, 1993-2000
[Continued]

Item	Unit	Calendar years							
		1993	1994	1995	1996	1997	1998	1999	2000
Turkeys									
Production[1]	Mil Lbs	4933	5136	5364	5612	5871	6124	6372	6622
Price[3]	Cents/Lb	62.6	67.2	72.3	77.2	77.2	77.2	79.3	80.9
Gross margin over feed costs									
Nominal	Cents/Lb	38.6	42.5	46.7	49.6	48.1	46.5	46.8	47.9
1982-84 $	Cents/Lb	26.7	28.4	30.0	30.5	28.4	26.3	25.4	24.9
Eggs									
Production	Mil Doz	5862	5786	5758	5791	5841	5861	5845	5829
Farm price	Cents/Doz	52.2	63.6	73.2	75.8	75.2	77.3	84.0	91.1
Gross margin over feed costs									
Nominal	Cents/Doz	24.5	35.1	44.0	44.7	42.1	42.2	46.8	53.4
1982-84 $	Cents/Doz	16.9	23.4	28.2	27.5	24.9	23.9	25.4	27.8

Source: "Projections of Variables Related to Poultry," *National-International Agricultural Outlook to the Year 2000*, Special Report 42, December, 1992, p. 21. Michigan State University Agricultural Experiment Station, East Lansing, Michigan. Figures from 1990 to 1992 are excluded. *Notes:* 1. Ready-to-cook weight. 2. 12-city average. 3. Eastern region, 8-16 pound young hens.

★ 39 ★

Red Meat and Poultry Consumption, 1990-2000

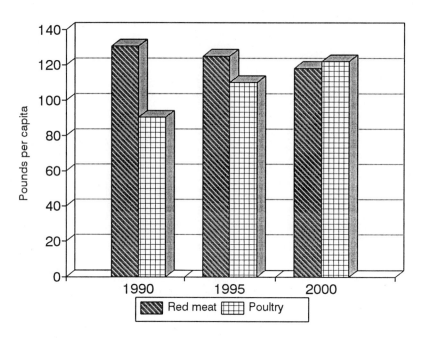

[Numbers in pounds]

Year	Red meat	Poultry
1990	130.5	90.4
1995[1]	125.0	110.0
2000[2]	118.0	122.0

Source: "Food Industry Must Earn Trust," *Food Engineering* 63, No. 1, January, 1991, p. 15. Primary source: "Red Meat & Poultry per capita Consumption (in Pounds)," Keith Rinehart, Perdue Farms, Inc. *Notes:* 1. USDA estimate. 2. Keith Rinehart's forecast.

★ 40 ★

Rice, 1993-2001

	1993-1994	1994-1995	1995-1996	1996-1997	1997-2001 Avg
Percent					
Program					
ARP rate	5.0	5.0	5.0	5.0	5.0
PLD rate	0.0	0.0	0.0	0.0	0.0
NFA rate	15.0	15.0	15.0	15.0	15.0
Participation rate	97.8	93.0	92.2	91.3	85.1

[Continued]

★ 40 ★

Rice, 1993-2001
[Continued]

	1993-1994	1994-1995	1995-1996	1996-1997	1997-2001 Avg
Million acres					
Area					
Base area	4.16	4.16	4.16	4.16	4.17
ARP/PLD/0-92	0.74	0.56	0.56	0.57	0.49
CRP idled	0.01	0.01	0.01	0.01	0.01
Net flexed area	-0.41	-0.30	-0.30	-0.32	-0.25
Payment planted	2.56	2.57	2.53	2.50	2.36
Planted area	2.74	2.86	2.88	2.87	2.96
Harvested area	2.71	2.83	2.85	2.84	2.93
Pounds per acre					
Yield					
Actual	5,754	5,778	5,831	5,896	6,047
Program	4,859	4,859	4,859	4,859	4,859
Million hundredweight					
Supply	190.0	194.7	198.9	201.2	214.2
Beginning stocks	28.6	25.4	26.6	27.7	30.0
Production	155.8	163.4	166.3	167.3	177.5
Imports	5.6	5.8	6.0	6.2	6.8
Domestic use	99.0	100.6	102.6	104.5	109.2
Food	70.5	71.4	72.7	73.9	76.6
Seed	3.8	3.8	3.8	3.8	4.0
Brewing	16.7	17.3	18.0	18.7	20.6
Residual	8.0	8.0	8.0	8.0	8.0
Exports	65.6	67.5	68.7	68.6	74.1
Total use	164.6	168.0	171.2	173.1	183.3
Ending stocks	25.4	26.6	27.7	28.1	31.0
CCC inventory	0.0	0.0	0.0	0.0	0.0
'Free' stocks	25.4	26.6	27.7	28.1	31.0
Dollars					
Price and returns					
Farm price/ctw	7.20	7.27	7.33	7.62	8.49
Loan rate/ctw	6.50	6.50	6.50	6.50	6.63
Target price/ctw	10.71	10.71	10.71	10.71	10.71
FOB Houston/mt	359.82	363.74	366.68	380.99	424.95
Variable expenses/a.	342.50	353.06	363.98	375.84	413.98
Partic. returns/a.	203.57	196.43	190.69	188.82	180.13
Nonpartic. returns/a.	71.57	67.24	63.59	73.28	99.95

Source: "U.S. Rice Supply and Utilization," *FAPRI 1992 U.S. Agriculture Outlook,* Food and Agriculture Policy Research Institute, Iowa State University and University of Missouri-Columbia, 1992, p. 63. Figures from 1989 to 1992 are excluded.

★ 41 ★

Sorghum, 1993-2001

	1993-1994	1994-1995	1995-1996	1996-1997	1997-2001 Avg
Percent					
Program					
ARP rate	7.5	7.5	5.0	5.0	7.5
PLD rate	0.0	0.0	0.0	0.0	0.0
NFA rate	15.0	15.0	15.0	15.0	15.0
Participation rate	77.9	76.6	77.3	76.1	76.6
Million acres					
Area					
Base area	13.4	13.3	13.2	13.4	15.2
ARP/PLD/0-92	2.5	2.3	2.2	2.1	3.2
CRP idled	2.5	2.6	2.7	2.4	0.7
Net flexed area	-0.9	-0.6	-0.7	-0.8	-1.1
Payment planted	6.0	6.0	6.2	6.2	6.4
Planted area	10.3	10.6	10.6	10.7	10.8
Harvested area	9.2	9.6	9.6	9.9	10.2
Bushels per acre					
Yield					
Actual	65.9	66.6	67.3	68.1	70.1
Program	57.7	57.7	57.7	57.7	57.7
Million bushels					
Supply	747	766	776	796	849
Beginning stocks	138	125	127	124	135
Production	608	641	649	672	715
Imports	0	0	0	0	0
Domestic use	396	413	422	435	443
Feed, residual	380	397	406	418	427
Food, seed, ind.	16	16	16	16	17
Exports	226	226	229	234	270
Total use	622	640	651	669	713
Ending stocks	125	127	124	128	136
FOR, special program	0	0	0	0	0
CCC inventory	0	0	0	0	0
9-month loan	6	5	4	5	7
'Free' stocks	119	122	120	123	129
Dollars					
Prices and returns					
Farm price/bu.	2.14	2.13	2.21	2.17	2.07
Loan rate/bu.	1.63	1.59	1.57	1.60	1.57
Target price/bu.	2.61	2.61	2.61	2.61	2.61
FOB Gulf price/mt	101.48	100.98	104.72	103.18	98.72
Variable expenses/a.	72.38	75.24	78.41	81.96	90.20

[Continued]

★ 41 ★

Sorghum, 1993-2001
[Continued]

	1993-1994	1994-1995	1995-1996	1996-1997	1997-2001 Avg
Partic. returns/a.	84.38	81.63	84.40	81.97	73.63
Nonpartic. returns/a.	68.38	66.32	70.28	66.06	55.23

Source: FAPRI 1992 U.S. Agriculture Outlook, Food and Agriculture Policy Research Institute, Iowa State University and University of Missouri-Columbia, 1992, p. 49. Figures from 1989 to 1992 are excluded.

★ 42 ★

Soybean Meal, 1993-2001

	1993-1994	1994-1995	1995-1996	1996-1997	1997-2001
Supply (000 tons)	30,117	30,747	31,231	31,582	33,066
Beginning stocks	286	300	303	299	311
Production	29,825	30,442	30,923	31,278	32,750
Imports	5	5	5	5	5
Domestic use	23,642	24,274	24,780	24,978	26,208
Exports	6,174	6,169	6,153	6,297	6,547
Total use	29,816	30,443	30,933	31,276	32,756
Ending stocks	300	303	299	306	310
Prices (dollars)					
Decatur/ton	189.26	189.58	196.82	191.56	169.01
Decatur/mt	208.62	208.97	216.96	211.15	186.30

Source: FAPRI 1992 U.S. Agriculture Outlook, Food and Agriculture Policy Research Institute, Iowa State University and University of Missouri-Columbia, 1992, p. 59. Figures from 1989 to 1992 are excluded.

★ 43 ★

Soybean Oil, 1993-2001

	1993-1994	1994-1995	1995-1996	1996-1997	1997-2001
Million Pounds					
Supply	16,412	16,765	17,049	17,249	18,015
Beginning stocks	2,333	2,396	2,453	2,485	2,557
Production	14,069	14,359	14,587	14,754	15,448
Imports	10	10	10	10	10
Domestic use	13,058	13,311	13,550	13,711	14,242
Exports	958	1,001	1,015	1,066	1,187
Total use	14,016	14,312	14,564	14,776	15,429

[Continued]

★ 43 ★

Soybean Oil, 1993-2001
[Continued]

	1993-1994	1994-1995	1995-1996	1996-1997	1997-2001
Ending stocks	2,396	2,453	2,485	2,472	2,586
Dollars					
Prices					
Decatur/cwt	16.44	17.16	18.13	19.50	22.18
Decatur/mt	362.48	378.25	399.77	429.80	488.90

Source: *FAPRI 1992 U.S. Agriculture Outlook*, Food and Agriculture Policy Research Institute, Iowa State University and University of Missouri-Columbia, 1992, p. 58. Figures from 1989 to 1992 are excluded.

★ 44 ★

Soybean-Related Variables, 1993-2000

Item	Unit	Crop years							
		1993	1994	1995	1996	1997	1998	1999	2000
Production	Mil Bu	2015	2024	2073	2161	2244	2276	2321	2355
Crushings	Mil Bu	1246	1290	1315	1342	1370	1400	1443	1471
Exports	Mil Bu	653	705	724	717	731	747	781	799
Ending stocks	Mil Bu	301	230	163	165	208	237	235	219
Ending stocks/utilization	Ratio	0.150	0.110	0.076	0.076	0.095	0.105	0.101	0.093
Farm price	$/Bu	5.69	6.01	6.91	7.01	6.63	6.57	6.69	7.00
Gross margin over variable costs									
Nominal	$/A	121	132	163	166	151	149	152	163
1982-84$	$/A	84	88	104	102	89	84	83	85
Soybean meal price	$/T	181	191	215	227	231	241	247	260
Soybean oil price[1]	Cents/Lb	21.3	22.4	26.2	25.3	21.7	19.7	20.2	21.0

Source: *National-International Agriculture Outlook to the Year 2000*, Special Report 42, December, 1992, p. 17. Michigan State University Agricultural Experiment Station, East Lansing, Michigan. Figures from 1990 to 1992 are excluded. *Note:* 1. At Decatur, Illinois.

★ 45 ★

Soybeans, 1993-2001

	1993-1994	1994-1995	1995-1996	1996-1997	1997-2001
Million acres					
Area					
CRP idled	4.5	4.7	5.0	4.7	1.7
Net flexed area	4.6	4.6	4.5	4.4	4.2
Planted area	60.1	60.3	60.2	60.7	62.6
Harvested area	59.0	59.2	59.0	59.5	61.3
Bushels per acre					
Yield	35.0	35.3	35.7	36.0	36.9
Million bushels					
Supply	2,367	2,415	2,438	2,465	2,616
Beginning stocks	301	319	325	316	351
Production	2,062	2,090	2,108	2,144	2,260
Imports	5	5	5	5	5
Domestic use	1,350	1,377	1,399	1,416	1,482
Crush	1,251	1,276	1,297	1,311	1,373
Seed, residual	99	100	102	104	108
Exports	698	713	724	731	778
Total use	2,048	2,090	2,123	2,147	2,260
Ending stocks	319	325	316	318	356
CCC inventory	0	0	0	0	0
9-month loan	66	66	52	51	82
'Free' stocks	254	259	264	267	275
Dollars					
Prices and returns					
Farm price/bu.	5.67	5.68	5.95	5.98	5.58
Loan rate/bu.	5.02	5.02	5.02	5.02	5.02
FOB Gulf price/mt	225.79	226.14	236.31	237.20	222.29
Bean/corn ratio	2.51	2.47	2.49	2.56	2.47
Variable expenses/a.	76.75	78.06	79.95	82.36	87.02
Net returns/a.	121.60	122.69	132.80	133.05	118.82
Meal price/ton	189.26	189.58	196.82	191.56	169.01
Oil price/cwt	16.44	17.16	18.13	19.50	22.18
Crushing margin/bu.	0.69	0.77	0.78	0.79	0.94

Source: FAPRI 1992 U.S. Agriculture Outlook, Food and Agriculture Policy Research Institute, Iowa State University and University of Missouri-Columbia, 1992, p. 57. Figures from 1989 to 1992 are excluded.

★ 46 ★

Sugar Production, 1993-2001

	1993-1994	1994-1995	1995-1996	1996-1997	1997-2001 Avg
Sugar beets					
Harv. area (1,000 lbs./a)	1,369	1,378	1,380	1,380	1,365
Yield (tons/a.)	20.59	20.74	20.89	21.04	21.48
Prod. (1,000 tons)	28,183	28,587	28,831	29,032	29,326
Sugarcane[1]					
Harv. area (1,000 a.)	855	861	867	873	864
Yield (tons/a)	36.04	36.14	36.24	36.34	36.64
Prod. (1,000 tons)	30,819	31,115	31,426	31,745	31,661

Source: FAPRI 1992 U.S. Agriculture Outlook, Food and Agriculture Policy Research Institute, Iowa State University and University of Missouri-Columbia, 1992, p. 67. Figures from 1989 to 1992 are excluded. *Note:* 1. Excludes sugarcane for seed.

★ 47 ★

Sugar Supply and Utilization, 1993-2001

	1993	1994	1995	1996	1997-2001 Avg
000 short tons, raw value					
Supply	13,046	13,104	13,165	13,202	13,338
Beginning stocks	3,403	3,423	3,439	3,456	3,489
Production	7,620	7,706	7,813	7,908	8,046
Imports	2,023	1,974	1,912	1,838	1,803
Utilization	9,623	9,664	9,709	9,735	9,834
Disappearance	9,009	9,050	9,095	9,121	9,220
Exports	614	614	614	614	614
Ending stocks	3,423	3,439	3,456	3,466	3,504
Cents per pound					
Prices (cents per pound)					
N.Y. spot raw sugar	21.75	21.75	21.75	21.75	21.75
Cane loan rate	18.00	18.00	18.00	18.00	18.00
Avg. refined retail	39.44	39.76	40.11	40.55	42.17

Source: FAPRI 1992 U.S. Agriculture Outlook, Food and Agriculture Policy Research Institute, Iowa State University and University of Missouri-Columbia, 1992, p. 67. Figures from 1989 to 1992 are excluded.

★ 48 ★

Turkeys, 1993-2001

	1993	1994	1995	1996	1997-2001 Avg
Supply (million pounds)					
Beginning stocks	344	378	388	425	514
Production	5,160	5,333	5,494	5,660	6,221
Change (%)	3.0	3.4	3.0	3.0	
Total	5,504	5,711	5,881	6,085	6,735
Change (%)	3.5	3.8	3.0	3.5	
Disappearance (million pounds)					
Domestic use	5,034	5,232	5,365	5,543	6,091
Change (%)	3.1	3.9	2.5	3.3	
Exports	92	92	92	92	92
Change (%)	0.0	0.0	0.0	0.0	
Total	5,126	5,324	5,457	5,635	6,183
Change (%)	3.0	3.9	2.5	3.3	
Ending stocks	378	388	425	450	552
Change (%)	9.9	2.58	9.6	5.9	
Per capita consumption (pounds)	19.44	20.02	20.37	20.88	22.44
Change (%)	2.1	3.0	1.7	2.5	
Prices (cents per pound)					
Wholesale price	61.71	64.46	65.87	62.34	66.45
Change (%)	5.0	4.4	2.2	-5.4	
Net returns	-1.03	1.31	2.08	-2.26	2.97

Source: FAPRI 1992 U.S. Agriculture Outlook, Food and Agriculture Policy Research Institute, Iowa State University and University of Missouri-Columbia, 1992, p. 76. Figures from 1989 to 1992 are excluded.

★ 49 ★

Wheat-Related Variables, 1993-2000

Item	Unit	Crop years							
		1993	1994	1995	1996	1997	1998	1999	2000
Production	Mil Bu	2614	2676	2744	2840	2931	3123	3187	3228
Utilization for food	Mil Bu	826	846	866	887	909	930	952	975
Fed to livestock	Mil Bu	262	322	324	358	343	378	400	367
Exports	Mil Bu	1298	1363	1455	1560	1701	1777	1822	1863

[Continued]

★ 49 ★

Wheat-Related Variables, 1993-2000
[Continued]

Item	Unit	Crop years							
		1993	1994	1995	1996	1997	1998	1999	2000
Ending stock	Mil Bu	710	797	834	804	715	678	614	558
Ending stocks/utilization	Ratio	0.285	0.302	0.303	0.275	0.233	0.211	0.186	0.168
Loan rate	$/Bu	2.45	2.34	2.30	2.23	2.38	2.43	2.49	2.60
Target price	$/Bu	4.00	4.00	4.00	4.00	4.00	4.00	4.00	4.00
Farm price	$/Bu	3.45	3.25	3.20	3.21	3.62	3.81	4.03	4.34
Gross margin over variable costs									
Participants[1]									
Nominal	$/A	83	77	76	75	77	80	81	92
1982-84 $	$/A	58	51	49	46	45	45	44	48
Nonparticipants[1]									
Nominal	$/A	67	58	55	54	69	74	81	92
1982-84 $	$/A	46	39	36	33	41	42	44	48

Source: National-International Agricultural Outlook to the Year 2000, Special Report 42, December, 1992, p. 16. Michigan State University Agricultural Experiment Station, East Lansing, Michigan. Figures from 1990 to 1992 are excluded. *Note:* 1. Wheat program.

★ 50 ★

Wheat, 1993-2001

	1993-1994	1994-1995	1995-1996	1996-1997	1997-2001 Avg
Percent					
Program					
ARP rate	5	5	5	5	5
PLD rate	0	0	0	0	0
NFA rate	15	15	15	15	15
Participation rate	81.4	88.2	87.0	81.7	76.2
Million acres					
Area					
Base area	78.7	78.4	78.0	78.6	86.2
ARP/PLD/0-92	7.7	9.2	9.2	8.4	9.8
CRP idled	11.0	11.3	11.7	11.1	3.5
Net flexed area	-0.5	-1.6	-1.4	-1.1	0.1
Payment planted	44.0	46.8	45.8	43.4	43.0
Planted area	74.6	72.1	71.9	73.2	79.2
Harvested area	64.0	61.4	61.1	62.4	67.2
Bushels per acre					
Yield					
Actual	38.0	38.3	38.6	39.0	39.3
Program	34.1	34.1	34.1	34.1	34.1

[Continued]

★ 50 ★

Wheat, 1993-2001
[Continued]

	1993-1994	1994-1995	1995-1996	1996-1997	1997-2001 Avg
Million bushels					
Supply	3,125	3,174	3,120	3,124	3,350
Beginning stocks	651	785	722	654	668
Production	2,435	2,349	2,359	2,431	2,643
Imports	40	40	40	40	40
Domestic use	1,241	1,263	1,261	1,260	1,278
Feed, residual	331	344	332	318	305
Seed	94	95	97	102	108
Food, other	815	824	833	841	865
Exports	1,100	1,190	1,205	1,235	1,400
Total use	2,340	2,453	2,466	2,495	2,678
Ending stocks	785	722	654	629	672
FOR, special program	25	0	0	0	0
CCC inventory	150	150	150	150	150
9-month loan	138	112	62	46	53
'Free' stocks	472	459	443	433	469
Dollars					
Price and returns					
Farm price/bu.	2.78	2.81	3.06	3.23	3.30
Loan rate/bu.	2.41	2.29	2.17	2.17	2.26
Target price/bu.	4.00	4.00	4.00	4.00	4.00
FOB Gulf price/mt	126.02	127.22	137.76	145.13	148.13
Variable expenses/a.	58.87	61.22	63.82	66.81	74.60
Partic. returns/a.	82.87	79.29	80.07	79.98	74.41
Nonpartic. returns/a.	50.86	50.19	58.02	62.82	58.95

Source: FAPRI 1992 U.S. Agriculture Outlook, Food and Agriculture Policy Research Institute, Iowa State University and University of Missouri-Columbia, 1992, p. 61. Figures from 1989 to 1992 are excluded.

Trade

★ 51 ★

Agricultural Trade Goals, 1995 and 2000 - I

This table shows assumptions underlying the projections in the following statistical table.

USDA analysts made the following specific assumptions for each category of agricultural exports through the year 2000:

Grain and feed	Export goals for grain and feed assume expansion in competitive production and exportable supplies,as well as steady growth in import demand, based on rising per capita consumption levels. USDA assumes there will be no major changes in U.S. policies or the status of credit and hard currency supply among less developed countries (LDCs), and no major international economic shocks (e.g. OPEC limits). Values are based on goal prices in current dollars, assuming normal rates of inflation and no domestic economic shocks to the U.S. grain/livestock markets.
Oilseeds and products	Oilseed and product export goals assume that in the long run assumption equals production and stock levels are constant. The United States will remain a residual supplier. Growth in U.S. exports will be a result of expanded consumption as opposed to reduction in competitor's exports. Future U.S. market share was forecast as equal to the 3-year average, derived from the most recent 5 years, after excluding high and low years. Export unit value was derived in the same manner.
Leaf tobacco	The United States currently maintains a 16-percent market share of world leaf exports. If the U.S. maintains this market share, U.S. leaf exports could increased about 1 percent annually in present value terms and 0.04 percent in volume through fiscal year 2000. This trend is supported by an expected 2-percent increase in total world leaf consumption, particularly in China, and a slight improvement in per capita consumption. The increase noted in world leaf consumption is supported by an expected 3-percent annual growth in world per capita GNP through fiscal year 2000. Moreover, given the growing competition abroad between U.S. cigarettes and foreign brands, increased foreign imports of quality U.S. leaf are expected for manufacturing domestic cigarettes to counter U.S. brand sales.
Tobacco products	U.S. cigarette exports account for over 90 percent of total manufactured tobacco product exports. By fiscal year 1995, this portion may reach 95 percent, and by year 2000, nearly 97 percent of U.S. manufactured tobacco exports could be in the form of cigarettes.

U.S. cigarette exports currently account for nearly 23 percent

---

[Continued]

★ 51 ★

Agricultural Trade Goals, 1995 and 2000 - I
[Continued]

of the world's cigarette trade. This market share is expected to reach nearly 40 percent by the year 2000. Given this trend, foreign sales of U.S. cigarettes are expected to improve 8 percent annually in present value terms and 11 percent in volume through year 2000.

The anticipated rise in U.S. cigarette exports is supported by an expected 3-percent annual growth in world GNP. In addition, improvements in world per capita consumption, particularly in China, and continued strength in U.S. cigarette sales to Asia, are expected to fuel U.S. cigarette exports.

Cotton linters

U.S. cotton exports are forecast to improve nearly 2 percent annually in volume and 1.2 percent in value through fiscal year 2000. The U.S. share of the world market is expected to reach 31 percent in 1990, but may go as high as 35 percent if world supplies remain tight.

Per capita consumption of cotton in the world is expected to improve through the year 2000 as a growing world GNP drives an increase in the demand for cotton over synthetic fibers. Furthermore, since the demand for cotton is fairly inelastic, world consumption of cotton is expected to grow as world population increases. Both of the above factors should advance U.S. cotton exports in the years to come.

Planting seeds

Over the last 20 years, U.S. planting seed exports have enjoyed excellent growth. By fiscal year 2000, the annual value of U.S. seed exports should reach nearly $635 million in present value terms, with the export volume increasing to 400,000 MT. So far in the 1980's, U.S. seed exports have increased a total of 28 percent. However, this trend is not expected to be maintained due to a variety of factors, including unpredictable weather patterns which cause enormous fluctuations in import requirements of many countries, and their desire and ability to become more self-sufficient.

Moreover, planting seeds have some unique attributes which make forecasting more difficult than for most commodities. Generally, consumption estimates can be made based on human and livestock demographics from which production and export forecasts can be made. However, in the case of planting seeds, individual commodity production forecasts are needed (but not available) to estimate consumption, and only then can seed production and export forecast be made. Furthermore, an aggregate planting seed estimate contains 63 separate kinds of seed plus three additional basket categories which lump the

[Continued]

★ 51 ★

Agricultural Trade Goals, 1995 and 2000 - I
[Continued]

seed of the countless other varieties marketed. Planting seeds also range in size and weight which can change from year to year thus adding to the complexity of forecasting volume and exports.

Solid wood products

Based on the following assumptions, the growth in export value of U.S. solid wood products between now and 2000 is projected to slightly exceed U.S. inflation which is assumed to average 3%. At least to the turn of the century, the use of tropical hardwood log bans and export quotas are expected to be more widely applied and/or more strictly enforced. The Philippines, Taiwan and Indonesia have either banned or severely restricted exports of logs. Recently, Taiwan and Thailand have banned logging altogether; while the Philippines has announced an export ban on rough lumber, in addition to its log ban. Malaysia has banned log exports from the mainland and is about to place prohibitive export taxes on rough lumber. In the United States, it is assumed that there will be no change in the current policy of prohibiting log exports from western Federal lands and that no other log bans will be enacted.

Tropical hardwood plywood production will remain relatively stable, increasing 1-3 percent per year as plants in Southeast Asia become more efficient and operate at a higher capacity. the EC plywood quota will remain at 650,000 cubic meters for the first 5 years and increase to 700,000 cubic meters the last 5 years.

Although there is increasingly world-wide pressure to restrict or ban imports of tropical wood products from "nonsustainable" forests, particularly in EC countries, no impact on supplies of tropical hardwood products is expected in the foreseeable future. More time, effort and funds will instead de devoted to better management and utilization of existing forests.

Horticultural and tropical products

Official trade figures supplied by the Bureau of the Census, Department of Commerce, significantly understate U.S. horticultural shipments to Canada, our leading export market.

FAS estimates that only 50 percent of exports to Canada are captured by Commerce. Commerce reportedly is making progress in correcting this problem. FAS has not factored this trade, uncounted by Commerce, into the forecasts. Once Commerce corrects this data collection deficiency, a surge in our export figures will take place. This increase will be distributed fairly evenly between fresh and processed fruits and vegetables.

[Continued]

★ 51 ★

Agricultural Trade Goals, 1995 and 2000 - I
[Continued]

Dairy, livestock and poultry	The dominant dairy, livestock and poultry export commodity group remains red meat, primarily beef and veal. Red meat exports are expected to grow by 38 percent over the ten year period 1991-2000. U.S. exports to Japan are expected to increase after a liberalization in 1991, but at a reduced rate compared to 1988 and 1989 exports. South Korea is also expected to liberalize its beef import market which will help boost U.S. beef exports into the 21st century.

U.S. tallow and grease, and hides and skins exports will remain strong over the next ten years, as the United States is expected to remain the world's largest surplus producer of these products. World demand for tallow and grease, and hides and skins, is expected to increase steadily over the 1991-2000 period facilitating increases in U.S. exports.

U.S. poultry meat exports are expected to grow by about one third over the ten year period 1991-2000 assuming that markets in the Far East for chicken parts continue to increase. U.S. exports of nonfat dry milk and cheese are expected to increase over the 1991-2000 period compared to the low level in 1989, while butter exports are expected to decline. U.S. dairy exports will depend heavily on Commodity Credit Corporation (CCC) stock levels and U.S. and EC dairy policies.

High value products	The basis for the estimates in the next table were analysis of a high-value/processed food subset of U.S. export data. This approach minimized duplication of forecasts emanating from other commodity program areas. In the process of assuring a minimum amount of possible duplication, we have revised the base year figures associated with last year's report; hence, comparisons with any trends associated with the October 1989 report will be misleading.

Exports of a select group of consumer-oriented high value products have grown substantially over the past two decades. Their total value stood at $2.2 billion during the base year of 1987; having grown from $185 million since 1962, the first year for which historical comparisons are available. Particularly noteworthy growth areas have included prepared breakfast foods; breads, biscuits and cakes; edible offal and dried meats; frozen vegetables; chocolate and products; non-alcoholic beverages; cider; beer, ale, porter and stout; and essential oils.

Source: U.S. Agricultural Trade Goals and Strategy Report, 1991, p. 1-9.

★ 52 ★

Agricultural Trade Goals, 1995 and 2000 - II

[Numbers in million metric tons (mmt) and billion dollars]

	1995		2000	
	Volume	Value	Volume	Value
Grains and feed, total[1]	121.2	17.5	139.7	20.4
Wheat and flour	41.0	6.5	46.0	7.5
Coarse grains	69.0	8.0	80.0	9.2
Rice	3.2	1.0	3.7	1.2
Other	8.0	2.0	10.0	2.5
Selected oilseeds and products	36.0	8.4	43.2	10.0
Soybeans	25.2	5.4	30.2	6.3
Soybean meal	8.4	1.6	9.9	1.9
Soybean oil	1.0	0.6	1.2	0.7
Sunflowerseed	0.3	0.2	0.5	0.3
Sunflowerseed oil	0.3	0.2	0.4	0.3
Cottonseed oil	0.3	0.1	0.4	0.2
Peanuts	0.5	0.3	0.6	0.3
Tobacco, total	[2]	4.9	[2]	6.9
Unmanufactured	0.2	1.3	0.2	1.3
Cigarettes (bil pieces)	181.2	3.6	275.3	5.6
Cotton and linters (mil bales)	8.6	2.7	9.3	2.9
Planting seeds	0.3	0.5	0.4	0.6
Solid wood products[3]	[2]	6.1	[2]	8.6
Selected horticultural products[4]	5.7	7.0	6.5	8.9
Fresh/processed fruit and juices	2.5	2.9	2.9	3.8
Fresh/processed vegetables	1.5	1.4	1.7	1.8
Tree nuts	0.3	1.0	0.3	1.3
Wine and malt beverages	[2]	0.3	[2]	0.4
Sugar and tropical products	1.1	1.4	1.2	1.6
Selected livestock products, total	[2]	4.9	[2]	5.2
Live animals (1,000 hd)	425.0	0.1	420.0	0.1
Red meat (1,000 cwe)[5]	0.7	2.7	0.8	3.2
Hides and skins (1,000)	0.9	1.7	0.8	1.5
Animal fats	1.4	0.4	1.4	0.4
Selected dairy products, total	350.0	0.6	380.0	0.6
Butter (1,000 mt)	25.0	[6]	30.0	0.1
Cheese (1,000 mt)	25.0	[6]	30.0	0.1
Nonfat dry milk (1,000 mt)	300.0	0.6	320.0	0.6
Poultry meat (1,000 mt)	550.0	0.6	580.0	0.6

[Continued]

★ 52 ★

Agricultural Trade Goals, 1995 and 2000 - II
[Continued]

	1995		2000	
	Volume	Value	Volume	Value
Selected high value products, total	[2]	3.2	[2]	3.6
Grand total	[2]	56.4	[2]	68.3

Source: U.S. Agricultural Trade Goals and Strategy Report, 1991, p. 14-18. *Notes:* 1. Includes pulses, feed ingredients and fodders. Also, because of rounding, the totals of some categories may differ from the sums of the commodities listed. 2. Volume totals are not meaningful. 3. Trade goals include wood products, which are not included in published U.S. Department of Agriculture export forecasts. 4. Excludes nursery products, vinegar, juice, and other beverages. 5. CWE = Carcass Weight Equivalent. 6. Less than $50 million.

★ 53 ★

Dairy-Product Exports, 1993-2001
[Numbers in thousands of metric tons]

	1993	1994	1995	1996	1997-2001 Avg
Butter					
Net exporters					
Australia	59	59	58	57	55
New Zealand	218	223	231	237	247
European Community	266	247	237	235	237
Other Europe	37	36	36	35	32
United States	88	86	77	68	59
Net importers					
Japan	17	19	20	21	22
Former USSR	314	298	282	273	254
Rest of World/residual	338	335	336	338	355
Cheese					
Net exporters					
Australia	32	34	33	31	25
New Zealand	104	114	123	127	135
European Community	345	328	324	333	375
Other Europe	94	95	95	95	92
Net importers					
Japan	122	127	131	135	148
United States	126	128	131	134	143
Former USSR	20	20	20	20	20
Rest of World/residual	307	296	294	297	316

[Continued]

★ 53 ★

Dairy-Product Exports, 1993-2001
[Continued]

	1993	1994	1995	1996	1997-2001 Avg
Nonfat dry milk					
Net exporters					
Australia	109	109	108	107	104
New Zealand	163	167	172	176	181
European Community	453	435	427	424	418
Other Europe	67	67	66	65	62
United States	65	56	44	33	19
Net importers					
Japan	107	111	112	113	110
Former USSR	0	0	0	0	0
Rest of world/residual	750	723	705	691	674

Source: FAPRI 1992 U.S. Agricultural Outlook, Food and Agriculture Policy Research Institute, Iowa State University and University of Missouri-Columbia, 1992, p. 43. Figures from 1989 to 1992 are excluded.

★ 54 ★

Export Quantity, 1993-2001

	1,000 Metric tons, fiscal year				
	1993	1994	1995	1996	97-2001 Avg.
Total	128,574	134,429	138,789	141,325	156,433
Animals, animal products	2,958	3,000	3,075	3,222	3,531
Grains, and feed	91,283	96,524	100,007	101,865	113,970
Wheat and flour	27,459	30,273	32,066	32,618	36,738
Rice	2,348	2,187	2,250	2,284	2,419
Feed grains and products	47,552	49,465	50,426	51,077	57,212
Other grains and feeds	13,924	14,599	15,265	15,887	17,601
Oilseeds and products	26,698	26,856	27,306	27,615	29,131
Cotton (excluding Linters)	1,556	1,579	1,649	1,655	1,818
Other products	6,079	6,470	6,751	6,968	7,983

Source: FAPRI 1992 U.S. Agricultural Outlook, Food and Agricultural Policy Research Institute, Iowa State University and University of Missouri-Columbia, 1992, p. 89. Figures from 1989 to 1992 are excluded.

★ 55 ★

Feed-Grain Exports, 1993-2001

	93/94	94/95	95/96	96/97	97/2001
		(000 metric tons)			
Net exporters					
Total non-U.S.	25,269	26,140	26,861	27,160	27,389
United State	47,810	48,825	49,345	50,877	57,592
(Trade share)	65.4%	65.1%	64.8%	65.2%	67.7%
Total	73,079	74,965	76,206	78,037	84,981
		(Dollars per metric ton)			
U.S. corn price					
(FOB Gulf)	102.66	104.20	108.01	105.91	102.63

Source: FAPRI 1992 U.S. Agricultural Outlook, Food and Agricultural Policy Research Institute, Iowa State University and University of Missouri-Columbia, 1992, p. 28. Figures from 1989 to 1992 are excluded.

★ 56 ★

Grain and Oilseed Exports, 1992-2001

[Numbers in millions of metric tons]

	Feed grains	Food grains	Soybean sector
1992-1993	47	30	25
1993-1994	49	33	25
1994-1995	50.5	36	25.5
1995-1996	51	36.5	25.7
1996-1997	53	37	26
1997-2001	59	42	27.5

Source: FAPRI 1992 U.S. Agriculture Outlook, Food and Agricultural Policy Research Institute, Iowa State University and University of Missouri-Columbia, 1992, p. 17. Figures from 1980 to 1991 are excluded. Magnitudes estimated from published chart.

★ 57 ★

Meat Exports, 1992-2001

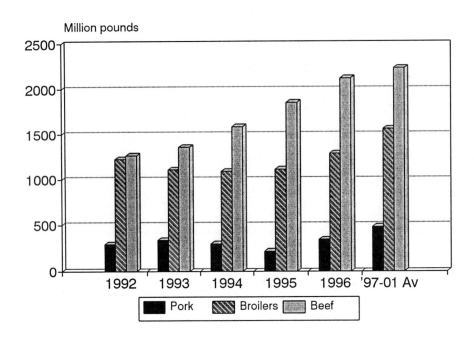

[Numbers in millions of pounds]

	Beef	Broilers	Pork
1992	1,266	1,225	291
1993	1,360	1,112	340
1994	1,587	1,095	297
1995	1,855	1,116	220
1996	2,118	1,293	343
1997-2001	2,228	1,561	484

Source: FAPRI 1992 U.S. Agriculture Outlook, Food and Agricultural Policy Research Institute, Iowa State University and University of Missouri-Columbia, 1992, p. 17. Figures from 1980 to 1991 are excluded. Magnitudes estimated from published chart.

★ 58 ★

Meat Exports, 1993-2001

	1993	1994	1995	1996	1997-2001 Avg
		1,000 metric tons			
Beef and veal					
Net exporters					
Argentina	371	362	343	334	321

[Continued]

★ 58 ★

Meat Exports, 1993-2001
[Continued]

	1993	1994	1995	1996	1997-2001 Avg
Australia	1,083	1,135	1,121	1,096	1,094
Brazil	212	190	161	145	129
Eastern Europe	23	22	18	24	79
European Community	653	510	578	566	517
New Zealand	409	408	416	423	428
Net importers					
Japan	658	703	768	821	923
United States	431	328	206	87	37
Former USSR	274	328	319	344	363
Rest of World/residual	1,388	1,369	1,345	1,337	1,245
Pork					
Net exporters					
Canada	296	281	321	332	335
China	230	230	230	230	230
Eastern Europe	351	401	444	384	340
European Community	565	515	472	462	496
Taiwan	216	227	239	238	237
Net importers					
Japan	615	643	670	706	808
United States	179	218	289	176	48
Former USSR	417	383	366	371	374
Rest of World/residual	448	409	381	394	406
Broiler meat					
Net exporters					
Brazil	380	403	423	427	474
Eastern Europe	59	62	65	60	65
European Community	330	341	344	349	335
Thailand	173	184	195	203	236
United States	505	497	506	586	708
Net importers					
Japan	351	391	432	493	613
Former USSR	168	158	147	153	186
Rest of world/residual	926	938	954	980	1,019

Dollars per hundredweight

	1993	1994	1995	1996	1997-2001 Avg
U.S. market price					
Omaha steers	72.22	70.94	68.90	69.82	81.78

[Continued]

★ 58 ★

Meat Exports, 1993-2001
[Continued]

	1993	1994	1995	1996	1997-2001 Avg
Barrows and gilts	44.98	52.04	56.71	51.67	53.88
12-city broilers	52.60	53.55	54.52	52.95	55.73

Source: FAPRI 1992 U.S. Agricultural Outlook, Food and Agriculture Policy Research Institute, Iowa State University and University of Missouri-Columbia, 1992, p. 41. Figures from 1989 to 1992 are excluded.

★ 59 ★

Rice Exports, 1993-2001

	93/94	94/95	95/96	96/97	97/2001
	1,000 metric tons				
Total non-U.S.	8,609	8,902	9,207	9,517	10,449
United States	1,910	1,964	1,996	1,988	2,142
(Trade share)	18.2%	18.1%	17.8%	17.3%	17.0%
Total	10,519	10,866	11,203	11,505	12,590

Source: FAPRI 1992 U.S. Agricultural Outlook, Food and Agricultural Policy Research Institute, Iowa State University and University of Missouri-Columbia, 1992, p. 39. Figures from 1989 to 1992 are excluded.

★ 60 ★

Soybean Exports, 1993-2001

	93/94	94/95	95/96	96/97	97/2001
	(000 metric tons)				
Net exporters					
Total non-U.S.	7,793	7,840	7,903	8,028	8,091
United States	18,868	19,272	19,569	19,767	21,047
(Trade share)	70.8%	71.1%	71.2%	71.1%	72.2%
Total	26,661	27,112	27,472	27,795	29,138

[Continued]

★ 60 ★

Soybean Exports, 1993-2001
[Continued]

	93/94	94/95	95/96	96/97	97/2001
(Dollars per metric ton)					
U.S. export price (FOB Gulf)	225.79	226.14	236.31	237.20	222.29

Source: FAPRI 1992 U.S. Agricultural Outlook, Food and Agricultural Policy Research Institute, Iowa State University and University of Missouri-Columbia, 1992, p. 31. Figures from 1989 to 1992 are excluded.

★ 61 ★

Soybean-Meal Exports, 1993-2001

	93/94	94/95	95/96	96/97	97/2001
(000 metric tons)					
Net exporters					
Total non-U.S.	15,610	15,955	16,286	16,641	17,738
United States	5,597	5,592	5,578	5,709	5,942
(Trade share)	26.4%	26.0%	25.5%	25.5%	25.1%
Total	21,207	21,547	21,864	22,350	23,680
(Dollars per metric ton)					
U.S. market price (Decatur)	208.62	208.97	216.96	211.15	186.30

Source: FAPRI 1992 U.S. Agricultural Outlook, Food and Agricultural Policy Research Institute, Iowa State University and University of Missouri-Columbia, 1992, p. 33. Figures from 1989 to 1992 are excluded.

★ 62 ★

Soybean-Oil Exports, 1993-2001

	93/94	94/95	95/96	96/97	97/2001
(000 metric tons)					
Net exporters					
Total non-U.S.	2,395	2,453	2,508	2,561	2,709
United States	430	450	456	479	534

[Continued]

★ 62 ★

Soybean-Oil Exports, 1993-2001
[Continued]

	93/94	94/95	95/96	96/97	97/2001
(Trade share)	15.2%	15.5%	15.4%	15.8%	16.4%
Total	2,825	2,903	2,964	3,040	3,243

(Dollars per metric ton)

U.S. market price (Decatur)	362.48	378.25	399.79	429.81	488.90

Source: FAPRI 1992 U.S. Agricultural Outlook, Food and Agricultural Policy Research Institute, Iowa State University and University of Missouri-Columbia, 1992, p. 35. Figures from 1989 to 1992 are excluded.

★ 63 ★

Value of Exports, 1993-2001

	(Million dollars, fiscal year)				
	1993	1994	1995	1996	97-2001 Avg.
Total	40,232	41,859	43,867	46,426	54,067
Animals, animal products	7,345	7,730	8,129	8,676	10,587
Meat, meat products	3,135	3,533	3,873	4,154	5,202
Poultry, poultry products	977	973	1,000	1,148	1,562
Dairy products	563	515	505	484	499
Hides and skins	1,515	1,523	1,526	1,607	1,843
Other animal products	1,155	1,185	1,225	1,283	1,481
Grains and feeds	12,390	12,916	13,557	14,447	16,605
Wheat and flour	3,686	3,636	3,894	4,289	5,147
Rice	689	729	759	782	947
Feed grains and products	5,189	5,550	5,735	6,013	6,488
Corn	4,300	4,655	4,800	5,030	5,348
Other feed grains	889	896	935	983	1,140
Other grains and feeds	2,826	3,001	3,170	3,363	4,024
Oilseeds and products	7,051	6,999	7,178	7,565	7,921
Soybeans	4,245	4,183	4,280	4,543	4,504
Other oilseeds, products	2,806	2,816	2,898	3,021	3,418
Cotton (excluding Linters)	2,356	2,344	2,445	2,500	2,925
Other products	11,090	11,870	12,558	13,238	16,029

Source: FAPRI 1992 U.S. Agricultural Outlook, Food and Agricultural Policy Research Institute, Iowa State University and University of Missouri-Columbia, 1992, p. 89. Figures from 1989 to 1992 are excluded.

★ 64 ★

Wheat Exports, 1993-2001

	93/94	94/95	95/96	96/97	97/2001
Million metric tons					
Total non-U.S.	60.53	60.73	62.13	63.56	67.06
United States	28.84	31.30	31.70	32.51	37.02
(Trade share)	32.3%	34.0%	33.8%	33.8%	35.5%
Total	89.36	92.03	93.83	96.07	104.08
Dollars per metric ton					
U.S. export (FOB Gulf)	126.02	127.22	137.76	145.13	148.13

Source: FAPRI 1992 U.S. Agricultural Outlook, Food and Agricultural Policy Research Institute, Iowa State University and University of Missouri-Columbia, 1992, p. 37. Figures from 1989 to 1992 are excluded.

Chapter 2
BUSINESS, BANKING, FINANCE, AND ECONOMICS

Business: The Automobile Industry

★ 65 ★

Exports of U.S. Automobiles Manufactured in Mexico, 1988-2000

Includes cars and light trucks.

[Numbers in millions of units]

1988	.23
1989	.25
1990	.31
1991	.45
1995	.89
2000	1.55

Source: "Detroit South," Stephen Baker, *Business Week*, No. 3256, March 16, 1992, p. 99. Primary sources: Mexican Automobile Industry Assn., National Autoparts Industry Assn., *BW*. *Note:* Magnitudes estimated from published chart.

★ 66 ★

Percent Change in Sales Growth of U.S. Automobiles Manufactured in Mexico, 1985-2000

"Mexico's car market is expected to grow far faster in the 1990s than northern markets, and that growth, say Big Three executives, should defuse criticism of their southern strategy. Mexico's production for its home market, they expect, will gobble up billions of dollars' worth of U.S. parts, which should eventually translate into more, not fewer, Rust Belt jobs."

U.S.	0.7
Canada	-1.0
Mexico	435.7

Source: "Detroit South," Stephen Baker, *Business Week*, No. 3256, March 16, 1992, p. 99. Primary sources: Mexican Automobile industry Association, National Autoparts Industry Association, *BW*.

★ 67 ★

Percentage of U.S. Passenger Car Market Held by General Motors, Ford, and Chrysler, 1960-2000

1960	92.0
1990	70.0
2000	57.0

Source: "Issues of the '90s," *Across the Board* XXVIII, No. 10, October, 1991, p. 20.

★ 68 ★

U.S. Automobile Production in Mexico, 1988-2000

Includes cars and light trucks.

[Numbers in millions of units]

1988	0.60
1989	0.70
1990	0.85
1991	1.10

[Continued]

★ 68 ★

U.S. Automobile Production in Mexico, 1988-2000
[Continued]

1995[1]	1.90
2000[1]	3.10

Source: "Detroit South," Stephen Baker, *Business Week*, No. 3256, March 16, 1992, p. 99. Primary sources: Mexican Automobile Industry Assn., National Autoparts Industry Assn., *BW*. Magnitudes estimated from published chart. *Note:* 1. Projections.

★ 69 ★

U.S. Share of European Car Market, 1990 and 2000

	1990	2000
Japanese (total)	12.6	19.5
Imported	12.0	10.5
Made in Europe	0.6	9.0
European	64.6	55.0
American	22.8	25.5

Source: "Getting Tough with the Japanese," Carla Rapoport, *Fortune* 125, No. 8, April 20, 1992, p. 149. Primary source: Euromotor Reports (1990), Industry Estimates (2000).

Business: The Communications Industry

★ 70 ★

Advertising Sales Forecast for Cable Television, 1991-1995
[Numbers in millions of dollars]

Year	Sales total	Percent increase	Network sales	Percent increase	Local sales	Percent increase
1991	1,970	10.1	1,500	9.1	470	13.3
1992	2,200	11.7	1,655	10.3	545	16.0
1993	2,500	13.6	1,855	12.1	645	18.3
1994	2,870	14.8	2,110	13.7	760	17.8
1995	3,180	10.8	2,300	9.0	880	15.8

Source: "Advertising Sales Forecast," *Cablevision* 16, No. 12, December 2, 1991, p. 41. Primary source: Veronis, Suhler & Associates/Wilkovsky Gruen Associates.

★ 71 ★

AM and FM Digital Fiber Sales in Cable TV, 1991-1999

"Actual system prices for AM gear (as opposed to list prices) will fall aggressively in the coming years. Our sales forecast assumes that transmitter output will increasingly be split between more than one receiver as the decade progresses."

	1991	1992	1993	1994	1995	1996	1997	1998	1999
Number of AM transmitters sold	1,600[1]	2,338[1]	3,218[1]	3,429[1]	6,262[2]	8,211[2]	6,120[3]	8,161[3]	11,292[3]
Number of AM receivers sold	2,000	2,922	4,022	5,196	7,544	9,893	12,241	14,589	16,937
Installed base of AM receivers	2,750	5,672	9,694	14,890	22,434	32,327	44,560	59,157	76,094
Typical cost of a single AM link[5]	14,400	11,520	10,368	4,216	8,295	7,373	6,636	5,898	5,308
Number of FM 60-ch. links sold	25[4]	24	21	15	12	9	9	6	6
Number of digital 60-ch. links sold	5	6	9	15	18	21	21	24	24
Cost-per-channel FM or digital with scrambling[3]	4,000	3,800	3,610	3,400	3,200	3,100	2,900	2,800	2,700
Number of FM or digital transmit site	10	10	10	10	10	10	10	10	10

Source: "Prices to Nosedive," Gary Kim, *Cablevision* 15, No. 16, February 11, 1991, p. 38. *Notes:* 1. Assumes 20% of transmitters have split output to two sites. 2. Assumes 33% of transmitters have split output to two sites. 3. Assumes 50% of transmitters have split output to three sites. 4. Assumes 89% of sales in 1991; 80% in 1992; 70% in 1993; 50% in 1994; 40% in 1995. 5. Cost in U.S. dollars.

★ 72 ★

Cable Network Revenue Forecast, 1992-1995

[Numbers in millions of dollars]

Year	Basic net system charges	Basic net ad revenue	Total basic revenue	Percent increase	Pay net system charges	Percent increase
1992	910	1,655	2,565	10.8	2,280	1.8
1993	1,015	1,855	2,870	11.9	2,330	2.2
1994	1,120	2,110	3,230	12.5	2,440	4.7
1995	1,230	2,300	3,530	9.3	2,495	2.3

Source: "Cable Network Revenue Forecast," *Cablevision* 16, No. 12, December 2, 1991, p. 41. Primary sources: Veronis, Suhler & Associates/Wilkovsky Gruen Associates. Figures from 1991 are excluded.

★ 73 ★

Cable Subscription Outlook, 1991-1995

[Number of households and subscribers in millions]

Year	Total TV homes	Homes passed	Basic subs	Basic percent of total TV homes	Pay subs	Pay units	Pay percent of total TV homes
1991	93.1	80.8	53.8	57.8	30.7	39.7	33.0
1992	94.4	82.3	55.4	58.7	31.9	40.0	33.8
1993	95.6	83.8	56.7	59.3	32.5	40.3	34.0
1994	96.8	85.4	58.2	60.1	33.3	41.1	34.4
1995	97.9	86.7	59.3	60.6	34.0	41.6	34.7

Source: "Cable Penetration Outlook," *Cablevision* 16, No. 12, December 2, 1991, p. 41. Primary sources: Veronis, Suhler & Associates/Wilkovsky Gruen Associates.

★ 74 ★

Cable Television Advertising Projections, 1991-2000

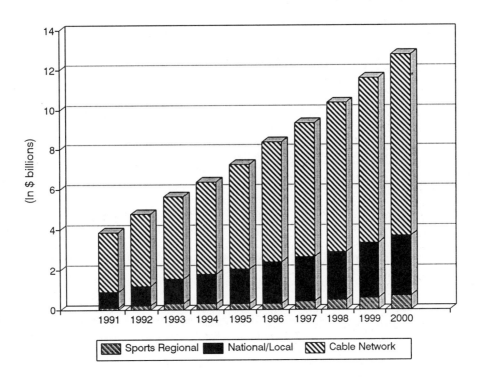

[Numbers in billions of dollars]

	1991	1992	1993	1994	1995	1996	1997	1998	1999	2000
Cable network	3.0	3.6	4.10	4.6	5.20	6.0	6.70	7.5	8.30	9.1
National/local	.8	1.0	1.25	1.5	1.75	2.1	2.25	2.4	2.75	3.0
Sports regional	.1	.2	.3	.3	.35	.4	.4	.5	.6	.7

Source: "The Next 10 Years," John Flinn, *Cablevision* 15, No. 23, May, 1991, p. 46A. Primary sources: CAB, with Paul Kagan Associates data. Magnitudes estimated from published chart.

★ 75 ★

Cellular/Personal Communications Network Market Forecast, 1996

[Numbers in billions of dollars]

Two-way PCN	3.2
One-way PCN	0.5
Dual-mode analog/digital	1.7
Analog	1.5
Digital	9.7

Source: "Cellular/Personal Communications Network Market Forecast for 1996," *Telephony* 222, No. 6, February 10, 1992, p. 14. Primary source: Frost & Sullivan, Inc.

★ 76 ★

Communications Industry Forecast, 1985-1995

"Study suggests broadcasting's current problems are mostly cyclical, not structural."

Industry segment	1985-90 compound annual growth (%)	1990 gross expenditures annual ($ million)	1990-95 compound growth (%)
Television broadcasting	5.2	25,490	6.0
TV networks	4.1	9,845	6.5
TV stations	6.0	15,645	5.8
Radio broadcasting	6.2	8,765	6.6
Radio networks	6.3	495	5.6
Radio stations	6.2	8,270	6.7
Cable television	13.2	15,115	8.2
Advertising	19.8	1,790	12.2
Subscriptions	12.4	13,325	7.6
Filmed entertainment	15.6	25,712	8.3
Box office	6.0	5,022	6.7
Home video	32.7	10,900	9.2
Television programs	9.4	8,640	7.8
Barter syndication	17.2	1,150	9.6
Total advertising	5.7	83,398	6.1
GNP	6.4	5,463,600	6.4

Source: "Renewed TV Network, Station Growth Ahead," *Broadcasting* 120, No. 25, June 24, 1991, p. 46. Primary sources: Veronis, Suhler and Associates, and Wilkofsky Gruen Associates.

★ 77 ★

Radio Spending for Advertisements, 1991-1995

[Numbers in percent]

1991	4.0
1992	6.5
1993	8.2
1994	7.8
1995	6.6
CAGR[1]	6.6

Source: "Radio Ad Revenue to Hit $12 Billion by 1995," *Broadcasting* 121, No. 17, October 21, 1991, p. 40. Primary source: Veronis, Suhler & Associates; Wilkofsky Gruen Associates. *Note:* 1. CAGR = Compound Annual Growth Rate.

★ 78 ★

Local and Spot Cable Ad Revenue Growth, 1984-1995

[Numbers in millions of dollars]

1984	98
1985	167
1986	195
1987	268
1988	374
1989	496
1990	635
1991	787
1992	953
1995	1,500

Source: "Local's Rapid Growth Curve," *Cablevision* 15, No. 28, April 8, 1991, p. 51. Primary source: Paul Kagan Associates, Inc. and CAB. figures for 1982 and 1983 are excluded.

★ 79 ★

Telecommunications Industry Revenues, 1978-1998

"The number of telephones operating in the United States increased more than 200 percent between 1960 and 1986. In spite of such growth, businesses hold a shrinking number of the total. In 1960, businesses held 28 percent of the phones in service. Today, only 26 percent of telephones are located in businesses."

[Numbers in millions of dollars]

	1978	1988	1998
Equipment	30.7	55.2	83.8
Services	61.4	141.4	244.7

Source: "Computers and Telecommunications," *Hospitals* 63, No. 22, November 20, 1989, p. 62. Primary source: CBEMA, 1989.

Business: The Computer Industry

★ 80 ★

Computer Industry Revenues, 1988-1998

"Since 1965, revenues from software and computer services have increased nearly 30,000 percent—or 28.1 percent annually compounded."

[Numbers in millions of dollars]

	1988	1998
Computer equipment	131.4	297.4
Processing services	26.8	64.3
Software products	19.9	68.9
Professional services	13.2	33.5

Source: "Computers and Telecommunications," *Hospitals* 63, No. 22, November 20, 1989, p. 62. Primary source: CBEMA, 1989.

★ 81 ★

Computer Induystry Sales, 1990 to 1994

[Numbers in billions of dollars]

	1990	1994
PCs	117.5	166.9
Minicomputers	75.0	105.0
Mainframes	30.0	35.0

Source: "Digital's Daring Comeback Plan," Stratford P. Sherman, *Fortune* 123, No. 1, January 14, 1991, p. 102. Primary source: International Data Corp.; Dataquest. Magnitudes estimated from published chart.

★ 82 ★

Laptop, Notebook, and Pocket Computer Sales, 1989-1994

[Numbers in millions of units]

U.S. market	1989	1990	1994
Laptop	967,000	1,100,000	1,900,000
Notebook	69,000	311,000	3,900,000
Hand-held	34,000	159,000	3,200,000

Source: "Where Sales Will Soar," Thayer C. Taylor, *Sales & Marketing Management* 143, No. 2, February, 1991, p. 56. Primary source: Dataquest and the Gartner Group.

★ 83 ★

Mobile Data Service Revenues, 1992-2000

Includes data over cellular networks; existing mobile data networks (Ram, Ardis); mobile satellite service; and specialized mobile radio.

[Numbers in millions of dollars]

1992	145
1994	303
1996	559
1998	715
2000	895

Source: "Mtorola Opens Ardis Protocols," Charles F. Mason, *Telephony* 222, No. 13, March 30, 1992, p. 8. Primary source: Datacom Research Co., Wilmette, Ill.

★ 84 ★

Percent of Personal Computers Sold to the Business Market by Type of Outlet, 1991 and 1995

	1991	1995
PC specialty stores	47.0	33.0
Superstores	2.0	20.0
Value-added resellers	13.0	15.0
Mass merchandisers	6.0	15.0
Mail order	13.0	8.0
Direct sales	16.0	5.0
Consumer electronic stores	1.0	3.0
Other	2.0	1.0

Source: "PC Purchases Not So Special," Christy Fisher, *Advertising Age* 62, No. 48, November 11, 1991, p. 5. Primary source: Dataquest.

★ 85 ★

Personal Computer Notebook Sales, 1990 and 1995

"The fastest growing segment of the portable computer market is notebooks."

	1990 mix	1995 mix
Transportables	200 million	90 million
Notebooks	800 million	4.7 billion

Source: "PC Notebook Sales to Surge," *Advertising Age* 62, No. 13, March 25, 1991, p. 1. Primary source: New Desktop Strategies Advisory Service.

★ 86 ★

Sales Force Automation Market Revenues, 1992-1997
[Numbers in millions of dollars]

	Software	Hardware	Total
1992	413	2,993	3,406
1993	659	3,937	4,596
1994	1,035	5,225	6,260
1995	1,536	6,836	8,372

[Continued]

★ 86 ★

Sales Force Automation Market Revenues, 1992-1997
[Continued]

	Software	Hardware	Total
1996	2,076	8,650	10,726
1997	2,527	10,445	12,972

Source: "SFA Revenues to Quadruple by 1997," Thayer C. Taylor, *Sales & Marketing Management* 144, No. 1, January, 1992, p. 73. Primary sources: *MIRC; Sales Automation Equipment Markets and End-User Strategies* and *Sales Automation Software Markets*.

★ 87 ★

Video Teleconferencing Revenues, 1990-1996

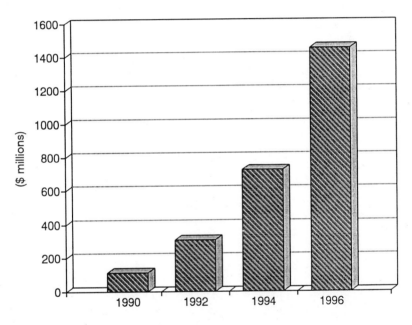

[Numbers in millions of dollars]

1990	113.3
1992	306.3
1994	723.2
1996	1,452

Source: "Videoconferencing Moves toward the Desktop," Dwight B. Davis, *Electronic Business* 16, No. 21, November 12990, p. 135. Primary source: Market Intelligence Research Corp.

Business: The Food Service Industry

★ 88 ★

Food Eaten at Home Versus Food Eaten Away From Home, 1970-2000

"In 1980, *Progressive Grocer*'s panel of supermarket executives predicted food-away-from-home would account for 50% of food spending by 1989. [The 1990] panel is making the same prediction again, but this time it's much more plausible."

[Numbers in percent of Food dollar]

	1970	1980	1988	2000
Food-at-home	76.0	71.0	67.0	50.0[1]
Food-away-from-home	24.0	29.0	33.0	50.0[1]

Source: "Supermarkets 2000: 45 'Insider' Predictions," Walter Heller, *Progressive Grocer* 69, No. 1, January, 1990, p. 28. Primary source: *Progressive Grocer Annual Reports. Note:* 1. Projection based on survey responses.

★ 89 ★

Food Service Industry Sales Summary, 1991-1996

Major market segments	1991 sales[1] ($ MM)	1991 purchases[2] ($ MM)	1991 vs. 1990 % sales growth		1996 sales[1] ($ MM)	1991-1996 % compound annual sales growth	
			Nominal	real		Nominal	real
Eating & drinking[3]	176,268	60,324	4.5	0.3	232,748	5.7	1.5
Eating places[3]	164,682	56,268	4.5	0.3	218,156	5.8	1.5
Limited menu	79,167	24,642	5.8	1.5	107,370	6.3	2.0
Full menu	77,875	28,814	3.2	-1.0	100,541	5.2	1.0
Retail market	11,974	4,421	6.1	1.8	15,921	6.0	1.7
Hotel/motel market	15,495	6,198	4.2	0.0	20,503	5.8	1.5
Leisure market	8,561	2,981	6.7	2.4	12,126	7.9	3.0
Business & industry	18,212	8,619	5.2	1.0	24,101	5.8	1.5
Health care market	11,580	5,790	4.1	0.9	13,548	3.2	1.0
Student market	16,450	7,765	3.5	0.5	20,116	4.1	1.1
Vending market	17,058	7,676	5.2	1.0	22,573	5.8	1.5
Airline market	4,675	2,338	7.3	3.0	6,987	8.4	4.0

Source: "Industry Report," Ralph D. Rush, *Restaurant Business* 90, No. 14, September 20, 1991, p. 74. *Notes:* 1. Sales estimates for Business & Industry, Health Care, Student, Vending, and Airline markets have been adjusted to reflect equivalent consumer expenditures. 2. Purchases include all food and nonalcoholic and alcoholic beverages. Alcohol beverage purchases have been excluded in Business & Industry, Health Care, Student, and Airline markets only. Student units were tabulated by number of school districts instead of number of schools as in previous years. 3. Full-menu and limited-menu restaurant sales are included in eating place sales. Eating place sales are included in eating and drinking place sales and should not be added with other major market segments to arrive at total market sales. Figures for 1990 are excluded.

★ 90 ★

Food Service Sales Real Growth Summary, 1990-1996

"The consumer price index for food-away-from-home is 4.7% for 1990 and 4.2% for 1991, except Primary/Secondary schools and Health Care where the rate is 2.3% and 2.0% respectively. Inflation for food-away-from-home is forecast to average 4.2% annually for the period 1991 through 1996 and 2.1% for health care and sales."

	1990 % real sales growth	1991 % real sales growth	1991-1996 % real compound annual growth rate
Total market	0.5	0.7	1.5
Commercial/contract/vending	0.4	0.6	1.6
Institutional/internal	1.3	0.7	0.7
Military	0.5	2.5	0.5
Major market segments			
Eating and drinking places	-0.1	0.3	1.5
Eating places	0.5	0.3	1.5
Limited menu	1.7	1.5	2.0
Full menu	-1.4	-1.0	1.0
Retail market	0.8	1.8	1.7
Hotel/motel market	0.5	0.0	1.0
Leisure market	3.0	2.4	3.0
Business & industry market	1.8	1.0	1.5
Health care market	1.3	0.9	1.0
Student market	0.5	0.5	1.1
Vending market	1.5	1.0	1.5
Airline market	5.0	3.0	4.0

Source: "Industry Report," Ralph D. Rush, *Restaurant Business* 90, No. 14, September 20, 1991, p. 75.

★ 91 ★

Share of Sales for Conventional Supermarkets vs. Superstores/Combos, 1979-2000

"Conventional stores' share of total grocery sales may continue to shrink, but many operators say these stores still have a place in the competitive arena."

	1979	1988	2000
Conventionals	83.2	50.1	30.0[1]
Superstores/combos	13.0	34.6	50.0[1]

Source: "Supermarkets 2000: 45 'Insider' Predictions," Walter Heller, *Progressive Grocer* 69, No. 1, January, 1990, p. 27. Primary source: *Progressive Grocer Annual Reports. Note:* 1. Projection based on survey responses.

★ 92 ★

Supermarket Sales, 1980-2000

Projections based on annual sales increases of 2%, 4%, and 6%. "If supermarket sales increase 6% a year—a rate just slightly above the gain posted in 1988—total volume will more than double by the year 2000."

[Numbers in billions of dollars]

	1980[1]	1988	2000
2 percent increase	157.0		304.9
4 percent increase			384.9
6 percent increase		240.4[2]	483.7

Source: "Supermarkets 2000: 45 'Insider' Predictions," Walter Heller, *Progressive Grocer* 69, No. 1, January, 1990, p. 25. Primary source: *Progressive Grocer Annual Reports. Notes:* 1. Represents actual sales. 2. Rate slightly below 6% in 1988.

★ 93 ★

Supermarket Share of Take-Out Market, 1989 and 1994

"Fast-food outlets, which command 67% of take-out sales in 1989, will see their share slashed 5% by 1994. Supermarkets, meanwhile, will gain 5%, capturing 17% of the market."

	1989	1994
Total ($)	57 billion	89 billion
Fast-food outlets	67.0	62.0
Supermarkets	12.0	17.0
C-stores	9.0	8.0
Other restaurants	12.0	13.0

Source: "Retails vs. Restaurants: The Food Service Fight Is on," Beth Lorenzini, *Restaurants & Institutions* 101, No. 20, 7 August, 1991, p. 43. Primary source: Find / SVP, New York.

Business: Various Industry Projections

★ 94 ★

Average Annual Percent Change in Capital Spending, 1950-2000

Measure of stock of industrial plant and equipment per worker. "As the labor force grows more slowly, companies will add plants and equipment to keep output and productivity rising."

1950-60	4.3
1960-70	3.6
1970-80	3.4
1980-90	1.8
1990-2000 Fortune estimates	3.5

Source: "A Coming Surge in Capital Spending," Joseph Spiers, *Fortune* 123, No. 8, April, 22, 1991, p. 114. Primary source: *Fortune* estimates. Magnitudes estimated from published chart.

★ 95 ★

Average Annual Percent Change in Shipments of Packaging Materials, 2000

Definition of categories: Aluminum—volume (pounds) of aluminum in packaging; Glass—volume (units) of glass containers; Paper—volume (real dollars) of paper in packaging; Plastics—volume (pounds) of plastics in packaging; Steel—volume (tons) of steel in containers, packaging and shipping material.

	Aluminum	Glass	Paper	Plastics	Steel
1985-1990	3.0	0.9	2.2	6.4	1.3
1990-1995	2.5	0.5	2.5	6.0	1.0
1995-2000	2.0	0.2	3.0	5.5	0.8

Source: "The Third Annual Packaging Forecast," Greg Erickson, ed., *Packaging* 37, No. 1, January, 1992, p. 38. Primary sources: Aluminum Assoc., U.S. Dept. of Commerce, Society of the Plastics Industry, and American Iron and Steel Institute.

★ 96 ★

Consumer Expenditures for the Publishing Industry by Type of Publication, 1985-1995

"Educational" includes elementary, high school, and college; "Professional & Reference" includes professional, university press, and subscription reference; "Pleasure" includes trade, religious, book club, and mass market paperback.

[Numbers in millions of dollars]

	1985	1990	1995
Educational	2990.6	4266.9	5914.7
Professional & reference	2558.2	3684.5	4925.9
Pleasure	6411.6	10339.8	15635.8

Source: "Domestic Consumer Expenditures," Book Industry Study Group, *Publishers Weekly* 238, No. 38, August 23, 1991, p. 12.

★ 97 ★

Consumer Expenditures for the Publishing Industry, 1985-1995 *

[Numbers in millions of dollars]

	Estimated expenditures		Projected expenditures
	1985	1990	1995
Trade (total)	3,660.0	6,497.0	10,548.8
Adult trade (total)	2,871.2	4,776.8	7,468.5
Hardbound	1,791.4	2,921.1	4,553.1
Paperbound	1,079.8	1,855.7	2,915.4
Juvenile trade (total)	788.8	1,721.0	3,080.3
Hardbound	572.1	1,234.4	2,215.2
Paperbound	216.7	486.6	865.1
Religious (total)	925.6	1,361.9	1,723.5
Hardbound	545.7	870.2	1,095.6
Paperbound	379.9	491.7	627.9
Professional (total)	2,043.4	2,956.8	4,018.5
Hardbound	1,452.2	2,119.3	2,883.6
Paperbound	591.2	837.5	1,134.98
Book Clubs (total)	581.5	704.7	910.6
Hardbound	454.5	560.1	714.4
Paperbound	127.0	144.6	196.2

[Continued]

★ 97 ★

Consumer Expenditures for the Publishing Industry, 1985-1995
[Continued]

	Estimated expenditures		Projected expenditures
	1985	1990	1995
Mail order publications	650.1	751.7	1,061.4
Mass market pprbk-rack size	1,244.5	1,775.4	2,452.9
University Press (total)	172.8	284.1	413.8
Hardbound	122.3	193.4	233.1
Paperbound	50.5	90.7	180.7
ELHI (Total)	1,415.3	1,947.9	2,582.8
Hardbound	820.9	1,072.8	1,443.7
Paperbound	594.4	875.1	1,139.1
College (total)	1,575.3	2,319.0	3,331.9
Hardbound	1,217.5	1,622.6	2,332.6
Paperbound	357.8	696.4	999.3
Subscription reference	342.0	443.6	493.6

Source: "Domestic Consumer Expenditures," Book Industry Study Group, *Publishers Weekly* 238, No. 38, August 23, 1991, p. 12.

★ 98 ★

Distribution of Institutions, 1990-2001

In business, the big get bigger, the small survive, and the middle-sized are squeezed out. (At Forecasting International, we somewhat ponderously call this the "bimodal distribution of institutions.") This trend appeared in the United States in the 1980s. It has now spread to Europe and will continue until virtually all of today's mid-sized corporations either have been absorbed by larger competitors or have been driven out of business.

1. Nine domestic U.S. airlines today control 80 percent of the market, leaving the smaller carriers with only 20 percent. By 2001 there will be only four major domestic carriers.

2. As of 1991, there are 20 major auto makers around the world with market shares ranging from 18.1 percent (GM) to 1.0 percent (BMW). By 2001, only five giant automobile firms will be left; production and assembly will be centered in the U.S., Korea, Italy, and Latin America.

[Continued]

★ 98 ★

Distribution of Institutions, 1990-2001
[Continued]

3. By 2000, there will be just three major corporations dominating the U.S. computer hardware industry: IBM, Digital, and Apple.

4. The 1990s will be the decade of "micro-segmentation" as more and more highly-specialized businesses and entrepreneurs search for even tinier markets.

5. The bimodal trend has hit almost all industries.

Source: "New U.S. Business Incorporations," from the book *CRYSTAL GLOBE: The Haves and Have-Nots of the New World Order,* by Marvin Cetron and Owen Davis, p. 358. Copyright (c) 1991. Reprinted with permission from St. Martin's Press, Inc., New York, N.Y.

★ 99 ★

Estimated Pet Food Market Share by Species, 1990 and 2000

[Numbers in percent]

	1990	2000
Dog food	57.5	51.5
Cat food	29.2	39.8
Specialty feeds	10.5	7.6
Other	7.8	1.0

Source: "Discounter Distinctions," *Discount Merchandiser* 31, No. 11, November, 1991, p. 61. Primary source: Business Trend Analysts, Commack, N.Y.

★ 100 ★

Consumer Electronics Market, 1992 and 2001

[Kenneth M. Bertaccini, president and CEO of AT&T Consumer Products] estimates that the market in which Consumer Products competes, $8 billion worldwide this year, will explode to $70 billion by 2001, thanks to new products arising from the convergence of computers, communications, and entertainment.

Source: "AT&T is Strutting Its Stuff in Consumer Goods," Peter Coy, *Business Week,* No. 3273, July 6, 1992, p. 70.

★ 101 ★

Distilled Spirits Sales, 1990 and 1995

[Numbers in thousands of nine-liter cases]

	1990	1995	ACGR[1]
License states			
Alaska	629	518	-3.8
Arizona	2,505	2,690	1.4
Arkansas	1,129	1,040	-1.6
California	19,705	16,925	-3.0
Colorado	2,411	1,988	-3.8
Connecticut	3,008	2,750	-1.8
Delaware	644	601	-1.4
District of Columbia	1,122	1,039	-1.5
Florida	11,053	10,628	-0.8
Georgia	4,973	4,906	-0.3
Hawaii	763	634	-3.6
Illinois	8,135	6,855	-3.4
Indiana	3,198	2,991	-1.3
Kansas	1,143	1,183	0.7
Kentucky	1,945	1,709	-2.6
Louisiana	2,717	2,642	-0.6
Maryland	3,618	3,331	-1.6
Massachusetts	5,115	4,614	-2.0
Minnesota	3,225	3,093	-0.8
Missouri	2,870	2,992	0.8
Nebraska	854	701	-3.9
Nevada	2,045	1,899	-1.5
New Jersey	6,188	5,399	-2.7
New Mexico	776	697	-2.1
New York	11,266	9,772	-2.8
North Dakota	498	382	-5.2
Oklahoma	1,551	1,333	-3.0
Rhode Island	714	653	-1.8
South Carolina	2,749	2,621	-0.9
South Dakota	487	422	-2.8
Tennessee	2,395	2,181	-1.9
Texas	7,656	6,669	-2.7
Wisconsin	4,086	3,441	-3.4
License state total	121,173	109,299	-2.0
Control states			
Alabama	2,032	1,864	-1.7
Idaho	470	403	-3.0
Iowa	1,161	924	-4.5
Maine	841	838	-0.1
Michigan	6,184	5,569	-2.1
Mississippi	1,339	1,218	-1.9
Montana	494	398	-4.2
New Hampshire	1,856	1,782	-0.8

[Continued]

★ 101 ★

Distilled Spirits Sales, 1990 and 1995
[Continued]

	1990	1995	ACGR[1]
North Carolina	3,591	3,391	-1.1
Ohio	4,671	3,997	-3.1
Oregon	1,687	1,469	-2.7
Pennsylvania	5,487	5,224	-1.0
Utah	584	586	0.1
Vermont	394	335	-3.2
Virginia	3,268	2,932	-2.1
Washington	2,992	2,948	-0.3
West Virginia	624	452	-6.2
Wyoming	329	262	-4.4
Control state total	38,002	34,592	-1.9
U.S. total	159,174	143,891	-2.0

Source: "The Projected Trend in Distilled Spirits Sales 1990-1995," *Jobson's Liquor Handbook 1991,* p. 16. Primary source: Jobson Beverage Alcohol Group; Steve L. Barsby & Associates, Inc. *Note:* 1. Annual Compound Growth Rate in percent.

★ 102 ★

Shipments of Packaging Machines, 2000

"Labeling and related machinery, representing 15% of the total market for packaging machinery in 1989, should see the fastest growth of all segments by 2000, at 2%."

	Share of market (%)	Change from 1989 (%)
Accumulating and other	23	1
Labeling	15	2
Wrapping and film packaging	14	1
Packaging machinery parts	11	-3
Cartoning and multipacking	9	0
Case fanning	9	0
Vacuum and filling	8	0
Form-fill-seal	6	0
Thermoforming	3	0
Capping, sealing, lidding	2	-1

Source: "The Third Annual Packaging Forecast," Greg Erickson, ed., *Packaging* 37, No. 1, January, 1992, p. 35. Primary source: The Freedonia Group.

★ 103 ★

Trends in Retail Shares of Apparel Sales, 1980-2000

Based on data from NPD's Consumer Panel.

[Numbers in percent]

	1980	1991	2000
Department stores	26.7	24.2	22.0
Specialty stores	26.3	19.8	22.0
National chains	18.6	14.8	12.0
Mass merchants	17.9	19.6	21.0
Other[1]	10.5	21.6	23.0

Source: "Retail Challenge: The Consumer of the 1990's," Elizabeth A. Germeroth, *Discount Merchandiser* 32, No. 5, May, 1992, p. 86. *Notes:* 1. Other includes mail order, factory outlets, warehouse clubs, off-price specialists, and food and drug outlets.

Banking

★ 104 ★

Decline in Number of Independent Banks, 1989-2100

By the year 2100, the number of U.S. banks will almost certainly be fewer than 100, compared with about 15,000 in 1985. This trend is easily predicted for several reasons.

First, the number and relative importance of small, independent banks has long been declining. The number of banking offices operated by U.S. chain banks grew almost steadily from 2,500 in 1925 to more than 40,000 in 1984, a period during which the number of one-office banks declined by more than 50%.

Second, chain banking has developed much further in advanced countries other than America. For instance, the five largest British banks have more than 10,000 branches and hold about 75% of all demand deposits (i.e., checking accounts). A similar concentration of commercial banking exists in most European nations, and in Canada there are only 71 such banks.

[Continued]

★ 104 ★

Decline in Number of Independent Banks, 1989-2100
[Continued]

There are more than ten times as many commercial banks in the United States as in any other Western country. More than half of American commercial bank assets are held in the 100 largest U.S. bank-holding companies, and the smallest 10,000 banks hold only about 10% of such assets. The chief reason there are still so many small banks is that the states, with federal approval and support, have protected small, mostly rural, banks by not allowing competition from out-of-state and/or big-city banks, despite the fact that the latter are more efficient.

Third, one-office banks are relatively inefficient. Whenever chain banks are allowed to compete with one-unit banks, they grow much faster than the latter because they can operate more cheaply. They enjoy all the economies of large-scale management and operation—volume purchasing of supplies, volume borrowing of funds, standardization of supplies and equipment, lower advertising costs, greater division of labor among both workers and machines, etc. The chain banks pass some of these savings on to their customers, who therefore increasingly prefer to deal with chain banks.

Fourth, restrictions on chain banking will gradually be weakened. The rise of chain or branch banking has been radically restricted by law in the United States. The National Bank Act of 1864 prohibited national banks from establishing branches. They are now allowed to have branches in states that allow state banks to do so, but about one-third of the states still allow only one-unit banks. As bankers, borrowers, voters, and politicians become more aware of the growing advantages of branch banking, they will gradually relax or end all legal restrictions on such banking. By 2050, all limitations on chain banking in the nation will probably have been eliminated.

Small-town bankers have long been the chief opponents of interstate chain banking. But the big chains have learned from experience that the best way to expand into new areas is to buy out small-bank stockholders. Since such stockholders have usually received generous prices for stock that was previously hard to sell, they are rapidly becoming reconciled to the probable future rise of national chain banking.

Chain banks can afford to offer generous and tempting bids for small banks because they know that these banks will become much more profitable when operated as branches of chain banks. It is highly probable, therefore, that most small U.S. banks that do not fail in the near future will be purchased by large chain banks before the year 2100.

Moreover, the continued concentration of agriculture and the declining number of U.S. farms will cause many small-town banks to fail or to reduce their dividends, and this will in turn help to persuade many small-bank stockholders to sell their stock to chain banks.

Source: "Eight Forecasts for U.S. Banking," Burnham P. Beckwith, *The Futurist* XXIII, No. 2, March-April, 1989, pp. 27-33.

★ 105 ★

U.S. Effective Exchange Rate, 1980-2001

[Index year: 1980 = 100]

1980	100.0
1981	112.0
1982	125.0
1983	132.0
1984	143.0
1985	149.0
1986	121.0
1987	107.0
1988	101.0
1989	105.0
1990	104.0
1991	100.0
1992	99.0
1993	97.0
1994	95.0
1995	93.0
1996	91.0
1997	90.0
1998	89.0
1999	88.5
2000	88.0
2001	87.0

Source: FAA Aviation Forecasts: Fiscal Years 1990-2001, U.S. Department of Transportation, Federal Aviation Administration, 1990, p. 21. Magnitudes estimated from published chart.

★ 106 ★

Exchange Rate of U.S. Dollar and Japanese Yen, 1980-2001

[Numbers in U.S. dollars per 1,000 Japanese yen]

1980	4.4
1985	4.2
1990	7.1
1995	9.5
2000	10.0
2001	10.1

Source: FAA Aviation Forecasts: Fiscal Years 1990-2001, U.S. Department of Transportation, Federal Aviation Administration, 1990, p. 21. Magnitudes estimated from published chart. Figures for 1981-1984, 1986-1989, 1991-1994, and 1996-1999 are excluded.

★ 107 ★

Exchange Rate of U.S. Dollar and German Deutsche Mark, 1980-2001

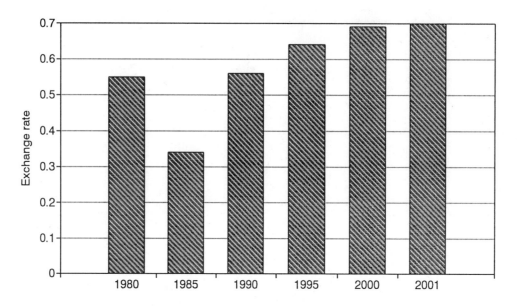

[Numbers in U.S. dollars per German mark]

1980	.55
1985	.34
1990	.56
1995	.64
2000	.69
2001	.70

Source: FAA Aviation Forecasts: Fiscal Years 1990-2001, U.S. Department of Transportation, Federal Aviation Administration, 1990, p. 21. Magnitudes estimated from published chart. Figures for 1981-1984, 1986-1989, 1991-1994, and 1996-1999 are excluded.

★ 108 ★

Potential Reduction of Bank Insurance Fund Costs Via Reforms, 1992-1997

"The savings would result partly from an improvement in bank earnings, increased cost efficiencies, diversified risk and an ability to raise new capital, producing a reduction in the rate at which new costs accrue. Savings would also result from reduced risk-raking with accrued deposits."

[Numbers in billions of dollars]

	1992	1993	1994	1995	1996	1997
Resolution Trust Corporation	40,437	32,503	-30,055	-26,008	-11,651	-18,996
Bank Insurance Fund	32,960	38,047	13,690	7,545	-4,508	-19,284
FSLIC Resolution Fund	7,020	6,383	253	240	432	297
Savings associations						
Insurance Fund	-	-1,012	-864	3,040	846	-1,652
National Credit Union Share Insurance Fund	-312	-227	-242	-257	-273	-288
All other	11	-2	-1	-1	-1	-1
Total	80,116	75,692	-17,219	-15,441	-15,155	-39,924

Source: Budget of the United States Government: Fiscal Year 1993, Part One, p. 262.

★ 109 ★

Restriction and Replacement of Cash by Checks, 1989-2100

The use of bank checks and check substitutes to make monetary payments has been growing almost steadily in the United States since 1800. It is estimated that in 1980 about 80% of all legal payments were made by check. This percentage will continue to rise until all payments of over $10, and many for smaller amounts, are made by check or by electronic fund transfer.

The use of checks has been growing, and will long continue to grow, because it is usually much cheaper and more convenient to send a check through the mail, or over a wire, than to send cash by mail or to deliver it in person. If one keeps or carries large sums of cash, they may be lost or stolen. Demand deposits cannot be lost or stolen, and stolen checks are much harder to spend than stolen currency. Moreover, checks can be quickly written for the exact amount required, and they serve as receipts when returned to the payee or entered in his bank account.

Growing restrictions on the use of cash, chiefly paper money, are inevitable as a cheap and effective method of crime prevention and detection. In recent years, several federal laws requiring banks to report large cash receipts have been enacted, and large fines have been imposed on some banks that violated these laws. In the future, these laws will become more and more restrictive, until nearly all nonessential acceptance of cash deposits by banks, and all use of cash to make payments over some small maximum amount, perhaps $10, will be illegal.

[Continued]

★ 109 ★

Restriction and Replacement of Cash by Checks, 1989-2100
[Continued]

One of the first new steps in this direction will be the gradual withdrawal from circulation of large-denomination paper money. By 2050, no paper money with a value (in 1985 values) of more than $10 will remain in circulation. This reform alone will have a significant effect on crime because many illegal payments are made in large-denomination paper money.

After all large-denomination paper money has been withdrawn from circulation or declared invalid, the U.S. government will gradually limit the use of cash to pay rent, buy autos, or make any other payment of more than some increasingly small maximum amount. By 2100, all such use of cash will be prohibited.

Source: "Eight Forecasts for U.S. Banking," Burnham P. Beckwith, *The Futurist* XXIII, No. 2, March-April, 1989, pp. 27-33.

★ 110 ★

Total Deposit Insurance Cash Outlays Assuming No Further Reforms, 1992-1997

"Deposit insurance cash outlays anticipated under current law, shown in [this table], reflect the problems that have afflicted many banks and thrifts."

[Numbers in millions of dollars]

	1992	1993	1994	1995	1996	1997
Resolution Trust Corporation	40,437	32,503	-30,055	-26,008	-11,651	-18,996
Bank Insurance Fund	32,960	38,047	13,690	7,545	-4,508	-19,284
FSLIC Resolution Fund	7,020	6,383	253	240	432	297
Savings associations						
Insurance Fund	-	-1,012	-864	3,040	846	-1,652
National Credit Union Share Insurance Fund	-312	-227	-242	-257	-273	-288
All other	11	-2	-1	-1	-1	-1
Total	80,116	75,692	-17,219	-15,441	-15,155	-39,924

Source: Budget of the United States Government: Fiscal Year 1993, Part One, p. 257.

Finance

★ 111 ★

Federal Debt Held by the Public, 1988-1997

[Numbers in billions of dollars]

	Current dollars	Constant 1987 dollars[1]	A percent of		Debt held by the public as a percent of total outlays[3]
			GDP	Credit market debt[2]	
1988	2,050.3	1,978.4	42.6	22.7	16.2
1989	2,190.3	2,023.8	42.4	22.4	16.5
1990	2,410.4	2,139.4	44.2	22.8	16.1
1991	2,687.2	2,295.0	47.8	24.3	16.2
1992 estimate	3,079.8	2,551.2	52.5	-	15.1
1993 estimate	3,433.2	2,752.3	55.1	-	15.6
1994 estimate	3,646.1	2,830.4	55.0	-	16.6
1995 estimate	3,841.3	2,886.7	54.4	-	16.5
1996 estimate	4,026.1	2,931.9	53.6	-	16.4
1997 estimate	4,213.7	2,973.3	53.0	-	16.0

Source: Budget of the United States Government: Fiscal Year 1993, Part One, p. 288. *Notes:* 1. Debt in current dollars deflated by the GDP deflator with index FY 1987 = 100. 2. Primary Source: Unpublished and preliminary estimates from the Federal Reserve Board flow of funds accounts. Total credit market debt owed by domestic nonfinancial sectors modified to be consistent with budget concepts for the measurement of Federal debt. Projections not available. 3. Interest on debt held by the public is estimated as the interest on the public debt less the "interest received by trust funds." It does not include the comparatively small amount of interest on agency debt or the offsets for other interest received by Government accounts. Figures from 1950 to 1987 are excluded.

★ 112 ★

Federal Funds Financing and Change in Debt Subject to Statutory Limit, 1991-1997

[Numbers in billions of dollars]

Description	1991 actual	Estimate					
		1992	1993	1994	1995	1996	1997
Financing							
Federal Funds surplus or deficit (-)	-381.0	-463.1	-450.6	-376.7	-368.3	-358.7	-379.8
(On budget)	(-379.7)	(-462.2)	(-449.0)	(-375.4)	(-367.3)	(-359.4)	(-380.8)
(Off budget)	(-1.3)	(-0.8)	(-1.6)	(-1.3)	(-1.1)	(0.7)	(1.0)
Means of financing other than borrowing:							
Decrease or increase(-) in Treasury operating cash balance	-1.3	10.2	-	-	-	-	-

[Continued]

★ 112 ★

Federal Funds Financing and Change in Debt Subject to Statutory Limit, 1991-1997
[Continued]

Description	1991 actual	Estimate					
		1992	1993	1994	1995	1996	1997
Increase or decrease (-) in:							
Checks outstanding, etc.[2]	-3.3	-4.4	-2.1	-	-	-	-
Deposit fund balances[3]	-0.3	-0.2	-1.4	-	-	-	-
Seigniorage on coins	0.4	0.3	0.4	0.4	0.4	0.3	0.3
Deduct (-): Net financing disbursements:							
Direct loan financing accounts	-	-3.1	-3.5	-4.8	-5.5	-6.2	-6.5
Guaranteed loan financing accounts	-	1.5	6.1	3.8	2.8	2.0	1.1
Insurance financing accounts	-	-34.2	-19.2	31.4	25.7	13.7	21.5
Total, means of financing other than borrowing	-4.4	-29.9	-19.7	30.7	23.3	9.8	16.4
Decrease or increase (-) in Federal debt held by Federal funds and deposit funds[4]	-7.2	11.7	4.0	1.1	-	-	-
Increase or decrease (-) in Federal debt not subject to limit	-15.0	-2.5	2.5	1.3	1.1	0.9	0.6
Total, requirement for Federal funds borrowing subject to debt limit	-407.6	-483.8	-463.8	-343.6	-343.9	-348.0	-362.7
Increase or decrease (-) in unamortized discounts (less premiums) on Treasury notes and bonds other than zero-coupon bonds	0.4	-	-	-	-	-	-
Adjustments including increase in debt subject to limit but not part of Federal debt	[1]	-	-	-	-	-	-
Increase in debt subject to limit	408.1	483.8	463.8	343.6	343.9	348.0	362.7
Addendum							
Debt subject to statutory limit[5]	3,569.3	4,053.1	4,516.9	4,860.5	5,204.4	5,552.4	5,915.1

Source: Budget of the United States Government: Fiscal Year 1993, Part One, p. 298. *Notes:* 1. $50 million or less. 2. Besides checks outstanding, includes accrued interest payable on Treasury debt, miscellaneous liability accounts, allocations of special drawing rights, and, as an offset, cash and monetary assets other than the Treasury operating cash balance, miscellaneous asset accounts, and profit on sale of gold. 3. Does not include investment in Federal debt securities by deposit funds classified as part of the public. 4. Only those deposit funds classified as Government accounts. 5. The statutory debt limit is $4,145 billion.

★ 113 ★

Federal Government Financing and Debt, 1991-1997
[Numbers in billions of dollars]

	1991 actual	Estimate					
		1992	1993	1994	1995	1996	1997
Financing							
Surplus or deficit (-)	-268.7	-366.7	-333.5	-243.6	-218.6	-194.6	-204.1
(On-budget)	(-320.9)	(-416.1)	(-395.3)	(-318.2)	(-304.4)	(-296.4)	(-320.1)
(Off-budget)	(52.2)	(49.4)	(61.8)	(74.5)	(85.8)	(101.8)	(116.0)
Means of financing other than borrowing from the public:							
Decrease or increase(-) in Treasury operating cash balance	-1.3	10.2	-	-	-	-	-

[Continued]

★ 113 ★

Federal Government Financing and Debt, 1991-1997
[Continued]

	1991 actual	Estimate					
		1992	1993	1994	1995	1996	1997
Increase or decrease (-) in:							
Checks outstanding, etc.[1]	-6.9	-0.3	-0.9	-	-	-	-
Deposit fund balances	-0.3	-0.2	-1.4	-	-	-	-
Seigniorage on coins	0.4	0.3	0.4	0.4	0.4	0.3	0.3
Deduct (-): Net financing disbursements:							
Direct loan financing accounts	-	-3.1	-3.5	-4.8	-5.5	-6.2	-6.5
Government loan financing accounts	-	1.5	6.1	3.8	2.8	2.0	1.1
Insurance financing accounts	-	-34.2	-19.2	31.4	25.7	13.7	21.5
Total, means of financing other than borrowing from the public	-8.1	-25.8	-18.5	30.7	23.3	9.8	16.4
Total, requirement for borrowing from the public	-276.8	-392.5	-352.1	-212.9	-195.2	-184.8	-187.7
Reclassification of debt[2]	-	-	-1.4	-	-	-	-
Change in debt held by the public	276.8	392.5	353.4	212.9	195.2	184.8	187.7
Debt, end of year							
Gross Federal debt:							
Debt issued by Treasury	3,581.2	4,065.0	4,528.9	4,872.5	5,216.4	5,564.4	5,927.1
Debt issued by other agencies	17.8	15.3	17.7	19.0	20.1	21.0	21.7
Total, gross Federal debt	3,599.0	4,080.3	4,546.6	4,891.5	5,236.5	5,585.4	5,948.8
Held by:							
Government accounts	911.8	1,000.5	1,113.4	1,245.5	1,395.2	1,559.3	1,735.0
The public	2,687.2	3,079.8	3,433.2	3,646.1	3,841.3	4,026.1	4,213.7
(Federal Reserve Banks)	(258.6)	-	-	-	-	-	-
(Other)	(2,428.7)	-	-	-	-	-	-
Debt subject to statutory limitation, end of year							
Debt issued by Treasury	3,581.2	4,065.0	4,528.9	4,872.5	5,216.4	5,564.4	5,927.1
Deduct (-): Treasury debt not subject to limitation[3]	-15.6	-15.6	-15.6	-15.6	-15.6	-15.6	-15.6
Agency debt subject to limitation	0.3	0.2	0.2	0.2	0.2	0.2	0.2
Unamortized discount (less premium) on Treasury notes and bonds other than zero-coupon bonds	3.4	3.4	3.4	3.4	3.4	3.4	3.4
Total debt subject to statutory limitation[4]	3,569.3	4,053.1	4,516.9	4,860.5	5,204.4	5,552.4	5,915.1

Source: Budget of the United States Government: Fiscal Year 1993, Part One, p. 289. *Notes:* Treasury securities held by the public are almost entirely measured in accrual value (i.e., sales price plus amortized discount or less amortized premium). Agency debt and Treasury securities held by Government accounts are almost entirely measured at face value. 1. Besides checks outstanding, includes accrued interest payable on Treasury debt, miscellaneous liability, allocations of special drawing rights, and, as an offset, cash and monetary assets other than the Treasury operating cash balance, miscellaneous asset accounts, and profit on sale of gold. 2. The Farm Credit System Financial Assistance Corporation is estimated to be reclassified from a Government sponsored enterprise to a Federal agency as of October 1, 1992, and its debt is accordingly reclassified as Federal agency debt. 3. Consists primarily of Federal Financing Bank debt. 4. The statutory debt limit is $4,145 billion.

★ 114 ★

Summary of Federal Direct Loans and Guaranteed Loans, 1990-1997
[Numbers in billions of dollars]

	Actual		Estimated					
	1990	1991	1992	1993	1994	1995	1996	1997
Direct loans								
Subsidy BA	n/a	n/a	2.0	1.5	1.4	1.4	1.4	1.4
Subsidy outlays	n/a	n/a	1.0	1.1	1.1	1.2	1.2	1.3
Loan obligations	16.2	16.1	18.1	17.8	17.4	17.3	17.3	17.2

[Continued]

★ 114 ★

Summary of Federal Direct Loans and Guaranteed Loans, 1990-1997
[Continued]

	Actual		Estimated					
	1990	1991	1992	1993	1994	1995	1996	1997
Loan disbursements	26.0	26.6	27.1	25.5	23.9	22.8	22.6	22.2
Guaranteed loans								
Subsidy BA	n/a	n/a	3.2	2.9	3.4	3.7	3.9	4.0
Subsidy outlays	n/a	n/a	1.7	2.1	2.8	3.2	3.4	3.6
Guaranteed commitments	105.4	106.9	122.0	129.7	131.1	134.5	136.7	139.8
Lender disbursements	96.3	97.1	102.9	115.6	118.2	121.5	124.3	127.0

Source: "Summary of Federal Direct Loans and Guaranteed Loans," *Budget of the United States Government: Fiscal Year 1993*, Appendix One, p. 123.

Economics

★ 115 ★

Annual Percent Change in Gross National Product (GNP), 1985-2001
[Percentages are based on 1982 dollars]

1985	3.7
1986	3.2
1987	2.8
1988	4.9
1989	3.2
1990	2.4
1991	3.0
1992	3.3
1993	3.2
1994	3.1
1995	3.0
1996	2.7
1997	2.6
1998	2.6
1999	2.6
2000	2.5
2001	2.5

Source: FAA Aviation Forecasts: Fiscal Years 1990-2001, U.S. Department of Transportation, Federal Aviation Administration, 1990. Magnitudes estimated from published chart.

★ 116 ★

Annual Percent Change in Consumer Price Index (CPI), 1985-2001

[Percentage changes based on constant dollars]

1985	3.7
1986	2.4
1987	1.8
1988	4.1
1989	4.7
1990	4.0
1991	4.0
1992	3.8
1993	3.6
1994	3.2
1995	3.1
1996	5.4
1997	5.3
1998	5.3
1999	5.4
2000	5.4
2001	5.4

Source: FAA Aviation Forecasts: Fiscal Years 1990-2001, p. 17, U.S. Department of Transportation, Federal Aviation Administration, 1990. Magnitudes estimated from published chart.

★ 117 ★

Domestic and Foreign Economic Projections, 1989-2001

	1989	1990	1991	1992	1993	1994	1995	1996	1997-2001 Avg
					Percent				
United States[1]									
Real GDP (change)	2.5	0.9	-0.6	2.3	3.2	3.1	3.5	3.4	2.8
GDP deflator (change)	4.1	4.1	3.6	1.8	2.5	3.0	3.1	3.8	4.3
CPI (change)	4.8	5.4	4.2	2.5	3.2	3.8	4.1	4.7	5.0
Unemployment rate	5.3	5.5	6.8	7.2	6.8	6.4	5.9	5.6	5.3
3-month Treasury bill rate	8.1	7.5	5.4	4.3	4.7	5.1	5.6	6.0	6.7
Moody's AAA corporate bond rate	9.3	9.3	8.8	8.2	8.5	8.8	9.2	9.6	9.1
MERM exchange rate (change)	4.5	-6.4	1.5	-1.8	-1.3	-1.2	-1.1	-1.3	-1.3
					Billion dollars				
Federal budget deficit	154.9	236.1	303.2	376.8	315.6	248.5	184.0	121.1	13.1
Current account	-106.3	-92.1	-13.3	-82.4	-99.8	-105.6	-113.9	-122.6	-143.9

[Continued]

★ 117 ★

Domestic and Foreign Economic Projections, 1989-2001

[Continued]

	1989	1990	1991	1992	1993	1994	1995	1996	1997-2001 Avg
					U.S. dollar per barrel				
Foreign[2]									
Average Arab oil	17.2	22.1	17.8	18.3	19.1	20.0	20.8	21.6	24.4
					Percent change				
Real GDP									
World	3.1	1.2	-0.2	2.5	2.9	3.7	3.3	3.7	3.4
Africa	2.8	3.3	2.4	3.2	3.0	2.9	2.9	3.2	3.2
Latin America	1.1	-0.3	2.4	3.5	4.2	4.8	4.6	4.5	4.1
Pacific Basin	6.8	6.3	5.6	6.2	6.6	6.6	6.5	6.1	6.4
Western Europe[3]	3.4	2.9	2.0	2.9	3.2	2.7	2.7	2.3	2.3
Eastern Europe	-1.2	-7.3	-13.8	-2.7	1.9	3.0	3.3	3.6	3.4
Former USSR	1.6	-2.0	-13.0	-5.9	-1.1	3.2	2.4	4.1	3.8
China	3.6	4.8	7.9	6.7	6.8	6.4	6.4	6.4	6.4
Foreign currency/U.S. dollar									
Argentina (real)	47.8	-41.3	-19.0	2.8	4.9	5.1	3.7	6.7	6.9
Brazil (real)	-20.9	-5.4	29.2	2.8	3.9	3.9	4.2	4.2	4.6
Canada	-3.8	-1.5	0.3	0.0	-0.4	-0.4	-0.4	-0.4	-0.4
Australia	-1.3	1.1	2.1	2.0	1.0	4.5	3.0	2.0	2.0
Thailand	1.6	-0.5	-0.1	0.0	0.0	0.0	0.0	0.0	0.0
Japan	7.7	5.0	-7.1	-3.6	-2.0	-2.0	-2.0	-2.0	-2.0
European Community	7.4	-13.4	4.3	-1.1	-1.3	-1.0	-0.5	-1.2	-1.3
South Korea	-8.2	5.4	3.0	2.5	2.8	0.2	0.3	0.0	-0.1
Taiwan	-7.7	1.9	-1.1	-2.1	-1.9	-1.1	-1.1	-1.0	-0.7

Source: FAPRI 1992 Agricultural Outlook, Food and Agricultural Policy Research Institute, Iowa State University and the University of Missouri-Columbia, 1992, p. 21. *Notes:* 1. The source for U.S. projections is the WEFA Group, January 1992. 2. The source for foreign projections is Project LINK, November and December, 1991. 3. Western Europe includes eastern Germany beginning in 1991.

★ 118 ★

Economic Trends, 1955-2000

| | 1955 | | 1970 | | 1985 | | 2000 | | | | | |
| | | | | | | | Base | | Low | | High | |
	Level	Change[1] %	Level	Change[1] %	Level	Change[1] %	Level	Change[1] %	Level	Change[1] %	Level	Change[1] %
Non-Communist World GDP (bil. 82 $)	NA	NA	4842	NA	7745	3.18	12204	3.1	9546	1.4	13057	3.5
U.S. GNP (bil. 82 $)	1495	NA	2416	3.25	3570	2.64	5463	2.9	4537	1.6	6431	4.0
U.S. GNP (bil. current $)	406	NA	1016	6.30	3988	9.55	9963	6.3	5344	2.0	12631	8.0
Unemployment rate (%)	4.4	-	4.9	-	7.1	-	7.0	-	9.9	-	5.9	-
GNP deflator (1982=100)	27.2	NA	42.0	2.94	111.7	6.74	182.4	3.3	117.8	0.4	196.4	3.8
Employment (millions)	62.2	NA	78.6	1.58	107.2	2.09	131.0	1.3	122.4	0.9	139.9	1.8
Manufacturing	16.9	NA	19.4	0.92	19.3	-0.02	17.2	-0.8	18.0	-0.4	18.1	-0.4
Commercial and other services	27.0	NA	38.2	2.34	62.0	3.29	84.3	2.1	76.5	1.4	88.7	2.4
Productivity (output/worker, 82 $)	24.1	NA	30.2	1.52	33.3	0.66	41.7	1.5	37.1	0.7	46.0	2.2
Manufacturing	19.4	NA	26.2	2.01	40.4	2.93	71.4	3.9	58.0	2.5	81.3	4.8
Commercial & other services	24.9	NA	30.6	1.41	29.9	-0.17	34.1	0.9	30.4	0.1	38.2	1.6

[Continued]

★ 118 ★

Economic Trends, 1955-2000
[Continued]

	1955		1970		1985		2000 Base		2000 Low		2000 High	
	Level	Change[1] %	Level	Change[1] %	Level	Change[1] %	Level	Change[1] %	Level	Change[1] %	Level	Change[1] %
Fed. surplus (bil. curr. $)	4.4	-	-12.4	-	-200.8	-	-110.0	-	-170.1	-	-40.7	-
Deficit/GNP (absolute number)	0.29	-	0.51	-	5.62	-	2.01	-	3.75	-	0.63	-
Current account balance (bil. curr. $)	0.4	-	2.3	-	-116.8	-	14.8	-	12.5	-	32.6	-
Exports (bil. 82 $)	76.9	NA	178.3	5.77	359.8	4.79	800.2	5.5	500.6	2.2	958.8	6.8
Imports (bil 82 $)	76.9	NA	208.3	6.87	467.8	5.54	773.9	3.4	482.4	0.2	952.5	4.9
Interest rates (moodys corp bond rate)[2]	3.1	NA	4.9	NA	10.0	NA	7.2	NA	5.1	NA	7.3	NA
Average compensation per worker (thou 82 $)	13.4	NA	18.7	2.27	19.8	0.39	25.6	1.7	22.0	0.7	27.6	2.2
Consumption per capita (thou. 82 $)	5.3	NA	7.3	2.13	9.6	1.89	12.5	1.8	10.7	0.7	14.3	2.7
Disposable income per capita (thou. 82 $)	5.7	NA	8.1	2.38	10.5	1.69	13.5	1.7	11.5	0.6	15.6	2.7

Source: "The U.S. Economy in the Year 2000," *Workforce 2000: Work and Workers for the Twenty-First Century*, William B. Johnston and Arnold E. Parker, Project Directors, Hudson Institute, Indianapolis, Indiana, June, 1987, p. 54. Primary source: Hudson Institute. *Notes:* 1. Average annual gain. 2. Average for period.

★ 119 ★

Economic Trends, 1985 and 2000

	1985 level	2000 (Three scenarios)					
		Base		Low		High	
		Level	Change[1]	Level	Change[1]	Level	Change[1]
World GDP (bill. 82$)	7745	12204	3.1	9546	1.4	13057	3.5
U.S. GNP (bill. 82$)	3570	5463	2.9	4537	1.6	6431	4.0
GNP deflator (1982-100)	111.7	182.4	3.3	117.8	0.4	196.4	3.8
Employment (millions)	107.2	131.0	1.3	122.4	0.9	139.9	1.8
Manufacturing	19.3	17.2	-0.8	18.0	-0.4	18.1	-0.4
Commercial & other services	62.0	84.3	2.1	76.5	1.4	88.7	2.4
Productivity (output/worker, 82$)	33.3	41.7	1.5	37.1	0.7	46.0	2.2
Manufacturing	40.4	71.4	3.9	58.0	2.5	81.3	4.8
Commercial & other services	29.9	34.1	0.9	30.4	0.1	38.2	1.6
Fed. surplus (bill. curr. $)	-200.8	-110.0	-	-170.1	-	-40.7	-
Curr. acct. bal. (bill. curr. $)	-116.8	14.0	-	12.5	-	32.6	-
Disp. income per capita (thou. 82$)	10.5	13.5	1.7	11.5	0.6	15.6	2.7

Source: "The U.S. Economy in the Year 2000," *Workforce 2000: Work and Workers for the Twenty-First Century*, William B. Johnston and Arnold E. Parker, Project Directors, Hudson institute, Indianapolis, Indiana, June, 1987, p. xvi. Figures measuring change in percent. *Note:* 1. Average annual gain.

★ 120 ★

Presidential Administration Economic Assumptions, 1989-1996

[Dollar amounts in billions]

	Actual 1989	Forecast			Assumptions			1996
		1990[1]	1991	1992	1993	1994	1995	
Major economic indicators								
Gross national product (percent change, fourth quarter over fourth quarter):								
Current dollars	5.6	4.5	5.3	7.5	7.1	6.8	6.5	6.4
Constant (1982) dollars	1.8	0	0.9	3.6	3.4	3.2	3.0	3.0
GNP deflator (percent change, Fourth quarter over fourth quarter)	3.7	4.5	4.3	3.8	3.6	3.5	3.4	3.3
Consumer Price Index (percent change, fourth quarter over fourth quarter)[2]	4.5	6.3	4.3	3.9	3.6	3.5	3.4	3.3
Unemployment rate (percent, fourth quarter)[3]	5.3	5.8	6.6	6.5	6.0	5.7	5.2	5.1
Annual economic assumptions								
Gross national product:								
Current dollars:								
Amount	5,201	5,465	5,689	6,095	6,536	6,990	7,451	7,931
Percent change, year over year	6.7	5.1	4.1	7.1	7.2	7.0	6.6	6.4
Constant (1982) dollars:								
Amount	4,118	4,152	4,140	4,267	4,415	4,560	4,699	4,840
Percent change, year over year	2.5	0.8	-0.3	3.1	3.5	3.3	3.1	3.0
Incomes:								
Personal income	4,384	4,644	4,856	5,182	5,524	5,887	6,259	6,655
Wages and salaries	2,573	2,700	2,802	3,006	3,235	3,467	3,703	3,950
Corporate profits before tax	308	300	294	335	379	419	447	484
Price level:								
GNP deflator:								
Level (1982 = 100), annual average	126.3	131.6	137.4	142.8	148.0	153.3	158.6	163.8
Percent change, year over year	4.1	4.2	4.4	3.9	3.6	3.5	3.4	3.3
Consumer price index[2]								
Level (1982-84 = 100), annual average	122.6	129.1	135.8	141.2	146.4	151.6	156.8	162.0
Percent change, year over year	4.8	5.3	5.2	4.0	3.7	3.5	3.4	3.3
Unemployment rates								
Total, annual average[3]	5.2	5.4	6.7	6.6	6.2	5.8	5.4	5.1
Federal pay raise, January (percent)	4.1	3.6	4.1	4.2	4.7	4.3	4.1	4.0
Interest rate, 91-day Treasury bills (percent)[4]	8.1	7.5	6.4	6.0	5.8	5.6	5.4	5.3
Interest rate, 10-year Treasury notes (percent)	8.5	8.5	7.5	7.2	6.8	6.6	6.4	6.3

Source: Congressional Quarterly Almanac: 102nd Congress, 1st Session, 1991, XLVII, p. 60. Primary source: Fiscal Year 1992 Budget. Notes: 1. Based on data available as of December 1990. 2. CPI for urban wage earners and clerical workers. Two versions of the CPI are now published. The index shown here is that currently used, as required by law, in calculating automatic cost of living increases for indexed federal programs. The manner in which this index measures housing costs changed significantly in January 1985. 3. Percent of total labor force, including armed forces residing in the United States. 4. Average rate on new issues within period, on a bank discount basis. These projections assume, by convention, that interest rates decline with the rate of inflation.

★ 121 ★

Presidential Administration Economic Forecasts, 1991-1997

Item	1991	1992	1993	1994	1995	1996	1997
	Percent change, fourth quarter to fourth quarter						
Policy forecast							
Real GDP	0.2	2.2	3.0	3.0	3.0	2.9	2.8
GDP deflator, 1987=100	3.2	3.2	3.4	3.3	3.3	3.2	3.2
Consumer price index	2.9	3.1	3.3	3.2	3.2	3.2	3.1
	Calendar year average, percent						
Unemployment rate	6.7	6.9	6.5	6.1	5.8	5.4	5.3
Interest rate, 91-day Treasury bills	5.4	4.1	4.9	5.3	5.3	5.2	5.1
Interest rate, 10-year Treasury notes	7.9	7.0	6.9	6.7	6.6	6.6	6.6
Civilian employment	116.8	117.4	119.6	121.7	123.7	125.8	127.8
	Percent change, fourth quarter to fourth quarter						
Business as usual forecast							
Real GDP	0.2	1.6	2.4	2.5	2.6	2.5	2.4
	Calendar year average, percent						
Unemployment rate	6.7	7.1	6.9	6.7	6.3	5.8	5.6
Interest rate, 91-day Treasury bills	5.4	4.2	5.1	5.5	5.5	5.4	5.3
Interest rate, 10-year Treasury notes	7.9	7.2	7.3	7.1	7.0	7.0	6.9

Source: Economic Report of the President, Transmitted to Congress, February, 1992, p. 76. Primary sources: Council of Economic Advisers, Department of Commerce, Department of Labor, Department of the Treasury, and Office Management and Budget.

★ 122 ★

GNP Growth Rate, 1979-2000

The projected rate of growth in real GNP for the 1988-2000 period is 2.3 percent per year, which will result in more than a 30 percent expansion of the economy over the period. This is a slower rate of GNP growth than the 2.9-percent annual rate that prevailed during the previous 12-year period, 1976-88, primarily because labor force growth—a major factor in changing the GNP—is projected to slow appreciably. Productivity—a second important catalyst—is projected to increase at a slightly faster rate than the average experienced over the 1976-88 period. The net effect of these two offsetting factors is that growth of real GNP will slow during 1988-2000, but not as much as it would if productivity were to increase less.

[Continued]

★ 122 ★

GNP Growth Rate, 1979-2000
[Continued]

Among the major categories of GNP, foreign trade is projected to change the most compared with long-term historical trends. From 1976 until 1986, imports grew faster than exports. At the same time, both of the components of foreign trade—exports and imports—increased faster than overall GNP. However, exports have grown faster than imports since 1986, reversing the trend. The projected rate of growth for foreign trade continues this very recent trend—primarily because of a slower projected growth for imports.

Another GNP category projected to break with the trend of the 1980's is the share of GNP devoted to defense expenditures. An increasing share of GNP was spent on defense over the 1979-86 period. An absolute decline is projected for real defense expenditures for 1988-2000.

Source: "The Major Trends," Ronald E. Kutscher, *Occupational Outlook Quarterly* 34, No. 1, Spring, 1990, pp. 2-7.

★ 123 ★

Projections for the U.S. Economy, 1999

"More than 6,000 readers entered *Forbes*'s second Decade Contest.... [The] pool of prophecies ranges all over the lot. Some contestants see steady growth, others fear wild inflation and some a 1930s depression-style deflation."

Category	1989	1999			
		Average	Median	High[2]	Low[2]
Value of $1	$1	0.56	0.55	2.50	0.04
Dow Jones Industrials	2753	4788	4343	15142	940
Average daily NYSE volume	165 mil	1,070 mil	260 mil	2,211 mil	40 mil
No. of Forbes Sales 500 cos of 1989 still on Forbes list	500	351	360	500	35
Gold (in 1989 dollars)	399/oz	585/oz	500/oz	3,192/oz	75/oz
Prime rate(in percent)	10.5	10.73	10.50	23.60	4.60
30-year Treasurys (in percent)	8.45	8.88	8.90	20.00	4.00
GNP (actual, in 1989 dollars)	5.2 tril	10.8 tril	9.3 tril	85.0 tril	3.2 tril
GNP (in 1989 dollars)	5.2 tril	7.3 tril	6.4 tril	40.0 tril	1.5 tril
National debt	3.0 tril	10.8 tril	4.5 tril	500 tril	0
Federal budget surplus (or deficit)	(152 bil)	(149 bil)	(62 bil)	2,000 bil	(2,000 bil)
U.S. trade surplus (or deficit)	(109 bil)	(60 bil)	(25 bil)	1,000 bil	(1,000 bil)
Consumer debt (excl mortgages)	717 bil	2,489 bil	1,000 bil	14,778 bil	1 bil
Per capita income	15,186[1]	27,121	25,000	109,760	5,000
Computers	52.4 mil	1,879.5 mil	107.1 mil	2,500.0 mil	12.6 mil
Fax machines	2.8 mil	81.2 mil	16.0 mil	3,300 mil	40 thou
Homes with high-definition TV	-	37 mil	9 mil	1,000 mil	0

[Continued]

★ 123 ★

Projections for the U.S. Economy, 1999
[Continued]

Category	1989	1999			
		Average	Median	High[2]	Low[2]
Cellular telephones	3.5 mil	39.0 mil	17.0 mil	600.0 mil	1.0 mil
Wristwatch telephones	-	8.7 mil	1.0 mil	323.0 mil	0

Source: "$100,000 Contest Concensus: There Ain't None," *Forbes* 147, No. 7, April 1, 1991, p. 27. Figures from some categories have been excluded. *Notes:* 1. Estimate. 2. Preliminary programming has selected high and low figures to remove distortions, such as leaving a category blank.

★ 124 ★

U.S. Deficit as a Percentage of GDP, 1992-2002

1992	5.2
1993	4.6
1994	3.8
1995	3.4
1996	3.6
1997	4.0
1998	4.1
1999	4.3
2000	4.6
2001	5.0
2002	5.3

Source: "Clinton's Plans to Cut Deficit Aren't Clear," *The Wall Street Journal*, October 26, 1992, p. 1. Magnitudes estimated from published chart. Primary source: Congressional Budget Office.

Chapter 3

CONSTRUCTION AND HOUSING

The Commercial Construction Market

★ 125 ★

Construction Expenditures by Type of Structure, 1988-1996

[1987 dollars in billions except as noted]

Item	1988	1989	1990	1991	1992	1996	Percent change		
							1990-91	1991-92	1991-96[1]
Total new construction	415.0	409.8	402.8	380.4	381.1	403.8	-6	0	1
New building construction	271.5	270.8	263.2	239.7	239.0	247.5	-9	0	0
New housing units	133.5	128.4	115.4	101.6	109.1	118.4	-12	7	3
Private nonresidential	103.0	105.7	106.4	93.8	85.9	83.2	-12	-8	-2
Publicly owned	35.0	36.7	41.3	44.3	44.0	46.0	7	-1	1
Other new structures	86.8	86.1	90.2	89.2	89.0	96.6	-1	0	1
Private nonresidential	31.1	31.7	32.8	33.3	33.0	36.0	2	-1	2
Publicly owned	55.7	54.4	57.4	55.9	56.0	59.7	-3	0	1
Home improvements[5]	56.8	52.9	49.5	51.5	53.0	60.6	4	3	3
Selected maintenance and Repair:[2]									
Residential[2]	39.4	39.8	41.0	42.2	43.1	46.6	3	2	2
Nonresidential buildings[2,3]	31.7	32.9	34.5	36.2	37.3	40.0	5	3	2
Highway[2]	19.6	20.1	20.7	21.3	22.0	24.7	3	3	3
Utility[2]	22.2	23.1	25.2	26.2	27.5	31.9	4	5	4
Nonresidential building Improvements[2,3,4,5]	55.3	57.0	59.9	62.9	66.0	69.4	5	5	2

Source: U.S. Industrial Outlook 1992: Business Forecasts for 350 Industries, U.S. Department of Commerce, January, 1992, p. 5-2. Primary source: U.S. Department of Commerce, Bureau of the Census and International Trade Administration (ITA). *Notes:* 1. Average annual rate of growth. 2. Estimates in constant 1987 dollars were derived by ITA, using current-dollar data developed by the Bureau of the Census, and the Census Fixed-Weight Composite Construction Cost Index as the deflator. 3. Excludes industrial and agricultural buildings, as well as buildings owned by the Federal Government or private utilities. Also excludes buildings of 1,000 square feet or less. 4. About half of all nonresidential building improvements are included in value of new construction. 5. Home improvements are included in the value of new construction put in place, but nonresidential building improvements are not included.

★ 126 ★

Electric-Utility Construction Outlays, 1991-2000[1]

"'The cost of building the new generating capacity that might be needed from 1991 to 2000 could vary by hundreds of billions of dollars,' comments [the Edison Electric Institute (EEI) in a draft report, 'Planning to Meet Future Electricity Needs'], which also points out that the industry's financial muscle has been shrinking since the oil embargo of 1973."

	1990	1991	1992	1993	1994	1995	2000
Construction work							
In progress	37,693	29,055	33,642	37,212	40,924	40,056	88,444
New plant in service	18,460	16,400	3540	1858	4215	13,595	14,897
Generating capacity							
Construction[2]	5189	4670	4036	4232	5309	7340	13,189
Oil/gas	460	581	893	1394	1579	2140	1504
Coal	2547	2306	1861	2028	3233	4859	11,635
Nuclear	1709	1331	784	400	194	72	-
Hydro	348	356	328	229	178	157	-
Other	125	96	170	181	125	112	50
AFUDC							
During construction	2115	1537	920	984	1188	1370	3062
Debt portion	841	611	367	397	494	606	1788
Equity portion	1274	926	553	587	694	764	1274
Transmission and distribution	14,255	15,364	16,626	17,985	19,455	21,106	32,061
Life extension	1969	836	887	941	997	1056	1396
Retrofit emission control	-	-	-	-	-	3167	30,823
Total	23,528	22,407	22,469	24,142	26,949	34,039	80,531
Cumulative total	23,527	45,935	68,404	92,546	119,495	153,534	391,129

Source: "An Uncertain Future Lies in Wait," *Electric World* 205, No. 10, October, 1991, p. 11. Primary source: DRI/McGraw-Hill. *Notes:* 1. Includes both private and public utilities. 2. Without allowance for funds used during construction.

★ 127 ★

Office and Industrial Construction Need, 1980-2000

[Square feet needed in millions]

	1980-1990	1990-2000
Primary office	2132.3	187.9
Factory	2213.7	1497.5
Other industrial	2075	1903.7

Source: "Past vs. Future Construction Needs," *Mortgage Banking* 51, No. 10, July, 1991, p. 18.

★ 128 ★

Office Space Added, 1960-1999

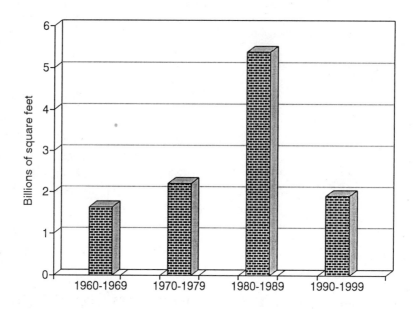

"Half the cities in the U.S. need not build another square foot of office space for the rest of the decade and could still meet demand, according to David Birch, president of Cognetics, who recently completed a study of future needs for the National Association of Industrial and Office Parks. The nation can expand office space at only about a third of the level of the previous decade, he believes."

[Numbers in billions of square feet]

1960-1969	1.63
1970-1979	2.21
1980-1989	5.38
1990-1999	1.90[1]

Source: "Real Estate's Low-Rise Future," Bill Saporito, *Fortune* 123, No. 2, January 28, 1991, p. 44. Primary source: *Statistical Abstract of the United States* and Cognetics. *Notes:* 1. Indicates projected office space needed to maintain a national average vacancy rate between 12% and 14%.

Value of New Construction, 1988-1996

[1987 dollars in billions except as noted]

Type of construction	1988	1989	1990	1991	1992	1996	Percent change		
							1990-91	1991-92	1991-96[1]
Total new construction	415.0	409.8	402.8	380.4	381.1	403.8	-6	0	1
Residential	190.3	181.3	164.9	153.0	162.1	178.1	-7	6	3
Single-family	112.0	107.8	98.1	90.3	97.5	104.6	-8	8	3
Multifamily	21.4	20.6	17.4	11.3	11.6	13.8	-35	3	4
Home improvement	56.8	52.9	49.5	51.5	53.0	59.7	4	3	3
Private nonresidential	134.1	137.4	139.2	127.2	118.9	119.1	-9	-6	-1
Manufacturing facilities	15.8	18.9	21.5	20.4	19.4	24.9	-5	-5	4
Office	29.8	29.3	25.9	22.0	18.7	14.5	-15	-15	-8
Hotels and motels	7.2	7.8	8.7	7.0	5.6	3.7	-20	-20	-12
Other commercial	31.9	31.5	30.8	24.6	21.7	18.1	-20	-12	-6
Religious	3.0	3.0	3.1	3.1	3.2	*	0	3	*
Educational	3.1	3.4	3.8	3.8	4.0	4.6	0	5	4
Hospital and institutional	7.7	7.7	8.5	8.9	9.4	10.3	5	5	3
Misc. buildings	4.6	4.1	4.1	4.0	4.0	*	-3	0	*
Telecommunications	9.5	8.5	8.5	8.9	8.9	10.3	5	0	3
Railroads	2.3	2.5	2.5	2.1	2.0	*	-15	-5	*
Electric utilities	11.2	11.8	11.3	11.6	11.9	12.9	3	2	2
Gas utilities	3.4	3.9	4.7	4.8	4.4	*	3	-10	*
Petroleum pipelines	0.4	0.3	0.4	0.4	0.4	*	0	0	*
Farm structures	2.2	2.1	2.4	2.4	2.4	*	0	2	*
Misc. structures	2.0	2.5	3.0	3.0	3.0	*	0	0	*
Public works	90.7	91.1	98.7	100.1	100.0	106.6	1	0	1
Housing and redevelopment	3.1	3.3	3.4	3.5	3.4	*	2	-2	*
Federal industrial	1.4	1.2	1.3	1.4	1.4	*	10	-2	*
Educational	13.9	15.8	18.5	21.1	22.1	23.3	14	5	2
Hospital	2.6	2.3	2.4	2.3	2.2	1.8	-5	-5	-5
Other public buildings	14.0	14.0	15.8	16.0	14.9	16.0	2	-7	0
Highways	27.6	26.1	28.2	27.4	26.8	30.2	-3	-2	2
Military facilities	3.4	3.3	2.5	2.0	1.7	1.4	-20	-15	-7
Conservation and development	4.6	4.6	4.2	4.6	5.1	5.1	10	11	2
Sewer systems	8.5	8.7	9.3	8.8	9.0	9.8	-5	2	2
Water supplies	3.9	3.8	4.6	5.1	5.3	6.2	10	5	4
Misc. public structures	7.7	8.0	8.6	8.0	8.0	*	-7	0	*

Source: U.S. Industrial Outlook 1992: Business Forecasts for 350 Industries, U.S. Department of Commerce, January, 1992, p. 5-2. Primary source: Department of Commerce, Bureau of the Census and International Trade Administration (ITA). Numbers for 1991 are estimates; numbers for 1992 and 1996 are projected. *Notes:* * Indicates long-term forecast not made separately. 1. Average annual rate.

Households

★ 130 ★

Age of Householders, 1990-2000

"Between now and 2000, the market will shift to older buyers as the number of households headed by 35-to 44-year olds jumps 16% to 24.4 million while younger households decline 16.9% to 16.8 million. Yet how many of those aging baby-boom households buy new homes will depend on local affordability and competition from existing stock, according to NAHB."

[Numbers in thousands]

Age of householder	1990	1995	2000
Under 25	4,573	4,151	4,375
25-34	20,693	19,114	16,782
35-44	21,028	23,416	24,356
45-64	27,143	30,946	36,496
65+	20,621	22,548	23,619

Source: "Starter Homes," Brad German, *Builder* 15, No. 1, January, 1992, p. 266. Primary source: Joint Center for Housing Studies.

★ 131 ★

Annual Household Growth Due to Aging, 1970-2000[1]

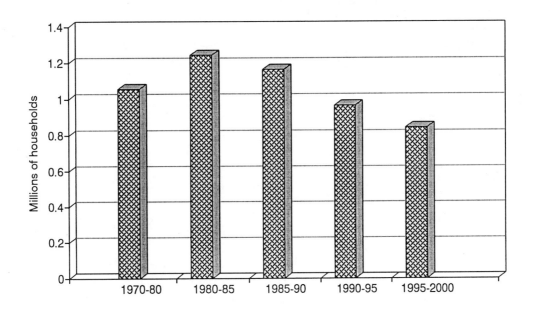

The effects "on household growth of the aging of the baby boom and baby bust generations can be seen in [the graph below] where calculations of trends and projections in the age structure factor in household growth are presented. The 1980-85 period was when the age structure factor exercised its biggest influence. Between 1990 and 1995 the effects of aging will decrease dramatically, and by the last five years of the century the age structure factor should account for almost 500 thousand fewer households annually than in 1980-85. Total household growth from all factors (age structure, migration and hardship) should fall to an average of just over one million per year by the end of the century, down from 1.7 million in the 1970s and 1.4 million per year in the 1980s."

[Numbers in millions of households]

1970-80	1.054
1980-85	1.243
1985-90	1.164
1990-95	0.964
1995-2000	0.843

Source: Working Paper W89-1 for the Joint Center for Housing Studies of Harvard University, *U.S. Household Trends: The 1980s and Beyond*, George S. Masnick, 1989. Primary source: George Masnick, "New Projections of Population and Households for States and Regions," Joint Center for Housing Studies, August 1989. 1. Includes aging of previous migrants.

★ 132 ★

Census Household Projections by Age of Head and Household Type, 2000-2010

Projections by household type to the year 2000 are shown in the top section of the table. The assumed annual rates of growth for the period 2000-2010 are shown in the next panel. These rates were used in calculating the percentage distribution of households by age of the head. This distribution is shown in the third section. Assuming that this distribution, as well as the targeted growth rates by type of household, are specifically achieved in 2010, the final projection of the number of households by type and age of head may be calculated as shown in the bottom panel.

[Numbers in thousands of households]

	Husband/ Wife	Female head	Male head	Female prime	Male prime	Total	Calculated total
All households	56,294	12,701	3,282	18,204	15,452	105,933	105,933
Under 25	1,064	813	232	1,077	1,256	4,442	4,442
25-29	3,251	1,132	259	1,148	2,011	7,801	7,801
30-34	5,010	1,474	423	1,341	1,955	10,203	10,203
35-44	14,947	3,632	934	1,806	4,020	25,339	25,339
45-54	13,557	2,958	768	1,930	2,390	21,603	21,603
55-64	8,805	1,124	358	2,198	1,417	13,903	13,902
65-74	5,922	718	165	3,581	1,129	11,516	11,515
75+	3,739	849	141	5,123	1,274	11,126	11,126
Calculated total	56,295	12,700	3,280	18,204	15,452	105,933	105,931

Assumed Annual Rate of Growth 2000-2010

	Husband/ Wife	Female head	Male head	Female prime	Male prime	Total	
All households	.0050	.0110	.0210	.0150	.0240	.0110	
Under 25	-.0065	.0370	.0498	.0416	.0320	.0266	
25-29	-.0475	-.0165	-.0115	-.0095	-.0108	-.0271	
30-34	-.0259	-.0054	.0120	.0167	.0093	-.0091	
35-44	-.0074	.0006	.0141	.0135	.0276	.0015	
45-54	.0323	.0438	.0463	.0416	.0580	.0380	
55-64	.0281	.0227	.0317	.0233	.0411	.0284	
65-74	-.0072	.0205	-.0179	-.0100	.0018	-.0081	
75+	.0205	.0107	.0000	.0236	.0258	.0215	

Percentage Distribution of Projected Households in 2010 by Age of Head

	Husband/ Wife	Female head	Male head	Female prime	Male prime	Total	
All households	.501	.120	.034	.179	.166	1.000	
Under 25	.016	.080	.091	.075	.086		
25-29	.033	.065	.056	.048	.090		
30-34	.063	.095	.115	.073	.107		
35-44	.227	.249	.260	.095	.263		
45-54	.305	.310	.292	.134	.209		
55-64	.190	.096	.118	.128	.106		
65-74	.090	.040	.033	.149	.057		
75+	.075	.064	.034	.298	.082		
Total	1.000	1.000	1.000	1.000	1.000		

Final Projection: Households in 2010 by Age of Head and Type

	Husband/ Wife	Female head	Male head	Female prime	Male prime	Total	Calculated total
All households	59,233	14,187	4,020	21,163	19,626	118,229	118,229

[Continued]

★ 132 ★

Census Household Projections by Age of Head and Household Type, 2000-2010
[Continued]

	Husband/ Wife	Female head	Male head	Female prime	Male prime	Total	Calculated total
Under 25	967	1,132	367	1,580	1,684		5,730
25-29	1,939	928	224	1,019	1,765		5,875
30-34	3,739	1,352	463	1,544	2,098		9,197
35-44	13,464	3,537	1,045	2,015	5,164		25,224
45-54	18,068	4,396	1,174	2,830	4,109		30,577
55-64	11,272	1,363	476	2,700	2,075		17,886
65-74	5,343	565	134	3,162	1,124		10,329
75+	4,441	915	137	6,312	1,607		13,413
Calculated total	59,233	14,187	4,020	21,163	19,626		118,229

Source: "Appendix C," Harold M. Katsura, Raymond J. Struyk, and Sandra J. Newman, *Housing for the Elderly in 2010: Projections and Policy Options*, Urban Institute Report 89-4. Washington, D.C.: The Urban Institute Press, 1989, pp. 145-46.

★ 133 ★

Distribution of Households by Household Type and Age of Head, 1985 and 2010

The table below provides the projected changes in the distribution of households among the household types and in the age of household heads. The data shows that a major decline in the percentage of households headed by married couples is likely over the period of 1985 to 2010. By 2010, married couples will head only 50 percent of all households as opposed to 58 percent in 1985. This change will be compensated by increases in other types of households, but the gain in households composed of males living alone is projected to be the biggest. The number of households headed by a person under age 35 is also expected to decline significantly when the largest age cohort—the baby boomers—jump to a higher age bracket, creating a 9 percent increase in the 45-64 age group. The projected rise in the percentage of households headed by persons 75 years of age or older is substantial as well, compensating for decreases in the age group 65-74, and this type of household will likely comprise 12 percent of all households by 2010.

[Numbers in percent]

	1985	2010
Household type		
Husband-wife	58.0	50.1
Male-headed families	2.6	3.4
Female-headed families	11.7	12.0
Male individual	12.3	16.6
Female individual	15.5	17.9
Age of household head		
Under 35	29.2	18.9
35-44	20.1	21.1

[Continued]

★ 133 ★

Distribution of Households by Household Type and Age of Head, 1985 and 2010

[Continued]

	1985	2010
45-64	29.7	38.7
65-74	12.6	9.3
75+	8.5	12.0

Source: "Projected Changes in the Characteristics and Housing Situation of the Elderly Population if Current Policies Continue," Harold M. Katsura, Raymond J. Struyk, and Sandra J. Newman, *Housing for the Elderly in 2010: Projections and Policy Options*, Urban Institute Report 89-4. Washington, D.C.: The Urban Institute Press, 1989, p. 16. Primary source: Tabulations of 1985 CPS file and Aged TRIM2 file.

Housing for the Elderly

★ 134 ★

Deficiencies and Housing Finances by Tenure, 1978 and 2010

The table below shows a slight increase in the percentage of structural and maintenance deficiencies for households and a small decrease in the percentage of households with excessive housing expenditures over the period of 1978 and 2010 and, using 1984 prices, provides the distribution of equity among elderly homeowners for each of those years.

[Numbers in percent]

	All households		Owners		Renters	
	1978	2010	1978	2010	1978	2010
Presence of dwelling Deficiencies						
Structural	9.4	12.1	8.8	11.7	11.0	13.3
Maintenance	2.2	2.3	1.6	1.8	3.6	3.6
Housing expenditures Greater than 30						
Percent of income	25.7	22.9	15.3	13.8	52.1	51.1
Home equity holdings[1]						
Under $50,000			46.5	34.1		
$50-90,000			35.9	48.7		
Over $90,000			17.7	17.3		

[Continued]

★ 134 ★

Deficiencies and Housing Finances by Tenure, 1978 and 2010
[Continued]

	All households		Owners		Renters	
	1978	2010	1978	2010	1978	2010
Percentage of owners with no mortgage debt			87.2	91.7		

Source: "Projected Changes in the Characteristics and Housing Situation of the Elderly Population if Current Policies Continue," Harold M. Katsura, Raymond J. Struyk, and Sandra J. Newman, *Housing for the Elderly in 2010: Projections and Policy Options*, Urban Institute Report 89-4, Washington, D.C.: The Urban Institute Press, 1989, p. 31. *Note:* 1. In 1984 dollars.

★ 135 ★

General Housing Attributes by Tenure, 1978 and 2010

This table considers attributes such as type of structure, whether the household in the unit receives housing assistance, and size of unit in projecting changes for the housing situation of the elderly population from 1978 to 2010.

[Numbers in percent]

	All households		Owners		Renters[4]	
	1987	2010	1978	2010	1987	2010
Building type						
house/apartment	93.5	93.4	92.4	92.4	96.5	96.9
mobile home	5.8	6.0	7.6	7.5	1.0	1.2
other	.7	.6	.1	.1	2.5	1.9
Number of units in structure						
1	71.4	73.5	90.0	91.1	20.5	18.9
2-4	13.2	9.4	7.1	5.4	29.9	22.0
5-9	3.6	3.9	.7	.8	11.7	13.6
10+	11.8	13.1	2.2	2.7	37.9	45.5
Household has lived in unit 5 years or more	77.3	85.4	86.1	92.2	53.3	64.2
Household receiving housing assistance[1]	21.2	30.8	--	--	21.2	30.8
Large unit[2]	18.7	15.2	18.6	14.4	19.0	17.6

[Continued]

★ 135 ★

General Housing Attributes by Tenure, 1978 and 2010
[Continued]

	All households		Owners		Renters[4]	
	1987	2010	1978	2010	1987	2010
Unit in 4+ story structure[3]	6.9	6.5	1.4	1.2	21.7	21.5

Source: "Projected Changes in the Characteristics and Housing Situation of the Elderly Population if Current Policies Continue," Harold M. Katsura, Raymond J. Struyk, and Sandra J. Newman, *Housing for the Elderly in 2010: Projections and Policy Options*, Urban Institute Report 89-4. Washington D.C.: The Urban Institute Press, 1989, p. 20. *Notes:* 1. Renters only. 2. 5 or more rooms for renters; 7 or more for owners. 3. Only for structures with 3+ units. 4. Cash renters only. .

The Housing Market

★ 136 ★

Average Annual Percent Change in the Real Price of Housing, 1991-2000

Two statistical models, called Bayesian vector autoregressions (BVARs), "were developed to forecast the real price of housing through the year 2000. Such models express each variable in the model in terms of its own past values and the past values of the other variables in the model. The first BVAR used the population aged 25-44 years to measure the homebuying population. The second BVAR differed only in that it used the population aged 25-64 years to measure the homebuying population. Each BVAR also included several economic influences on the real price of housing: the after-tax mortgage rate, real disposable income, the GNP implicit price deflator, real residential investment spending, and the real wage of construction workers."

	BVAR with population aged 25-44 years	BVAR with population aged 25-64 years
5-year periods		
1991-1995	-.5	.8
1996-2000	2.9	-1.2
10-year period		
1991-2000	-1.7	-.2

Source: "Will the Real Price of Housing Drop Sharply in the 1990s?" C. Alan Garner, *Economic Review* 77, No. 1, First Quarter, 1992, p. 65.

★ 137 ★

Factory-Built Housing Market Growth, 1976-2000

"By 1993, factory-built housing will account for 27 percent of all housing. As product is upgraded, demand will increase.... Modular housing is an ideal product for inner-city sites, where labor is scarce, pilferage is a serious problem and too many potential homeowners are still renters. In rural areas, where many live in substandard housing, modulars can be erected easily and quickly, providing a safe, decent and affordable form of shelter."

Item (000 units)	1976	1988	1993	2000	% Annual growth	
					1988/1970	1993/1988
Total housing starts						
(both stick and factory built)	1835	1706	1825	1725	-0.4%	1.4%
Factory-built housing	532	437	500	550	-1.1%	2.7%
By type:						
Manufactured housing	401	218	250	250	-3.3%	2.8%
Modular/sectional	27	69	85	105	5.4%	4.3%
Panelized	88	113	120	135	1.4%	1.2%
Pre-cut packages	16	37	45	60	4.8%	4.0%
By market:						
Single-family	529	403	450	475	-1.5%	2.2%
Multifamily	3	34	50	75	14.4%	8.0%

Source: Professional Builder 55, No. 14, August, 1990, p. 101. Primary source: The Freedonia Group Inc.

★ 138 ★

Long-Term Forecast for Key Economic Variables Affecting Housing Outlook in the 1990s

"One of the major demographic forces causing the slowdown in housing is a deceleration in population growth over the next decade. From 1991 to 2000, population aged 16 and over is expected to grow at a compound annual rate of 0.9%, which is below the 1.1% rate recorded from 1981 to 1990. Embedded in this slowdown is a decline in the segment of the population aged 25 to 44. After increasing 2.7% in the Seventies and Eighties, this segment of the population is expected to shrink by 0.1% in the Nineties. This decline signifies the passage of the baby-boom generation through the age group with the highest household formation rates. The generation to follow, known as the baby-bust generation, will be fewer in number and consequently will have less of a demand for housing."

	1990	1991	1992	1993	1994	1995	1996-2000
Real GNP	1.0	-0.5	2.3	3.3	2.7	2.0	2.7
Unemployment	5.5	6.7	6.7	6.0	5.9	6.0	5.9
Consumer price index	5.4	4.2	3.1	3.4	3.4	3.6	3.4
3-Month treasury bill	7.5	5.5	5.0	5.2	5.3	5.4	5.4

[Continued]

★ 138 ★

Long-Term Forecast for Key Economic Variables Affecting Housing Outlook in the 1990s
[Continued]

	1990	1991	1992	1993	1994	1995	1996-2000
30-Yr government bond	8.6	8.1	7.6	7.4	7.0	7.0	7.0
30-Yr fixed mortgage	10.1	9.3	8.4	8.2	7.6	7.6	7.6
Housing starts	1,203	1,000	1,198	1,357	1,327	1,277	1,205
Single family	901	828	970	1,061	1,026	977	886
Multifamily	302	172	228	296	299	300	319

Source: "Beyond the Recession: Look at the Nineties," Kimberly A. Martin, *Real Estate Outlook*, December, 1991, p. 13. Due to data availability, researchers were unable to incorporate the short-term forecast as a starting point for the long-term forecast. Consequently, there are some minor differences between the forecasts for 1991-93.

★ 139 ★

Multifamily Housing Starts, 1992-2000

"Multifamily starts are expected to grow faster than renter households to offset unusually weak production years from 1989 to 1992. NAHB says multi starts will peak at 400,000 units in 1995, and then average 272,000 a year through 2000."

[Numbers in millions]

	Multifamily	Total
1992	200,000	1.280
1993	254,000	1.425
1994	370,000	1.550
1995	400,000	1.590
1996	325,000	1.335
1997	255,000	1.235
1998	320,000	1.450
1999	250,000	1.310
2000	210,000	1.200

Source: "Multi Demand is Picking Up," Brad German, *Builder* 15, No. 9, August, 1992, p. 90. Primary source: NAHB.

★ 140 ★

Projections for Housing Starts in the 1990s in Relation to Personal Income Growth

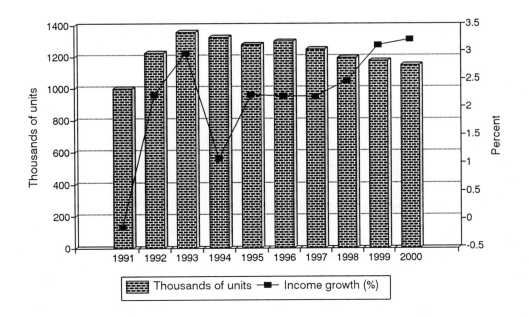

"The outlook for housing is shaped by personal income growth and demographics. Housing starts will continue to be constrained early on in the forecast period by the lingering recession. In 1991, personal income is expected to post its first decline since 1974, and consequently, housing starts will average 1.0 million units, the lowest level recorded in more than 20 years..." According to the forecast, housing starts will peak in 1993 at 1.357 million units, below the 1.488 million unit average recorded in the 1980s. Underlying this weakness are small gains in personal income, huge consumer debt burdens, and major shifts in the demographic composition of the United States. These factors will limit growth in housing starts, which are expected to average 1.22 million units over the coming decade.

[Personal income growth measured by percentage and housing starts in thousands of units]

	Percent	Thousands of units
1991	0.12	1000
1992	2.25	1225
1993	3.00	1357
1994	1.1	1325
1995	2.25	1280
1996	2.23	1300
1997	2.22	1250
1998	2.5	1195

[Continued]

★ 140 ★

Projections for Housing Starts in the 1990s in Relation to Personal Income Growth
[Continued]

	Percent	Thousands of units
1999	3.15	1175
2000	3.25	1150

Source: "Beyond the Recession: A look at the Nineties," Kimberly A. Martin, *Real Estate Outlook*, December, 1991, p. 13. Magnitudes estimated from published chart.

★ 141 ★

Single-Family Housing Starts, 1970-1999

"House prices in the years ahead are likely to move roughly in line with overall inflation. Whether they increase more or less than inflation will depend on the strength of regional markets along with a number of other contributing factors."

	Prices
1970-79	11,430,000
1980-89	9,870,000
1990-99	9,000,000

Source: "Nearly 106 Million U.S. Households by Turn of Century," Kent W. Colton, *Builder* 13, No. 4, April, 1990, p. S-42.

★ 142 ★

Summary of Projections of Population and Housing Consumption, 1975-2000

"The forecasts that appear in [the table below] are taken from Pitkin and Masnick (1980). Pitkin and Masnick employ a new methodology to develop their estimates of future housing demand, an approach that directly relates housing consumption by dwelling size and tenure type to age cohorts and then follows these cohorts (and their resulting housing consumption patterns) through time. Because of the flexibility of their technique and the wide range of assumptions that it can consider, a great diversity of forecasts is possible. Reproduced here is a middle-range projection predicated on total fertility rate of 1.8 births per woman and extrapolation to the year 2000 of cohort housing choice trends typical of the 1960-1970 period."

	Total households	Tenure		Structure type			
		Owners	Renters	Mobile	1 family	2 to 4 family	5+ family
All households (thousands)							
1975	72,482	46,894	25,588	3,368	49,737	8,901	10,510
1980	79,114	50,535	28,578	4,188	52,346	9,990	12,623
1985	86,338	55,052	31,286	5,049	55,830	10,862	14,628
1990	92,717	59,468	33,249	5,818	59,099	11,368	16,461
1995	97,513	63,546	33,967	6,557	61,839	11,578	17,568
2000	101,697	67,275	34,423	7,301	64,284	11,688	18,455
Percentage							
1975	100.0	64.7	35.3	4.6	68.6	12.3	14.5
1980	100.0	63.9	36.1	5.3	66.2	12.6	16.0
1985	100.0	63.8	36.2	5.8	64.7	12.6	16.9
1990	100.0	64.1	35.9	6.3	63.7	12.3	17.8
1995	100.0	65.2	34.8	6.7	63.4	11.9	18.0
2000	100.0	66.2	33.8	7.2	63.2	11.5	18.1
Five-year change (thousands)							
1975-1980	6,632	3,641	2,990	820	2,609	1,089	2,113
1980-1985	7,225	4,517	2,708	861	3,484	872	2,005
1985-1990	6,379	4,417	1,962	769	3,269	506	1,653
1990-1995	4,796	4,077	719	739	2,739	210	1,107
1995-2000	4,184	3,729	456	744	2,446	110	887
Five-year change (%)							
1975-1980	9.1	7.8	11.7	24.3	5.2	12.2	20.1
1980-1985	9.1	8.9	9.5	20.6	6.7	8.7	15.9
1985-1990	7.4	8.0	6.3	15.2	5.9	4.7	12.5
1990-1995	5.2	6.9	2.2	12.7	4.6	1.8	6.7
1995-2000	4.3	5.9	1.3	11.3	4.0	0.9	5.0

Source: "Summary of Projections of U.S. Population and Housing Consumption, 1980-2000," Philip W. Brown, *North American Housing Markets into the Twenty-First Century*, edited by George W. Gau and Michael A. Goldberg, Cambridge, Mass.: Ballinger Publishing Company, 1983, p. 28. Primary source: Pitkin and Masnick, 1980: table 1.3.

Chapter 4
CRIME, LAW ENFORCEMENT, AND PRISONS

Criminal Justice: Budget

★ 143 ★

Federal Criminal Justice Budget Authorities and Outlays, Fiscal Year 1991 (Actual) and 1992-95 (Estimated)

"These data are from the budget submitted by the President to Congress in February 1992. The budget authority (actual or estimated) for each fiscal year includes appropriations for that year, as well as for future years, that have been approved by Congress. The outlays (actual or estimated) for the corresponding year are funded partially by the budget authority and partially through unspent funds allocated in previous years. 'Outlays' are defined as values of checks issued, interest accrued on public debt, or other payments made, and net of refunds and reimbursements. These data do not include various fees and program changes that may reduce actual expenditures."

[Numbers in millions of dollars]

Type of program	1991 actual		1992 estimate		1993 estimate		1994 estimate		1995 estimate	
	Budget authority	Outlays	Budget authority	Outlays	Budget authority	Outlays	Budget authority	Outlays	Budget authority	Outlays
Federal law enforcement activities, total	$6,596	$6,304	$7,325	$7,118	$7,771	$7,364	$7,748	$7,698	$7,742	$7,736
Criminal investigations	2,770	2,566	3,052	2,948	3,273	2,929	3,270	3,246	3,270	3,276
Alcohol, tobacco, and firearms investigations	308	300	337	332	357	355	357	357	357	357
Border enforcement activities	2,519	2,482	2,767	2,691	2,939	2,908	2,950	2,921	2,944	2,924
Protection activities (Secret Service)	445	443	512	494	510	503	510	503	510	503
Other enforcement	554	513	657	653[1]	692	669	661	671	661	676
Federal litigative and judicial activities, total	4,613	4,353	5,051	5,028	5,724	5,649	5,763	5,740	5,785	5,775
Civil and criminal prosecution and representation	2,146	1,975	2,285	2,264	2,530[1]	2,488[1]	2,557[1]	2,541[1]	2,569[1]	2,567[1]
Federal judicial activities	2,118	2,011	2,393	2,394	2,835	2,788	2,846	2,837	2,855	2,847
Representation of indigents in civil cases	328	344	350	346	350	350	350	350	350	350
Other	21	23	23	24	9	23	10	12	11	11
Federal correctional activities	1,728	1,600	2,051	1,901	2,187	2,202	2,187	2,284	2,187	2,111
Criminal justice assistance	853	663	870	709	774	876	780	993	780	781
Total	13,790	12,920	15,297	14,756	16,456	16,091	16,478	16,715	16,494	16,403

Source: Sourcebook of Criminal Justice Statistics-1991, Timothy J. Flanagan and Kathleen Maguire, eds., U.S. Department of Justice, Bureau of Justice Statistics, Washington, D.C., 1992, p. 16, Table 1.12. *Note:* 1. Includes proposed legislation.

Juvenile Crime and Correctional Facilities

★ 144 ★

Estimated Cost of Operating a Juvenile Correctional Facility in Fiscal Year 1993

Forty agency budgets for FY '93 were estimated to average $46,326,227. Capital budget estimates averaged $5,577,111 in 28 agencies and operating budgets averaged $42,422,249 in forty agencies. In twenty-nine agencies food budget estimates averaged $1,892,825 and in 28 agencies medical estimates averaged $1,279,804.

Budget	($) Total	($)Capital	($)Operating	($)Food	($) Medical
AL	24,535,793		24,535,793		
AR	10,291,000	86,000	10,205,000	225,000	280,000
CA	352,000,000	6,933,000	345,067,000	27,657,000	15,735,000
CO[1]	37,900,846	55,000	37,845,846	801,529	268,357
CT	15,629,983	75,000	15,554,983	334,107	208,000
DE	17,500,000	1,100,000	16,400,000	450,000	335,000
HI	4,259,383		4,259,383		
IL	46,534,700	2,243,000	44,291,700	1,225,200	2,510,900
IN	22,778,545		22,778,545		
IA	13,400,000		13,400,000		
LA[2]	54,661,364	346,602	54,314,762	713,476	88,146
MD	90,994,684		90,994,684		
MA	51,690,000	170,000	51,520,000	750,000	694,000
MN	8,116,000	32,000	8,084,000	390,500	206,300
MS	11,323,155	87,744	11,235,411		
MO	21,747,674	226,100	21,521,574	728,642	
MT	6,987,826	90,746	6,897,080	459,613	122,870
NE	7,485,726	60,000	7,425,726	571,887	302,456
NV	6,577,219	3,030,000	3,547,219	215,367	44,970
NJ	30,827,000		30,827,000	535,111	68,000
NM	28,996,000	1,944,400	27,051,600	746,400	227,500
NY[3]	152,400,800	32,033,000	120,367,800		
NC	48,801,600	411,964	48,389,636	891,339	1,424,351
ND	5,265,000	166,200	5,098,800	130,000	70,500
OH	226,296,032	90,476,373	135,819,659	7,156,283	2,112,502
OK[4]	46,753,824		46,753,824		
OR	23,006,630	25,408	22,981,222	1,514,589	1,081,933
PA	52,000,000		52,000,000		
RI	14,184,740		14,184,740	388,048	408,000
SC[5]	38,578,317		38,578,317	732,570	1,546,060
SD	4,071,934	164,573	3,907,361	226,428	52,230
TN	47,825,700		47,825,700	653,700	1,071,700
TX	76,418,115	513,364	75,904,751	2,635,904	4,310,550
UT	20,761,018		20,761,018		
VT	10,330,953	10,000	10,320,953	47,642	30,000
VA	114,086,415	10,329,147	103,757,268	3,218,041	2,121,825

[Continued]

113

★ 144 ★

Estimated Cost of Operating a Juvenile Correctional Facility in Fiscal Year 1993
[Continued]

Budget	($) Total	($)Capital	($)Operating	($)Food	($) Medical
WA	63,846,038	3,150,000	60,696,038		
WV	3,000,000	300,000	2,700,000	171,000	81,000
WI	33,040,200	199,500	32,840,700	892,600	73,000
WY	8,144,860	1,900,000	6,244,860	429,939	359,355
Average	$46,326,227	$5,577,111	$42,422,249	$1,892,825	$1,279,804

Source: The Corrections Yearbook, 1992: Juvenile Corrections, George M. and Camille Grapham Camp, Criminal Justice Institute, South Salem, N.Y., 1992, pp. 36-37. Primary source: Survey questionnaire returned to the Criminal Justice Institute by 50 to 51 juvenile corrections agencies in the United States. *Notes:* 1. Food and medical excludes personnel costs. 2. Medical includes only supplies. 3. Excludes $121,158,000 in state aid and $255,000,000 in reappropriations. 4. Pending legislative approval. 5. Capital, food, and medical estimates.

★ 145 ★

Juvenile Homicide Projected to Rise Dramatically toward the End of the Century

Homicides by juveniles are on the rise, and they may triple or even quadruple by the end of the century. This dire prediction comes from Charles Patrick Ewing, a professor of law and clinical associate professor of psychology at the State University of New York at Buffalo.

The number of homicides committed by juveniles in the United States has been increasing steadily for several years and is now up to 2,000 annually. But that number could skyrocket to some 8,000 a year within a decade, says Ewing. He suggests that an increase in child abuse is the key underlying factor. Juvenile killers suffer psychological trauma from witnessing or experiencing abuse, and/or become violent in direct response to the abuse, killing their abuser.

Other trends fueling juvenile homicide are an increase in juvenile poverty, worsening substance abuse, and easier juvenile access to guns, including automatic weapons, Ewing points out in *Kids Who Kill* (Lexington Books, 1990). In addition, the juvenile population is expected to rise during the 1990s.

Source: "Future Scope: Rapid Rise of Juvenile Homicide," *The Futurist* 26, No. 4, July-August 1992, p. 8. Primary source: Charles Patrick Ewing, *Kids Who Kill*, Lexington Books, 1990, as reported by the News Bureau, State University of New York at Buffalo.

★ 146 ★

Number of Juvenile Beds Added During 1991 and Status of Planned Beds, as of January 1, 1992

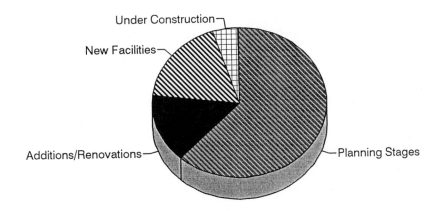

Planning stages	3,300
New facilities	969
Additions/renovations	798
Under construction	247

Source: The Corrections Yearbook, 1992: Juvenile Corrections, George M. and Camille Graham Camp, Criminal Justice Institute, South Salem, N.Y., 1992, p. 33. Primary source: Survey questionnaire returned to the Criminal Justice Institute by 50 of 51 juvenile corrections agencies in the United States.

Prisons: Future Trends in Capacity, Populations, and Costs

★ 147 ★

Capacity of Federal Prisons, 1989-1997

All years referred to are fiscal years, unless otherwise noted. Detail in the table may not add to the totals due to rounding. "To insure that adequate space is available [to incarcerate convicted criminals for the full term of their sentence], the Federal Government has invested over $2 billion in prison construction since 1989. This investment is now paying off as many new prisons open in the next five years. In 1993 space for an estimated 4,200 prisoners will be added to the Federal prison system." The Federal Budget for 1993 is slated to spend $339 million for prison construction and rehabilitation projects. When completed, these new prisons will add nearly 3,400 new prison beds to the system.

[Numbers of beds in thousands]

	Number	Percent of Prisoners over Capacity
1989	31,727	61.0
1991	42,531	51.0
1993	53,402	48.0
1995	71,955	39.0
1997	85,804	35.0

Source: Budget of the United States Government, Fiscal Year 1993, Washington, D.C., 1992, Part One, p. 202. Primary source: Department of Justice, Bureau of Prisons.

★ 148 ★

New Prisons Under Construction, Prisons Being Enlarged, and Projected Total Prison Beds by Type of Security, as of 1992

Grand totals equal data concerning state and Federal prisons added together. As of 1992, 110 new facilities were under construction in 27 jurisdictions; 105 facilities were being added to in 27 jurisdictions. A total of 107,089 beds were being added, of which 32,219 were maximum security, 57,602 were medium security, and 14,117 were minimum security. 23 agencies were slated to spend $2.3 billion to add facilities and beds.

[Costs in millions of dollars]

	Institutions		Beds				($) cost
	New	Exist	Total	Max.	Med.	Min.	
Arizona	2		1,050		1,050		33,085,000
Arkansas	1		600		600		
California	4		11,508	3,000	7,284	1,224	
Colorado[1]	2		750	500	250		
Connecticut	7	2	3,086		2,578	508	328,009,000
Delaware	2		440				
District of Columbia	1						
Florida[2]	4	4	4,758	4,630			64,201,000
Georgia[3]	13	10	12,074	5,051	5,080	1,943	256,000,000
Hawaii		2	136			136	3,600,000
Idaho		1	40				120,000
Illinois[4]	6	2	2,056		979	950	
Indiana	1	3	374	144	150	80	12,850,000
Iowa		4	430		100	330	17,000,000
Kansas	1		150	150			
Kentucky	1		500		500		
Louisiana		3	1,728		1,728		18,000,000
Maine[5]	1	1	100	100			13,000,000
Maryland	1	2	908	768		140	13,800,000
Massachusetts	2	5	966	258	588	120	93,422,738
Michigan	3		1,724	764	720	240	
Minnesota		2	250		250		5,572,000
Missouri		1	200			200	2,865,000
New Hampshire		1	300		150	150	2,000,000
New Jersey		2	682	394		288	51,996,528
New York		2	116	56		60	9,000,000
North Carolina[6]	8	12	6,969	1,872	3,627	1,470	220,859,331
Ohio[7]	3	1	1,225	750		475	90,637,241
Oklahoma		1	350			350	5,500,000
Pennsylvania[8]	5	2	8,188	828	6,406	750	
Rhode Island[9]		5	1,326	726	600		123,000,000
South Carolina	4	4	3,990	50	3,460	480	
South Dakota	1		288		192	96	
Tennessee	2						
Texas	10		15,000	9,000	6,000		
Virginia[10]	3	1	4,822	697	4,125		
Washington[11]	2	4	4,043		2,872	1,171	
Wisconsin		1	50			50	3,310,000

[Continued]

★ 148 ★

New Prisons Under Construction, Prisons Being Enlarged, and Projected Total Prison Beds by Type of Security, as of 1992

[Continued]

	Institutions		Beds				($) cost
	New	Exist	Total	Max.	Med.	Min.	
Federal prisons[12]	20	27	15,912	2,481	8,313	2,906	899,615,000
Total	110	105	107,089	32,219	57,602	14,117	2,267,442,838

Source: The Corrections Yearbook, 1992: Adult Corrections, George M. and Camille Graham Camp, Criminal Justice Institute, South Salem, N.Y., 1992, pp. 42-43. Primary source: Survey questionnaire returned to the Criminal Justice Institute by state and Federal adult correctional agencies in the United States. *Notes:* 1. Med. is a mixed special needs unit. 2. Total includes 128 other beds. 3. Existing institutions include four county correctional institutions; Max. is close; and cost excludes counties' share. 4. New includes four work camps, one community center, and one prison; total includes 127 beds added to existing facilities at cost of $3.5 million. 5. 52 min. beds may be added in future. 6. Max. includes close. 7. Max. includes 500 close. 8. Total includes 204 beds to two existing facilities. 9. Cost estimated. 10. Total excludes 375 replacement beds at cost of $11 million; maximum is close and minimum is dormitory. 11. Total includes 2,219 beds to existing facility at cost of $103 million. 12. Existing institution excludes satellite camps and total includes 2,212 administrative beds.

★ 149 ★

Numbers of New Prison Beds in Planning, but Not Under Construction, and Total Projected Cost, as of 1992

Figures include planned beds in both Federal and state prisons. As of 1992, 24,085 beds were planned in 32 systems. Thirty-five systems reported projected costs of $1.4 billion.

Planned beds	Beds	Cost
Mobile County, AL		17,930,815
Maricopa County, AZ	554	4,100,000
Fresno County, CA	128	4,200,000
Monterey County, CA	204	20,800,000
San Mateo County, CA		50,000,000
Stanislaus County, CA		29,849,215
Ventura County, CA	750	54,000,000
El Paso County, CO[1]	96	21,300
Alachua County, FL	512	32,000,000
Brevard County, FL	560	23,500,000
Broward County, FL	250	
Collier County, FL	256	
Hillsborough County, FL	1,024	40,000,000
Escambia County, FL	600	5,000,000
Marion County, FL		1,700,000
Dade County, FL	1,250	
Orange County, FL	7,503	131,400,513
Cook County, IL	1,600	230,000,000
Marion County, IN	192	7,000,000
Lexington-Fayette County, KY	350	4,000,000
Caddo County, LA		31,000,000
Baltimore County, MD	216	17,000,000

[Continued]

★ 149 ★

Numbers of New Prison Beds in Planning, but Not Under Construction, and Total Projected Cost, as of 1992
[Continued]

Planned beds	Beds	Cost
Montgomery County, MD	400	48,000,000
Prince George's County, MD	384	18,000,000
Hennepin County, MN	1,440	180,000,000
St. Louis, MO	228	15,000,000
Las Vegas, NV	134	101,048
Hudson County, NJ	250	
Monmouth County, NJ	560	37,000,000
Monroe County, NY[2]		15,000,000
Mecklenburg County, NC	600	
Cuyahoga County, OH		52,000,000
Tulsa County, OK	96	4,000,000
Lancaster County, PA[2]	320	64,000
Philadelphia Prisons, PA	1,000	97,000,000
Nueces County, TX [3]	192	700,000
Smith County, TX	240	1,500,000
Salt Lake County, UT	150	
Fairfax County, VA	750	77,123,000
King County, WA[4]	896	150,000,000
Snohomish County, WA	400	13,000,000
Total	24,085	1,411,989,891

Source: The Corrections Yearbook, 1992: Jail Systems, George M. and Camille Graham Camp, Criminal Justice Institute, South Salem, N.Y., 1992, pp. 31-32. Primary source: Survey questionnaire returned to the Criminal Justice Institute by state and Federal adult correctional agencies in the United States. *Notes:* 1. Through double-bunking. 2. Cost estimated. 3. Dorms only. 4. Projected cost excludes 344 beds planned for the year 2000 and includes cost of 23 court rooms and offices.

★ 150 ★

Growth in Prison Populations in Selected States, 1989-1994

According to the NCCD's 1989 national prison population forecast, "the current War on Drugs will overwhelm the nation's correctional systems" by 1994. The projected 68 percent inmate population increase by 1994 (averaging a 13 percent increase per year) translates into an additional 460,000 inmates, for a total of 1,133,000 prison inmates by 1994. "With average operating costs of $25,000 per inmate per year and a construction cost of $50,000 per cell, states will require at least an additional $35 billion to build and operate their prisons over the next five years." In 1991 California became the first state to exceed 100,000 inmates. By 1994 it will have over 136,000 inmates. Florida's prison population will grow faster than that of any other state, reaching over 100,000 inmates by 1994. "The primary reason for the dramatic increase in prison populations is the War on Drugs, which is not only increasing the number of prison admissions but is also increasing the rate of parole violations."

State	1989	1990	1991	1992	1993	1994	% change
California	82,855	94,995	107,250	117,775	127,725	136,640	64.9
Florida	39,085	68,436	80,469	88,977	95,371	100,855	158.0
Illinois	22,894	26,079	28,623	30,552	32,559	34,373	50.1
Louisiana	16,324	16,700	17,084	17,477	17,878	18,290	12.0
Massachusetts	7,738	8,491	8,948	9,411	9,678	10,065	30.1
Michigan[1]	27,619	31,773	35,146	38,519	41,892	45,265	63.9
Nevada	5,249	5,909	6,906	7,734	8,686	9,500	81.0
Ohio	28,332	32,051	35,005	38,096	41,048	42,852	51.2
Oklahoma	11,274	12,003	12,843	13,874	14,846	15,823	40.3
Oregon	5,355	5,906	6,466	7,192	7,903	8,748	63.4
Tennessee	9,774	10,083	10,239	10,125	10,049	10,088	3.2
Virginia	15,288	17,033	18,853	20,981	23,046	25,120	64.1
Total	271,787	329,459	367,832	400,713	430,681	457,619	68.4

Source: "The 1989 NCCD Prison Population Forecast: The Impact of the War on Drugs," James Austin and Aaron David McVey, *NCCD Focus,* The National Council on Crime and Delinquency, December, 1989, p. 4. *Note:* 1. Projected prison populations for 1992-94 are extrapolated estimates and are not officia

★ 151 ★

Numbers of Inmates Confined to Prisons by State, 1993 and 1994, and Percent Change Compared to 1992

Table includes inmate projections for Federal prisons as final item. From January 1, 1992, fifty-one jurisdictions projected an average growth of 9.1 percent by January 1, 1993, and fifty projected 16.6 percent growth by January 1, 1994.

	1/1/93	% change	1/1/94	% change
Alabama	17,284	19.6	19,347	39.2
Alaska	2,530	3.9	2,600	6.9
Arizona	16,541	7.6	17,680	15.7
Arkansas	8,035	8.1	8,035	8.8
California	104,763	8.7	109,395	14.4

[Continued]

★ 151 ★

Numbers of Inmates Confined to Prisons by State, 1993 and 1994, and Percent Change Compared to 1992
[Continued]

	1/1/93	% change	1/1/94	% change
Colorado[1]	8,855	17.1	9,042	23.2
Connecticut	11,342	6.8	11,742	11.1
Delaware	3,926	5.3	4,051	9.0
District of Columbia	11,690	16.9	11,930	22.8
Florida	48,660	4.4	51,885	11.5
Georgia	29,453	19.7	33,214	40.5
Hawaii	2,667	8.4	2,745	12.3
Idaho	2,378	13.5	2,528	23.0
Illinois	31,451	7.4	33,106	13.7
Indiana	13,919	6.5	14,893	14.5
Iowa	4,900	7.6	5,200	14.9
Kansas	5,996	3.7	6,208	7.5
Kentucky	11,205	20.4	11,946	33.9
Louisiana	15,880	8.6		
Maine	1,786	12.4	1,893	21.0
Maryland	20,781	11.5	21,569	17.3
Massachusetts	9,309	-7.3	9,579	-4.1
Michigan	34,651	9.0	35,721	13.3
Minnesota	3,774	8.5	4,112	19.1
Mississippi	9,545	6.6	10,017	12.4
Missouri	16,067	3.7	16,667	7.8
Montana	1,649	12.6	1,759	22.1
Nebraska	2,567	1.1	2,610	2.8
Nevada	6,149	4.9	6,574	12.4
New Hampshire	1,675	5.1	1,800	13.2
New Jersey	18,600	3.1	18,800	4.3
New York	61,000	5.1	61,000	5.4
North Carolina	20,182	5.3	21,785	14.0
North Dakota	560	4.6	570	6.7
Ohio	38,045	6.8	40,018	12.9
Oklahoma[2]	12,650	15.5	13,454	25.8
Oregon	6,752	3.8	6,939	6.9
Pennsylvania	25,871	11.9	27,724	21.6
Rhode Island	3,355	17.0	3,726	33.9
South Carolina	17,440	8.5	18,664	16.9
South Dakota[3]	1,564	11.1	1,645	18.3
Tennessee[4]	15,600	8.7	16,250	14.1
Texas	59,917	15.7	64,742	28.2
Utah	3,170	11.7	3,476	24.2
Vermont	1,287	13.9	1,352	22.0
Virginia	19,204	11.8	20,605	21.7
Washington	9,194	9.3	9,751	16.9
West Virginia	1,700	9.8	1,825	19.0
Wisconsin	9,069	15.2	10,112	31.6
Wyoming	950	3.2	967	5.1

[Continued]

★ 151 ★

Numbers of Inmates Confined to Prisons by State, 1993 and 1994, and Percent Change Compared to 1992

[Continued]

	1/1/93	% change	1/1/94	% change
Federal	72,000	7.7	81,000	21.9
Projections	857,538	9.1	892,253	16.6

Source: The Corrections Yearbook, 1992: Adult Corrections, George M. and Camille Graham Camp, Criminal Justice Institute, South Salem, N.Y., 1992, pp. 9-10. Primary source: Survey questionnaire returned to the Criminal Justice Institute by state and Federal adult correctional agencies in the United States. *Notes:* 1. Includes off-grounds. 2. June 30, 1993. 3. Fiscal year 1993. 4. All incarcerated felons.

★ 152 ★

Projected Capital and Operating Costs of Prison Systems by State in Fiscal Year 1993

"Proposed budgets were estimated by forty-seven agencies to exceed $12.5 billion for operations and $937 million for capital expenditures for a projected total of $15.7 billion."

1993 projected budgets	Total	Capital	Operating
Alabama	130,759,047		130,759,047
Alaska	105,000,000		105,000,000
Arizona[1]	290,000,000	20,000,000	270,000,000
Colorado	184,794,308	757,600	184,036,708
Connecticut	361,530,938	65,500,000	296,030,938
Delaware	77,878,800	504,700	77,374,100
District of Columbia	312,364,000	56,500,000	255,864,000
Florida	1,401,621,421	123,713,940	1,277,907,481
Georgia[2]	529,583,998	11,600,000	517,983,998
Hawaii	88,790,964	2,800,000	85,990,964
Idaho	48,037,900	6,844,900	41,193,000
Illinois	514,943,000	27,663,000	487,280,000
Indiana	304,545,854		304,545,854
Iowa	123,353,076	3,795,023	119,558,053
Kansas	175,204,900	8,631,900	166,573,000
Louisiana[3]	174,899,798	2,847,842	172,051,956
Maine	44,200,000		44,200,000
Maryland	388,143,952	27,890,500	360,253,452
Massachusetts[4]	320,192,700	50,000,000	270,192,700
Michigan[5]	937,073,100		937,073,100
Minnesota	103,128,000		103,128,000
MIssissippi	87,686,132		87,686,132
Missouri	213,451,895	4,546,040	208,905,855
Montana	44,441,570	15,499,210	28,942,360
Nebraska	53,740,633	351,350	53,389,283
Nevada	92,889,192	165,806	92,723,386

[Continued]

★ 152 ★

Projected Capital and Operating Costs of Prison Systems by State in Fiscal Year 1993

[Continued]

1993 projected budgets	Total	Capital	Operating
New Hampshire	35,828,972		35,828,972
New Jersey	640,800,000	2,300,000	638,500,000
New Mexico	112,499,415	4,289,015	108,210,400
New York	1,289,803,700	131,395,000	1,158,408,700
North Carolina	500,583,981		500,583,981
North Dakota	8,266,000	400,000	7,866,000
Ohio	659,194,581	79,919,227	579,275,354
Oklahoma	223,017,712		223,017,712
Oregon[1]	110,000,000		110,000,000
Rhode Island	104,022,086	14,314,952	89,707,134
South Carolina	336,472,729	88,415,647	248,057,082
South Dakota	30,698,246	499,757	30,198,489
Tennessee	306,511,800	24,000,000	282,511,800
Texas	811,376,034	8,398,093	802,977,941
Vermont	37,717,650	1,600,000	36,117,650
Virginia	398,634,466		398,634,466
Washington	450,785,206	151,434,206	299,351,000
West Virginia	22,000,000		22,000,000
Wisconsin	286,300,000		286,300,000
Wyoming	18,269,368	1,188,815	17,080,553
Federal system	2,246,031,000	399,963,000	1,846,068,000
Total	15,737,068,124	937,766,523	12,553,270,601

Source: The Corrections Yearbook, 1992: Adult Corrections, George M. and Camille Graham Camp, Criminal Justice Institute, South Salem, N.Y., 1992, pp. 48-49. Primary source: Survey questionnaire returned to the Criminal Justice Institute by state and Federal adult correctional agencies in the United States. *Notes:* 1. Estimated. 2. Excludes $11.6 million bond. 3. Recommended executive budget for adult institutions. 4. Based on requested budget. 5. Proposed budget.

Chapter 5

EDUCATION

Elementary and Secondary School Enrollment

★ 153 ★

Elementary Enrollment Rates by Age and Sex, 1989 and 1991-2002

The following projections were based on projected enrollment rates by age and sex, which were applied to population projections developed by the U.S. Bureau of the Census for individuals aged 5 to 21 in elementary grades 1-8. These projections were based on the assumption that recent rates will remain constant through the year 2002. Several of the rates exceed 100 percent, as a result of several factors.

[Numbers in percent]

Age	Boys		Girls	
	1989	1991-2002	1989	1991-2002
5	4.3	5.3	6.9	6.5
6	80.8	81.9	86.6	87.7
7	99.6	100.3	99.6	100.0
8	102.4	101.9	101.7	102.0
9	101.2	100.7	102.1	101.3
10	102.0	100.4	101.8	102.4
11	103.4	102.5	103.5	101.8
12	103.3	100.7	102.5	102.6
13	93.3	94.2	94.9	92.3
14	37.0	37.4	26.6	23.8
15	6.6	7.2	4.0	3.7
16	0.6	0.6	0.8	0.5
17	0.1	0.1	0	0
18	0	0	0	0

Source: Projections of Education Statistics to 2002, U.S. Department of Education, Office of Educational Research and Improvement, December, 1991, p. 153.

★ 154 ★

Enrollment in Elementary and Secondary Schools by Organizational Level and Control of Institution, Fall 1977 to Fall 2002

[Numbers in thousands]

Year	Total			Public			Private		
	K-12[1]	Elementary	Secondary	K-12[1]	Elementary	Secondary	K-12[1]	Elementary	Secondary
1977	48,717	28,788	19,929	43,577	24,991	18,586	5,140	3,797	1,343
1978	47,636	28,749	18,887	42,550	25,017	17,534	5,086	3,732	1,353
1979	46,645	28,591	18,054	41,645	24,891	16,754	5,000[2]	3,700	1,300
1980	46,249	28,212	18,037	40,918	24,220	16,698	5,331	3,992	1,339
1981	45,522	28,174	17,348	40,022	24,074	15,948	5,500[2]	4,100	1,400
1982	45,166	28,023	17,142	39,566	23,823	15,742	5,600[2]	4,200	1,400
1983	44,967	28,264	16,703	39,252	23,949	15,303	5,715	4,315	1,400
1984	44,908	28,395	16,513	39,208	24,095	15,113	5,700[2]	4,300	1,400
1985	44,979	28,470	16,509	39,422	24,275	15,147	5,557	4,195	1,362
1986	45,205	28,266	16,939	39,753	24,150	15,603	5,452[2]	4,116	1,336
1987	45,487	28,537	16,950	40,008	24,305	15,703	5,479[3]	4,232	1,247
1988	45,430	28,451	16,980	40,189	24,415	15,774	5,241[3]	4,036	1,206
1989	45,881	28,782	17,099	40,526	24,620	15,906	5,355[3]	4,162	1,193
1990[3]	46,221	29,680	16,541	41,026	25,614	15,412	5,195	4,066	1,129
Projected									
1991	46,841	30,070	16,772	41,575	25,943	15,632	5,266	4,127	1,140
1992	47,601	30,442	17,159	42,250	26,250	16,000	5,351	4,192	1,159
1993	48,410	30,800	17,610	42,971	26,550	16,421	5,439	4,250	1,189
1994	49,279	31,130	18,149	43,749	26,830	16,919	5,530	4,300	1,230
1995	50,054	31,460	18,594	44,442	27,115	17,327	5,612	4,345	1,267
1996	50,759	31,817	18,942	45,074	27,433	17,641	5,685	4,384	1,301
1997	51,331	32,081	19,251	45,585	27,659	17,926	5,746	4,422	1,325
1998	51,750	32,364	19,386	45,955	27,899	18,056	5,795	4,465	1,330
1999	52,110	32,551	19,559	46,276	28,061	18,215	5,834	4,490	1,344
2000	52,406	32,691	19,715	46,539	28,175	18,364	5,867	4,516	1,351
2001	52,679	32,764	19,915	46,782	28,229	18,553	5,897	4,535	1,362
2002	52,996	32,783	20,213	47,068	28,238	18,830	5,928	4,545	1,383

Source: Projections of Education Statistics to 2002, National Center for Education Statistics, December, 1991, p. 10. Primary source: U.S. Department of Education, National Center for Education Statistics, *Statistics of Public Elementary and Secondary Schools*; Common Core of Data surveys; "Selected Public and Private Elementary and Secondary Education Statistics," *NCES Bulletin*, December, 1984; 1985 Private School Survey; "Key Statistics for Private Elementary and Secondary Education: School Year 1988-89," *Early Estimates*; "Key Statistics for Public and Private Elementary and Secondary Education: School Year 1989-90," *Early Estimates*; and "Key Statistics for Public and Private Elementary and Secondary Education: School Year 1990-91," *Early Estimates*. Some data have been revised from previously published figures. Projections are based on data through 1989. Because of rounding, details may not add to totals. As of April 1991. *Notes:* 1. Includes most kindergarten and nursery school enrollment. 2. Estimated by NCES. 3. Estimate.

★ 155 ★

Enrollment of Grades 9 through 12 in Public Schools by Region and State, Fall 1990 to Fall 1996

[Numbers in thousands]

Region and state	Estimate 1990	Projected					
		1991	1992	1993	1994	1995	1996
United States	11,284	11,389	11,587	11,880	12,298	12,660	13,006
Northeast	2,052	2,075	2,100	2,140	2,197	2,249	2,305
Connecticut	120	120	120	122	125	128	130
Maine	62	60	60	63	64	65	68
Massachusetts	223	225	226	230	237	244	252
New Hampshire	41	46	48	50	54	57	59
New Jersey	300	300	302	309	318	327	341
New York	750	768	779	793	812	826	843
Pennsylvania	494	493	500	509	522	532	541
Rhode Island	37	37	37	38	39	41	42
Vermont	25	26	26	26	27	28	29
Midwest	2,801	2,836	2,883	2,948	3,044	3,111	3,157
Illinois	515	517	521	531	546	560	575
Indiana	275	280	285	290	298	301	301
Iowa	145	141	145	148	153	155	154
Kansas	117	120	125	128	133	138	142
Michigan	432	436	440	449	462	471	475
Minnesota	209	215	222	230	241	247	251
Missouri	222	232	237	244	254	263	273
Nebraska	77	77	78	79	82	84	85
North Dakota	32	33	34	35	36	39	40
Ohio	514	514	519	529	543	553	561
South Dakota	34	35	36	37	40	42	43
Wisconsin	228	235	241	248	256	259	258
South	3,966	3,938	3,992	4,092	4,243	4,377	4,521
Alabama	199	195	197	199	205	208	212
Arkansas	121	123	125	127	132	135	138
Delaware	26	27	29	29	30	32	33
District of Columbia	19	20	19	20	21	24	26
Florida	498	467	479	504	534	563	587
Georgia	298	304	310	319	331	342	350
Kentucky	179	177	181	184	187	187	187
Louisiana	202	194	197	203	211	220	232
Maryland	186	190	196	203	213	222	232
Mississippi	134	132	135	136	141	145	150
North Carolina	301	302	306	314	328	341	356
Oklahoma	157	156	158	162	167	171	176
South Carolina	171	171	174	179	186	190	195
Tennessee	225	225	227	233	241	249	254
Texas	885	887	892	902	922	941	968
Virginia	265	269	274	283	297	312	330
West Virginia	100	97	95	96	97	95	94

[Continued]

★ 155 ★

Enrollment of Grades 9 through 12 in Public Schools by Region and State, Fall 1990 to Fall 1996

[Continued]

Region and state	Estimate 1990	Projected					
		1991	1992	1993	1994	1995	1996
West	2,467	2,539	2,614	2,701	2,814	2,923	3,022
Alaska	30	28	29	30	31	33	35
Arizona	115	165	172	179	188	196	202
California	1,352	1,373	1,410	1,449	1,503	1,559	1,615
Colorado	155	155	159	163	172	180	189
Hawaii	45	47	49	52	57	61	68
Idaho	66	60	62	65	67	69	69
Montana	43	43	42	43	46	47	49
Nevada	52	54	56	60	62	64	66
New Mexico	92	93	95	97	101	106	113
Oregon	143	137	141	144	149	154	156
Utah	123	126	133	140	148	154	155
Washington	225	232	240	250	262	269	275
Wyoming	29	27	27	28	29	31	31

Source: Projections of Education Statistics to 2002, U.S. Department of Education, Office of Educational Research and Improvement, December, 1991, pp. 119-20. Primary source: U.S. Department of Education, National Center for Education Statistics, Common Core of Data Surveys and "Key Statistics for Public and Private Elementary and Secondary Education: School Year 1990-1991," *Early Estimates. Notes:* As of June 1. Includes most kindergarten and some nursery school enrollment. Source also includes actual data for 1984-1989.

★ 156 ★

Enrollment of Grades 9 through 12 in Public Schools by Region and State, Fall 1997 to Fall 2002

[Numbers in thousands]

Region and state	Projected					
	1997	1998	1999	2000	2001	2002
United States	13,242	13,294	13,433	13,507	13,610	13,823
Northeast	2,346	2,371	2,562	2,604	2,662	2,735
Connecticut	132	132	128	131	135	138
Maine	70	71	71	74	75	76
Massachusetts	257	263	260	268	276	285
New Hampshire	60	62	62	64	66	70
New Jersey	353	365	403	412	425	442
New York	859	866	990	1,003	1,022	1,047
Pennsylvania	544	541	573	576	585	598
Rhode Island	42	41	41	43	44	44
Vermont	30	30	33	33	35	35
Midwest	3,138	3,086	3,087	3,065	3,088	3,113
Illinois	584	585	633	628	631	638

[Continued]

★ 156 ★

Enrollment of Grades 9 through 12 in Public Schools by Region and State, Fall 1997 to Fall 2002

[Continued]

Region and state	Projected					
	1997	1998	1999	2000	2001	2002
Indiana	295	286	284	283	287	289
Iowa	148	139	143	139	137	135
Kansas	142	140	138	135	135	134
Michigan	466	455	468	469	481	491
Minnesota	248	242	227	227	228	230
Missouri	277	279	274	273	276	280
Nebraska	84	83	78	77	75	74
North Dakota	41	42	41	39	37	36
Ohio	556	548	523	521	525	532
South Dakota	46	46	46	45	44	43
Wisconsin	251	242	231	230	230	230
South	4,660	4,726	4,676	4,705	4,715	4,784
Alabama	213	213	209	209	210	212
Arkansas	141	141	139	138	137	137
Delaware	33	34	33	33	34	36
District of Columbia	29	32	36	37	37	37
Florida	613	628	616	638	655	681
Georgia	358	364	356	363	370	380
Kentucky	184	180	176	174	171	172
Louisiana	246	252	268	261	255	250
Maryland	244	254	266	275	284	294
Mississippi	152	152	158	156	155	153
North Carolina	373	384	387	395	403	416
Oklahoma	180	181	173	168	160	155
South Carolina	199	202	195	196	198	202
Tennessee	258	256	249	249	249	253
Texas	998	1,002	958	949	928	924
Virginia	350	366	370	378	385	398
West Virginia	91	86	88	86	86	86
West	3,098	3,111	3,109	3,132	3,145	3,191
Alaska	39	41	43	44	43	45
Arizona	206	207	197	201	205	209
California	1,660	1,673	1,669	1,695	1,717	1,760
Colorado	199	203	203	201	198	198
Hawaii	76	82	92	92	91	90
Idaho	69	67	65	64	63	62
Montana	49	49	48	48	46	44
Nevada	65	62	56	56	55	56
New Mexico	118	121	156	158	159	162
Oregon	154	149	141	140	141	141
Utah	157	155	156	151	147	146

[Continued]

★ 156 ★

Enrollment of Grades 9 through 12 in Public Schools by Region and State, Fall 1997 to Fall 2002

[Continued]

Region and state	Projected					
	1997	1998	1999	2000	2001	2002
Washington	276	270	253	252	250	250
Wyoming	32	33	31	30	29	28

Source: Projections of Education Statistics to 2002, U.S. Department of Education, Office of Educational Research and Improvement, December, 1991, pp. 119-20. Primary source: U.S. Department of Education, National Center for Education Statistics, Common Core of Data Surveys and "Key Statistics for Public and Private Elementary and Secondary Education: School Year 1990-1991," *Early Estimates. Notes:* As of June 1. Includes most kindergarten and some nursery school enrollment. Source also includes actual data for 1984-1989.

★ 157 ★

Enrollment of Grades Kindergarten through 12 in Public Elementary and Secondary Schools by Region and State, Fall 1990 to Fall 1996

[Numbers in thousands]

Region and state	Estimate 1990	Projected					
		1991	1992	1993	1994	1995	1996
United States	41,026	41,575	42,250	42,971	43,749	44,442	45,074
Northeast	7,233	7,339	7,461	7,608	7,737	7,862	7,982
Connecticut	469	477	488	500	508	517	524
Maine	216	218	220	226	231	237	244
Massachusetts	829	846	863	885	903	922	941
New Hampshire	171	181	189	197	205	213	219
New Jersey	1,083	1,101	1,126	1,161	1,195	1,230	1,268
New York	2,563	2,599	2,633	2,674	2,702	2,728	2,755
Pennsylvania	1,668	1,680	1,701	1,721	1,743	1,761	1,775
Rhode Island	138	139	142	145	147	149	150
Vermont	96	97	99	100	103	105	107
Midwest	9,899	9,973	10,055	10,133	10,266	10,364	10,434
Illinois	1,803	1,811	1,826	1,849	1,884	1,918	1,952
Indiana	956	962	968	970	980	986	989
Iowa	484	477	475	471	473	468	463
Kansas	436	442	448	452	457	461	463
Michigan	1,577	1,589	1,601	1,615	1,631	1,644	1,652
Minnesota	752	767	779	789	802	810	814
Missouri	810	826	838	850	869	886	902
Nebraska	274	274	275	274	277	278	278
North Dakota	117	117	117	117	118	119	119
Ohio	1,770	1,775	1,787	1,798	1,818	1,832	1,844
South Dakota	129	131	132	133	137	139	141
Wisconsin	791	802	810	814	821	822	817

[Continued]

★ 157 ★

Enrollment of Grades Kindergarten through 12 in Public Elementary and Secondary Schools by Region and State, Fall 1990 to Fall 1996
[Continued]

Region and state	Estimate 1990	Projected					
		1991	1992	1993	1994	1995	1996
South	14,761	14,889	15,117	15,379	15,677	15,960	16,242
Alabama	728	726	730	735	745	755	764
Arkansas	435	438	441	443	449	454	458
Delaware	100	102	106	108	111	114	117
District of Columbia	80	81	81	84	85	86	88
Florida	1,862	1,894	1,967	2,049	2,119	2,184	2,242
Georgia	1,152	1,179	1,208	1,239	1,271	1,303	1,337
Kentucky	630	623	621	618	620	621	621
Louisiana	779	767	766	770	779	790	802
Maryland	715	739	766	797	824	849	875
Mississippi	500	496	497	498	504	510	518
North Carolina	1,083	1,099	1,121	1,150	1,184	1,220	1,258
Oklahoma	579	574	572	570	568	565	560
South Carolina	622	628	636	645	658	669	679
Tennessee	822	827	835	845	860	873	886
Texas	3,353	3,379	3,408	3,433	3,463	3,488	3,514
Virginia	998	1,025	1,056	1,095	1,138	1,182	1,229
West Virginia	323	313	306	300	298	296	293
West	9,135	9,374	9,617	9,851	10,070	10,256	10,415
Alaska	112	111	114	116	118	122	127
Arizona	590	660	685	709	728	745	757
California	4,963	5,101	5,260	5,415	5,546	5,660	5,763
Colorado	569	576	586	596	606	616	625
Hawaii	171	176	182	190	198	205	214
Idaho	221	215	214	213	215	216	216
Montana	152	151	150	150	151	151	150
Nevada	197	206	214	221	226	229	230
New Mexico	300	305	311	318	327	336	346
Oregon	485	482	488	491	499	503	506
Utah	445	445	449	451	461	469	475
Washington	832	852	872	889	903	911	914
Wyoming	98	94	93	91	92	92	92

Source: Projections of Education Statistics to 2002, U.S. Department of Education, Office of Educational Research and Improvement, December, 1991, pp. 113-14. Primary source: U.S. Department of Education, National Center for Education Statistics, Common Core of Data Surveys and "Key Statistics for Public and Private Elementary and Secondary Education: School Year 1990-1991," *Early Estimates. Notes:* As of June 1. Includes most kindergarten and some nursery school enrollment. Source also includes actual data for 1984-1989.

★ 158 ★

Enrollment of Grades Kindergarten through 12 in Public Elementary and Secondary Schools by Region and State, Fall 1997 to Fall 2002

[Numbers in thousands]

Region and state	Projected					
	1997	1998	1999	2000	2001	2002
United States	45,585	45,955	46,276	46,539	46,782	47,068
Northeast	8,091	8,184	8,591	8,662	8,728	8,791
Connecticut	530	535	545	549	551	552
Maine	248	254	257	261	264	266
Massachusetts	957	972	972	983	992	1,000
New Hampshire	224	230	233	239	243	249
New Jersey	1,306	1,341	1,459	1,480	1,499	1,516
New York	2,781	2,800	3,009	3,025	3,042	3,058
Pennsylvania	1,785	1,789	1,849	1,856	1,864	1,874
Rhode Island	151	151	156	157	159	159
Vermont	109	110	111	113	115	116
Midwest	10,460	10,443	10,485	10,489	10,520	10,538
Illinois	1,983	2,005	2,130	2,135	2,144	2,153
Indiana	988	983	975	979	985	990
Iowa	453	439	444	437	432	427
Kansas	461	458	459	455	454	451
Michigan	1,653	1,647	1,721	1,728	1,742	1,750
Minnesota	812	806	769	770	772	773
Missouri	916	926	914	917	924	930
Nebraska	277	273	260	258	255	252
North Dakota	119	119	114	110	107	105
Ohio	1,849	1,850	1,781	1,783	1,790	1,797
South Dakota	144	144	143	142	142	141
Wisconsin	807	793	776	774	772	769
South	16,496	16,720	16,623	16,738	16,826	16,953
Alabama	772	779	769	772	775	779
Arkansas	462	464	458	458	457	457
Delaware	119	122	121	123	127	129
District of Columbia	91	94	102	101	101	100
Florida	2,296	2,345	2,299	2,356	2,406	2,459
Georgia	1,369	1,402	1,380	1,409	1,436	1,464
Kentucky	619	617	618	617	615	615
Louisiana	812	819	862	850	837	828
Maryland	901	926	939	958	974	989
Mississippi	523	529	544	546	548	550
North Carolina	1,297	1,336	1,361	1,384	1,406	1,430
Oklahoma	553	546	521	507	492	481
South Carolina	690	699	682	688	694	702
Tennessee	896	903	911	917	922	928
Texas	3,528	3,534	3,394	3,369	3,333	3,316
Virginia	1,276	1,322	1,373	1,397	1,418	1,441

[Continued]

★ 158 ★

Enrollment of Grades Kindergarten through 12 in Public Elementary and Secondary Schools by Region and State, Fall 1997 to Fall 2002

[Continued]

Region and state	Projected					
	1997	1998	1999	2000	2001	2002
West Virginia	289	285	290	288	286	285
West	10,538	10,608	10,578	10,649	10,708	10,787
Alaska	132	138	139	141	143	145
Arizona	767	773	757	771	784	796
California	5,848	5,907	5,932	5,998	6,057	6,128
Colorado	633	637	627	621	613	609
Hawaii	223	231	250	251	251	251
Idaho	215	213	208	207	206	205
Montana	150	148	146	144	142	139
Nevada	228	225	214	215	217	218
New Mexico	356	364	395	399	402	406
Oregon	504	499	482	481	481	481
Utah	480	483	488	488	488	491
Washington	910	898	851	846	841	836
Wyoming	92	92	88	87	85	83

Source: *Projections of Education Statistics to 2002*, U.S. Department of Education, Office of Educational Research and Improvement, December, 1991, pp. 113-14. Primary source: U.S. Department of Education, National Center for Education Statistics, Common Core of Data Surveys and "Key Statistics for Public and Private Elementary and Secondary Education: School Year 1990-1991," *Early Estimates. Notes:* As of June 1. Includes most kindergarten and some nursery school enrollment. Source also includes actual data for 1984-1989.

★ 159 ★

Enrollment of Grades Kindergarten through 8 and 9-12 in Elementary and Secondary Schools by Control of Institution, Fall 1977 to Fall 2002

[Numbers in thousands]

Year	Total			Public			Private	
	K-12[1]	K-8[1]	9-12	K-12[1]	K-8[1]	9-12	K-12[1]	K-8[1]
1977	48,717	33,133	15,583	43,577	29,336	14,240	5,140	3,797
1978	47,636	32,157	15,478	42,550	28,425	14,125	5,086	3,732
1979	46,645	31,631	15,014	41,645	27,931	13,714	5,000[2]	3,700
1980	46,249	31,669	14,581	40,918	27,677	13,242	5,331	3,992
1981	45,522	31,370	14,152	40,022	27,270	12,752	5,500[2]	4,100
1982	45,166	31,358	13,807	39,566	27,158	12,407	5,600[2]	4,200
1983	44,967	31,294	13,674	39,252	26,979	12,274	5,715	4,315
1984	44,908	31,200	13,708	39,208	26,900	12,308	5,700[2]	4,300
1985	44,979	31,225	13,754	39,422	27,030	12,392	5,557	4,195

[Continued]

★ 159 ★

Enrollment of Grades Kindergarten through 8 and 9-12 in Elementary and Secondary Schools by Control of Institution, Fall 1977 to Fall 2002
[Continued]

Year	Total			Public			Private	
	K-12[1]	K-8[1]	9-12	K-12[1]	K-8[1]	9-12	K-12[1]	K-8[1]
1986	45,205	31,536	13,669	39,753	27,420	12,333	5,452[2]	4,116
1987	45,487	32,164	13,323	40,008	27,932	12,076	5,479[3]	4,232
1988	45,430	32,539	12,892	40,189	28,503	11,686	5,241[3]	4,036
1989	45,881	33,320	12,562	40,526	29,158	11,369	5,355[3]	4,162
1990[3]	46,221	33,808	12,413	41,026	29,742	11,284	5,195	4,066
Projected								
1991	46,841	34,313	12,529	41,575	30,186	11,389	5,266	4,127
1992	47,601	34,855	12,746	42,250	30,663	11,587	5,351	4,192
1993	48,410	35,341	13,069	42,971	31,091	11,880	5,439	4,250
1994	49,279	35,751	13,528	43,749	31,451	12,298	5,530	4,300
1995	50,054	36,127	13,927	44,442	31,782	12,660	5,612	4,345
1996	50,759	36,452	14,307	45,074	32,068	13,006	5,685	4,384
1997	51,331	36,765	14,567	45,585	32,343	13,242	5,746	4,422
1998	51,750	37,126	14,624	45,955	32,661	13,294	5,795	4,465
1999	52,110	37,333	14,777	46,276	32,843	13,433	5,834	4,490
2000	52,406	37,548	14,858	46,539	33,032	13,507	5,867	4,516
2001	52,679	37,707	14,972	46,782	33,172	13,610	5,897	4,535
2002	52,996	37,790	15,206	47,068	33,245	13,823	5,928	4,545

Source: Projections of Education Statistics to 2002, National Center for Education Statistics, December, 1991, p. 9. Primary source: U.S. Department of Education, National Center for Education Statistics, *Statistics of Public Elementary and Secondary Schools*; Common Core of Data surveys; "Selected Public and Private Elementary and Secondary Education Statistics," *NCES Bulletin*, December, 1984; 1985 Private School Survey; "Key Statistics for private Elementary and Secondary Education: School Year 1988-89," *Early Estimates*; "Key Statistics for Public and Private Elementary and Secondary Education: School Year 1989-90," *Early Estimates*; and "Key Statistics for Public and Private Elementary and Secondary Education: School Year 1990-91," *Early Estimates*. Some data have been revised from previously published figures. Projections are based on data through 1989. Because of rounding, details may not add to totals. *Notes:* Prepared April 1991. 1. Includes most kindergarten and nursery school enrollment. 2. Estimated by NCES. 3. Estimate.

★ 160 ★

Enrollment of Grades Kindergarten through 8 in Public Schools by Region and State, Fall 1990 to Fall 1996
[Numbers in thousands]

Region and state	Estimate 1990	Projected					
		1991	1992	1993	1994	1995	1996
United States	29,742	30,186	30,663	31,091	31,451	31,782	32,068
Northeast	5,181	5,264	5,361	5,468	5,539	5,613	5,5678
Connecticut	349	357	367	378	383	389	394
Maine	154	157	160	163	167	172	176
Massachusetts	606	621	637	655	667	679	689
New Hampshire	130	136	141	147	151	155	160

[Continued]

★ 160 ★

Enrollment of Grades Kindergarten through 8 in Public Schools by Region and State, Fall 1990 to Fall 1996
[Continued]

Region and state	Estimate 1990	Projected					
		1991	1992	1993	1994	1995	1996
New Jersey	783	800	824	852	877	903	928
New York	1,813	1,831	1,854	1,881	1,890	1,902	1,912
Pennsylvania	1,174	1,188	1,201	1,213	1,221	1,229	1,234
Rhode Island	101	102	105	106	107	108	108
Vermont	71	71	72	74	75	77	78
Midwest	7,098	7,137	7,173	7,185	7,222	7,253	7,277
Illinois	1,288	1,294	1,305	1,318	1,338	1,358	1,377
Indiana	681	682	682	680	682	685	689
Iowa	339	336	330	323	319	314	309
Kansas	319	322	323	324	324	323	321
Michigan	1,145	1,153	1,161	1,166	1,169	1,173	1,177
Minnesota	543	552	558	559	562	564	563
Missouri	588	594	601	606	615	623	630
Nebraska	197	197	196	195	195	194	193
North Dakota	85	84	83	82	82	80	79
Ohio	1,256	1,262	1,268	1,269	1,274	1,279	1,283
South Dakota	95	96	96	96	97	97	98
Wisconsin	563	567	569	566	565	563	559
South	10,795	10,952	11,125	11,287	11,434	11,583	11,721
Alabama	529	531	533	536	540	547	553
Arkansas	314	315	316	316	317	319	320
Delaware	74	76	76	79	81	82	84
District of Columbia	61	61	62	64	63	63	62
Florida	1,364	1,426	1,488	1,545	1,585	1,621	1,655
Georgia	854	875	898	920	940	962	987
Kentucky	451	445	440	434	433	434	434
Louisiana	577	573	570	567	568	570	569
Maryland	529	549	571	594	611	627	643
Mississippi	366	364	362	361	363	365	368
North Carolina	782	796	815	836	856	879	902
Oklahoma	422	418	415	408	402	394	384
South Carolina	451	456	462	467	472	478	484
Tennessee	597	602	608	612	619	624	632
Texas	2,468	2,493	2,516	2,532	2,542	2,547	2,545
Virginia	733	755	782	812	840	870	899
West Virginia	223	216	210	204	202	201	199
West	6,668	6,835	7,003	7,150	7,256	7,333	7,393
Alaska	82	84	84	86	88	89	91
Arizona	475	495	513	530	540	548	555
California	3,611	3,728	3,850	3,967	4,043	4,102	4,148
Colorado	414	421	428	432	434	436	436

[Continued]

★ 160 ★

Enrollment of Grades Kindergarten through 8 in Public Schools by Region and State, Fall 1990 to Fall 1996

[Continued]

Region and state	Estimate 1990	Projected					
		1991	1992	1993	1994	1995	1996
Hawaii	126	129	133	138	141	144	145
Idaho	155	155	152	149	148	147	146
Montana	109	108	108	106	105	104	102
Nevada	145	151	158	162	164	165	164
New Mexico	208	212	216	221	226	229	234
Oregon	342	345	347	347	350	350	350
Utah	322	319	316	311	313	316	320
Washington	607	620	632	639	641	642	639
Wyoming	69	67	66	64	63	62	62

Source: Projections of Education Statistics to 2002, U.S. Department of Education, Office of Educational Research and Improvement, December, 1991, pp. 116-17. Primary source: U.S. Department of Education, National Center for Education Statistics, Common Core of Data Surveys and "Key Statistics for Public and Private Elementary and Secondary Education: School Year 1990-1991," *Early Estimates. Notes:* As of June 1. Includes most kindergarten and some nursery school enrollment. Source also includes actual data for 1984-1989.

★ 161 ★

Enrollment of Grades Kindergarten through 8 in Public Schools by Region and State, Fall 1997 to Fall 2002

[Numbers in thousands]

Region and state	Projected					
	1997	1998	1999	2000	2001	2002
United States	32,343	32,661	32,843	33,032	33,172	33,245
Northeast	5,745	5,812	6,029	6,058	6,066	6,056
Connecticut	398	403	417	418	416	414
Maine	179	183	185	187	188	191
Massachusetts	700	709	712	715	716	715
New Hampshire	164	168	171	175	178	180
New Jersey	953	976	1,056	1,067	1,073	1,074
New York	1,922	1,934	2,020	2,022	2,020	2,011
Pennsylvania	1,241	1,248	1,276	1,279	1,279	1,276
Rhode Island	109	111	114	115	115	115
Vermont	79	80	78	79	80	81
Midwest	7,323	7,357	7,398	7,424	7,432	7,425
Illinois	1,399	1,421	1,497	1,506	1,513	1,515
Indiana	694	698	691	696	699	701
Iowa	305	300	300	299	295	291
Kansas	319	318	321	320	318	316
Michigan	1,186	1,192	1,253	1,259	1,261	1,259
Minnesota	564	565	542	543	544	543

[Continued]

★ 161 ★

Enrollment of Grades Kindergarten through 8 in Public Schools by Region and State, Fall 1997 to Fall 2002
[Continued]

Region and state	Projected					
	1997	1998	1999	2000	2001	2002
Missouri	639	646	640	645	648	650
Nebraska	192	190	182	181	180	178
North Dakota	78	77	73	72	70	69
Ohio	1,293	1,302	1,258	1,262	1,265	1,265
South Dakota	98	98	97	97	97	97
Wisconsin	556	552	545	544	542	539
South	11,835	11,994	11,947	12,033	12,111	12,169
Alabama	559	566	560	563	565	567
Arkansas	322	323	318	319	320	320
Delaware	86	88	88	90	92	93
District of Columbia	62	63	66	64	64	62
Florida	1,684	1,717	1,683	1,717	1,750	1,778
Georgia	1,011	1,038	1,024	1,046	1,066	1,084
Kentucky	435	437	442	443	444	443
Louisiana	566	567	595	589	583	578
Maryland	657	672	673	682	690	695
Mississippi	371	376	386	390	393	397
North Carolina	925	952	974	989	1,003	1,014
Oklahoma	373	365	348	339	333	326
South Carolina	491	498	487	491	496	499
Tennessee	638	646	662	668	673	676
Texas	2,531	2,532	2,436	2,421	2,406	2,392
Virginia	927	956	1,003	1,019	1,033	1,043
West Virginia	199	199	202	201	200	199
West	7,439	7,497	7,469	7,517	7,563	7,595
Alaska	94	97	96	97	100	100
Arizona	561	567	561	570	578	587
California	4,188	4,234	4,263	4,303	4,339	4,368
Colorado	434	434	424	420	415	411
Hawaii	147	149	159	158	160	161
Idaho	146	146	143	143	143	142
Montana	101	99	98	96	95	94
Nevada	164	163	158	160	161	162
New Mexico	239	244	239	241	243	244
Oregon	350	350	341	340	340	339
Utah	323	329	332	337	341	345

[Continued]

★ 161 ★

Enrollment of Grades Kindergarten through 8 in Public Schools by Region and State, Fall 1997 to Fall 2002

[Continued]

Region and state	Projected					
	1997	1998	1999	2000	2001	2002
Washington	634	628	598	594	590	586
Wyoming	60	60	57	57	56	56

Source: Projections of Education Statistics to 2002, U.S. Department of Education, Office of Educational Research and Improvement, December, 1991, pp. 116-17. Primary source: U.S. Department of Education, National Center for Education Statistics, Common Core of Data Surveys and "Key Statistics for Public and Private Elementary and Secondary Education: School Year 1990-1991," *Early Estimates. Notes:* As of June 1. Includes most kindergarten and some nursery school enrollment. Source also includes actual data for 1984-1989.

★ 162 ★

Enrollment Rates in Public Schools by Age and Grade Level, 1989-2002

[Numbers in percent]

Grade level	Population base age	1989	Projected	
			1997	2002
Kindergarten	5	96.8	93.4	93.4
Grade 1	6	94.8	94.5	94.5
Elementary ungraded and special	5-13	1.7	1.7	1.7
Secondary ungraded and special	14-17	2.0	2.0	2.0
Postgraduate	18	0.2	0.2	0.2

Source: Projections of Education Statistics to the Year 2002, U.S. Deparmtnet of Education, Office of Educational Research and Improvement, December, 1991, p. 157.

★ 163 ★

Percent Change in Enrollment of Grades 9-12 in Public Schools by Region and State, Fall 1984 to Fall 2002

[Numbers in thousands]

Region and state	Actual	Projected		
	1984 to 1990	1990 to 1996	1996 to 2002	1990 to 2002
United States	-8.3	15.2	6.3	22.5
Northeast	-19.3	12.3	18.6	33.3
Connecticut	-17.3	8.4	6.5	15.4
Maine	-6.8	10.8	11.4	23.4
Massachusetts	-23.8	12.9	13.0	27.6

[Continued]

★ 163 ★

Percent Change in Enrollment of Grades 9-12 in Public Schools
by Region and State, Fall 1984 to Fall 2002
[Continued]

Region and state	Actual 1984 to 1990	Projected		
		1990 to 1996	1996 to 2002	1990 to 2002
New Hampshire	-22.4	43.1	18.2	69.1
New Jersey	-21.6	13.7	29.8	47.6
New York	-19.7	12.3	24.2	39.5
Pennsylvania	-17.5	9.5	10.5	21.0
Rhode Island	-16.6	15.4	4.5	20.6
Vermont	-6.0	13.9	20.6	37.3
Midwest	-12.2	12.7	-1.4	11.1
Illinois	-11.2	11.7	10.8	23.8
Indiana	-11.6	9.3	-3.8	5.2
Iowa	-10.5	6.2	-12.0	-6.6
Kansas	-4.9	20.9	-5.2	14.6
Michigan	-16.7	9.8	3.4	13.5
Minnesota	-12.0	19.9	-8.3	10.0
Missouri	-10.8	22.7	2.6	26.0
Nebraska	-4.5	9.4	-12.8	-4.6
North Dakota	-9.5	26.4	-9.9	13.9
Ohio	-12.1	9.1	-5.1	3.5
South Dakota	-6.7	29.2	-0.1	29.0
Wisconsin	-15.8	13.2	-10.9	0.9
South	-3.8	14.0	5.8	20.6
Alabama	0.2	6.2	-0.1	6.1
Arkansas	-5.4	14.4	-0.8	13.4
Delaware	-11.7	24.8	8.4	35.2
District of Columbia	-21.9	37.7	44.2	98.6
Florida	7.7	18.0	16.0	36.9
Georgia	-5.6	17.3	8.7	27.4
Kentucky	-7.5	4.7	-8.2	-3.9
Louisiana	-8.9	14.9	7.8	23.8
Maryland	-18.3	24.6	26.4	57.5
Mississippi	-5.1	11.9	2.0	14.1
North Carolina	-10.0	18.5	16.7	38.3
Oklahoma	-9.4	12.1	-12.0	-1.4
South Carolina	-5.7	14.4	3.8	18.7
Tennessee	-4.6	12.8	-0.6	12.2
Texas	4.0	9.4	-4.6	4.3
Virginia	-11.2	24.8	20.5	50.3
West Virginia	-7.1	-6.3	-9.0	-14.7
West	0.7	22.5	5.6	29.3
Alaska	-0.8	18.0	27.2	50.1
Arizona	-27.1	76.6	3.4	82.6
California	3.6	19.4	9.0	30.2

[Continued]

★ 163 ★

Percent Change in Enrollment of Grades 9-12 in Public Schools
by Region and State, Fall 1984 to Fall 2002
[Continued]

Region and state	Actual	Projected		
	1984 to 1990	1990 to 1996	1996 to 2002	1990 to 2002
Colorado	-8.6	22.3	4.8	28.2
Hawaii	-14.2	52.9	32.4	102.4
Idaho	11.0	5.7	-9.9	-4.8
Montana	-5.2	13.8	-8.5	4.2
Nevada	9.7	28.2	-15.8	7.9
New Mexico	19.9	22.0	43.8	75.4
Oregon	1.4	9.1	-9.3	-1.1
Utah	21.8	26.0	-6.0	18.4
Washington	-5.8	22.0	-8.9	11.2
Wyoming	3.1	5.8	-9.8	-4.6

Source: Projections of Education Statistics to 2002, U.S. Department of Education, Office of Educational Research and Improvement, December, 1991, p. 121. Primary source: U.S. Department of Education, National Center for Education Statistics, Common Core of Data Surveys and "Key Statistics for Public and Private Elementary and Secondary Education: School Year 1990-1991," *Early Estimates. Note:* As of June 1. Includes most kindergarten and some nursery school enrollment.

★ 164 ★

Percent Change in Enrollment of Grades 9-12 in Public Schools by State, Fall 1990 to Fall 2002

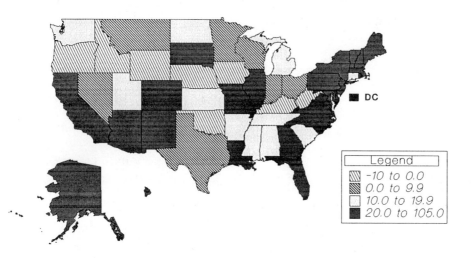

"While public high school enrollment declined during the latter half of the 1980s, it is expected to show sizable increases between 1990 and 2002. This expected increase reflects the changes in the high school age group that will occur during the 1990s, rather than shifts in the graduation rate from public high schools. During the 1990s and beyond, the high school enrollment decreases of the 1980s are expected to reverse as larger numbers of students enter the high school grades, but changes in the regions of the country are expected to differ. High school enrollment in the Northeast is expected to rise by 33 percent between 1990 and 2002, while enrollment in the West will rise by 29 percent. Lower increases in public high school enrollment have been projected for the South and Midwest between 1990 and 2002, 21 percent and 11 percent, respectively."

State	Percent change
Alabama	0.0 to 9.9
Alaska	20.0 to 105.0
Arizona	20.0 to 105.0
Arkansas	10.0 to 19.9
California	20.0 to 105.0
Colorado	20.0 to 105.0
Connecticut	10.0 to 19.9
Delaware	20.0 to 105.0
District of Columbia	20.0 to 105.0
Florida	20.0 to 105.0
Georgia	20.0 to 105.0
Hawaii	20.0 to 105.0
Idaho	-10.0 to 0.0
Illinois	20.0 to 105.0
Indiana	0.0 to 9.9
Iowa	-10.0 to 0.0

[Continued]

★ 164 ★

Percent Change in Enrollment of Grades 9-12 in Public Schools by State, Fall 1990 to Fall 2002

[Continued]

State	Percent change
Kansas	10.0 to 19.9
Kentucky	-10.0 to 0.0
Louisiana	20.0 to 105.0
Maine	20.0 to 105.0
Maryland	20.0 to 105.0
Massachusetts	20.0 to 105.0
Michigan	10.0 to 19.9
Minnesota	10.0 to 19.9
Mississippi	10.0 to 19.9
Missouri	20.0 to 105.0
Montana	0.0 to 9.9
Nebraska	-10.0 to 0.0
Nevada	0.0 to 9.9
New Hampshire	20.0 to 105.0
New Jersey	20.0 to 105.0
New Mexico	20.0 to 105.0
New York	20.0 to 105.0
North Carolina	20.0 to 105.0
North Dakota	10.0 to 19.9
Ohio	0.0 to 9.9
Oklahoma	-10.0 to 0.0
Oregon	-10.0 to 0.0
Pennsylvania	20.0 to 105.0
Rhode Island	20.0 to 105.0
South Carolina	10.0 to 19.9
South Dakota	20.0 to 105.0
Tennessee	10.0 to 19.9
Texas	0.0 to 9.9
Utah	10.0 to 19.9
Vermont	20.0 to 105.0
Virginia	20.0 to 105.0
Washington	10.0 to 19.9
West Virginia	-10.0 to 0.0
Wisconsin	0.0 to 9.9
Wyoming	-10.0 to 0.0

Source: Projections of Education Statistics to 2002, U.S. Department of Education, Office of Educational Research and Improvement, December, 1991, p. 108.

★ 165 ★

Percent Change in Enrollment of Grades Kindergarten through 12 in Public Schools by Region and State, Fall 1984 to Fall 2002

[Numbers in thousands]

Region and state	Actual 1984 to 1990	Projected		
		1990 to 1996	1996 to 2002	1990 to 2002
United States	4.6	9.9	4.4	14.7
Northeast	-2.2	10.4	10.1	21.5
Connecticut	0.2	11.7	5.5	17.8
Maine	3.8	12.8	9.3	23.3
Massachusetts	-3.5	13.5	6.3	20.6
New Hampshire	7.5	28.0	13.8	45.7
New Jersey	-4.1	17.1	19.5	40.0
New York	-3.1	7.5	11.0	19.3
Pennsylvania	-2.0	6.4	5.5	12.3
Rhode Island	3.0	9.0	5.9	15.4
Vermont	6.7	11.3	8.5	20.7
Midwest	0.1	5.4	1.0	6.5
Illinois	-1.7	8.3	10.3	19.4
Indiana	-1.7	3.5	0.0	3.5
Iowa	-1.4	-4.4	-7.7	-11.8
Kansas	7.7	6.1	-2.6	3.3
Michigan	-2.0	4.8	5.9	11.0
Minnesota	7.1	8.3	-5.0	2.8
Missouri	2.0	11.4	3.1	14.9
Nebraska	3.0	1.4	-9.2	-7.9
North Dakota	-1.7	1.7	-11.7	-10.2
Ohio	-1.9	4.2	-2.6	1.5
South Dakota	4.9	9.3	-0.2	9.1
Wisconsin	3.0	3.3	-5.9	-2.8
South	5.7	10.0	4.4	14.9
Alabama	2.1	5.0	1.9	7.0
Arkansas	0.5	5.4	-0.3	5.1
Delaware	8.7	17.2	10.0	28.9
District of Columbia	-8.0	10.2	13.0	24.5
Florida	22.2	20.4	9.7	32.1
Georgia	8.5	16.0	9.5	27.1
Kentucky	-2.2	-1.4	-1.0	-2.4
Louisiana	-2.7	2.9	3.3	6.4
Maryland	6.1	22.4	13.0	38.3
Mississippi	7.3	3.5	6.3	10.0
North Carolina	-0.6	16.2	13.6	32.0
Oklahoma	-1.9	-3.3	-14.1	-17.0
South Carolina	3.2	9.2	3.3	12.8
Tennessee	0.6	7.7	4.8	12.9
Texas	10.3	4.8	-5.6	-1.1
Virginia	3.4	23.1	17.3	44.4
West Virginia	-11.0	-9.1	-3.0	-11.8

[Continued]

★ 165 ★

Percent Change in Enrollment of Grades Kindergarten through 12 in Public Schools by Region and State, Fall 1984 to Fall 2002

[Continued]

Region and state	Actual 1984 to 1990	Projected		
		1990 to 1996	1996 to 2002	1990 to 2002
West	14.8	14.0	3.6	18.1
Alaska	6.7	13.0	14.7	29.6
Arizona	11.3	28.3	5.1	34.9
California	19.6	16.1	6.3	23.5
Colorado	4.4	9.9	-2.7	7.0
Hawaii	4.3	24.9	17.6	46.9
Idaho	6.3	-2.4	-5.1	-7.4
Montana	-1.3	-1.1	-7.8	-8.8
Nevada	29.6	16.9	-5.5	10.5
New Mexico	10.3	15.5	17.2	35.4
Oregon	8.5	4.4	-5.0	-0.9
Utah	14.1	6.7	3.3	10.2
Washington	12.3	9.8	-8.5	0.5
Wyoming	-3.0	-6.0	-9.5	-14.9

Source: Projections of Education Statistics to 2002, U.S. Department of Education, Office of Educational Research and Improvement, December, 1991, p. 115. Primary source: U.S. Department of Education, National Center for Education Statistics, Common Core of Data Surveys and "Key Statistics for Public and Private Elementary and Secondary Education: School Year 1990-1991," *Early Estimates. Note:* As of June 1. Includes most kindergarten and some nursery school enrollment.

★ 166 ★

Percent Change in Enrollment of Grades Kindergarten through 12 in Public Schools by State, Fall 1990 to Fall 2002

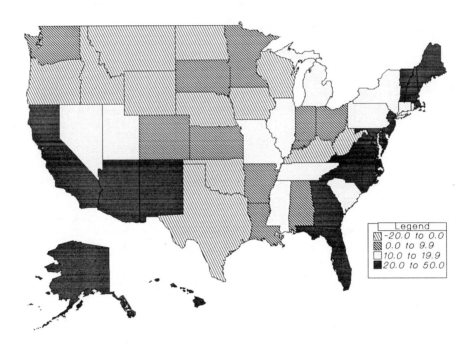

"Public elementary and secondary school enrollment is projected to rise steadily between 1990 and the year 2002, but these increases will vary widely across the Nation. Enrollment will increase most rapidly in the Northeastern and Western regions, where public school enrollment is projected to rise 22 percent and 18 percent, respectively. An increase of 15 percent is projected for the Southern region, while a smaller increase of 7 percent is expected in the Midwestern region. The greatest growth will occur at the secondary level."

State	Percent change
Alabama	0.0 to 9.9
Alaska	20.0 to 50.0
Arizona	20.0 to 50.0
Arkansas	0.0 to 9.9
California	20.0 to 50.0
Colorado	0.0 to 9.9
Connecticut	10.0 to 19.9
Delaware	20.0 to 50.0
District of Columbia	20.0 to 50.0
Florida	20.0 to 50.0
Georgia	20.0 to 50.0
Hawaii	20.0 to 50.0
Idaho	-20.0 to 0.0
Illinois	10.0 to 19.9

[Continued]

★ 166 ★

Percent Change in Enrollment of Grades Kindergarten through 12 in Public Schools by State, Fall 1990 to Fall 2002
[Continued]

State	Percent change
Indiana	0.0 to 9.9
Iowa	-20.0 to 0.0
Kansas	0.0 to 9.9
Kentucky	-20.0 to 0.0
Louisiana	0.0 to 9.9
Maine	20.0 to 50.0
Maryland	20.0 to 50.0
Massachusetts	20.0 to 50.0
Michigan	10.0 to 19.9
Minnesota	0.0 to 9.9
Mississippi	10.0 to 19.9
Missouri	10.0 to 19.9
Montana	-20.0 to 0.0
Nebraska	-20.0 to 0.0
Nevada	10.0 to 19.9
New Hampshire	20.0 to 50.0
New Jersey	20.0 to 50.0
New Mexico	20.0 to 50.0
New York	10.0 to 19.9
North Carolina	20.0 to 50.0
North Dakota	-20.0 to 0.0
Ohio	0.0 to 9.9
Oklahoma	-20.0 to 0.0
Oregon	-20.0 to 0.0
Pennsylvania	10.0 to 19.9
Rhode Island	10.0 to 19.9
South Carolina	10.0 to 19.9
South Dakota	0.0 to 9.9
Tennessee	10.0 to 19.9
Texas	-20.0 to 0.0
Utah	10.0 to 19.9
Vermont	20.0 to 50.0
Virginia	20.0 to 50.0
Washington	0.0 to 9.9
West Virginia	-20.0 to 0.0
Wisconsin	-20.0 to 0.0
Wyoming	-20.0 to 0.0

Source: Projections of Education Statistics to 2002, U.S. Department of Education, Office of Educational Research and Improvement, December, 1991, p. 98.

★ 167 ★

Percent Change in Enrollment of Grades Kindergarten through 8 in Public Schools by Region and State, Fall 1984 to Fall 2002

[Numbers in thousands]

Region and state	Actual 1984 to 1990	Projected		
		1990 to 1996	1996 to 2002	1990 to 2002
United States	10.6	7.8	3.7	11.8
Northeast	6.8	9.6	6.7	16.9
Connecticut	8.1	12.8	5.1	18.6
Maine	8.8	13.7	8.5	23.3
Massachusetts	7.0	13.7	3.8	18.0
New Hampshire	22.5	23.2	12.2	38.2
New Jersey	4.9	18.4	15.8	37.1
New York	5.9	5.5	5.2	11.0
Pennsylvania	6.4	5.2	3.4	8.7
Rhode Island	12.6	6.6	6.4	13.5
Vermont	12.1	10.3	4.0	14.7
Midwest	6.0	2.5	2.0	4.6
Illinois	2.7	6.9	10.1	17.7
Indiana	2.9	1.1	1.7	2.9
Iowa	3.1	-9.0	-5.6	-14.1
Kansas	13.1	0.6	-1.4	-0.8
Michigan	5.0	2.8	7.0	10.0
Minnesota	17.0	3.8	-3.6	0.1
Missouri	7.9	7.1	3.3	10.6
Nebraska	6.3	-1.7	-7.6	-9.2
North Dakota	1.6	-7.5	-12.6	-19.2
Ohio	2.9	2.2	-1.4	0.7
South Dakota	9.7	2.4	-0.2	2.1
Wisconsin	13.2	-0.7	-3.6	-4.3
South	9.7	8.6	3.8	12.7
Alabama	2.8	4.6	2.6	7.3
Arkansas	2.9	1.9	-0.1	1.8
Delaware	18.6	14.5	10.6	26.6
District of Columbia	-2.8	1.8	0.1	1.9
Florida	28.5	21.3	7.4	30.3
Georgia	14.4	15.6	9.8	27.0
Kentucky	0.1	-3.8	2.1	-1.8
Louisiana	-0.4	-1.3	1.5	0.2
Maryland	18.5	21.7	8.1	31.5
Mississippi	12.7	0.4	8.1	8.6
North Carolina	3.6	15.3	12.4	29.6
Oklahoma	1.3	-9.0	-15.1	-22.7
South Carolina	7.0	7.3	3.1	10.6
Tennessee	2.7	5.8	7.0	13.2
Texas	12.7	3.1	-6.0	-3.0
Virginia	9.9	22.6	16.1	42.3
West Virginia	-12.7	-10.4	-0.1	-10.5

[Continued]

★ 167 ★

Percent Change in Enrollment of Grades Kindergarten through 8 in Public Schools by Region and State, Fall 1984 to Fall 2002
[Continued]

Region and state	Actual 1984 to 1990	Projected		
		1990 to 1996	1996 to 2002	1990 to 2002
West	21.0	10.9	2.7	13.9
Alaska	9.7	11.1	9.9	22.2
Arizona	27.5	16.7	5.8	23.4
California	26.9	14.9	5.3	20.9
Colorado	10.2	5.3	-5.9	-0.9
Hawaii	12.8	15.1	10.7	27.3
Idaho	4.3	-5.8	-2.8	-8.5
Montana	0.3	-6.9	-7.5	-13.9
Nevada	38.5	12.9	-1.3	11.4
New Mexico	6.5	12.6	4.5	17.6
Oregon	11.8	2.4	-3.1	-0.8
Utah	11.4	-0.6	7.8	7.1
Washington	20.9	5.3	-8.3	-3.5
Wyoming	-5.3	-10.9	-9.3	-19.2

Source: Projections of Education Statistics to 2002, U.S. Department of Education, Office of Educational Research and Improvement, December, 1991, p. 118. Primary source: U.S. Department of Education, National Center for Education Statistics, Common Core of Data Surveys and "Key Statistics for Public and Private Elementary and Secondary Education: School Year 1990-1991," *Early Estimates. Note:* As of June 1. Includes most kindergarten and some nursery school enrollment.

★ 168 ★

Percent Change in Enrollment of Grades Kindergarten through 8 in Public Schools by State, Fall 1990 to Fall 2002

"Public elementary school enrollment in kindergarten through grade 8 is expected to grow 1 percent annually between 1990 and 2002, resulting in an increase of about 12 percent for the entire period. All of the regions of the country are expected to show increases, ranging from 17 percent in the Northeastern region to about 5 percent in the Midwestern region. Elementary enrollment is projected to grow by 14 percent in the West and by 13 percent in the South. Enrollment increases are expected for most states; 15 states are expected to have elementary enrollment decreases between 1990 and 2002."

State	Percent change
Alabama	0.0 to 9.9
Alaska	20.0 to 45.0
Arizona	20.0 to 45.0
Arkansas	0.0 to 9.9
California	20.0 to 45.0
Colorado	-25.0 to 0.0
Connecticut	10.0 to 19.9

[Continued]

★ 168 ★

Percent Change in Enrollment of Grades Kindergarten through 8 in Public Schools by State, Fall 1990 to Fall 2002

[Continued]

State	Percent change
Delaware	20.0 to 45.0
District of Columbia	-25.0 to 0.0
Florida	20.0 to 45.0
Georgia	20.0 to 45.0
Hawaii	20.0 to 45.0
Idaho	-25.0 to 0.0
Illinois	10.0 to 19.9
Indiana	0.0 to 9.9
Iowa	-25.0 to 0.0
Kansas	-25.0 to 0.0
Kentucky	-25.0 to 0.0
Louisiana	0.0 to 9.9
Maine	20.0 to 45.0
Maryland	20.0 to 45.0
Massachusetts	10.0 to 19.9
Michigan	10.0 to 19.9
Minnesota	0.0 to 9.9
Mississippi	0.0 to 9.9
Missouri	10.0 to 19.9
Montana	-25.0 to 0.0
Nebraska	-25.0 to 0.0
Nevada	10.0 to 19.9
New Hampshire	20.0 to 45.0
New Jersey	20.0 to 45.0
New Mexico	10.0 to 19.9
New York	10.0 to 19.9
North Carolina	20.0 to 45.0
North Dakota	-25.0 to 0.0
Ohio	0.0 to 9.9
Oklahoma	-25.0 to 0.0
Oregon	-25.0 to 0.0
Pennsylvania	0.0 to 9.9
Rhode Island	10.0 to 19.9
South Carolina	10.0 to 19.9
South Dakota	0.0 to 9.9
Tennessee	10.0 to 19.9
Texas	-25.0 to 0.0
Utah	0.0 to 9.9
Vermont	10.0 to 19.9
Virginia	20.0 to 45.0
Washington	-25.0 to 0.0
West Virginia	-25.0 to 0.0

[Continued]

★ 168 ★

Percent Change in Enrollment of Grades Kindergarten through 8 in Public Schools by State, Fall 1990 to Fall 2002

[Continued]

State	Percent change
Wisconsin	-25.0 to 0.0
Wyoming	-25.0 to 0.0

Source: Projections of Education Statistics to 2002, U.S. Department of Education, Office of Educational Research and Improvement, December, 1991, p. 103.

★ 169 ★

Public School Grade Retention Rates, 1989-2002

"Several of the rates in [the table below] exceed one hundred percent, as a result of several factors. The enrollment data by age were prorated to agree with NCES totals. The Bureau of the Census does not revise enrollment estimates by age, but population estimates are revised regularly."

Grade	1989	Projected	
		1997	2002
1 to 2	95.1	94.7	94.7
2 to 3	100.4	100.0	100.0
3 to 4	100.5	100.2	100.2
4 to 5	100.5	100.3	100.3
5 to 6	101.4	101.2	101.2
6 to 7	103.1	103.4	103.4
7 to 8	98.2	98.1	98.1
8 to 9	109.5	109.1	109.1
9 to 10	92.3	92.7	92.7
10 to 11	90.8	91.0	91.0
11 to 12	90.0	90.3	90.3

Source: Projections of Education Statistics to the Year 2002, U.S. Department of Education, Office of Educational Research and Improvement, December, 1991, p. 157.

★ 170 ★

Secondary Enrollment Rates by Age and Sex, 1989 and 1991-2002

The following projections were based on projected enrollment rates by age and sex, which were applied to population projections developed by the U.S. Bureau of the Census for individuals aged 12 to 34 in secondary grades 9-12. These projections were based on the assumption that recent rates will remain constant through the year 2002.

[Numbers in percent]

Age	Boys		Girls	
	1989	1991-2002	1989	1991-2002
12	0.2	0.3	0.4	0.4
13	4.9	5.5	6.2	7.1
14	61.3	64.6	71.1	74.2
15	90.8	87.5	91.4	91.0
16	92.7	92.2	91.5	91.4
17	81.7	80.4	80.0	79.4
18	25.4	25.8	19.4	17.0
19	6.7	5.9	2.8	3.0
20	0.5	1.0	0.9	1.0
21	0.6	0.7	1.2	0.8
22	0.3	0.4	0.3	0.3
23	0.5	0.3	0.3	0.2
24	0.3	0.3	0.2	0.3
25-29	0.2	0.2	0.4	0.4
30-34	0.2	0.2	0.3	0.3

Source: Projections of Education Statistics to 2002, U.S. Department of Education, Office of Educational Research and Improvement, December, 1991, p. 153.

★ 171 ★

Shifting Enrollment in Elementary and Secondary Schools, 1985-1986 and 1994-1995

"[This] report focuses on five groups: blacks, American Indians and Alaska natives, Asians and Pacific Islanders, Hispanic students, and non-Hispanic whites. It made the following projections for those groups: Asians and Pacific Islanders are expected to increase by 70 percent in elementary and secondary school enrollment to about 1.6 million by 1994 from about 940,000 in 1985. Hispanic enrollment is expected to increase by 54 percent, to an estimated 5.1 million in 1994 from about 3.3 million in 1985. Black students will remain the second-largest racial or ethnic group in the public schools, behind whites, but are expected to increase by only 13 percent to about 6.7 million in 1994 from about 5.9 million in 1985. American Indians and Alaska natives enrolled in school are expected to increase by 29 percent, but still remain the smallest group, with about 414,000 students in 1994, up from about 321,000 in 1985. By 1995, the report projects, more than 29 percent of the public high school graduates in 16 states and the District of Columbia will be non-white or Hispanic."

[Numbers in percent]

	1985-1986	1994-1995
White	71	68
Black	16	17
Hispanic	8	13
Asian	3	4
American Indian	1	2

Source: "Large Increase Is Predicted in Minorities in U.S. Schools, " Karen De Witt *New York Times*, September 13, 1991, p. A14. Primary source: Western Interstate Commission for Higher Education and the College Board. Magnitudes estimated from published chart.

Expenditures and Financial Aspects of Education

★ 172 ★

Alumni Contributions to Institutions of Higher Education, 1990 and 2010

For purposes of the forecast, the author broke total alumni giving into two components: "the number of living alumni and the dollars given per alumnus. Actually, the increased giving over the past 40 years was driven by the rising values of both components, but because each variable is influenced by quite different factors, it is better to examine the sources of increase separately."

[Numbers for Alumni Base and Total Giving in millions]

Year	Alumni base	Dollars per alumnus	Total giving (millions)
1990	28.7 mil	$94.93	$2,726
2010	43.8 mil	$116.52	$5,105
Percent change	+53%	+23%	+87%
Growth rate/year	$2.1%	$1.0%	+3.2%

Source: "How Much Will Alumni Give in the Future?" Ralph Bristol, Jr., *Planning for Higher Education* 20, Winter 1991-1992, p. 7. Primary source: Council for Aid to Education, annual surveys, 1950-1989; American Stock Exchange Index.

★ 173 ★

Average Annual Salaries of Classroom Teachers in Public Elementary and Secondary Schools with Alternative Projections, 1991-2002

Prepared May 1991. "Teacher salaries are seen as being related to current expenditures and enrollments. Also like current expenditures, these projections depend on the projections of these inputs, and assume that the relationships that have existed among the variables in the past will continue throughout the projection period."

Year ending	Constant 1989-90 dollars[1]	Current dollars[2]
1991	31,204	33,015
	Middle-high alternative projections	
1992	31,911	35,080
1993	32,515	37,034

[Continued]

★ 173 ★

Average Annual Salaries of Classroom Teachers in Public Elementary and Secondary Schools with Alternative Projections, 1991-2002
[Continued]

Year ending	Constant 1989-90 dollars[1]	Current dollars[2]
1994	33,219	39,586
1995	33,903	42,409
1996	34,585	45,358
1997	35,114	-
1998	35,546	-
1999	35,819	-
2000	36,035	-
2001	36,314	-
2002	36,675	-
Low alternative projections		
1992	31,649	34,553
1993	32,102	36,407
1994	32,687	38,802
1995	33,263	41,496
1996	33,825	44,321
1997	34,211	-
1998	34,552	-
1999	34,784	-
2000	35,002	-
2001	35,275	-
2002	35,529	-
Middle-low alternative projections		
1992	31,670	34,814
1993	32,177	36,649
1994	32,815	39,104
1995	33,440	41,830
1996	34,043	44,647
1997	34,489	-
1998	34,875	-
1999	35,160	-
2000	35,429	-
2001	35,767	-
2002	36,089	-
High alternative projections		
1992	32,046	34,948
1993	32,741	37,016
1994	33,660	39,719

[Continued]

★ 173 ★

Average Annual Salaries of Classroom Teachers in Public Elementary and Secondary Schools with Alternative Projections, 1991-2002
[Continued]

Year ending	Constant 1989-90 dollars[1]	Current dollars[2]
1995	34,629	42,779
1996	35,506	45,897
1997	36,158	-
1998	36,607	-
1999	36,895	-
2000	37,239	-
2001	37,641	-
2002	38,138	-

Source: "Expenditures of Public Elementary and Secondary Schools," *Projections of Education Statistics to 2002*, U.S. Department of Education, Office of Educational Research and Improvement, National Center for Education Statistics, December 1991, pp. 90-91, Table 36. Primary source: National Education Association, annual *Estimates of State School Statistics*. (Latest edition 1990-91). Copyright 1991 by the National Education Association. All rights reserved. Original table also includes data for 1977-1990. *Notes:* 1. Based on the Consumer Price Index for all urban consumers, Bureau of Labor Statistics, U.S. Department of Labor. 2. Projections in current dollars are not shown after 1996 due to the uncertain behavior of inflation over the long term.

★ 174 ★

Current Expenditures and Current Expenditures per Pupil in Average Daily Attendance (ADA) in Public Elementary and Secondary Schools, with Alternative Projections, 1977-2002

Prepared May 1991. "The economic climate of the nation and the amount of revenue receipts from state government to local government for education are important factors in determining the level of spending on elementary and secondary education (and revenue receipts from states are influenced by the state of the economy). Regression equations were used to develop the forecasts for current expenditures, with a measure of the state of the economy (disposable income per capita) and the amount of revenue receipts from state sources for education used as two of the factors influencing current expenditures. Several plausible growth paths for disposable income per capita and revenue receipts from state sources were used to produce alternative sets of projections for current expenditures.... Four sets of projections are presented in this table for current expenditures. These sets of forecasts are based on alternative projections for disposable income per capita and local government revenue receipts from states sources per capita. The forecasts for disposable income per capita were developed by the WEFA Group, an economic consulting firm, and the forecasts for revenue receipts from state sources were developed [by the NCES] using forecasts from The WEFA Group...."

Year ending	ADA (in thousands)	Current expenditures			
		Constant 1989-90 dollars[1]		Current dollars[2]	
		Total (in billions)	Per pupil in ADA	Total (in billions)	Per pupil in ADA
1977	40,832	$144.7	$3,543	$66.9	$1,638
1978	40,080	148.2	3,698	73.1	1,823
1979	39,076	146.4	3,747	79.0	2,020
1980	38,289	142.4	3,719	87.0	2,272
1981	37,704	138.3	3,669	94.3	2,502
1982	37,095	136.4	3,678	101.1	2,726
1983	36,636	140.1	3,824	108.3	2,955
1984	36,363	144.0	3,960	115.4	3,173
1985	36,404	151.7	4,167	126.3	3,470
1986	36,523	160.0	4,381	137.2	3,756
1987	36,864	167.2	4,536	146.6	3,976
1988	37,051	172.2	4,647	157.1	4,240
1989	37,282	181.2	4,860	172.9	4,639
1990[3]	37,511	185.2	4,938	185.2	4,938
1991[4]	37,974	188.1	4,953	199.0	5,240
		Middle-high alternative projections			
1992	38,482	192.3	4,996	211.4	5,492
1993	39,107	199.2	5,095	226.9	5,803
1994	39,774	206.6	5,195	246.2	6,191
1995	40,494	214.6	5,299	268.4	6,629
1996	41,136	222.5	5,409	291.8	7,094
1997	41,721	230.2	5,518	-	-
1998	42,194	236.8	5,611	-	-
1999	42,536	242.2	5,693	-	-
2000	42,833	247.2	5,771	-	-

[Continued]

★ 174 ★

Current Expenditures and Current Expenditures per Pupil in Average Daily Attendance (ADA) in Public Elementary and Secondary Schools, with Alternative Projections, 1977-2002

[Continued]

| Year ending | ADA (in thousands) | Current expenditures | | | |
| | | Constant 1989-90 dollars[1] | | Current dollars[2] | |
		Total (in billions)	Per pupil in ADA	Total (in billions)	Per pupil in ADA
2001	43,077	252.0	5,850	-	-
2002	43,302	257.7	5,951	-	-
			Low alternative projections		
1992	38,482	190.0	4,937	207.4	5,389
1993	39,107	195.6	5,001	221.8	5,671
1994	39,774	201.8	5,074	239.6	6,023
1995	40,494	208.7	5,153	260.3	6,429
1996	41,136	215.4	5,236	282.2	6,860
1997	41,721	221.6	5,312	-	-
1998	42,194	227.2	5,384	-	-
1999	42,536	232.1	5,457	-	-
2000	42,833	237.1	5,535	-	-
2001	43,077	241.8	5,613	-	-
2002	43,302	246.4	5,689	-	-
			Middle-low alternative projections		
1992	38,482	190.1	4,941	209.0	5,432
1993	39,107	196.2	5,018	233.5	5,715
1994	39,774	203.0	5,103	241.9	6,081
1995	40,494	210.3	5,194	263.1	6,497
1996	41,136	217.4	5,285	285.1	6,932
1997	41,721	224.3	5,375	-	-
1998	42,194	230.3	5,458	-	-
1999	42,536	235.8	5,543	-	-
2000	42,833	241.3	5,633	-	-
2001	43,077	246.6	5,725	-	-
2002	43,302	251.9	5,817	-	-
			High alternative projections		
1992	38,482	193.4	5,027	211.0	5,482
1993	39,107	201.3	5,146	227.5	5,818
1994	39,774	210.6	5,296	248.5	6,249
1995	40,494	221.3	5,465	273.4	6,751
1996	41,136	231.1	5,619	298.8	7,264
1997	41,721	240.1	5,756	-	-
1998	42,194	247.0	5,853	-	-
1999	42,536	252.6	5,939	-	-

[Continued]

★ 174 ★

Current Expenditures and Current Expenditures per Pupil in Average Daily Attendance (ADA) in Public Elementary and Secondary Schools, with Alternative Projections, 1977-2002

[Continued]

Year ending	ADA (in thousands)	Current expenditures			
		Constant 1989-90 dollars[1]		Current dollars[2]	
		Total (in billions)	Per pupil in ADA	Total (in billions)	Per pupil in ADA
2000	42,833	258.9	6,045	-	-
2001	43,077	265.0	6,152	-	-
2002	43,302	272.1	6,284	-	-

Source: "Expenditures of Public Elementary and Secondary Schools," *Projections of Education Statistics to 2002*, U.S. Department of Education, Office of Educational Research and Improvement, National Center for Education Statistics, pp. 77-78 and 86-87, Table 34. Primary source: U.S. Department of Education, National Center for Education Statistics, *Statistics of State School Systems*; *Revenues and Expenditures for Public Elementary and Secondary Education*; Common Core of Data survey; and "Key Statistics for Public Elementary and Secondary Education: School Year 1990-91," *Early Estimates*; and National Education Association, annual *Estimates of State School Statistics*. (Latest edition 1990-91. Copyright 1991 by the National Education Association. All rights reserved). *Notes:* 1. Based on the Consumer Price Index for all urban consumers, Bureau of Labor Statistics, U.S. Department of Labor. 2. Projections in current dollars are not shown after 1996 due to the uncertain behavior of inflation over the long term. 3. Current expenditures are early estimates. Average daily attendance is estimated on the basis of past data. 4. Estimated on the basis of past data.

★ 175 ★

Current Expenditures and Current Expenditures per Pupil in Fall Enrollment in Public Elementary and Secondary Schools, with Alternative Projections, 1990-2002

Prepared May 1991. "Current expenditures are projected to increase by 37 percent ... between school years 1991-92 and 2001-2002 in the middle high set of projections presented [here]. The projections are based on assumptions concerning economic growth and assistance by state governments to local governments.... Other sets of projections [are] based on alternative economic scenarios.... Enrollments are projected to increase steadily during the forecast period."

Year ending	Fall enrollment[1] (in thousands)	Current expenditures			
		Constant 1989-90 dollars[2]		Current dollars[3]	
		Total (in billions)	Per pupil in fall enrollment	Total (in billions)	Per pupil in fall enrollment
1990[4]	40,526	185.2	4,571	185.2	4,571
1991[5]	41,026	188.1	4,584	199.0	4,850
Middle-high alternative projections					
1992	41,575	192.3	4,625	211.4	5,084
1993	42,250	199.2	4,716	226.9	5,371

[Continued]

★ 175 ★

Current Expenditures and Current Expenditures per Pupil in Fall Enrollment in Public Elementary and Secondary Schools, with Alternative Projections, 1990-2002
[Continued]

Year ending	Fall enrollment[1] (in thousands)	Current expenditures			
		Constant 1989-90 dollars[2]		Current dollars[3]	
		Total (in billions)	Per pupil in fall enrollment	Total (in billions)	Per pupil in fall enrollment
1994	42,971	206.6	4,809	246.2	5,730
1995	43,749	214.6	4,905	268.4	6,136
1996	44,442	222.5	5,007	291.8	6,566
1997	45,074	230.2	5,107	-	-
1998	45,585	236.8	5,194	-	-
1999	45,955	242.2	5,270	-	-
2000	46,276	247.2	5,342	-	-
2001	46,539	252.0	5,415	-	-
2002	46,782	257.7	5,508	-	-
Low alternative projections					
1992	41,575	190.0	4,569	207.4	4,988
1993	42,250	195.6	4,629	221.8	5,249
1994	42,971	201.8	4,696	239.6	5,575
1995	43,749	208.7	4,770	260.3	5,951
1996	44,442	215.4	4,846	282.2	6,350
1997	45,074	221.6	4,917	-	-
1998	45,585	227.2	4,984	-	-
1999	45,955	232.1	5,051	-	-
2000	46,276	237.1	5,124	-	-
2001	46,539	241.8	5,195	-	-
2002	46,782	246.4	5,266	-	-
Middle-low alternative projections					
1992	41,575	190.1	4,574	209.0	5,028
1993	42,250	196.2	4,645	223.5	5,290
1994	42,971	203.0	4,723	241.9	5,629
1995	43,749	210.3	4,807	263.1	6,014
1996	44,442	217.4	4,892	285.1	6,416
1997	45,074	224.3	4,975	-	-
1998	45,585	230.3	5,052	-	-
1999	45,955	235.8	5,131	-	-
2000	46,276	241.3	5,214	-	-
2001	46,539	246.6	5,299	-	-
2002	46,782	251.9	5,384	-	-

[Continued]

★ 175 ★

Current Expenditures and Current Expenditures per Pupil in Fall Enrollment in Public Elementary and Secondary Schools, with Alternative Projections, 1990-2002
[Continued]

| Year ending | Fall enrollment[1] (in thousands) | Current expenditures | | | |
| | | Constant 1989-90 dollars[2] | | Current dollars[3] | |
		Total (in billions)	Per pupil in fall enrollment	Total (in billions)	Per pupil in fall enrollment
		High alternative projections			
1992	41,575	193.4	4,653	211.0	5,074
1993	42,250	201.3	4,764	227.5	5,386
1994	42,971	210.6	4,902	248.5	5,784
1995	43,749	221.3	5,058	273.4	6,249
1996	44,442	231.1	5,201	298.8	6,723
1997	45,074	240.1	5,328	-	-
1998	45,585	247.0	5,418	-	-
1999	45,955	252.6	5,497	-	-
2000	46,276	258.9	5,596	-	-
2001	46,539	265.0	5,695	-	-
2002	46,782	272.1	5,817	-	-

Source: "Expenditures of Public Elementary and Secondary Schools," *Projections of Education Statistics to 2002*, U.S. Department of Education, Office of Educational Research and Improvement, National Center for Education Statistics, December 1991, pp. 88-89, Table 35. Primary source: U.S. Department of Education, National Center for Education Statistics, *Statistics of State School Systems; Revenues and Expenditures for Public Elementary and Secondary Education Statistics of Public Elementary and Secondary Education; Statistics of Public and Secondary Schools;* "Selected Public and Private Elementary and Secondary Education Statistics," NCES Bulletin, October 23, 1979; Common Core of Data survey; and "Key Statistics for Public Elementary and Secondary Education: School Year 1990-91," *Early Estimates;* and National Education Association, annual *Estimates of State School Statistics* (Latest edition 1990-91. Copyright 1991 by the National Education Association. All rights reserved). Original chart also includes data for 1977-1989. *Notes:* 1. Each enrollment is for the fall of the school year ending in the school year shown in column 1. Hence, the enrollment number listed for 1977 is for Fall 1976. the Consumer Price Index for all urban consumers, Bureau of Labor Statistics, U.S. Department of Labor. 2. Projections in current dollars are not shown after 1996 due to the uncertain behavior of inflation over the long term. 3. Current expenditures are early estimates.

★ 176 ★

Disposable Personal Income, with Alternative Projections, 1992-2002

Prepared April 1991. The trend alternative projections for disposable income are from The WEFA Group's trend scenario. "The trend scenario shows the real economy, after coming out of a recession during 1991, growing at historical averages in relation to population growth. In this scenario, disposable income per capita rises each year from 1991-92 to 2001-2002 at rates between 0.3 and 2.1 percent." The low projections for disposable income are from WEFA's pessimistic scenario, in which growth is lower, with the change in disposable income per capita ranging between minus 0.3 and 1.7 percent during the period from 1991-92 to 2001-2002. The high projections for disposable income per capita are from WEFA's optimistic scenario, in which disposable income per capita rises each year from 1991-92 to 2001-2002 at rates between 0.4 and 2.4 percent.

[Numbers in constant 1989-90 dollars]

Year ending	Trend alternative projections[1]	Pessimistic alternative projections	Optimistic alternative projections
1992	$15,164	$15,133	$15,298
1993	15,437	15,323	15,615
1994	15,718	15,527	15,978
1995	16,044	15,778	16,358
1996	16,371	16,043	16,748
1997	16,664	16,245	17,116
1998	16,899	16,414	17,435
1999	17,116	16,554	17,724
2000	17,346	16,710	18,034
2001	17,583	16,851	18,352
2002	17,820	16,991	18,670

Source: "Appendix B: Supplementary Tables," *Projections of Education Statistics to 2002*, U.S. Department of Education, Office of Educational Research and Improvement, National Center for Education Statistics, December 1991, p. 189, Table B5. Primary source: The WEFA Group, "Offline U.S. Economic Service: Longterm Option." Original table also includes data for 1977-1990.

★ 177 ★

Education Revenue Receipts per Capita From State Source, with Alternative Projections, 1992-2002

Prepared May 1991. Two alternative projections were generated for revenue receipts from state sources, based on two different sets of projections for personal taxes, business taxes, and the rate of change in the inflation rate. "The middle set of projections was produced using the values for these variables from the WEFA Group's trend scenario, and high set of projections was produced using the values from WEFA's optimistic scenario."

[Numbers in constant 1989-1990 dollars]

Year ending	Middle alternative projections	Low alternative projections	High alternative projections
1992	$404	$397	$405
1993	412	403	415
1994	420	410	428
1995	429	417	443
1996	438	424	456
1997	447	431	467
1998	455	437	474
1999	461	444	479
2000	466	450	485
2001	471	456	492
2002	478	462	501

Source: "Appendix B: Supplementary Tables," *Projections of Education Statistics to 2002*, U.S. Department of Education, Office of Educational Research and Improvement, National Center for Education Statistics, December 1991, p. 190, Table B6. Primary source: U.S. Department of Education, National Center for Education Statistics, *Statistics of State School Systems; Revenues and Expenditures for Public Elementary and Secondary Education*, Common Core of Data survey, and "Key Statistics for Public Elementary and Secondary Education: School Year 1990-91," *Early Estimates;* and National Association, annual *Estimates of State School Statistics.* (Latest edition 1990-91. Copyright 1991 by the National Education Association. All rights reserved.) Source also contains data for 1977-1989. Revenue per capita based on the Consumer Price Index for all urban consumers, Bureau of Labor Statistics, U.S. Department of Labor.

★ 178 ★

Indirect Business Taxes and Tax Accruals, Excluding Property Taxes, for State and Local Governments, Per Capita with Alternative Projections, 1977-2002

Prepared April 1991. The alternative projections were based on the WEFA Group's optimistic and trend scenarios for growth of the economy.

[Numbers in constant 1989-1990 dollars]

Year ending	Indirect business taxes and tax accruals, excluding property taxes, for state and local governments per capita[1]	
1977	$728	-
1978	747	-
1979	754	-
1980	726	-
1981	720	-
1982	710	-
1983	725	-
1984	790	-
1985	833	-
1986	865	-
1987	880	-
1988	887	-
1989	887	-
1990	886	-
1991[2]	887	-
	Trend alternative projections	Optimistic alternative projections
1992	910	$911
1993	943	947
1994	974	980
1995	1,000	1,009
1996	1,025	1,035
1997	1,047	1,059
1998	1,065	1,079
1999	1,080	1,096
2000	1,092	1,110
2001	1,103	1,123
2002	1,114	1,135

Source: "Appendix B: Supplementary Tables," *Projections of Education Statistics to 2002,* U.S. Department of Education, Office of Educational Research and Improvement, National Center for Education Statistics, December 1991, p. 194, Table B10. Primary source: The WEFA Group, "Off-line U.S. Economic Service: Longterm Option." Source also contains data for 1977-1990. *Notes:* 1. Based on the Consumer Price Index for all urban consumers, Bureau of Labor Statistics, U.S. Department of Labor. 2. Projected.

★ 179 ★

Personal Tax and Nontax Payments to State and Local Governments, Per Capita with Alternative Projections, 1992-2002

Prepared April 1991. The alternative projections were based on the WEFA Group's optimistic and trend scenarios for growth of the economy.

[Numbers in constant 1989-1990 dollars]

Year ending	Trend alternative projections[1]	Optimistic alternative projections
1992	$817	$827
1993	839	852
1994	857	874
1995	871	892
1996	884	909
1997	896	915
1998	904	919
1999	912	931
2000	920	944
2001	938	967
2002	961	996

Source: "Appendix B: Supplementary Tables," *Projections of Education Statistics to 2002*, U.S. Department of Education, Office of Educational Research and Improvement, National Center for Education Statistics, December 1991, p. 193, Table B9. Primary source: The WEFA Group, "Offline U.S. Economic Service: Longterm Option." Source also contains data for 1977-1990. *Note:* 1. Based on the Consumer Price Index for all urban consumers, Bureau of Labor Statistics, U.S. Department of Labor.

★ 180 ★

Rate of Change of the Inflation Rate, Based on the Consumer Price Index, with Alternative Projections, 1992-2002

Prepared April 1991. The alternative projections for the rate of inflation were based on The WEFA Group's optimistic, pessimistic, and trend scenarios for growth of the economy.

Year ending	Trend alternative projections	Pessimistic alternative projections	Optimistic alternative projections
1992	-0.328	-0.196	-0.218
1993	-0.075	-0.029	-0.056
1994	0.282	0.203	0.192
1995	0.074	0.090	0.072
1996	-0.026	-0.011	-0.011
1997	-0.004	-0.006	-0.012

[Continued]

★ 180 ★

Rate of Change of the Inflation Rate, Based on the Consumer Price Index, with Alternative Projections, 1992-2002
[Continued]

Year ending	Trend alternative projections	Pessimistic alternative projections	Optimistic alternative projections
1998	0.000	0.004	-0.012
1999	-0.003	0.001	-0.000
2000	0.002	-0.002	-0.002
2001	-0.002	-0.004	-0.004
2002	-0.002	0.004	0.000

Source: "Appendix B: Supplementary Tables," *Projections of Education Statistics to 2002,* U.S. Department of Education, Office of Educational Research and Improvement, National Center for Education Statistics, December 1991, p. 192, Table B8. Primary source: The WEFA Group, "Off-line U.S. Economic Service: Longterm Option." Source also contains data for 1977-1990.

General Education Statistics

★ 181 ★

Average Daily Attendance (ADA) in Public Elementary and Secondary Schools, Change in ADA, the Population, and ADA as a Proportion of Population, 1990-2002

Prepared May 1991.

[Numbers for Average Daily Attendance in thousands; Population in millions]

Year ending	ADA[1] (in thousands)	Change in ADA	Population (in millions)	ADA as a proporation of the population
1990[2]	37,511	229,708	250.1	0.150
1991[3]	37,974	462,921	252.7	0.150
Projected				
1992	38,482	507,696	255.2	0.151
1993	39,107	624,784	257.7	0.152
1994	39,774	667,362	260.0	0.153
1995	40,494	720,122	262.1	0.154
1996	41,136	641,445	264.2	0.156
1997	41,721	584,983	266.2	0.157
1998	42,194	472,985	268.2	0.157
1990	42,536	342,474	270.1	0.157

[Continued]

★ 181 ★

Average Daily Attendance (ADA) in Public Elementary and Secondary Schools, Change in ADA, the Population, and ADA as a Proportion of Population, 1990-2002

[Continued]

Year ending	ADA[1] (in thousands)	Change in ADA	Population (in millions)	ADA as a proporation of the population
2000	42,833	297,120	272.0	0.157
2001	43,077	243,434	273.9	0.157
2002	43,302	224,922	275.8	0.157

Source: Projections of Education Statistics to 2002, U.S. Department of Education, Office of Educational Research and Improvement, December 1991, p. 188. Table B4. Primary source: U.S. Department of Education, National Center for Education Statistics, *Statistics of State School Systems; Revenues and Expenditures for Public Elementary and Secondary Education;* Common Core of Data survey; and "Key Statistics for Public Elementary and Secondary Education: School Year 1990-91," *Early Estimates*; The WEFA Group, "Off-line U.S. Economic Service: Long-term Option," and National Education Association, annual *Estimates of State School Statistics* (Latest edition 1990-91. Copyright 1991 by the National Education Association. All rights reserved. Original table also includes data for 1977-1989. *Notes*: 1. Projections of average daily attendance were made by multiplying the forecasts for enrollment reported in *Projections of Education Statistics to 2002* (December 1991) by the average value of the ratio of average daily attendance to the enrollment from 1980 to 1989; this average was approximately 0.93. 2. Average daily attendance is estimated on the basis of past data. 3. Projected.

★ 182 ★

College-Age Populations 1993-2002

[Numbers in thousands]

Year (July 1)	18 years old	18-24 years old	25-29 years old	30-34 years old	35-44 years old
			Projected		
1993	3,334	25,330	20,008	22,705	40,917
1994	3,287	24,976	19,576	22,578	41,752
1995	3,438	24,694	19,386	22,306	42,574
1996	3,470	24,368	19,471	21,750	43,327
1997	3,581	24,447	19,346	21,189	43,897
1998	3,712	24,838	19,116	20,627	44,292
1999	3,772	25,363	18,738	20,194	44,518
2000	3,822	25,851	18,363	20,001	44,491

[Continued]

★ 182 ★

College-Age Populations 1993-2002
[Continued]

Year (July 1)	18 years old	18-24 years old	25-29 years old	30-34 years old	35-44 years old
2001	3,843	25,734	17,848	19,988	44,199
2002	3,784	26,756	17,777	19,965	43,657

Source: "Appendix B: Supplementary Tables." *Projections of Education Statistics to 2002*, U.S. Department of Education, Office of Educational Research and Improvement, National Center for Education Statistics, December 1991, p. 187, Table B3. Primary source: "United States Population Estimates, by Age, Sex, Race and Hispanic Origin: 1980 to 1988," U.S. Department of Commerce, Bureau of the Census, *Current Population Reports*, Series P-25, No. 1045, January 1990; "Projections of the Population of the United States, by Age, Sex, and Race: 1988 to 2080," *Current Population Reports*, Series P-25, No. 1018, January 1989. Table also includes data for 1977-1992.

★ 183 ★

College Enrollment among Persons 18-24 by Sex, 1976-2000

Cohorts = members of the same gender having the same birth year. "For males ... the model incorporates three types of influence on college enrollment rates—a long-run cyclical effect captured by cohort size; a trend effect, based on the real income of the prospective student's father; and a variable that captures the irregular short-term effects of the draft-plus an error term.... Cohort size would be expected to affect the enrollment rates of females in the same way as for males.... The real income effect, too, would be expected to operate in the same direction as for males. The variable that is peculiar to the female model is the state of the marriage market."

[Numbers in thousands]

	Percent married	Actual 1976	Projected 1985	1990	1995	2000
Assuming 0.5% income growth per annum						
Total	A. Decreases	7181	8295	8476	8629	9977
	B. Constant	7181	7931	7956	7947	9091
	C. Increases	7181	7622	7519	7381	8331
Males 18-19		1391	1510	1670	1664	2067
20-24		2282	2775	2574	2547	2715
Females 18-19	A. Decreases	1546	1533	1672	1656	2077
20-24		1962	2477	2560	2762	3118
18-19	B. Constant	1546	1475	1580	1538	1901
20-24		1962	2171	2131	2198	2408

[Continued]

★ 183 ★

College Enrollment among Persons 18-24 by Sex, 1976-2000

[Continued]

	Percent married	Actual 1976	Projected			
			1985	1990	1995	2000
18-19	C. Increases	1546	1431	1509	1445	1760
20-24		1962	1906	1766	1725	1789

Assuming 1.5% income growth per annum

Total	A. Decreases	7181	8998	9594	10109	12144
	B. Constant	7181	8624	9065	9430	11266
	C. Increases	7181	8322	8632	8861	10514
Males						
18-19		1391	1674	1940	2017	2634
20-24		2282	3023	2963	3070	3424
Females						
18-19	A. Decreases	1546	1671	1899	1953	2558
20-24		1962	2630	2792	3069	3528
18-19	B. Constant	1546	1613	1807	1838	2382
20-24		1962	2314	2355	2505	2826
18-19	C. Increases	1546	1566	1740	1742	2249
20-24		1962	2059	1989	2032	2207

Source: "The Outlook for Higher Education: A Cohort Size Model of Enrollment of the College Age Population, 1948-2000," Dennis Ahlburg, Eileen M. Crimmins, and Richard A. Easterlin, *Review of Public Data* 9, No. 3, November 1981, pp. 223-25. Primary source: Census Bureau projections, U.S. Bureau of the Census (1977, 1978).

★ 184 ★

Comparisons of Different Projected College Enrollment Rates of Persons Aged 18-24 by Sex, 1985-2000

Cohorts = members of the same sex sharing the same birth year. "Census Age-Sex specific enrollment rates for Series C and E population projections computed using projected populations and enrollments from Census Bureau projections in U.S. Bureau of the Census (1970). These rates differ slightly in 1990 and 2000 by population series because of distribution of age within age groups. Rates used are average of two population series. For comparability, these were applied to more recent population projections from U.S. Bureau of the Census (1977)."

[Numbers in thousands]

Source	Assumption	1985	1990	2000
	Males			
Goldberg and Anderson (1974)		32.9	36.3	N.A.
Census Bureau[1]	(1)	40.4	44.0	49.2
	(2)	35.7	38.0	40.2
	(3)	31.0	31.9	32.0
	Income increase			
Cohort size model	0.5%	30.5	32.0	38.3
	1.5%	33.5	36.9	48.6
	Females			
Goldberg and Anderson (1974)		24.1	27.8	N.A.
Census Bureau[1]	(1)	26.5	30.0	34.5
	(2)	22.7	25.0	27.2
	(3)	18.9	19.9	19.9
	Income increase			
	0.5%			

[Continued]

★ 184 ★

Comparisons of Different Projected College Enrollment Rates of Persons Aged 18-24 by Sex, 1985-2000

[Continued]

Source	Assumption	1985	1990	2000
Cohort size model	Marriage down	29.0	33.9	42.7
	Marriage constant	26.4	29.8	35.4
	Marriage up	24.1	26.3	29.1
	Income increase 1.5% Marriage down	31.1	37.6	50.0
	Marriage constant	28.4	33.4	42.8
	Marriage up	26.2	29.9	36.6

Source: "The Outlook for Higher Education: A Cohort Size Model of Enrollment of the College Age Population, 1948-2000," Dennis Ahlburg, Eileen M. Crimmins, and Richard A. Easterlin, *Review of Public Data* 9, No. 3, November 1981, p. 224. Primary source: D. Goldberg and A. Anderson, *Projections of Population and College Enrollments in Michigan, 1970-2000*, The Governor's Commission on Higher Education, 1974: Table 12. *Notes*: N.A. = Not available. 1. Census Bureau assumptions: enrollment rates (a) Increase annually at 1950-52 to 1969-70 rate. (b) Rates are average of (a) and 1969-1970 level. (c) Constant at 1970 level.

★ 185 ★

Comparisons of Different Projections of Percent Change in College Enrollment Rates, 1980-2000

Cohorts = Persons of the same sex sharing the same birth year.

Projection			1980-1990	1990-2000
	Enrollment change			
Cohort size model	Parental income growth 1.5%	Marriage Down	13.3	26.6
	1.5%	Constant	8.9	24.3
	1.5%	Up	5.1	21.8

[Continued]

★ 185 ★

Comparisons of Different Projections of Percent Change in College Enrollment Rates, 1980-2000
[Continued]

Projection			1980-1990	1990-2000
	0.5%	Down	3.5	17.7
	0.5%	Constant	-1.3	14.3
	0.5%	Up	-5.2	10.8
Census bureau[1]	(1)		3.5	7.8
	(2)		-3.6	3.4
	(3)		-11.6	-3.6
Carnegie commission[2]				
	Projection I (1971)		-2.8	30.9
	Projection II (1973)		-7.8	25.1
	Projection III (1973)		-2.3	25.4
	Projection IV (1974)		2.6	8.3
Dresch[3]			-45.8	-11.9
Population change				
Population 18 years old			-19.4	-15.1
18-24 years old			-12.6	-6.7

Source: "The Outlook for Higher Education: A Cohort Size Model of Enrollment of the College Age Population, 1948-2000," Dennis Ahlburg, Eileen M. Crimmins, and Richard A. Easterlin, *Review of Public Data* 9, No. 3, November 1981, pp. 223-25. Primary source: U.S. Bureau of the Census, Census Bureau projections, (1970, 1977); Carnegie Commission on Higher Education, *Priorities for Action: Final Report of the Carnegie Commission on Higher Education*, 1973, Table A-5, Projections, I, II, III; The Carnegie Foundation, *More Than Survival*, 1975: Table 5, Projection IV; S.P. Dresch, "Demography, Technology, and Higher Education," *Journal of Political Economy* 83, 1975, pp. 535-69. *Notes*: 1. Census Bureau assumptions: enrollment rates (a) increase annually at 1950-52 to 1969-70 rate (b) rates are average of (a) and 1969-70 level (c) constant at 1970 level. 2. Includes 18-34 year olds. 3. Includes only degree credit enrollments.

★ 186 ★

Educational Requirements for Jobs Available through 2000

Trends in Education:

1. Education will be the major public agenda item into the twenty-first century.

[Continued]

★ 186 ★

Educational Requirements for Jobs Available through 2000
[Continued]

2. Education will continue to be viewed as the key to economic growth.

3. Technology, coupled with flexible home, work, and learning schedules, will provide more productive time for schooling, training, and working.

4. There is a growing mismatch between the literacy (vocabulary, reading and writing skills) of the labor force and the competency required by the jobs available.

Both ill-prepared new entrants and employed workers, who cannot adapt to changing requirements that new technologies bring to their jobs, contribute to this mismatch.

The mismatch will be greatest among the 'best' jobs, where educational demands are greatest. Three-quarters of new entrants will be qualified for only 40% of new jobs created between 1985 and 2000.

Source: "Appendix A: Seventy-Five Trends in Education," *Educational Renaissance: Our Schools at the Turn of the Century*, Marvin J. Cetron and Margaret Evans Gayle, (c) 1991, St. Martin's Press, New York, 1991, pp. 221-22. Copyright (c) 1991 by Marvin Cetron and Margaret Gayle.

★ 187 ★

Enrollment in Educational Institutions by Level and Control of Institution, Fall 1869 to Fall 2002

Prepared April 1991. Elementary and secondary enrollment includes pupils in local public school systems and in most private schools (religiously affiliated and nonsectarian), but generally excludes pupils in subcollegiate departments of institutions of higher education, residential schools for exceptional children, and Federal schools. Elementary enrollment includes some prekindergarten pupils. Higher education enrollment includes students in colleges, universities, professional schools, teachers colleges, and 2-year colleges. Higher education enrollment by the National Center for Education Statistics. Some data have been revised from previously published figures. Because of rounding, details may not add to totals.

[Numbers in thousands]

Year	Total enrollment, all levels	Elementary and secondary, total	Public elementary and secondary schools			Private elementary and secondary schools[1]			Higher education[2]		
			Total	Kinder-garten through grade 8	Grades 9 through 12	Total	Kinder-garten through grade 8	Grades 9 through 12	Total	Public	Private
1869-70	-	-	6,872	6,792	80	-	-	-	52	-	-
1879-80	-	-	9,868	9,757	110	-	-	-	116	-	-
1889-90	14,491	14,334	12,723	12,520	203	1,611	1,516	95	157	-	-
1899-1900	17,092	16,855	15,503	14,984	519	1,352	1,241	111	238	-	-
1909-10	19,728	19,372	17,814	16,899	915	1,558	1,441	117	355	-	-
1919-20	23,876	23,278	21,578	19,378	2,200	1,699	1,486	214	598	-	-
1929-30	29,430	28,329	25,678	21,279	4,399	2,651	2,310	341	1,101	-	-
1939-40	29,539	28,045	25,434	18,832	6,601	2,611	2,153	458	1,494	797	698

[Continued]

★ 187 ★

Enrollment in Educational Institutions by Level and Control of Institution, Fall 1869 to Fall 2002
[Continued]

Year	Total enrollment, all levels	Elementary and secondary, total	Public elementary and secondary schools			Private elementary and secondary schools[1]			Higher education[2]		
			Total	Kinder-garten through grade 8	Grades 9 through 12	Total	Kinder-garten through grade 8	Grades 9 through 12	Total	Public	Private
1949-50	31,151	28,492	25,111	19,387	5,725	3,380	2,708	672	2,659	1,355	1,304
Fall 1959	44,497	40,857	35,182	26,911	8,271	5,675	4,640	1,035	3,640	2,181	1,459
Fall 1964	52,996	47,716	41,416	30,025	11,391	6,300[3]	5,000[3]	1,300	5,280	3,468	1,812
Fall 1965	54,394	48,473	42,173	30,563	11,610	6,300	4,900	1,400	5,921	3,970	1,951
Fall 1966	55,629	49,239	43,039	31,145	11,894	6,200[3]	4,800[3]	1,400[3]	6,390	4,349	2,041
Fall 1967	56,803	49,891	43,891	31,641	12,250	6,000[3]	4,600[3]	1,400[3]	6,912	4,816	2,096
Fall 1968	58,257	50,744	44,944	32,226	12,718	5,800	4,400	1,400	7,513	5,431	2,082
Fall 1969	59,124	51,119	45,619	32,597	13,022	5,500[3]	4,200[3]	1,300[3]	8,005	5,897	2,108
Fall 1970	59,853	51,272	45,909	32,577	13,332	5,363	4,052	1,311	8,581	6,428	2,153
Fall 1971	60,230	51,281	46,081	32,265	13,816	5,200[3]	3,900[3]	1,300[3]	8,949	6,804	2,144
Fall 1972	59,959	50,744	45,744	31,831	13,913	5,000[3]	3,700[3]	1,300[3]	9,215	7,071	2,144
Fall 1973	60,031	50,429	45,429	31,353	14,077	5,000[3]	3,700[3]	1,300[3]	9,602	7,420	2,183
Fall 1974	60,277	50,053	45,053	30,921	14,132	5,000[3]	3,700[3]	1,300[3]	10,224	7,989	2,235
Fall 1975	60,976	49,791	44,791	30,487	14,304	5,000[3]	3,700[3]	1,300[3]	11,185	8,835	2,350
Fall 1976	60,496	49,484	44,317	30,006	14,311	5,167	3,825	1,342	11,012	8,653	2,359
Fall 1977	60,003	48,717	43,577	29,336	14,240	5,140	3,797	1,343	11,286	8,847	2,439
Fall 1978	58,896	47,636	42,550	28,425	14,125	5,086	3,732	1,353	11,260	8,786	2,474
Fall 1979	58,215	46,645	41,645	27,931	13,714	5,000[3]	3,700[3]	1,300[3]	11,570	9,037	2,533
Fall 1980	58,346	46,249	40,918	27,677	13,242	5,331	3,992	1,339	12,097	9,457	2,640
Fall 1981	57,894	45,522	40,022	27,270	12,752	5,500[3]	4,100[3]	1,400[3]	12,372	9,647	2,725
Fall 1982	57,591	45,166	39,566	27,158	12,407	5,600[3]	4,200[3]	1,400[3]	12,426	9,696	2,730
Fall 1983	57,432	44,967	39,252	26,979	12,274	5,715	4,315	1,400	12,465	9,683	2,782
Fall 1984	57,150	44,908	39,208	26,901	12,308	5,700[3]	4,300[3]	1,400[3]	12,242	9,477	2,765
Fall 1985	57,226	44,979	39,422	27,030	12,392	5,557	4,195	1,362	12,247	9,479	2,768
Fall 1986	57,709	45,205	39,753	27,421	12,333	5,452[3]	4,116[3]	1,336[3]	12,504	9,714	2,790
Fall 1987	58,254	45,487	40,008	27,932	12,076	5,479	4,232	1,247	12,767	9,973	2,793
Fall 1988	58,485	45,430	40,189	28,503	11,686	5,241	4,036	1,206	13,055	10,161	2,894
Fall 1989[4]	59,339	45,881	40,526	29,158	11,369	5,355	4,162	1,193	13,458	10,515	2,943
Fall 1990[5]	60,172	46,221	41,026	29,742	11,284	5,195	4,066	1,129	13,951	10,912	3,039
Fall 1991[6]	60,946	46,841	41,575	30,186	11,389	5,267	4,127	1,140	14,105	10,982	3,123
Fall 1992[6]	61,836	47,601	42,250	30,663	11,587	5,351	4,192	1,159	14,235	11,083	3,152
Fall 1993[6]	62,776	48,410	42,971	31,091	11,880	5,439	4,250	1,189	14,366	11,187	3,179
Fall 1994[6]	63,791	49,279	43,749	31,451	12,298	5,530	4,300	1,230	14,512	11,305	3,207
Fall 1995[6]	64,675	50,054	44,442	31,782	12,660	5,612	4,345	1,267	14,621	11,393	3,228
Fall 1996[6]	65,561	50,759	45,074	32,068	13,006	5,685	4,384	1,301	14,802	11,537	3,266
Fall 1997[6]	66,309	51,331	45,585	32,343	13,242	5,746	4,422	1,325	14,978	11,673	3,305
Fall 1998[6]	66,977	51,750	45,955	32,661	13,294	5,795	4,465	1,330	15,227	11,864	3,363
Fall 1999[6]	67,572	52,110	46,276	32,843	13,433	5,834	4,490	1,344	15,462	12,043	3,419
Fall 2000[6]	68,098	52,406	46,539	33,032	13,507	5,867	4,516	1,351	15,692	12,220	3,472

[Continued]

★ 187 ★

Enrollment in Educational Institutions by Level and Control of Institution, Fall 1869 to Fall 2002
[Continued]

Year	Total enrollment, all levels	Elementary and secondary, total	Public elementary and secondary schools			Private elementary and secondary schools[1]			Higher education[2]		
			Total	Kinder-garten through grade 8	Grades 9 through 12	Total	Kinder-garten through grade 8	Grades 9 through 12	Total	Public	Private
Fall 2001[6]	68,544	52,679	46,782	33,172	13,610	5,897	4,535	1,362	15,865	12,355	3,510
Fall 2002[6]	69,026	52,996	47,068	33,245	13,823	5,928	4,545	1,383	16,030	12,478	3,552

Source: "All Levels of Education," *Digest of Education Statistics: 1991*, U.S. Department of Education, Office of Educational Research and Improvement, National Center for Education Statistics, November, 1991, p. 14. Table 3. Primary source: U.S. Department of Education, National Center for Education Statistics, *Statistics of State School Systems; Statistics of Public Elementary and Secondary School Systems; Statistics of Nonpublic Elementary and Secondary Schools; Projections of Education Statistics to 2002;* Common Core of Data and "Fall Enrollment in Institutions of Higher Education"; and Integrated Postsecondary Education Data Systems (IPEDS); "Fall Enrollment" surveys. *Notes:* 1. Beginning in Fall 1980, data include estimates for an expanded universe of private schools. Therefore, these totals may differ from figures shown in other tables, and direct comparisons with earlier years should be avoided. 2. Data for 1869-70 through 1949-50 include resident degree-credit students enrolled at any time during the academic year. Beginning in 1959, data include all resident and extension students enrolled at the beginning of the fall term. 3. Estimated. 4. Preliminary data. 5. Based on "Early Estimates" surveys. 6. Projected. - Data not available.

★ 188 ★

Enrollment in Educational Institutions by Level and Control of Institution, Fall 1980 to Fall 2000

Higher education enrollment projections are based on the middle alternative projections published by the National Center for Education Statistics. Because of rounding, details may not add to totals. Some data have been revised from previously published figures. "College enrollment rose to a record level of 14.0 million in Fall 1990, reflecting a significant increase in public college enrollment. Enrollment is expected to rise during the 1990s because of the high attendance rates of younger age groups and the large number of older students."

[Numbers in thousands]

Level of instruction and type of control	Fall 1980	Fall 1983	Fall 1984	Fall 1985	Fall 1986	Fall 1987	Fall 1988	Fall 1989[1]	Estimated fall 1990	Projected fall 1995	Projected fall 2000
All levels	58,346	57,432	57,150	57,226	57,709	58,254	58,485	59,339	60,172	64,675	68,098
Public	50,376	48,935	48,686	48,901	49,467	49,981	50,350	51,041	51,938	55,835	58,759
Private	7,971	8,497	8,465	8,325	8,242	8,273	8,135	8,298	8,234	8,840	9,339
Elementary and secondary education[2]	46,249	44,967	44,908	44,979	45,205	45,487	45,430	45,881	46,221	50,054	52,406
Public	40,918	39,252	39,208	39,422	39,753	40,008	40,189	40,526	41,026	44,442	46,539
Private	5,331	5,715	5,700[3]	5,557	5,452[3]	5,479	5,241	5,355	5,195	5,612	5,867
Grades K-8[4]	31,669	31,294	31,201	31,225	31,537	32,164	32,539	33,320	33,808	36,127	37,548
Public	27,677	26,979	26,901	27,030	27,421	27,932	28,503	29,158	29,742	31,782	33,032
Private	3,992	4,315	4,300[3]	4,195	4,116[3]	4,232	4,036	4,162	4,066	4,345	4,516
Grades 9-12	14,581	13,674	13,708	13,754	13,669	13,323	12,892	12,562	12,413	13,927	14,858
Public	13,242	12,274	12,308	12,392	12,333	12,076	11,686	11,369	11,284	12,660	13,507
Private	1,339	1,400	1,400[3]	1,362	1,336[3]	1,247	1,206	1,193	1,129	1,267	1,351
Higher education[5]	12,097	12,465	12,242	12,247	12,504	12,767	13,055	13,458	13,951	14,621	15,692
Public	9,457	9,683	9,477	9,479	9,714	9,973	10,161	10,515	10,912	11,393	12,220
Undergraduate[6]	8,442	8,697	8,493	8,477	8,661	8,919	9,103	9,425	9,803	10,065	10,841
First-professional	114	113	114	112	112	110	109	113	115	136	143

[Continued]

★ 188 ★

Enrollment in Educational Institutions by Level and Control of Institution, Fall 1980 to Fall 2000

[Continued]

Level of instruction and type of control	Fall 1980	Fall 1983	Fall 1984	Fall 1985	Fall 1986	Fall 1987	Fall 1988	Fall 1989[1]	Estimated fall 1990	Projected fall 1995	Projected fall 2000
Graduate[7]	901	872	870	890	941	945	949	978	994	1,192	1,236
Private	2,640	2,782	2,765	2,768	2,790	2,793	2,894	2,943	3,039	3,228	3,472
Undergraduate[6]	2,033	2,149	2,125	2,120	2,137	2,128	2,213	2,241	2,350	2,384	2,595
First-professional	163	165	165	162	158	158	158	161	158	194	205
Graduate[7]	443	468	475	486	494	507	522	541	531	650	672

Source: "All Levels of Education," *Digest of Education Statistics: 1991*, U.S. Department of Education, Office of Educational Research and Improvement, National Center for Education Statistics, November, 1991, p. 11, Table 2. Primary source: U.S. Department of Education, National Center for Education Statistics, Common Core of Data and "Fall Enrollment in Institutions of Higher Education" surveys, and *Projections of Education Statistics to 2002. Notes*: 1. Preliminary. 2. Includes enrollments in local public school systems and in most private schools (religiously affiliated and nonsectarian). Excludes subcollegiate departments of institutions of higher education, residential schools for exceptional children, and Federal schools. Excludes preprimary pupils in schools that do not offer first grade or above. 3. Estimated. 4. Includes kindergarten and some nursery school pupils. 5. Includes full-time and part-time students enrolled in degree-credit and nondegree-credit programs in universities and 2-year colleges. 6. Includes unclassified students below the baccalaureate level. 7. Includes unclassified postbaccalaureate students.

★ 189 ★

Needs of American Education, 2000

"The class of 2000 will need a far better education simply to get a decent job; by 2010, virtually every job in the country will require some skill with information-processing technology. Beyond that, simply living in modern society will raise the level of education we all need. By 2000, new technology will change our work lives so fast we will need constant retraining. Knowledge itself will double four times by the year 2000. In that one year, the class of 2000 will be exposed to more information than their grandparents experienced in a lifetime.

"Schools will have to meet these demands. Today, schools offer adult education as a community service or in hope of earning sorely needed revenue. In the future, they will be teaching adults because they haven't any choice. Many public schools will be open 24 hours a day, retraining adults from 4 p.m. to midnight, and renting out their costly computer and communicating systems to local businesses during the graveyard shift.

"Fortunately, American schools can provide top-quality education when they make the effort; unfortunately, examples of this remain rare bright spots in a bleak educational picture. There is all too much evidence that American schools are failing many students, and the failure is not limited to tough subjects like math. By the year 2000, according to one estimate, the literacy rate in America will be only 30 percent."

Source: "Preparing Education for the Year 2000," Marvin J. Cetron, *The Education Digest* LIV, No. 8, April, 1989, pp. 3-4.

★ 190 ★

Percentage of Large Companies Offering Remedial Education for Employees, 1980-2000

In the table below, companies represented are those with 10,000 or more employees. The United Way of America's Strategic Institute has identified the development of the information-based economy as one of nine major trends in society for the 1990s. Increasingly reliant on high technology, the productivity of employees within this economy will demand more company-sponsored education in the workplace. "The information-based economy will take many decades to become full-blown, but the magnitude of its impact should be kept in mind when examining information technology trends."

1980	15%
1989	30%
2000	65%

Source: "Nine Forces Reshaping America," *The Futurist,* July-August, 1990, p. 12. Primary source: American Society for Training and Development, 1989.

★ 191 ★

Preprimary School-Age Populations, 1993-2002

[Numbers in thousands]

Year (July 1)[1]	3 years old	4 years old	5 years old	3-5 years old
1993	3,907	3,917	3,857	11,681
1994	3,924	3,956	3,920	11,800
1995	3,920	3,974	3,960	11,854
1996	3,909	3,969	3,977	11,855
1997	3,898	3,959	3,972	11,829
1998	3,889	3,948	3,962	11,799
1999	3,883	3,939	3,951	11,773
2000	3,882	3,933	3,942	11,757
2001	3,886	3,931	3,936	11,753
2002	3,897	3,937	3,935	11,769

Source: "Appendix B: Supplementary Tables," *Projections of Education Statistics to 2002,* National Center for Education Statistics, December 1991, p. 185. Primary source: "United States Population Estimates, by Age, Sex, Race and Hispanic Origin: 1980 to 1988," U.S. Department of Commerce, Bureau of the Census, *Current Population Reports,* Series P-25, No. 1045, January 1990; "Projections of the Population of the United States, by Age, Sex, and Race: 1988 to 2080," *Current Population Reports,* Series P-25, No. 1018, January 1989. Original table includes data for 1977-1992. *Note:* 1. Projected.

★ 192 ★

Projections of College Enrollment, Degrees, and High School Graduates, 1991-2002

	1991	1992	1993	1994	1995	1996	1997	1998	1999	2000	2001	2002
College enrollment												
Total	14,105,000	14,235,000	14,366,000	14,512,000	14,621,000	14,803,000	14,978,000	15,227,000	15,462,000	15,692,000	15,865,000	16,030,000
Men	6,473,000	6,516,000	6,531,000	6,549,000	6,575,000	6,674,000	6,691,000	6,774,000	6,853,000	6,922,000	6,991,000	7,052,000
Women	7,632,000	7,719,000	7,835,000	7,963,000	8,046,000	8,156,000	8,287,000	8,453,000	8,609,000	8,770,000	8,874,000	8,978,000
Public	10,982,000	11,083,000	11,187,000	11,305,000	11,393,000	11,537,000	11,673,000	11,864,000	12,043,000	12,220,000	12,355,000	12,478,000
Private	3,123,000	3,152,000	3,179,000	3,207,000	3,228,000	3,266,000	3,305,000	3,363,000	3,419,000	3,472,000	3,510,000	3,552,000
Full-time	7,844,000	7,871,000	7,895,000	7,949,000	7,988,000	8,095,000	8,212,000	8,408,000	8,588,000	8,770,000	8,906,000	9,035,000
Part-time	6,261,000	6,364,000	6,471,000	6,563,000	6,633,000	6,708,000	6,766,000	6,819,000	6,874,000	6,922,000	6,959,000	6,995,000
Full-time equivalent[1]	10,106,000	10,171,000	10,232,000	10,321,000	10,385,000	10,519,000	10,656,000	10,871,000	11,070,000	11,270,000	11,418,000	11,561,000
Four-year institutions												
Total	8,844,000	8,923,000	8,990,000	9,066,000	9,120,000	9,227,000	9,334,000	9,500,000	9,655,000	9,810,000	9,927,000	10,041,000
Public	5,993,000	6,045,000	6,088,000	6,139,000	6,175,000	6,247,000	6,320,000	6,434,000	6,539,000	6,646,000	6,727,000	6,803,000
Private	2,851,000	2,878,000	2,902,000	2,927,000	2,945,000	2,980,000	3,014,000	3,066,000	3,116,000	3,164,000	3,200,000	3,238,000
Two-year institutions												
Total	5,261,000	5,312,000	5,376,000	5,446,000	5,501,000	5,576,000	5,644,000	5,727,000	5,807,000	5,882,000	5,938,000	5,989,000
Public	4,989,000	5,038,000	5,099,000	5,166,000	5,218,000	5,290,000	5,353,000	5,430,000	5,504,000	5,574,000	5,628,000	5,675,000
Private	272,000	274,000	277,000	280,000	283,000	286,000	291,000	297,000	303,000	308,000	310,000	314,000
Undergraduate												
Total	12,084,000	12,165,000	12,247,000	12,356,000	12,449,000	12,610,000	12,768,000	12,998,000	13,216,000	13,436,000	13,598,000	13,748,000
Public	9,747,000	9,818,000	9,892,000	9,987,000	10,065,000	10,196,000	10,322,000	10,501,000	10,670,000	10,841,000	10,969,000	11,084,000
Private	2,337,000	2,347,000	2,355,000	2,369,000	2,384,000	2,414,000	2,446,000	2,497,000	2,546,000	2,595,000	2,629,000	2,664,000
Graduate												
Total	1,712,000	1,752,000	1,793,000	1,826,000	1,842,000	1,859,000	1,872,000	1,888,000	1,901,000	1,908,000	1,915,000	1,926,000
Public	1,108,000	1,134,000	1,160,000	1,182,000	1,192,000	1,204,000	1,212,000	1,223,000	1,231,000	1,236,000	1,241,000	1,248,000
Private	604,000	618,000	633,000	644,000	650,000	655,000	660,000	665,000	670,000	672,000	674,000	678,000
Professional												
Total	309,000	318,000	326,000	330,000	330,000	334,000	338,000	341,000	345,000	348,000	352,000	356,000
Public	127,000	131,000	135,000	136,000	136,000	137,000	139,000	140,000	142,000	143,000	145,000	146,000
Private	182,000	187,000	191,000	194,000	194,000	197,000	199,000	201,000	203,000	205,000	207,000	210,000
Degrees												
Associate												
Total	470,000	477,000	476,000	478,000	480,000	487,000	491,000	500,000	507,000	519,000	529,000	539,000
Men	200,000	205,000	204,000	204,000	203,000	204,000	205,000	208,000	209,000	213,000	216,000	219,000
Women	270,000	272,000	272,000	274,000	277,000	283,000	286,000	292,000	298,000	306,000	313,000	320,000
Bachelor's												
Total	1,064,000	1,081,000	1,101,000	1,100,000	1,100,000	1,098,000	1,100,000	1,102,000	1,114,000	1,129,000	1,164,000	1,189,000
Men	492,000	495,000	514,000	511,000	510,000	507,000	5035,000	505,000	507,000	509,000	523,000	528,000
Women	572,000	586,000	587,000	589,000	590,000	591,000	595,000	599,000	607,000	620,000	641,000	661,000
Master's												
Total	327,000	338,000	343,000	350,000	354,000	354,000	355,000	357,000	362,000	368,000	376,000	383,000
Men	150,000	157,000	159,000	162,000	165,000	164,000	164,000	165,000	168,000	173,000	179,000	184,000
Women	177,000	181,000	184,000	188,000	189,000	190,000	191,000	192,000	194,000	195,000	197,000	199,000
Doctorate												
Total	38,700	39,300	39,800	40,000	40,200	40,400	40,600	40,900	41,100	41,200	41,400	41,400
Men	24,200	24,300	24,400	24,100	23,800	23,600	23,400	23,300	23,200	22,900	22,700	22,400
Women	14,500	15,000	15,400	15,900	16,400	16,800	17,200	17,600	17,900	18,300	18,700	19,000
First-professional												
Total	73,800	80,100	82,600	85,500	87,800	88,100	88,100	89,100	90,900	92,200	92,900	94,400
Men	44,200	49,000	50,400	51,500	52,500	52,800	52,800	53,500	54,600	55,300	56,000	57,000
Women	29,600	31,100	32,300	34,000	35,300	35,300	35,400	35,600	36,300	36,900	36,900	37,400
High-school graduates												
Total	2,465,000	2,446,000	2,470,000	2,464,000	2,563,000	2,615,000	2,719,000	2,831,000	2,885,000	2,932,000	2,943,000	2,882,000
Public	2,210,000	2,193,000	2,215,000	2,209,000	2,298,000	2,345,000	2,438,000	2,538,000	2,587,000	2,629,000	2,639,000	2,584,000
Private	2,337,000	2,347,000	2,355,000	2,369,000	2,384,000	2,414,000	2,446,000	2,497,000	2,546,000	2,595,000	2,629,000	2,664,000
Graduate												
Total	1,712,000	1,752,000	1,793,000	1,826,000	1,842,000	1,859,000	1,872,000	1,888,000	1,901,000	1,908,000	1,915,000	1,926,000
Public	1,108,000	1,134,000	1,160,000	1,182,000	1,192,000	1,204,000	1,212,000	1,223,000	1,231,000	1,236,000	1,241,000	1,248,000
Private	604,000	618,000	633,000	644,000	650,000	655,000	660,000	665,000	670,000	672,000	674,000	678,000
Professional												
Total	309,000	318,000	326,000	330,000	330,000	334,000	338,000	341,000	345,000	348,000	352,000	356,000
Public	127,000	131,000	135,000	136,000	136,000	137,000	139,000	140,000	142,000	143,000	145,000	146,000
Private	182,000	187,000	191,000	194,000	194,000	197,000	199,000	201,000	203,000	205,000	207,000	210,000
Degrees												
Associate												
Total	470,000	477,000	476,000	478,000	480,000	487,000	491,000	500,000	507,000	519,000	529,000	539,000

[Continued]

★ 192 ★

Projections of College Enrollment, Degrees, and High School Graduates, 1991-2002
[Continued]

	1991	1992	1993	1994	1995	1996	1997	1998	1999	2000	2001	2002
Men	200,000	205,000	204,000	204,000	203,000	204,000	205,000	208,000	209,000	213,000	216,000	219,000
Women	270,000	272,000	272,000	274,000	277,000	283,000	286,000	292,000	298,000	306,000	313,000	320,000
Bachelor's												
Total	1,064,000	1,081,000	1,101,000	1,100,000	1,100,000	1,098,000	1,100,000	1,102,000	1,114,000	1,129,000	1,164,000	1,189,000
Men	492,000	495,000	514,000	511,000	510,000	507,000	505,000	503,000	507,000	509,000	523,000	528,000
Women	572,000	586,000	587,000	589,000	590,000	591,000	595,000	599,000	607,000	620,000	641,000	661,000
Master's												
Total	327,000	338,000	343,000	350,000	354,000	354,000	355,000	357,000	362,000	368,000	376,000	383,000
Men	150,000	157,000	159,000	162,000	165,000	164,000	164,000	165,000	168,000	173,000	179,000	184,000
Women	177,000	181,000	184,000	188,000	189,000	190,000	191,000	192,000	194,000	195,000	197,000	199,000
Doctorate												
Total	38,700	39,300	39,800	40,000	40,200	40,400	40,600	40,900	41,100	41,200	41,400	41,400
Men	24,200	24,300	24,400	24,100	23,800	23,600	23,400	23,300	23,200	22,900	22,700	22,400
Women	14,500	15,000	15,400	15,900	16,400	16,800	17,200	17,600	17,900	18,300	18,700	19,000
First-professional												
Total	73,800	80,100	82,600	85,500	87,800	88,100	88,100	89,100	90,900	92,200	92,900	94,400
Men	44,200	49,000	50,400	51,500	52,500	52,800	52,800	53,500	54,600	55,300	56,000	57,000
Women	29,600	31,100	32,200	34,000	35,300	35,300	35,300	35,600	36,300	36,900	36,900	37,400
High-school graduates												
Total	2,465,000	2,446,000	2,470,000	2,464,000	2,563,000	2,615,000	2,719,000	2,831,000	2,885,000	2,932,000	2,943,000	2,882,000
Public	2,210,000	2,193,000	2,215,000	2,209,000	2,298,000	2,345,000	2,438,000	2,538,000	2,587,000	2,629,000	2,639,000	2,584,000
Private	255,000	253,000	255,000	255,000	265,000	270,000	281,000	293,000	298,000	303,000	304,000	298,000

Source: "Fact File: Projections of College Enrollment, Degrees and High-School Graduates, 1991-2002," *The Chronicle of Higher Education* XXXVIII, No. 20, January 22, 1992, p. A36. Primary source: U.S. Department of Education. Details may not add to totals because of rounding. *Note:* 1. Estimate based on full-time enrollment plus the full-time equivalent of part-time enrollment as reported by institutions.

★ 193 ★

School-Age Populations, 1991-2002
[Numbers in thousands]

Year (July 1)	5 years old	6 years old	5-13 years old	14-17 years old
		Projected		
1991	3,740	3,762	33,000	13,402
1992	3,782	3,750	33,402	13,710
1993	3,857	3,792	33,934	13,873
1994	3,920	3,867	34,310	14,305
1995	3,960	3,931	34,673	14,647
1996	3,977	3,969	34,994	15,005
1997	3,972	3,987	35,290	15,272
1998	3,962	3,982	35,642	15,346
1999	3,951	3,972	35,844	15,497
2000	3,942	3,960	36,044	15,585

[Continued]

★ 193 ★

School-Age Populations, 1991-2002
[Continued]

Year (July 1)	5 years old	6 years old	5-13 years old	14-17 years old
2001	3,936	3,949	36,200	15,790
2002	3,935	3,945	36,283	15,935

Source: "Appendix B: Supplementary Tables." *Projections of Education Statistics to 2002,* National Center for Education Statistics, December 1991, p. 186, Table B3. Primary source: "United States Population Estimates, by Age, Sex, Race and Hispanic Origin: 1980 to 1988," U.S. Department of Commerce, Bureau of the Census, *Current Population Reports,* Series P-25, No. 1045, January 1990; "Projections of the Population of the United States, by Age, Sex, and Race: 1988 to 2080," *Current Population Reports,* Series P-25, No. 1018, January 1989.

High School Graduates and Earned Degrees Conferred

★ 194 ★

Annual Number of Bachelor's Degrees Awarded by Sex of Recipient, with Alternative Projections, 1990-2002

Prepared April 1991. Projections are based on data through 1988-1989. Because of rounding, details may not add to totals. "Three alternative projections of earned degrees by level and [gender] were developed. The number of degrees was related to college-age populations and higher education enrollment by level enrolled and attendance status."

Year ending	Total	Men	Women
1990[1]	1,043,000	485,000	558,000
	Middle alternative projections		
1991	1,064,000	492,000	572,000
1992	1,081,000	495,000	586,000
1993	1,101,000	514,000	587,000
1994	1,100,000	511,000	589,000
1995	1,100,000	510,000	590,000
1996	1,098,000	507,000	591,000
1997	1,100,000	505,000	595,000
1998	1,102,000	503,000	599,000
1999	1,114,000	507,000	607,000
2000	1,129,000	509,000	620,000
2001	1,164,000	523,000	641,000
2002	1,189,000	528,000	661,000

[Continued]

★ 194 ★

Annual Number of Bachelor's Degrees Awarded by Sex of Recipient, with Alternative Projections, 1990-2002
[Continued]

Year ending	Total	Men	Women
Low alternative projections			
1991	1,064,000	492,000	572,000
1992	1,081,000	495,000	586,000
1993	1,065,000	496,000	569,000
1994	1,057,000	493,000	564,000
1995	1,050,000	491,000	559,000
1996	1,047,000	487,000	560,000
1997	1,045,000	483,000	562,000
1998	1,050,000	481,000	569,000
1999	1,061,000	483,000	578,000
2000	1,078,000	486,000	592,000
2001	1,109,000	499,000	610,000
2002	1,130,000	501,000	629,000
High alternative projections			
1991	1,064,000	492,000	572,000
1992	1,081,000	495,000	586,000
1993	1,153,000	522,000	631,000
1994	1,185,000	529,000	656,000
1995	1,217,000	537,000	680,000
1996	1,211,000	536,000	675,000
1997	1,206,000	539,000	667,000
1998	1,197,000	531,000	666,000
1999	1,214,000	544,000	670,000
2000	1,224,000	548,000	676,000
2001	1,254,000	564,000	690,000
2002	1,277,000	571,000	706,000

Source: "Earned Degrees Conferred," *Projections of Education Statistics to 2002*, U.S. Department of Education, Office of Educational Research and Improvement, National Center for Education Statistics, December 1991, p. 63, Table 28. Primary source: U.S. Department of Education, National Center for Education Statistics, "Degrees and Other Formal Awards Conferred" survey; Integrated and Postsecondary Education Data System (IPEDS), "Completions" survey; and "National Higher Education Statistics: Fall 1990," *Early Estimates*. Source also contains data for 1977-1989. *Note*: 1. Estimate.

★ 195 ★

Annual Number of Graduates From Public High School by Region and State with Projections, 1984-1985 to 1992-1993

Prepared June 1991.

Region and state	Actual					Estimate	Projected		
	1984-85	1985-86	1986-87	1987-88	1988-89	1989-90	1990-91	1991-92	1992-93
United States	2,414,201	2,382,616	2,428,803	2,500,192	2,456,139	2,324,035	2,210,030	2,192,980	2,215,070
Northeast	511,189	496,104	495,738	503,042	475,232	442,511	411,120	402,300	401,490
Connecticut	32,126	33,571	31,141	32,383	30,862	30,000	26,160	25,950	25,670
Maine	13,924	13,006	13,692	13,808	13,857	13,323	12,460	12,220	12,280
Massachusetts	63,411	60,360	61,010	59,515	54,892	54,954	48,960	48,010	46,260
New Hampshire	11,052	10,648	10,796	11,685	11,340	10,357	9,680	9,660	9,440
New Jersey	81,547	78,781	79,376	80,863	76,263	68,445	64,700	62,970	62,070
New York	166,752	162,165	163,765	165,379	154,580	142,400	132,620	130,160	131,610
Pennsylvania	127,226	122,871	121,219	124,376	118,921	109,630	103,860	100,610	101,700
Rhode Island	9,382	8,908	8,771	8,856	8,554	7,708	7,490	7,530	7,280
Vermont	5,769	5,794	5,968	6,177	5,963	5,694	5,190	5,190	5,180
Midwest	668,475	647,462	657,067	675,571	663,225	617,784	583,380	574,230	586,180
Illinois	117,027	114,319	116,075	119,090	116,660	108,119	102,030	100,950	102,330
Indiana	63,308	59,817	60,364	64,037	63,571	59,415	56,870	54,450	56,790
Iowa	36,087	34,279	34,580	35,218	34,294	31,780	29,460	29,530	30,890
Kansas	25,983	25,587	26,933	27,036	26,848	25,108	24,540	24,320	25,160
Michigan	105,908	101,042	102,725	106,151	101,784	93,000	88,120	86,480	85,960
Minnesota	53,352	51,988	53,533	54,645	53,122	48,502	46,600	46,990	48,530
Missouri	51,290	49,204	50,840	51,316	51,968	48,457	46,480	46,090	46,930
Nebraska	18,036	17,845	18,129	18,300	18,690	18,556	16,510	16,760	17,390
North Dakota	8,146	7,610	7,821	8,432	8,077	7,690	7,640	7,400	7,470
Ohio	122,281	119,561	121,121	124,503	125,036	114,513	107,700	104,620	107,060
South Dakota	8,206	7,870	8,074	8,415	8,181	7,650	7,250	7,340	7,700
Wisconsin	58,851	58,340	56,872	58,428	54,994	54,994	50,180	49,300	49,970
South	789,445	790,924	807,348	833,532	836,564	807,843	771,190	761,490	758,820
Alabama	40,002	39,620	42,463	43,799	43,437	36,555	39,840	38,470	38,940
Arkansas	26,342	26,227	27,101	27,776	28,162	27,343	25,910	25,790	25,500
Delaware	5,893	5,791	5,895	5,963	6,104	6,111	5,220	5,290	5,440
District of Columbia	3,940	3,875	3,842	3,882	3,565	3,626	3,050	3,200	2,790
Florida	81,140	83,029	82,184	89,206	90,759	89,000	86,850	87,760	78,640
Georgia	58,654	59,082	60,018	61,765	61,937	56,605	57,460	57,320	58,580
Kentucky	37,999	37,288	36,948	39,484	38,883	38,693	34,760	33,090	34,080
Louisiana	39,742	39,965	39,084	39,058	37,198	35,899	34,570	33,090	33,600
Maryland	48,299	46,700	46,107	47,175	45,791	41,566	39,200	38,380	38,690
Mississippi	25,315	25,134	26,201	27,896	24,241	25,039	23,520	23,000	23,180
North Carolina	67,245	65,865	65,421	67,836	69,300	64,521	62,250	60,110	60,720
Oklahoma	34,626	34,452	35,514	36,145	36,773	35,606	32,770	32,310	30,300
South Carolina	34,500	34,500	36,000	36,113	37,020	34,600	33,390	32,630	33,130
Tennessee	43,293	43,263	44,731	47,904	48,553	47,500	43,720	43,480	43,710
Texas	159,234	161,150	168,430	171,436	176,951	182,057	169,700	169,950	174,660
Virginia	60,959	63,113	65,008	65,688	65,004	61,268	57,680	56,990	56,520

[Continued]

Annual Number of Graduates From Public High School by Region and State with Projections, 1984-1985 to 1992-1993

[Continued]

Region and state	Actual					Estimate	Projected		
	1984-85	1985-86	1986-87	1987-88	1988-89	1989-90	1990-91	1991-92	1992-93
West Virginia	22,262	21,870	22,401	22,406	22,886	21,854	21,300	20,630	20,340
West	445,092	448,126	468,650	488,047	481,118	455,898	444,340	454,960	468,580
Alaska	5,184	5,464	5,692	5,907	5,631	5,437	5,260	5,270	5,260
Arizona	27,877	27,533	29,549	29,777	31,638	32,103	28,240	29,170	29,690
California	225,448	229,026	237,414	249,617	244,629	229,353	227,120	234,890	243,550
Colorado	32,255	32,621	34,200	35,977	35,520	32,967	31,340	30,400	31,400
Hawaii	10,092	9,958	10,371	10,575	10,404	9,905	9,560	9,180	9,490
Idaho	12,148	12,059	12,243	12,425	12,520	11,642	11,640	12,150	12,280
Montana	10,016	9,761	10,073	10,311	10,490	9,375	9,020	9,060	9,220
Nevada	8,572	8,784	9,506	9,404	9,464	9,462	9,270	9,560	9,890
New Mexico	15,622	15,468	15,701	15,868	15,481	14,884	14,770	15,130	15,400
Oregon	26,870	26,286	27,165	28,058	26,903	25,564	24,490	24,940	25,530
Utah	19,890	19,774	20,930	22,226	22,934	22,511	23,280	24,220	24,860
Washington	45,431	45,805	49,873	51,754	49,425	46,872	44,730	45,340	46,340
Wyoming	5,687	5,587	5,933	6,148	6,079	5,823	5,620	5,650	5,670

Source: "Public High School Graduates," *Projections of Education Statistics to 2002,* U.S. Department of Education, Office of Educational Research and Improvement, National Center for Education Statistics, December 1991, pp. 129-30, Table 43. Primary source: U.S. Department of Education, National Center for Education Statistics, Common Core of Data surveys and "Key Statistics for Public and Private Elementary and Secondary Education: School Year 1990-1991," *Early Estimates.*

Annual Number of Graduates From Public High School by Region and State with Projections, 1993-1994 to 2001-2002

Prepared June 1991.

Region and state	1993-94	1994-95	1995-96	1996-97	1997-98	1998-99	1999-2000	2000-2001	2001-2002
United States	2,209,050	2,298,020	2,345,000	2,438,040	2,538,020	2,587,040	2,629,030	2,639,040	2,583,990
Northeast	396,870	407,190	416,600	428,030	437,730	448,580	456,960	460,220	455,420
Connecticut	25,250	26,140	26,800	27,760	28,680	29,740	30,520	30,920	31,020
Maine	11,890	12,140	12,630	13,030	13,160	13,750	14,000	13,560	13,740
Massachusetts	45,650	46,770	47,800	49,140	51,000	52,730	54,190	54,330	54,970
New Hampshire	9,390	9,820	10,280	10,910	11,630	12,490	13,010	13,070	13,150
New Jersey	61,340	62,900	62,860	64,980	65,590	66,210	67,510	68,400	69,270
New York	131,370	133,890	136,580	139,130	140,590	143,260	145,860	146,650	143,970
Pennsylvania	99,540	102,600	106,390	109,280	112,670	115,510	116,650	117,520	114,050
Rhode Island	7,270	7,570	7,790	8,120	8,570	8,790	9,000	9,270	8,980
Vermont	5,170	5,360	5,470	5,680	5,840	6,100	6,220	6,500	6,270
Midwest	577,810	602,990	613,940	636,830	661,490	662,570	660,830	656,930	641,210

[Continued]

Annual Number of Graduates From Public High School by Region and State with Projections, 1993-1994 to 2001-2002

[Continued]

Region and state	1993-94	1994-95	1995-96	1996-97	1997-98	1998-99	1999-2000	2000-2001	2001-2002
Illinois	102,740	106,690	107,020	111,840	116,370	112,470	110,840	108,560	108,110
Indiana	55,350	57,640	58,610	59,680	61,920	61,740	61,950	61,370	59,460
Iowa	30,570	31,870	32,440	33,400	34,830	35,080	34,150	33,840	32,040
Kansas	25,500	26,600	27,080	28,080	29,600	30,430	30,280	30,710	29,640
Michigan	83,340	86,100	87,870	90,390	92,300	92,980	93,900	93,690	92,010
Minnesota	48,660	51,060	53,630	56,200	59,550	61,580	62,590	62,540	60,610
Missouri	46,090	48,660	50,170	51,630	53,270	52,650	52,500	54,640	52,730
Nebraska	16,790	17,550	17,880	18,460	19,400	19,750	19,490	19,000	18,730
North Dakota	7,470	7,760	7,780	7,810	7,930	8,110	8,010	7,860	7,520
Ohio	104,290	107,660	108,400	113,120	116,920	117,340	116,480	114,040	111,700
South Dakota	7,920	8,210	8,290	8,670	8,990	9,040	8,990	8,550	8,570
Wisconsin	49,090	53,190	54,770	57,550	60,410	61,400	61,650	62,130	60,090
South	753,420	781,780	795,010	825,220	857,650	871,550	883,770	884,920	867,000
Alabama	38,330	39,490	39,750	40,510	42,030	41,040	40,640	39,790	39,540
Arkansas	25,460	26,160	26,000	26,920	27,590	27,370	27,110	26,780	26,450
Delaware	5,450	5,710	5,950	6,450	6,730	7,140	7,100	6,970	6,970
District of Columbia	2,730	2,640	2,670	2,700	2,620	2,660	2,580	2,540	2,670
Florida	84,000	86,960	90,490	99,330	105,810	113,220	121,100	126,590	124,940
Georgia	58,090	60,420	62,760	66,110	70,600	72,460	71,540	71,440	71,540
Kentucky	34,100	35,920	35,940	36,480	37,180	36,330	35,680	35,610	33,170
Louisiana	32,260	32,830	33,120	33,220	33,150	32,570	32,010	30,670	30,190
Maryland	38,390	41,230	42,440	44,520	47,080	48,860	51,250	51,680	52,730
Mississippi	23,110	24,570	24,430	24,740	25,620	25,870	25,450	24,370	23,520
North Carolina	57,940	60,070	60,380	61,670	63,070	63,530	64,260	64,440	63,790
Oklahoma	31,510	32,750	33,000	33,720	34,990	35,430	36,100	36,530	33,360
South Carolina	31,870	33,530	33,980	35,240	36,600	36,940	37,390	37,050	36,020
Tennessee	41,760	43,620	43,960	45,010	45,340	45,910	46,810	46,380	44,870
Texas	172,930	177,210	180,840	187,970	195,950	198,650	200,390	201,970	193,850
Virginia	55,610	58,160	59,370	61,780	63,830	64,670	65,920	65,650	67,250
West Virginia	19,880	20,510	19,930	18,850	19,460	18,900	18,440	17,460	16,140
West	480,950	506,060	519,450	547,960	581,150	604,340	627,470	636,970	620,360
Alaska	5,490	5,690	5,860	6,030	6,320	6,600	6,670	6,200	6,410
Arizona	31,190	33,590	34,930	38,400	41,340	43,430	46,590	48,570	47,120
California	249,860	263,060	272,110	285,780	307,110	323,290	337,520	346,890	340,070
Colorado	31,310	31,920	32,640	34,260	35,710	36,810	37,540	37,360	36,170
Hawaii	9,860	10,090	10,130	10,480	10,970	11,130	11,400	11,530	11,580
Idaho	12,620	13,060	13,380	13,780	13,850	13,610	13,690	13,220	12,460
Montana	9,310	9,570	9,680	9,660	9,960	9,990	9,870	9,650	9,260
Nevada	10,500	11,440	12,050	13,300	14,700	15,740	16,760	17,490	16,740
New Mexico	15,170	15,710	16,170	16,500	17,450	17,880	18,080	18,210	17,710
Oregon	26,340	27,430	28,070	29,080	29,060	29,860	31,240	31,009	29,650
Utah	26,950	28,220	26,800	29,290	30,100	29,130	29,230	27,660	26,181

[Continued]

★ 196 ★

Annual Number of Graduates From Public High School by Region and State with Projections, 1993-1994 to 2001-2002

[Continued]

Region and state	1993-94	1994-95	1995-96	1996-97	1997-98	1998-99	1999-2000	2000-2001	2001-2002
Washington	46,860	50,590	52,080	55,470	58,620	61,130	63,230	63,660	62,170
Wyoming	5,490	5,690	5,550	5,930	5,960	5,640	5,650	5,520	4,840

Source: "Public High School Graduates," *Projections of Education Statistics to 2002*, U.S. Department of Education, Office of Educational Research and Improvement, National Center for Education Statistics, December 1991, pp. 129-30, Table 43. Primary source: U.S. Department of Education, National Center for Education Statistics, Common Core of Data surveys and "Key Statistics for Public and Private Elementary and Secondary Education: School Year 1990-1991," *Early Estimates.*

★ 197 ★

Annual Number of Master's Degrees Awarded by Sex of Recipient, with Alternative Projections, 1990-2002

Prepared April 1991. Projections are based on data through 1988-1989. Because of rounding, details may not add to totals. "Three alternative projections of earned degrees by level and [gender] were developed. The number of degrees was related to college-age populations and higher education enrollment by level enrolled and attendance status."

Year ending	Total	Men	Women
1990[1]	319,000	149,000	170,000

Middle alternative projections

Year ending	Total	Men	Women
1991	327,000	150,000	177,000
1992	338,000	157,000	181,000
1993	343,000	159,000	184,000
1994	350,000	162,000	188,000
1995	354,000	165,000	189,000
1996	354,000	164,000	190,000
1997	355,000	164,000	191,000
1998	357,000	165,000	192,000
1999	362,000	168,000	194,000
2000	368,000	173,000	195,000
2001	376,000	179,000	197,000
2002	383,000	184,000	199,000

Low alternative projections

Year ending	Total	Men	Women
1991	321,000	150,000	171,000
1992	324,000	152,000	172,000
1993	325,000	152,000	173,000
1994	328,000	153,000	175,000
1995	331,000	155,000	176,000
1996	329,000	151,000	178,000
1997	328,000	148,000	180,000

[Continued]

★ 197 ★

Annual Number of Master's Degrees Awarded by Sex of Recipient, with Alternative Projections, 1990-2002
[Continued]

Year ending	Total	Men	Women
1998	328,000	146,000	182,000
1999	330,000	146,000	184,000
2000	333,000	147,000	186,000
2001	337,000	149,000	188,000
2002	342,000	152,000	190,000
High alternative projections			
1991	334,000	150,000	184,000
1992	351,000	163,000	188,000
1993	363,000	170,000	193,000
1994	373,000	176,000	197,000
1995	381,000	184,000	197,000
1996	386,000	188,000	198,000
1997	390,000	191,000	199,000
1998	395,000	195,000	200,000
1999	401,000	199,000	202,000
2000	410,000	207,000	203,000
2001	421,000	216,000	205,000
2002	430,000	223,000	207,000

Source: "Earned Degrees Conferred," *Projections of Education Statistics to 2002*, U.S. Department of Education, Office of Educational Research and Improvement, National Center for Education Statistics, December 1991, p. 64, Table 29. Primary source: U.S. Department of Education, National Center for Education Statistics, "Degrees and Other Formal Awards Conferred" survey; Integrated and Postsecondary Education Data System (IPEDS), "Completions" survey; and "National Higher Education Statistics: Fall 1990," *Early Estimates*. Source also contains data for 1977-1989. *Note*: 1. Estimate.

★ 198 ★

Annual Numbers of Associate Degrees Awarded by Sex of Recipient, with Alternative Projections, 1990-2002

Prepared April 1991. Projections are based on data through 1988-1989. Because of rounding, details may not add to totals. "The historical growth in enrollment of women in institutions of higher education led to an increase in the number of earned degrees conferred [during the period under study]. Over the projection period [1994 to 2002], the number of degrees awarded to women will continue to rise at all levels. With the exception of doctor's degrees, the trends in the [declining] number of degrees awarded to men will reverse and increase over the same period. Three alternative projections of earned degrees by level and [gender] were developed. The number of degrees was related to college-age populations and higher education enrollment by level enrolled and attendance status."

Year ending	Total	Men	Women
1990[1]	445,000	185,000	260,000
Middle alternative projections			
1991	470,000	200,000	270,000
1992	477,000	205,000	272,000
1993	476,000	204,000	272,000
1994	478,000	204,000	274,000
1995	480,000	203,000	277,000
1996	487,000	204,000	283,000
1997	491,000	205,000	286,000
1998	500,000	208,000	292,000
1999	507,000	209,000	298,000
2000	519,000	213,000	306,000
2001	529,000	216,000	313,000
2002	539,000	219,000	320,000
Low alternative projections			
1991	470,000	200,000	270,000
1992	462,000	198,000	264,000
1993	457,000	196,000	261,000
1994	453,000	194,000	259,000
1995	454,000	193,000	261,000
1996	457,000	193,000	264,000
1997	463,000	194,000	269,000
1998	470,000	195,000	275,000
1999	479,000	197,000	282,000
2000	489,000	200,000	289,000
2001	499,000	202,000	297,000
2002	510,000	205,000	305,000
High alternative projections			
1991	470,000	200,000	270,000
1992	495,000	208,000	287,000

[Continued]

★ 198 ★

Annual Numbers of Associate Degrees Awarded by Sex of Recipient, with Alternative Projections, 1990-2002

[Continued]

Year ending	Total	Men	Women
1993	505,000	210,000	295,000
1994	516,000	212,000	304,000
1995	520,000	213,000	307,000
1996	524,000	216,000	308,000
1997	524,000	214,000	310,000
1998	536,000	221,000	315,000
1999	543,000	224,000	319,000
2000	555,000	229,000	326,000
2001	566,000	234,000	332,000
2002	576,000	238,000	338,000

Source: "Earned Degrees Conferred," *Projections of Education Statistics to 2002*, U.S. Department of Education, Office of Educational Research and Improvement, National Center for Education Statistics, December 1991, p. 62, Table 27. Primary source: U.S. Department of Education, National Center for Education Statistics, "Degrees and Other Formal Awards Conferred," survey; Integrated and Postsecondary Education Data System (IPEDS), "Completions" survey; and "National Higher Education Statistics: Fall 1990," *Early Estimates*. Source also contains data for 1977-1989. *Note:* 1. Estimate.

★ 199 ★

Average Annual Change in Number of High School Graduates in Percent, 1976-2002

"Over the projection period [1989-90 to 2001-2002], the total number of high school graduates is expected to fluctuate and then decrease to 2.5 million in 1993-94. Thereafter, it is projected to rise to 2.9 million by 2001-2002, an increase of 11 percent from 1989-90, or an average annual growth rate of 0.9 percent. During the projection period, the growth rate will be lower in the first half of the period (1989-90 to 1995-96) than in the second half (1995-96 to 2001-2002)."

	1976-77 to 1983-84	1983-84 to 1989-90	Projected	
			1989-90 to 1995-96	1995-96 to 2001-2002
Total	-1.9	-1.1	0.1	1.6
Public	-1.8	-1.2	0.1	1.6
Private	-2.1	-0.2	0.1	1.7

Source: "High School Graduates," *Projections of Education Statistics to 2002*, U.S. Department of Education, Office of Educational Research and Development, National Center for Education Statistics, December, 1991, p. 51.

★ 200 ★

Average Annual Growth Rate in Number of High School Graduates, 1977-2002

[Numbers in percent]

	Public	Private
1977-1984	-1.8	-2.1
1984-1990	-1.2	-0.2
1990-1996	0.1	0.1
1996-2002	1.6	1.7

Source: "High School Graduates," *Projections of Education Statistics to 2002*, U.S. Department of Education, Office of Educational Research and Improvement, National Center for Education Statistics, December, 1991, p. 53, Fig. 30.

★ 201 ★

Doctoral Degrees Awarded by Sex of Recipient, with Alternative Projections, 1990-2002

Prepared April 1991. Projections are based on data through 1988-1989. Because of rounding, details may not add to totals. Doctor's degrees are defined here as earned degrees carrying the title of doctor. These include the Doctor of Philosophy, as well as specialized degrees awarded within certain professional fields, such as education (Ed.D.), musical arts (D.M.A.), business administration (D.B.A.) and engineering (D.Eng.). "Three alternative projections of earned degrees by level and [gender] were developed. The number of degrees was related to college-age populations and higher education enrollment by level and attendance status.... Most notable are the trends in degrees awarded to men and women." Under the middle alternative projection the number of doctoral degrees awarded to men is expected to decline by 7 percent between 1989-90 and 2001-2002. For women, according to the middle alternative projection, the number of degrees conferred is expected to increase by 36 percent between 1989-90 and 2001-2002. Among total doctoral degrees conferred in 2001-2002, women are projected to receive 46 percent and men 54 percent.

Year ending	Total	Men	Women
1990[1]	38,000	24,000	14,000

Middle alternative projections

Year ending	Total	Men	Women
1991	38,700	24,200	14,500
1992	39,300	24,300	15,000
1993	39,800	24,400	15,400
1994	40,000	24,100	15,900
1995	40,200	23,800	16,400
1996	40,400	23,600	16,800
1997	40,600	23,400	17,200

[Continued]

★ 201 ★

Doctoral Degrees Awarded by Sex of Recipient, with Alternative Projections, 1990-2002
[Continued]

Year ending	Total	Men	Women
1998	40,900	23,300	17,600
1999	41,100	23,200	17,900
2000	41,200	22,900	18,300
2001	41,400	22,700	18,700
2002	41,400	22,400	19,000
Low alternative projections			
1991	37,400	23,000	14,400
1992	37,500	22,700	14,800
1993	38,000	22,800	15,200
1994	37,700	22,100	15,600
1995	37,500	21,500	16,000
1996	37,300	20,800	16,500
1997	37,300	20,400	16,900
1998	37,200	19,900	17,300
1999	37,100	19,400	17,700
2000	37,000	18,900	18,100
2001	36,900	18,400	18,500
2002	36,700	17,900	18,800
High alternative projections			
1991	40,000	25,400	14,600
1992	41,100	25,900	15,200
1993	42,200	26,600	15,600
1994	43,000	26,900	16,100
1995	43,700	27,100	16,600
1996	44,200	27,200	17,000
1997	44,800	27,400	17,400
1998	45,500	27,700	17,800
1999	46,200	28,100	18,100
2000	46,600	28,100	18,500
2001	47,400	28,500	18,900
2002	50,300	30,000	20,300

Source: "Earned Degrees Conferred," *Projections of Education Statistics to 2002*, U.S. Department of Education, Office of Educational Research and Improvement, National Center for Education Statistics, December 1991, p. 65, Table 30. Primary source: U.S. Department of Education, National Center for Education Statistics, "Degrees and Other Formal Awards Conferred," survey; Integrated and Postsecondary Education Data System (IPEDS), "Completions" survey; and "National Higher Education Statistics: Fall 1990," *Early Estimates*. Source also contains data for 1977-1989. *Note*: 1. Estimates.

★ 202 ★

First-Professional Degrees Awarded by Sex of Recipient with Alternative Projections, 1977-2002

Prepared April 1991. Projections are based on data through 1988-1989. Because of rounding, details may not add to totals. The first-professional degree has been defined by the National Center for Education Statistics as a degree signifying both completion of the academic requirements for beginning practice in a given profession and a level of professional skill beyond that normally required for a bachelor's degree. Examples are the degrees awarded in dentistry (D.D.S. or D.M.D.), medicine (M.D.) and law (LL.B). "Three alternative projections of earned degrees by level and [gender] were developed. The number of degrees was related to college-age populations and higher education enrollment by level enrolled and attendance status."

Year ending	Total	Men	Women
1977	64,359	52,374	11,985
1978	66,581	52,270	14,311
1979	68,848	52,652	16,196
1980	70,131	52,716	17,415
1981	71,956	52,792	19,164
1982	72,032	52,223	19,809
1983	73,136	51,310	21,826
1984	74,407	51,334	23,073
1985	75,063	50,455	24,608
1986	73,910	49,261	24,649
1987	72,750	47,460	25,290
1988	70,735	45,484	25,251
1989	70,758	45,067	25,691
1990[1]	71,000	43,000	28,000
Middle alternative projections			
1991	73,800	44,200	29,600
1992	80,100	49,000	31,100
1993	82,600	50,400	32,200
1994	85,500	51,500	34,000
1995	87,800	52,500	35,300
1996	88,100	52,800	35,300
1997	88,100	52,800	35,300
1998	89,100	53,500	35,600
1999	90,900	54,600	36,300
2000	92,200	55,300	36,900
2001	92,900	56,000	36,900
2002	94,400	57,000	37,400
Low alternative projections			
1991	71,600	44,200	27,400
1992	76,500	48,000	28,500
1993	77,700	48,700	29,000
1994	78,500	49,000	29,500
1995	80,300	49,700	30,600

[Continued]

★ 202 ★

First-Professional Degrees Awarded by Sex of Recipient with Alternative Projections, 1977-2002
[Continued]

Year ending	Total	Men	Women
1996	80,300	49,700	30,600
1997	80,000	49,400	30,600
1998	80,600	49,000	31,600
1999	81,200	49,400	31,800
2000	82,100	49,700	32,400
2001	83,000	50,100	32,900
2002	83,300	50,100	33,200
	High alternative projections		
1991	75,300	44,200	31,100
1992	84,400	50,400	34,000
1993	89,100	52,200	36,900
1994	92,900	54,200	38,700
1995	95,300	56,000	39,300
1996	96,600	57,300	39,300
1997	97,900	58,400	39,500
1998	99,200	59,400	39,800
1999	100,600	60,800	39,800
2000	102,800	62,500	40,300
2001	104,600	64,300	40,300
2002	106,300	65,700	40,600

Source: "Earned Degrees Conferred," *Projections of Education Statistics to 2002*, U.S. Department of Education, Office of Educational Research and Improvement, National Center for Education Statistics, December, 1991, p. 66, Table 31. Primary source: U.S. Department of Education, National Center for Education Statistics, "Degrees and Other Formal Awards Conferred" survey; Integrated Postsecondary Education Data System (IPEDS), "Completions" survey; and "National Higher Education Statistics: Fall 1990," *Early Estimates*. *Note*: 1. Estimate.

★ 203 ★

Number of High School Graduates by Control of Institution, with Annual Projections, 1990-2002

Because of rounding, details may not add to totals. "Over the projection period (1991-2002) the number of both public and private high school graduates is expected to show an increase of 11 percent from 1989-90, or an average growth rate of 0.9 percent."

[Numbers in thousands]

Year ending	Total	Public	Private
1990[1]	2,592	2,324	268
		Projected	
1991	2,465	2,210	255
1992	2,446	2,193	253
1993	2,470	2,215	255
1994	2,464	2,209	255
1995	2,563	2,298	265
1996	2,615	2,345	270
1997	2,719	2,438	281
1998	2,831	2,538	293
1999	2,885	2,587	298
2000	2,932	2,629	303
2001	2,943	2,639	304
2002	2,882	2,584	298

Source: "High School Graduates," *Projections of Education Statistics to 2002*, U.S. Department of Education, Office of Educational Research and Improvement, National Center for Education Statistics, December, 1991, p. 54. Table 26. Primary source: U.S. Department of Education, National Center for Education Statistics, *Statistics of Public Elementary and Secondary Schools*; Common Core of Data surveys; "Selected Public and Private Elementary and Secondary Education Statistics," *NCES Bulletin*, October 23, 1979; "Private Elementary and Secondary Education, 1983: Enrollment, Teachers, and Schools, " *NCES Bulletin*, December 1984; 1985 Private School Survey; Key Statistics for Private Elementary and Secondary Education: School Year 1988-89," *Early Estimates*; "Key Statistics for Private Elementary and Secondary Education: School Year 1989-90," *Early Estimates*; and "Key Statistics for Public and Private Elementary and Secondary Education: School Year 1990-91," *Early Estimates*. Prior to 1989 and 1990, numbers for private high school graduates were estimated by NCES. Source also contains data for 1977-1989. *Note*: 1. Estimate.

★ 204 ★

Percent Change in Annual Number of High School Graduates by State, 1989-1990 to 2001-2002

Among the 50 states, 37 are expected to show increases in the numbers of public high school graduates during the period between 1989-90 and 2001-2002. A substantial increase is expected in the West (36%) and smaller increases are projected for the South (7% overall), the Midwest (4%) and the Northeast (3%).

[Numbers in percent]

Alabama	0.0 to 9.9
Alaska	10.0 to 19.9
Arizona	20.0 to 77.0
Arkansas	-27.0 to -0.0
California	20.0 to 77.0
Colorado	0.0 to 9.9
Connecticut	0.0 to 9.9
Delaware	0.0 to 9.9
District of Columbia	-27.0 to -0.0
Florida	20.0 to 77.0
Georgia	20.0 to 77.0
Hawaii	10.0 to 19.9
Idaho	0.0 to 9.9
Illinois	0.0 to 9.9
Indiana	0.0 to 9.9
Iowa	0.0 to 9.9
Kansas	10.0 to 19.9
Kentucky	-27.0 to -0.0
Louisiana	-27.0 to -0.0
Maine	0.0 to 9.9
Maryland	0.0 to 9.9
Massachusetts	0.0 to 9.9
Michigan	-27.0 to -0.0
Minnesota	20.0 to 77.0
Mississippi	-27.0 to -0.0
Missouri	0.0 to 9.9
Montana	-27.0 to -0.0
Nebraska	0.0 to 9.9
Nevada	20.0 to 77.0
New Hampshire	20.0 to 77.0
New Jersey	0.0 to 9.9
New Mexico	10.0 to 19.9
New York	0.0 to 9.9
North Carolina	-27.0 to -0.0
North Dakota	-27.0 to -0.0
Ohio	-27.0 to -0.0
Oklahoma	-27.0 to -0.0
Oregon	10.0 to 19.9
Pennsylvania	0.0 to 9.9
Rhode Island	10.0 to 19.9

[Continued]

★ 204 ★

Percent Change in Annual Number of High School Graduates by State, 1989-1990 to 2001-2002

[Continued]

South Carolina	0.0 to 9.9
South Dakota	10.0 to 19.9
Tennessee	-27.0 to -0.0
Texas	0.0 to 9.9
Utah	10.0 to 19.9
Vermont	10.0 to 19.9
Virginia	0.0 to 9.9
Washington	20.0 to 77.0
West Virginia	-27.0 to -0.0
Wisconsin	0.0 to 9.9
Wyoming	-27.0 to -0.0

Source: "Public High School Graduates," *Projections of Education Statistics to 2002*, U.S. Department of Education, Office of Educational Research and Improvement, National Center for Education Statistics, December, 1991, p. 124, fig. 88.

★ 205 ★

Percent Change in Annual Number of Public High School Graduates by Region and State with Projections, 1984-1985 to 2001-2002

Prepared June 1991. Among the 50 states, 37 are expected to show increases in the numbers of public high school graduates during the period between 1989-90 and 2001-2002. A substantial increase is expected in the West (36%) and smaller increases are projected for the South (7% overall), the Midwest (4%) and the Northeast (3%).

Region and state	Actual 1984-85 to 1989-90	Projected		
		1989-90 to 1995-96	1995-96 to 2001-2002	1989-90 to 2001-2002
United States	-3.7	0.9	10.2	11.2
Northeast	-13.4	-5.9	9.3	2.9
Connecticut	-6.6	-10.7	15.8	3.4
Maine	-4.3	-5.2	8.8	3.2
Massachusetts	-13.3	-13.0	15.0	0.0
New Hampshire	-6.3	-0.8	27.9	26.9
New Jersey	-16.1	-8.2	10.2	1.2
New York	-14.6	-4.1	5.4	1.1
Pennsylvania	-13.8	-3.0	7.2	4.0
Rhode Island	-16.2	1.1	15.3	16.5
Vermont	-1.3	-3.9	14.7	10.2
Midwest	-7.6	-0.6	4.4	3.8

[Continued]

193

★ 205 ★

Percent Change in Annual Number of Public High School Graduates by Region and State with Projections, 1984-1985 to 2001-2002
[Continued]

Region and state	Actual 1984-85 to 1989-90	Projected		
		1989-90 to 1995-96	1995-96 to 2001-2002	1989-90 to 2001-2002
Illinois	-7.6	-1.0	1.0	-0.0
Indiana	-6.1	-1.4	1.5	0.1
Iowa	-11.9	2.1	-1.2	0.8
Kansas	-3.4	7.8	9.5	18.1
Michigan	-12.2	-5.5	4.7	-1.1
Minnesota	-9.1	10.6	13.0	25.0
Missouri	-5.5	3.5	5.1	8.8
Nebraska	2.9	-3.6	4.7	0.9
North Dakota	-5.6	1.2	-3.4	-2.3
Ohio	-6.4	-5.3	3.0	-2.5
South Dakota	-6.8	8.4	3.4	12.1
Wisconsin	-6.6	-0.4	9.7	9.3
South	2.3	-1.6	9.1	7.3
Alabama	-8.6	8.7	-0.5	8.2
Arkansas	3.8	-4.9	1.7	-3.3
Delaware	3.7	-2.7	17.3	14.1
District of Columbia	-8.0	-26.3	-0.0	-26.3
Florida	9.7	1.7	38.1	40.4
Georgia	-3.5	10.9	14.0	26.4
Kentucky	1.8	-7.1	-7.7	-14.3
Louisiana	-9.7	-7.8	-8.8	-15.9
Maryland	-13.9	2.1	24.2	26.9
Mississippi	-1.1	-2.4	-3.8	-6.1
North Carolina	-4.1	-6.4	5.6	-1.1
Oklahoma	2.8	-7.3	1.1	-6.3
South Carolina	0.3	-1.8	6.0	4.1
Tennessee	9.7	-7.5	2.1	-5.5
Texas	14.3	-0.7	7.2	6.5
Virginia	0.5	-3.1	13.3	9.8
West Virginia	-1.8	-8.8	-19.0	-26.1
West	2.4	13.9	19.4	36.1
Alaska	4.9	7.7	9.4	17.9
Arizona	15.2	8.8	34.9	46.8
California	1.7	18.6	25.0	48.3
Colorado	2.2	-1.0	10.8	9.7
Hawaii	-1.9	2.3	14.3	16.9
Idaho	-4.2	15.0	-6.9	7.0
Montana	-6.4	3.2	-4.3	-1.2
Nevada	10.4	27.3	38.9	76.9

[Continued]

★ 205 ★

Percent Change in Annual Number of Public High School Graduates by Region and State with Projections, 1984-1985 to 2001-2002

[Continued]

Region and state	Actual 1984-85 to 1989-90	Projected 1989-90 to 1995-96	Projected 1995-96 to 2001-2002	Projected 1989-90 to 2001-2002
New Mexico	-4.7	8.7	9.5	19.0
Oregon	-4.9	9.8	5.6	16.0
Utah	13.2	19.0	-2.2	16.4
Washington	3.2	11.1	19.4	32.6
Wyoming	2.4	-4.6	-12.9	-16.9

Source: "Public High School Graduates," *Projections of Educational Statistics to 2002*, U.S. Department of Education, Office of Educational Research and Improvement, National Center for Education Statistics, December, 1991 p. 131, Table 44. Primary source: U.S. Department of Education, National Center for Education Statistics, Common Core of Data surveys and "Key Statistics for Public and Private Elementary and Secondary Education: School Year 1990-91," *Early Estimates*.

★ 206 ★

Projected Number of High-School Graduates by Racial and Ethnic Group and State, 1986-1995

Nationwide, the proportion of graduates who are minority-group members is expected to rise from 22 percent in 1986 to 28 percent in 1995. High school dropout rates used in projections were compiled by the U.S. Department of Education. Statistics shown in the table include only high school students graduating from public schools (89 percent of all high school graduates). "The projections of enrollments and graduates are based on birth records and historical data on elementary and secondary school enrollments by grade. The study assumes that migration rates will remain at current levels."

	American Indian	Asian	Black	Hispanic	White	Total
Alabama	589	242	12,986	176	26,211	40,204
Alaska	1,017	261	287	121	4,214	5,900
Arizona	2,416	702	1,372	7,640	22,463	34,593
Arkansas	47	173	5,863	111	20,019	26,213
California	2,105	39,696	17,801	77,027	125,507	262,136
Colorado	244	836	1,484	4,151	24,915	31,630
Connecticut	28	635	2,691	1,851	20,357	25,562
Delaware	6	71	1,374	101	4,571	6,123
District of Columbia	0	37	2,571	212	70	2,890
Florida	112	2,237	18,324	13,806	58,038	92,517
Georgia	10	384	20,670	237	38,481	59,782
Hawaii	35	8,069	218	218	2,170	10,710
Idaho	119	144	25	448	12,535	13,271

[Continued]

★ 206 ★

Projected Number of High-School Graduates by Racial and Ethnic Group and State, 1986-1995

[Continued]

	American Indian	Asian	Black	Hispanic	White	Total
Illinois	119	3,983	16,865	7,932	76,643	105,542
Indiana	87	451	5,026	1,040	50,659	57,263
Iowa	34	304	628	250	30,391	31,607
Kansas	232	452	1,905	1,172	22,912	26,673
Kentucky	11	305	2,962	70	33,402	36,750
Louisiana	136	435	14,828	371	20,076	35,846
Maine	39	78	80	79	11,662	11,938
Maryland	59	1,275	11,438	599	28,019	41,390
Massachusetts	58	2,191	3,313	3,333	38,068	46,963
Michigan	745	899	10,807	1,402	71,053	84,906
Minnesota	475	1,755	1,127	809	46,322	50,488
Mississippi	34	87	12,246	28	12,374	24,769
Missouri	38	336	5,601	255	42,158	48,388
Montana	296	66	31	59	9,062	9,514
Nebraska	80	188	540	323	16,257	17,388
Nevada	161	438	852	636	8,852	10,939
New Hampshire	5	157	80	241	9,642	10,125
New Jersey	70	4,152	9,370	6,451	45,293	65,336
New Mexico	1,423	266	346	6,435	7,645	16,115
New York	420	8,201	19,948	12,217	96,004	136,790
North Carolina	840	733	17,119	572	41,644	60,908
North Dakota	342	43	26	79	7,213	7,703
Ohio	48	599	12,083	830	94,277	107,837
Oklahoma	3,066	393	2,902	698	24,272	31,331
Oregon	438	888	547	1,112	24,356	27,341
Pennsylvania	63	2,037	9,312	1,562	89,855	102,829
Rhode Island	15	106	253	122	6,867	7,363
South Carolina	46	342	12,967	279	19,746	33,380
South Dakota	321	26	14	28	7,782	8,171
Tennessee	13	523	8,218	145	35,023	43,922
Texas	299	4,683	23,846	52,210	92,736	173,774
Utah	346	724	131	807	26,395	28,403
Vermont	34	126	70	50	6,212	6,492
Virginia	65	2,954	12,342	1,225	42,608	59,194
Washington	909	3,307	1,585	2,410	40,800	49,011
West Virginia	22	98	686	125	20,182	21,113
Wisconsin	478	978	2,323	943	48,188	52,910

[Continued]

★ 206 ★

Projected Number of High-School Graduates by Racial and Ethnic Group and State, 1986-1995

[Continued]

	American Indian	Asian	Black	Hispanic	White	Total
Wyoming	62	23	34	288	5,181	5,588
Total	18,657	98,089	308,117	213,286	1,669,382	2,307,531

Source: "Study Predicts Dramatic Shifts in Enrollments," Jean Evangelauf, *The Chronicle of Higher Education* XXXVIII, No. 4, September 18, 1991, p. A40. Source also contains percent proportions of minority students. Primary source: Western Interstate Commission for Higher Education.

Higher Education Enrollment

★ 207 ★

Average Annual Growth Rates for Full-Time Equivalent Enrollment, 1977-2002

[Average annual percent]

1977-1984	0.9
1984-1990	1.9
1990-1996	0.8
1996-2002	1.6

Source: Projections of Education Statistics to 2002, U.S. Department of Education, Office of Educational Research and Improvement, December 1991, p. 24. *Note:* Growth distributions are based on middle alternative projections.

★ 208 ★

Average Annual Growth Rates for Higher Education Enrollment by Attendance Status, 1977-2002

[Average annual percent]

	Full-time	Part-time
1977-1984	0.6	2.0
1984-1990	1.6	2.9
1990-1996	0.6	1.6
1996-2002	1.8	0.8

Source: *Projections of Education Statistics to 2002*, National Center for Education Statistics, December, 1991, p. 19. *Note:* Growth distributions are based on middle alternative projections.

★ 209 ★

Average Annual Growth Rates for Higher Education Enrollment by Control of Institution, 1977-2002

[Average annual percent]

	Public institutions	Private institutions
1977-1984	1.0	1.8
1984-1990	2.3	1.9
1990-1996	1.0	0.9
1996-2002	1.3	1.4

Source: *Projections of Education Statistics to 2002*, National Center for Education Statistics, December, 1991, p. 20. *Note:* Growth distributions are based on middle alternative projections.

★ 210 ★

Average Annual Growth Rates for Total Higher Education Enrollment by Type of Institution, 1977-2002

[Average annual percent]

	4-year institutions	2-year institutions
1977-1984	0.9	1.6
1984-1990	2.1	2.3
1990-1996	0.9	1.2
1996-2002	1.4	1.2

Source: Projections of Education Statistics to 2002, U.S. Department of Education, Office of Educational Research and Improvement, December, 1991, p. 21. *Note:* Growth distributions are based on middle alternative projections.

★ 211 ★

Average Annual Growth Rates for Postbaccalaureate Enrollment, 1977-2002

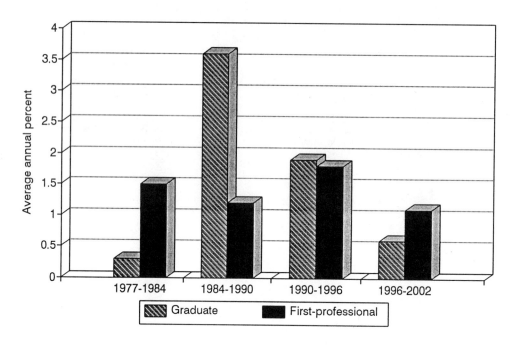

[Average annual percent]

	Graduate	First-professional
1977-1984	0.3	1.5
1984-1990	3.6	1.2
1990-1996	1.9	1.8
1996-2002	0.6	1.1

Source: Projections of Education Statistics to 2002, U.S. Department of Education, Office of Educational Research and Improvement, December, 1991, p. 23. *Note:* Growth distributions are based on middle alternative projections.

★ 212 ★

Average Annual Growth Rates for Total Higher Education Enrollment, 1977-2002

[Average annual percent]

1977-1984	1.2
1984-1990	2.2
1990-1996	1.0
1996-2002	1.3

Source: Projections of Education Statistics to 2002, National Center for Education Statistics, December, 1991, p. 17. *Note:* Growth distributions are based on middle alternative projections.

★ 213 ★

Average Annual Growth Rates for Total Higher Education Enrollment by Sex, 1977-2002

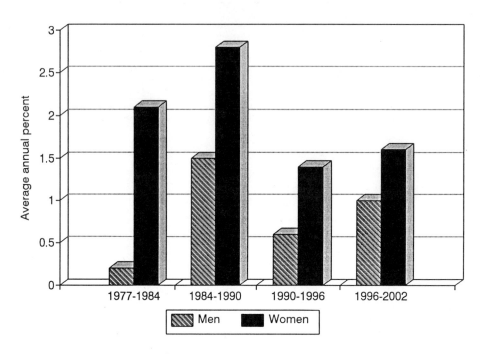

[Average annual percent]

	Men	Women
1977-1984	0.2	2.1
1984-1990	1.5	2.8
1990-1996	0.6	1.4
1996-2002	1.0	1.6

Source: Projections of Education Statistics to 2002, National Center for Education Statistics, December, 1991, p. 18. *Note:* Growth distributions are based on middle alternative projections.

★ 214 ★

Average Annual Growth Rates for Undergraduate Enrollment, 1977-2002

[Average annual percent]

1977-1984	1.3
1984-1990	2.0
1990-1996	0.9
1996-2002	1.5

Source: Projections of Education Statistics to 2002, U.S. Department of Education, Office of Educational Research and Improvement, December, 1991, p. 22. *Note:* Growth distributions are based on middle alternative projections.

★ 215 ★

Average Annual Rate of Growth in Higher Education Institutions, with Alternative Projections, 1977-1990 and 1990-2002

"Under the low alternative, college enrollment is projected to increase from an estimated 13.9 million in 1990 to 15.2 million by the year 2002....This alternative assumes that enrollment rates will either remain the same as the middle alternative or increase at a slower rate. Under the high alternative, college enrollment is expected to increase from an estimated 13.9 million in 1990 to 17.4 million by the year 2002.... This high level is expected to be maintained during the 1990s and beyond if the enrollment rates remain well above their 1990 levels."

[In percent]

	1977-90	1990-2002		
		Low	Middle	High
Total	1.6	0.8	1.2	1.9
Men	0.8	0.2	0.8	1.9
Women	2.4	1.2	1.5	1.8
Full-time	1.1	0.8	1.2	1.8
Part-time	2.4	0.8	1.1	1.9
Public	1.6	0.8	1.2	1.9
Private	1.8	0.7	1.2	1.9
4-year	1.5	0.8	1.2	1.9
2-year	1.9	0.8	1.2	1.9
Undergraduate	1.6	0.8	1.2	1.8
Graduate	1.8	0.6	1.2	2.1
First-professional	1.4	0.5	1.4	2.5
Full-time equivalent	1.4	0.7	1.2	1.9

Source: Projections of Education Statistics to 2002, National Center for Education Statistics, December 1991, p. 12.

★ 216 ★

Average Annual Rate of Growth in Higher Education Institutions, 1977-2002

[In percent]

	1977-84	1984-90	Projected	
			1990-96	1996-2002
Total	1.2	2.2	1.0	1.3
Men	0.2	1.5	0.6	1.0
Women	2.1	2.8	1.4	1.6
Full-time	0.6	1.6	0.6	1.8
Part-time	2.0	2.9	1.6	0.8
Public	1.0	2.3	1.0	1.3
Private	1.8	1.9	0.9	1.4
4-year	0.9	2.1	0.9	1.4
2-year	1.6	2.3	1.2	1.2
Undergraduate	1.3	2.0	0.9	1.5
Graduate	0.3	3.6	1.9	0.6
First-professional	1.5	1.2	1.8	1.1
Full-time equivalent	0.9	1.9	0.8	1.6

Source: Projections of Education Statistics to 2002, National Center for Education Statistics, December 1991, p. 12. *Note:* Projections are based on middle alternative series.

★ 217 ★

College Enrollment Rates by Age, Sex, and Attendance Status, 1989-2002

"Projections of full-time and part-time college enrollments were considered only for ages 16 and over. (College enrollment is negligible for earlier ages.) Three alternative projections were made using various assumptions."

[Numbers in percent]

Age, sex, and attendance status	1989	Low alternative		Middle alternative		High alternative	
		1997	2002	1997	2002	1997	2002
Men							
Full-time							
16	0.1	0.2	0.2	0.2	0.2	0.2	0.2
17	3.0	3.1	3.1	3.1	3.1	3.1	3.1
18	27.8	32.5	31.7	32.5	31.7	32.5	31.7
19	34.8	32.0	31.1	36.0	36.0	41.2	41.2
20	27.1	29.8	27.9	29.8	27.9	29.8	27.9
21	25.6	27.3	28.9	30.7	30.7	31.3	31.3
22	16.7	17.9	17.9	18.5	18.5	19.0	19.0
23	11.9	12.2	12.6	12.2	12.6	14.6	16.3
24	9.0	8.7	8.9	8.7	8.9	15.1	19.0

[Continued]

★ 217 ★

College Enrollment Rates by Age, Sex, and Attendance Status, 1989-2002

2002
[Continued]

Age, sex, and attendance status	1989	Low alternative		Middle alternative		High alternative	
		1997	2002	1997	2002	1997	2002
25-29	3.6	3.6	3.6	3.6	3.6	4.0	4.3
30-34	1.5	1.5	1.5	1.5	1.5	1.5	1.5
35-44	1.0	1.2	1.4	1.6	2.0	1.6	2.0
Part-time							
16	0.0	0.1	0.1	0.1	0.1	0.6	0.6
17	0.6	0.7	0.7	0.7	0.7	1.0	1.1
18	2.5	3.9	4.0	3.9	4.0	3.9	4.0
19	3.2	4.5	4.8	4.5	4.8	4.5	4.8
20	5.4	6.9	7.6	6.9	7.6	6.9	7.6
21	5.0	6.0	6.6	6.0	6.6	6.4	7.3
22	8.5	9.2	9.9	9.8	10.3	12.5	12.5
23	6.0	6.3	6.6	6.8	6.9	8.0	9.1
24	4.6	4.6	4.8	4.6	4.8	4.9	5.1
25-29	5.8	5.3	5.3	6.1	6.1	7.8	9.1
30-34	3.9	4.0	4.0	4.0	4.0	4.0	4.0
35-44	3.7	3.9	4.0	4.5	4.5	4.6	5.1
Women							
Full-time							
16	0.4	0.3	0.3	0.6	0.7	1.0	1.0
17	4.8	4.9	4.9	4.9	4.9	4.9	4.9
18	32.1	37.3	37.6	37.3	37.6	37.3	37.6
19	38.1	40.6	42.6	40.6	42.6	44.1	44.1
20	28.0	31.5	33.9	31.5	33.9	31.5	33.9
21	28.7	31.0	32.8	31.0	33.5	35.0	35.0
22	15.4	16.4	18.4	19.0	20.0	21.9	21.9
23	10.2	10.8	12.0	13.3	13.3	13.5	13.5
24	7.9	8.4	9.2	8.9	10.9	12.3	12.3
25-29	2.9	3.1	3.2	3.3	3.5	3.7	4.2
30-34	1.7	1.9	2.1	2.0	2.2	2.0	2.2
35-44	1.7	1.9	2.1	2.4	2.4	2.6	2.6
Part-time							
16	0.1	0.1	0.1	0.1	0.1	0.1	0.1
17	0.6	1.0	1.0	1.0	1.0	1.0	1.0
18	4.4	6.2	6.9	6.2	6.9	6.2	6.9
19	5.3	6.2	7.0	6.2	7.0	6.2	7.0
20	5.7	7.0	7.4	7.0	7.4	7.0	7.4
21	5.9	7.2	8.1	7.2	8.1	7.2	8.1
22	11.4	10.9	11.8	10.9	11.8	14.4	14.4
23	7.5	7.8	8.4	9.2	9.2	9.6	9.6
24	5.9	6.1	6.4	7.5	7.5	7.5	8.6
25-29	6.7	6.8	7.1	8.1	8.1	8.8	8.8

[Continued]

★ 217 ★

College Enrollment Rates by Age, Sex, and Attendance Status, 1989-2002

[Continued]

Age, sex, and attendance status	1989	Low alternative		Middle alternative		High alternative	
		1997	2002	1997	2002	1997	2002
30-34	5.0	5.4	5.6	5.4	5.6	5.4	5.6
35-44	6.7	7.7	8.3	7.7	8.3	7.7	8.3

Source: *Projections of Education Statistics to the Year 2002*, National Center for Education Statistics, December, 1991, p. 154.

★ 218 ★

College Enrollment, 1977-2002

"In findings that present a rosier outlook for college enrollments than previous studies did, the U.S. Department of Education estimates that the number of college students will climb from 14.1 million in 1991 to 16 million in 2002. The projected 13 percent increase is largely the result of rising college-enrollment rates and the growth, beginning in 1996, of the 18-to 24-year-old population."

[Numbers in millions]

1977	11.2
1982	12.5
1987	13.8
1992	14.3
1997	14.9
2002	16.2

Source: "Enrollment Projections Revised Upward in New Government Analysis," Jean Evangelauf, *Chronicle of Higher Education* 38, No. 20, January 22, 1992, p. A1. Primary source: U.S. Department of Education. *Note:* Numbers estimated from published chart.

★ 219 ★

Enrollment in All Institutions of Higher Education by Age, Sex, and Attendance Status, with High Alternative Projections, 1990-2002

Prepared April 1991. "Under the high alternative, college enrollment is projected to increase from an estimated 13.9 million in 1990 to 17.4 million by the year 2002....This high level is expected to be maintained during the 1990s and beyond if the enrollment rates remain well above their 1990 levels." Source also contains data for 1982 and 1987.

[Numbers in thousands]

Age	1990 (projected)			1997 (projected)			2002 (projected)		
	Total	Full-time	Part-time	Total	Full-time	Part-time	Total	Full-time	Part-time
Total	13,931	7,828	6,103	16,047	8,873	7,174	17,399	9,738	7,661
14 to 17 years	172	141	30	209	170	39	222	179	43
18 to 19 years	2,994	2,647	347	3,170	2,796	374	3,466	3,025	442
20 to 21 years	2,553	2,101	451	2,701	2,221	480	3,109	2,512	596
22 to 24 years	2,126	1,322	804	2,620	1,650	970	2,995	1,893	1,102
25 to 29 years	2,073	712	1,360	2,344	743	1,601	2,344	749	1,596
30 to 34 years	1,406	362	1,044	1,373	372	1,001	1,328	372	956
35 years and over	2,605	540	2,065	3,631	922	2,709	3,935	1,008	2,927
Men	6,419	3,879	2,540	7,287	4,244	3,043	8,044	4,697	3,347
14 to 17 years	69	56	13	82	63	20	89	66	23
18 to 19 years	1,455	1,317	138	1,506	1,354	153	1,631	1,455	176
20 to 21 years	1,262	1,047	216	1,318	1,082	236	1,477	1,180	297
22 to 24 years	1,072	703	369	1,281	843	438	1,519	1,015	503
25 to 29 years	1,017	395	622	1,150	391	759	1,207	383	824
30 to 34 years	622	167	455	588	160	429	557	153	404
35 years and over	920	194	726	1,362	353	1,009	1,564	444	1,121
Women	7,512	3,949	3,563	8,760	4,629	4,131	9,355	5,041	4,314
14 to 17 years	102	85	17	126	107	19	133	113	20
18 to 19 years	1,540	1,330	209	1,664	1,443	221	1,835	1,569	266
20 to 21 years	1,290	1,055	236	1,383	1,140	244	1,632	1,332	300
22 to 24 years	1,054	619	435	1,339	807	532	1,476	878	598
25 to 29 years	1,056	318	739	1,194	352	842	1,138	365	772
30 to 34 years	784	195	589	784	212	573	771	219	552
35 years and over	1,685	347	1,338	2,269	569	1,700	2,371	565	1,806

Source: Projections of Education Statistics to 2002, U.S. Department of Education, Office of Educational Research and Improvement, December, 1991, p. 33. Primary source: U.S. Department of Education, National Center for Education Statistics, Fall Enrollment in Colleges and Universities surveys and Integrated Postsecondary Education Data System (IPEDS) surveys; and U.S. Bureau of the Census, *Current Population Reports*, series P-25, No. 1018. Projections include all 50 States and Washington, D.C. Because of rounding, details may not add to totals.

★ 220 ★

Enrollment in All Institutions of Higher Education by Age, Sex, and Attendance Status, with Low Alternative Projections, 1990-2002

Prepared April 1991. "Under the low alternative, college enrollment is projected to increase from an estimated 13.9 million in 1990 to 15.2 million by the year 2002....This alternative assumes that enrollment rates will either remain the same as the middle alternative or increase at a slower rate." Source also contains data for 1982 and 1987.

[Numbers in thousands]

Age	1990 (projected)			1997 (projected)			2002 (projected)		
	Total	Full-time	Part-time	Total	Full-time	Part-time	Total	Full-time	Part-time
Total	13,931	7,828	6,103	14,117	7,751	6,366	15,243	8,557	6,686
14 to 17 years	172	141	30	191	157	34	202	166	36
18 to 19 years	2,994	2,647	347	2,937	2,564	374	3,231	2,789	442
20 to 21 years	2,553	2,101	451	2,557	2,084	473	3,005	2,421	584
22 to 24 years	2,126	1,322	804	2,040	1,272	768	2,357	1,468	889
25 to 29 years	2,073	712	1,360	1,816	647	1,169	1,707	605	1,102
30 to 34 years	1,406	362	1,044	1,363	362	1,001	1,313	357	956
35 years and over	2,605	540	2,065	3,214	667	2,547	3,428	751	2,678
Men	6,419	3,879	2,540	6,237	3,698	2,539	6,589	3,959	2,630
14 to 17 years	69	56	13	78	63	15	82	66	16
18 to 19 years	1,455	1,317	138	1,337	1,185	153	1,425	1,249	176
20 to 21 years	1,262	1,047	216	1,241	1,012	229	1,416	1,132	285
22 to 24 years	1,072	703	369	1,018	670	348	1,141	741	400
25 to 29 years	1,017	395	622	872	353	519	803	325	478
30 to 34 years	622	167	455	586	158	429	553	149	404
35 years and over	920	194	726	1,105	259	846	1,169	297	872
Women	7,512	3,949	3,563	7,880	4,053	3,827	8,654	4,598	4,056
14 to 17 years	102	85	17	114	95	19	120	100	20
18 to 19 years	1,540	1,330	209	1,600	1,379	221	1,806	1,540	266
20 to 21 years	1,290	1,055	236	1,315	1,072	244	1,588	1,289	300
22 to 24 years	1,054	619	435	1,022	602	420	1,217	728	489
25 to 29 years	1,056	318	739	944	294	650	904	280	624
30 to 34 years	784	195	589	777	204	573	760	208	552
35 years and over	1,685	347	1,338	2,109	409	1,700	2,259	454	1,806

Source: Projections of Education Statistics to 2002, U.S. Department of Education, Office of Educational Research and Improvement, December, 1991, p. 32. Primary source: U.S. Department of Education, National Center for Education Statistics, Fall Enrollment in Colleges and Universities surveys and Integrated Postsecondary Education Data System (IPEDS) surveys; and U.S. Bureau of the Census, *Current Population Reports*, series P-25, No. 1018. Projections include all 50 States and Washington, D.C. Because of rounding, details may not add to totals.

★ 221 ★

Enrollment in All Institutions of Higher Education by Age, Sex, and Attendance Status, with Middle Alternative Projections, 1990-2002

[Numbers in thousands]

Age	1990 (projected)			1997 (projected)			2002 (projected)		
	Total	Full-time	Part-time	Total	Full-time	Part-time	Total	Full-time	Part-time
Total	13,931	7,828	6,103	14,978	8,212	6,766	16,030	9,035	6,995
14 to 17 years	172	141	30	196	162	34	210	174	36
18 to 19 years	2,994	2,647	347	3,010	2,637	374	3,331	2,889	442
20 to 21 years	2,553	2,101	451	2,616	2,143	473	3,055	2,471	584
22 to 24 years	2,126	1,322	804	2,208	1,375	833	2,500	1,565	935
25 to 29 years	2,073	712	1,360	2,035	666	1,369	1,890	632	1,258
30 to 34 years	1,406	362	1,044	1,371	369	1,001	1,324	368	956
35 years and over	2,605	540	2,065	3,541	858	2,683	3,723	939	2,785
Men	6,419	3,879	2,540	6,691	3,924	2,767	7,052	4,234	2,818
14 to 17 years	69	56	13	78	63	15	82	66	16
18 to 19 years	1,455	1,317	138	1,410	1,258	153	1,525	1,349	176
20 to 21 years	1,262	1,047	216	1,300	1,071	229	1,453	1,168	285
22 to 24 years	1,072	703	369	1,046	680	367	1,164	752	412
25 to 29 years	1,017	395	622	946	353	594	871	325	546
30 to 34 years	622	167	455	586	158	429	553	149	404
35 years and over	920	194	726	1,324	342	982	1,405	426	979
Women	7,512	3,949	3,563	8,287	4,288	3,999	8,978	4,801	4,177
14 to 17 years	102	85	17	118	99	19	128	108	20
18 to 19 years	1,540	1,330	209	1,600	1,379	221	1,806	1,540	266
20 to 21 years	1,290	1,055	236	1,316	1,072	244	1,602	1,302	300
22 to 24 years	1,054	619	435	1,162	696	466	1,336	813	523
25 to 29 years	1,056	318	739	1,089	313	776	1,019	307	711
30 to 34 years	784	195	589	784	212	573	771	219	552
35 years and over	1,685	347	1,338	2,217	516	1,700	2,318	513	1,806

Source: Projections of Education Statistics to 2002, U.S. Department of Education, Office of Educational Research and Improvement, December, 1991, p. 31. Primary source: U.S. Department of Education, National Center for Education Statistics, Fall Enrollment in Colleges and Universities surveys and Integrated Postsecondary Education Data System (IPEDS) surveys; and U.S. Bureau of the Census, *Current Population Reports*, series P-25, No. 1018. Projections include all 50 States and Washington, D.C. Because of rounding, details may not add to totals. Prepared April 1991.

★ 222 ★

Enrollment in Institutions of Higher Education by Race/Ethnicity: Asian or Pacific Islander, American Indian/Alaskan Native, and Nonresident Alien, Fall 1976 to Fall 2000

[Numbers in thousands]

Year	Asian or Pacific Islander			American Indian/Alaskan Native			Nonresident alien		
	Total	Men	Women	Total	Men	Women	Total	Men	Women
1976	282	108	174	76	38	38	219	154	65
1978	331	126	205	78	37	41	253	180	73
1980	391	151	240	84	38	46	305	211	94
1982	457	189	268	88	40	48	331	230	101
1984	491	210	281	83	37	46	334	230	104
1986	567	239	328	90	39	51	345	233	112
1988	629	259	370	92	39	53	361	235	126
1990[1]	717	300	416	98	42	56	386	252	134
Projected									
1991	771	326	445	99	42	57	390	254	136
1992	824	351	473	100	42	58	393	255	138
1993	879	375	503	101	42	58	396	256	140
1994	911	400	511	102	43	59	399	257	142
1995	918	401	517	103	43	60	402	258	144
1996	930	406	524	104	43	61	406	261	146
1997	941	409	532	105	44	62	410	262	148
1998	956	414	543	107	44	63	417	265	151
1999	971	418	553	109	45	64	423	269	154
2000	986	423	563	110	45	65	428	271	157

Source: Projections of Education Statistics to the Year 2002, National Center for Education Statistics, December, 1991, p. 142. Primary source: U.S. department of Commerce, Bureau of the Census, "United States Population Estimates, by Age, Sex, Race, and Hispanic Origin: 1980 to 1988," *Current Population Reports*, series P-25, No. 1045, January, 1990, *Current Population Reports*, series P-25, No. 1057, March, 1990, "Projections of the Population of the United States, by Age, Sex, and Race: 1988 to 2080," *Current Population Reports*, series P-25, No. 1018, January, 1989, and "Projections of the Hispanic Population: 1983-2080," *Current Population Reports*, series P-25, No. 995, November, 1986; and U.S. Department of Education, National Center for Education Statistics, Fall Enrollment in Colleges and Universities; Integrated Postsecondary Education Data System (IPEDS) surveys; and unpublished tabulations. Projections are based on data through 1989 and have been adjusted to sum to the middle alternative projections of higher education enrollment by sex. Because of rounding, details may not add to totals. Includes all fifty states and Washington, D.C.

★ 223 ★

Enrollment in Institutions of Higher Education by Race/Ethnicity: Black, White, and Hispanic, Fall 1976 to Fall 2000

[Numbers in thousands]

Year	White, non-Hispanic			Black, non-Hispanic			Hispanic		
	Total	Men	Women	Total	Men	Women	Total	Men	Women
1976	9,076	4,814	4,262	1,033	470	563	384	210	174
1978	9,194	4,613	4,581	1,054	453	601	417	212	205
1980	9,833	4,773	5,060	1,107	464	643	472	232	240
1982	9,997	4,830	5,167	1,102	458	644	520	252	268

[Continued]

★ 223 ★

Enrollment in Institutions of Higher Education by Race/Ethnicity:
Black, White, and Hispanic, Fall 1976 to Fall 2000
[Continued]

Year	White, non-Hispanic			Black, non-Hispanic			Hispanic		
	Total	Men	Women	Total	Men	Women	Total	Men	Women
1984	9,814	4,690	5,124	1,076	437	639	535	254	281
1986	9,921	4,647	5,274	1,082	436	646	618	290	328
1988	10,284	4,712	5,572	1,130	443	687	680	310	370
1990[1]	10,750	4,910	5,840	1,274	553	721	707	362	345
Projected									
1991	10,826	4,919	5,907	1,289	559	730	731	374	357
1992	10,757	4,870	5,887	1,367	592	775	794	406	388
1993	10,889	4,895	5,994	1,318	566	752	786	398	388
1994	10,838	4,818	6,021	1,402	598	803	859	433	426
1995	11,020	4,885	6,135	1,339	568	771	839	419	420
1996	11,019	4,878	6,140	1,431	604	827	913	455	458
1997	11,259	4,967	6,292	1,376	573	802	887	436	451
1998	11,310	4,965	6,345	1,478	615	862	961	472	489
1999	11,476	5,019	6,457	1,499	622	877	984	479	504
2000	11,637	5,069	6,568	1,521	627	895	1,010	488	522

Source: Projections of Education Statistics to the Year 2002, National Center for Education Statistics, December, 1991, p. 141. Primary source: U.S. Department of Commerce, Bureau of the Census, "United States Population Estimates, by Age, Sex, Race, and Hispanic Origin: 1980 to 1988," *Current Population Reports*, series P-25, No. 1045, January, 1990, "U.S. Population Estimates by Age, Sex, Race, and Hispanic Origin: 1980," *Current Population Reports*, series P-25, No. 1057, March, 1990, "Projections of the Population of the United States, by Age, Sex, and Race: 1988 to 2080," *Current Population Reports*, series P-25, No. 1018, January, 1989, and "Projections of the Hispanic Population: 1983-2080," *Current Population Reports*, series P-25, No. 995, November, 1986; and U.S. Department of Education, National Center for Education Statistics, Fall Enrollment in Colleges and Universities; Integrated Postsecondary Education Data System surveys; and unpublished tabulations. Projections are based on data through 1989 and have been adjusted to sum to middle alternative projections of higher education enrollment by sex. Because of rounding, details may not add to totals. Includes all fifty states and Washington, D.C.

★ 224 ★

First-Professional Enrollment in All Institutions of Higher Education by Sex and Attendance Status, with Alternative Projections, Fall 1977 to Fall 2002

Prepared April 1991. "Under the low alternative, college enrollment is projected to increase from an estimated 13.9 million in 1990 to 15.2 million by the year 2002....This alternative assumes that enrollment rates will either remain the same as the middle alternative or increase at a slower rate. Under the high alternative, college enrollment is expected to increase from an estimated 13.9 million in 1990 to 17.4 million by the year 2002....This high level is expected to be maintained during the 1990s and beyond if the enrollment rates remain well above their 1990 levels."

[Numbers in thousands]

Year	Total	Men		Women	
		Full-time	Part-time	Full-time	Part-time
1977	251	173	18	53	7
1978	257	175	17	58	7
1979	263	176	17	63	7
1980	278	181	18	70	9
1981	275	175	18	73	9
1982	278	174	17	78	9
1983	279	169	19	81	10
1984	279	166	19	83	10
1985	274	162	17	84	10
1986	270	159	15	87	9
1987	268	154	16	88	10
1988	267	151	16	90	10
1989	274	152	16	95	10
1990[1]	300	167	19	103	11
Middle alternative projections					
1991	309	171	19	107	12
1992	318	174	20	111	13
1993	326	177	20	116	13
1994	330	178	20	119	13
1995	330	178	20	119	13
1996	334	180	21	119	14
1997	338	183	21	120	14
1998	341	185	21	121	14
1999	345	187	21	123	14
2000	348	190	21	123	14
2001	352	192	21	125	14
2002	356	195	21	126	14
Low alternative projections					
1991	292	166	18	97	11
1992	297	167	19	99	12
1993	301	169	19	101	12
1994	303	169	19	103	12
1995	303	168	19	103	13
1996	302	167	19	103	13
1997	305	168	19	105	13
1998	307	169	19	106	13
1999	310	170	19	108	13

[Continued]

★ 224 ★

First-Professional Enrollment in All Institutions of Higher Education by Sex and Attendance Status, with Alternative Projections, Fall 1977 to Fall 2002

[Continued]

Year	Total	Men		Women	
		Full-time	Part-time	Full-time	Part-time
2000	312	170	19	110	13
2001	315	171	19	111	14
2002	320	173	19	114	14
High alternative projections					
1991	327	176	20	118	13
1992	342	182	20	127	13
1993	353	187	21	132	13
1994	360	191	21	134	14
1995	363	194	21	134	14
1996	366	197	22	133	14
1997	371	201	22	134	14
1998	378	206	24	134	14
1999	385	211	24	136	14
2000	389	215	24	136	14
2001	396	220	25	137	14
2002	402	225	25	138	14

Source: Projections of Education Statistics to 2002, U.S. Department of Education, Office of Educational Research and Improvement, December, 1991, p. 45. Primary source: U.S. Department of Education, National Center for Education Statistics, Fall Enrollment in Colleges and Universities surveys and Integrated Postsecondary Education Data System (IPEDS) surveys. Projections are based on data through 1989 and include all 50 States and Washington, D.C. Because of rounding, details may not add to totals. *Note:* 1. Projected.

★ 225 ★

First-Professional Enrollment in Private Institutions of Higher Education by Sex and Attendance Status, with Alternative Projections, Fall 1977 to Fall 2002

Prepared April 1991. "Under the low alternative, college enrollment is projected to increase from an estimated 13.9 million in 1990 to 15.2 million by the year 2002....This alternative assumes that enrollment rates will either remain the same as the middle alternative or increase at a slower rate. Under the high alternative, college enrollment is expected to increase from an estimated 13.9 million in 1990 to 17.4 million by the year 2002....This high level is expected to be maintained during the 1990s and beyond if the enrollment rates remain well above their 1990 levels."

[Numbers in thousands]

Year	Total	Men		Women	
		Full-time	Part-time	Full-time	Part-time
1977	148	99	15	30	5
1978	152	100	14	32	6
1979	157	102	15	35	6
1980	163	104	16	38	7
1981	162	101	14	40	7

[Continued]

★ 225 ★

First-Professional Enrollment in Private Institutions of Higher Education by Sex and Attendance Status, with Alternative Projections, Fall 1977 to Fall 2002

[Continued]

Year	Total	Men		Women	
		Full-time	Part-time	Full-time	Part-time
1982	165	101	14	43	7
1983	165	97	16	44	8
1984	164	96	16	43	8
1985	162	93	14	46	8
1986	158	91	12	48	7
1987	158	88	14	48	8
1988	158	87	14	49	8
1989	161	87	14	52	9
1990[1]	177	96	16	56	9
Middle alternative projections					
1991	182	98	16	58	10
1992	187	100	17	60	10
1993	191	101	17	63	10
1994	194	102	17	65	10
1995	194	102	17	65	10
1996	197	103	18	65	11
1997	199	105	18	65	11
1998	201	106	18	66	11
1999	203	107	18	67	11
2000	205	109	18	67	11
2001	207	110	18	68	11
2002	210	112	18	69	11
Low alternative projections					
1991	172	95	15	53	9
1992	176	96	16	54	10
1993	178	97	16	55	10
1994	179	97	16	56	10
1995	178	96	16	56	10
1996	178	96	16	56	10
1997	179	96	16	57	10
1998	181	97	16	58	10
1999	182	97	16	59	10
2000	183	97	16	60	10
2001	185	98	16	60	11
2002	188	99	16	62	11
High alternative projections					
1991	192	101	17	64	10
1992	200	104	17	69	10
1993	207	107	18	72	10
1994	211	109	18	73	11
1995	213	111	18	73	11
1996	215	113	19	72	11
1997	218	115	19	73	11
1998	222	118	20	73	11

[Continued]

★ 225 ★

First-Professional Enrollment in Private Institutions of Higher Education by Sex and Attendance Status, with Alternative Projections, Fall 1977 to Fall 2002

[Continued]

Year	Total	Men		Women	
		Full-time	Part-time	Full-time	Part-time
1999	226	121	20	74	11
2000	228	123	20	74	11
2001	233	126	21	75	11
2002	236	129	21	75	11

Source: *Projections of Education Statistics to 2002*, U.S. Department of Education, Office of Educational Research and Improvement, December, 1991, p. 47. Primary source: U.S. Department of Education, National Center for Education Statistics, Fall Enrollment in Colleges and Universities surveys and Integrated Postsecondary Education Data System (IPEDS) surveys. Projections are based on data through 1989 and include all 50 States and Washington, D.C. Because of rounding, details may not add to totals. *Note:* 1. Projected.

★ 226 ★

First-Professional Enrollment in Public Institutions of Higher Education by Sex and Attendance Status, with Alternative Projections, Fall 1977 to Fall 2002

Prepared April 1991. "Under the low alternative, college enrollment is projected to increase from an estimated 13.9 million in 1990 to 15.2 million by the year 2002....This alternative assumes that enrollment rates will either remain the same as the middle alternative or increase at a slower rate. Under the high alternative, college enrollment is expected to increase from an estimated 13.9 million in 1990 to 17.4 million by the year 2002....This high level is expected to be maintained during the 1990s and beyond if the enrollment rates remain well above their 1990 levels."

[Numbers in thousands]

Year	Total	Men		Women	
		Full-time	Part-time	Full-time	Part-time
1977	103	75	4	24	2
1978	105	75	3	25	1
1979	106	74	2	27	1
1980	114	79	4	32	2
1981	112	75	3	33	2
1982	113	73	3	35	2
1983	113	71	3	37	2
1984	114	70	3	38	2
1985	111	69	3	38	2
1986	112	67	3	39	2
1987	110	65	3	40	2
1988	109	64	2	41	2
1989	113	65	2	43	2
1990[1]	123	71	3	47	2
Middle alternative projections					
1991	127	73	3	49	2
1992	131	74	3	51	3

[Continued]

★ 226 ★

First-Professional Enrollment in Public Institutions of Higher Education by Sex and Attendance Status, with Alternative Projections, Fall 1977 to Fall 2002
[Continued]

Year	Total	Men		Women	
		Full-time	Part-time	Full-time	Part-time
1993	135	76	3	53	3
1994	136	76	3	54	3
1995	136	76	3	54	3
1996	137	77	3	54	3
1997	139	78	3	55	3
1998	140	79	3	55	3
1999	142	80	3	56	3
2000	143	81	3	56	3
2001	145	82	3	57	3
2002	146	83	3	57	3
Low alternative projections					
1991	120	71	3	44	2
1992	121	71	3	45	2
1993	123	72	3	46	2
1994	124	72	3	47	2
1995	125	72	3	47	3
1996	124	71	3	47	3
1997	126	72	3	48	3
1998	126	72	3	48	3
1999	128	73	3	49	3
2000	129	73	3	50	3
2001	130	73	3	51	3
2002	132	74	3	52	3
High alternative projections					
1991	135	75	3	54	3
1992	142	78	3	58	3
1993	146	80	3	60	3
1994	149	82	3	61	3
1995	150	83	3	61	3
1996	151	84	3	61	3
1997	153	86	3	61	3
1998	156	88	4	61	3
1999	159	90	4	62	3
2000	161	92	4	62	3
2001	163	94	4	62	3
2002	166	96	4	63	3

Source: *Projections of Education Statistics to 2002*, U.S. Department of Education, Office of Educational Research and Improvement, December, 1991, p. 46. Primary source: U.S. Department of Education, National Center for Education Statistics, Fall Enrollment in Colleges and Universities surveys and Integrated Postsecondary Education Data System (IPEDS) surveys. Projections are based on data through 1989 and include all 50 States and Washington, D.C. Because of rounding, details may not add to totals. *Note:* 1. Projected.

Full-Time Enrollment by Level and Type of Institution as a Percent of Total Enrollment for Each Age and Sex Classification, 1989-2002

[Numbers in percent]

Age	Men			Women		
	1989	1997[1]	2002[1]	1989	1997[1]	2002[1]
Undergraduate, 4-year institutions						
16-17 years old	78.5	70.6	70.6	62.5	69.4	69.4
18-19 years old	68.2	67.6	67.6	66.7	68.0	68.0
20-21 years old	78.2	80.0	80.0	83.1	83.1	83.1
22-24 years old	67.7	65.9	65.9	67.6	65.0	65.0
25-29 years old	38.7	40.1	40.1	42.3	41.2	41.2
30-34 years old	28.3	29.6	29.6	38.0	38.6	38.6
35 years and over	29.1	29.7	29.7	44.6	40.7	40.7
Undergraduate, 2-year institutions						
16-17 years old	21.5	28.8	28.8	37.5	30.6	30.6
18-19 years old	31.8	32.4	32.4	33.3	32.0	32.0
20-21 years old	21.8	20.0	20.0	16.9	16.9	16.9
22-24 years old	13.8	14.6	14.6	13.1	15.3	15.3
25-29 years old	15.0	15.4	15.4	21.9	23.6	23.6
30-34 years old	20.4	19.5	19.5	34.3	33.1	33.1
35 years and over	23.0	21.8	21.8	30.4	32.4	32.4
Postbaccalaureate, 4-year institutions						
16-17 years old	-	-	-	-	-	-
18-19 years old	-	-	-	-	-	-
20-21 years old	-	-	-	-	-	-
22-24 years old	18.5	19.5	19.5	19.3	19.7	19.7
25-29 years old	46.4	44.6	44.6	35.8	35.2	35.2
30-34 years old	51.3	50.9	50.9	27.7	28.3	28.3
35 years and over	47.9	48.4	48.4	25.0	27.0	27.0

Source: Projections of Education Statistics to the Year 2002, National Center for Education Statistics, December, 1991, p. 158. *Notes:* - Not applicable. 1. Projections adjusted to add to 100 percent.

★ 228 ★

Full-Time-Equivalent Enrollment in All Institutions of Higher Education by Level of Student and Type of Institution, with Alternative Projections, Fall 1977 to Fall 2002

Prepared April 1991. "Under the low alternative, college enrollment is projected to increase from an estimated 13.9 million in 1990 to 15.2 million by the year 2002....This alternative assumes that enrollment rates will either remain the same as the middle alternative or increase at a slower rate. Under the high alternative, college enrollment is expected to increase from an estimated 13.9 million in 1990 to 17.4 million by the year 2002....This high level is expected to be maintained during the 1990s and beyond if the enrollment rates remain well above their 1990 levels."

[Numbers in thousands]

| Year | Total | Undergraduate | | Graduate | First-profes- |
		4-year	2-year	4-year	sional - 4 year
1977	8,415	4,919	2,480	776	240
1978	8,348	4,906	2,416	779	248
1979	8,487	4,989	2,471	778	249
1980	8,819	5,109	2,658	790	263
1981	9,015	5,188	2,765	801	262
1982	9,092	5,194	2,843	790	266
1983	9,166	5,254	2,841	805	266
1984	8,952	5,215	2,659	814	263
1985	8,943	5,204	2,649	829	261
1986	9,064	5,241	2,704	859	259
1987	9,230	5,363	2,743	868	256
1988	9,467	5,517	2,802	892	256
1989	9,734	5,621	2,930	919	263
1990[1]	10,033	5,761	2,991	995	286
Middle alternative projections					
1991	10,106	5,781	3,006	1,024	295
1992	10,171	5,794	3,024	1,050	303
1993	10,232	5,793	3,052	1,076	311
1994	10,321	5,819	3,091	1,096	315
1995	10,385	5,847	3,120	1,103	315
1996	10,519	5,922	3,168	1,111	318
1997	10,656	6,004	3,211	1,119	322
1998	10,871	6,144	3,270	1,132	325
1999	11,070	6,274	3,326	1,141	329
2000	11,270	6,413	3,377	1,148	332
2001	11,418	6,513	3,415	1,154	336
2002	11,561	6,607	3,449	1,165	340
Low alternative projections					
1991	9,691	5,554	2,887	971	279
1992	9,668	5,525	2,878	982	283
1993	9,687	5,512	2,890	998	287
1994	9,709	5,512	2,908	1,000	289
1995	9,781	5,547	2,940	1,006	288
1996	9,900	5,617	2,983	1,012	288
1997	10,050	5,711	3,029	1,020	290
1998	10,243	5,836	3,087	1,028	292
1999	10,436	5,962	3,142	1,037	295

[Continued]

★ 228 ★

Full-Time-Equivalent Enrollment in All Institutions of Higher Education by Level of Student and Type of Institution, with Alternative Projections, Fall 1977 to Fall 2002

[Continued]

| Year | Total | Undergraduate | | Graduate | First-profes- |
		4-year	2-year	4-year	sional - 4 year
2000	10,647	6,106	3,198	1,046	297
2001	10,810	6,212	3,242	1,056	300
2002	10,970	6,318	3,281	1,066	305
High alternative projections					
1991	10,663	6,127	3,151	1,073	312
1992	10,928	6,270	3,215	1,116	327
1993	11,021	6,273	3,254	1,157	337
1994	11,101	6,291	3,291	1,175	344
1995	11,128	6,285	3,307	1,189	347
1996	11,321	6,391	3,379	1,202	349
1997	11,464	6,469	3,424	1,217	354
1998	11,693	6,606	3,493	1,233	361
1999	11,923	6,746	3,558	1,251	368
2000	12,149	6,892	3,619	1,266	372
2001	12,334	7,005	3,667	1,284	378
2002	12,504	7,107	3,709	1,304	384

Source: Projections of Education Statistics to 2002, U.S. Department of Education, Office of Educational Research and Improvement, December, 1991, p. 48. Primary source: U.S. Department of Education, National Center for Education Statistics, Fall Enrollment in Colleges and Universities surveys and Integrated Postsecondary Education Data System (IPEDS) surveys. Projections are based on data through 1989 and include all 50 States and Washington, D.C. Because of rounding, details may not add to totals. *Note:* 1. Projected.

★ 229 ★

Full-Time-Equivalent Enrollment in Private Institutions of Higher Education by Level of Student and Type of Institution, with Alternative Projections, Fall 1977 to Fall 2002

Prepared April 1991. "Under the low alternative, college enrollment is projected to increase from an estimated 13.9 million in 1990 to 15.2 million by the year 2002....This alternative assumes that enrollment rates will either remain the same as the middle alternative or increase at a slower rate. Under the high alternative, college enrollment is expected to increase from an estimated 13.9 million in 1990 to 17.4 million by the year 2002....This high level is expected to be maintained during the 1990s and beyond if the enrollment rates remain well above their 1990 levels."

[Numbers in thousands]

| Year | Total | Undergraduate | | Graduate | First-profes- |
		4-year	2-year	4-year	sional - 4 year
1977	2,019	1,503	123	253	139
1978	2,069	1,531	133	259	146
1979	2,095	1,552	138	259	146
1980	2,177	1,585	174	268	150
1981	2,233	1,612	192	277	152

[Continued]

★ 229 ★

Full-Time-Equivalent Enrollment in Private Institutions of Higher Education by Level of Student and Type of Institution, with Alternative Projections, Fall 1977 to Fall 2002
[Continued]

| Year | Total | Undergraduate | | Graduate | First-profes- |
		4-year	2-year	4-year	sional - 4 year
1982	2,241	1,596	213	276	156
1983	2,285	1,619	226	285	155
1984	2,267	1,610	212	293	152
1985	2,276	1,603	221	300	151
1986	2,286	1,613	221	303	149
1987	2,292	1,632	201	311	148
1988	2,370	1,690	210	321	149
1989	2,397	1,701	213	332	151
1990[1]	2,504	1,758	223	357	166
Middle alternative projections					
1991	2,524	1,764	222	368	170
1992	2,543	1,768	223	377	175
1993	2,558	1,767	225	387	179
1994	2,578	1,775	228	393	182
1995	2,592	1,784	230	396	182
1996	2,622	1,807	233	398	184
1997	2,656	1,832	237	401	186
1998	2,712	1,875	243	406	188
1999	2,763	1,915	248	410	190
2000	2,813	1,957	252	412	192
2001	2,850	1,988	254	414	194
2002	2,889	2,017	258	417	197
Low alternative projections					
1991	2,418	1,694	214	349	161
1992	2,414	1,686	212	352	164
1993	2,418	1,681	213	358	166
1994	2,422	1,682	214	359	167
1995	2,435	1,692	216	361	166
1996	2,463	1,714	220	363	166
1997	2,499	1,743	223	366	167
1998	2,547	1,781	229	368	169
1999	2,594	1,820	233	371	170
2000	2,648	1,864	238	375	171
2001	2,690	1,897	242	378	173
2002	2,732	1,929	245	382	176
High alternative projections					
1991	2,671	1,870	236	385	180
1992	2,743	1,914	240	401	188
1993	2,766	1,915	242	415	194
1994	2,785	1,920	245	422	198
1995	2,790	1,918	245	427	200
1996	2,832	1,949	251	431	201
1997	2,869	1,974	254	437	204
1998	2,925	2,015	259	443	208

[Continued]

★ 229 ★

Full-Time-Equivalent Enrollment in Private Institutions of Higher Education by Level of Student and Type of Institution, with Alternative Projections, Fall 1977 to Fall 2002

[Continued]

| Year | Total | Undergraduate | | Graduate | First-profes- |
		4-year	2-year	4-year	sional - 4 year
1999	2,983	2,058	264	449	212
2000	3,041	2,102	270	455	214
2001	3,091	2,138	273	462	218
2002	3,134	2,168	276	469	221

Source: Projections of Education Statistics to 2002, U.S. Department of Education, Office of Educational Research and Improvement, December, 1991, p. 50. Primary source: U.S. Department of Education, National Center for Education Statistics, Fall Enrollment in Colleges and Universities surveys and Integrated Postsecondary Education Data System (IPEDS) surveys. Projections are based on data through 1989 and include all 50 States and Washington, D.C. Because of rounding, details may not add to totals. *Note:* 1. Projected.

★ 230 ★

Full-Time-Equivalent Enrollment in Public Institutions of Higher Education by Level of Student and Type of Institution, with Alternative Projections, Fall 1977 to Fall 2002

Prepared April 1991. "Under the low alternative, college enrollment is projected to increase from an estimated 13.9 million in 1990 to 15.2 million by the year 2002....This alternative assumes that enrollment rates will either remain the same as the middle alternative or increase at a slower rate. Under the high alternative, college enrollment is expected to increase from an estimated 13.9 million in 1990 to 17.4 million by the year 2002....This high level is expected to be maintained during the 1990s and beyond if the enrollment rates remain well above their 1990 levels."

[Numbers in thousands]

| Year | Total | Undergraduate | | Graduate | First-profes- |
		4-year	2-year	4-year	sional - 4 year
1977	6,396	3,416	2,357	523	101
1978	6,279	3,375	2,283	519	101
1979	6,393	3,438	2,333	519	103
1980	6,642	3,524	2,484	522	113
1981	6,781	3,575	2,573	524	110
1982	6,851	3,597	2,630	514	110
1983	6,881	3,635	2,616	520	111
1984	6,685	3,605	2,447	521	111
1985	6,668	3,601	2,428	529	110
1986	6,778	3,629	2,483	556	110
1987	6,938	3,731	2,542	557	108
1988	7,097	3,827	2,592	571	107
1989	7,337	3,920	2,718	587	112
1990[1]	7,529	4,003	2,768	637	121
Middle alternative projections					
1991	7,583	4,017	2,785	656	125
1992	7,628	4,026	2,801	673	128

[Continued]

★ 230 ★

Full-Time-Equivalent Enrollment in Public Institutions of Higher Education by Level of Student and Type of Institution, with Alternative Projections, Fall 1977 to Fall 2002

[Continued]

| Year | Total | Undergraduate | | Graduate | First-profes- |
		4-year	2-year	4-year	sional - 4 year
1993	7,675	4,026	2,827	690	132
1994	7,743	4,044	2,863	703	133
1995	7,794	4,064	2,890	707	133
1996	7,897	4,115	2,935	713	134
1997	7,999	4,172	2,974	717	136
1998	8,161	4,270	3,028	726	137
1999	8,308	4,359	3,078	732	139
2000	8,456	4,455	3,125	736	140
2001	8,569	4,525	3,161	741	142
2002	8,672	4,590	3,191	748	143
Low alternative projections					
1991	7,274	3,860	2,674	622	118
1992	7,254	3,839	2,666	630	119
1993	7,268	3,830	2,677	640	121
1994	7,288	3,830	2,694	642	122
1995	7,346	3,855	2,724	645	122
1996	7,436	3,903	2,763	649	121
1997	7,550	3,967	2,806	654	123
1998	7,697	4,055	2,859	660	123
1999	7,842	4,142	2,909	666	125
2000	7,999	4,242	2,960	671	126
2001	8,120	4,316	3,000	677	127
2002	8,238	4,389	3,036	684	129
High alternative projections					
1991	7,993	4,258	2,915	688	132
1992	8,184	4,356	2,974	715	139
1993	8,256	4,359	3,012	742	143
1994	8,317	4,371	3,046	754	146
1995	8,339	4,368	3,061	763	147
1996	8,488	4,442	3,127	771	148
1997	8,596	4,495	3,171	780	150
1998	8,767	4,591	3,233	790	153
1999	8,939	4,687	3,294	802	156
2000	9,108	4,790	3,349	811	158
2001	9,244	4,868	3,394	822	160
2002	9,371	4,939	3,434	835	163

Source: Projections of Education Statistics to 2002, U.S. Department of Education, Office of Educational Research and Improvement, December, 1991, p. 49. Primary source: U.S. Department of Education, National Center for Education Statistics, Fall Enrollment in Colleges and Universities surveys and Integrated Postsecondary Education Data System (IPEDS) surveys. Projections are based on data through 1989 and include all 50 States and Washington, D.C. Because of rounding, details may not add to totals. *Note:* 1. Projected.

★ 231 ★

Full-Time-Equivalent of Part-Time Enrollment as a Percent of Part-Time Enrollment, by Level Enrolled and by Type and Control of Institution, 1989-2002

For each enrollment category by level enrolled and by type and control of institution, "the table below measures the percent of persons enrolled part-time, but who completed the full-time equivalent, to persons who were enrolled only part-time."

[Numbers in percent]

Enrollment category	1989	1997	2002
Public, 4-year, undergraduate	40.0	40.0	40.0
Public, 2-year, undergraduate	33.6	33.6	33.6
Private, 4-year, undergraduate	39.9	39.8	39.8
Private, 2-year, undergraduate	40.0	40.2	40.2
Public, 4-year, graduate	36.2	36.2	36.2
Private, 4-year, graduate	38.1	38.1	38.1
Public, 4-year, first-professional	50.0	52.0	52.0
Private, 4-year, first-professional	52.2	54.5	54.5

Source: Projections of Education Statistics to the Year 2002, National Center for Education Statistics, December, 1991, p. 160.

★ 232 ★

Graduate Enrollment as a Percent of Total Postbaccalaureate Enrollment by Sex, Attendance Status, and by Type and Control of Institution, 1989-2002

"For each enrollment category by sex and enrollment level, and by type and control of institution, the percent that graduate enrollment was of postbaccalaureate enrollment was projected."

Enrollment category	Men			Women		
	1989	1997	2002	1989	1997	2002
Full-time, 4-year, public	74.7	74.2	74.2	79.5	79.6	79.6
Part-time, 4-year, public	99.2	99.0	99.0	99.5	9.4	99.4
Full-time, 4-year, private	56.5	55.3	55.3	63.6	63.4	63.4
Part-time, 4-year, private	91.9	92.0	92.0	95.2	95.2	95.2

Source: Projections of Education Statistics to the Year 2002, National Center for Education Statistics, December, 1991, p. 160.

★ 233 ★

Graduate Enrollment in All Institutions of Higher Education by Sex and Attendance Status, with Alternative Projections, Fall 1977 to Fall 2002

Prepared April 1991. "Under the low alternative, college enrollment is projected to increase from an estimated 13.9 million in 1990 to 15.2 million by the year 2002....This alternative assumes that enrollment rates will either remain the same as the middle alternative or increase at a slower rate. Under the high alternative, college enrollment is expected to increase from an estimated 13.9 million in 1990 to 17.4 million by the year 2002....This high level is expected to be maintained during the 1990s and beyond if the enrollment rates remain well above their 1990 levels."

[Numbers in thousands]

Year	Total	Men		Women	
		Full-time	Part-time	Full-time	Part-time
1977	1,319	289	411	184	434
1978	1,312	280	402	188	442
1979	1,309	280	389	196	444
1980	1,343	281	394	204	466
1981	1,343	277	397	207	462
1982	1,322	280	390	205	447
1983	1,340	286	391	211	452
1984	1,345	286	386	215	459
1985	1,376	289	388	220	479
1986	1,435	294	399	228	514
1987	1,452	294	400	233	525
1988	1,472	304	393	249	526
1989	1,518	309	401	263	547
1990[1]	1,662	325	460	280	597
Middle alternative projections					
1991	1,712	331	475	291	615
1992	1,752	337	485	303	627
1993	1,793	343	493	315	642
1994	1,826	345	500	324	657
1995	1,842	347	507	324	664
1996	1,859	350	514	324	671
1997	1,872	353	516	326	677
1998	1,888	358	516	332	682
1999	1,901	363	516	335	687
2000	1,908	367	514	337	690
2001	1,915	372	512	338	693
2002	1,926	378	511	342	695
Low alternative projections					
1991	1,631	320	449	265	597
1992	1,647	323	450	271	603
1993	1,672	328	455	277	612
1994	1,681	326	457	277	621
1995	1,694	325	460	280	629
1996	1,707	324	462	282	639
1997	1,722	325	465	285	647
1998	1,735	326	466	289	654

[Continued]

★ 233 ★

Graduate Enrollment in All Institutions of Higher Education by Sex and Attendance Status, with Alternative Projections, Fall 1977 to Fall 2002

[Continued]

Year	Total	Men		Women	
		Full-time	Part-time	Full-time	Part-time
1999	1,749	328	468	293	660
2000	1,763	330	469	298	666
2001	1,775	333	470	303	669
2002	1,787	336	470	309	672
High alternative projections					
1991	1,777	342	482	320	633
1992	1,838	352	495	343	648
1993	1,899	363	509	361	666
1994	1,935	371	523	361	680
1995	1,961	377	536	362	686
1996	1,986	383	549	361	693
1997	2,014	390	563	362	699
1998	2,039	399	572	364	704
1999	2,067	408	583	367	709
2000	2,090	415	593	370	712
2001	2,114	426	600	373	715
2002	2,142	437	610	378	717

Source: *Projections of Education Statistics to 2002*, U.S. Department of Education, Office of Educational Research and Improvement, December, 1991, p. 42. Primary source: U.S. Department of Education, National Center for Education Statistics, Fall Enrollment in Colleges and Universities surveys and Integrated Postsecondary Education Data System (IPEDS) surveys. Projections are based on data through 1989 and include all 50 States and Washington, D.C. Because of rounding, details may not add to totals. *Note:* 1. Projected.

★ 234 ★

Graduate Enrollment in Private Institutions of Higher Education by Sex and Attendance Status, with Alternative Projections, Fall 1977 to Fall 2002

Prepared April 1991. "Under the low alternative, college enrollment is projected to increase from an estimated 13.9 million in 1990 to 15.2 million by the year 2002....This alternative assumes that enrollment rates will either remain the same as the middle alternative or increase at a slower rate. Under the high alternative, college enrollment is expected to increase from an estimated 13.9 million in 1990 to 17.4 million by the year 2002....This high level is expected to be maintained during the 1990s and beyond if the enrollment rates remain well above their 1990 levels."

[Numbers in thousands]

Year	Total	Men		Women	
		Full-time	Part-time	Full-time	Part-time
1977	416	98	144	59	115
1978	418	97	144	61	116
1979	424	98	144	63	119
1980	442	100	147	67	128
1981	456	100	155	69	132
1982	453	100	153	69	131
1983	468	103	156	71	138
1984	476	104	156	75	142
1985	486	108	156	76	147
1986	494	106	155	78	156
1987	507	108	156	82	161
1988	522	111	157	86	168
1989	541	113	159	91	177
1990[1]	587	119	182	97	189
Middle alternative projections					
1991	604	121	188	101	194
1992	618	123	192	105	198
1993	633	126	195	109	203
1994	644	126	198	112	208
1995	650	127	201	112	210
1996	655	128	203	112	212
1997	660	129	204	113	214
1998	665	131	204	115	215
1999	670	133	204	116	217
2000	672	134	203	117	218
2001	674	136	202	117	219
2002	678	138	202	118	220
Low alternative projections					
1991	576	117	178	92	189
1992	580	118	178	94	190
1993	589	120	180	96	193
1994	592	119	181	96	196
1995	597	119	182	97	199
1996	601	118	183	98	202
1997	607	119	184	99	205
1998	610	119	184	100	207

[Continued]

★ 234 ★

Graduate Enrollment in Private Institutions of Higher Education by Sex and Attendance Status, with Alternative Projections, Fall 1977 to Fall 2002

[Continued]

Year	Total	Men		Women	
		Full-time	Part-time	Full-time	Part-time
1999	615	120	185	101	209
2000	621	121	186	103	211
2001	624	122	186	105	211
2002	628	123	186	107	212
High alternative projections					
1991	626	125	190	111	200
1992	649	129	196	119	205
1993	670	133	201	125	211
1994	683	136	207	125	215
1995	692	138	212	125	217
1996	701	140	217	125	219
1997	712	143	223	125	221
1998	721	146	226	126	223
1999	731	149	231	127	224
2000	740	152	235	128	225
2001	748	156	237	129	226
2002	759	160	241	131	227

Source: *Projections of Education Statistics to 2002*, U.S. Department of Education, Office of Educational Research and Improvement, December, 1991, p. 44. Primary source: U.S. Department of Education, National Center for Education Statistics, Fall Enrollment in Colleges and Universities surveys and Integrated Postsecondary Education Data System (IPEDS) surveys. Projections are based on data through 1989 and include all 50 States and Washington, D.C. Because of rounding, details may not add to totals. *Note:* 1. Projected.

★ 235 ★

Graduate Enrollment in Public Institutions of Higher Education by Sex and Attendance Status, with Alternative Projections, Fall 1977 to Fall 2002

Prepared April 1991. "Under the low alternative, college enrollment is projected to increase from an estimated 13.9 million in 1990 to 15.2 million by the year 2002....This alternative assumes that enrollment rates will either remain the same as the middle alternative or increase at a slower rate. Under the high alternative, college enrollment is expected to increase from an estimated 13.9 million in 1990 to 17.4 million by the year 2002....This high level is expected to be maintained during the 1990s and beyond if the enrollment rates remain well above their 1990 levels."

[Numbers in thousands]

Year	Total	Men		Women	
		Full-time	Part-time	Full-time	Part-time
1977	900	190	267	124	319
1978	894	183	258	127	326
1979	884	182	246	133	325
1980	900	180	245	137	337
1981	887	177	242	138	329
1982	870	180	237	136	317
1983	872	184	235	140	313
1984	870	182	229	142	317
1985	891	181	232	144	333
1986	941	188	244	150	358
1987	945	185	244	152	364
1988	949	193	236	163	357
1989	978	195	242	171	369
1990[1]	1,075	206	278	183	408
Middle alternative projections					
1991	1,108	210	287	190	421
1992	1,134	214	293	198	429
1993	1,160	217	298	206	439
1994	1,182	219	302	212	449
1995	1,192	220	306	212	454
1996	1,204	222	311	212	459
1997	1,212	224	312	213	463
1998	1,223	227	312	217	467
1999	1,231	230	312	219	470
2000	1,236	233	311	220	472
2001	1,241	236	310	221	474
2002	1,248	240	309	224	475
Low alternative projections					
1991	1,055	203	271	173	408
1992	1,067	205	272	177	413
1993	1,083	208	275	181	419
1994	1,089	207	276	181	425
1995	1,097	206	278	183	430
1996	1,106	206	279	184	437
1997	1,115	206	281	186	442
1998	1,125	207	282	189	447

[Continued]

★ 235 ★

Graduate Enrollment in Public Institutions of Higher Education by Sex and Attendance Status, with Alternative Projections, Fall 1977 to Fall 2002

[Continued]

Year	Total	Men		Women	
		Full-time	Part-time	Full-time	Part-time
1999	1,134	208	283	192	451
2000	1,142	209	283	195	455
2001	1,151	211	284	198	458
2002	1,159	213	284	202	460
High alternative projections					
1991	1,151	217	292	209	433
1992	1,189	223	299	224	443
1993	1,229	230	308	236	455
1994	1,252	235	316	236	465
1995	1,269	239	324	237	469
1996	1,285	243	332	236	474
1997	1,302	247	340	237	478
1998	1,318	253	346	238	481
1999	1,336	259	352	240	485
2000	1,350	263	358	242	487
2001	1,366	270	363	244	489
2002	1,383	277	369	247	490

Source: Projections of Education Statistics to 2002, U.S. Department of Education, Office of Educational Research and Improvement, December, 1991, p. 43. Primary source: U.S. Department of Education, National Center for Education Statistics, Fall Enrollment in Colleges and Universities surveys and Integrated Postsecondary Education Data System (IPEDS) surveys. Projections are based on data through 1989 and include all 50 States and Washington, D.C. Because of rounding, details may not add to totals. *Note:* 1. Projected.

★ 236 ★

Part-Time Enrollment by Level and Type of Institution as a Percent of Total Enrollment for Each Age and Sex Classification, 1989-2002

[Numbers in percent]

Age	Men			Women		
	1989	1997[1]	2002[1]	1989	1997[1]	2002[1]
Undergraduate, 4-year institutions						
16-17 years old	6.4	18.6	18.6	14.0	16.8	16.8
18-19 years old	23.8	19.4	19.4	16.8	18.5	18.5
20-21 years old	29.0	24.1	24.1	28.7	28.0	28.0
22-24 years old	32.3	32.7	32.7	25.4	28.3	28.3
25-29 years old	31.2	31.4	31.4	32.7	30.0	30.0
30-34 years old	26.7	29.1	29.1	26.1	26.0	26.0
35 years and over	24.7	26.9	26.9	26.9	26.8	26.8

[Continued]

★ 236 ★

Part-Time Enrollment by Level and Type of Institution as a Percent of Total Enrollment for Each Age and Sex Classification, 1989-2002
[Continued]

Age	Men			Women		
	1989	1997[1]	2002[1]	1989	1997[1]	2002[1]
Undergraduate, 2-year institutions						
16-17 years old	88.2	75.6	75.6	80.8	79.1	79.1
18-19 years old	70.1	73.7	73.7	77.9	76.7	76.7
20-21 years old	64.6	70.2	70.2	64.5	66.3	66.3
22-24 years old	54.8	54.1	54.1	61.9	58.2	58.2
25-29 years old	51.3	49.7	49.7	46.9	49.9	49.9
30-34 years old	51.5	49.2	49.2	57.0	56.2	56.2
35 years and over	50.8	46.8	46.8	53.2	52.9	52.9
Postbaccalaureate, 4-year institutions						
16-17 years old	5.4	5.8	5.8	5.2	4.2	4.2
18-19 years old	6.0	6.9	6.9	5.3	4.8	4.8
20-21 years old	6.4	5.7	5.7	6.9	5.8	5.8
22-24 years old	12.9	13.2	13.2	12.7	13.5	13.5
25-29 years old	17.5	19.0	19.0	20.3	20.1	20.1
30-34 years old	21.8	21.7	21.7	16.8	17.8	17.8
35 years and over	24.5	26.2	26.2	19.9	20.3	20.3

Source: Projections of Education Statistics to the Year 2002, National Center for Education Statistics, December, 1991, p. 159. *Note:* 1. Projections adjusted to add to 100 percent.

★ 237 ★

Percentage Distribution of Enrollment in Institutions of Higher Education by Age Group, 1990 and 2002

	1990	2002
Under 25	56.3	56.7
25 to 29	14.9	11.8
30 to 34	10.1	8.3
35+	18.7	23.2

Source: Projections of Education Statistics to 2002, U.S. Department of Education, Office of Educational Research and Improvement, December 1991, p. 25. The age distribution for 2002 is based on middle alternative projections.

★ 238 ★

Percentage Distribution of Men Enrolled in Institutions of Higher Education by Age Group, 1990 and 2002

	1990	2002
Under 25	60.1	59.9
25 to 29	15.8	12.3
30 to 34	9.7	7.8
35 +	14.3	19.9

Source: Projections of Education Statistics to 2002, U.S. Department of Education, Office of Educational Research and Improvement, December 1991, p. 26. The age distribution for 2002 is based on middle alternative projections.

★ 239 ★

Percentage Distribution of Women Enrolled in Institutions of Higher Education by Age Group, 1990 and 2002

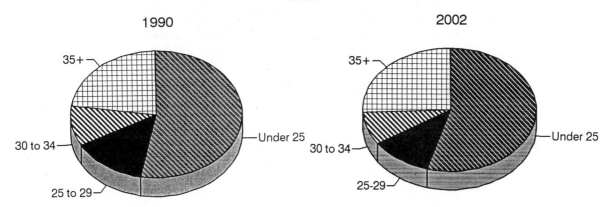

	1990	2002
Under 25	53.1	54.3
25 to 29	14.1	11.3
30 to 34	10.4	8.6
35 +	22.4	25.8

Source: Projections of Education Statistics to 2002, U.S. Department of Education, Office of Educational Research and Improvement, December 1991, p. 27. The age distribution for 2002 is based on middle alternative projections.

★ 240 ★

Projected Numbers of Male and Female Doctorate
Recipients, 1976-2001

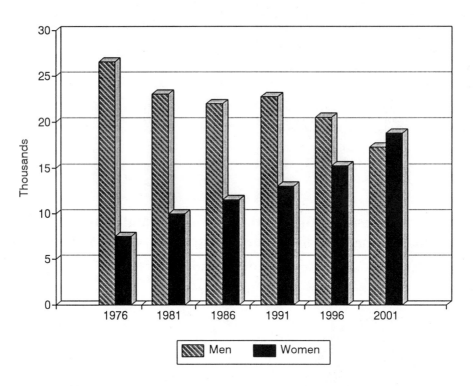

"By the year 2001, the number of doctorate degrees awarded to women is projected to surpass the number awarded to men. The number of doctorate degrees awarded to women increased by more than 70 percent between 1975-76 and 1990-91, while the number conferred on men dropped about 10 percent during the same period. These trends are projected to continue through 2001. The growth in the number of doctorate degrees awarded to women reflects the rising enrollment of women in graduate schools. Between 1976 and 1988, their numbers increased from 619,000 to 774,000, an increase of 25 percent. In contrast, the graduate enrollment of men decreased 2 percent, from 714,000 to 698,000. Over the projection period, these patterns are expected to continue."

[Numbers in thousands]

	1976	1981	1986	Projected		
				1991	1996	2001
Men	26.5	23.0	22.0	22.75	20.50	17.25
Women	7.5	10.0	11.5	13.00	15.25	18.75

Source: Occupational Outlook Quarterly 35, No. 1, Spring, 1991. Primary source: U.S. Department of Education, National Center for Education Statistics, "Projections of Education Statistics to 2001, an Update." Magnitudes estimated from published chart.

★ 241 ★

Public School Enrollment as a Percent of Total Enrollment by Attendance Status, Sex, Level Enrolled, and Type of Institution, 1989-2002

"For each enrollment category—sex, attendance status, level enrolled, and type of institution—the percent that public enrollment was of total enrollment was projected."

[Numbers in percent]

Enrollment category	Men			Women		
	1989	1997	2002	1989	1997	2002
Full-time, undergraduate, 4-year institutions	69.7	69.5	69.5	69.3	69.0	69.0
Part-time, undergraduate, 4-year institutions	72.8	72.8	72.8	70.1	70.1	70.1
Full-time, undergraduate, 2-year institutions	91.3	91.0	91.0	89.4	88.8	88.8
Part-time, undergraduate, 2-year institutions	96.6	96.9	96.9	97.9	98.0	98.0
Full-time, postbaccalaureate, 4-year institutions	56.6	56.4	56.4	60.1	60.1	60.1
Part-time, postbaccalaureate, 4-year institutions	58.5	58.7	58.7	66.6	67.5	67.5

Source: *Projections of Education Statistics to the Year 2002*, National Center for Education Statistics, December, 1991, p. 160.

★ 242 ★

Total Enrollment in 2-Year Institutions of Higher Education by Sex, Attendance Status, and Control of Institution, with Alternative Projections, Fall 1977 to Fall 2002

Prepared April 1991. "Under the low alternative, college enrollment is projected to increase from an estimated 13.9 million in 1990 to 15.2 million by the year 2002....This alternative assumes that enrollment rates will either remain the same as the middle alternative or increase at a slower rate. Under the high alternative, college enrollment is expected to increase from an estimated 13.9 million in 1990 to 17.4 million by the year 2002....This high level is expected to be maintained during the 1990s and beyond if the enrollment rates remain well above their 1990 levels."

[Numbers in thousands]

Year	Total	Sex		Attendance status		Control	
		Men	Women	Full-time	Part-time	Public	Private
1977	4,043	1,965	2,077	1,654	2,388	3,902	141
1978	4,028	1,885	2,143	1,558	2,470	3,874	154
1979	4,217	1,924	2,294	1,591	2,627	4,057	160
1980	4,526	2,047	2,479	1,754	2,772	4,329	198
1981	4,716	2,124	2,591	1,796	2,919	4,481	236
1982	4,772	2,170	2,602	1,840	2,932	4,520	252
1983	4,723	2,131	2,592	1,827	2,897	4,459	264
1984	4,531	2,017	2,514	1,704	2,827	4,279	252
1985	4,531	2,002	2,529	1,691	2,840	4,270	261
1986	4,680	2,061	2,619	1,696	2,983	4,414	266
1987	4,776	2,073	2,703	1,709	3,068	4,541	235
1988	4,875	2,090	2,785	1,744	3,132	4,615	260

[Continued]

★ 242 ★

Total Enrollment in 2-Year Institutions of Higher Education by Sex, Attendance Status, and Control of Institution, with Alternative Projections, Fall 1977 to Fall 2002

[Continued]

Year	Total	Sex		Attendance status		Control	
		Men	Women	Full-time	Part-time	Public	Private
1989	5,083	2,187	2,897	1,831	3,252	4,821	263
1990[1]	5,193	2,227	2,966	1,867	3,326	4,921	272
Middle alternative projections							
1991	5,261	2,248	3,013	1,856	3,405	4,989	272
1992	5,312	2,262	3,050	1,857	3,455	5,038	274
1993	5,376	2,271	3,105	1,867	3,509	5,099	277
1994	5,446	2,282	3,164	1,890	3,556	5,166	280
1995	5,501	2,299	3,202	1,905	3,596	5,218	283
1996	5,576	2,329	3,247	1,939	3,637	5,290	286
1997	5,644	2,347	3,297	1,970	3,674	5,353	291
1998	5,727	2,376	3,351	2,017	3,710	5,430	297
1999	5,807	2,403	3,404	2,060	3,747	5,504	303
2000	5,882	2,426	3,456	2,099	3,783	5,574	308
2001	5,938	2,447	3,491	2,128	3,810	5,628	310
2002	5,989	2,466	3,523	2,153	3,836	5,675	314
Low alternative projections							
1991	5,061	2,145	2,916	1,778	3,283	4,799	262
1992	5,063	2,138	2,925	1,763	3,300	4,803	260
1993	5,096	2,137	2,959	1,765	3,331	4,834	262
1994	5,131	2,138	2,993	1,774	3,357	4,868	263
1995	5,187	2,146	3,041	1,794	3,393	4,921	266
1996	5,256	2,163	3,093	1,824	3,432	4,985	271
1997	5,329	2,182	3,147	1,856	3,473	5,055	274
1998	5,416	2,208	3,208	1,899	3,517	5,136	280
1999	5,502	2,235	3,267	1,938	3,564	5,217	285
2000	5,589	2,260	3,329	1,979	3,610	5,298	291
2001	5,658	2,285	3,373	2,009	3,649	5,362	296
2002	5,720	2,306	3,414	2,037	3,683	5,421	299
High alternative projections							
1991	5,467	2,303	3,164	1,969	3,498	5,180	287
1992	5,576	2,344	3,232	2,010	3,566	5,283	293
1993	5,668	2,377	3,291	2,023	3,645	5,372	296
1994	5,749	2,413	3,336	2,037	3,712	5,450	299
1995	5,801	2,437	3,364	2,034	3,767	5,500	301
1996	5,912	2,508	3,404	2,086	3,826	5,604	308
1997	5,999	2,555	3,444	2,111	3,888	5,688	311
1998	6,107	2,613	3,494	2,159	3,948	5,789	318
1999	6,213	2,670	3,543	2,203	4,010	5,890	323
2000	6,316	2,723	3,593	2,243	4,073	5,986	330

[Continued]

★ 242 ★

Total Enrollment in 2-Year Institutions of Higher Education by Sex, Attendance Status, and Control of Institution, with Alternative Projections, Fall 1977 to Fall 2002

[Continued]

Year	Total	Sex		Attendance status		Control	
		Men	Women	Full-time	Part-time	Public	Private
2001	6,397	2,773	3,624	2,274	4,123	6,063	334
2002	6,476	2,822	3,654	2,298	4,178	6,138	338

Source: Projections of Education Statistics to 2002, U.S. Department of Education, Office of Educational Research and Improvement, December, 1991, p. 30. Primary source: U.S. Department of Education, National Center for Education Statistics, Fall Enrollment in Colleges and Universities surveys and Integrated Postsecondary Education Data System (IPEDS) surveys. Projections are based on data through 1989 and include all 50 States and Washington, D.C. Because of rounding, details may not add to totals. *Note:* 1. Projected.

★ 243 ★

Total Enrollment in 4-Year Institutions of Higher Education by Sex, Attendance Status, and Control of Institution, with Alternative Projections, Fall 1977 to Fall 2002

Prepared April 1991. "Under the low alternative, college enrollment is projected to increase from an estimated 13.9 million in 1990 to 15.2 million by the year 2002....This alternative assumes that enrollment rates will either remain the same as the middle alternative or increase at a slower rate. Under the high alternative, college enrollment is expected to increase from an estimated 13.9 million in 1990 to 17.4 million by the year 2002....This high level is expected to be maintained during the 1990s and beyond if the enrollment rates remain well above their 1990 levels."

[Numbers in thousands]

Year	Total	Sex		Attendance status		Control	
		Men	Women	Full-time	Part-time	Public	Private
1977	7,243	3,823	3,419	5,138	2,104	4,945	2,298
1978	7,232	3,755	3,476	5,109	2,122	4,912	2,320
1979	7,353	3,762	3,591	5,202	2,151	4,980	2,373
1980	7,571	3,827	3,743	5,344	2,226	5,129	2,442
1981	7,655	3,852	3,805	5,387	2,270	5,166	2,489
1982	7,654	3,861	3,793	5,381	2,273	5,176	2,478
1983	7,741	3,893	3,849	5,434	2,307	5,223	2,518
1984	7,711	3,847	3,864	5,395	2,317	5,198	2,513
1985	7,716	3,816	3,900	5,385	2,331	5,210	2,506
1986	7,824	3,824	4,000	5,423	2,401	5,300	2,524
1987	7,990	3,859	4,131	5,522	2,468	5,432	2,558
1988	8,180	3,912	4,268	5,693	2,487	5,546	2,634
1989	8,374	3,969	4,406	5,795	2,579	5,694	2,680
1990[1]	8,738	4,192	4,546	5,961	2,777	5,923	2,815
Middle alternative projections							
1991	8,844	4,225	4,619	5,988	2,856	5,993	2,851
1992	8,923	4,254	4,669	6,014	2,909	6,045	2,878
1993	8,990	4,260	4,730	6,028	2,962	6,088	2,902
1994	9,066	4,267	4,799	6,059	3,007	6,139	2,927
1995	9,120	4,276	4,844	6,083	3,037	6,175	2,945

[Continued]

★ 243 ★

Total Enrollment in 4-Year Institutions of Higher Education by Sex, Attendance Status, and Control of Institution, with Alternative Projections, Fall 1977 to Fall 2002

[Continued]

Year	Total	Sex		Attendance status		Control	
		Men	Women	Full-time	Part-time	Public	Private
1996	9,227	4,318	4,909	6,156	3,071	6,247	2,980
1997	9,334	4,344	4,990	6,242	3,092	6,320	3,014
1998	9,500	4,398	5,102	6,391	3,109	6,434	3,066
1999	9,655	4,450	5,205	6,528	3,127	6,539	3,116
2000	9,810	4,496	5,314	6,671	3,139	6,646	3,164
2001	9,927	4,544	5,383	6,778	3,149	6,727	3,200
2002	10,041	4,586	5,455	6,882	3,159	6,803	3,238
Low alternative projections							
1991	8,476	4,050	4,426	5,738	2,738	5,746	2,730
1992	8,474	4,043	4,431	5,716	2,758	5,742	2,732
1993	8,499	4,036	4,463	5,712	2,787	5,758	2,741
1994	8,518	4,020	4,498	5,707	2,811	5,770	2,748
1995	8,574	4,012	4,562	5,738	2,836	5,809	2,765
1996	8,665	4,027	4,638	5,802	2,863	5,872	2,793
1997	8,788	4,055	4,733	5,895	2,893	5,955	2,833
1998	8,937	4,100	4,837	6,021	2,916	6,059	2,878
1999	9,092	4,147	4,945	6,149	2,943	6,165	2,927
2000	9,262	4,191	5,071	6,295	2,967	6,281	2,981
2001	9,392	4,240	5,152	6,406	2,986	6,371	3,021
2002	9,523	4,283	5,240	6,520	3,003	6,461	3,062
High alternative projections							
1991	9,303	4,344	4,959	6,371	2,932	6,306	2,997
1992	9,546	4,431	5,115	6,545	3,001	6,467	3,079
1993	9,648	4,481	5,167	6,570	3,078	6,533	3,115
1994	9,731	4,540	5,191	6,587	3,144	6,587	3,144
1995	9,769	4,553	5,216	6,581	3,188	6,612	3,157
1996	9,919	4,662	5,257	6,683	3,236	6,715	3,204
1997	10,048	4,732	5,316	6,762	3,286	6,800	3,248
1998	10,233	4,835	5,398	6,904	3,329	6,926	3,307
1999	10,424	4,938	5,486	7,052	3,372	7,055	3,369
2000	10,614	5,029	5,585	7,201	3,413	7,186	3,428
2001	10,771	5,129	5,642	7,326	3,445	7,291	3,480
2002	10,923	5,222	5,701	7,440	3,483	7,394	3,529

Source: Projections of Education Statistics to 2002, U.S. Department of Education, Office of Educational Research and Improvement, December, 1991, p. 29. Primary source: U.S. Department of Education, National Center for Education Statistics, Fall Enrollment in Colleges and Universities surveys and Integrated Postsecondary Education Data System (IPEDS) surveys. Projections are based on data through 1989 and include all 50 States and Washington, D.C. Because of rounding, details may not add to totals. *Note:* 1. Projected.

★ 244 ★

Total Enrollment in All Institutions of Higher Education by Sex and Attendance Status, with Alternative Projections, Fall 1977 to Fall 2002

Prepared April 1991. "Under the low alternative, college enrollment is projected to increase from an estimated 13.9 million in 1990 to 15.2 million by the year 2002....This alternative assumes that enrollment rates will either remain the same as the middle alternative or increase at a slower rate. Under the high alternative, college enrollment is expected to increase from an estimated 13.9 million in 1990 to 17.4 million by the year 2002....This high level is expected to be maintained during the 1990s and beyond if the enrollment rates remain well above their 1990 levels."

[Numbers in thousands]

Year	Total	Men		Women	
		Full-time	Part-time	Full-time	Part-time
1977	11,286	3,650	2,138	3,142	2,354
1978	11,260	3,527	2,113	3,140	2,479
1979	11,570	3,544	2,142	3,249	2,636
1980	12,097	3,689	2,185	3,409	2,814
1981	12,372	3,714	2,262	3,469	2,927
1982	12,426	3,753	2,278	3,468	2,927
1983	12,465	3,760	2,264	3,501	2,940
1984	12,242	3,648	2,216	3,451	2,927
1985	12,247	3,608	2,211	3,468	2,961
1986	12,504	3,599	2,285	3,521	3,098
1987	12,767	3,611	2,321	3,620	3,214
1988	13,055	3,662	2,340	3,775	3,278
1989	13,458	3,728	2,428	3,899	3,403
1990[1]	13,931	3,879	2,540	3,949	3,563
Middle alternative projections					
1991	14,105	3,867	2,606	3,977	3,655
1992	14,235	3,868	2,648	4,003	3,716
1993	14,366	3,855	2,676	4,040	3,795
1994	14,512	3,854	2,695	4,095	3,868
1995	14,621	3,852	2,723	4,136	3,910
1996	14,803	3,893	2,754	4,202	3,954
1997	14,978	3,924	2,767	4,288	3,999
1998	15,227	3,995	2,779	4,413	4,040
1999	15,462	4,061	2,792	4,527	4,082
2000	15,692	4,122	2,800	4,648	4,122
2001	15,865	4,183	2,808	4,723	4,151
2002	16,030	4,234	2,818	4,801	4,177
Low alternative projections					
1991	13,537	3,720	2,475	3,796	3,546
1992	13,537	3,700	2,481	3,779	3,577
1993	13,595	3,681	2,492	3,796	3,626
1994	13,649	3,660	2,498	3,821	3,670
1995	13,761	3,651	2,507	3,881	3,722
1996	13,921	3,670	2,520	3,956	3,775
1997	14,117	3,698	2,539	4,053	3,827
1998	14,353	3,755	2,553	4,165	3,880

[Continued]

★ 244 ★

Total Enrollment in All Institutions of Higher Education by Sex and Attendance Status, with Alternative Projections, Fall 1977 to Fall 2002

[Continued]

Year	Total	Men		Women	
		Full-time	Part-time	Full-time	Part-time
1999	14,594	3,806	2,576	4,281	3,931
2000	14,851	3,857	2,594	4,417	3,983
2001	15,050	3,912	2,613	4,503	4,022
2002	15,243	3,959	2,630	4,598	4,056
High alternative projections					
1991	14,770	3,992	2,655	4,348	3,775
1992	15,122	4,057	2,718	4,498	3,849
1993	15,316	4,073	2,785	4,520	3,938
1994	15,480	4,112	2,841	4,512	4,015
1995	15,570	4,084	2,906	4,531	4,049
1996	15,831	4,196	2,974	4,573	4,088
1997	16,047	4,244	3,043	4,629	4,131
1998	16,340	4,343	3,105	4,720	4,172
1999	16,637	4,440	3,168	4,815	4,214
2000	16,930	4,522	3,230	4,922	4,256
2001	17,168	4,618	3,284	4,982	4,284
2002	17,399	4,697	3,347	5,041	4,314

Source: Projections of Education Statistics to 2002, U.S. Department of Education, Office of Educational Research and Improvement, December, 1991, p. 34. Primary source: U.S. Department of Education, National Center for Education Statistics, Fall Enrollment in Colleges and Universities surveys and Integrated Postsecondary Education Data System (IPEDS) surveys. Projections are based on data through 1989 and include all 50 States and Washington, D.C. Because of rounding, details may not add to totals. *Note:* 1. Projected.

★ 245 ★

Total Enrollment in All Institutions of Higher Education by Sex, Attendance Status, and Control of Institution, with Alternative Projections, Fall 1977 to Fall 2002

Prepared April 1991. "Under the low alternative, college enrollment is projected to increase from an estimated 13.9 million in 1990 to 15.2 million by the year 2002....This alternative assumes that enrollment rates will either remain the same as the middle alternative or increase at a slower rate. Under the high alternative, college enrollment is expected to increase from an estimated 13.9 million in 1990 to 17.4 million by the year 2002....This high level is expected to be maintained during the 1990s and beyond if the enrollment rates remain well above their 1990 levels."

[Numbers in thousands]

Year	Total	Sex		Attendance status		Control	
		Men	Women	Full-time	Part-time	Public	Private
1977	11,286	5,789	5,497	6,793	4,493	8,847	2,439
1978	11,260	5,641	5,619	6,668	4,592	8,786	2,474
1979	11,570	5,683	5,887	6,794	4,776	9,037	2,533
1980	12,097	5,874	6,223	7,098	4,999	9,457	2,640

[Continued]

★ 245 ★

Total Enrollment in All Institutions of Higher Education by Sex, Attendance Status, and Control of Institution, with Alternative Projections, Fall 1977 to Fall 2002

[Continued]

Year	Total	Sex		Attendance status		Control	
		Men	Women	Full-time	Part-time	Public	Private
1981	12,372	5,975	6,397	7,181	5,190	9,647	2,725
1982	12,426	6,031	6,394	7,221	5,205	9,696	2,730
1983	12,465	6,024	6,441	7,261	5,204	9,683	2,782
1984	12,242	5,864	6,378	7,098	5,144	9,477	2,765
1985	12,247	5,818	6,429	7,075	5,172	9,479	2,768
1986	12,504	5,885	6,619	7,120	5,384	9,714	2,790
1987	12,767	5,932	6,836	7,231	5,536	9,973	2,793
1988	13,055	6,002	7,053	7,437	5,619	10,161	2,894
1989	13,458	6,155	7,302	7,627	5,830	10,515	2,943
1990[1]	13,931	6,419	7,512	7,828	6,103	10,844	3,087
Middle alternative projections							
1991	14,105	6,473	7,632	7,844	6,261	10,982	3,123
1992	14,235	6,516	7,719	7,871	6,364	11,083	3,152
1993	14,366	6,531	7,963	7,895	6,563	11,305	3,207
1994	14,512	6,549	7,963	7,949	6,563	11,187	3,179
1995	14,621	6,575	8,046	7,988	6,633	11,393	3,228
1996	14,803	6,647	8,156	8,095	6,708	11,537	3,266
1997	14,978	6,691	8,287	8,212	6,766	11,673	3,305
1998	15,227	6,774	8,453	8,408	6,819	11,864	3,363
1999	15,462	6,853	8,609	8,588	6,874	12,043	3,419
2000	15,692	6,922	8,770	8,770	6,922	12,220	3,472
2001	15,865	6,991	8,874	8,906	6,959	12,355	3,510
2002	16,030	7,052	8,978	9,035	6,995	12,478	3,552
Low alternative projections							
1991	13,537	6,195	7,342	7,516	6,021	10,545	2,992
1992	13,537	6,181	7,356	7,479	6,058	10,545	2,992
1993	13,595	6,173	7,422	7,477	6,118	10,592	3,003
1994	13,649	6,158	7,491	7,481	6,168	10,638	3,011
1995	13,761	6,158	7,603	7,532	6,229	10,730	3,031
1996	13,921	6,190	7,731	7,626	6,295	10,857	3,064
1997	14,117	6,237	7,880	7,751	6,366	11,010	3,107
1998	14,353	6,308	8,045	7,920	6,433	11,195	3,158
1999	14,594	6,382	8,212	8,087	6,507	11,382	3,212
2000	14,851	6,451	8,400	8,274	6,577	11,579	3,272
2001	15,050	6,525	8,525	8,415	6,635	11,733	3,317
2002	15,243	6,589	8,654	8,557	6,686	11,882	3,361
High alternative projections							
1991	14,770	6,647	8,123	8,340	6,530	11,486	3,284
1992	15,122	6,775	8,347	8,555	6,567	11,750	3,372
1993	15,316	6,858	8,458	8,593	6,723	11,905	3,411
1994	15,480	6,953	8,527	8,624	6,856	12,037	3,443
1995	15,570	6,990	8,580	8,615	6,955	12,112	3,458
1996	15,831	7,170	8,661	8,769	7,062	12,319	3,512
1997	16,047	7,287	8,760	8,873	7,174	12,488	3,559

[Continued]

★ 245 ★

Total Enrollment in All Institutions of Higher Education by Sex, Attendance Status, and Control of Institution, with Alternative Projections, Fall 1977 to Fall 2002

[Continued]

Year	Total	Sex		Attendance status		Control	
		Men	Women	Full-time	Part-time	Public	Private
1998	16,340	7,448	8,892	9,063	7,277	12,715	3,625
1999	16,637	7,608	9,029	9,255	7,382	12,945	3,692
2000	16,930	7,752	9,178	9,444	7,486	13,172	3,758
2001	17,168	7,902	9,266	9,600	7,568	13,354	3,814
2002	17,399	8,044	9,355	9,738	7,661	13,532	3,867

Source: Projections of Education Statistics to 2002, U.S. Department of Education, Office of Educational Research and Improvement, December, 1991, p. 28. Primary source: U.S. Department of Education, National Center for Education Statistics, Fall Enrollment in Colleges and Universities surveys and Integrated Postsecondary Education Data System (IPEDS) surveys. Projections are based on data through 1989 and include all 50 States and Washington, D.C. *Note:* 1. Projected.

★ 246 ★

Total Enrollment in Private 2-Year Institutions of Higher Education by Sex and Attendance Status, with Alternative Projections, Fall 1977 to Fall 2002

Prepared April 1991. "Under the low alternative, college enrollment is projected to increase from an estimated 13.9 million in 1990 to 15.2 million by the year 2002....This alternative assumes that enrollment rates will either remain the same as the middle alternative or increase at a slower rate. Under the high alternative, college enrollment is expected to increase from an estimated 13.9 million in 1990 to 17.4 million by the year 2002....This high level is expected to be maintained during the 1990s and beyond if the enrollment rates remain well above their 1990 levels."

[Numbers in thousands]

Year	Total	Men		Women	
		Full-time	Part-time	Full-time	Part-time
1977	141	47	14	63	16
1978	154	48	15	72	20
1979	160	48	14	76	22
1980	198	68	15	90	24
1981	236	71	34	95	35
1982	252	80	45	99	28
1983	264	88	41	105	30
1984	252	79	37	106	29
1985	261	84	38	110	30
1986	266	83	43	108	32
1987	235	76	30	102	29
1988	260	73	40	103	44
1989	263	75	45	103	40
1990[1]	272	81	42	109	40
Middle alternative projections					
1991	272	79	43	109	41
1992	274	79	43	110	42

[Continued]

★ 246 ★

Total Enrollment in Private 2-Year Institutions of Higher Education by Sex and Attendance Status, with Alternative Projections, Fall 1977 to Fall 2002

[Continued]

Year	Total	Men		Women	
		Full-time	Part-time	Full-time	Part-time
1993	277	79	44	111	43
1994	280	79	44	114	43
1995	283	79	45	115	44
1996	286	80	45	117	44
1997	291	81	45	120	45
1998	297	83	46	123	45
1999	303	85	46	126	46
2000	308	86	46	129	47
2001	310	87	46	130	47
2002	314	88	47	132	47
Low alternative projections					
1991	262	76	41	105	40
1992	260	75	41	104	40
1993	262	75	41	105	41
1994	263	75	41	106	41
1995	266	75	41	108	42
1996	271	76	42	110	43
1997	274	76	42	113	43
1998	280	78	42	116	44
1999	285	79	43	119	44
2000	291	80	43	123	45
2001	296	81	44	125	46
2002	299	82	44	127	46
High alternative projections					
1991	287	82	44	119	42
1992	293	83	45	122	43
1993	296	83	46	123	44
1994	299	84	46	124	45
1995	301	83	48	125	45
1996	308	86	49	127	46
1997	311	87	50	128	46
1998	318	89	51	131	47
1999	323	91	52	133	47
2000	330	93	53	136	48
2001	334	95	54	137	48
2002	338	96	55	138	49

Source: Projections of Education Statistics to 2002, U.S. Department of Education, Office of Educational Research and Improvement, December, 1991, p. 38. Primary source: U.S. Department of Education, National Center for Education Statistics, Fall Enrollment in Colleges and Universities surveys and Integrated Postsecondary Education Data System (IPEDS) surveys. Projections are based on data through 1989 and include all 50 States and Washington, D.C. Because of rounding, details may not add to totals. *Note:* 1. Projected.

★ 247 ★

Total Enrollment in Private 4-Year Institutions of Higher Education by Sex and Attendance Status, with Alternative Projections, Fall 1977 to Fall 2002

Prepared April 1991. "Under the low alternative, college enrollment is projected to increase from an estimated 13.9 million in 1990 to 15.2 million by the year 2002....This alternative assumes that enrollment rates will either remain the same as the middle alternative or increase at a slower rate. Under the high alternative, college enrollment is expected to increase from an estimated 13.9 million in 1990 to 17.4 million by the year 2002....This high level is expected to be maintained during the 1990s and beyond if the enrollment rates remain well above their 1990 levels."

[Numbers in thousands]

Year	Total	Men		Women	
		Full-time	Part-time	Full-time	Part-time
1977	2,298	925	329	734	309
1978	2,320	919	327	755	319
1979	2,373	924	329	784	336
1980	2,442	936	333	816	357
1981	2,489	939	344	830	376
1982	2,478	933	341	824	380
1983	2,518	935	350	834	399
1984	2,513	926	345	839	401
1985	2,506	917	340	844	403
1986	2,524	910	343	856	415
1987	2,558	908	346	878	426
1988	2,634	933	347	918	436
1989	2,680	929	358	932	461
1990[1]	2,815	977	395	956	487
Middle alternative projections					
1991	2,851	978	406	966	501
1992	2,878	981	414	973	510
1993	2,902	979	419	982	522
1994	2,927	978	423	994	532
1995	2,945	977	428	1,003	537
1996	2,980	986	433	1,017	544
1997	3,014	994	434	1,037	549
1998	3,066	1,010	435	1,068	553
1999	3,116	1,026	436	1,096	558
2000	3,164	1,041	435	1,126	562
2001	3,200	1,057	434	1,144	565
2002	3,238	1,071	435	1,164	568
Low alternative projections					
1991	2,730	942	384	919	485
1992	2,732	940	386	916	490
1993	2,741	936	388	920	497
1994	2,748	930	390	925	503
1995	2,765	926	391	938	510
1996	2,793	929	392	955	517
1997	2,833	936	395	978	524
1998	2,878	949	395	1,004	530
1999	2,927	961	398	1,032	536

[Continued]

★ 247 ★

Total Enrollment in Private 4-Year Institutions of Higher Education by Sex and Attendance Status, with Alternative Projections, Fall 1977 to Fall 2002
[Continued]

Year	Total	Men		Women	
		Full-time	Part-time	Full-time	Part-time
2000	2,981	973	400	1,066	542
2001	3,021	987	401	1,087	546
2002	3,062	999	402	1,112	549
High alternative projections					
1991	2,997	1,009	413	1,058	517
1992	3,079	1,028	424	1,098	529
1993	3,115	1,035	435	1,103	542
1994	3,144	1,045	446	1,100	553
1995	3,157	1,041	455	1,103	558
1996	3,204	1,066	466	1,110	562
1997	3,248	1,079	477	1,124	568
1998	3,307	1,103	486	1,145	573
1999	3,369	1,128	496	1,168	577
2000	3,428	1,149	504	1,194	581
2001	3,480	1,175	511	1,210	584
2002	3,529	1,197	520	1,225	587

Source: Projections of Education Statistics to 2002, U.S. Department of Education, Office of Educational Research and Improvement, December, 1991, p. 37. Primary source: U.S. Department of Education, National Center for Education Statistics, Fall Enrollment in Colleges and Universities surveys and Integrated Postsecondary Education Data System (IPEDS) surveys. Projections are based on data through 1989 and include all 50 States and Washington, D.C. Because of rounding, details may not add to totals. *Note:* 1. Projected.

★ 248 ★

Total Enrollment in Public 2-Year Institutions of Higher Education by Sex and Attendance Status, with Alternative Projections, Fall 1977 to Fall 2002

Prepared April 1991. "Under the low alternative, college enrollment is projected to increase from an estimated 13.9 million in 1990 to 15.2 million by the year 2002....This alternative assumes that enrollment rates will either remain the same as the middle alternative or increase at a slower rate. Under the high alternative, college enrollment is expected to increase from an estimated 13.9 million in 1990 to 17.4 million by the year 2002....This high level is expected to be maintained during the 1990s and beyond if the enrollment rates remain well above their 1990 levels."

[Numbers in thousands]

Year	Total	Men		Women	
		Full-time	Part-time	Full-time	Part-time
1977	3,902	805	1,099	739	1,259
1978	3,874	738	1,084	700	1,351
1979	4,057	739	1,123	728	1,468
1980	4,329	812	1,152	784	1,581
1981	4,481	827	1,192	803	1,658

[Continued]

★ 248 ★

Total Enrollment in Public 2-Year Institutions of Higher Education by Sex and Attendance Status, with Alternative Projections, Fall 1977 to Fall 2002
[Continued]

Year	Total	Men		Women	
		Full-time	Part-time	Full-time	Part-time
1982	4,520	851	1,195	810	1,664
1983	4,459	827	1,175	807	1,650
1984	4,279	762	1,138	756	1,623
1985	4,270	743	1,138	754	1,635
1986	4,414	742	1,193	764	1,715
1987	4,541	744	1,225	787	1,785
1988	4,615	746	1,231	822	1,817
1989	4,821	785	1,282	868	1,885
1990[1]	4,921	810	1,294	867	1,950
Middle alternative projections					
1991	4,989	800	1,326	868	1,995
1992	5,038	795	1,345	873	2,025
1993	5,099	792	1,356	885	2,066
1994	5,166	795	1,364	902	2,105
1995	5,218	797	1,378	914	2,129
1996	5,290	810	1,394	932	2,154
1997	5,353	818	1,403	951	2,181
1998	5,430	835	1,412	976	2,207
1999	5,504	850	1,422	999	2,233
2000	5,574	863	1,431	1,021	2,259
2001	5,628	875	1,439	1,036	2,278
2002	5,675	884	1,447	1,049	2,295
Low alternative projections					
1991	4,799	765	1,263	832	1,939
1992	4,803	757	1,265	827	1,954
1993	4,834	752	1,269	833	1,980
1994	4,868	751	1,271	842	2,004
1995	4,921	753	1,277	858	2,033
1996	4,985	760	1,285	878	2,062
1997	5,055	768	1,296	899	2,092
1998	5,136	781	1,307	924	2,124
1999	5,217	792	1,321	948	2,156
2000	5,298	803	1,334	973	2,188
2001	5,362	813	1,347	990	2,212
2002	5,421	821	1,359	1,007	2,234
High alternative projections					
1991	5,180	826	1,351	942	2,061
1992	5,283	835	1,381	970	2,097
1993	5,372	836	1,412	981	2,143
1994	5,450	845	1,438	984	2,183
1995	5,500	835	1,471	991	2,203
1996	5,604	867	1,506	1,006	2,225
1997	5,688	877	1,541	1,019	2,251
1998	5,789	899	1,574	1,040	2,276

[Continued]

★ 248 ★

Total Enrollment in Public 2-Year Institutions of Higher Education by Sex and Attendance Status, with Alternative Projections, Fall 1977 to Fall 2002

[Continued]

Year	Total	Men		Women	
		Full-time	Part-time	Full-time	Part-time
1999	5,890	919	1,608	1,060	2,303
2000	5,986	935	1,642	1,079	2,330
2001	6,063	952	1,672	1,090	2,349
2002	6,138	965	1,706	1,099	2,368

Source: Projections of Education Statistics to 2002, U.S. Department of Education, Office of Educational Research and Improvement, December, 1991, p. 36. Primary source: U.S. Department of Education, National Center for Education Statistics, Fall Enrollment in Colleges and Universities surveys and Integrated Postsecondary Education Data System (IPEDS) surveys. Projections are based on data through 1989 and include all 50 States and Washington, D.C. Because of rounding, details may not add to totals. *Note:* 1. Projected.

★ 249 ★

Total Enrollment in Public 4-Year Institutions of Higher Education by Sex and Attendance Status, with Alternative Projections, Fall 1977 to Fall 2002

Prepared April 1991. "Under the low alternative, college enrollment is projected to increase from an estimated 13.9 million in 1990 to 15.2 million by the year 2002....This alternative assumes that enrollment rates will either remain the same as the middle alternative or increase at a slower rate. Under the high alternative, college enrollment is expected to increase from an estimated 13.9 million in 1990 to 17.4 million by the year 2002....This high level is expected to be maintained during the 1990s and beyond if the enrollment rates remain well above their 1990 levels."

[Numbers in thousands]

Year	Total	Men		Women	
		Full-time	Part-time	Full-time	Part-time
1977	4,945	1,873	696	1,606	770
1978	4,912	1,822	687	1,613	789
1979	4,980	1,833	676	1,661	810
1980	5,129	1,873	685	1,719	851
1981	5,166	1,877	692	1,741	858
1982	5,176	1,889	698	1,734	855
1983	5,223	1,910	698	1,755	860
1984	5,198	1,880	694	1,749	874
1985	5,210	1,864	693	1,760	893
1986	5,300	1,865	706	1,792	937
1987	5,432	1,882	723	1,854	973
1988	5,546	1,910	722	1,932	982
1989	5,694	1,938	743	1,996	1,017
1990[1]	5,923	2,011	809	2,017	1,086
Middle alternative projections					
1991	5,993	2,010	831	2,034	1,118
1992	6,045	2,013	846	2,047	1,139

[Continued]

★ 249 ★

Total Enrollment in Public 4-Year Institutions of Higher Education by Sex and Attendance Status, with Alternative Projections, Fall 1977 to Fall 2002

[Continued]

Year	Total	Men		Women	
		Full-time	Part-time	Full-time	Part-time
1993	6,088	2,005	857	2,062	1,164
1994	6,139	2,002	864	2,085	1,188
1995	6,175	1,999	872	2,104	1,200
1996	6,247	2,017	882	2,136	1,212
1997	6,320	2,031	885	2,180	1,224
1998	6,434	2,067	886	2,246	1,235
1999	6,539	2,100	888	2,306	1,245
2000	6,646	2,132	888	2,372	1,254
2001	6,727	2,164	889	2,413	1,261
2002	6,803	2,191	889	2,456	1,267
Low alternative projections					
1991	5,746	1,937	787	1,940	1,082
1992	5,742	1,928	789	1,932	1,093
1993	5,758	1,918	794	1,938	1,108
1994	5,770	1,904	796	1,948	1,122
1995	5,809	1,897	798	1,977	1,137
1996	5,872	1,905	801	2,013	1,153
1997	5,955	1,918	806	2,063	1,168
1998	6,059	1,947	809	2,121	1,182
1999	6,165	1,974	814	2,182	1,195
2000	6,281	2,001	817	2,255	1,208
2001	6,371	2,031	821	2,301	1,218
2002	6,461	2,057	825	2,352	1,227
High alternative projections					
1991	6,306	2,075	847	2,229	1,155
1992	6,467	2,111	868	2,308	1,180
1993	6,533	2,119	892	2,313	1,209
1994	6,587	2,138	911	2,304	1,234
1995	6,612	2,125	932	2,312	1,243
1996	6,715	2,177	953	2,330	1,255
1997	6,800	2,201	975	2,358	1,266
1998	6,926	2,252	994	2,404	1,276
1999	7,055	2,302	1,012	2,454	1,287
2000	7,186	2,345	1,031	2,513	1,297
2001	7,291	2,396	1,047	2,545	1,303
2002	7,394	2,439	1,066	2,579	1,310

Source: Projections of Education Statistics to 2002, U.S. Department of Education, Office of Educational Research and Improvement, December, 1991, p. 35. Primary source: U.S. Department of Education, National Center for Education Statistics, Fall Enrollment in Colleges and Universities surveys and Integrated Postsecondary Education Data System (IPEDS) surveys. Projections are based on data through 1989 and include all 50 States and Washington, D.C. Because of rounding, details may not add to totals. *Note:* 1. Projected.

★ 250 ★

Undergraduate Enrollment in All Institutions of Higher Education by Sex and Attendance Status, with Alternative Projections, Fall 1977 to Fall 2002

Prepared April 1991. "Under the low alternative, college enrollment is projected to increase from an estimated 13.9 million in 1990 to 15.2 million by the year 2002....This alternative assumes that enrollment rates will either remain the same as the middle alternative or increase at a slower rate. Under the high alternative, college enrollment is expected to increase from an estimated 13.9 million in 1990 to 17.4 million by the year 2002....This high level is expected to be maintained during the 1990s and beyond if the enrollment rates remain well above their 1990 levels."

[Numbers in thousands]

Year	Total	Men		Women	
		Full-time	Part-time	Full-time	Part-time
1977	9,717	3,188	1,709	2,906	1,914
1978	9,691	3,072	1,694	2,895	2,030
1979	9,998	3,087	1,734	2,993	2,185
1980	10,475	3,227	1,773	3,135	2,340
1981	10,755	3,261	1,848	3,188	2,458
1982	10,825	3,299	1,871	3,184	2,470
1983	10,846	3,304	1,854	3,210	2,478
1984	10,618	3,195	1,812	3,153	2,459
1985	10,597	3,156	1,806	3,163	2,471
1986	10,798	3,146	1,871	3,206	2,575
1987	11,046	3,164	1,905	3,299	2,677
1988	11,317	3,206	1,931	3,436	2,743
1989	11,666	3,267	2,011	3,542	2,846
1990[1]	11,969	3,387	2,061	3,566	2,955
Middle alternative projections					
1991	12,084	3,365	2,112	3,579	3,028
1992	12,165	3,357	2,1	3,589	3,076
1993	12,247	3,335	2,163	3,609	3,140
1994	12,356	3,331	2,175	3,652	3,198
1995	12,449	3,327	2,196	3,693	3,233
1996	12,610	3,363	2,219	3,759	3,269
1997	12,768	3,388	2,230	3,842	3,308
1998	12,998	3,452	2,242	3,960	3,344
1999	13,216	3,511	2,255	4,069	3,381
2000	13,436	3,565	2,265	4,188	3,418
2001	13,598	3,619	2,275	4,260	3,444
2002	13,748	3,661	2,286	4,333	3,468
Low alternative projections					
1991	11,614	3,234	2,008	3,434	2,938
1992	11,593	3,210	2,012	3,409	2,962
1993	11,622	3,184	2,018	3,418	3,002
1994	11,665	3,165	2,022	3,441	3,037
1995	11,764	3,158	2,028	3,498	3,080
1996	11,912	3,179	2,039	3,571	3,123
1997	12,090	3,205	2,055	3,663	3,167
1998	12,311	3,260	2,068	3,770	3,213
1999	12,535	3,308	2,089	3,880	3,258

[Continued]

★ 250 ★

Undergraduate Enrollment in All Institutions of Higher Education by Sex and Attendance Status, with Alternative Projections, Fall 1977 to Fall 2002

[Continued]

Year	Total	Men		Women	
		Full-time	Part-time	Full-time	Part-time
2000	12,776	3,357	2,106	4,009	3,304
2001	12,960	3,408	2,124	4,089	3,339
2002	13,136	3,450	2,141	4,175	3,370
High alternative projections					
1991	12,666	3,474	2,153	3,910	3,129
1992	12,942	3,523	2,203	4,028	3,188
1993	13,064	3,523	2,255	4,027	3,259
1994	13,185	3,550	2,297	4,017	3,321
1995	13,246	3,513	2,349	4,035	3,349
1996	13,479	3,616	2,403	4,079	3,381
1997	13,662	3,653	2,458	4,133	3,418
1998	13,923	3,738	2,509	4,222	3,454
1999	14,185	3,821	2,561	4,312	3,491
2000	14,451	3,892	2,613	4,416	3,530
2001	14,658	3,972	2,659	4,472	3,555
2002	14,855	4,035	2,712	4,525	3,583

Source: Projections of Education Statistics to 2002, U.S. Department of Education, Office of Educational Research and Improvement, December, 1991, p. 39. Primary source: U.S. Department of Education, National Center for Education Statistics, Fall Enrollment in Colleges and Universities surveys and Integrated Postsecondary Education Data System (IPEDS) surveys. Projections are based on data through 1989 and include all 50 States and Washington, D.C. Because of rounding, details may not add to totals. *Note:* 1. Projected.

★ 251 ★

Undergraduate Enrollment in Private Institutions of Higher Education by Sex and Attendance Status, with Alternative Projections, Fall 1977 to Fall 2002

Prepared April 1991. "Under the low alternative, college enrollment is projected to increase from an estimated 13.9 million in 1990 to 15.2 million by the year 2002....This alternative assumes that enrollment rates will either remain the same as the middle alternative or increase at a slower rate. Under the high alternative, college enrollment is expected to increase from an estimated 13.9 million in 1990 to 17.4 million by the year 2002....This high level is expected to be maintained during the 1990s and beyond if the enrollment rates remain well above their 1990 levels."

[Numbers in thousands]

Year	Total	Men		Women	
		Full-time	Part-time	Full-time	Part-time
1977	1,872	775	184	708	205
1978	1,905	770	184	734	217
1979	1,951	772	184	762	233
1980	2,033	800	185	801	246
1981	2,106	809	209	816	272

[Continued]

★ 251 ★

Undergraduate Enrollment in Private Institutions of Higher Education by Sex and Attendance Status, with Alternative Projections, Fall 1977 to Fall 2002

[Continued]

Year	Total	Men		Women	
		Full-time	Part-time	Full-time	Part-time
1982	2,112	812	219	811	270
1983	2,149	823	219	824	283
1984	2,124	805	212	827	280
1985	2,120	800	210	832	278
1986	2,137	796	219	839	284
1987	2,128	788	204	850	286
1988	2,213	807	217	886	304
1989	2,241	804	230	892	315
1990[1]	2,323	843	239	912	329
Middle alternative projections					
1991	2,337	838	245	916	338
1992	2,347	837	248	918	344
1993	2,355	831	251	921	352
1994	2,369	829	252	931	357
1995	2,384	827	255	941	361
1996	2,414	835	257	957	365
1997	2,446	841	257	979	369
1998	2,497	856	259	1,010	372
1999	2,546	871	260	1,039	376
2000	2,595	884	260	1,071	380
2001	2,629	898	260	1,089	382
2002	2,664	909	262	1,109	384
Low alternative projections					
1991	2,244	806	232	879	327
1992	2,236	801	233	872	330
1993	2,236	794	233	874	335
1994	2,240	789	234	879	338
1995	2,256	786	234	893	343
1996	2,285	791	235	911	348
1997	2,321	797	237	935	352
1998	2,367	811	237	962	357
1999	2,415	823	240	991	361
2000	2,468	835	241	1,026	366
2001	2,508	848	243	1,047	370
2002	2,545	859	244	1,070	372
High alternative projections					
1991	2,466	865	250	1,002	349
1992	2,523	878	256	1,032	357
1993	2,534	878	262	1,029	365
1994	2,549	884	267	1,026	372
1995	2,553	875	273	1,030	375
1996	2,596	899	279	1,040	378
1997	2,629	908	285	1,054	382
1998	2,682	928	291	1,077	386

[Continued]

★ 251 ★

Undergraduate Enrollment in Private Institutions of Higher Education by Sex and Attendance Status, with Alternative Projections, Fall 1977 to Fall 2002

[Continued]

Year	Total	Men		Women	
		Full-time	Part-time	Full-time	Part-time
1999	2,735	949	297	1,100	389
2000	2,790	967	302	1,128	393
2001	2,833	988	307	1,143	395
2002	2,872	1,004	313	1,157	398

Source: Projections of Education Statistics to 2002, U.S. Department of Education, Office of Educational Research and Improvement, December, 1991, p. 41. Primary source: U.S. Department of Education, National Center for Education Statistics, Fall Enrollment in Colleges and Universities surveys and Integrated Postsecondary Education Data System (IPEDS) surveys. Projections are based on data through 1989 and include all 50 States and Washington, D.C. Because of rounding, details may not add to totals. *Note:* 1. Projected.

★ 252 ★

Undergraduate Enrollment in Public Institutions of Higher Education by Sex and Attendance Status, with Alternative Projections, Fall 1977 to Fall 2002

Prepared April 1991. "Under the low alternative, college enrollment is projected to increase from an estimated 13.9 million in 1990 to 15.2 million by the year 2002....This alternative assumes that enrollment rates will either remain the same as the middle alternative or increase at a slower rate. Under the high alternative, college enrollment is expected to increase from an estimated 13.9 million in 1990 to 17.4 million by the year 2002....This high level is expected to be maintained during the 1990s and beyond if the enrollment rates remain well above their 1990 levels."

[Numbers in thousands]

Year	Total	Men		Women	
		Full-time	Part-time	Full-time	Part-time
1977	7,842	2,413	1,524	2,197	1,708
1978	7,786	2,302	1,510	2,161	1,813
1979	8,046	2,316	1,551	2,229	1,952
1980	8,441	2,426	1,588	2,334	2,093
1981	8,648	2,452	1,639	2,373	2,185
1982	8,713	2,487	1,653	2,373	2,201
1983	8,697	2,482	1,635	2,385	2,195
1984	8,494	2,390	1,600	2,325	2,179
1985	8,478	2,357	1,596	2,331	2,193
1986	8,661	2,351	1,652	2,367	2,291
1987	8,919	2,375	1,701	2,449	2,393
1988	9,103	2,399	1,714	2,550	2,439
1989	9,425	2,463	1,781	2,650	2,531
1990[1]	9,646	2,544	1,822	2,654	2,626
Middle alternative projections					
1991	9,747	2,527	1,867	2,663	2,690
1992	9,818	2,520	1,895	2,671	2,732

[Continued]

★ 252 ★

Undergraduate Enrollment in Public Institutions of Higher Education by Sex and Attendance Status, with Alternative Projections, Fall 1977 to Fall 2002

[Continued]

Year	Total	Men		Women	
		Full-time	Part-time	Full-time	Part-time
1993	9,892	2,504	1,912	2,688	2,788
1994	9,987	2,502	1,923	2,721	2,841
1995	10,065	2,500	1,941	2,752	2,872
1996	10,196	2,528	1,962	2,802	2,904
1997	10,322	2,547	1,973	2,863	2,939
1998	10,501	2,596	1,983	2,950	2,972
1999	10,670	2,640	1,995	3,030	3,005
2000	10,841	2,681	2,005	3,117	3,038
2001	10,969	2,721	2,015	3,171	3,062
2002	11,084	2,752	2,024	3,224	3,084
Low alternative projections					
1991	9,370	2,428	1,776	2,555	2,611
1992	9,357	2,409	1,779	2,537	2,632
1993	9,386	2,390	1,785	2,544	2,667
1994	9,425	2,376	1,788	2,562	2,699
1995	9,508	2,372	1,794	2,605	2,737
1996	9,627	2,388	1,804	2,660	2,775
1997	9,769	2,408	1,818	2,728	2,815
1998	9,944	2,449	1,831	2,808	2,856
1999	10,120	2,485	1,849	2,889	2,897
2000	10,308	2,522	1,865	2,983	2,938
2001	10,452	2,560	1,881	3,042	2,969
2002	10,591	2,591	1,897	3,105	2,998
High alternative projections					
1991	10,200	2,609	1,903	2,908	2,780
1992	10,419	2,645	1,947	2,996	2,831
1993	10,530	2,645	1,993	2,998	2,894
1994	10,636	2,666	2,030	2,991	2,949
1995	10,693	2,638	2,076	3,005	2,974
1996	10,883	2,717	2,124	3,039	3,003
1997	11,033	2,745	2,173	3,079	3,036
1998	11,241	2,810	2,218	3,145	3,068
1999	11,450	2,872	2,264	3,212	3,102
2000	11,661	2,925	2,311	3,288	3,137
2001	11,825	2,984	2,352	3,329	3,160
2002	11,983	3,031	2,399	3,368	3,185

Source: Projections of Education Statistics to 2002, U.S. Department of Education, Office of Educational Research and Improvement, December, 1991, p. 40. Primary source: U.S. Department of Education, National Center for Education Statistics, Fall Enrollment in Colleges and Universities surveys and Integrated Postsecondary Education Data System (IPEDS) surveys. Projections are based on data through 1989 and include all 50 States and Washington, D.C. Because of rounding, details may not add to totals. *Note:* 1. Projected.

Teachers

★ 253 ★

Annual Demand for Newly Hired Teachers in the Public School System, 1990-2000

"Trends in Education: Class-size policies, school enrollment projections, and the expected attrition of the aging teacher force will be major factors determining the numbers of new teachers required to staff the nation's schools. The supply of newly graduated teaching candidates is expected to satisfy only about 60% of the 'new hire' demand [through 2001]. By 1995, most states will implement alternative routes to certification ... as a solution to teacher shortages, especially in the sciences."

[Numbers in thousands]

1990	230
1995	220
2000	245

Source: "Appendix A: Seventy-Five Trends in Education," *Educational Renaissance: Our Schools at the Turn of the Century,* Marvin J. Cetron and Margaret Evans Gayle, (c) 1991, St. Martin's Press, Inc., New York, 1991, p. 225. Copyright (c) 1991 by Marvin Cetron and Margaret Gayle. Parameters estimated from published graph. Source also contains additional data for 1989, 1991-1994, and 1996-1999.

★ 254 ★

Average Annual Percent Rate of Growth in Numbers of Classroom Teachers, 1977-2002

Between 1990 and 2002, the number of classroom teachers is projected to rise primarily due to the increase in school enrollment. The number of secondary school teachers will increase at a faster rate than that of elementary teachers. The numbers of public and private teachers will grow at similar rates. Percentages shown represent Middle Alternative projections. "Three alternative projections of the numbers of classroom teachers were developed to indicate a range of possible outcomes. These alternatives are based on different assumptions about the growth paths for two of the key variables in the teacher model—disposable personal income per capita and local education revenue receipts from state governments per capita. Under the middle alternative, disposable personal income per capita is projected to increase by 16 percent between 1990 and 2002, while local education revenue receipts from state governments per capita will rise by 21 percent during this period."

	1977-84	1984-90	Projected	
			1990-96	1996-2002
Total	0.1	1.5	1.6	1.3
Elementary	0.7	2.0	1.4	1.2
Secondary	-0.7	0.8	1.9	1.4
Public	-0.3	1.6	1.6	1.3
Private	2.9	0.6	1.5	1.3

Source: "Classroom Teachers," *Projections of Education Statistics to 2002*, U.S. Department of Education, Office of Educational Research and Improvement, National Center for Education Statistics, December 1991, p. 67. Primary source: *Projections of Education Statistics to 2002*, December 1991, p. 189, Table B5 and p. 190, Table B6.

★ 255 ★

Average Annual Percent Rate of Growth in Numbers of Classroom Teachers by Control of Institution, 1977-2002

Percentages shown for 1990-96 and 1996-2002 represent Middle Alternative projections. "Three alternative projections of the numbers of classroom teachers were developed to indicate a range of possible outcomes. These alternatives are based on different assumptions about the growth paths for two of the key variables in the teacher model-disposable personal income per capita is projected to increase by 16 percent between 1990 and 2002, while local education revenue receipts from state government per capita will rise by 21 percent during this period."

[Numbers in percentages]

	Public	Private
1977-1984	-0.3	2.9
1984-1990	1.6	0.6
1990-1996	1.6	1.5
1996-2002	1.3	1.3

Source: "Classroom Teachers," *Projections of Education Statistics to 2002*, U.S. Department of Education, Office of Educational Research and Improvement, National Center for Education Statistics, December 1991, p. 73, Fig. 46.

★ 256 ★

Numbers of Classroom Teachers in Elementary and Secondary Schools by Control of Institutions and by Level of Institution, with Alternative Projections, Fall 1977 to Fall 2002

Prepared April 1991. The numbers of elementary and secondary teachers reported separately by the National Education Association were prorated to the NCES totals for each year. Projections are based on data through 1989. Because of rounding, details may not add to totals. The economic climate of the nation and the amount of revenue receipts from state government to local government for education are important factors in determining the level of spending on elementary and secondary education.

[Numbers in thousands]

Year	Total			Public			Private		
	K-12	Elementary	Secondary	K-12	Elementary	Secondary	K-12	Elementary	Secondary
Middle alternative projections									
1990[1]	2,744	1,632	1,112	2,391	1,379	1,012	353	253	100
1991	2,826	1,631	1,194	2,465	1,378	1,087	360	253	107
1992	2,791	1,645	1,146	2,433	1,389	1,043	358	255	103
1993	2,847	1,674	1,173	2,482	1,414	1,067	365	260	105
1994	2,902	1,704	1,198	2,530	1,439	1,090	372	264	108
1995	2,958	1,736	1,222	2,579	1,467	1,112	379	269	110
1996	3,015	1,770	1,245	2,628	1,495	1,133	387	275	112
1997	3,066	1,799	1,267	2,673	1,520	1,153	393	279	114

[Continued]

★ 256 ★

Numbers of Classroom Teachers in Elementary and Secondary Schools by Control of Institutions and by Level of Institution, with Alternative Projections, Fall 1977 to Fall 2002

[Continued]

Year	Total			Public			Private		
	K-12	Elementary	Secondary	K-12	Elementary	Secondary	K-12	Elementary	Secondary
1998	3,107	1,824	1,283	2,709	1,541	1,167	398	283	115
1999	3,145	1,846	1,299	2,742	1,559	1,182	403	286	117
2000	3,181	1,866	1,316	2,774	1,576	1,198	408	289	118
2001	3,217	1,884	1,333	2,805	1,592	1,213	412	292	120
2002	3,254	1,903	1,351	2,838	1,608	1,230	417	295	122

Low alternative projections

Year	K-12	Elementary	Secondary	K-12	Elementary	Secondary	K-12	Elementary	Secondary
1991	2,825	1,631	1,194	2,465	1,378	1,087	360	253	107
1992	2,785	1,639	1,146	2,428	1,385	1,043	357	254	103
1993	2,831	1,662	1,170	2,469	1,404	1,064	363	258	105
1994	2,878	1,686	1,192	2,509	1,424	1,085	369	261	107
1995	2,925	1,713	1,212	2,550	1,447	1,103	375	266	109
1996	2,974	1,742	1,232	2,593	1,471	1,121	381	270	111
1997	3,015	1,764	1,251	2,629	1,490	1,139	386	274	113
1998	3,049	1,784	1,265	2,658	1,507	1,151	390	277	114
1999	3,079	1,801	1,278	2,685	1,521	1,163	394	279	115
2000	3,109	1,817	1,292	2,711	1,535	1,176	398	282	116
2001	3,137	1,830	1,306	2,725	1,547	1,189	401	284	117
2002	3,167	1,843	1,324	2,762	1,557	1,205	405	286	119

High alternative projections

Year	K-12	Elementary	Secondary	K-12	Elementary	Secondary	K-12	Elementary	Secondary
1991	2,836	1,639	1,196	2,474	1,385	1,089	362	254	108
1992	2,802	1,654	1,148	2,442	1,397	1,045	360	257	103
1993	2,862	1,687	1,176	2,495	1,425	1,070	367	262	106
1994	2,927	1,724	1,203	2,552	1,456	1,095	376	267	108
1995	2,991	1,764	1,227	2,607	1,490	1,117	384	274	110
1996	3,056	1,803	1,253	2,664	1,524	1,140	392	280	113
1997	3,118	1,838	1,280	2,718	1,553	1,164	400	285	115
1998	3,171	1,868	1,302	2,764	1,578	1,185	407	290	117
1999	3,217	1,893	1,324	2,804	1,600	1,205	413	294	119
2000	3,263	1,919	1,343	2,844	1,622	1,222	419	298	121
2001	3,304	1,944	1,360	2,881	1,643	1,238	424	302	122
2002	3,348	1,969	1,379	2,919	1,664	1,255	430	305	124

Source: "Classroom Teachers," *Projections of Education Statistics to 2002*, U.S. Department of Education, Office of Educational Research and Improvement, National Center for Education Statistics, December 1991, p. 75, Table 32. Primary source: U.S. Department of Education, National Center for Education Statistics, *Statistics of Public Elementary and Secondary Schools*; Common Core of Data surveys; "Selected Public and Private Elementary and Secondary Education Statistics," *NCES Bulletin*, October 23, 1979; "Private Elementary and Secondary Education, 1983: Enrollment, Teachers, and Schools," *NCES Bulletin*, December 1984; 1985 Private School Survey; Key Statistics for Private Elementary and Secondary Education: School Year 1988-89," *Early Estimates*; and "Key Statistics for Public and Private Elementary and Secondary Education: School Year 1989-90," *Early Estimates*; Key Statistics for Public and Private Elementary and Secondary Education: School Year 1990-91," *Early Estimates*. Source also contains data for 1977-1989. *Note*: 1. Estimate.

★ 257 ★

Pupil-Teacher Ratios in Elementary and Secondary Schools by Control of Institution and by Level with Alternative Projections, Fall 1977 to Fall 2002

Prepared April 1991. The pupil-teacher ratios were derived from *Projections of Education Statistics to 2002*, December 1991, p. 10, Table 2 and p. 7, Table 3. Some data have been revised from previously published figures. Projections are based on data through 1989. Because of rounding, details may not add to totals. "Three alternative projections of the numbers of classroom teachers were developed to indicate a range of possible outcomes. These alternatives are based on different assumptions about the growth paths for two of the key variables in the teacher model-disposable personal income per capita and local education revenue receipts from state governments per capita."

Year	Total		Public		Private	
	Elementary	Secondary	Elementary	Secondary	Elementary	Secondary
1990[1]	18.2	14.9	18.6	15.2	16.1	11.3
Middle alternative projections						
1991	18.4	14.0	18.8	14.4	16.3	10.6
1992	18.5	15.0	18.9	15.3	16.4	11.2
1993	18.4	15.0	18.8	15.4	16.4	11.3
1994	18.3	15.1	18.6	15.5	16.3	11.4
1995	18.1	15.2	18.5	15.6	16.1	11.5
1996	18.0	15.2	18.3	15.6	16.0	11.6
1997	17.8	15.2	18.2	15.5	15.8	11.6
1998	17.7	15.1	18.1	15.5	15.8	11.5
1999	17.6	15.1	18.0	15.4	15.7	11.5
2000	17.5	15.0	17.9	15.3	15.6	11.4
2001	17.4	14.9	17.7	15.3	15.5	11.4
2002	17.2	15.0	17.6	15.3	15.4	11.4
Low alternative projections (Based on high alternative projections of teachers)						
1991	18.3	14.0	18.7	14.4	16.2	10.6
1992	18.4	14.9	18.8	15.3	16.3	11.2
1993	18.3	15.0	18.6	15.3	16.2	11.2
1994	18.1	15.1	18.4	15.4	16.1	11.4
1995	17.8	15.1	18.2	15.5	15.9	11.5
1996	17.6	15.1	18.0	15.5	15.7	11.6
1997	17.5	15.0	17.8	15.4	15.5	11.5
1998	17.3	14.9	17.7	15.2	15.4	11.4
1999	17.2	14.8	17.5	15.1	15.3	11.3
2000	17.0	14.7	17.4	15.0	15.2	11.2
2001	16.9	14.6	17.2	15.0	15.0	11.1
2002	16.6	14.7	17.0	15.0	14.9	11.2
High alternative projections (Based on low alternative projections of teachers)						
1991	18.4	14.0	18.8	14.4	16.3	10.6
1992	18.6	15.0	19.0	15.3	16.5	11.3
1993	18.5	15.1	18.9	15.4	16.5	11.3
1994	18.5	15.2	18.8	15.6	16.4	11.5

[Continued]

★ 257 ★

Pupil-Teacher Ratios in Elementary and Secondary Schools by Control of Institution and by Level with Alternative Projections, Fall 1977 to Fall 2002
[Continued]

Year	Total		Public		Private	
	Elementary	Secondary	Elementary	Secondary	Elementary	Secondary
1995	18.4	15.3	18.7	15.7	16.4	11.6
1996	18.3	15.4	18.6	15.7	16.2	11.7
1997	18.2	15.4	18.6	15.7	16.2	11.8
1998	18.1	15.3	18.5	15.7	16.1	11.7
1999	18.1	15.3	18.4	15.7	16.1	11.7
2000	18.0	15.3	18.4	15.6	16.0	11.6
2001	17.9	15.2	18.3	15.6	16.0	11.6
2002	17.8	15.3	18.1	15.6	15.9	11.6

Source: "Classroom Teachers," *Projections of Education Statistics to 2002*, U.S. Department of Education, Office of Educational Research and Improvement, National Center for Education Statistics, December 1991, p. 75, Table 32. Primary source: U.S. Department of Education, National Center for Education Statistics, *Statistics of Public Elementary and Secondary Schools*; Common Core of Data surveys; "Selected Public and Private Elementary and Secondary Education Statistics," *NCES Bulletin*, October 23, 1979; "Private Elementary and Secondary Education, 1983: Enrollment, Teachers, and Schools," *NCES Bulletin*, December 1984; 1985 Private School Survey; "Key Statistics for Private Elementary and Secondary Education: School Year 1988-89," *Early Estimates*; and "Key Statistics for Public and Private Elementary and Secondary Education: School Year 1989-90," *Early Estimates*; and "Key Statistics for Public and Private Elementary and Secondary Education: School Year 1990-91," *Early Estimates*. Source also contains data for 1977-1989. *Note*: 1. Estimate.

Chapter 6
ENVIRONMENTAL ISSUES AND NATURAL RESOURCES

Costs of Environmental Protection

★ 258 ★

Average Annual Household Payments for Environmental Services for a Sample of 8,032 Cities, Towns, and Townships, 1987 and 2000

"If current trends continue, the average household will spend $647 a year by the year 2000 for environmental services including drinking water, wastewater treatment, and solid waste management. This is 54 percent more than the average household payment for such services in 1987. The largest increment, $599 a year in 2000, is attributable to simply maintaining the current level of environmental and service standards. The average annual cost of complying with new regulations is estimated to be an additional $48."

[Numbers in 1988 dollars]

City size	Average payments in 1987	Additional payments to maintain current levels of environmental quality in 2000	Additional payments to comply with new environmental and service standards in 2000	Total estimated household payments for environmental protection in 2000
500 or less	670	593	317	1,580
500-2,500	473	223	67	763
2,500-10,000	433	143	29	605
10,000-50,000	444	197	24	665
50,000-100,000	373	142	24	539
100,000-250,000	291	111	34	436
250,000-500,000	335	126	68	529

[Continued]

★ 258 ★

Average Annual Household Payments for Environmental Services for a Sample of 8,032 Cities, Towns, and Townships, 1987 and 2000

[Continued]

City size	Average payments in 1987	Additional payments to maintain current levels of environmental quality in 2000	Additional payments to comply with new environmental and service standards in 2000	Total estimated household payments for environmental protection in 2000
500,000 or more	393	140	93	626
Population weighted average	419	180	48	647

Source: A Preliminary Analysis of the Public Costs of Environmental Protection: 1981-2000, Environmental Protection Agency, May, 1990, p. 30. Primary source: Apogee Research, from U.S. Bureau of Census, 1986 Survey of Community Water Systems, and data compiled by the Environmental Law Institute from EPA Regulatory Impact Analyses. The terms expenditures, spending, and outlays are used interchangeably in this report, which examines two kinds of expenditures: (1) federal, state, and local spending to maintain current levels of environmental quality and (2) local spending to comply with new regulations. Costs of new regulations, which were derived from Regulatory Impact Analyses (RIAs) prepared for EPA program offices in 1988, include only those for local governments. Full compliance is assumed in estimating costs of new regulations. The future costs of maintaining current levels of environmental quality were estimated for each program area and level of government by regressing five years of historical spending trends against time. The projections assume that factors contributing to recent spending trends will continue to do so in the future. Such factors include population growth, implementation of current policies, rates of compliance, replacement of current capital facilities, and budget cutbacks. Significant changes in any of these factors could have an important effect on costs.

★ 259 ★

Comparison of EPA and Local Government Capital Expenditures, 1981-2000

"Local demands for capital are expected to increase by 97 percent between 1987 and 2000. Concurrently, EPA's capital grants for local environmental services are scheduled to end by 1995. To a large extent, the substitution of local for federal capital results from the phasing-out of EPA construction grants for wastewater treatment facilities. Capital grants are expected to decline from 4.5 billion in 1981 to zero when grants to capitalize state wastewater treatment revolving funds expire in 1994."

[Numbers in millions of 1988 dollars]

Year	EPA capital outlays	Local capital outlays
1981	$4,511	$8,374
1982	$4,071	$6,877
1983	$3,250	$7,883
1984	$2,848	$7,853
1985	$3,126	$8,650
1986	$3,258	$9,810
1987	$2,967	$9,547

[Continued]

★ 259 ★

Comparison of EPA and Local Government Capital Expenditures, 1981-2000
[Continued]

Year	EPA capital outlays	Local capital outlays
1988	$2,566	$12,461
1989	$2,362	$16,260
1990	$2,325	$16,683
1991	$2,288	$19,829
1992	$1,689	$22,004
1993	$1,108	$17,905
1994	$545	$17,983
1995	$0	$17,635
1996	$0	$17,934
1997	$0	$18,859
1998	$0	$18,736
1999	$0	$19,982
2000	$0	$18,696

Source: A Preliminary Analysis of the Public Costs of Environmental Protection: 1981-2000, Environmental Protection Agency, May, 1990, p. 55. Primary source: Apogee Research, from U.S. Bureau of the Census, Government Finances (various years); Bureau of Economic Analysis, Pollution Abatement and Control Expenditures (various years), U.S. EPA, Justification of Appropriation Estimates for Committee on Appropriations (various years). and data prepared by the Environmental Law Institute from Regulatory Impact Analyses for the water quality and solid waste programs. Costs of new regulations for the water quality program are the preliminary analysis for the "Estimates of the Total Benefit and Total Costs Associated with the 1986 Amendments to the Safe Drinking Water Act," November, 1989. The terms expenditures, spending, and outlays are used interchangeably in this report, which examines two kinds of expenditures: (1) federal, state and local spending to maintain current levels of environmental quality and (2) local spending to comply with new regulations. Costs of new regulations, which were derived from Regulatory Impact Analyses (RIAs) prepared for EPA program offices in 1988, include only those for local governments. Full compliance is assumed in estimating costs of new regulations. The future costs of maintaining current levels of environmental quality were estimated for each program area and level of government by regressing five years of historical spending trends against time. The projections assume that factors contributing to recent spending trends will continue to do so in the future. Such factors include population growth, implementation of current policies, rates of compliance, replacement of current capital facilities, and budget cutbacks. Significant changes in any of these factors could have an important effect on costs.

★ 260 ★

Cost of Environmental Protection Per Household as a Percentage of Household Income by City Size, 1987 and 2000

"The difference in costs between households based on city size is ... dramatic when examined as a percentage of household income. For the smallest cities, with lower household income and higher costs per household, the cost of environmental protection as a percentage of household income will increase from 2.8 percent in 1987 to 5.6 percent in 2000. For medium-sized cities the percentage is expected to change slightly during the period 1987-2000, from 1.0 to 1.2 percent, and in large cities, to change from 1.1 to 1.5 percent."

[Numbers in 1988 dollars]

City size	1987			2000		
	Average household costs of environmental programs	Average household income	Cost as a percentage of household income	Average household cost of environmental programs[1]	Average household income	Cost as a percentage household income
500 or less	$670	$24,277	2.8%	$1,580	$28,357	5.6%
500 - 2,500	$473	$26,361	1.8%	$763	$30,792	2.5%
2,500 - 10,000	$433	$30,546	1.4%	$605	$35,680	1.7%
10,000 - 50,000	$444	$31,685	1.4%	$665	$37,010	1.8%
50,000 - 100,000	$373	$37,189	1.0%	$539	$43,440	1.2%
100,000 - 250,000	$291	$33,769	0.9%	$436	$39,445	1.1%
250,000 - 500,000	$335	$31,943	1.0%	$529	$37,312	1.4%
500,000 or more	$393	$34,756	1.1%	$626	$40,597	1.5%
Population weighted average	$419	$31,617	1.3%	$647	$36,931	1.8%

Source: A Preliminary Analysis of the Public Costs of Environmental Protection: 1981-2000, Environmental Protection Agency, May, 1990, p. 32. Primary source: Apogee Research from U.S. Bureau of the Census, 1986 Survey of Community Water Systems, and data compiled by the Environmental Law Institute from EPA Regulatory Impact Analyses. The terms expenditures, spending, and outlays are used interchangeably in this report, which examines two kinds of expenditures: (1) federal, state and local spending to maintain current levels of environmental quality and (2) local spending to comply with new regulations. Costs of new regulations, which were derived from Regulatory Impact Analyses (RIAs) prepared for EPA program offices in 1988, include only those for local governments. Full compliance is assumed in estimating costs of new regulations. The future costs of maintaining current levels of environmental quality were estimated for each program area and level of government by regressing five years of historical spending trends against time. The projections assume that factors contributing to recent spending trends will continue to do so in the future. Such factors include population growth, implementation of current policies, rates of compliance, replacement of current capital facilities, and budget cutbacks. Significant changes in any of these factors could have an important effect on costs. 1. Includes cost of maintaining 1987 levels of environmental quality plus costs of new regulations.

★ 261 ★

Cost of Restoration of Prince William Sound and Gulf of Alaska after Exxon Valdez Oil Spill, 1992-2001

Numbers represent federal offsetting collections.

[Dollars in millions]

	1992	1993	1994	1995-2001	Total
Criminal fines and restitution	62	-	-	-	62
Civil restoration	18	45	45	250	358
Total	80	45	45	250	420

Source: Budget of the United States Government, Fiscal Year 1993, section 10, part 1, p. 213.

★ 262 ★

Distribution of Public Expenditures to Maintain 1987 Levels of Environmental Quality, 1987 and 2000

"Spending in some programs...will increase more substantially than in others. Spending for drinking water and solid waste programs will increase as a percentage of total spending; water quality expenditures will decrease as a percentage of the total."

	1987	2000
Water quality	41.0	46.0
Drinking water	38.0	40.0
Solid waste	15.0	15.0
Air	2.0	3.0
Others	4.0	7.0
Billion $	40.0	55.0

Source: *A Preliminary Analysis of the Public Costs of Environmental Protection: 1981-2000*, Environmental Protection Agency, May, 1990, p. 5. Primary source: U.S. Bureau of the Census, *Government Finances* (various years); Bureau of Economic Analysis, *Pollution Abatement and Control Expenditures* (various years); Bureau of the Census, *Pollution Abatement Cost and Expenditure Survey* (various years); and U.S. EPA, *Justification of Appropriation Estimates for Committee on Appropriations* (various years). Original chart also includes expenditures for 1981. The terms expenditures, spending, and outlays are used interchangeably in this report, which examines two kinds of expenditures: (1) federal, state, and local spending to maintain current levels of environmental quality and (2) local spending to comply with new regulations. Costs of new regulations, which were derived from Regulatory Impact Analyses (RIAs) prepared for EPA program offices in 1988, include only those for local governments. Full compliance is assumed in estimating costs of new regulations. The future costs of maintaining current levels of environmental quality were estimated for each program area and level of government by regressing five years of historical spending trends against time. The projections assume that factors contributing to recent spending trends will continue to do so in the future. Such factors include population growth, implementation of current policies, rates of compliance, replacement of current capital facilities, and budget cutbacks. Significant changes in any of these factors could have an important effect on costs. Public expenditures comprise EPA, State, and local government spendishown in 1988 dollars. Includes costs to delivery services.

★ 263 ★

EPA, State, and Local Government Expenditures to Maintain Current Levels of Environmental Quality by Media, 1981-2000

"With the exception of the air quality program, expenditures to maintain [1988] levels of environmental quality have steadily increased in the 1980s and are expected to continue to do so in the 1990s. Rapid growth for spending for 'other' environmental programs is attributable largely to steady increases in Superfund program activities."

[Numbers in millions of 1988 dollars]

Year	Air	DW	WQ	SW	Others	Total
1981	887	12,253	15,647	4,984	837	34,608
1987	896	15,002	16,339	6,056	1,456	39,749
2000	867	21,906	20,339	8,336	3,873	55,320

Source: A Preliminary Analysis of the Public Costs of Environmental Protection: 1981-2000, Environment Protection Agency, May, 1990, p. 48. Primary source: U.S. Bureau of the Census, *Government Finances* (various years); Bureau of Economic Analysis, *Pollution Abatement and Control Expenditures* (various years); Bureau of the Census, *Pollution Abatement Costs and Expenditure Survey* (various years); and U.S. EPA, *Justification of Appropriation Estimates for Committee on Appropriations* (various years). The terms expenditures, spending, and outlays are used interchangeably in this report, which examines two kinds of expenditures: (1) federal, state, and local spending to maintain current levels of environmental quality and (2) local spending to comply with new regulations. Costs of new regulations, which were derived from Regulatory Impact Analyses (RIAs) prepared for EPA program offices in 1988, include only those for local governments. Full compliance is assumed in estimating costs of new regulations. The future costs of maintaining current levels of environmental quality were estimated for each program area and level of government by regressing five years of historical spending trends against time. The projections assume that factors contributing to recent spending trends will continue to do so in the future. Such factors include population growth, implementation of current policies, rates of compliance, replacement of current capital facilities, and budget cutbacks. Significant changes in any of these factors could have an important effect on costs. *Notes*: DW = Drinking water; WQ = Water Quality; SW = Solid Waste.

★ 264 ★

Increase in Annual Household User Charges to Maintain Existing Levels of Environmental Quality and to Comply with New Regulations, 2000

"Household costs of each environmental program, including those to maintain levels of environmental quality and to comply with new regulations in the year 2000, differ by city size category. Households in smaller cities will pay comparatively more than households in either large or medium-sized cities."

[Numbers in 1988 dollars]

Municipality size category	Average payment in 1987	Additional fees by program in the year 2000				
		Wastewater treatment	Drinking water	Solid waste	Other	Total additional fees
500 or less	$670	$259	$366	$218	$67	$910
500 - 2,500	$473	$174	$59	$43	$14	$290
2,500 - 10,000	$433	$85	$59	$19	$9	$172
10,000 - 50,000	$444	$124	$71	$19	$7	$221
50,000 - 100,000	$373	$77	$64	$20	$5	$166
100,000 - 250,000	$291	$63	$63	$14	$5	$145
250,000 - 500,000	$335	$114	$43	$33	$4	$194
500,000 or more	$393	$146	$42	$40	$5	$233

Source: A Preliminary Analysis of the Public Costs of Environmental Protection: 1981-2000, Environmental Protection Agency, May, 1990, p. 32. Primary source: Apogee Research from U.S. Bureau of the Census, 1986 Survey of Community Water Systems, and data compiled by the Environmental Law Institute from EPA Regulatory Impact Analyses. The terms expenditures, spending, and outlays are used interchangeably in this report, which examines two kinds of expenditures: (1) federal, state and local spending to maintain current levels of environmental quality and (2) local spending to comply with new regulations. Costs of new regulations, which were derived from Regulatory Impact Analyses (RIAs) prepared for EPA program offices in 1988, include only those for local governments. Full compliance is assumed in estimating costs of new regulations. The future costs of maintaining current levels of environmental quality were estimated for each program area and level of government by regressing five years of historical spending trends against time. The projections assume that factors contributing to recent spending trends will continue to do so in the future. Such factors include population growth, implementation of current policies, rates of compliance, replacement of current capital facilities, and budget cutbacks. Significant changes in any of these factors could have an important effect on costs.

★ 265 ★

Local Capital Expenditures to Maintain Current Levels of Environmental Quality and to Comply with New Regulations, 1981-2000

"Local demands for capital are estimated to increase from 9.5 billion a year in 1987 to $16.5 billion a year in 2000. State demands for capital are expected to remain stable over the same period and are relatively small, averaging about $680 million per year. Estimated local capital costs of new regulations add an average of $3 billion a year to local capital needs associated with current environmental regulations. As a result, localities are expected to have capital needs of nearly $19 billion a year by 2000."

[Numbers in millions of 1988 dollars]

Year	Current capital expenditures	New capital costs	Total capital
1981	$8,374	$0	$8,374
1982	$6,877	$0	$6,877
1983	$7,883	$0	$7,883
1984	$7,853	$0	$7,853
1985	$8,650	$0	$8,650
1986	$9,810	$0	$9,810
1987	$9,547	$0	$9,547
1988	$10,262	$2,199	$12,461
1989	$13,379	$2,881	$16,260
1990	$13,689	$2,994	$16,683
1991	$16,517	$3,313	$19,830
1992	$16,112	$5,892	$22,004
1993	$15,728	$2,177	$17,905
1994	$15,366	$2,617	$17,983
1995	$15,024	$2,610	$17,634
1996	$15,337	$2,597	$17,934
1997	$15,650	$3,209	$18,859
1998	$15,962	$2,774	$18,736
1999	$16,275	$3,707	$19,982
2000	$16,587	$2,110	$18,697

Source: A Preliminary Analysis of the Public Costs of Environmental Protection: 1981-2000, Environmental Protection Agency, May, 1990, p. 53. Primary source: Apogee Research, from U.S. Bureau of the Census, Government Finances (various years); Bureau of Economic Analysis, Pollution Abatement and Control Expenditures (various years), U.S. EPA, Justification of Appropriation Estimates for Committee on Appropriations (various years). and data prepared by the Environmental Law Institute from Regulatory Impact Analyses for the water quality and solid waste programs. Costs of new regulations for the water quality program are the preliminary analysis for the "Estimates of the Total Benefit and Total Costs Associated with the 1986 Amendments to the Safe Drinking Water Act," November, 1989. The terms expenditures, spending, and outlays are used interchangeably in this report, which examines two kinds of expenditures: (1) federal, state and local spending to maintain current levels of environmental quality and (2) local spending to comply with new regulations. Costs of new regulations, which were derived from Regulatory Impact Analyses (RIAs) prepared for EPA program offices in 1988, include only those for local governments. Full compliance is assumed in estimating costs of new regulations. The future costs of maintaining current levels of environmental quality were estimated for each program area and level of government by regressing five years of historical spending trends against time. The projections assume that factors contributing to recent spending trends will continue to do so in the future. Such factors include population growth, implementation of current policies, rates of compliance, replacement of current capital facilities, and budget cutbacks. Significant changes in any of these factors could have an important effect on costs.

★ 266 ★

Local Government Capital and O&M Expenditures to Maintain 1988 Levels of Environment Quality and to Comply with New Regulations, 198190-2000

"[As] operating expenses grow, local governments could be expected to rely more heavily on borrowed funds to finance their capital needs. Annual operating and maintenance expenditures are expected to increase by 52 percent, from about $23 billion in 1987 to $35 billion in 2000. This rate of increase in operating expenditures, 3.6 percent a year, is almost three times the rate of population growth expected over this period. New environmental programs will add another 10 to 20 percent to these totals."

[Numbers in millions of 1988 dollars]

Year	Local capital	Local O&M	Local total
1981	$8,374	$17,966	$26,340
1982	$6,877	$18,803	$25,680
1983	$7,883	$19,794	$27,677
1984	$7,853	$20,546	$28,399
1985	$8,650	$21,379	$30,029
1986	$9,810	$23,034	$32,581
1988	$12,461	$23,969	$36,430
1989	$16,260	$24,659	$40,919
1990	$16,683	$25,700	$42,384
1991	$19,830	$26,564	$46,394
1992	$22,004	$27,838	$49,842
1993	$17,905	$29,429	$47,334
1994	$17,983	$30,224	$48,207
1995	$17,634	$31,040	$48,674
1996	$17,934	$31,846	$49,781
1997	$18,859	$32,631	$51,490
1998	$18,736	$33,459	$52,195
1999	$19,982	$34,242	$54,223
2000	$18,697	$35,017	$53,714

Source: A Preliminary Analysis of the Public Costs of Environmental Protection: 1981-2000, Environmental Protection Agency, May, 1990, p. 54. Primary source: Apogee Research, from U.S. Bureau of the Census, Government Finances (various years); Bureau of Economic Analysis, Pollution Abatement and Control Expenditures (various years), U.S. EPA, Justification of Appropriation Estimates for Committee on Appropriations (various years). and data prepared by the Environmental Law Institute from Regulatory Impact Analyses for the water quality and solid waste programs. Costs of new regulations for the water quality program are the preliminary analysis for the "Estimates of the Total Benefit and Total Costs Associated with the 1986 Amendments to the Safe Drinking Water Act," November, 1989. The terms expenditures, spending, and outlays are used interchangeably in this report, which examines two kinds of expenditures: (1) federal, state and local spending to maintain current levels of environmental quality and (2) local spending to comply with new regulations. Costs of new regulations, which were derived from Regulatory Impact Analyses (RIAs) prepared for EPA program offices in 1988, include only those for local governments. Full compliance is assumed in estimating costs of new regulations. The future costs of maintaining current levels of environmental quality were estimated for each program area and level of government by regressing five years of historical spending trends against time. The projections assume that factors contributing to recent spending trends will continue to do so in the future. Such factors include population growth, implementation of current policies, rates of compliance, replacement of current capital facilities, and budget cutbacks. Significant changes in any of these factors could have an important effect on costs.

Local Government Expenditures to Maintain 1988 Levels of Environmental Quality and to Comply with New Environmental Standards by Media, 1981-2000 - I

"Local costs of new water quality regulations will average $2.6 billion per year in the 1990s. Most of these costs are for building new or upgrading existing facilities to meet the secondary treatment requirements of the Clean Water Act. EPA estimated in 1988 that $83.5 billion would be required to bring all municipal wastewater treatment facilities into compliance with minimum national standards."

[Numbers in millions of 1988 dollars]

| Year | Drinking water | | |
	Current programs[1] (1988 $MM)	New programs (1988 $MM)	Total (1988 $MM)
1981	12,073	0	12,073
1982	12,087	0	12,087
1983	12,547	0	12,547
1984	12,533	0	12,533
1985	13,625	0	13,625
1986	14,873	0	14,873
1987	14,816	0	14,816
1988	15,348	0	15,348
1989	15,879	1	15,880
1990	16,411	24	16,435
1991	16,942	26	16,968
1992	17,474	35	17,509
1993	18,005	94	18,099
1994	18,537	539	19,076
1995	19,068	580	19,648
1996	19,600	625	20,225
1997	20,131	1,296	21,427
1998	20,663	951	21,614
1999	21,194	1,030	22,224
2000	21,726	497	22,223

Source: A Preliminary Analysis of the Public Costs of Environmental Protection: 1981-2000, Environment Protection Agency, May, 1990, p. 51. Primary source: Apogee Research, from U.S. Bureau of the Census, *Government Finances* (various years); Bureau of Economic Analysis, *Pollution Abatement and Control Expenditures* (various years); U.S. EPA, *Justification of Appropriation Estimates for Committee on Appropriations* (various years); and data prepared by the Environmental Law Institute from Regulatory Impact Analyses for the water quality and solid waste programs. Costs of new regulations for the water quality program are from the preliminary analysis for the "Estimates of the Total Benefits and Total Costs Associated with the 1986 Amendments to the Safe Drinking Water Act," November, 1989. The terms expenditures, spending, and outlays are used interchangeable in this report, which examines two kinds of expenditures: (1) federal, state, and local spending to maintain current levels of environmental quality and (2) local spending to comply with new regulations. Costs of new regulations, which were derived from Regulatory Impact Analyses (RIAs) prepared for EPA program offices in 1988, include only those for local governments. Full compliance is assumed in estimating costs of new regulations. The future costs of maintaining current levels of environmental quality were estimated for each program area and level of government by regressing five years of historical spending trends against time. The projections assume that factors contributing to recent spending trends will continue to do so in the future. Such factors include population growth, implementation of current policies, rates of compliance, replacement of current capital facilities, and budget cutbacks. Significant changes in any of these factors could have an important effect on costs. *Note:* 1. Includes costs to deliver services.

★ 268 ★

Local Government Expenditures to Maintain 1988 Levels of Environmental Quality and to Comply with New Environmental Standards by Media, 1981-2000 - II

"Local costs of new water quality regulations will average $2.6 billion per year in the 1990s. Most of these costs are for building new or upgrading existing facilities to meet the secondary treatment requirements of the Clean Water Act. EPA estimated in 1988 that $83.5 billion would be required to bring all municipal wastewater treatment facilities into compliance with minimum national standards."

[Numbers in millions of 1988 dollars]

| Year | Water quality | | |
	Current programs[1] (1988 $MM)	New programs (1988 $MM)	Total (1988 $MM)
1981	9,086	0	9,086
1982	8,309	0	8,309
1983	9,693	0	9,693
1984	10,169	0	10,169
1985	10,295	0	10,295
1986	10,967	0	10,967
1987	11,376	0	11,376
1988	12,148	2,052	14,200
1989	15,288	2,130	17,418
1990	15,605	2,266	17,871
1991	18,433	2,305	20,738
1992	18,054	2,506	20,560
1993	17,710	2,499	20,209
1994	17,322	2,574	19,896
1995	16,938	2,650	19,588
1996	17,192	2,725	19,917
1997	17,429	2,800	20,299
1998	17,651	2,875	20,526
1999	17,858	2,951	20,809
2000	18,052	3,026	21,078

Source: A Preliminary Analysis of the Public Costs of Environmental Protection: 1981-2000, Environment Protection Agency, May, 1990, p. 51. Primary source: Apogee Research, from U.S. Bureau of the Census, *Government Finances* (various years); Bureau of Economic Analysis, *Pollution Abatement and Control Expenditures* (various years); U.S. EPA, *Justification of Appropriation Estimates for Committee on Appropriations* (various years); and data prepared by the Environmental Law Institute from Regulatory Impact Analyses for the water quality and solid waste programs. Costs of new regulations for the water quality program are from the preliminary analysis for the "Estimates of the Total Benefits and Total Costs Associated with the 1986 Amendments to the Safe Drinking Water Act," November, 1989. The terms expenditures, spending, and outlays are used interchangeably in this report, which examines two kinds of expenditures: (1) federal, state, and local spending to maintain current levels of environmental quality and (2) local spending to comply with new regulations. Costs of new regulations, which were derived from Regulatory Impact Analyses (RIAs) prepared for EPA program offices in 1988, include only those for local governments. Full compliance is assumed in estimating costs of new regulations. The future costs of maintaining current levels of environmental quality were estimated for each program area and level of government by regressing five years of historical spending trends against time. The projections assume that factors contributing to recent spending trends will continue to do so in the future. Such factors include population growth, implementation of current policies, rates of compliance, replacement of current capital facilities, and budget cutbacks. Significant changes in any of these factors could have an important effect on costs. *Note:* 1. Includes costs to deliver services.

★ 269 ★

Local Government Expenditures to Maintain 1988 Levels of Environmental Quality and to Comply with New Environmental Standards by Media, 1981-2000 - III

"Local costs of new water quality regulations will average $2.6 billion per year in the 1990s. Most of these costs are for building new or upgrading existing facilities to meet the secondary treatment requirements of the Clean Water Act. EPA estimated in 1988 that $83.5 billion would be required to bring all municipal wastewater treatment facilities into compliance with minimum national standards."

[Numbers in millions of 1988 dollars]

Year	Solid waste		
	Current programs[1] (1988 $MM)	New programs (1988 $MM)	Total (1988 $MM)
1981	4,948	0	4,948
1982	5,043	0	5,043
1983	5,163	0	5,163
1984	5,384	0	5,384
1985	5,771	0	5,771
1986	5,858	0	5,858
1987	6,050	0	6,050
1988	6,233	0	6,233
1989	6,426	0	6,426
1990	6,617	0	6,617
1991	6,804	357	7,161
1992	6,987	3,194	10,181
1993	7,166	1,035	8,201
1994	7,340	1,069	8,410
1995	7,510	1,104	8,614
1996	7,675	1,138	8,813
1997	7,836	1,172	9,009
1998	7,994	1,234	9,228
1999	8,150	1,297	9,447
2000	8,302	1,361	9,663

Source: A Preliminary Analysis of the Public Costs of Environmental Protection: 1981-2000, Environment Protection Agency, May, 1990, p. 51. Primary source: Apogee Research, from U.S. Bureau of the Census, *Government Finances* (various years); Bureau of Economic Analysis, *Pollution Abatement and Control Expenditures* (various years); U.S. EPA, *Justification of Appropriation Estimates for Committee on Appropriations* (various years); and data prepared by the Environmental Law Institute from Regulatory Impact Analyses for the water quality and solid waste programs. Costs of new regulations for the water quality program are from the preliminary analysis for the "Estimates of the Total Benefits and Total Costs Associated with the 1986 Amendments to the Safe Drinking Water Act," November, 1989. The terms expenditures, spending, and outlays are used interchangeable in this report, which examines two kinds of expenditures: (1) federal, state, and local spending to maintain current levels of environmental quality and (2) local spending to comply with new regulations. Costs of new regulations, which were derived from Regulatory Impact Analyses (RIAs) prepared for EPA program offices in 1988, include only those for local governments. Full compliance is assumed in estimating costs of new regulations. The future costs of maintaining current levels of environmental quality were estimated for each program area and level of government by regressing five years of historical spending trends against time. The projections assume that factors contributing to recent spending trends will continue to do so in the future. Such factors include population growth, implementation of current policies, rates of compliance, replacement of current capital facilities, and budget cutbacks. Significant changes in any of these factors could have an important effect on costs. *Note:* 1. Includes costs to deliver services.

★ 270 ★

Percentage of Public Expenditures by Level of Government to Maintain 1987 Levels of Environmental Quality, 1987 and 2000

"The future cost of maintaining current levels of environmental quality falls unevenly on different levels of government, with municipalities expected to underwrite a growing share in the future. While EPA expenditures are expected to decline by a third between 1981 and 2000, local spending could almost double."

[Numbers in percent except where indicated]

	1987	2000
Local	82.0	87.0
EPA	13.0	8.0
State	5.0	5.0
Total spending (billion $)	40.0	55.0

Source: A Preliminary Analysis of the Public Costs of Environmental Protection: 1981-2000, Environmental Protection Agency, May, 1990, p. 10. Primary source: U.S. Bureau of the Census, *Government Finances* (various years); Bureau of Economic Analysis, *Pollution Abatement and Control Expenditures* (various years); Bureau of the Census, *Pollution Abatement Cost and Expenditure Survey* (various years); and U.S. EPA, *Justification of Appropriation Estimates for Committee on Appropriations* (various years). This study documents recent EPA, state and local government expenditures for environmental protection and projects future costs to the year 2000. Original chart also contains data for 1981. The terms expenditures, spending, and outlays are used interchangeably in this report, which examines two kinds of expenditures: (1) federal, state, and local spending to maintain current levels of environmental quality and (2) local spending to comply with new regulations. Costs of new regulations, which were derived from Regulatory Impact Analyses (RIAs) prepared for EPA program offices in 1988, include only those for local governments. Full compliance is assumed in estimating costs of new regulations. The future costs of maintaining current levels of environmental quality were estimated for each program area and level of government by regressing five years of historical spending trends against time. The projections assume that factors contributing to recent spending trends will continue to do so in the future. Such factors include population growth, implementation of current policies, rates of compliance, replacement of current capital facilities, and budget cutbacks. Significant changes in any of these factors could have an important effect on costs.

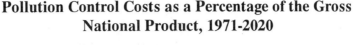

★ 271 ★

Pollution Control Costs as a Percentage of the Gross National Product, 1971-2020

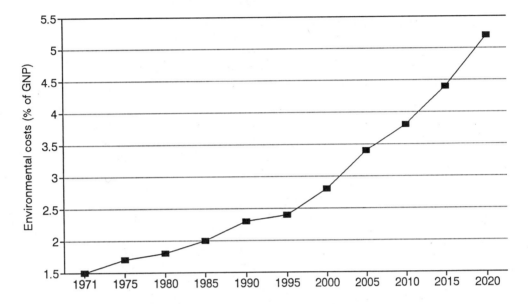

"If the model is correct, the environmental maintenance costs will be a steadily increasing portion of our GNP and a substantial growing burden on the economy, exceeding the projected defense budget in 2020."

1971	1.5
1975	1.7
1980	1.8
1985	2.0
1990	2.3
1995	2.4
2000	2.8
2005	3.4
2010	3.8
2015	4.4
2020	5.2

Source: The Next 200 Years: A Scenario for America and the World, Herman Kahn, William Brown, and Leon Martel: William Morrow, New York, 1976, p. 149. Magnitudes estimated from published charts. Primary source: "Future Environmental Needs and Costs," S. Fred Singer, *Economics of a Clean Environment*, Mitre Corp., Virginia, July, 1974, p. 21.

★ 272 ★

Projected EPA, State, and Local Government Expenditures to Maintain 1987 Levels of Environmental Quality Compared to Current Environmental Expenditures, 1981-2000

"In 1987, EPA, states, and local governments spent an estimated $40 billion for environmental protection. If recent trends continue, environmental expenditures by all levels of government are expected to increase to $55.6 billion in the year 2000 just to maintain current levels of environmental quality."

[Numbers in millions of 1988 dollars]

Year	Total	Spending to maintain existing levels of environmental quality in addition to existing expenditures (1987)
1981	$34,608	$0
1982	$33,293	$0
1983	$34,316	$0
1984	$36,765	$0
1985	$36,958	$0
1986	$39,312	$0
1987	$39,749	$0
1988	$41,160	$1,411
1989	$45,508	$5,759
1990	$46,478	$6,729
1991	$50,418	$10,669
1992	$50,240	$10,491
1993	$50,115	$10,367
1994	$49,956	$10,207
1995	$49,814	$10,065
1996	$50,957	$11,208
1997	$52,078	$12,329
1998	$53,178	$13,429

[Continued]

★ 272 ★

Projected EPA, State, and Local Government Expenditures to Maintain 1987 Levels of Environmental Quality Compared to Current Environmental Expenditures, 1981-2000

[Continued]

Year	Total	Spending to maintain existing levels of environmental quality in addition to existing expenditures (1987)
1999	$54,258	$14,509
2000	$55,320	$15,571

Source: A Preliminary Analysis of the Public Costs of Environmental Protection: 1981-2000, Environmental Protection Agency, May, 1990, p. 47. Primary source: U.S. Bureau of the Census, *Government Finances* (various years); Bureau of Economic Analysis, *Pollution Abatement and Control Expenditures* (various years); Bureau of Census, *Pollution Abatement Cost and Expenditure Survey* (various years); and U.S. EPA, *Justification of Appropriation Estimates for Committee on Appropriations* (various years). The terms expenditures, spending, and outlays are used interchangeably in this report, which examines two kinds of expenditures: (1) federal, state and local spending to maintain current levels of environmental quality and (2) local spending to comply with new regulations. Costs of new regulations, which were derived from Regulatory Impact Analyses (RIAs) prepared for EPA program offices in 1988, include only those for local governments. Full compliance is assumed in estimating costs of new regulations. The future costs of maintaining current levels of environmental quality were estimated for each program area and level of government by regressing five years of historical spending trends against time. The projections assume that factors contributing to recent spending trends will continue to do so in the future. Such factors include population growth, implementation of current policies, rates of compliance, replacement of current capital facilities, and budget cutbacks. Significant changes in any of these factors could have an important effect on costs.

★ 273 ★

Projected Local Government Expenditures to Maintain 1988 Levels of Environmental Quality and to Comply with New Environmental Standards, 1981-2000

"The costs to local governments associated with new regulations are projected to reach $5.3 billion by the year 2000. The report assumes that costs of municipal waste combustion air standards, $2.5 billion, would be incurred in 1992, resulting in a large peak in that year. A more likely scenario is that these costs will be even more evenly distributed over several years."

[In millions of 1988 dollars]

Year	Current level of local spending	Additional spending to maintain current environmental quality	Additional spending to comply with standards
1981	26,340	0	0
1982	25,680	0	0
1983	27,677	0	0
1984	28,399	0	0
1985	30,029	0	0
1986	32,036	0	0
1987	32,581	0	0
1988	34,068	1,487	2,362
1989	37,933	5,352	2,986
1990	38,973	6,392	3,411
1991	42,520	9,939	3,874
1992	42,857	10,276	6,985
1993	43,223	10,642	4,111
1994	43,542	10,961	4,665
1995	43,859	11,278	4,815
1996	44,810	12,229	4,970
1997	45,740	13,159	5,750
1998	46,652	14,071	5,542

[Continued]

★ 273 ★

Projected Local Government Expenditures to Maintain 1988 Levels of Environmental Quality and to Comply with New Environmental Standards, 1981-2000
[Continued]

Year	Current level of local spending	Additional spending to maintain current environmental quality	Additional spending to comply with standards
1999	47,546	14,965	6,677
2000	48,424	15,843	5,297

Source: A Preliminary Analysis of the Public Costs of Environmental Protection: 1981-2000, Environment Protection Agency, May, 1990, p. 50. Primary source: Apogee Research, from U.S. Bureau of the Census, *Government Finances* (various years); Bureau of Economic Analysis, *Pollution Abatement and Control Expenditures* (various years); U.S. EPA, *Justification of Appropriation Estimates for Committee on Appropriations* (various years); and data prepared by the Environmental Law Institute from Regulatory Impact Analyses for the water quality and solid waste programs. Costs of new regulations for the water quality program are from the preliminary analysis for the "Estimates of the Total Benefits and Total Costs Associated with the 1986 Amendments to the Safe Drinking Water Act," November, 1989. The terms expenditures, spending, and outlays are used interchangeable in this report, which examines two kinds of expenditures: (1) federal, state, and local spending to maintain current levels of environmental quality and (2) local spending to comply with new regulations. Costs of new regulations, which were derived from Regulatory Impact Analyses (RIAs) prepared for EPA program offices in 1988, include only those for local governments. Full compliance is assumed in estimating costs of new regulations. The future costs of maintaining current levels of environmental quality were estimated for each program area and level of government by regressing five years of historical spending trends against time. The projections assume that factors contributing to recent spending trends will continue to do so in the future. Such factors include population growth, implementation of current policies, rates of compliance, replacement of current capital facilities, and budget cutbacks. Significant changes in any of these factors could have an important effect on costs.

★ 274 ★

Public Expenditures (Capital and O&M) by Level of Government to Maintain 1988 Levels of Environmental Quality, 1981-2000

"While EPA expenditures are expected to decline by a third between 1981 and 2000, local spending could almost double."

[Numbers in billions of 1988 dollars]

Year	EPA		State		Local		Total	
	Amount	Percent share	Amount	Percent share	Amount	Percent share	Amount	Percent share
1981	6.3	18	2.0	6	26.3	76	34.6	100
1987	5.0	13	2.1	5	32.6	82	39.7	100
2000	4.3	8	2.6	5	48.4	87	55.3	100

Source: A Preliminary Analysis of the Public Costs of Environmental Protection: 1981-2000, Environment Protection Agency, May, 1990, p. 49. The terms expenditures, spending, and outlays are used interchangeably in this report, which examines two kinds of expenditures: (1) federal, state, and local spending to maintain current levels of environmental quality and (2) local spending to comply with new regulations. Costs of new regulations, which were derived from Regulatory Impact Analyses (RIAs) prepared for EPA program offices in 1988, include only those for local governments. Full compliance is assumed in estimating costs of new regulations. The future costs of maintaining current levels of environmental quality were estimated for each program area and level of government by regressing five years of historical spending trends against time. The projections assume that factors contributing to recent spending trends will continue to do so in the future. Such factors include population growth, implementation of current policies, rates of compliance, replacement of current capital facilities, and budget cutbacks. Significant changes in any of these factors could have an important effect on costs.

Summary of Local Government Environmental Expenditures by Media, 1987 and 2000

"Adding the local costs of new regulations to the costs of maintaining current levels of environmental quality results in a small change in the proportion spent for each environmental program between 1987 and 2000. The most important shift between 1987 and 2000 is the 4 percent increase in water quality expenditures from 35 to 39 percent of total expenditures and a corresponding 4 percent reduction in the percentage that is expended for drinking water, from 45 to 41 percent.... [While] local spending on water quality is increasing, the total public sector spending for water quality is expected to decrease by 5 percent between 1987 and 2000 (from 41 percent to 36 percent). The percentage increase for other programs is largely due to costs imposed by new regulations (Underground Storage Tanks Standards, Asbestos in Schools, and SARA Title III Requirements)."

[Numbers in billions of 1988 dollars]

Program	1987	Percentage of Total	2000[2]	Percentage of total	Percentage increase 1987-2000
Water quality	$11.4	35.0%	$21.1	39.3%	85%
Drinking water[1]	$14.8	45.4%	$22.2	41.4%	50%
Solid waste[1]	$6.1	18.7%	$9.7	18.0%	59%
Others	$0.3	0.9%	$0.7	1.3%	133%
Total local spending	$32.6	100.0%	$53.7	100.0%	65%

Source: A Preliminary Analysis of the Public Costs of Environmental Protection: 1981-2000, Environmental Protection Agency, May, 1990, p. 14. Primary source: Apogee Research from U.S. Bureau of the Census and data prepared in 1988 by the Environmental Law Institute from EPA Regulatory Impact Analyses. The terms expenditures, spending, and outlays are used interchangeably in this report, which examines two kinds of expenditures: (1) federal, state and local spending to maintain current levels of environmental quality and (2) local spending to comply with new regulations. Costs of new regulations, which were derived from Regulatory Impact Analyses (RIAs) prepared for EPA program offices in 1988, include only those for local governments. Full compliance is assumed in estimating costs of new regulations. The future costs of maintaining current levels of environmental quality were estimated for each program area and level of government by regressing five years of historical spending trends against time. The projections assume that factors contributing to recent spending trends will continue to do so in the future. Such factors include population growth, implementation of current policies, rates of compliance, replacement of current capital facilities, and budget cutbacks. Significant changes in any of these factors could have an important effect on costs. *Notes*: 1. Includes costs to deliver services. 2. Cost of maintaining 1987 levels of environmental quality plus costs of new regulations.

★ 276 ★

Total Capital Expenditures by EPA, States, and Local Governments to Maintain 1988 Levels of Environmental Quality and Local Capital Spending to Comply with New Regulations, 1981-2000

"Capital formation by EPA, states, and local government to maintain [1988] levels of environment quality is expected to fluctuate between $13 billion and $20 billion a year between 1987 and the year 2000. If recent trends continue, by the year 2000 most of the demand for capital to maintain current programs will be accounted for by local governments."

[Numbers in millions of dollars]

Year	Total capital expenditures to maintain current levels of environment quality	Local capital cost to comply with new regulations
1981	$13,274	$0
1982	$11,334	$0
1983	$11,399	$0
1984	$11,010	$0
1985	$12,205	$0
1986	$13,468	$0
1987	$12,935	$0
1988	$13,267	$2,199
1989	$16,433	$2,881
1990	$16,718	$2,994
1991	$19,749	$3,313
1992	$18,640	$5,892
1993	$17,574	$2,177
1994	$16,550	$2,617
1995	$15,567	$2,610
1996	$15,892	$2,597
1997	$16,217	$3,209
1998	$16,541	$2,774

[Continued]

★ 276 ★

Total Capital Expenditures by EPA, States, and Local Governments to Maintain 1988 Levels of Environmental Quality and Local Capital Spending to Comply with New Regulations, 1981-2000
[Continued]

Year	Total capital expenditures to maintain current levels of environment quality	Local capital cost to comply with new regulations
1999	$16,865	$3,707
2000	$17,188	$2,110

Source: A Preliminary Analysis of the Public Costs of Environmental Protection: 1981-2000, Environmental Protection Agency, May, 1990, p. 52. Primary source: Apogee Research, from U.S. Bureau of the Census, *Government Finances* (various years); Bureau of Economic Analysis, *Pollution Abatement and Control Expenditures* (various years); U.S. EPA, *Justification of Appropriation Estimates for Committee on Appropriations* (various years); and data prepared by the Environmental Law Institute from Regulatory Impact Analyses for the water quality and solid waste programs. Costs of new regulations for the water quality program are the preliminary analysis for the "Estimates of the Total Benefit and Total Costs Associated with the 1986 Amendments to the Safe Drinking Water Act," November, 1989. The terms expenditures, spending, and outlays are used interchangeably in this report, which examines two kinds of expenditures: (1) federal, state and local spending to maintain current levels of environmental quality and (2) local spending to comply with new regulations. Costs of new regulations, which were derived from Regulatory Impact Analyses (RIAs) prepared for EPA program offices in 1988, include only those for local governments. Full compliance is assumed in estimating costs of new regulations. The future costs of maintaining current levels of environmental quality were estimated for each program area and level of government by regressing five years of historical spending trends against time. The projections assume that factors contributing to recent spending trends will continue to do so in the future. Such factors include population growth, implementation of current policies, rates of compliance, replacement of current capital facilities, and budget cutbacks. Significant changes in any of these factors could have an important effect on costs.

★ 277 ★

Total Costs to Control Pollution, 1987 and 1997

"The U.S. currently spends $115 billion a year, or 2.1% of its gross national product, on pollution control. By the year 2000 the cost of such protection could rise to as high as $185 billion a year (in 1990 dollars), or 2.8% of GNP, the Environmental Protection Agency estimates."

[Values in percent]

	Water	Land	Air & radiation	Chemicals	Multimedia
1987 Capital and operating costs[1] ($77 billion)	43	26	29	1	1
1997 Capital and operating costs[1] ($119 billion)	36	34	27	2	1

Source: "Rising Pollution Control Costs May Alter EPA's Regulatory Direction," Lois R. Ember, *Chemical and Engineering News* 69, No.7, February 18, 1991, p. 26. Primary source: Environmental Protection Agency. *Note*: 1. Assuming full implementation of programs, includin quality standard for ozone and satisfying U.S.'s wastewater treatment needs (1986 dollars).

Impacts of Environmental Destruction

★ 278 ★

Comparative Global Rates of Species Extinctions, c. 70,000,000 BC-2000 AD

"Arguably, extinctions are part of the natural process of Darwinian evolution, but the current number of extinctions is compounded exponentially by manmade environmental changes and destruction."

Time	Rates of extinction
70,000,000 years ago (disappearance of the dinosaurs)	1 species/1000 years
1 AD to 1650	1 species mammal or bird/82 years
1650 to 1850	1 species mammal or bird/5 years
1850 to 1900	1 species mammal or bird/9.5 months
1900 to 1950	1 species mammal or bird/8 months
Present	All plant and animal life, 1 to 6 species/day
2000	All plant and animal life, 1 species/hour

Source: "Zoo Veterinarians: Doctors on the Ark?," R. Eric Miller, *Journal of the American Veterinary Medical Association* 20, No. 5, March 1, 1992, p. 643.

★ 279 ★

Potential Exhaustion of Selected Minerals, 1980-2128

"It is our view that very few important materials in the world—perhaps none—will become unduly scarce, although the distribution of the prime sources of many of them is so uneven that unless we are careful cartels might occasionally be able to extract higher prices than usual from consumers, thus causing local needs for conservation, substitution and redesign."

Resources	Average annual growth in use (%)	Year exhausted	
		Low estimate	High estimate
Aluminum	6.4	2007	2023
Chromium	2.6	2089	2111
Coal	4.1	2092	2106
Cobalt	1.5	2064	2106
Copper	4.6	2001	2020
Gold	4.1	1980	1991
Iron	1.8	2128	n.a.
Lead	2.0	2002	2093
Manganese	2.9	2080	2097

[Continued]

★ 279 ★

Potential Exhaustion of Selected Minerals, 1980-2128
[Continued]

Resources	Average annual growth in use (%)	Year exhausted Low estimate	High estimate
Mercury	2.6	1993	2018
Molybdenum	4.5	2039	2066
Natural gas	4.7	1993	2032
Nickel	3.4	2024	2049
Petroleum	3.9	1997	2017
Platinum	3.8	2015	2023
Silver	2.7	1989	1997
Tin	1.1	2036	2066
Tungsten	2.5	2001	n.a.
Zinc	2.9	2050	2089

Source: The Next 200 Years: A Scenario for America and the World, Herman Kahn, William Brown, and Leon Martel, New York: William Morrow, 1976, p. 89. Primary source: *Dynamics of Growth in a Finite World*, Dennis L. Morrows et al., Wright-Allen Press, Cambridge, 1974, pp. 372-73. Years estimated from published table.

Impacts of Global Climate Change

★ 280 ★

Dryland Loss by 2100 without Shore Protection

"Given the high property values of developed coastlines in the United States, it is likely that measures would be taken to hold back the sea along most developed shores. Preliminary estimates suggest that the cumulative capital cost (including response to current sea level rise) of protecting currently developed areas would be $73 to $111 billion (in 1988 dollars) through 2100 for a 1-meter global rise (compared with $4 to $6 billion to protect developed areas from current trends in sea level rise). A 1-meter sea level rise would lead to a cumulative inundation of 7,000 square miles of dryland-an area the size of Massachussetts. If the oceans continue to rise at current rates, approximately 3,000 square miles of dryland would be lost."

[Numbers in thousands of square miles]

	Sea level rise scenario			
	Baseline	50 CM	100 CM	200 CM
South Atlantic	5.0	11.0	16.2	25.9
South & West Florida	2.8	7.7	13.0	20.7
Mid-Atlantic	4.5	9.0	12.1	18.0
West	1.0	5.2	9.1	18.0
Louisiana	12.0	13.7	14.0	16.7

[Continued]

★ 280 ★

Dryland Loss by 2100 without Shore Protection
[Continued]

	Sea level rise scenario			
	Baseline	50 CM	100 CM	200 CM
Other Gulf	5.7	9.0	11.0	15.2
Northeast	.4	1.5	2.3	4.9

Source: United States Environmental Protection Agency, Office of Policy, Planning, and Evaluation and Office of Research and Development, *The Potential Effects of Global Climate Change on the United States*, December, 1989, p. xxxvi. Magnitudes estimated from published chart.

★ 281 ★

Dryland Loss by 2100 with Protection of Developed Areas

"Given the high property values of developed coastlines in the United States, it is likely that measures would be taken to hold back the sea along most developed shores. Preliminary estimates suggest that the cumulative capital cost (including response to current sea level rise) of protecting currently developed areas would be $73 to $111 billion (in 1988 dollars) through 2100 for a 1-meter global rise (compared with $4 to $6 billion to protect developed areas from current trends in sea level rise). A 1-meter sea level rise would lead to a cumulative inundation of 7,000 square miles of dryland-an area the size of Massachussetts. If the oceans continue to rise at current rates, approximately 3,000 square miles of dryland would be lost."

[Numbers in thousands of square miles]

	Sea level rise scenario			
	Baseline	50 CM	100 CM	200 CM
South Atlantic	5.0	9.0	12.9	20.2
South & West Florida	2.8	7.1	12.0	19.2
West	.8	4.5	8.9	15.9
Louisiana	11.8	12.2	12.9	14.7
Other Gulf	5.9	8.0	9.8	14.0
Mid-Atlantic	4.5	7.1	9.3	13.9
Northeast	.3	.7	1.2	2.8

Source: United States Environmental Protection Agency, Office of Policy, Planning, and Evaluation and Office of Research and Development, *The Potential Effects of Global Climate Change on the United States*, December, 1989, p. xxxvi. Magnitudes estimated from published chart.

★ 282 ★

Global Warming Potentials Normalized to Carbon Dioxide, 2010-2490

"Value (shown) is the potential impact on global warming caused by 1 kilogram of the gas for the time period noted compared to 1 kilogram of carbon dioxide. For example, in the [2090] time horizon a kilogram of methane will have a global warming potential equal to 21 kilograms of carbon dioxide."

	2010	2090	2490
Carbon dioxide	1	1	1
Methane (including indirect)	63	21	9
Nitrous oxide	270	290	190
CFC-11	4,500	3,500	1,500
CFC-12	7,100	7,300	4,500
HCFC-22	4,100	1,500	510

Source: *National Energy Strategy: Powerful Ideas for America*, February, 1991, p. 177. Primary source: *IPCC Scientific Assessment*, August, 1990. Years estimated from published table.

★ 283 ★

Estimated Economic Welfare Effects of Climate-Induced Agricultural Yield Changes, 2050

The estimates in the table below "are largely illustrative because of the high degree of uncertainty concerning the regional yield effects of climate change; note in particular that ... the impact on U.S. yield is negative. This analysis predicts a climate-induced increase in world corn and soybean prices of about 10 percent since most production of these crops occurs in mid-latitude countries that may be adversely affected by climate changes. The prices of all other primary agricultural commodities are expected to decline though prices of oil and meal would rise. As [the table below] shows, these estimated price changes would lead to small increases in net U.S. and global welfare. Global welfare rises because decreased production in some regions is more than offset by increases in others. From the perspective of any individual country, large domestic yield effects do not necessarily translate into large welfare effects; welfare effects depend on prices determined in world markets and on flows of imports and exports. Thus, even though yields are assumed to fall in the United States, U.S. net welfare is estimated to increase by just under 4200 million in 2050. (These estimates do not consider adaptation costs, such as the possible need to increase irrigated acreage)."

[Numbers in percent]

Country/region	Assumed percentage changes in yields of major crops	Estimated net welfare change (1986 $ million)
United States	-10 to -15	+194
Canada	-10 to +5	-167
European Community	-5 to -10	-763
Northern Europe	+10 to +30	-51
Japan	-5 to +15	-1,209
Australia	+10 to +15	+66
China	+10	+2,882
USSR	+10 to +15	+658
Brazil	No change	-47
Argentina	No change	+95
Pakistan	No change	-50
Thailand	No change	-33
Rest of World	No change	-67

Source: United States Department of Energy, Office of Policy, Planning, and Analysis, *The Economics of Long-Term Global Climate Change: A Preliminary Assessment*, September, 1990, p. 11. Primary source: USEPA (1989) Rapidly Changing World Scenario.

★ 284 ★

Eventual Loss of Coastal Wetlands From a One-Meter Rise in Sea Level

"Historically, wetlands have kept pace with a slow rate of sea level rise. However, in the future, sea level will probably rise too fast for some marshes and swamps to keep pace. Although some wetlands can survive by migrating inland, a study on coastal wetlands estimated that for a 1-meter rise, 26 to 66% of wetlands would be lost, even if wetland migration were not blocked. A majority of these losses would be in the South. Efforts to protect coastal development would increase wetland losses, because bulkheads and levees would prevent new wetlands from forming inland. If all shorelines are protected, 50 to 82% of wetlands would be lost."

Region	Current wetlands area (mi^2)	All dryland protected (% loss)	Current development protected (% loss)	No protection (% loss)
Northeast	600	16	10	2
Mid-Atlantic	746	70	46	38
South Atlantic	3,813	64	44	39
South and West Florida	1,869	44	8	7
Louisiana[1]	4,835	77	77	77
Other Gulf	1,218	85	76	75
West	64	56	gain[2]	gain[2]
United States	13,145	50-82	29-69	26-66

Source: United States Environmental Protection Agency, Office of Policy, Planning, and Evaluation and Office of Research and Development, *The Potential Effects of Global Climate Change on the United States*, December, 1989, p. xxxv. Primary source: Adapted from Park et al. *Notes:* 1. Louisiana projections do not consider potential benefits of restoring flow of sediment and freshwater. 2. Potential gain in wetland acreage not shown because principal author suggested that no confidence could be attributed to those estimates. West Coast sites constituted less than 0.5% of wetlands in study sample.

★ 285 ★

Nationwide Impacts of Sea Level Rise by 2100

"A rise in sea level is one of the more probable impacts of climate change. Higher global temperatures will expand ocean water and melt some mountain glaciers, and may eventually cause polar ice sheets to discharge ice.... Published estimates of sea level rise due to global warming generally range from 0.5 to 2.0 meters (1.5 to 7 feet) by 2100m. Sea level rise could be greater than or less than this range because uncertainties exist regarding the rate of atmospheric warming, glacial processes, oceanic uptake of heat, precipitation in polar areas, and other variables. [This study estimates] the potential nationwide loss of wetlands, and the cost of defending currently developed areas from a rising sea, for three scenarios (50, 100, and 200 cm) of sea level rise by the year 2100. The scenarios are based on quantitative estimates of sea level rise, but no probabilities have been attributed to them. Wetland loss estimates were based on remote-sensing data and topographic maps for a sample of sites along the U.S. coast. The cost of holding back the sea was based on (1) the quantity of sand necessary to elevate beaches and coastal barrier islands as sea level rises; (2) rebuilding roads and elevating structures; and (3) constructing levees and bulkheads to protect developed lowlands along sheltered waters."

Alternative	Baseline[1]	Sea level rise by 2100		
		50 cm	100 cm	200 cm
If densely developed areas are protected				
Shore protection costs (billions of 1986 dollars)	4-6	32-43	73-111	169-309
Dryland lost (mi^2)	1,500-4,700	2,200-6,100	4,100-9,200	6,400-13,500
Wetlands lost (%)	9-25	20-45	29-69	33-80
If no shores are protected				
Dryland lost (mi^2)	N.C.	3,300-7,300	5,100-10,300	8,200-15,400
Wetlands lost (%)	N.C.	17-34	26-66	29-76
If all shores are protected				
Wetlands lost (%)	N.C.	38-61	50-82	66-90

Source: United States Environmental Protection Agency, Office of Policy, Planning, and Evaluation and Office of Research and Development, *The Potential Effects of Global Climate Change on the United States*, December, 1989, p. xxxv. Primary source: Assembled by Titus and Greene. *Notes:* N.C.=Not calculated. 1. Baseline assumes current global sea level rise trend of 12 cm per century. Given coastal subsidence trends, this implies about a 1-foot rise in relative sea level along most of the U.S. coast.

★ 286 ★

Potential Global Carbon Dioxide Anthropogenic Emissions, 1985-2050

"Measurements of carbon dioxide (CO_2) levels show atmospheric concentrations increasing from somewhere between 250 and 295 parts per million (ppm) at the beginning of the 19th century to 346 ppm in 1986. Good data are available on fossil fuel CO_2 emissions and (the far smaller) emissions from cement production; data on the impacts of land-use changes (primarily tropical deforestation) are fair to poor. It is important to keep in mind that natural flows of carbon into and out of the atmosphere are roughly ten to twenty times larger than the (anthropogenic) flows associated with human activity. [The table below] provides historical and projected anthropogenic emissions data by region and by source assuming no mitigation. These projections are uncertain because of uncertainties about future population and economic growth, sectorial composition of gross natural product (GNP), and sector-specific energy efficiencies. Nonetheless, it is important to note that because energy-related sources of CO_2 emissions are expected to grow comparatively rapidly, and chlorofluorocarbons (CFCs) are expected to be controlled significantly, CO_2 is expected to account for a larger share of increased radiative forcing in the future than in the past. The U.S. now accounts for about 21 percent of total anthropogenic CO_2 emissions, but that share is expected to shrink to around 12 percent by the middle of the next century. Despite the attention paid to tropical deforestation, most anthropogenic CO_2 emissions are and will be the result of combustion of fossil fuels."

[Numbers in percentage shares]

Source	1985	Projections		
		2000	2015	2050
Countries				
United States	21	19	16	12
Rest of OECD	22	19	16	12
USSR & Eastern Europe	22	22	19	18
Centrally Planned Asia	10	13	161	
Other developing	25	28	32	37
	100	100	100	100
Sectors				
Commercial energy	86	87	89	92
Tropical deforestation	12	11	9	6
Other	2	2	2	2
	100	100	100	100
Total scenario emissions (10^9 metric tons of carbon)	5.99	8.05	10.27	16.95
Average Annual Growth rate	1.6%	1.6%	1.6%	1.6%

Source: United States Department of Energy, Office of Policy, Planning, and Analysis, *The Economics of Long-Term Global Climate Change: A Preliminary Assessment*, September, 1990, p. 2. Primary source: USEPA (1989) Rapidly Changing World Scenario.

★ 287 ★

Potential Global Chlorofluorocarbon Emissions Assuming No Further Controls Beyond Original Montreal Protocol, 1985-2050

"Chlorofluorocarbons (CFCs) are entirely man-made and were invented during the 20th century. The concentrations of CFC-11 and CFC-12 were 226 parts per trillion (ppt) and 392 ppt, respectively, in 1986 and have been rising at 4 percent annually. [The table below] gives projected regional emissions of these two gases assuming implementation of the Montreal Protocol (aimed at reducing stratospheric ozone depletion) as it existed prior to June, 1990, with 100 percent participation by developed countries and 75 percent participation elsewhere. In June, 1990, the parties agreed to a total phaseout of CFC's by the year 2000 in place of the 50-percent emissions reduction [in the table below]. [The] United States and other developed nations now account for well over half of emissions of CFCs and related gases, but, even under the original terms of the Montreal Protocol, the shares of developing nations would have been expected to increase sharply. The recent revisions to the Protocol will reduce the emissions of signatory nations by a substantial further amount. The extent of developing country participation phaseout of CFCs is uncertain and will significantly affect future shares and quantities of emissions."

[Numbers in percentage shares]

Source	1985	Projections		
		2000	2015	2050
United States	24	18	17	12
Other developed	41	24	24	21
USSR & Eastern Europe	16	14	14	13
0.2Kg Nations[1]	6	14	15	19
Other developing	12	30	30	36
	100	100	100	100
Total scenario emissions (10^3 tonnes CFC)	642.1	837.8	755.1	828.5
Average annual growth rate	0.4%	0.4%	0.4%	0.4%

Source: United States Department of Energy, Office of Policy, Planning and Analysis, *The Economics of Long-Term Global Climate Change: A Preliminary Assessment*, September, 1990, p. 4. Primary source: USEPA (1989) Rapidly Changing World Scenario. *Note:* 1. Nations with CFC use between 0.1 and 0.2 kilograms per capita and likely to reach the 0.3 kilogram per capita limit in the Montreal Protocol prior to 1999.

★ 288 ★

Potential Global Methane Anthropogenic Emissions, 1985-2050

"Atmospheric concentrations of methane (CH_4) were relatively constant prior to the middle of the last century at about 700 parts per billion (ppb); by 1987 CH_4 concentrations had increased to 1,675 ppb. Recently, atmospheric concentrations of methane have been increasing at an observed rate of about 1.1 percent annually. The contributions of the different sources of methane that together account for aggregate emissions remain uncertain. Anthropogenic emissions of CH_4 are thought to account for roughly two-thirds of all emissions. [Figures in the table below] should be treated as uncertain. The United States now contributes about 12 percent of anthropogenic emissions of CH_4; this share is expected to decline to about 8 percent. Over half of total anthropogenic emissions of methane are produced by domestic animals (enteric fermentation) and rice cultivation. The centrally planned and developing nations account for the bulk of these methane emissions. Energy-related methane emissions occur in coal mining, and when natural gas is gathered, transmitted, distributed, or vented."

[Numbers in percentage shares]

Source	1985	Projections		
		2000	2015	2050
Countries				
United States	12	11	9	8
Rest of OECD	13	12	12	10
USSR & Eastern Europe	13	14	14	15
Centrally Planned Asia	17	16	17	19
Other developing	46	47	49	48
	100	100	100	100
Sectors				
Fuel production	18	22	26	32
Enteric fermentation	23	24	23	22
Rice cultivation	34	31	29	24
Landfills	9	10	10	14
Tropical deforestation	6	6	5	4
Other	9	7	7	5
	100	100	100	100
Total scenario emissions (10^6 metric tons of CH_4)	320.1	399.5	476.8	710.5
Average Annual Growth rate	1.2%	1.2%	1.2%	1.2%

Source: United States Department of Energy, Office of Policy, Planning, and Analysis, *The Economics of Long-Term Global Climate Change: A Preliminary Assessment*, September, 1990, p. 3. Primary source: USEPA (1989) Rapidly Changing World Scenario.

★ 289 ★

Potential Global Nitrous Oxide Anthropogenic Emissions, 1985-2050

"Atmospheric concentrations of N_2O averaged about 285 ppb from 1600 to 1800, began to rise slowly at the start of this century and more rapidly after 1940, and are now around 310 parts per billion (ppb). Data on natural and anthropogenic sources of N_2O emissions are poor, and the data in [the table below] should be considered as approximate at best. The Department of Energy believes that N_2O emissions associated with energy processes may be overestimated by an order of magnitude. As in the case of methane, most N_2O emissions are associated with agricultural activity and with developing nations. Increased fertilizer use has both raised N_2O emissions and dramatically increased food supplies in many developing nations. The U.S. share of world N_2O emissions is only about 14 percent and is expected to fall below 10 percent by mid-century."

[Numbers in percentage shares]

Source	1985	Projections		
		2000	2015	2050
Countries				
United States	14	12	11	9
Rest of OECD	13	14	14	12
USSR & Eastern Europe	14	15	14	13
Centrally Planned Asia	13	16	14	15
Other developing	46	47	47	52
	100	100	100	100
Sectors				
Coal combustion	25	26	29	36
Fertilizer use	38	43	44	41
Gain of cultivated land	10	8	8	6
Tropical deforestation	13	11	10	9
Fuelwood & Ind. Biomass	5	4	3	2
Agricultural Wastes	10	8	7	6
	100	100	100	100
Total scenario emissions (10^6 tonnes N_2O)	4.21	5.85	6.87	8.85
Average annual growth rate	1.2%	1.2%	1.2%	1.2%

Source: United States Department of Energy, Office of Policy, Planning and Analysis, *The Economics of Long-Term Global Climate Change: A Preliminary Assessment*, September, 1990, p. 5. Primary source: USEPA (1989) Rapidly Changing World Scenario.

★ 290 ★

Proposed Reduction in Chlorofluorocarbon Production Levels, 1991-1999

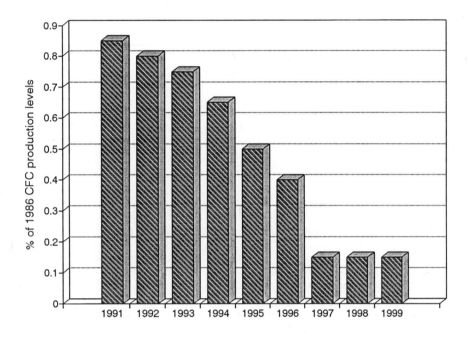

Percentages represent reduction from 1986 CFC production levels each year. By 2000, no production of CFCs will be allowed.

1991	85.0
1992	80.0
1993	75.0
1994	65.0
1995	50.0
1996	40.0
1997	15.0
1998	15.0
1999	15.0

Source: "Death and Taxes for CFCs," Warren Thayer, *Progressive Grocer*, December, 1990, p. 74.

★ 291 ★

Tax Assessments for Chlorofluorocarbon Production, 1991-1999

	1991	1992	1993	1994	1995	1996	1997	1998	1999
R-12 tax per pound	1.37	1.67	2.65	2.65	3.10	3.55	4.00	4.45	4.90
R-502 tax per pound	0.41	0.50	0.80	0.80	0.93	1.07	1.20	1.34	1.47

Source: "Death and Taxes for CFCs," Warren Thayer, *Progressive Grocer*, December, 1990, p. 74.

Impacts of Pollution Controls

★ 292 ★

Estimates of Sulfur Dioxide Emissions and Emission Ceilings for Electricity Generators, 1980-2010

"When fossil fuels are burned to produce electricity, a variety of gases and particulates, if not removed by pollution control equipment, are released into the atmosphere. Among these gases are sulfur dioxide (SO_2) and nitrogen oxides (NO_x) which under the proper conditions, react with other chemicals in the atmosphere to form sulfuric acid and nitric acid, respectively. These acids are either deposited directly onto the Earth as 'acid deposition' or absorbed by rain droplets, forming 'acid rain.' According to the National Acid Precipitation Assessment Program Emissions Inventory, in 1980 man-made sources released 26 million tons of SO_2 and 21 million tons of NO_x into the atmosphere. Generators of electricity were responsible for 67 percent of the SO_2 and 30 percent of the NO_x. Although SO_2 and NO_x emissions by generators of electricity have been regulated for 20 years, concern about acid deposition has led to calls for new, more stringent regulation. As a result, the Clean Air Act Amendments of 1990 established a new emission-reduction program. The goals of that program are to reduce annual SO_2 emissions by 10 million tons and annual NO_x emissions by 2 million tons from 1980 levels for all man-made sources. Generators of electricity will be responsible for 87 percent of the annual SO_2 reductions and all of the annual NO_x reductions, which are to be fully achieved by 2010."

[Tons in millions]

Region	SO_2 emissions		Estimated SO_2 emission ceilings		
	NAPAP estimates 1980	EIA estimates 1989[1]	1995	2000	2010
New England	0.40	0.43	0.47	0.29	0.28
New York/New Jersey	0.58	0.52	0.61	0.37	0.35
Mid-Atlantic	2.91	2.85	2.50	1.32	1.28
South Atlantic	4.75	4.26	3.89	2.49	2.38
Midwest	6.17	5.67	3.93	2.43	2.25
Southwest	0.47	0.92	0.94	1.10	1.06
Central	1.62	1.29	1.12	0.64	0.57
North Central	0.36	0.45	0.52	0.51	0.48

[Continued]

★ 292 ★

Estimates of Sulfur Dioxide Emissions and Emission Ceilings for Electricity Generators, 1980-2010

[Continued]

Region	SO_2 emissions		Estimated SO_2 emission ceilings		
	NAPAP estimates 1980	EIA estimates 1989[1]	1995	2000	2010
West	0.20	0.21	0.23	0.31	0.29
Northwest	0.07	0.07	0.09	0.05	0.04
Total United States	17.53	16.66	14.31	9.50	8.99

Source: Annual Outlook for U.S. Electric Power 1991: Projections through 2010, Energy Information Administration, July, 1991, p. 35. Primary source: 1980 Emissions Estimates: National Acid Precipitation Program, *Interim Assessment: The Causes and Effects of Acidic Deposition*, Vol. II, "Emissions and Control" (September, 1987), pp. 1-35 and 1-52. 1989 Emissions Estimates: Energy Information Administration, *Electric Power Annual 1989*, January, 1991, p. 75. Emission Ceilings: Energy Information Administration, Office of Coal, Nuclear, Electric, and Alternative Fuels. All emissions data shown is estimated; actual emissions data have not been collected. Estimates of 1980 emissions were prepared by the National Acid Precipitation Assessment Program (NAPAP). Estimates of 1989 emissions were prepared by the Energy Information Administration (EIA). Alaska is excluded from the Northwest region, and Hawaii is excluded from the West region. Totals may not equal sum of components due to independent rounding. *Note:* 1. SO_2 emissions were developed using EPA emission factors.

★ 293 ★

Fossil Steam Plant Life Extension, 1991-2010

"Fossil steam plants with nameplate capacities greater than or equal to 100 megawatts and with no reported retirement dates are considered for life extension. Only plants of 100 megawatts or larger were considered eligible for life extension because economies of scale favor the refurbishment of large generating units.... Two categories of life extension are established. Super critical units and units currently operated at a capacity factor greater than 35 percent would be fully life-extended while the remaining units would be partially life-extended. Fully life-extended units are assumed to perform as new units. Partially life-extended units will not be able to perform as new units and their maximum capacity factor will be limited to 40 percent since many of the units currently being used in the cycling mode could not be economically operated as baseload units; consequently, utilities are expected to spend less money refurbishing them."

[Numbers in gigawatts]

Status	Capacity
Fully life-extended	275.9
Partially life-extended	70.4
Total	346.3

Source: Assumptions for the Annual Energy Outlook 1992, Energy Information Administration, January, 1992, p. 77. Primary source: Energy Information Administration, Office of Integrated Analysis and Forecasting.

★ 294 ★

Fuel Consumption Shares for CAA, 1995-2010

Fuel shares	1995	2000	2005	2010
Coal consumption shares (percent)				
Low sulfur	43.9	52.1	52.4	45.0
Mid sulfur	40.3	34.7	32.4	33.0
High sulfur	15.8	13.3	15.2	22.0
Oil consumption shares (percent)				
Low sulfur	79.7	75.2	74.6	100.0
High sulfur	20.3	24.8	25.4	0.0
Capacity retrofitted with scrubbers (Gigawatts)	9.1	9.1	9.1	12.0

Source: *Assumptions for the Annual Energy Outlook 1992*, Energy Information Administration, January, 1992, p. 85. Primary source: Energy Information Administration, Office of Integrated Analysis and Forecasting.

★ 295 ★

Heavy-Duty Truck Engine Emission Standards to Comply with the 1990 Clean Air Act (CAA), 1990-1998

[g/bhp.h measured during EPA heavy-duty engine test]

Model year	NO_x	HC	CO	PM
1990	6.0	1.3	15.5	0.60
1991	5.0	1.3	15.5	0.25
1994	5.0	1.3	15.5	0.10
1998	4.0	1.3	15.5	0.10

Source: "Cellular Ceramic Products Help Curb Diesel Engine Emissions," Nitin S. Kulkarn, *Automotive Engineering* 100, No. 1, January, 1992, p. 23. Notes: NO_x = Nitrogen oxides; HC = Hydrocarbons; CO = Carbon Monoxide; PM = Per Million.

★ 296 ★

Major National Energy Strategies to Improve Environmental Quality, 2000 and 2030

[Numbers in percent]

Strategy action	Air pollutants						Water Suspended solids		Wastes			
	SO$_2$		NO$_x$		VOC				Coal ash		Petroleum hazardous wastes	
	2000	2030	2000	2030	2000	2030	2000	2030	2000	2030	2000	2030
Clean Air Act, including clean coal	39	37	15	14	11	16	1	1	2	5	2	1
Alternative vehicles and fuels	*	1	0	1	1	2	1	3	0	0	3	8
Transportation technology R&D	0	0	3	9	10	27	0	8	0	0	1	20
Industrial energy-efficiency R&D	0	5	0	3	0	1	0	6	0	5	0	1
Integrated resource planning	1	5	1	3	0	0	1	3	1	10	1	0
Expanded nuclear energy	0	11	0	6	0	0	0	6	0	24	0	1
Natural gas reform	3	1	1	0	0	0	1	1	1	1	2	1

Source: National Energy Strategy: Powerful Ideas for America, February, 1991, p. 153. Value is percent reduction below current policy resulting from the National Energy Strategy action. The combined effect of these actions will be less than the sum of the individual expected benefits. *Note:* * indicates less than 0.5 percent.

★ 297 ★

National Environmental Markups for Gasoline and Distillate Fuel Oil by Sector and Fuel Type, 1995-2010

"Congress' recent amendments to the CAA require that gasoline sold in nine U.S. cities beginning in 1995 must be 'reformulated' and that beginning in 1992, for at least 4 months per year, gasoline sold in about 40 cities must be 'oxygenated'.... Reformulated gasoline is estimated to cost an additional 8.0 cents per gallon while oxygenated gasoline is estimated to cost an additional 2.0 cents per gallon."

[Numbers in 1990 dollars per million BTU]

Year	Commercial Gasoline	Trans-portation		Industrial Gasoline
		Gasoline	Distillate fuel oil	
1995	0.33	0.33	0.38	0.33
2000	0.47	0.47	0.38	0.47
2005	0.66	0.66	0.38	0.66
2010	0.76	0.76	0.38	0.76

Source: Assumptions for the Annual Energy Outlook 1992, Energy Information Administration, January, 1992, p. 49. Primary source: Markups derived from U.S. Environmental Protection Agency (EPA), Office of Underground Storage Tanks, "Regulatory Impact Analysis of Technical Standards for Underground Storage Tanks," August 24, 1988; EPA, final rule "Regulations of Fuel Sold in 1993 and Later Calendar Years," August 8, 1990; *Federal Register* 55, No. 112, June 11, 1990, p. 23663; American Petroleum Institute, *Costs of Congressionally Reformulated Gasoline*, Editorial and Special Issues Department, Public Affairs Group, May 4, 1990; 101st Congress, Second Session, *Congressional Record*, October 26, 1990, p. 12857; and Congressional *Proposed Standards*, September, 1990, p. 1.

★ 298 ★

National Impacts of the CAA, 1995-2010

	1995	2000	2010
Scrubber retrofits (gigawatts)	7.8	10.6	12.0
Coal production (million tons)			
Low sulfur	16	59	77
Medium sulfur	-1	-12	-22
High sulfur	-16	-52	-64
Utility residual oil consumption (million barrels)			
Low sulfur	0	0	57
High sulfur	0	0	-76
Utility natural gas consumption (billion cubic feet)	1	-2	214
Electricity price (1990 cents per kilowatt-hour)	0.03	0.05	0.10

Source: Annual Outlook for U.S. Electric Power 1991: Projections through 2010, Energy Information Administration, July 1991, p. 37. Primary source: Energy Information Administration, AEO 1991 Forecasting System. The values in the table represent the difference within each year in results from two scenarios, one incorporating the CAA, the other without the CAA.

★ 299 ★

Nitrogen Oxides Standards for Highway Trucks, 1985-2000

"Since 1985, federal regulations have forced ... diesel-engine makers to slash in half two big pollutants: smog-causing nitrogen oxides and particulates like traces of carbon and partly burned fuel.... For 1994, U.S. diesel-engine makers must meet standards that call for cutting particulates to less than half 1991's reduced levels.... [A further challenge will occur] in 1998, when nitrogen oxides must be cut by another 20%."

[Tons in thousands]

1985-1990	10.7
1990-1991	6.0
1991-1998	5.0
1998-2000	4.0

Source: "Truck-Engine Research Has Its Mr. Clean," Robert L. Rose, *The Wall Street Journal*, December 15, 1992, p. B5. Primary source: Cummins Engine Co.

★ 300 ★

Purchases of Wastewater Treatment Equipment by Industry, 1987-1995

[Numbers in millions of 1987 dollars]

Sector	1987	1989	1991	1993	1995
Chemicals	160	190	206	238	263
Iron and steel	98	97	95	91	88
Metal finishing	59	58	56	56	50
Petroleum refining	37	55	78	83	88
Total for industry	662	745	845	907	958
Chemical industry wastewater expenses:					
Design/engineering	49	58	63	73	80
Equipment	160	190	206	238	263
Instruments	34	40	44	51	56
Construction	414	465	503	544	611
Total	657	754	816	906	1,010

Source: "Water Supply and Disposal Date," Gerald Parkinson and Nicholas Basta, *Chemical Engineering* 98, No. 4, April, 1991, p. 39. Primary source: William T. Lorenz & Co.

★ 301 ★

Savings in Fuel and Power Use and Costs Due to Compliance with OTA Controls, 2015

"The cost effectiveness of these measures (i.e., tons of carbon avoided per dollar of net costs) varies widely. Between about one-third to one-half of the reductions either save money or are of very low cost. About one-quarter of the reductions have costs exceeding $200 per ton of carbon avoided."

	1987	Energy (trillion Btu)			Cost (billion 1987 $, 2015 prices)		
		Base 2015	Change:		Base 2015	Change:	
			Moderate 2015	Tough 2015		Moderate 2015	Tough 2015
Residential buildings:							
Natural gas	4,462	4,198	-639	-1,320	$48	-$7	-$15
Electricity	2,854	3,323	-597	-1,067	$110	-$20	-$35
Oil	1,590	1,124	-174	-374	$11	-$2	-$4
Coal	74	62	-8	-13	$0	-$0	-$0
Wood	837	1,516	-353	-897			
Total	8,980	8,707	-1,418	-2,774	$169	-$29	-$54
Commercial buildings:							
Natural gas	2,421	3,387	-416	387	$36	-$4	$4
Electricity	2,525	4,264	-1,572	-2,922	$119	-$44	-$81
Oil	1,086	922	-259	-649	$9	-$3	-$6
Coal	107	114	-23	-43	$0	-$0	-$0

[Continued]

★ 301 ★

Savings in Fuel and Power Use and Costs Due to Compliance with OTA Controls, 2015
[Continued]

	1987	Energy (trillion Btu)			Cost (billion 1987 $, 2015 prices)		
		Base 2015	Change:		Base 2015	Change:	
			Moderate 2015	Tough 2015		Moderate 2015	Tough 2015
Total	6,139	8,687	-2,270	-3,226	$164	-$51	-$84
Industry:							
Coal	2,678	4,598	-1,299	-3,088	$13	-$4	-$9
Natural gas	7,044	7,685	-227	-24	$69	-$2	-$0
Oil	4,725	5,041	-627	-1,742	$40	-$5	-$14
Biomass	2,230	3,520	-298	-1,370			
Electric	2,679	4,398	-685	-1,686	$97	-$15	-$37
Total	19,355	25,242	-3,136	-7,909	$219	-$26	-$60
Transportation:							
Gasoline	13,393	16,380	-2,008	-6,927	$244	-$30	-$103
Distillate oil	3,338	5,140	-420	-1,586	$51	-$4	-$16
Jet fuel	2,872	4,686	-317	-1,327	$70	-$5	-$20
Aviation gas	45	48	0	0	$1	$0	$0
Residual oil	817	1207	0	0	$10	$0	$0
Natural gas	571	724	0	0	$8	$0	$0
Electricity	17	28	0	104	$1	$0	$3
Total	21,053	28,213	-2,745	-9,736	$383	-$39	-$136
Exogenous electricity	0	2,527	-632	-1,263	$69	-$17	-$35
All sectors:							
Natural gas	14,497	15,994	-1,282	-957	$160	-$14	-$11
Electricity	8,074	12,013	-2,855	-5,571	$396	-$96	-$186
Oil	27,866	34,548	-3,805	-12,605	$436	-$48	-$163
Coal	2,859	4,774	-1,330	-3,143	$14	-$4	-$9
Biomass	3,067	5,036	-651	-2,267			
Total	56,364	72,365	-9,923	-24,543	$1,006	-$162	-$369

Source: U.S. Congress, Office of Technology Assessment, *Changing by Degrees: Steps to Reduce Greenhouse Gases*, February, 1991, p. 321. Primary source: Office of Technology Assessment, 1991.

★ 302 ★

Urban Bus Heavy-Duty Engine Emission Standards to Comply with the 1990 Clean Air Act (CAA), 1990-1994

"Cities have already discussed the possibility of banning diesel buses from their streets because of the sooty, smelly exhaust they produce. And the EPA has legislated strict diesel particulate emissions regulations for busses and heavy-duty trucks that take effect in 1993 and 1994, respectively, and get tighter through the year 2000."

[g/bhp.h measured during EPA heavy-duty engine test]

Model year	NO_x	HC	CO	PM
1990	6.0	1.3	15.5	0.60
1991	5.0	1.3	15.5	0.25
1993	5.0	1.3	15.5	0.10
1994	5.0	1.3	15.5	0.05

Source: "Cellular Ceramic Products Help Curb Diesel Engine Emissions," Nitin S. Kulkarn, *Automotive Engineering* 100, No. 1, January, 1992, p. 23. *Notes*: NO_x = Nitrogen oxides; HC = Hydrocarbons; CO = Carbon monoxide; PM = Per Million.

New Technologies and Renewable Resources

★ 303 ★

Alternative-Fuel Vehicle Sales, 2010

[Numbers in thousands]

	Oil price case		
	Low oil price ($23)	Mid-level price ($34)	High oil price ($45)
Light-duty vehicles	235	234	612
Medium-duty trucks	0	4	8
Heavy-duty trucks	0	3	7

Source: Assumption for the Annual Energy Outlook 1992, Energy Information Administration, January, 1992, p. 28. Primary source: Tables 16, 18, and 20.

★ 304 ★

Energy From the Combustion of Municipal Solid Waste Using Heat Recovery, 1990-2010

[Numbers in percent]

Year	Low economic growth case	Reference base case	High economic growth case
1990	16	16	16
1995	23	30	30
2000	26	40	47
2005	30	50	63
2010	30	55	80

Source: Assumptions for the Annual Energy Outlook 1992, Energy Information Administration, January, 1992, p. 23. Primary source: Energy Information Administration, Office of Integrated Analysis and Forecasting, Energy Supply and Conversion Division.

★ 305 ★

Impacts of 100 Percent of Electric Cars on Employment and Payroll by Industry, 1980-2000

Industry	Standard industrial code	Employment change, thousands			Payroll change, millions of 1977 dollars		
		1980	1990	2000	1980	1990	2000
Independent of battery type							
Carburetor, piston, valve manufacturing	3592	-24	-31	-37	-345	-450	-554
Electric controls manufacturing	3622	33	38	41	425	497	459
ICE electric equipment manufacturing	3694	15	14	11	425	230	187
Motor vehicle body and parts manufacturing	3711, 3714	-56	-57	-54	-1000	-1173	1227
Motor vehicle parts distribution	5012	-57	-55	-84	-854	-819	-1360
Petroleum wholesalers	5171, 5172	-35	-22	-28	-505	-339	-455
Automotive supply stores	5531	-67	-87	-107	-640	-858	-1075
Automotive service stations	5541	-293	-350	-410	-1741	-2112	-2499
Automotive repair shops	7538, 7539	-93	-118	-143	-757	-948	-1141
Subtotal		-576	-667	-810	-5191	-5972	-7665
Lead-acid batteries							
Lead and zinc mining, smelting	1031, 3332	73	86	107	994	1,254	1,665
Storage battery manufacturing	3691	196	214	224	2,648	2,985	3,212
Battery distribution and sales	-	432	454	467	5,753	6,536	7,099
Subtotal		701	754	798	9,395	10,775	11,976
Nickel-zinc batteries							
Lead and zinc mining and smelting	1031, 3332	55	60	57	744	868	892
Nickel and cobalt mining	-	43	37	35	796	915	1,332
Storage battery manufacturing	3691	518	587	622	6,996	8,197	8,903
Battery distribution and sales	-	1,084	1,140	1,172	14,438	16,404	17,818

[Continued]

★ 305 ★

Impacts of 100 Percent of Electric Cars on Employment and Payroll by Industry, 1980-2000
[Continued]

Industry	Standard industrial code	Employment change, thousands			Payroll change, millions of 1977 dollars		
		1980	1990	2000	1980	1990	2000
Subtotal	1,700	1,823	1,887	22,973	26,384	28,946	
Lithium-sulfur batteries							
Nickel and cobalt mining	-			11			408
Lithium mining	-			27			863
Molybdenum mining	-			12			402
Storage battery manufacturing	3691			699			10,005
Battery distribution and sales	-			1,317			20,010
Subtotal				2,066			31,694

Source: Congress of the United States, Office of Technology Assessment, *Synthetic Fuels for Transportation: The Future Potential of Electric and Hybrid Vehicles,* January, 1982, p. 183. Primary source: Baseline projections made by least-squares regression analysis of historical data published in *County Business Patterns.* Adjustments were made to the portion of activity estimated to be affected by electric vehicle production and use.

★ 306 ★

National Use of Energy without and with 20 Percent Electrification of Light-Duty Vehicular Travel, 1990-2010

"Assumptions: Total energy use projections without EHVs were derived from the President's National Energy Plan II, submitted to Congress in the spring of 1979. These projections were selected because they assume 'medium world oil prices' by 2000, continuing to 2010. They also assume that various transitional and ultimate energy technologies will be developed, such as the use of direct petroleum substitutes, e.g., heavy oils, tar sands, synthetic liquids, and solar power."

[Numbers in quadrillion Btus per year]

	1990			2000			2010		
	Without	With	Percent change	Without	With	Percent change	Without	With	Percent change
Nuclear	11	11.17	+1.6	17	17.35	+2.0	22	22.52	+2.4
Coal	28	29.01	+3.6	39	40.24	+3.2	49	50.30	+2.7
Oil	37	35.60	-3.8	32	30.79	-3.8	26	24.90	-4.2
Other	26	26.11	+0.4	29	29.07	+0.3	32	32.07	+0.2
	102	101.89	-0.1	117	117.45	+0.4	129	129.79	+0.6

Source: Congress of the United States, Office of Technology Assessment, *Synthetic Fuels for Transportation: The Future Potential of Electric and Hybrid Vehicles,* January, 1982, p. 166. Primary source: *National Energy Plan 1,* 1979, and the Recharge Capacity Projection System (RECAPS), General Research Corporation.

★ 307 ★

Percent Contribution of Automobiles and Power Plants to Emissions without Electric and Hybrid Vehicles, 1980-2010

"Assumptions: Industrial growth projections were for 1977, and were obtained from the Department of Commerce OBERS model. Base year emissions data were for 1975, and were obtained from the National Emission Data System (NEDS). Electric utility growth projections were based on the Recharge Capacity Projection System (RECAPS) output generated both with and without EHV [Electric and Hybrid Vehicles] use. Emissions from facilities built prior to 1978 were assumed to be controlled to the level defined in NEDS. These projections, therefore, do not fully reflect the effect of the 1977 Amendments to the Clean Air Act which require that states submit revised State Implementation Plans (SIPs) which assure that future air quality will satisfy the national primary standard. Analysis was based on the 24 most populated air quality control regions (AQCRs) in the United States. The results reflect population-weighted averages."

Pollutant	Contribution of vehicles, percent				Contribution of power plants, percent			
	1980	1990	2000	2010	1980	1990	2000	2010
Total Suspended particulates	10	9	9	9	10	7	6	5
Sulfur oxides	0	0	0	0	38	32	26	20
Nitrogen oxides	20	14	14	14	23	21	20	19
Total hydrocarbons	25	13	12	11	0	0	0	0
Carbon monoxide	54	38	38	38	0	0	1	2

Source: Congress of the United States, Office of Technology Assessment, *Synthetic Fuels for Transportation: The Future Potential of Electric and Hybrid Vehicles,* January 1982, p. 168. Primary source: Regional Emissions Projection System (REPS), General Research Corporation.

★ 308 ★

Projection of Annual Electric Vehicle Sales under Alternative Policies, 1985 and 1995

Incentives	1985		1995	
	Number	Percent increase	Number	Percent increase
Base case (no incentives)	20,300	--	36,900	--
$300 purchase subsidy	38,000	38	50,900	38
$1,000 purchase subsidy	59,600	194	107,400	191
$3,000 purchase subsidy	503,000	2378	867,800	2252
Off-peak electricity pricing	27,100	33	49,900	35
50-cent gas tax	51,900	156	102,400	178
10-cent gas tax	25,300	25	45,500	23
Doubling of range	55,900	175	114,200	209
Operating subsidy of one-third of most life cycle costs	240,100	108	465,500	1161
Combination of 50-cent gas tax and doubling of range	144,800	613	313,400	749
Combination of 50-cent gas tax and operating subsidy	601,700	2860	1,221,000	3209

Source: Congress of the United States, Office of Technology Assessment, *Synthetic Fuels for Transportation: The Future Potential of Electric and Hybrid Vehicles,* January, 1982, p. 153. Primary source: C. Upton and C. Agnew, *An Analysis of Federal Incentives to Stimulate Consumer Acceptance of Electric Vehicles,* Machtech, September, 1977.

★ 309 ★

Representative Future Electric Cars by 2000

"Assumptions: Electricity Price: $0.03 per kilowatt-hour; Gasoline price (for ICE vehicles): $1.25 per gallon; Electric vehicle life: 12 years; ICE vehicle life: 10 years; Annual travel: 10,000 miles; Acceleration capability: 0-40 mph in 10 seconds; Passenger capacity: Four persons plus luggage."

Battery type	ETV-1 (1980) Pb-acid (lead-acid)	Near-term (by 1990)					Advanced (by 2000)		
		Pb-acid (lead-acid)	Ni-Fe (nickel-iron)	Ni-Zn (nickel-zinc)	Zn-Cl$_2$ (zinc-chlorine)	(ICE)[2]	Zn-Cl$_2$ (zinc-chlorine)	Li-MS (lithium-metal sulfide)	(ICE)[2]
Battery specific energy, Wh/lb[1]	16.9	22.7	27.2	31.8	34.0	-	45.4	68.0	-
Nominal range (urban), mi	60	100	100	100	100	-	150	150	-
Curb weight, lb	3,260	4,090	3,290	3,030	2,960	2,010	2,300	2,260	1,810
Battery system weight, lb	1,140	1,580	1,050	890	-	840	600	400	
Sticker price, mid-1980 dollars	8,480	8,520	8,400	8,130	8,120	4,740	7,050	6,810	5,140
Life-cycle cost, 1980 cents/mi	26.1	23.9	24.9	26.6	22.0	21.4	19.4	20.1	21.8
Electricity use, KWh/mi	0.38	0.40	0.44	0.33	0.45	-	0.31	0.30	-
Fuel economy, mpg (urban driving)	-	-	-	-	-	33.0	-	-	35.6

Source: Congress of the United States, Office of Technology Assessment, *Synthetic Fuels for Transportation: The Future Potential of Electric and Hybrid Vehicles,* January, 1982, p. 50. Prepared under contract by the General Research Corporation. Primary source: General Research Corporation. Performance cost estimates for all vehicles were based on computer models. Costs are in mid-1980 dollars and are based on mass production of all vehicles (300,000 units or more per year). *Notes:* 1. Energy delivered by the battery in a full discharge over three hours, in watt-hours per pound of battery weight. 2. Internal combustion engine.

★ 310 ★

Utility and Nonutility Electric Capability for Renewable Technologies, 1990-2010

[Numbers in gigawatts]

Renewables	1990		1995		2000		2005		2010	
	Utility	Nonutility	Utility	Nonutility	Utility	Nonutility	Utility	Nonutility	Utility	Nonutility
Conventional hydro	73.6	2.1	74.9	3.5	74.9	3.6	74.9	3.6	74.9	3.8
Pumped storage	17.3	0.0	18.7	0.0	20.3	1.5	20.3	1.5	20.3	1.5
Wind	0.0	2.0	0.0	2.6	0.0	3.5	0.0	4.3	0.0	5.2
Solar thermal	0.0	0.4	0.1	1.2	0.1	1.2	0.1	1.3	0.1	1.6
Geothermal	1.6	1.0	1.8	1.4	2.7	2.6	3.8	4.0	4.1	4.3
Photovaltaic	0.0	0.0	0.0	0.1	0.1	0.0	0.0	0.0	0.0	0.0
Wood	0.3	5.0	0.3	5.7	0.4	6.0	0.4	6.2	0.5	6.4
Municipal solid waste	0.4	2.0	0.5	4.7	0.8	7.0	1.0	9.7	1.2	11.7
Total	93.2	12.4	96.1	19.0	99.0	25.3	100.5	30.5	101.1	34.3

Source: Assumptions for the Annual Energy Outlook 1992, Energy Information Administration, January, 1992, p. 75. Primary source: Energy Information Administration, Office of Integrated Analysis and Forecasting. *Notes*: 1990 numbers are estimated. Totals may not equal sum of components due to independent rounding.

Solid Waste Management

★ 311 ★

Average Rates of Increase or Decrease of Generation of Materials in Municipal Solid Waste, 1960-2000[1]

[Numbers in annual percent by weight]

	1960-1970	1970-1980	1980-1990	1990-2000
Paper & paperboard	4.5	2.1	3.4	1.6
Glass	6.8	1.9	0.0	0.2
Metals	2.7	0.5	1.0	0.6
Plastics	27.5	12.1	8.3	4.4
Wood	2.8	6.6	7.7	2.7
All other materials[2]	4.3	4.0	3.5	4.5
Food wastes	0.3	0.3	0.0	0.0
Yard trimmings	1.3	1.6	2.4	-2.5
Total MSW	3.5	2.3	2.8	1.3
Population	1.2	1.1	1.0	0.7

Source: U.S. Environmental Protection Agency, Municipal and Industrial Solid Waste Division, Office of Solid Waste, *Characterization of Municipal Solid Waste in the United States: 1992 Update,* July 1992, 4-6. Primary source: Franklin Associates, Ltd., Prairie Village, Kansas. Details may not add to totals due to rounding. *Notes:* 1. Rates are based on 10-year trend lines for each decade. 2. Rubber and leather, textiles, electrolytes in batteries, wood pulp and moisture in disposable diapers, miscellaneous inorganics.

★ 312 ★

Chemical Industry's Hazardous Waste Output, 1990 and 1995

[Pounds in billions]

	1990	1995
Chemicals & allied products	373	470
Primary metals	119	143
Petroleum and coal	88	110
Fabricated metal	68	86
Rubber & plastic	42	60
Other	71	90
Total	761	959

Source: "Hazardous Waste Management Industry to Grow," Ann Thayer, *Chemical and Engineering News* 69, No. 8, February 25, 1991, p. 12. Primary source: Leading Edge Reports.

★ 313 ★

Energy From the Combustion of Municipal Solid Waste, 1990-2010

[BTU in quadrillions]

Year	Low economic growth case	Reference base case	High economic growth case
1990	0.26	0.29	0.32
1995	0.42	0.64	0.70
2000	0.50	0.95	1.22
2005	0.63	1.32	1.82
2010	0.66	1.58	2.53

Source: *Assumptions for the Annual Energy Outlook 1992*, Energy Information Administration, January, 1992, p. 23. Primary source: Energy Information Administration, Office of Integrated Analysis and Forecasting, Energy Supply and Conversion Division.

★ 314 ★

Heat Value of Municipal Solid Waste, 1990-2010

[Numbers in BTUs per pound]

Year	Low economic growth case	Reference base case	High economic growth case
1990	4,503	5,004	5,504
1995	4,792	5,325	5,857
2000	4,950	5,500	6,050
2005	5,084	5,649	6,214
2010	5,171	5,745	6,320

Source: *Assumptions for the Annual Energy Outlook 1992*, Energy Information Administration, January, 1992, p. 22. Primary source: Energy Information Administration, Office of Integrated Analysis and Forecasting, Energy Supply and Conversion Division.

★ 315 ★

Methods of Solid Waste Disposal, 1990-2000

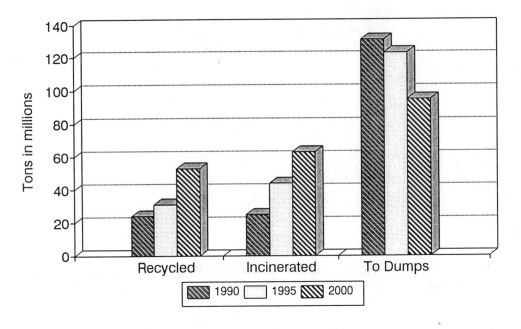

"Even as garbage increases, the need for dumps could decline."

[Tons in millions]

	1990	1995	2000
To dumps	131	123	95
Incinerated	25	44	63
Recycled	24	31	53

Source: "Gallatin National's Expectations Are Down for Its Dump: Changes in Trash Disposal Market Pose Problems for Newcomers," Jeff Bailey, *Wall Street Journal*, October 21, 1992, p. B4. Primary source: Browning-Ferris Industries Inc. Magnitudes estimated from published chart.

★ 316 ★

Municipal Solid Waste Discards, 1960-2000

"Past landfilling practices have caused serious threats to public health and the environment. Reports of explosions and fires caused by methane gas build-up from decaying garbage, and the contamination of groundwater from leaking substances are more and more common. For decades, all types of waste—hazardous and nonhazardous—were dumped directly on the ground or into large pits. While this practice caused minimal damage a century ago, the addition of toxic substances from industries and households has proved disastrous to underlying groundwater."

Year	Gross annual discards (in million tons)	Per capita discards (pounds per day)
1960	87.5	2.65
1965	102.3	2.88
1970	120.5	3.22
1975	125.3	3.18
1980	142.6	3.43
1981	144.8	3.45
1982	142.0	3.35
1983	148.4	3.47
1984	153.6	3.56
1985	152.5	3.49
1986	157.7	3.58
1990	167.4	3.67
1995	180.1	3.80
2000	192.7	3.94

Source: "Total Municipal Solid Waste Discards: 1970-2000," Carol Andress, *Waste Not, Want Not: State and Federal Roles in Source Reduction and Recycling of Solid Waste*, February, 1989, p. 3. Primary source: Environmental Protection Agency, *Characterization of Municipal Solid Waste in the United States, 1960-2000*, March 1988, pp. 18-19.

★ 317 ★

Outlook for Medical-Waste Disposal Market, 1992-2000

Includes hospital and non-hospital medical waste sent off-site for disposal. "Arthur D. Little Inc., a consulting firm, expects a growing percentage of medical waste to be handled off-site, or commercially, as the total volume grows.... [In] many markets disposal capacity exceeds demand, and competitors have aggressively cut prices to get business.... The price decline has been so precipitous that Arthur D. Little slashed revenue expectations for the medical-waste business in the year 2000 to less than $1 billion from more than $2 billion."

[Tons in thousands]

	Hospital	Non-hospital
1992	215	270
1993	230	290
1994	250	320
1995	270	345
1996	285	365
1997	300	380
1998	315	405
1999	330	420
2000	345	455

Source: "How Two Garbage Giants Fought Over Medical Waste," Jeff Baily, *The Wall Street Journal*, November 17, 1992, p. B6. Primary source: Projections by Arthur D. Little Inc. Magnitudes estimated from published chart.

★ 318 ★

Projections of Categories of Products Generated in the Municipal Waste Stream, 1990-2000[1]

Products	Millions of tons			% of total generation		
	1990	1995	2000	1990	1995	2000
Durable goods	27.9	30.3	33.8	14.3%	14.6%	15.2%
Nondurable goods	52.3	58.6	64.4	26.7%	28.2%	29.0%
Containers and packaging	64.4	69.1	74.7	32.9%	33.2%	33.6%
Total product waste[2]	144.6	158.0	172.9	73.9%	76.0%	77.8%
Other wastes						
Food wastes	13.2	13.2	13.2	6.7%	6.3%	5.9%
Yard trimmings	35.0	33.7	32.9	17.9%	16.2%	14.8%
Miscellaneous inorganic wastes	2.9	3.0	3.1	1.5%	1.4%	1.4%

[Continued]

★ 318 ★

Projections of Categories of Products Generated in the Municipal Waste Stream, 1990-2000
[Continued]

Products	Millions of tons			% of total generation		
	1990	1995	2000	1990	1995	2000
Total other wastes	51.1	49.9	49.2	26.1%	24.0%	22.2%
Total MSW generated	195.7	207.9	222.1	100.0%	100.0%	100.0%

Source: U.S. Environmental Protection Agency, Municipal and Industrial Solid Waste Division, Office of Solid Waste, *Characterization of Municipal Solid Waste in the United States: 1992 Update*, July, 1992, 4-6. Primary source: Franklin Associates, Ltd., Prairie Village, Kansas. Details may not add to totals due to rounding. *Notes*: 1. Generation before materials recovery or combustion. 2. Other than food products.

★ 319 ★

Projections of Materials Generated in the Municipal Waste Stream, 1990-2000[1]

Materials	Millions of Tons			% of total generation		
	1990	1995	2000	1990	1995	2000
Paper and paperboard	73.3	79.2	84.7	37.5%	38.1%	38.1%
Glass	13.2	13.6	13.5	6.7%	6.5%	6.1%
Metals						
Ferrous	12.3	12.0	12.1	6.3%	5.8%	5.4%
Aluminum	2.7	3.1	3.6	1.4%	1.5%	1.6%
Other nonferrous	1.2	1.4	1.5	0.6%	0.7%	0.7%
Total metals	16.2	16.5	17.1	8.3%	7.9%	7.7%
Plastics	16.2	20.0	24.8	8.3%	9.6%	11.2%
Rubber and leather	4.6	5.9	6.5	2.4%	2.8%	2.9%
Textiles	5.6	5.9	6.7	2.9%	2.9%	3.0%
Wood	12.3	13.5	16.0	6.3%	6.5%	7.2%
Other	3.2	3.4	3.7	1.6%	1.7%	1.6%
Total materials in products	144.6	158.0	172.9	73.9	76.0	77.8
Other wastes						
Food wastes	13.2	13.2	13.2	6.7%	6.3%	5.9%
Yard trimmings	35.0	33.7	32.9	17.9%	16.2%	14.8%
Miscellaneous inorganic wastes	2.9	3.0	3.1	1.5%	1.4%	1.4%
Total other wastes	51.1	49.9	49.2	26.1%	24.0%	22.2%
Total MSW generated	195.7	207.9	222.1	100.0%	100.0%	100.0%

Source: U.S. Environmental Protection Agency, Municipal and Industrial Solid Waste Division, Office of Solid Waste, *Characterization of Municipal Solid Waste in the United States: 1992 Update*, July, 1992, 4-2. Primary source: Franklin Associates, Ltd., Prairie Village, Kansas. Details may not add to totals due to rounding. *Note*: 1. Generation before materials recovery or combustion.

★ 320 ★

Projections of Products Generated in the Municipal Waste Stream
(with Detail on Containers and Packaging), 1990-2000[1]

Products	Millions of tons			% of total generation		
	1990	1995	2000	1990	1995	2000
Durable goods	27.9	30.3	33.8	14.3	14.6	15.2
Nondurable goods	52.3	58.6	64.4	26.7	28.2	29.0
Containers and packaging						
Glass packaging						
Beer and soft drinks bottles	5.7	5.7	5.6	2.9%	2.7%	2.5%
Wine and liquor bottles	2.1	2.2	2.2	1.1%	1.1%	1.0%
Food and other bottles & jars	4.1	4.2	4.1	2.1%	2.0%	1.9%
Total glass packaging	11.9	12.1	11.9	6.1%	5.8%	5.4%
Steel packaging						
Beer and soft drink cans	0.1	0.1	0.1	0.1%	0.1%	0.1%
Food and other cans	2.5	2.4	2.3	1.3%	1.1%	1.0%
Other steel packaging	0.2	0.2	0.2	0.1%	0.1%	0.1%
Total steel packaging	2.9	2.7	2.6	1.5%	1.3%	1.2%
Aluminum packaging						
Beer and soft drink cans	1.6	1.7	2.0	0.8%	0.8%	0.9%
Other cans	0.0	0.1	0.1	0.0%	0.0%	0.0%
Foil and closures	0.3	0.4	0.4	0.2%	0.2%	0.2%
Total aluminum pkg.	1.9	2.2	2.5	1.0%	1.1%	1.1%
Paper & paperboard pkg.						
Corrugated boxes	23.9	25.3	27.0	12.2%	12.2%	12.2%
Milk cartons	0.5	0.5	0.5	0.3%	0.2%	0.2%
Folding cartons	4.3	4.5	4.7	2.2%	2.2%	2.1%
Other paperboard packaging	0.3	0.3	0.3	0.1%	0.1%	0.1%
Bags and sacks	2.4	2.5	2.5	1.2%	1.2%	1.1%
Wrapping papers	0.1	0.1	0.1	0.1%	0.1%	0.1%
Other paper packaging	1.0	1.0	1.0	0.5%	0.5	0.5%
Total paper & board pkg.	32.6	34.3	36.2	16.7%	16.5%	16.3%
Plastics packaging						
Soft drink bottles	0.4	0.6	0.7	0.2%	0.3%	0.3%
Milk bottles	0.4	0.5	0.5	0.2%	0.2%	0.2%
Other containers	1.8	2.8	3.5	0.9%	1.3%	1.6%
Bags and sacks	0.9	1.2	1.4	0.5%	0.6%	0.6%
Wraps	1.5	1.7	2.0	0.8%	0.8%	0.9%
Other plastics packaging	1.9	2.1	2.6	1.0%	1.0%	1.2%
Total plastics packaging	7.0	8.7	10.7	3.6%	4.2%	4.8%
Wood packaging	7.9	8.9	10.6	4.0%	4.3%	4.8%
Other misc. packaging	0.2	0.2	0.2	0.1%	0.1%	0.1%
Total containers & pkg.	64.4	69.1	74.7	32.9%	33.2%	33.6%
Total product wastes[2]	144.6	158.0	172.9	73.9%	76.0%	77.8%
Other wastes						
Food wastes	13.2	13.2	13.2	6.7%	6.3%	5.9%

[Continued]

★ 320 ★

Projections of Products Generated in the Municipal Waste Stream (with Detail on Containers and Packaging), 1990-2000

[Continued]

Products	Millions of tons			% of total generation		
	1990	1995	2000	1990	1995	2000
Yard trimmings	35.0	33.7	32.9	17.9%	16.2%	14.8%
Miscellaneous inorganic wastes	2.9	3.0	3.1	1.5%	1.4%	1.4%
Total other wastes	51.1	49.9	49.2	26.1%	24.0%	22.2%
Total MSW generated	195.7	207.9	222.1	100.0%	100.0%	100.0%

Source: U.S. Environmental Protection Agency, Municipal and Industrial Solid Waste Division, Office of Solid Waste, *Characterization of Municipal Solid Waste in the United States: 1992 Update*, July, 1992, 4-11. Primary source: Franklin Associates, Ltd., Prairie Village, Kansas. Details may not add to totals due to rounding. *Notes*: 1. Generation before materials recovery or combustion. 2. Other than food products.

★ 321 ★

Projections of Products Generated in the Municipal Waste Stream (with Detail on Durable Goods), 1990-2000

Products generated before materials recovery or combustion.

Products	Millions of tons			% of total generation		
	1990	1995	2000	1990	1995	2000
Durable goods						
Major appliances	2.8	3.2	3.4	1.4	1.5	1.5
Furniture and furnishings	7.4	7.7	9.1	3.8	3.7	4.1
Carpets and rugs	1.7	2.3	2.8	0.9	1.1	1.3
Rubber tires	1.8	2.3	2.4	0.9	1.1	1.1
Batteries, lead-acid	1.7	2.0	2.2	0.9	1.0	1.0
Miscellaneous durables	12.5	12.8	13.9	6.4	6.2	6.3
Total durable goods	27.9	30.3	33.8	14.3	14.6	15.2
Nondurable goods	52.3	58.6	64.4	26.7	28.2	29.0
Containers and packaging	64.4	69.1	74.7	32.9	33.2	33.6
Total waste products[1]	144.6	158.0	172.9	73.9	76.0	77.8
Other wastes						
Food wastes	13.2	13.2	13.2	6.7	6.3	5.9
Yard trimmings	35.0	33.7	32.9	17.9	16.2	14.8
Miscellaneous inorganic wastes	2.9	3.0	3.1	1.5	1.4	1.4
Total other wastes	51.1	49.9	49.2	26.1	24.0	22.2
Total MSW generated	195.7	207.9	222.1	100.0	100.0	100.0

Source: U.S. Environmental Protection Agency, Municipal and Industrial Solid Waste Division, Office of Solid Waste, *Characteristics of Municipal Solid Waste in the United States: 1992 Update*, July, 1992, pp. 4-8. Primary source: Franklin Associates, Ltd., Prairie Village, Kansas. Details may not add to totals due to rounding. *Note:* 1. Other than food products.

★ 322 ★

Projections of Products Generated in the Municipal Waste Stream (with Detail on Nondurable Goods), 1990-2000

Products generated before materials recovery or combustion.

Products	Millions of tons			% of total generation		
	1990	1995	2000	1990	1995	2000
Durable goods	27.9	30.3	33.8	14.3	14.6	15.2
Nondurable goods						
Newspapers	12.9	14.1	15.1	6.6	6.8	6.8
Books	1.0	1.1	1.2	0.5	0.5	0.5
Magazines	2.8	3.3	3.8	1.4	1.6	1.7
Office papers	6.4	7.5	8.1	3.3	3.6	3.6
Telephone books	0.5	0.6	0.7	0.3	0.3	0.3
Third class mail	3.8	4.2	4.6	2.0	2.0	2.0
Other commercial printing	5.5	5.9	6.5	2.8	2.8	2.9
Tissue paper and towels	3.2	3.5	3.8	1.6	1.7	1.7
Paper plates and cups	0.7	0.7	0.7	0.3	0.3	0.3
Plastic plates and cups	0.3	0.5	0.6	0.2	0.2	0.3
Trash bags	0.8	1.1	1.3	0.4	0.5	0.6
Disposable diapers	2.6	2.8	2.9	1.4	1.3	1.3
Other nonpackaging paper	3.8	3.9	4.1	1.9	1.9	1.9
Clothing and footwear	3.7	3.9	4.5	1.9	1.9	2.0
Towels, sheets, & pillowcases	1.0	1.1	1.2	0.5	0.5	0.5
Other misc. nondurables	3.2	4.4	5.5	1.6	2.1	2.5
Total nondurable goods	52.3	58.6	64.4	26.7	28.2	29.0
Containers and packaging	64.4	69.1	74.7	32.9	33.2	33.6
Total product wastes[1]	144.6	158.0	172.9	73.9	76.0	77.8
Other wastes						
Food wastes	13.2	13.2	13.2	6.7	6.3	5.9
Yard trimmings	35.0	33.7	32.9	17.9	16.2	14.8
Miscellaneous inorganic wastes	2.9	3.0	3.1	1.5	1.4	1.4
Total other wastes	51.1	49.9	49.2	26.1	24.0	22.2
Total MSW generated	195.7	207.9	222.1	100.0	100.0	100.0

Source: U.S. Environmental Protection Agency, Municipal and Industrial Solid Waste Division, Office of Solid Waste, *Characteristics of Municipal Solid Waste in the United States: 1992 Update,* July, 1992, pp. 4-9. Primary source: Franklin Associates, Ltd., Prairie Village, Kansas. Details may not add to totals due to rounding. *Note:* 1. Other than food products.

★ 323 ★

Quantities of Municipal Solid Waste, 1990-2010

[Tons in millions]

Year	Low economic growth case	Reference case	High economic growth case
1990	182.0	182.0	182.0
1995	189.8	199.8	199.8
2000	194.4	216.0	216.0
2005	205.3	233.0	233.0
2010	213.0	250.6	250.6

Source: Assumptions for the Annual Energy Outlook 1992, Energy Information Administration, January, 1992, p. 22. Primary source: Energy Information Administration, Office of Integrated Analysis and Forecasting, Energy Supply and Conversion Division.

Trends in Recycling

★ 324 ★

Average Recycling Growth Rates, 1989 and 1994

	1989		1994		Average annual
	%	Million tons	%	Million tons	growth rate, %
Glass	20.0	0.75	40.0	1.7	17.8
Metal	19.5	2.60	25.9	4.0	9.0
Paper	25.0	12.0	28.7	15.4	5.1
Paperboard	32.3	11.0	37.7	13.2	3.6
Plastics	5.0	0.1	13.0	0.4	31.0

Source: Modern Plastics, January, 1990, p. 143. Primary source: Business Communications Co.

★ 325 ★

Fiber Reuse in Recycled Printing and Writing Paper, 1990-1995

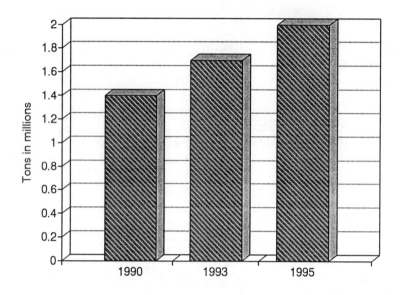

"Printing and writing papers consume about 1.4 million tons of waste stream recovered fiber.... As part of the pulp and paper industry commitment to increase the reuse of paper to 40%, a voluntary commitment by this industry, the Franklin Study projects this figure will increase to 2.0 million tons by 1995. This will still represent only about 6% of total printing and writing production capacity in that year."

[Tons in millions]

Year	Tons
1990	1.4
1993	1.7
1995	2.0

Source: "Strategies for the Reuse of Paper," Thomas C. Norris, *Graphic Arts Monthly* 63, No. 6, June, 1991, p. 84. Primary source: API & Franklin Associates.

★ 326 ★

Growth in Materials Recycling, 1989 and 1994

"According to a new report from Business Communications Co., Inc., recycling rates for plastics, glass, metal and paperboard will rise significantly between now and 1994. Although lowest of the four materials in total tonnage recycled, plastics will lead the group in rate of change, rising 31 percent. In comparison, the total amount of paperboard recycled annually is 33 times as great as that of plastics, but the recycling rate of paperboard will rise less than four percent by 1994."

[Tons in millions]

	1989	1994
Plastics	.3	.8
Glass	1.2	2.0
Metal	2.3	3.5
Paperboard	10.0	13.8

Source: "Firm Foresees Rise in Recycling," *Packaging* 35, No. 1, January, 1990, p. 39. Primary source: Business Communications Co., Inc. Magnitudes estimated from published chart. Numbers may not sum to percentage rates due to rounding.

★ 327 ★

Market for Old Newspapers (ONP), Old Magazines (OMG), Old Corrugated Containers (OCC), and Office Wastepaper (OWP), 1991-1995

"Major changes in the markets for recycled paper recovered by municipalities (old newspapers and old magazines) and by commercial establishments (old corrugated containers and office wastepaper) are projected over the next few years, according to Andover International Associates (AIA).... Some of AIA's definitions of wastepaper differ from the typical definitions used by the [recycling] industry. AIA includes inserts and flyers in with newspaper in the category of old newspapers (ONP), and catalogs are included with magazines in old magazines (OMG). In this way, AIA's figures reflect conditions encountered in the field by both collectors and users of recycled paper, and the categories are determined by what is actually obtained in municipal and commercial collections."

	1991	1993	1995
Number of ONP-consuming mills	158	163	175
Number of mills consuming 50,000 tons per year or more of ONP	12	17	29
Number of OMG-consuming mills	78	82	94
Number of mills consuming 30,000 tons per year or more of OMG	46	50	58
Number of OCC-consuming mills	205	209	217
Number of mills consuming 75,000 tons per year or more of OCC	46	50	58

[Continued]

★ 327 ★

Market for Old Newspapers (ONP), Old Magazines (OMG), Old Corrugated Containers (OCC), and Office Wastepaper (OWP), 1991-1995

[Continued]

	1991	1993	1995
Number of OWP-consuming mills	222	228	238
Number of mills consuming 30,000 tons per year or more of OWP	27	33	43

Source: "Wastepaper Market Evolving as Demand Changes Collection Infrastructure," *Pulp and Paper* 66, No. 5, May, 1992, pp. 91-94. Primary source: Andover International Associates. Compiled from four published tables that also provide information on Canadian markets for waste paper and total North American consumption of waste paper.

★ 328 ★

Production and Fiber Composition of Printing and Writing Paper, 1990 and 1995

[Tons in millions]

	1990	1995
Production	21.8	26.8
Woodpulp requirement	16.3	18.7-19.9
Recycled fiber requirement	1.2	1.4-2.7
Recycled fiber content	6.8%	6.8-12.9%

Source: "New Recycled Definitions Stir the Market," Michael J. Ducey, *Graphic Arts Monthly* 64, No. 5, May, 1992, p. 128. Primary source: Andover International Associates.

★ 329 ★

Projected Generation of Municipal Solid Waste and Ranges of Recovery , 2000[1]

"The range of projected recovery rates for materials in MSW under three recovery scenarios in the year 2000 is shown.... Continued increases in recovery in every category will be required to reach the scenarios shown."

[Numbers in millions of tons and percent of generation of each material]

Materials	Recovery						
	Million tons				% of generation		
	Generation	25%	30%	35%	25%	30%	35%
Paper and paperboard	84.7	28.0	33.8	36.2	33.1%	39.9%	42.7%
Glass	13.5	3.8	4.7	5.3	28.1%	34.8%	39.3%
Metals							
Ferrous	12.1	3.3	3.8	4.4	27.3%	31.4%	36.4%
Aluminum	3.6	1.4	1.5	1.6	38.9%	41.7%	44.4%
Other nonferrous[2]	1.5	1.1	1.1	1.1	71.0%	73.3%	73.3%
Total metals	17.1	5.8	6.4	7.1	33.7%	37.4%	41.5%
Plastics	24.8	1.9	2.5	2.9	7.7%	10.1%	11.7%
Rubber & Leather	6.5	0.3	0.4	0.2	4.6%	6.2%	3.1%
Clothing, other textiles	6.7	0.4	0.6	0.9	6.0%	9.0%	13.4%
Wood	16.0	1.1	1.6	2.1	6.9%	10.0%	13.1%
Yard trimmings	32.9	13.2	15.8	21.1	40.1%	48.0%	64.1%
Other materials[3]	19.9	1.0	1.0	1.8	5.0%	5.0%	9.0%
Totals	222.1	55.5	66.8	77.6	25.0%	30.0%	35.0%

Source: U.S. Environmental Protection Agency, Municipal and Industrial Solid Waste Division, Office of Solid Waste, *Characterization of Municipal Solid Waste in the United States: 1992 Update*, July, 1992, 4-15. Primary source: Franklin Associates, Ltd., Prairie Village, Kansas. Details may not add to totals due to rounding. *Notes:* 1. Recovery of postconsumer wastes; does not include converting/fabrication scrap. Does not include recovery for mixed MSW composting. 2. Includes some nonferrous metals other than battery lead. 3. Food wastes, miscellaneous inorganic wastes, other.

★ 330 ★

Recovered Waste Paper Utilization Rates by Major Grade, 1989 and 1995

Rates of recovered paper consumption are indicated as a percentage of production.

	1989	1995
Newsprint	24.6	36.5
Printing/writing	6.3	7.0
Packaging/converting	3.7	5.2
Tissue	49.0	49.4

[Continued]

★ 330 ★

Recovered Waste Paper Utilization Rates by Major Grade, 1989 and 1995

[Continued]

	1989	1995
Paperboard	35.6	43.0
Total	25.4	33.1

Source: "A Pulp Market Portrait," Ronald J. Slinn, *Graphic Arts Monthly* 63, No. 5, May, 1991, p. 134. Primary source: API & Franklin Associates.

★ 331 ★

Recovery and Composting Rates of Selected Products, 1995

[Tons in millions; generation of each material in percent]

Products	Million tons		% of generation	
	Low	High	Low	High
Paper and paperboard				
Newspaper	6.8	8.3	45.0	55.0
Books and magazines	1.0	1.7	15.0	25.0
Office papers	2.0	2.9	20.0	30.0
Commercial printing	0.9	1.4	15.0	25.0
Corrugated boxes	15.2	17.4	55.0	63.0
Other paper and paperboard	0.6	0.9	2.9	4.4
Total paper and paperboard	26.5	32.6	31.0	38.0
Glass containers				
Beer and soft drink bottles	1.3	1.7	35.0	45.0
Other glass containers	0.8	1.4	13.0	17.5
Total glass containers	2.1	3.1	22.0	32.0
Ferrous metals				
Beer and soft drink cans	<0.1	<0.1	45.0	55.0
Other steel containers	1.0	1.2	45.0	55.0
Ferrous in durables	0.5	1.1	6.8	16.8
Total ferrous metals	1.5	2.4	12.8	20.5
Aluminum				
Beer and soft drink cans	1.1	1.4	60.0	75.0
Other aluminum packaging	<0.1	<0.1	6.5	17.5
Total aluminum packaging	1.1	1.4	50.0	64.0
Plastics				
Soft drink bottles	0.1	0.2	25.0	40.0
Milk/water bottles	<0.1	0.1	10.0	25.0
Other plastic packaging	0.2	0.7	3.8	11.5
Total plastic packaging	0.4	1.1	6.0	15.0

[Continued]

★ 331 ★

Recovery and Composting Rates of Selected Products, 1995
[Continued]

Products	Million tons		% of generation	
	Low	High	Low	High
Batteries (lead only)	0.8	0.9	85.0	95.0
Composting				
Food wastes	0.0	1.0	0.0	7.6
Yard wastes	6.6	11.0	20.0	33.3
Other materials[1]	1.2	2.2	-	-
Total recovery	40.1	55.3	20.0	27.7

Primary source: *Characterization of Municipal Solid Waste in the United States: 1990 Update*, U.S. Environmental Protection Agency, June, 1990, p. 65, Franklin Associates Ltd. *Note:* 1. Plastic and other materials in batteries, rubber, wood, and textiles.

★ 332 ★

Solvent Recycling, 1990-2000
[Gallons in billions]

Item	1990	1995	2000	% Annual growth 95/90
Solvent recycling (billions of $)	15.2	18.0	20.0	3.4
$/gallon	0.24	0.29	0.34	3.9
Solvents demand	159.9	153.4	145.4	-0.8
% recyclable	50.0	48.9	48.1	-
Potentially recycled solvents	80.0	75.0	70.0	-1.3
% recycled	78.1	82.0	85.0	-
Solvent recycled (total)	62.5	61.5	59.5	-0.3
Halogenated hydrocarbons	16.0	14.0	12.0	-2.6
Hydrocarbons	14.7	14.0	13.0	-1.0
Alcohols	12.3	13.5	14.0	1.9
Esters and ethers	10.0	10.4	10.8	0.8
Ketones	9.5	9.6	9.7	0.2
On-site	51.0	49.2	46.8	-0.7
Commercial	11.5	12.3	12.7	1.4

Source: "Recycling Everything, Part 4: The Recycling Loop Closes for Solvents," Nicholas Basta with Kent Gilges, *Chemical Engineering* 98, No. 6, June, 1991, p. 45. Primary source: The Freedonia Group.

★ 333 ★

Waste Stream Recycling Goals for U.S. States, 1991-2005

As of October 1, 1989.

Alabama	No set goals
Alaska	No set goals
Arizona	No set goals
Arkansas	No set goals
California	50.0
Colorado	No set goals
Connecticut	25%
Delaware	No set goals
District of Columbia	25.0
Florida	30.0
Georgia	No set goals
Hawaii	No set goals
Idaho	No set goals
Illinois	No set goals
Indiana	25.0
Iowa	50.0
Kansas	No set goals
Kentucky	No set goals
Louisiana	20.0
Maine	50.0
Maryland	20.0
Massachusetts	20.0
Michigan	50.0
Minnesota	25.0
Mississippi	No set goals

[Continued]

★ 333 ★

Waste Stream Recycling Goals for U.S. States, 1991-2005

[Continued]

Missouri	No set goals
Montana	No set goals
Nebraska	No set goals
Nevada	No set goals
New Hampshire	No set goals
New Jersey	25.0
New Mexico	No set goals
New York	50.0
North Carolina	25.0
North Dakota	No set goals
Ohio	25.0
Oklahoma	No set goals
Oregon	No set goals
Pennsylvania	25.0
Rhode Island	15.0
South Carolina	No set goals
South Dakota	No set goals
Tennessee	No set goals
Texas	No set goals
Utah	No set goals
Vermont	40.0
Virginia	25.0
Washington	50.0
West Virginia	30.0
Wisconsin	No set goals
Wyoming	No set goals

Source: ENR, February 22, 1990, p. 54, from National Solid Waste Management Association.

Chapter 7
HEALTH, MEDICAL CARE, AND HUMAN SERVICES

Advances in National Health

★ 334 ★

Predictions for the Creation of Revolutionary Medical Treatments by the Year 2000

"New insights into human diseases would spur the creation of elegant new treatments. For instance, Leroy Hood, a brilliant Caltech immunologist, says that by the year 2000 it should be essentially possible to prevent such autoimmune diseases as rheumatoid arthritis, multiple sclerosis, and insulin-dependent diabetes, in which the body mistakenly attacks its own tissue. Clones of immune system cells gone haywire do the damage. Hood and his associates are already designing ways to remove such undesirable cell families in mice.

"One of the experts' most startling predictions is that by the year 2000 it should be possible to regrow whole organs, or parts of them, in the body instead of replacing them with transplants."

Source: "Technology in the Year 2000," Gene Bylinsky, *Fortune,* July 18, 1988, p. 97.

★ 335 ★

Estimated Impact of Projected and Targeted Changes in Death Rates for Individual and Group Causes of Death, 2000

The table below shows the effect of trend and target changes based on national health objectives for each cause of death on added years of life expected at birth, assuming no changes in mortality for other causes. "The potential changes in heart disease will have the largest impact on the increase in life expectancy (0.8 to 1.2 years), followed by stroke (0.3-0.4 years) and infant mortality (0.2 to 0.3 years). This should be compared to a range of 1.5 to 3.6 years of potential increase in [added years of life expected at birth]. Cancer mortality trends are increasing slightly, and the effect of meeting the target would change a 0.1 year decrease in life expectancy to an increase of 0.1 year. With only two exceptions ... none of the variants of the other causes of death lead to a change in life expectancy of more than 0.2 years." The table "also shows the effect on [the increase in the percentage of individuals surviving to age 65] for each cause of death, assuming no changes in mortality for other causes. The same causes as above are also the most prominent in their effect on [the increase in the percentage of individuals surviving to age 65]. Unintentional injury deaths, however, achieve more prominence."

Causes of death	Projected changes			Targeted changes	
	High mortality trend	Low mortality trend	PHS targets	Target and no change in residual	Target and residual trend
Added years of life expected at birth					
All causes	1.6	3.6	2.1	1.8	1.5
Chronic diseases	1.3	1.9	1.5	1.3	1.1
Heart disease	1.2	1.2	1.2	0.9	0.8
Cancer	-0.1	0.0	0.1		
Stroke	0.3	0.4	0.3		
COPD[1]	-0.2	0.0	-0.1		
Diabetes	0.0	0.1	0.0		
Cirrhosis	0.1	0.1	0.1		
Injuries	0.3	0.4	0.2		
Suicide	0.0	0.0	0.0		
Homicide	0.0	0.1	0.0		
Unintentional injuries	0.3	0.3	0.1		
Infant mortality	0.2	0.3	0.2		
Other causes of death	-0.2	0.7	0.1	0.1	0.0
Pneumonia and influenza	-0.1	0.1	0.1		
All other causes	-0.1	0.5	0.0	0.0	-0.1
Increase in percentage surviving to age 65					
All causes	1.7	3.7	2.3	2.1	1.8
Chronic diseases	1.3	1.9	1.6	1.4	1.2
Heart disease	1.2	1.3	1.2	1.0	0.8
Cancer	-0.1	0.0	0.1		
Stroke	0.2	0.3	0.2		
COPD[1]	-0.2	0.0	-0.2		
Diabetes	0.0	0.1	0.0		

[Continued]

★ 335 ★

Estimated Impact of Projected and Targeted Changes in Death Rates for Individual and Group Causes of Death, 2000
[Continued]

Causes of death	Projected changes		Targeted changes		
	High mortality trend	Low mortality trend	PHS targets	Target and no change in residual	Target and residual trend
Cirrhosis	0.2	0.2	0.2		
Injuries	0.5	0.7	0.4		
Suicide	0.0	0.0	0.1		
Homicide	0.1	0.2	0.1		
Unintentional injuries	0.5	0.5	0.2		
Infant mortality	0.2	0.3	0.2		
Other causes of death	-0.2	0.8	0.0	0.0	0.0
Pneumonia and influenza	-0.1	0.1	0.0		
All other causes	-0.1	0.7	0.0	0.0	-0.1

Source: "National Health Objectives for the Year 2000: The Demographic Impact of Health Promotion and Disease Prevention," Michael A. Stoto, *American Journal of Public Health* 81, No. 11, November, 1991, p. 1460. *Note:* 1. COPD stands for chronic obstructive pulmonary disease.

★ 336 ★

Percentage of Smoke-free Offices, 1992 and 2020

"Facilities managers predict the workplace of the future will be virtually smoke-free."

1992	56.0
2020	96.0

Source: "Smoke-free Workplace," Sam Ward, *USA Today*, September 24, 1992, p. B1. Primary source: International Facility Management Association survey of 2,470 managers.

★ 337 ★

Predicted Rise in Number of Health-Active Consumers, 1975-2000

Most of us grew up under the old "Marcus Welby" health-care system, in which the physician was all-powerful. But with the coming of the information age in the mid-1970s, that system began to produce diminishing returns. It is now being supplemented by a new health-care system in which more informed consumers will increasingly get to play the hero. "Market researcher John Fiorillo of New York's Health Strategy Group and Yale cancer surgeon and best-selling author Bernie Siegel have described three categories of health consumers: 1. Passive patients. These consumers regard health matters with a grim resignation. They feel that there is little they can do to improve their health or to manage illness. Siegel notes that, when passive patients get cancer, they often give up without a fight.... 2. Concerned consumers. These are the 'A-students' of traditional medical practice. While they sometimes ask questions and may occasionally seek out a second opinion, they will almost always go along with whatever their doctor recommends. Concerned consumers see themselves as operating under the umbrella of the physician's authority.... 3. Health-active, health-responsible consumers. These highly motivated men and women are determined to play an active role in their own health. They will not hesitate to disagree with their health advisors, and they frequently choose to explore alternative and holistic therapies. They understand that medical treatments involve substantial costs and hazards as well as potential benefits. If they aren't satisfied with a doctor's recommendation, they may seek a second, third, fourth, or even fifth opinion."

	1975	1988	2000
Concerned	5-10	30-35	40-50
Passive	85-95	55-65	30-40
Active and responsible	1-2	5-8	20-25

Source: "Patient, Heal Thyself: Health in the Information Age," Tom Ferguson, *The Futurist* 26, No. 1, January-February, 1992, p. 10. Primary source: Health Strategy Group, New York. Reproduced, with permission, from *The Futurist*, published by the World Future Society, 7910 Woodmont Avenue, Suite 450, Bethesda, Maryland, 20814.

★ 338 ★

Rapid Growth in Managed Health Care Systems, 1977-1997

"By 1997, as much as 90 percent of health care will be delivered under some form of managed care system, reports Hewitt Associates, Lincolnshire, IL."

	1977	1987	1997
Indemnity plans	96.0	73.0	10.0
Managed care	4.0	27.0	90.0

Source: "Managed Care," *Hospitals* 64, No. 17, September 5, 1990, p. 24. Primary source: Hewitt Associates, 1990.

Health Care Costs and Revenues

★ 339 ★

Hospital Financial Performance, 1990 and 1995

"A panel of 28 health care finance experts predicts that hospitals will see continued declines in their financial performance through 1995. Those declines will result primarily from Medicare and Medicaid reimbursement shortfalls, and also from a growing inability to cost-shift to make up for those losses."

[Numbers in percent]

	1990[1]	1995
Operating margin	2.70	2.00
Return on equity	8.90	7.30
Current ratio	2.00	1.90
Days in patient accounts receivable	75.00	75.30
Days cash on hand	19.90	17.40
Long-term debt-to-equity	0.63	0.64
Debt service coverage	3.20	3.00
Total asset turnover	0.93	0.94
Average age of plant	7.60	8.10
Replacement viability	0.44	0.43
Profit per discharge	20.00	16.00
Net price per discharge	4,395.00	6,304.00
Net price per visit	161.00	232.00
Bad debt and charity care	5.00	5.50
Outpatient revenue	22.50	30.30
Occupancy	58.80	59.50
Length of stay	6.40	6.20
Cost per discharge	4,307.00	6,138.00
FTEs per occupied bed	4.55	4.66
Inpatient man-hours per discharge, adjusted for case mix	142	148

Source: "Panel Predicts Worsening Hospital Financial Picture," Howard J. Anderson, *Hospitals* 66, No. 6, March 20, 1992, p. 82. Primary source: Healthcare Financial Management Association. *Note*: 1. Figures for 1990 are based on HFMA's study of 3,400 hospitals' audited financial statements and an annual survey of 1,700 hospitals.

★ 340 ★

Inflation in Labor Costs, 1990 and 1995

"The composite forecast pegs labor cost inflation at 6.8 percent in 1990, falling to 6 percent in 1995. Even with the decrease, forecasters say that salaries for health care workers will increase much faster than for other types of workers. There is a wide range in the forecasts, however. The low 1990 forecast is 4 percent, while the high hits 9 percent. In 1995, the low forecast is also 4 percent, with a high forecast of 8.8 percent."

	1990	1995
Minimum forecast	4.0	4.0
Mean forecast	6.8	6.0
Maximum forecast	9.0	8.8

Source: "Health Care in the 1990s: Forecasts by Top Analysts," *Hospitals* 63, No. 14, July 20, 1989, p. 36.

★ 341 ★

Inflation in the Cost of Products, 1990 and 1995

"The composite forecast for inflation in the cost of products purchased by hospitals is 5.4 percent in both 1990 and 1995, although there is considerably more variation in the 1995 forecasts. The range of 1990 forecasts spans 5.1 percentage points, while the range of 1995 forecasts spans 7.5 percentage points."

	1990	1995
Minimum forecast	3.0	2.5
Mean forecast	5.4	5.4
Maximum forecast	8.1	10.0

Source: "Health Care in the 1990s: Forecasts by Top Analysts," *Hospitals* 63, No. 14, July 20, 1989, p. 39.

★ 342 ★

Inflation in the Cost of Services, 1990 and 1995

"Inflation in the services purchased by hospitals will increase slightly from 1990 to 1995, from 5.1 percent to 5.3 percent, according to the composite forecast. The increase is forecast despite an intervening recession, which most participants predict. This implies a shift toward increased use of services.... But the forecasters split in their appraisal: seven forecast an increase in inflation in services, six forecast no change, and four forecast a decline. There is also a wide variation between the high and low forecasts in each year, with a spread of 6.3 percentage points in 1990 and a spread of 6.5 percentage points in 1995."

	1990	1995
Minimum forecast	1.5	1.5
Mean forecast	5.1	5.3
Maximum forecast	7.8	8.0

Source: "Health Care in the 1990s: Forecasts by Top Analysts," *Hospitals* 63, No. 14, July 20, 1989, p. 39.

★ 343 ★

Percentage of Net Patient Revenue From Outpatient Care, 1991-2000

1991	30.0
1992	33.0
1993	36.0
2000	49.0

Source: "Ambulatory Care Directors Help Hospitals Gear Up for Growth" *Hospitals* 66, No. 6, March 20, 1992, p. 52. Primary source: Survey of 506 hospital CEOs, Hamiliton/KSA, 1992. *Note:* Figures are median responses to questions asking for estimates.

Health Care Employment

★ 344 ★

Demand for Registered Nurses, 1990-2020

"An examination of projections for the required number of registered nurses by practice site," as presented in the table, "shows that by the year 2020 the total supply of nurses would be sufficient to meet registered nurse staffing needs only in hospital settings, leaving physician offices, nursing homes, and other settings with a shortfall of nearly one million registered nurses."

[Numbers in millions]

1990	1.60
2000	1.98
2010	2.14
2020	2.30

Source: Environmental Assessment 91/92, American Hospital Association, 1991, p. 33. Data are for full-time equivalents. Magnitudes estimated from published chart.

★ 345 ★

Estimated and Projected Numbers of Physicians and Dentists, 1982-2000

[Numbers in thousands]

Year	Total U.S. population (millions)	Physicians			Dentists
		Total	Medical doctors	Osteopaths	
Actual					
1982	232.5	483.7	465.0	18.7	132.0
1983	234.8	501.2	481.5	19.7	135.1
1984	237.0	506.5	485.7	20.8	138.0
1985	239.3	520.7	498.8	21.9	140.8
1986	241.7	534.8	511.6	23.2	143.2
1987	243.9	548.5	524.1	24.4	145.5
1988	246.3	562.0	536.3	25.7	147.4
Projections					
1990	248.7	587.7	559.5	28.2	150.8

[Continued]

★ 345 ★

Estimated and Projected Numbers of Physicians and Dentists, 1982-2000

[Continued]

Year	Total U.S. population (millions)	Physicians			Dentists
		Total	Medical doctors	Osteopaths	
1995	255.2	645.5	611.1	34.4	156.8
2000	259.6	696.5	656.1	40.0	161.2

Source: "Health Services, Resources, and Utilization," *Source Book of Health Insurance Data,* 1991, p. 91. Primary source: U.S. Department of Health and Human Services, Health Care Financing Administration. Original chart also includes data for 1950-1981.

★ 346 ★

Number of Active Post-Residency Physicians and Number of Full-Time-Equivalent Post-residency Patient Care Physicians by Age, Specialty, and Country of Graduation, 1970-2010

The table below "presents historical and projected data for the number of active post-residency physicians and the number of active post-residency patient care physicians. Both measures show that physician supply is growing rapidly. Projected growth is slightly slower for the full-time-equivalent measure."

	Historical		Projected	
	1970	1986	2000	2010
Active Post-residency physicians	262,694	438,935	567,300	611,100
Full-time-equivalent post-residency patient care physicians	233,400	393,500	495,700	522,100
Ratio of full-time-equivalent post-residency patient care physicians to active post-residency physicians	.888	.896	.873	.854

Source: "The Growing Proportion of Female Physicians: Implications for U.S. Physician Supply," Phillip R. Kletke, William D. Marder, and Anne B. Silberger, *American Journal of Public Health* 80, No. 3, March, 1990, pp. 300-304. Primary source: AMA Physician Masterfile, 1970-86, Department of Data Release Services, Division of Survey and Data Resources; AMA Demographic Model of the Physician Population, AMA Center for Health Policy Research, 1988.

★ 347 ★

Percent Change in Demand for Allied Health Professionals, 1988-2000

"Health professions expected to grow most rapidly in the 1990s are in the allied health sector. The Bureau of Labor Statistics projects a 50 percent increase in the number of jobs in this field by the year 2000."

Home health aides	68
Radiologic technologists/technicians	66
Medical records technicians	60
Physical therapists	57
Occupational therapists	49
Respiratory therapists	41
Speech pathologists/audiologists	28
Dieticians/nutritionists	28
Lab technologists/technicians	19
Emergency medicine technicians	13

Source: *Environmental Assessment, 91/92*, American Hospital Association, 1991, p. 35.

★ 348 ★

Percent Change in Number of Professionally Active Medical Doctors per 100,000 Residents, 1986-2000

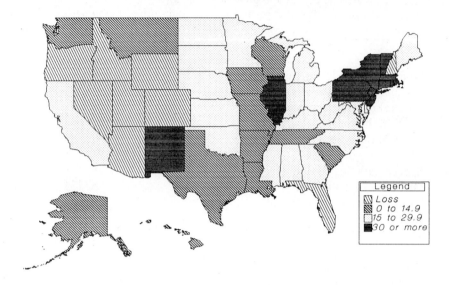

"Between 1986 and 2000, the number of medical doctors for every 100,000 U.S. residents is expected to increase 15 percent, from 216 to 248. But nine states should have fewer doctors per 100,000 residents in 2000."

State	Percent
Alabama	15 - 29.9
Alaska	0-14.9
Arizona	loss
Arkansas	0-14.9
California	15-29.9
Colorado	loss
Connecticut	30 or more
Delaware	15-29.9
District of Columbia	15-29.9
Florida	loss
Georgia	15-29.9
Hawaii	0-14.9
Idaho	loss
Illinois	30 or more
Indiana	15-29.9
Iowa	0-14.9
Kansas	15-29.9
Kentucky	15-29.9
Louisiana	0-14.9
Maine	15-29.9
Maryland	15-29.9
Massachusetts	30 or more
Michigan	15-29.9

[Continued]

★ 348 ★

Percent Change in Number of Professionally Active Medical Doctors per 100,000 Residents, 1986-2000

[Continued]

State	Percent
Minnesota	15-29.9
Mississippi	15-29.9
Missouri	0-14.9
Montana	0-14.9
Nebraska	15-29.9
Nevada	loss
New Hampshire	loss
New Jersey	30 or more
New Mexico	30 or more
New York	30 or more
North Carolina	15-29.9
North Dakota	15-29.9
Ohio	15-29.9
Oklahoma	15-29.9
Oregon	loss
Pennsylvania	30 or more
Rhode Island	30 or more
South Carolina	0-14.9
South Dakota	15-29.9
Tennessee	0-14.9
Texas	0-14.9
Utah	loss
Vermont	30 or more
Virginia	15-29.9
Washington	0-14.9
West Virginia	15-29.9
Wisconsin	0-14.9
Wyoming	loss

Source: "Where is the Doctor?," *American Demographics* 14, No. 1, January, 1992, p. 10. Primary source: U.S. Congress, Office of Technology Assessment, Health Care in Rural America, OTA-H-434, September, 1990.

★ 349 ★

Percent Change in Projected Growth of Physician Supply, 1986-2000

"Some analysts have suggested that there may be an oversupply of as many as 100,000 doctors by the year 2000. These projections, however, are aggregate figures and do not reflect the disparities in supply across states or the shortages of physicians in many rural and inner-city communities. Nor do they reflect current and projected differences in supply across specialties."

Gastroenterology	79.6
Pulmonary diseases	71.4
Cardiovascular disease	67.6
Diagnostic radiology	62.0
Physical medicine/rehabilitation	53.3
Pediatric specialties	38.6
General pediatrics	35.7
Obstetrics/gynecology	32.0
Internal medicine	23.6
Surgical specialties	23.1
Psychiatry/child psych.	18.4
General/family practice	16.1
Public health	-34.2
Occupational medicine	-16.9

Source: Environmental Assessment, 91/92, American Hospital Association, 1991, p. 38.

★ 350 ★

Percent Change in the Number of Active Post-Residency Physicians and the Number of Full-Time-Equivalent Post-Residency Patient Care Physicians, 1986-2000 and 1986-2010

The table below "shows the percent growth in the two supply measures for the various components of the physician population in 1970-86 and 1986-2010. Both measures indicate that: the percent growth is substantially larger for female physicians than for male physicians; growth rates for emergency medicine, general internal medicine, and pediatrics are greater than for other specialties; and the number of physicians over 65 will grow faster than the physician population as a whole. More important for this analysis are the subtle differences between the two measures attributable to changes in the composition of the physician population. In both time periods, the percent increase of active post-residency physicians is several percentage points greater than their full-time equivalents, i.e., the growth of effective physician supply. For almost all the components of the physician population, the percent increase in active physicians exceeds the percent increase in full-time-equivalent patient care physicians. Female physicians are an important exception. Between 1986 and 2000, disproportionate numbers of female physicians will enter the middle age categories when they spend the most time in patient care. On the other hand, male physicians will be entering the older age categories and thus are expected to work fewer hours per week. Due to this difference, the sex differential in the rate at which physicians provide patient care will decrease in the future."

	1986-2000		1986-2010	
	All active	Full-time-equivalent patient care	All active	Full-time-equivalent patient care
Total	29.2	26.0	39.2	32.7
Sex				
Male	15.6	13.8	15.1	11.5
Female	120.0	120.7	199.3	197.4
Country of graduation				
USMG	34.7	32.0	49.5	43.6
FMG	11.6	6.8	5.9	-2.1
USFMG	64.3	62.1	92.4	85.5
Foreign-born FMG	3.7	-1.7	-7.1	-15.7
Age (years)				
<36	-19.5	-21.3	-21.1	-23.0
36-45	16.0	13.8	2.6	-1.3
46-55	76.0	73.0	71.8	67.1
56-65	30.6	30.0	100.2	97.2
>65	71.2	67.9	121.1	115.5
Specialty				
General/family practice	11.8	10.7	17.0	14.4
General internal medicine	54.1	51.1	72.5	64.6
Medical subspecialties	38.4	32.7	58.7	47.4
General surgery	25.7	24.0	25.5	21.5
Surgical subspecialties	18.4	15.2	21.2	15.8
Pediatrics	47.1	41.3	67.9	56.5
Obstetrics/gynecology	26.6	21.2	37.6	28.4
Radiology	30.9	26.3	41.5	33.9
Psychiatry	13.8	8.9	15.7	7.8
Anesthesiology	41.5	37.9	58.9	51.9

[Continued]

★ 350 ★

Percent Change in the Number of Active Post-Residency Physicians and the Number of Full-Time-Equivalent Post-Residency Patient Care Physicians, 1986-2000 and 1986-2010
[Continued]

	1986-2000		1986-2010	
	All active	Full-time-equivalent patient care	All active	Full-time-equivalent patient care
Pathology	14.4	8.5	12.0	3.2
Emergency medical	57.6	53.0	87.4	77.4
Other specialties	20.0	15.8	22.4	14.4

Source: "The Growing Proportion of Female Physicians: Implications for U.S. Physician Supply," Phillip R. Kletke, William D. Marder, and Anne B. Silberger, *American Journal of Public Health* 80, No. 3, March, 1990, pp. 300-304. Primary source: Modified from AMA Physician Masterfile, 1970-86, Department of Data Release Services, Division of Survey and Data Resources; AMA Demographic Model of the Physician Population, AMA Center for Health Policy Research, 1988.

★ 351 ★

Projected Supply of Registered Nurses, 1990-2020
[Numbers in millions]

1990	1.400
1995	1.525
2000	1.625
2005	1.650
2010	1.625
2015	1.525
2020	1.400

Source: Environmental Assessment 91/92, American Hospital Association, 1991, p. 33. Data are for full-time equivalents. Magnitudes estimated from published chart.

★ 352 ★

Proportion of Active Female Physicians by Age, Specialty, and Country of Graduation, 1970-2010

The chart prepared by the AMA "shows that the proportion of women physicians increased from 7.1 percent to 15.3 percent between 1970 and 1986, and is projected to reach almost 30 percent by the year 2010. Consequently, women physicians are concentrated in the younger age categories. In 1970 and 1986, female physicians were disproportionately represented among foreign medical graduates not born in the U.S., but the relationship between sex and country of graduation reverses during the projection period due to the growing number of females graduating from U.S. medical schools. Female physicians are concentrated in pediatrics and psychiatry and are underrepresented in general surgery and the surgical subspecialties. These patterns appear in both the 1970 and 196 data as well as the projection estimates for 2000 and 2010."

[Numbers in percent]

	Historical		Projected	
	1970	1986	2000	2010
Total	7.1	15.3	24.1	29.4
Country of graduation				
U.S. Medical Graduates	5.4	14.0	24.7	30.7
Foreign Medical Graduates	14.6	20.0	21.7	23.0
U.S. Foreign Med. Grads	4.2	10.7	13.0	14.0
Foreign-born Foreign Medical Graduates	16.0	21.7	24.0	25.9
Age (years)				
<36	9.5	24.5	36.5	37.3
36-45	6.4	15.6	30.3	37.1
46-55	6.3	9.5	20.5	30.9
56-65	5.0	7.1	12.8	21.4
>65	5.4	5.9	8.8	13.8
Specialty				
General/family practice	4.4	12.9	22.9	28.8
General internal medicine	5.8	17.4	26.5	31.5
Medical subspecialties	5.0	10.2	18.4	22.8
General surgery	1.1	5.8	10.6	14.0
Surgical subspecialties	1.3	3.9	6.8	8.9
Pediatrics	21.4	35.3	47.5	54.1
Obstetrics/gynecology	7.2	19.6	35.9	45.6
Radiology	5.3	12.1	19.7	24.4
Psychiatry	13.2	22.4	34.0	41.8
Anesthesiology	14.3	17.4	23.2	26.6
Pathology	12.9	21.8	29.2	34.7
Emergency medical	-	12.9	20.5	24.3
Other specialties	9.6	18.1	26.4	31.7

Source: "The Growing Proportion of Female Physicians: Implications for U.S. Physician Supply," Phillip R. Kletke, William D. Marder, and Anne B. Silberger, *American Journal of Public Health* 80, No. 3, March, 1990, pp. 300-304. Primary source: Modified from AMA Physician Masterfile, 1970-86, Department of Data Release Services, Division of Survey and Data Resources; AMA Demographic Model of the Physician Population, AMA Center for Health Policy Research, 1988.

Health Care Expenditures

★ 353 ★

Effect of Delaying Medical Cost Control Efforts: Medical Expenditures in 2025 as a Ratio to Gross Domestic Product

According to the report, "the importance of immediate efforts to contain costs is illustrated in the table. The column for 1980 indicates the ratio of medical expenditure to GDP in 2025 *if, as of 1980*, the medical costs variable were to rise no faster than productivity. The remaining columns indicate the expenditure ratios that would prevail in 2025.... Delay of such efforts to contain costs to the year 2000 would add approximately 0.7 percent points of GDP in medical care expenditure, using ... historically conservative cost factors ... delay to the year 2010 would add 1.2-1.5 percentage points of GDP. This assumption of delay highlights the importance of the efforts for cost containment currently underway in these countries—and which are likely to be emphasized even more as the demographic situation changes."

Country	Growth in medical costs held to rate of productivity growth as of[1]			
	1980	2000	2010	2025
Canada	5.5	6.3	6.7	7.2
France	7.5	8.3	8.7	9.4
Germany, Fed. Rep. of	7.7	8.4	8.9	9.7
Italy	5.8	6.1	6.4	6.7
Japan	6.4	7.1	7.5	8.1
United Kingdom	6.1	6.9	7.3	8.0
United States	4.4	5.5	5.9	6.6
(Relative to 1980 ratio to GDP)				
Canada	127	144	153	166
France	112	124	130	140
Germany, Fed. Rep. of	126	137	145	159
Italy	118	125	130	137
Japan	134	149	157	169
United Kingdom	112	127	133	146
United States	132	167	178	200

Source: Aging and Social Expenditures in the Major Industrial Countries, 1980-2025, Peter S. Heller, Richard Hemming, Peter W. Kohnert et. al., International Monetary Fund, September, 1986, p. 42. Primary source: Fund staff estimates. *Notes:* Gross Domestic Product excludes expenditure on medical research and education, administration, and capital investment in the medical sector. 1. Relative to 1980 ratio of GDP.

★ 354 ★

Health Care as a Percentage of GNP, 1990 and 1995

"Health care will consume an increasing proportion of the nation's income as measured by the Gross National Product, the forecasters predict. The composite [mean] forecast pegs health care as a percent of the GNP rising from 11.9 percent in 1990 to 13.1 percent in 1995."

[Numbers in percent]

	1990	1995
Minimum forecast	11.3	11.6
Mean forecast	11.9	13.1
Maximum forecast	12.5	15.0

Source: "Health Care in the 1990s: Forecasts by Top Analysts," *Hospitals* 63, No. 14, July 20, 1989, p. 34.

★ 355 ★

Health Spending as a Percentage of GNP, 2000 and 2030

"'Total health spending has grown from less than 6 percent of the Gross National Product [GNP] three decades ago to about 12 percent today,'" President George Bush's budget director Richard G. Darman said at a hearing of the Senate Finance Committee. "'It is currently expected to reach 17 percent by the year 2000 and 37 percent of GNP by 2030.'"

Source: "Darman Forecasts Dire Health Costs," Robert Rear, *New York Times*, April 17, 1991, p. A14.

★ 356 ★

Medical Spending as a Percentage of GNP, 1970-2000
[Numbers in billions of dollars]

	Cost	Percent
1970	74	7.3
1992	809	13.4
2000	1,616	16.4

Source: "U.S. Medical Spending," *Fortune*, March 23, 1992, p. 47.

★ 357 ★

National Health Care Expenditures, 1965-2000

[Numbers in billions of dollars]

1965	42.0
1990	670.9
1991	730.2
2000	1,600.0

Source: Statistical Bulletin 72, No. 4, October-December, 1991, p. 14. Primary source: U.S. Health Care Financing Administration.

★ 358 ★

Percentages of U.S. Biotech Drug Sales by Category, 1991 and 1996

"Many analysts expect biotech drug sales to multiply like bacteria in a laboratory dish. Biggest likely gainers: anticancer medications and monoclonal antibodies that help control immune systems diseases."

	1991	1996
Cancer	24.0	44.0
Cardiovascular including t-PA	38.0	22.0
Hormones growth factors, insulin	30.0	14.0
Monoclonal antibodies	1.0	12.0
Vaccines including AIDS, herpes, and hepatitis B	7.0	4.0
Other		4.0
Total	1.67 billion	5.44 billion

Source: "Biotech Firms Tackle the Giants," Gene Bylinsky, *Fortune* 124, No. 4, July 18, 1988, pp. 78-81.

★ 359 ★

Real Government Expenditure on Medical Care, 1980-2025

The table provided by the researchers "presents, in index form, the effects of demographic developments on the absolute level of medical care expenditure, assuming no increase in real expenditure per recipient in any age group or in coverage (i.e., simply the effect on outlays of the change in size and structure of the population). There is a sharp divergence in growth across countries, ranging from only a modest increase in the Federal Republic of Germany, Italy, and the United Kingdom to a substantial increase in Canada, Japan, and the United States. The development of real spending reflects two factors: changes in the age structure and the absolute size of the population. Thus, while a more aging population tends to have more rapidly growing expenditure, if other things remain constant, this can be offset by the scale factor. The Federal Republic of Germany's population ages much faster than that of France, Italy, and the United Kingdom, but it shows a smaller expenditure growth because of a declining population size. Medical expenditure in France will grow much faster than in the United Kingdom, despite slower aging and a lower initial expenditure share on the elderly, because of faster growth in the population. It is also interesting to compare Canada and the United States. Canada's population is aging more rapidly and will have a slightly faster growth in its total population, yet in the United States expenditure on medical care will grow somewhat more rapidly. The reason lies in the much higher share of government expenditure that is allocated to the elderly in the United States. Neither scenario would be particularly worrisome for any country if demographic factors alone were the only influence on the growth of real medical expenditure. Such a growth in expenditure would be small in comparison to the growth in total output, so that the ratio of medical expenditure to GDP would drop to 70 percent of its present value by the year 2000 and would be even lower in subsequent years. This scenario would be extremely unlikely, given the historical evidence that suggests that medical costs per capita will continue to rise in real terms."

[1980 = 100]

Country	1980	2000	2010	2025
Baseline demographic scenario				
Canada	100	128	140	174
France	100	117	125	130
Germany, Fed. Rep. of	100	104	107	103
Italy	100	113	117	121
Japan	100	130	140	147
United Kingdom	100	105	105	115
United States	100	130	144	180
"Greater aging" demographic scenario				
Canada	100	130	142	174
France	100	120	129	149
Germany, Fed. Rep. of	100	103	105	100
Italy	100	114	118	123
Japan	100	139	150	153

[Continued]

★ 359 ★

Real Government Expenditure on Medical Care, 1980-2025
[Continued]

Country	1980	2000	2010	2025
United Kingdom	100	106	108	119
United States	100	132	148	188

Source: *Aging and Social Expenditure in the Major Industrial Countries, 1980-2025*, Peter S. Heller, Richard Hemming, Peter W. Kohnert et al., International Monetary Fund, September, 1986, p. 40. Primary source: Fund staff estimates. Gross Domestic Product excludes expenditure on medical research and education, administration, and capital investment in the medical sector; assumes no increase in real expenditure per capita by age group over 1980 levels.

★ 360 ★

Real National Health Care Expenditures, 1981-2000
[Numbers in billions of 1987 dollars]

Year	Real national health expenditures
1981	365
1982	386
1983	407
1984	426
1985	447
1986	467
1987	489
1988	518
1990	568
2000	840

Source: Congressional Budget Office, *Trends in Health Expenditures by Medicare and the Nation*, January, 1991, p. 60. Primary source: Congressional Budget Office calculations based on data from the Health Care Financing Administration, Office of the Actuary, and Committee on Ways and Means, staff projections for 1990 and 2000. The latter are based on assumed rates of increase in health expenditures from the National Institute of Aging, Macroeconomic-Demographic model. The projections assume an average annual real rate of growth of 5.1 percent between 1988 and 1990 and of 4.0 percent between 1990 and 2000.

★ 361 ★

Real Per Capita Health Expenditures, 1980-2000

[Numbers in 1987 dollars]

1980	1,465
1981	1,537
1982	1,607
1983	1,681
1984	1,739
1985	1,810
1986	1,872
1987	1,941
1988	2,038
1990	2,183
2000	3,021

Source: U.S. Congressional Budget Office, *Trends in Health Expenditures by Medicare and the Nation*, January, 1991, p. 61. Congressional Budget Office calculations based on data from the Health Care Financing Administration, Office of the Actuary, and Committee on Ways and Means, staff projections for 1990 and 2000. The latter are based on assumed rates of increase in health expenditures from the National Institute of Aging, Macroeconomic-Demographic model. The projections assume an average annual real rate of growth of 4.0 percent between 1988 and 1990 and of 3.3 percent between 1990 and 2000.

★ 362 ★

Sales of Products on Drug Market, 1991-2001

[Numbers in millions of dollars]

	1991	1996	2001
Cardiovascular	600	1145	2250
Erythropoietin	350[1]	800	1300
Tissue plasminogen activator	225[1]	225	450
Blood factors	25[1,2]	50	100
Superoxide dimutase	0	20	100
Others	0	50	300
Cancer	145	685	1850
Colony-stimulating factors	20[1,2]	250	650
Interferons	125[1]	200	350
Interleukins	0	210	550
Others	0	25	200
Hormones/growth factors	420	890	1605
Epidermal growth factor	0	65	230
Human growth hormone	250[1]	470	650
Human insulin	170[1]	250	325
Others	0	105	400
Vaccines	15	170	825
AIDS	0	50	300

[Continued]

★ 362 ★

Sales of Products on Drug Market, 1991-2001
[Continued]

	1991	1996	2001
Herpes	0	15	150
Hepatitis B, others	15[1]	105	375
Monoclonal antibodies			
Therapeutics	20	200	490
Others	0	210	680
Total	1200	3300	7700

Source: "Erythropoietin Leads U.S. Biotech Drug Market," *Chemical and Engineering News* 69, No. 8, February 25, 1991, p. 32. Primary source: Consulting Resources Corp. and *Chemical and Engineering News* estimates. *Notes:* 1. Some *Chemical and Engineering News* estimates based on analyst reports and company projections. 2. Some drugs not yet approved but may reach market in 1991.

★ 363 ★

Total U.S. Spending on Health, 1975-2000

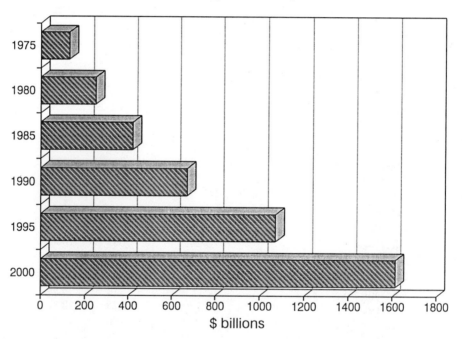

$ billions

[Numbers in billions of dollars]

1975	132
1980	249
1985	420
1990	671

[Continued]

★ 363 ★

Total U.S. Spending on Health, 1975-2000
[Continued]

1995	1.073[1]
2000	1.616[1]

Source: "No Simple Cure for Sick System," Judi Hasson, *USA Today*, October 15, 1992, p. 5A. Primary source: Health Care Financing Administration, Public Opinion Strategies and Mellman & Lazarus, Public Citizen Health Research Group, Office of Management and Budget, Families USA. *Note:* 1. Numbers in trillions of dollars.

Health Care for the Elderly

★ 364 ★

Elderly Americans in Need of Long-Term Care, 1980-2040

"Advances in medical technology have increased life expectancy, but living longer brings increased chances of illness and dependency. In 1985, the average life expectancy for women was 78.5 years and 71.5 years for men. By 2005, life expectancy will increase to 81 years for women and 74.1 for men. The incidence and impact of chronic illness increases with age. As chronic illnesses are 'managed' rather than cured, they often require ongoing assistance and attention. In 1989, there were an estimated 7.1 million disabled elderly. By the year 2000, this number will increase to 8.9 million."

[Numbers in millions]

	Percent needing long-term care
1980	5.5
2000	9.0
2020	12.0
2040	20.0

Source: "Failing America's Caregivers: Status Report on Women Who Care," Suzanne Jackson, *Older Women's League*, 1989 Mother's Day Report, p. 5. Primary source: Manroe and Saldo, "Dynamics of Health Changes in the Oldest Old: New Perspectives and Evidence," *Milbank Memorial Fund Quarterly* 63, No. 2, Spring, 1985; and unpublished tabulations from the author. Magnitudes estimated from published graph.

★ 365 ★

Percentage of Government Medical Care Expenditure on the Elderly Population, Compared to Other Countries, as Projected in the Baseline Scenarios, 1980-2025

According to the table below, "with the shift in the age structure of the population, an associated change will take place in the underlying structure of demand for services, creating imbalances between available physical capacity and professional manpower resources and the structure of demand. This change will undoubtedly create short-term transitional adjustment difficulties. For example, the share of government expenditure on medical care consumed by the age group 65 and over will substantially increase. In the Federal Republic of Germany, Italy, and the United Kingdom, it will increase by 7-9 percentage points between 1980 and 2025; in Canada, Japan, and the United States, the increase will be even more dramatic. This increased share will be reflected in a change in the demand for particular services, with obviously increased needs for nursing home facilities and for professionals and paraprofessionals trained in geriatric care. An associated problem will be the need to 'retool' plants and retrain professionals in specialties less in demand."

Country	1980	2000	2010	2025
Canada	33.3	38.0	40.9	53.1
France	-	-	-	-
Germany, Fed. Rep. of[1]	33.1	33.6	39.0	42.6
Italy	31.8	36.2	37.4	40.6
Japan	27.4	37.7	43.8	48.3
United Kingdom	42.1	44.1	44.3	49.4
United States	50.0	54.4	55.6	64.6

Source: Aging and Social Expenditure in the Major Industrial Countries, 1980-2025, Peter S. Heller, Richard Hemming, Peter W. Kohnert et. al., International Monetary Fund, September, 1986, p. 45. Primary source: Fund staff estimates. Table 7. *Notes:* Gross Domestic Product excludes expenditure on medical research and education, administration, and capital investment in the medical sector. 1. People included are those over age sixty.

★ 366 ★

Projected Nursing Home Population, 1985-2050

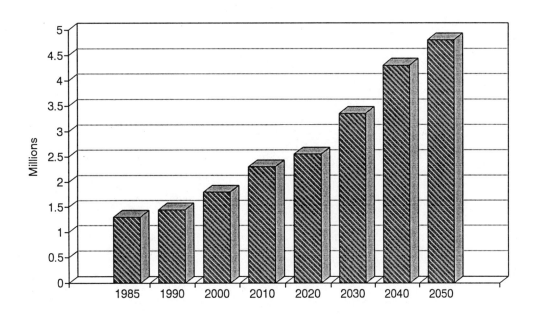

"The likelihood that institutional care will be required in old age is widely debated, with recent estimates ranging from a 36 percent chance. Projections indicate that during the next 40 years, the nursing home population will more than double from its current level of 1.5 million." Published chart also includes age-specific data.

[Numbers in millions]

1985	1.30
1990	1.45
2000	1.80
2010	2.30
2020	2.55
2030	3.35
2040	4.30
2050	4.80

Source: Environmental Assessment, 91/92, American Hospital Association, 1991, p. 25. Magnitudes estimated from published chart.

Projections of Statistics on AIDS

★ 367 ★

Economic Cost of the AIDS Epidemic by 2000, as Compared to Canada and Latin America

"By the end of the decade, [AIDS] could wreak havoc on the [U.S.] economy."

[In billions of dollars and percent of GDP lost]

	Cost		Percentage	
	Best case	Worst case	Best case	Worst case
United States	81	107	0.9	1.1
Canada	8	11	0.8	1.0
Latin America	13	24	0.8	1.4

Source: "The Hidden Cost of AIDS," Robert F. Black, *U.S. News & World Report* 113, No. 4, July 27, 1992, p. 50. Primary source: Global AIDS Policy Coalition-Harvard University, World Health Organization, DRI/McGraw-Hill, *USN&WR* estimates. Published chart also includes percentage estimates of GDP lost.

★ 368 ★

Estimated Increases in the Frequency of AIDS and Projections on Causes, 2000

"The World Health Organization (WHO) ... predicted a cumulative global total of at least 6 million cases of AIDS by the year 2000, with 'an alarming rate' of increase of new infections in developing countries.

"Also, 15 million to 20 million people around the world could be infected with the human immuno-deficiency virus that causes AIDS by the year 2000 because of the soaring rate of new infections in developing countries, WHO said in updating its worldwide AIDS projections....

"As of this year, about 60% of all global infections had resulted from heterosexual intercourse. WHO predicted that by the year 2000, 75% to 80% of all HIV infections will result from heterosexual intercourse.

Source: "Alarming Increase in AIDS Reported," Marlene Cimons, *Los Angeles Times*, June 13, 1990, p. A4. Primary source: World Health Organization.

★ 369 ★

Estimated Increases in the Frequency of AIDS by 2002

The Hudson Institute predicts that "if current trends continue unchecked, as many as 14.5 million people in the United States could be infected with the AIDS-causing human immunodeficiency virus (HIV) by the year 2002....

"The Hudson Institute's study explored worst, best, and middle scenarios for the progression of the AIDS epidemic in America. In a worst-case situation, the cumulative number of HIV infections by the year 2002 would be 14.5 million, with nearly a million active AIDS cases, causing immense strain on the nation's health-care system. A most likely, even a best-case situation would be over 1.5 million Americans infected with HIV since the disease's discovery, with nearly 200,000 active cases of AIDS and a cumulative total of 863,000 AIDS deaths....

"Blacks and the poor—those least likely to have adequate health-care insurance—will be hit especially hard by the AIDS epidemic in the United States. Under the most likely scenario, some 15% of all blacks between the ages of 15 and 50 will carry the virus by 2002."

Source: "Grim Scenarios: The Spread of AIDS," *The Futurist* XXV, No. 2, March-April, 1991, p. 47. Primary source: *The Catastrophe Ahead: AIDS and the Case for a New Public Policy*, William B. Johnston and Kevin R. Hopkins, Praeger, 1990; this work is based on a two-year study by the Hudson Institute.

★ 370 ★

People Receiving Medical Treatment for AIDS or HIV, 1992-1996

	1992	1994	1996
Low projection	141,000	191,000	231,000
High projection	357,000	525,000	636,000

Source: "AIDS: Increasing Patient Survival," Diana Sterne, *Challenges in Health Care: A Chartbook Perspective*, 1991, p. 42.

★ 371 ★

Projected Cost of Treating People with HIV and/or AIDS in the United States, 1991-1994

"The total estimated cost of treating all people with the human immunodeficiency virus (HIV) is expected to increase 21 percent between 1991 and 1994," according to a study performed by Dr. Fred Hellinger and cited by the Blue Cross and Blue Shield Association.

[Numbers in billions of 1990 dollars]

	1991	1992	1993	1994
Cost of treating people with AIDS	4.398	5.444	6.572	7.859
Cost of treating people with HIV but without AIDS	1.412	1.753	2.116	2.530
Cost of treating all people with HIV	5.810	7.197	8.688	10.389

Source: "Study: 21% Rise in HIV Treatment Costs by 1994," *Hospitals* 66, No. 2, January 20, 1992, p. 18. Primary source: *Inquiry*, Blue Cross and Blue Shield Association, 1991.

★ 372 ★

Projected Number of AIDS Cases in the United States, 1991-1994

"The number of AIDS cases diagnosed is expected to increase from 62,470 during 1991 to 100,648 in 1994," according to a study performed by Dr. Fred Hellinger and cited by the Blue Cross and Blue Shield Association.

	1991	1992	1993	1994
Number of AIDS cases diagnosed during year	62,470	74,299	87,026	100,648
Number of people alive with AIDS during any part of calendar year	137,433	170,145	205,380	245,580

Source: "Study: 21% Rise in HIV Treatment Costs by 1994," *Hospitals* 66, No. 2, January 20, 1992, p. 18. Primary source: *Inquiry*, Blue Cross and Blue Shield Association, 1991.

★ 373 ★

Proportion of Women to Men as Victims of AIDS, 2000

"Women are now catching AIDS almost as fast as men, and by the year 2000 they will make up the majority of victims. One reason: in many societies, women have no influence on their husbands' sexual behavior and cannot force them to wear condoms."

Source: "Troubling Dispatches From the AIDS Front," *Time* 140, No. 5, August 3, 1992, p. 28. Primary source: The Eighth International Conference on AIDS.

Trends in Hospital Health Care

★ 374 ★

Average Length of Stay in Hospitals, 1990 and 1995

"Average length of stay will not change from 1990 to 1995: the composite forecast shows the average length of stay at 6.7 days in both years. But individual forecasters are divided on whether this measure of occupancy will rise or fall. Although most of the group believes that the length of stay will rise through 1995, more than one-third see length of stay falling or holding steady."

[Numbers in days]

	1990	1995
Minimum forecast	6.0	5.8
Mean forecast	6.7	6.7
Maximum forecast	7.1	7.4

Source: "Health Care in the 1990s: Forecasts by Top Analysts," *Hospitals* 63, No. 14, July 20, 1989, p. 42.

★ 375 ★

Hospital Operating Margins, 1990 and 1995

"Hospitals will face tighter financial constraints as operating margins fall to 1.3 percent in 1990, according to the composite forecast. Margins are forecast to rebound slightly to 1.9 percent by 1995, but that figure may be deceptive. Margins will fall below the 1990 level and will rebound only after a reduction in industry capacity, many forecasters say."

	1990	1995
Minimum forecast	-1.0	0.0
Mean forecast	1.3	1.9
Maximum forecast	2.3	3.0

Source: "Health Care in the 1990s: Forecasts by Top Analysts," *Hospitals* 63, No. 14, July 20, 1989, p. 40.

★ 376 ★

Percent Occupancy of Staffed Beds, 1990 and 1995

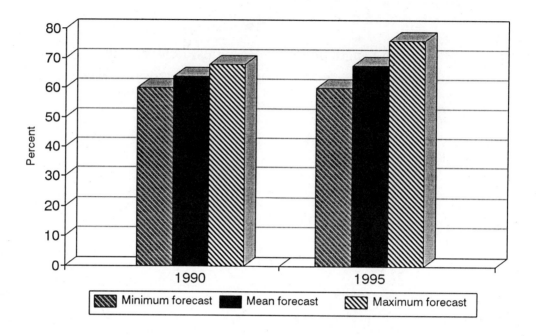

"All but two of the forecasters predict that occupancy of staffed beds will increase in the period from 1990 to 1995, while the two dissenters simply predict no change. The composite forecast shows occupancy increasing from 64 percent in 1990 to 67.6 percent in 1995."

	1990	1995
Minimum forecast	60.0	60.0
Mean forecast	64.0	67.6
Maximum forecast	68.0	76.0

Source: "Health Care in the 1990s: Forecasts by Top Analysts," *Hospitals* 63, No. 14, July 20, 1989, p. 42.

Human Services

★ 377 ★

Estimated Government Savings Through Cuts in Retirement Benefits and Medicare, 1992-1997

[Numbers in billions of dollars]

	1992	1993	1994	1995	1996	1997
Retirement benefits	353	371	392	414	439	465
Medicare	128	142	158	176	196	218
Total	481	513	550	590	635	683
Proposed ways to cut costs						
Eliminate cost-of-living increase for one year, to save		6.5	8.9	8.9	8.8	8.5
Eliminate income thresholds and tax 85 percent of retirement benefits to raise		10.4	23.8	24.7	25.8	27.0
Raise Medicare premiums from 25 percent of cost to 30 percent of cost, to save		1.4	2.0	2.9	4.9	7.2

Source: "Entitlements for the Retired Take Ever More Money," *New York Times*, August 30, 1992, p. 4E. Primary source: Congressional Budget Office.

★ 378 ★

Financial Support of the Elderly, 2025

"By 2025 what economists call the dependency ratio—the proportion of pensioners 60 or older to all workers—will have roughly doubled in Japan, the U.S., and West Germany. If the present benefit systems are kept in place, U.S. programs for the elderly could consume 50% of the federal budget by then."

	1990	2025
W. Germany	3.9	7.0
Japan	2.2	4.4
U.S.	2.7	4.3

Source: "Many More Elderly to Carry," *Fortune* 121, No. 8, April 9, 1990, p. 71.

★ 379 ★

Health Care Expenditures Under Different Demographic and Economic Scenarios, 1990-2065

"Selected projections of health care expenditures under the three different demographic and economic scenarios, using structural forecasts of health price inflation appropriate to the scenarios, are shown in [the table below]. Under the optimistic projection, shown in the middle panel, the share of GNP devoted to health expenditures increases from 12 percent to about 26 percent in 2065. This growth owes to the continued rapid rate of health price inflation, as well as to the aging of the population. Medicare expenditures increase from 2 to 5 percent of GNP. Under the pessimistic projection, shown in the bottom panel, the share of GNP devoted to health care increases to almost 37 percent, while Medicare expenditures increase to over 8 percent. Clearly, the more pronounced aging present in the pessimistic projection is the cause for the higher health expenditures."

[Numbers as a percent of GNP, Structural Forecast]

	Total expenditures	Medicare expenditures
Intermediate		
1990	12.0	2.9
2015	20.3	3.6
2035	25.5	5.6
2065	28.9	6.5
Optimistic		
1990	12.0	2.0
2015	20.1	3.4
2035	24.3	4.9
2065	25.9	5.1
Pessimistic		
1990	12.0	2.6
2015	20.0	3.7
2035	25.7	6.0
2065	31.7	8.1

Source: Board of Governors of the Federal Reserve System, Division of Research and Statistics, Fiscal Analysis Section, Mark J. Warshawsky, *Projections of Health Care Expenditures as a Share of GNP: Actuarial and Economic Approaches*, November, 1991.

★ 380 ★

Medicare and Medicaid Beneficiaries, 1983-1995

The table below demonstrates that "there were substantial increases in the number of Medicaid beneficiaries between 1968 and 1974, the early years of the program. Since then, the numbers have remained fairly steady between 21.5 and 23.5 million. The Census Bureau's Current Population Survey indicates that between 1980 and 1988 the number of Medicaid beneficiaries who were below the poverty line was also fairly constant at 12 to 13 million."

[Number of beneficiaries in thousands]

Fiscal year	Medicare aged benef.	Medicare disabled benef.	Medicaid benef.
1983	26,670	2,918	21,554
1984	27,112	2,884	21,607
1985	27,123	2,944	21,814
1986	27,728	2,986	22,515
1987	28,239	3,042	23,109
1988	28,779	3,115	22,907
1989	29,358	3,200	23,511
1990[1]	29,951	3,251	24,600
1991[1]	30,480	3,297	25,600
1995[1]	32,277	3,597	

Source: Medicare and Medicaid's 25th Anniversary—Much Promised, Accomplished, and Left Unfinished: A Report Presented by the Chairman of the Select Committee on Aging, U.S. Government Printing Office, 1990. Primary source: Health Care Financing Administration and Congressional Budget Office, 1990. Original table also includes data for 1967-1985. *Note:* 1. Estimate.

★ 381 ★

Number of Workers Paying into Social Security for Each Person Receiving Benefits, 1970-2040

1970	3.7
1980	3.2
1990	3.4
2000	3.2
2010	2.9
2020	2.4
2030	2.0
2040	2.0

Source: "Entitlements for the Retired Take Ever More Money," *New York Times,* August 30, 1992, p. 4E. Primary source: Social Security Administration; Tax Foundation (tax increases).

★ 382 ★

Percent of Federal Budget Spent on the Medicaid and Social Security Programs, 1980-1997

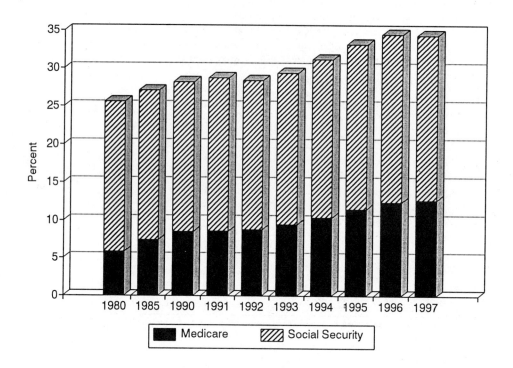

	1980	1985	1990	1991	1992	1993	1994	1995	1996	1997
Total Social Security and Medicare	25.5	27.1	28.3	28.8	28.4	29.4	31.2	33.2	34.5	34.4
Social Security	19.8	19.7	19.7	20.2	19.6	19.9	20.8	21.7	22.1	21.7
Medicare	5.8	7.4	8.5	8.6	8.8	9.5	10.4	11.5	12.4	12.7

Source: "Entitlements for the Retired Take Ever More Money," *New York Times*, August 30, 1992, p. 4E. Primary source: Congressional Budget Office. Original graph also contains data for 1970 and 1975. *Note:* Numbers may not add due to rounding.

★ 383 ★

Projected Growth in Medicare Costs, 1991-1997

"Federal spending on Medicaid is projected to nearly triple and Medicare nearly double between 1991 and 1997."

[Numbers in billions of dollars]

	1991	1992	1993	1994	1995	1996	1997
Medicare	102.0 .0	120.0	135.0	145.0	165.0	185.0	197.7
Medicaid	52.5	80.0	90.0	105.0	120.0	140.0	150.7

Source: "No Simple Cures for Sick System," Judi Hasson, *USA Today*, October 15, 1992, p. 5A. Primary source: Health Care Financing Administration, Public Opinion Strategies and Mellman & Lazarus, Public Citizen Health Research Group, Office of Management and Budget, Families USA. Some magnitudes estimated from published chart.

★ 384 ★

Projected Percent Increase in Spending on Medicare and Social Security Each Fiscal Year, 1992-1997

	1992	1993	1994	1995	1996	1997
Medicare	12.3	10.9	11.3	11.4	11.4	11.2
Social Security	6.7	5.6	5.6	5.7	5.4	5.6

Source: "Entitlements for the Retired Take Ever More Money," *New York Times*, August 30, 1992, p. 4E. Primary source: Social Security Administration.

★ 385 ★

Proportion of Children with Medical Insurance Provided Through a Parent's Employer, 1977-2000

According to a report completed by a Washington-based advocacy group, the Children's Defense Fund, "almost 40 percent of all children, or 25 million youngsters under the age of 18, are not covered by health insurance through a parent's employer. In 1977, the study says, 72.8 percent of all children were covered by health insurance through an employer-provided plan. By 1987, that proportion had dropped to 62.9 percent. If the trend continues, the study estimates, about half of all children, and 80 percent of black children, will not be covered by employer-based health insurance by the end of the decade."

	1977	1987	2000
Total	72.8	62.9	50.0
Black	52.5	38.1	19.4
Two-parent, one wage earner families	83.0	73.3	60.7
Low income	63.4	47.0	25.7
Middle income	83.6	79.0	73.0

Source: "Shrinking Number of Children Found Covered by Employer Health Insurance," Ellen Flax, *Education Week* XI, No. 17, January 15, 1992, p. 10. Primary source: Children's Defense Fund. *Note:* Data are based on an average annual rate of change, 1977-1987.

★ 386 ★

Real Medicare Spending per Enrollee, 1986-1995

"[This table] indicates the growth in Medicare expenditures between 1967 and 1989 with projections through 1995. In constant 1990 dollars, expenditures will have increased from $1,104 per enrollee in 1969 to $4,228 in 1995, a four-fold increase. For that period, the growth rate was fairly steady between 1975 and 1984 at around 7 percent and then decreased to 3.1 percent for 1985-1991 due to a decrease in hospital expenditures. Based on current law, the rate is projected at 6.2 percent for the 1991-1995 period."

[In constant 1990 dollars]

	Medicare spending
Fiscal year	
1986	2,817
1987	2,886
1988	2,960
1989	3,079
Congressional Budget Office projections	
1990	3,230
1991	3,328
1992	3,576
1993	3,794

[Continued]

★ 386 ★

Real Medicare Spending per Enrollee, 1986-1995
[Continued]

	Medicare spending
1994	4,012
1995	4,228

Source: Medicare and Medicaid's 25th Anniversary—Much Promised, Accomplished, and Left Unfinished: A report Presented by the Chairman of the Select Committee on Aging, U.S. Government Printing Office, 1990. Primary source: Health Care Financing Administration and Congressional Budget Office, 1990. Original table also includes data for 1967-1985.

★ 387 ★

Total Support Ratio, Aged Support Ratio, and Young Support Ratio: Actual and Projected, 1900-2050

Concern has been "expressed about the number of workers compared to the number of non-working persons in the society, sometimes referred to as the 'dependency [or support] ratio.' It [has been] noted that in the long term, approximately the year 2010, the number of retired persons will jump as the baby-boomers begin to reach retirement age. But for the short-term, the cost-benefit question of employment of elderly and handicapped is related directly to the expenses of maintaining children under eighteen, the retired, the frail elderly, non-working handicapped, economically dependent children and the families of the chronically unemployed.... While the current support ratio is not expected to change significantly in the immediate future, interest [has been] expressed in finding ways to keep the statistics under control, especially in relation to reducing the incidence of teenage pregnancy, functional illiteracy, teenage unemployment and other social dysfunctioning. Comparable efforts need to be made to increase the self-sufficiency of physically and mentally disabled persons, and creating employment opportunities for all who want to work."

[Number of persons per 100 aged 18 to 64 years]

	1900	1920	1940	1960	1980	1982	1990	2000	2025	2050
Total support ratio (under 18 and 65 and over)	83.65	75.69	62.84	81.95	64.39	62.86	62.57	61.86	71.00	74.46
Aged support ratio (65 years and over)	7.35	7.99	10.90	16.84	18.59	18.82	20.70	21.16	33.31	37.85
Young support ratio (under 18)	76.30	67.70	51.94	65.11	45.80	44.04	41.87	40.70	37.69	36.61

Source: "Employment Opportunities for Special Groups," *Proceedings of a Symposium on Social Services in the Year 2000*, Office of Human Development Services, U.S. Department of Health and Human Services, November 26-28, 1984, p. 25. Primary source: U.S. Bureau of the Census, "Projections of the Population of the United States: 1982 to 2050" (Advance Report), Series P-25, No. 922, October, 1982, and "Estimates of the Population of the United States by Single Years of Age, Color and Sex: 1900 to 1959," Series P-25, No. 311, July 2, 1965. Projections are the middle series. In *Social Services in the Year 2000*, The Future Group, Glastonbury, CT, 1984, p. 44.

★ 388 ★

Welfare Measures: Projections of Consumption Per Capita Assuming Moderate Gross Investment, 1990-2065

[Consumption in 1990 dollars]

	1990	2015	2040	2065
One percent capital deepening				
Consumption per capita	16,626	20,806	23,083	25,791
All other consumption per capita	14,092	17,454	19,191	21,764
Memo: ratio of capital to labor--all other	60.6	62.8	52.9	39.2
Two percent capital deepening				
Consumption per capita	16,626	20,567	22,184	23,116
All other consumption per capita	14,092	17,216	18,292	19,990
Memo: ratio of capital to labor--all other	60.5	60.1	45.4	25.8
Two-and-a-half percent capital deepening				
Consumption per capita	16,626	20,426	21,512	20,135
All other consumption per capita	14,092	17,074	17,620	16,108
Memo: ratio of capital to labor--all other	60.5	58.5	40.3	15.0

Source: Board of Governors of the Federal Reserve System, Division of Research and Statistics, Fiscal Analysis Section, Mark J. Warshawsky, *Projections of Health Care Expenditures as a Share of GNP: Actuarial and Economic Approaches*, November, 1991. Primary source: Author's calculations, assuming gross investment is 21 percent of GNP.

★ 389 ★

Welfare Measures: Projections of Consumption Per Capita, 1990-2065, Assuming Low Gross Investment

[Consumption per capita in 1990 dollars]

	1990	2015	2040	2065
One percent capital deepening				
Consumption per capita	17,047	20,771	22,910	25,495
All other consumption per capita	14,513	17,420	19,018	21,468
Memo: ratio of capital to labor--all other	60.6	56.7	46.7	34.1
Two percent capital deepening				
Consumption per capita	17,047	20,514	21,902	22,393
All other consumption per capita	14,513	17,252	18,010	18,367
Memo: ratio of capital to labor--all other	60.5	54.1	39.2	20.7
Two-and-a-half percent capital deepening				
Consumption per capita	17,047	20,361	21,141	18,633
All other consumption per capita	14,513	17,009	17,249	14,606
Memo: ratio of capital to labor--all other	60.5	52.5	34.1	10.0

Source: Board of Governors of the Federal Reserve System, Division of Research and Statistics, Fiscal Analysis Section, Mark J. Warshawsky, *Projections of Health Care Expenditures as a Share of GNP: Actuarial and Economic Approaches*, November, 1991. Primary source: Author's calculations, assuming gross investment is 19 percent of GNP.

Chapter 8

INCOME, PRICES, AND SPENDING

Corporate and Governmental Income

★ 390 ★

Corporate Income Tax Receipts, Total and as a Percentage of Federal Receipts and GNP, 1985-1996

Fiscal year	Receipts[1] (millions)	Receipts as percent of total Federal receipts	Receipts as percent of GNP
1985	61,331	8.4	1.6
1986	63,143	8.2	1.5
1987	83,926	9.8	1.9
1988	94,508	10.4	2.0
1989	103,291	10.4	2.0
1990	93,507	9.1	1.7
1991 (estimate)	95,866	8.8	1.7
1992 (estimate)	101,913	8.7	1.7
1993 (estimate)	109,913	8.7	1.7
1994 (estimate)	120,578	8.8	1.8
1995 (estimate)	130,024	8.9	1.8
1996 (estimate)	138,285	8.9	1.8

Source: "Corporate Income Tax Receipts, Total and as Percent of Federal Receipts and Percent of GNP, 1934-96," *Overview of the Federal Tax System*, U.S. Government Printing Office, Washington, D.C., 1991. Primary source: Office of Management and Budget, *Budget of the United States Government*, Fiscal Year 1992, tables 2.1, 2.2, and 2.3. Source also contains information for 1934-1984. *Notes:* 1. Beginning in 1987, includes trust fund receipts for the hazardous substance superfund. The trust amounts are as follows (in millions of dollars): 1987: 196; 1988: 313; 1989: 292; 1990: 461; 1991: 320; 1992: 394; 1993: 465; 1994: 548; 1995: 662; 1996: 750.

Income: Personal

★ 391 ★

Annual Maximum Taxable Earnings and Contribution Rate: Employers and Employees, 1984-2000 and Beyond

OASDI = old-age and survivor disability insurance program; HI = hospital insurance program; OASI = old-age and survivor insurance; DI = disability insurance program.

Beginning-	Annual maximum taxable earnings OASDI	Annual maximum taxable earnings HI	Contribution rate (percent of covered earnings)			
			Total	OASI	DI	HI
1984[1]	37,800	37,800	7.0	5.2	.5	1.3
1985	39,600	39,600	7.05	5.2	.5	1.35
1986	42,000	42,000	7.15	5.2	.5	1.45
1987	43,800	43,800	7.15	5.2	.5	1.45
1988	45,000	45,000	7.51	5.53	.53	1.45
1989	48,000	48,000	7.51	5.53	.53	1.45
1990	51,300	51,300	7.65	5.6	.60	1.45
1991	53,400	125,000[2]	7.65	5.6	.60	1.45
1992-1999	[3]	[3]	7.65	5.6	.60	1.45
2000 and thereafter	[3]	[3]	7.65	5.49	.71	1.45

Source: "Social Security Payroll Taxes," *Overview of the Federal Tax System*, Committee on Ways and Means, U.S. House of Representatives, April 10, 1991, Washington, D.C., p. 179. Primary source: Social Security Bulletin, Annual Statistical Supplement, 1990. Table also includes data for 1937-1983. *Notes*: 1. Tax credits apply for 1984. 2. Based on 1990 legislation. 3. Subject to automatic increase.

★ 392 ★

Annual Maximum Taxable Earnings and Contribution Rate: Self-Employed, 1984-2000 and Beyond

Beginning-	Annual maximum OASDI taxable earnings	Annual maximum taxable earnings HI	Contribution rate (percent of covered earnings)			
			Total	OASI	DI	HI
1984[1]	37,800	37,800	14.0	10.4	1.0	2.6
1985[1]	39,600	39,600	14.1	10.4	1.0	2.7
1986[1]	42,000	42,000	14.3	10.4	1.0	2.9
1987[1]	43,800	43,800	14.3	10.4	1.0	2.9

[Continued]

★ 392 ★

Annual Maximum Taxable Earnings and Contribution Rate: Self-Employed, 1984-2000 and Beyond

[Continued]

Beginning-	Annual maximum OASDI taxable earnings	Annual maximum taxable earnings HI	Contribution rate (percent of covered earnings)			
			Total	OASI	DI	HI
1988[1]	45,000	45,000	15.02	11.06	1.06	2.9
1989[1]	48,000	48,000	15.02	11.06	1.06	2.9
1990	51,300	51,300	15.3	11.2	1.2	2.9
1991	53,400	125,000	15.3	11.2	1.2	2.9
1992-99	[2]	[2]	15.3	11.2	1.2	2.9
2000 and thereafter	[2]	[2]	15.3	10.98	1.42	2.9

Source: "Social Security Payroll Taxes," *Overview of the Federal Tax System*, Committee on Ways and Means, U.S. House of Representatives, April 10, 1991, Washington, D.C., p. 181. Primary source: Social Security Bulletin, Annual Statistical Supplement, 1990. Table also includes statistics for 1937-1983. 1. Tax credits apply for 1984 to 1989. 2. Subject to automatic increase.

★ 393 ★

Economic Climate, 1990-2000

E. Fabian Linden is author of a report released late last month by the Conference Board that seems to contradict the pessimistic figures that cascade across his desk every month as well as the pessimistic prophecies from America's departments of economics. "The Great Income Reshuffle" predicts that the 90's will be a period of economic growth, expanded personal and household income and increased opportunity. "The idea that we are losing the middle class and the American dream is tarnished has no basis in reality," Mr. Linden said.

Mr. Linden argues that the United States has demographics on its side: a huge segment of the 78 million member baby boom generation is about to hit its so called peak earning years of 45 to 55, which will expand higher income brackets; the numbers of women entering the labor force will continue to grow and , as they gain experience, they will achieve wage parity with men. And, Mr. Linden predicts, the young segment of the baby boom cohort, which hasn't married yet, will soon start to marry in droves, creating multi-paycheck households.

Source: "Is the Forecast Too Good to be True?" Barbara Presley Noble, *The New York Times* CXLI, No. 48,927, April 5, 1992, p. III 27.

★ 394 ★

The Future of Wealth and Power, 1990-2000

What do futurists expect for the international class system in the 1990s and thereafter? Many technoliberals ... think that in the long run it will grow more egalitarian. But they are in a minority. If present-day trends continue, with no fundamental structural changes in the world-system, we may assume that by the middle of the next century, the gap between the rich and the poor nations will have grown much wider. The nations in the top 10 percent will enjoy not a 100-1 lead, as they do now, but a 200-1 lead in per capita income over the nations in the bottom quintile.

Source: "The Future of Wealth and Power," *The Next Three Futures*, W. Warren Wagar, Greenwood Press, New York, p. 81.

★ 395 ★

Income in the 21st Century

There will be fewer millionaires as tax reforms are finally made [in the 21st century], there will also be fewer people living in poverty as new kinds of jobs open up and hiring reforms are made when the Democrats return to power.... The richest people in America will be entertainers and professional athletes, who will be in such demand because of cable television that their incomes will be three times what they are today.

Salaries will begin to equalize, as they have in Sweden, where nobody makes more than two and one half times what anybody else makes. By 1990, the percentage of Americans making less than $10,000 a year will drop from the 34 percent it is today to 29 percent. The lowest-paid semi-professional and professional Americans will continue to be policemen, firemen and schoolteachers.

Source: "Social Shock," *Encounters with the Future: A Forecast of Life into the 21st Century*, Marvin Cetron and Thomas O'Toole, McGraw-Hill Book Company, New York, 1982, p. 32-33.

★ 396 ★

Personal Income by Metropolitan Area, 1988-2000

	Total personal income				Per capita personal income 1982 dollars		
	Millions of 1982 dollars			Average annual growth rate (percent)			
	1988	1995	2000	1988-2000	1988	1995	2000
United States[1]	3,255,648	3,756,405	4,108,386	2.0	13,245	14,469	15,345
Consolidated metropolitan statistical areas[2]							
Buffalo, NY	15,195	16,667	17,626	1.2	12,926	13,979	14,687
Chicago, IL	123,857	139,196	150,207	1.6	15,140	16,306	17,173
Cincinnati, OH	22,805	25,786	27,864	1.7	13,193	14,494	15,379
Cleveland, OH	38,442	43,041	46,255	1.6	13,883	15,250	16,227
Dallas, TX	54,099	63,362	69,860	2.2	14,365	15,818	16,866
Denver, CO	27,244	32,350	36,125	2.4	14,664	15,877	16,782
Detroit, MI	69,418	77,671	83,416	1.5	15,025	16,402	17,366
Houston, TX	47,174	54,694	60,077	2.0	12,955	14,217	15,172
Los Angeles, CA	209,456	249,879	278,161	2.4	15,211	16,345	17,189
Miami, FL	44,157	51,892	57,328	2.2	14,716	16,033	17,002
Milwaukee, WI	22,376	25,319	27,326	1.7	14,237	15,531	16,464
New York, NY	319,944	359,018	386,270	1.6	17,789	19,789	20,357
Philadelphia, PA	89,303	101,489	110,289	1.8	14,975	16,261	17,198
Pittsburgh, PA	29,736	32,925	35,189	1.4	13,019	14,187	15,008
Portland, OR	18,681	22,077	24,439	2.3	13,209	14,385	15,235
San Francisco, CA	109,107	129,239	143,307	2.3	18,059	19,676	20,875
Seattle, WA	36,046	43,094	48,019	2.4	14,890	16,216	17,188

Source: "Metropolitan Statistical Area Projections of Income, Employment, and Population to the Year 2000," *Survey of Current Business* 70, No. 10, October, 1990, p. 27. *Notes:* 1. The U.S. total includes metropolitan and nonmetropolitan counties. The U.S. population estimate for 1988 differs slightly from the estimate shown in the article on regional and State projections in the May 1990 *Survey of Current Business*. The U.S. total for metropolitan statistical areas and nonmetropolitan counties results from summing Census Bureau county-level population estimates, which were used in making the population projections for substate areas. The U.S. total for States is from revised State-level population estimates made by the Census Bureau after the county-level estimates were made. The Census Bureau has not revised the county-level population estimates to agree with the State-level estimates. 2. Only the name of the largest metropolitan area in each consolidated metropolitan statistical area (CMSA) is shown.

★ 397 ★

Projected Income for Hispanics, 1975-2000

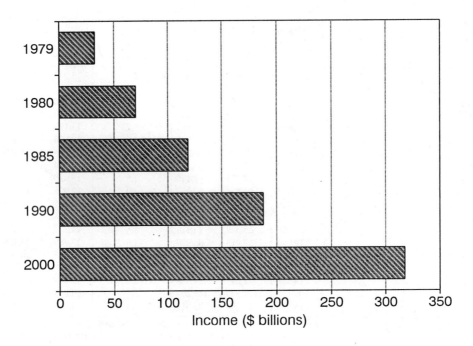

[Numbers in billions]

Year	Income
1975	32.8
1980	71.1
1985	119.5
1990	188.3
2000	318[1]

Source: "U.S. Hispanic Population and Hispanic Money Income," *Hispanic Business* 13, No. 12, December, 1991, p. 27. Primary source: U.S. Bureau of the Census, "Money Income of Households, Families and Persons in the United States" and decennial Census data. Hispanic Business Inc. *Notes:* 1. Forecast for the year 2000 is the average of high and low series projections.

★ 398 ★

State Rankings in Employment, Personal Income, and Business, 1988-2000 - I

State	Nonagricultural employment-Con. Manufacturing employees 1989		Union membership in manufacturing 1988		Personal income			
			Percent of manufacturing employees	Rank	Projected change, 1988-2000		Per capita, 1989	
	Percent	Rank			Percent	Rank	Amount (Dol.)	Rank
United States	17.9	X	24.9	X	26. 2	X	13,546	X
Alabama	24.2	9	15.3	28	22.5	39	10,489	43
Alaska	7.0	46	25.5	12	15.6	50	16,671	4
Arizona	12.9	39	3.8	48	40.6	2	12,165	29
Arkansas	25.8	5	12.0	32	24.2	31	9,931	48
California	17.2	29	22.6	17	33.0	7	15,342	8
Colorado	13.1	38	10.0	38	32.8	8	13,513	18
Connecticut	21.4	13	15.6	27	19.6	45	19,002	1
Delaware	21.1	14	20.5	20	27.5	16	14,229	12
District of Columbia	2.3	X	NA	X	17.0	X	18,084	X
Florida	10.3	42	8.9	40	37.3	3	13,585	16
Georgia	19.3	19	12.0	32	31.2	11	12,358	27
Hawaii	4.2	50	41.4	3	33.2	6	14,220	13
Idaho	16.5	30	8.6	41	28.9	14	10,552	40
Illinois	19.0	21	33.3	7	21.6	41	14,491	11
Indiana	26.0	3	37.6	6	24.4	29	12,147	30
Iowa	19.5	18	20.8	19	23.7	34	11,922	32
Kansas	17.3	28	11.4	34	24.4	28	12,701	21
Kentucky	19.8	16	23.0	16	22.5	38	10,580	39
Louisiana	11.5	40	20.4	21	17.8	47	9,947	47
Maine	19.6	17	18.7	23	25.5	24	12,508	26
Maryland	9.7	43	30.0	9	25.1	26	16,176	6
Massachusetts	18.1	24	19.9	22	20.3	44	17,070	3
Michigan	24.8	7	53.6	1	21.8	40	13,429	19
Minnesota	19.1	20	18.1	24	25.4	25	13,593	15
Mississippi	26.4	2	8.1	43	23.6	35	9,025	50
Missouri	19.0	21	32.4	8	24.2	30	12,542	25
Montana	7.6	44	25.1	13	23.3	36	10,838	38
Nebraska	13.4	37	9.9	39	26.9	21	11,891	33
Nevada	4.4	49	6.2	45	46.2	1	14,834	9
New Hampshire	21.6	12	6.8	44	28.4	15	15,602	7
New Jersey	17.6	27	24.8	14	23.0	37	18,305	2
New Mexico	7.5	45	10.4	36	33.6	5	10,115	45
New York	14.4	33	48.2	2	19.2	46	16,222	5
North Carolina	28.3	1	4.6	47	27.4	17	11,700	34
North Dakota	6.3	47	10.1	37	27.2	18	10,441	44

[Continued]

★ 398 ★

State Rankings in Employment, Personal Income, and Business, 1988-2000 - I
[Continued]

State	Nonagricultural employment-Con. Manufacturing employees 1989		Union membership in manufacturing 1988		Personal income			
			Percent of manufacturing employees	Rank	Projected change, 1988-2000		Per capita, 1989	
	Percent	Rank			Percent	Rank	Amount (Dol.)	Rank
Ohio	23.3	11	40.9	4	20.7	43	12,604	23
Oklahoma	14.1	36	17.1	25	24.9	27	10,896	37
Oregon	18.0	25	21.4	18	29.1	13	12,255	28
Pennsylvania	20.5	15	40.7	5	21.4	42	13,294	20
Rhode Island	23.5	10	11.1	35	24.1	32	13,818	14
South Carolina	26.0	3	3.1	49	26.2	23	10,496	42
South Dakota	11.5	40	2.7	50	26.5	22	10,535	41
Tennessee	24.3	8	13.5	30	29.7	12	11,312	35
Texas	14.2	35	15.1	29	26.9	20	12,088	31
Utah	14.9	31	5.0	46	36.3	4	10,069	46
Vermont	18.4	23	8.3	42	27.2	19	12,603	24
Virginia	14.9	31	12.2	31	31.4	9	14,570	10
Washington	17.7	26	28.2	11	31.3	10	13,585	16
West Virginia	14.3	34	29.8	10	16.1	49	9,503	49
Wisconsin	24.9	6	24.3	15	24.0	33	12,663	22
Wyoming	4.5	48	15.9	26	16.5	48	11,169	36

Source: State and Metropolitan Area Data Book, 1991, U.S. Bureau of the Census, Washington, D.C., 1991, p. xviii.

★ 399 ★

State Rankings in Employment, Personal Income, and Business, 1988-2000 - II

State	Women-owned firms, percent change, 1982-1987		U.S. exports by State of origin			
			Amount[1], 1990 (Mil. dol.)	Rank	Percent change 1989-1990	Rank
	Percent	Rank				
United States	57.5	X	315,065[1]	X	15.9	X
Alabama	55.6	27	2,834	27	-3.9	48
Alaska	47.3	35	2,850	26	40.8	4
Arizona	72.6	6	3,729	22	13.0	33
Arkansas	45.0	41	920	39	26.3	12
California	57.8	19	44,520	1	10.7	37
Colorado	55.8	25	2,274	29	5.6	43
Connecticut	71.9	7	4,356	19	18.8	25

[Continued]

★ 399 ★

State Rankings in Employment, Personal Income, and Business, 1988-2000 - II

[Continued]

State	Women-owned firms, percent change, 1982-1987		U.S. exports by State of origin			
	Percent	Rank	Amount[1], 1990 (Mil. dol.)	Rank	Percent change 1989-1990	Rank
Delaware	70.6	9	1,344	36	59.9	1
District of Columbia	23.5	X	320	X	39.6	X
Florida	76.5	4	11,634	9	14.1	30
Georgia	65.3	12	5,763	15	18.6	26
Hawaii	50.5	31	179	50	11.7	35
Idaho	41.6	47	898	40	19.7	24
Illinois	60.6	18	12,965	8	24.3	18
Indiana	45.0	40	5,273	16	24.2	19
Iowa	48.5	34	2,189	30	0.8	47
Kansas	45.5	39	2,113	31	26.2	13
Kentucky	46.2	36	3,175	23	26.5	11
Louisiana	45.8	37	14,199	6	-5.6	49
Maine	65.3	13	870	41	25.8	14
Maryland	69.3	19	2,592	28	6.2	42
Massachusetts	76.3	5	9,501	10	10.2	38
Michigan	53.7	28	18,474	5	24.1	20
Minnesota	56.7	22	5,091	18	15.4	28
Mississippi	42.0	45	1,605	33	9.5	40
Missouri	62.1	15	3,130	24	29.6	7
Montana	39.1	48	229	48	-19.1	50
Nebraska	41.9	46	693	42	3.5	46
Nevada	61.3	17	394	44	39.2	5
New Hampshire	90.7	1	973	38	4.0	45
New Jersey	85.6	2	7,633	14	17.6	27
New Mexico	55.9	24	249	47	29.4	8
New York	61.4	16	22,072	4	12.7	34
North Carolina	63.0	14	8,010	13	21.9	21
North Dakota	44.7	42	360	45	20.1	23
Ohio	50.3	32	13,378	7	31.5	6
Oklahoma	29.5	49	1,646	32	15.3	29
Oregon	45.6	38	4,065	20	4.8	44
Pennsylvania	57.7	20	8,491	12	24.7	17
Rhode Island	80.7	3	595	43	13.1	32
South Carolina	57.5	21	3,116	25	8.4	41
South Dakota	42.8	44	205	49	59.6	2

[Continued]

★ 399 ★

State Rankings in Employment, Personal Income, and Business, 1988-2000 - II

[Continued]

State	Women-owned firms, percent change, 1982-1987		U.S. exports by State of origin			
	Percent	Rank	Amount[1], 1990 (Mil. dol.)	Rank	Percent change 1989-1990	Rank
Tennessee	51.1	30	3,746	21	28.4	9
Texas	49.2	33	32,931	2	9.7	39
Utah	56.3	23	1,596	34	43.2	3
Vermont	71.6	8	1,154	37	13.6	31
Virginia	66.0	11	9,333	11	21.9	22
Washington	52.3	29	24,432	3	26.6	10
West Virginia	43.4	43	1,550	35	25.5	15
Wisconsin	55.8	26	5,158	17	24.9	16
Wyoming	28.6	50	264	46	11.3	36

Source: State and Metropolitan Area Data Book, 1991, U.S. Bureau of the Census, Washington, D.C., 1991, p. xviii. *Note*: 1. Excludes exports that are not identified as to the State of origin in the amount of $75,329 million.

★ 400 ★

Total and Per Capita Personal Income in Constant (1982) Dollars, 1979-2000

	Personal income						Personal income per capita[1]					
	1979 (mil. dol.)	1988 (mil. dol.)	1995 (mil. dol.)	2000 (mil. dol.)	Average annual percent change		1979 (dol.)	1988 (dol.)	1995 (dol.)	2000 (dol.)	Average annual percent change	
					1979-1988	1988-2000					1979-1988	1988-2000
U.S.	2,594,003	3,255,648	3,756,405	4,108,386	2.56	1.96	11,551	13,245	14,469	15,345	1.53	1.23

Source: "Total and Per Capita Personal Income in Constant (1982) Dollars, 1979 and 1988; and Projections: 1995 to 2000," *Statistical Abstract of the United States*, 1991, p. 443. Primary source: U.S. Bureau of Economic Analysis, *Survey of Current Business*, May, 1990. *Note:* 1. Based on U.S. Bureau of the Census population as of July 1, 1990.

★ 401 ★

Total Per Capita Personal Income and Earnings by Region and State, 1988 and 2000

Region, division, and state	Personal income (Constant 1982 dollars)			
	Total (Bil. dol.)		Per capita (Dol.)	
	1988	2000	1988	2000
United States	3,255.6	4,108.4	13,245	15,345
Northeast	780.8	944.5	15,432	17,635
New England	210.1	255.4	16,206	18,155
Maine	14.6	18.3	12,126	14,014
New Hampshire	16.8	21.5	15,449	17,363
Vermont	6.9	8.7	12,305	14,193
Massachusetts	98.6	118.6	16,736	18,694
Rhode Island	13.4	16.7	13,540	15,555
Connecticut	59.8	71.5	18,500	20,503
Middle Atlantic	570.7	689.1	15,166	17,449
New York	277.1	330.4	15,470	17,852
New Jersey	137.3	168.8	17,780	19,932
Pennsylvania	156.4	189.9	13,028	15,173
Midwest	768.9	944.4	12,840	14,938
East North Central	549.3	670.3	13,042	15,098
Ohio	135.5	163.6	12,486	14,531
Indiana	66.3	82.5	11,937	14,031
Illinois	164.1	199.4	14,126	16,131
Michigan	122.8	149.5	13,288	15,361
Wisconsin	60.6	75.2	12,490	14,575
West North Central	219.5	274.1	12,362	14,562
Minnesota	57.6	72.2	13,378	15,508
Iowa	33.4	41.3	11,777	13,849
Missouri	63.8	79.3	12,414	14,592
North Dakota	6.8	8.7	10,254	12,461
South Dakota	7.3	9.2	10,244	12,330
Nebraska	19.0	24.1	11,882	14,322
Kansas	31.6	39.3	12,645	14,986
South	1,006.1	1,288.7	11,885	13,975
South Atlantic	548.4	716.0	12,927	15,009
Delaware	9.4	12.0	14,217	15,747
Maryland	72.7	90.9	15,727	17,665
District of Columbia	10.6	12.4	17,149	19,823
Virginia	85.3	112.1	14,189	16,345
West Virginia	17.6	20.5	9,393	10,921

[Continued]

★ 401 ★

Total Per Capita Personal Income and Earnings by Region and State, 1988 and 2000
[Continued]

Region, division, and state	Personal income (Constant 1982 dollars)			
	Total (Bil. dol.)		Per capita (Dol.)	
	1988	2000	1988	2000
North Carolina	74.5	94.9	11,481	13,481
South Carolina	36.0	45.4	10,372	12,304
Georgia	77.8	102.0	12,262	14,297
Florida	164.5	225.8	13,340	15,496
East South Central	158.7	198.5	10,340	12,272
Kentucky	38.4	47.1	10,304	12,178
Tennessee	54.5	70.7	11,138	13,192
Alabama	42.3	51.9	10,318	12,247
Mississippi	23.4	28.9	8,936	10,631
West South Central	299.0	374.1	11,122	13,206
Arkansas	23.5	29.2	9,812	11,594
Louisiana	43.5	51.3	9,876	11,680
Oklahoma	34.7	43.3	10,700	12,937
Texas	197.3	250.3	11,716	13,851
West	699.9	930.8	13,811	15,844
Mountain	155.9	210.9	11,694	13,698
Montana	8.3	10.3	10,364	12,474
Idaho	10.1	13.1	10,119	12,181
Wyoming	5.3	6.1	10,956	12,898
Colorado	43.6	57.9	13,220	15,311
New Mexico	15.1	20.2	10,037	11,949
Arizona	42.0	59.0	12,029	13,926
Utah	16.5	22.5	9,791	11,605
Nevada	14.8	21.7	14,076	15,855
Pacific	544.1	720.0	14,566	16,607
Washington	61.5	80.7	13,228	15,316
Oregon	33.1	42.7	11,953	13,908
California	426.7	567.6	15,070	17,113
Alaska	8.0	9.3	15,302	16,765
Hawaii	14.8	19.7	13,449	15,219

Source: State and Metropolitan Area Data Book, 1991, U.S. Bureau of the Census, Washington, D.C., 1991, p. 249.

★ 402 ★

Total Per Capita Personal Income and Earnings by Industry Sector, Region, and State, 1988 and 2000

Region, division, and State	Personal income (Constant 1982 dollars) Earnings (Bil. dol.)											
	Total[1]		Private								Government[3]	
			Total[1]		Manufacturing		Retail trade		Services[2]			
	1988	2000	1988	2000	1988	2000	1988	2000	1988	2000	1988	2000
United States	2,388.8	3,009.0	1,978.5	2,537.0	484.7	555.5	227.9	286.8	583.4	854.8	373.5	433.3
Northeast	570.7	690.0	492.0	602.0	113.8	120.9	50.4	61.7	153.1	213.4	76.6	85.8
New England	154.5	187.6	135.1	165.8	35.3	37.8	15.5	19.0	40.7	57.3	18.8	21.3
Maine	10.4	12.9	8.5	10.8	2.3	2.7	1.2	1.6	2.2	3.3	1.8	2.0
New Hampshire	11.4	14.5	10.1	13.0	2.8	3.2	1.4	1.9	2.6	4.0	1.2	1.5
Vermont	4.9	6.3	4.2	5.3	1.1	1.3	0.5	0.7	1.2	1.7	0.7	0.8
Massachusetts	74.8	90.5	65.9	80.4	15.7	16.4	7.3	8.6	22.1	30.8	8.8	10.0
Rhode Island	9.5	11.9	8.0	10.2	2.3	2.5	1.0	1.2	2.4	3.6	1.4	1.6
Connecticut	43.5	51.6	38.5	46.1	11.1	11.7	4.1	4.9	10.1	14.0	4.8	5.3
Middle Atlantic	416.3	502.4	356.9	436.3	78.5	83.0	34.9	42.7	112.3	156.0	57.9	64.5
New York	213.9	254.5	181.6	219.1	33.4	35.4	16.0	19.3	60.1	80.8	31.7	34.8
New Jersey	92.2	114.2	79.8	100.0	18.9	19.9	8.5	10.8	23.5	34.2	12.2	13.9
Pennsylvania	110.1	133.7	95.4	117.1	26.2	27.8	10.4	12.6	28.8	41.0	13.9	15.7
Midwest	562.9	690.5	475.9	591.3	150.4	169.5	51.8	62.6	124.6	178.7	76.4	87.3
East North Central	403.0	491.3	347.2	427.4	117.6	130.6	36.5	43.8	89.7	128.1	52.1	59.4
Ohio	99.3	119.6	85.7	104.2	30.5	33.8	9.2	10.7	22.3	31.3	12.9	14.7
Indiana	48.7	60.0	42.0	52.2	16.3	18.8	4.6	5.6	9.1	13.0	6.2	7.2
Illinois	121.9	149.2	105.7	130.8	26.1	28.8	10.9	13.3	30.4	43.4	15.2	17.3
Michigan	90.0	109.3	77.8	95.3	31.5	33.9	7.9	9.6	19.1	27.9	11.8	13.3
Wisconsin	43.1	53.1	36.0	44.9	13.1	15.3	3.9	4.6	8.8	12.5	6.0	6.9
West North Central	159.9	199.3	128.7	163.8	32.8	38.8	15.3	18.7	34.8	50.6	24.3	27.9
Minnesota	43.7	55.0	36.4	46.5	10.3	12.4	4.2	5.2	9.6	14.0	6.1	7.0
Iowa	23.0	28.4	17.9	22.6	5.1	6.0	2.1	2.6	4.8	6.9	3.5	4.1
Missouri	47.4	59.0	40.2	50.8	10.4	11.8	4.6	5.6	11.0	15.9	6.5	7.4
North Dakota	4.7	5.9	3.4	4.3	0.3	0.4	0.5	0.6	1.1	1.5	1.0	1.1
South Dakota	5.0	6.2	3.5	4.5	0.5	0.7	0.5	0.6	1.1	1.5	1.0	1.1
Nebraska	14.2	17.4	10.2	13.3	1.9	2.3	1.3	1.6	2.9	4.2	2.5	2.8
Kansas	22.0	27.4	17.1	21.8	4.2	5.2	2.1	2.6	4.5	6.7	3.8	4.4
South	736.1	939.3	588.2	769.8	131.1	157.1	74.6	95.0	170.2	254.9	133.5	155.3
South Atlantic	398.6	516.7	315.6	421.2	66.8	80.7	41.2	53.4	96.2	146.5	77.3	90.1
Delaware	7.6	9.5	6.4	8.2	2.3	2.5	0.7	0.9	1.5	2.2	1.0	1.2
Maryland	47.9	60.2	37.6	48.5	5.3	5.9	5.4	6.7	13.3	19.6	10.0	11.3
District of Columbia	19.5	23.7	11.2	14.9	0.6	0.6	0.7	0.9	7.1	10.0	8.3	8.8
Virginia	61.5	80.3	46.3	62.6	9.4	11.3	5.7	7.6	14.5	22.5	14.8	17.2
West Virginia	11.7	13.5	9.6	11.1	2.2	2.4	1.2	1.3	2.3	3.1	2.0	2.3
North Carolina	58.2	73.8	47.3	61.5	16.4	19.9	5.8	7.4	10.3	15.5	9.4	11.0
South Carolina	27.0	33.9	21.3	27.4	7.4	9.0	2.8	3.4	4.8	7.2	5.5	6.2
Georgia	60.7	79.5	49.8	66.7	11.6	14.3	6.0	7.9	12.5	19.6	9.9	11.7
Florida	104.5	142.4	86.0	120.2	11.7	14.7	12.9	17.4	29.9	46.8	16.4	20.4
East South Central	116.3	146.4	93.2	120.2	28.0	33.7	11.5	14.5	23.7	34.6	20.0	23.0
Kentucky	27.3	33.7	22.0	27.6	6.2	7.3	2.8	3.4	5.4	7.8	4.6	5.3
Tennessee	41.7	54.0	34.8	45.8	10.2	12.2	4.3	5.5	9.2	13.8	6.2	7.5
Alabama	31.0	38.4	24.1	30.9	7.5	9.1	2.8	3.6	6.2	8.9	6.0	6.7
Mississippi	16.3	20.3	12.3	15.9	4.1	5.1	1.6	2.0	2.9	4.1	3.2	3.6

[Continued]

★ 402 ★

Total Per Capita Personal Income and Earnings by Industry Sector, Region, and State, 1988 and 2000

[Continued]

Region, division, and State	Personal income (Constant 1982 dollars) Earnings (Bil. dol.)											
	Total[1]		Private								Government[3]	
			Total[1]		Manufacturing		Retail trade		Services[2]			
	1988	2000	1988	2000	1988	2000	1988	2000	1988	2000	1988	2000
West South Central	221.1	276.2	179.4	228.4	36.4	42.7	21.9	27.1	50.3	73.8	36.3	42.2
Arkansas	16.7	20.7	12.9	16.6	4.0	4.9	1.7	2.1	3.1	4.4	2.5	2.9
Louisiana	31.0	36.7	25.1	30.1	4.4	4.9	3.0	3.6	7.5	10.2	5.3	5.9
Oklahoma	24.0	30.4	18.4	23.9	3.8	4.5	2.4	3.1	5.1	7.4	4.8	5.6
Texas	149.4	188.4	123.0	157.8	24.2	28.4	14.8	18.3	34.7	51.7	23.7	27.8
West	519.1	689.1	422.5	573.8	89.4	108.1	51.1	67.6	135.5	207.9	86.9	104.9
Mountain	113.4	153.7	89.5	124.9	15.2	19.5	11.7	15.8	29.2	45.6	21.6	26.1
Montana	5.4	6.8	4.0	5.1	0.5	0.5	0.6	0.8	1.3	1.8	1.2	1.3
Idaho	7.2	9.4	5.5	7.4	1.3	1.6	0.7	1.0	1.5	2.3	1.3	1.5
Wyoming	3.8	4.4	2.7	3.3	0.2	0.2	0.3	0.4	0.6	0.8	1.0	1.0
Colorado	32.6	43.2	26.1	35.6	5.0	6.1	3.2	4.3	8.0	12.3	5.9	7.0
New Mexico	10.7	14.3	7.6	10.5	0.8	1.1	1.1	1.5	2.7	4.2	2.9	3.5
Arizona	29.9	41.9	24.2	34.9	4.8	6.3	3.3	4.5	7.5	12.2	5.2	6.5
Utah	12.6	17.4	9.8	14.0	2.2	2.9	1.2	1.7	2.9	4.6	2.6	3.2
Nevada	11.3	16.2	9.6	14.2	0.5	0.8	1.1	1.6	4.8	7.4	1.6	2.0
Pacific	405.7	535.4	332.9	448.9	74.2	88.6	39.4	51.8	106.3	162.3	65.3	78.8
Washington	43.9	57.8	34.7	47.1	9.3	11.7	4.3	5.7	9.4	14.4	8.2	9.5
Oregon	23.9	30.6	19.3	25.2	5.1	6.2	2.5	3.2	5.3	8.0	3.8	4.5
California	319.7	424.5	266.4	360.3	58.9	69.8	30.6	40.6	87.3	133.6	47.9	58.8
Alaska	6.8	7.6	4.6	5.3	0.4	0.4	0.6	0.6	1.2	1.6	2.2	2.3
Hawaii	11.3	14.9	8.0	11.0	0.5	0.6	1.3	1.7	3.1	4.7	3.1	3.6

Source: State and Metropolitan Area Data Book, 1991, U.S. Bureau of the Census, Washington, D.C., 1991, p. 249. *Notes:* 1. Includes industries not shown separately. 2. Includes agricultural services services. 3. includes Federal civilian and military, State and local.

Income: U.S. Government

★ 403 ★

Composition of Social Insurance Taxes Contributions, 1981-1995 - I

"Unless otherwise noted, all receipts shown in this table are trust funds and on-budget."

[Numbers in millions of dollars]

	1981	1982	1983	1984	1985	1986	1987	1988	1989
Employment taxes and contributions:									
Old-age and survivors insurance (Off-Budget)	117,757	122,840	128,972	150,312	169,822	182,518	194,541	220,337	240,595
Disability insurance (Off-Budget)	12,418	20,626	18,348	15,763	16,348	17,711	18,861	21,154	23,071
Hospital insurance	30,340	34,301	35,641	40,262	44,871	51,335	55,992	59,859	65,396
Railroad retirement/pension fund	2,457	2,917	2,805	3,321	2,213	2,103	2,220	2,326	2,391
Railroad social security equivalent account	[1]	[1]	[1]	[1]	1,391	1,395	1,414	1,417	1,407
Total[2]	162,973	180,686	185,766	209,658	234,646	255,062	273,028	305,028	332,859

[Continued]

★ 403 ★

Composition of Social Insurance Taxes Contributions, 1981-1995 - I
[Continued]

	1981	1982	1983	1984	1985	1986	1987	1988	1989
Unemployment insurance	15,763	16,600	18,799	25,138	25,758	24,098	25,575	24,584	22,011
Other retirement contributions:									
Employees retirement-employee contributions	3,908	4,140	4,351	4,494	4,672	4,645	4,613	4,537	4,428
Contributions for non-Federal employees	76	72	78	86	87	96	102	122	119
Total	3,984	4,212	4,429	4,580	4,759	4,742	4,715	4,658	4,656
Total social insurance taxes and contributions[2]	182,720	201,498	208,994	239,376	265,163	283,901	303,318	334,335	359,416

Source: "Social Security Payroll Taxes," *Overview of the Federal Tax System*, Committee on Ways and Means, U.S. House of Representatives, April 10, 1991, Washington, D.C., pp. 189-91. Primary source: Budget of the United States Government, Fiscal Year 1991. Table also includes information for years 1940-1080. *Notes*: 1. $500 thousand or less. 2. On-budget and off-budget.

★ 404 ★

Composition of Social Insurance Taxes Contributions, 1981-1995 - II

"Unless otherwise noted, all receipts shown in this table are trust funds and on-budget."

[Numbers in millions of dollars]

	1990 estimate	1991 estimate	1992 estimate	1993 estimate	1994 estimate	1995 estimate
Employment taxes and contributions:						
Old-age and survivors insurance (Off-Budget)	258,457	284,139	304,849	326,772	350,815	370,942
Disability insurance (Off-Budget)	26,977	30,402	32,542	35,175	37,584	39,753
Hospital insurance	69,324	77,122	82,479	89,042	95,075	100,451
Railroad retirement/pension fund	2,395	2,452	2,500	2,543	2,593	2,634
Railroad social security equivalent account	1,445	1,483	1,506	1,530	1,557	1,578
Total[1]	358,598	395,598	423,876	455,062	487,624	515,358
Unemployment insurance	22,029	21,054	21,035	21,558	22,088	22,300
Other retirement contributions:						
Employees retirement-employee contributions	4,617	4,641	4,650	4,642	4,655	4,639
Contributions for non-Federal employees	118	156	160	164	187	190
Total	4,734	4,797	4,810	4,806	4,842	4,830
Total social insurance taxes and contributions[1]	385,362	421,449	449,721	481,426	514,554	542,487

Source: "Social Security Payroll Taxes," *Overview of the Federal Tax System*, Committee on Ways and Means, U.S. House of Representatives, April 10, 1991, Washington, D.C., pp. 189-91. Primary source: Budget of the United States Government, Fiscal Year 1991. Table also includes information for years 1940-1080. *Note:* 1. On-budget and off-budget.

★ 405 ★

Individual Income Tax Returns by Type, 1992 and 1999

Detail may not add to totals because of rounding.

[Numbers in millions of returns]

Type of return	1992	1999
Total	114	126
Form 1040	78	94
Form 1040A	20	17
Form 1040EZ	17	15

Source: "Projections of Returns to be Filed in Calendar Years 1992-1999," Carolyn De Wilde, *SOI Bulletin* 11, No. 3, Winter, 1991-1992, Figure C.

★ 406 ★

Number of Returns to Be Filed with the Internal Revenue Service, Calendar Years 1990-1999

Detail may not add to totals because of rounding.

[Numbers of returns in thousands]

Type of return	Actual 1990 (1)	Estimated 1991[2] (2)	Projected 1992 (3)	1993 (4)	1994 (5)	1995 (6)	1996 (7)	1997 (8)	1998 (9)	1999 (10)
Grand total[1]	203,223	205,516	207,698	207,582	211,303	214,763	217,857	220,676	223,346	226,113
Primary returns, total	192,966	194,725	196,613	200,152	203,698	206,973	209,880	212,510	214,993	217,574
Individual income tax, total	112,596	113,894	114,458	116,601	118,814	120,767	122,394	123,787	124,901	126,115
Forms 1040, 1040A, and 1040EZ, total	112,305	113,599	114,155	116,278	118,471	120,406	122,015	123,340	124,485	125,677
Form 1040	74,489	74,594	77,960	82,420	86,102	88,870	90,891	92,391	93,556	94,249
Form 1040A	18,380	21,688	19,635	17,980	16,991	16,528	16,395	16,465	16,464	16,692
Form 1040EZ	19,436	17,317	16,559	15,878	15,378	15,008	14,729	14,484	14,465	14,736
Other[3]	291	295	303	323	343	361	379	397	416	438
Individual estimated tax	39,363	39,609	40,398	41,211	42,027	42,843	43,659	44,474	45,290	46,106
Fiduciary income tax[4]	2,681	2,851	2,934	3,000	3,076	3,154	3,228	3,305	3,385	3,472
Fiduciary estimated tax	667	704	724	741	760	779	797	816	836	857
Partnership	1,751	1,734	1,724	1,715	1,705	1,696	1,686	1,677	1,667	1,658
Corporation income tax[5]	4,320	4,375	4,510	4,587	4,678	4,782	4,893	4,999	5,103	5,205
Estate tax	61	66	71	77	83	90	97	104	112	121
Gift tax	148	167	174	179	185	189	194	198	201	205
Employment tax[6]	28,911	28,665	28,909	29,202	29,460	29,700	29,897	30,105	30,339	30,613
Form 1042[7]	22	23	24	24	25	26	27	28	30	31
Tax-exempt organization[8]	487	497	516	531	544	555	556	575	586	596
Employee plan[9]	1,108	1,133	1,183	1,224	1,258	1,291	1,322	1,353	1,384	1,416
Excise tax[10]	852	1,008	989	1,059	1,084	1,102	1,120	1,138	1,158	1,180
Supplemental documents, total	10,257	10,791	11,086	7,430	7,605	7,790	7,978	8,165	8,352	8,539
Form 1040X	1,393	1,799	1,638	1,564	1,525	1,498	1,478	1,462	1,447	1,433
Form 4868[11]	5,278	5,314	5,672	1,985	2,094	2,200	2,304	2,407	2,508	2,608
Form 2688	1,623	1,651	1,695	1,744	1,793	1,842	1,889	1,934	1,978	2,021
Form 1120X	36	28	26	25	24	23	22	20	19	18

[Continued]

★ 406 ★

Number of Returns to Be Filed with the Internal Revenue Service, Calendar Years 1990-1999
[Continued]

Type of return	Actual 1990 (1)	Estimated 1991[2] (2)	Projected								
			1992 (3)	1993 (4)	1994 (5)	1995 (6)	1996 (7)	1997 (8)	1998 (9)	1999 (10)
Form 7004	1,897	1,965	2,019	2,075	2,131	2,187	2,244	2,300	2,356	2,412
Form 1041A	31	35	35	37	38	39	41	42	44	46

Source: "Projections of Returns to be Filed in Calendar Years 1992-1999," Carolyn De Wilde, *SOI Bulletin* 11, No. 3, Winter 1991-92, Table I. *Notes*: 1. Excluded from all totals are the following "Non-Master File" returns: Form CT-2, 941M, 990BL, and 1120-IC-DISC. Also excluded are withholding information documents, including Forms such as W-2 and the 1099 series and related forms. 2. Estimate, including that for some corporations, is based on returns processed through part of 1991. The actual number filed in CY 1991 was unavailable when this table was compiled. 3. Includes Forms 1040NR, 1040PR, 1040SS, and 1040C. 4. Includes forms 1041 and 1041S. 5. Includes Forms 1120, 1120A, 1120F, 1120H, 1120L, 1120POL, 1120S, 1120DF, 1120FSC, 1120PC, 1120REIT, and 1120 RIC. 6. Includes Forms 940, 940EZ, 940PR, 941, 941E, 941PR, 941SS, 942, 942 PR, 943, 943 PR, and CT-1. 7. Annual Withholding Tax Return for U.S. Source Income of Foreign Persons. 8. Includes Forms 990, 990C, 990 PF, 990T, 4720, 5227, and 990EZ. 9. Includes Forms 5500, 5500C, 5500EZ, 5500R. 10. Includes Forms 11C, 720, 730, 2290, and (starting Calendar Year 1991) 8752; excludes Forms 11 and 5000.24 which are filed with the Bureau of Alcohol, Tobacco and Firearms, U.S. Department of the Treasury, instead of with the Internal Revenue Service. 11. Form 4868 projections reflect the new APEX system to take place in CY 1993.

★ 407 ★

Percentage Composition of Receipts by Source, Selected Years, 1980-1995
[Numbers indicate percentages]

	1980	1985	1989	1995 (estimate)
Individual income tax	47.2	45.6	45.0	46.9
Corporation income tax	12.5	8.4	10.5	8.9
Social insurance taxes and contributions	30.5	36.1	36.3	36.4
On-budget	(8.6)	(10.8)	(9.7)	(9.8)
Off-budget	(21.9)	(25.4)	(26.6)	(26.6)
Excise taxes	4.7	4.9	3.4	3.7
Other	5.1	5.0	4.8	4.1
Total	100.0	100.0	100.0	100.0
On-budget	(78.1)	(74.6)	(73.4)	(73.4)
Off-budget	(21.9)	(25.4)	(26.6)	(26.6)

Source: "The Federal Tax System," *Overview of the Federal Tax System*, Committee on Ways and Means, U.S. House of Representatives, April 10, 1991, Washington, D.C., p. 58. Primary source: Budget of the United States Government for Fiscal Year 1992.

★ 408 ★

Projected Average Annual Percent Change in the Number of Returns Filed by Type of Return, 1992-1999

"The projections for the grand total of all returns call for an annual average increase of 1-2 percent through 1999."

[Numbers indicate percentage change]

Grand total	1.20
Primary returns, total	1.40
Individual income tax, total	1.28
Form 1040, 1040A, 1040EZ,total	1.27
Form 1040	2.96
Form 1040A	-3.03
Form 1040EZ	-1.98
Individual income tax, other	5.07
Individual estimated tax	1.92
Fiduciary income tax	2.50
Fiduciary estimated tax	2.50
Partnership	-0.56
Corporation income tax	2.19
Estate tax	7.85
Gift tax	2.59
Employment tax	0.83
Tax-exempt organization	2.29
Employee plan	2.83
Excise tax	2.02
Supplemental documents	-2.02

Source: "Projections of Returns to be Filed in Calendar Years 1992-1999," Carolyn De Wilde, *SOI Bulletin* 11, No. 3, Winter 1991-92, Figure A.

★ 409 ★

Tax Receipts by Source, 1990-1996

[Numbers in billions of dollars]

Source	1990 actual	Estimate					
		1991	1992	1993	1994	1995	1996
Individual income taxes	466.9	492.6	529.5	572.0	632.9	688.9	742.1
Corporation income taxes	93.5	95.9	101.9	109.0	120.6	130.0	138.3
Social insurance taxes and contributions	380.0	402.0	429.4	463.8	501.0	534.1	568.5
On-budget	(98.4)	(103.7)	(114.1)	(125.1)	(135.5)	(144.2)	(151.3)

[Continued]

★ 409 ★

Tax Receipts by Source, 1990-1996
[Continued]

Source	1990 actual	Estimate					
		1991	1992	1993	1994	1995	1996
Off-budget	(281.7)	(298.3)	(315.3)	(338.7)	(365.5)	(389.8)	(417.2)
Excise taxes	35.3	44.8	47.8	50.1	52.0	53.6	47.8
Estate and gift taxes	11.5	12.2	13.3	14.1	13.7	14.6	15.7
Customs duties and fees	16.7	17.7	19.3	20.8	22.0	22.7	23.9
Miscellaneous receipts	27.3	26.2	23.9	22.8	23.2	23.5	24.5
Total receipts	1,031.3	1,091.4	1,165.0	1,252.7	1,365.3	1,467.3	1,560.7
On-budget	(749.7)	(793.2)	(849.8)	(914.0)	(999.8)	(1,077.5)	(1,143.5)
Off-budget	(281.7)	(298.3)	(315.3)	(338.7)	(365.5)	(389.8)	(417.2)

Source: "The Federal Tax System," *Overview of the Federal Tax System*, Committee on Ways and Means, U.S. House of Representatives, April 10, 1991, Washington, D.C., p. 58. Primary source: Budget of the United States Government, Fiscal Year 1992.

★ 410 ★

Tax Receipts by Source as Percentages of the GNP, 1990-1996

Fiscal year	Individual income taxes	Corporation income taxes	Social insurance taxes and contributions			Excise taxes	Other	Total receipts		
			Total	On budget	Off budget			Total	On budget	Off budget
1990	8.6	1.7	7.0	(1.8)	(5.2)	.7	1.0	19.1	(13.9)	(5.2)
1991 estimate	8.8	1.7	7.2	(1.8)	(5.3)	.8	1.0	19.4	(14.1)	(5.3)
1992 estimate	8.8	1.7	7.2	(1.9)	(5.3)	.8	.9	19.5	(14.2)	(5.3)
1993 estimate	8.9	1.7	7.2	(1.9)	(5.3)	.8	.9	19.5	(14.2)	(5.3)
1994 estimate	9.2	1.8	7.3	(2.0)	(5.3)	.8	.9	19.9	(14.5)	(5.3)
1995 estimate	9.4	1.8	7.3	(2.0)	(5.3)	.7	.8	20.0	(14.7)	(5.3)
1996 estimate	9.5	1.8	7.3	(1.9)	(5.3)	.6	.8	20.0	(14.6)	(5.3)

Source: "Historical Tables," *Overview of the Federal Tax System*, Committee on Ways and Means, U.S. House of Representatives, April 10, 1991, Washington, D.C., pp. 242-44. Table also includes data for 1934-1989. Primary source: Office of Management and Budget, Budget of the United States Government, Fiscal Year 1992.

Prices

★ 411 ★

Inflation, 1990-2000

Since February, 1991, core inflation is running at an annual rate of only 3.1%, according to the latest government figures (charts). That's down from 5.2% in 1990. Inflation next year, most forecasters say, will run between 3.5% and 3.8%. "Core inflation is drifting down, and we've broken the 4% barrier," observes Donald Ratajczak, an economist at Georgia State University and a leading price watcher.

The inflation slowdown could last well into the 1990s. The key reason for optimism: Service-sector inflation, troublesome for most of the past decade, at last appears to be moderating. In part, that's because the recent recession forced a wide range of service businesses, from restaurants to apartment buildings to hair styling, to hold down prices. But even as the economy starts to recover, banks, insurers, ad agencies, and others are being forced to become more competitive by cutting costs and laying off workers with a vengeance. This promises to boost productivity, lower costs, and lessen the need to increase prices. As a result, says Morgan Stanley & Co. senior economist Stephen S. Roach, "we could be moving into an era of 3%- to-3.5% inflation."

Source: "Mom, What's Inflation?," Michael J. Mandel, *Business Week*, No. 3228, August 26, 1991, p. 20.

★ 412 ★

Monthly Subscriptions for Cable Television, 1991-1995
[Number of dollars in millions]

Year	Basic service fee	Percent increase	Pay service fee	Percent increase
1991	15.60	7.6	9.40	1.1
1992	16.70	7.1	9.50	1.1
1993	17.80	6.6	9.65	1.6
1994	18.90	6.2	9.90	2.6
1995	20.00	5.8	10.00	1.0

Source: "Monthly Sub Charge Forecast," *Cablevision* 16, No. 12, December 2, 1991, p. 41. Primary source: Veronis, Suhler & Associates/Wilkovsky Gruen Associates.

★ 413 ★

National Health Care Costs, 1987-2000

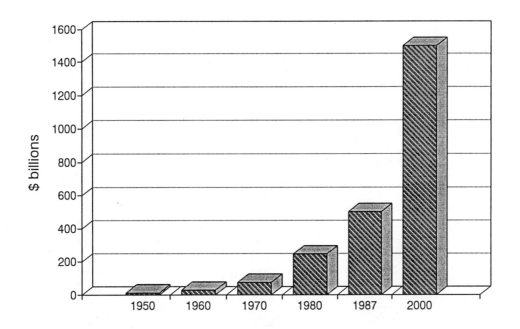

"The United States currently spends about $1.5 billion a day on health care, or nearly 12% of the gross national product, and that proportion is expected to reach 15% by the year 2000. The health of Americans on average has been improving, but the exceptions—among the poor and minorities—will be of growing concern in the coming years."

Year	
1950	12.7 billion
1960	26.9 billion
1970	75.0 billion
1980	248.1 billion
1987	500 billion
2000	1.5 trillion

Source: "Nine Forces Reshaping America," *The Futurist* XXIV, No. 4, July-August, 1990, p. 13. Primary source: National Leadership Commission on Health Care, 1989.

★414★

Projected Yearly Expenditures in Current Dollars on a Child Born in 1990 by Income Group for Married-Couple Families, 1990-2007

"According to the Census Bureau's March 1990 Current Population Survey, a clear majority (60 percent) of households headed by baby boomers (persons aged 25 to 44) contained children under age 18. During the 1990s, an ever-increasing share of baby boomer spending will go toward feeding, clothing, schooling, and entertaining their children."

Year	Age of child	Income group		
		low	middle	high
1990	Under 1	4,330	6,140	8,770
1991	1	4,590	6,510	9,300
1992	2	4,870	6,900	9,850
1993	3	5,510	7,790	11,030
1994	4	5,850	8,260	11,690
1995	5	6,200	8,750	12,390
1996	6	6,550	9,220	12,950
1997	7	6,950	9,770	13,730
1998	8	7,360	10,360	14,550
1999	9	7,570	10,690	15,120
2000	10	8,020	11,340	16,030
2001	11	8,500	12,020	16,990
2002	12	10,360	14,190	19,680
2003	13	10,980	15,040	20,860
2004	14	11,640	15,940	22,110
2005	15	13,160	17,950	24,610
2006	16	13,950	19,030	26,090
2007	17	14,780	20,170	27,650
Total		151,170	210,070	293,400

Source: "The Costs of Growing Up," Thomas Exter, *American Demographics*, August, 1991, p. 59.

Spending: Consumer Goods

★ 415 ★

Anticipated Apparel Spending, 1990-2000

Table shows the percent of apparel spending for the years 1990 and 2000 for ten cohort groups. These divisions, determined by a study conducted by DuPont and Management Horizons, segment the consuming public by common values set during the ages of 7-21. McAllister Isaacs III projects that "women's apparel spending will increase (in today's dollars) from $120-billion in 1990 to $215-billion in 2000," and that "men's apparel spending will increase from $58-billion in 1990 to $105-billion in 2000."

Cohort (Birth)	1990			2000		
	Age span	Percent of U.S. population	Percent of apparel spending	Age span	Percent of U.S. population	Percent of apparel spending
World War I Babies (1910-1919)	71-80	5.3	4.0	81-90	2.6	0.7
Roaring 20's Babies (1920-1929)	61-70	8.2	8.1	71-80	5.7	3.8
Depression Babies (1930-1939)	51-60	8.8	9.5	61-70	7.3	6.7
World War II Babies (1940-1945)	45-50	6.5	6.2	55-60	5.9	6.1
Mature Boomers (1946-1950)	40-44	7.1	8.6	50-54	6.5	6.8
Mid-Boomers (1951-1957)	33-39	11.6	13.8	43-49	10.7	10.0
Young Boomers (1958-1964)	26-32	12.4	13.1	36-42	11.6	14.1
Mature Busters (1965-1970)	20-25	9.1	9.6	30-35	8.8	11.3
Young Busters (1971-1976)	14-19	8.3	10.7	24-29	7.9	9.7
Mature Boomlets (1977-1982)	8-13	8.5	6.7	18-23	8.2	9.1

Source: "Focus on Everybody's Customer—The Consumer," McAllister Isaacs III, *Textile World* 139, No. 11, November, 1989, p. 74.

★ 416 ★

Credit Cards: Holders, Numbers, Spending, and Debt, 1980-2000

Type of credit card	Cardholders (mil.)			Number of cards (mil.)			Credit card spending (bil. dol.)			Credit card debt (bil. dol.)		
	1980	1989	2000 proj.	1980	1989	2000 proj.	1980	1989	2000 proj.	1980	1989	2000 proj.
Total[1]	86.1	109.5	118.3	526.0	956.9	1,167.0	201.2	430.3	893.0	80.2	206.7	435.7
Bank	63.3	75.2	87.5	110.6	200.0	272.0	52.9	217.6	495.9	25.0	133.4	307.1
Oil company	68.5	82.1	90.2	110.0	122.0	134.0	28.9	24.0	40.6	2.2	3.0	5.1
Phone	(NA)	103.6	111.0	(NA)	109.0	124.0	(NA)	8.7	16.9	(NA)	1.0	2.2
Retail store	83.0	95.4	112.2	276.5	454.9	535.0	74.4	73.3	107.0	47.3	48.0	71.7
Travel and entertainment	10.5	22.7	34.5	10.4	27.0	41.0	21.2	83.5	182.3	2.7	9.8	27.4
Other[2]	13.4	8.2	9.0	18.5	44.0	61.0	23.8	23.2	50.2	3.0	11.5	22.4

Source: "Credit Cards—Holders, Numbers, Spending, and Debt, 1980 and 1989, and Projections, 2000," *Statistical Abstract of the United States*, 1991, p. 510. Primary source: HSN Consultants Inc., Santa Monica, CA, *The Nilson Report*, bimonthly. *Notes:* 1. Cardholders may hold more than one type of card. 2. Includes airline, automobile rental, Discover (except for cardholders), hotel, motel, and other miscellaneous credit cards.

★ 417 ★

Expenditures for Wholesale Membership Clubs, 1989-1995

"Degen forecasts that sales will soar from $23.4 billion in 1980 to $77.1 billion by 1995. At the same time, the number of clubs will climb from 425 units to 875. The average sales per unit of $55.1 million will increase to $88.1 million. What will fuel that increase in average club sales is the expansion into more perishables such as bakery, produce, and fresh meats, which today only account for minor sales."

[Numbers in billions]

	1989	1990	1991	1992	1993	1994	1995
Units	367	425	500	575	660	760	875
Retail sales							
Food	8.3	11.8	16.0	20.7	26.9	35.0	44.6
Non-food	9.8	11.6	14.2	17.9	22.1	27.7	32.5
Total	18.1	23.4	30.2	38.6	49.0	62.7	77.1
Avg. sales/unit	49.3	55.1	60.4	67.8	74.2	81.2	88.1

Source: "Wholesale Clubs: A Unique Class of Trade," *Discount Merchandiser* 31, No. 3, March, 1991, p. 76. *Selling & Marketing to Membership Warehouse Clubs*, James M. Degen & Company, Inc., Santa Barbara, Cal.

★ 418 ★

Percentage of Total Food Expenditures for Food Eaten at and Away From Home, 1965-2000

Magnitudes estimated from published chart. Food eaten away from home includes take-out food. "Americans spent more than $500 billion on food products in 1989. Only 54 percent of that money was spent on food prepared at home, a decline from 70 percent in 1965. If this trend continues, spending on restaurants and take-out stands will overtake the nation's grocery bill by 1996."

	1965	1970	1975	1980	1985	1990
Food eaten at home	70.0	67.0	65.0	60.0	58.0	65.0
Food eaten away from home	30.0	35.0	37.0	39.0	42.0	47.0

Source: "Eating Out, Going Up," *American Demographics* 14, No. 1, January, 1992, p. 55. Primary source: *National Live Stock and Meat Board*, 1965-1989, *American Demographics*, 1990-2000.

★ 419 ★

Projected Distilled Spirits Consumption by Category, 1990-1995

[Numbers in thousands of nine-liter cases]

Category	1990[1]	1995[1]	ACGR[2]
Straight	16,607	14,303	-2.9
Blend	9,578	7,154	-5.7
Canadian	20,213	17,969	-2.3
Scotch	13,316	11,016	-3.7
Irish & other imp whiskey	278	248	-2.2
Gin	13,470	11,221	-3.6
Vodka	35,362	33,402	-1.1
Rum	13,564	12,805	-1.1
Tequila	4,410	4,923	2.2
Brandy & Cognac	7,539	7,061	-1.3
Cordials & Liqueurs	17,636	16,453	-1.4
Prepared cocktails	7,200	7,336	0.4
Total	159,174	143,891	-2.0

Source: "Projected Distilled Spirits Consumption by Category 1990-1995," *Jobson's Liquor Handbook 1991*, p. 17. Primary source: Jobson Beverage Alcohol Group; Steve L. Barsby & Associates, Inc. *Notes:* Projections take into account trends toward smaller average case size and assume no further FET increase. 1. Estimated. 2. Annual compound growth rate.

Spending: Corporate

★ 420 ★

Cable Television Spending, 1989 and 1994

[Numbers in billions of dollars]

	1989	1994	Compound annual growth
Network TV advertising	$9.3	$12.8	6.6%
Spot	$7.4	$9.9	6.0%
Local TV advertising	$7.8	$11.2	7.7%
Total TV advertising	$24.5	$33.9	6.8%
Pay cable subscriptions	$4.1	$5.1	4.5%
Basic rate subscriptions	$7.6	$11.4	8.5%
National cable advertising	$1,225	$2,310	13.5%
Local cable advertising	$.340	$.665	14.3%
Total cable TV spending	$13.3	$19.5	8.0%

[Continued]

★ 420 ★

Cable Television Spending, 1989 and 1994
[Continued]

	1989	1994	Compound annual growth
Network radio advertising	$.500	$.700	8.1%
Spot radio advertising	$1,560	$2,340	8.4%
Local radio advertising	$6,350	$9,300	7.9%
TV network program buying	$4,125	$5,925	7.5%
TV station program buying	$1,750	$2,500	7.4%
Cable TV program buying	$2,050	$3,225	9.5%
Barter syndication program	$1,215	$2,450	15.1%
Total program expenditures	$9,140	$14.1	9.1%

Source: "Things Are Looking up for Network Advertising," Joe Flint, *Broadcasting* 119, No. 4, July 23, 1990, p. 68. Primary source: Veronis, Suhler & Associates.

★ 421 ★

Corporate Tax Expenditures, 1987-1996
[Numbers in millions of dollars]

Fiscal year	Corporate tax expenditures
1987	97,100[1]
1988	62,000
1989	37,300
1990	38,700
1991	40,700
1992	46,900
1993	47,200
1994	48,200
1995	49,300
1996	50,600

Source: "Corporate Income Tax," *Overview of the Federal Tax System*, Committee on Ways and Means, U.S. House of Representatives, April 10, 1991, Washington, D.C., p. 76. Table also includes data for 1980-1986. Primary source: Staff of the Joint Committee on Taxation. *Note:* 1. Estimated prior to enactment of the Tax Reform Act of 1986.

★ 422 ★

Growth in Radio Spending, 1991-1995

[Numbers in percent]

1991	4.0
1992	6.5
1993	8.2
1994	7.8
1995	6.6
CAGR[1]	6.6

Source: "Radio Ad Revenue to Hit $12 Billion by 1995," Lucia Cobo, *Broadcasting* 121, No. 17, October 21, 1991, p. 40. Primary source: Veronis, Suhler & Associates. *Note*: 1. Compound annual growth rate.

Spending: Personal

★ 423 ★

End-User Spending on Media and Entertainment, 1984-1994

"Cable is on the verge of slowing its rate of growth."

[Numbers in millions]

Category	1984 Spending	'84-'89 Compound annual growth (%)	1989 Spending	'89-'94 Compound annual growth (%)	1994 Spending
Cable TV	$6,980	10.9	$11,710	7.2	$16,545
Box office	4,030	4.5	5,022	5.3	6,500
Home video	1,375	47.5	9,600	8.8	14,645
Program syndication	4,990	9.7	7,925	8.0	11,650
Record music	4,370	8.1	6,464	5.3	8,350
Newspapers	7,617	4.3	9,405	5.9	12,500
Books	11,599	9.2	18,036	8.3	26,905
Magazines	4,881	9.1	7,555	7.9	11,070
Business information	12,449	11.4	21,314	8.6	32,210
Total	58,291	10.7	97,031	7.7	140,375

Source: "Veronis Suhler Predicts Slowdown in Cable Growth," Tom Kerver, *Cablevision* 15, No. 3, July 30, 1990, p. 33. Primary source: 1990 Communications Industry Forecast, Veronis Suhler & Associates.

★ 424 ★

Growth in Users for Selected Supermarket Product Categories, 2000 versus 1988

	% Change		% Change
Products showing fastest growth		Products showing slower growth	
Homemakers		Homemakers	
Ground coffee	+19.4	Infant formula	-2.4
English muffins	+18.5	Disposable diapers	-1.9
Drain cleaners	+18.3	Baby foods	NC
Outdoor insecticides	+17.2	Powdered fruit/soft drinks	+7.4
Dried fruit	+17.1	Toaster products	+8.7
Disposable plates	+16.7	Pizza mixes	+9.1
Cottage cheese	+16.2	Charcoal	+9.1
Turkey, frozen	+16.1	Cotton swabs	+9.2
Metal polish	+16.1	Meat snacks	+9.5
Canned dog food	+15.7	Table syrup/molasses	+9.5
Salt substitute	+15.4	Canned pasta	+9.6
Adults		Adults	
Denture cleaners	+18.8	Tooth brushes	+9.5
Artificial sweeteners	+14.9	Nuts, snacks	+9.6
Laxatives	+14.9	Motor oil additives	+9.9
Vitamins	+13.8	Diet soft drinks	+9.9
Mouthwash	+13.0	Adhesive bandages	+10.3
Men		Men	
Hair tonic/dressing	+15.3	Hair conditioners	+5.5
Hair coloring	+15.0	Shampoo	+6.3
Pipe tobacco	+14.7	Deodorants/anti-perspirants	+9.0
Hair sprays	+14.4	Facial cleansers	+9.0
Pre-electric shave lotion	+12.3	Hair conditioning treatment	+9.4
Women		Women	
Hair coloring	+14.5	Tampons	+3.8
Lipstick/lip gloss	+13.8	Shampoo	+4.2
Face creams/lotions	+13.3	Blusher	+6.5
Deod.-colognes/body sprays	+12.7	Eye shadow	+6.7
Fem. hygiene deod. sprays	+12.7	Nail polish	+7.5

Source: "Looking Toward the 1990s," Robert Dietrich, *Supermarket Business* 44, No. 3, March, 1989, p. 37.

★ 425 ★

Growth of Major Supermarket Departments, 2000

[Numbers measure average change in number of users]

Female homemakers	
Produce	+15.6
Oils/dressings/condiments	+14.5
Household cleaning	+14.5
Desserts/baking ingredients	+14.2
Laundry supplies	+14.0
Household supplies	+13.5
Fruits/vegetables, canned	+13.4
Refrigerated meats	+13.4
Baked goods	+13.3
Dairy	+13.2
Soaps, non-laundry	+13.0
Pet products	+12.9
Frozen foods	+12.8
Sauces	+12.8
Spices/extracts	+12.7
Paper/plastic products	+12.7
Packaged specialty foods	+12.6
Family beverages	+12.1
Snacks	+11.9
Breakfast foods	+11.2
Baby/children's HBA	+1.7
Baby foods	-1.3

Source: "Looking Toward the 1990s," Robert Dietrich, *Supermarket Business* 44, No. 3, March, 1989, p. 36.

★ 426 ★

Popular Supermarket Products, 2000

Products expected to be "hot" or not in 2000. "By the year 2000, your supermarket may be stocking more English muffins and less infant formula. Why? Because the sizable baby-boom generation will be changing their buying habits as they grow older...."

To be	Not to be
Coffee	Beer
Whole turkey	Pizza mixes
Diet colas	Regular colas
Popcorn	Meat snacks

[Continued]

★ 426 ★

Popular Supermarket Products, 2000
[Continued]

Grapefruit juice	Powdered drinks
English muffins	Garlic bread
Dessert-type wines	Wine and spirit coolers
Canned hash	Canned pasta
Dried fruit	Baby foods
Cottage cheese	Ready-to-serve dips
Regular ice cream	Ice cream novelties
Cough drops	Chewing gum
Disposable plates	Disposable diapers
Drain cleaners	Car wax and polish
Outdoor insecticides	Charcoal
Pipe tobacco	Smokeless tobacco
Face creams	Blusher and mascara
Hair coloring	Hair conditioners
Mouthwash	Breath fresheners
Laxatives	Diet pills

Source: "Shopping in the Year 2000," Robert Dietrich, *The Futurist* XXIII, No. 6, November/December, 1989, p. 44. Primary source: *Supermarket Business.*

★ 427 ★

Sepnding in the 21st Century

We shall [in the 21st century] enter a checkless, cashless society. Only diehards will use cash, paying a penalty for the privilege because cash will require special handling, a cash register, a safe and all the worry and concern those things entail. Funds will be transferred by voiceprint. Nobody with a voiceprint identification card or number will have to shop in person. Dial a store through your two-way television at home or in the office, check prices on your screen and order by credit card or checking account number. The merchant will push a button that lights up green if you have the funds in your account, red if you don't and yellow if you're in the process of transferring funds to your account.

Source: "Social Shock," *Encounters with the Future: A Forecast of Life into the 21st Century,* Marvin Cetron and Thomas O'Toole, McGraw-Hill Book Company, New York, 1982, p. 32.

★ 428 ★

Spending on Household Appliances, 1990 and 2000

Numbers may not add perfectly because of rounding.

[All dollar figures are yearly totals in millions]

	1990		2000		% = Expenditures
	Expenditures	Market share	Expenditures	Market share	
Washing machines	$3,191	100	$4,362	100	36.7
18-34 Years old	$786	24.6	$1,085	24.9	38
35-64 Years old	$1,573	49.3	$2,106	48.3	33.9
65+ Years old	$832	26.1	$1,171	26.8	40.7
Clothes dryers	$1,847	100	$2,551	100	38.1
18-34 Years old	$404	21.9	$525	20.6	30
35-64 Years old	$975	52.8	$1,319	51.7	35.3
65+ Years old	$468	25.3	$707	27.7	51.1
Electric floor cleaners	$1,384	100	$2,073	100	49.8
18-34 Years old	$384	27.7	$571	27.5	48.7
35-64 Years old	$812	58.7	$1,216	58.7	49.8
65+ Years old	$188	13.6	$286	13.8	52.1
Sewing machines	$721	100	$998	100	38.4
18-34 Years old	$130	18	$126	12.6	-3.1
35-64 Years old	$401	55.6	$597	59.8	48.9
65+ Years old	$190	26.4	$274	27.5	44.2
Room air-conditioners	$1,715	100	$2,275	100	32.7
18-34 Years old	$232	13.5	$212	9.3	-8.6
35-64 Years old	$767	44.7	$1,057	46.5	37.8
65+ Years old	$716	41.7	$1,006	44.2	40.5

Source: "Projected Consumer Spending in the 90s," James Stevens, *Appliances* 47, No. 12, December, 1990, p. 13. Primary source: A *Preventive Magazine* report based on information from the U.S. Bureau of Labor Statistics.

★ 429 ★

Supermarket Beer Purchases by Grade, 2000

"Among the product classes whose base group is adults, beer shows the poorest prospects for growth between now and 2000."

Beer Base = Adults	Percent who use (1988)	Use by Age (vs. average) by percentage						Growth in users (vs. 1988, in pct.)	
		18-24	25-34	35-44	45-54	55-64	65+	1955	2000
Beer, Domestic, regular (HU)[1]	12.8	+42	+21	-2	-16	-20	-41	+3.0	+6.2
Beer, Domestic, low calorie	16.6	+41	+36	+7	-7	-42	-64	+3.2	+5.8
Ale	3.6	+46	+33	-1	-31	-33	-42	+2.2	+4.4
Beer, low alcohol	1.2	-3	+48	-16	-49	-15	-	+2.2	+3.6
Beer, Imported	14.4	+65	+43	-5	-25	-43	-68	+1.4	+3.3
Malt liquor	2.3	+65	+50	-3	-35	-47	-70	+0.9	+2.3

Source: "Looking toward the 1990s," Robert Dietrich, *Supermarket Business* 44, No. 3, March, 1989, p. 42-3. *Note:* 1. (HU) = Heavy users.

★ 430 ★

Supermarket Breakfast Foods Purchases by Type, 2000

"Overall, the product categories that comprise breakfast foods are projected to show lackluster gains between now and the year 2000 compared to other dry grocery department sections.... The best performer promises to be jams and jellies, whose popularity peaks among the fast-growing 45-54 group, 11.0% of whom are heavy users (two jars or more in the last 30 days). The relatively new breakfast bars and toaster products categories have found relatively little favor among those over 45."

Breakfast Foods (Base = Female homemakers)	Percent who use (1988)	Use by age (vs. average) by percentage						Growth in users (vs. 1988, in pct.)	
		18-24	25-34	35-44	45-54	55-64	65+	1955	2000
Jams, jellies (HU)[1]	11.0	-52	-	-4	+16	+11	+8	+8.7	+14.0
Honey	32.5	-25	+3	4	+4	+9	+3	+7.7	+12.5
Pancake, waffle mix	44.9	+1	+8	+9	+6	-8	-21	+7.6	+12.0
Peanut butter (HU)	7.1	+11	+12	+19	+9	-15	-38	+7.6	+11.9
Cold breakfast cereals (HU)	22.6	-32	+18	+30	-6	-6	-31	+7.8	+11.7
Hot breakfast cereals (HU)	11.0	-35	-2	-22	-24	+35	+36	+6.4	+11.0
Breakfast/snack/nutritional bars	21.6	+9	+41	+22	-1	-30	-59	+7.1	+9.9
Table syrup/Molasses (HU)	4.8	-26	+31	+5	-16	-2	-20	+6.3	+9.5
Toaster products (HU)	6.3	+38	+37	+32	-13	-47	-59	+6.3	+8.7

Source: "Looking toward the 1990s," Robert Dietrich, *Supermarket Business* 44, No. 3, March, 1989, p. 43. *Note:* 1. (HU) = Heavy users.

★ 431 ★

Supermarket Pet Products Purchases by Type, 2000

"For cats, the 35-to-44 group are the best customers for canned, moist and dry food as well as cat litter. Slack performance among that other fast growing group (45-to-54), however, suppresses the prospects for these products to the average level.... Products to feed dogs find favor with both the 35-to-44 and 45-to-54 groups, pushing their forecasts up to the top of the list."

Pet products (Base = Female homemakers)	Percent who use (1988)	Use by age (vs. average) by percentage						Growth in users (vs. 1988, in pct.)	
		18-24	25-34	35-44	45-54	55-64	65+	1955	2000
Dog food, canned	14.4	-33	-11	+22	+28	+2	-16	+9.8	+15.7
Dog food, moist	6.1	-30	-12	+23	+12	+20	-18	+8.9	+14.6
Dog biscuits/treats	18.9	-24	-	+26	+16	+4	-31	+8.8	+14.0
Flea/tick care products for dogs/cats	24.1	-15	+4	+32	+13	+3	-45	+8.4	+13.3
Dog food, dry	28.7	-17	+10	+33	+15	-7	-48	+8.5	+13.1
Cat food, canned	13.9	-3	+3	+23	+12	-13	-28	+8.4	+13.1
Cat food, moist	7.8	+2	+3	+20	+8	-7	-28	+8.0	+12.7
Cat food, dry	20.6	+3	+14	+34	-4	-20	-38	+7.7	+11.5
Cat litter	15.9	+22	+20	+22	+7	-23	-50	+7.3	+11.1
Cat treats	6.8	+61	+10	+9	-9	-6	-41	+5.8	+9.8

Source: "Looking toward the 1990s," Robert Dietrich, *Supermarket Business* 44, No. 3, March, 1989, p. 56.

Spending: U.S. Government

★ 432 ★

Actual and Projected Changes in Support Ratio (Relative to 1990): Four Alternative Measures, 1990-2065

	Earnings-weighted population/ needs-weighted consumption	Unweighted population aged 20-64 needs-weighted consumption	Earnings-weighted population/ unweighted consumption	Unweighted population aged 20-64/ unweighted consumption
1990	.995	.995	1.005	.995
2000	1.025	1.01	1.03	1.04
2010	1.01	1.02	1.025	1.01
2020	.95	.96	.97	.99
2030	.905	.905	.94	.94
2040	.89	.91	.925	.94

[Continued]

★ 432 ★

Actual and Projected Changes in Support Ratio (Relative to 1990): Four Alternative Measures, 1990-2065

[Continued]

	Earnings-weighted population/ needs-weighted consumption	Unweighted population aged 20-64 needs-weighted consumption	Earnings-weighted population/ unweighted consumption	Unweighted population aged 20-64/ unweighted consumption
2050	.89	.905	.93	.94
2060	.88	.89	.925	.93

Source: "An Aging Society: Opportunity or Challenge?, David M. Cutler, James M. Poterba, Louise M. Sheiner, Laurence H. Summers, *Brookings Papers on Economic Activity*, No. 1, 1990, p. 14. Table also includes data for 1970-1990. Magnitudes estimated for published chart.

★ 433 ★

Changes in Support Ratio Relative to 1990, 1950-2060

"The earnings-weighted labor force measure uses contemporaneous and projected labor force participation rates and the 1987 age-earnings profiles of men and women to form effective labor forces."

[Numbers in percent]

Year	Unweighted population age 20-64/ unweighted consumption	Earnings-weighted population/ unweighted consumption	Unweighted population age 20-64/ needs-weighted consumption	Earnings-weighted population/ needs-weighted consumption
1950	-1.4	-11.5	1.4	-9.0
1960	-10.9	-16.5	-7.4	-13.2
1970	-10.8	-16.9	-7.7	-14.0
1980	-3.3	-7.0	-2.0	-5.8
1990	0.0	0.0	0.0	0.0
2000	1.3	3.7	0.8	3.2
2010	3.8	2.8	2.3	1.4
2020	-0.5	-2.3	-3.1	-4.8
2030	-5.9	-6.0	-9.5	-9.6
2040	-6.2	-6.6	-10.0	-10.5

[Continued]

★ 433 ★

Changes in Support Ratio Relative to 1990, 1950-2060
[Continued]

Year	Unweighted population age 20-64/ unweighted consumption	Earnings-weighted population/ unweighted consumption	Unweighted population age 20-64/ needs-weighted consumption	Earnings-weighted population/ needs-weighted consumption
2050	-6.5	-7.3	-10.4	-11.2
2060	-7.4	-7.8	-11.5	-11.8

Source: "An Aging Society: Opportunity or Challenge?" David M. Cutler, James M. Poterba, Louise M. Sheiner, Laurence H. Summers, *Brookings Papers on Economic Activity*, No. 1, 1990, p. 13. Magnitudes estimated from published chart. Primary source: Board of Trustees of the Federal Old-Age and Survivors Insurance and Disability Insurance Trust Funds (1988).

★ 434 ★

Consumption Response with Induced Productivity, 1990-2065

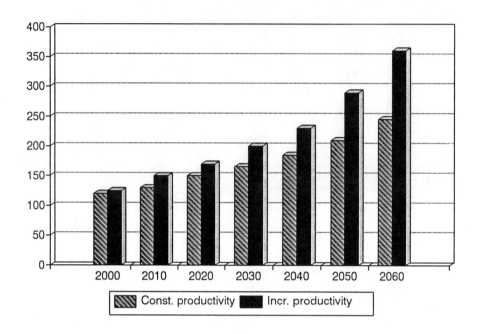

"For increasing productivity, it is assumed that productivity grows 0.5 percent for each 1 percent decline in annual labor force. The consumption measure is needs-weighted, and the labor force is earnings-weighted. The simulations assume unit elasticities of substitution in production and consumption."

[Per capita consumption (index, 1990 = 100)]

Year	Constant productivity	Increasing productivity
2000	120	125
2010	130	150
2020	150	170
2030	165	200
2040	185	230
2050	210	290
2060	245	360

Source: "An Aging Society: Opportunity or Challenge?, "David M. Cutler, James M. Poterba, Louise M. Sheiner, Laurence H. Summers, *Brookings Papers on Economic Activity*, No. 1, 1990, p. 45. Magnitudes estimated from published chart. Primary source: Authors' calculations.

★ 435 ★

Costs of Federal Regulations, 1990 and 2000

"The costs are broken out into major categories and show that the predicted increase in the costs of social regulation (mainly regulations risk to health, safety and the environment), is the primary explanation for the expected increase in the overall costs of regulation for the year 2000."

[Numbers in billions of 1990 dollars]

	1990	2000
Environmental regulation	109	184
Other social regulation	32	52
Economic regulation	155-261	155-261
Process regulation	134-160	151-191
Total costs	430-562	542-688

Source: "Reforming Regulation and Managing Risk Reduction," *Budget of the United States Government, Fiscal Year 1993*, Washington, D.C., p. 397. Primary source: "Cost of Regulation," Thomas D. Hopkins, Rochester Institute of Technology Working Paper, December, 1991.

★ 436 ★

Current Services Outlay Projections for Federal Physical Capital Spending, in Constant 1987 Dollars, 1991-1997

[Numbers in billions of dollars]

	1991 Actual	Estimate					
		1992	1993	1994	1995	1996	1997
Nondefense:							
Transportation-related categories:							
Roadways and bridges	13.1	14.0	14.4	14.4	14.1	14.1	14.1
Airports and airway facilities	2.9	3.0	3.3	3.3	3.3	3.3	3.3
Mass transportation systems	2.9	2.7	2.7	2.5	2.3	2.3	2.3
Railroads	0.2	0.2	0.3	0.4	0.3	0.3	0.3
Subtotal, transportation	19.1	20.1	20.6	20.5	20.1	20.1	20.1
Housing and buildings categories:							
Federally assisted housing	0.1	0.1	0.4	0.9	1.3	1.3	1.3
Hospitals	1.1	1.3	1.4	1.4	1.3	1.3	1.3
Public buildings[1]	1.5	2.1	2.7	3.1	2.7	2.7	2.7
Subtotal, housing and buildings	2.7	3.4	4.4	5.3	5.2	5.2	5.2
Other nondefense categories:							
Wastewater treatment and related facilities	2.3	2.1	2.0	2.0	1.9	1.9	1.9
Water resources projects	2.9	2.8	2.7	2.7	2.7	2.7	2.7
Space and communications facilities	3.3	4.0	3.7	3.6	3.5	3.5	3.5
Energy programs	2.3	2.6	3.3	3.5	3.1	3.1	3.1
Community development programs	2.9	3.1	2.9	3.0	2.6	2.6	2.6

[Continued]

★ 436 ★

Current Services Outlay Projections for Federal Physical Capital Spending, in Constant 1987 Dollars, 1991-1997

[Continued]

	1991 Actual	Estimate					
		1992	1993	1994	1995	1996	1997
Other nondefense	3.1	3.3	3.3	3.3	3.2	3.2	3.2
Subtotal, other nondefense	16.8	17.9	17.9	18.1	17.1	17.1	17.1
Subtotal, nondefense	38.7	41.4	42.0	43.9	42.3	42.3	42.3
National defense	80.5	72.0	66.6	62.1	59.9	59.9	59.9
Total	119.2	113.4	108.6	106.0	102.3	102.3	102.3

Source: "Physical and Other Capital Presentation," Budget of the United States Government, Fiscal Year 1993, p. 45. Note: 1. Excludes outlays for public buildings that are included in other categories in this table.

★ 437 ★

Current Services Outlay Projections for Federal Physical Capital Spending, 1991-2001

[Numbers in billions of dollars]

	1991 Actual	Estimate									
		1992	1993	1994	1995	1996	1997	1998	1999	2000	2001
Nondefense:											
Transportation-related categories:											
Roadways and bridges	14.6	16.1	17.0	17.6	18.0	18.6	19.2	19.8	20.4	21.1	21.7
Airports and airway facilities	3.2	3.5	3.8	4.0	4.2	4.3	4.4	4.6	4.7	4.9	5.0
Mass transportation systems	3.2	3.1	3.2	3.1	2.9	3.0	3.1	3.2	3.3	3.4	3.6
Railroads	0.2	0.3	0.4	0.4	0.4	0.4	0.4	0.4	0.4	0.4	0.4
Subtotal, transportation	21.2	23.0	24.5	25.2	25.5	26.3	27.1	28.0	28.9	29.8	30.8
Housing and buildings categories:											
Federally assisted housing	0.1	0.1	0.4	1.1	1.6	1.6	1.7	1.8	1.8	1.9	1.9
Hospitals	1.3	1.4	1.6	1.6	1.6	1.7	1.7	1.8	1.8	1.9	2.0
Public buildings[1]	1.6	2.4	3.2	3.7	3.3	3.4	3.5	3.6	3.8	3.9	4.0
Subtotal, housing and buildings	3.0	3.9	5.2	6.5	6.5	6.7	6.9	7.2	7.4	7.6	7.9
Other nondefense categories:											
Wastewater treatment and related facilities	2.5	2.4	2.4	2.4	2.4	2.5	2.6	2.7	2.8	2.8	2.9
Water resources projects	3.2	3.1	3.1	3.2	3.4	3.5	3.6	3.7	3.8	3.9	4.1
Space and communications facilities	3.7	4.6	4.3	4.4	4.4	4.5	4.7	4.8	5.0	5.1	5.3
Energy programs	2.6	3.0	3.9	4.2	3.9	4.0	4.1	4.3	4.4	4.5	4.7
Community development programs	3.2	3.5	3.5	3.6	3.3	3.4	3.5	3.7	3.8	3.9	4.0
Other nondefense	3.4	3.8	3.9	4.0	4.0	4.2	4.3	4.4	4.6	4.7	4.9
Subtotal, other nondefense	18.5	20.4	21.1	21.9	21.4	22.1	22.8	23.6	24.3	25.1	25.9
Subtotal, nondefense	42.7	47.2	50.7	53.6	53.4	55.1	56.9	58.7	60.6	62.5	64.5

[Continued]

★ 437 ★

Current Services Outlay Projections for Federal Physical Capital Spending, 1991-2001
[Continued]

	1991 Actual	Estimate									
		1992	1993	1994	1995	1996	1997	1998	1999	2000	2001
National defense	87.3	80.5	77.0	74.1	74.8	77.2	79.6	82.2	84.8	87.5	90.3
Total	130.1	127.7	127.7	127.7	128.2	132.3	136.5	140.9	145.4	150.0	154.8

Source: "Physical and Other Capital Presentation," *Budget of the United States Government, Fiscal Year 1993*, p. 45. *Note:* 1. Excludes outlays for public buildings that are included in other categories in this table.

★ 438 ★

Current Services Outlays by Agency, 1991-1993
[Numbers in billions of dollars]

	1991 actual	Current services	
		1992 estimate	1993 estimate
Legislative branch	2.3	2.8	2.7
The judiciary	2.0	2.3	2.4
Executive Office of the President	0.2	0.2	0.2
Funds appropriated to the President	11.7	10.7	11.0
Department of Agriculture	54.1	61.8	59.8
Department of Commerce	2.6	2.9	2.7
Department of Defense-Military	261.9	295.0	283.7
Department of Defense-Civil	26.5	27.9	29.3
Department of Education	25.3	26.8	30.1
Department of Energy	12.5	15.7	16.3
Department of Health and Human Services, except Social Security	218.0	263.5	291.9
Department of Health and Human services, Social Security	266.4	280.7	295.7
Department of Housing and Urban Development	22.8	24.2	27.9
Department of Interior	6.1	7.5	6.9
Department of Justice	8.2	9.4	9.3
Department of Labor	34.0	48.9	38.6
Department of State	4.3	4.6	4.9
Department of Transportation	30.5	33.4	34.6
Department of the Treasury	274.3	290.5	312.0
Department of Veterans Affairs	31.2	33.6	34.5
Environmental Protection Agency	5.8	5.9	6.0
General Services Administration	0.5	0.4	1.2
National Aeronautics and Space Administration	13.9	13.8	13.6
Office of Personnel Management	34.8	36.1	37.8
Small Business Administration	0.6	0.5	0.5
Other independent agencies	83.1	67.4	78.7
Allowances	[1]	[1]	.2
Undistributed offsetting receipts	-110.6	-116.0	-123.2

[Continued]

★ 438 ★

Current Services Outlays by Agency, 1991-1993
[Continued]

	1991 actual	Current services	
		1992 estimate	1993 estimate
Total outlays	1,323.0	1,450.4	1,509.4
On-budget	(1,081.3)	(1,198.9)	(1,245.9)
Off-budget	(241.7)	(251.5)	(263.5)

Source: "Current Services Estimates," *Budget of the United States Government, Fiscal Year 1993*, Washington, D.C., Appendix 2, p. 16. *Note*: 1. $50 million or less.

★ 439 ★

Estimated U.S. Government Subsidy Rates, Budget Authority, and Outlays for Direct Loans, 1993-1995

[Numbers in millions of dollars]

Agency and program	1993 Weighted-average subsidy as a percent of disbursements	In millions of dollars					
		Subsidy budget authority			Subsidy outlays		
		1993	1994	1995	1993	1994	1995
Funds appropriated to the President:							
Foreign military financing	17.5	63	63	63	10	33	52
Overseas Private Investment Corporation	13.9	4	4	4	2	4	4
AID Private Sector Investment Program	6.4	1	1	1	1	1	1
Agriculture:							
Agriculture credit insurance fund	19.7	111	100	98	106	96	93
Rural development insurance fund	13.7	96	83	73	6	5	4
Rural development loan fund	52.3	20	20	19	2	2	2
Rural housing insurance fund	38.5	392	380	370	342	362	364
Public Law 480 export credits	67.1	318	318	318	335	318	318
Rural Electrification Administration:							
Rural electric and telephone	11.3	181	128	124	118	93	107
Rural telephone bank	2.1	10	9	8	1	3	5
Housing and Urban Development: Restore loans	50	50	50	50	17	33	50
Interior: Bureau of Reclamation loan program	48.5	1	1	1	1	1	1
State Department: repatriation loans	80	1	1	1	1	1	1
Veterans affairs:							
Direct loan revolving fund	5.4	1	1	1	1	1	1
Loan guaranty revolving fund	8.4	67	52	41	67	52	41
Guaranty and indemnity fund	7.7	16	25	35	16	25	35
Vocational rehabilitation	2.9	1	1	1	1	1	1
Education loan fund	12.4	1	1	1	1	1	1

[Continued]

★ 439 ★

Estimated U.S. Government Subsidy Rates, Budget Authority, and Outlays for Direct Loans, 1993-1995

[Continued]

Agency and program	1993 Weighted-average subsidy as a percent of disbursements	In millions of dollars					
		Subsidy budget authority			Subsidy outlays		
		1993	1994	1995	1993	1994	1995
Transitional housing loans	10.0	1	1	1	1	1	1
Small Business Administration:							
Disaster loans	8.2	24	24	24	61	34	24
Business loans: handicapped assistance	18.7	1	1	1	7	2	1
Export-Import Bank	6.1	128	128	128	34	71	105
Total, direct loan subsidies[2]	9.4	1,489	1,394	1,359	1,126	1,135	1,207

Source: "Identifying Long-Term Obligations and Reducing Underwriting Risks," *Budget of the United States Government, Fiscal Year 1993,* Washington, D.C., Part 1, p. 271.
Note: 1. $500 thousand or less. 2. Weighted average.

★ 440 ★

Federal Grant Payments by Function, 1991-1997

"The functions with the largest amount of grants are health and income security, with combined estimated grant outlays of $132.6 billion or 67 percent of total grant outlays in 1993."

[Numbers in billions of dollars]

Function	Actual 1991	Estimate					
		1992	1993	1994	1995	1996	1997
National defense	0.2	0.2	0.1	0.1	0.1	0.1	0.1
Energy	0.5	0.4	0.4	0.4	0.4	0.4	0.4
Natural resources and environment	4.0	4.0	4.0	4.1	4.0	3.6	3.2
Agriculture	1.2	1.3	1.3	1.3	1.3	1.3	1.2
Transportation	19.9	21.3	22.3	23.4	22.5	22.6	22.5
Community and regional development	4.3	4.7	4.9	4.5	4.0	3.8	3.7
Education, training, employment, and social services	26.0	28.7	29.9	31.5	31.8	32.2	32.6
Health	55.8	76.2	88.5	102.5	118.0	135.4	155.1
Income security	36.9	42.0	44.1	47.4	50.0	51.5	52.7
Veterans benefits and services	0.1	0.2	0.2	0.2	0.2	0.2	0.2
Administration of justice	0.9	1.0	1.1	1.2	1.0	1.1	1.1
General government	2.2	2.3	2.3	3.6	2.3	3.1	2.3
Total outlays	152.0	182.2	199.1	220.1	235.5	255.1	275.2

Source: "Federal Grant Outlays by Function," *Budget of the United States Government: Fiscal Year 1993,* p. 436.

★ 441 ★

Federal Health Spending (Outlays and Tax Expenditures in 1993 Dollars), 1965-1995

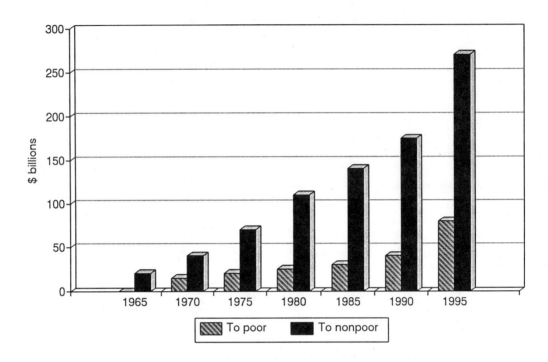

The table below reports "Federal spending for Medicare, Medicaid, hospital and medical care for veterans, and other payments to individuals for health purposes; and tax expenditures for employment-provided health plans and for deductions of health expenses. Spending share to poor reflects percent of recipients with money incomes below poverty thresholds."

[Numbers in billions of dollars]

	To poor	To nonpoor
1965	.0	.20
1970	.15	.40
1975	.20	.70
1980	.25	.110
1985	.30	.140
1990	.40	.175
1995	.80	.270

Source: "Director's Introduction," *Budget of the United States Government, Fiscal Year 1993*, p. 20. Magnitudes estimated from published chart. Primary source: Census Bureau publication on receipt of noncash benefits.

★ 442 ★

Indices of the Growth in Real Pension Expenditure and the Ratio of Pension Expenditure to GDP, as Projected in the Baseline Scenarios, 1980-2025

[Index 1980 = 100]

Country	1980	2000	2010	2025
	Index of real pension expenditure			
Canada	100	154	189	317
France	100	175	230	325
Germany, Fed. Rep. of	100	180	218	300
Italy	100	198	285	498
Japan	100	430	787	1,314
United Kingdom	100	159	199	290
United States	100	145	178	306
	Index of the ratio of pension expenditure to GDP			
Canada	100	89	89	123
France	100	110	115	130
Germany, Fed. Rep. of	100	129	140	154
Italy	100	121	138	171
Japan	100	229	307	319
United Kingdom	100	115	124	144
United States	100	92	90	110

Source: "Pensions," *Aging and Social Expenditure in the Major Industrial Countries, 1980-2025*, Peter S. Heller, Richard Hemming, Peter W. Kohnert, International Monetary Fund, Washington, D.C., 1986, p. 31. Primary source: Fund staff estimates.

★ 443 ★

Percentage of Government Spending on Social Programs as Compared to That of Other Countries, 1980-2025

Social programs include pensions, medical care, education, unemployment insurance and other welfare payments.

Country	Spending as percentage of GDP			
	1980	2000	2010	2025
United States	18.0	16.0	17.0	19.0
Canada	20.0	17.0	17.0	21.0
Japan	15.0	21.0	26.0	27.0
United Kingdom	23.0	23.0	24.0	27.0

[Continued]

★ 443 ★

Percentage of Government Spending on Social Programs as Compared to That of Other Countries, 1980-2025

[Continued]

Country	Spending as percentage of GDP			
	1980	2000	2010	2025
France	31.0	32.0	33.0	35.0
West Germany	31.0	33.0	35.0	39.0

Source: "Government Spending on Social Programs as a Percentage of Gross Domestic Product," *America in the 21st Century: A Demographic Overview*, 1989, p. 20 (Washington, D.C.: Population Reference Bureau, 1989). Primary source: International Monetary Fund, *Aging and Social Expenditures in the Major Industrial Countries, 1980-2025*, Occasional paper No. 47, 1986.

★ 444 ★

Projected Government Expenditures as a Percentage of GNP, 1990-2060

This table was compiled under the assumption that "age specific expenditure patterns remain at 1989 levels for the next 60 years."

Year	Social Security and disability	Health care	Education	Other	Total
1990	4.7	4.1	4.7	18.0	31.8
2000	4.5	5.3	4.9	18.0	32.9
2010	4.6	5.9	4.9	18.0	33.4
2020	5.6	6.5	4.8	18.0	35.0
2030	6.5	7.4	4.9	18.0	36.7
2040	6.5	7.8	4.9	18.0	37.1
2050	6.5	7.8	4.9	18.0	37.1
2060	6.5	7.8	4.9	18.0	37.0

Source: "An Aging Society: Opportunity or Challenge?" David M. Cutter and James M. Poterba, et. al., *Brookings Papers on Economic Activity*, No. 1, 1990, p. 49.

★ 445 ★

Projected Government Expenditures, United States, 1990-2060

"Social security and disability spending are predicted from projected population growth rates. For health care spending, we combined four types of spending (Medicare, Medicaid, Division of National Cost Estimates, and government spending). Finally, for age-specific spending on education, we obtained 1986 age-specific enrollment rates in school as well as the aggregate amounts spent on primary and secondary education, and higher education."

[Numbers are percent of GNP]

Year	Social security and disability	Health care	Education	Other	Total
1990	4.7	4.1	4.7	18.0	31.8
2000	4.5	5.3	4.9	18.0	32.9
2010	4.6	5.9	4.9	18.0	33.4
2020	5.6	6.5	4.8	18.0	35.0
2030	6.5	7.4	4.9	18.0	36.7
2040	6.5	7.8	4.9	18.0	37.1
2050	6.5	7.8	4.9	18.0	37.1
2060	6.5	7.8	4.9	18.0	37.0

Source: "An Aging Society: Opportunity or Challenge?" David M. Cutler, James M. Poterba, Louise M. Sheiner, Laurence H. Summers, *Brookings Papers on Economic Activity*, No. 1, 1990, p. 49.

★ 446 ★

Proposed Federal Block Grant Spending, 1992-1997

[Numbers in millions of dollars]

Department/programs	1992 Enacted BA	O	Proposed 1993 BA	1993 O	1994 BA	1994 O	1995 BA	1995 O	1996 BA	1996 O	1997 BA	1997 O
Education:												
Chapter 2	450	517	450	478	450	453	450	450	450	450	450	450
College assistance migrant program	2	2	2	2	2	2	2	2	2	2	2	2
High school equivalency	8	7	8	8	8	8	8	8	8	8	8	8
Drug free schools and community act	624	654	654	648	654	649	654	653	654	654	654	654
Vocational education	1,135	859	1,138	961	1,138	1,131	1,138	1,145	1,138	1,138	1,138	1,138
Education for homeless youth	25	10	25	22	25	25	25	25	25	25	25	25
Follow-through program	9	7	-	7	-	2	-	-	-	-	-	-
Adult education act (State grants)	236	175	261	202	261	254	261	262	261	261	261	261
Foreign language assistance	10	5	-	8	-	2	-	-	-	-	-	-
Student literacy corps	5	4	-	4	-	1	-	-	-	-	-	-
Workplace literacy partnership	19	16	19	16	19	19	19	19	19	19	19	19
Literacy training for the homeless	10	8	10	8	10	10	10	10	10	10	10	10
Environment:												
Construction grants	2,011	2,196	2,030	2,110	1,500	2,044	700	1,889	200	1,609	-	1,162
Health and Human Services:												
Maternal and child health block grant	650	553	674	674	674	674	674	674	674	674	674	674
Social services block grant	2,800	2,800	2,800	2,800	2,800	2,800	2,800	2,800	2,800	2,800	2,800	2,800

[Continued]

★ 446 ★

Proposed Federal Block Grant Spending, 1992-1997
[Continued]

Department/programs	1992 Enacted BA	O	Proposed									
			1993		1994		1995		1996		1997	
			BA	O	BA	O	BA	O	BA	O	BA	O
State welfare administration expenses:												
Medicaid	2,649	2,649	2,868	2,802	2,868	3,164	3,521	3,521	3,922	3,922	4,374	4,374
AFDC	1,369	1,403	1,483	1,466	1,587	1,567	1,598	1,600	1,650	1,643	1,685	1,681
Food stamps	1,410	1,457	1,470	1,456	1,511	1,507	1,564	1,560	1,620	1,615	1,677	1,672
Justice:												
Drug control	498	341	496	502	496	496	496	496	496	496	496	496
Juvenile justice	72	68	8	58	9	28	8	9	8	8	8	8
Other programs:												
Job training for the homeless	9	11	17	11	17	15	17	17	17	17	17	17
ASCS cost share	194	204	125	171	125	164	125	139	125	135	125	127
Community service employment for older Americans	87	84	75	85	75	77	75	75	75	75	75	75
National and community services act	73	38	73	57	73	70	73	73	73	73	73	73
Total	14,355	14,068	14,686	14,622	14,598	15,162	14,218	15,427	14,227	15,634	14,571	15,726

Source: "Encouraging Experimentation," *Budget of the United States Government, Fiscal Year 1993*, Washington, D.C., p. 417. *Notes*: BA = Budget Authority; O = Outlays.

★ 447 ★

Proposed Spending by Agency (Excluding Comprehensive Health Reform), 1992 and 1993
[Numbers in billions of dollars]

Agency	1992[1]				1993			
	Discretionary		Mandatory outlays	Total outlays	Discretionary		Mandatory outlays	Total outlays
	BA	Outlays			BA	Outlays		
Cabinet agencies:								
Agriculture	14.9	14.0	47.8	61.8	14.4	14.4	45.0	59.4
Commerce	3.0	3.0	-0.1	2.9	2.9	3.0	-0.1	2.9
Defense-Military	282.0	300.5	-5.8	294.7	267.9	278.7	-0.8	277.9
Education	22.6	20.9	5.6	26.5	24.3	22.6	7.8	30.4
Energy	18.9	17.8	-1.9	16.0	19.4	18.4	-1.9	16.5
Health & Human services	29.9	30.3	513.8	544.1	29.3	30.8	554.4	585.2
Housing & Urban development	24.7	22.9	1.3	24.2	23.7	25.5	2.7	28.1
Interior	7.1	7.2	[2]	7.2	6.5	6.7	[2]	6.7
Justice	8.8	8.3	1.1	9.4	9.7	9.3	1.1	10.4
Labor	9.4	9.5	34.7	44.2	9.4	9.5	28.3	37.8
State	4.3	4.2	0.3	4.5	5.0	4.8	0.4	5.2
Transportation	14.2	33.1	0.3	33.4	12.8	34.2	0.3	34.5
Treasury	9.6	9.6	2.1	11.6	10.2	10.2	2.7	12.9
Veterans Affairs	15.6	15.2	18.4	33.6	16.3	16.1	18.1	34.1
Major Agencies:								
Corps of Engineers	3.6	3.4	[2]	3.4	3.5	3.5	[2]	3.5
Deposit Insurance	[2]	0.1	80.1	80.2	[2]	0.1	75.7	75.8
Environmental Protection Agency	6.7	6.1	-0.1	5.9	7.0	6.4	-0.2	6.2
General Services Administration	0.4	0.6	-0.2	0.4	0.5	1.4	-0.2	1.2
National Aeronautics and Space Administration	14.3	13.8	[2]	13.8	15.0	14.1	[2]	14.1
Office of Personnel Management	0.1	0.2	35.9	36.1	[2]	0.1	37.5	37.6
Small Business Administration	0.8	0.7	-0.2	0.5	0.5	0.6	-0.3	0.3
Other agencies:								
Executive Office of the President	0.2	0.2	[2]	0.2	0.3	0.3	[2]	0.3
Foreign Assistance and related programs	26.7	12.9	-0.7	12.2	13.7	12.7	-0.7	12.0
Judicial Branch	2.2	2.2	0.2	2.4	2.6	2.6	0.2	2.8
Legislative Branch	2.4	2.4	0.4	2.8	2.5	2.5	0.3	2.8

[Continued]

★ 447 ★

Proposed Spending by Agency (Excluding Comprehensive Health Reform), 1992 and 1993
[Continued]

| Agency | 1992[1] | | | | 1993 | | | |
| | Discretionary | | Mandatory | Total | Discretionary | | Mandatory | Total |
	BA	Outlays	outlays	outlays	BA	Outlays	outlays	outlays
Other Independent Agencies	11.2	10.3	33.0	43.3	10.7	10.7	35.9	46.6
Allowances	0.0	0.0	-0.1	-0.1	-0.5	-0.4	0.0	-0.4
Undistributed offsetting receipts	0.0	0.0	-38.8	-38.8	-1.4	-1.4	-40.1	-41.5
Net Interest	0.0	0.0	198.8	198.8	0.0	0.0	213.8	213.8
Total	533.9	549.2	926.0	1,475.1	506.3	537.0	979.7	1,516.7

Source: "Director's Introduction," *Budget of the United States Government, Fiscal Year 1993*, p. 29. *Notes*: 1. Includes impact of supplements and recessions. 2. $50 million or less.

★ 448 ★

Ratio of Expenditures to GDP for Total Government Social Expenditure as Compared to Other Major Industrial Countries, 1980-2025

"In brief, the projections to the year 2025 indicate a significant increase in the ratio of government social expenditure to GDP in most of the countries except Canada, and particularly sharp increases in most of the European countries and Japan.... In Canada and the United States, the expenditures ratio will decrease until 2010. In both countries the ratio would then increase in the following 15 years, but in Canada the increase would still be very limited."

[Numbers in percent]

	1980	2000	2010	2025
Canada				
Baseline demographic and economic scenario	21.0	17.5	17.5	21.0
Greater aging demographic/baseline economic scenario	21.0	16.5	17.0	20.0
Greater aging demographic/pessimistic economic scenario	21.0	18.0	18.75	22.0
France				
Baseline demographic and economic scenario	31.0	32.5	33.0	35.0
Greater aging demographic/baseline economic scenario	31.0	31.0	32.0	38.0
Greater aging demographic/pessimistic economic scenario	31.0	32.5	35.0	41.0
Federal Republic of Germany				
Baseline demographic and economic scenario	31.25	33.0	35.0	38.75
Greater aging demographic/baseline economic scenario	-	32.5	34.0	-
Greater aging demographic/pessimistic economic scenario	-	-	-	39.0
Italy				
Baseline demographic and economic scenario	25.0	27.25	30.0	35.0
Greater aging demographic/baseline economic scenario		27.25	30.5	37.25
Greater aging demographic/pessimistic economic scenario		27.5	31.0	37.28
Japan				
Baseline demographic and economic scenario	15.0	21.0	25.5	27.25
Greater aging demographic/baseline economic scenario	-	22.0	27.5	28.75
Greater aging demographic/pessimistic economic scenario	-	22.25	27.5	29.0
United Kingdom				
Baseline demographic and economic scenario	22.5	22.5	23.75	26.25
Greater aging demographic/baseline economic scenario	-	23.0	24.0	28.0

[Continued]

★ 448 ★

Ratio of Expenditures to GDP for Total Government Social Expenditure as Compared to Other Major Industrial Countries, 1980-2025

[Continued]

	1980	2000	2010	2025
Greater aging demographic/pessimistic economic scenario	-	23.0	24.0	28.0
United States				
Baseline demographic and economic scenario	17.5	16.25	16.50	19.0
Greater aging demographic/baseline economic scenario	-	16.25	16.50	21.0
Greater aging demographic/pessimistic economic scenario	-	17.25	17.50	21.50

Source: "Ratio of Expenditure to GDP for Total Government Social Expenditure, 1980-2025," *Aging and Social Expenditure in the Major Industrial Countries, 1980-2025*, Peter S. Heller, Richard Hemming, and Peter W. Kohnert, International Monetary Fund, Washington, D.C., 1986, p. 4. Magnitudes estimated from published chart.

★ 449 ★

Real Government Expenditures on Medical Care as Compared to Other Major Industrial Countries, 1980-2025

[Index: 1980 = 100]

Country	1980	2000	2010	2025
Baseline demographic scenario				
Canada	100	128	140	174
France	100	117	125	130
Germany, Fed. Rep. of	100	104	107	103
Italy	100	113	117	121
Japan	100	130	140	147
United Kingdom	100	105	105	115
United States	100	130	144	180
"Greater aging" demographic scenario				
Canada	100	130	142	174
France	100	120	129	149
Germany, Fed. Rep. of	100	103	105	100
Italy	100	114	118	123
Japan	100	139	150	153
United Kingdom	100	106	108	119
United States	100	132	148	188

Source: "Real Government Expenditure on Medical Care, 1980-2025," *Aging and Social Expenditure in the Major Industrial Countries, 1980-2025*, Peter S. Heller, Richard Hemming, and Peter W. Kohnert, International Monetary Fund, Washington, D.C., 1986, p. 40. *Notes:* Excluding expenditures on medical research and education, administration, and capital investment in the medical sector; assumes no increase in real expenditure per capita by age group over 1980 levels.

★ 450 ★

Sum of Tax Expenditure by Type of Taxpayer, Fiscal Years 1992-1996

[Numbers in billions of dollars]

Fiscal year	Corporations	Individuals	Total
1992	46.9	328.0	374.9
1993	47.2	351.7	398.9
1994	48.2	376.3	424.5
1995	49.3	402.5	451.8
1996	50.6	432.2	482.8

Source: "Federal Tax Expenditures," *Overview of the Federal Tax System*, Committee on Ways and Means, U.S. House of Representatives, April 10, 1991, Washington, D.C., p. 266.

★ 451 ★

Tax Expenditure Estimates by Budget Function, Fiscal Years 1992-1996

[Numbers in billions of dollars]

Function	Corporations					Individuals					Total
	1992	1993	1994	1995	1996	1992	1993	1994	1995	1996	1992-96
National defense											
Exclusion of benefits and allowances to Armed Forces personnel	...	...	...	...	...	2.0	2.1	2.2	2.3	2.3	10.9
Exclusion of military disability benefits	...	...	...	...	...	0.1	0.1	0.1	0.1	0.1	0.5
International affairs											
Exclusion of income earned abroad by U.S. citizens	...	...	...	...	...	1.5	1.5	1.6	1.6	1.7	7.9
Exclusion of certain allowances for Federal employees abroad	...	...	...	...	...	0.2	0.2	0.2	0.2	0.2	1.0
Exclusion of income of foreign sales corporations (FSCs)	0.9	1.0	1.1	1.1	1.2	...	...	...	...	...	5.3
Deferral of income of controlled foreign corporations	0.2	0.2	0.3	0.3	0.3	...	...	...	...	...	1.2
Inventory property sales source rule exception	3.2	3.4	3.7	3.8	3.9	...	...	...	...	...	18.0
Interest allocation rules for certain non-financial institutions	0.2	0.2	0.2	0.2	0.2	...	...	...	...	...	0.9
General science, space, and technology											
Expensing of research and development expenditures	1.6	1.7	1.9	2.0	2.1	...	...	...	...	...	9.3
Credit for increasing research activities	0.7	0.8	0.8	0.8	0.9	...	...	...	...	...	4.0
Energy											
Expensing of exploration and development costs:											
Oil and gas	[2]	0.1	0.1	0.2	0.2	0.6	0.7	0.7	0.8	0.8	4.2
Other fuels	[1]	[1]	[1]	[1]	[1]						0.2
Excess of percentage over cost depletion:											
Oil and gas	0.1	0.1	0.1	0.2	0.2	0.4	0.4	0.5	0.5	0.6	3.1
Other fuels	0.2	0.2	0.2	0.2	0.2	[1]	[1]	[1]	[1]	[1]	1.1
Credit for enhanced oil recovery costs	[1]	[1]	[1]	[1]	[1]	[1]	[1]	[1]	[1]	[1]	0.2
Alternative fuel production credit	0.3	0.4	0.4	0.4	0.3	0.1	0.1	0.1	0.1	0.1	2.4
Alcohol fuel credits[3]	0.1	0.1	0.2	0.2	0.3	...	...	...	...	...	1.0
Exclusion of interest on State and local government industrial development bonds for energy production facilities	[2]	[2]	[2]	[2]	[2]	0.2	0.2	0.2	0.2	0.2	1.0

[Continued]

★ 451 ★

Tax Expenditure Estimates by Budget Function, Fiscal Years 1992-1996
[Continued]

Function	Corporations					Individuals					Total
	1992	1993	1994	1995	1996	1992	1993	1994	1995	1996	1992-96
Expensing of tertiary injectants	[1]	[1]	[1]	[1]	[1]	[1]	[1]	[1]	[1]	[1]	0.1
Business energy tax credits	[1]	[2]	[2]	...	...	...	...	...	...	...	1
Natural resources and environment											
Expensing of exploration and development costs nonfuel minerals	[1]	[1]	0.1	0.1	0.1	[1]	[1]	[1]	[1]	[1]	0.4
Excess of percentage over cost depletion, nonfuel minerals	0.3	0.3	0.3	0.3	0.3	[1]	[1]	[1]	[1]	[1]	1.6
Investment credit and 7-year amortization for reforestation expenditures	[1]	[1]	[1]	[1]	[1]	[1]	[1]	[1]	[1]	[1]	0.1
Expensing multiperiod timber-growing costs	0.4	0.4	0.4	0.4	0.5	[1]	[1]	[1]	[1]	[1]	2.2
Exclusion of interest on State and local government sewage, water, and hazardous waste facilities bonds	-0.4	-0.4	-0.4	-0.5	-0.5	1.8	1.9	2.0	2.0	2.1	7.6
Investment tax credit for rehabilitation of historic structures	[1]	[1]	[1]	[1]	[1]	0.1	0.1	0.1	0.1	0.1	0.5
Special rules for mining reclamation reserves	[1]	[1]	[1]	[1]	[1]	[1]	[1]	[1]	[1]	[1]	0.2
Agriculture											
Expensing certain multiperiod production costs	[1]	[1]	[1]	[1]	[1]	0.2	0.2	0.2	0.2	0.2	1.2
Deductibility of patronage dividends and certain other items of cooperatives	0.3	0.3	0.3	0.4	0.4	-0.1	-0.1	-0.1	-0.1	-0.1	1.4
Exclusion of cost-sharing payments	...	...	...	...	...	[1]	[1]	[1]	[1]	[1]	0.1
Exclusion of cancellation of indebtedness income of farmers	...	...	...	...	...	0.1	0.1	0.1	0.1	0.1	0.5
Cash accounting for agriculture	0.1	0.1	0.1	0.1	0.1	0.2	0.2	0.2	0.2	0.2	1.5
Commerce and housing											
Financial institutions:											
Bad-debt reserves of financial institutions	0.1	0.1	0.2	0.2	0.2	...	...	...	...	...	0.8
Merger rules for banks and thrift institutions	2.6	1.7	1.2	9.0	0.6	...	...	...	...	...	7.0
Exemption of credit union income	0.6	0.7	0.8	0.9	0.9	...	...	...	...	...	3.9
Insurance companies:											
Exclusion of investment income on life insurance and annuity contracts	0.1	0.1	0.1	0.1	0.1	7.8	8.5	9.3	10.2	11.2	47.4
Exclusion of investment income from structured settlement amounts	[1]	[1]	[1]	[1]	[1]	...	...	...	...	...	0.1
Small life insurance company taxable income adjustment	0.1	0.1	0.1	0.1	0.1	...	...	...	...	...	0.5
Treatment of life insurance company reserves	0.7	0.7	0.8	0.8	0.9	...	...	...	...	...	3.8
Deduction of unpaid loss reserves for property and casualty insurance companies	1.6	1.4	1.3	1.1	1.0	...	...	...	...	...	6.4
Special alternative tax on small property and casualty insurance companies	[1]	[1]	[1]	[1]	[1]	...	...	...	...	...	0.1
Tax exemption for certain insurance companies	[1]	[1]	[1]	[1]	[1]	...	...	...	...	...	0.1
Special deduction for Blue Cross and Blue Shield companies	0.1	0.1	[1]	[1]	[1]	...	...	...	...	...	0.2
Housing:											
Deductibility of mortgage interest on owner-occupied residences	...	...	...	...	...	38.8	42.2	45.9	50.0	54.4	231.2
Deductibility of property tax on owner-occupied residences	...	...	...	...	...	11.0	12.3	13.6	15.2	16.9	69.0
Deferral of capital gains on sales of principal residences	...	...	...	...	...	11.5	12.1	12.7	13.6	15.5	65.3
Exclusion of capital gains on sales principal residences for persons age 55 and over ($125,000 exclusion)	...	...	...	...	...	3.8	4.0	4.2	4.5	5.2	21.8
Exclusion of interest on State and local government bonds for owner-occupied housing	0.3	0.3	0.3	0.3	0.3	1.4	1.3	1.2	1.1	1.0	7.5
Depreciation of rental housing in excess of alternative depreciation system	1.1	1.1	1.1	1.2	1.2	0.5	0.5	0.6	0.6	0.6	8.5

[Continued]

★ 451 ★

Tax Expenditure Estimates by Budget Function, Fiscal Years 1992-1996

[Continued]

Function	Corporations					Individuals					Total 1992-96
	1992	1993	1994	1995	1996	1992	1993	1994	1995	1996	1992-96
Low-income housing tax credit	0.1	0.1	0.1	0.1	0.1	1.0	1.0	1.0	1.0	1.0	5.6
Exclusion of interest on State and local goverment bonds for rental housing	0.2	0.3	0.3	0.3	0.3	0.6	0.6	0.7	0.7	0.7	4.7
Other business and commerce:											
Maximum 28% tax rate on long-term capital gains	...	...	...	...	...	4.5	5.1	5.6	6.0	6.5	27.7
Depreciation on buildings other than rental housing in excess of alternative depreciation system	5.1	5.3	5.5	5.7	5.9	1.9	2.0	2.0	2.1	2.2	37.7
Depreciation on equipment in excess of alternative depreciation system	14.1	14.6	15.1	15.6	16.2	4.0	4.1	4.3	4.4	4.6	97.0
Investment credit other than ESOPs, rehabilitation of structures, reforestation, and energy property	0.9	0.3	0.1	0.1	0.1	0.1	[1]	[1]	[1]	[1]	1.6
Expensing up to $10,000 depreciable business property	0.1	0.1	0.1	0.1	0.1	0.1	0.1	0.1	0.1	0.1	1.0
Exclusion of capital gains at death:											
Capital gains at death	...	...	...	...	...	10.5	11.6	12.7	14.0	15.4	64.2
Carryover basis on gifts	...	...	...	...	...	1.1	1.3	1.4	1.4	1.5	6.7
Amortization of business startup costs	[1]	[1]	[1]	[1]	[1]	0.2	0.2	0.2	0.2	0.2	1.0
Reduced rates on first $75,000 of corporate taxable income	3.0	3.1	3.2	3.3	3.5	...	...	...	...	...	16.1
Permanent exemption from imputed interest rules	[1]	[1]	[1]	[1]	[1]	0.2	0.2	0.2	0.2	0.2	1.0
Expensing of magazine circulation expenditures	[1]	[1]	[1]	[1]	[1]	[1]	[1]	[1]	[1]	[1]	0.1
Special rules for magazine, paperback, and record returns	[1]	[1]	[1]	[1]	[1]	[1]	[1]	[1]	[1]	[1]	0.1
Deferral of gain on non-dealer installment sales	0.1	0.1	0.1	0.1	0.1	[1]	[1]	[1]	[1]	[1]	0.8
Completed contract rules	0.2	0.3	0.3	0.3	0.3	[1]	[1]	[1]	[1]	[1]	1.2
Cash accounting, other than agriculture	[1]	[1]	[1]	[1]	[1]	[1]	[1]	[1]	[1]	[1]	0.3
Exclusion of interest on State and local government small-issue bonds	-0.1	-0.1	-0.1	-0.1	-0.1	2.4	2.4	2.4	2.4	2.4	11.5
Deferral of gain on like-kind exchanges	0.3	0.2	0.2	0.4	0.4	0.2	0.2	0.2	0.2	0.2	2.7
Exception from net operating loss limitations for corporations in bankruptcy proceedings	0.2	0.2	0.2	0.2	0.2	...	...	...	...	...	1.0
Gain from sale or exchange to effectuate policies of the FCC	0.2	0.2	0.1	0.1	0.1	[1]	[1]	[1]	[1]	[1]	0.7
Exemption of RIC expenses from miscellaneous deduction floor	...	...	...	...	...	0.5	0.6	0.7	0.8	0.8	3.4
Transportation											
Deferral of tax on capital construction funds of shipping companies	0.1	0.1	0.1	0.1	0.1	...	...	...	...	...	0.5
Exclusion of interest on State and local government bonds for mass transit commuting vehicles	[2]	[2]	[2]	[2]	[2]	[1]	[1]	[1]	[1]	[1]	0.1
Exclusion of interest on State and local government bonds for high-speed inter-urban rail facilities	[2]	[2]	[2]	[2]	[2]	0.1	0.1	0.2	0.2	0.2	0.8
Community and regional development											
Investment credit for rehabilitation of structures, other than historic structures	[1]	[1]	[1]	[1]	[1]	[1]	[1]	[1]	[1]	[1]	0.4
Exclusion of interest on State and local government bonds for private airports and docks	-0.1	-0.1	-0.2	-0.2	-0.2	0.8	0.8	0.8	0.9	0.9	3.4
Education, training, employment, and social services											
Education and training:											
Exclusion of scholarship and fellowship income	...	...	...	...	...	0.6	0.6	0.6	0.7	0.7	3.2
Parental personal exemption for students age 19 to 23	...	...	...	...	...	0.3	0.3	0.4	0.5	0.5	2.0
Exclusion of interest on State and local government student loan bonds	[1]	[1]	[1]	[1]	[1]	0.4	0.4	0.4	0.4	0.4	2.0
Exclusion of interest on State and local government bonds for private educational facilities	[1]	[1]	[1]	[1]	[1]	0.3	0.3	0.3	0.3	0.3	1.5
Deductibility of charitable contributions for education	0.5	0.6	0.6	0.6	0.6	1.6	1.7	1.9	2.0	2.1	12.2
Educational savings bonds	...	...	...	...	...	0.1	0.2	0.2	0.3	0.3	1.1

[Continued]

★ 451 ★

Tax Expenditure Estimates by Budget Function, Fiscal Years 1992-1996
[Continued]

Function	Corporations					Individuals					Total
	1992	1993	1994	1995	1996	1992	1993	1994	1995	1996	1992-96
Employment:											
Targeted jobs tax credit	0.2	0.1	1	1	1	1	1	1	...	...	0.4
Exclusion of employee meals and lodging											
(other than military)	...	...	...	...	...	0.8	0.8	0.9	0.9	0.9	4.3
Employee stock ownership plans (ESOPs)	0.9	1.0	1.1	1.2	1.2	1	1	1	1	1	5.3
Exclusion for benefits provided under cafeteria plans	...	...	...	...	...	2.6	2.9	3.1	3.2	3.3	15.1
Exclusion of rental allowances for ministers' homes	...	...	...	...	...	0.2	0.2	0.2	0.2	0.3	1.1
Exclusion of miscellaneous fringe benefits	...	...	...	...	...	4.1	4.3	4.6	4.9	5.2	23.1
Exclusion of employee awards	...	...	...	...	...	0.1	0.1	0.1	0.1	0.1	0.6
Exclusion of income earned by benefit organizations:											
Supplemental unemployment benefits trusts	...	...	...	...	...	1	1	1	1	1	0.1
Voluntary employees' beneficiary associations	...	...	...	...	...	0.5	0.5	0.5	0.5	0.6	2.7
Social services:											
Deductibility of charitable contributions, other											
than for education and health	0.5	0.6	0.6	0.6	0.6	12.5	13.3	14.2	15.1	16.1	74.1
Credit for child and dependent care expenses	...	...	...	...	...	3.1	3.3	3.4	3.5	3.7	17.0
Exclusion for employer-provided child care	...	...	...	...	...	0.3	0.4	0.5	0.5	0.6	2.3
Exclusion for certain foster care payments	...	...	...	...	...	1	1	1	1	1	0.1
Expensing costs of removing architectural barriers	0.1	0.1	0.1	0.1	0.1	1	1	1	1	1	0.3
Tax credit for disabled access expenditures	0.1	0.1	0.1	0.1	0.1	...	...	...	...	...	0.5
Health											
Exclusion of employer contributions for medical											
insurance premiums and medical care	...	...	...	...	...	37.7	41.3	45.1	49.0	53.2	226.4
Deductibility of medical insurance premiums by											
the self employed	...	...	...	...	...	0.1	...	...	...	...	0.1
Credit for child medical insurance premiums[4]	...	...	...	...	...	0.1	0.1	0.1	0.1	0.1	0.5
Deductibility of medical expenses	...	...	...	...	...	2.9	3.3	3.8	4.4	5.0	19.4
Exclusion of interest on State and local government											
bonds for private hospital facilities	0.1	0.1	0.1	0.1	0.1	2.6	2.9	3.2	3.5	3.7	16.4
Deductibility of charitable contributions for health	0.2	0.2	0.2	0.2	0.2	1.6	1.7	1.8	1.9	2.0	10.0
Tax credit for orphan drug research	1	1	1	1	1	...	...	...	...	...	1
Medicare											
Exclusion of untaxed medicare benefits:											
Hospital insurance	...	...	...	...	...	7.1	7.7	8.3	9.0	9.8	41.8
Supplementary medical insurance	...	...	...	...	...	4.0	4.5	5.0	5.7	6.4	25.5
Income security											
Exclusion of workers' compensation benefits	...	...	...	...	...	2.9	3.1	3.2	3.4	3.6	16.1
Exclusion of special benefits for disabled coal miners	...	...	...	...	...	0.1	0.1	0.1	0.1	0.1	0.6
Exclusion of cash public assistance benefits	...	...	...	...	...	0.4	0.4	0.4	0.4	0.5	2.1
Net exclusion of pension contributions and earnings	...	...	...	...	...	54.0	57.0	59.0	61.0	64.0	295.0
Individual retirement plans	...	...	...	...	...	6.2	6.5	6.9	7.3	7.8	34.7
Keogh plans	...	...	...	...	...	2.9	3.0	3.2	3.4	3.6	16.1
Exclusion of other employee benefits:											
Premiums on group term life insurance	...	...	...	...	...	2.2	2.3	2.5	2.6	2.7	12.4
Premiums on accident and disability insurance	...	...	...	...	...	0.1	0.1	0.1	0.1	0.1	0.6
Exclusion for employer-provided death benefits	...	...	...	...	...	1	1	1	1	1	0.1
Additional standard deduction for the blind and											
the elderly	...	...	...	...	...	1.7	1.8	1.9	1.9	2.0	9.3
Tax credit for the elderly and disabled	...	...	...	...	...	.1	.1	.1	.1	.1	.5
Deductibility of casualty and theft losses	...	...	...	...	...	.3	.4	.5	.6	.7	2.5
Earned income credit[5]	...	...	...	...	...	.9	.9	1.2	1.4	1.5	5.9
Social security and railroad retirement											
Exclusion of untaxed social security-railroad											
retirement benefits	...	...	...	...	...	25.6	27.0	28.4	29.9	31.4	142.3
Veterans' benefits and services											
Exclusion of veterans' disability compensation	...	...	...	...	...	1.4	1.5	1.5	1.6	1.7	7.7
Exclusion of veterans' pensions	...	...	...	...	...	0.1	0.1	0.1	0.1	0.1	0.6

[Continued]

★ 451 ★

Tax Expenditure Estimates by Budget Function, Fiscal Years 1992-1996
[Continued]

Function	Corporations					Individuals					Total 1992-96
	1992	1993	1994	1995	1996	1992	1993	1994	1995	1996	
Exclusion of GI bill benefits	...	...	...	...	...	0.1	0.1	0.1	0.1	0.1	0.4
Exclusion of interest on State and local government veterans' housing bonds	1	1	1	1	1	0.2	0.2	0.2	0.2	0.2	1.1
General purpose fiscal assistance											
Exclusion of interest on public purpose State and local government debt	1.5	1.4	1.4	1.3	1.3	10.0	10.9	11.8	13.0	13.7	66.3
Deduction of nonbusiness State and local government income and personal property taxes	...	...	...	...	...	23.8	25.5	27.4	29.5	31.7	137.9
Tax credit for corporations with possessions source income	2.9	3.0	3.1	3.2	3.3	...	...	...	...	...	15.5
Interest											
Deferral of interest on savings bonds	...	...	...	...	...	1.0	1.0	1.0	1.0	1.0	5.0

Source: "Federal Tax Expenditures," *Overview of the Federal Tax System*, Committee on Ways and Means, U.S. House of Representatives, April 10, 1991, Washington, D.C., pp. 257-66. Primary source: Joint Committee on Taxation, "Estimates of Federal Tax Expenditures for Fiscal Years 1992-1996," (JCS-4-91), March 11, 1991. *Notes*: 1. Positive tax expenditure of less than $50 million. 2. Negative tax expenditure of less than $50 million. 3. In addition, the 5.4 cents-per-gallon exemption from excise tax for alcohol fuels results in a reduction in excise tax receipts, net of income tax effect, of $0.4 billion per year for 1992 and 1993, $0.5 billion per year for 1994 and 1995, and $0.6 billion for 1996. 4. The figures in the table show the effect of the child medical insurance credit on receipts. The increase in outlays is $0.5 billion in 1992, $0.5 billion per year in 1993 and 1994, and $0.7 billion per year in 1995 and 1996. 5. The figures in the table show the effect of the earned income credit on receipts. The increase in outlays is: $7.8 billion in 1992, $8.5 billion in 1993, $10.6 billion in 1994, $12.3 billion in 1995, and 13.2 billion in 1996.

★ 452 ★

Trends in Federal Grants to State and Local Governments, 1960-1997 - I
[Numbers in billions of dollars except where noted]

	Actual							
	1960	1965	1970	1975	1980	1985	1990	1991
A. Percentage distribution of grants by function:								
Natural resources and environment	2%	2%	2%	5%	6%	4%	3%	3%
Agriculture	3	5	3	1	1	2	1	1
Transportation	43	38	19	12	14	16	14	13
Community and regional development	2	6	7	6	7	5	4	3
Education, training, employment and social services	7	10	27	24	24	17	17	17
Health	3	6	16	18	17	23	32	37
Income security	38	32	24	19	20	26	26	24
General government	2	2	2	14	9	6	2	1
Other functions	*	1	1	2	1	1	1	1
Total	100%	100%	100%	100%	100%	100%	100%	100%
B. Composition:								
Current dollars:								
Payments for individuals	2.5	3.7	8.7	16.8	32.7	49.4	77.1	89.9
Physical capital[1]	3.3	5.0	7.0	10.9	22.5	24.8	25.7	26.5
Other grants	1.2	2.2	8.3	22.2	36.3	31.7	32.5	35.6
Total	7.0	10.9	24.1	49.8	91.5	105.9	135.4	152.0

[Continued]

413

★ 452 ★

Trends in Federal Grants to State and Local Governments, 1960-1997 - I
[Continued]

	Actual							
	1960	1965	1970	1975	1980	1985	1990	1991
Percentage of total grants:								
Payments for individuals	35%	34%	36%	34%	36%	47%	57%	59%
Physical capital[1]	47	46	29	22	25	23	19	17
Other grants	17	20	34	45	40	30	24	23
Total	100%	100%	100%	100%	100%	100%	100%	100%
Constant (FY 1987) dollars:								
Payments for individuals	9.0	12.5	24.7	35.1	46.3	53.0	67.4	75.0
Physical capital[1]	13.8	19.5	21.9	20.6	27.6	25.8	23.6	23.8
Other grants	6.4	9.8	26.7	49.6	53.7	34.2	28.7	30.1
Total	29.1	41.8	73.6	105.4	127.6	113.0	119.7	129.0
C. Total grants as a percent of:								
Federal outlays:								
Total	8%	9%	12%	15%	15%	11%	11%	11%
Domestic programs[2]	18%	18%	23%	22%	22%	18%	17%	17%
State and local expenditures	15%	16%	20%	24%	28%	23%	20%	N/A
Gross domestic product	1%	2%	2%	3%	3%	3%	2%	3%
D. As a share of total State and local capital spending:								
Federal capital grants	25%	25%	25%	27%	37%	31%	21%	N/A
State and local own-source financing	75	75	75	73	63	69	79	N/A
Total	100%	100%	100%	100%	100%	100%	100%	100%

Source: "Providing Federal Aid to State and Local Governments," *Budget of the United States Government, Fiscal Year 1993,* Washington, D.C., Part 1, p. 438. *Notes*: 1. Excludes capital grants that are included as payments for individuals. 2. Excludes national defense, international affairs, net interest, and undistributed offsetting receipts.

★ 453 ★

Trends in Federal Grants to State and Local Governments, 1960-1997 - II
[Numbers in billions of dollars except where noted]

	Estimate					
	1992	1993	1994	1995	1996	1997
A. Percentage distribution of grants by function:						
Natural resources and environment	2%	2%	2%	2%	1%	1%
Agriculture	1	1	1	1	*	*
Transportation	12	11	11	10	9	8
Community and regional development	3	2	2	2	1	1
Education, training, employment and social services	16	15	14	13	13	12
Health	42	44	47	50	53	56
Income security	23	22	22	21	20	19

[Continued]

★ 453 ★

Trends in Federal Grants to State and Local Governments, 1960-1997 - II
[Continued]

	Estimate					
	1992	1993	1994	1995	1996	1997
General government	1	1	2	1	1	1
Other functions	1	1	1	1	1	1
Total	100%	100%	100%	100%	100%	100%
B. Composition:						
Current dollars:						
Payments for individuals	114.6	128.8	145.5	163.5	182.4	203.4
Physical capital[1]	28.1	29.4	28.6	29.1	29.1	30.5
Other grants	39.5	40.9	45.9	42.9	43.6	41.2
Total	182.2	199.1	220.1	235.5	255.1	275.2
Percentage of total grants:						
Payments for individuals	63%	65%	66%	69%	71%	74%
Physical capital[1]	15	15	13	12	11	11
Other grants	22	21	21	18	17	15
Total	100%	100%	100%	100%	100%	100%
Constant (FY 1987) dollars:						
Payments for individuals	93.0	101.3	110.9	120.7	130.5	141.0
Physical capital[1]	24.5	24.8	23.3	22.9	22.1	22.4
Other grants	32.4	32.4	35.2	31.7	31.1	28.3
Total	149.9	158.4	169.3	175.3	183.7	191.7
C. Total grants as a percent of:						
Federal outlays:						
Total	13%	13%	15%	15%	16%	16%
Domestic programs[2]	19%	20%	22%	22%	23%	23%
State and local expenditures	N/A	N/A	N/A	N/A	N/A	N/A
Gross domestic product	3%	3%	3%	3%	3%	3%
D. As a share of total State and local capital spending:						
Federal capital grants	N/A	N/A	N/A	N/A	N/A	N/A
State and local own-source financing	N/A	N/A	N/A	N/A	N/A	N/A
Total	100%	100%	100%	100%	100%	100%

Source: "Providing Federal Aid to State and Local Governments," *Budget of the United States Government, Fiscal Year 1993*, Washington, D.C., Part 1, p. 438. *Notes*: 1. Excludes capital grants that are included as payments for individuals. 2. Excludes national defense, international affairs, net interest, and undistributed offsetting receipts.

Employment Opportunities for Selected Industries

★ 454 ★

Employment by Industry, 1975-2005

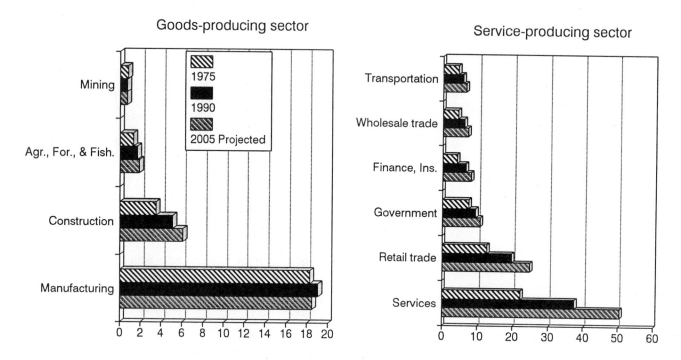

Goods-producing sector

Service-producing sector

"Within the goods-producing sector, agriculture and construction will increase and offset the decline in manufacturing and mining. All service sectors will increase, but most of the growth will be in two industry divisions—services and retail trade."

[Numbers in millions]

	1975	1990	2005 projected
Goods-producing sector			
Manufacturing	18.3	19.1	18.5
Construction	3.5	5.1	6.1
Agriculture, forestry and fishing	1.3	1.7	1.9
Mining	.8	.7	.7
Service-producing sector			
Services	22.1	37.5	50.5
Retail trade	12.6	19.7	24.8
Government	7.5	9.5	10.8
Finance, insurance, and real estate	4.2	6.7	8.1
Wholesale trade	4.4	6.2	7.2
Transportation, communications, and public utilities	4.5	5.8	6.7

Source: "Outlook 1990-2005," *Occupational Outlook Quarterly* 35, No. 3, Fall, 1991, p. 18.

★ 455 ★

Percentage and Numerical Changes in Employment: Administrative Support Occupations Including Clerical, 1990-2005

Occupation	Estimated employment, 1990	Percent change in employment, 1990-2005	Numerical change in employment, 1990-2005
Adjusters, investigators, and collectors	1,088,000	24.0	264,000
Bank tellers	517,000	-5.0	-25,000
Clerical supervisors and managers	1,218,000	22.0	263,000
Computer and peripheral equipment operators	320,000	13.0	42,000
Credit clerks and authorizers	240,000	24.0	58,000
General Office clerks	2,737,000	24.0	670,000
Information clerks	1,418,000	41.0	584,000
Hotel and motel desk clerks	118,000	34.0	40,000
Interviewing and new accounts clerks	250,000	28.0	71,000
Receptionists and information clerks	900,000	47.0	422,000
Reservation and transportation ticket agents and travel clerks	150,000	34.0	52,000
Mail clerks and messengers	280,000	9.0	26,000
Material recording, scheduling, dispatching, and distributing occupations	3,756,000	12.0	443,000
Dispatchers	209,000	29.0	60,000
Stock clerks	2,191,000	12.0	257,000
Traffic, shipping, and receiving clerks	762,000	13.0	97,000
Postal clerks and mail carriers	607,000	17.0	101,000
Record clerks	3,809,000	[1]	-15,000
Billing clerks	413,000	4.0	18,000
Bookkeeping, accounting, and auditing clerks	2,276,000	-6.0	-133,000
Brokerage clerks and statement clerks	93,000	10.0	9,000
File clerks	271,000	11.0	29,000
Library assistants and bookmobile drivers	117,000	11.0	13,000
Order clerks	291,000	3.0	8,700
Payroll and timekeeping clerks	171,000	3.0	4,700
Personnel clerks	129,000	21.0	27,000
Secretaries	3,576,000	15.0	540,000
Stenographers and court reporters	132,000	-5.0	-7,100
Teacher aides	808,000	34.0	278,000
Telephone operators	325,000	-32.0	-104,000
Typists, word processors, and data entry keyers	1,448,000	-3.0	-46,000

Source: "The Job Outlook in Brief: 1990-2000," *Occupational Outlook Quarterly* 36, No. 1, Spring, 1992, pp. 26-8. Also in source: description of employment prospects for each occupation. Primary source: U.S. Department of Labor, Bureau of Labor Statistics, industry-occupation matrix. *Note:* 1. Less than one.

★ 456 ★

Percentage and Numerical Changes in Employment: Agriculture, Forestry, Fishing, and Related Occupations, 1990-2005

Occupation	Estimated employment, 1990	Percent change in employment, 1990-2005	Numerical change in employment, 1990-2005
Farm operators and managers	1,223,000	-16.0	-200,000
Fishers, hunters, and trappers	61,000	13.0	7,800
Timber cutting and logging workers	108,000	-2.0	-1,800

Source: "The Job Outlook in Brief: 1990-2000," *Occupational Outlook Quarterly* 36, No. 1, Spring, 1992, p. 31. Also in source: a description of employment prospects for each occupation. Primary source: U.S. Department of Labor, Bureau of Labor Statistics, industry-occupation matrix.

★ 457 ★

Percentage and Numerical Changes in Employment: Construction Trades and Extractive Occupations, 1990-2005

Occupation	Estimated employment, 1990	Percent change in employment, 1990-2005	Numerical change in employment, 1990-2005
Bricklayers and stonemasons	152,000	20.0	31,000
Carpenters	1,077,000	14.0	154,000
Carpet installers	73,000	21.0	15,000
Concrete masons and terrazzo workers	113,000	13.0	15,000
Drywall workers and lathers	143,000	23.0	33,000
Electricians	548,000	29.0	158,000
Glaziers	42,000	22.0	9,300
Insulation workers	70,000	24.0	17,000
Painters and paperhangers	453,000	24.0	111,000
Plasterers	28,000	13.0	3,700
Plumbers and pipefitters	379,000	21.0	80,000
Roofers	138,000	23.0	31,000
Roustabouts	38,000	-4.0	-1,400
Sheet-metal workers	98,000	23.0	22,000
Structural and reinforcing ironworkers	92,000	21.0	20,000
Tilesetters	28,000	24.0	6,700
Numerical-control machine-tool operations	70,000	23.0	16,000

Source: "The Job Outlook in Brief: 1990-2000," *Occupational Outlook Quarterly* 36, No. 1, Spring, 1992, pp. 35-6. Also in source: a prose description of employment prospects for each occupation. Primary source: U.S. Department of Labor, Bureau of Labor Statistics, industry-occupation matrix.

★ 458 ★

Employment Growth of Education Services Industry, 1990-2005

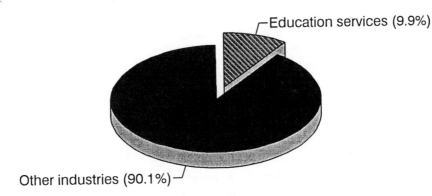

Education services (9.9%)

Other industries (90.1%)

"Employment in public and private education will grow by 2.3 million, almost 10 percent of total job growth."

[Numbers in millions]

Education services	2.3
Other industries	20.9

Source: "Outlook 1990-2005," *Occupational Outlook Quarterly* 35, No. 3, Fall, 1991, p. 24.

★ 459 ★

Growth of Selected Occupations in Education Services, 1990-2005

[Numbers in percent]

Teachers, special education	40
Bus drivers, school	35
Counselors	35
Teachers, secondary school	34
Registered nurses	33
Teacher aides and educational assistants	33
Teachers, vocational education	29
Education administrators	24
Teachers, elementary school	23
Teachers, preschool and kindergarten	23

[Continued]

★ 459 ★

Growth of Selected Occupations in Education Services, 1990-2005

[Continued]

Speech-language pathologists	21
College faculty	19

Source: "Outlook 1990-2005," Occupational Outlook Quarterly 35, No. 3, Fall, 1991, p. 24.

★ 460 ★

Percentage and Numerical Changes in Employment: Executive, Administrative, and Managerial Occupations, 1990-2005

Occupation	Estimated employment, 1990	Percent change in employment, 1990-2005	Numerical change in employment 1990-2005
Accountants and auditors	985,000	34.0	340,000
Administrative services managers	221,000	23.0	52,000
Budget analysts	64,000	22.0	14,000
Construction and building inspectors	60,000	19.0	11,000
Construction contractors and managers	183,000	33.0	60,000
Cost estimators	173,000	24.0	42,000
Education administrators	348,000	24.0	85,000
Employment interviewers	83,000	23.0	19,000
Engineering, science, and data processing managers	315,000	34.0	108,000
Financial managers	701,000	28.0	193,000
General managers and top executives	3,086,000	19.0	598,000
Government chief executives and legislators	71,000	4.0	3,100
Health service managers	257,000	42.0	108,000
Hotel managers and assistants	102,000	44.0	45,000
Industrial production managers	210,000	20.0	41,000
Inspectors and compliance officers	156,000	30.0	46,000
Management analysts and consultants	151,000	52.0	79,000
Marketing, advertising, and public relations managers	427,000	47.0	203,000
Personnel, training, and labor specialists and managers	456,000	32.0	144,000
Property and real estate managers	225,000	34.0	76,000
Purchasing agents and managers	300,000	23.0	69,000
Restaurant and food service managers	556,000	32.0	177,000
Underwriters	105,000	24.0	25,000
Wholesale and retail buyers and merchandise managers	361,000	19.0	68,000

Source: "The Job Outlook in Brief: 1990-2000," Occupational Outlook Quarterly 36, No. 1, Spring, 1992, pp. 12-14. Also in source: a description of employment prospects for each occupation. Primary source: U.S. Department of Labor, Bureau of Labor Statistics industry-occupation matrix.

★ 461 ★

Percentage and Numerical Changes in Employment: Handlers, Equipment Cleaners, Helpers, and Laborers, 1990-2005

Occupation	Estimated employment 1990	Percent change in employment 1990-2005	Numerical change in employment 1990-2005
Handlers, equipment cleaners, helpers, and laborers	4,935,000	8.0	396,000

Source: "The Job Outlook in Brief: 1990-2000," *Occupational Outlook Quarterly* 36, No. 1, Spring, 1992, p. 41. Also in source: a prose description of employment prospects. Primary source: U.S. Department of Labor, Bureau of Labor Statistics industry-occupation matrix.

★ 462 ★

Employment Growth of Health Professions, 1990-2005

[Numbers in millions]

Health services, total	3.90
Hospitals	1.30
Offices of physicians	.90
Nursing and personal care facilities	.70
Home health care services	.30
Office of other health practitioners	.20
Health and allied services not elsewhere classified	.15
Offices of dentists	.15
Medical and dental laboratories	.10

Source: "Outlook 1990-2005," *Occupational Outlook Quarterly* 35, No. 3, Fall, 1991, p. 20.

★ 463 ★

Growth of Selected Occupations in Health Services, 1990-2005

"Occupations concentrated in the health services industry will be among the most rapidly growing occupations."

[Numbers in percent]

Home health aides	96.0
Physical therapists	87.0
Medical scientists	87.0
Medical assistants	77.0
Psychologists	76.0
Radiologic technicians	72.0
Occupational therapists	65.0
Receptionists	65.0
Human services workers	64.0
Speech-language pathologists	62.0
Medical records technicians	58.0
Surgical technicians	55.0
Respiratory therapists	53.0
Social workers	53.0
General managers	52.0
Recreation workers	50.0
Registered nurses	49.0
Nurse aides, orderlies, and attendants	48.0
Opticians, dispensing	44.0
Physicians	44.0
Licensed practical nurses	42.0
Dental hygienists	41.0
Pharmacists	35.0
Dental assistants	35.0
Clinical laboratory technicians	26.0

Source: "Outlook 1990-2005," *Occupational Outlook Quarterly* 35, No. 3, Fall, 1991, p. 21.

★ 464 ★

Employment Opportunities for Managers and Professionals, 1990-2005

Occupation	Rate of increase, 1990-2005	Median weekly earnings (1990)[1]
Mathematical and computer scientists	73.0	734
Registered nurses and other health therapists	43.0	600
Lawyers and judges	34.0	1,052
Primary, secondary, and special education teachers	30.0	522
Health diagnosticians	29.0	824
Executives, administrators, and managers	27.0	604
Engineers	26.0	809
Natural scientists	26.0	661
Technical specialists	23.0	509
College and university teachers	19.0	747

Source: Richman, Louis S., "America's Tough New Job Market," *Fortune,* February 24, 1992, p. 58. Primary source: Bureau of Labor Statistics. *Note:* 1. Excludes self-employed workers.

★ 465 ★

Distribution of Employment: Manufacturing and All Other Industries, 2005

"Manufacturing employment will decline by 600,000 jobs over the 1990-2005 period, but the industry will still account for almost 14 percent of total employment."

Manufacturing	13.7
Other industries	86.3

Source: "Outlook 1990-2005," *Occupational Outlook Quarterly* 35, No. 3, Fall, 1991, p. 26.

★ 466 ★

Employment Change in Manufacturing, Major Occupational Groups, and Selected Occupations, 1990-2005

"Overall, employment in manufacturing will decline by 36 percent, but some occupations will have much greater declines and others will increase."

Executive, administrative, and managerial occupations	8
Industrial production managers	20
Marketing, advertising, and public relations managers	23
All other managers and administrators	
Professional specialty occupations	16
Accountants	10
Engineers	12
Petroleum engineers	-17
Life scientists	32
Systems analysts	42
Writers and editors, including technical writers	25
Technicians and related occupations	9
Engineering and science technicians	5
Drafters	-14
Computer programmers	25
Marketing and sales occupations	27
Sales persons, retail	-7
Administrative support workers	-8
Payroll and timekeeping clerks	-14
Receptionists and information clerks	17
Service occupations	-6
Guards	-11
Agriculture, forestry, and fishing occupations	2
Fellers and buckers	-6
Precision production, craft, and repair occupations	-2
Plumbers, pipefitters, and steamfitters	-7
Industrial machinery mechanics	5
Printing workers	22
Woodworkers, precision	15
Operators, fabricators, and laborers	-10
Numerical control machine tool operators	22
Combination machine tool operators	22
Printing press operators	18
Textile machine setters and setup operators	-30
Woodworking machine operators	12
Truck drivers	5

Source: "Outlook 1990-2005," *Occupational Outlook Quarterly* 35, No. 3, Fall, 1991, p. 27. Some magnitudes estimated from published chart.

★ 467 ★

Manufacturing Employment Growth by City, 1990-2000

MSAs ranked by projected growth in manufacturing employment, in thousands, 1990-2000. "In the Information Age, service and information-based industries are supposed to grow while the share of manufacturing jobs declines. But service and information companies need customers, just like everyone else. And most of their customers are in the business of making things. That's why growth in manufacturing employment predicts growth in information and service jobs. During the 1990s, the 50 metropolitan areas with the largest absolute growth in manufacturing employment will range from Los Angeles-Long Beach (population 8,863,164) to Hickory-Morganton, North Carolina (population 221,700). Leading the pack is Anaheim-Santa Ana, California, already a hotbed of manufacturing activity. Close behind is Silicon Valley (San Jose, California), the home port of manufacturing in the Information Age. In third place is Seattle, where aircraft companies like Boeing promote information by making the world seem smaller. The top 50 in absolute growth include 2 metros where the rate of increase should exceed 50 percent: Merced, California (54.7 percent), and Ocala, Florida (53 percent)."

	Rank	1990	2000	Change	Percent change
Anaheim-Santa Ana, CA	1	277.8	343.4	65.6	23.6
San Jose, CA	2	274.6	338.5	63.9	23.3
Seattle, WA	3	207.8	240.7	32.9	15.8
San Diego, CA	4	132.4	164.3	31.9	24.1
Dallas, TX	5	227.9	256.7	28.8	12.6
Phoenix, AZ	6	146.2	172.7	26.5	18.1
Atlanta, GA	7	193.3	217.3	24.0	12.4
Washington, DC-MD-VA	8	95.3	118.4	23.1	24.3
Minneapolis-St. Paul, MN-WI	9	269.6	288.6	19.0	7.0
Riverside-San Bernardino, CA	10	91.9	108.4	16.5	17.9
Raleigh-Durham, NC	11	63.7	79.4	15.7	24.6
Tampa-St. Petersburg-Clearwater, FL	12	99.7	115.1	15.4	15.4
Fort Worth-Arlington, TX	13	122.8	135.7	12.9	10.5
Orlando, FL	14	60.6	73.2	12.6	20.9
Salt Lake City-Ogden, UT	15	66.8	79.2	12.4	18.6
Elkhart-Goshen, IN	16	60.1	71.9	11.8	19.6
Fort Lauderdale-Hollywood-Pompano Beach, FL	17	49.0	60.8	11.8	24.0
Los Angeles-Long Beach, CA	18	917.5	929.1	11.6	1.3
Huntsville, AL	19	33.3	44.0	10.7	32.0
Charlotte-Gastonia-Rock Hill, NC-SC	20	160.0	170.5	10.5	6.6
Denver, CO	21	96.4	106.6	10.2	10.6
Nashville, TN	22	89.4	99.3	9.9	11.1
Oxnard-Ventura, CA	23	33.3	42.8	9.5	28.7
West Palm Beach-Boca Ratan-Delray Beach, FL	24	37.0	46.1	9.1	24.6
El Paso, TX	25	42.1	50.9	8.8	20.9
Sacramento, TX	26	45.5	53.9	8.4	18.5
Austin, TX	27	43.7	52.0	8.3	19.1
Hickory-Morganton, NC	28	69.1	77.3	8.2	11.8
Grand Rapids, MI	29	103.6	111.7	8.1	7.9
Wichita, KS	30	63.3	70.9	7.6	12.0
Colorado Springs, CO	31	24.3	31.9	7.6	31.1
Boulder-Longmont, CO	32	31.0	38.6	7.6	24.5
Norfolk-Virginia Beach-Newport News, VA	33	68.4	75.8	7.4	10.8
Greensboro-Winston-Salem-High Point, NC	34	158.4	165.2	6.8	4.3

[Continued]

★ 467 ★

Manufacturing Employment Growth by City, 1990-2000

[Continued]

	Rank	1990	2000	Change	Percent change
Santa Barbara-Santa Maria-Lompoc, CA	35	23.6	30.1	6.5	27.5
Santa Rosa-Petaluma, CA	36	20.3	26.6	6.3	30.9
Tucson, AZ	37	32.3	38.5	6.2	19.2
Ocala, FL	38	11.5	17.6	6.1	53.0
Merced, CA	39	11.0	17.0	6.0	54.7
Portland, OR	40	105.8	111.6	5.8	5.4
Fort Smith, AR-OK	41	28.4	33.9	5.5	19.4
Greenville-Spartanburg, SC	42	104.2	109.1	4.9	4.7
Boise City, ID	43	14.9	19.7	4.8	32.2
Richland-Kennewick-Pasco, WA	44	14.7	19.4	4.7	32.0
Santa Cruz, CA	45	15.4	19.9	4.5	29.3
Appleton-Oshkosh-Neenah, WI	46	53.3	57.7	4.4	8.3
Modesto, CA	47	26.0	30.4	4.4	16.8
Madison, WI	48	26.2	30.5	4.3	16.4
Columbia, SC	49	30.9	35.2	4.3	13.9
McAllen-Edinburg-Mission, TX	50	13.0	17.3	4.3	32.7

Source: "Makers and Movers," Thomas Exter, *American Demographics*, 13, No. 10, October 1991, .Note: *MSA = Metropolitan Statistical Area.*

★ 468 ★

Decline in Goods Production Employment, 1985-2000

"Between 1985 and 2000, employment and output in goods production will continue to decline. By the year 2000, manufacturing will employ 2.2 million fewer workers than it does today, and only 14 percent of all U.S. employees will work in manufacturing industries. Both durables and nondurables will shed more than one million workers, with the biggest losses coming in primary metals (-346,000), textiles (-243,000), and motor vehicles (-143,000)."

[Millions of workers]

	1985		2000		Change (1985-2000)	
	Number[1]	Share	Number	Share	Number	Percent
Total	107.16	100.00	130.96	100.00	23.81	22.22
Goods						
Total	28.21	26.32	25.74	19.65	-2.47	-8.76
Farm, forest, fishing	3.14	2.93	2.67	2.04	-0.47	-14.88
Mining	0.97	0.90	0.79	0.60	-0.18	-18.68
Construction	4.66	4.35	5.06	3.86	0.40	8.52
Manufacturing	19.44	18.14	17.22	13.15	-2.22	-11.42
Durable	11.58	10.81	10.51	8.02	-1.08	-9.28
Nondurable	7.86	7.34	6.72	5.13	-1.15	-14.57
Services						
Total	72.62	67.77	96.51	73.96	23.89	32.90

[Continued]

★ 468 ★

Decline in Goods Production Employment, 1985-2000
[Continued]

	1985		2000		Change (1985-2000)	
	Number[1]	Share	Number	Share	Number	Percent
Fin. Ins. & Real Estate	5.92	5.53	8.12	6.20	2.19	37.02
Wholesale & Retail Trade	23.19	21.64	30.37	23.19	7.18	30.95
Regulated Industries	5.29	4.94	5.76	4.40	0.47	8.92
Other Services	21.92	20.46	32.16	24.56	10.24	46.71
Government	16.30	15.21	20.10	15.35	3.81	23.37

Source: Workforce 2000: Work and Workers for the Twenty-First Century, Hudson Institute, Indianapolis, Indiana, 1987, p. 58.
Note: 1. Excludes self-employment.

★ 469 ★

Percentage and Numerical Changes in Employment: Marketing and Sales Occupations, 1990-2005

Occupation	Estimated employment, 1990	Percent change in employment, 1990-2005	Numerical change in employment 1990-2005
Cashiers	2,633,000	26.0	685,000
Counter and rental clerks	215,000	34.0	74,000
Insurance agents and brokers	439,000	20.0	88,000
Manufacturers' and wholesale sales representatives	1,944,000	15.0	284,000
Real estate agents, brokers, and appraisers	413,000	19.0	79,000
Retail sales workers	4,754,000	29.0	1,881,000
Securities and financial services sales representatives	191,000	40.0	76,000
Services sales representatives	588,000	55.0	325,000
Travel agents	132,000	62.0	82,000

Source: "The Job Outlook in Brief: 1990-2000," *Occupational Outlook Quarterly* 36, No. 1, Spring, 1992, p. 25. Also in source: a prose description of employment prospects for each occupation. Primary source: U.S. Department of Labor, Bureau of Labor Statistics industry-occupation matrix.

★ 470 ★

Percentage and Numerical Changes in Employment: Mechanics, Installers, and Repairers, 1990-2005

Subgroup Occupation	Estimated employment, 1990	Percent change in employment, 1990-2005	Numerical change in employment, 1990-2005
Aircraft mechanics and engine specialists	122,000	24.0	29,000
Automotive body repairers	219,000	22.0	48,000
Automotive mechanics	757,000	22.0	166,000
Diesel mechanics	268,000	22.0	58,000
Electronic equipment repairers	444,000	1.0	4,100
Commercial and industrial electronic equipment repairers	75,000	17.0	13,000
Communications equipment mechanics	125,000	-38.0	-48,000
Computer and office machine repairers	156,000	38.0	60,000
Electronic home entertainment repairers	41,000	13.0	5,100
Telephone installers and repairers	47,000	-55.0	-26,000
Elevator installers and repairers	19,000	17.0	3,100
Farm equipment mechanics	48,000	9.0	4,500
General maintenance mechanics	1,128,000	22.0	251,000
Heating, air-conditioning, and refrigeration technicians	219,000	21.0	46,000
Home appliance and power tool repairers	71,000	-1.0	-700
Industrial machinery repairers	474,000	10.0	46,000
Line installers and cable splicers	232,000	-14.0	-32,000
Millwrights	73,000	12.0	8,900
Mobile heavy equipment mechanics	104,000	13.0	13,000
Motorcycle, boat,and small engine mechanics	50,000	10.0	4,900
Musical instrument repairers and tuners	8,700	2.0	[1]
Vending machine servicers and repairers	26,000	-1.0	[1]

Source: "The Job Outlook in Brief: 1990-2000," *Occupational Outlook Quarterly* 36, No. 1, Spring, 1992, pp. 32-4. Also in source: a description of employment prospects for each occupation. Primary source: U.S. Department of Labor, Bureau of Labor Statistics, industry-occupation matrix. *Note:* 1. Less than 500.

★ 471 ★

Percentage and Numerical Changes in Employment: Production Occupations, 1990-2005

Subgroup Occupation	Estimated employment, 1990	Percent change in employment, 1990-2005	Numerical change in employment, 1990-2005
Assemblers			
Precision assemblers	352,000	-33.0	-116,000
Blue-collar worker supervisors	1,792,000	7.0	120,000
Food processing occupations			
Butchers and meat, poultry, and fish cutters	355,000	[1]	1,200
Inspectors, testers, and graders	668,000	-1.0	-9,200
Metalworking and plastics-working occupations			
Boilermakers	22,000	3	700
Jewelers	40,000	20.0	8,000
Machinists	386,000	10.0	41,000
Metalworking and plastics-working machine operators	1,473,000	-8.0	-122,000
Tool and die makers	141,000	3.0	3,900
Welders, cutters, and welding machine operators	427,000	4.0	18,000
Plant and systems operators			
Electric power generating plant operators and power distributors and dispatchers	44,000	9.0	3,900
Stationary engineers	35,000	1.0	[2]
Water and wastewater treatment plant operators	78,000	29.0	23,000
Printing occupations			
Prepress workers	186,000	22.0	40,000
Printing press operators	251,000	19.0	49,000
Bindery workers	78,000	11.0	8,900
Textile, apparel, and furnishings occupations			
Apparel workers	1,037,000	-8.0	-81,000
Shoe an leather workers and repairers	27,000	-19.0	-5,200
Textile machinery operators	289,000	-28.0	-81,000
Upholsterers	64,000	10.0	6,100
Woodworking occupations	349,000	12.0	43,000
Miscellaneous production occupations			
Dental laboratory technicians	57,000	4.0	2,500
Ophthalmic laboratory technicians	19,000	29.0	5,600
Painting and coating machine operators	160,000	-1.0	-1,600
Photographic process workers	76,000	19.0	14,000

Source: "The Job Outlook in Brief: 1990-2000," *Occupational Outlook Quarterly* 36, No. 1, Spring, 1992, pp. 37-9. Also in source: description of employment prospects for each occupation. Primary source: U.S. Department of Labor, Bureau of Labor Statistics, industry-occupation matrix. *Notes:* 1. Less than one. 2. Less than 500.

★ 472 ★

Percentage and Numerical Changes in Employment: Professional Specialty Occupations, 1990-2005

Subgroup Occupation	Estimated employment, 1990	Percent change in employment, 1990-2005	Numerical change in employment 1990-2005
Engineers	1,519,000[2]	26.0	400,000
Aerospace engineers	73,000	20.0	15,000
Chemical engineers	48,000	12.0	5,600
Civil engineers	198,000	30.0	59,000
Electrical and electronics engineers	426,000	34.0	145,000
Industrial engineers	135,000	19.0	26,000
Mechanical engineers	233,000	24.0	56,000
Metallurgical, ceramic, and materials engineers	18,000	21.0	3,900
Mining engineers	4,200	4.0	[1]
Nuclear engineers	18,000	0.0	[2]
Petroleum engineers	17,000	1.0	[2]
Architects and surveyors			
Architects	108,000	24.0	26,000
Landscape architects	20,000	31.0	6,200
Surveyors	108,000	14.0	15,000
Computer, mathematical, and operations research occupations			
Actuaries	13,000	34.0	4,400
Computer systems analysts	463,000	79.0	366,000
Mathematicians	22,000	9.0	2,000
Operations research analysts	57,000	73.0	42,000
Statisticians	16,000	12.0	1,800
Life scientists			
Agricultural scientists	25,000	27.0	6,600
Biological scientists	62,000	34.0	21,000
Foresters and conservation scientists	29,000	12.0	3,600
Physical scientists			
Chemists	83,000	16.0	13,000
Geologists and geophysicists	48,000	22.0	11,000
Meteorologists	5,500	30.0	1,600
Physicists and astronomers	20,000	5.0	1,000
Lawyers and judges	633,000	34.0	217,000
Social scientists and urban planners			
Economists and marketing research analysts	37,000	21.0	8,000
Psychologists	125,000	64.0	79,000
Sociologists	[3]	[3]	[3]
Urban and regional planners	23,000	19.0	4,400

[Continued]

★ 472 ★

Percentage and Numerical Changes in Employment: Professional Specialty Occupations, 1990-2005

[Continued]

Subgroup Occupation	Estimated employment, 1990	Percent change in employment, 1990-2005	Numerical change in employment 1990-2005
Social and recreation workers			
Human services workers	145,000	71.0	103,000
Social workers	438,000	34.0	150,000
Recreation workers	194,000	24.0	47,000
Religious workers			
Protestant ministers	255,000[4]	[3]	[3]
Rabbis	2,700[4]	[3]	[3]
Roman Catholic priests	53,000[4]	[3]	[3]
Teachers, librarians, and counselors			
Adult education teachers	517,000	29.0	152,000
Archivists and curators	17,000	21.0	3,700
College and university faculty	712,000	19.0	134,000
Counselors	144,000	34.0	49,000
Kindergarten and elementary school teachers	1,521,000	23.0	350,000
Librarians	149,000	11.0	17,000
Secondary school teachers	1,280,000	34.0	437,000
Health diagnosing occupations			
Chiropractors	42,000	[3]	[3]
Dentists	174,000	12.0	21,000
Optometrists	37,000	20.0	7,600
Physicians	580,000	34.0	196,000
Podiatrists	16,000	46.0	7,300
Veterinarians	47,000	31.0	14,000
Health assessment and treating occupations			
Dietitians and nutritionists	45,000	24.0	11,000
Occupational therapists	36,000	55.0	20,000
Pharmacists	169,000	21.0	35,000
Physical therapists	88,000	76.0	67,000
Physician assistants	53,000	34.0	18,000
Recreational therapists	32,000	39.0	13,000
Registered nurses	1,727,000	44.0	767,000
Respiratory therapists	60,000	52.0	31,000
Speech-language pathologists and audiologists	68,000	34.0	23,000
Communications occupations			
Public relations specialists	109,000	19.0	21,000
Radio and television announcers and newscasters	57,000	20.0	11,000
Reporters and correspondents	67,000	20.0	14,000

[Continued]

★ 472 ★

Percentage and Numerical Changes in Employment: Professional Specialty Occupations, 1990-2005

[Continued]

Subgroup Occupation	Estimated employment, 1990	Percent change in employment, 1990-2005	Numerical change in employment 1990-2005
Writers and editors	232,000	26.0	60,000
Visual arts occupations			
Designers	339,000	26.0	89,000
Photographers and camera operators	120,000	23.0	28,000
Visual artists	230,000	32.0	73,000
Performing arts occupations			
Actors, directors, and producers	95,000	41.0	39,000
Dancers and choreographers	8,600	38.0	3,300
Musicians	252,000	9.0	24,000

Source: "The Job Outlook in Brief: 1990-2000," *Occupational Outlook Quarterly* 36, No. 1, Spring, 1992, pp. 15-22. Also in source: a description of employment prospects for each occupation. Primary source: U.S. Department of Labor, Bureau of Labor Statistics industry-occupation matrix. *Notes:* 1. Total exceeds the sum of the individual estimates because not all branches of engineering are covered separately. 2. Less than 500. 3. Estimates not available. 4. Includes only those who serve congregations.

★ 473 ★

Employment Growth of Retail Trade Industry, 1990-2005

"Employment in retail trade will increase by 5.1 million, about 22 percent of total job growth."

[Numbers in millions]

Retail trade	5.1
Other industries	16.1

Source: "Outlook 1990-2005," *Occupational Outlook Quarterly* 35, No. 3, Fall, 1991, p. 25.

★ 474 ★

Employment Growth in Retail Trade Occupations, 1990-2005

Industry	Number (thousands)	Growth rate (percent)
Total	5,121	26
Eating and drinking places	2,147	33
Food stores	671	21
Miscellaneous retail stores	534	21
Automotive dealers and service stations	470	22
Apparel and accessory stores	433	37
Department stores	323	15
Building materials and garden supplies	228	30
Furniture and home furnishings stores	217	26

Source: "Outlook 1990-2005," *Occupational Outlook Quarterly* 35, No. 3, Fall, 1991, p. 25.

★ 475 ★

Growth of Selected Occupations in Retail Trade, 1990-2005

"Employment in eating and drinking places will increase by 2.1 million and account for about 40 percent of the total growth of retail trade and 8 percent of total employment growth. Food stores, with an increase of 671,000 jobs, will also account for a large share of the growth."

[Numbers in percent]

Food service and lodging managers	52
Cooks, restaurant	47
Dining room attendants	38
Food counter, fountain, and related workers	37
Food preparation workers	34
Cooks, short order and fast food	33
Truck drivers	29
Salespersons, retail	26
Cashiers	26
Auto mechanics	26
Waiters and waitresses	25
General managers	18
Stock clerks, sales floor	17

Source: "Outlook 1990-2005," *Occupational Outlook Quarterly* 35, No. 3, Fall, 1991, p. 25.

★ 476 ★

Percentage and Numerical Changes in Employment: Service Occupations, 1990-2005

Occupation	Estimated employment, 1990	Percent change in employment, 1990-2005	Numerical change in employment, 1990-2005
Protective service occupations			
Correction officers	230,000	61.0	142,000
Firefighting occupations	280,000	24.0	68,000
Guards	883,000	34.0	298,000
Police, detectives, and special agents	655,000	24.0	160,000
Food and beverage preparation and service occupations			
Chefs, cooks, and other kitchen workers	3,069,000	34.0	1,035,000
Food and beverage service workers	4,400,000	28.0	1,223,000
Health service occupations			
Dental assistants	176,000	34.0	60,000
Medical assistants	165,000	74.0	122,000
Nursing aides and psychiatric aides	1,374,000	43.0	587,000
Personal service and cleaning occupations			
Animal caretakers except farm	106,000	38.0	40,000
Barbers and cosmetologists	713,000	22.0	156,000
Flight attendants	101,000	59.0	59,000
Gardeners and groundskeepers	874,000	40.0	348,000
Homemaker-home health aides	391,000	88.0	343,000
Janitors and cleaners	3,007,000	18.0	555,000
Preschool workers	990,000	49.0	490,000
Private household workers	782,000	-29.0	-227,000

Source: "The Job Outlook in Brief: 1990-2000," *Occupational Outlook Quarterly* 36, No. 1, Spring, 1992, pp. 29-30. Also in source: description of employment prospects for each occupation. Primary source: U.S. Department of Labor, Bureau of Labor Statistics, industry-occupation matrix.

★ 477 ★

Productivity Gains in Service Industries, 1955-2000

	1955-1970	1970-1985	1985-2000
Productivity			
Services & other	35.7	-	33.0
Manufacturing	13.1	20.0	30.0
Employment			
Services & other	45.0	78.3	36.6
Manufacturing	6.0	-	-

Source: "Productivity Gains in Services Are the Key to Future Economic Growth," *Workforce 2000: Work and Workers for the Twenty-First Century,* Hudson Institute, Indianapolis, Indiana, 1987, p. 65.

★ 478 ★

Percentage and Numerical Changes in Employment: Technicians and Related Support Occupations, 1990-2005

Subgroup Occupation	Estimated employment, 1990	Percent change in employment, 1990-2005	Numerical change in employment 1990-2005
Health technologists and technicians			
Clinical laboratory technologists	258,000	24.0	63,000
Dental hygienists	97,000	41.0	40,000
Dispensing opticians	64,000	37.0	24,000
EEG technologists	6,700	57.0	3,800
EKG technicians	16,000	-5.0	-800
Emergency medical technicians	89,000	30.0	26,000
Licensed practical nurses	644,000	42.0	269,000
Medical record technicians	52,000	54.0	28,000
Nuclear medicine technologists	10,000	53.0	5,500
Radiologic technologists	149,000	70.0	103,000
Surgical technologists	38,000	55.0	21,000
Technicians except health			
Aircraft pilots	90,000	34.0	31,000
Air traffic controllers	32,000	7.0	2,200
Broadcast technicians	33,000	4.0	1,200
Computer programmers	565,000	56.0	317,000
Drafters	326,000	13.0	44,000
Engineering technicians	755,000	28.0	210,000
Library technicians	65,000	11.0	7,300
Paralegals	90,000	85.0	77,000

[Continued]

★ 478 ★

Percentage and Numerical Changes in Employment: Technicians and Related Support Occupations, 1990-2005
[Continued]

Subgroup Occupation	Estimated employment, 1990	Percent change in employment, 1990-2005	Numerical change in employment 1990-2005
Science technicians	246,000	24.0	58,000
Tool programmers, numerical control	7,800	6.0	[1]

Source: "The Job Outlook in Brief: 1990-2000," *Occupational Outlook Quarterly* 36, No. 1, Spring, 1992, pp. 23-4. Also in source: a prose description of employment prospects for each occupation. Primary source: U.S. Department of Labor, Bureau of Labor Statistics industry-occupation matrix. *Note:* 1. Less than 500.

★ 479 ★

Percentage and Numerical Changes in Employment: Transportation and Material Moving Occupations, 1990-2005

Subgroup Occupation	Estimated employment, 1990	Percent change in employment, 1990-2005	Numerical change in employment 1990-2005
Busdrivers	561,000	32.0	177,000
Material moving equipment operators	1,019,000	12.0	123,000
Rail transportation workers	107,000	-4.0	-4,600
Truckdrivers	2,701,000	24.0	659,000
Water transportation occupations	49,000	-13.0	-6,600

Source: "The Job Outlook in Brief: 1990-2000," *Occupational Outlook Quarterly* 36, No. 1, Spring, 1992, p. 40. Also in source: a description of employment prospects for each occupation. Primary source: U.S. Department of Labor, Bureau of Labor Statistics industry-occupation matrix.

Labor Force and Occupational Employment by Selected Characteristics

★ 480 ★

Civilian Labor Force, 1975-2005

"Employment will increase by 24 million from 1990 to 2005."

[Numbers in millions]

1975	94
1990	125
2005	151

Source: "Outlook 1990-2005," *Occupational Outlook Quarterly* 35, No. 3, Fall, 1991, p. 6.

★ 481 ★

Future Trends in Labor

The world's labor force will grow by only 1.5 percent per year during the 1990s, much less quickly than in recent decades, but fast enough to provide most countries with the workers they need. In contrast, the United States faces shortages of labor in general, especially of low wage-rate workers.

In the 1990s, the American economy will create about one million new jobs in the less-skilled and labor categories.

Institutions of higher education, business, and the military will vie for youths 16 to 24 years old as this group shrinks from 20 percent of the U.S. labor force in 1985 to 16 percent in 2000.

Unions will continue to lose their hold on labor.

Union membership is declining steadily in the United States. It reached 17.5 percent in 1986. According to the United Auto Workers, it will fall to 14 percent by 1990, 12 percent by 1995, and less than 10 percent by 2000.

Increased use of robots, CAD/CAM, flexible manufacturing complexes can cut a company's workforce by up to one-third.

Changing careers will become increasingly common. By the early 21st century, the average worker will change his career every ten years.

[Continued]

★ 481 ★

Future Trends in Labor
[Continued]

Two-income couples are also on the rise. In 1960, only 28.5 percent of American couples both held jobs. By 1970, the number was 37.7 percent. A decade later, it was 46.2 percent, and by 1985 it had climbed to 49.0 percent. Forecasting International believes the figure will reach 75 percent by 2000.

The long-standing trend toward specialization will continue.

In the 1990s, close to six million jobs will open up in the United States alone in the highly skilled executive, professional, and technical occupations.

The growth of information industries will move the developed countries toward an "information society."

By the year 2000, Forecasting International believes that 85 percent of the labor force will be working in the service sector, many of them in information industries, and many others working with computerized equipment.

Computer competence will approach 100 percent in U.S. urban areas by 2000.

Seventy percent of U.S. homes will have computers in 2001, compared with 24 percent now; more than three-fourths will be equipped to permit communication with the public data network.

High technology industries are being encouraged in many states' economic development plans, yet these industries account for only 4 to 5 percent of the new jobs created each year in the United States. Far more new jobs are opening up in businesses that use computers and other high-tech equipment.

The rise of knowledge industries will make Western society far more dependent on information.

About half of all service workers (43 percent of U.S. labor force by 2000) will be involved in collecting, analyzing, synthesizing, structuring, storing, or retrieving information.

Half of these people will opt for "flex-time, flex-place" arrangements that allow them to work at home, communicating with the office via computer terminals.

Developers of hardware and software will still enjoy vast opportunities. Five of the ten fastest growing careers between now and 2001 will be computer-related, with the demand for programmers and systems analysts growing by 70 percent.

The wave of new entrepreneurs that appeared in the United States during the 1970s and '80s is just the leading edge of a much broader trend.

[Continued]

★ 481 ★

Future Trends in Labor
[Continued]

Mid-career professionals increasingly will found their own businesses as new management techniques squeeze many of the executives out of large companies. For many, it will be the only career advancement possible: by 2001 only one American in fifty will be promoted; in 1987, it was one in twenty.

By 2000, 85 percent of the U.S. labor force will be working for firms employing fewer than two-hundred people.

Throughout the developed world, employment in the service sector will continue to grow rapidly.

The U.S. Bureau of Labor Statistics projects that service industries will employ 74.4 percent American workers by 1995, 77.4 percent by 2000. Forecasting International's estimate for 2000 is about 85 percent.

In contrast, employment in the agricultural and manufacturing sectors will continue to plummet in the industrialized lands.

There will be 1.25 million farmers in the U.S. in 2000; this is 900,000 fewer than in 1991.

Construction and manufacturing will continue their steady decline. In 1990, they employed 23.2 percent of American workers. By 1995, the number will be 22.6 percent. Five years later, it will have fallen to 19.6 percent. Similar trends can be found in Europe, and even Japan. In contrast, farm laborers are streaming off the land and into factories throughout the developing economies of the Pacific Rim, just as American and European workers did earlier in this century.

The projections above come from the U.S. Bureau of Labor Statistics. Forecasting International believes they are far too optimistic. By 2000, agriculture and mining will employ only 2.7 percent of American workers, fabrication only 13 percent.

By 2001, only 9.7 percent of the American labor force will hold jobs in manufacturing, down from 18 percent in 1987. However, productivity will have increased by 500 percent in those industries which have automated, added robotics, and implemented flexible manufacturing technology.

Source: "90 Major Trends Now Changing Our World: Labor & Lifestyle." From the book *Crystal Globe: The Haves and Have-Nots of the New World Order*, by Marvin Cetron and Owen Davis. Copyright (c) 1991. Reprinted with permission from St. Martin's Press, Inc., New York, 1991, pp. 339-48. This section contains numerous other projections and speculations as well as several tables and charts.

★ 482 ★

Labor Force Growth, 1975-1990 and 1990-2005

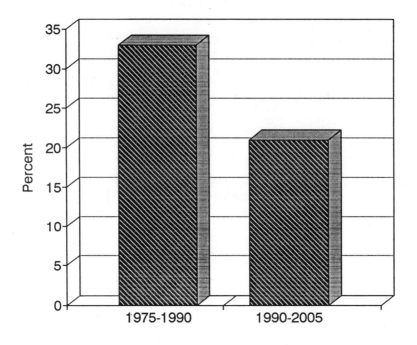

[Numbers in percent]

1975-90	33.0
1990-2005	21.0

Source: "Outlook 1990-2005," *Occupational Outlook Quarterly* 35, No. 3, Fall, 1991, p. 6.

★ 483 ★

Effects of Increased Productivity on Slow Work Force Growth through 2000

"The Key to Domestic Economic Growth is a Rebound in Productivity, Particularly in Services: The similarity in economic growth rates between 1955-1970, 1970-1985, and 1985-2000 masks dramatic changes in the economy. To offset the decline in the rate of labor force growth, the nation must substantially increase its productivity. In the baseline scenario, output per worker, which was an anemic 0.7 percent from 1970 to 1985, more than doubles to 1.5 percent per year, equal to the rate that prevailed from 1955-1970. This rebound stems from a modest improvement in manufacturing productivity, from 3.4 percent per year in the most recent 15-year period to 3.9 percent from 1985-2000. This is coupled with a sharp turnaround in service industry productivity, which climbs from -0.2 percent to +0.9 percent. By contrast, in the deflation scenario, productivity continues to stumble along at the rates of the 1970-1985 period, causing the economy to grow by less than 2 percent per year. This projected gain in productivity is the key, not only to the performance of the economy over the next 13 years, but to the increases that are forecast in compensation, personal income, and the quality of the jobs of the year 2000."*

[Annual percent gain]

	1955-1970	1970-1985	1985-2000
GNP	3.2	2.6	2.9
Employment	1.6	2.1	1.3
Output per worker	1.5	0.7	1.5

Source: "U.S. Productivity Rebounds Offsetting Slower Labor force Growth," *Workforce 2000: Work and Workers for the Twenty-First Century*, Hudson Institute, Indianapolis, Indiana, 1987, p. 55. Primary source: Wharton Econometrics, Hudson Institute.

★ 484 ★

Labor Force Growth, 1950-2000

Year	Labor force (millions)	Gains from previous period (millions)
1950	62.2	9.5
1960	69.6	7.4
1970	82.8	13.2
1980	106.9	24.1
1990	124.6	18.0
2000	140.5	15.6

Source: Workforce 2000: Work and Workers for the Twenty-First Century, Hudson Institute, Indianapolis, Indiana, 1987, p. 78. Primary source: Bureau of Labor Statistics, *Handbook of Labor Statistics, 1985*, Table 4, and Hudson Institute.

★ 485 ★

The Labor Force of the Year 2000

Everyone who will be working in the year 2000 has already been born, and two-thirds of them are at work today. Similarly, most of today's jobs will still exist in the year 2000.

Source: "Work and Workers in the Year 2000," *Workforce 2000: Work and Workers for the Twenty-first Century*, Hudson Institute, Indianapolis, Indiana, 1987, p. 75.

★ 486 ★

Projected Average Annual Labor Force Growth Rate, 1990-2060

"LF1 assumes that all people aged 20-64 are in the labor force. Those individuals 19 and under or 65 and over are not. LF2 recognizes that both human capital and labor force participation rates vary by age. We use data on the average 1989 earnings of people of each age (measured in five year intervals), along with Social Security Administration forecasts of age-specific labor force participation rates, to estimate LF2."

[Numbers in percent]

Period	Labor force	
	Population 20-64 (LF1)	Earnings weighted population (LF2)
1990-2000	0.83	1.07
2000-2010	0.80	0.48
2010-2020	0.06	-0.03
2020-2030	-0.26	-0.10
2030-2040	0.11	0.07
2040-2050	0.00	-0.03
2050-2060	-0.06	-0.02

Source: "An Aging Society: Opportunity of Challenge?" David M. Cutler, et. al., *Brookings Papers on Economic Activity*, No. 1, 1990, p. 12. Also in source: actual figures for 1950-1960, 1960-1970, 1970-1980, and 1980-1990. Primary source: Board of Trustees of the Federal Old-Age and Survivors Insurance and Disability Insurance Trust Funds (1988). Projected data for 1990-2060 use alternative IIb.

★ 487 ★

Rate of Labor Force Participation, 2000

Combining the highest rates of immigration projected by the Census Bureau with the highest plausible rates of labor force participation projected by the Bureau of Labor Statistics would produce a labor force of 147 million in 2000. In contrast, the lowest projections would cause the labor force to rise to only 129 million. In other words, the workforce could increase by as little as 12 percent—the slowest rate in the country's history—or by as much as 28 percent—almost as fast as during the 1970s.

Source: "Work and Workers in the Year 2000," *Workforce 2000: Work and Workers for the Twenty-first Century*, Hudson Institute, Indianapolis, Indiana, 1987, p. 78.

★ 488 ★

Civilian Labor Force Participation Rates, 1980-2000

For civilian noninstitutionalized population 16 years old and over. Annual averages of monthly figures. Rates are based on annual average civilian noninstitutional population of each specified group and represent proportion of each specified group in the civilian labor force. Based on Current Population Survey.

Race, sex, and age	Civilian labor force (millions)					Participation rate (percent)				
	1980	1985	1988	1989	2000	1980	1985	1988	1989	2000
Total[1]	106.9	115.5	121.7	123.9	141.1	63.8	64.8	65.9	66.5	69.0
White	93.6	99.9	104.8	106.4	119.0	64.1	65.0	66.2	66.7	69.5
Male	54.5	56.5	58.3	59.0	63.3	78.2	77.0	76.9	77.1	76.6
Female	39.1	43.5	46.4	47.4	55.7	51.2	54.1	56.4	57.2	62.9
Black	10.9	12.4	13.2	13.5	16.5	61.0	62.9	63.8	64.2	66.5
Male	5.6	6.2	6.6	6.7	8.0	70.6	70.8	71.0	71.0	71.4
Female	5.3	6.1	6.6	6.8	8.5	53.2	56.5	58.0	58.7	62.5
Hispanic[2]	6.1	7.7	9.0	9.3	14.3	64.0	64.6	67.4	67.6	69.9
Male	3.8	4.7	5.4	5.6	8.3	81.4	80.3	81.9	82.0	80.3
Female	2.3	3.0	3.6	3.7	6.0	47.4	49.3	53.2	53.5	59.4
Male	61.5	64.4	66.9	67.8	74.3	77.4	76.3	76.2	76.4	75.9
16-19 years	5.0	4.1	4.2	4.1	4.4	60.5	56.8	56.9	57.9	59.0
16 and 17 years	2.1	1.7	1.7	1.6	1.9	50.1	45.1	46.1	46.3	48.9
18 and 19 years	2.9	2.5	2.4	2.5	2.5	71.3	68.9	68.1	69.2	69.7
20-24 years	8.6	8.3	7.6	7.5	6.9	85.9	85.0	85.0	85.3	86.5
25-34 years	17.0	18.8	19.7	19.9	16.6	95.2	94.7	94.3	94.4	94.1
35-44 years	11.8	14.5	16.1	16.6	20.2	95.5	95.0	94.5	94.5	94.3
45-54 years	9.9	9.9	10.6	10.9	16.4	91.2	91.0	90.9	91.1	90.5
55-64 years	7.2	7.1	6.8	6.8	7.8	72.1	67.9	67.0	67.2	68.1
65 years and over	1.9	1.8	2.0	2.0	2.0	19.0	15.8	16.5	16.6	14.7
Female	45.5	51.1	54.7	56.0	66.8	51.5	54.5	56.6	57.4	62.6

[Continued]

443

★ 488 ★

Civilian Labor Force Participation Rates, 1980-2000
[Continued]

Race, sex, and age	Civilian labor force (millions)					Participation rate (percent)				
	1980	1985	1988	1989	2000	1980	1985	1988	1989	2000
16-19 years	4.4	3.8	3.9	3.8	4.4	52.9	52.1	53.6	53.9	59.5
16 and 17 years	1.8	1.5	1.6	1.5	1.8	43.6	42.1	44.0	44.5	49.8
18 and 19 years	2.6	2.3	2.3	2.3	2.6	61.9	61.7	62.9	62.5	69.0
20-24 years	7.3	7.4	6.9	6.7	6.7	68.9	71.8	72.7	72.4	77.9
25-34 years	12.3	14.7	15.8	16.0	15.1	65.5	70.9	72.7	73.5	82.4
35-44 years	8.6	11.6	13.4	14.0	18.6	65.5	71.8	75.2	76.0	84.9
45-54 years	7.0	7.5	8.5	9.0	14.4	59.9	64.4	69.0	70.5	76.5
55-64 years	4.7	4.9	5.0	5.1	6.1	41.3	42.0	43.5	45.0	49.0
65 years and over	1.2	1.2	1.3	1.4	1.4	8.1	7.3	7.9	8.4	7.6

Source: "Civilian Labor Force and Participation Rates by Race, Hispanic Origin, Sex, and Age, 1980 to 1989, and Projections, 2000," *Statistical Abstract of the United States,* 1991, p. 384. Primary source: U.S. Bureau of Labor Statistics, *Employment and Earnings, Monthly Labor Review,* November, 1989, and unpublished data. *Notes:* 1. Includes other races not shown separately. 2. Persons of Hispanic origin may be of any race.

★ 489 ★

Changes in the Occupational Structure, 1984-2000

"The job prospects for professional and technical, managerial, sales, and service jobs will far outstrip the opportunities in other fields. In contrast to the average gain of about 25 percent across all occupational categories, the fastest growing fields—lawyers, scientists, and health professionals—will grow two to three times as fast. On the other hand, jobs as machine tenders, assemblers, miners, and farmers actually will decline."

Occupation	Current jobs (000)	New jobs (000)	Rate of growth (%)
Total	105,008	25,952	25.0
Service occupations	16,059	5,957	37.0
Managerial and management-related	10,893	4,280	39.0
Marketing and sales	10,656	4,150	39.0
Administrative support	18,483	3,620	20.0
Technicians	3,146	1,389	44.0
Health diagnosing and treating occupations	2,478	1,384	53.0
Teachers, librarians, and counselors	4,437	1,381	31.0
Mechanics, installers, and repairers	4,264	966	23.0
Transportation and heavy equipment operators	4,604	752	16.0
Engineers, architects, and surveyors	1,447	600	41.0
Construction trades	3,127	595	19.0
Natural, computer, and mathematical scientists	647	442	68.0
Writers, artists, entertainers, and athletes	1,092	425	39.0
Other professionals and paraprofessionals	825	355	43.0
Lawyers and judges	457	326	71.0
Social, recreational, and religious workers	759	235	31.0
Helpers and laborers	4,168	205	5.0
Social scientists	173	70	40.0

[Continued]

★ 489 ★

Changes in the Occupational Structure, 1984-2000
[Continued]

Occupation	Current jobs (000)	New jobs (000)	Rate of growth (%)
Precision production workers	2,790	61	2.0
Plant and system workers	275	36	13.0
Blue collar supervisors	1,442	-6	0.0
Miners	175	-28	-16.0
Hand workers, assemblers, and fabricators	2,604	-179	-7.0
Machine setters, operators, and tenders	5,527	-448	-8.0
Agriculture, forestry, and fisheries	4,480	-538	-12.0

Source: "The Changing Occupational Structure, 1984-2000," *Workforce 2000: Work and Workers for the Twenty-First Century*, Hudson Institute, Indianapolis, Indiana, 1987, p. 97.

★ 490 ★

Employment Increase, 1990-2005

Total employment is projected to increase by 20 percent, or by 24.6 million jobs, between 1990 to 2005, according to the Bureau of Labor Statistics' moderate growth scenario for the U.S. economy. This rate of growth is just slightly more than half that of the previous 15-year period, 1975-90, largely because of the expected slowing of labor force growth. Projected changes in the industrial composition of employment and changes in technology, combined with the overall slowing of employment growth, cause the projected employment trends of some of the major occupational groups and numerous detailed occupations to depart from their historical growth rates.

Source: "Occupational Employment Projections,"George Silvestri and John Lukasiewicz, *Monthly Labor Review* 114, No. 11, November, 1991, p. 64. Primary source: Office of Employment Projections, Bureau of Labor Statistics. Also in source: a 13-page chart listing employment figures for more than 500 occupations for 1990 and projections to 2005 under low, medium, and high economic growth scenarios.

★ 491 ★

Civilian Employment by Occupation under Low, Medium, and High Scenarios for Economic Growth, 1990-2005 - I

[Numbers in thousands]

Occupation	Total employment				1990-2005 employment change					
	1990	Projected, 2005			Number			Percent		
		Low	Moderate	High	Low	Moderate	High	Low	Moderate	High
Total, all occupations	122,573	136,806	147,191	154,543	14,233	24,618	31,969	12	20	26
Executive, administrative, and managerial occupations	12,451	14,782	15,866	16,625	2,331	3,414	4,173	19	27	34
Managerial and administrative occupations	8,838	10,417	11,174	11,703	1,579	2,336	2,865	18	26	32
Administrative services manager	221	252	273	287	31	52	66	14	23	30

[Continued]

★ 491 ★

Civilian Employment by Occupation under Low, Medium, and High Scenarios for Economic Growth, 1990-2005 - I

[Continued]

Occupation	Total employment				1990-2005 employment change					
	1990	Projected, 2005			Number			Percent		
		Low	Moderate	High	Low	Moderate	High	Low	Moderate	High
Communication, transportation, and utilities operations manager	143	175	189	199	32	45	55	22	32	39
Construction managers	183	223	243	260	40	60	77	22	33	42
Education administrators	348	400	434	465	52	85	116	15	24	33
Engineering, mathematical, and natural science managers	315	387	423	441	72	108	126	23	34	40
Financial managers	701	828	894	939	127	193	238	18	28	34
Food service and lodging managers	595	762	793	819	166	198	224	28	33	38
Funeral directors and morticians	35	39	41	43	4	6	8	10	17	23
General managers and top executives	3,086	3,409	3,684	3,871	323	598	784	10	19	25
Government chief executives and legislators	71	68	74	80	-3	3	9	-4	4	12
Industrial production managers	210	227	251	260	17	41	50	8	20	24
Marketing, advertising, and public relations managers	427	582	630	659	154	203	232	36	47	54
Personnel, training, and labor relations managers	178	217	235	246	38	57	68	22	32	38
Property and real estate managers	225	288	302	311	62	78	86	28	34	38
Purchasing managers	248	275	298	312	26	49	64	11	20	26
All other managers and administrators	1,850	2,287	2,412	2,512	437	562	662	24	30	36
Management support occupations	3,613	4,364	4,691	4,922	752	1,079	1,309	21	30	36
Accountants and auditors	985	1,235	1,325	1,385	250	340	400	25	34	41
Budget analysts	64	73	78	82	9	14	18	14	22	28
Claims examiners, property and casualty insurance	30	37	40	42	7	9	12	21	31	38
Construction and building inspectors	60	65	71	76	6	11	16	9	19	27
Cost estimators	173	197	215	228	24	42	55	14	24	32
Credit analysts	36	43	46	48	7	10	21	19	27	34
Employment interviewers, private or public employment service	83	94	102	108	11	19	25	13	23	30
Inspectors and compliance officers, except construction	156	190	202	214	34	46	58	22	30	37
Loan officers and counselors	172	205	219	230	33	47	58	19	28	34
Management analysts	151	218	230	240	67	79	88	44	52	58
Personnel, training, and labor relations specialists	278	339	366	384	61	87	105	22	31	38
Purchasing agents, except wholesale, retail, and farm products	218	246	266	276	28	47	58	13	22	27
Tax examiners and revenue agents	62	66	70	73	5	8	11	8	13	18
Underwriters	105	121	130	138	16	25	33	16	24	31
Wholesale and retail buyers, except farm products	194	218	235	246	24	41	52	13	21	27
All other management support workers	846	1,017	1,097	1,153	171	251	307	20	30	36
Professional specialty occupations	15,800	19,379	20,907	22,140	3,578	5,107	6,340	23	32	40
Engineers	1,519	1,748	1,919	2,001	229	400	482	15	26	32
Aeronautical and astronautical engineers	73	81	88	91	8	15	18	11	20	24
Chemical engineers	48	50	54	57	1	6	8	2	12	17
Civil engineers, including traffic engineers	198	235	257	274	37	59	78	19	30	39
Electrical and electronics engineers	426	519	571	693	93	145	167	22	34	39
Industrial engineers, except safety engineers	135	145	160	166	11	26	31	8	19	23
Mechanical engineers	233	263	289	301	30	56	68	13	24	29
Metallurgists and metallurgical, ceramic, and materials engineer	18	20	22	2	2	4	5	10	21	26
Mining engineers, including mine safety engineers	4	4	4	5	-0	0	0	-4	4	10
Nuclear engineers	18	17	18	19	-1	-0	1	-7	-0	4
Petroleum engineers	17	16	18	18	-2	0	1	-10	1	3
All other engineers	347	397	436	454	50	89	107	14	26	31
Architects and surveyors	236	260	284	300	24	48	64	10	20	27
Architects, except landscape and marine	108	124	134	142	15	26	334	14	24	31
Landscape architects	20	24	26	27	5	6	7	23	31	37
Surveyors	108	112	123	131	4	15	23	4	14	21
Life scientists	174	215	230	241	42	56	67	24	32	39
Agricultural and food scientists	25	30	32	33	5	7	8	20	27	31
Biological scientists	62	78	83	87	16	21	25	26	34	39
Foresters and conservation scientists	29	31	32	34	2	4	5	7	12	18
Medical scientists	19	29	31	33	10	12	14	55	66	74
All other life scientists	39	47	51	55	8	12	16	21	32	41
Computer, mathematical, and operations research analysts	571	916	987	1,030	345	416	459	60	73	80
Actuaries	13	16	18	19	3	4	5	24	34	41
Systems analysts and computer scientists statisticians	436	769	829	864	306	366	401	66	79	87
Statisticians	16	16	18	18	1	2	3	5	12	16
Mathematicians and all other mathematical scientists	22	22	24	25	0	2	3	1	9	15
Operations research analysts	57	92	100	104	35	42	47	60	73	81
Physical scientists	200	223	241	251	24	41	51	12	21	26

[Continued]

★ 491 ★

Civilian Employment by Occupation under Low, Medium, and High Scenarios for Economic Growth, 1990-2005 - I

[Continued]

Occupation	Total employment				1990-2005 employment change					
	1990	Projected, 2005			Number			Percent		
		Low	Moderate	High	Low	Moderate	High	Low	Moderate	High
Chemists	83	89	96	100	6	13	17	7	16	21
Geologists, geophysicists, and oceanographers	48	54	58	60	6	11	13	13	22	27
Meteorologists	5	7	7	7	1	2	2	22	30	34
Physicists and astronomers	20	20	21	22	-0	1	2	-2	5	9
All other physical scientists	44	54	59	62	11	15	18	24	34	41
Social scientists	224	301	320	336	77	96	112	34	43	50
Economists	37	43	45	47	5	8	10	14	21	26
Psychologists	125	193	204	214	68	79	90	55	64	72
Urban and regional planners	23	25	28	30	2	4	6	9	19	28
All other social scientists	38	40	43	45	1	4	6	4	11	17
Social, recreational, and religious workers	1,049	1,278	1,376	1,460	230	327	412	22	31	39
Clergy	209	214	228	240	5	19	31	2	9	15
Directors, religious activities and education	62	65	69	73	3	7	11	4	12	18
Human services workers	145	231	249	264	85	103	119	59	71	82
Recreational workers	194	224	241	257	30	47	63	15	24	32
Social workers	438	545	588	626	107	150	188	25	34	43
Lawyers and judicial workers	633	798	850	892	165	217	259	26	34	41
Judges, magistrates, and other judicial workers	46	53	57	61	7	11	15	14	24	33
Lawyers	587	745	793	830	158	206	244	27	35	42
Teachers, librarians, and counselors	5,687	6,701	7,280	7,813	1,014	1,593	2,126	18	28	37
Teachers, elementary	1,362	1,538	1,675	1,803	176	313	441	13	23	32
Teachers, preschool and kindergarten	425	555	598	636	130	173	211	31	41	50
Teachers, special education	332	428	467	503	96	134	170	29	40	51
Teachers, secondary school	1,280	1,575	1,717	1,849	296	437	570	23	34	45
College and university faculty	712	776	846	911	64	134	200	9	19	35
Other teachers and instructors	757	895	963	1,024	138	206	267	18	27	35
Farm and home management advisors	18	18	19	21	-1	1	2	-4	4	12
Instructors and coaches, sports and physical training	221	254	274	293	32	53	72	15	24	32
Adult and vocational education teachers	517	623	669	710	106	152	193	21	29	37
Instructors, adult (nonvocational) education	219	273	289	304	54	70	85	25	32	39
Teachers and instructors, vocational education and training	298	350	380	407	52	82	109	18	27	36
All other teachers and instructors	511	586	636	681	75	125	170	15	24	33
Librarians, archivists, curators, and related workers	166	172	187	200	6	21	34	4	12	20
Curators, archivists, museum technicians, and restorers	17	20	21	22	2	4	5	13	21	28

Source: "Occupational Employment Projections," George Silvestri and John Lukasiewicz, *Monthly Labor Review* 114, No. 11, November, 1991, pp. 68-80.

★ 492 ★

Civilian Employment by Occupation under Low, Medium, and High Scenarios for Economic Growth, 1990-2005 - II

[Numbers in thousands]

Occupation	Total employment				1990-2005 employment change					
	1990	Projected, 2005			Number			Percent		
		Low	Moderate	High	Low	Moderate	High	Low	Moderate	High
Librarians, professional	149	152	165	177	4	17	29	3	11	19
Counselors	144	177	192	206	33	49	63	23	34	44
Health diagnosing occupations	855	1,039	1,101	1,158	185	247	303	22	29	35
Dentists	174	186	196	205	12	21	30	7	12	17
Optometrists	37	42	45	47	5	8	10	13	20	27
Physicians	580	730	776	818	150	196	238	26	34	41
Podiatrists	16	22	23	24	6	7	8	39	46	53
Veterinarians and veterinary inspectors	47	59	62	64	12	14	17	26	31	35
Health assessment and treating occupations	2,305	3,072	3,304	3,505	767	999	1,201	33	43	52

[Continued]

★ 492 ★

Civilian Employment by Occupation under Low, Medium, and High Scenarios for Economic Growth, 1990-2005 - II
[Continued]

| Occupation | Total employment | | | | 1990-2005 employment change | | | | | |
| | 1990 | Projected, 2005 | | | Number | | | Percent | | |
		Low	Moderate	High	Low	Moderate	High	Low	Moderate	High
Dietitians and nutritionists	45	52	56	59	7	11	14	16	24	32
Pharmacists	169	190	204	215	21	35	46	13	21	27
Physician assistants	53	67	72	76	13	18	23	25	34	42
Registered nurses	1,727	2,318	2,494	2,648	591	767	921	34	44	53
Therapists	311	446	479	508	135	168	197	43	54	63
Occupational therapists	36	52	56	60	16	20	24	44	55	65
Physical therapists	88	145	155	164	57	67	76	65	76	86
Recreational therapists	32	42	45	48	10	13	15	30	39	47
Respiratory therapists	60	84	91	97	25	31	37	41	52	62
Speech pathologists and audiologists	68	85	91	97	17	23	29	24	34	43
All other therapists	26	37	40	42	11	13	16	41	51	60
Writers, artists, and entertainers	1,542	1,799	1,915	1,995	257	373	454	17	24	29
Artists and commercial artists	230	288	303	313	58	73	84	25	32	36
Athletes, coaches, umpires, and referees	32	41	43	46	9	11	13	27	34	41
Dancers and choreographers	9	11	12	12	3	3	4	29	38	45
Designers	339	399	428	447	60	89	108	18	26	32
Designers, except interior designers	270	311	335	349	42	65	80	16	24	30
Interior designers	69	88	93	98	18	24	28	26	34	40
Musicians	252	260	276	288	8	24	36	3	9	14
Photographers and camera operators	120	140	148	154	20	28	35	16	23	29
Camera operators, television, motion picture, video	13	16	17	18	3	5	5	28	37	43
Photographers	107	123	131	36	16	23	29	15	22	27
Producers, directors, actors, and entertainers	95	125	134	139	31	39	45	32	41	47
Public relations specialists and publicity writers	109	121	130	137	12	21	28	11	19	25
Radio and TV announcers and newscasters	57	63	68	71	7	11	14	12	20	26
Reporters and correspondents	67	76	81	84	9	14	17	13	20	25
Writers and editors, including technical writers	232	274	292	303	42	60	71	18	26	31
All other professional workers	808	1,028	1,102	1,158	221	294	350	27	36	43
Technicians and related support occupations	4,204	5,317	5,754	6,063	1,113	1,550	1,859	26	37	44
Health technicians and technologists	1,833	2,413	2,595	2,752	580	763	919	32	42	50
Clinical lab technologists and technicians	258	299	321	341	41	63	83	16	24	32
Dental hygienists	97	127	137	145	30	40	48	31	41	50
EEG technologists	7	10	11	11	3	4	4	46	57	67
EKG technicians	16	14	15	16	-2	-1	0	-12	-5	1
Emergency medical technicians	89	107	116	123	18	26	34	20	30	38
Licensed practical nurses	644	849	913	968	205	269	324	32	42	60
Medical records technician	52	74	80	84	23	28	33	44	54	63
Nuclear medicine technicians	10	15	16	17	4	6	7	42	53	63
Opticians, dispensing and measuring	64	81	88	93	18	24	29	28	37	45
Radiologic technologists and technicians	149	234	252	268	86	103	119	58	70	80
Surgical technologists	38	55	59	63	17	21	25	44	55	65
All other health professionals, paraprofessionals, and technicians	409	547	588	623	138	179	214	34	44	52
Engineering and science technicians and technologists	1,327	1,498	1,640	1,718	170	312	391	13	24	29
Engineering technicians	755	881	965	1,008	126	210	253	17	28	33
Electrical and electronic technicians/technologists	363	444	488	508	81	125	145	22	34	40
All other engineering technicians and technologists	392	437	477	500	45	85	108	11	22	28
Drafters	326	335	370	391	8	44	65	3	13	20
Science and mathematics technicians	246	282	305	320	36	58	73	14	24	30
Technicians, except health and engineering and science	1,044	1,406	1,519	1,592	363	475	548	35	46	53
Aircraft pilots and flight engineers	90	111	120	126	21	31	37	24	34	41
Air traffic controllers	32	33	34	35	2	2	3	5	7	9
Broadcast technicians	33	31	34	35	-1	1	3	-3	4	8
Computer programmers	565	811	882	923	246	317	359	44	56	63

[Continued]

★ 492 ★

Civilian Employment by Occupation under Low, Medium, and High Scenarios for Economic Growth, 1990-2005 - II

[Continued]

Occupation	Total employment				1990-2005 employment change					
	1990	Projected, 2005			Number			Percent		
		Low	Moderate	High	Low	Moderate	High	Low	Moderate	High
Legal assistants and technicians, except clerical	220	309	329	345	89	109	125	40	49	57
Paralegals	90	156	167	176	66	7	85	73	85	95
Title examiners and searchers	29	32	33	35	2	4	5	7	13	18
All other legal assistants, including law clerks	100	121	129	134	21	28	34	21	28	34
Programmers, numerical, tool, and process control	8	7	8	9	-0	0	1	-5	6	9
Technical assistants, library	65	66	72	77	1	7	13	2	11	20
All other technicians	33	38	40	42	5	7	10	15	23	29
Marketing and sales occupations	14,088	16,288	17,489	18,313	2,200	3,401	4,226	16	24	30
Cashiers	2,633	3,094	3,318	3,474	461	685	842	18	26	32
Counter and rental clerks	215	268	289	303	53	74	88	25	34	41
Insurance sales workers	439	496	527	553	57	88	114	13	20	26
Real estate agents, brokers, and appraisers	413	471	492	508	58	79	95	14	19	23
Brokers, real estate	69	79	83	85	10	14	16	15	20	24
Real estate appraisers	44	51	54	57	8	11	13	18	24	29
Sales agents, real estate	300	340	355	366	40	55	66	13	18	22
Salesperson, retail	3,619	4,180	4,506	4,728	561	887	1,109	15	24	31
Securities and financial services sales workers	191	250	267	279	59	76	88	31	40	46
Stock clerks, sales floor	1,242	1,343	1,451	1,524	101	209	282	8	17	23
Travel agents	132	199	214	224	68	82	92	51	62	70
All other sales and related workers	5,204	5,987	6,426	6,719	783	1,222	1,515	15	23	29
Administrative support occupations, including clerical	21,951	22,996	24,835	26,158	1,044	2,884	4,207	5	13	19
Adjusters, investigators, and collectors	1,058	1,218	1,313	1,384	160	255	326	15	24	31
Adjustment clerks	320	360	390	409	40	70	89	12	22	28
Bill and account collectors	183	226	244	256	43	60	72	23	33	39
Insurance claims and policy processing occupations	423	486	521	550	62	98	127	15	23	30
Insurance adjusters, examiners, and investigators	147	177	189	200	29	42	52	20	28	35
Insurance claims clerks	104	119	128	135	15	24	31	15	23	30
Insurance policy processing clerks	172	190	204	216	18	32	44	10	19	25
Welfare eligibility workers and interviewers	93	102	111	119	9	18	26	10	19	28
All other adjusters and investigators	38	43	47	50	5	9	12	14	23	31
Communications equipment operators	345	219	236	248	-126	-108	-96	-37	-31	-28
Telephone operators	325	205	221	232	-120	-104	-93	-37	-32	-28
Central office operators	53	20	22	23	-33	-31	-30	-62	-59	-57
Directory assistance operators	26	10	11	11	-16	-16	-15	-62	-59	-57
Switchboard operators	246	176	189	198	-71	-57	-47	-29	-23	-19
All other communications equipment operators	20	14	15	16	-5	-5	-4	-28	-23	-20
Computer operators and peripheral equipment operators	320	334	361	379	14	42	59	4	13	19
Computer operators, except peripheral equipment	282	296	320	336	13	38	53	5	13	19

Source: "Occupational Employment Projections," George Silvestri and John Lukasiewicz, *Monthly Labor Review* 114, No. 11, November, 1991, pp. 68-80.

★ 493 ★

Civilian Employment by Occupation under Low, Medium, and High Scenarios for Economic Growth, 1990-2005 - III

[Numbers in thousands]

| Occupation | Total employment | | | | 1990-2005 employment change | | | | | |
| | 1990 | Projected, 2005 | | | Number | | | Percent | | |
		Low	Moderate	High	Low	Moderate	High	Low	Moderate	High
Peripheral equipment operators	37	38	41	43	1	4	6	2	10	16
Financial records processing occupations	2,860	2,555	2,750	2,887	-305	-110	28	-11	-4	1
Billing, cost, and rate clerks	318	308	332	350	-11	14	32	-3	5	10
Billing, posting, and calculating machine operators	95	91	99	104	-4	4	9	-4	4	10
Bookkeeping, accounting, and auditing clerks	2,276	1,994	2,143	2,248	-281	-133	-27	-12	-6	-1
Payroll and timekeeping clerks	171	162	176	185	-9	5	13	-5	3	8
Information clerks	1,418	1,861	2,003	2,104	443	584	686	31	41	48
Hotel desk clerks	118	150	158	162	32	40	45	27	34	38
Interviewing clerks, except personnel and social welfare	144	185	200	209	41	56	66	29	39	46
New accounts clerks, banking	106	113	121	127	6	14	21	6	13	19
Receptionists and information clerks	900	1,228	1,322	1,394	328	422	494	36	47	55
Reservation and transportation ticket agents and travel clerks	150	186	2052	212	36	52	62	24	34	41
Mail clerks and messengers	280	285	306	321	5	26	41	2	9	15
Mail clerks, except mail machine operators and postal service	137	136	146	153	-1	9	16	-0	7	12
Messengers	143	149	160	168	6	17	25	4	12	18
Postal clerks and mail carriers	439	479	519	548	40	80	109	9	18	25
Postal mail carriers	305	350	380	401	45	74	96	15	24	31
Postal service clerks	134	129	140	147	-5	6	14	-4	4	10
Material recording, scheduling, dispatching, and distributing occupations	2,513	2,534	2,754	2,888	21	241	375	1	10	15
Dispatchers	209	249	269	285	40	60	76	19	29	36
Dispatchers, except police, fire, and ambulance	138	168	181	191	30	43	53	22	31	38
Dispatchers, police, fire, an ambulance	71	80	87	94	10	17	23	14	24	33
Meter readers, utilities	50	35	37	39	-15	-12	-10	-30	-25	-20
Order fillers, wholesale and retail sales	197	195	211	222	-1	14	25	-1	7	13
Procurement clerks	56	48	51	53	-8	-4	-2	-14	-8	-4
Production, planning, and expediting clerks	237	217	239	248	-20	1	10	-9	1	4
Stock clerks, stockroom, warehouse, or yard	752	726	786	824	-26	34	72	-4	4	10
Traffic, shipping, and receiving clerks	762	788	860	901	26	97	138	3	13	18
Weighers, measurers, checkers, and samplers, recordkeeping	37	35	38	40	-2	1	3	-5	4	8
All other material recording, scheduling, and distribution workers	214	242	263	276	28	50	63	13	23	29
Records processing occupations, except financial	949	966	1,045	1,100	17	96	151	2	10	16
Advertising clerks	18	19	21	21	1	3	4	8	15	20
Brokerage clerks	60	63	68	71	3	8	11	5	13	19
Correspondence clerks	30	34	37	39	4	7	9	13	22	29
File clerks	271	278	300	317	7	29	46	2	11	17
Library assistants and bookmobile drivers	117	119	130	139	2	13	23	2	11	19
Order clerks, materials, merchandise, and service	291	276	300	314	-16	9	23	-5	3	8
Personnel clerks, except payroll and timekeeping	129	145	155	162	16	27	34	13	21	26
Statement clerks	33	32	34	36	-1	1	3	-4	3	9
Secretaries, stenographers, and typists	4,680	4,735	5,110	5,387	55	429	706	1	9	15
Secretaries	3,576	3,813	4,116	4,338	237	540	762	7	15	21
Legal secretaries	281	385	413	435	104	133	154	37	47	55
Medical secretaries	232	363	390	415	131	158	183	57	68	79
Secretaries, except legal and medical	3,064	3,065	3,312	3,488	2	248	425	0	8	14
Stenographers	132	116	125	132	-16	-7	0	-12	-5	0
Typists and word processors	972	805	869	916	-166	-103	-55	-17	-11	-6
Other clerical and administrative support workers	7,090	7,811	8,439	8,912	721	1,349	1,822	10	19	26
Bank tellers	517	459	492	518	-58	-25	1	-11	-5	0
Clerical supervisors and managers	1,218	1,373	1,481	1,559	155	263	341	13	22	28
Court clerks	47	53	58	62	6	11	16	14	24	33
Credit authorizers, credit checkers, and loan and credit clerks	240	278	298	313	38	58	73	16	24	30
Credit authorizers	21	24	26	27	3	5	6	15	24	31
Credit checkers	48	55	60	63	7	12	15	16	24	31
Loan and credit clerks	151	175	187	197	25	37	46	16	24	31
Loan interviewers	20	23	25	26	3	4	6	13	21	27
Customer service representatives, utilities	109	111	120	126	2	11	17	2	10	15
Data entry keyers, except composing	456	471	510	536	14	54	79	3	12	17
Data entry keyers, composing	19	21	23	24	2	4	5	11	20	25
Duplicating, mail, and other office machine operators	169	176	191	200	7	22	31	4	13	18
General office clerks	2,737	3,149	3,407	3,597	411	670	859	15	24	31
Municipal clerks	22	25	27	29	3	5	7	13	23	33
Proofreaders and copy markers	29	26	28	29	-4	-2	-0	-12	-5	-1

[Continued]

★ 493 ★

Civilian Employment by Occupation under Low, Medium, and High Scenarios for Economic Growth, 1990-2005 - III

[Continued]

Occupation	Total employment				1990-2005 employment change					
	1990	Projected, 2005			Number			Percent		
		Low	Moderate	High	Low	Moderate	High	Low	Moderate	High
Real estate clerks	29	32	34	35	3	5	6	12	17	21
Statistical clerks	85	50	54	57	-35	-31	-28	-41	-36	-33
Teacher aides and educational assistants	808	999	1,086	1,165	192	278	358	24	34	44
All other clerical and administrative support workers	604	587	629	662	-17	25	58	-3	4	10
Service occupations	19,204	23,374	24,806	25,951	4,170	5,602	6,747	22	29	35
Cleaning and building service occupations, except										
private household	3,435	3,804	4,068	4,261	369	633	826	11	18	24
Institutional cleaning supervisors	142	166	177	185	24	35	43	17	24	30
Janitors and cleaners, including maids and housekeeping										
cleaners	3,007	3,322	3,562	3,728	326	555	721	11	18	24
Pest controllers and assistants	51	52	55	57	1	4	6	2	8	13
All other cleaning and building service workers	235	254	274	291	19	39	56	8	17	24
Food service preparation and service occupations	7,705	9,582	10,031	10,387	1,877	2,325	2,681	24	30	35
Chiefs, cooks, and other kitchen workers	3,069	3,906	4,104	4,264	837	1,035	1,195	27	34	39
Cooks, except short order	1,170	1,512	1,594	1,661	342	424	491	29	36	42
Bakers, bread and pastry	140	180	192	200	40	52	60	28	37	43
Cooks, institution or cafeteria	415	493	530	563	78	115	149	19	28	36
Cooks, restaurant	615	840	872	898	225	257	283	37	42	46
Cooks, short order and fast food	743	953	989	1,018	209	246	274	28	33	37
Food preparation workers	1,156	1,442	1,521	1,585	286	365	429	25	32	37
Food and beverage service occupations	4,400	5,392	5,623	5,803	992	1,223	1,403	23	28	32
Bartenders	400	404	422	436	3	21	35	1	5	9
Dining room and cafeteria attendants and bar helpers	461	592	619	641	131	158	180	28	34	39
Food counter, fountain, and related workers	1,607	2,067	2,158	2,229	459	550	622	29	34	39
Hosts and hostesses, restaurant, lounge, or coffee shop	184	220	229	235	36	44	51	19	24	28
Waiters and waitresses	1,747	2,110	2,196	2,262	363	449	515	21	26	29
All other food preparation and service workers	236	283	304	319	47	67	83	20	29	35
Health service occupations	1,972	2,636	2,832	3,002	664	860	1,030	34	44	52
Ambulance drivers and attendants, except EMT's	12	14	15	16	1	2	3	11	20	28
Dental assistants	176	220	26	250	44	60	74	25	34	42
Medical assistants	165	268	287	306	102	122	140	62	74	85
Nursing aides and psychiatric aides	1,374	1,824	1,960	2,077	450	587	703	33	43	51
Nursing aides, orderlies, and attendants	1,274	1,700	1,826	1,934	426	552	660	33	43	52
Psychiatric aides	100	124	134	143	24	34	43	24	34	43
Occupational therapy assistants and aides	10	14	15	16	4	5	6	46	57	67
Pharmacy assistants	83	94	101	107	11	18	24	13	22	29
Physical and corrective therapy assistants and aides	45	68	74	78	24	29	33	53	64	74
All other health workers	107	134	144	153	27	37	46	25	35	43
Personal service occupations	2,192	2,983	3,164	3,316	790	972	1,124	36	44	51
Amusement and recreation attendants	184	213	228	241	29	44	57	16	24	31

Source: "Occupational Employment Projections," George Silvestri and John Lukasiewicz, *Monthly Labor Review* 114, No. 11, November, 1991, pp. 68-80.

★ 494 ★

Civilian Employment by Occupation under Low, Medium, and High Scenarios for Economic Growth, 1990-2005 - IV

[Numbers in thousands]

Occupation	Total employment				1990-2005 employment change					
	1990	Projected, 2005			Number			Percent		
		Low	Moderate	High	Low	Moderate	High	Low	Moderate	High
Personal service occupations										
Baggage porters and bellhops	31	39	42	43	8	10	12	25	33	37
Barbers	77	73	76	79	-4	-1	2	-5	-1	2
Child care workers	725	1,027	1,078	1,123	303	353	398	42	49	55
Cosmetologists and related workers	636	751	793	830	115	157	194	18	25	30

[Continued]

★ 494 ★

Civilian Employment by Occupation under Low, Medium, and High Scenarios for Economic Growth, 1990-2005 - IV

[Continued]

| Occupation | Total employment | | | | 1990-2005 employment change | | | | | |
| | 1990 | Projected, 2005 | | | Number | | | Percent | | |
		Low	Moderate	High	Low	Moderate	High	Low	Moderate	High
Hairdressers, hairstylists, and cosmetologists	597	703	742	775	106	145	178	18	24	30
Manicurists	25	33	35	37	8	10	11	30	38	45
Shampooers	14	16	17	18	2	3	4	13	21	29
Flight attendants	101	146	159	168	46	59	67	45	59	67
Homemaker-home health aides	391	682	733	776	291	343	385	75	88	99
Home health aides	287	512	550	582	224	263	295	78	92	103
Personal and home care aides	103	170	183	194	67	79	90	64	77	87
Ushers, lobby attendants, and ticket takers	48	51	55	57	3	6	9	6	13	19
Private household workers	782	514	555	584	-268	-227	-198	-34	-29	-25
Child care workers, private household	314	176	190	200	-138	-124	-114	-44	-40	-36
Cleaners and servants, private household	411	287	310	326	-124	-101	-85	-30	-25	-21
Cooks, private household	12	9	10	11	-3	-2	-1	-22	-16	-12
Housekeepers and butlers	45	42	45	48	-3	0	3	-7	1	6
Protective service occupations	2,266	2,765	2,995	3,185	500	729	920	22	32	41
Firefighting occupations	280	321	348	374	41	68	95	15	24	34
Firefighters	210	241	262	281	31	51	71	15	24	34
Firefighting and prevention supervisors	58	66	72	77	8	14	20	15	24	34
Fire inspection occupations	12	13	15	16	2	3	4	14	24	34
Law enforcement occupations	886	1,093	1,187	1,277	208	302	392	23	34	44
Correction officers	230	342	372	400	112	142	170	49	61	74
Police and detectives	655	751	815	877	96	160	222	15	24	34
Police and detectives supervisor	93	105	113	122	11	20	28	12	21	30
Police detectives and investigators	69	77	83	88	8	14	19	12	20	27
Police patrol officers	384	455	495	533	71	111	149	18	29	39
Sheriffs and deputy sheriffs	72	74	81	87	2	9	15	3	12	21
Other law enforcements occupations	37	40	43	47	3	7	10	9	18	27
Other protective service workers	1,101	1,352	1,460	1,534	251	359	433	23	33	39
Detectives, except public	47	61	66	69	14	19	22	31	41	47
Guards	883	1,094	1,181	1,238	211	298	354	24	34	40
Crossing guards	54	52	57	61	-2	2	7	-4	4	13
All other protective service workers	116	145	157	167	28	40	50	24	34	43
All other service workers	852	1,090	1,161	1,216	238	309	364	28	36	43
Agriculture, forestry, fishing, and related occupations	3,506	3,514	3,665	3,799	7	158	293	0	5	8
Animal caretakers, except farm	106	138	145	151	32	40	45	31	38	43
Farm occupations	901	802	828	853	-99	-73	-48	-11	-8	-5
Farm workers	837	723	745	766	-114	-92	-71	-14	-11	-8
Nursery workers	64	78	83	86	15	19	23	23	30	36
Farm operators and managers	1,223	990	1,023	1,054	-233	-200	-169	-19	-16	-14
Farmers	1,074	822	850	876	-252	-224	-198	-23	-21	-18
Farm managers	149	168	173	177	19	24	28	13	16	19
Fishers, hunters, and trappers	61	66	69	71	5	8	10	8	13	16
Captains and other officers, fishing vessels	8	9	10	10	1	1	2	13	18	21
Fishers, hunters and trappers	53	57	60	61	4	6	8	7	12	15
Forestry and logging occupations	148	144	150	158	-4	1	9	-3	1	6
Forest and conservation workers	40	41	43	45	1	3	5	4	8	13
Timber cutting and logging occupations	108	102	106	113	-6	-2	4	-5	-2	4
Fallers and buckers	36	34	35	37	-2	-1	1	-6	-3	2
Logging tractor operators	29	29	30	32	-0	1	3	-1	3	9
Log handling equipment operators	16	16	17	18	-0	1	2	-0	4	11
All other timber cutting and related logging workers	27	23	24	26	-3	-2	-1	-12	-9	-4
Gardeners and groundskeepers, except farm	874	1,158	1,222	1,275	284	348	401	33	40	46
Supervisors, farming, forestry, and agricultural related occupations	65	69	72	74	4	7	9	6	10	14
All other agricultural, forestry, fishing, and related workers	129	146	156	164	18	27	35	14	21	27
Precision production, craft, and repair occupations	14,124	14,710	15,909	16,698	586	1,785	2,574	4	13	18
Blue-collar worker supervisors	1,792	1,760	1,912	2,003	-32	120	211	-2	7	12
Construction trades	3,763	4,244	4,557	4,818	481	794	1,055	13	21	28
Bricklayers and stone masons	152	169	183	194	18	31	42	12	20	28
Carpenters	1,057	1,134	1,209	1,274	76	152	216	7	14	20
Carpet installers	73	84	88	92	11	15	19	15	21	26
Ceiling tile installers and acoustical carpenters	20	20	22	23	0	2	4	2	11	19
Concrete and terrazzo finishers	113	118	128	137	5	15	24	4	13	21

[Continued]

Civilian Employment by Occupation under Low, Medium, and High Scenarios for Economic Growth, 1990-2005 - IV

[Continued]

Occupation	Total employment				1990-2005 employment change					
	1990	Projected, 2005			Number			Percent		
		Low	Moderate	High	Low	Moderate	High	Low	Moderate	High
Drywall installers and finishers	143	163	175	186	20	33	43	14	23	30
Electricians	548	652	706	748	104	158	200	19	29	36
Glazers	42	47	51	55	5	9	12	13	22	30
Hard tile setters	28	33	35	37	4	7	9	16	24	30
Highway maintenance workers	151	172	188	202	22	37	52	14	24	34
Insulation workers	70	80	87	93	10	17	23	15	24	33
Painters and paperhangers, construction and maintenance	453	533	564	590	80	111	137	18	24	30
Paving, surfacing, and tamping equipment operators	73	87	95	102	14	22	29	19	30	39
Pipelayers and pipelaying fitters	55	67	72	77	11	17	22	20	31	40
Plasters	28	30	32	34	1	4	6	5	13	20
Plumbers, pipefitters, and steamfitters	379	426	459	485	47	80	106	12	21	28
Roofers	138	158	169	179	20	31	41	14	23	30
Structural and reinforcing metal workers	80	87	95	102	8	16	22	10	20	28
All other construction trades workers	160	184	198	209	25	38	49	15	24	31
Extractive and related workers, including blasters	237	223	247	257	-14	9	20	-6	4	8
Oil and gas extraction occupations	80	68	78	80	-12	-2	-0	-15	-2	-1
Roustabouts	38	31	36	37	-6	-1	-1	-17	-4	-2
All other oil and gas extraction occupations	42	37	42	43	-6	-0	0	-14	-1	1
Mining, quarrying, and tunneling occupations	24	19	20	21	-6	-5	-4	-24	-19	-15
All other extraction and related workers	133	137	148	157	4	15	24	3	12	18
Mechanics, installers, and repairers	4,900	5,262	5,669	5,946	362	769	1,046	7	16	21
Communications equipment mechanics, installers, and repairers	125	71	77	81	-54	-48	-44	-43	-38	-35
Central office and PBX installers and repairers	80	43	46	48	-38	-34	-32	-47	-43	-40
Frame wires, central office	11	4	5	5	-7	-7	-7	-63	-60	-58
Radio mechanics	13	12	13	14	-1	-0	1	-9	-1	4
Signal or track switch maintainers	4	2	2	3	-2	-2	-2	-44	-40	-37
All other communications equipment mechanics, installers, and repairers	16	10	11	11	-6	-5	-5	-38	-33	-30
Electrical and electronic equipment mechanics, installers, and repairers	530	502	540	565	-28	10	35	-5	2	7
Data processing equipment repairers	84	123	134	140	40	50	56	48	60	67
Electrical powerline installers and repairers	99	101	108	113	2	9	14	2	9	14
Electronic home entertainment equipment repairers	41	43	46	48	2	5	7	5	13	18
Electronics repairers, commercial and industrial equipment	75	83	88	92	8	13	16	10	17	22
Station installers and repairers, telephone	47	20	21	22	-27	-26	-25	-58	-55	-53
Telephone and cable TV line installers and repairers	133	85	92	98	-48	-40	-35	-36	-30	-26
All other electrical and electronic equipment mechanics, installers, and repairers	52	47	51	53	-5	-1	1	-9	-2	2

Source: "Occupational Employment Projections," George Silvestri and John Lukasiewicz, *Monthly Labor Review* 114, No. 11, November, 1991, pp. 68-80.

★ 495 ★

Civilian Employment by Occupation under Low, Medium, and High Scenarios for Economic Growth, 1990-2005 - V

[Numbers in thousands]

Occupation	Total employment				1990-2005 employment change					
	1990	Projected, 2005			Number			Percent		
		Low	Moderate	High	Low	Moderate	High	Low	Moderate	High
Machinery and related mechanics, installers and repairers	1,675	1,834	1,980	2,074	159	305	400	9	18	24
Industrial machinery mechanics	474	477	520	542	3	46	68	1	10	14
Maintenance repairers, general utility	1,128	1,283	1,379	1,447	154	251	319	14	22	28
Millwrights	73	75	82	86	2	9	13	2	12	18
Vehicle and mobile equipment mechanics and repairers	1,568	1,762	1,892	1,987	194	324	419	12	21	27
Aircraft mechanics and engine specialists	122	140	151	158	18	29	36	15	24	29
Aircraft engine specialists	17	19	21	21	2	4	4	15	22	27

[Continued]

★ 495 ★

Civilian Employment by Occupation under Low, Medium, and High Scenarios for Economic Growth, 1990-2005 - V

[Continued]

Occupation	Total employment				1990-2005 employment change					
	1990	Projected, 2005			Number			Percent		
		Low	Moderate	High	Low	Moderate	High	Low	Moderate	High
Aircraft mechanics	105	121	131	136	16	26	31	15	24	30
Automotive body and related repairers	219	249	267	281	30	48	62	14	22	28
Automotive mechanics	757	861	923	969	104	166	212	14	22	28
Bus and truck mechanics and diesel engine specialists	268	302	326	343	34	58	76	13	22	28
Farm equipment mechanics	48	49	52	55	1	4	7	3	9	14
Mobile heavy equipment mechanics	104	109	117	123	5	13	19	5	13	18
Motorcycle, boat, and small engine mechanics	50	51	55	58	1	5	7	3	10	15
Motorcycle repairers	12	12	13	13	0	1	2	4	11	16
Small engine specialists	39	39	42	44	1	4	6	2	9	14
Other mechanics, installers, and repairers	1,002	1,093	1,180	1,240	91	177	237	9	18	24
Bicycle repairers	15	16	17	18	1	2	2	5	11	16
Camera and photographic equipment repairers	7	8	9	9	1	1	2	10	17	21
Coin and vending machine servicers and repairers	26	24	26	27	-2	-0	1	-8	-1	4
Electric meter installers and repairers	14	15	16	17	1	2	3	11	18	24
Electromedical and biomedical equipment repairers	8	11	12	13	3	4	5	40	51	60
Elevator installers and repairers	19	20	22	23	1	3	5	7	17	24
Heat, air conditioning, and refrigeration mechanics and installers	219	246	266	280	27	46	61	12	21	28
Home appliance and power tool repairers	71	65	70	73	-6	-1	3	-8	-1	4
Musical instrument repairers and tuners	9	8	9	9	-0	0	1	-4	2	7
Office and cash register servicers	73	76	82	86	3	9	14	5	13	19
Precision instrument repairers	50	50	54	56	-0	4	6	-0	8	12
Riggers	14	13	14	15	-1	-0	1	-6	-0	4
Tire repairers and changers	81	88	95	100	7	14	19	9	17	23
Watchmakers	7	4	5	5	-3	-2	-2	-37	-33	-30
All other mechanics, installers, and repairers	390	447	484	508	57	94	118	15	24	30
Production occupations, precision	3,134	2,928	3,208	3,338	-206	74	204	-7	2	7
Assemblers, precision	352	209	236	243	-143	-116	-109	-41	-33	-31
Aircraft assemblers, precision	32	31	34	35	-1	2	3	-3	6	9
Electrical and electronic equipment assemblers, precision	171	78	90	92	-93	-81	-79	-55	-48	-46
Electromechanical equipment assemblers, precision	49	27	31	32	-21	-18	-17	-44	-37	-35
Fitters, structural metal, precision	15	12	13	14	-3	-2	-1	-21	-14	-9
Machine builders and other precision machine assemblers	50	37	42	43	-13	-8	-7	-25	-17	-14
All other precision assemblers	34	23	26	27	-11	-8	-7	-32	-24	-21
Food workers, precision	301	271	286	297	-30	-15	-4	-5	-1	-1
Bakers, manufacturing	34	32	32	33	-2	-1	-0	-6	-4	-1
Butchers and meatcutters	234	207	220	229	-27	-14	-4	-12	-6	-2
All other precision food and tobacco workers	34	33	34	35	-1	0	1	-2	1	3
Inspectors, testers, and graders, precision	668	592	659	683	-77	-9	15	-11	-1	2
Metal workers, precision	936	930	1,021	1,065	-6	85	-129	-1	9	14
Boilermakers	22	21	23	24	-1	1	2	-4	3	9
Jewelers and silversmiths	40	44	48	50	4	8	10	9	20	24
Machinists	386	389	427	444	3	41	58	1	10	15
Sheet metal workers and duct installers	233	242	263	278	9	30	44	4	13	19
Shipfitters	13	12	12	13	-1	-0	-0	-9	-4	-1
Tool and die makers	141	130	145	150	-11	4	9	-7	3	6
All other precision metal workers	101	92	103	106	-9	2	6	-9	2	6
Printing workers, precision	161	181	195	203	20	33	41	12	21	26
Bookbinders	7	8	8	8	0	1	1	5	13	18
Compositors and typesetters, precision	14	13	14	15	-1	-0	0	-8	-2	1
Job printers	15	17	18	19	2	3	4	14	23	28
Paste-up workers	30	32	34	36	2	4	5	5	13	18
Electronic pagination systems workers	12	14	16	16	3	4	5	24	33	39
Photoengravers	8	9	9	10	0	1	1	5	13	17
Camera operators	17	19	20	21	2	4	4	13	21	26
Strippers, printing	32	40	43	44	8	11	13	25	34	40
Platemakers	14	16	17	18	2	3	4	15	23	29
All other printing workers, precision	12	14	15	16	2	3	3	15	23	28
Textile, apparel, and furnishings workers, precision	272	274	302	313	2	29	41	1	11	15
Custom tailors and sewers	116	129	137	143	13	21	27	11	18	23
Patternmakers and layout workers, fabric and apparel	16	12	15	15	-4	-1	-0	-23	-4	-2
Shoe and leather workers and repairers, precision	27	16	22	23	-11	-5	-4	-40	-19	-15

[Continued]

★ 495 ★

Civilian Employment by Occupation under Low, Medium, and High Scenarios for Economic Growth, 1990-2005 - V

[Continued]

Occupation	Total employment				1990-2005 employment change					
	1990	Projected, 2005			Number			Percent		
		Low	Moderate	High	Low	Moderate	High	Low	Moderate	High
Upholsterers	64	65	70	72	1	6	8	1	10	13
All other precision textile, apparel, and furnishings workers	50	52	57	60	2	7	10	5	15	20
Woodworkers, precision	213	223	240	251	10	27	39	5	13	18
Cabinetmakers and bench carpenters	107	114	122	128	7	14	21	6	13	19
Furniture finishers	34	35	38	39	1	4	6	3	12	17
Wood machinists	46	48	51	54	1	5	8	3	12	17
All other precision woodworkers	25	26	29	30	1	3	4	3	13	17
Other precision workers	231	249	270	283	18	39	52	8	17	23
Dental lab technicians, precision	57	56	59	63	-1	3	6	-2	4	10
Optical goods workers, precision	19	22	25	26	3	6	6	14	29	34
Photographic process workers, precision	18	19	21	22	2	3	4	8	16	21
All other precision workers	137	152	165	173	15	28	36	11	21	26
Plant and systems occupations	297	294	317	335	-4	19	37	-1	6	12
Chemical plant and system operators	35	28	30	31	-7	-5	-3	-21	-14	-10
Electric power generating plant operators, distributors, and dispatchers	44	45	48	50	1	4	6	2	9	14
Power distributors and dispatchers	18	18	19	20	-0	1	2	-1	6	11
Power generating and reactor plant operators	26	27	29	31	1	3	4	3	11	17
Gas and petroleum plant system occupations	31	25	27	28	-5	-3	-3	-18	-11	-9
Stationary engineers	35	33	36	37	-2	0	2	-5	1	7
Water and liquid waste treatment plant and system operators	78	93	101	109	15	23	30	19	29	39
All other plant and system operators	74	69	75	79	-5	1	4	-7	1	6
Operators, fabricators, and laborers	17,245	16,448	17,961	18,796	-797	716	1,550	-5	4	9
Machine setters, set-up operators, operators, and tenders	4,905	4,104	4,579	4,754	-800	-326	-151	-16	-7	-3
Numerical control machine tool operators and tenders, metal and plastic	70	78	87	90	7	16	19	11	23	27
Combination machine tool setters, set-up operators, operators, and tenders	93	102	113	118	10	21	25	11	23	27
Machine tool cut and form setters, operators, and tenders, metal and plastic	765	529	585	609	-236	-179	-156	-31	-23	-20
Drilling and boring machine tool setters and set-up operators, metal and plastic	52	35	39	40	-17	-13	-12	-33	-26	-23
Grinding machine setters and set-up operators, metal and plastic	72	49	54	56	-24	-18	-16	-33	-25	-22
Lathe and turning machine tool setters and set-up operators, metal and plastic	80	55	61	63	-26	-20	-17	-32	-24	-22
Machine forming operators and tenders, metal and plastic	174	119	131	137	-55	-43	-37	-32	-25	-21
Machine tool cutting operators and tenders, metal and plastic	145	93	104	107	-52	-42	-38	-36	-29	-26
Punching machine setters and set-up operators, metal and plastic	52	38	42	44	-14	-10	-8	-27	-18	-15
All other machine tool cutting and forming, etc.	189	140	155	161	-49	-34	-28	-26	-18	-15
Metal fabricating machine setters, operators, and related workers	140	136	149	156	-5	9	16	-3	6	11
Metal fabricators, structural metal products	34	35	37	40	1	4	6	2	11	18
Soldering and brazing machine operators and tenders	11	10	11	11	-1	-0	0	-12	-1	2
Welding machine setters, operators, and tenders	95	92	101	105	-4	6	10	-4	6	10
Metal and plastic processing machine setters, operators, and related workers	393	355	396	411	-38	3	18	-10	1	5
Electrolytic plating machine operators and tenders, setters and set-up operators, metal and plastic	43	34	38	39	-10	-6	-4	-22	-13	-10
Foundry mold assembly and shakeout workers	10	6	7	7	-3	-3	-2	-33	-26	-23
Furnace operators and tenders	22	19	27	22	-3	-0	0	-12	-2	2
Heaters, metal and plastic	5	4	5	5	-0	0	0	-9	1	6

Source: "Occupational Employment Projections," George Silvestri and John Lukasiewicz, *Monthly Labor Review* 114, No. 11, November, 1991, pp. 68-80.

★ 496 ★

Civilian Employment by Occupation under Low, Medium, and High Scenarios for Economic Growth, 1990-2005 - VI

[Numbers in thousands]

Occupation	Total employment				1990-2005 employment change					
	1990	Projected, 2005			Number			Percent		
		Low	Moderate	High	Low	Moderate	High	Low	Moderate	High
Heating equipment setters and set-up operator, metal and plastic	7	6	7	7	-1	-0	0	-10	-0	4
Heat treating machine operators and tenders, metal and plastic	21	19	21	22	-2	0	1	-10	0	4
Metal molding machine operators and tenders, setters, and set-up operators	38	28	31	32	-10	-7	-6	-26	-18	-15
Nonelectrolytic plating machine operators and tenders, setters, and set-up operators metal and plastic	7	5	6	6	-2	-1	-1	-22	-15	-11
Plastic molding machine operators and tenders, setters, and set-up operators	143	155	173	180	12	31	37	8	21	26
All other metal and plastic machine setters, operators, and related work	99	79	88	91	-20	-11	-8	-20	-11	-8
Printing, binding, and related workers	393	430	466	484	37	72	90	9	18	23
Bindery machine operators and set-up operators	71	73	79	82	2	8	11	3	11	16
Printing press operators	224	249	268	279	24	44	54	11	19	24
Letterpress operators	16	13	14	15	-3	-2	-1	-16	-10	-6
Offset lithographic press operators	91	113	122	127	22	31	36	25	34	39
Printing press machine setters, operators, and tenders	104	106	15	120	3	12	16	3	11	16
All other printing press setters and set-up operators	14	16	17	17	2	3	3	13	20	25
Photoengraving and lithographing machine operators, and photographers	98	108	119	123	10	21	25	10	21	25
Photoengraving and lithographic machine operators and tenders	6	6	7	7	1	1	1	11	20	25
Screen printing machine setters and set-up operators	26	28	31	32	2	5	6	6	19	22
Typesetting and composing machine operators and tenders	26	30	32	33	4	6	7	14	23	28
All other printing, binding, and related workers	40	44	48	50	4	8	10	11	21	26
Textile and related setters, operators, a nd related workers	1,090	751	912	936	-339	-178	-153	-31	-16	-14
Extruding and forming machine operators and tenders, synthetic or glass fibers	21	18	20	21	-3	-1	0	-12	-3	1
Pressing machine operators and tenders, textile, garment, and related materials	84	85	96	100	0	12	16	0	14	19
Sewing machine operators, garment	585	368	469	478	-217	-116	-106	-37	-20	-18
Sewing machine operators, nongarment	131	121	138	142	-10	7	11	-8	5	8
Textile bleaching and dyeing machine operators and tenders	28	17	20	21	-11	-8	-7	-39	-28	-26
Textile draw-out and winding machine operators and tenders	199	116	138	142	-82	-61	-57	-41	-31	-29
Textile machine setters and set-up operators	42	26	30	31	-16	-11	-10	-38	-27	-25
Woodworking machine setters, operators, and other related workers	136	142	152	160	6	16	24	4	12	17
Head sawyers and sawing machine operators and tenders, setters and set-up operators	72	75	80	85	3	8	13	4	11	17
Woodworking machine operators and tenders, setters, and set-up operators	64	67	72	75	3	8	11	4	12	18
Other machine setters, set-up operators, operators, and tenders	1,825	1,582	1,718	1,790	-243	-106	-35	-13	-6	-2
Boiler operators and tenders, low pressure	21	20	22	23	-2	0	1	-7	0	6
Cement and gluing machine operators and tenders	35	25	28	29	-10	-7	-6	-28	-20	-16
Chemical equipment controllers, operators, and tenders	75	56	61	63	-19	-14	-11	-25	-19	-15
Cooking and roasting machine operators and tenders, food and tobacco	31	26	26	27	-6	-5	-4	-18	-16	-14
Crushing and mixing operators and tenders	135	134	145	151	-1	10	16	-1	7	12
Cutting and slicing machine setters, operators, and tenders	88	81	89	92	-7	1	4	-8	1	5
Dairy processing equipment operators, including setters	18	15	16	16	-3	-2	-2	-15	-13	-11
Electronic semiconductor processors	32	19	22	22	-13	-10	-10	-41	-31	-30
Extruding and forming machine setters, operators, and tenders	94	85	93	97	-9	-1	3	-10	-1	3
Furnace, kiln, or kettle operators and tenders	56	48	53	55	-8	-4	-1	-15	-6	-2
Laundry and drycleaning machine operators and tenders, except pressing	173	198	212	223	26	39	50	15	23	29
Motion picture projectionists	13	11	12	12	-2	-1	-1	-15	-9	-5
Packaging and filling machine operators and tenders	324	278	297	308	-46	-27	-16	-14	-8	-5
Painting and coating machine operators	160	143	158	165	-16	-2	5	-10	-1	3
Coating, painting, and spraying machine. Coating, painting and spraying machine operators, tenders, setters, and set-up operators	117	103	115	119	-14	-3	2	-12	-2	2
Painters, transportation equipment	42	40	43	45	-2	1	3	-4	3	8
Paper goods machine setters and set-up operators	59	53	57	59	-6	-2	1	-10	-3	1
Photographic processing machine operators and tenders	58	64	69	73	6	11	15	11	20	25
Separating and still machine operators and tenders	26	19	21	21	-6	-5	-4	-25	-20	-17

[Continued]

Civilian Employment by Occupation under Low, Medium, and High Scenarios for Economic Growth, 1990-2005 - VI

[Continued]

Occupation	Total employment				1990-2005 employment change					
	1990	Projected, 2005			Number			Percent		
		Low	Moderate	High	Low	Moderate	High	Low	Moderate	High
Shoe sewing machine operators and tenders	18	5	10	10	-13	-8	-8	-71	-46	-43
Tire building machine operators	14	8	9	9	-6	-5	-45	-38	-34	
All other machine operators, tenders, setters, and set-up operators	396	294	320	334	-102	-75	-62	-26	-19	-16
Hand workers, including assemblers and fabricators	2,675	2,100	2,307	2,394	-575	-368	-281	-21	-14	-11
Cannery workers	78	70	73	74	-8	-6	-4	-10	-7	-5
Coil winders, tapers, and finishers	20	11	13	13	-8	-6	-6	-41	-33	-31
Cutters and trimmers, hand	59	48	55	57	-11	-4	-2	-19	-6	-3
Electrical and electronic assemblers	232	112	128	131	-121	-105	-101	-52	-45	-44
Grinders and polishers, hand	84	59	65	67	-25	-19	-16	-30	-23	-20
Machine assemblers	50	40	44	46	-11	-6	-4	-21	-12	-9
Meat, poultry, and fish cutters and trimmers, hand	121	132	136	140	11	15	19	9	12	15
Metal pourers and casters, basic shapes	12	10	11	11	-2	-1	-1	-18	-9	-6
Painting, coating, and decorating workers, hand	46	46	50	52	0	4	6	0	9	14
Portable machine cutters	13	10	12	13	-3	-0	-0	-24	-4	-2
Pressers, hand	17	15	18	19	-2	1	1	-14	4	8
Sewers, hand	16	11	15	15	-5	-1	-1	-28	-7	-5
Solderers and brazers	28	21	24	24	-7	-5	-4	-25	-16	-13
Welders and cutters	332	317	344	360	-15	13	29	-4	4	9
All other assemblers and fabricators	1,192	888	980	1,018	-304	-212	-173	-26	-18	-15
All other hand workers	375	311	339	352	-64	-36	-23	-17	-10	-6
Transportation and material moving machine and vehicle operators	4,730	5,329	5,743	6,043	599	1,013	1,312	13	21	28
Motor vehicle operators	3,417	3,997	4,301	4,522	580	883	1,105	17	26	32
Bus drivers	561	680	738	789	118	177	228	21	32	41
Bus drivers	159	183	198	210	23	39	51	15	24	32
Bus drivers, school	402	497	541	579	95	138	177	24	34	44
Taxi drivers and chauffeurs	108	132	140	146	24	32	38	22	29	35
Truckdrivers	2,701	3,126	3,360	3,522	425	659	821	16	24	30
Driver/sales workers	339	359	381	397	20	42	58	6	12	17
Truckdrivers, light and heavy	2,362	2,767	2,979	3,125	405	617	763	17	26	32
All other motor vehicle operators	47	58	62	65	12	16	18	25	33	40
Rail transportation workers	107	95	102	108	-12	-5	2	-11	-4	2
Locomotive engineers	16	14	15	16	-2	-1	-0	-12	-6	-0
Railroad brake, signal, and switch operators	35	27	29	31	-8	-6	-5	-23	-18	-13
Railroad conductors and yardmasters	28	22	24	25	-6	-4	-3	-20	-14	-9
Rail yard engineers, dinkey operators, and hostlers	8	7	8	8	-1	-0	0	-12	-5	1
Subway and streetcar operators	14	21	23	24	7	9	11	53	66	79
All other rail vehicle operators	6	3	3	4	-2	-2	-2	-42	-38	-35
Water transportation and related workers	140	135	144	153	-5	4	13	-4	3	10
Able seamen, ordinary seamen and marine oilers	22	16	17	18	-6	-5	-4	-28	-24	-18
Captains and pilots, ship	14	13	14	15	-1	0	1	-4	1	9
Mates, ship, boat, and barge	7	6	7	7	-1	-0	0	-9	-4	4
Ship engineers	7	5	5	6	-1	-1	-1	-23	-19	-13
All other transportation and related workers	91	94	102	108	4	11	17	4	12	18
Material moving equipment operators	1,019	1,053	1,142	1,202	34	123	183	3	12	18
Crane and tower operators	51	50	54	57	-1	4	6	-2	7	13
Excavation and loading machine operators	74	77	83	88	2	9	14	3	12	19
Grader, dozer, and scraper operators	93	96	104	110	2	11	17	3	11	18
Hoist and winch operators	11	12	13	13	1	1	2	4	13	19
Industrial truck and tractor operators	431	433	469	492	2	38	60	0	9	14
Operating engineers	157	186	201	214	28	44	57	18	28	36
All other material moving equipment operators	201	200	218	227	-0	17	26	-0	8	13
All other transportation and material moving equipment operators	47	50	54	57	3	7	10	5	14	21

Source: "Occupational Employment Projections," George Silvestri and John Lukasiewicz, *Monthly Labor Review* 114, No. 11, November, 1991, pp. 68-80.

★ 497 ★

Civilian Employment by Occupation under Low, Medium, and High Scenarios for Economic Growth, 1990-2005 - VII

[Numbers in thousands]

Occupation	Total employment				1990-2005 employment change					
	1990	Projected, 2005			Number			Percent		
		Low	Moderate	High	Low	Moderate	High	Low	Moderate	High
Helpers, laborers, and material movers, hand	4,935	4,914	5,332	5,606	-21	396	670	-0	8	14
Freight, stock, and material movers, hand	884	912	990	1,037	28	106	153	3	12	17
Hand packers and packagers	667	685	744	774	18	77	107	3	12	16
Helpers, construction trades	552	583	636	679	32	84	128	6	15	23
Machine feeders and offbearers	255	229	249	260	-26	-6	5	-10	-2	2
Parking lot attendants	50	57	61	64	7	11	15	14	23	29
Refuse collectors	124	120	129	137	-4	5	13	-4	4	10
Service station attendants	246	212	229	240	-34	-17	-6	-14	-7	-2
Vehicle washers and equipment cleaners	240	274	295	310	34	55	70	14	23	29
All other helpers, laborers, and material movers, hand	1,918	1,842	1,999	2,103	-76	80	185	-4	4	10

Source: "Occupational Employment Projections," George Silvestri and John Lukasiewicz, *Monthly Labor Review* 114, No. 11, November, 1991, pp. 68-80.

★ 498 ★

Employment Change Classified by Occupational Employment Change Factors, 1990-2005

Employment in millions.

Factors	Total projected change	Change due to -		Number of occupations
		Industrial related component	Occupational structure	
Total, all factor combinations	24.6	24.6	0.0[1]	507
Increases from both industry and structure change	19.4	14.6	4.9	233
Decreases from both industry and structure change	-1.1	-.5	-.6	50
Increase from industry change and decrease from structure change	6.4	11.1	-4.7	175
Decrease from industry change and increase from structure change	-.1	-.5	.4	49

Source: "Occupational Employment Projections," George Silvestri and John Lukasiewicz, *Monthly Labor Review* 114, No. 11, November, 1991, p. 87. Also in source: a 13-page chart listing employment figures for more than 500 occupations for 1990 and projections to 2005 under low, medium, and high economic growth scenarios. Primary source: Office of Employment Projections, Bureau of Labor Statistics. *Notes:* 1. At the total, all factor combinations level, the net change due to occupational structure is zero because changes to any detailed occupation must be counterbalanced by a change in the opposite direction to one or more different occupations.

★ 499 ★

Distribution of Labor Force by Age, 1975-2005

"By 2005, the baby-boomers will be concentrated in the 45-54 age group, which will increase by 15 million from its level in 1990. The decline in the birth rate in the late 1960s will cause a decline in the 25-34 age group between 1990 and 2005. The children of the baby-boom generation will be entering the labor force from 1990 to 2005. As a result, the 16-24 year age group will increase ... (as early as) the mid-1990s."

[Numbers in millions]

Age group	1975	1990	2005	Percent change	
				1975-90	1990-2005
Total, all ages	94	125	151	33.0	21.0
16-24 years	23	21	24	-6.0	16.0
25-34 years	23	36	32	57.0	-12.0
35-44 years	17	32	37	88.0	16.0
45-54 years	17	20	36	20.0	75.0
55 and older	14	15	22	8.0	44.0

Source: "Outlook 1990-2005," *Occupational Outlook Quarterly* 35, No. 3, Fall, 1991, p. 11.

★ 500 ★

Percent Distribution of Labor Force by Age, 1975-2005

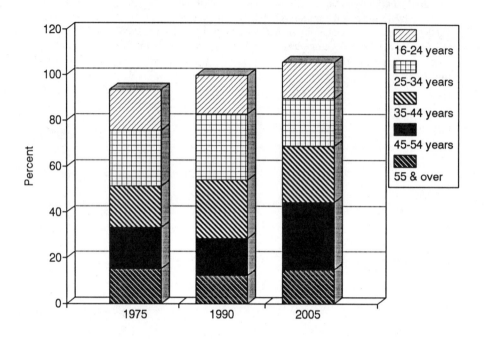

"The changing age of the baby-boom generation over time will continue to have a major impact on the age distribution of the labor force."

[Numbers in percent]

	1975	1990	2005
16-24 years	18.0	17.0	16.0
25-34 years	24.4	28.8	21.0
35-44 years	18.0	25.5	24.5
45-54 years	18.2	16.4	29.8
55 and over	15.3	12.3	14.7

Source: "Outlook 1990-2005," *Occupational Outlook Quarterly* 35, No. 3, Fall, 1991, p. 11.

★ 501 ★

Percent Change in Age of Labor Force, 1970-2000

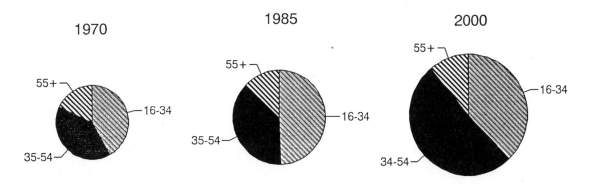

"The age of the labor force will closely track the population, rising from a median of 35 years in 1984 to about 39 in 2000. All of the gains will come in the middle years of worklife, while the numbers at the two extremes decline. The number of workers age 35-54 will rise by more than 25 million, approximately equal to the total increase in the workforce."

Age	1970	1985	2000
Total	82,900,000	115,460,000	140,460,000
Percent of total			
16-34	42.0	50.0	38.0
35-54	40.0	38.0	51.0
55+	18.0	13.0	11.0

Source: Workforce 2000: Work and Workers for the Twenty-First Century, Hudson Institute, Indianapolis, Indiana, 1987, p. 81.

★ 502 ★

Change in Age of Labor through 2010

The rapid growth of the U.S. labor force has been pushed by the baby boomers who have now matured into working-age adults. Between 1990 and 2000, the number of people between 35 and 44 will jump by 16%, and those between the ages of 45 and 54 will increase by 46%, compared with an overall expected population growth of 7.1%.

Source: "Future Work," Joseph F. Coates, Jennifer Jarratt, and John B. Mahaffie, *The Futurist* 25, No. 3, May-June, 1991 p. 10.

★ 503 ★

Occupational Employment and Selected Employment Characteristics, 1986-2000 - I

[Numbers in thousands]

Matrix occupation	Employment		Employment change 1986-2000[1]		Worker characteristics (Percent of employees)						
					Separation rate (Annual)	Part-time	Age		55 and over	Female	Black
	1986	2000	Number	Percent			16-24	25-54			
Managerial and Management Related Occupations											
Managerial and administrative occupations											
Education administrators	288	325	37	12.9	6.9	7.3	3.6	80.2	16.2	47.7	8.9
Financial managers	638	792	154	24.1	8.2	1.9	4.8	84.0	11.1	38.4	3.0
Food service and lodging managers	509	663	154	30.4							
General managers and top executives	2,383	2,965	582	24.4							
Marketing, advertising, and public relations managers	323	427	105	32.5	10.7	2.0	5.3	84.1	10.6	24.9	2.5
Personnel, training, and labor relations managers	151	194	43	28.3	9.5	1.9	4.7	82.5	12.7	48.8	5.5
Postmasters and mail superintendents	28	30	2	8.3	3.2						
Property and real estate managers and administrators	128	178	50	38.8	15.8	16.4	7.3	67.3	25.4	44.2	5.2
Public administration chief executives, legislative, and general administration	66	75	9	13.7							
Purchasing managers	230	260	30	13.1	6.3	1.2	4.2	82.6	13.2	29.4	4.1
All other managers and administrators	2,627	3,532	905	34.5							
Management support occupations											
Accountants and auditors	945	1,322	376	39.8	12.1	5.5	12.4	76.5	11.1	44.9	5.6
Claims examiners, property and casualty insurance	34	45	11	33.3							
Inspectors and compliance officers, except construction	125	142	17	13.3	12.7	3.4	4.0	77.9	18.2	20.5	13.6
Construction and building inspectors	50	55	5	10.8	15.6	5.0	6.9	72.2	21.0	5.0	4.5
Cost estimators	157	188	31	19.6							
Employment interviewers, personnel and labor relations specialists	305	407	102	33.5	11.6	6.6	6.9	81.5	11.6	55.2	11.9
Employment interviewers, private or public employment service	75	129	54	71.2							
Personnel, training, and labor relations specialists	230	278	49	21.1							
Loan officers and counselors	98	131	33	34.2							
Management analysts	126	165	40	31.5	16.5	15.9	5.0	72.2	22.8	30.9	5.9
Purchasing agents, except wholesale, retail, and farm products	188	193	5	2.8	20.0	2.8	8.3	78.5	13.3	39.9	4.6
Tax examiners, collectors, and revenue agents	57	67	10	17.1							
Underwriters	99	134	34	34.2	12.3	.9	9.4	84.5	6.1	47.3	6.0
Wholesale and retail buyers, except farm products	192	209	17	8.7	17.6	8.0	10.1	77.2	12.7	50.2	3.2
All other management support workers	837	1,117	280	33.4							
Professional specialty occupations											
Engineers, architects, and surveyors											
Aeronautical and astronautical engineers	53	58	6	11.1	4.6	0.6	6.2	73.9	19.9	7.1	4.0
Chemical engineers	52	60	8	15.5	11.8	2.1	9.3	76.0	14.7	8.1	.7
Civil engineers, including traffic engineers	199	249	50	25.2	6.6	2.2	4.8	79.3	16.0	2.7	4.3
Electrical and electronics engineers	401	592	192	47.8	7.1	1.2	9.3	79.4	11.3	6.9	4.2
Industrial engineers, except safety engineers	117	152	35	29.7	11.5	1.3	6.0	78.7	15.2	10.9	4.1
Mechanical engineers	233	309	76	32.7	4.6	1.3	6.8	78.1	15.1	3.5	3.6
Metallurgists and metal, ceramic, and material engineers	18	22	5	25.4							
Mining engineers, including mine safety engineers	5	5	0	.2							
Nuclear engineers	14	14	0	0.7							
Petroleum engineers	22	23	2	7.9							
All other engineers	257	328	71	27.6							
Architects, except landscape and marine	84	108	25	29.8	3.0	3.3	7.6	77.2	15.1	9.7	3.2
Landscape architects	18	25	7	38.2							
Surveyors	94	113	19	20.1	5.2	4.1	18.4	75.1	6.6	8.6	3.7
Natural, computer, and mathematical scientists											
Computer systems analysts, electronic data processing	331	582	251	75.6	8.2	4.4	9.6	86.7	3.7	34.4	6.6
Life scientists											
Agricultural and food scientists	28	35	6	22.0							
Biological scientists	61	75	14	22.7	.7	6.8	5.6	87.4	7.0	37.6	1.4
Foresters and conservation scientists	24	26	2	9.7							
Life scientists											
All other life scientists	27	34	7	27.2							
Mathematical scientists, actuaries and statisticians											
Actuaries	9	14	5	48.4							
Statisticians	18	22	4	24.2							
Mathematicians and all other mathematical scientists	20	25	5	23.9							
Operations and systems researchers	38	59	21	54.1	10.6	2.4	5.3	87.5	7.2	39.4	7.6
Physical scientists											
Chemists	86	96	10	11.4	10.5	2.2	6.8	80.0	13.2	22.8	3.6
Geologists, geophysicists, and oceanographers	44	50	6	13.2	12.3	5.8	7.6	79.6	12.8	14.0	1.2
Meteorologists	6	7	2	28.7							
Physicists and astronomers	22	26	4	16.8							
All other physical scientists	22	26	3	14.9							

[Continued]

★ 503 ★

Occupational Employment and Selected Employment Characteristics, 1986-2000 - I

[Continued]

Matrix occupation	Employment 1986	Employment 2000	Employment change 1986-2000[1] Number	Percent	Worker characteristics (Percent of employees) Separation rate (Annual)	Part-time	Age 16-24	25-54	55 and over	Female	Black
Social scientists											
Economists	37	50	13	34.1	16.0	7.1	9.6	81.6	8.8	39.3	3.0
Psychologists	110	148	37	34.0	5.0	23.5	3.1	83.5	13.3	52.5	6.8
Urban and regional planners	20	24	4	19.4							
All other social scientists	31	36	5	16.6							
Social, recreational, and religious workers											
Clergy	295	304	9	3.2	6.6	7.8	2.2	69.9	27.9	7.2	5.5
Directors, religious activities and education	46	45	-1	-2.9							
Recreation workers	164	196	33	20.0	24.8	23.7	36.6	53.8	9.6	68.3	15.6
Social service technicians	88	122	34	38.1							
Social workers	365	485	120	32.7	10.1	9.8	7.1	83.5	9.4	65.0	17.8
Lawyers and judicial workers											
Judges, magistrates, and other judicial workers	38	47	9	23.3							
Lawyers	527	718	191	36.3	5.7	6.3	2.0	83.7	14.3	18.0	2.9
Teachers, librarians, and counselors											
Teachers, preschool, kindergarten and elementary	1,702	2,066	363	21.3	12.4	14.7	6.6	84.8	8.6	87.9	11.4
Teachers preschool	176	240	64	36.3							
Teachers, kindergarten and elementary	1,527	1,826	299	19.6							
Teachers, secondary school	1,128	1,280	152	13.4	9.1	9.5	3.7	85.5	10.7	54.9	7.8
College and university faculty	754	722	-32	-4.2							
Farm and home management advisors	22	21	-2	-7.0							
Adult and vocational education teachers											
Instructors, adult (nonvocational) education	202	241	39	19.3							
Teachers and instructors, vocational education and training	225	268	43	19.0							
All other teachers and instructors	647	810	163	25.2							
Curators, archivists, museum technicians, and restorers	8	10	2	22.3							
Librarians, professional	136	155	18	13.5	13.2	25.2	8.1	71.4	20.5	85.9	7.5
Counselors	123	148	25	20.6	11.1	12.0	6.4	80.9	12.6	53.9	12.9
Health and treating occupations											
Dentists	151	196	45	29.6	.4	17.1	.5	72.4	27.0	4.4	5.5
Dietitians and nutritionists	40	54	14	33.8							
Optometrists	37	55	18	49.2							
Pharmacists	151	187	36	24.2	7.4	13.9	5.7	79.0	15.3	31.4	4.0
Podiatrists	13	23	10	77.2							
Physician assistants	26	41	15	56.7							
Physicians and surgeons	491	679	188	38.2	3.8	4.6	.8	82.0	17.1	17.6	3.3
Registered nurses	1,406	2,018	612	43.6	7.6	25.5	6.8	83.2	10.0	94.3	6.7
Therapists											
Occupational therapists	29	45	15	52.2							
Physical therapists	61	115	53	87.4	4.9	19.8	11.4	84.4	4.2	71.8	4.1
Recreational therapists	29	43	14	48.8							
Respiratory therapists	56	76	19	34.2	5.6	14.5	8.1	90.8	1.1	59.9	13.8
Speech pathologists and audiologists	45	61	15	34.2	8.5	26.9	5.9	91.8	2.3	90.8	3.9
All other therapists	19	28	8	42.9							
Veterinarians and veterinary inspectors	37	54	17	45.6							
Writers, artists, and entertainers											
Artists and commercial artists	176	235	59	33.6	18.4	23.5	9.7	76.4	13.9	51.0	6.3
Dancers and choreographers	14	18	4	30.6							
Designers	259	343	84	32.4	13.0	17.5	12.1	77.0	10.9	49.7	3.8
Musicians	189	231	42	22.5	24.8	55.8	15.7	69.6	32.0	8.3	
Camera operators, television and motion picture	9	12	3	37.9							
Photographers	100	133	33	33.1	11.0	20.2	19.3	67.5	13.1	31.9	5.7
Producers, directors, actors, and entertainers	73	97	24	33.7	22.1	17.6	13.6	80.0	6.4	38.9	5.5
Public relations specialists and publicity writers	87	122	35	39.5	27.4	13.2	11.0	76.1	12.8	51.7	6.9
Radio and TV announcers and newscasters	61	76	15	23.9	37.7	35.4	34.6	61.9	3.5	20.0	8.3
Reporters, writers and editors[2]	288	374	86	29.9	14.6	20.2	11.0	74.0	15.0	49.6	3.6
Reporters and correspondents	75	88	13	17.8							
Writers and editors, including technical writers	214	287	73	34.1							
Technician Occupations											
Health technicians and technologists											
Dental hygienists	87	141	54	62.6	1.8	47.1	20.7	78.2	1.2	99.5	.5
Dietetic technicians	17	22	5	27.8							
Electrocardiographic technicians/technologists	18	21	3	15.6							
Electroencephalograph technicians	6	8	2	41.7							
Emergency medical technicians	65	75	10	15.0							
Licensed practical nurses	631	869	238	37.7	8.7	25.6	7.7	82.1	10.1	97.5	17.2
Medical and clinical lab technologists and technicians	239	296	57	23.8	8.3	16.6	12.8	81.9	5.3	76.5	10.8
Medical records technicians	40	70	30	75.0	12.8	13.6	18.5	66.9	14.6	93.3	16.0

[Continued]

★ 503 ★

Occupational Employment and Selected Employment Characteristics, 1986-2000 - I

[Continued]

Matrix occupation	Employment		Employment change 1986-2000[1]		Worker characteristics (Percent of employees)						
					Separation rate (Annual)	Part-time	Age		55 and over	Female	Black
	1986	2000	Number	Percent			16-24	25-54			
Nuclear medicine and radiologic technologists and technicians[2]	125	202	77	61.5	4.0	13.5	13.6	80.7	5.7	67.1	9.0
Nuclear medicine technologists	10	12	2	23.0							
Radiologic technologists and technicians	115	190	75	64.7							
Opticians, dispensing and measuring	50	72	23	46.0	23.4	12.2	26.9	64.8	8.3	55.9	3.5
Surgical technicians	37	49	12	33.1							
All other health professionals and paraprofessionals	283	435	152	53.8							
Engineering and science technologists											
Electrical and electronic technicians and technologists	313	459	145	46.4	10.5	3.1	15.9	76.1	8.0	12.6	7.0
Engineering technicians and technologists, except electrical and electronic	376	475	99	26.4							
Drafters	348	354	5	1.6	12.3	7.3	20.4	67.5	12.2	19.4	4.3
Physical and life science technicians and technologists, and mathematical technicians	227	262	35	15.4	16.2	9.8	18.1	73.2	8.7	27.9	7.0
Technicians, except health and engineering and science											
Air traffic controllers	26	28	2	8.1							
Broadcast technicians	27	33	5	19.8							
Computer programmers	479	813	335	69.9	11.4	6.7	20.9	76.4	2.7	34.0	5.9
Legal assistants and technicians, except clerical	170	272	102	60.0							
Paralegal personnel	61	125	64	103.7							
Title examiners and searchers	30	36	6	21.7							
All other legal assistants, including law clerks	79	111	32	40.5							
Programmers, numerical, tool, and process control	9	10	1	14.6							
Technical assistants, library	51	57	7	12.9							
All other technicians	26	29	2	9.0							
All other professionals, paraprofessionals, and technicians	714	842	128	17.9							
Marketing and sales occupations											
Cashiers	2,165	2,740	575	26.5	36.1	53.2	52.2	40.6	7.2	82.9	12.3
Counter and rental clerks	178	238	60	33.6	17.8	40.8	38.5	46.6	15.0	72.5	8.5
Insurance sales workers	463	565	102	22.1	11.3	8.0	7.9	76.5	15.6	28.7	5.8
Real estate sales occupations[2]	412	593	181	43.8	14.8	16.0	4.3	72.1	23.7	50.6	2.1
Brokers, real estate	63	91	28	44.8							
Sales agents, real estate	313	451	138	43.9							
Real estate appraisers	36	51	15	41.4							
Salespersons, retail	3,579	4,780	1,201	33.5	30.5	41.9	34.8	48.8	16.4	61.1	5.4
Travel agents	105	154	49	46.4							
Securities and financial services sales workers	197	279	82	41.6	7.0	6.6	9.3	79.0	11.6	24.5	3.1
Stock clerks, sales floor	1,087	1,312	225	20.6							
All other sales and related workers	4,419	5,673	1,255	28.4							
Administrative support occupations, including clerical											
Adjusters, investigators, and collectors											
Adjustment clerks, credit authorizers and clerks[2]	355	434	79	22.2	18.9	9.5	20.6	71.7	7.7	74.4	9.9
Adjustment clerks	136	165	29	21.1							
Credit authorizers	19	17	-1	-7.7							
Credit checkers	41	45	4	9.8							
Loan and credit clerks	159	207	47	29.8							
Bill and account collectors	126	167	42	33.2	22.3	12.0	16.3	71.5	12.2	67.2	7.8
Insurance claims and policy processing occupations	355	385	30	8.5	6.9	3.7	17.7	72.0	10.3	66.6	12.5
Insurance adjusters, examiners, and investigators	119	154	36	30.2							
Insurance claims clerks	85	88	3	3.6							
Insurance policy processing clerks	151	142	-9	-5.7							
Welfare eligibility workers and interviewers	86	100	14	16.2	15.7	11.7	8.7	79.4	11.9	90.4	18.1
All other adjusters and investigators	60	77	18	29.5							
Communications equipment operators											
Telephone operators	353	391	38	10.7	13.2	14.9	18.8	66.4	14.9	87.9	17.4
Central office operators	42	34	-8	-17.9							
Directory assistance operators	32	27	-6	-17.7							
Switchboard operators	279	330	51	18.3							
All other communications equipment operators	12	13	1	9.5							
Computer operators and peripheral equipment operators	309	457	148	47.7	15.4	11.8	26.8	67.1	6.1	68.5	14.0
Computer operators, except peripheral equipment	263	387	124	47.2							
Peripheral EDP equipment operators	46	70	24	50.8							
Duplicating, mail, and other office machine operators	166	178	12	7.0	18.5	19.4	27.3	62.7	10.1	61.8	16.9
Financial records processing occupations											
Billing, cost, and rate clerks	307	313	5	1.7	15.1	13.0	21.0	68.2	10.8	84.3	11.5
Billing, posting, and calculating machine operators	105	114	9	8.8	22.2	30.3	31.4	61.7	6.9	86.7	9.2
Bookkeeping, accounting, and auditing clerks	2,116	2,208	92	4.3	18.4	25.8	13.4	68.3	18.3	91.8	4.1
Payroll and timekeeping clerks	204	180	-25	-12.0	12.6	12.6	12.2	69.2	18.5	89.0	10.5
General office clerks	2,361	2,824	462	19.6	24.4	23.0	24.4	61.1	14.4	80.5	13.0
Information clerks											
Hotel desk clerks	109	156	47	42.6	32.0	19.3	36.6	52.6	10.8	72.1	9.2

[Continued]

★ 503 ★

Occupational Employment and Selected Employment Characteristics, 1986-2000 - I
[Continued]

Matrix occupation	Employment		Employment change 1986-2000[1]		Worker characteristics (Percent of employees)						
					Separation rate (Annual)	Part-time	Age			Female	Black
	1986	2000	Number	Percent			16-24	25-54	55 and over		
Interviewing clerks, except personnel and social welfare	104	150	46	44.7	24.2	25.5	23.9	64.8	11.3	85.8	9.3
New accounts clerks, banking	94	117	23	24.3							
Receptionists and information clerks	682	964	282	41.4	28.1	35.6	31.9	55.5	12.6	94.4	8.0
Reservation and transportation ticket agents and travel clerks	122	146	24	20.1	16.0	10.9	18.1	74.5	7.4	68.3	9.4
Mail and message distribution workers											
Mail clerks, except postal service	136	145	9	6.3	31.6	22.6	32.7	54.3	13.0	48.9	18.4
Messengers	101	123	22	22.3	31.3	34.5	35.6	48.7	15.8	26.8	17.8
Postal mail carriers	269	291	22	8.3	8.0	5.6	6.4	77.7	15.9	20.6	12.9
Postal service clerks	370	388	18	4.7	6.9	8.4	7.3	80.5	12.2	43.5	29.8
Material records, scheduling, dispatching, and distribution occupations											
Dispatchers	185	215	30	16.2	11.7	6.8	18.1	70.0	11.9	50.7	7.7
Dispatchers, except police, fire, and ambulance	124	146	22	17.7							
Dispatchers, police, fire, and ambulance	61	69	8	13.0							
Meter readers, utilities	48	43	-5	-9.5	27.7	5.7	20.6	69.9	9.5	9.7	15.3
Order fillers, procurement and stock clerks[2]	961	946	-15	-1.6	20.8	14.5	22.8	65.9	11.3	39.9	14.2
Order fillers, wholesale and retail sales	195	208	13	6.6							
Procurement clerks	41	35	-5	-12.8							
Stock clerks, stockroom, warehouse, or yard	726	703	-23	-3.1							
Production, planning, and expediting clerks	213	228	15	7.3	16.1	10.3	13.2	75.0	11.7	51.5	8.4
Traffic, shipping, and receiving clerks	548	585	38	6.8	23.5	8.5	23.6	66.1	10.3	26.1	11.7
Weighers, measurers, checkers, and samplers, recordkeeping	40	39	0	-1.1	14.6	16.8	21.2	63.8	15.0	45.2	14.2
All other material recorders, schedulers, and distribution workers	179	207	28	15.5							
Records processing occupations, except financial											
Advertising clerks	13	18	4	32.4							
Brokerage and statement clerks	102	132	30	29.7	19.4	11.7	19.9	64.2	16.0	81.5	11.9
Brokerage clerks	58	75	16	28.0							
Statement clerks	43	57	14	32.0							
File clerks	242	274	32	13.3	28.5	31.0	40.4	47.5	12.1	84.5	17.6
Library assistants and bookmobile drivers	102	114	12	11.8	27.4	59.4	43.4	43.5	13.2	76.0	13.1
Order clerks[2]	373	376	3	.7	12.8	10.5	15.3	75.7	9.0	76.0	12.3
Order clerks, materials, merchandising, and service	271	277	6	2.0							
Customer service representative, utilities	102	99	-3	-2.8							
Personnel clerks, except payroll and timekeeping	119	126	7	5.5	17.7	10.0	14.3	68.9	16.8	92.5	12.6
Secretaries, stenographers, and typists											
Secretaries	3,234	3,658	424	13.1	14.6	16.9	18.5	69.9	11.6	99.0	6.9
Stenographers	178	128	-50	-28.2	5.1	14.1	9.8	67.2	23.0	89.8	6.8
Typists and word processors	1,002	862	-140	-13.9	20.7	23.7	25.6	64.4	10.0	95.2	16.3
Other clerical and administrative support workers											
Bank tellers	539	610	71	13.2	24.4	22.6	35.4	59.1	5.5	91.8	7.8
Court clerks	40	51	10	25.7							
Data entry keyers[2]	429	378	-51	-11.9	21.7	13.1	25.5	68.1	6.4	91.1	19.6
Data entry keyers, except composing	400	334	-66	-16.4							
Data entry keyers, composing	29	43	15	50.8							
First line supervisors and managers	956	1,161	205	21.4	11.6	2.6	6.3	80.3	13.3	59.3	10.8
Municipal clerks	18	20	2	12.8							
Real estate clerks	26	36	10	39.3							
Statistical clerks	71	52	-19	-26.4	15.7	14.8	15.5	68.1	16.4	77.3	13.5
Teacher aides and educational assistants	648	773	125	19.3	22.4	48.4	12.9	75.2	11.9	94.2	17.9
All other clerical and administrative support workers	684	757	73	10.7							
Service occupations											
Cleaning and building service occupations, except private household											
Housekeepers, institutional	123	165	42	34.0							
Janitors and cleaners, including maids/housekeeping cleaners	2,676	3,280	604	22.6	24.5	32.0	20.3	58.7	21.0	42.7	24.4
Pest controllers and assistants	50	58	8	16.1	35.0	6.6	20.8	66.1	13.0	2.7	4.4
All other cleaning and building service workers	258	316	58	22.5							
Food preparation and service occupations											
Cooks, except for short order	1,023	1,378	355	34.7	27.8	38.8	39.7	47.6	12.7	50.6	17.2
Bakers, bread and pastry	114	162	48	42.0							
Cooks, institution or cafeteria	389	457	68	17.3							
Cooks, restaurant	520	759	240	46.2							
Cooks, short order and fast food	591	775	184	31.2	38.0	60.4	63.9	32.2	3.9	36.8	22.6
Food preparation workers	949	1,273	324	34.1	35.3	51.9	43.6	46.1	10.3	76.3	18.2
Bartenders	396	553	157	39.8	25.5	30.5	22.2	69.5	8.3	48.8	3.1
Dining room and cafeteria attendants and barroom helpers	433	631	197	45.6	47.0	65.6	68.9	24.5	6.6	39.2	15.1
Food counter, fountain, and related workers	1,500	1,949	449	29.9	46.7	74.4	80.7	16.5	2.8	78.5	12.6
Hosts and hostesses, restaurant/lounge/coffee shop	172	245	73	42.3							
Waiters and waitresses	1,702	2,454	752	44.2	34.0	52.4	46.0	48.7	5.3	85.1	5.1
All other food preparation and service workers	337	446	109	32.3							

[Continued]

★ 503 ★

Occupational Employment and Selected Employment Characteristics, 1986-2000 - I
[Continued]

Matrix occupation	Employment		Employment change 1986-2000[1]		Worker characteristics (Percent of employees)						
	1986	2000	Number	Percent	Separation rate (Annual)	Part-time	Age 16-24	Age 25-54	55 and over	Female	Black
Health service occupations											
Ambulance drivers and attendants, except EMTs	15	17	2	10.5							
Dental assistants	155	244	88	57.0	17.4	30.4	35.0	62.2	2.8	99.0	4.2
Medical assistants	132	251	119	90.4							
Nursing aides and psychiatric aides	1,312	1,750	437	33.3	23.0	26.3	19.3	66.8	13.9	90.5	29.5
Nursing aides, orderlies, and attendants	1,224	1,658	433	35.4							
Psychiatric aides	88	92	4	4.6							
Occupational therapy assistants and aides	9	13	4	48.5							
Pharmacy assistants	64	79	15	24.2							
Physical and corrective therapy assistants and aides	36	65	29	81.6							
All other health service workers	96	131	35	35.9							
Personal service occupations											
Amusement and recreation attendants	184	239	55	30.0	43.1	43.5	46.4	44.6	9.0	43.1	8.3
Baggage porters and bellhops	31	41	10	32.1							
Barbers	80	81	1	.9	7.9	21.1	6.0	60.5	33.5	16.6	9.6
Child care workers	589	708	118	20.1	35.2	40.8	19.4	68.0	12.6	96.5	11.4
Cosmetologists and related workers	595	702	107	18.0	11.3	33.8	21.7	68.1	10.3	88.8	7.3
Hairdressers, hairstylists, and cosmetologists	562	662	99	17.7							
Manicurists	21	27	6	29.2							
Shampooers	12	14	2	12.7							
Flight attendants	80	105	26	32.0	14.5	36.4	12.3	85.5	2.2	77.1	7.3
Social welfare service and home health aides											
Home health aides	138	249	111	80.1							
Social welfare service aides	59	88	29	48.8	24.5	52.3	12.1	60.1	27.8	91.7	22.5
Ushers, lobby attendants, and ticket takers	42	46	4	9.2							
Private household workers											
Cooks, private household	16	16	0	2.2							
Housekeepers and butlers	34	35	1	2.2							
Child care workers, private household	400	362	-38	-9.6	51.5	60.9	59.2	30.3	10.5	97.4	8.3
Cleaners and servants, private household	531	543	12	2.2	32.8	67.5	11.5	57.6	31.0	95.3	35.3
Protective service occupations											
Correction officers and jailers	176	236	60	34.2	9.1	1.3	12.1	78.9	9.0	18.7	22.4
Firefighting occupations											
Fire fighters	223	260	37	16.8	4.8	1.6	8.8	86.2	5.0	1.9	7.8
Fire fighting and prevention supervisors	45	52	8	16.8							
Fire inspection occupations	11	13	2	16.0							
Police and detectives											
Police and detective supervisors	84	100	17	19.7	2.9	.5	.4	93.0	6.6	4.8	7.1
Police detectives and patrol officers [2]	405	476	70	17.3	7.9	1.6	7.0	89.5	3.5	7.0	11.7
Police detectives and investigators	57	67	10	17.2							
Police patrol officers	349	409	61	17.4							
Crossing guards	52	56	4	7.7	20.5	90.9	2.6	49.9	47.5	76.5	17.5
Guards	794	1,177	383	48.3	26.5	18.5	19.8	56.1	24.1	12.5	20.1
All other protective service workers	266	330	64	24.1							
All other service workers	671	929	258	38.5							
Farming, forestry, fishing, and related occupations											
Animal caretakers, except farm	80	104	24	30.2	35.3	35.2	35.6	54.3	10.1	65.9	5.0
Gardeners and groundskeepers, except farm	767	1,005	238	31.1	29.4	36.0	36.6	47.8	15.6	5.2	12.1
Supervisors, farming, forestry, and agriculture related occupations	65	62	-3	-4.2	24.3	8.3	20.9	66.0	13.1	7.4	6.5
Farm occupations											
Farm workers	940	750	-190	-20.3	27.4	24.7	35.5	51.1	13.4	23.6	8.6
Nursery workers	46	57	11	23.8							
Farm operators and managers											
Farmers	1,182	850	-332	-28.1	13.3	14.4	4.4	55.9	39.7	14.1	1.5
Farm managers	154	201	47	30.8	15.2	8.2	11.1	67.0	21.8	13.8	1.2
Fishers, hunters, trappers, and fishing vessel officers											
Captains and other officers, fishing vessels	12	16	4	34.3							
Fishers, hunters, and trappers	65	81	16	24.2	18.0	16.1	20.0	68.2	11.9	10.5	.0
Forestry and logging occupations											
Forest and conservation workers	36	42	5	14.7							
Timber cutting and logging occupations except logging tractor operators[2]	74	68	-6	-8.6	17.2	16.3	21.8	67.7	10.5	1.3	18.0
Fallers and buckers	36	32	-4	-11.4							
Log hauling equipment operators	16	15	-1	-4.8							
All other timber cutters and related logging workers	23	21	-2	-7.0							
All other agriculture, forestry, fishery, and related workers	106	129	23	21.9							
Precision production, craft, and repair occupations											
Blue collar worker supervisors	1,823	1,967	144	7.9	12.1	1.9	5.8	79.7	14.6	10.3	6.6

[Continued]

★ 503 ★

Occupational Employment and Selected Employment Characteristics, 1986-2000 - I
[Continued]

Matrix occupation	Employment		Employment change 1986-2000[1]		Worker characteristics (Percent of employees)						
					Separation rate (Annual)	Part-time	Age		55 and over	Female	Black
	1986	2000	Number	Percent			16-24	25-54			
Construction trades											
Bricklayers and stone masons	161	187	26	16.3	15.1	7.1	16.2	70.8	13.1	.2	15.3
Carpenters	1,010	1,192	182	18.1	20.4	8.2	20.9	68.5	10.5	1.4	5.3

Source: "Selected Occupational Data, 1986 and Projected 2000," *Occupational Projections and Training Data: A Statistical and Research Supplement to the 1988-89 Occupational Outlook Handbook,* U.S. Department of Labor, 1988, pp. 21-64. Source also contains data on industry distribution of employees. *Notes:* 1. Calculated on unrounded data. 2. This title does not appear in the National Industry-Occupation Matrix, but was formed by combining several matrix occupations in order to achieve CPS comparability. The matrix occupations used in the combination appear as a subgroup of this title.

★ 504 ★

Occupational Employment and Selected Employment Characteristics, 1986-2000 - II
[Numbers in thousands]

Matrix occupation	Employment		Employment change 1986-2000[1]		Worker characteristics (Percent of employees)						
					Separation rate (annual)	Part-time	Age		55 and over	Female	Black
	1986	2000	Number	Percent			16-24	25-54			
Precision production, craft, and repair occupations											
Construction trades											
Carpent installers	66	83	17	25.9	13.5	10.9	24.5	69.0	6.5	.9	8.4
Ceiling tile installers and acoustical carpenters	24	29	6	24.1							
Concrete and terrazzo finishers	118	142	24	20.5	22.5	8.5	19.6	73.6	6.8	.9	31.3
Drywall installers and finishers	154	191	37	23.9	19.4	8.4	24.5	72.1	3.4	2.4	5.4
Electricians	556	644	89	15.9	11.9	3.3	14.7	74.5	10.8	1.3	6.2
Glaziers	47	56	9	19.4	20.8	4.1	16.6	73.9	9.6	3.3	3.3
Hard tile setters	32	39	8	24.8	10.3	7.3	19.8	71.3	8.8	.6	2.9
Highway maintenance workers	167	188	22	12.9							
Insulation workers	62	75	13	21.7	33.0	3.2	34.0	58.8	7.3	2.2	10.3
Painters and paperhangers, construction and maintenance	412	502	90	21.9	25.5	19.4	22.6	67.4	10.0	7.0	8.8
Paving, surfacing, and tamping equipment operators	59	69	11	18.1			·				
Pipelayers and pipelaying fitters	52	59	8	14.5							
Plasterers	28	31	3	11.9							
Plumbers, pipefitters, and steamfitters	402	471	69	17.2	15.4	3.8	13.0	75.9	11.1	.7	7.2
Roofers	142	181	39	27.6	20.2	13.3	30.1	65.1	4.7	1.4	9.5
Structural and reinforcing metal workers	86	104	17	20.2	19.3	2.0	11.2	81.7	7.2	.5	6.6
All other construction trades workers	187	196	9	5.0							
Extractive and related workers, including blasters											
Roustabouts	56	52	-4	-7.5							
Oil and gas extraction occupations, except roustabouts	52	58	6	12.5							
Mining, quarrying, and tunneling occupations	21	18	-3	-14.2							
All other extraction and related workers	114	139	25	21.9							
Communications equipment mechanics, installers, and repairers											
Central office and PBX installers and repairers	74	57	-17	-23.1							
Frame wires, central office	13	10	-3	-23.5							
Radio mechanics	7	7	1	8.1							
Signal or track switch maintainers	8	4	-4	-4							
All other communications equipment mechanics, installers, and repairers	8	9	1	6.9							
Electrical and electronic equipment mechanics, installers, and repairers											
Data processing equipment repairers	69	125	56	80.4	8.6	2.7	16.5	80.5	3.0	11.1	9.6
Electrical powerline installers and repairers	108	118	11	9.9	12.1	.5	7.3	83.5	9.3	1.4	7.1
Electronic home entertainment equipment repairers	49	59	10	20.2							
Electronics repairers, commercial and industrial equipment	81	104	23	2802							
Station installers and repairers, telephone	58	40	-18	-31.8							
Telephone and cable TV line installers and repairers	119	108	-11	-9.1	.6	1.0	5.8	90.7	3.5	6.2	9.6
All other electrical and electronic equipment mechanics, installers, and repairers	49	60	11	23.3							
Machinery and related mechanics, installers, and repairers											
Industrial machinery mechanics	421	447	26	6.2	12.3	2.5	8.0	77.7	14.3	2.6	7.6
Maintenance repairers, general utility	1,039	1,270	232	22.3							
Millwrights	86	93	7	8.4	15.9	1.4	5.3	77.9	16.9	1.3	6.2

[Continued]

★ 504 ★

Occupational Employment and Selected Employment Characteristics, 1986-2000 - II
[Continued]

Matrix occupation	Employment		Employment change 1986-2000[1]		Worker characteristics (Percent of employees)						
					Separation rate (annual)	Part-time	Age			Female	Black
	1986	2000	Number	Percent			16-24	25-54	55 and over		
Vehicle and mobile equipment mechanics and repairers											
Aircraft mechanics and engine specialists	107	129	22	20.1	11.5	2.1	7.3	80.8	11.9	3.1	9.9
Aircraft engine specialists	16	19	3	18.0							
Aircraft mechanics	91	109	19	20.5							
Automotive body and related repairers	214	239	25	11.6	12.7	5.5	20.3	70.4	9.3	1.4	3.3
Automotive mechanics	748	808	60	8.0	12.4	6.6	22.4	68.4	9.2	1.0	7.6
Bus and truck mechanics and diesel engine specialists	263	325	63	23.9	9.1	3.4	15.1	73.7	11.2	.7	6.3
Farm equipment mechanics	52	54	2	3.7							
Mobile heavy equipment mechanics, except engines, and rail car repairs[2]	126	144	18	14.5	12.4	3.2	9.7	79.2	11.0	0.6	6.8
Mobile heavy equipment mechanics, except engines	102	127	25	24.3							
Rail car repairers	24	17	-7	-27.5							
Motorcycle repairers	11	12	1	11.4							
Small engine specialists	38	48	9	23.8	29.4	7.5	24.1	64.1	11.8	.3	2.8
Other mechanics, installers, and repairers											
Bicycle repairers	12	14	3	22.2							
Camera, musical instrument, and watch repairers[2]	25	28	3	11.8							
Camera and photographic equipment repairers	7	8	1	21.8							
Musical instrument repairers and tuners	8	9	1	7.3							
Watchmakers	10	11	1	8.6							
Coin and vending machine servicers and repairers	27	30	3	11.5							
Electric meter installers	18	20	2	11.1							
Electromedical and biomedical equipment repairers	7	9	2	24.2							
Elevator installers and repairers	15	18	3	22.4							
Heating, a/c, and refrigeration mechanics and installers	222	272	50	22.3	12.1	4.0	17.6	73.0	9.3	0.3	6.1
Home appliance and power tool repairers	76	84	8	10.1	5.3	10.4	23.2	61.4	15.4	1.6	7.4
Office machine and cash register servicers	56	78	22	40.0	8.4	3.7	14.2	81.1	4.8	1.6	9.7
Precision instrument repairers	49	52	3	5.1							
Riggers	19	20	0	.3							
All other mechanics, installers, and repairers	322	368	46	14.4							
Precision food workers											
Bakers, manufacturing	38	35	-3	-7.0							
Butchers and meatcutters	248	259	11	4.5	22.6	10.8	21.0	65.1	13.9	21.5	16.1
All other precision food and tobacco workers	31	28	-3	-11.1							
Precision metal workers											
Boilermakers	30	32	2	5.2							
Jewelers and silversmiths	36	44	8	22.4							
Machinists	378	373	-5	-1.4	9.1	2.0	12.9	73.2	13.9	3.7	5.7
Sheet metal workers	222	240	19	8.4	10.4	1.6	17.4	72.3	10.3	6.2	7.1
Shipfitters	13	10	-3	-21.6							
Tool and die makers	160	168	8	5.2	8.7	2.6	8.2	69.5	22.3	1.6	2.3
All other precision metal workers	100	95	-6	-5.6							
Precision printing workers											
Bookbinders	11	12	1	8.0							
Compositors and typesetters[2]	67	61	-6	-9.3	15.0	16.7	19.1	71.3	9.7	72.4	1.5
Compositors, typesetters, and arrangers, precision	30	25	-5	-17.1							
Typesetting and composing machine operators and tenders	37	36	-1	-2.8							
Job printers	18	21	3	15.7							
Lithographers and photoengravers[2]	78	97	19	25.1	2.9	.4	9.6	76.4	13.9	19.6	6.1
Lithography and photoengraving workers, precision	48	59	11	22.4							
Photoengraving and lithographic machine operators and photographers	29	38	9	29.4							
All other precision printing workers	5	5	1	15.1							
Precision textile, apparel, and furnishings workers											
Sewers, hand	15	13	-2	-13.0							
Custom tailors and sewers	108	123	15	13.4							
Patternmakers and layout workers, fabric and apparel	13	11	-2	-14.9							
Shoe and leather workers and repairers, precision	35	29	-6	-16.9							
Upholsterers	74	82	8	10.3	16.1	13.6	15.9	64.0	20.0	24.6	8.6
All other precision textile, apparel, and furnishings workers	55	61	7	12.2							
Precision woodworkers	204	234	30	14.6	12.0	11.6	17.9	64.6	17.5	16.8	3.6
Inspectors, testers, and graders	694	692	-3	-.4	18.8	4.7	12.0	73.6	14.4	46.1	13.0
Other precision workers											
Dental lab technicians, precision	46	64	18	39.2	8.4	16.1	11.9	71.2	16.9	39.4	8.7
Optical goods worker, precision	24	30	6	27.0							
Photographic process workers, precision	17	24	7	41.0							
All other precision workers	136	149	13	9.4							

[Continued]

Occupational Employment and Selected Employment Characteristics, 1986-2000 - II
[Continued]

Matrix occupation	Employment		Employment change 1986-2000[1]		Worker characteristics (Percent of employees)						
					Separation rate (annual)	Part-time	Age			Female	Black
	1986	2000	Number	Percent			16-24	25-54	55 and over		
Operator, fabricator, and laborer occupations											
Machine setters, set-up operators, and tenders											
Numerical control machine tool operators and tenders, metal and plastic	56	60	4	6.7							
Combination machine tool setters, set-up operators, and tenders	92	97	5	5.8							
Machine tool cutting and forming setters, operators, and tenders, metal and plastic	822	737	-85	-10.3	17.0	2.6	13.2	74.2	12.7	18.5	11.7
Drilling machine tool setters and set-up operators, metal and plastic	63	57	-6	-9.5							
Grinding machine setters and set-up operators, metal and plastic	88	80	-8	-9.3							
Lathe machine tool setters and set-up operators, metal and plastic	96	86	-9	-9.8							
Machine forming operators and tenders, metal and plastic	170	156	-15	-8.6							
Machine tool cutting operators and tenders, metal and plastic	167	148	-19	-11.2							
Punching machine setters and set-up operators, metal and plastic	61	55	-6	-9.4							
All other machine tool cutting and forming workers	177	155	-22	-12.6							
Metal fabricating machine setters, operators, and related workers											
Metal fabricators, structural metal products	37	38	1	3.9							
Soldering and brazing machine operators and hand workers[2]	42	44	1	3.3							
Soldering and brazing machine operators and setters	17	17	0	-1.8							
Solderers and brazers	25	27	2	6.8							
Welding machine operators and hand workers[2]	414	418	5	1.1	17.7	2.4	13.8	77.6	8.6	5.1	9.4
Welding machine setters, operators, and tenders	126	112	-15	-11.6							
Welders and cutters	287	307	19	6.7							
Metal and plastic process machine setters, operators, and related workers											
Plating machine operators[2]	59	57	-2	-2.8							
Electric plating machine operators, setters and set-up operators, metal and plastic	47	45	-1	-2.7							
Nonelectric plating machine operators, setters and set-up operators, metal and plastic	13	12	0	-3.4							
Foundry mold assembly and shakeout workers	5	4	-1	-27.7							
Heat treating equipment operators[2]	52	44	-8	-15.0							
Furnace operators and tenders	20	15	-4	-22.5							
Heaters, metal and plastic	5	4	-1	-13.1							
Heating equipment setters and set-up operators, metal and plastic	7	7	-1	-8.8							
Heat treating machine operators and tenders, metal and plastic	20	18	-2	-10.3							
Metal molding machine operators and tenders, setters and set-up operators	37	33	-4	-12.1	16.4	0.9	18.6	71.0	10.4	29.8	7.9
Plastic molding machine operators and tenders, setters and set-up operators	147	183	36	24.6							
All other metal/plastic machine setters, operators, and related workers	90	89	-2	-1.8							
Printing, binding, and related workers											
Bindery machine operators, setters and set-up operators	72	90	17	24.2							
Printing press operators	222	262	40	18.0	9.4	5.9	22.0	67.5	10.5	14.5	7.4
Letterpress setters and set-up operators	22	20	-2	-7.5							
Offset lithographic press and set-up operators	73	96	23	31.9							
Printing press machine setters, operators and tenders	115	131	17	14.7							
All other printing press setters and set-up operators	13	15	2	12.5							
Screen printing machine setters and set-up operators	14	14	0	-2.6							
All other printing, binding, and related workers	37	38	1	3.0							
Textile and related setters, operators, and related workers											
Extruding and forming machine operators and tenders, synthetic or glass fibers	14	12	-2	-14.2							
Pressing machine operators and tenders, textile, garment and related workers	89	88	-1	-1.6	25.8	16.1	19.2	66.0	14.8	71.9	33.7
Sewing machine operators[2]	767	666	-101	-13.2	19.1	7.4	12.3	73.3	14.4	90.6	17.1
Sewing machine operators, garment	633	541	-92	-14.5							
Sewing machine operators, nongarment	135	125	-10	-7.3							
Textile bleaching and dyeing machine operators and tenders	22	19	-3	-13.8							
Textile draw-out and winding machine operators and tenders	219	164	-55	-25.2							
Textile machine setters and set-up operators	54	47	-7	-12.5							

[Continued]

★ 504 ★

Occupational Employment and Selected Employment Characteristics, 1986-2000 - II

[Continued]

Matrix occupation	Employment		Employment change 1986-2000[1]		Worker characteristics (Percent of employees)						
					Separation rate (annual)	Part-time	Age			Female	Black
	1986	2000	Number	Percent			16-24	25-54	55 and over		
Woodworking machine setters, operators, and other related workers											
Head sawyers and sawing machine operators and tenders, setters and set-up operators	74	78	5	6.5	33.8	5.1	22.9	65.5	11.5	13.5	15.3
Woodworking machine operators and tenders, setters and set-up operators	74	81	7	9.4	22.0	5.6	21.6	60.3	18.1	22.2	14.1
Other machine setters, set-up operators, operators, and tenders											
Boiler operators and stationary engineers[2]	63	64	1	1.9	13.3	2.3	4.4	75.3	20.4	2.5	10.6
Boiler operators and tenders, low pressure	22	22	-1	-3.2							
Stationary engineers	41	42	2	4.7							
Cementing and gluing machine operators and tenders	42	41	-1	-1.9							
Chemical equipment controllers, operators and tenders	73	52	-22	-29.7							
Cooking and roasting machine operators and tenders, food and tobacco	26	22	-4	-14.2							
Crushing and mixing machine operators and tenders	132	123	-9	-7.1	19.7	3.9	22.2	68.5	9.2	13.5	15.7
Cutting and slicing machine setters, operators and tenders	82	82	0	.2	24.7	6.0	23.3	62.9	13.9	24.7	13.3
Dairy processing equipment operators, including setters	16	12	-4	-25.1							
Electronic semiconductor processors	29	14	-15	-51.1							
Extruding and forming machine setters, operators and tenders	100	96	-3	-3.5							
Furnace, kiln, or kettle operators and tenders	58	53	-5	-8.4	17.3	2.5	12.6	71.1	16.3	4.1	10.7
Laundry and drycleaning machine operators and tenders, except presser	140	170	31	21.9	20.3	23.3	18.6	59.2	22.2	65.5	23.7
Motion picture projectionists	13	12	-1	-8.3							
Packaging and filling machine operators and tenders	299	293	-5	-1.8	24.3	9.6	21.7	67.3	11.0	60.1	21.8
Painting and paint spraying machine operators	100	102	1	1.4	17.2	3.3	25.3	66.4	8.2	17.4	13.6
Painting machine operators, tenders, setters, and set-up operators	66	68	2	3.2							
Painters, transportation equipment	35	34	-1	-2.0							
Paper goods machine setters and set-up operators	60	60	0	.0							
Photographic processing machine operators and tenders	39	48	9	24.1							
Separating and still machine operators and tenders	26	23	-3	-11.8	10.9	2.2	9.0	82.2	8.8	13.6	11.9
Shoe sewing machine operators and tenders	27	18	-9	-32.1							
Tire building machine operators	13	8	-5	-36.5							
All other machine operators, tenders, setters, and set-up operators	403	416	13	3.1							
Assemblers and other handworking occupations											
Aircraft assemblers	24	19	-5	-19.2							
Electrical, electronic, and electromechanical equipment assemblers[2]	478	349	-129	-26.9	17.0	3.5	18.5	70.6	10.8	68.7	12.8
Electrical and electronic equipment assemblers, precision	170	171	1	.7							
Electromechanical equipment assemblers, precision	59	62	4	6.6							
Electrical and electronic assemblers	249	116	-134	-53.7							
Fitters, structural metal, precision	20	19	-1	-3.7							
Machine builders and other precision machine assemblers	50	48	-2	-3.7							
All other precision assemblers	28	27	-1	-1.9							
Other hand workers, including assemblers and fabricators											
Cannery workers	78	72	-5	-7.1							
Coil winders, tapers, and finishers	34	28	-6	-18.5							
Cutters and trimmers, hand	50	50	0	.8							
Grinders and polishers, hand	73	69	-4	-6.0							
Machine assemblers	50	49	-1	-2.0							
Meat, poultry, and fish cutters and trimmers, hand	101	106	4	4.4							
Metal pourers and casters, basic shapes	11	8	-3	-23.9							
Painting, coating, and decorating workers, hand	42	46	4	8.6	24.9	21.6	16.3	63.6	20.1	42.5	7.8
Portable machine cutters	17	14	-3	-16.8							
Pressers, hand	21	18	-2	-10.7							
All other assemblers and fabricators	1,019	1,006	-13	-1.3							
All other hand workers	278	312	34	12.4							
Plant and system occupations											
Chemical plant and system operators	33	23	-10	-29.6							
Electric power generation plant operators, distributors, and dispatchers	45	50	5	11.0	7.0	2.6	7.8	85.5	6.8	6.3	7.8
Power distributors and dispatchers	20	22	2	7.7							
Power generating and reactor plant operators	25	28	3	13.6							
Gas and petroleum plant and system occupations	31	20	-11	-34.3							
Water and liquid waste treatment plant and system operators	74	85	11	15.3	17.2	1.1	9.4	77.3	13.3	5.7	5.0
All other plant and system operators	68	75	7	9.9							
Transportation and material moving machine and vehicle operators											
Aircraft pilots and flight engineers	76	98	22	28.6	10.6	23.6	1.3	86.4	12.3	1.5	.9

[Continued]

★ 504 ★

Occupational Employment and Selected Employment Characteristics, 1986-2000 - II
[Continued]

Matrix occupation	Employment		Employment change 1986-2000[1]		Worker characteristics (Percent of employees)						
					Separation rate (annual)	Part-time	Age			Female	Black
	1986	2000	Number	Percent			16-24	25-54	55 and over		
Motor vehicle operators											
Bus drivers	478	555	77	16.2	15.1	44.8	7.6	73.1	19.2	50.4	24.0
Bus drivers, other than school	143	177	34	23.5							
Bus drivers, school	334	378	44	13.1							
Taxi drivers and chauffeurs	88	94	6	7.2	27.9	23.0	13.8	65.2	21.0	12.5	21.9
Truck drivers											
Driver/sales workers	252	232	-20	-7.9	10.8	5.4	13.7	77.3	9.0	7.5	5.8
Truck drivers light and heavy	2,211	2,736	525	23.8	18.3	9.5	16.0	71.9	12.1	4.3	13.4
All other motor vehicle operators	61	76	15	23.8							
Rail transportation workers											
Locomotive and rail yard engineers, and all other rail vehicle operators[2]	46	31	-15	-32.1	10.2	1.4	.4	84.4	15.2	1.7	4.9
Locomotive engineers	17	10	-7	-40.7							
Rail yard engineers, dinkey operators, and hostlers	11	7	-4	-36.1							
All other rail vehicle operators	18	14	-4	-21.5							
Railroad brake, signal, and switch operators	42	25	-17	-39.9	20.1	8.0	.2	92.5	7.2	3.6	5.2
Railroad conductors and yardmasters	29	17	-12	-40.9							
Water transportation and related workers											
Able seamen, ordinary seamen, and marine oilers	22	20	-2	-8.4							
Captains and pilots, ship	16	15	-1	-6.3							
Mates, ship, boat, and barge	6	5	0	-6.7							
Ship engineers	7	6	-1	-8.3							
Other transportation related workers											
Parking lot attendants	30	37	7	21.5	41.9	35.2	46.2	37.4	16.3	7.2	20.8
Service station attendants and tire repairers[2]	382	388	6	1.6	31.1	29.7	54.1	35.5	10.3	5.8	10.3
Service station attendants	299	285	-14	-4.7							
Tire repairers and changers	83	103	20	24.1							
All other transportation and related workers	86	99	13	14.9							
Material moving equipment operators											
Crane and tower operators	58	60	3	5.0	13.4	1.6	4.4	81.6	13.9	.8	17.6
Excavation and loading machine operators	70	79	9	13.4	17.1	5.2	11.1	76.6	12.2	.5	6.1
Grader, dozer, and scraper operators	92	104	11	12.4	9.5	4.4	9.4	73.0	17.6	1.9	7.6
Hoist and winch operators	19	22	2	11.0							
Industrial and logging truck and tractor operators[2]	455	311	-144	-31.6	22.0	2.9	18.8	73.8	7.4	5.0	19.4
Industrial truck and tractor operators	426	283	-143	-33.6							
Material moving equipment operators											
Logging tractor operators	28	28	-1	-1.8							
Operating engineers	150	172	23	15.1	9.8	1.3	7.9	80.3	11.8	1.0	7.7
All other material moving equipment operators	182	184	2	1.0							
All other transportation and material moving equipment operators	43	52	10	22.4							
Helpers, laborers, and material movers, hand											
Freight, stock, and material movers, hand	831	812	-19	-2.3	31.8	38.8	52.5	41.8	5.7	15.2	15.7
Hand packers and packagers	566	639	73	12.8	27.1	16.4	25.3	63.5	11.2	64.1	16.8
Helpers, construction trade	519	587	68	13.1	36.1	17.1	51.1	44.7	4.2	4.8	15.6
Machine feeders and offbearers	278	262	-16	-5.6	21.5	9.3	23.9	67.1	8.9	35.0	22.3
Refuse collectors	113	135	22	19.1	20.0	10.9	19.0	68.2	12.8	2.7	40.3
Vehicle washers and equipment cleaners	189	203	14	7.4	29.4	24.2	43.1	49.7	7.3	14.8	20.8
All other helpers, laborers, and material movers, hand	1,777	1,885	108	6.1	22.1	14.6	28.3	61.0	10.7	17.7	18.0

Source: "Selected Occupational Data, 1986 and Projected 2000," *Occupational Projections and Training Data: A Statistical and Research Supplement to the 1988-89 Occupational Outlook Handbook,* U.S. Department of Labor, 1988, pp. 21-64. Source also contains data on industry distribution of employees. *Notes:* 1. Calculated on unrounded data. 2. This title does not appear in the National Industry-Occupation Matrix, but was formed by combining several matrix occupations in order to achieve CPS comparability. The matrix occupations used in the combination appear as a subgroup of this title.

★ 505 ★

Rankings of All Occupations by Selected Characteristics, 1986-2000 - I

National Industry-Occupation Matrix occupation	Employment		Employment change 1986-2000		Median weekly earnings of full-time workers	Unemployment rate	Separation rate (Annual)	Percent of employees		Significant sources of training[1]
	1986	2000	Number	Percent				Working part-time	Age 16-24	
Managerial and management related occupations										
Education administrators	H	H	H	A	VH	VL	VL	A	L	CD
Financial managers	VH	VH	VH	H	VH	L	VL	VL	L	PS, CD
Marketing, advertising, and public relations managers	H	VH	VH	VH	VH	L	L	VL	L	PS, CD
Personnel, training, and labor relations managers	H	H	H	H	VH	L	L	VL	L	PS, CD
Postmasters and mail superintendents	VL	VL	L	L	VH	VL	VL	L	L	
Property and real estate managers and administrators	H	H	H	VH	A	L	A	H	L	PS
Purchasing managers	H	H	H	A	VH	L	VL	VL	L	CD
Accountants and auditors	VH	VH	VH	VH	H	L	L	L	A	CD
Inspectors and compliance officers, except construction	A	A	A	A	H	L	L	L	L	E, CD
Construction and building inspectors	L	L	L	L	H	A	A	L	L	E
Employment interviewers, personnel and labor relations specialists	H	VH	VH	VH	H	A	L	L	L	PS, CD
Management analysts	H	H	H	H	VH	L	A	H	L	CD
Purchasing agents, except wholesale, retail, and farm products	H	H	L	L	H	L	H	VL	L	PS
Underwriters	A	A	H	VH	A	L	L	VL	L	CD
Wholesale and retail buyers, except farm products	H	H	A	L	A	L	A	A	L	PS
Professional specialty occupations										
Aeronautical and astronautical engineers	L	L	L	L	VH	VL	VL	VL	L	CD
Chemical engineers	L	L	A	A	VH	L	L	VL	L	CD
Civil engineers, including traffic engineers	H	H	H	H	VH	L	VL	VL	L	CD
Electrical and electronic engineers	VH	VH	VH	VH	VH	VL	VL	VL	L	CD
Industrial engineers, except safety engineers	A	A	H	H	VH	L	L	VL	L	CD
Mechanical engineers	H	H	VH	VH	VH	L	VL	VL	L	CD
Architects, except landscape and marine	A	A	H	H	VH	L	VL	VL	L	CD
Surveyors	A	A	H	A	A	A	VL	L	H	E, PS, CD
Computer systems analysts, electronic data processing	H	VH	VH	VH	VH	VL	VL	L	L	CD
Biological scientists	A	A	A	H	A	L	VL	L	L	CD
Operations and systems researchers	L	L	H	VH	VH	VL	L	VL	L	CD
Chemists	A	A	A	L	VH	L	L	VL	L	CD
Geologists, geophysicists, and oceanographers	L	L	L	A	VH	A	L	L	L	CD
Economists	L	L	A	VH	VH	L	A	A	L	CD
Psychologists	A	A	H	VH	H	L	VL	H	L	CD
Clergy	H	H	A	L	A	VL	VL	A	L	CD
Recreation workers	H	H	H	A	VL	VH	H	H	H	CD
Social workers	VH	VH	VH	VH	A	A	L	A	L	CD
Lawyers	VH	VH	VH	VH	VH	VL	VL	L	L	CD
Teachers, preschool, kindergarten and elementary	VH	VH	VH	A	A	L	L	H	L	CD
Teachers, secondary school	VH	VH	VH	A	H	VL	L	A	L	CD
Librarians, professional	H	H	H	A	H	L	A	VH	L	CD
Counselors	A	A	H	A	H	L	L	A	L	CD
Dentists	H	H	H	H	VH	VL	VL	H	L	CD
Pharmacists	H	H	H	H	VH	VL	VL	H	L	CD
Physicians and surgeons	VH	VH	VH	VH	VH	VL	VL	L	L	CD
Registered nurses	VH	VH	VH	VH	H	VL	VL	VH	L	PS, CD
Physical therapists	A	A	H	VH	H	VL	VL	H	A	CD
Respiratory therapists	L	A	H	VH	A	L	VL	H	L	PS
Speech pathologists and audiologists	L	L	A	VH	H	VL	VL	VH	L	CD
Artists and commercial artists	H	H	VH	VH	A	L	H	H	L	PS
Designers	H	H	VH	H	H	A	L	H	A	PS, CD
Musicians	H	H	H	H	A	H	H	VH	A	HS, CD
Photographers	A	A	H	VH	A	L	L	H	H	E, PS
Producers, directors, actors, and entertainers	A	A	H	VH	H	VH	H	H	A	PS, CD
Public relations specialists and publicity writers	A	A	H	VH	H	L	VH	A	L	PS, CD
Radio and TV announcers and newscasters	L	A	A	H	L	A	VH	VH	H	PS, CD
Reporters, writers, and editors	H	H	VH	H	H	L	A	H	L	CD
Technical occupations										
Dental hygienists	A	A	H	VH	A	VL	VL	VH	H	PS
Licensed practical nurse	VH	VH	VH	VH	L	A	VL	VH	L	PS
Medical and clinical laboratory technologists and technicians	H	H	H	H	A	L	VL	H	A	PS, CD
Medical records technician	L	A	H	VH	L	A	L	A	H	PS
Nuclear medicine and radiologic technologists and technicians	A	H	VH	VH	A	L	VL	A	A	PS
Opticians, dispensing and measuring	L	A	H	VH	L	L	H	A	H	E, PS
Electrical and electronic technicians/technologists	H	VH	VH	VH	H	L	L	VL	A	E, PS
Drafters	H	H	L	L	A	A	L	A	H	HS, PS
Physical and life science technicians, technologists and mathematical technicians	H	H	H	A	A	A	A	A	H	PS
Computer programmers	VH	VH	VH	VH	H	L	L	L	H	PS, CD

[Continued]

472

★ 505 ★

Rankings of All Occupations by Selected Characteristics, 1986-2000 - I

[Continued]

National Industry-Occupation Matrix occupation	Employment		Employment change 1986-2000		Median weekly earnings of full-time workers	Unemployment rate	Separation rate (Annual)	Percent of employees		Significant sources of training[1]
	1986	2000	Number	Percent				Working part-time	Age 16-24	
Marketing and sales occupations										
Cashiers	VH	VH	VH	H	VL	H	VH	VH	H	
Counter and rental clerks	H	H	VH	VH	VL	H	A	VH	H	
Insurance sales workers	VH	VH	VH	H	H	L	L	A	L	E
Real estate sales occupations	VH	VH	VH	VH	H	VL	A	H	L	E, PS
Salesperson, retail	VH	VH	VH	VH	VL	A	VH	VH	H	
Securities and financial services sales workers	H	H	VH	VH	VH	VL	VL	L	L	E, CD
Administrative occupations										
Adjustment clerks, credit authorizers and clerks	VH	VH	VH	H	L	L	H	A	H	
Bill and account collectors	A	H	H	VH	L	A	H	A	A	
Insurance claims and policy processing occupations	H	H	H	L	A	L	VL	L	H	E
Welfare eligibility workers and interviewers	A	A	A	A	L	A	A	A	L	PS
Telephone operators	H	VH	H	L	L	A	L	H	H	E
Computer operators and peripheral equipment operators	H	VH	VH	VH	L	A	A	A	H	HS, E, PS
Duplicating, mail, and other office machine operators	H	H	A	L	L	H	H	H	H	
Billing, cost, and rate clerks	H	H	L	L	L	A	A	A	H	HS
Billing, posting, and calculating machine operators	A	A	A	L	VL	H	H	VH	H	
Bookkeeping, accounting, and auditing clerks	VH	VH	VH	L	L	A	A	VH	A	HS, PS

Source: "Occupational Comparisons," *Occupational Projections and Training Data: A Statistical and Research Supplement to the 1988-89 Occupational Outlook Handbook,* U.S. Department of Labor, 1988, pp. 8-12. Rankings are based on all occupations in the National-Industry-Occupation Matrix and the Current Population Survey. *Notes:* The information compared in this chapter is derived from two sources: the National Industry-Occupation Matrix and the Current Population Survey (CPS). The matrix is the source of data on 1986 employment and 1986-2000 employment change. All other data are derived from the Current Population Survey. However, the CPS data used are for different time periods. Information on earnings and unemployment is for 1983-86; the separation rate is based on 1986-87 data, part-time work and age data are 1986 annual averages, while information about the type of training is derived from supplemental questions added to the January 1983 CPS survey. 1. Codes for describing the variables are: VH = "Very High," H = "High," A = "Average," L = "Low," and VL = "Very low." Codes for source of training are: HS = high school vocational training programs, E = formal education, PS = postsecondary school training, but less than a bachelor's degree, CD = 4-year college degree program.

★ 506 ★

Rankings of All Occupations by Selected Characteristics, 1986-2000 - II

National Industry-Occupation Matrix occupation	Employment		Employment change 1986-2000		Median weekly earnings of full-time workers	Unemployment rate	Separation rate (Annual)	Percent of employees		Significant sources of training[1]
	1986	2000	Number	Percent				Working part-time	Age 16-24	
Administrative Occupations										
Payroll and timekeeping clerks	H	H	VL	VL	L	A	L	A	A	HS, PS
General office clerks	VH	VH	VH	A	L	A	H	H	H	HS
Hotel desk clerks	A	H	H	VH	VL	H	VH	H	H	
Interviewing clerks, except personnel and social welfare	A	A	H	VH	L	A	H	VH	H	PS
Receptionists and information clerks	VH	VH	VH	VH	VL	H	VH	VH	H	HS
Reservation and transportation ticket agents and travel clerks	A	A	H	A	A	L	A	A	H	E
Mail clerks, except mail machine operators and postal service	H	A	A	L	VL	H	VH	H	H	
Messengers	A	A	H	H	VL	H	VH	VH	H	
Postal mail carriers	H	H	H	L	H	VL	VL	L	L	
Postal service clerks	VH	H	A	L	H	L	VL	A	L	
Dispatchers	H	H	H	A	L	A	L	L	H	
Meter readers, utilities	L	L	VL	VL	A	VL	VH	L	H	
Order fillers, procurement and stock clerks	VH	VH	VL	VL	L	H	H	H	H	
Production, planning, and expediting clerks	H	H	A	L	A	A	A	A	A	
Traffic, shipping, and receiving clerks	VH	VH	H	L	L	H	H	A	H	
Weighers, measurers, checkers, and samplers, recordkeeping	L	L	VL	L	L	H	A	H	H	
Brokerage and statement clerks	A	A	H	H	L	A	H	A	H	HS
File clerks	H	H	H	A	VL	H	VH	VH	H	HS
Library assistants and bookmobile drivers	A	A	A	A	VL	A	VH	VH	H	
Order clerks	VH	H	L	L	A	L	L	A	A	
Personnel clerks, except payroll and timekeeping	A	A	A	L	L	L	A	A	A	
Secretaries	VH	VH	VH	A	L	A	A	H	H	HS, PS
Stenographers	H	A	VL	VL	A	L	VL	H	L	HS, PS
Typists and word processors	VH	VH	VL	VL	L	H	H	H	H	HS

[Continued]

★ 506 ★

Rankings of All Occupations by Selected Characteristics, 1986-2000 - II
[Continued]

National Industry-Occupation Matrix occupation	Employment		Employment change 1986-2000		Median weekly earnings of full-time workers	Unemployment rate	Separation rate (Annual)	Percent of employees		Significant sources of training[1]
	1986	2000	Number	Percent				Working part-time	Age 16-24	
Bank tellers	VH	VH	VH	A	VL	L	H	H	H	E
Data entry keyers	VH	H	VL	VL	L	H	H	A	H	HS, E
First-line supervisors and managers	VH	VH	VH	A	H	L	L	VL	L	E
Statistical clerks	A	L	VL	VL	A	L	A	H	A	HS
Teacher aides and educational assistants	VH	VH	VH	A	VL	A	H	VH	A	PS
Service occupations										
Janitors and cleaners	VH	VH	VH	H	VL	VH	H	VH	H	
Pest controllers	L	L	A	A	L	H	VH	L	H	
Cooks, except short order	VH	VH	VH	VH	VL	H	VH	VH	H	E, PS
Cooks, short order and fast food	VH	VH	VH	H	VL	VH	VH	VH	H	
Food preparation workers	VH	VH	VH	VH	VL	H	VH	VH	H	
Bartenders	VH	VH	VH	VH	VL	VH	H	VH	H	
Dining room and cafeteria attendants and barroom helpers	VH	VH	VH	VH	VL	VH	VH	VH	H	
Food counter, fountain, and related workers	VH	VH	VH	H	VL	VH	VH	VH	H	
Waiters and waitresses	VH	VH	VH	VH	VL	VH	VH	VH	H	
Dental assistants	H	H	VH	VH	VL	A	A	VH	H	
Nursing aides and psychiatric aides	VH	VH	VH	VH	VL	H	H	VH	H	E
Amusement and recreation attendants	H	H	H	H	VL	VH	VH	VH	H	
Barbers	A	A	L	L	VL	VL	VL	H	L	PS
Child care workers	VH	VH	VH	A	VL	A	VH	VH	H	
Cosmetologists and related workers	VH	VH	VH	A	VL	L	L	VH	H	PS
Flight attendants	A	A	H	H	H	A	A	VH	A	E
Social welfare service aides	L	A	H	VH	VL	H	H	VH	A	
Child care workers, private household	VH	H	VL	VL	VL	A	VH	VH	H	
Cleaners and servants, private household	VH	VH	A	L	VL	H	VH	VH	H	
Correction officers and jailers	H	H	VH	VH	A	L	L	VL	A	E
Firefighters	H	H	H	A	H	VL	VL	VL	L	E
Police and detective supervisors	A	A	A	A	VH	VL	VL	VL	L	E, PS
Police detectives and patrol officers	VH	VH	VH	A	H	VL	VL	VL	L	E, PS
Crossing guards	L	L	L	L	L	L	H	VH	L	
Guards	VH	VH	VH	VH	VL	H	VH	H	H	
Farming, forestry, and fishing										
Animal caretakers, except farm	A	A	H	H	VL	H	VH	VH	H	
Gardeners and groundskeepers, except farm	VH	VH	VH	H	VL	VH	VH	VH	H	
Supervisors, farming, forestry, and agriculture-related occupations	A	L	VL	VL	L	H	H	A	H	
Farm workers	VH	VH	VL	VL	VL	VH	VH	VH	H	
Farmers	VH	VH	VL	VL	VL	VL	A	H	L	
Farm managers	H	H	H	H	L	L	A	A	L	
Fishers, hunters, and trappers	A	A	A	H	L	VH	A	H	H	
Timber cutting and logging occupations, except logging tractor operators	A	L	VL	VL	L	VH	A	H	H	
Precision production, craft, and repair occupations										
Blue-collar worker supervisors	VH	VH	VH	L	H	L	L	VL	L	E
Bricklayers and stone masons	H	H	H	A	A	VH	A	A	A	E
Carpenters	VH	VH	VH	A	A	VH	H	A	H	E
Carpet installers	A	A	A	H	L	H	A	A	H	E
Concrete and terrazzo finishers	A	A	H	A	A	VH	H	A	H	E
Drywall installers and finishers	H	H	H	H	A	VH	H	A	H	E
Electronics	VH	VH	VH	A	H	H	L	VL	A	E
Glaziers	L	L	A	A	A	A	H	L	A	E
Hard tile setters	L	L	A	H	A	H	L	A	H	
Insulation workers	A	A	A	H	A	VH	VH	VL	H	
Painters and paperhangers, construction and maintenance	VH	VH	VH	H	L	VH	H	H	H	
Plumbers, pipefitters, and steamfitters	VH	VH	VH	A	H	H	A	L	A	E
Roofers	H	H	H	H	L	VH	H	A	H	
Structural and reinforcing metal workers	A	A	A	A	H	VH	H	VL	A	E
Data processing equipment repairers	A	A	H	VH	H	L	VL	VL	A	E, PS
Electrical powerline installers and repairers	A	A	A	L	H	A	L	VL	L	E
Telephone and cable TV line installers and repairers	A	A	VL	VL	VH	L	VL	VL	L	E
Industrial machinery mechanics	VH	VH	H	L	H	A	L	VL	L	E
Millwrights	A	A	A	L	H	VH	A	VL	L	E
Aircraft mechanics and engine specialists	A	A	H	A	H	A	L	VL	L	E, PS
Automotive body and related repairers	H	H	H	A	L	H	L	L	H	E
Automotive mechanics	VH	VH	VH	L	L	A	L	L	H	HS, E, P S
Bus and truck mechanics and diesel engine specialists	H	H	VH	H	A	A	L	L	A	E, PS

[Continued]

★ 506 ★

Rankings of All Occupations by Selected Characteristics, 1986-2000 - II
[Continued]

National Industry-Occupation Matrix occupation	Employment		Employment change 1986-2000		Median weekly earnings of full-time workers	Unemployment rate	Separation rate (Annual)	Percent of employees		Significant sources of training[1]
	1986	2000	Number	Percent				Working part-time	Age 16-24	
Mobile heavy equipment mechanics, except engines, and rail car repairers	H	A	H	A	H	H	L	VL	L	E
Small engine specialists	L	L	A	H	L	H	VH	A	H	E
Heating, a/c, and refrigeration mechanics and installers	H	H	H	H	A	A	L	L	H	E, PS
Home appliance and power tool repairers	A	A	A	L	A	L	VL	A	H	E, PS
Office machine and cash register servicers	L	A	H	VH	A	L	VL	L	A	E, PS
Butchers and meatcutters	H	H	A	L	L	H	H	A	H	E
Machinists	VH	H	VL	VL	H	H	L	VL	A	HS, E
Sheet-metal workers	H	H	H	L	H	H	L	VL	H	E
Tool and die makers	H	H	A	L	H	L	L	VL	L	HS, E
Compositors and typesetters	A	L	VL	VL	L	L	A	H	H	HS, E
Lithographers and photoengravers	A	A	H	H	H	A	VL	VL	L	HS, E
Upholsterers	A	A	A	L	L	A	A	A	A	E
Precision woodworkers	H	H	H	A	L	H	L	A	H	HS, E
Inspectors, testers, and graders	VH	VH	VL	L	L	H	H	L	A	E
Dental laboratory technicians, precision	L	L	A	VH	A	A	VL	H	A	E, PS

Source: "Occupational Comparisons," *Occupational Projections and Training Data: A Statistical and Research Supplement to the 1988-89 Occupational Outlook Handbook,* U.S. Department of Labor, 1988, pp. 8-12. Rankings are based on all occupations in the National-Industry-Occupation Matrix and the Current Population Survey. *Notes:* The information compared in this chapter is derived from two sources: the National Industry-Occupation Matrix and the Current Population Survey (CPS). The matrix is the source of data on 1986 employment and 1986-2000 employment change. All other data are derived from the Current Population Survey. However, the CPS data used are for different time periods. Information on earnings and unemployment is for 1983-86; the separation rate is based on 1986-87 data, part-time work and age data are 1986 annual averages, while information about the type of training is derived from supplemental questions added to the January 1983 CPS survey. 1. Codes for describing the variables are: VH = "Very High," H = "High," A = "Average," L = "Low," and VL = "Very low." Codes for source of training are: HS = high school vocational training programs, E = formal education, PS = postsecondary school training, but less than a bachelor's degree, CD = 4-year college degree program.

★ 507 ★

Rankings of All Occupations by Selected Characteristics, 1986-2000 - III

National Industry-Occupation Matrix occupation	Employment		Employment change 1986-2000		Median weekly earnings of full-time workers	Unemployment rate	Separation rate (Annual)	Percent of employees		Significant sources of training[1]
	1986	2000	Number	Percent				Working part-time	Age 16-24	
Operator, fabricator, and laborer occupations										
Machine tool cutting and forming operators, metal and plastic	VH	VH	VL	VL	A	VH	A	VL	A	
Welding machine operators and hand workers	VH	VH	L	L	A	VH	A	VL	A	E
Metal molding machine operators and tenders, setters, and set-up operators	L	L	VL	VL	L	VH	A	VL	H	
Printing press operators	H	H	H	A	A	A	L	L	H	HS, E
Pressing machine operators and tenders, textile, garment, and related materials	A	A	VL	VL	VL	VH	VH	H	H	
Sewing machine operators	VH	VH	VL	VL	VL	VH	H	A	A	
Head sawyers and sawing machine operators and tenders, setters, and set-up operators	A	A	L	L	VL	H	VH	L	H	
Woodworking machine operators and tenders, setters, and set-up operators	A	A	A	L	VL	VH	H	L	H	
Boiler operators and stationary engineers	A	L	L	L	H	A	A	VL	L	E, PS
Crushing and mixing operators and tenders	H	A	VL	VL	L	VH	H	L	H	
Cutting and slicing machine setters, operators, and tenders	A	A	L	L	L	VH	H	L	H	
Furnace, kiln, or kettle operators and tenders	L	L	VL	VL	A	H	A	VL	A	
Laundry and drycleaning machine operators and tenders, except pressers	H	H	H	H	VL	H	H	H	H	
Packaging and filling machine operators and tenders	H	H	VL	VL	VL	VH	H	A	H	
Painting and paint spraying machine operators	A	A	L	L	L	VH	A	VL	H	
Separating and still machine operators and tenders	VL	VL	VL	VL	H	A	L	VL	L	
Electrical, electronic, and electromechanical equipment assemblers	VH	H	VL	VL	VL	VH	A	L	H	
Painting, coating, and decorating workers, hand	L	L	L	L	L	H	H	H	A	
Electric power generation plant operators, distributors, and dispatchers	L	L	L	L	VH	VL	VL	VL	L	E

[Continued]

★ 507 ★

Rankings of All Occupations by Selected Characteristics, 1986-2000 - III
[Continued]

National Industry-Occupation Matrix occupation	Employment		Employment change 1986-2000		Median weekly earnings of full-time workers	Unemployment rate	Separation rate (Annual)	Percent of employees		Significant sources of training[1]
	1986	2000	Number	Percent				Working part-time	Age 16-24	
Water and liquid waste treatment plant and system operators	A	A	A	A	A	A		VL	L	E, PS
Aircraft pilots and flight engineers	A	A	H	H	VH	L	L	H	L	PS, CD
Bus drivers	VH	VH	VH	A	A	A	A	VH	L	E
Taxi drivers and chauffeurs	A	A	A	L	L	H	VH	H	A	
Driver/sales workers	H	H	VL	VL	A	A	L	L	A	
Truck drivers, light and heavy	VH	VH	VH	H	A	H	A	A	A	
Locomotive and rail yard engineers and all other rail vehicle operators	L	L	VL	VL	VH	A	L	VL	L	E
Railroad brake, signal, and switch operators	L	VL	VL	VL	VH	H	H	A	L	
Parking lot attendants	L	L	A	H	VL	H	VH	VH	H	
Service station attendants and tire repairers	VH	H	L	L	VL	VH	VH	VH	H	
Crane and tower operators	L	L	L	L	H	VH	A	VL	L	E
Excavation and loading machine operators	A	A	A	A	A	H	A	L	L	E
Grader, dozer, and scraper operators	A	A	A	A	A	H	L	L	L	E
Industrial and logging truck and tractor operators	VH	H	VL	VL	L	VH	H	VL	H	
Operating engineers	H	H	H	A	A	VH	L	VL	L	E
Freight, stock, and material movers, hand	VH	VH	VL	VL	L	H	VH	VH	H	
Hand packers and packagers	VH	VH	VH	A	VL	VH	VH	H	H	
Helpers, construction trades	VH	VH	VH	A	VL	VH	VH	H	H	
Machine feeders and offbearers	H	H	VL	VL	L	VH	H	A	H	
Refuse collectors	A	A	H	A	VL	VH	H	A	H	
Vehicle washers and equipment cleaners	H	H	A	L	VL	VH	VH	H	H	
All other helpers, laborers, and material movers, hand	VH	VH	VH	L	L	VH	H	H	H	

Source: "Occupational Comparisons," *Occupational Projections and Training Data: A Statistical and Research Supplement to the 1988-89 Occupational Outlook Handbook,* U.S. Department of Labor, 1988, pp. 8-12. Rankings are based on all occupations in the National-Industry-occupation Matrix and the Current Population Survey. *Notes:* The information compared in this chapter is derived from two sources: the National Industry-Occupation Matrix and the Current Population Survey (CPS). The matrix is the source of data on 1986 employment and 1986-2000 employment change. All other data are derived from the Current Population Survey. However, the CPS data used are for different time periods. Information on earnings and unemployment is for 1983-86; the separation rate is based on 1986-87 data, part-time work and age data are 1986 annual averages, while information about the type of training is derived from supplemental questions added to the January 1983 CPS survey. 1. Codes for describing the variables are: VH = "Very High," H = "High," A = "Average," L = "Low," and VL = "Very low." Codes for source of training are: HS = high school vocational training programs, E = formal education, PS = postsecondary school training, but less than a bachelor's degree, CD = 4-year college degree program.

★ 508 ★

Selected Occupational Groups Ranked by Projected Percentage Rate of Employment Growth, Levels of Educational Attainment, and Median Weekly Earnings, 1990-2005

As of 1990.

Occupation	1990-2005 rates of employment change	Levels of educational attainment (Percent of occupational employment)				Median weekly earnings
		less than high school	High school	1-3 years of college	4 or more of college	
Total, all occupations	20	15	39	22	24	415
Mathematical and computer scientists	73	0	10	24	66	734
Personal service	44	18	52	22	8	252
Health service	44	19	52	23	5	263
Health assessment and treating	43	1	87	34	58	600
Health technologists and technicians	42	2	31	42	25	398
Lawyers and judges	34	0	2	2	96	1,052
Protective service	32	9	42	34	15	468
Food preparation and service	30	36	42	17	5	220
Teachers, except college and university	30	1	6	9	84	522
Health diagnosing	29	1	2	2	96	824

[Continued]

★ 508 ★

Selected Occupational Groups Ranked by Projected Percentage Rate of Employment Growth, Levels of Educational Attainment, and Median Weekly Earnings, 1990-2005

[Continued]

Occupation	1990-2005 rates of employment change	Levels of educational attainment (Percent of occupational employment)				Median weekly earnings
		less than high school	High school	1-3 years of college	4 or more of college	
Executive, administrative, and managerial	27	4	27	24	45	604
Engineers	26	1	8	17	74	809
Natural scientists	26	1	4	7	88	661
Sales	24	12	39	25	24	401
Engineering and related technologists and technicians	23	4	36	40	21	509
Supervisors, administrative support	22	4	42	29	24	497
Transportation and material moving	21	26	54	15	4	413
Construction trades	21	25	51	18	6	479
Teachers, college and university	19	1	2	7	90	747
Cleaning and building service	18	40	45	11	3	272
Mechanics and repairers	16	19	54	22	6	476
Mail and message distributing	15	8	50	31	11	514
Computer equipment operators	13	4	47	34	15	374
Secretaries, stenographers, and typists	9	3	53	34	10	342
Handlers, equipment cleaners, helpers, and laborers	8	35	48	14	3	298
Farming, forestry, and fishing	5	37	41	14	8	257
Financial records processing	-4	4	55	29	12	338
Machine operators, assemblers, and inspectors	-9	31	54	12	4	325
Private household workers	-29	50	36	10	4	172

Source: "Occupational Employment Projections," George Silvestri and John Lukasiewicz, *Monthly Labor Review* 114, No. 11, November, 1991, p. 90.

★ 509 ★

Occupational Growth, 1990-2005, and Distribution by Educational Attainment, 1990

"On average, job growth will be fastest in occupational groups requiring the most education. Managerial, professional, and technician occupations have the highest proportion of workers with 4 years of college or 1-3 years of college; these occupations will grow faster than average. In contrast, precision production, operators, and agriculture occupations have the lowest proportion of workers with college training, and these occupations are projected to have the slowest employment growth."

[Numbers in percent]

Occupational group	Projected change 1990-2005	Educational attainment of workers, 1990[1]			4 years of college or more
		Less than high school	High school	1 to 3 years of college	
All occupations	20	15	39	22	24
Managerial	27	4	27	24	45
Professional specialty	32	1	8	16	74
Technicians	37	3	28	37	33
Marketing and sales	24	12	39	25	24
Administrative support	13	6	51	31	13
Services	29	28	45	19	6
Precision production	13	21	53	20	6

[Continued]

★ 509 ★

Occupational Growth, 1990-2005, and Distribution by Educational Attainment, 1990

[Continued]

Occupational group	Projected change 1990-2005	Educational attainment of workers, 1990[1]			4 years of college or more
		Less than high school	High school	1 to 3 years of college	
Operators	4	31	52	13	3
Agriculture-related	5	35	41	14	8

Source: "Outlook 1990-2005," *Occupational Outlook Quarterly* 35, No. 3, Fall, 1991, p. 29. *Note:* 1. Rows may not sum to 100 because of rounding.

★ 510 ★

Self-Employed Workers in Occupations with 50,000 Workers or More, 1990-2005

"The number of self-employed workers is expected to grow by 1.5 million, or a total of 15 percent, between 1990 and 2005."

[Numbers in thousands]

Occupation	1990			2005			Change in self-employed, 1990-2005	
	Total employment	Self-employed workers	Percent of total employment	Total employment	Self-employed workers	Percent of total employment	Number	Percent
Total, all occupations	122,573	10,161	8.3	147,191	11,663	7.9	1,502	14.8
Executive, administrative, and managerial occupations	12,451	1,598	12.8	15,866	2,106	13.3	508	31.8
Managerial and administrative occupations	8,838	1,328	15.0	11,174	1,778	15.9	450	33.9
Food service and lodging managers	595	247	41.5	793	280	35.3	33	13.4
Property and real estate managers	225	89	39.5	302	110	36.5	21	23.6
Management support occupations	3,613	270	7.5	4,691	328	7.0	58	21.5
Accountants and auditors	985	102	10.4	1,325	110	8.3	8	7.8
Management analysts	151	68	4.9	230	100	43.4	32	47.1
Professional specialty occupations	15,800	1,446	9.2	20,907	1,727	8.3	281	19.4
Social scientists	224	65	29.0	320	106	33.1	41	63.1
Psychologists	125	51	40.9	204	90	44.1	39	76.5
Lawyers and judicial workers	633	198	31.3	850	205	24.1	7	3.5
Lawyers	587	198	33.8	793	205	25.9	7	3.5
Teachers, librarians, and counselors	5,687	134	2.4	7,280	165	2.3	31	23.1
Other teachers and instructors	757	108	14.3	963	135	14.0	27	25.0
Adult and vocational education teachers	517	108	20.9	669	135	20.2	27	25.0
Instructors, adult (nonvocational) education	219	108	49.3	289	135	46.7	27	25.0
Health diagnosing occupations	855	271	31.7	1,101	310	28.1	39	14.4
Dentists	174	92	52.7	196	103	52.6	11	12.0
Physicians	580	139	24.0	776	160	20.6	21	15.1
Health assessment and treating occupations	2,305	69	3.0	3,304	89	2.7	20	29.0
Writers, artists, and entertainers	1,542	517	33.5	1,915	603	31.5	86	16.6
Artists and commercial artists	230	143	62.2	303	190	62.8	47	32.9
Designers	339	114	33.6	428	123	28.7	9	7.9
Designers, except interior designers	270	86	31.9	335	90	26.9	4	4.7
Musicians	252	75	29.7	276	85	30.8	10	13.3
Writers and editors, including technical writers	232	78	33.6	292	89	30.5	11	14.1
Technicians and related support occupations	4,204	107	2.5	5,754	132	2.3	25	22.9
Marketing and sales occupations	14,088	1,831	13.0	17,489	1,903	10.9	72	4.0
Insurance sales workers	439	139	31.7	527	150	28.5	11	7.9
Real estate agents, brokers, and appraisers	413	255	61.8	492	281	57.2	26	10.4
Sales agents, real estate	300	199	66.3	355	220	62.0	21	10.6
Salesperson, retail	3,619	187	5.2	4,506	200	4.4	13	7.0
Administrative support occupations, including clerical	21,951	338	1.5	24,835	382	1.5	44	13.0
Financial records processing occupations	2,860	147	5.1	2,750	164	6.0	17	11.6
Bookkeeping, accounting, and auditing clerks	2,276	143	6.3	2,143	160	7.5	17	11.9
Secretaries, stenographers, and typists	4,680	88	1.9	5,110	110	2.2	22	25.0
Service occupations	19,204	1,220	6.4	24,805	1,662	6.7	442	36.2
Cleaning and building service occupations, except private household	3,435	238	6.9	4,068	352	8.7	114	47.9
Janitors and cleaners, including maids and housekeeping cleaners	3,007	221	7.4	3,562	332	9.3	111	50.2
Food preparation and service occupations	7,706	79	1.0	10,031	80	.8	1	1.3
Chefs, cooks, and other kitchen workers	3,069	50	1.6	4,104	55	1.3	5	10.0

[Continued]

★ 510 ★

Self-Employed Workers in Occupations with 50,000 Workers or More, 1990-2005
[Continued]

Occupation	1990			2005			Change in self-employed, 1990-2005	
	Total employment	Self-employed workers	Percent of total employment	Total employment	Self-employed workers	Percent of total employment	Number	Percent
Personal service occupations	2,192	824	37.6	3,164	1,112	35.1	288	34.9
Barbers	77	59	76.6	76	59	77.8	0	0.0
Child care workers	725	466	64.3	1,078	676	62.7	210	45.0
Cosmetologists and related workers	636	296	46.5	793	374	47.1	78	26.4
Hairdressers, hairstylists, and cosmetologists	597	287	48.1	742	363	48.9	76	26.5
Agriculture, forestry, fishing, and related occupations	3,506	1,380	39.4	3,665	1,250	34.1	-131	-9.5
Farm operators and managers	1,223	1,074	87.8	1,023	850	83.1	-224	-20.9
Farmers	1,074	1,074	100.0	850	850	100.0	-224	-20.9
Gardeners and groundskeepers, except farm	874	166	19.0	1,222	250	20.5	84	50.6
Precision production, craft, and repair occupations	14,124	1,686	11.9	15,909	1,932	12.1	246	14.6
Blue-collar worker supervisors	1,792	130	7.3	1,912	143	7.5	13	10.0
Construction trades	3,763	936	24.9	4,557	1,158	25.4	222	23.7
Carpenters	1,057	373	35.3	1,209	450	37.2	77	20.6
Electricians	548	58	10.6	706	75	10.6	17	29.3
Painters and paperhangers, construction and maintenance	453	214	47.2	564	289	51.2	75	35.0
Plumbers, pipefitters, and steamfitters	379	65	17.2	459	75	16.4	10	15.4
Mechanics, installers, and repairers	4,900	407	8.3	5,669	411	7.3	4	1.0
Machinery and related mechanics, installers, and repairers	1,675	56	3.3	1,980	65	3.3	9	16.1
Vehicle and mobile equipment mechanics and repairers	1,568	240	15.3	1,892	225	11.9	-15	-6.3
Automotive mechanics	757	152	20.1	923	145	15.7	-7	-4.6
Other mechanics, installers, and repairers	1,002	73	7.3	1,180	77	6.5	4	5.5
Production occupations, precision	3,134	205	6.5	3,208	212	6.6	7	3.4
Textile, apparel, and furnishings workers, precision	272	90	33.0	302	96	31.8	6	6.7
Custom tailors and sewers	116	61	52.7	137	70	51.0	9	14.8
Operators, fabricators, and laborers	17,245	555	3.2	17,961	570	3.2	15	2.7
Machine setters, set-up operators, operators, and tenders	4,905	93	1.9	4,579	97	2.1	4	4.3
Hand workers, including assemblers and fabricators	2,675	103	3.9	2,307	119	5.2	16	15.5
Transportation and material moving machine and vehicle operators	4,730	285	6.0	5,743	278	4.8	-7	-2.5
Motor vehicle operators	3,417	248	7.3	4,301	242	5.6	-6	-2.4
Truckdrivers	2,701	196	7.3	3,360	174	5.2	-22	-11.2
Truckdrivers, light and heavy	2,362	182	7.7	2,979	160	5.4	-22	-12.1
Helpers, laborers, and material movers, hand	4,935	74	1.5	5,332	76	1.4	2	2.7

Source: "Occupational Employment Projections," George Silvestri and John Lukasiewicz, *Monthly Labor Review* 114, No. 11, November, 1991, pp. 85-86.

Employee Earnings and Benefits

★ 511 ★

Average Earnings per Worker, 1970, 1985, and 2000

	1970		1985		2000					
					Base		Low		High	
	Level	% change	Level	% change	Level	% change	Level	% change	Level	% change
Average compensation per worker in thousands	18.7	2.27	19.8	0.39	25.6	1.7	22.0	0.7	27.6	2.2

Source: Workforce 2000: Work and Workers for the Twenty-First Century, Hudson Institute, Indianapolis, Indiana, 1987, p. 54. Also in source: data on the U.S. Gross National Product, Unemployment, Deflation, Employment in manufacturing and commercial and other services, productivity per worker in manufacturing and commercial and other services, the federal surplus, the federal deficit, import and export balances, interest rates, consumption per capita, and disposable income per capita for the years 1955, 1970, 1985, and projections to 2000.

★ 512 ★

Earnings: Business and Financial Services, 1991 and 2000

Occupation	Salary (average unless other- wise noted) 1991	Salary (average unless other- wise noted) 2000
Accountant/Auditor	28,400 (starting)	43,000 (starting)
Bank Loan Officer	26,250 to 44,000 (starting)	40,000 to 65,000 (starting)
Bank Marketer	36,382 to 220,000	50,000 to 300,000
Corporate Financial Analyst	73,867	101,400
Court Reporter	26,460	37,000.
Economist	27,000 (starting with bachelor's degree)	40,512 (starting with bachelor's degree)
Financial Planner	18,900 to 31,500 (starting)	30,000 to 50,000 (starting)
Insurance Claim Examiner	22,176	32,260
Investment Banker	45,000 to 50,000 (starting)	77,000 to 86,000 (starting)
Lawyer	57,170	88,000
Management Consultant	40,021 to 45,510	60,000 to 72,000
Paralegal	30,171	39,840
Real Estate Agent/Broker	30,870	46,200 +
Real Estate Appraiser	33,075	50,000
Underwriter	31,303	45,427

Source: "The Top Jobs: Business and Financial Services," *The 100 Best Jobs for the 1990s and Beyond*, Carol Kleiman, Dearborn Financial Publishing, Chicago, IL., 1992. Primary source: *Projections 2000: A Look at Occupational Employment in the Year 2000*, George T. Silvestri and John M. Lukasiewicz, Division of Occupational Outlook, U.S. Department of Labor, Bureau of Labor Statistics, September, 1987; and *Occupational Outlook Handbook*, April, 1990. Data are also drawn from other published and unpublished sources.

★ 513 ★

Earnings: Education, Government, and Social Services, 1991 and 2000

Occupation	Salary (average unless other- wise noted) 1991	Salary (average unless other- wise noted) 2000
Corrections Officer/Guard/Jailer	17,000 to 21,000	21,000 to 35,000
Educational Administrator	55,125	70,000
Firefighter	30,870	42,000
Librarian	28,665 to 88,200	40,300 to 124,000
Mathematician/Statistician	29,900 (starting with bachelor's degree)	45,000 (starting with bachelor's degree)
Police Officer	30,870	42,750
Psychologist/Counselor	36,225 to 55,125	45,000 to 75,000

[Continued]

★ 513 ★

Earnings: Education, Government, and Social Services, 1991 and 2000

[Continued]

Occupation	Salary (average unless otherwise noted) 1991	Salary (average unless otherwise noted) 2000
Social Worker	32,793	45,000
Teacher/Professor	32,202 (teacher)	46,733 (teacher)
	43,720 (professor)	71,211 (professor)

Source: "The Top Jobs: Education, Government, and Social Services," *The 100 Best Jobs for the 1990s and Beyond*, Carol Kleiman, Dearborn Financial Publishing, Chicago, IL., 1992. Primary source: *Projections 2000: A Look at Occupational Employment in the Year 2000*, George T. Silvestri and John M. Lukasiewicz, Division of Occupational Outlook, U.S. Department of Labor, Bureau of Labor Statistics, September, 1987; and *Occupational Outlook Handbook*, April, 1990. Data are also drawn from other published and unpublished sources.

★ 514 ★

Earnings: Engineering and Computer Technology, 1991 and 2000

Occupation	Salary (average) 1991	Salary (average) 2000
Computer Operator	20,466 to 27,707	33,000 to 42,000
Computer Programmer	31,900	52,632
Computer Service Technician	34,177	52,000
Computer Systems Analyst	31,200 to 42,997	48,000 to 67,000
Database Manager	38,587	50,000
Drafter	16,537 to 40,000	20,000 to 60,000
Engineer	34,300 (with bachelor's degree)	68,000 (with bachelor's degree)
Information Systems Manager	146,081	225,250
Manufacturing Specialist (CAD/CAM and CAI)	34,177	45,000
Operations/Systems Research Analyst	40,633	62,500
Peripheral Electronic Data Processing Equipment Operator	22,050	30,000

Source: "The Top Jobs: Health Care Professions," *The 100 Best Jobs for the 1990s and Beyond*, Carol Kleiman, Dearborn Financial Publishing, Chicago, IL., 1992. Primary source: *Projections 2000: A Look at Occupational Employment in the Year 2000*, George T. Silvestri and John M. Lukasiewicz, Division of Occupational Outlook, U.S. Department of Labor, Bureau of Labor Statistics, September, 1987; and *Occupational Outlook Handbook*, April, 1990. Data are also drawn from other published and unpublished sources.

★ 515 ★

Earnings: Health Care Professions, 1991 and 2000

Occupation	Salary (average unless otherwise noted) 1991	Salary (average unless otherwise noted) 2000
Dental Hygienist	27,397	39,800
Dentist	79,065	125,000
Dietitian	27,562 to 71,662	40,000 to 80,000
Health Services Administrator	38,587 to 66,150	71,250
Home Health Aide	15,435	20,000
Licensed Practical Nurse	23,152	42,000
Medical Records Administrator	43,549	64,000
Occupational Therapist	29,767	51,000
Opthalmic Laboratory Technician	12,763 to 19,143	16,785 to 26,000
Optician	28,665	40,000
Paramedic	26,460	36,000
Pharmacist	44,000	60,605
Physical Therapist	31,421 to 66,150	45,000 to 96,000
Physician	157,500	233,906
Physician Assistant	35,000 to 60,000	47,250
Podiatrist	44,100 (starting)	68,412 (starting)
Radiologic Technologist	25,358 (starting)	41,000 (starting)
Registered Nurse	27,000 (starting)	50,000 (starting)
Speech Pathologist/Audiologist	31,421	46,000
Veterinarian	25,000 (starting)	34,000 (starting)

Source: "The Top Jobs: Health Care Professions," *The 100 Best Jobs for the 1990s and Beyond,* Carol Kleiman, Dearborn Financial Publishing, Chicago, IL., 1992. Primary source: *Projections 2000: A Look at Occupational Employment in the Year 2000,* George T. Silvestri and John M. Lukasiewicz, Division of Occupational Outlook, U.S. Department of Labor, Bureau of Labor Statistics, September, 1987; and *Occupational Outlook Handbook,* April, 1990. Data are also drawn from other published and unpublished sources.

★ 516 ★

Earnings: Hospitality Industry, 1991 and 2000

Occupation	Salary (average unless otherwise noted) 1991	Salary (average unless otherwise noted) 2000
Cook/Chef	13,230 (cook, starting) 40,000 (chef, starting)	26,000 (cook, starting) 60,000 (chef, starting)
Flight Attendant	24,888 to 43,989	34,000 to 53,422
Flight Engineer	46,305	65,000
Hotel Manager/Assistant	55,252	80,000 +
Pilot	92,610	125,000
Restaurant/Food Service Manager	40,792	65,000
Travel Agent	21,110	27,000

Source: "The Top Jobs: Hospitality Industry," *The 100 Best Jobs for the 1990s and Beyond*, Carol Kleiman, Dearborn Financial Publishing, Chicago, IL., 1992. Primary source: *Projections 2000: A Look at Occupational Employment in the Year 2000*, George T. Silvestri and John M. Lukasiewicz, Division of Occupational Outlook, U.S. Department of Labor, Bureau of Labor Statistics, September, 1987; and *Occupational Outlook Handbook*, April, 1990. Data are also drawn from other published and unpublished sources.

★ 517 ★

Earnings: Management and Office Personnel, 1991 and 2000

Occupation	Salary (average unless otherwise noted) 1991	Salary (average unless otherwise noted) 2000
Clerical Supervisor/Office Manager	19,845 to 44,000	25,000 to 60,000
Corporate Personnel Trainer	30,870	50,000
Employment Interviewer	17,640 to 30,000 (starting)	25,000 to 48,000 (starting)
Human Resources Manager/Executive	81,585	122,160

[Continued]

★ 517 ★

Earnings: Management and Office Personnel, 1991 and 2000

[Continued]

Occupation	Salary (average unless otherwise noted) 1991	Salary (average unless otherwise noted) 2000
Labor Relations Specialist	40,091	61,818
Secretary/Office Administrator	19,361	24,000

Source: "The Top Jobs: Management and Office Personnel," *The 100 Best Jobs for the 1990s and Beyond*, Carol Kleiman, Dearborn Financial Publishing, Chicago, IL., 1992. Primary source: *Projections 2000: A Look at Occupational Employment in the Year 2000*, George T. Silvestri and John M. Lukasiewicz, Division of Occupational Outlook, U.S. Department of Labor, Bureau of Labor Statistics, September, 1987; and *Occupational Outlook Handbook*, April, 1990. Data are also drawn from other published and unpublished sources.

★ 518 ★

Earnings: Manufacturing, Repair, Construction, Agriculture, and Transportation, 1991 and 2000

Occupation	Salary (average unless otherwise noted) 1991	Salary (average unless otherwise noted) 2000
Aircraft Technician	23,152 to 31,972	30,000 to 45,000
Appliance/Power Tool Repairer	27,562	40,000
Architect	39,946	61,596
Automotive Mechanic	26,460	36,000
Carpenter	23,152	34,650
Farm Manager	18,742	30,000
Industrial Designer	26,823 (starting)	45,000 (starting)
Landscape Architect	23,152 to 28,662 (starting)	35,000 to 42,600 (starting)
Office/Business Machine Repairer	25,809	37,565
Operations Manager/Manufacturing	85,000	95,000
Radio/TV Service Technician	17,867 to 25,525	24,000 to 35,000
Truck Driver	17,867 to 25,525	24,000 to 35,000

Source: "The Top Jobs: Manufacturing, Repair, Construction, Agriculture, and Transportation," *The 100 Best Jobs for the 1990s and Beyond*, Carol Kleiman, Dearborn Financial Publishing, Chicago, IL., 1992. Primary source: *Projections 2000: A Look at Occupational Employment in the Year 2000*, George T. Silvestri and John M. Lukasiewicz, Division of Occupational Outlook, U.S. Department of Labor, Bureau of Labor Statistics, September, 1987; and *Occupational Outlook Handbook*, April, 1990. Data are also drawn from other published and unpublished sources.

★ 519 ★

Earnings: Media and the Arts, 1991 and 2000

Occupation	Salary (average unless otherwise noted) 1991	Salary (average unless otherwise noted) 2000
Actor/Director/Producer	6,614 to 100,000 (actor) 38,587 to 100,000 + (director) 66,150 to 100,000 + (producer)	12,000 to 150,000 (actor) 70,000 to 200,000 + (director) 95,000 to 200,000 + (producer)
Accounting and Marketing Supervisor	48,041	70,000
Arts Administrator	20,000 (starting)	50,000 (starting)
Commercial and Graphic Artists	27,562	35,000
Editor/Writer	35,059	50,000
Interior Designer	31,972	47,000
Photographer/Camera Operator	25,357	35,882
Public relations Specialist	31,972	50,000
Radio/TV New Reporter	28,972 (starting)	44,000 (starting)
Reporter/Correspondent	16,537 to 60,637	30,000 to 100,000

Source: "The Top Jobs: Media and the Arts," *The 100 Best Jobs for the 1990s and Beyond*, Carol Kleiman, Dearborn Financial Publishing, Chicago, IL., 1992. Primary source: *Projections 2000: A Look at Occupational Employment in the Year 2000*, George T. Silvestri and John M. Lukasiewicz, Division of Occupational Outlook, U.S. Department of Labor, Bureau of Labor Statistics, September, 1987; and *Occupational Outlook Handbook*, April, 1990. Data are also drawn from other published and unpublished sources.

★ 520 ★

Earnings: Sales and Personal Services, 1991 and 2000

Occupation	Salary (average) 1991	Salary (average) 2000
Cosmetologist	13,325	18,000
Insurance Salesperson	54,000	86,400
Retail Salesperson	13,781 to 18,522	20,000 to 27,000
Wholesale Sales Representative	27,364	40,000

Source: "The Top Jobs: Sales and Personal Services," *The 100 Best Jobs for the 1990s and Beyond,* Carol Kleiman, Dearborn Financial Publishing, Chicago, IL., 1992. Primary source: *Projections 2000: A Look at Occupational Employment in the Year 2000,* George T. Silvestri and John M. Lukasiewicz, Division of Occupational Outlook, U.S. Department of Labor, Bureau of Labor Statistics, September, 1987; and *Occupational Outlook Handbook,* April, 1990. Data are also drawn from other published and unpublished sources.

★ 521 ★

Earnings: Science, 1991 and 2000

Occupation	Salary (average unless otherwise noted) 1991	Salary (average unless otherwise noted) 2000
Agricultural Scientist	23,835	45,000
Biological Scientist	33,075 (average)	50,000 (average)
Chemist	33,000	64,000
Environmental Scientist	39,060	68,200
Food Scientist	25,000	35,000
Physicist/Astronomer	44,000	62,000

Source: "The Top Jobs: Science," *The 100 Best Jobs for the 1990s and Beyond,* Carol Kleiman, Dearborn Financial Publishing, Chicago, IL., 1992. Primary source: *Projections 2000: A Look at Occupational Employment in the Year 2000,* George T. Silvestri and John M. Lukasiewicz, Division of Occupational Outlook, U.S. Department of Labor, Bureau of Labor Statistics, September, 1987; and *Occupational Outlook Handbook,* April, 1990. Data are also drawn from other published and unpublished sources.

★ 522 ★

Employee Benefits, 1990-2000

Percent of International Foundation of Employee Benefits Plan member companies surveyed that offer or will offer selected benefits, in 1990 or by 2000. IFEBP obtained responses from 463 of its 1,865 member organizations. About 21 percent of respondents represented organizations with fewer than 500 employees, 49 percent had between 500 and 4,999 employees, and the remainder had 5,000 or more. About 28 percent were manufacturing firms, 26 percent were in financial or insurance services, and the rest were in transportation, health, trade, or other industries.

	Offered in 1990	Will offer by 2000
Child/elder care		
Child care resource/referral	29.0	74.0
Subsidization of child care expenses	12.0	52.0
On- or near-site child care facility	7.0	35.0
Sick child facility/home based care	3.0	28.0
School/camp advisory services	3.0	14.0
Elder services resource/referral	11.0	64.0
Subsidization of elder care expenses	3.0	23.0
Elder respite care	1.0	19.0
Adult day care	1.0	11.0
Other life cycle benefits		
Financial planning	22.0	69.0
Long term care insurance	8.0	68.0
Special health/life benefits for older workers	7.0	41.0
Training/education/awareness		
Tuition reimbursement	91.0	97.0
Technical/management/professional training	84.0	95.0
Basic skills training	47.0	73.0
Retraining	38.0	70.0
Sex/minority workshops	27.0	56.0
Literacy training	19.0	50.0
Sabbaticals	14.0	33.0
Counseling		
Family counseling	49.0	69.0
Mentor/career counseling	29.0	67.0
Immigration counseling/legal assistance	11.0	25.0
Housing assistance resource/referral	21.0	37.0
Work environment		
Affirmative action program	72.0	83.0
Special work stations for disabled	30.0	67.0
Multilingual worksites	15.0	29.0
Work schedule/location		
Part-time employment	80.0	94.0
Flextime	52.0	86.0

[Continued]

★ 522 ★

Employee Benefits, 1990-2000
[Continued]

	Offered in 1990	Will offer by 2000
Family leave	49.0	84.0
Seasonal hours/school work year	27.0	46.0
Job sharing	24.0	67.0
Compressed workweek	22.0	51.0
Telecommuting	15.0	52.0

Source: "Meet the New Boss," Judith Waldrop, *American Demographics* 13, No. 6, June, 1991, p. 29. Primary source: International Foundation of Employee Benefits Plans, Brookfield, WI.

Ethnic and Gender-Related Demographics

★ 523 ★

Civilian Labor Force Participation Rates of Women by Race and Ethnicity, 1988 and 2000

Group	1988	2000
White women	56.4	62.9
Black women	58.0	62.5
Hispanic women	53.2	59.4
Asian women	56.5	57.5

Source: A Changing Nation—Its Changing Labor Force, Everett Crawford, Carol J. Romero, and Burt S. Barnow, Research Report Number 91-04. National Commission for Employment Policy, November 1991, p. 55. Also in source: data from 1970, 1976, and 1980. Primary source: U.S. Bureau of the Census, *Statistical Abstract of the United States: 1988*, Washington, D.C., 1987, and U.S. Bureau of Labor Statistics, *Employment and Earnings*, Annual Averages - 1990, Washington, D.C., 1991. Howard N. Fullerton, Jr. (1989), "New Labor Force Projections, Spanning 1988 to 2000, *Monthly Labor Review*, Volume 112, No. 11, November 1989, Table 4. U.S. Commission on Civil Rights (1990), *The Economic Status of Black Women: An Exploratory Investigation*, Washington, D.C.; The Commission, Table 1.2.

★ 524 ★

Minority Share in the Labor Force, 1970-2000

"Non-whites will comprise 29 percent of the net additions to the workforce between 1985 and 2000 and will be more than 15 percent of the workforce in the year 2000. Black women will comprise the largest share of the increase in the non-white labor force. In fact, by the year 2000, black women will outnumber black men in the labor force."

[Numbers in millions, shares in percent]

	1970	1985	2000
Working age population (16 +)	137.1	184.1	213.7
Non-white share	10.9	13.6	15.7
Labor force	82.8	115.5	140.4
Non-white share	11.1	13.1	15.5
Labor force increase			
Over previous period	x	32.7	25.0
Non-white share	x	18.4	29.0

Source: "Non-Whites are a Growing Share of the Workforce," *Workforce 2000: Work and Workers for the Twenty-First Century*, Hudson Institute, Indianapolis, Indiana, 1987, p. 89. Primary source: Bureau of Labor Statistics, *Handbook of Labor Statistics, 1985*, Tables 4 and 5, and Hudson Institute. *Note:* X stands for not available.

★ 525 ★

Net Change in the Ethnic Composition of the Civilian Labor Force, 1988-2000

	Net change (1,000)	Percent of total
White non-Hispanic men	2,256	11.6
White non-Hispanic women	6,939	35.7
Black non-Hispanic men	1,302	6.7
Black non-Hispanic women	1,754	9.0
Asian and other men	950	4.9
Asian and other women	910	4.7
Hispanic men	2,877	14.8
Hispanic women	2,464	12.7
Total	19,461	100.0

Source: A Changing Nation—Its Changing Labor Force, Everett Crawford, Carol J. Romero, and Burt S. Barrow, Research Report November 91-04, National Commission for Employment Policy, November 1991, p. 7. Primary source: Bureau of Labor Statistics, U.S. Department of Labor, "New Labor Force Projections, Spanning 1988 to 2000," *Monthly Labor Review* 112, No. 11, 1989. *Note:* Data are for persons 16 years and older.

★ 526 ★

Sharing the Job Market: Whites, Non-Whites, Women, and Immigrants, 1985-2000

"Non-whites, women, and immigrants will make up more than five-sixths of the net additions to ... the workforce between now and the year 2000, though they make up only about half of it today."

	1985 labor force	Net new workers 1985-2000
Total	115,461,000	25,000,000
Percent distribution		
Native white men	47.0	15.0
Native white women	36.0	42.0
Native non-white men	5.0	7.0
Native non-white women	5.0	13.0
Immigrant men	4.0	13.0
Immigrant women	3.0	9.0

Source: Workforce 2000: Work and Workers for the Twenty-First Century, Hudson Institute, Indianapolis, Indiana, 1987, p. xxi.

★ 527 ★

Non-White, Female, and Immigrant Entrants to the Labor Force, 1985-2000

"The cumulative impact of the changing ethnic and racial composition of the labor force will be dramatic. The small net growth of workers will be dominated by women, blacks, and immigrants. White males will comprise only 15 percent of the net additions to the labor force between 1985 and 2000."

[Numbers are in percent]

	Labor force 1985	Increase 1985-2000
Native white males	47.0	15.0
Native white females	36.0	42.0
Native non-white males	5.0	7.0
Native non-white females	5.0	13.0
Immigrant males	4.0	13.0
Immigrant females	3.0	9.0

Source: "Most New Entrants to the Labor Force Will be Non-White, Female, or Immigrants," *Workforce 2000: Work and Workers for the Twenty-First Century*, Hudson Institute, Indianapolis, Indiana, 1987, p. 95.

★ 528 ★

Sharing the Job Market: Women, Blacks, and Hispanics, 1985-2000

Shares are in percent.

Group	Share of current jobs	Implied share of new jobs (1985-2000)	Share of labor force growth
Women	45.0	50.5	59.3
Blacks	9.9	9.5	19.7
Black men	4.9	3.8	7.7
Black women	5.1	5.6	12.0
Hispanics	6.4	5.0	22.0
Ages 16-24	19.1	17.9	-9.6
25-44	51.6	53.0	44.8
45 +	29.3	29.1	64.8

Source: "Black Men and Hispanics Face the Greatest Difficulties in the Emerging Job Markets," *Workforce 2000: Work and Workers for the Twenty-First Century*, Hudson Institute, Indianapolis, Indiana, 1987, p. 102.

★ 529 ★

Growth in Women's Share of the Labor Force, 1950-2000

"By the year 2000, approximately 47 percent of the workforce will be women, and 61 percent of women will be at work. Women will comprise about three fifths of the new entrants into the labor force between 1985 and 2000."

[Numbers in thousands, except percent]

	1950	1960	1970	1980	1990	2000
Women in the workforce	18,389	23,240	31,543	45,487	57,230	66,670
Female labor force participation rate	33.9	37.7	43.3	51.5	57.5	61.1
Female share of the workforce	29.6	33.4	38.1	42.5	45.8	47.5

Source: Workforce 2000: Work and Workers for the Twenty-First Century, Hudson Institute, Indianapolis, Indiana, 1987, p. 85.

★ 530 ★

Distribution of Entrants to the Labor Force by Sex, Race, and Hispanic Origin, 1990-2005

"White non-Hispanic men and women will account for the majority of entrants to the labor force."

[Numbers in percent]

	Men	Women
White, non-Hispanic	32.2	33.1
Black, non-Hispanic	6.2	6.8
Hispanic, all races	9.1	6.6
Asian and other	3.0	3.0

Source: "Outlook 1990-2005," *Occupational Outlook Quarterly* 35, No. 3, Fall, 1991, p. 15.

★ 531 ★

Distribution of the Labor Force by Race and Hispanic Origin, 1990 and 2005

"For Asians and others, [faster growth will occur] primarily due to immigration. The number of Hispanics will increase because of immigration and a higher historic birth rate. Blacks will grow faster than whites because the birth rates for blacks declined more slowly than for whites during the 1970s."

[Numbers in percent]

	1990	2005
White, non-Hispanics	78.5	73.0
Blacks	10.7	11.6
Hispanics	7.7	11.1
Asians	3.1	4.3

Source: "Outlook 1990-2005," *Occupational Outlook Quarterly* 35, No. 3, Fall, 1991, p. 12. The Asians and others group includes Asians, Pacific Islanders, American Indians, and Alaskan Natives.

★ 532 ★

Labor Force Growth by Race and Hispanic Origin, 1990-2005

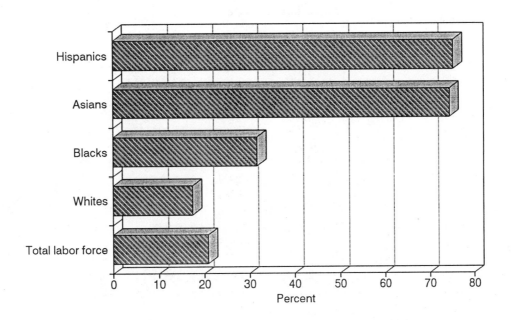

"Blacks, Hispanics, Asians, and others will continue to increase in number faster than the average growth of the labor force as a whole. Although minority groups will account for an increasing share of the labor force, the vast majority of workers will continue to be white non-Hispanics."

[Numbers in percent]

Hispanics	75.3
Asians and other races	74.5
Blacks	31.7
Whites	17.4
Total labor force	20.8

Source: "Outlook 1990-2005," *Occupational Outlook Quarterly* 35, No. 3, Fall, 1991, p. 12. The Asians and others group includes Asians, Pacific Islanders, American Indians, and Alaskan Natives.

★ 533 ★

Labor Force Entrants and Separations by Race, Ethnicity, and Gender, 1990-2005

Group	Labor force, 1990	Entrants, 1990-2005	Leavers, 1990-2005	Labor force, 2005
Number (in thousands)				
Total	124,786	55,798	29,851	150,732
Men	68,232	28,197	17,090	79,339
Women	56,554	27,601	12,761	71,394
White, non-Hispanic	98,013	36,425	24,423	110,015
Men	53,784	17,965	14,204	57,545
Women	44,229	18,460	10,219	52,470
Black	13,340	7,250	3,144	17,447
Men	6,628	3,461	1,553	8,537
Women	6,712	3,789	1,591	8,910
Hispanic	9,577	8,768	1,556	16,789
Men	5,756	5,085	939	9,902
Women	3,822	3,683	617	6,888
Asian and other	3,855	3,354	728	6,482
Men	2,064	1,686	395	3,356
Women	1,791	1,668	333	3,126
Share (percent)				
Total	100.0	100.0	100.0	100.0
Men	54.7	50.5	57.3	52.6
Women	45.3	49.5	42.7	47.4
White, non-Hispanic	78.5	65.3	81.8	73.0
Men	43.1	32.2	47.6	38.2
Women	35.4	33.1	34.2	34.8
Black	10.7	13.0	10.5	11.6
Men	5.3	6.2	5.2	5.7
Women	5.4	6.8	5.3	5.9
Hispanic	7.7	15.7	5.2	11.1
Men	4.6	9.1	3.1	6.6
Women	3.1	6.6	2.1	4.6
Asian and other	3.1	6.0	2.4	4.3
Men	1.7	3.0	1.3	2.2
Women	1.4	3.0	1.1	2.1

Source: "Civilian Labor Force, 1990 and Projected to 2005, and Projected Entrants and Leavers, 1990-2005," Howard N. Fullerton, Jr., *Monthly Labor Review* 114, No. 11, November, 1991, p. 41 Primary source: Bureau of Labor Statistics, Office of Employment Projections.

★ 534 ★

Percent Change in Employment for Selected Occupations, 1990-2005, and Percent of Employment Composed of Women, Blacks, and Hispanics, 1990

Occupation	Percent change, 1990-2005	Percent in 1990 composed of --		Hispanics
		Women	Blacks	
Total, all occupations	20	45	10	8
Executive, administrative, and managerial	27	40	6	4
Professional specialty occupations	32	51	7	3
Engineers	26	9	3	3
Mathematical and computer scientists	73	37	7	3
Natural scientists	26	26	3	4
Health diagnosing occupations	29	18	3	4
Health assessment and treating occupations	43	86	7	3
Teachers, college and university	19	38	5	3
Teachers, except college and university	30	74	9	4
Lawyers and judges	34	21	3	3
Technicians and related support	37	49	9	4
Health technologists and technicians	42	84	14	5
Engineering and related technologists and technicians	23	20	7	5
Sales occupations	24	49	6	5
Administrative support, including clerical	13	80	11	7
Supervisors, administrative support	22	58	12	7
Computer equipment operators	13	66	13	7
Secretaries, stenographers, and typists	9	98	9	5
Financial records processing	-4	92	6	5
Mail and message distributing	15	45	25	5
Service occupations	29	60	17	11
Private household	-29	60	17	11
Protective service	32	15	17	6
Food preparation and service	30	60	12	13
Health service	44	90	26	6
Cleaning and building service	18	44	22	17
Personal service	44	82	12	7
Precision, production, craft, and repair	13	9	8	9
Mechanics and repairers	16	4	8	7
Construction trades	21	2	7	9
Operators, fabricators, and laborers	4	26	15	12
Machine operators, assemblers, and inspectors	-9	40	14	14
Transportation and material moving	21	9	15	9
Handlers, equipment cleaners, helpers, and laborers	8	18	16	13
Farming, forestry, and fishing	5	16	6	14

Source: "Occupational Employment Projections," George Silvestri and John Lukasiewicz, *Monthly Labor Review* 114, No. 11, November, 1991, p. 92.

Occupations by Educational Requirement

★ 535 ★

Percent of Occupations by Educational Requirement, 1984-2000

"Of all the new jobs that will be created over the 1984-2000 period, more than half will require some education beyond high school, and almost a third will be filled by college graduates. The median years of education required by the new jobs created between 1984 and 2000 will be 13.5, compared to 12.8 for the current workforce."

[Numbers are in percent]

	Current jobs	New jobs
Total	100.0	100.0
8 years or less	6.0	4.0
1-3 years of High School	12.0	10.0
4 years of High School	40.0	35.0
1-3 years of college	20.0	22.0
4 years of college or more	22.0	30.0
Median years of school	12.8	13.5

Source: "The Occupations of the Future Will Require More Education," *Workforce 2000: Work and Workers for the Twenty-First Century*, Hudson Institute, Indianapolis, Indiana, 1987, p. 98. Primary source: Bureau of Labor Statistics, Hudson Institute.

★ 536 ★

Decline in Low-Skilled Jobs, 1987-2000

In percent.

Skill ratings	Existing jobs	Jobs in the year 2000
0.7-1.4	9.0	4.0
1.5-2.4	31.0	23.0
2.5-3.4	35.0	34.0
3.5-4.4	18.0	28.0
4.5-5.4	5.0	11.0
5.5-6.4	1.0	2.0

Source: "Low Skilled Jobs Are Declining," *Workforce 2000: Work and Workers for the Twenty-First Century*, Hudson Institute, Indianapolis, Indiana, 1987, p. 100.

★ 537 ★

Projected Growth Occupations by Level of Education Required, 1990-2005

Group I: Occupations generally requiring a bachelor's degree or more education

System analysts and computer scientists
Physical therapists
Operations research analysts
Psychologists
Computer programmers
Occupational therapists
Management analysts
Marketing, advertising, and public relations managers
General managers and top executives
Teachers, secondary school
Teachers, elementary school
Accountants and auditors
Lawyers

Group II: Occupations generally requiring some postsecondary training or extensive employer training

Paralegals
Radiologic technologists and technicians
Medical assistants
Physical and corrective therapy assistants and aides
Data processing equipment repairers
Medical records technicians
Surgical technicians
Cooks, restaurant
Respiratory therapists
Licensed practical nurses
Maintenance repairers, general utility
Teacher aides and educational assistants

Registered nurses
Legal secretaries
Medical secretaries

Group III: Occupations generally requiring high school graduation or less education

Home health aides
Human services worker
Personal and home care aides
Correction officers
Travel agents
Flight attendants
Salespersons, retail
General office clerks
Cashiers
Food counter, fountain, and related workers
Truckdrivers, light and heavy
Nursing aides, orderlies, and attendants
Janitors and cleaners, including maids and housekeeping cleaners
Waiters and waitresses
Food preparation workers
Receptionists and information clerks
Gardeners and groundskeepers, except farm
Guards
Child care workers
Secretaries, except legal and medical
Cooks, short order and fast food
Clerical supervisors and managers
Stock clerks, sales floor

Source: "Occupational Employment Projections," George Silvestri and John Lukasiewicz, *Monthly Labor Review* 114, No. 11, November, 1991, 83.

★ 538 ★

Fastest Growing Occupations Requiring a High School Diploma or Less Education, 1990-2005

"Service occupations account for nearly half of the 20 fastest growing occupations requiring a high school graduation or less education; these jobs often require some on-the-job training."

[Numbers in percent]

Home health aides	92.0
Personal home care aides	77.0
Human service workers	71.0
Medical secretaries	68.0
Subway and streetcar operators	66.0
Travel agents	62.0
Correction officers	61.0
Flight attendants	59.0
Childcare workers	49.0
Receptionists and information clerks	47.0
Nursing aides, orderlies, and attendants	43.0
Detectives except public	41.0
Gardeners and groundskeepers	40.0
Interviewing clerks	39.0
Manicurists	38.0
Animal caretakers	38.0
Camera operators, television and motion picture	37.0
Bakers, bread and pastry	37.0
Teacher aides and educational assistants	34.0
Bus drivers, school	34.0

Source: "Outlook, 1990-2005," *Occupational Outlook Quarterly* 35, No. 3, Fall, 1991, p. 35.

★ 539 ★

Rankings of Occupations for Which Formal Employer Training is Significant by Selected Characteristics, 1986-2000

National Industry-Occupation Matrix occupation	Employment		Employment change 1986-2000		Median weekly earnings of full-time workers	Unemployment rate	Separation rate (Annual)	Percent of employees	
	1986	2000	Number	Percent				Working part-time	Age 16-24
Managerial and management related occupations									
Inspectors and compliance officers, except construction[1]	A	A	L	L	VH	VL	A	A	L
Construction and building inspectors	VL	VL	VL	L	H	A	H	A	L
Professional specialty occupations									
Surveyors[2]	L	L	A	H	A	A	VL	A	H
Photographers[3]	L	A	H	VH	A	L	L	VH	H
Technician occupations									
Opticians, dispensing and measuring[3]	VL	VL	A	VH	VL	L	VH	VH	H
Electrical and electronic technicians/technologists[3]	H	H	VH	VH	H	L	L	L	A

[Continued]

Rankings of Occupations for Which Formal Employer Training is Significant by Selected Characteristics, 1986-2000

[Continued]

National Industry-Occupation Matrix occupation	Employment		Employment change 1986-2000		Median weekly earnings of full-time workers	Unemployment rate	Separation rate (Annual)	Percent of employees	
	1986	2000	Number	Percent				Working part-time	Age 16-24
Marketing and sales occupations									
Insurance sales workers	VH	VH	VH	H	A	VL	L	H	L
Real estate sales workers[3]	H	VH	VH	VH	H	VL	H	VH	L
Securities and financial services sales workers[1]	A	H	VH	VH	VH	VL	VL	H	L
Administrative support occupations									
Insurance claims and policy processing occupations	H	H	H	L	L	L	VL	A	H
Telephone operators	H	H	H	L	VL	H	A	VH	H
Computer operators and peripheral equipment operators[4]	H	H	VH	VH	VL	A	H	H	H
Reservation and transportation ticket agents and travel clerks	A	A	A	H	A	VL	H	H	H
Bank tellers	VH	VH	VH	L	VL	L	VH	VH	H
Data entry keyers[5]	VH	H	VL	VL	VL	H	VH	VH	H
First-line supervisors and managers	VH	VH	VH	H	H	VL	L	L	L
Service occupations									
Cooks, except short order[3]	VH	VH	VH	VH	VL	VH	VH	VH	H
Nursing aides and psychiatric aides	VH	VH	VH	VH	VL	H	VH	VH	H
Flight attendants	L	L	A	VH	H	A	H	VH	A
Correction officers and jailers	A	A	H	VH	L	VL	L	VL	A
Firefighters	H	H	H	A	H	VL	VL	VL	L
Police and detective supervisors[3]	L	L	L	H	VH	VL	VL	VL	L
Police detectives and patrol officers[3]	H	VH	H	A	H	VL	VL	VL	L
Precision production, craft, and repair occupations									
Blue collar worker supervisors	VH	VH	VH	VL	VH	L	A	L	L
Bricklayers and stone masons	A	A	A	A	A	VH	H	H	A
Carpenters	VH	VH	VH	A	L	VH	VH	H	H
Carpet installers	VL	L	L	H	VL	H	A	H	H
Concrete and terrazzo finishers	A	A	A	H	L	VH	VH	H	H
Drywall installers and finishers	A	A	H	H	A	VH	VH	H	H
Electricians	VH	VH	VH	A	H	H	A	L	A
Glaziers	VL	VL	L	A	L	A	VH	A	H
Plumbers, pipefitters, and steamfitters	H	H	H	A	H	H	H	A	A
Structural and reinforcing metal workers	L	L	L	H	VH	VH	VH	L	A
Data processing equipment repairers[3]	VL	L	H	VH	VH	VL	VL	L	H
Electrical powerline installers and repairers	L	L	L	L	VH	L	A	VL	L
Telephone and cable TV line installers and repairers	A	L	VL	VL	VH	L	VL	VL	L
Industrial machinery mechanics	VH	H	A	VL	A	A	A	L	L
Millwrights	L	L	VL	L	VH	VH	H	VL	L
Aircraft mechanics and engine specialists[3]	L	L	A	H	VH	L	L	L	L
Automotive body and related repairers	A	A	A	L	L	H	A	A	H
Automotive mechanics[4]	VH	VH	H	L	L	H	A	H	H
Bus and truck mechanics and diesel engine specialists[3]	H	H	H	H	A	A	L	A	A
Mobile heavy equipment mechanics, except engines, and rail car repairers	A	A	A	A	H	H	A	L	L
Small engine specialists	VL	VL	L	H	VL	H	VH	H	H
Heating, a/c, and refrigeration mechanics and installers[3]	H	H	H	H	A	A	A	A	H
Home appliance and power tool repairers[3]	L	L	L	L	A	L	VL	H	H
Office machine and cash register servicers[3]	VL	VL	A	VH	A	VL	VL	A	A
Butchers and meatcutters	H	A	L	VL	VL	H	VH	H	H
Machinists[5]	H	H	VL	VL	A	H	L	L	A
Sheet-metal workers	A	A	A	L	H	VH	L	VL	H
Tool and die makers[5]	A	A	L	VL	VH	L	L	L	L
Compositors and typesetters[5]	VL	VL	VL	VL	VL	L	H	VH	H
Lithographers and photoengravers[5]	L	L	A	H	H	A	VL	VL	L
Upholsterers	L	VL	VL	L	VL	A	H	VH	A
Precision woodworkers[5]	A	A	H	A	VL	H	A	H	H
Inspectors, testers, and graders	VH	VH	VL	VL	L	H	VH	A	A
Dental laboratory technicians, precision[3]	VL	VL	L	VH	L	A	VL	VH	A
Operator, fabricator, and laborer occupations									
Welding machine operators and hand workers	H	H	VL	VL	L	VH	H	L	A
Printing press operators[5]	H	H	H	A	L	A	L	A	H
Boiler operators and stationary engineers[3]	VL	VL	VL	VL	H	L	A	L	L
Electric power generation plant operators, distributors, and dispatchers	VL	VL	VL	L	VH	VL	VL	L	L
Water and liquid waste treatment plant and system operators[3]	L	L	L	A	A	L	H	VL	L
Bus drivers, commercial and school bus	VH	VH	VH	A	L	A	H	VH	L
Locomotive and rail yard engineers and all other rail vehicle operators	VL	VL	VL	VL	VH	A	L	VL	L
Crane and tower operators	VL	VL	VL	VL	H	VH	A	VL	L
Excavation and loading machine operators	L	VL	L	A	L	VH	H	A	L

[Continued]

★ 539 ★

Rankings of Occupations for Which Formal Employer Training is Significant by Selected Characteristics, 1986-2000
[Continued]

National Industry-Occupation Matrix occupation	Employment		Employment change 1986-2000		Median weekly earnings of full-time workers	Unemployment rate	Separation rate (Annual)	Percent of employees	
	1986	2000	Number	Percent				Working part-time	Age 16-24
Grader, dozer, and scraper operators	L	L	L	L	L	VH	L	A	L
Operating engineers	A	A	A	A	A	VH	L	VL	L

Source: "Occupational Comparisons," *Occupational Projections and Training Data: A Statistical and Research Supplement to the 1988-89 Occupational Outlook Handbook,* U.S. Department of Labor, 1988, pp. 17-18. Codes for describing the variables are: VH = "Very High," H = "High," A = "Average," L = "Low," and VL = "Very low." *Notes:* The information compared in this chapter is derived from two sources: the National Industry-Occupation Matrix and the Current Population Survey (CPS). The matrix is the source of data on 1986 employment and 1986-2000 employment change. All other data are derived from the Current Population Survey. However, the CPS data used are for different time periods. Information on earnings and unemployment is for 1983-86; the separation rate is based on 1986-87 data, part-time work and age data are 1986 annual averages, while information about the type of training is derived from supplemental questions added to the January 1983 CPS survey. 1. A 4-year college degree program is an alternative source of training for this occupation. 2. Postsecondary school training, but less than a bachelor's degree or a 4-year college degree program, are alternative sources of training for this occupation. 3. Postsecondary school training, but less than a bachelor's degree, is an alternative source of training for this occupation. 4. A high school training program or postsecondary school training, but less than a bachelor's degree, are alternate sources of training for this occupation. 5. A high school vocational training program is an alternative source of training for this occupation.

★ 540 ★

Rankings of Occupations for Which High School Vocational Training Is Useful by Selected Characteristics, 1986-2000

National Industry-Occupation Matrix occupation	Employment		Employment change, 1986-2000		Median weekly earnings of full-time workers	Unemployment rate	Separation rate (Annual)	Percent of employees	
	1986	2000	Number	Percent				Working part-time	Age 16-24
Professional specialty occupations									
Musicians[1]	L	L	H	H	H	H	VH	VH	L
Technician occupations									
Drafters[2]	H	A	L	L	VH	A	L	L	A
Administrative support occupations									
Computer operators and peripheral equipment operators[3]	A	H	VH	VH	A	L	A	L	H
Billing, cost, and rate clerks	A	A	L	L	L	A	A	A	H
Bookkeeping, accounting, and auditing clerks[2]	VH	VH	H	A	L	L	H	VH	L
Payroll and timekeeping clerks[2]	L	L	VL	VL	A	L	L	A	L
General office clerk	VH	VH	VH	H	VL	H	VH	H	H
Receptionists and information clerks	H	VH	VH	VH	VL	VH	VH	VH	H
Brokerage and statement clerks	VL	L	A	VH	L	A	H	L	A
File clerks	A	A	H	H	VL	VH	VH	VH	H
Secretaries[2]	VH	VH	VH	A	L	L	A	H	A
Stenographers[2]	L	VL	VL	VL	H	VL	VL	A	L
Typists and word processors	VH	H	VL	VL	VL	VH	H	H	H
Date Entry Keyers[4]	H	H	VL	L	L	H	H	A	H
Statistical clerks	VL	VL	L	VL	H	VL	H	H	L
Precision production, craft, and repair occupations									
Automotive mechanics[3]	H	H	H	A	H	H	L	L	H
Machinists[4]	H	H	L	L	VH	VH	VL	VL	L
Tool and die makers[4]	L	L	A	A	VH	VL	VL	VL	L
Operator, fabricator, and laborer occupations									
Compositors and typesetters[4]	VL	VL	L	L	A	VL	A	H	A
Lithographers and photoengravers[4]	VL	VL	A	VH	VH	A	VL	VL	L

[Continued]

★ 540 ★

Rankings of Occupations for Which High School Vocational Training Is Useful by Selected Characteristics, 1986-2000

[Continued]

National Industry-Occupation Matrix occupation	Employment		Employment change, 1986-2000		Median weekly earnings of full-time workers	Unemployment rate	Separation rate (Annual)	Percent of employees	
	1986	2000	Number	Percent				Working part-time	Age 16-24
Precision woodworkers[4]	L	L	A	H	A	H	L	L	L
Printing press operators[4]	A	A	H	H	H	L	L	VL	H

Source: "Occupational Comparisons," *Occupational Projections and Training Data: A Statistical and Research Supplement to the 1988-89 Occupational Outlook Handbook,* U.S. Department of Labor, 1988, p. 19. Codes for describing the variables are: VH = "Very High," H = "High," A = "Average," L = "Low," and VL = "Very low." *Notes:* The information compared in this chapter is derived from two sources: the National Industry-Occupation Matrix and the Current Population Survey (CPS). The matrix is the source of data on 1986 employment and 1986-2000 employment change. All other data are derived from the Current Population Survey. However, the CPS data used are for different time periods. Information on earnings and unemployment is for 1983-86; the separation rate is based on 1986-87 data, part-time work and age data are 1986 annual averages, while information about the type of training is derived from supplemental questions added to the January 1983 CPS survey. 1. A 4-year college degree program is an alternative source of training for this occupation. 2. Postsecondary school training, but less than a bachelor's degree, is an alternative source of training for this occupation. 3. Formal employer training or postsecondary school training, but less than a bachelor's degree, are alternate sources of training for this occupation. 4. Formal employer training is an alternate source of training for this occupation.

★ 541 ★

Fastest-Growing Occupations Requiring Some Postsecondary Training or Extensive Employer Training, 1990-2005

"Health services occupations are a sizable proportion of the fastest growing occupations requiring some postsecondary training or extensive employer training."

[Numbers in percent]

Paralegals	85.0
Medical assistants	74.0
Radiologic technologists and technicians	70.0
Physical and corrective therapy assistants	64.0
Data processing equipment repairers	60.0
EEG technologists	57.0
Occupational therapy assistants and aides	55.0
Surgical technologists	55.0
Medical records technicians	54.0
Nuclear medicine technologists	53.0
Respiratory therapists	52.0
Electromedical and biomedical equipment repairers	51.0
Legal secretaries	47.0
Registered nurses	44.0
Licensed practical nurses	42.0
Cooks, restaurant	42.0
Producers, directors, actors, and entertainers	41.0
Dental hygienists	41.0

[Continued]

★ 541 ★

Fastest-Growing Occupations Requiring Some Postsecondary Training or Extensive Employer Training, 1990-2005

[Continued]

Dancers and choreographers	38.0
Opticians, dispensing	37.0

Source: "Outlook 1990-2005," *Occupational Outlook Quarterly* 35, No. 3, Fall, 1991, p. 34.

★ 542 ★

Rankings of Occupations for Which Postsecondary School Training but Less Than a Bachelor's Degree Is Significant by Selected Characteristics, 1986-2000

National Industry-Occupation Matrix occupation	Employment		Employment change, 1986-2000		Median weekly earnings of full-time workers	Unemployment rate	Separation rate (Annual)	Percent of employees	
	1986	2000	Number	Percent				Working part-time	Age 16-24
Managerial and management related occupations									
Financial managers[1]	VH	VH	VH	A	VH	VL	L	VL	L
Marketing, advertising, and public relations managers[1]	H	H	H	A	VH	L	A	VL	L
Personnel, training, and labor relations managers[1]	A	A	A	A	VH	A	L	VL	L
Property and real estate managers and administrators	A	A	A	H	L	L	H	H	L
Employment interviewers, personnel and labor relations specialists[1]	H	H	H	A	H	H	A	L	L
Purchasing agents, except wholesale, retail, and farm products	A	A	VL	VL	H	A	VH	VL	L
Wholesale and retail buyers, except farm products	A	A	L	VL	A	L	H	L	A
Professional specialty occupations									
Surveyors[2]	L	L	L	L	A	VH	VL	L	H
Registered nurses[1]	VH	VH	VH	H	H	VL	VL	VH	L
Respiratory therapists	VL	VL	L	H	L	L	VL	A	L
Artists and commercial artists	A	A	H	H	A	L	VH	H	L
Designers[1]	H	H	H	A	H	H	H	H	A
Photographers[3]	L	L	A	A	A	A	A	H	H
Producers, directors, actors, and entertainers[1]	VL	L	L	H	H	VH	VH	H	A
Public relations specialists and publicity writers[1]	L	L	A	H	VH	L	VH	A	A
Radio and TV announcers and newscasters[1]	VL	VL	VL	A	VL	VH	VH	VH	H
Technician occupations									
Dental hygienists	L	A	A	VH	A	VL	VL	VH	H
Licensed practical nurses	VH	VH	VH	H	L	H	L	VH	L
Medical and clinical laboratory technologists and technicians[1]	H	H	A	A	L	VL	L	H	A
Medical records technicians	VL	VL	A	VH	VL	H	A	A	H
Nuclear medicine and radiologic technologists and technicians	A	A	H	VH	A	L	VL	A	A
Opticians, dispensing and measuring[3]	VL	VL	L	VH	VL	A	VH	A	H
Electrical and electronic technicians/technologists[3]	H	H	VH	VH	H	A	L	L	H
Drafters[4]	H	H	VL	VL	H	VH	A	L	H
Physical and life science technicians/technologists and mathematical technicians	A	A	A	L	H	H	H	A	H
Computer programmers[1]	VH	VH	VH	VH	VH	VL	A	L	H
Marketing and sales occupations									
Real estate sales occupations[3]	H	H	VH	VH	H	VL	H	H	L
Administrative support occupations									
Welfare eligibility workers and interviewers	L	L	VL	L	L	H	H	A	L
Computer operators and peripheral equipment operators[5]	H	H	VH	VH	L	H	H	A	H
Bookkeeping, accounting, and auditing clerks[4]	VH	VH	H	VL	VL	A	VH	VH	A
Payroll and timekeeping clerks[4]	A	A	VL	VL	L	VH	A	A	A
Interviewing clerks, except personnel and social welfare	L	A	A	VH	VL	VH	VH	VH	H
Secretaries[4]	VH	VH	VH	L	VL	H	H	H	H
Stenographers[4]	A	L	VL	VL	L	VL	VL	A	L
Teacher aides and educational assistants	VH	VH	VH	L	VL	VH	VH	VH	A
Service occupations									
Cooks, except short order[3]	VH	VH	VH	H	VL	VH	VH	VH	H
Barbers	L	VL	VL	VL	VL	VL	VL	H	L
Cosmetologists and related workers	VH	VH	H	L	VL	A	A	VH	H

[Continued]

★ 542 ★

Rankings of Occupations for Which Postsecondary School Training but Less Than a Bachelor's Degree Is Significant by Selected Characteristics, 1986-2000

[Continued]

National Industry-Occupation Matrix occupation	Employment		Employment change, 1986-2000		Median weekly earnings of full-time workers	Unemployment rate	Separation rate (Annual)	Percent of employees	
	1986	2000	Number	Percent				Working part-time	Age 16-24
Police and detective supervisors[3]	L	L	L	L	VH	VL	VL	VL	L
Police detectives and patrol officers[3]	H	H	H	L	H	VL	VL	VL	L
Precision production, craft, and repair occupations									
Data processing equipment repairers[3]	VL	L	A	VH	VH	L	L	VL	H
Aircraft mechanics and engine specialists[3]	A	L	L	L	VH	A	A	VL	L
Automotive mechanics[5]	VH	VH	H	VL	L	VH	A	L	H
Bus and truck mechanics and diesel engine specialists[3]	H	H	H	A	A	VH	L	L	H
Heating, a/c, an refrigeration mechanics and installers[3]	A	A	A	A	A	H	A	L	H
Home appliance and power tool repairers[3]	L	VL	VL	VL	A	A	VL	A	H
Office machine and cash register servicers[3]	VL	VL	L	H	A	L	L	L	A
Dental laboratory technicians, precision[3]	VL	VL	L	H	L	H	L	H	A
Operator, fabricator, and laborer occupations									
Boiler operators and stationary engineers[3]	VL	VL	VL	VL	VH	A	H	VL	L
Water and liquid waste treatment and system operators[3]	VL	VL	VL	L	A	A	H	VL	L
Aircraft pilots and flight engineers[1]	L	L	L	A	VH	L	L	VH	L

Source: "Occupational Comparisons," *Occupational Projections and Training Data: A Statistical and Research Supplement to the 1988-89 Occupational Outlook Handbook*, U.S. Department of Labor, 1988, pp. 15-16. Codes for describing the variables are: VH = "Very High," H = "High," A = "Average," L = "Low," and VL = "Very low." *Notes:* The information compared in this chapter is derived from two sources: the National Industry-Occupation Matrix and the Current Population Survey (CPS). The matrix is the source of data on 1986 employment and 1986-2000 employment change. All other data are derived from the Current Population Survey. However, the CPS data used are for different time periods. Information on earnings and unemployment is for 1983-86; the separation rate is based on 1986-87 data, part-time work and age data are 1986 annual averages, while information about the type of training is derived from supplemental questions added to the January 1983 CPS survey. 1. A 4-year college degree program is an alternative source of training for this occupation. 2. Formal employer training or a 4-year college degree program, are alternative sources of training for this occupation. 3. Formal employer training is alternate source of training for this occupation. 4. A high school vocational training program is an alternative source of training for this occupation. 5. A high school vocational training program or formal employer training are alternative sources of training for this occupation.

★ 543 ★

Fastest-Growing Occupations Requiring a College Degree or More Education, 1990-2005

"Of the 20 fastest growing occupations requiring a bachelor's degree or more education, the top seven are tied to the health services industry or computer technology."

[Numbers in percent]

Systems analysts and computer scientists	79.0
Physical therapists	76.0
Operations research analysts	73.0
Medical scientists	66.0
Psychologists	64.0
Computer programmers	56.0
Occupational therapists	55.0
Management analysts	52.0
Marketing, advertising, and public relations managers	47.0
Podiatrists	46.0
Teachers, preschool and kindergarten	41.0
Teachers, special education	40.0
Securities and financial services sales representatives	40.0

[Continued]

★ 543 ★

Fastest-Growing Occupations Requiring a College Degree or More Education, 1990-2005
[Continued]

Recreational therapists	39.0
Lawyers	35.0
Accountants and auditors	34.0
Aircraft pilots and flight engineers	34.0
Social workers	34.0
Engineering, mathematics, and natural science managers	34.0
Teachers, secondary school	34.0

Source: "Outlook 1990-2005," *Occupational Outlook Quarterly* 35, No. 3, Fall, 1991, p. 33.

★ 544 ★

Rankings of Occupations Generally Requiring a 4-Year College Degree by Selected Characteristics, 1986-2000

National Industry-Occupation Matrix occupation	Employment		Employment change, 1986-2000		Median weekly earnings of full-time workers	Unemployment rate	Separation rate (Annual)	Percent of employees	
	1986	2000	Number	Percent				Working part-time	Age 16-24
Managerial and management related occupations									
Education administrators	H	H	A	VL	A	VL	L	A	L
Financial managers[1]	VH	VH	VH	L	A	L	L	VL	L
Marketing, advertising, and public relations managers[1]	H	H	H	A	VH	A	A	VL	L
Personnel, training, and labor relations managers[1]	A	A	A	A	A	H	A	VL	L
Purchasing managers	A	A	L	VL	H	L	L	VL	L
Accountants and auditors	VH	VH	VH	VH	L	A	H	L	H
Inspectors and compliance officers, except construction[2]	L	L	VL	VL	A	H	H	L	L
Employment interviewers, personnel and labor relations specialists[1]	H	H	H	H	L	VH	H	A	A
Management analysts	A	A	A	A	H	L	VH	H	L
Underwriters	L	L	L	H	VL	A	H	VL	H
Professional specialty occupations									
Aeronautical and astronautical engineers	VL	VL	VL	VL	VH	VL	VL	VL	A
Chemical engineers	VL	VL	VL	VL	VH	L	H	VL	H
Civil engineers, including traffic engineers	A	A	A	A	H	H	L	L	L
Electrical and electronics engineers	VH	VH	VH	VH	VH	L	L	VL	H
Industrial engineers, except safety engineers	L	L	A	A	H	H	H	VL	L
Mechanical engineers	H	H	H	H	VH	A	VL	VL	A
Architects, except landscape and marine	L	L	L	A	A	A	VL	L	A
Surveyors[3]	L	L	L	L	VL	VH	VL	L	H
Computer systems analysts, electronic data processing	H	H	VH	VH	H	L	L	L	H
Biological scientists	VL	VL	VL	L	A	H	VL	A	L
Operations and systems researchers	VL	VL	L	VH	H	L	A	L	L
Chemists	L	VL	VL	VL	A	H	A	L	A
Geologists, geophysicists, and oceanographers	VL	VL	VL	VL	VH	VH	H	L	A
Economists	VL	VL	VL	H	H	H	VH	A	H
Psychologists	L	L	A	H	L	A	VL	VH	L
Clergy	H	H	VL	VL	VL	VL	L	A	L
Recreation workers	A	A	L	L	VL	VH	VH	VH	H
Social workers	H	H	H	H	VL	VH	A	A	A
Lawyers	VH	VH	VH	H	VH	VL	VL	A	L
Teachers, preschool, kindergarten and elementary	VH	VH	VH	L	VL	A	H	H	A
Teachers, secondary school	VH	VH	H	VL	L	L	A	A	L
Librarians, professional	A	A	L	VL	VL	A	VH	VH	H
Counselors	L	L	L	L	A	A	A	H	A
Dentists	A	A	A	A	VH	VL	VL	H	L
Pharmacists	A	A	A	L	H	VL	L	H	L
Physicians and surgeons	VH	VH	VH	H	H	VL	VL	L	L
Registered nurses[1]	VH	VH	VH	VH	L	L	L	VH	A

[Continued]

★ 544 ★

Rankings of Occupations Generally Requiring a 4-Year College Degree by Selected Characteristics, 1986-2000

[Continued]

National Industry-Occupation Matrix occupation	Employment		Employment change, 1986-2000		Median weekly earnings of full-time workers	Unemployment rate	Separation rate (Annual)	Percent of employees	
	1986	2000	Number	Percent				Working part-time	Age 16-24
Physical therapists	VL	L	H	VH	L	VL	VL	H	H
Speech pathologists and audiologists	VL	VL	VL	H	L	VL	A	VH	L
Designers[1]	H	H	H	A	L	VH	H	H	H
Musicians[4]	A	A	A	L	VL	VH	VH	VH	H
Producers, directors, actors, and entertainers[1]	VL	VL	L	H	L	VH	VH	H	H
Public relations specialists and publicity writers[1]	L	L	A	VH	A	H	VH	H	H
Radio and TV announcers and newscasters[1]	VL	VL	VL	L	VL	VH	VH	VH	H
Reporters, writers, and editors	H	H	H	A	L	H	VH	VH	H
Technician occupations									
Medical and clinical laboratory technologists and technicians[1]	H	H	H	L	VL	A	A	H	H
Computer programmers[1]	VH	VH	VH	VH	A	L	H	A	H
Marketing and sales occupations									
Securities and financial services sales workers[2]	A	A	H	VH	H	VL	L	A	H
Operator, fabricator, and laborer occupations									
Aircraft pilots and flight engineers[1]	L	L	L	A	VH	H	A	VH	L

Source: "Occupational Comparisons," *Occupational Projections and Training Data: A Statistical and Research Supplement to the 1988-89 Occupational Outlook Handbook,* U.S. Department of Labor, 1988, pp. 13-14. Codes for describing the variables are: VH = "Very High," H = "High," A = "Average," L = "Low," and VL = "Very low." *Notes:* The information compared in this chapter is derived from two sources: the National Industry-Occupation Matrix and the Current Population Survey (CPS). The matrix is the source of data on 1986 employment and 1986-2000 employment change. All other data are derived from the Current Population Survey. However, the CPS data used are for different time periods. Information on earnings and unemployment is for 1983-86; the separation rate is based on 1986-87 data, part-time work and age data are 1986 annual averages, while information about the type of training is derived from supplemental questions added to the January 1983 CPS survey. 1. Postsecondary school training, but less than a bachelor's degree is an alternative source of training for this occupation. 2. Formal employer training is an alternative source of training for this occupation. 3. Formal employer training or postsecondary school training, but less than a bachelor's degree, are alternate sources of training for this occupation. 4. A high school vocational training program is an alternative source of training for this occupation.

Projections of Growth and Decline for Selected Occupations

★ 545 ★

Percent Distribution of Employment by Occupation, 1990-2005

Occupation	1990	2005		
		Low	Moderate	High
Total, all occupations	100.0	100.0	100.0	100.0
Executive, administrative, and managerial occupations	10.2	10.8	10.8	10.8
Professional specialty	12.9	14.2	14.2	14.3
Technicians and related support	3.5	3.9	3.9	3.9
Marketing and sales	11.5	11.9	11.9	11.8
Administrative support occupations, including clerical	17.9	16.8	16.9	16.9
Service occupations	15.7	17.1	16.9	16.8
Agricultural, forestry, and fishing	2.9	2.6	2.5	2.5

[Continued]

★ 545 ★

Percent Distribution of Employment by Occupation, 1990-2005
[Continued]

Occupation	1990	2005		
		Low	Moderate	High
Precision production, craft, and repair	11.5	10.8	10.8	10.8
Operators, fabricators, and laborers	14.0	12.0	12.2	12.2

Source: "Percentage Distribution of Employment by Occupation, 1990 and 2005," George Silvestri and John Lukasiewicz, *Monthly Labor Review* 114, No. 11, November, 1991, p. 93. Also in source: a 13-page chart listing employment figures for more than 500 occupations for 1990 and projections to 2005 under low, medium, and high economic growth scenarios. Primary source: Office of Employment Projections, Bureau of Labor Statistics.

★ 546 ★

Annual Average Rates of Employment Growth for Selected Occupations, 1988-2000 - I

[Numbers in percent]

Occupation	Annual average rate of growth in employment (percent)
Total all occupations	1.2
Executive administrative and managerial occupations	1.7
Administrative services managers	2.0
Communication transportation and utilities operations manager	1.3
Construction managers	2.0
Education administrators	1.5
Engineering mathematical and natural sciences managers	2.4
Financial managers	1.5
Food service and lodging managers	2.1
General managers and top executives	1.2
Government chief executives and legislators	0.2
Industrial production managers	1.4
Marketing advertising and public relations managers	1.9
Personnel training and labor relations managers	1.6
Property and real estate managers	1.4
Purchasing managers	1.1
Management support occupations	1.7
Accountants and auditors	1.7
Budget analysts	1.3
Claims examiners property and casualty insurance	1.8
Construction and building inspectors	1.1
Cost estimators	1.2
Employment interviewers private or public employment service	2.8
Inspectors and compliance officers except construction	1.1
Loan officers and counselors	1.6

[Continued]

★ 546 ★

Annual Average Rates of Employment Growth for Selected Occupations, 1988-2000 - I

[Continued]

Occupation	Annual average rate of growth in employment (percent)
Management analysts	2.6
Personnel training and labor relations specialists	1.6
Purchasing agents except wholesale retail and farm products	1.1
Underwriters	2.2
Wholesale and retail buyers except farm products	0.5
Professional specialty occupations	1.8
Aeronautical and astronautical engineers	1.0
Chemical engineers	1.3
Civil engineers including traffic engineers	1.4
Electrical and electronic engineers	2.8
Industrial engineers except safety engineers	1.3
Mechanical engineers	1.5
Architects except landscape and marine	1.8
Surveyors	0.9
Agricultural food scientists	1.5
Biological scientists	2.0
Foresters and conservation scientists	0.9
Computer systems analysts	3.6
Operations research analysts	3.7
Chemists	1.3
Geologists geophysicists and oceanographers	1.3
Economists	1.9
Psychologists	2.0
Clergy	0.6
Directors religious activities and education	0.9
Human service workers	3.1
Recreational workers	1.4
Social workers	2.1
Judges magistrates and other judicial workers	1.4
Lawyers	2.3
Teachers special education	1.2
Teachers preschool	2.2
Teachers kindergarten and elementary school	1.2
Teachers secondary school	1.5
College and university faculty	0.2
Librarians archivists curators and related workers	0.9
Counselors	2.0
Dentists	1.0
Optometrists	1.3
Physicians	2.1
Veterinarians and veterinary inspectors	1.8

[Continued]

★ 546 ★

Annual Average Rates of Employment Growth for Selected Occupations, 1988-2000 - I
[Continued]

Occupation	Annual average rate of growth in employment (percent)
Dietitians and nutritionists	2.0
Pharmacists	2.0
Physician assistants	2.2
Registered nurses	2.8
Therapists	3.0
Writers artists and entertainers	1.7
Artists and commercial artists	2.0
Designers	2.1
Musicians	0.8
Photographers and camera operators	1.5
Producers directors actors and entertainers	2.2
Public relations specialists and publicity writers	1.2
Radio and tv announcers and newscasters	1.4
Reporters and correspondents	1.3
Writers and editors including technical writers	1.9
Technicians and related support occupations	2.3
Clinical lab technologists and technicians	1.5
Dental hygienists	1.4
Emergency medical technicians	1.0
Licensed practical nurses	2.6
Medical records technicians	4.0
Opticians dispensing and measuring	2.4
Radiologic technologists and technicians	4.3
Surgical technologists	3.8
Engineering technicians	2.1
Drafters	1.0
Science and mathematics technicians	1.4
Aircraft pilots and flight engineers	2.2
Air traffic controllers	1.2
Broadcast technicians	-2.9
Computer programmers	3.3
Legal assistants and technicians except clerical	3.1
Technical assistants library	0.7

Source: Georgia Business and Economic Conditions, pp. 12-15. Primary source: Annual average rates of employment growth were calculated by the Selig Center for Economic Growth, College of Business Administration, the University of Georgia. Base employment data for 1988 and 2000 were obtained from the U.S. Department of Labor, Bureau of Labor Statistics.

★ 547 ★

Annual Average Rates of Employment Growth for Selected Occupations, 1988-2000 - II

[Numbers in percent]

Occupation	Annual average rate of growth in employment (percent)
Marketing and sales occupations	1.5
Counter and retail clerks	2.1
Insurance sales workers	1.1
Real estate agents brokers an appraisers	1.3
Salespersons retail	1.5
Securities and financial services sales workers	3.7
Stock clerks sales floor	1.2
Travel agents	3.7
Administrative support occupations including clerical	0.9
Adjustment clerks	1.6
Bill and account collectors	2.3
Insurance claims and policy processing occupations	1.0
Communications equipment operators	1.2
Computer and peripheral equipment operators	2.2
Financial records processing occupations	0.0
Information clerks	2.4
Mail clerks and messengers	0.8
Postal clerks and mail carriers	0.5
Dispatchers	1.1
Meter readers utilities	-0.7
Order fillers wholesale and retail sales	0.7
Procurement clerks	0.9
Production planning and expediting clerks	0.7
Stock clerks stockroom warehouse or storage yard	0.7
Traffic shipping and receiving clerks	0.8
Weighers measurers checkers an samplers recordkeeping	1.0
Brokerage clerks	0.3
Correspondence clerks	2.1
File clerks	0.8
Library assistants and bookmobile drivers	0.5
Order clerks materials merchandise and service	-0.1
Personnel clerks except payroll and timekeeping	0.7
Statement clerks	0.3
Secretaries	1.3
Stenographers	-2.2
Typists and word processors	-0.5
Bank tellers	0.4
Clerical supervisors and managers	0.9
Court clerks	1.6
Credit authorizers credit checkers and loan and credit clerks	2.0
Customer service representatives utilities	1.4

[Continued]

★ 547 ★

Annual Average Rates of Employment Growth for Selected Occupations, 1988-2000 - II

[Continued]

Occupation	Annual average rate of growth in employment (percent)
Data entry keyers except composing	-0.4
Duplicating mail and other office machines operators	0.8
General office clerks	1.4
Proofreaders and copy markers	-0.5
Real estate clerks	0.6
Statistical clerks	-0.1
Teacher aides and educational assistants	1.6
Service occupations	1.7
Housekeepers institutional	2.7
Janitors and cleaners including maids and housekeeping cleaners	1.5
Pest controllers and assistants	1.3
Chefs cooks and other kitchen workers	1.6
Cooks short order and fast food	1.1
Food preparation workers	1.7
Bartenders	1.7
Dining room and cafeteria attendants and bar helpers	2.1
Food counter fountain and related workers	1.2
Hosts and hostesses restaurant lounge or coffee shop	2.2
Waiters and waitresses	2.3
Dental assistants	1.4
Medical assistants	4.5
Nursing aides and psychiatric aides	2.3
Pharmacy assistants	2.0
Physical and corrective therapy assistants and aides	3.7
Amusement and recreation attendants	1.8
Baggage porters and bellhops	1.9
Barbers	0.0
Child care workers	2.1
Cosmetologists and related workers	1.0
Flight attendants	2.8
Homemaker home health aides	4.2
Users lobby attendants and ticket takers	0.7
Child care workers private household	-0.6
Cleaners and servants private household	-0.2
Housekeepers and butlers	-0.2
Correction officers and jailers	2.9
Firefighting occupations	0.8
Police and detectives	1.0
Crossing guards	0.6
Guards	2.3
Other protective service workers	1.3

[Continued]

★ 547 ★

Annual Average Rates of Employment Growth for Selected Occupations, 1988-2000 - II

[Continued]

Occupation	Annual average rate of growth in employment (percent)
Agriculture forestry fishing and related occupations	-0.4
Animal caretakers except farm	1.2
Farm workers	-1.5
Nursery workers	1.5
Farm operators and managers	-1.7
Fishers hunters and trappers	0.9
Forestry and logging occupations	-0.4
Gardens and groundskeepers except farm	1.8

Source: Georgia Business and Economic Conditions, pp. 12-15. Primary source: Annual average rates of employment growth were calculated by the Selig Center for Economic Growth, College of Business Administration, the University of Georgia. Base employment data for 1988 and 2000 were obtained from the U.S. Department of Labor, Bureau of Labor Statistics.

★ 548 ★

Annual Average Rates of Employment Growth for Selected Occupations, 1988-2000 - III

[Numbers in percent]

Occupation	Annual average rate of growth in employment (percent)
Construction trades	1.3
Bricklayers and stone masons	1.2
Carpenters	1.3
Carpet installers	1.6
Concrete and terrazzo finishers	1.4
Drywall installers and finishers	1.3
Electricians	1.4
Glaziers	1.4
Hard tile setters	1.7
Highway maintenance workers	0.7
Insulation workers	1.6
Painters and paperhangers construction and maintenance	1.3
Paving surfacing and tamping equipment operators	1.3
Pipelayers and pipelaying fitters	1.1
Plasters	0.9
Plumbers pipefitters and steamfitters	1.4
Roofers	1.5

[Continued]

511

★ 548 ★

Annual Average Rates of Employment Growth for Selected Occupations, 1988-2000 - III

[Continued]

Occupation	Annual average rate of growth in employment (percent)
Structural and reinforcing metal workers	1.4
Extractive and related workers including blasters	0.3
Mechanics installers and repairers	1.0
Communications equipment mechanics installers and repairers	-1.5
Electrical and electronic equipment mechanics installers and repairers	0.8
Industrial machinery mechanics	1.3
Maintenance repairers general utility	1.4
Millwrights	1.3
Vehicle and mobile equipment mechanics and repairers	1.3
Other mechanics installers and repairers	0.3
Coin and vending machine servicers and repairers	0.0
Heat air conditioning and refrigeration mechanics and installers	1.3
Home appliance and power tool repairers	0.0
Office machine and cash register servicers	0.1
Precision instrument repairers	0.7
Tire repairers and changers	1.1
Production occupations precision	0.0
Assemblers precision	-2.4
Food workers precision	0.2
Inspectors testers and graders precision	-0.5
Metal workers precision	0.5
Printing workers precision	0.7
Textile apparel and furnishing workers precision	0.7
Woodworkers precision	0.8
Chemical plant and system operators	-1.8
Electric power generating plant operators distributors and dispatchers	1.0
Gas and petroleum plant and system occupations	-2.6
Stationary engineers	0.0
Water and treatment plant and system operators	1.1
Operators fabricators and laborers	0.1
Machine setters set up operators operators and tenders	-0.3
Numerical control machine tool operators and tenders metal and plastic	0.7
Combination machine tool setters set up operators and tenders	0.7
Machine tool cut and form setters operators and tenders metal and plastic	-0.5
Metal fabricating machine setters operators and related workers	-0.9

[Continued]

★ 548 ★

Annual Average Rates of Employment Growth for Selected Occupations, 1988-2000 - III

[Continued]

Occupation	Annual average rate of growth in employment (percent)
Metal and plastic processing machine setters operators and related workers	0.2
Printing binding and related workers	1.1
Textile and related setters operators and related workers	-0.9
Woodworking machine setters operators and other related workers	0.6
Other machine setters set up operators operators and tenders	-0.4
Hand workers including assemblers and fabricators	-0.9
Cannery workers	-0.1
Cutters and trimmers hand	0.3
Electrical and electronic assemblers	-4.6
Grinders and polishers hand	-1.1
Machine assemblers	-1.1
Meat poultry and fish cutters and trimmers hand	1.3
Painting coating and decorating workers hand	-0.4
Solderers and brazers	-0.6
Welders and cutters	-0.4
Transportation and material moving machine and vehicle operators	0.9
Motor vehicle operators	1.2
Rail transportation workers	-1.4
Water transportation and related workers	0.1
Material moving equipment operators	0.3
Helpers laborers and material movers hand	0.2
Freight stock and material movers hand	0.2
Hand packers and packagers	-1.0
Helpers construction trades	1.1
Machine feeders and offbearers	-1.1
Parking lot attendants	1.2
Refuse collectors	0.0
Service station attendants	0.6
Vehicle washers and equipment cleaners	0.6

Source: Georgia Business and Economic Conditions, pp. 12-15. Primary source: Annual average rates of employment growth were calculated by the Selig Center for Economic Growth, College of Business Administration, the University of Georgia. Base employment data for 1988 and 2000 were obtained from the U.S. Department of Labor, Bureau of Labor Statistics.

★ 549 ★

Employment Growth, 1975-1990 and 1990-2005

"Reflecting the declining growth of the labor force, job growth will slow. The rate of employment growth will be half the rate of growth during the previous 15 years."

[Numbers in percent]

1975-90	40
1990-2005	20

Source: "Outlook 1990-2005," *Occupational Outlook Quarterly* 35, No. 3, Fall, 1991, p. 7.

★ 550 ★

Employment Growth of Health Services Industry, 1990-2005

"Employment in the health services industry will grow by 3.9 million, 17 percent of total employment growth. Health services, which accounted for 7 percent of total wage and salary worker employment in 1975 and 8 percent in 1990, will approach 9 percent of total employment by 2005."

[Numbers in millions]

Health services	3.9
All other industries	19.3

Source: "Outlook 1990-2005," *Occupational Outlook Quarterly* 35, No. 3, Fall, 1991, p. 20.

★ 551 ★

Range of Projected Employment for Detailed Occupations under Alternative Growth Scenarios, 1990-2005

"The range of total employment in 2005 from the low-trend alternative to the high-trend alternative is 17.7 million workers. Therefore, the range in projected employment for detailed occupations can be very large, particularly for occupations of large size."

[Numbers in thousands]

Occupation	1990 employment	Moderate-trend employment change, 1990-2005	Low- to high-trend employment difference 2005
All other sales workers	5,204	1,222	732
Salespersons, retail	3,619	887	548
General managers and top executives	3,086	598	461
General office clerks	2,737	670	448
Secretaries, except legal and medical	3,064	248	423
Janitors and cleaners	3,007	555	396
Cashiers	2,633	685	381
Truckdrivers, light and heavy	2,362	617	358
Registered nurses	1,727	767	331
Teachers, secondary school	1,280	437	274

Source: "Occupational Employment Projections," George Silvestri and John Lakasiewicz, *Monthly Labor Review* 114, No. 11, November, 1991, p. 94.

★ 552 ★

Occupational Growth, 1988-2000 - I

[Numbers in thousands]

Occupation	1988	2000	% change
Adjusters, investigators, and collectors	961.0	1,133.0	18.0
Aircraft mechanics and engine specialists	124.0	144.0	16.0
Animal caretakers, except farm	92.0	106.0	16.0
Apparel workers	1,104.0	1,026.0	-7.0
Automotive body repairers	214.0	270.0	26.0
Automotive mechanics	771.0	897.0	16.0
Bank tellers	552.0	546.0	5.0
Barbers	46.0	<46.5	0.0
Billing clerks and related workers	421.0	422.4	0.0
Bindery workers	73.0	80.9	11.0
Blue-collar worker supervisors	1,797.0	1,930.0	7.0
Boilermakers	25.0	27.2	9.0
Bookkeeping, accounting, and auditing clerks	2,252.0	2,272.0	1.0
Bricklayers and stonemasons	167.0	192.0	16.0

[Continued]

★ 552 ★

Occupational Growth, 1988-2000 - I
[Continued]

Occupation	1988	2000	% change
Brokerage clerks and statement clerks	96.0	98.8	3.0
Busdrivers	506.0	594.0	17.0
Butchers and meat, poultry, and fish cutters	368.0	398.0	8.0
Carpenters	1,106.0	1,286.0	16.0
Carpet installers	56.0	68.0	21.0
Chefs, cooks, and other kitchen workers	2,277.0	3,341.0	21.0
Childcare workers	670.0	856.0	30.0
Clerical supervisors and managers	1,183.0	1,319.0	12.0
Commercial and industrial electronic equipment repairers	78.8	91.8	17.0
Communications equipment mechanics	113.0	95.0	-16.0
Compositors and typesetters	86.0	<86.5	1.0
Computer and office machine repairers	128.0	172.0	35.0
Computer and peripheral equipment operators	316.0	408.0	29.0
Concrete masons and terrazzo workers	114.0	133.0	17.0
Corrections officers	186.0	262.0	41.0
Cosmetologists and related workers	649.0	731.0	13.0
Credit clerks and authorizers	229.0	290.0	27.0
Dental assistants	166.0	197.0	19.0
Dental laboratory technicians	51.0	56.2	10.0
Diesel mechanics	269.0	312.0	16.0
Dispatchers	202.0	231.0	14.0
Drywall workers and lathers	52.0	178.0	17.0
Electric power generating plant operators and power distributors and dispatchers	45.0	51.4	14.0
Electricians	542.0	638.0	18.0
Electronic home entertainment equipment repairers	44.0	49.5	13.0
Elevator installers and repairers	13.0	15.3	17.0
Farm equipment mechanics	54.0	54.8	1.0
Farm operators and managers	1,272.0	1,035.0	-19.0
File clerks	263.0	290.0	10.0
Financial records processors	2,849.0	2,867.0	1.0
Firefighting occupations	291.0	320.0	10.0
Fishers, hunters, and trappers	54.0	59.7	10.0
Flight attendants	88.0	122.0	39.0
Food and beverage service workers	4,458.0	5,526.0	24.0
Gardeners and groundskeepers	760.0	942.0	24.0
General maintenance mechanics	1,080.0	1,282.0	19.0
General office clerks	2,519.0	2,974.0	18.0
Glaziers	49.0	57.6	18.0
Guards	795.0	1,051.0	32.0
Handlers, equipment cleaners, helpers, and laborers	4,894.0	4,999.0	2.0
Heating, air-conditioning, and refrigeration mechanics	225.0	263.0	17.0
Home appliance and power tool repairers	76.0	<76.5	0.0

[Continued]

516

★ 552 ★

Occupational Growth, 1988-2000 - I
[Continued]

Occupation	1988	2000	% change
Homemaker-home health aides	327.0	534.0	63.0
Hotel and motel clerks	113.0	142.0	26.0
Industrial machinery repairers	463.0	538.0	16.0
Information clerks	1,316.0	1,757.0	34.0
Inspectors, testers, and graders	676.0	634.0	-6.0
Insulation workers	65.0	77.0	19.0
Interviewing and new account clerks	237.0	280.0	18.0
Janitors and cleaners	2,895.0	3,451.0	19.0
Jewelers	35.0	40.7	16.0
Library assistants and bookmobile drivers	105.0	111.1	6.0
Line installers and cable splicers	231.0	221.0	-4.0
Lithographic and photoengraving workers	67.0	79.0	18.0
Machinists	397.0	433.0	9.0
Mail clerks and messengers	259.0	285.0	10.0
Material moving equipment operators	1,010.0	1,047.0	4.0
Material recording, scheduling, dispatching, and distributing occupations	2,889.0	3,227.0	12.0
Medical assistants	149.0	253.0	70.0
Metalworking and plasticworking machine operators	1,405.0	1,365.0	-3.0
Metalworking machine operators	1,252.0	1,182.0	-6.0
Millwrights	77.0	90.0	17.0
Mobile heavy equipment mechanics	108.0	124.0	14.0
Motorcycle, boat, and small-engine mechanics	58.0	65.7	13.0
Musical instrument repairers and tuners	7.5	8.1	8.0
Nursing aides and psychiatric aides	1,289.0	1,703.0	31.0
Numerical-control machine-tool operators	64.0	69.9	9.0
Order clerks	293.0	288.6	-2.0
Ophthalmic laboratory technicians	25.0	33.3	28.0
Painting and coating machine operators	159.0	167.5	5.0
Painters and paperhangers	431.0	501.0	16.0
Payroll and timekeeping clerks	176.0	171.8	-2.0
Personnel clerks	129.0	141.0	9.0
Photographic process workers	67.0	81.0	21.0
Plasters	27.0	29.2	8.0
Plastic-working machine operators	144.0	176.0	22.0
Plumbers and pipefitters	396.0	469.0	18.0
Police, detectives, and special agents	515.0	583.0	13.0
Postal clerks and mail carriers	665.0	706.0	6.0
Precision assemblers	354.0	344.9	-26.0
Printing press operators	239.0	274.0	15.0
Private household workers	902.0	860.0	-5.0
Railroad transportation workers	106.0	90.0	-16.0
Receptionists	833.0	1,164.0	40.0
Records clerks	886.0	930.0	5.0

[Continued]

★ 552 ★

Occupational Growth, 1988-2000 - I
[Continued]

Occupation	1988	2000	% change
Reservation and transportation ticket agents and travel clerks	133.0	170.0	28.0
Roofers	123.0	147.0	19.0
Roustabouts	39.0	<39.5	1.0
Secretaries	3,373.0	3,944.0	17.0
Sheet-metal workers	97.0	115.0	19.0
Shoe and leather workers and repairers	32.0	<32.5	0.0
Stationary engineers	36.0	35.5	-1.0
Stenographers	159.0	123.0	-23.0
Steel workers	8.9	7.2	-19.0
Stock clerks	2,152.0	2,406.0	12.0
Structural and reinforcing ironworkers	91.0	108.0	19.0
Teachers aides	682.0	827.0	21.0
Telephone installers and repairers	58.0	46.0	-20.0
Telephone operators	330.0	378.0	15.0
Textile machinery operators	310.0	273.0	-12.0
Tilesetters	26.0	31.8	22.0
Timber cutting and logging workers	106.0	96.0	-10.0
Tool and die makers	152.0	158.8	4.0
Traffic, shipping, and receiving clerks	535.0	591.0	10.0
Truckdrivers	2,641.0	3,023.0	14.0
Typists, word processors, and data entry keyers	1,416.0	1,334.0	-6.0
Upholsterers	73.0	81.1	11.0
Vending machine servicers and repairers	27.0	<27.5	1.0
Water and wastewater treatment plant operators	76.0	87.0	14.0
Water transportation occupations	49.0	43.2	12.0
Welders, cutters, and welding machine operators	424.0	394.0	-7.0
Woodworking occupations	375.0	409.0	9.0

Source: "Projected Occupational Growth from 1988 to 2000 (Occupations in Alphabetical Order)," *Vocational Careers Sourcebook: Where to Find Help Planning Careers in Skilled, Trade, and Nontechnical Vocations,* Kathleen M. Savage and Karen Hill, eds., Gale Research Inc., Detroit, Michigan, 1992, pp. 1080-820. Primary source: Bureau of Labor Statistics' industry-occupation matrix, 1990.

★ 553 ★

Occupational Growth, 1988-2000 - II

Annual figures are in thousands.

	1988	2000	% change
Accountants and Auditors	963	1,174	22.0
Actuaries	16	24	53.6
Administrative Services Managers	217	274	26.2
Adult and Vocational Education Teachers	467	523	12.1
Aeronautical and Astronautical Engineers	78	88	12.7

[Continued]

★ 553 ★

Occupational Growth, 1988-2000 - II
[Continued]

	1988	2000	% change
Agricultural and Food Scientists	25	30	20.9
Air Traffic Controllers	27	31	15.5
Aircraft Pilots and Flight Engineers	83	108	30.9
Architects	105	132	25.7
Architects, except Landscape and Marine	86	107	24.7
Artists and Commercial Artists	216	274	27.1
Biological Scientists	57	72	26.0
Broadcast Technicians	27	19	-31.1
Budget Analysts	62	72	16.5
Camera Operators, Television and Motion Picture	11	14	29.1
Chemical Engineers	49	57	16.4
Chemists	80	93	16.7
Civil Engineers, including Traffic Engineers	186	219	17.4
Claims Examiners, Property and Casualty Insurance	30	37	23.5
Clergy	185	199	7.2
Clinical Lab Technologists and Technicians	242	288	19.2
College and university Faculty	846	869	2.8
Communication, Transportation, and Utilities Operations Managers	167	194	16.3
Computer Programmers	519	769	48.1
Computer Systems Analysts	403	617	53.3
Construction and Building Inspectors	56	64	14.2
Construction Managers	187	236	26.0
Cost Estimators	169	194	15.4
Counselors	124	157	26.9
Curators, Archivists, Museum Technicians, and Restorers	16	19	16.5
Dancers and Choreographers	11	13	19.2
Dental Hygienists	91	107	17.6
Dentists	167	189	13.1
Designers	309	395	27.9
Dietitians and Nutritionists	40	51	27.8
Directors, Religious Activities and Education	56	62	9.8
Drafters	319	358	12.2
Economists	36	45	27.3
Education Administrators	320	382	19.4
Electrical and Electronics Engineering Technicians and Technologists	341	471	38.2
Electrical and Electronics Engineers	439	615	40.0
Electrocardiograph Technicians and Technologists	18	20	10.2
Electroencephalograph Technicians and Technologists	6	10	50.4
Emergency Medical Technicians	76	86	13.0
Employment Interviewers and Personnel Specialists	333	418	25.5
Employment Interviewers, Private or Public Employment Service	81	113	40.5
Engineering and Science Technicians and Technologists	1,273	1,559	22.4

[Continued]

★ 553 ★

Occupational Growth, 1988-2000 - II
[Continued]

	1988	2000	% change
Engineering, Mathematical, and Natural Sciences Managers	258	341	32.0
Engineering Technicians	722	926	28.2
Engineering Technicians and Technologists (all other)	381	454	19.2
Engineers	1,411	1,762	24.9
Engineers (all other)	247	299	21.2
Executive, Administrative, and Managerial Occupations	12,104	14,762	22.0
Farm and Home Management Advisors	23	22	-6.2
Financial Managers	673	802	19.3
Food Service and Lodging Managers	560	721	28.8
General Managers and Top Executives	3,030	3,509	15.8
Geologists, Geophysicists, and Oceanographers	42	49	15.7
Government Chief Executives and Legislators	69	71	3.0
Health Assessment and Treating Occupations	2,084	2,876	38.0
Health Diagnosing Occupations	801	995	24.2
Health Professionals, Paraprofessionals, and Technicians (all other)	313	419	33.9
Health Technicians and Technologists	1,645	2,211	34.4
Human Services Workers	118	171	44.9
Industrial Engineers, except Safety Engineers	132	155	18.0
Industrial Production Managers	215	254	18.0
Inspectors and Compliance Officers, except Construction	130	148	13.9
Judges, Magistrates, and other Judicial Workers	40	47	17.9
Landscape Architects	19	25	28.9
Lawyers	582	763	31.0
Lawyers and Judicial Workers	622	810	30.2
Legal Assistants and Technicians, except Clerical	200	290	45.0
Legal Assistants (all other) including Law Clerks	90	113	25.4
Librarians, Archivists, Curators, and related workers	159	176	10.7
Librarians, Professional	143	157	10.0
Licensed Practical Nurses	626	855	36.6
Life Scientists	154	189	22.2
Life Scientists (all other)	45	57	26.6
Loan Officers and Counselors	172	209	21.5
Management Analysts	130	176	35.0
Management Support Occupations	3,428	4,187	22.1
Management Support Workers (all other)	869	1,104	27.1
Managerial and administrative Occupations	8,675	10,575	21.9
Managers and Administrators (all other)	1,925	2,515	30.7
Marketing, Advertising, and Public Relations Managers	406	511	25.7
Mathematicians and all other Mathematical Scientists	16	19	19.4
Mechanical Engineers	225	269	19.8
Medical Records Technicians	47	75	59.9
Metallurgists and Metallurgical, Ceramic, and Materials Engineers	19	22	13.0

[Continued]

★ 553 ★

Occupational Growth, 1988-2000 - II
[Continued]

	1988	2000	% change
Meteorologists	6	8	29.6
Mining Engineers, including Mine Safety Engineers	5	6	5.8
Musicians	229	251	9.5
Nuclear Engineers	15	15	3.0
Nuclear Medicine and Radiologic Technicians and Technologists	142	231	62.7
Nuclear Medicine Technologists	10	13	29.6
Occupational Therapists	33	48	48.8
Operations research Analysts	55	85	55.4
Opticians, Dispensing and Measuring	49	65	31.5
Optometrists	37	43	16.5
Paralegals	83	145	75.3
Personnel, Training, and Labor Relations Managers	171	208	22.1
Personnel, Training, and Labor Relations Specialists	252	305	21.2
Petroleum Engineers	17	18	6.9
Pharmacists	162	206	26.9
Photographers	94	111	17.5
Photographers and Camera Operators	105	125	18.7
Physical Scientists	184	215	16.9
Physical Scientists (all other)	37	44	18.6
Physical Therapists	68	107	57.0
Physician Assistants	48	62	28.1
Physicians	535	684	27.8
Physicists and Astronomers	18	21	12.3
Podiatrists	17	22	34.6
Producers, Directors, Actors, and Entertainers	80	104	29.6
Professional Specialty Occupations	14,628	18,137	24.0
Professional Workers (all other)	774	980	26.6
Programmers, Numerical, Tool, and Process Control	8	10	26.3
Property and Real Estate Managers	225	267	19.0
Psychologists	104	132	27.0
Public Relations Specialists and Publicity Writers	91	105	15.4
Purchasing Agents, except Wholesale, Retail, and Farm Products	206	236	14.6
Purchasing Managers	252	289	14.4
Radio and TV Announcers and Newscasters	57	67	18.6
Radiologic Technologists and Technicians	132	218	66.0
Recreation Workers	186	221	18.9
Recreational Therapists	26	35	36.9
Registered Nurses	1,577	2,190	38.8
Reporters and Correspondents, Writers and Editors	289	356	23.2
Reporters and Correspondents	70	82	16.4
Respiratory Therapists	56	79	41.3
Science and Mathematics Technicians	232	275	18.6
Social, Recreational, and Religious Workers	931	1,147	23.3
Social Scientists	194	239	23.5
Social Workers	385	495	28.5

[Continued]

★ 553 ★

Occupational Growth, 1988-2000 - II
[Continued]

	1988	2000	% change
Social Workers and Human Services Workers	503	666	32.4
Speech-Language Pathologists and Audiologists	53	68	27.8
Statisticians	15	18	22.5
Surgical Technologists	35	55	56.4
Surveyors	100	112	11.9
Teachers and Instructors, Vocational Education and Training	239	255	6.6
Teachers and Instructors (all other)	725	900	24.0
Teachers, Kindergarten and Elementary	1,359	1,567	15.3
Teachers, Librarians, and Counselors	5,379	6,228	15.8
Teachers, Preschool	238	309	30.2
Teachers, Preschool, Kindergarten and Elementary	1,597	1,876	17.5
Teachers, Secondary School	1,164	1,388	19.3
Teachers, Special Education	275	317	15.6
Teachers and Instructors (other)	490	545	11.2
Technical Assistants, Library	54	59	8.8
Technicians and related Support Occupations	3,867	5,089	31.6
Technicians, except Health and Engineering and Science	949	1,319	39.0
Technicians (all other)	30	33	8.7
Therapists	256	367	43.3
Therapists (all other)	20	29	42.2
Title Examiners and Searchers	27	31	17.3
Underwriters	103	134	29.4
Urban and Regional Planners	20	23	14.8
Veterinarians and Veterinary Inspectors	46	57	25.5
Wholesale and Retail Buyers, except Farm Products	207	220	6.3
Writers, Artists, and Entertainers	1,387	1,690	21.9
Writers and Editors, including Technical Writers	219	274	25.3

Source: "Occupational Growth from 1988 to 2000 (Occupations in Alphabetical Order)," *Professional Careers Sourcebook: Where to Find Help Planning Careers that Require College or Technical Degrees*, Kathleen M. Savage and Annette Novello, eds., Gale Research Co., Detroit, Mich., 1992, pp. 1111-13. Primary source: Bureau of Labor Statistics.

★ 554 ★

Occupations by Percentage of Change, 1988-2000 - I

Below is an extract from the Bureau of Labor Statistics' Industry - Occupation Matrix (1990). Annual employment figures are in thousands (000s).

Occupation	1988	2000	% change
Medical assistants	149.0	253.0	70.0
Homemaker-home health aides	327.0	534.0	63.0
Corrections officers	186.0	262.0	41.0
Receptionists	833.0	1,164.0	40.0

[Continued]

★ 554 ★

Occupations by Percentage of Change, 1988-2000 - I
[Continued]

Occupation	1988	2000	% change
Flight attendants	88.0	122.0	39.0
Computer and office machine repairers	128.0	172.0	35.0
Information clerks	1,316.0	1,757.0	34.0
Guards	795.0	1,051.0	32.0
Nursing aides and psychiatric aides	1,289.0	1,703.0	31.0
Childcare workers	670.0	856.0	30.0
Computer and peripheral equipment operators	316.0	408.0	29.0
Opthalmic laboratory technicians	25.0	33.3	28.0
Reservation and transportation ticket agents and clerks	133.0	170.0	28.0
Credit clerks and authorizers	229.0	290.0	27.0
Automotive body repairers	214.0	270.0	26.0
Hotel and motel clerks	113.0	142.0	26.0
Food and beverage service workers	4,458.0	5,526.0	24.0
Gardeners and groundskeepers	760.0	942.0	24.0
Plastic-working machine operators	144.0	176.0	22.0
Tilesetters	26.0	31.8	22.0
Chefs, cooks, and other kitchen workers	2,755.0	3,341.0	21.0
Teacher aides	682.0	827.0	21.0
Photographic process workers	67.0	81.0	21.0
Carpet installers	56.0	68.0	21.0
Janitors and cleaners	2,895.0	3,451.0	19.0
General maintenance mechanics	1,080.0	1,282.0	19.0
Dental assistants	166.0	197.0	19.0
Roofers	123.0	147.0	19.0
Sheet-metal workers	97.0	115.0	19.0
Structural and reinforcing ironworkers	91.0	108.0	19.0
Insulation workers	65.0	77.0	19.0
General office clerks	2,519.0	2,974.0	18.0
Adjusters, investigators, and collectors	961.0	1,133.0	18.0
Electricians	542.0	638.0	18.0
Plumbers and pipefitters	396.0	469.0	18.0
Interviewing and new accounts clerks	237.0	280.0	18.0
Lithographic and photoengraving workers	67.0	79.0	18.0
Glaziers	49.0	57.6	18.0
Secretaries	3,373.0	3,944.0	17.0
Busdrivers	506.0	594.0	17.0
Heating, air-conditioning, and refrigeration mechanics	225.0	263.0	17.0
Drywall workers and lathers	152.0	178.0	17.0
Concrete masons and terrazzo workers	114.0	133.0	17.0
Commercial and industrial electronic equipment repairers	78.8	91.8	17.0
Millwrights	77.0	90.0	17.0
Elevators installers and repairers	13.0	15.3	17.0
Carpenters	1,106.0	1,286.0	16.0

[Continued]

★ 554 ★

Occupations by Percentage of Change, 1988-2000 - I
[Continued]

Occupation	1988	2000	% change
Automotive mechanics	771.0	897.0	16.0
Industrial machinery repairers	463.0	538.0	16.0
Painter and paperhangers	431.0	501.0	16.0
Diesel mechanics	269.0	312.0	16.0
Bricklayers and stonemasons	167.0	192.0	16.0
Aircraft mechanics and engine specialists	124.0	144.0	16.0
Animal caretakers, except farm	92.0	106.0	16.0
Jewelers	35.0	40.7	16.0
Telephone operators	330.0	378.0	15.0
Printing press operators	239.0	274.0	15.0
Truckdrivers	2,641.0	3,023.0	14.0
Dispatchers	202.0	231.0	14.0
Mobile heavy equipment mechanics	108.0	124.0	14.0
Water and wastewater treatment plant operators	76.0	87.0	14.0
Electric power generating plant operators and power distributors and dispatchers	45.0	51.4	14.0
Cosmetologists and related workers	649.0	731.0	13.0
Police, detectives, and special agents	515.0	583.0	13.0
Motorcycle, boat, and small-engine mechanics	58.0	65.7	13.0
Electric home entertainment equipment repairers	44.0	49.5	13.0
Material recording, scheduling, dispatching, and distributing occupations	2,889.0	3,227.0	12.0
Stock clerks	2,152.0	2,406.0	12.0
Clerical supervisors and managers	1,183.0	1,319.0	12.0
Upholsterers	73.0	81.1	11.0
Bindery workers	73.0	80.9	11.0
Traffic, shipping, and receiving clerks	535.0	591.0	10.0
Firefighting occupations	291.0	320.0	10.0
File clerks	263.0	290.0	10.0
Mail clerks and messengers	259.0	285.0	10.0
Fishers, hunters, and trappers	54.0	59.7	10.0
Dental laboratory technicians	51.0	56.2	10.0
Machinists	397.0	433.0	9.0
Woodworking occupations	375.0	409.0	9.0
Personnel clerks	129.0	141.0	9.0
Numerical-control machine-tool operators	64.0	69.9	9.0
Boilermakers	25.0	27.2	9.0
Butchers and meat, poultry, and fish cutters	368.0	398.0	8.0
Plasterers	27.0	29.2	8.0
Musical instrument repairers and tuners	7.5	8.1	8.0
Blue-collar worker supervisors	1,797.0	1,930.0	7.0
Postal clerks and mail carriers	665.0	706.0	6.0
Library assistants and bookmobile drivers	105.0	111.1	6.0
Records clerks	886.0	930.0	5.0

[Continued]

★ 554 ★

Occupations by Percentage of Change, 1988-2000 - I
[Continued]

Occupation	1988	2000	% change
Bank tellers	522.0	546.0	5.0
Painting and coating machine operators	159.0	167.5	5.0
Material moving equipment operators	1,010.0	1,047.0	4.0
Tool and die makers	152.0	158.8	4.0
Brokerage clerks and statement clerks	96.0	98.8	3.0
Handlers, equipment cleaners, helpers, and laborers	4,894.0	4,999.0	2.0
Financial records processors	2,849.0	2,867.0	1.0
Bookkeeping, accounting, and auditing clerks	2,252.0	2,272.0	1.0
Compositors and typesetters	86.0	<86.5	1.0
Farm equipment mechanics	54.0	54.8	1.0
Roustabouts	39.0	<39.5	1.0
Vending machine machine servicers	27.0	<27.5	1.0
Billing clerks and related workers	421.0	422.4	0.0
Home appliance and power tool repairers	76.0	<76.5	0.0
Barbers	46.0	<46.5	0.0
Shoe and leather workers and repairers	32.0	<32.5	0.0
Stationary engineers	36.0	35.5	-1.0
Order clerks	293.0	288.6	-2.0
Payroll and timekeeping clerks	176.0	171.8	-2.0
Metalworking and plasticworking machine operators	1,405.0	1,365.0	-3.0
Line installers and cable splicers	231.0	221.0	-4.0
Private household workers	902.0	860.0	-5.0
Typists, word processors, and data entry keyers	1,416.0	1,334.0	-6.0
Metalworking machine operators	1,252.0	1,182.0	-6.0
Inspectors, testers, and graders	676.0	634.0	-6.0
Apparel workers	1,104.0	1,026.0	-7.0
Welders, cutters, and welding machine operators	424.0	394.0	-7.0
Timbers cutting, and logging workers	106.0	96.0	-10.0
Textile machinery operators	310.0	273.0	-12.0
Water transportation occupations	49.0	43.2	-12.0
Communications equipment mechanics	113.0	95.0	-16.0
Railroad transportation workers	106.0	90.0	-16.0
Farm operators and managers	1,272.0	1,035.0	-19.0
Steel workers	8.9	7.2	-19.0
Telephone installers and repairers	58.0	46.0	-20.0
Stenographers	159.0	123.0	-23.0
Precision assemblers	354.0	344.9	-26.0

Source: "Projected Occupational Growth from 1988 to 2000 (Occupations by Percentage of Change)," *Vocational Careers Sourcebook: Where to Find Help Planning Careers in Skilled, Trade, and Nontechnical Vocations,* Kathleen M. Savage and Karen Hill, eds., Gale Research Inc., Detroit, Michigan, 1992, pp. 1079-80. Primary source: Bureau of Labor Statistics' industry-occupation matrix, 1990.

★ 555 ★

Occupations by Percentage of Change, 1988-2000 - II

Annual figures are presented in thousands.

	1988	2000	% change
Paralegal Personnel	83	145	75.3
Radiologic Technologists and Technicians	132	218	66.0
Nuclear Medicine and Radiologic Technicians and Technologists	142	231	62.7
Medical Records Technicians	47	75	59.9
Physical Therapists	68	107	57.0
Surgical Technologists	35	55	56.4
Operations Research Analysts	55	85	55.4
Actuaries	16	24	53.6
Computer Systems Analysts	403	617	53.3
Computer, Mathematical and Operations Research Analysts	503	763	51.5
Electroencephalograph Technicians and Technologists	6	10	50.4
Occupational Therapists	33	48	48.8
Computer Programmers	519	769	48.1
Legal Assistants and Technicians, except Clerical	200	290	45.0
Human Services Workers	118	171	44.9
Therapists	256	367	43.3
All other Therapists	20	29	42.2
Respiratory Therapists	56	79	41.3
Employment Interviewers, Private or Public Employment Service	81	113	40.5
Electrical and Electronics Engineers	439	615	40.0
Technicians, except Health and Engineering and Science	949	1,319	39.0
Registered Nurses	1,577	2,190	38.8
Electrical and Electronics Engineering Technicians and Technologists	341	471	38.2
Health Assessment and Treating Occupations	2,084	2,876	38.0
Recreational Therapists	26	35	36.9
Licensed Practical Nurses	626	855	36.6
Management Analysts	130	176	35.0
Podiatrists	17	22	34.6
Health Technicians and Technologists	1,645	2,211	34.4
All other Health Professionals, Paraprofessionals, and Technicians	313	419	33.9
Social Workers and Human Services Workers	503	666	32.4
Engineering, Mathematical, and Natural Sciences Managers	258	341	32.0
Technicians and related Support Operations	3,867	5,089	31.6
Opticians, Dispensing and Measuring	49	65	31.5
Lawyers	582	763	31.0
Aircraft Pilots and Flight Engineers	83	108	30.9
All other Managers and Administrators	1,925	2,515	30.7
Lawyers and Judicial Workers	622	810	30.2
Teachers, Preschool	238	309	30.2
Meteorologists	6	8	29.6

[Continued]

★ 555 ★

Occupations by Percentage of Change, 1988-2000 - II
[Continued]

	1988	2000	% change
Nuclear Medicine Technologists	10	13	29.6
Producers, Directors, Actors and Entertainers	80	104	29.6
Underwriters	103	134	29.4
Camera Operators, Television and Motion Picture	11	14	29.1
Landscape Architects	19	25	28.9
Food Service and Lodging Managers	560	721	28.8
Social Workers	385	495	28.5
Engineering Technicians	722	926	28.2
Physicians Assistants	48	62	28.1
Designers	309	395	27.9
Dietitians and Nutritionists	40	51	27.8
Physicians	535	684	27.8
Speech-Language Pathologists and Audiologists	53	68	27.8
Economists	36	45	27.3
Artists and Commercial Artists	216	274	27.1
All other Management Support Workers	869	1,104	27.1
Psychologists	104	132	27.0
Counselors	124	157	26.9
Pharmacists	162	206	26.9
All other Life Scientists	45	57	26.6
All other Professional Workers	774	980	26.6
Programmers, Numerical, Tool, and Process Control	8	10	26.3
Administrative Services Managers	217	274	26.2
Biological Scientists	57	72	26.0
Construction Managers	187	236	26.0
Architects	105	132	25.7
Marketing, Advertising, and Public Relations Managers	406	511	25.7
Employment Interviewers and Personnel Specialists	333	418	25.5
Veterinarians and Veterinary Inspectors	46	57	25.5
All other Legal Assistants, including Law Clerks	90	113	25.4
Writers, Editors, including Technical Writers	219	274	25.3
Engineers	1,411	1,762	24.9
Architects, except Landscape and Marine	86	107	24.7
Health Diagnosing Occupations	801	995	24.2
Professional Specialty Occupations	14,628	18,137	24.0
All other Teachers and Instructors	725	900	24.0
Claims Examiners, Property and Casualty Insurance	30	37	23.5
Social Scientists	194	239	23.5
Social, Recreational, and Religious Workers	931	1,147	23.3
Reporters and Correspondents, Writers and Editors	289	356	23.2
Statisticians	15	18	22.5
Engineering and Science Technicians and Technologists	1,273	1,559	22.4
Life Scientists	154	189	22.2
Management Support Occupations	3,428	4,187	22.1
Personnel, Training, and Labor Relations Managers	171	208	22.4

[Continued]

★ 555 ★

Occupations by Percentage of Change, 1988-2000 - II
[Continued]

	1988	2000	% change
Accountants and Auditors	963	1,174	22.0
Executive, Administrative, and Managerial Occupations	12,104	14,762	22.0
Managerial and Administrative Occupations	8,675	10,575	21.9
Writers, Artists, and Entertainers	1,387	1,690	21.9
Loan Officers and Counselors	172	209	21.5
Personnel, Training, and Labor Relations Specialists	252	305	21.2
All other Engineers	247	299	21.2
Agricultural and Food Scientists	25	30	20.9
Mechanical Engineers	225	269	19.8
Education Administrators	320	382	19.4
Mathematicians and all other Mathematical Scientists	16	19	19.4
Financial Managers	673	802	19.3
Teachers, Secondary School	1,164	1,388	19.3
Clinical Lab Technologists and Technicians	242	288	19.2
Dancers and Choreographers	11	13	19.2
All other Engineering Technicians and Technologists	381	454	19.2
Property and Real Estate Managers	225	267	19.0
Architects and Surveyors	205	244	18.9
Recreation Workers	186	221	18.9
Photographers and Camera Operators	105	125	18.7
Radio and TV Announcers and Newscasters	57	67	18.6
Science and Mathematics Technicians	232	275	18.6
All other Physical Scientists	37	44	18.6
Industrial Engineers except Safety Engineers	132	155	18.0
Industrial Production Managers	215	254	18.0
Instructors, Adult (nonvocational) Education	227	268	17.9
Judges, Magistrates, and other Judicial Workers	40	47	17.9
Dental Hygienists	91	107	17.6
Photographers	94	111	17.5
Teachers, Preschool, Kindergarten and Elementary	1,597	1,876	17.5
Civil Engineers, including Traffic Engineers	186	219	17.4
Title Examiners and Searchers	27	31	17.3
Physical Scientists	184	215	16.9
Chemists	80	93	16.7
Budget Analysts	62	72	16.5
Curators, Archivists, Museum Technicians, and Restorers	16	19	16.5
Optometrists	37	43	16.5
Chemical Engineers	49	57	16.4
Reporters and Correspondents	70	82	16.4
Communication, Transportation and Utilities Operations Managers	167	194	16.3
General Managers and Top Executives	3,030	3,509	15.8
Teachers, Librarians, and Counselors	5,379	6,228	15.8
Geologists, Geophysicists, and Oceanographers	42	49	15.7
Teachers, Special Education	275	317	15.6

[Continued]

★ 555 ★

Occupations by Percentage of Change, 1988-2000 - II
[Continued]

	1988	2000	% change
Air Traffic Controllers	27	31	15.5
Cost Estimators	169	194	15.4
Public Relations Specialists and Publicity Writers	91	105	15.4
Teachers, Kindergarten and Elementary	1,359	1,567	15.3
Urban and regional Planners	20	23	14.8
Purchasing Agents, except Wholesale, Retail and Farm Products	206	236	14.6
Purchasing Managers	252	289	14.4
Construction and Building Inspectors	56	64	14.2
Inspectors and Compliance Officers, except Construction	130	148	13.9
All other Social Scientists	33	38	13.7
Dentists	167	189	13.1
Emergency Medical Technicians	76	86	13.0
Metallurgists and Metallurgical, Ceramic, and Materials Engineers	19	22	13.0
Aeronautical and Astronautical Engineers	78	88	12.7
Physicists and Astronomers	18	21	12.3
Drafters	319	358	12.2
Adult and Vocational Teachers	467	523	12.1
Surveyors	100	112	11.9
Other Teachers and Instructors	490	545	11.2
Librarians, Archivists, Curators, and related workers	159	176	10.7
Electrocardiograph Technicians and technologists	18	20	10.2
Librarians, Professional	143	157	10.0
Directors, Religious Activities and Education	56	62	9.8
Musicians	229	251	9.5
Technical Assistants, Library	54	59	8.8
All other Technicians	30	33	8.7
Foresters and Conservation Scientists	27	30	8.3
Clergy	185	199	7.2
Petroleum Engineers	17	18	6.9
Teachers and Instructors, Vocational Education and Training	239	255	6.6
Wholesale and Retail Buyers, except Farm Products	207	220	6.3
Mining Engineers, including Mine Safety Engineers	5	6	5.8
Government Chief Executives and Legislators	69	71	3.0
Nuclear Engineers	15	15	3.0
College and University Faculty	846	869	2.8
Farm and Home Management Advisors	23	22	-6.2
Broadcast Technicians	27	19	-31.1

Source: "Occupational Growth from 1988 to 2000 (Occupations by Percentage of Change)," *Professional Careers Sourcebook: Where to Find Help Planning Careers that Require College or Technical Degrees*, Kathleen M. Savage and Annette Novello, eds., Gale Research Co., Detroit, Mich., 1992, pp. 1109-11. Primary source: Bureau of Labor Statistics.

★ 556 ★

Job Openings by Major Occupational Group, 1990-2005

"Jobs will be available at all levels of education because of the large size of the occupation groups requiring less than college training and the need to replace workers who will leave their jobs from 1990 to 2005."

[Numbers in thousands]

Occupational group	Job openings due to replacement needs	Job openings due to employment increases	Total job openings
All occupations	38,851	26,892	65,743
Managerial	3,085	3,414	6,499
Professional specialty	4,281	5,107	9,388
Technicians	1,200	1,551	2,751
Marketing and sales	5,379	3,401	8,780
Administrative support	6,413	3,309	9,722
Service	7,403	5,830	13,233
Precision production	4,764	2,068	6,832
Operators	5,449	1,734	7,183
Agriculture-related	863	477	1,340

Source: "Outlook 1990-2005," *Occupational Outlook Quarterly* 35, No. 3, Fall, 1991, p. 29.

★ 557 ★

Fastest Growing Occupations, 1990 and 2005

Occupation	Employment, in thousands		Change
	1990	2005	
Home health aides	287	550	92.0
Paralegals	90	167	85.0
Systems analysts and computer scientists	463	829	79.0
Personal and home care aides	103	183	77.0
Physical therapists	88	155	76.0
Medical assistants	165	287	74.0
Operations research analysts	57	100	73.0
Human services workers	145	249	71.0
Radiologic technologists and technicians	149	252	70.0
Medical secretaries	232	390	68.0

Source: Richman, Louis S., "America's Tough New Job Market," *Fortune*, February 24, 1992, p. 54. Primary source: Bureau of Labor Statistics.

★ 558 ★

Occupations with the Largest Job Growth, 1990-2005

[Numbers in thousands]

Occupation	Employment, in thousands		Numerical Change	Percent change
	1990	2005		
Salespersons, retail	3,619	4,506	887	24.5
Registered nurses	1,727	2,494	767	44.4
Cashiers	2,633	3,318	685	26.0
General office clerks	2,737	3,407	670	24.5
Truckdrivers, light and heavy	2,362	2,979	617	26.1
General managers and top executives	3,086	3,684	598	19.4
Janitors and cleaners, including maids and housekeeping cleaners	3,007	3,562	555	18.5
Nursing aides, orderlies, and attendants	1,274	1,826	552	43.4
Food counter, fountain, and related workers	1,607	2,158	550	34.2
Waiters and waitresses	1,747	2,196	449	25.7
Teachers, secondary school	1,280	1,717	437	34.2
Receptionists and information clerks	900	1,322	422	46.9
Systems analysts and computer scientists	463	829	366	78.9
Food preparation workers	1,156	1,521	365	31.6
Child care workers	725	1,078	353	48.8
Gardeners and groundskeepers, except farm	874	1,222	348	39.8
Accountants and auditors	985	1,325	340	34.5
Computer programmers	565	882	317	56.1
Teachers, elementary	1,362	1,675	313	23.0
Guards	883	1,181	298	33.7
Teacher aides and educational assistants	808	1,086	278	34.4
Licensed practical nurses	844	913	269	41.9
Clerical supervisors and managers	1,218	1,481	263	21.6
Home health aides	287	550	263	91.7
Cooks, restaurant	615	872	257	41.8
Maintenance repairers, general utility	1,128	1,379	251	22.2
Secretaries, except legal and medical	3,064	3,312	248	8.1
Cooks, short order and fast food	743	989	246	33.0
Stock clerks, sales floor	1,242	1,451	209	16.8
Lawyers	587	793	206	35.1

Source: "Occupational Employment Projections," George Silvestri and John Lukasiewicz, *Monthly Labor Review* 114, No. 11, November, 1991, p. 82.

★ 559 ★

Occupations with the Greatest Numerical Increases, 1990-2005

"Among 500 occupations for which projections were developed, 30 will account for half of total employment growth over the 1990-2005 period."

[Numbers in thousands]

Salespersons, retail	887
Registered nurses	767
Cashiers	685
General office clerks	670
Truck drivers, light and heavy	617
General managers and top executives	598
Janitors and cleaners	555
Nursing aides, orderlies, and attendants	552
Food counter, fountain, and related workers	550
Waiters and waitresses	449
Teachers, secondary school	437
Receptionists and information clerks	422
Systems analysts and computer scientists	366
Food preparation workers	365
Childcare workers	353
Gardeners and groundskeepers	348
Accountants and auditors	340
Computer programmers	317
Teachers, elementary school	313
Guards	298
Teachers aides and educational assistants	278
Licensed practical nurses	269
Clerical supervisors and managers	263
Home health aides	263
Cooks, restaurants	257
Maintenance repairers, general utility	251
Secretaries except legal and medical	248
Cooks, short order and fast food	246
Stock clerks, sales floor	209
Lawyers	206

Source: "Outlook 1990-2005," *Occupational Outlook Quarterly* 35, No. 3, Fall, 1991, p. 30.

★ 560 ★

Fastest Growing Occupations, 1990-2005

[Numbers in thousands].

Occupation	Employment		Numerical change	Percent change
	1990	2005		
Home health aides	287	550	263	91.7
Paralegals	90	167	77	85.2
Systems analysts and computer scientists	463	829	366	78.9
Personal and home care aides	103	183	79	76.7
Physical therapists	88	155	67	76.0
Medical assistants	165	287	122	73.9
Operations research analysts	57	100	42	73.2
Human services workers	145	249	103	71.2
Radiologic technologists and technicians	149	252	103	69.5
Medical secretaries	232	390	158	68.3
Physical and corrective therapy assistants and aides	45	74	29	64.0
Psychologists	125	204	79	63.6
Travel agents	132	214	82	62.3
Correction officers	230	372	142	61.4
Data processing equipment repairers	84	134	50	60.0
Flight attendants	101	159	59	58.5
Computer programmers	565	882	317	56.1
Occupational therapists	36	56	20	55.2
Surgical technologists	38	59	21	55.2
Medical records technicians	52	80	28	54.3
Management analysts	151	230	79	52.3
Respiratory therapists	60	91	31	52.1
Child care workers	725	1,078	353	48.8
Marketing, advertising, and public relations managers	427	630	203	47.4
Legal secretaries	281	413	133	47.4
Receptionists and information clerks	900	1,322	422	46.9
Registered nurses	1,727	2,494	767	44.4
Nursing aides, orderlies, and attendants	1,274	1,826	552	43.4
Licensed practical nurses	644	913	269	41.9
Cooks, restaurant	615	872	257	41.8

Source: "Occupational Employment Projections," George Silvestri and John Lukasiewicz, *Monthly Labor Review* 114, No. 11, November, 1991, p. 81. Also in source: a 13-page chart listing employment figures for more than 500 occupations for 1990 and projections to 2005 under low, medium, and high economic growth scenarios. Primary source: Office of Employment Projections, Bureau of Labor Statistics.

★ 561 ★

Occupations with the Largest Growth, 1988-2000

Numbers in thousands.

Occupation	Employment		Change in employment 1988-2000	
	1988	Projected 2000	Number	Percent
Salespersons, retail	3,834	4,564	730	19.0
Registered nurses	1,577	2,190	613	38.8
Janitors and cleaners, including maids and housekeeping cleaners	2,895	3,450	556	19.2
Waiters and waitresses	1,786	2,337	551	30.9
General managers and top executives	3,030	3,509	479	5.8
General office clerks	2,519	2,974	455	18.1
Secretaries, except legal and medical	2,903	3,288	385	13.2
Nursing aides, orderlies, and attendants	1,184	1,562	378	31.9
Truckdrivers, light and heavy	2,399	2,768	369	15.4
Receptionists and information clerks	833	1,164	331	39.8
Cashiers	2,310	2,614	304	13.2
Guards	795	1,050	256	32.2
Computer programmers	519	769	250	48.1
Food counter, fountain, and related workers	1,626	1,866	240	14.7
Food preparation workers	1,027	1,260	234	22.8
Licensed practical nurses	626	855	229	36.6
Teachers, secondary school	1,164	1,388	224	19.5
Computer systems analysts	403	617	214	53.3
Accountants and auditors	963	1,174	211	22.0
Teachers, kindergarten and elementary	1,359	1,567	208	15.3

Source: "The Major Trends," Ronald E. Kutscher, Occupational Outlook Quarterly 34, No. 1, Spring, 1990, p. 7.

★ 562 ★

Selected Occupations with Small Projected Staffing Increases, 2000

Occupation	Reason for change	Projected change in total employment
Biological scientists	Increased expenditures for research and development	Faster than average
Busdrivers, school	Demographic trends	Faster than average
Camera and photographic equipment repairers	Technological advances	About as fast as average
Cooks, restaurant	Changes in business practices	Faster than average

[Continued]

★ 562 ★

Selected Occupations with Small Projected Staffing Increases, 2000
[Continued]

Occupation	Reason for change	Projected change in total employment
Cost estimators	Changes in business practices	About as fast as average
Dentists	Changes in business practices	About as fast as average
Dining room and cafeteria attendants and bartender helpers	Changes in business practices	Faster than average
Economists	Changes in business practices	Faster than average
Electricians	Technological advances	About as fast as average
Electronics repairers, commercial and industrial equipment	Technological advances	About as fast as average
Flight attendants	Other	Much faster than average
Gardeners and groundskeepers, except farm	Other	Faster than average
Hosts and hostesses, restaurant/lounge/coffee shop	Changes in business practices	Much faster than average
Insurance adjusters, examiners, and investigators	Changes in business practices	Faster than average
Locomotive engineers	Technological advances	Decline
Machinists	Technological advances	More slowly than average
Marketing, advertising, and public relations managers	Changes in business practices	Faster than average
Mining engineers, including mine safety engineers	Other	More slowly than average
Nursery workers	Other	Faster than average
Occupational therapy assistants and aides	Changes in the way medical care is provided	Much faster than average
Optical goods workers, precision	Changes in business practices	Faster than average
Personnel training, and labor relations managers and specialist	Changes in business practices	Faster than average
Pharmacists	Changes in the way medical care is provided	Faster than average
Rail yard engineers, dinkey operators, and hostlers	Technological advances	Decline

[Continued]

★ 562 ★

Selected Occupations with Small Projected Staffing Increases, 2000
[Continued]

Occupation	Reason for change	Projected change in total employment
Registered nurses	Changes in the way medical care is provided	Much faster than average
Science and mathematics technicians	Increased expenditures for research and development	About as fast as average
Social workers	Other	Faster than average
Statisticians	Changes in business practices	Faster than average
Teachers, secondary school	Demographic trends	About as fast as average
Tool and die makers	Technological advances	More slowly than average
Waiters and waitresses	Changes in business practices	Much faster than average

Source: "Occupational Staffing Patterns Within Industries Through the Year 2000," Liesel Brand, *Occupational Outlook Quarterly* 34, No. 2, Summer 1990, p. 44.

★ 563 ★

Selected Occupations with Moderate Projected Staffing Increases, 2000

Occupation	Reason for change	Projected change in total employment
Administrative services managers	Changes in business practices	Faster than average
Advertising clerks	Changes in business practices	Faster than average
Agricultural and food scientists	Increased expenditures for research and development	Faster than average
Air traffic controllers	Other	About as fast as average
Automotive body and related repairers	Technological advances	Faster than average
Camera operators	Technological advances	Faster than average
Chemical engineers	Increased expenditures for research and development	About as fast as average
Chemists	Increased expenditures for research and development	About as fast as average
Claims examiners, property and casualty insurance	Changes in business practices	Faster than average
Combination machine tool setters, set-up operators, operators, and tenders	Changes in business practices	More slowly than average
Construction managers	Changes in business practices	Faster than average
Counselors	Changes in business practices	Faster than average

[Continued]

★ 563 ★

Selected Occupations with Moderate Projected Staffing Increases, 2000
[Continued]

Occupation	Reason for change	Projected change in total employment
Court clerks	Trends in law, law enforcement and government regulations	Faster than average
Detectives and investigators, except public protective service workers	Trends in law, law enforcement and government regulations	Much faster than average
EEG technologists	Changes in the way medical care is provided	Much faster than average
Electromedical and biomedical equipment repairers	Changes in the way medical care is provided	Much faster than average
Engineering, mathematics, and natural science managers	Increased expenditures for research and development	Much faster than average
Food service and lodging managers	Changes in business practices	Faster than average
Geologists, geophysicists, and oceanographers	Increased expenditures for research and development	About as fast as average
Guards	Other	Much faster than average
Human services workers	Other	Much faster than average
Industrial engineers, except safety engineers	Technological advances	About as fast as average
Industrial machinery mechanics	Technological advances	About as fast as average
Industrial production managers	Changes in business practices	About as fast as average
Inspectors and compliance officers, except construction	Trends in law, law enforcement and government regulations	About as fast as average
Judges, magistrates, and other judicial workers	Trends in law, law enforcement and government regulations	About as fast as average
Lawyers	Trends in law, law enforcement and government regulations	Much faster than average
Log handling equipment operators	Technological advances	Decline
Manicurists	Other	Faster than average
Meat, poultry, and fish cutters and trimmers, hand	Changes in business practices	About as fast as average
Mechanical engineers	Increased expenditures for research and development	Faster than average
Metallurgists and metallurgical, ceramic, and materials engineers	Increased expenditures for research and development	About as fast as average
Numerical control machine tool operators and tenders, metal and plastic	Technological advances	More slowly than average
Occupational therapists	Changes in the way medical care is provided	Much faster than average
Offset lithograph press operators	Technological advances	Faster than average
Opticians, dispensing and measuring	Changes in business practices	Much faster than average
Petroleum engineers	Other	More slowly than average
Pharmacy assistants	Changes in the way medical care is provided	Faster than average
Photographers	Changes in business practices	About as fast as average
Physical therapists	Changes in the way medical care is provided	Much faster than average

[Continued]

★ 563 ★

Selected Occupations with Moderate Projected Staffing Increases, 2000
[Continued]

Occupation	Reason for change	Projected change in total employment
Physicists and astronomers	Increased expenditures for research and development	About as fast as average
Property and real estate managers	Changes in business practices	About as fast as average
Radiologic technologists and technicians	Changes in the way medical care is provided	Much faster than average
Respiratory therapists	Demographic trends	Much faster than average
Securities and financial services sales workers	Changes in business practices	Much faster than average
Typesetting and composing machine operators and tenders	Technological advances	About as fast as average
Underwriters	Changes in business practices	Faster than average

Source: "Occupational Staffing Patterns Within Industries Through the Year 2000," Liesel Brand, *Occupational Outlook Quarterly* 34, No. 2, Summer 1990, pp. 45-6.

★ 564 ★

Selected Occupations with Significant Projected Staffing Increases, 2000

Occupation	Reason for change	Projected change in total employment
Actuaries	Changes in business practices	Much faster than average
Bakers, bread and pastry	Changes in business practices	Much faster than average
Computer programmers	The growing use of computers	Much faster than average
Computer systems analysts	The growing use of computers	Much faster than average
Correction officers and jailers	Trends in law, law enforcement and government regulations	Much faster than average
Data processing equipment repairers	The growing use of computers	Much faster than average
Electrical and electronics engineers	Increased expenditures for research and development	Much faster than average
Electrical and electronics technicians and technologists	Increased expenditures for research and development	Much faster than average
Farm managers	Changes in business practices	Faster than average
Management analysts and consultants	Changes in business practices	Much faster than average

[Continued]

★ 564 ★

Selected Occupations with Significant Projected Staffing Increases, 2000
[Continued]

Occupation	Reason for change	Projected change in total employment
Medical record technicians	Changes in business practices	Much faster than average
Meteorologists	Other	Faster than average
Millwrights	Technological advances	About as fast as average
Operations research analysts	Changes in business practices	Much faster than average
Paralegals	Changes in business practices and trends in law, law enforcement, and government regulations	Much faster than average
Photographic process workers, precision	Changes in business practices	Much faster than average
Programmers, numerical, tool, and process control	Technological advances	Faster than average
Shoe and leather workers and repairers	Demographic trends	Little change
Subway and streetcar operators	Other	Much faster than average
Surgical technologists	Changes in the way medical care is provided	Much faster than average

Source: "Occupational Staffing Patterns Within Industries Through the Year 2000," Liesel Brand, *Occupational Outlook Quarterly* 34, No. 2, Summer 1990, p. 47.

★ 565 ★

Jobs in Decline, 1990-2005

[Numbers in thousands].

Occupation	Employment		Numerical change	Percent change
	1990	2005		
Farmers	1,074	850	-224	-20.9
Bookkeeping, accounting, and auditing clerks	2,276	2,143	-133	-5.8
Child care workers, private household	314	190	-124	-39.5
Sewing machine operators, garment	585	469	-116	-19.8
Electrical and electronic assemblers	232	128	-105	-45.1
Typists and word processors	972	869	-103	-10.6
Cleaners and servants, private household	411	310	-101	-24.5

[Continued]

★ 565 ★

Jobs in Decline, 1990-2005
[Continued]

Occupation	Employment		Numerical	Percent
	1990	2005	change	change
Farm workers	837	745	-92	-11.0
Electrical and electronic equipment assemblers, precision	171	90	-81	-47.5
Textile draw-out and winding machine operators and tenders	199	138	-61	-30.6
Switchboard operators	246	189	-57	-23.2
Machine forming operators and tenders, metal and plastic	174	131	-43	-24.5
Machine tool cutting operators and tenders, metal and plastic	145	104	-42	-28.6
Telephone and cable TV line installers and repairers	133	92	-40	-30.4
Central office and PBX installers and repairers	80	46	-34	-42.5
Central office operators	53	22	-31	-59.2
Statistical clerks	85	54	-31	-36.1
Packaging and filling machine operators and tenders	324	297	-27	-8.3
Station installers and repairers, telephone	47	21	-26	-55.0
Bank tellers	517	492	-25	-4.8
Lathe and turning machine tool setters and set-up operators, metal and plastic	80	61	-20	-24.4
Grinders and polishers, hand	84	65	-19	-22.5
Electromechanical equipment assemblers, precision	49	31	-18	-36.5
Grinding machine setters and set-up operators metal and plastic	72	54	-18	-25.1
Service station attendants	246	229	-17	-7.1
Directory assistance operators	26	11	-16	-59.4
Butchers and meatcutters	234	220	-14	-5.9
Chemical equipment controllers, operators, and tenders	75	61	-14	-19.1
Drilling and boring machine tool setters and set-up operators, metal and plastic	52	39	-13	-25.6
Meter readers, utilities	50	37	-12	-24.8

Source: "Occupations With the Largest Job Declines, 1990-2005, Moderate Alternative Projections," George Silvestri and John Lukasiewicz, *Monthly Labor Review* 114, No. 11, November, 1991, p. 84. Also in source: 13-page chart listing employment figures for more than 500 occupations for 1990 and projections to 2005 under low, medium, and high economic growth scenarios. Primary source: Office of Employment Projections, Bureau of Labor Statistics.

★ 566 ★

Occupations with Greatest Declines, 1990-2005

"Occupations with the greatest declines in employment are concentrated in declining industries or affected by technological change. Some occupations are affected by both factors. About half the declining occupations are concentrated in manufacturing."

[Numbers in thousands]

Farmers	-224
Bookkeeping, accounting, and auditing clerks	-133
Childcare workers, private household	-124
Sewing machine operators, garment	-116
Electrical and electronic assemblers	-105
Typists and word processors	-103
Cleaners and servants, private household	-101
Farm workers	-92
Electrical and electronic equipment assembler	-81
Textile draw-out and winding machine operators	-61
Switchboard operators	-57
Machine-forming operators	-43
Machine tool cutting operators	-42
Telephone and cable TV line installers and repairers	-40
Central office and PBX installers and repairers	-34
Central office operators	-31
Statistical clerks	-31
Packaging and filling machine operators	-27
Station installers and repairers, telephone	-26
Bank tellers	-25
Lathe turning machine tool setters	-20
Grinders and polishers, hand	-19
Electromechanical equipment assemblers	-18
Grinding machine setters	-18
Service station attendants	-17
Directory assistance operators	-16
Butchers and meatcutters	-14
Chemical equipment controllers	-14
Drilling and boring machine tool setters	-13
Meter readers, utilities	-12

Source: "Outlook 1990-2005," *Occupational Outlook Quarterly* 35, No. 3, Fall, 1991, p. 32.

★ 567 ★

Selected Occupations with Small Projected Staffing Decreases, 2000

Occupation	Reason for change	Projected change in total employment
Bank tellers	Productivity increases due to the use of computers and office automation	More slowly than average
Bookbinders	Productivity increases due to automation of manufacturing	More slowly than average
Butchers and meatcutters	Productivity increases due to automation of manufacturing	More slowly than average
Cannery workers	Productivity increases due to automation of manufacturing	Little change
Cashiers	Productivity increases due to the use of computers and office automation	About as fast as average
Coil winders, tapers, and finishers	Productivity increases due to automation of manufacturing	Decline
Cooks, institution or cafeteria	Changes in business practices	About as fast as average
Drafters	Productivity increases due to the use of computers and office automation	About as fast as average
Electrolytic plating machine operators and tenders, setters, and set-up operators, metal and plastic	Productivity increases due to automation of manufacturing	Decline
Fitters, structural metal, precision	Productivity increases due to automation of manufacturing	Decline
Freight, stock, and material movers, hand	Productivity increases due to automation of manufacturing	Little change
Heaters, metal and plastic	Productivity increases due to automation of manufacturing	Decline
Heat treating machine operators and tenders, metal and plastic	Productivity increases due to automation of manufacturing	Decline
Industrial truck and tractor operators	Productivity increases due to automation of manufacturing	Decline
Inspectors, testers, and graders	Productivity increases due to	

[Continued]

★ 567 ★

Selected Occupations with Small Projected Staffing Decreases, 2000
[Continued]

Occupation	Reason for change	Projected change in total employment
	automation of manufacturing	Decline
Insurance claims clerks	Productivity increases due to the use of computers and office automation	About as fast as average
Insurance policy processing clerks	Productivity increases due to the use of computers and office automation	More slowly than average
Interviewing clerks, except personnel and welfare	Changes in business practices	About as fast as average
Janitors and cleaners	Changes in business practices	About as fast as average
Legal secretaries	Changes in business practices	Faster than average
Licensed practical nurses	Changes in the way medical care is provided	Much faster than average
Machine tool cutting operators and tenders metal and plastic	Productivity increases due to automation of manufacturing	Decline
Metal fabricators, structural metal products	Productivity increases due to automation of manufacturing	Little change
Mining, quarrying, and tunneling occupations	Productivity increases due to automation of manufacturing	Decline
Nonelectrolytic plating machine operators and tenders, setters, and set-up operators, metal and plastic	Productivity increases due to automation of manufacturing	Decline
Nursing aides, orderlies, and attendants	Changes in the way medical care is provided	Much faster than average
Order fillers, wholesale and retail trade	Productivity increases due to the use of computers and office automation	More slowly than average
Painters, transportation equipment	Productivity increases due to automation of manufacturing	Little change
Physicians	Changes in the way medical care is provided	Faster than average

[Continued]

★ 567 ★

Selected Occupations with Small Projected Staffing Decreases, 2000
[Continued]

Occupation	Reason for change	Projected change in total employment
Plasterers	Changes in business practices	More slowly than average
Police patrol officers	Trends in law, law enforcement and government regulations	About as fast as average
Pressers, hand	Productivity increases due to automation of manufacturing	Decline
Real estate clerks	Productivity increases due to the use of computers and office automation	More slowly than average
Refuse collectors	Other	Little change
Roustabouts	Technological advances	Little change
Secretaries, except legal and medical	Productivity increases due to the use of computers and office automation	About as fast as average
Service station attendants	Changes in business practices	More slowly than average
Sheriffs and deputy sheriffs	Trends in law, law enforcement and government regulations	Little change
Signal or track switch maintainers	Technological advances	Decline
Sodering and brazing machine operators and setters	Productivity increases due to automation of manufacturing	Decline
Statement clerks	Productivity increases due to the use of computers and office automation	Little change
Stationary engineers	Technological advances	Little change
Stockclerks, stockroom, warehouse, or yard	Productivity increases due to the use of computers and office automation	More slowly than average
Surveyors	Technological advances and changes in business practices	About as fast as average

[Continued]

★ 567 ★

Selected Occupations with Small Projected Staffing Decreases, 2000
[Continued]

Occupation	Reason for change	Projected change in total employment
Teachers and instructors, vocational education and training	Demographic trends	More slowly than average
Tire building machine operators	Productivity increases due to automation of manufacturing	Decline
Tire repairers and changers	Other	About as fast as average
Vehicle washers and equipment cleaners	Technological advances	More slowly than average
Watchmakers	Technological advances	More slowly than average
Welders and cutters	Productivity increases due to automation of manufacturing	Decline
Welding machine setters, operators, and tenders	Productivity increases due to automation of manufacturing	Decline

Source: "Occupational Staffing Patterns Within Industries Through the Year 2000," Liesel Brand, *Occupational Outlook Quarterly* 34, No. 2, Summer 1990, pp. 48-9.

★ 568 ★

Selected Occupations with Moderate Projected Staffing Decreases, 2000

Occupation	Reason for change	Projected change in total employment
Animal caretakers, except farm	Other	About as fast as average
Bicycle repairers	Changes in business practices	More slowly than average
Billing, cost, and rate clerks	Productivity increases due to the use of computers and office automation	Little change
Bookkeeping, accounting, and auditing clerks	Productivity increases due to the use of computers and office automation	Little change
Cement and gluing machine operators	Productivity increases due to automation of manufacturing	Decline

[Continued]

★ 568 ★

Selected Occupations with Moderate Projected Staffing Decreases, 2000
[Continued]

Occupation	Reason for change	Projected change in total employment
Central office operators	Productivity increases due to the use of computers and office automation	Decline
Chemical equipment controllers, operators, and tenders	Productivity increases due to automation of manufacturing	Decline
Chemical plant and systems operators	Productivity increases due to automation of manufacturing	Decline
Clinical laboratory technologists and technicians	Changes in the way medical care is provided	About as fast as average
College and university faculty	Demographic trends	Little change
Compositors, typesetters, and arrangers, precision	Productivity increases due to the use of computers and office automation	Decline
Cooking and roasting machine operators and tenders, food and tobacco	Productivity increases due to automation of manufacturing	Decline
Cooks, short order and fast food	Changes in business practices	About as fast as average
Crushing and mixing machine operators and tenders	Productivity increases due to automation of manufacturing	Decline
Cutting and slicing machine setters, operators, and tenders	Productivity increases due to automation of manufacturing	Decline
Duplicating, mail, and other office machine operators	Productivity increases due to the use of computers and office automation	More slowly than average
EKG technicians	Changes in the way medical care is provided	More slowly than average
Electromechanical equipment assemblers, precision	Productivity increases due to automation of manufacturing	Decline
Electronic home entertainment equipment repairers	Technological advances	About as fast as average
Electronic semiconductor processors	Productivity increases due to automation of manufacturing	Decline

[Continued]

★ 568 ★

Selected Occupations with Moderate Projected Staffing Decreases, 2000
[Continued]

Occupation	Reason for change	Projected change in total employment
Farm equipment mechanics	Other	Little change
Farm and home management advisors	Other	Decline
File clerks	Productivity increases due to the use of computers and office automation	More slowly than average
Food counter, fountain, and related workers	Changes in business practices	About as fast as average
Foundry mold assembly and shakeout workers	Productivity increases due to automation of manufacturing	Decline
Furnace, kiln, or kettle operators and tenders	Productivity increases due to automation of manufacturing	Decline
Gas and petroleum plant and system occupations	Productivity increases due to automation of manufacturing	Decline
Grinders and polishers, hand	Productivity increases due to automation of manufacturing	Decline
Handpackers and packagers	Productivity increases due to automation of manufacturing	Decline
Home appliance and power tool repairers	Technological advances and changes in business practices	Little change
Jewelers and silversmiths	Other	About as fast as average
Letterpress operators	Productivity increases due to automation of manufacturing	Decline
Library assistants and bookmobile drivers	Productivity increases due to the use of computers and office automation	More slowly than average
Machine assemblers	Productivity increases due to automation of manufacturing	Decline
Machine builders and other precision machine assemblers	Productivity increases due to automation of manufacturing	Decline
Machine feeders and offbearers	Productivity increases due to	

[Continued]

547

★ 568 ★

Selected Occupations with Moderate Projected Staffing Decreases, 2000
[Continued]

Occupation	Reason for change	Projected change in total employment
	automation of manufacturing	Decline
Machine forming operators and tenders, metal and plastic	Productivity increases due to automation of manufacturing	Decline
Mail clerks, except mail machine operators and postal service	Productivity increases due to the use of computers and office automation	Little change
Messengers	Productivity increases due to the use of computers and office automation	About as fast as average
Metal pourers and casters, basic shapes	Productivity increases due to automation of manufacturing	Decline
Meter readers, utilities	Technological advances	Decline
Musical instrument repairers and tuners	Other	More slowly than average
Office machine and cash register services	Productivity increases due to the use of computers and office automation	Little change
Optometrists	Changes in business practices	About as fast as average
Order clerks, materials, merchandise, and service	Productivity increases due to the use of computers and office automation	Little change
Packaging and filling machine operators and tenders	Productivity increases due to automation of manufacturing	Decline
Painting, coating, and decorating workers, hand	Productivity increases due to automation of manufacturing and changes in business practices	Decline
Payroll and timekeeping clerks	Productivity increases due to the use of computers and office automation	Little change
Pest controllers and assistants	Other	About as fast as average

[Continued]

★ 568 ★

Selected Occupations with Moderate Projected Staffing Decreases, 2000

[Continued]

Occupation	Reason for change	Projected change in total employment
Photographic processing machine operators and tenders	Other	About as fast as average
Physician assistants	Other	Faster than average
Printing press machine operators and tenders	Productivity increases due to automation of manufacturing	More slowly than average
Public relations specialists	Other	About as fast as average
Separating and still machine operators and tenders	Productivity increases due to automation of manufacturing	Decline
Shoe sewing machine operators and tenders	Productivity increases due to automation of manufacturing	Decline
Solderers and brazers	Productivity increases due to automation of manufacturing	Decline
Title examiners and searchers	Productivity increases due to the use of computers and office automation	About as fast as average
Wholesale and retail buyers, except farm products	Changes in business practices	More slowly than average

Source: "Occupational Staffing Patterns Within Industries Through the Year 2000," Liesel Brand, *Occupational Outlook Quarterly* 34, No. 2, Summer 1990, pp. 50-1.

★ 569 ★

Selected Occupations with Small Significant Staffing Decreases, 2000

Occupation	Reason for change	Projected change in total employment
Billing, posting, and calculating machine operators	Productivity increases due to the use of computers and office automation	Decline
Broadcast technicians	Technological advances and changes in business practices	Decline

[Continued]

★ 569 ★

Selected Occupations with Small Significant Staffing Decreases, 2000
[Continued]

Occupation	Reason for change	Projected change in total employment
Brokerage clerks	Productivity increases due to the use of computers and office automation	Little change
Central office and PBX installers and repairers	Technological advances	Decline
Data entry keyers, composing	Productivity due to the use of computers and office automation	Decline
Data entry keyers, except composing	Productivity increases due to the use of computers and office automation	Decline
Dental laboratory technicians, precision	Other	More slowly than average
Directory assistance operators	Productivity increases due to the use of computers and office automation	Decline
Electrical and electronic equipment assemblers, precision	Productivity increases due to automation of manufacturing	Decline
Frame wirers, central office	Technological advances	Decline
Nuclear engineers	Other	Little change
Podiatrists	Other	Much faster than average
Proofreaders and copy markers	Productivity increases due to the use of computers and office automation	Decline
Station installers and repairers, telephone	Technological advances	Decline
Statistical clerks	Productivity increases due to the use of computers and office automation	Little change
Stenographers	Productivity increases due to the use of computers and office automation	Decline

[Continued]

★ 569 ★

Selected Occupations with Small Significant Staffing Decreases, 2000

[Continued]

Occupation	Reason for change	Projected change in total employment
Telephone and cable TV line installers and repairers	Technological advances	Decline
Typists and word processors	Productivity increases due to the use of computers and office automation	Decline

Source: "Occupational Staffing Patterns Within Industries Through the Year 2000," Liesel Brand, *Occupational Outlook Quarterly* 34, No. 2, Summer 1990, p. 52.

★ 570 ★

Separations From and Entrants to the Labor Force, 1990 and 2005

"The total number of labor force entrants will be much larger than labor force growth because of the large number of people needed to replace workers who die or leave the labor force to retire, pursue leisure activities, care for their family, or emigrate."

[Numbers in millions]

	1990	2005
In labor force	95	95
Separations 1990-2200	30	-
Entrant, replacements	-	30
Entrants, growth		26

Source: "Outlook 1990-2005," *Occupational Outlook Quarterly* 35, No. 3, Fall, 1991, p. 14.

★ 571 ★

Total Job Opportunities Due to Replacements and Projected Occupational Employment Change, 1990-2005

"Of the total number of job openings in 2005, more are expected to result from net replacement needs than from employment growth in the economy."

[Jobs in thousands]

Occupational title	1990 total employment	Job openings due to net replacements 1990-2005	Job openings due to growth 1990-2005[1]	Total job openings 1990-2005	Opportunity ratio
Total, all occupations	122,573	38,851	26,892	65,743	0.54
Executive, administrative, and managerial	12,451	3,085	3,414	6,499	.52
Professional specialty occupations	15,800	4,281	5,107	9,388	.59
Engineers, architects, and surveyors	1,755	571	448	1,019	.58
Mathematical and computer scientists	571	82	416	498	.87
Natural scientists	373	171	97	268	.72
Health diagnosing occupations	855	307	247	554	.65
Health assessment and treating occupations	2,305	591	999	1,590	.69
Teachers, college and university	712	339	134	473	.66
Teachers, except college and university	4,666	1,107	1,389	2,496	.54
Counselors, educational and vocational	144	41	49	90	.63
Librarians, archivists, and curators	166	52	21	73	.44
Social scientists and urban planners	224	50	96	146	.65
Social, recreational, and religious workers	1,049	186	327	513	.49
Lawyers and judges	633	191	217	408	.64
Writers, artists, and entertainers	1,542	440	373	813	.53
Technicians and related support	4,204	1,200	1,551	2,751	.65
Health technologists and technicians	1,833	434	763	1,197	.65
Engineering and related technologists and technicians	1,081	368	254	622	.58
Science technicians	246	97	58	155	.63
Technicians, except health, engineering, and science	1,044	300	475	775	.74
Sales occupations	14,088	5,379	3,401	8,780	.62
Administrative support, including clerical	21,951	6,413	3,389	9,722	.44
Supervisors, administrative support	1,218	444	263	707	.58
Computer equipment operators	320	43	42	85	.26
Secretaries, stenographers, and typists	4,680	1,524	540	2,064	.44
Information clerks	1,418	350	584	934	.66
Records processing occupations, except financial	949	393	96	489	.51
Financial records processing occupations	2,860	951	23	974	.34
Duplicating, mail, and other office machine operators	169	81	22	103	.61
Communications equipment operators	345	132	0	132	.38
Mail and message distributing occupations	718	231	107	338	.47
Material recording, scheduling, distribution company	2,513	720	257	977	.39
Adjusters and investigators	1,058	170	255	425	.40
Miscellaneous administrative support	5,703	1,374	1,121	2,495	.44
Service occupations	19,204	7,403	5,830	13,233	.69
Private household	782	249	0	249	.32
Protective service occupations	2,266	936	729	1,665	.73
Food preparation and service occupations	7,705	4,149	2,325	6,474	.84
Health service occupations	1,972	403	860	1,263	.64
Cleaning and building service occupations	3,435	990	633	1,623	.47
Personnel service occupations	2,192	475	973	1,448	.66
Precision production, craft, and repair	14,124	4,764	2,068	6,832	.48
Mechanics and repairers	4,900	1,569	887	2,456	.50
Construction trades	3,763	1,114	794	1,908	.51
Extractive occupations	237	62	15	77	.33
Precision production occupations	3,134	1,189	74	1,263	.40
Operators, fabricators, and laborers	17,245	5,449	1,734	7,183	.42
Machine operators, assemblers, and inspectors	7,580	2,455	281	2,736	.36
Transportation and material moving occupations	4,730	1,262	1,033	2,295	.49

[Continued]

★ 571 ★

Total Job Opportunities Due to Replacements and Projected Occupational Employment Change, 1990-2005

[Continued]

Occupational title	1990 total employment	Job openings due to net replacements 1990-2005	Job openings due to growth 1990-2005[1]	Total job openings 1990-2005	Opportunity ratio
Handlers, equipment cleaners, helpers, and laborers	4,935	1,732	420	2,152	.44
Farming, forestry, and fishing	3,506	863	477	1,340	.38

Source: "Occupational Employment Projections," George Silvestri and John Lukasiewicz, *Monthly Labor Review* 114, No. 11, November, 1991, p. 88. *Notes:* 1. Job openings due to growth are a result of summing the employment increases for detailed occupations within each of the occupational groups shown in this table.

★ 572 ★

Employment Change for Selected Occupations, 1990-2005

"Examples of jobs projected to have the fastest growth between 1990 and 2005, and some expected to have the greatest decline."

Occupation	% change
Home health aides	92.0
Paralegals	85.0
Systems analysts	79.0
Physical therapists	76.0
Operations research analysts	73.0
Psychologists	64.0
Travel agents	62.0
Corrections officers	61.0
Flight attendants	59.0
Management analysts	52.0
Telephone operators	-59.0
Electrical equipment assemblers	-48.0
Private child care helpers	-40.0
Precision assembly workers	-37.0
Textile machine operators	-31.0
Utilities meter readers	-25.0
Machine tool operators	-24.0
Farm workers	-21.0
Garment sewers	-20.0
Bank tellers	-5.0

Source: Howard Banks, "What's Ahead for Business: Job Trends Across the Millennia," *Forbes*, January 6, 1992, p. 35. Primary source: Bureau of Labor Statistics.

★ 573 ★

Occupations with Projected Employment Changes in the National Industry-Occupation Matrix, 1986-2000 - I

Occupation	Projected changes and reasons
Agricultural and food scientists	Small increases in all industries except miscellaneous business services due to the expected increase in research opportunities created by biotechnology. A moderate decrease in miscellaneous business services because the segment of the industry where these workers are concentrated is expected to grow more slowly than the rest of the industry.
Cashiers	Small increases in grocery and apparel stores to reflect the growing importance of discount operations that require more cashiers relative to other workers. A small decrease in gasoline service stations due to the growth of self-service stations and expected spread of automated gas pumps.
General managers and top executives	Small increases in all industries due to the expected increasing complexity of business operations.
Geologists, geophysicists, and oceanographers	Small increases in all industries except miscellaneous business services and engineering, architectural, and surveying services due to expected increase in exploration for petroleum and minerals. Little or no change is expected in the industries listed as exceptions.
Marketing, advertising, and public relations managers	Small increases in all industries due to the expectation that an increasingly competitive economy will result in a greater demand for these workers.
Medical assistants	A small increase in offices of physicians due to the expectation that these workers will increasingly perform tasks previously performed by other employees.
Pharmacists	A small increase in drug stores to reflect the growing use of part-time

[Continued]

★ 573 ★

Occupations with Projected Employment Changes in the National Industry-Occupation Matrix, 1986-2000 - I

[Continued]

	workers and the trend toward offering pharmacy services on a 24-hour basis.
Physical and life science technicians and technologists	Small increases in all industries except miscellaneous business services and engineering, architectural, and surveying due to expected increases in research and development expenditures. Little or no change is expected in the two industries listed above because the segments of the industries where these workers are concentrated are not expected to grow as fast as other parts of these industries.
Property and real estate managers	Small increases in all industries to reflect the increasing complexity of real estate operations.
Salespersons, retail	Small increases in all industries to reflect growing use of part-time workers and more attention to customer service.
Securities and financial services salesworkers	Small increases in banks and other financial institutions due to a wider range and growing complexity of financial services that are expected to be offered to the public.
Tax examiners, collectors, and revenue agents	Small increases in Federal, State, and local government due to the expected greater enforcement of tax laws.
Teacher aides and educational assistants	A small increase in educational services due to the expected rise in student enrollments. A moderate increase in religious organizations due to expected large increases in enrollments in religious schools.
Teachers and instructors, vocational education and training	A small increase in educational services to reflect the projected number of 18- to 22-year-olds and other adults who will need vocational training and retraining.

[Continued]

555

★ 573 ★

Occupations with Projected Employment Changes in the National Industry-Occupation Matrix, 1986-2000 - I
[Continued]

Teachers, kindergarten and elementary	A small increase in educational services as kindergarten and elementary school enrollments are expected to become a larger proportion of total school enrollments.

Moderate increases

Accountants and auditors	Moderate increases in all industries except accounting, auditing, and bookkeeping services to reflect the greater use of financial data in day-to-day business decisionmaking. Only a small increase is expected in accounting, auditing, and bookkeeping services.
Actuaries	Moderate increases in all industries due to expected greater demand for these workers as consultants to analyze revisions to State insurance plans and to appraise the impact of tax law changes on the financial soundness of companies
Aeronautical and astronautical engineers	Moderate increases in all industries except miscellaneous business services due to the expectation that aircraft and space vehicles will continue to become more technologically advanced and, therefore, require a higher level of design and research and development efforts. Little or no change is expected in miscellaneous business services because these workers are not concentrated in the fastest growing segment of that industry.
Bakers, bread and pastry	Moderate increases in grocery stores, eating and drinking places, and hotels and other lodging places to reflect a greater volume of baked goods prepared on the premises of establishments in these industries. A small decrease in hospitals to reflect the trend toward contracting out food service functions.

[Continued]

★ 573 ★

Occupations with Projected Employment Changes in the National Industry-Occupation Matrix, 1986-2000 - I
[Continued]

Bartenders	A moderate increase in hotels to reflect the trend toward larger hotels, which provide more lounges and full-service restaurants.
Biological scientists	Moderate increases in all industries except miscellaneous business services due to expected increase in research and development funds for biological and medical research. A significant decrease in miscellaneous business services due to projected slower growth in the segment of the industry where these workers are concentrated than in the rest of the industry.
Bus drivers	A moderate increase in local government and small increases in local and suburban transportation and intercity buses to reflect an increasing trend toward more part-time bus drivers.
Chemical engineers	Moderate increases in all industries except miscellaneous business services due to the expected growth in research and development expenditures. Little or no change is expected in miscellaneous business services because of projected slower growth in the segment of the industry where these workers are concentrated than in the rest of the industry.
Child care workers	A moderate increase in religious organizations to reflect expected enrollment increases in religiously affiliated day care centers and schools.
Combination machine tool setters, set-up operators, operators, and tenders	Moderate increases in all industries due to increased use of numerical control machine tools and flexible manufacturing systems.
Computer operators, except peripheral equipment	Moderate increases in all industries reflecting the rising use of computers throughout the economy.

[Continued]

★ 573 ★

Occupations with Projected Employment Changes in the National Industry-Occupation Matrix, 1986-2000 - I
[Continued]

Cooks, restaurant	A moderate increase in hotels and other lodging places to reflect the trend toward larger hotels, which are expected to provide more full-service dining.
Correction officers and jailers	Moderate increases in Federal, State, and local governments due to increasing public concern about crime and expected increases in expenditures for construction of new correctional facilities.
Court clerks	Moderate increases in Federal, State, and local governments due to increasing concern about law and order and the need to reduce the backlog of cases waiting to be heard.
Electroencephalograph technicians	A moderate increase in hospitals to reflect more sophisticated and specialized medical treatments. A significant increase in offices of physicians to reflect the trend toward large group practices that will require the services of specialized personnel.
Electronic repairers, commercial and industrial equipment	Moderate increases in all industries to reflect a greater volume of electronic industrial equipment in use by firms to automate offices and production processes.
Food service and lodging managers	A moderate increase in eating and drinking places due to expected growth of chain restaurants, which will require more salaried managers and fewer self-employed managers. A moderate increase in hotels and other lodging places due to the expected trend toward larger, chain-affiliated hotels, which will require more salaried managers. Small decreases in hospitals and educational services to reflect the trend toward contracting out food service functions in these industries to the eating and drinking places industry.

[Continued]

★ 573 ★

Occupations with Projected Employment Changes in the National Industry-Occupation Matrix, 1986-2000 - I
[Continued]

Gardeners and groundskeepers, except farm	A moderate increase in agricultural services due to expected faster growth in demand for landscaping services than in demand for other services in this industry. A moderate decrease in private households due to the expectation that individuals will increasingly use firms offering gardening and related services rather than directly employing gardeners.
Guards	A moderate increase in miscellaneous business services and moderate decreases in all other industries as more and more firms contract out for security services.
Industrial machinery mechanics	Moderate increases in all industries to reflect an expanding number of industrial machines in use.
Judges, magistrates, and other judicial workers	A moderate increase in State government to reflect concern about law and order to reflect efforts to reduce the backlog of cases waiting to be heard.
Lawyers	Moderate increases in industries other than legal services as more legal work is expected to be done in-house.
Millwrights	Moderate increases in all industries to reflect an expanding number of industrial machines in use.
Occupational therapy assistants and aides	A moderate increase in hospitals due to an expected greater volume of therapy services that will be offered.
Offset lithographic press setters and setup operators	A moderate increase in commercial printing and business forms to reflect the continuing trend toward lithography as the dominant form of printing in this industry.
Operations and systems researchers and analysts	Moderate increases in all industries to reflect the growing importance of quantitative analysis.

[Continued]

★ 573 ★

Occupations with Projected Employment Changes in the National Industry-Occupation Matrix, 1986-2000 - I

[Continued]

Peripheral electronic data processing equipment operators	Moderate increases in virtually all industries to reflect the rising use of computers throughout the economy.
Physical and corrective therapy assistants and aides	A moderate increase in hospitals due to an expected greater volume of therapy services that will be offered.
Programmers, numerical, tool, and process control	Moderate increases in all industries due to the growing use of numerical control machine tools.
Public relations specialist	Moderate increases in all industries to reflect the growing importance of public relations activities throughout the economy.
Radiologic technologists and technicians	A moderate increase in hospitals due to expected advances in technology and increased use of radiologic diagnostic techniques. A significant increase in offices of physicians due to the increasing trend toward large group practices and more scans performed on an outpatient basis. A significant increase in outpatient care facilities, reflecting very rapid growth of Health Maintenance Organizations, specialty medical clinics, and diagnostic imaging centers that employ these workers.

Source: "Reasons Underlying Changes to the 1986 Coefficients in the National Industry-Occupation Matrix," *Occupational Projections and Training Data: A Statistical and Research Supplement to the 1988-89 Occupational Outlook Handbook,* U.S. Department of Labor, 1988, pp. 100-110.

★ 574 ★

Occupations with Projected Employment Changes in the National Industry-Occupation Matrix, 1986-2000 - II

Occupation	Projected changes and reasons
Registered nurses	A moderate increase in hospitals due to the expectation that nurses will be given greater responsibilities. A moderate

[Continued]

★ 574 ★

Occupations with Projected Employment Changes in the National Industry-Occupation Matrix, 1986-2000 - II
[Continued]

	increase in offices of physicians because of the increasing size of physician practices and the greater use of sophisticated technology. A moderate increase in nursing and personal care facilities due to the expectation that more patients will be released from hospitals to nursing homes to convalesce. A moderate increase in outpatient care facilities due to the expected growth in rehabilitation centers which rely heavily on registered nurses.
Respiratory therapists	A moderate increase in hospitals due to an expected increase in the volume of surgery performed and more patients with cardiopulmonary illnesses who require respiratory care. A moderate increase in outpatient care facilities due to the expected growth of Health Maintenance Organization, surgicenters, and other medical facilities which employ these workers. A moderate increase in offices of physicians due to an expected increase in large group practices and an expected increase in outpatient surgery done in physicians' offices.
Shoe and leather workers and repairers, precision	Moderate increase in the leather footwear industry. These workers are concentrated in the manufacture of custom-made shoes, a sector which is not expected to be as adversely affected by imports as the rest of the footwear industry.
Surgical technicians	A moderate increase in hospitals due to expected increases in the volume of both inpatient and outpatient surgery.
Significant increases	
Computer programmers	Significant increases in virtually all industries due to the rising use of computers throughout the economy. Only a moderate increase is expected in computer and data processing services. In the

[Continued]

★ 574 ★

Occupations with Projected Employment Changes in the National Industry-Occupation Matrix, 1986-2000 - II
[Continued]

	Federal Government, where there is an increasing trend toward contracting out computer services, little or no change in the occupational coefficient is expected.
Computer systems analysts, electronic data processing	Significant increases in all industries except Federal Government due to the expected rising use of computers throughout the economy. Improvements to hardware and software are expected to make computers more versatile, cheaper, and easier to use. No change is expected in Federal Government because of the trend toward contracting out computer services.
Data entry keyers, composing	Significant increases in newspapers and commercial printing and business forms due to expected increasing use of computerized typesetting technology.
Data processing equipment repairers	Significant increases in all industries to reflect the increasing use of computers throughout the economy as improvements to hardware and software make computers more versatile, cheaper, and easier to use.
Electrical and electronics engineers	Significant increases in all industries except miscellaneous business services due to the expectation that the pace of innovation in electronic devices will accelerate. A moderate increase is expected in miscellaneous business services.
Electrical and electronics technicians and technologists	Significant increases in all manufacturing industries due to the expectation that the pace of innovation in electronic devices will accelerate, and the period between new products will shorten. Moderate increases in all other industries except miscellaneous business services, which is expected to show little or no change in the occupational coefficient.

[Continued]

★ 574 ★

Occupations with Projected Employment Changes in the National Industry-Occupation Matrix, 1986-2000 - II

[Continued]

Farm managers	A significant increase in crops, livestock products to reflect the increasing number of large farms and farms with absentee owners. A moderate decrease in agricultural services since farm managers are concentrated in the part of the industry that is not expected to grow as fast as other parts.
Industrial engineers, except safety engineers	Significant increases in all industries except miscellaneous business services due to the expected need to incorporate increasingly sophisticated production methods such as robots and computers into production systems. Little or no change in miscellaneous business services because industrial engineers are not concentrated in one of the faster growing segments of this rapidly growing industry.
Mechanical engineers	Significant increases in all industries except miscellaneous business services and engineering, architectural, and surveying services. Research and development expenditures are expected to increase significantly in virtually all other industries. Only a small increase is expected in engineering, architectural, and surveying services. No change is expected in miscellaneous business services because these workers are not concentrated in one of the fastest growing segments of this industry.
Medical records technician	Significant increases in hospitals, outpatient care facilities, and offices of physicians due to continued emphasis on cost containment, which entails much greater documentation and recordkeeping for reimbursement, clinical, and management purposes.
Metallurgists and metallurgical ceramic, and materials engineers	Significant increases in all industries except engineering, architectural, and

[Continued]

★ 574 ★

Occupations with Projected Employment Changes in the
National Industry-Occupation Matrix, 1986-2000 - II
[Continued]

	surveying services and miscellaneous business services. Research and development expenditures for materials research are expected to increase more than expenditures for other research and development. Only a small increase is expected in engineering, architectural, and surveying services. No change is expected in miscellaneous business services because these workers are not concentrated in one of the faster growing segments of this industry.
Meteorologists	A significant increase in Federal Government due to the expected higher level of funding for meteorological activities. A significant decrease in miscellaneous business services, reflecting much slower expected growth in the segment of the industry where these workers are concentrated than in the rest of the industry.
Occupational therapist	A significant increase in hospitals, reflecting more outpatient therapy services.
Paralegal personnel	A significant increase in legal services due to the growing acceptance of these workers as cost-effective members of the legal service team. Moderate increases in Federal, State, and local governments due to the expected greater use of these workers in legal work.
Physical therapists	A significant increase in hospitals, reflecting more outpatient therapy services. A significant increase in offices of "other health practitioners" to reflect the trend by physical therapists to separate themselves from physicians and set up their own private and group practices. Consequently, a significant decrease in offices of physicians is expected. A moderate increase in outpatient care facilities

[Continued]

★ 574 ★

Occupations with Projected Employment Changes in the National Industry-Occupation Matrix, 1986-2000 - II
[Continued]

	due to the expected greater demand for physical therapy services on an outpatient basis.

Small decreases

Animal caretakers, except farm	A small decrease in agricultural services due to expected slower growth in demand for animal and veterinary services than for other services provided by this industry.
Architects, except landscape and marine	A small decrease in engineering, architectural, and surveying services due to the expected slower rate of growth in the demand for architectural services than for the other services provided by this industry.
Artists and commercial artists	Small decreases in all detailed printing and publishing industries and in mailing, reproduction, and commercial art due to the expected negative impact that computer graphics will have on these workers.
Bookbinders	Small decreases in all industries due to expected continued automation of bookbinding activities.
Broadcast technicians	A small decrease in radio and television broadcasting due to expected advances in broadcasting technology.
Construction and building inspectors	Small decreases in State and local governments due to the expectation that some intermediate inspection functions will be done by maintenance supervisors and engineers.
Cooks, institution or cafeteria	A small decrease in educational services and moderate decreases in hospitals, residential care, nursing homes, and Federal, State, and local governments due to expected contracting out food service functions. A significant increase in the

[Continued]

★ 574 ★

Occupations with Projected Employment Changes in the National Industry-Occupation Matrix, 1986-2000 - II
[Continued]

	eating and drinking places industry, which will provide food service functions on a contractual basis to the above industries.
Dental laboratory technicians, precision	A small decrease in medical and dental laboratories because the demand for dental services is not expected to grow as fast as the demand for medical services in this industry.
Dining room and cafeteria attendants and bartender helpers	Small decreases in nursing homes, hospitals, educational services, and residential care to reflect contracting out of food service functions to reduce cost. A small increase in eating and drinking places as other industries contract out food services. A small increase in hotels to reflect the trend toward larger hotels, which are expected to provide more lounges and full-service restaurants.
Electrocardiograph (EKG) technicians and technologists	A small decrease in hospitals due to the expectation that registered nurses and other technicians will do some of the work performed by EKG technicians. A moderate increase in offices of physicians due to the expected continuation of the trend toward large group practices, which will employ more of these workers.
Electronic home entertainment equipment repairers	Small decreases in all industries to reflect the lower maintenance requirements of equipment made with microelectronic circuitry.
Food, counter, fountain, and	A small decrease in eating and drinking places due to expected slower growth in fast-food restaurants, where these workers are concentrated, than in other types of eating establishments.
Foundry mold assembly and shakeout workers	Small decreases in blast furnaces and basic steel products and iron and steel

[Continued]

★ 574 ★

Occupations with Projected Employment Changes in the National Industry-Occupation Matrix, 1986-2000 - II

[Continued]

	foundries to reflect increased use of continuous casting and robots within the steel mill.
Frame wirers, central office	Small decreases in all industries due to increased use of microelectronics that permit more telephone circuits to be transmitted on one wire.
Grinding machine setters and set-up operators, metal and plastic	Small decreases in all industries due to greater use of computer controls and flexible manufacturing systems.
Housekeepers, institutional	Small decreases in all industries except hotels and other lodging places due to expected contracting out of housekeeping services.
Janitors and cleaners	Small decreases in all industries except services to buildings due to a continuation of contracting out of janitorial services. Little or no change is expected in services to buildings.
Jewelers and silversmiths	A small decrease in miscellaneous shopping goods stores due to the expectation that many retail outlets that sell jewelry will no longer repair what they sell but rather will contract out for repair services.

Source: "Reasons Underlying Changes to the 1986 Coefficients in the National Industry-Occupation Matrix," *Occupational Projections and Training Data: A Statistical and Research Supplement to the 1988-89 Occupational Outlook Handbook*, U.S. Department of Labor, 1988, pp. 100-110.

★ 575 ★

Occupations with Projected Employment Changes in the National Industry-Occupation Matrix, 1986-2000 - III

Occupation	Projected changes and reasons
Lathe machine tool setters and set-up operators, metal and plastic	Small decreases in all industries to reflect advances in technology such as computer-controlled machines and flexible

[Continued]

★ 575 ★

Occupations with Projected Employment Changes in the National Industry-Occupation Matrix, 1986-2000 - III

[Continued]

	manufacturing systems.
Librarians	A small decrease in local government to reflect anticipated reductions in expenditures for library services.
Library assistants and bookmobile drivers	A small decrease in local government due to expected reductions in expenditures for library services.
Machine forming operators and tenders, metal and plastic	Small decreases in all industries to reflect increased use of computer-controlled machine tools and flexible manufacturing systems.
Machinists	Small decreases in all industries due to advances in manufacturing processes such as flexible manufacturing systems, numerical control machine tools, and greater use of computers.
Motorcycle repairers	A small decrease in boat and miscellaneous vehicle dealers due to expected slow growth or even a possible decline in the number of motorcycles in operation.
Personnel clerks	Small decrease in all industries due to computerization of employment records and information concerning employee benefits and basic personnel practices.
Physicians and surgeons	A small decrease in offices of physicians to reflect the trend toward large medical group practices which require more clerical and clinical support staff relative to the number of physicians. A small decrease in hospitals to reflect cost-containment efforts, which are expected to result in a greater utilization of physician assistants and nurse practitioners relative to physicians.
Pressing machine operators and tenders, textile, garment, and	Small decreases in laundry, cleaning, and garment services and apparel

[Continued]

★ 575 ★

Occupations with Projected Employment Changes in the
National Industry-Occupation Matrix, 1986-2000 - III
[Continued]

related workers	manufacturing to reflect new pressing technologies that are expected to reduce the demand for these workers.
Purchasing agents, except wholesale, retail, and farm products	Small decreases in all industries due to the expectation that computerization of purchasing tasks and more efficient purchasing methods will result in less demand for these workers.
Purchasing managers	Small decreases in all industries except State and local governments due to the expected increasing computerization of purchasing tasks and more efficient purchasing methods. Moderate increases in State and local governments due to the expected growth of purchasing departments in these sectors.
Radio mechanics	Small decreases in all industries to reflect increased use of durable and easy-to-maintain microelectronic circuitry in radios.
Recreation workers	A small decrease in local government due expected reduction in expenditures for noncritical services. A moderate increase in civic, social, and fraternal organizations to reflect growing membership in recreation clubs, day camps, sports instruction schools, and health clubs.
Sewing machine operators, nongarment	Small decreases in household furniture, knitting mills, floor covering mills, apparel, miscellaneous textile goods, and miscellaneous fabricated textile products due to expected advances in the application of industrial robots to sewing functions.
Shipfitters	Small decreases in all industries to reflect declining demand for new vessels.
Signal or track switch maintainers	A small decrease in railroad transportation due to computerization of

[Continued]

★ 575 ★

Occupations with Projected Employment Changes in the
National Industry-Occupation Matrix, 1986-2000 - III
[Continued]

	track switching operations.
Surveyors	A small decrease in engineering, architectural and surveying services due to the expected slower growth in the demand for surveying services than for the other services provided by this industry.
Technical assistants, library	A small decrease in local government due to expected reduction in expenditures for library services.

Moderate decreases

Automotive body and related repairers	A moderate decrease in automobile repair shops due to increased use of plastics in vehicle bodies.
Automotive mechanics	A moderate decrease in gasoline service stations due to the continuing trend toward self-service stations that do not provide vehicle repair and maintenance services.
Bank tellers	Moderate decreases in all industries due to expected increases in automatic teller machines and the assumption of some banking functions by other financial industries.
Barbers	A moderate decrease in beauty shops due to expected slower growth in the demand for the services of barbers than for other services provided by this industry.
Billing, posting, and calculating machine operators	Moderate decreases in all industries due to the widespread use of computers and other aspects of office automation.
Billing, rate, and cost clerks	Moderate decreases in all industries due to an expected greater use of computerized office equipment.
Bookkeeping, accounting, and auditing clerks	Moderate decreases in all industries except finance, insurance, and real

[Continued]

★ 575 ★

Occupations with Projected Employment Changes in the National Industry-Occupation Matrix, 1986-2000 - III
[Continued]

	estate due to the widespread use of computers in bookkeeping and accounting functions. Little or no change is expected in finance, insurance, and real estate because a fairly high level of computerization has already been achieved.
Child care workers, private household	A moderate decrease in private households due to a projected decline in the number of children under age 5 and the trend toward formal daycare services rather than in-home child care.
Coil winders, tapers, and finishers	Moderate decreases in all industries due to the expected effect of automation on these workers.
College and university faculty	A moderate decrease in educational services since college and university enrollments are expected to decline as a portion of total enrollments in educational services.
Cooks, short order	A moderate decrease in eating and drinking places due to expected slower growth in fast-food restaurants relative to other types of restaurants.
Credit authorizers	Moderate decreases in all industries except department stores to reflect the growing use of computers to directly access credit files. A significant decrease in department stores due to the phasing out of chain store credit cards.
Credit checkers	Moderate decreases in all industries except department stores to reflect the computerization and centralization of financial data. A significant decrease in department stores to reflect the industry trend away from offering credit to customers.
Dietetic technicians	A moderate decrease in hospitals due to expected staffing cuts and increased use

[Continued]

★ 575 ★

Occupations with Projected Employment Changes in the National Industry-Occupation Matrix, 1986-2000 - III
[Continued]

	of food service contractors.
Drill machine tool setters and set-up operators, metal and plastic	Moderate decreases in all industries due to greater use of computers and flexible manufacturing systems.
Driver-salesworker	Moderate decreases in all industries as employers are expected to continue to separate the sales and delivery functions of these jobs, employing salesworkers and delivery drivers instead.
Duplicating, mail, and other office machine operators	Moderate decreases in all industries due to expected advances in duplicating machine technology. in addition, other aspects of office automation, such as electronic mail, copiers, and facsimile transmission, are expected to reduce the demand for these workers.
Farm and home management advisors	Moderate decreases in all industries due to the projected decline in the number of farmers who rely on the services of these workers.
File clerks	Moderate decreases in all industries due to expected greater use of electronic filing systems.
Food preparation workers	Moderate decreases in nursing homes, hospitals, and residential care and a small decrease in educational services due to contracting out of food service functions to reduce costs. A moderate increase in grocery stores to reflect a greater range of products and services offered to customers. A moderate increase in hotels due to the trend toward larger hotels, which are expected to offer more full-service dining.
Freight, stock, and material movers, hand	Moderate decreases in all industries due to technological advances in material handling equipment.
Furnace operators and tenders	Moderate decreases in blast furnaces and

[Continued]

★ 575 ★

Occupations with Projected Employment Changes in the National Industry-Occupation Matrix, 1986-2000 - III

[Continued]

	basic steel products and iron and steel foundries due to expected investment expenditures in basic oxygen process and electric arc furnaces.
Heaters, metal and plastic	Moderate decreases in blast furnaces and basic steel products and iron and steel foundries to reflect the introduction of continuous casting and computers.
Insurance claims clerks	Moderate decreases in all industries due to the expected impact of computer technology on these workers.
Laundry and drycleaning machine operators and tenders	Moderate decreases in nursing and personal care facilities and hospitals due to expected contracting out of laundry services and greater use of disposable products. A small decrease in hotels and other lodging places for the same reasons.
Licensed practical nurses	A moderate decrease in hospitals to reflect cost-containment efforts, which are expected to result in greater use of registered nurses at the expense of these workers. A moderate increase in nursing homes as these facilities increasingly provide more medical care.
Mail clerks, except mailing machine operators and postal service	Moderate decreases in all industries due to the expected introduction of robotic devices into mail handling systems and the expected greater use of electronic mail.
Medical and clinical laboratory technologists and technicians	A moderate decrease in hospitals due to the expectation that hospitals will send medical tests to central laboratories in an effort to contain costs. A significant decrease in offices of physicians due to the expectation that medical assistants, registered nurses, and clerical staff in this industry may perform medical tests. A moderate increase in medical and dental laboratories due to the expected growth

[Continued]

573

★ 575 ★

Occupations with Projected Employment Changes in the National Industry-Occupation Matrix, 1986-2000 - III
[Continued]

	in the number and complexity of medical tests being performed in this sector. A significant increase in outpatient care facilities due to the expectation that clinics will choose to perform a greater volume of medical tests in-house.
Optometrists	A moderate decrease in offices of "other health practitioners" as the demand for vision care is not expected to keep pace with the demand for other services provided by this industry.
Order clerks, materials, merchandise, and services	Moderate decreases in all industries to reflect the increasing trend toward transmitting orders electronically.
Order fillers, wholesale and retail trade	Moderate decreases in all industries to reflect increasing use of electronic ordering systems.
Procurement clerks	Moderate decreases in all industries to reflect increasing use by purchasing departments of computerized data bases to obtain information about products, and also to reflect the increasing use of computers to write up routine purchase orders.

Source: "Reasons Underlying Changes to the 1986 Coefficients in the National Industry-Occupation Matrix," *Occupational Projections and Training Data: A Statistical and Research Supplement to the 1988-89 Occupational Outlook Handbook,* U.S. Department of Labor, 1988, pp. 100-110.

★ 576 ★

Occupations with Projected Employment Changes in the National Industry-Occupation Matrix, 1986-2000 - IV

Occupation	Projected changes and reasons
Psychiatric aides	A moderate decrease in hospitals because State mental hospitals, where these workers are concentrated, are not expected to grow as fast as other hospitals.

[Continued]

Occupations with Projected Employment Changes in the National Industry-Occupation Matrix, 1986-2000 - IV
[Continued]

Roustabouts	Moderate decreases in crude petroleum, natural gas, and gas liquids, and in oil and gas field services due to continued mechanization and greater use of new equipment.
Secretaries	Moderate decreases in all industries except personnel supply services, offices of physicians, and legal services. Secretaries are expected to be negatively affected by office automation, but the effect is expected to be moderated by the fact that these workers have many tasks that cannot be completely automated or delegated to other people. Little or no change is expected in the industries listed as exceptions since secretaries are expected to grow about as fast as total employment in these sectors.
Station installers and repairers, telephone	Moderate decreases in all industries due to a proliferation of telephones that are cheaper to replace than to repair. Also, modular plugs allow consumers to install their own telephones.
Stock clerks, stockroom, warehouse, or yard	Moderate decreases in all industries due to computerized inventory control and automated materials handling equipment.
Switchboard operators	Moderate decreases in all industries reflecting the greater use of automatic telephone switching equipment.
Telephone and cable television line installers and repairers	Moderate decreases in telephone communication and in telegraph and communication services not elsewhere classified, to reflect the switch from traditional cable lines to microwave transmission and the greater efficiency obtained from using fiber optic cable.
Textile draw-out and winding machine operators and tenders	Moderate decreases in all detailed textile industries due to expected expenditures on laborsaving devices such as industrial robots, automated material

[Continued]

★ 576 ★

Occupations with Projected Employment Changes in the National Industry-Occupation Matrix, 1986-2000 - IV

[Continued]

	handling systems, and computer-controlled machinery.
Tire building machine operators	A moderate decrease in tires and inner tubes due to the expected effect of automation.
Title examiners and searchers	A moderate decrease in pension funds and insurance not elsewhere classified due to the increasing use of computers in assessing title information.
Watchmakers	Moderate decreases in all industries reflecting a trend toward disposable watches and toward clocks that do not require repair work.
Welders and cutters	Moderate decreases in fabricated metal products nonelectrical machinery, aircraft and parts, and miscellaneous transportation equipment due to expected automation of welding functions. A significant decrease in motor vehicles and parts manufacturing because this industry has been one of the leaders in introducing industrial robots.
Wholesale and retail buyers, except farm products	Moderate decreases in all industries due to the expectation that firms increasingly will order directly from manufacturers through electronic ordering systems.

Significant decreases

Butchers and meatcutters	A significant decrease in grocery stores and a moderate increase in meat products manufacturing, reflecting the continued shift in the processing of beef from retail to manufacturing establishments.
Chemical equipment controllers, operators, and tenders	Significant decreases in all industries due to expected advances in computerized and automated control systems.
Chemical plant and system	Significant decreases in all industries

[Continued]

★ 576 ★

Occupations with Projected Employment Changes in the National Industry-Occupation Matrix, 1986-2000 - IV

[Continued]

operators	due to expected advances in computerized and automated control systems.
Compositors, typesetters, and arrangers	Significant decreases in newspapers, commercial printing and business forms, and printing trade services to reflect the growing availability of low-cost computer technology.
Data entry keyers, except composing	Significant decreases in all industries due to expected advances in data entry technologies, such as on-line processing and optical character and voice recognition technologies.
Drafters	Significant decreases in all industries due to the expected widespread implementation of computer-aided design technology.
Electrical and electronic equipment assemblers	Significant decreases in all industries due to the expectation that most electronic assembly will be done by industrial robots or other automated processes.
Electronic semiconductor processors	Significant decreases in all industries due to expected automation of the duties of these workers and a shift towards having much of the work done abroad.
Farm equipment mechanics	A significant decrease in wholesale trade in machinery and equipment due to much slower expected growth in the farm equipment dealer segment than in the rest of the industry. A moderate increase in crops, livestock products to reflect the trend toward larger farms and increasingly complex farm equipment.
Gas and petroleum plant and system occupations	Significant decreases in all industries due to expected advances in computerized and automated control systems.
Industrial truck and tractor operators	Significant decreases in all industries due to expected continuing implementation

[Continued]

★ 576 ★

Occupations with Projected Employment Changes in the National Industry-Occupation Matrix, 1986-2000 - IV
[Continued]

	of automated material handling equipment in factories and warehouses.
Insurance policy processing clerks	Significant decrease in all industries due to the expected effect of the greater use of automated equipment.
Letterpress setters and setup operators	Significant decreases in commercial printing and business forms and newspapers to reflect the trend toward lithography as the dominant form of printing in these industries.
Meter readers, utilities	Significant decreases in all industries except local government due to expected advances in computerized meter reading. Little or no change expected in local government.
Nuclear engineers	Significant decreases are expected in heavy construction, except highway and street; fabricated structural metal products; miscellaneous business services; and engineering, architectural, and surveying services as a result of the slowdown in nuclear power plant construction and the expected slowdown in the rate of increase in defense expenditures.
Nursing aides, orderlies, and attendants	Significant decreases in hospitals and personnel supply services. Hospitals are expected to continue to eliminate many lesser skilled jobs that can be performed by more highly skilled personnel. The demand for nursing aides in personnel supply services is not expected to keep up with the demand for other services provided by this industry.
Opticians, dispensing and measuring	A significant decrease in offices "other health practitioners" due to the expectation that optometrists' offices, where optician employment is concentrated, will grow more slowly than the rest of the industry.

[Continued]

★ 576 ★

Occupations with Projected Employment Changes in the National Industry-Occupation Matrix, 1986-2000 - IV
[Continued]

Painters, transportation	Significant decreases in motor vehicle and equipment manufacturing and aircraft and parts due to increased use of robots to perform painting functions on assembly lines. Small decreases in motor vehicle dealers and automotive repair shops due to greater use of plastic body panels in automobiles, which are less likely to require repainting after minor damage.
Payroll and timekeeping clerks	Significant decreases in all industries due to increasing computerization of payroll and timekeeping functions.
Pest controllers and assistants	A significant decrease in services to buildings because the demand for the services of pest controllers is not expected to grow as fast as the demand for other services in this industry.
Photographic process workers, precision	A significant decrease in miscellaneous business services because these workers are concentrated in a slower growing segment of this industry.
Podiatrists	A significant decrease in offices of "other health practitioners" because the demand for the services of podiatrists is not expected to grow as fast as the demand for services provided by other practitioners in this industry.
Statistical clerks	Significant decreases in all industries due to the increasing use of computers, especially personal computers, in performing all types of statistical analyses.
Stenographers	Significant decreases in all industries except Federal, State, and local governments due to the widespread use of increasingly sophisticated dictation equipment. Little or no change is expected in the three levels of government because any negative effect of office automation is expected to be

[Continued]

★ 576 ★

Occupations with Projected Employment Changes in the National Industry-Occupation Matrix, 1986-2000 - IV
[Continued]

	offset by an increased demand for stenographers who work as court reporters and stenotype operators.
Typesetting and composing machine operators and tenders	A significant decrease in newspapers due to expected advances in computerized typesetting. Moderate decreases in all other industries for this reason.
Typists and word processors	Significant decreases in all industries except personnel supply services due to the expectation that more and more of the work of typists will be performed by word processors. the demand for word processors is expected to increase but is not expected to offset the decreased demand for typists. Therefore, the coefficient for the combined occupation is expected to decrease. No change is expected in personnel supply services due to the expectation that typists and word processors will continue to account for a large proportion of temporary jobs.
Welding machine setters, operators, and tenders	A significant decrease in motor vehicle manufacturing and moderate decreases in metal forgings and stampings farm and garden machinery and equipment and construction and related machinery and equipment due to increased use of industrial robots to perform welding functions on assembly lines.

Source: "Reasons Underlying Changes to the 1986 Coefficients in the National Industry-Occupation Matrix," *Occupational Projections and Training Data: A Statistical and Research Supplement to the 1988-89 Occupational Outlook Handbook,* U.S. Department of Labor, 1988, pp. 100-110.

★ 577 ★

Employment Change, 1988-2000

"As changes occur in demand for certain occupations, businesses will have to take more responsibility for preparing their future labor force by forming partnerships with schools."

[Jobs in millions]

Total, all occupations	18.1
Services	4.2
Professional specialty	3.5
Executive, administrative, managerial	2.7
Marketing and sales	2.6
Administrative support and clerical	2.5
Precision production, crafts	1.4
Technicians & support	1.2
Operators, fabricators, laborers	0.2
Agricultural, forestry, fishing	-0.2

Source: "Skills Lacking for Tomorrow's Jobs," *USA Today*, December, 1990, p. 12.

★ 578 ★

Employment Growth, 1975-2005

"Employment will increase by 24 million from 1990 to 2005, much less than the 35 million increase from 1975 to 1990."

[Numbers in millions]

1975	88
1990	123
2005	147

Source: "Outlook 1990-2005," *Occupational Outlook Quarterly* 35, No. 3, Fall, 1991, p. 7.

Chapter 10

MILITARY AFFAIRS

Military and Business

★ 579 ★

Estimate of Average Annual Job Changes Resulting From Alternative Use of Defense Expenditure, 1991-1994

Indicates jobs gained from civilian spending and lost from military spending cuts.

Branch	Gained	Lost	Net
Durable goods	138,150	280,600	-142,450
Non-durable goods	86,150	56,450	+29,700
Construction	258,400	40,850	+217,550
Transportation, utilities & mining	86,550	71,850	+14,700
Finance, real estate & insurance	93,500	54,550	+38,950
Wholesale & retail trade	255,450	177,950	+77,550
Services	1,016,880	302,400	+714,480
Federal government civilian personnel	49,350	205,250	-155,900
Federal government military personnel	-	498,500	-498,500
State & local government	180,850	-	+180,850
Total	2,165,280	1,688,400	+476,880

Source: "Of Arms and the Man: Possible Employment Consequences of Disarmament," Peter Richards, *International Labour Review* 130, No. 3, 1991, pp. 275-89. Primary source: M. Anderson, G. Bischak, and M. Oden: *Converting the American Economy*, p. 27.

★ 580 ★

Military Force Structure Reduction Impact on Investment, 1991-1995

[Numbers in billions]

	Fiscal 1991	Fiscal 1992	Fiscal 1993	Fiscal 1994	Fiscal 1995
Aircraft	25.3	29.9	35.2	34.3	38.7
Ships	11.2	10.1	10.5	10.8	10.9
Missiles/space	17.0	19.2	19.5	18.2	19.2
Combat vehicles	2.2	.8	.5	.8	.5
Other	19.7	19.6	18.1	21.5	19.5
Total	75.4	79.6	83.8	85.6	88.7
R&D	38.4	39.9	41.5	43.2	44.9

Source: "Cheney's 25% Force Reduction Plan Could Spur Further Spending Cuts," John D. Morrocco, *Aviation Week and Space Technology* 132, No. 26, June 25, 1990, pp. 24-5.

Military Employment

★ 581 ★

Defense Employment Levels, 1980-2001

[Numbers in millions]

	Military personnel	DoD civilians	Defense industry
1980	2.0	3.2	4.8
1985	2.2	3.4	6.2
1990	2.0	3.2	6.0
1995	1.5	2.5	4.5
2001	1.2	2.0	3.5

Source: "Introduction," *After the Cold War: Living with Lower Defense Spending*, Congress of the United States: Office of Technology Assessment, Washington, D.C., 1992, p. 6. Table also includes statistics for 1950-1980. Magnitudes are estimated. Primary source: Department of Defense, Office of the Comptroller, *National Defense Budget Estimate for FY 1992*. Future year estimates by Office of Technology Assessment.

★ 582 ★

Active Duty Military Personnel, 1975-1997

"Reductions in forces can be accomplished by two means—attrition and involuntary separation (layoff). Attrition is exceptionally effective as a means of downsizing in the armed forces. In an average recent year, roughly 290,000 members left the ranks of the armed forces (a turnover rate of about 15 percent). Most of those voluntarily leaving are young enlisted personnel who did not plan a career in the military. With this rate of attrition, it might seem that the reduction of forces could be accomplished simply by massively curtailing accessions (new entrants). While this approach might avoid displacement, it is not a viable option from the perspective of force structure management or long-term security."

[Numbers in thousands]

	Enlisted	Officer
1975	1800	2100
1980	1750	2100
1985	1800	2200
1990	1700	2000
1995	1400	1600

Source: "Veterans' Adjustment," *After the Cold War: Living With Lower Defense Spending*, Congress of the United States: Office of Technology Assessment, Washington, D.C., 1992, p. 134. Magnitudes are estimated. Primary source: Department of Defense, Office of the Comptroller, *National Defense Budget Estimates for FY 1992*, and projections from the Office of the Assistant Secretary of Defense, Force Management and Personnel, unpublished data.

★ 583 ★

Active Navy Shipbuilding Base Labor Projection, 1988-1998

"Projection on 10/1/91 for 16 yards."

[Thousands of workers]

	1988	1989	1990	1991	1992	1993	1994	1995	1996	1997	1998
Total employment	84	89	90	90	92	85	70	50	40	42	43
New construction[1]	50	51	55	55	57	55	50	30	25	27	30
New construction[2]	50	51	55	55	54	48	40	25	20	15	10
Repair & non-ship work	11	10	10	10	12	15	14	12	12	12	10

Source: "Shipbuilding and Repair," *U.S. Industrial Outlook '92: Business Forecasts for 350 Industries*, U.S. Department of Commerce. Washington, D.C., 1992, p. 22-6. Magnitudes are estimated. Primary source: U.S. Department of Transportation, Maritime Administration. *Notes:* Total employment reflects actual number of workers employed; other data refers to number of shipyard production workers expressed in 8-hour equivalent work units. 1. Projected. 2. Contracted.

★ 584 ★

Projected Annual Declines in Defense Industry Employment, 1992-1997

[Numbers in thousands]

1992	-180
1993	-340
1994	-200
1995	-110
1996	-120
1997	-110

Source: "Some Defense Spending Funds Go Elsewhere, But Clinton's Comments Leave Goals Ill-Defined," Thomas E. Ricks, *The Wall Street Journal*, November 16, 1992, p. A 12. Magnitudes are estimated. Primary source: Defense Budget Project, Washington, D.C.

★ 585 ★

Defense Spending and Employment Levels, 1991-2001

Total employment in this table includes Department of Defense civilian and military personnel stationed overseas. "These figures may overstate the number of jobs that will actually be lost.... [It] is likely that at least half of the loss of civilian jobs in the DoD can be taken care of by attrition without the need for layoffs. Many private defense jobs are in industries that provide goods and services not specifically and uniquely military. Assuming healthy economic growth, some defense jobs in those industries will never disappear at all, because commercial customers will take the place of defense procurement. This could be the case, for example, in such diverse sectors as banking, textile manufacture, and steelmaking. Defense companies that also make commercial products—especially in aircraft and electronics—might expand that side of the business and move some employees over from the military side. In addition, normal attrition—people moving to new jobs, retiring, or otherwise voluntarily leaving the work force—could moderate the impact of some of the job loss. On the other hand, these numbers do not count jobs generated by the pay of defense workers—anything from grocery store clerk to school psychologist. In communities hit hard by defense cutbacks such jobs could disappear without much hope of early replacement."

[Numbers in constant 1991 dollars]

Year	Total defense outlays (051) (billions)	Active duty military (thousands)	DoD civilians (thousands)	Defense industry employment (thousands)	Defense employment (thousands)
1991 DoD estimate	287.5	2,049	1,044	2,900	5,993
1995 DoD estimate	235.7	1,653	940	2,280 to 2,370	4,873 to 4,963
Loss from 1991	51.8	396	104	530 to 620	1,030 to 1,120
Percent loss	18.0	19.0	10.0	18.0 to 21.0	17.0 to 19.0
1995 faster paced reduction	218.0	1,653	940	1,980 to 2,080	4,573 to 4,673
Loss from 1991	69.5	396	104	820 to 920	1,320 to 1,420
Percent loss	24.0	19.0	10.0	28.0 to 32.0	22.0 to 24.0
2001 faster paced reduction	168.6	1,340	697	1,500 to 1,620	3,537 to 3,657
Loss from 1991	118.9	709	347	1,280 to 1,400	2,336 to 2,456

[Continued]

★ 585 ★

Defense Spending and Employment Levels, 1991-2001
[Continued]

Year	Total defense outlays (051) (billions)	Active duty military (thousands)	DoD civilians (thousands)	Defense industry employment (thousands)	Defense employment (thousands)
Percent loss	41.0	35.0	33.0	44.0 to 48.0	39.0 to 41.0
Loss from 1995	49.4	313	243	360 to 580	916 to 1,136
Percent loss	23.0	19.0	26.0	18.0 to 28.0	20.0 to 24.0

Source: "Summary and Findings," *After the Cold War: Living with Lower Defense Spending*, Congress of the United States: Office of Technology Assessment, Washington, D.C., 1992, p. 19. Primary source: DoD estimates from the Office of the Assistant Secretary of Defense (Public Affairs), "FY 1992-93 Department of Defense Budget Request," News release No. 52-91, Feb. 4, 1991; except defense industry employment, which is estimated by the Office of Technology Assessment based on DoD projection of defense purchases. Faster pace alternative budget estimates from William Kauffman, *Glasnost, Perestroika, and U.S. Defense Spending*; and William Kauffman and John Steinbruner, *Decisions for Defense*. The 2001 alternative uses projections of troop and civilian personnel levels given by Kauffman in *Glasnost, Perestroika, and U.S. Defense Spending* (Kauffman's scenario D). Industry employment levels estimated by the Office of Technology Assessment from budget estimates given by Kauffman. The 1995 budget estimates are from Kauffman and Steinbruner, *Decisions for Defense*, and reflect savings through reductions in procurement of new systems and a reduction in nuclear forces, assuming no additional reduction in the estimates of manpower given by DoD. Industry employment for 1995 was estimated by the Office of Technology Assessment based on level of defense purchases.

★ 586 ★

Total Reduction in End Strength, 1990-1997

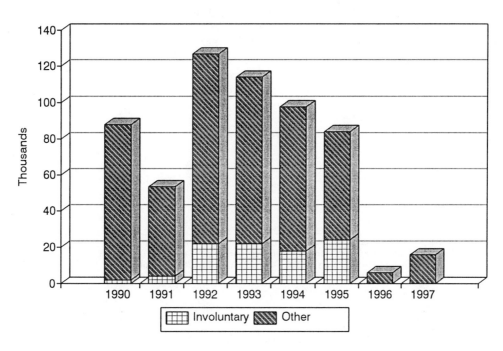

"Projections of involuntary separations were made before the new voluntary separation incentive was enacted. This number may overstate the actual number of involuntary separations that will take place."

[Numbers in thousands]

	Involuntary	Other
1990	2	86
1991	4	50
1992	22	105
1993	22	92
1994	18	80
1995	24	60
1996	-	6
1997	-	16

Source: "Veterans' Adjustment," *After the Cold war: Living with Lower Defense Spending*, Congress of the United States: Office of Technology Assessment, Washington, D.C., 1992, p. 135. Magnitudes are estimated. Primary source: Office of the Assistant Secretary of Defense, Force Management and Personnel, unpublished data.

★ 587 ★

Reduction in Enlisted End Strength, 1990-1997

"Projections of involuntary separations were made before the new voluntary separation incentive was enacted. This number may overstate the actual number of involuntary separations that will take place."

[Numbers in thousands]

	Involuntary	Other
1990	-	81
1991	2	42
1992	13	40
1993	14	78
1994	12	64
1995	20	52
1996	-	5
1997	-	10

Source: "Veterans' Adjustment," *After the Cold War: Living with Lower Defense Spending,* Congress of the United States: Office of Technology Assessment, Washington, D.C., 1992, p. 135. Magnitudes are estimated. Primary source: Office of the Assistant Secretary of Defense, Force Management and Personnel, unpublished data.

★ 588 ★

Reduction in Officer End Strength, 1990-1997

"Projections of involuntary separations were made before the new voluntary separation incentive was enacted. This number may overstate the actual number of involuntary separations that will take place."

[Numbers in thousands]

	Involuntary	Other
1990	1.0	6.1
1991	1.2	5.9
1992	8.5	14.2
1993	7.5	14.0
1994	5.8	10.0
1995	6.0	8.0
1996	0	0
1997	-	2.0

Source: "Veterans' Adjustment," *After the Cold War: Living with Lower Defense Spending,* Congress of the United States: Office of Technology Assessment, Washington, D.C., 1992, p. 135. Magnitudes are estimated. Primary source: Office of the Assistant Secretary of Defense, Force Management and Personnel, unpublished data.

Military Expenditures

★ 589 ★

Department of Defense Discretionary Levels Compared to Summit Baseline, 1992-1997

[Numbers in billions of dollars]

	1992	1993	1994	1995	1996	1997	Cumulative 1992-97
Summit baseline[1]							
Budget authority	278.2	278.6	279.0	281.5	283.4	288.2	1,688.9
Outlays	283.9	279.7	274.0	275.3	279.4	284.8	1,677.1
Inflation adjustment							
Budget authority	-	-2.3	-2.4	-2.4	-2.7	-2.8	-12.5
Outlays	-	-1.0	-1.7	-2.0	-2.4	-2.6	-9.7
Adjusted baseline							
Budget authority	278.2	276.3	276.6	279.1	280.7	285.4	1,676.4
Outlays	283.9	278.7	272.3	273.3	276.9	282.2	1,667.4
Proposed defense savings							
Budget authority	-6.6	-7.9	-8.0	-8.4	-9.4	-10.0	-50.4
Outlays	-0.6	-5.2	-4.1	-4.6	-5.2	-7.7	-27.4
Proposed levels (excluding Operation Desert Shield/Desert Storm)							
Budget authority	271.6	268.4	268.6	270.7	271.3	275.5	1,626.0
Outlays	283.3	273.5	268.2	268.7	271.7	274.5	1,639.9

Source: "Preserving National Security and Advancing America's Interests Abroad," *Budget of the United States Government, Fiscal Year 1993*, Washington, D.C., Part One, p. 242. *Notes:* 1. Defined as January 1991 budget levels extended to 1997 and adjusted for 1992 Congressional action and technical corrections.

★ 590 ★

Impacts of Military Cuts, 1990-2000

The United States economy can absorb large cuts in military spending without serious damage, economists say, although for a while, at least tens of thousands of Americans will lose their jobs.

That will happen mostly because military spending will shrink faster than the civilian sector can expand to take up the slack. By most estimates, the process could temporarily idle up to 100,000 people a year in the 1990s, most of them discharged from the military service against their wishes or laid off at weapons plants which would then go unused.

[Continued]

★ 590 ★

Impacts of Military Cuts, 1990-2000
[Continued]

The proposed military cuts, some calling for reductions that would reach more than $100 billion a year by the late 1990s, would mark the fourth big cutback in military spending since World War II. But it would differ from the others in two significant ways. Never before on the eve of a major reduction has the military represented so small a portion of the national economy, less than 6 percent of the total wealth created in the nation last year. As a result, the cutback will scarcely show up in the statistics that measure economic strength.

Source: "Economy Expected to Absorb Effects of Military Cuts," Louis Uchitelle, *The New York Times*, CXXXIX, No. 48,206, p. I 20.

★ 591 ★

Funding Summary for National Defense and International Affairs, 1989-1993
[Numbers in billions of dollars]

	1989 actual	1992 enacted[1]	1992 proposed	1993 proposed	Dollar change: 1992 enacted to 1993	Percent change: 1992 enacted to 1993
National Defense (050)[2]						
Budget authority	299.6	290.4	283.8	281.0	-9.4	-3.0
Outlays	303.6	295.8	295.2	285.8	-9.9	-3.0
Department of Defense--Military (051)[2]						
Budget authority	(290.8)	(277.5)	(270.9)	(267.6)	(-9.8)	(-4.0)
Outlays	(294.9)	(283.1)	(282.5)	(272.8)	(-10.4)	(-4.0)
International affairs (150)						
Budget authority	17.3	21.0[3]	21.0	20.6	-0.4	-2.0
Outlays	9.6	17.8	17.8	18.0	+0.2	+1.0
Total						
Budget authority	316.8	311.4	304.8	301.5	-9.8	-3.0
Outlays	313.1	313.6	313.0	303.8	-9.8	-3.0

Source: "Preserving National Security and Advancing America's Interests Abroad," *Budget of the United States Government, Fiscal Year 1993*, Washington, D.C., Part One, p. 239. Includes both discretionary and mandatory programs. *Notes:* 1. A portion of the funds for International Affairs programs is covered by a continuing resolution. 2. Funding for Operation Desert Shield/Desert Storm is excluded. 3. Excludes International Monetary Fund quota increase.

★ 592 ★

Military Budget Projections, 1991-2001

"A single cap applies to the three categories of discretionary spending in Fiscal 1994 and 1995. The discretionary caps in later years are Congressional Budget Office extrapolations."

[Numbers in billions of dollars]

	1991	1992	1993	1994	1995	1996	1997	1998	1999	2000	2001
Defense discretionary	322	314	295	-	-	-	-	-	-	-	-
International discretionary	20	20	21	-	-	-	-	-	-	-	-
Domestic discretionary	197	215	225	-	-	-	-	-	-	-	-
Total discretionary	539	549	541	539	544	563	585	608	633	658	684
Deficit	279	362	278	234	157	182	208	238	269	303	

Source: "Nuclear Arms Cuts Spur Drive in Congress to Renegotiate Budget," David F. Bond, *Aviation Week and Space Technology* 135, No. 5, October 14, 1991, pp. 22-3. Primary source: Congressional Budget Office.

★ 593 ★

Downsizing of the Military, 1990-1995

[Military personnel in millions]

	1990	1995
Military personnel	2.1	1.65
Active duty Army divisions	18	12
Navy ships	545	451
Air Force fighter wings	24	15

Source: "Fact and Comment," Malcom S. Forbes, Jr., *Forbes* 147, No. 9, April 29, 1991, pp. 23-4.

★ 594 ★

National Defense Budget Authority by Function and Program, 1989-1997

[Numbers in billions of dollars]

	1989 actual	1992 enacted	Proposed					
			1992	1993	1994	1995	1996	1997
National Defense Discretionary excluding Operation Desert Shield/Desert Storm								
Department of Defense--Military	291.5	278.2	271.6	268.4	268.6	270.7	271.3	275.5
Atomic energy defense activities	8.1	12.0	12.0	12.1	12.7	13.4	14.1	14.8
Defense-related activities	0.5	0.8	0.8	1.0	1.0	0.9	0.9	0.9
Subtotal, discretionary	300.1	291.0	284.4	281.6	282.3	285.0	286.3	291.2

[Continued]

★ 594 ★

National Defense Budget Authority by Function and Program, 1989-1997
[Continued]

	1989 actual	1992 enacted	Proposed					
			1992	1993	1994	1995	1996	1997
National Defense Mandatory								
Department of Defense--Military	-0.7	-0.7	-0.7	-0.8	-0.8	-0.8	-0.8	-0.8
Defense-related activities	0.1	0.2	0.2	0.2	0.2	0.2	0.2	0.2
Subtotal, Mandatory	-0.6	-0.6	-0.6	-0.6	-0.6	-0.6	-0.6	-0.6
National Defense totals								
Department of Defense--Military	290.8	277.5	270.9	267.6	267.8	269.9	270.4	274.6
Atomic energy defense activities	8.1	12.0	12.0	12.1	12.7	13.4	14.1	14.8
Defense-related activities	0.6	1.0	1.0	1.2	1.1	1.1	1.1	1.1
Total	299.6	290.4	283.8	281.0	281.6	284.3	285.7	290.6
National Defense Operation Desert Shield/Desert Storm	-	10.4	10.4	-	-	-	-	-
Offsetting foreign cash contributions	-	-5.0[1]	-5.0	-	-	-	-	-
Net Budget authority	-	5.4	5.4	-	-	-	-	-

Source: "Preserving National Security and Advancing America's Interests Abroad," *Budget of the United States Government, Fiscal Year 1993*, Washington, D.C., Part One, p. 240. *Note:* 1. Estimate.

★ 595 ★

National Defense Outlays by Function and Program, 1989-1997
[Numbers in billions of dollars]

	1989 actual	1992 enacted	Proposed					
			1992	1993	1994	1995	1996	1997
National Defense Discretionary excluding Operation Desert Shield/Desert Storm								
Department of Defense - Military	295.6	283.9	283.3	273.5	268.2	268.7	271.7	274.5
Atomic energy defense activities	8.1	11.7	11.7	11.9	12.5	13.0	13.7	14.4
Defense-related activities	0.4	0.8	0.8	1.0	0.9	0.9	0.9	0.9
Subtotal discretionary	304.1	296.4	295.8	286.4	281.6	282.7	286.4	289.8
National Defense Mandatory								
Department of Defense - Military	-0.7	-0.8	-0.8	-0.8	-0.8	-0.8	-0.8	-0.8
Defense-related activities	0.1	0.2	0.2	0.2	0.2	0.2	0.2	0.2
Subtotal, Mandatory	-0.6	-0.6	-0.6	-0.6	-0.6	-0.6	-0.6	-0.6
National Defense Totals								
Department of Defense - Military	294.9	283.1	282.5	272.8	267.4	267.9	270.9	273.6
Atomic energy defense activities	8.1	11.7	11.7	11.9	12.5	13.0	13.7	14.4
Defense-related activities	0.6	1.0	1.0	1.2	1.1	1.1	1.1	1.1
Total	303.6	295.8	295.2	285.8	281.0	282.1	285.8	289.2

[Continued]

★ 595 ★

National Defense Outlays by Function and Program, 1989-1997

[Continued]

	1989 actual	1992 enacted	Proposed					
			1992	1993	1994	1995	1996	1997
National Defense Operation Desert Shield/ Desert Storm	-	17.1	17.1	5.5	2.4	1.1	0.5	0.1
Offsetting foreign cash contributions	-	-5.0[1]	-5.0	-	-	-	-	-
Net outlays	-	12.1	12.1	5.5	2.4	1.1	0.5	0.1

Source: "Preserving National Security and Advancing America's Interests Abroad," *Budget of the United States Government, Fiscal Year 1993,* Washington, D.C., Part One, p. 241. *Note:* 1. Estimate.

★ 596 ★

National Defense Spending, 1975-2001

[Numbers in billions of 1991 dollars]

	Historical	DoD estimate	Kauffman estimate
1975	210	-	-
1980	225	-	-
1985	325	-	-
1990	310	-	-
1995	-	225	210
2001	-	-	180

Source: "Introduction," *After the Cold War: Living With Lower Defense Spending,* Congress of the United States: Office of Technology Assessment, Washington, D.C., 1992, p. 4. Table also includes statistics for 1950-1975. Primary source: Steven Alexis Cain, *Analysis of the FY 1992-93 Defense Budget Request, with Historical Budget Tables*; and Office of Technology Assessment projections based on William Kauffman, *Glasnost, Perestroika, and U.S. Defense Spending.*

★ 597 ★

U.S. Defense Spending as Percent of GNP, 1940-1995

1940	3.0
1945	39.0
1950	5.5
1955	11.5
1960	10.0
1965	8.0

[Continued]

★ 597 ★

U.S. Defense Spending as Percent of GNP, 1940-1995
[Continued]

1970	8.0
1975	5.5
1980	5.0
1985	6.0
1990	5.5
1995	4.0

Source: "Converting Machines, and Minds," Thom Shanker, *Chicago Tribune*, February 25, 1990, I, 18. Primary source: Office of Management and Budget. Figures are presented in percent of gross national product per fiscal year. Magnitudes estimated from published chart.

Military Theory

★ 598 ★

The Military Forecasters: Air Force, 1985-2025

Innovation Task Force 2025 tried to balance technology considerations with innovative concepts in operations, organization, and management. The participants of this effort were assigned to generate and implement ideas on how the Air Force could best prepare itself for the first quarter of the next century and to find ways for the Air Force to sustain innovation.

The four phases of Innovation Task Force 2025 were: scenario development, led by The Futures Group of Glastonbury, Connecticut; idea development, in which members of the Air Staff and Air Force Systems Command developed 600 ideas on technology concepts, organization, and resources; idea selection, in which the most promising ideas developed were presented to the Air Force Chief of Staff; and recommendation development, in which suggestions were made on how the Air Force could meet the challenges identified in the previous phases.

One of the more novel forecasting initiatives took place in May 1985 during a three day conference at Wright-Patterson Air Force Base in Ohio. The participants consisted of a diverse group of advanced-concept engineers, scientists, and 40 prominent science-fiction writers, including Greg Benford (author of *If the Stars Are Gods*), Joe Haldeman (*The Forever War*), Larry Niven (*Tales of Known Space*), and Jerry Pournelle (*A Spaceship for the King*).

[Continued]

★ 598 ★

The Military Forecasters: Air Force, 1985-2025
[Continued]

The purpose of Futurist II was to expose the advanced-concepts researchers to some of the creative thinking coming from the authors, most of whom were also well versed in technology and weapons systems. The researchers and the writers found this forecasting approach to be professionally useful as well as a personally rewarding experience.

Several of the ideas generated by the writers appeared to captivate the interest of the Air Force researchers, including; using genetically tailored organisms, towing an asteroid to Earth orbit for metal resources, attacking enemy information processing facilities with "cybernetic infections," and having satellite power stations beam energy down to combat vehicles, eliminating the need for their own internal fuel supplies.

Several concepts had been evolving among both the defense researchers and the writers, but they each had been unaware of what the other had been working on until the conference. The Air Force participants were quite surprised as to the level of sophisticated thought that science-fiction writers displayed about pilotless aircraft featuring remote heads-up and sensory-response technologies. And the writers were astonished as to the research progress made by the Air Force in the virtual cockpit program to develop systems of advanced cockpit displays and arrangement to assist pilots. By and large, the benefit to the writers came in terms of specific details rather than the broad concepts.

Source: "The Military Forecasters," Earl D. Cooper and Steven M. Shaker, *The Futurist* XXII, No. 3, May/ June, 1988, pp. 37-43. Reproduced, with permission, from THE FUTURIST, published by the World Future Society, 7910 Woodmont Avenue, Suite 450, Bethesda, Maryland 20814.

★ 599 ★

The Military Forecasters: Army, 1995-2015

[Air Land Battle 2000 (later renamed Army 21 to avoid confusion with the Air Land Battle Doctrine)] was to serve as a base line by which to guide future weapons acquisition destined for the 1995-2015 time frame. As with the Air Land Battle Doctrine, the broad operational concepts were translated into requirements that in turn guided weapons development.

Air Land Battle 2000 depicted a scenario in which battles would encompass the full depth of enemy formations, up to 300 kilometers. Numerous surveillance, reconnaissance, and target-acquisition systems would be operating from the air and space. In order to fight successfully, the Army would need to use dispersed and highly mobile forces in a conventional as well as a nuclear/biological/chemical warfare environment. Electronic warfare would also play an important factor on a battlefield in which the U.S. Army may not have a significant advantage in weaponry.

Source: "The Military Forecasters," Earl D. Cooper and Steven M. Shaker, *The Futurist* XXII, No. 3, May/June, 1988, pp. 37-43. Reproduced, with permission, from THE FUTURIST, published by the World Future Society, 7910 Woodmont Avenue, Suite 450, Bethesda, Maryland 20814.

★ 600 ★

The Military Forecasters: Navy, 2000

A comprehensive study of the U.S. Navy in the next century has been undertaken by the NAS Naval Studies Board. This work is plotting the shape that the Navy must take to meet potential future threats. Navy 21 is also addressing the use of rapidly advancing technology for solving projected Navy problems and for providing new or improved weapons systems that will significantly enhance operations.

Navy 21 is noteworthy from several perspectives. First, it is probably the most comprehensive Navy futures study ever undertaken. In the past, Navy studies of such magnitude and scope have been difficult to initiate and accomplish because of internal Navy competitive forces. Second, it is a "top down" effort with guidance emanating from the Chief of Naval Operations himself. Third, the study is not nearsighted, but looks reasonably far into the future—circa, the end of the first quarter of the new century.

Source: "The Military Forecasters," Earl D. Cooper and Steven M. Shaker, *The Futurist* XXII, No. 3, May/June, 1988, pp. 37-43. Reproduced, with permission, from THE FUTURIST, published by the World Future Society, 7910 Woodmont Avenue, Suite 450, Bethesda, Maryland 20814.

★ 601 ★

American Military Power after the Cold War, 1990-2000

A number of observers assume that the emerging world can best be described as multipolar, and some theorists have argued that the flexible shifting of alliances associated with the classical multipolar balance of power will be a new source of stability in global politics. But the development of a true multipolarity between, say, five countries with similar levels of power resources does not seem likely in the 1990s. Other major countries are likely to be deficient in significant power resources, and the mix of relevant power resources is changing. The USSR is declining, China remains a less developed country, Japan lacks military and ideological power, and Europe lacks unity. The US economy is five times the size of a unified Germany.

So the US is likely to remain "No. 1," but being No. 1 won't be what it used to be. New issues in international politics—ecology, debt, drugs, AIDS, terrorism—involve a diffusion of power away from larger states to weaker states and private actors. Unilateral action and hard power resources such as military force cannot solve these problems. Instead, they require cooperative responses. The US and other countries will have to pay much more attention to the problems of organizing cooperation through a wide variety of multilateral arrangements.

Source: "Soviet Decline and America's Soft Power," Joseph S. Nye, Jr., *The Christian Science Monitor* 82, No. 181, August 14, 1990, p. 19.

Military Technology

★ 602 ★

Estimated Strategic Forces under Strategic Arms Reduction Talks, 1990-2000

SLCM = submarine-launched cruise missiles; ALCM = air-launched cruise missiles; SRAM = short-range attack missiles; ICBM = inter-continental ballistic missiles; SLBM = submarine-launched ballistic missiles.

	United States	Soviet Union
Current strategic force levels		
ICBM warheads	2,450	6,595
SLBM warheads	5,056	2,810
Bombs & SRAMs	2,608	616
ALCMs	1,600	720
SLCMs	367	100
Total warheads	12,081	10,841

[Continued]

★ 602 ★

Estimated Strategic Forces under Strategic Arms Reduction Talks, 1990-2000

[Continued]

	United States	Soviet Union
Estimated post-START strategic force levels, late 1990s		
ICBM warheads	1,423	3,228
SLBM warheads	3,456	1,672
Bombs & SRAMs	2,736	960
ALCMs	1,900	1,300
SLCMs[1]	880	880
Total warheads	10,395	8,040

Source: "Appendix A," *The Future of the U.S.- Soviet Nuclear Relationship*, Committee on International Security and Arms Control, National Academy of Sciences, National Academy Press, Washington, D.C., 1991, p. 53. Magnitudes are estimated. *Note*: 1. The permitted ceiling on long-range nuclear SLCMs is 880; current U.S. plans call for 637. To date, the Soviet Union has reportedly deployed only about 100 SS-N-21 SLCMs.

★ 603 ★

The "Star Wars" Market: The Strategic Defense Initiative Fiscal Year Budget, 1995-2005

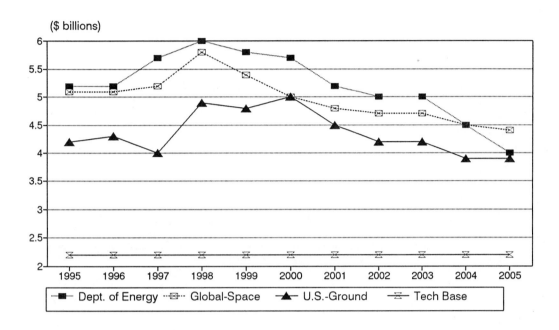

"What remains under the program officially known as the Strategic Defense Initiative is a much more down-to-earth plan for advanced ground-based missiles and special satellites to monitor attacks and manage the response. And even those programs are being stretched out under budget pressures."

[Numbers in billions of dollars]

	1995	1996	1997	1998	1999	2000	2001	2002	2003	2004	2005
Global - Space	5.1	5.1	5.2	5.8	5.4	5.0	4.8	4.7	4.7	4.5	4.4
Department of Energy	5.2	5.2	5.7	6.0	5.8	5.7	5.2	5.0	5.0	4.0	4.0
U.S. Ground	4.2	4.3	4.0	4.9	4.8	5.0	4.5	4.2	4.2	3.9	3.9
Tech Base/Follow-on	2.2	2.2	2.2	2.2	2.2	2.2	2.2	2.2	2.2	2.2	2.2

Source: "Defense Contractors Are Keeping the 'Star Wars' Faith—though Thinner, Program's Funds May be Crucial in Lean Years Ahead," Jeff Cole, *The Wall Street Journal*, September 9, 1993, p. B3. Chart also includes statistics for 1985-1994. Magnitudes are estimated. Primary source: Strategic Defense Initiative Organization.

★ 604 ★

Weapons Production as Compared to Other Countries, 2000

Major independent weapon production	Indigenous production of a wide range of weapons	Limited production of many types of weapons	Limited production of a few types of weapons	Minimal weapon production capability
United States	Brazil	Chile	Argentina	Algeria
Soviet Union	India	Greece	Egypt	Iraq
France	Israel	Indonesia	North Korea	Libya
Germany	Yugoslavia	Iran	Taiwan	Morocco
United Kingdom	South Korea	Malaysia	Canada[1]	Syria
China	South Africa	Singapore		
Poland	Spain[1]	Pakistan		
Czechoslovakia		Thailand		
Italy		Turkey		
Sweden				
Japan[1]				

Source: "Table 1," *American Military Power: Future Needs, Future Choices,* Congress of the United States, Office of Technology Assessment, Washington, D.C., October, 1991, p. 7. Primary source: Briefing by David Louscher, "Patterns of Demand and Supply of Weapons." *Note:* 1. Additional estimates by Office of Technology Assessment.

Chapter 11

POPULATION, THE FAMILY, AND VITAL STATISTICS

Population Projections by Age, Sex, and Race

★ 605 ★

Population Growth, 1950-2000

"By the year 2000, the U.S. population will reach 275 million, an increase of 15 percent over the 240 million U.S. residents in 1985."

Year	Total	Increase compared to previous census
1950	151.3	19.1
1960	179.3	28.0
1970	203.2	24.0
1980	226.5	23.2
1990	252.7	26.2
2000	275.2	22.5

Source: "Work and Workers in the Year 2000," *Workforce 2000: Work and Workers for the Twenty-First Century*, Hudson Institute, Indianapolis, Indiana, 1987, p. 76. Primary source: U.S. Bureau of the Census, Decennial Censuses and *Current Population Reports*, series P-25, No. 937, Table 1. Numbers in millions.

★ 606 ★

Total Population Projections by Age, Sex, and Race, 1995-2010

Age, sex, and race	Population (1,000)				Percent distribution		Percent change	
	1995	2000	2005	2010	2000	2010	1990-2000	2000-2010
Total	260,138	268,266	275,604	282,575	100.0	100.0	7.1	5.3
Under 5 years old	17,799	16,898	16,611	16,899	6.3	6.0	-8.2	(Z)
5-17 years old	48,374	48,815	47,471	45,747	18.2	16.2	7.0	-6.3

[Continued]

★ 606 ★

Total Population Projections by Age, Sex, and Race, 1995-2010
[Continued]

Age, sex, and race	Population (1,000)				Percent distribution		Percent change	
	1995	2000	2005	2010	2000	2010	1990-2000	2000-2010
18-24 years old	24,281	25,231	26,918	27,155	9.4	9.6	-3.5	7.6
25-34 years old	40,962	37,149	35,997	37,572	13.8	13.3	-15.4	1.1
35-44 years old	42,336	43,911	40,951	37,202	16.4	13.2	15.9	-15.3
45-54 years old	31,297	37,223	41,619	43,207	13.9	15.3	46.0	16.1
55-64 years old	21,325	24,158	29,762	35,430	9.0	12.5	13.1	46.7
65-74 years old	18,930	18,243	18,410	21,039	6.8	7.4	-0.7	15.3
75 years old and over	14,834	16,639	17,864	18,323	6.2	6.5	26.2	10.1
16 years old and over	201,018	210,134	219,301	227,390	78.3	80.5	8.9	8.2
Male, total	127,123	131,191	134,858	138,333	100.0	100.0	7.3	5.4
Under 5 years old	9,118	8,661	8,517	8,668	6.6	6.3	-8.1	0.1
5-17 years old	24,787	25,027	24,350	23,473	19.1	17.0	7.1	-6.2
18-24 years old	12,290	12,770	13,628	13,752	9.7	9.9	-3.4	7.7
25-34 years old	20,579	18,662	18,091	18,878	14.2	13.6	-15.5	1.2
35-44 years old	21,104	21,945	20,458	18,586	16.7	13.4	16.8	-15.3
45-54 years old	15,292	18,296	20,585	21,432	13.9	15.5	47.5	17.1
55-64 years old	10,149	11,557	14,321	17,173	8.8	12.4	14.4	48.6
65-74 years old	8,476	8,242	8,407	9,691	6.3	7.0	0.9	17.6
75 years old and over	5,326	6,032	6,501	6,681	4.6	4.8	28.9	10.8
16 years old and over	96,834	101,392	105,984	110,024	77.3	79.5	9.2	8.5
Female, total	133,016	137,076	140,746	144,241	100.0	100.0	7.0	5.2
Under 5 years old	8,681	8,237	8,094	8,231	6.0	5.7	-8.3	-0.1
5-17 years old	23,587	23,788	23,121	22,274	17.4	15.4	6.9	-6.4
18-24 years old	11,991	12,461	13,290	13,402	9.1	9.3	-3.6	7.6
25-34 years old	20,384	18,487	17,906	18,694	13.5	13.0	-15.4	1.1
35-44 years old	21,233	21,966	20,493	18,616	16.0	12.9	14.9	-15.3
45-54 years old	16,005	18,927	21,034	21,775	13.8	15.1	44.7	15.0
55-64 years old	11,175	12,601	15,441	18,257	9.2	12.7	11.9	44.9
65-74 years old	10,454	10,001	10,004	11,348	7.3	7.9	-2.0	13.5
75 years old and over	9,507	10,607	11,364	11,642	7.7	8.1	24.7	9.8
16 years old and over	104,184	108,742	113,317	117,366	79.3	81.4	8.6	7.9
White, total	216,820	221,514	225,424	228,978	100.0	100.0	5.2	3.4
Under 5 years old	14,251	13,324	12,936	13,084	6.0	5.7	-10.5	-1.8
5-17 years old	38,493	38,569	37,118	35,258	17.4	15.4	5.6	-8.6
18-24 years old	19,452	19,998	21,188	21,298	9.0	9.3	-6.2	6.5
25-34 years old	33,680	29,988	28,603	29,585	13.5	12.9	-18.1	-1.3
35-44 years old	35,635	36,574	33,639	29,997	16.5	13.1	13.2	-18.0
45-54 years old	26,879	31,618	34,911	35,860	14.3	15.7	44.0	13.4
55-64 years old	18,327	20,667	25,407	29,913	9.3	13.1	10.9	44.7
65-74 years old	16,681	15,811	15,708	17,875	7.1	7.8	-3.5	13.1

[Continued]

★ 606 ★

Total Population Projections by Age, Sex, and Race, 1995-2010
[Continued]

Age, sex, and race	Population (1,000)				Percent distribution		Percent change	
	1995	2000	2005	2010	2000	2010	1990-2000	2000-2010
75 years old and over	13,421	14,965	15,914	16,108	6.8	7.0	25.1	7.6
16 years old and over	169,665	175,579	181,478	186,417	79.3	81.4	6.8	6.2
Male	106,365	108,774	110,785	112,610	49.1	49.2	5.4	3.5
Female	110,455	112,739	114,639	116,368	50.9	50.8	4.9	3.2
Black, total	33,199	35,129	37,003	38,833	100.0	100.0	12.8	10.6
Under 5 years old	2,790	2,748	2,764	2,820	7.8	7.3	-2.3	2.6
5-17 years old	7,697	7,895	7,889	7,809	22.5	20.1	10.1	-1.1
18-24 years old	3,703	3,924	4,198	4,314	11.2	11.1	2.9	9.9
25-34 years old	5,534	5,264	5,299	5,590	15.0	14.4	-7.4	6.2
35-44 years old	5,041	5,481	5,332	5,076	15.6	13.1	30.2	-7.4
45-54 years old	3,261	4,106	4,928	5,369	11.7	13.8	52.9	30.8
55-64 years old	2,288	2,578	3,155	3,995	7.3	10.3	19.6	55.0
65-74 years old	1,762	1,848	1,994	2,277	5.3	5.9	14.9	23.2
75 years old and over	1,122	1,283	1,445	1,584	3.7	4.1	27.7	23.5
16 years old and over	23,860	25,708	27,638	29,467	73.2	75.9	15.7	14.6
Male	15,840	16,787	17,707	18,602	47.8	47.9	13.2	10.8
Female	17,359	18,342	19,296	20,231	52.2	52.1	12.4	10.3
Other races, total	10,119	11,624	13,177	14,764	100.0	100.0	34.5	27.0
Under 5 years old	758	826	911	995	7.1	6.7	17.8	20.4
5-17 years old	2,184	2,350	2,464	2,680	20.2	18.2	22.2	14.1
18-24 years old	1,126	1,309	1,532	1,542	11.3	10.4	31.1	17.9
25-34 years old	1,748	1,897	2,095	2,396	16.3	16.2	17.1	26.3
35-44 years old	1,660	1,856	1,980	2,129	16.0	14.4	34.5	14.7
45-54 years old	1,156	1,500	1,780	1,979	12.9	13.4	76.2	32.0
55-64 years old	711	912	1,200	1,523	7.8	10.3	59.9	67.1
65-74 years old	487	584	708	886	5.0	6.0	51.9	51.8
75 years old and over	290	391	506	632	3.4	4.3	79.3	61.8
16 years old and over	7,493	8,847	10,186	11,506	76.1	77.9	40.5	30.1
Male	4,918	5,629	6,366	7,122	48.4	48.2	33.3	26.5
Female	5,202	5,995	6,811	7,642	51.6	51.8	35.6	27.5

Source: "Projections of the Total Population by Age, Sex, and Race: 1995 to 2010," *Statistical Abstract of the United States*, 1991, p. 16. Primary source: U.S. Bureau of the Census, *Current Population Reports*, series P-25, No. 1018. As of July 1. Includes armed forces overseas. Data are for middle series. *Note:* - indicates decrease. (Z) indicates less than .05 percent.

★ 607 ★

Total Population as Compared to Populations of Other Major Industrial Countries, 1980-2025

Baseline projections are based on middle demographic data from census and public pension sources used by the countries concerned. "For the United States, the 'greater aging' scenario reflects the official 'pessimistic' scenario of the Social Security Administration, which suggests a decline in the fertility rate from 1.86 to 1.6 over the next 25 years."

[Numbers in millions]

Country	1980	2000	2010	2025
Canada				
Baseline scenario	24.0	29.0	31.0	32.5
Greater aging	24.0	29.0	30.5	31.5
France				
Baseline scenario	54.0	58.0	60.0	61.0
Greater aging	54.0	58.0	60.0	61.0
Federal Republic of Germany				
Baseline scenario	62.0	60.0	58.0	53.0
Greater aging	62.0	58.0	56.0	50.0
Italy				
Baseline scenario	56.5	58.0	58.0	57.0
Greater aging	56.5	57.5	57.0	55.0
Japan				
Baseline scenario	115.0	133.0	134.0	131.0
Greater aging	115.0	127.0	131.0	127.0
United Kingdom				
Baseline scenario	56.0	57.0	57.5	58.5
Greater aging	56.0	56.5	57.0	57.5
United States				
Baseline scenario	236.0	278.0	292.0	310.0
Greater aging	236.0	272.0	281.0	286.0

Source: "Population Dynamics in Seven Major Industrial Countries," *Aging and Social Expenditure in the Major Industrial Countries, 1980-2025*, Peter S. Heller et al, International Monetary Fund, Washington, D.C., September, 1986, pp. 27-8. Magnitudes estimated from published chart.

★ 608 ★

Population by Percent Distribution of Age, 1900-2050

Age	1900	1950	1990[1]	2050[1]
All ages	100.0	100.0	100.0	100.0
Under 15	34.4	26.9	21.6	16.4
15-24	19.7	14.7	14.4	11.6
25-44	28.1	30.0	32.7	24.7

[Continued]

★ 608 ★

Population by Percent Distribution of Age, 1900-2050

[Continued]

Age	1900	1950	1990[1]	2050[1]
45-64	13.7	20.3	18.7	24.4
65 & over	4.1	8.1	12.6	22.9

Source: "Historical Perspectives," *Statistical Bulletin* 71, No. 3, July-September, 1990, p. 33. Primary source: U.S. Bureau of the Census. As of July 1. *Note:* 1. Includes Armed Forces overseas.

★ 609 ★

Population Distribution by Age, 1900-2050

[Numbers in thousands]

Age	1900	1950	1990[1]	2050[1]
All ages	76,212	151,326	250,409	299,847
Under 15	26,171	40,673	54,070	49,420
15-24	14,930	22,221	36,107	34,754
25-44	21,386	45,413	81,822	74,043
45-64	10,422	30,724	46,851	73,098
65 and over	3,085	12,295	31,559	68,532

Source: "Historical Perspectives," *Statistical Bulletin* 71, No. 3, July-September, 1990, p. 33. Primary source: U.S. Bureau of the Census. As of July 1. *Note:* 1. Includes Armed Forces overseas.

★ 610 ★

Ratio of Children to the Elderly, 1940-2030

"By the year 2030, with the older population continuing to grow faster than the younger, there will be nearly equal numbers of American children and elderly."

Year	Number of children[1]
1940	447
1950	381
1960	387
1970	347
1980	248
1988	210
2000	194
2010	170

[Continued]

★ 610 ★

Ratio of Children to the Elderly, 1940-2030

[Continued]

Year	Number of children[1]
2020	135
2030	110

Source: "America's Children: Mixed Prospects," by Susan M. Bianchi, *Population Bulletin* 45, No. 1, June, 1990, p. 7. Primary source: U.S. Bureau of the Census, *Current Population Reports*, series P-25, Nos. 1018, 952, and 1045; and author's estimates based on published and unpublished data. *Note:* 1. Children under age 18 per 100 persons age 65+.

★ 611 ★

Projections of the Youth Population, 1990-2010

Magnitudes estimated from published chart. "These projections are based on the Census Bureau's Series 18, dating from 1988. Series 18 was selected because it represents an age structure in 1990 that most closely matches that found in the 1990 census."

[Numbers in millions]

	1990	1995	2000	2005	2010
Under 5	19.0	19.3	19.3	20.0	21.2
5 to 9	18.5	19.4	20.0	19.8	20.4
10 to 14	17.3	18.9	20.0	20.7	20.7
15 to 19	17.5	17.8	19.4	20.4	21.0
20 to 24	18.9	17.8	18.0	19.7	20.7

Source: "Youth to 2010," *American Demographics* 14, No. 2, February, 1992, p. 55.

★ 612 ★

18-Year Olds by Sex and Race, 1981-2050

[Numbers in thousands]

Year	All races			Black & other races			Black		
	Total	Men	Women	Total	Men	Women	Total	Men	Women
1981	4,234	2,156	2,078	706	356	350	605	303	302
1982	4,188	2,140	2,049	712	361	351	606	306	301
Series II projections[1]									
1983	4,015	2,046	1,969	701	353	348	595	299	296
1984	3,774	1,926	1,848	672	339	333	569	286	283
1985	3,658	1,863	1,795	643	324	319	540	270	269
1990	3,431	1,752	1,679	634	319	315	517	260	257

[Continued]

★ 612 ★

18-Year Olds by Sex and Race, 1981-2050
[Continued]

Year	All races			Black & other races			Black		
	Total	Men	Women	Total	Men	Women	Total	Men	Women
1995	3,332	1,702	1,603	620	313	307	496	250	246
2000	3,751	1,916	1,836	773	391	382	613	309	304
2025	3,675	1,878	1,797	855	432	422	667	334	328
2050	3,650	1,865	1,784	920	465	455	688	348	341

Source: "18 Year Olds by Sex and Race, Selected Years, 1950-2050," *Professional Women and Minorities: A Manpower Data Resource Service,* Commission on Professionals in Science and Technology, December, 1989, p. 7. Primary source: U.S. Bureau of the Census; National Center for Education Statistics; and Commission on Professionals in Science and Technology. *Notes:* Total population, including armed forces overseas as of July 1. 1. Series II projections use a fertility assumption of 1.9 lifetime births per woman. Projections reflect the results of the 1980 Census. Original table also includes data for 1950-1980.

★ 613 ★

Projected Annual Average Percent Change of the Population Aged 18 to 64 Years, 1980-2010

"These projections suggest that population growth of [Americans] ... ages 18 to 64, will slow down ... in the five years starting 1990, to a rate almost half the 1980 to 1988 level. The situation will be a bit better in the next five years (1995 to 2000)—when growth picks up slightly—but will still remain below the rate of the 1980s."

Period	Population aged 18 to 64 years	Population aged less than 18 and more than 64
1980 to 1988	1.18	0.63
1990 to 1995	0.69	0.89
1995 to 2000	0.92	0.13
2000 to 2010	0.74	0.14

Source: "Ordinary Life Sales: Why the Decline?" Khan H. Zahid, *Best's Review 92,* No. 2, June, 1991, p. 117. Primary source: U.S. Bureau of the Census, *Current Population Reports.*

★ 614 ★

Ratio of the Middle-Aged to the Youth Population, 1990-2020

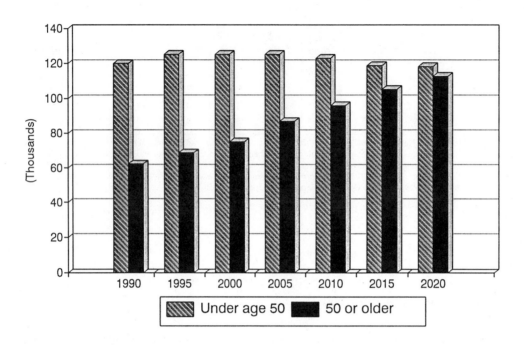

Includes total adult population under age 50 and aged 50 and older, 1990-2020. Magnitudes estimated from published chart. "Over the next thirty years, the number of young adults will remain stable, while the number of older adults will grow rapidly."

[Numbers in thousands]

	1990	1995	2000	2005	2010	2015	2020
Under age 50	120,000	125,000	125,000	125,000	123,000	118,750	118,000
50 or older	62,500	68,750	75,000	87,000	96,000	105,000	112,500

Source: "Business's Mid-Life Cycle," David B. Wolfe, *American Demographics* 14, No. 9, September, 1992, p. 42. Primary source: Census Bureau, 1990 census and "Projections of the Population of the United States, by Age, Sex, and Race: 1988 to 2080."

★ 615 ★

Projected Decline in Median-Age Populations, 1976-2000

[Numbers in percent]

Age group	1976-88	1988-2000
18-24	-5.9	-1.7
25-34	33.4	-12.8
35-44	52.6	26.2

Source: "The Job Outlook for College Graduates to the Year 2000: A 1990 Update," Jon Sargent and Janet Pfleeger, *Occupational Outlook Quarterly* 34, No. 2, Summer, 1990, p. 5. Primary source: U.S. Bureau of the Census.

★ 616 ★

Change in Median Age of Population, 1920-2000

"Maturing, rather than aging, may be the best description for the population trends of the next decade and a half. The number of young people will decline both relatively and absolutely. The numbers between 20 and 29, for example, will shrink from 41 million in 1980 to 34 million in 2000, and their share of the population will drop from 18 to 13 percent."

Year	Median age
1920	28.20
1930	26.75
1940	29.00
1950	30.20
1960	29.50
1970	28.00
1980	29.50
1990	32.50
2000	36.00

Source: "Work and Workers in the Year 2000," *Workforce 2000: Work and Workers for the Twenty-first Century*, William P. Johnston and Arnold E. Packer, Hudson Institute, Indianapolis, Indiana, June, 1987. Primary source: U.S. Bureau of the Census, *Current Population Reports*, series P-23, No. 138, Table 2-9. Magnitudes estimated from published chart.

★ 617 ★

Population at Retirement Age, 2008-2020

"Between July 2008 and July 2009, 3.5 million people will celebrate their 62nd birthday as the first baby boomers pass this milestone. That's 37 percent more than in the previous year, and 63 percent more than in 1990. Economic incentives could push the average age of retirement up as much as seven years. But despite delayed retirement plans, the boom will continue for several decades and peak around 2020."

Source: "You'll Know It's the 21st Century When...," Judith Waldrop, *American Demographics* 12, No. 12, December, 1990, p. 25.

★ 618 ★

Population 65 Years and Older by Race, 1950-2020

[Numbers in percent]

Race and age	1950	1960	1970	1980	1990	2000	2010	2020
White								
65 +	8.4	9.6	10.2	11.9	13.6	14.0	14.9	18.6
70 +	5.0	6.0	6.7	7.9	9.3	10.4	10.5	12.7
75 +	2.7	3.3	3.9	4.7	5.9	7.0	7.3	7.9
80 +	1.2	1.5	1.9	2.5	3.2	4.1	4.7	4.7
85 +	0.4	0.5	0.7	1.1	1.5	2.7	3.4	3.5
Black								
65 +	5.7	6.3	6.8	7.8	8.2	8.4	8.9	11.6
70 +	3.0	3.7	4.1	4.9	5.6	6.0	6.1	7.4
75 +	1.6	1.9	2.2	2.8	3.5	3.9	4.1	4.5
80 +	0.8	0.9	1.1	1.4	1.8	2.3	2.6	2.7
85 +	0.3	0.4	0.5	0.6	0.9	1.2	1.4	1.5

Source: "Black Americans' Health," *A Common Destiny: Blacks and American Society*, Gerald David Jaynes and Robin M. Williams, eds., National Academy Press, Washington, D.C., 1989, p. 426. Primary source: Decennial censuses and Census Bureau projections.

★ 619 ★

Population 65 Years Old and Over by Age Group and Sex, 1960-2000

Age group and sex	Number (1,000)					Percent distribution				
	1960	1970	1980	1989	2000 proj.	1960	1970	1980	1989	2000 proj.
Persons 65 years and over	16,675	20,107	25,704	30,984	34,882	100.0	100.0	100.0	100.0	100.0
65-69 years old	6,280	7,026	8,812	10,170	9,491	37.7	34.9	34.3	32.8	27.2
70-74 years old	4,773	5,467	6,841	8,012	8,752	28.6	27.2	26.6	25.9	25.1
75-79 years old	3,080	3,871	4,828	6,033	7,282	18.5	19.3	18.8	19.5	20.9
80-84 years old	1,601	2,312	2,954	3,728	4,735	9.6	11.5	11.5	12.0	13.6
85 years old and over	940	1,430	2,269	3,042	4,622	5.6	7.1	8.8	9.8	13.2
Males, 65 yrs. and over	7,542	8,413	10,366	12,636	14,273	100.0	100.0	100.0	100.0	100.0
65-69 years old	2,936	3,139	3,919	4,631	4,382	38.9	37.3	37.8	36.7	30.7
70-74 years old	2,197	2,322	2,873	3,464	3,860	29.1	27.6	27.7	27.4	27.0
75-79 years old	1,370	1,573	1,862	2,385	2,971	18.2	18.7	18.0	18.9	20.8
80-84 years old	673	883	1,026	1,306	1,739	8.9	10.5	9.9	10.3	12.2
85 years old and over	366	496	688	850	1,322	4.9	5.9	6.6	6.7	9.3
Females, 65 yrs. and over	9,133	11,693	15,338	18,348	20,608	100.0	100.0	100.0	100.0	100.0
65-69 years old	3,344	3,887	4,894	5,538	5,109	36.6	33.2	31.9	30.2	24.8
70-74 years old	2,577	3,145	3,968	4,549	4,892	28.2	26.9	25.9	24.8	23.7
75-79 years old	1,711	2,298	2,966	3,648	4,311	18.7	19.7	19.3	19.9	20.9
80-84 years old	928	1,429	1,928	2,422	2,996	10.2	12.2	12.6	13.2	14.5
85 years old and over	574	934	1,582	2,192	3,300	6.3	8.0	10.3	11.9	16.0

Source: "Population 65 Years Old and Over, by Age Group and Sex, 1960 to 1989, and Projections, 2000," *Statistical Abstract of the United States*, 1991, p. 37. Primary source: U.S. Bureau of the Census, *Current Population Reports*, series P-25, Nos. 519, 917, 1018, and 1057. As of July 1. Includes Armed Forces overseas. Projections are for middle series. These projections were prepared prior to the release of 1990 census results and are therefore not based on 1990 census data.

★ 620 ★

Projected Growth Rate of Population Over Age 65, 1950-2000

[Numbers in thousands]

	Total over 65	Increase	Percent increase
1950	12,397	x	x
1960	16,675	4,278	34.5
1970	20,087	3,412	20.5
1980	25,708	5,621	28.0

[Continued]

★ 620 ★

Projected Growth Rate of Population Over Age 65, 1950-2000

[Continued]

	Total over 65	Increase	Percent increase
1990	31,680	5,972	23.2
2000	35,410	3,730	11.8

Source: "Work and Workers in the Year 2000," *Workforce 2000: Work and Workers for the Twenty-First Century*, William B. Johnston and Arnold E. Packer, Hudson Institute, Indianapolis, Indiana, June, 1987, p. 80. Primary source: U.S. Bureau of the Census, *Current Population Reports*, series P-23, No. 138, Table 2-1, Hudson Institute.

★ 621 ★

Projected Percentage of Total Population by Race, 1985-2000

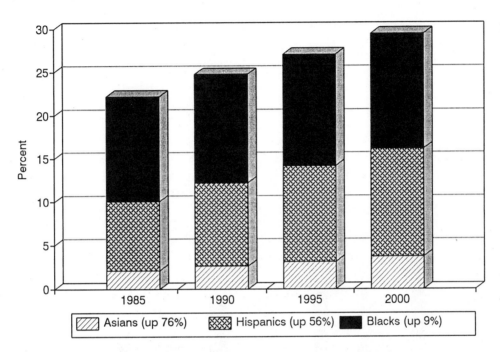

| | Asians (up 76%) | | Hispanics (up 56%) | | Blacks (up 9%) |

"Nearly one in three Americans will be a minority by year 2000."

[Numbers in percent]

	1985	1990	1995	2000
Blacks (up 9%)	12.2	12.6	12.9	13.3
Hispanics (up 56%)	8.0	9.6	11.1	12.5
Asians (up 76%)	2.1	2.6	3.1	3.7

Source: "Nine Forces Reshaping America," United way Strategic Institute, *The Futurist XXIV*, No. 4, July-August, 1990, p. 11. Primary source: Population Reference Bureau, 1986.

★ 622 ★

Financial Support of the Elderly, 2025

"By 2025 what economists call the dependency ratio—the proportion of pensioners 60 or older to all workers—will have roughly doubled in Japan, the U.S., and West Germany. If the present benefit systems are kept in place, U.S. programs for the elderly could consume 50% of the federal budget by then."

Source: "Many More Elderly to Carry," *Fortune* 121, No. 8, April 9, 1990, p. 71.

★ 623 ★

Share of Age Group 75 and Over in U.S. Population as Compared to Other Major Industrial Nations, 1980-2025

(In percent)

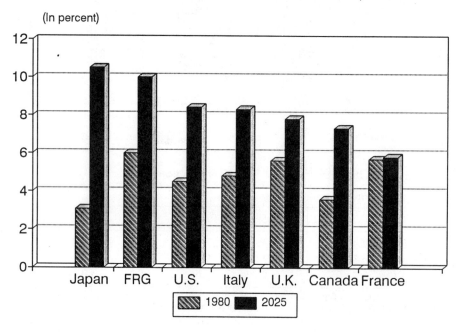

"[Worldwide, the] share of the very old (i.e., 75 and over) among the elderly will rise on average from 38 percent in 1980 to 42 percent by the year 2000."

[In percent]

	1980	2025
Japan	3.1	10.5
Federal Republic of Germany	6.0	10.0
United States	4.5	8.4
Italy	4.8	8.3
United Kingdom	5.6	7.8

[Continued]

★ 623 ★

Share of Age Group 75 and Over in U.S. Population as Compared to Other Major Industrial Nations, 1980-2025
[Continued]

	1980	2025
Canada	3.6	7.3
France	5.7	5.8

Source: "Population Dynamics in Seven Major Industrial Countries," *Aging and Social Expenditure in the Major Industrial Countries, 1980-2025,* Peter S. Heller et al, International Monetary Fund, Washington, D.C., September, 1986, p. 27. Projections are based on middle demographic data from census and public pension sources used by the countries concerned. Magnitudes estimated from published chart.

★ 624 ★

Population 85 Years and Older, 1990 and 2080

"If the Census Bureau is right, the number of people aged 85 or older will grow from 3.3 million today to 18.7 million in 2080. But if a Duke University demographer working with the National Institute on Aging is correct, the number of these oldest old in 2080 could actually be 72 million, a figure nearly four times as great as the Census Bureau projection."

1990	3.3 million
2080	
Estimate by Dr. Gregory Spencer, Census Bureau	18.7 million
Estimate by Dr. James Vaupel, Duke University	72 million

Source: "New Views on Life Spans Alter Forecasts on Elderly," Gina Kolata, *The New York Times* CXLII, No. 49, 152, November 16, 1992, p. A1. Primary source: First projection by Dr. Gregory Spencer, U.S. Bureau of the Census; second by Dr. James Vaupel, Duke university.

★ 625 ★

Female Population 18 to 34 Years Old, 1960-2080
[Numbers in thousands]

Year	Total	White	Black	Other races
Estimates				
1960	19,625	17,179	2,233	213
1965	21,415	18,709	2,438	269
1970	25,048	21,745	2,922	382
1975	29,704	25,501	3,607	596
1980	33,905	28,642	4,359	905

[Continued]

★ 625 ★

Female Population 18 to 34 Years Old, 1960-2080
[Continued]

Year	Total	White	Black	Other races
1985	35,284	29,357	4,791	1,136
1987	35,191	29,134	4,848	1,211
Projections				
1990	34,772	28,569	4,908	1,296
1995	32,375	26,189	4,759	1,426
2000	30,948	24,634	4,713	1,601
2005	31,195	24,530	4,851	1,816
2010	32,096	25,073	5,053	1,969
2020	31,799	24,417	5,181	2,200
2030	30,624	22,964	5,169	2,491
2040	31,031	22,994	5,275	2,760
2050	30,403	22,237	5,217	2,948
2080	28,783	20,579	4,841	3,363

Source: "Projections of the Population of the United States by Age, Sex, and Race: 1988 to 2080," *Current Population Reports*, series P-25, No. 1018, p. 12. Primary source: *Current Population Reports*, Series P-25, Nos. 519, 917, 1022; table 4; and unpublished data. Projection data from middle series. As of July 1. Includes Armed Forces overseas.

★ 626 ★

Female Proportion of Elderly Population, 1985-2020

[In percent].

Age	1985	2000	2020
Total 65 +	60.1	60.1	57.6
65-74 years	56.5	55.1	53.3
75-84 years	63.0	61.9	60.0
85+	72.0	73.3	72.0

Source: Personnel for Health Needs of the Elderly Through Year 2020, September 1987 Report to Congress, U.S. Department of Health and Human Services. Primary source: Social Security Administration, 1985.

★ 627 ★

Components of Population Change by Race, 1995-2025

Year and race	Population at start of period (1,000)	Total (Jan. 1-Dec. 31)					Per 1000 midyear population					
		Net increase[1]		Natural Increase		Net civilian immigration (1,000)	Net growth rate[1]	Natural increase				Net civil. immigr. rate
		Total (1,000)	Percent[2]	Births (1,000)	Deaths (1,000)			Total	Birth rate	Death rate	
All races												
1995	259,238	1,767	0.68	3,517	2,275	525	6.8	4.8	13.5	8.7	2.0
2000	267,498	1,522	0.57	3,389	2,367	500	5.7	3.8	12.6	8.8	1.9
2005	274,884	1,433	0.52	3,399	2,465	500	5.2	3.4	12.3	8.9	1.8
2010	281,894	1,351	0.48	3,485	2,634	500	4.8	3.0	1.23	9.3	1.8
2025	297,926	622	0.21	3,357	3,235	500	2.1	0.4	11.3	10.9	1.7
White												
1995	216,267	1,074	0.50	2,744	1,966	296	5.0	3.6	12.7	9.1	1.4
2000	221,087	837	0.38	2,602	2,038	273	3.8	2.5	11.7	9.2	1.2
2005	225,048	746	0.33	2,583	2,110	273	3.3	2.1	11.5	9.4	1.2
2010	228,637	674	0.29	2,639	2,238	273	2.9	1.8	11.5	9.8	1.2
2025	235,317	79	0.03	2,490	2,684	273	0.3	-0.8	10.6	11.4	1.2
Black												
1995	33,000	396	1.20	601	262	56	11.9	10.2	18.1	7.9	1.7
2000	34,939	379	1.08	597	272	54	10.8	9.2	17.0	7.7	1.5
2005	36,816	372	1.01	604	286	54	10.1	8.6	16.3	7.7	1.5
2010	38,653	358	0.93	616	312	54	9.2	7.8	15.9	8.0	1.4
2025	43,348	247	0.57	602	410	54	5.7	4.5	13.9	9.5	1.3
Other races												
1995	9,971	298	2.98	172	48	174	29.4	12.2	17.0	4.7	17.2
2000	11,472	305	2.66	190	58	173	26.3	11.4	16.4	5.0	14.9
2005	13,020	315	2.42	211	69	173	23.9	10.8	16.0	5.2	13.1
2010	14,604	319	2.18	230	84	173	21.6	9.9	15.6	5.7	11.7
2025	19,261	296	1.54	265	142	173	15.5	6.4	13.9	7.4	9.0

Source: "Projected Components of Population Change, by Race: 1995 to 2025," *Statistical Abstract of the United States*, 1991, p. 15. Primary source: U.S. Bureau of the Census, *Current Population Reports*, series P-25, No. 1018. *Notes:* Includes U.S. Armed Forces overseas. Projections are for middle series (series 14). 1. Includes overseas admissions into, less discharges from Armed Forces, not shown separately. 2. Percent of population at beginning of period.

★ 628 ★

Total Population by Race, 1994-2025

Year	By race (middle series)					
	Number (1,000)			Percent distribution		
	White	Black	Other races	White	Black	Other races
1994	215,714	32,801	9,923	83.5	12.7	3.8
1995	216,820	33,199	10,119	83.3	12.8	3.9
1996	217,862	33,592	10,418	83.2	12.8	4.0
1997	218,845	33,981	10,717	83.0	12.9	4.1
1998	219,773	34,366	11,017	82.9	13.0	4.2
1999	220,661	34,749	11,320	82.7	13.0	4.2
2000	221,514	35,129	11,624	82.6	13.1	4.3

[Continued]

★ 628 ★

Total Population by Race, 1994-2025
[Continued]

Year	By race (middle series)					
	Number (1,000)			Percent distribution		
	White	Black	Other races	White	Black	Other races
2005	225,424	37,003	13,177	81.8	13.4	4.8
2010	228,978	38,833	14,764	81.0	13.7	5.2
2015	232,081	40,564	16,352	80.3	14.0	5.7
2020	234,330	42,128	17,906	79.6	14.3	6.1
2025	235,369	43,473	19,410	78.9	14.6	6.5

Source: "Projections of Total Population, by Race: 1991 to 2025," *Statistical Abstract of the United States*, 1991, p. 15. Primary source: U.S. Bureau of the Census, *Current Population Reports*, series P-25, No. 1018. As of July 1. Includes Armed Forces abroad. For the series shown, the following assumptions were made about fertility (ultimate lifetime births per woman), mortality (ultimate lifetime expectancy in 2080), and immigration (ultimate yearly net immigration). Lowest series: 1.5 births per woman, 77.9 years, and 300,000 net immigration. Middle series: 1.8 births per woman, 81.2 years, and 500,000 immigration. Highest series: 2.2 births per woman, 88.0 years, and 800,000 net immigration. Zero migration series: 1.8 births per woman, 81.2 years. These projections were prepared prior to the release of 1990 census results and are therefore not based on 1990 census data. Original table also includes data for 1991-93.

★ 629 ★

Population by Race and Sex, 1988-2000

	1988	2000
Total females	125,995,000	137,076,000
Total males	120,054,000	131,191,000
Percent distribution		
Total population	100.0	100.0
White females	43.1	42.0
White males	41.3	40.5
Black females	6.5	6.8
Black males	5.9	6.3
Other females	1.7	2.2
Other males	1.6	2.1

Source: "American Women Today: A Statistical Portrait," *The American Woman, 1990-1991*, edited by Sara E. Rix, W. W. Norton & Company, Inc., New York, 1990, p. 364. Primary source: U.S. Bureau of the Census, January 1989, table 4. As of January 1989. Includes Armed Forces overseas. These projections were prepared prior to the release of 1990 census results and are therefore not based on 1990 census data.

★ 630 ★

Population Trends by Percent of Race, 1980 and 2080

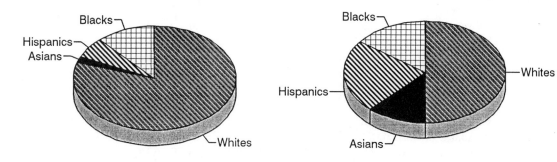

"Immigration and birth-rate trends of the 1980s are pointing toward dramatic changes in the U.S. population mix over the next century. If current patterns hold, slightly more than half of all Americans will be Hispanics, Asians and blacks by the year 2080."

	1980	2080
Whites	79.9	49.9
Hispanics	6.4	23.4
Blacks	11.7	14.7
Asians, others	2.0	12.0

Source: "Profile of Tomorrow's New U.S.," *U.S. News and World Report* 101, No. 21, November 24, 1986, p. 32. Primary source: U.S. News and World Report—Basic data: Population Reference Bureau, Inc.

★ 631 ★

African-American Age Distribution, 1985-2000

[Numbers in millions except where noted]

Age range	1985		1990		2000	
	Number	Percent	Number	Percent	Number	Percent
All ages	29.1	100.0	31.4	100.0	35.8	100.0
Male	13.8		14.9		17.0	
Female	15.3		16.5		18.7	
Infants/toddlers						
Under 5	3.1	11.0	3.2	10.0	3.1	9.0
Male	1.5		1.6		1.6	
Female	1.5		1.6		1.5	

[Continued]

★ 631 ★

African-American Age Distribution, 1985-2000
[Continued]

Age range	1985		1990		2000	
	Number	Percent	Number	Percent	Number	Percent
Childhood						
5-9 years	2.5	8.0	3.1	10.0	3.2	9.0
Male	1.3		1.6		1.6	
Female	1.2		1.5		1.6	
Early adolescence						
10-14 years	2.5	8.0	2.5	8.0	3.2	9.0
Male	1.3		1.3		1.6	
Female	1.2		1.2		1.6	
Late adolescence						
15-19 years	2.7	9.0	2.5	8.0	3.1	9.0
Male	1.4		1.3		1.6	
Female	1.3		1.3		1.5	
Young adulthood						
20-24 years	3.0	10.0	2.7	9.0	2.6	7.0
Male	1.5		1.4		1.3	
Female	1.5		1.4		1.3	
Adulthood						
25-39 years	7.1	24.0	8.2	26.0	8.3	23.0
Male	3.4		3.9		4.1	
Female	3.8		4.3		4.2	
Middle Years						
40-64	5.8	20.0	6.5	21.0	9.2	26.0
Male	2.7		2.8		4.2	
Female	3.1		3.7		5.0	
Seniors						
65-84 years	2.2	8.0	2.2	7.0	2.6	7.0
Male	1.0		.8		.9	
Female	1.3		1.4		1.7	
Elders						
85-over	189[1]	1.0	257[1]	1.0	412[1]	1.0
Male	60[1]		77[1]		110[1]	
Female	129[1]		180[1]		302[1]	
Median	26.2		27.7		30.2	

Source: "Understanding African-American Family Diversity," Andrew Billingsley, *State of Black America*, Janet Dewart, ed., National Urban League, Inc., 1990, p. 107. Primary source: U.S. Bureau of the Census, *Current Population Reports*, series P-25, No. 952. *Note:* 1. Numbers in thousands.

★ 632 ★

Blacks as a Percentage of the Total Population by Age Group, 1940-2020

"The Bureau of the Census predicts that the black proportion will rise from about one in eight in the 1980s to one in six by the middle of the next century, a change that will occur most rapidly at the younger ages."

Year	All	Under 15	25-54	65 and over
1940	9.7	11.5	9.4	6.8
1960	10.5	12.7	8.7	7.0
1980	11.7	14.8	10.7	8.2
2000	13.3	17.0	13.0	8.5
2020	14.9	18.4	15.3	9.9

Source: "Children and Families," *A Common Destiny: Blacks and American Society*, edited by Gerald David Jaynes and Robin M. Williams, Jr., National Academy Press, Washington, D.C., 1989, p. 548. Primary source: Decennial censuses (for 1940-1980) and U.S. Bureau of the Census projections (for 2000 and 2020).

★ 633 ★

Projections of the Total Hispanic Population, 1970-2000

1970	9,073,237
1980	14,608,673
1990	22,354,059
2000	29,500,000[1]

Source: "30 Million in 9 Years," *Hispanic Business* 13, No. 12, December, 1991 p. 27. Primary source: U.S. Bureau of the Census, *Decennial Censuses 1970-1990. Note:* 1. Forecast for the year 2000 is the average of high and low series projections.

★ 634 ★

Projections of the Hispanic Population by Age and Sex, 1995-2010

Age and sex	Population (1,000)				Percent distribution		Percent change	
	1995	2000	2005	2010	2000	2010	1990-2000	2000-2010
Total	22,550	25,223	27,959	30,795	100.0	100.0	26.8	22.1
Under 5 years old	2,412	2,496	2,644	2,852	9.9	9.3	9.4	14.3
5-17 years old	5,555	6,207	6,551	6,848	24.6	22.2	28.6	10.3
18-24 years old	2,511	2,767	3,254	3,599	11.0	11.7	15.9	30.1

[Continued]

★ 634 ★

Projections of the Hispanic Population by Age and Sex, 1995-2010
[Continued]

Age and sex	Population (1,000)				Percent distribution		Percent change	
	1995	2000	2005	2010	2000	2010	1990-2000	2000-2010
25-34 years old	3,717	3,804	4,036	4,526	15.1	14.7	4.8	19.0
35-44 years old	3,430	3,803	3,894	3,983	15.1	12.9	36.4	4.7
45-54 years old	2,165	2,811	3,440	3,806	11.1	12.4	68.5	35.4
55-64 years old	1,342	1,619	2,093	2,704	6.4	8.8	36.9	67.0
65-74 years old	894	1,041	1,183	1,432	4.1	4.7	47.2	37.6
75 years old and over	525	678	864	1,045	2.7	3.4	61.8	54.1
16 years old and over	15,322	17,419	19,753	22,131	69.0	71.9	29.5	27.1
Male	11,285	12,627	14,000	15,419	50.1	50.1	26.9	22.1
Female	11,265	12,596	13,960	15,376	49.9	49.9	26.7	22.1

Source: "Projections of the Hispanic Population, by Age and Sex: 1995 to 2010," *Statistical Abstract of the United States*, 1991, p. 14. Primary source: U.S. Bureau of the Census, *Current Population Reports*, series P-25, No. 995. As of July 1. Includes Armed Forces overseas. Data are for the middle series with the following assumptions about fertility (ultimate lifetime births per woman), mortality (ultimate life expectancy in 2080), and immigration (yearly net immigration): 1.9 births per woman, 81.0 years, and 143,000 net immigration. These projections were prepared prior to the release of 1990 census results and are therefore not based on 1990 census data.

Population Projections for U.S. States, Regions, and Major Cities

★ 635 ★

Population and Average Annual Rates of Growth for Major U.S. Cities, 1989-2000

City	Rank	Midyear population (1,000)				Average annual growth rate (percent)			Area (square miles)	Density 1989 (pop. per square mile)
		1989	1990	1995	2000	1989-1990	1990-1995	1995-2000		
New York	1	14,618	14,622	14,638	14,648	0.03	0.02	0.01	1,274	11,473
Los Angeles	2	9,974	10,060	10,414	10,714	0.86	0.69	0.57	1,110	8,985
Chicago	3	6,523	6,526	6,541	6,568	0.05	0.05	0.08	762	8,560
Philadelphia	4	4,011	4,007	3,988	3,979	-0.09	-0.10	-0.05	471	8,515
San Francisco	5	3,924	3,958	4,104	4,214	0.87	0.72	0.53	428	9,167
Miami	6	3,359	3,421	3,679	3,894	1.82	1.45	1.14	448	7,498
Detroit[1]	7	3,022	2,995	2,865	2,735	-0.90	-0.89	-0.93	468	6,457
Dallas	8	2,689	2,743	2,972	3,257	1.98	1.60	1.83	419	6,418
Washington	9	2,529	2,547	2,637	2,707	0.73	0.69	0.52	357	7,082
Boston	10	2,473	2,475	2,480	2,485	0.08	0.04	0.04	303	8,162
Houston	11	2,258	2,298	2,456	2,651	1.74	1.33	1.53	310	7,284

Source: "Population and Average Annual Rates of Growth for World's 94 Largest Cities: 1989 to 2000," *Statistical Abstract of the United States*, 1991, pp. 835-36. Primary source: U.S. Bureau of the Census, *World Population Profile: 1989. Notes:* - Represents zero. Cities are defined as population clusters of continuous built-up area with a population density of at least 50,000 persons per square mile. Original table also includes data for world's 94 largest cities. 1. Includes Windsor, Canada.

★ 636 ★

A Projection of Population Growth in U.S. Cities as Compared to Those in Other Countries, 1950 and 2000

"By the year 2000 there will be twenty-two cities of over 10 million people. In 1950 five of the ten largest cities in the world were in Europe and the United States. By the year 2000 there will be only one: New York City."

Source: "Triumph of the Individual," *Megatrends 2000: Ten New Directions for the 1990s,* by John Naisbitt and Patricia Aburdene, William Morrow and Company, Inc., New York, 1990, p. 307.

★ 637 ★

Projections of White and Black Populations by State, 2000

Region, division, and state	White Number (1,000)				Black Number (1,000)				Black Percent of total population			
	Series A	Series B	Series C	Series D	Series A	Series B	Series C	Series D	Series A	Series B	Series C	Series D
U.S.	221,146	221,146	221,146	221,146	35,005	35,005	35,005	35,005	13.1	13.1	13.1	13.1
Northeast	44,433	43,201	43,805	45,202	6,355	6,277	6,285	6,691	12.1	12.3	12.2	12.5
New England	12,981	12,511	12,791	12,623	705	688	695	735	5.0	5.1	5.0	5.4
Maine	1,320	1,292	1,337	1,240	5	4	5	5	0.4	0.3	0.3	0.4
New Hampshire	1,375	1,227	1,341	1,124	11	9	10	8	0.8	0.7	0.8	0.7
Vermont	608	584	608	584	3	3	3	3	0.5	0.5	0.5	0.5
Massachusetts	5,650	5,437	5,473	5,685	337	317	324	350	5.5	5.4	5.4	5.7
Rhode Island	972	937	970	967	45	44	45	49	4.3	4.3	4.3	4.7
Connecticut	3,056	3,034	3,062	3,023	303	311	308	320	8.9	9.1	9.0	9.4
Mid Atlantic	31,451	30,690	31,014	32,579	5,650	5,590	5,590	5,956	14.7	14.9	14.8	14.9
New York	14,041	13,695	13,716	15,085	3,165	3,123	3,112	3,469	17.6	17.8	17.7	17.9
New Jersey	6,717	6,503	6,601	6,639	1,315	1,300	1,304	1,273	15.7	16.0	15.8	15.5
Pennsylvania	10,693	10,492	10,697	10,855	1,169	1,167	1,174	1,214	9.7	9.8	9.7	9.9
Midwest	52,551	53,278	53,692	55,925	6,570	6,632	6,673	6,723	10.9	10.8	10.8	10.5
East North Central	36,024	36,200	36,845	38,426	5,606	5,648	5,696	5,705	13.2	13.2	13.1	12.6
Ohio	9,502	9,438	9,648	9,983	1,294	1,299	1,310	1,311	11.8	12.0	11.8	11.5
Indiana	5,102	5,105	5,227	5,311	525	524	533	526	9.2	9.2	9.1	8.9
Illinois	9,289	9,406	9,436	10,153	2,020	2,035	2,032	2,115	17.2	17.2	17.1	16.6
Michigan	7,652	7,610	7,923	8,174	1,495	1,505	1,540	1,478	16.0	16.1	15.9	15.0
Wisconsin	4,478	4,641	4,610	4,805	272	285	282	275	5.6	5.7	5.7	5.3
West North Central	16,527	17,078	16,847	17,500	964	985	977	1,018	5.4	5.3	5.3	5.3
Minnesota	4,328	4,327	4,372	4,418	79	82	82	84	1.7	1.8	1.8	1.8
Iowa	2,465	2,709	2,581	2,909	56	65	60	63	2.2	2.3	2.3	2.1
Missouri	4,782	4,746	4,808	4,718	609	600	606	627	11.1	11.1	11.0	11.5
North Dakota	562	658	580	688	4	4	4	4	0.6	0.6	0.6	0.6
South Dakota	634	662	641	690	3	4	3	3	0.4	0.5	0.5	0.4
Nebraska	1,458	1,570	1,497	1,632	56	62	59	66	3.6	3.8	3.7	3.8
Kansas	2,300	2,407	2,369	2,444	157	167	163	171	6.2	6.3	6.2	6.3
South	75.003	74,835	74,040	71,405	18,493	18,463	18,408	18,239	19.3	19.4	19.5	19.9
South Atlantic	39,859	36,239	38,010	33,803	10,902	10,515	10,739	10,123	21.0	22.0	21.5	22.5
Delaware	617	537	582	549	164	151	158	139	20.4	21.4	20.8	19.7

[Continued]

★ 637 ★

Projections of White and Black Populations by State, 2000
[Continued]

Region, division, and state	White Number (1,000)				Black Number (1,000)				Black Percent of total population			
	Series A	Series B	Series C	Series D	Series A	Series B	Series C	Series D	Series A	Series B	Series C	Series D
Maryland	3,844	3,403	3,638	3,414	1,535	1,476	1,520	1,326	27.4	29.1	28.3	26.9
District of Columbia	180	179	179	192	405	399	396	455	68.1	67.9	67.7	69.0
Virginia	5,682	5,207	5,492	5,004	1,373	1,338	1,364	1,254	18.9	19.8	19.3	19.4
West Virginia	1,597	1,817	1,660	1,886	43	51	45	59	2.6	2.7	2.6	3.0
North Carolina	5,821	5,410	5,633	5,043	1,685	1,620	1,655	1,574	21.8	22.4	22.1	23.1
South Carolina	2,729	2,663	2,718	2,515	1,187	1,189	1,194	1,181	30.0	30.5	30.2	31.6
Georgia	5,734	5,171	5,504	4,824	2,152	2,056	2,117	1,950	26.9	28.1	27.4	28.3
Florida	13,657	11,852	12,603	10,375	2,358	2,235	2,289	2,184	14.5	15.6	15.1	17.1
East South Central	12,739	13,090	13,113	12,754	3,353	3,360	3,367	3,504	20.6	20.2	20.2	21.3
Kentucky	3,376	3,557	3,490	3,638	289	304	297	306	7.8	7.8	7.8	7.7
Tennessee	4,464	4,445	4,570	4,220	908	891	910	884	16.7	16.5	16.4	17.1
Alabama	3,175	3,276	3,297	3,140	1,133	1,148	1,150	1,197	26.0	25.7	25.6	27.3
Mississippi	1,724	1,813	1,756	1,757	1,023	1,017	1,010	1,117	36.9	35.6	36.2	38.5
West South Central	22,405	25,505	22,917	24,848	4,238	4,587	4,302	4,612	15.5	14.8	15.4	15.2
Arkansas	2,068	2,174	2,124	2,053	401	402	399	452	16.0	15.4	15.6	17.8
Louisiana	2,686	3,262	2,777	3,254	1,380	1,510	1,402	1,567	33.3	31.0	32.9	31.8
Oklahoma	2,440	3,035	2,539	2,921	205	250	213	259	7.0	6.9	7.0	7.4
Texas	15,211	17,035	15,477	16,621	2,252	2,426	2,288	2,333	12.6	12.2	12.6	12.0
West	49,160	49,833	49,610	48,614	3,587	3,633	3,639	3,352	6.1	6.1	6.1	5.8
Mountain	13,884	14,555	13,992	13,764	419	431	423	413	2.8	2.7	2.8	2.7
Montana	693	836	712	799	2	2	2	2	0.2	0.2	0.2	0.2
Idaho	977	1,163	1,023	1,121	5	6	6	6	0.5	0.5	0.5	0.5
Wyoming	391	557	411	528	4	5	4	5	0.9	0.8	0.9	0.9
Colorado	3,182	3,583	3,294	3,379	141	162	147	151	4.1	4.2	4.2	4.1
New Mexico	1,513	1,585	1,509	1,483	29	30	29	31	1.7	1.7	1.7	1.8
Arizona	4,154	3,711	3,987	3,404	126	113	120	115	2.7	2.7	2.7	3.0
Utah	1,757	1,973	1,833	2,056	12	14	13	16	0.6	0.7	0.7	0.7
Nevada	1,219	1,146	1,223	994	101	98	101	87	7.2	7.4	7.2	7.5
Pacific	35,275	35,278	35,617	34,850	3,168	3,202	3,217	2,939	7.2	7.3	7.2	6.8
Washington	4,666	4,973	4,921	4,527	125	140	137	142	2.4	2.5	2.5	2.8
Oregon	2,688	2,968	2,856	2,754	50	56	54	52	1.7	1.8	1.7	1.7
California	27,032	26,401	26,994	26,718	2,945	2,958	2,981	2,700	7.7	7.9	7.9	6.8
Alaska	446	488	401	463	22	23	21	22	3.6	3.5	3.8	3.6
Hawaii	444	448	446	388	25	24	24	22	1.8	1.8	1.8	1.8

Source: "White and Black Population Projections, by State: 2000," *Statistical Abstract of the United States*, 1991, p. 26. Primary source: U.S. Bureau of the Census, *Current Population Reports*, series P-25, No. 1053. As of July 1. These projections were prepared prior to the release of 1990 census results and are therefore not based on 1990 census data. Series projections derive from such data as births and deaths, school statistics from State departments of education and parochial school systems, and Federal income tax returns.

★ 638 ★

State Population Projections by Age, 2000

[Numbers in thousands]

Region, division, and state	Under 18 years				18-64 years				65 years and over			
	Series A	Series B	Series C	Series D	Series A	Series B	Series C	Series D	Series A	Series B	Series C	Series D
U.S.	65,713	65,715	65,716	65,714	167,156	167,147	167,152	167,149	34,884	34,884	34,876	34,880
Northeast	12,229	11,787	12,006	12,148	32,841	31,892	32,329	33,617	7,351	7,323	7,328	7,817
New England	3,249	3,082	3,181	3,044	8,869	8,516	8,720	8,652	1,885	1,886	1,888	1,950
Maine	333	319	335	296	834	817	845	789	176	178	179	176
New Hampshire	351	303	339	268	906	804	881	736	153	148	153	143
Vermont	156	147	155	143	391	375	392	379	72	71	72	72
Massachusetts	1,393	1,317	1,336	1,360	3,913	3,738	3,775	3,935	854	853	849	895
Rhode Island	236	224	235	232	660	633	657	660	152	152	153	157
Connecticut	780	772	781	745	2,165	2,149	2,170	2,153	478	484	482	507
Mid Atlantic	8,980	8,705	8,825	9,104	23,972	23,376	23,609	24,965	5,466	5,437	5,440	5,867
New York	4,200	4,085	4,091	4,496	11,307	11,024	11,040	12,178	2,459	2,439	2,431	2,738
New Jersey	2,003	1,922	1,961	1,868	5,228	5,053	5,131	5,161	1,152	1,143	1,146	1,200
Pennsylvania	2,777	2,698	2,773	2,740	7,437	7,299	7,438	7,626	1,855	1,855	1,863	1,929
Midwest	15,138	15,393	15,553	15,755	37,375	37,865	38,171	39,934	8,012	8,086	8,089	8,541
East North Central	10,682	10,731	10,975	11,037	26,398	26,527	26,981	28,224	5,478	5,520	5,542	5,913
Ohio	2,694	2,671	2,746	2,741	6,766	6,723	6,867	7,131	1,469	1,475	1,483	1,563
Indiana	1,427	1,424	1,469	1,428	3,542	3,538	3,624	3,713	727	734	738	769
Illinois	2,981	3,016	3,031	3,210	7,265	7,355	7,372	7,927	1,477	1,485	1,484	1,628
Michigan	2,365	2,350	2,468	2,386	5,860	5,832	6,061	6,237	1,140	1,148	1,163	1,255
Wisconsin	1,215	1,270	1,261	1,272	2,965	3,079	3,057	3,216	665	678	674	698
West North Central	4,456	4,662	4,578	4,718	10,977	11,340	11,190	11,710	2,534	2,566	2,547	2,628
Minnesota	1,148	1,146	1,164	1,150	2,834	2,835	2,864	2,916	584	588	587	606
Iowa	608	692	650	727	1,536	1,700	1,613	1,848	404	416	408	438
Missouri	1,352	1,335	1,358	1,327	3,351	3,320	3,366	3,336	769	771	771	771
North Dakota	145	183	153	189	366	427	377	445	85	88	85	94
South Dakota	190	202	194	208	421	439	427	459	103	105	103	109
Nebraska	385	430	402	438	925	998	951	1,053	228	233	229	238
Kansas	628	674	657	679	1,544	1,621	1,592	1,653	361	365	364	372
South	23,259	23,271	22,936	22,756	59,581	59,452	58,900	57,113	12,735	12,660	12,649	11,881
South Atlantic	12,190	10,891	11,543	10,406	32,445	29,816	31,135	28,154	7,294	7,063	7,167	6,405
Delaware	199	169	186	170	501	440	475	439	101	98	100	94
Maryland	1,373	1,207	1,299	1,119	3,613	3,266	3,459	3,194	622	600	612	624
District of Columbia	106	102	102	148	409	407	405	427	80	79	79	85
Virginia	1,734	1,554	1,660	1,457	4,734	4,394	4,603	4,233	807	793	803	791
West Virginia	375	446	397	453	1,025	1,171	1,067	1,229	251	264	254	276
North Carolina	1,809	1,641	1,729	1,525	4,910	4,601	4,769	4,353	997	984	994	924
South Carolina	987	960	982	929	2,505	2,465	2,504	2,369	469	469	470	446
Georgia	2,087	1,861	1,995	1,741	5,094	4,661	4,919	4,365	825	808	820	776
Florida	3,520	2,951	3,193	2,864	9,654	8,411	8,934	7,545	3,142	2,968	3,035	2,389
East South Central	3,992	4,091	4,109	4,055	10,116	10,349	10,371	10,242	2,135	2,163	2,156	2,122
Kentucky	887	948	926	967	2,312	2,437	2,390	2,504	491	501	496	507
Tennessee	1,256	1,233	1,283	1,184	3,453	3,436	3,529	3,275	714	717	721	698
Alabama	1,093	1,130	1,140	1,090	2,687	2,757	2,774	2,722	578	587	585	571
Mississippi	756	780	760	814	1,664	1,719	1,678	1,741	352	358	354	346
West South Central	7,077	8,289	7,284	8,295	17,020	19,287	17,394	18,717	3,306	3,434	3,326	3,354
Arkansas	618	647	633	639	1,512	1,577	1,545	1,540	379	391	384	365
Louisiana	1,105	1,356	1,147	1,381	2,536	2,991	2,608	3,015	501	521	504	531
Oklahoma	683	919	724	861	1,818	2,253	1,890	2,173	423	452	427	448
Texas	4,671	5,367	4,780	5,414	11,154	12,466	11,351	11,989	2,003	2,070	2,011	2,010

[Continued]

★ 638 ★

State Population Projections by Age, 2000

[Continued]

Region, division, and state	Under 18 years				18-64 years				65 years and over			
	Series A	Series B	Series C	Series D	Series A	Series B	Series C	Series D	Series A	Series B	Series C	Series D
West	15,087	15,264	15,221	15,055	37,359	37,938	37,752	36,485	6,786	6,815	6,810	6,641
Mountain	4,025	4,268	4,065	4,118	9,410	9,865	9,485	9,245	1,776	1,788	1,772	1,680
Montana	179	231	187	212	465	561	478	537	100	105	100	110
Idaho	276	347	294	334	614	728	641	697	118	127	120	124
Wyoming	109	169	116	152	263	372	276	352	38	41	38	46
Colorado	813	940	849	882	2,242	2,534	2,325	2,376	370	386	373	390
New Mexico	485	513	483	474	1,057	1,105	1,051	1,032	193	200	193	194
Arizona	1,188	1,031	1,131	996	2,796	2,502	2,688	2,297	649	616	638	514
Utah	651	743	683	789	1,036	1,172	1,084	1,213	159	167	161	163
Nevada	324	294	322	279	937	891	942	741	149	146	149	139
Pacific	11,062	10,996	11,156	10,937	27,949	28,073	28,267	27,240	5,010	5,027	5,038	4,961
Washington	1,225	1,333	1,316	1,192	3,364	3,584	3,547	3,281	602	618	613	602
Oregon	689	781	745	704	1,839	2,033	1,955	1,901	375	393	385	381
California	8,664	8,379	8,626	8,601	21,471	21,135	21,516	20,847	3,829	2,813	3,838	3,770
Alaska	174	191	158	176	397	437	367	398	29	27	26	40
Hawaii	310	312	311	264	878	884	882	813	175	176	176	168

Source: "Population Projections, by Age—States: 2000," *Statistical Abstract of the United States*, 1991, p. 25. Primary source: U.S. Bureau of the Census, *Current Population Reports*, series P-25, No. 1053. As of July 1. These projections were prepared prior to the release of 1990 census results and are therefore not based on 1990 census data. Series projections derive from such data as births and deaths, school statistics from State departments of education and parochial school systems, and Federal income tax returns.

★ 639 ★

State Population Projections, 1995 and 2000

[Numbers in thousands]

Region, division, and state	1995				2000			
	Series A	Series B	Series C	Series D	Series A	Series B	Series C	Series D
U.S.	259,620	259,620	259,620	259,620	267,748	267,748	267,748	267,748
Northeast	51,665	50,976	51,357	52,553	52,419	51,005	51,662	53,583
New England	13,575	13,320	13,498	13,427	14,002	13,486	13,788	13,647
Maine	1,295	1,275	1,301	1,243	1,344	1,313	1,359	1,262
New Hampshire	1,276	1,196	1,270	1,128	1,410	1,255	1,373	1,148
Vermont	597	582	597	582	619	594	619	593
Massachusetts	6,032	5,913	5,939	6,096	6,159	5,909	5,959	6,190
Rhode Island	1,021	1,005	1,027	1,030	1,048	1,010	1,046	1,049
Connecticut	3,354	3,349	3,363	3,348	3,422	3,405	3,432	3,405
Mid Atlantic	38,090	37,656	37,859	39,126	38,417	37,519	37,874	39,936
New York	17,909	17,724	17,727	18,857	17,966	17,548	17,563	19,412
New Jersey	8,100	7,991	8,062	8,050	8,382	8,119	8,238	8,229
Pennsylvania	12,080	11,942	12,070	12,219	12,069	11,852	12,073	12,295
Midwest	60,712	60,914	61,213	62,665	60,528	61,342	61,815	64,231
East North Central	42,678	42,631	43,066	44,079	42,557	42,779	43,499	45,176
Ohio	10,958	10,889	11,027	11,237	10,930	10,869	11,096	11,436
Indiana	5,688	5,656	5,738	5,785	5,696	5,697	5,831	5,910

[Continued]

State Population Projections, 1995 and 2000

[Continued]

Region, division, and state	1995				2000			
	Series A	Series B	Series C	Series D	Series A	Series B	Series C	Series D
Illinois	11,759	11,795	11,814	12,337	11,722	11,856	11,887	12,765
Michigan	9,364	9,317	9,534	9,653	9,365	9,331	9,692	9,879
Wisconsin	4,908	4,974	4,954	5,067	4,844	5,027	4,993	5,186
West North Central	18,035	18,283	18,146	18,586	17,971	18,563	18,316	19,055
Minnesota	4,501	4,481	4,513	4,542	4,566	4,568	4,615	4,672
Iowa	2,703	2,825	2,741	2,949	2,549	2,808	2,671	3,013
Missouri	5,353	5,320	5,369	5,331	5,473	5,425	5,495	5,434
North Dakota	631	687	635	705	596	698	615	728
South Dakota	719	733	720	751	715	746	723	775
Nebraska	1,582	1,641	1,595	1,682	1,539	1,660	1,583	1,730
Kansas	2,546	2,597	2,574	2,626	2,534	2,658	2,613	2,703
South	91,227	91,317	90,781	89,132	95,575	95,382	94,483	91,750
South Atlantic	47,859	45,767	47,034	44,106	51,930	47,770	49,843	44,966
Delaware	739	690	723	690	802	706	760	704
Maryland	5,180	4,908	5,090	4,830	5,608	5,073	5,370	4,936
District of Columbia	592	593	590	645	595	588	586	660
Virginia	6,758	6,475	6,676	6,320	7,275	6,741	7,066	6,482
West Virginia	1,749	1,883	1,779	1,929	1,651	1,882	1,717	1,958
North Carolina	7,197	6,943	7,102	6,702	7,717	7,226	7,492	6,803
South Carolina	3,772	3,733	3,769	3,645	3,962	3,894	3,956	3,743
Georgia	7,288	6,949	7,196	6,682	8,005	7,329	7,733	6,882
Florida	14,583	13,593	14,110	12,663	16,315	14,330	15,162	12,798
East South Central	15,978	16,125	16,146	16,020	16,242	16,603	16,636	16,419
Kentucky	3,740	3,832	3,785	3,886	3,689	3,887	3,813	3,978
Tennessee	5,239	5,199	5,288	5,068	5,424	5,386	5,533	5,156
Alabama	4,282	4,331	4,345	4,279	4,358	4,474	4,498	4,383
Mississippi	2,717	2,764	2,727	2,787	2,772	2,856	2,791	2,902
West South Central	27,390	29,425	27,602	29,006	27,402	31,009	28,004	30,365
Arkansas	2,473	2,528	2,501	2,486	2,509	2,615	2,562	2,544
Louisiana	4,274	4,690	4,316	4,725	4,141	4,868	4,258	4,927
Oklahoma	3,072	3,466	3,105	3,389	2,924	3,624	3,042	3,481
Texas	17,572	18,741	17,680	18,406	17,828	19,903	18,142	19,413
West	56,015	56,412	56,269	55,271	59,226	60,019	59,788	58,186
Mountain	14,515	14,940	14,581	14,381	15,207	15,922	15,326	15,048
Montana	774	861	780	839	744	897	766	858
Idaho	1,018	1,126	1,036	1,093	1,008	1,202	1,056	1,156
Wyoming	439	546	446	523	409	582	430	550
Colorado	3,407	3,656	3,460	3,525	3,424	3,861	3,548	3,649
New Mexico	1,639	1,697	1,642	1,624	1,735	1,818	1,727	1,701
Arizona	4,149	3,899	4,097	3,692	4,633	4,149	4,457	3,809

[Continued]

★ 639 ★

State Population Projections, 1995 and 2000

[Continued]

Region, division, and state	1995				2000			
	Series A	Series B	Series C	Series D	Series A	Series B	Series C	Series D
Utah	1,807	1,930	1,841	1,963	1,845	2,082	1,929	2,166
Nevada	1,283	1,225	1,279	1,122	1,409	1,331	1,414	1,159
Pacific	41,500	41,473	41,688	40,890	44,019	44,097	44,462	43,138
Washington	5,052	5,185	5,157	4,919	5,191	5,535	5,477	5,076
Oregon	2,887	3,032	2,960	2,906	2,903	3,206	3,086	2,986
California	31,749	31,390	31,780	31,307	33,963	33,328	33,981	33,218
Alaska	560	609	538	578	599	655	550	614
Hawaii	1,253	1,256	1,253	1,180	1,362	1,373	1,368	1,244

Source: "State Population Projections: 1995 and 2000," *Statistical Abstract of the United States*, 1991, p. 24. Primary source: U.S. Bureau of the Census, *Current Population Reports*, series P-25, No. 1053. As of July 1. These projections were prepared prior to the release of 1990 census results and are therefore not based on 1990 census data. Series projections derive from such data as births and deaths, school statistics from State departments of education and parochial school systems, and Federal income tax returns.

★ 640 ★

State Population Projections, 2000-2010

[Numbers in thousands]

Region, division, and state	2000	2010
U.S.	269,838	284,752
Northeast	51,811	52,496
N.E.	13,776	14,243
ME	1,271	1,308
NH	1,333	1,455
VT	591	608
MA	6,087	6,255
RI	1,049	1,085
CT	3,445	3,532
M.A.	38,035	38,253
NY	17,986	18,139
NJ	8,546	8,980
PA	11,503	11,134
Midwest	59,595	59,018
E.N.C.	41,745	41,111
OH	10,629	10,397
IN	5,502	5,409
IL	11,580	11,495
MI	9,250	9,097
WI	4,784	4,713

[Continued]

★ 640 ★

State Population Projections, 2000-2010
[Continued]

Region, division, and state	2000	2010
W.N.C.	17,850	17,907
MN	4,490	4,578
IA	2,549	2,382
MO	5,383	5,521
ND	629	611
SD	714	722
NE	1,556	1,529
KS	2,529	2,564
South	99,009	107,614
S.A.	50,002	55,111
DE	734	790
MD	5,274	5,688
DC	634	672
VA	6,877	7,410
WV	1,722	1,617
NC	7,483	8,154
SC	3,906	4,205
GA	7,957	9,045
FL	15,415	17,530
E.S.C.	16,286	16,847
KY	3,733	3,710
TN	5,266	5,500
AL	4,410	4,609
MS	2,877	3,028
W.S.C.	32,721	35,656
AR	4,618	5,319
LA	4,516	4,545
OK	3,376	3,511
TX	20,211	22,281
West	59,423	65,624
Mt	16,023	17,680
MT	794	794
ID	1,047	1,079
WY	489	487
CO	3,813	4,098
NM	1,968	2,248
AZ	4,618	5,319
UT	1,991	2,171
NV	1,303	1,484
Pac	43,400	47,944
WA	4,991	5,282

[Continued]

★ 640 ★

State Population Projections, 2000-2010
[Continued]

Region, division, and state	2000	2010
OR	2,877	2,991
CA	33,500	37,347
AK	687	765
HI	1,345	1,559

Source: Almanac of the 50 States: Basic Data Profiles with Comparative Tables, Edith R. Horner, ed., Information Publications, Palo Alto, California, 1992, p. 424. Primary source: U.S. Bureau of the Census, *Current Population Reports*, series P-25, No. 1053.

★ 641 ★

State Populations Under Age 18, Ranked by Percent Minority, 1990-2010

Minorities include blacks, Asians, and other races as well as white Hispanics. Since the Census Bureau's state population projections include only "whites" and "blacks," projections for racial minorities were estimated "by subtracting 'whites' from the total population in each state"; white Hispanics were then reallocated from "white" to "minority" using the bureau's Hispanic population projections series (*Current Population Reports*, series P-25, No. 995). Using middle series projections, white Hispanics under age 18 in 1990, 2000, and 2010 were "distributed among the states according to the 1980 census distribution of white and 'other' Hispanics," and the percent white Hispanic was added "to the percent black and 'other' races in order to estimate the minority share of the population under age 18 in each state."

[Numbers in thousands]

| | 1990 | | 2000 | | 2010 | | Change from 1990 to 2010 | |
	All children under 18	Percent minority	All children under 18	Percent minority	All children under 18	Percent minority	All children under 18 (percent change)	Minority share (percentage point change)
Total	64,031	30.7	65,717	34.0	62,644	38.2	-2.2	7.5
District of Columbia	121	89.7	111	90.9	105	93.2	-13.2	3.6
Hawaii	284	75.5	296	76.4	310	79.5	9.2	4.0
New Mexico	487	67.0	569	70.0	595	76.5	22.2	9.5
Texas	5,065	47.1	5,415	51.9	5,418	56.9	7.0	9.8
California	7,581	46.4	8,402	51.4	8,520	56.9	12.4	10.5
Florida	2,807	46.4	3,244	48.6	3,270	53.4	16.5	7.0
New York	4,246	39.9	4,189	45.8	3,862	52.8	-9.0	12.9
Louisiana	1,324	43.9	1,229	47.3	1,118	50.3	-15.6	6.4
Mississippi	800	47.6	791	48.8	749	49.9	-6.4	2.4
New Jersey	1,861	36.6	2,037	40.2	1,935	45.7	4.0	9.0
Maryland	1,149	38.5	1,267	40.2	1,220	42.7	6.2	4.2
Illinois	3,031	32.7	2,947	36.8	2,684	41.7	-11.4	9.0
South Carolina	946	39.9	968	39.6	931	40.1	-1.6	0.2
Georgia	1,804	36.2	2,056	36.4	2,116	37.9	17.3	1.7
Arizona	1,015	32.3	1,191	33.6	1,229	37.1	21.1	4.8
Delaware	165	29.7	179	32.9	177	37.0	7.3	7.3
Alabama	1,119	34.5	1,111	34.8	1,046	35.6	-6.5	1.1
Nevada	257	27.4	286	30.0	288	33.4	12.1	6.0

[Continued]

★ 641 ★

State Populations Under Age 18, Ranked by Percent Minority, 1990-2010
[Continued]

	1990		2000		2010		Change from 1990 to 2010	
	All children under 18	Percent minority	All children under 18	Percent minority	All children under 18	Percent minority	All children under 18 (percent change)	Minority share (percentage point change)
North Carolina	1,635	32.3	1,723	32.3	1,684	33.2	3.0	0.9
Colorado	886	25.3	924	28.9	893	33.1	0.8	7.7
Alaska	176	27.5	201	29.5	208	32.7	18.2	5.2
Virginia	1,485	28.5	1,607	29.4	1,549	31.1	4.3	2.6
Michigan	2,440	22.8	2,347	25.5	2,094	29.2	-14.2	6.3
Oklahoma	873	22.1	838	24.8	795	27.5	-8.9	5.4
Connecticut	751	20.8	781	23.4	715	27.0	-4.8	6.1
Arkansas	643	25.5	621	26.1	576	26.8	-10.4	1.3
Tennessee	1,237	23.2	1,204	24.1	1,125	25.3	-9.1	2.1
Ohio	2,783	16.7	2,631	18.6	2,349	20.8	-15.6	4.2
Wyoming	151	12.3	137	17.8	125	20.2	-17.2	7.9
Missouri	1,330	17.3	1,331	18.5	1,236	19.9	-7.1	2.6
South Dakota	200	14.4	193	16.2	180	19.8	-10.0	5.3
Washington	1,173	14.7	1,163	16.9	1,098	19.5	-6.4	4.8
Kansas	654	14.5	633	17.1	585	19.3	-10.6	4.9
Indiana	1,456	14.8	1,382	16.7	1,242	19.2	-14.7	4.3
Pennsylvania	2,765	15.4	2,609	16.7	2,260	18.7	-18.3	3.3
Rhode Island	228	12.9	236	15.5	222	18.6	-2.6	5.7
Massachusetts	1,315	13.5	1,368	15.5	1,267	18.2	-3.7	4.7
Oregon	692	11.8	677	14.1	637	16.8	-7.9	4.9
Wisconsin	1,262	11.5	1,208	13.7	1,067	16.6	-15.5	5.1
Montana	220	10.9	198	13.2	181	15.4	-17.7	4.5
Kentucky	979	11.3	906	12.6	818	14.1	-16.4	2.8
Nebraska	423	9.4	398	10.8	358	13.1	-15.4	3.6
Utah	673	9.3	715	11.2	740	12.4	10.0	3.1
Minnesota	1,131	7.7	1,138	9.1	1,042	11.2	-7.9	3.5
Idaho	309	7.2	291	9.4	275	11.0	-11.0	3.8
North Dakota	182	8.3	157	8.6	138	10.0	-24.2	1.7
Iowa	715	5.6	622	7.0	529	8.7	-26.0	3.1
West Virginia	469	5.9	401	6.7	344	7.3	-26.7	1.4
New Hampshire	284	3.9	329	4.8	317	5.5	11.6	1.6
Vermont	144	3.8	150	4.7	138	5.4	-4.2	1.6
Maine	305	2.8	310	3.0	284	3.1	-6.9	0.3

Source: "All Our Children," Joe Schwartz and Thomas Exter, *American Demographics* 11, No. 5, May, 1989, pp. 36-7. Primary source: *American Demographics* estimates and "Projections of the Population of States by Age, Sex, and Race: 1988 to 2010," *Current Population Reports*, series P-25, No. 1017, U.S. Bureau of the Census, 1988.

Fertility and Birth Rates

★ 642 ★

Decrease in American Fertility Rates, 1960-2025

"An American woman reaching childbearing age in 1960 would expect 3.6 children; an identical woman in 1990 would expect only 1.9 children. The dramatic demographic change makes it almost inevitable that the American population will age rapidly over the next fifty years. By 2025, the share of the American population that is 65 or older will exceed the share of Florida's population that is of retirement age today."

Source: "An Aging Society: Opportunity or Challenge?" by David M. Cutler and others, *Brookings Papers on Economic Activity*, No. 1, 1990, p. 1.

★ 643 ★

Fertility Rates: Total Rates and Projections, 1960-2080
[Rates per 1,000 women.]

Year	Total	White	Black	Other races
Estimates				
1960	3,606	3,510	4,238[1]	(NA)
1965	2,882	2,764	3,624	(NA)
1970	2,432	2,338	2,949	(NA)
1975	1,770	1,685	2,184	(NA)
1980	1,849	1,745	2,211	(NA)
1985	1,840	1,752	2,170	(NA)
1987	1,824	1,749	2,156	2,147
1990	1,850	1,781	2,170	2,175
1995	1,849	1,779	2,130	2,137
2000	1,846	1,780	2,095	2,110
2005	1,845	1,783	2,064	2,083
2010	1,849	1,791	2,040	2,059
2020	1,846	1,800	1,987	2,003
2030	1,832	1,800	1,925	1,936
2040	1,817	1,800	1,862	1,868
2050	1,800	1,800	1,800	1,800
2080	1,800	1,800	1,800	1,800

Source: "Total Fertility Rates: 1960 to 2080," *Projections of the Population of the United States, by Age, Sex, and Race: 1988 to 2080*, p. 11. Primary source: National Center for Health Statistics, *Vital Statistics of the United States*, 1985, Vol. I, Natality (1988); tables A-4 to A-6; and unpublished data. *Notes:* NA stands for not available. 1. Black and other races. Projection data from middle series.

★ 644 ★

Projections in Fertility Rates, 1990-2010

Birth rates represent live births per 1,000 women in age group indicated. Projections are based on middle fertility assumptions (1.8 births per woman).

Age group	All races			White			Black			Other races		
	1990	2000	2010	1990	2000	2010	1990	2000	2010	1990	2000	2010
Total fertility rate	1,850	1,846	1,849	1,781	1,780	1,791	2,170	2,095	2,040	2,175	2,110	2,059
Birth rates												
10-14 years old	0.8	0.9	0.8	0.4	0.5	0.5	3.0	2.8	2.3	0.4	0.5	0.5
15-19 years old	49.3	46.6	45.2	41.5	40.3	40.0	90.8	80.2	71.6	39.9	39.0	38.9
20-24 years old	105.5	104.1	102.2	102.2	100.4	99.2	132.0	124.6	118.4	98.6	97.5	96.9
25-29 years old	110.9	113.0	115.0	111.4	113.3	115.2	104.6	107.5	110.5	124.9	124.7	124.5
30-34 years old	72.3	73.9	75.4	71.6	72.9	74.3	67.3	69.4	71.4	108.8	104.5	100.1
35-39 years old	26.0	26.2	26.7	24.4	24.7	25.1	29.5	29.0	28.6	48.9	45.3	41.9
40-44 years old	5.0	4.3	4.2	4.5	3.8	3.8	6.8	5.4	5.1	12.6	9.6	8.4
45-49 years old	0.2	0.2	0.2	0.1	0.1	0.1	0.2	0.2	0.2	1.0	0.9	0.7

Source: "Projected Fertility Rates, by Race and Age Group: 1990 to 2010," *Statistical Abstract of the United States*, 1991, p. 65. Primary source: U.S. Bureau of the Census, *Current Population Reports*, series P-25, No. 1018.

★ 645 ★

Total Fertility Rate Projections by Alternative, 1990-2011

Includes the populations of Puerto Rico, Guam, American Samoa, the Virgin Islands, and U.S. citizens living abroad. The total fertility rate is defined as "the average number of children that would be born to a woman if she were to survive the childbearing period and were to experience the age-specific central birth rates for the tabulated year throughout the period." Alternatives in the table below are "based on three different sets of assumptions about future net immigration, birth rates, and death rates.... Alternative I is designated as optimistic because among the three projections the assumptions selected produce the most favorable financial effect for the OASDI program. Conversely, the assumptions chosen for Alternative III, designated pessimistic, produce the most unfavorable financial effect."

[Per thousand women]

Calendar year	Total fertility rate		
	Alternative I	Alternative II	Alternative III
1990	1,914.9	1,864.0	1,791.4
1991	1,933.7	1,870.4	1,780.7
1992	1,952.6	1,876.8	1,770.1
1993	1,971.3	1,883.3	1,759.9
1994	1,990.1	1,889.9	1,750.1
1995	2,008.9	1,896.5	1,740.3
1996	2,027.7	1,903.2	1,730.8

[Continued]

★ 645 ★

Total Fertility Rate Projections by Alternative, 1990-2011
[Continued]

Calendar year	Total fertility rate		
	Alternative I	Alternative II	Alternative III
1997	2,046.5	1,909.7	1,721.3
1998	2,065.2	1,916.2	1,712.1
1999	2,083.9	1,922.7	1,703.0
2000	2,102.3	1,929.2	1,694.0
2001	2,120.6	1,935.7	1,685.1
2002	2,138.7	1,942.2	1,676.2
2003	2,156.8	1,948.8	1,667.4
2004	2,175.0	1,955.3	1,658.7
2005	2,193.2	1,962.0	1,650.2
2006	2,211.3	1,968.5	1,641.8
2007	2,229.2	1,975.0	1,633.4
2008	2,247.0	1,981.4	1,625.0
2009	2,264.8	1,987.6	1,616.6
2010	2,282.6	1,993.9	1,608.3
2011	2,300.0	2,000.0	1,600.0

Source: "Social Security Area Population Projections," Alice H. Wade (Office of the Actuary, Social Security Administration), *Social Security Bulletin* 51, No. 2, February, 1988, p. 6.

★ 646 ★

Adjusted Birth Rate Projections Based on Actual 1990 Birth Rate, 1960-2000

In the table below, University of Southern California demographer Richard Easterlin predicts a much higher birth rate for the year 2000 than that projected by the U.S. Census Bureau. "In its most recent estimate, published in 1989, the bureau predicted 3.7 million births in 1990. Actual result: 4.2 million, the most since the late baby-boom year of 1961 when 4.3 million children entered the world."

[Number of births in millions]

	Actual	Census projection	Easterlin projection
1960	4.3	-	-
1970	3.7	-	-
1980	3.6	-	-
1990	4.2	3.7[1]	-
2000	-	3.4[1]	5.0

Source: "The Baby Boomlet Is for Real," Joseph Spires, *Fortune* 125, No. 3, February 10, 1992, pp. 101-02. *Note:* 1. Projection made in 1989.

★ 647 ★

Central Birth Rate Projections by Age and Alternative, 1985-2011

Includes the populations of Puerto Rico, Guam, American Samoa, the Virgin Islands, and U.S. citizens living abroad. The central birth rate is defined as "the ratio of the number of births during the year for mothers at the tabulated age to the midyear female population at that age." Alternatives in the table below are "based on three different sets of assumptions about future net immigration, birth rates, and death rates.... Alternative I is designated as optimistic because among the three projections the assumptions selected produce the most favorable financial effect for the OASDI program. Conversely, the assumptions chosen for Alternative III, designated pessimistic, produce the most unfavorable financial effect."

[Per thousand women]

Alternative and age	Calendar year									
	1985	1986	1987	1988	1989	1990	1995	2000	2005	2011
Alternative I										
14	6.4	6.4	6.5	6.6	6.7	6.8	7.3	7.8	8.3	8.5
15	17.1	17.1	17.3	17.5	17.7	17.9	18.9	19.9	20.9	21.5
16	32.2	32.2	32.5	32.8	33.1	33.4	34.9	36.4	37.9	39.4
17	51.7	51.6	52.1	52.6	53.1	53.6	56.1	58.6	61.1	63.6
18	72.0	71.8	72.5	73.2	73.9	74.6	78.1	81.6	85.1	88.8
19	88.1	87.9	88.8	89.7	90.5	91.3	95.3	99.3	103.3	107.9
20	99.9	99.7	100.7	101.7	102.7	103.7	108.4	112.9	117.4	122.7
21	106.5	106.3	107.4	108.5	109.6	110.6	115.6	120.6	125.6	131.5
22	111.3	111.0	112.1	113.2	114.3	115.4	120.9	126.3	131.5	138.0
23	114.8	114.5	115.7	116.9	118.1	119.3	125.0	130.5	136.0	142.6
24	116.7	116.5	117.7	118.9	120.1	121.3	127.3	132.9	138.4	145.1
25	116.8	116.6	117.8	119.0	120.2	121.4	127.4	133.3	138.8	145.7
26	115.1	114.8	115.9	117.1	118.3	119.5	125.5	131.4	136.9	143.6
27	111.8	111.5	112.6	113.7	114.8	116.0	122.0	127.7	133.2	139.8
28	106.6	106.4	107.5	108.6	109.7	110.8	116.3	121.8	127.3	133.9
29	99.4	99.1	100.1	101.1	102.1	103.1	108.5	113.9	118.9	124.9
30	89.8	89.6	90.5	91.4	92.3	93.2	98.0	103.0	107.6	113.0
31	79.0	78.9	79.7	80.5	81.3	82.1	86.3	90.8	94.9	99.7
32	67.8	67.7	68.4	69.1	69.8	70.5	74.0	77.9	81.4	85.6
33	57.1	56.9	57.5	58.1	58.7	59.3	62.3	65.3	68.3	71.9
34	46.8	46.7	47.2	47.7	48.2	48.7	51.2	53.7	56.2	59.2
35	37.1	37.0	37.4	37.8	38.2	38.6	40.6	42.6	44.6	47.0
36	28.7	28.7	29.0	29.3	29.6	29.9	31.4	32.9	34.4	36.2
37	22.0	21.9	22.1	22.4	22.7	23.0	24.2	25.3	26.8	28.5
38	16.3	16.3	16.5	16.7	16.9	17.1	18.1	19.1	20.1	21.3
39	11.8	11.8	11.9	12.0	12.1	12.2	12.7	13.2	13.7	14.3
40	8.1	8.1	8.2	8.3	8.4	8.5	9.0	9.5	10.0	10.6
41	5.3	5.3	5.3	5.3	5.3	5.4	5.9	6.4	6.9	7.5
42	3.5	3.5	3.5	3.5	3.5	3.5	3.5	3.5	3.5	3.5
43	2.3	2.3	2.3	2.3	2.3	2.3	2.3	2.3	2.3	2.3
44	1.2	1.2	1.2	1.2	1.2	1.2	1.2	1.2	1.2	1.2
45	.6	.6	.6	.6	.6	.6	.6	.6	.6	.6
46	.1	.1	.1	.1	.1	.1	.1	.1	.1	.1
47	.0	.0	.0	.0	.0	.0	.0	.0	.0	.0
48	.0	.0	.0	.0	.0	.0	.0	.0	.0	.0
49	.0	.0	.0	.0	.0	.0	.0	.0	.0	.0

[Continued]

★ 647 ★

Central Birth Rate Projections by Age and Alternative, 1985-2011
[Continued]

Alternative and age	Calendar year									
	1985	1986	1987	1988	1989	1990	1995	2000	2005	2011
Alternative II										
14	6.4	6.4	6.4	6.4	6.4	6.4	6.4	6.4	6.4	6.4
15	17.1	17.1	17.2	17.3	17.4	17.5	18.0	18.5	19.0	19.3
16	32.2	32.2	32.3	32.4	32.5	32.6	33.1	33.6	34.1	34.7
17	51.7	51.6	51.8	52.0	52.2	52.4	53.4	54.4	55.4	56.4
18	72.0	71.8	72.1	72.4	72.7	73.0	74.4	75.4	76.6	77.8
19	88.1	87.9	88.2	88.5	88.8	89.1	90.6	92.1	93.6	95.3
20	99.9	99.7	100.1	100.5	100.9	101.3	103.3	104.9	106.5	108.4
21	106.5	106.3	106.7	107.1	107.5	107.9	109.9	111.9	113.9	116.2
22	111.3	111.0	111.4	111.8	112.2	112.6	114.6	116.6	118.6	121.0
23	114.8	114.5	114.9	115.3	115.7	116.1	118.1	120.1	122.1	124.5
24	116.7	116.5	116.9	117.3	117.7	118.1	120.1	122.1	124.1	126.5
25	116.8	116.6	117.0	117.4	117.8	118.3	120.3	122.3	124.3	126.7
26	115.1	114.8	115.2	115.6	116.0	116.4	118.4	120.4	122.4	124.8
27	111.8	111.5	111.9	112.3	112.7	113.1	115.1	117.1	119.1	121.5
28	106.6	106.4	106.7	107.0	107.4	107.8	109.8	111.8	113.8	116.2
29	99.4	99.1	99.4	99.7	100.0	100.3	102.3	104.3	106.3	108.7
30	89.8	89.6	89.9	90.2	90.5	90.8	92.5	94.1	95.6	94.1
31	79.0	78.9	79.1	79.3	79.5	79.8	81.3	82.8	84.3	86.1
32	67.8	67.7	67.9	68.1	68.3	68.5	69.6	71.1	72.6	74.0
33	57.1	56.9	57.1	57.3	57.5	57.7	58.7	59.7	60.7	61.9
34	46.8	46.7	46.8	46.9	47.0	47.1	47.9	48.9	49.9	51.1
35	37.1	37.0	37.1	37.2	37.3	37.4	37.9	38.4	38.9	39.5
36	28.7	28.7	28.7	28.8	28.9	29.0	29.5	30.0	30.5	31.1
37	22.0	21.9	21.9	21.9	21.9	22.0	22.5	23.0	23.5	24.1
38	16.3	16.3	16.3	16.3	16.3	16.3	16.3	16.8	17.3	17.9
39	11.8	11.8	11.7	11.7	11.7	11.7	11.7	11.7	11.7	11.7
40	8.1	8.1	8.0	8.0	8.0	8.0	8.0	8.0	8.0	8.0
41	5.3	5.3	5.2	5.2	5.2	5.2	5.2	5.2	5.2	5.2
42	3.5	3.5	3.4	3.4	3.4	3.4	3.4	3.4	3.4	3.4
43	2.3	2.3	2.3	2.3	2.3	2.3	2.3	2.3	2.3	2.3
44	1.2	1.2	1.2	1.2	1.2	1.2	1.2	1.2	1.2	1.2
45	.6	.6	.6	.6	.6	.6	.6	.6	.6	.6
46	.1	.1	.1	.1	.1	.1	.1	.1	.1	.1
47	.0	.0	.0	.0	.0	.0	.0	.0	.0	.0
48	.0	.0	.0	.0	.0	.0	.0	.0	.0	.0
49	.0	.0	.0	.0	.0	.0	.0	.0	.0	.0
Alternative III										
14	6.4	6.4	6.4	6.4	6.4	6.4	6.4	6.4	6.4	6.4
15	17.1	17.1	17.0	16.9	16.8	16.7	16.2	15.7	15.2	14.6
16	32.2	32.2	32.0	31.8	31.6	31.4	30.4	29.4	28.4	27.7
17	51.7	51.6	51.3	51.0	50.7	50.4	48.9	47.4	46.1	44.9
18	72.0	71.8	71.4	71.0	70.6	70.2	68.2	66.4	64.7	62.9
19	88.1	87.9	87.4	86.9	86.4	85.9	83.6	81.6	79.6	77.2
20	99.9	99.7	99.2	98.7	98.2	97.7	95.2	92.7	90.2	87.3

[Continued]

★ 647 ★

Central Birth Rate Projections by Age and Alternative, 1985-2011
[Continued]

Alternative and age	Calendar year									
	1985	1986	1987	1988	1989	1990	1995	2000	2005	2011
21	106.5	106.3	105.7	105.1	104.5	103.9	101.1	98.6	96.1	93.1
22	111.3	111.0	110.4	109.8	109.2	108.6	105.6	102.9	100.4	97.4
23	114.8	114.5	113.9	113.3	112.7	112.1	109.1	106.1	103.5	100.5
24	116.7	116.5	115.9	115.3	114.7	114.1	111.1	108.1	105.1	101.6
25	116.8	116.6	115.9	115.3	114.7	114.1	111.1	108.1	105.2	102.0
26	115.1	114.8	114.1	113.5	112.9	112.3	109.3	106.3	103.5	100.5
27	111.8	111.5	110.8	110.1	109.5	108.9	105.9	102.9	100.4	97.4
28	106.6	106.4	105.7	105.0	104.4	103.8	100.8	98.3	95.8	92.8
29	99.4	99.1	98.4	97.8	97.2	96.6	94.1	91.6	89.1	86.1
30	89.8	89.6	88.9	88.3	87.7	87.2	84.7	82.3	80.3	77.9
31	79.0	78.9	78.3	77.7	77.2	76.7	74.5	72.5	70.5	68.1
32	67.8	67.7	67.1	66.6	66.1	65.6	63.6	62.1	60.6	58.8
33	57.1	56.9	56.4	55.9	55.5	55.1	53.4	51.9	50.4	48.6
34	46.8	46.7	46.2	45.8	45.4	45.0	43.5	42.5	41.5	40.3
35	37.1	37.0	36.5	36.1	35.8	35.5	34.3	33.3	32.3	31.1
36	28.7	28.7	28.3	27.9	27.6	27.3	26.3	25.6	25.1	24.5
37	22.0	21.9	21.5	21.2	20.9	20.7	19.9	19.4	18.9	18.3
38	16.3	16.3	16.0	15.7	15.5	15.3	14.7	14.2	13.7	13.1
39	11.8	11.8	11.5	11.3	11.1	10.9	10.4	9.9	9.4	9.1
40	8.1	8.1	7.9	7.7	7.5	7.4	6.9	6.7	6.7	6.7
41	5.3	5.3	5.1	5.0	4.9	4.8	4.5	4.5	4.5	4.5
42	3.5	3.5	3.4	3.3	3.2	3.1	2.9	2.9	2.9	2.9
43	2.3	2.3	2.2	2.1	2.0	1.9	1.9	1.9	1.9	1.9
44	1.2	1.2	1.1	1.1	1.1	1.1	1.1	1.1	1.1	1.1
45	.6	.6	.6	.6	.6	.6	.6	.6	.6	.6
46	.1	.1	.1	.1	.1	.1	.1	.1	.1	.1
47	.0	.0	.0	.0	.0	.0	.0	.0	.0	.0
48	.0	.0	.0	.0	.0	.0	.0	.0	.0	.0
49	.0	.0	.0	.0	.0	.0	.0	.0	.0	.0

Source: "Social Security Area Population Projections," Alice H. Wade (Office of the Actuary, Social Security Administration), *Social Security Bulletin* 51, No. 2, February, 1988, pp. 8-9.

★ 648 ★

Distribution of Births by Race, 1980-2080

Year	Births to all women		Births to White women		Births to Black women		Births to other races women	
	Under age 20	Age 35 and over	Under age 20	Age 35 and over	Under age 20	Age 35 and over	Under age 20	Age 35 and over
1980	15.7	4.6	13.6	4.6	26.7	4.1	11.4	8.0
1985	12.8	6.5	10.9	6.6	23.0	5.0	9.2	10.4
Projections								
1987	12.1	7.4	10.4	7.3	21.5	6.5	8.2	13.7
1990	11.6	8.4	9.9	8.2	20.5	7.5	8.4	14.5
1995	11.7	9.6	10.1	9.5	20.0	8.7	8.6	14.4
2000	13.0	9.8	11.4	9.7	20.8	8.9	9.8	13.6
2005	13.0	8.9	11.7	8.8	20.0	8.2	9.0	12.5
2010	12.2	8.0	11.0	7.8	18.4	7.6	8.7	12.0
2020	11.2	8.8	10.2	8.6	16.1	8.3	9.3	12.5
2030	11.6	9.0	11.0	8.9	14.9	8.4	9.9	10.7
2040	11.0	8.4	10.7	8.2	12.8	8.2	10.0	9.6
2050	10.6	8.6	10.5	8.7	10.9	8.4	10.5	8.7
2080	10.7	8.7	10.7	8.6	10.8	8.6	10.5	8.8

Source: "Percent Distribution of Births, by Age and Race: 1965 to 2080," *Projections of the Population of the United States by Age, Sex, and Race: 1988 to 2080*, p. 12. Primary source: U.S. Bureau of the Census, *Current Population Reports*, series P-25, No. 952; and unpublished data. Projection data are from middle series. Births are adjusted for underregistration in all years. Original table also includes data for 1965, 1970, and 1975.

★ 649 ★

Percent Distribution of Births by Age and Race of Mother, 1965-2080

[In percent]

Year	Births to all women		Births to White women		Births to Black women		Births to other races women	
	Under age 20	Age 35 and over	Under age 20	Age 35 and over	Under age 20	Age 35 and over	Under age 20	Age 35 and over
Estimates								
1965	15.9	9.9	14.3	9.9	25.1	9.4	11.1	12.5
1970	17.6	6.3	15.2	6.2	31.3	6.5	13.8	9.2
1975	19.0	4.6	16.3	4.6	33.1	4.6	14.1	7.0
1980	15.7	4.6	13.6	4.6	26.7	4.1	11.4	8.0
1985	12.8	6.5	10.9	6.6	23.0	5.0	9.2	10.4
Projections								
1987	12.1	7.4	10.4	7.3	21.5	6.5	8.2	13.7
1990	11.6	8.4	9.9	8.2	20.5	7.5	8.4	14.5
1995	11.7	9.6	10.1	9.5	20.0	8.7	8.6	14.4
2000	13.0	9.8	11.4	9.7	20.8	8.9	9.8	13.6
2005	13.0	8.9	11.7	8.8	20.0	8.2	9.0	12.5

[Continued]

★ 649 ★

Percent Distribution of Births by Age and Race of Mother, 1965-2080

[Continued]

Year	Births to all women		Births to White women		Births to Black women		Births to other races women	
	Under age 20	Age 35 and over	Under age 20	Age 35 and over	Under age 20	Age 35 and over	Under age 20	Age 35 and over
2010	12.2	8.0	11.0	7.8	18.4	7.6	8.7	12.0
2020	11.2	8.8	10.2	8.6	16.1	8.3	9.3	12.5
2030	11.6	9.0	11.0	8.9	14.9	8.4	9.9	10.7
2040	11.0	8.4	10.7	8.2	12.8	8.2	10.0	9.6
2050	10.6	8.6	10.5	8.7	10.9	8.4	10.5	8.7
2080	10.7	8.7	10.7	8.6	10.8	8.6	10.5	8.8

Source: "Projections of the Population of the United States, by Age, Sex, and Race: 1988 to 2080," *Current Population Reports*, series P-25, No. 1018, p. 12. Primary source: *Current Population Reports*, series P-25, No. 952, and unpublished data. Projection data are from middle series. Births are adjusted for underregistration for all years.

Mortality and Life Expectancy Rates

★ 650 ★

Age-Adjusted Central Death Rate Projections by Age, Sex, and Alternative, 1990-2080

Includes the populations of Puerto Rico, Guam, American Samoa, the Virgin Islands, and U.S. citizens living abroad. The age-adjusted central death rate is defined as "the weighted average of the age-specific central death rates for a particular sex and year. The weights are the number of people in the corresponding age groups in the 1980 U.S. census population." Alternatives in the table below are "based on three different sets of assumptions about future net immigration, birth rates, and death rates.... Alternative I is designated as optimistic because among the three projections the assumptions selected produce the most favorable financial effect for the OASDI program. Conversely, the assumptions chosen for Alternative III, designated pessimistic, produce the most unfavorable financial effect."

[Per hundred thousand]

Calendar year	Alternative I		Alternative II		Alternative III	
	Male	Female	Male	Female	Male	Female
1990	1,070.5	629.7	1,033.5	605.5	998.0	582.6
1991	1,065.5	626.1	1,020.1	596.7	977.3	569.0
1992	1,060.6	622.7	1,007.3	588.2	957.7	556.3
1993	1,055.9	619.5	995.0	580.1	939.2	544.3
1994	1,051.4	616.3	983.3	572.4	921.7	533.0
1995	1,047.0	613.3	872.2	565.1	905.3	522.6
1996	1,042.8	610.4	961.8	558.4	890.1	512.9

[Continued]

★ 650 ★

Age-Adjusted Central Death Rate Projections by Age, Sex, and Alternative, 1990-2080

[Continued]

Calendar year	Alternative I		Alternative II		Alternative III	
	Male	Female	Male	Female	Male	Female
1997	1,038.8	607.6	952.1	552.1	876.2	504.0
1998	1,304.9	604.9	943.3	546.4	863.4	496.0
1999	1,031.2	602.4	935.3	541.2	851.9	488.7
2000	1,027.6	600.0	928.2	536.7	841.5	482.1
2005	1,011.7	589.8	902.2	519.8	799.0	454.7
2010	998.0	581.4	882.2	506.5	762.5	430.8
2015	985.1	573.6	863.4	493.9	728.2	408.3
2020	972.6	566.0	845.2	481.8	695.6	387.3
2025	960.5	558.6	827.6	470.1	664.8	367.5
2030	948.6	551.4	810.5	458.8	635.5	348.9
2035	937.1	544.4	794.0	447.8	607.6	331.3
2040	925.8	537.6	777.9	437.2	581.2	314.9
2045	914.8	530.9	762.3	426.9	556.1	299.3
2050	904.1	524.5	747.1	416.9	532.2	284.7
2055	893.7	518.2	732.4	407.3	509.5	270.9
2060	883.6	512.1	718.1	397.9	487.9	258.0
2065	873.7	506.2	704.2	388.8	467.4	245.7
2070	864.0	500.4	690.7	380.0	447.9	234.2
2075	854.6	494.8	677.6	371.5	429.3	223.2
2080	845.5	489.3	664.8	363.2	4411.6	213.0

Source: "Social Security Area Population Projections," Alice H. Wade (Office of the Actuary, Social Security Administration), *Social Security Bulletin* 51, No. 2, February, 1988, p. 10.

★ 651 ★

Age-Sex-Adjusted Central Death Rate Projections by Alternative, 1990-2080

Includes the populations of Puerto Rico, Guam, American Samoa, the Virgin Islands, and U.S. citizens living abroad. The age-sex-adjusted central death rate is defined as "the weighted average of the age-sex-specific central death rates for a particular year. The weights are the number of people in the corresponding age and sex groups in the U.S. census population." Alternatives in the table below are "based on three different sets of assumptions about future net immigration, birth rates, and death rates.... Alternative I is designated as optimistic because among the three projections the assumptions selected produce the most favorable financial effect for the OASDI program. Conversely, the assumptions chosen for Alternative III, designated pessimistic, produce the most unfavorable financial effect."

[Per hundred thousand]

Calendar year	Alternative I	Alternative II	Alternative III
1990	838.9	808.4	779.2
1991	834.1	796.8	761.7
1992	829.5	785.7	745.1
1993	825.0	775.0	729.4
1994	820.6	764.9	714.6
1995	816.4	755.3	700.8
1996	812.3	746.2	688.0
1997	808.5	737.8	676.2
1998	804.8	730.1	665.6
1999	801.2	723.3	655.9
2000	797.9	717.1	647.2
2005	783.9	695.0	612.0
2010	772.8	678.4	582.1
2015	762.6	663.0	554.3
2020	752.6	648.0	528.0
2025	742.9	633.6	503.1
2030	733.5	619.5	479.6
2035	724.3	606.0	457.3
2040	715.4	592.8	436.3
2045	706.6	580.0	416.3
2050	698.2	567.6	397.5
2055	689.9	555.6	379.6
2060	681.9	544.0	362.7
2065	674.0	532.7	346.6
2070	666.4	521.7	331.4
2075	659.0	511.0	317.0
2080	651.7	500.6	303.3

Source: "Social Security Area Population Projections," Alice H. Wade (Office of the Actuary, Social Security Administration), *Social Security Bulletin* 51, No. 2, February, 1988, p. 11.

★ 652 ★

Age-Specific Death Rates, 1990-2065

The table below "shows the shapes of the age profiles that we forecast for 2030 and 2065. Two trends stand out in relation to the earlier profiles, which are also shown. First, the hump in mortality at young adult ages becomes more pronounced; second, by 2065 the death rates for age groups 1-4, 5-9, and 10-14 become virtually identical. The reader can assess the plausibility of these patterns."

[Numbers per 100,000 births]

Age group	Date								
	1990	1995	2000	2010	2020	2030	2040	2050	2065
0-1	932	790	669	481	345	248	178	128	78
1-4	35	28	23	15	10	7	5	3	2
5-9	19	16	14	10	7	5	4	3	2
10-14	20	17	15	11	8	6	4	3	2
15-19	67	62	57	48	40	34	28	24	18
20-24	86	78	71	58	48	40	33	27	20
25-29	84	75	68	54	44	35	28	23	16
30-34	97	87	78	62	50	40	32	25	18
35-39	138	124	111	90	72	58	47	38	27
40-44	221	201	182	150	124	102	84	69	52
45-49	370	341	315	267	227	193	164	139	109
50-54	613	572	533	464	403	351	305	265	215
55-59	965	907	853	754	666	589	520	460	382
60-64	1,511	1,432	1,357	1,218	1,094	982	882	792	674
65-69	2,233	2,119	2,010	1,810	1,629	1,466	1,320	1,188	1,015
70-74	3,361	3,187	3,022	2,718	2,444	2,198	1,976	1,777	1,515
75-79	4,979	4,693	4,423	3,930	3,491	3,102	2,756	2,448	2,050
80-84	7,748	7,323	6,921	6,182	5,523	4,933	4,407	3,936	3,323
85-89	12,267	11,687	10,609	10,108	9,177	8,331	7,564	6,868	5,942
90-94	19,099	18,341	16,915	16,246	14,987	13,827	12,758	11,774	10,439
95-99	29,744	28,864	27,188	26,390	24,869	23,442	22,102	20,844	19,095
100-04	46,334	45,554	44,053	43,329	41,933	40,600	39,325	38,104	36,364
105-09	72,195	72,100	71,956	71,906	71,845	71,831	71,861	71,930	72,097

Source: "Modeling and Forecasting U.S. Mortality," Ronald D. Lee and Lawrence R. Carter, *Journal of the American Statistical Association* 87, No. 419, September, 1992, p. 666. Forecasts of the mortality index are based on a model fit to data from 1900-1989; for explanation, see original source.

★ 653 ★

Central Death Rate Projections by Age, Sex, and Alternative, 1985-2080

Includes the populations of Puerto Rico, Guam, American Samoa, the Virgin Islands, and U.S. citizens living abroad. The central death rate is defined as "the ratio of the number of deaths during the year for persons at the tabulated age to the midyear population at that age." Alternatives in the table below are "based on three different sets of assumptions about future net immigration, birth rates, and death rates.... Alternative I is designated as optimistic because among the three projections the assumptions selected produce the most favorable financial effect for the OASDI program. Conversely, the assumptions chosen for Alternative III, designated pessimistic, produce the most unfavorable financial effect."

[Per hundred thousand]

Alternative, sex, and age group	Calendar year										
	1985	1990	2000	2010	2020	2030	2040	2050	2060	2070	2080
Alternative I:											
Male:											
0	1,177.6	1,042.1	890.7	834.4	795.5	759.5	726.2	695.4	666.8	640.4	615.8
1-4	56.8	53.0	48.1	46.1	44.9	43.9	42.9	41.9	41.0	40.1	39.3
5-9	31.3	28.3	24.4	23.3	22.8	22.4	22.0	21.7	21.3	21.0	20.6
10-14	35.2	32.4	28.4	27.2	26.7	26.2	25.8	25.3	24.9	24.4	24.0
15-19	116.4	110.5	102.1	98.3	96.4	94.6	92.8	91.0	89.3	87.6	86.0
20-24	163.6	156.1	145.1	140.0	137.2	134.6	132.0	129.5	127.0	124.7	122.3
25-29	172.5	168.0	161.4	157.3	154.3	151.5	148.7	146.0	143.3	140.8	138.3
30-34	185.6	177.3	165.3	159.7	156.7	153.8	151.0	148.2	145.6	143.0	140.5
35-39	236.5	219.6	196.2	187.7	183.8	180.1	176.5	173.0	169.7	166.5	163.4
40-44	348.1	321.2	284.1	270.9	264.9	259.1	253.6	248.4	243.3	238.4	233.8
45-49	509.0	473.1	423.7	404.9	395.5	386.7	378.2	370.2	362.5	355.1	348.1
50-54	844.7	796.2	730.7	704.6	688.7	673.5	659.1	645.4	632.3	619.8	608.0
55-59	1,316.2	1,238.8	1,134.0	1,092.9	1,068.3	1,045.0	1,022.8	1,001.7	981.6	962.5	944.4
60-64	2,078.4	1,965.1	1,831.3	1,750.8	1,710.6	1,672.5	1,636.3	1,601.9	1,569.2	1,538.2	1,508.6
65-69	3,186.6	3,081.1	2,953.8	2,872.9	2,806.5	2,743.5	2,683.7	2,626.9	2,572.9	2,521.6	2,472.9
70-74	4,792.8	4,674.9	4,550.5	4,437.7	4,330.8	4,229.4	4,133.2	4,041.9	3,955.3	3,873.1	3,795.0
75-79	7,308.7	7,172.3	7,057.8	6,895.1	6,720.3	6,554.6	6,397.6	6,248.7	6,107.5	5,973.6	5,846.5
80-84	10,935.3	10,761.4	10,666.1	10,416.8	10,135.6	9,869.1	9,616.6	9,377.3	9,150.4	8,935.3	8,731.3
85-89	15,749.1	15,506.5	15,402.8	15,024.7	14,594.9	14,187.7	13,802.0	13,436.5	13,090.1	12,761.8	12,450.3
90-94	22,547.1	22,142.2	21,867.5	21,261.9	20,605.5	19,984.0	19,395.6	18,838.3	18,310.4	17,810.1	17,335.9
Alternative II:											
Male:											
0	1,177.6	955.9	714.1	644.5	593.7	549.0	509.7	474.9	444.1	416.7	392.3
1-4	56.8	50.3	41.3	38.4	36.7	35.1	33.7	32.3	31.1	29.9	28.8
5-9	31.3	26.5	19.9	18.6	17.9	17.4	16.8	16.3	15.8	15.3	14.8
10-14	35.2	30.6	24.0	22.4	21.6	20.9	20.3	19.6	19.0	18.4	17.9
15-19	116.4	106.8	91.9	86.7	84.0	81.4	78.9	76.5	74.2	72.0	69.8
20-24	163.6	151.3	131.8	124.6	120.7	117.1	113.5	110.1	106.8	103.6	100.5
25-29	172.5	165.1	153.2	146.8	142.3	138.0	133.8	129.8	125.9	122.1	118.5
30-34	185.6	172.0	150.9	142.9	138.4	134.1	130.0	126.1	122.2	118.6	115.0
35-39	236.5	209.0	169.3	158.3	152.8	147.7	142.7	138.0	133.5	129.2	125.1
40-44	348.1	304.4	242.1	225.3	216.9	209.0	201.5	194.4	187.5	181.1	174.9
45-49	509.0	450.8	368.0	343.8	330.5	317.9	306.1	294.8	284.1	274.0	264.3
50-54	844.7	763.7	648.9	613.3	589.6	567.3	546.1	526.0	506.9	488.9	471.7
55-59	1,316.2	1,188.8	1,009.5	954.5	917.5	882.6	849.6	818.3	788.6	760.5	733.8
60-64	2,078.4	1,887.9	1,618.8	1,532.1	1,471.8	1,414.9	1,361.1	1,310.3	1,262.2	1,216.5	1,173.3
65-69	3,186.6	2,980.5	2,680.3	2,551.5	2,449.7	2,353.8	2,263.2	2,177.6	2,096.7	2,020.1	1,947.5
70-74	4,792.8	4,532.9	4,155.2	3,965.0	3,803.0	3,650.4	3,506.5	3,370.8	3,242.6	3,121.5	3,006.9
75-79	7,308.7	6,960.9	6,461.3	6,177.6	5,917.8	5,673.5	5,443.6	5,227.0	5,022.9	4,830.3	4,648.4
80-84	10,935.3	10,419.9	9,699.7	9,264.7	8,860.3	8,480.8	8,124.3	7,789.1	7,473.7	7,176.6	6,896.6
85-89	15,749.1	14,995.6	13,961.2	13,316.9	12,714.6	12,150.1	11,620.6	11,123.5	10,656.4	10,217.2	9,803.8
90-94	22,547.1	21,433.4	19,867.4	18,878.2	17,978.1	17,136.1	16,347.8	15,609.3	14,916.7	14,266.7	13,656.2

[Continued]

★ 653 ★

Central Death Rate Projections by Age, Sex, and Alternative, 1985-2080
[Continued]

Alternative, sex, and age group	Calendar year										
	1985	1990	2000	2010	2020	2030	2040	2050	2060	2070	2080
Alternative III:											
Male:											
0	1,177.6	877.8	593.9	525.4	473.6	429.2	391.1	358.1	329.5	304.4	282.4
1-4	56.8	47.7	35.6	31.8	29.4	27.2	25.3	23.5	21.9	20.4	19.0
5-9	31.3	24.7	16.4	14.6	13.6	12.7	11.8	11.1	10.3	9.7	9.1
10-14	35.2	28.9	20.2	18.1	16.8	15.7	14.7	13.7	12.8	12.0	11.2
15-19	116.4	103.2	82.8	75.4	70.7	66.4	62.3	58.5	55.0	51.7	48.6
20-24	163.6	146.6	119.9	109.4	102.7	96.5	90.7	85.2	80.1	75.3	70.8
25-29	172.5	162.3	145.8	135.5	127.3	119.7	112.5	105.8	99.6	93.7	88.2
30-34	185.6	166.9	138.2	126.3	118.5	111.1	104.3	98.0	92.0	86.5	81.3
35-39	236.5	199.0	146.7	131.5	122.4	114.0	106.3	99.2	92.6	86.6	80.9
40-44	348.1	288.5	207.3	184.0	169.6	156.6	144.7	133.8	123.9	114.8	106.5
45-49	509.0	429.6	322.5	287.8	262.5	239.7	219.1	200.5	183.6	168.4	154.6
50-54	844.7	732.9	580.1	519.9	471.8	428.6	389.7	354.6	323.1	294.7	269.0
55-59	1,316.2	1,141.3	905.4	810.7	733.5	664.2	602.0	546.2	496.0	450.8	410.2
60-64	2,078.4	1,814.6	1,454.6	1,302.8	1,178.1	1,066.3	966.0	876.0	795.1	722.4	657.0
65-69	3,186.6	2,883.8	2,436.7	2,194.7	1,988.9	1,804.2	1,638.3	1,489.2	1,355.1	1,134.4	1,125.7
70-74	4,792.8	4,396.1	3,798.6	3,438.3	3,123.6	2,840.8	2,586.5	2,357.5	2,151.4	1,965.5	1,797.9
75-79	7,308.7	6,757.2	5,922.5	5,392.9	4,915.1	4,484.8	4,097.1	3,747.6	3,432.2	3,147.2	2,889.7
80-84	10,935.5	10,091.0	8,833.9	8,060.1	7,365.4	6,738.9	6,173.4	5,662.7	5,200.9	4,783.0	4,404.4
85-89	15,749.1	14,504.1	12,679.2	11,589.3	10,613.2	9,731.5	8,934.5	8,213.3	7,560.2	6,968.0	6,430.5
90-94	22,547.1	20,751.7	18,096.4	16,522.4	15,139.5	13,889.7	12,759.1	11,735.3	10,807.3	9,965.3	9,200.6
Alternative I:											
Female:											
0	927.0	763.5	575.3	516.3	473.3	435.5	402.4	373.1	347.3	324.4	304.1
1-4	45.1	39.3	31.4	29.0	27.5	26.1	24.9	23.7	22.6	21.6	20.6
5-9	23.0	19.6	14.9	13.8	13.2	12.7	12.2	11.7	11.2	10.8	10.4
10-14	21.4	18.8	15.0	13.9	13.3	12.8	12.3	11.8	11.3	10.9	10.4
15-19	43.0	39.5	34.4	32.4	31.1	29.9	28.7	27.6	26.5	25.5	24.5
20-24	51.4	47.6	42.3	40.1	38.5	37.0	35.6	34.2	32.8	31.6	30.4
25-29	60.2	54.4	46.2	43.4	41.7	40.1	38.6	37.1	35.7	34.3	33.1
30-34	72.1	61.9	48.2	44.8	43.1	41.5	39.9	38.5	37.1	35.7	34.4
35-39	107.5	90.3	67.9	62.8	60.4	58.1	55.9	53.8	51.8	49.9	48.1
40-44	175.7	150.6	116.5	107.9	103.6	99.5	95.7	92.0	88.6	85.2	82.1
45-49	281.8	248.6	200.8	186.6	179.1	172.0	165.3	158.9	152.8	147.0	141.5
50-54	465.8	426.5	368.4	347.2	333.3	320.1	307.6	295.8	284.5	273.8	263.5
55-59	713.2	663.8	592.8	564.7	542.1	520.6	500.2	480.9	462.4	444.9	428.2
60-64	1,146.3	1,090.1	1,014.2	973.3	933.2	895.3	859.3	825.2	792.9	762.1	732.9
65-69	1,700.4	1,640.3	1,568.4	1,510.5	1,446.3	1,385.7	1,328.2	1,273.9	1,222.4	1,173.6	1,127.3
70-74	2,610.8	2,457.8	2,259.4	2,158.2	2,060.7	1,968.9	1,882.4	1,800.9	1,723.9	1,651.1	1,582.3
75-79	4,057.2	3,729.8	3,285.1	3,103.4	2,951.7	2,809.7	2,676.5	2,551.5	2,434.1	2,323.8	2,219.9
80-84	6,644.2	6,060.2	5,241.0	4,906.9	4,647.1	4,405.0	4,179.0	3,967.9	3,770.5	3,585.8	3,412.7
85-89	11,545.8	10,592.4	9,218.3	8,596.0	8,116.3	7,670.7	7,256.1	6,869.9	6,509.8	6,173.8	5,860.0
90-94	18,288.9	17,052.4	15,203.3	14,172.1	13,346.3	12,580.7	11,869.6	11,208.4	10,593.3	10,020.4	9,486.4
Alternative II:											
Female:											
0	927.0	827.5	712.3	666.4	634.2	604.3	576.8	551.2	527.6	505.6	485.4
1-4	45.1	41.7	37.4	35.8	34.8	34.0	33.2	32.4	31.6	30.9	30.3
5-9	23.0	20.9	18.1	17.3	17.0	16.7	16.4	16.1	15.8	15.6	15.4
10-14	21.4	19.8	17.6	16.9	16.5	16.2	16.0	15.7	15.4	15.2	14.9
15-19	43.0	40.9	37.9	36.7	36.0	35.3	34.7	34.0	33.4	32.9	32.3
20-24	51.4	49.0	45.9	44.6	43.8	43.0	42.2	41.4	40.7	40.0	39.3
25-29	60.2	56.6	51.8	50.0	49.1	48.3	47.4	46.6	45.8	45.1	44.4
30-34	72.1	65.8	57.5	55.1	54.2	53.4	52.6	51.8	51.1	50.3	49.6
35-39	107.5	96.8	83.0	79.4	78.2	77.0	75.9	74.8	73.8	72.8	71.9

[Continued]

Central Death Rate Projections by Age, Sex, and Alternative, 1985-2080
[Continued]

Alternative, sex, and age group	Calendar year										
	1985	1990	2000	2010	2020	2030	2040	2050	2060	2070	2080
40-44	175.7	160.1	139.6	133.6	131.4	129.4	127.5	125.6	123.9	122.2	120.6
45-49	281.8	261.3	233.2	223.9	220.2	216.7	213.5	210.3	207.4	204.5	201.9
50-54	465.8	261.3	233.2	223.9	220.2	216.7	213.5	210.3	207.4	204.5	201.9
55-59	713.2	684.0	644.7	628.6	618.2	608.4	599.0	590.1	581.6	573.6	565.9
60-64	1,146.3	1,123.2	1,104.5	1,087.3	1,068.0	1,049.7	1,032.3	1,015.7	1,000.0	985.1	970.9
65-69	1,700.4	1,694.7	1,723.7	1,704.8	1,671.8	1,640.5	1,610.7	1,582.5	1,555.6	1,530.2	1,505.9
70-74	2,610.8	2,551.0	2,510.0	2,459.9	2,403.3	2,349.7	2,298.8	2,250.5	2,204.8	2,161.4	2,120.2
75-79	4,057.2	3,884.3	3,682.2	3,565.8	3,467.0	3,373.6	3,285.2	3,201.5	3,122.2	3,047.2	2,976.1
80-84	6,644.2	6,320.2	5,913.5	5,679.2	5,497.0	5,325.0	5,162.5	5,008.9	4,863.6	4,726.2	4,596.2
85-89	11,545.8	11,029.6	10,382.5	9,946.2	9,598.7	9,271.1	8,961.7	8,669.3	8,393.1	8,132.0	7,885.2
90-94	18,288.9	17,673.7	16,939.1	16,249.2	15,644.9	15,075.2	14,537.2	14,029.0	13,548.9	13,095.2	12,666.3
Alternative III:											
Female											
0	927.0	705.0	479.6	420.2	376.1	338.5	306.4	278.9	255.1	234.4	216.4
1-4	45.1	37.0	26.5	23.4	21.3	19.5	17.8	16.4	15.0	13.8	12.8
5-9	23.0	18.3	12.3	10.8	9.9	9.1	8.4	7.7	7.1	6.6	6.1
10-14	21.4	17.8	12.9	11.3	10.4	9.5	8.7	8.0	7.4	6.8	6.3
15-19	43.0	38.3	31.4	28.3	26.1	24.0	22.1	20.4	18.8	17.3	16.0
20-24	51.4	46.2	39.3	36.0	33.1	30.4	28.0	25.8	23.8	22.0	20.3
25-29	60.2	52.3	41.6	37.3	34.2	31.4	28.9	26.6	24.5	22.6	20.9
30-34	72.1	58.3	40.6	35.5	32.3	29.4	26.9	24.6	22.5	20.6	18.9
35-39	107.5	84.2	55.7	47.9	43.1	38.8	34.9	31.6	28.6	25.9	23.5
40-44	175.7	141.6	97.3	83.6	74.6	66.7	59.7	53.6	48.2	43.4	39.2
45-49	281.8	236.5	173.2	149.3	132.8	118.3	105.6	94.4	84.6	75.9	68.3
50-54	465.8	412.0	334.6	294.9	261.2	231.7	206.0	183.4	163.6	146.2	131.0
55-59	713.2	644.6	546.0	483.7	428.5	380.2	338.0	301.0	268.6	240.2	215.2
60-64	1,146.3	1,058.3	930.8	832.4	741.0	660.9	590.6	528.8	474.4	426.5	384.2
65-69	1,700.4	1,587.9	1,424.1	1,282.5	1,146.8	1,027.4	922.3	829.5	747.6	675.2	611.0
70-74	2,610.8	2,368.8	2,037.8	1,832.6	1,644.7	1,478.8	1,332.2	1,202.6	1,087.7	985.7	895.1
75-79	4,057.2	3,582.9	2,949.1	2,645.8	2,384.8	2,153.6	1,948.6	1,766.4	1,604.3	1,459.8	1,330.9
80-84	6,644.2	5,821.8	4,676.8	4,180.5	3,776.0	3,416.8	3,097.2	2,812.6	2,558.7	2,331.7	2,128.7
85-89	11,545.8	10,174.8	8,232.7	7,355.4	6,659.0	6,039.2	5,486.4	4,992.6	4,550.8	4,155.0	3,799.8
90-94	18,288.9	16,455.4	13,697.0	12,255.8	11,106.3	10,081.2	9,165.1	8,345.2	7,610.4	6,950.8	6,357.9

Source: "Social Security Area Population Projections," Alice H. Wade (Office of the Actuary, Social Security Administration), *Social Security Bulletin* 51, No. 2, February, 1988, pp. 14-15.

★ 654 ★

Life Expectancy at Birth by Sex and Alternative, 1987-2080

Includes the populations of Puerto Rico, Guam, American Samoa, the Virgin Islands, and U.S. citizens living abroad. Life expectancy is defined as "the average number of years of life remaining to a person if he or she were to experience the age-specific mortality rates for the tabulated year throughout the remainder of his or her life." Alternatives in the table below are "based on three different sets of assumptions about future net immigration, birth rates, and death rates.... Alternative I is designated as optimistic because among the three projections the assumptions selected produce the most favorable financial effect for the OASDI program. Conversely, the assumptions chosen for Alternative III, designated pessimistic, produce the most unfavorable financial effect."

[Numbers in years]

Calendar year	Alternative I		Alternative II		Alternative III	
	Male	Female	Male	Female	Male	Female
1987	71.5	78.6	71.6	78.7	71.8	78.8
1988	71.6	78.6	71.8	78.9	72.1	79.1
1989	71.7	78.7	72.1	79.1	72.4	79.5
1990	71.8	78.8	72.3	79.3	72.8	79.7
1991	71.9	78.9	72.5	79.5	73.1	80.0
1992	72.0	79.0	72.7	79.6	73.4	80.3
1993	72.0	79.0	72.9	79.8	73.7	80.6
1994	72.1	79.1	73.1	80.0	73.9	80.8
1995	72.2	79.2	73.2	80.1	74.2	81.1
1996	72.3	79.2	73.4	80.3	74.5	81.3
1997	72.4	79.3	73.6	80.4	74.7	81.5
1998	72.4	79.3	73.7	80.6	74.9	81.7
1999	72.5	79.4	73.8	80.7	75.1	81.9
2000	72.6	79.4	73.9	80.8	75.2	82.0
2005	72.8	79.6	74.3	81.1	75.9	82.7
2010	73.0	79.8	74.6	81.4	76.5	83.3
2015	73.1	80.0	74.9	81.7	77.0	83.9
2020	73.3	80.1	75.1	82.0	77.6	84.5
2025	73.4	80.3	75.4	82.3	78.1	85.1
2030	73.6	80.4	75.7	82.6	78.7	85.7
2035	73.7	80.6	75.9	82.9	79.2	86.2
2040	73.9	80.7	76.2	83.1	79.8	86.8
2045	74.0	80.8	76.4	83.4	80.3	87.3
2050	74.2	81.0	76.7	83.7	80.9	87.9
2055	74.3	81.1	76.9	84.0	81.4	88.5
2060	74.5	81.3	77.1	84.2	82.0	89.0
2065	74.6	81.4	77.4	84.5	82.5	89.5
2070	74.7	81.5	77.6	84.8	83.0	90.1
2075	74.9	81.7	77.9	85.1	83.6	90.6
2080	75.0	81.8	78.1	85.3	84.1	91.1

Source: "Social Security Area Population Projections," Alice H. Wade (Office of the Actuary, Social Security Administration), Social Security Bulletin 51, No. 2, February, 1988, p. 16.

★ 655 ★

Life Expectancy at Age 65 by Sex and Alternative, 1990-2080

Includes the populations of Puerto Rico, Guam, American Samoa, the Virgin Islands, and U.S. citizens living abroad. Life expectancy is defined as "the average number of years of life remaining to a person if he or she were to experience the age-specific mortality rates for the tabulated year throughout the remainder of his or her life." Alternatives in the table below are "based on three different sets of assumptions about future net immigration, birth rates, and death rates.... Alternative I is designated as optimistic because among the three projections the assumptions selected produce the most favorable financial effect for the OASDI program. Conversely, the assumptions chosen for Alternative III, designated pessimistic, produce the most unfavorable financial effect."

[Numbers in years]

Calendar year	Alternative I		Alternative II		Alternative III	
	Male	Female	Male	Female	Male	Female
1990	14.7	18.9	14.9	19.2	15.2	19.5
1991	14.7	18.9	15.0	19.3	15.3	19.7
1992	14.7	19.0	15.1	19.4	15.4	19.9
1993	14.7	19.0	15.1	19.5	15.6	20.0
1994	14.7	19.0	15.2	19.6	15.7	20.2
1995	14.8	19.0	15.3	19.7	15.8	20.3
1996	14.8	19.1	15.4	19.8	15.9	20.5
1997	14.8	19.1	15.4	19.9	16.0	20.6
1998	14.8	19.1	15.5	19.9	16.1	20.7
1999	14.8	19.2	15.5	20.0	16.2	20.9
2000	14.8	19.2	15.6	20.1	16.3	21.0
2005	14.9	19.3	15.8	20.3	16.7	21.5
2010	15.0	19.4	16.0	20.6	17.1	21.9
2015	15.1	19.5	16.1	20.8	17.5	22.4
2020	15.2	19.7	16.3	21.0	17.9	22.8
2025	15.3	19.8	16.5	21.2	18.3	23.3
2030	15.4	19.9	16.7	21.5	18.7	23.7
2035	15.5	20.0	16.9	21.7	19.1	24.2
2040	15.6	20.1	17.0	21.9	19.6	24.6
2045	15.7	20.3	17.2	22.1	20.0	25.1
2050	15.8	20.4	17.4	22.4	20.4	25.5
2055	15.9	20.5	17.6	22.6	20.8	26.0
2060	16.0	20.6	17.7	22.8	21.2	26.4
2065	16.1	20.7	17.9	23.0	21.6	26.9
2070	16.2	20.8	18.1	23.3	22.0	27.3
2075	16.3	20.9	18.3	23.5	22.5	27.7
2080	16.4	21.1	18.5	23.7	22.9	28.2

Source: "Social Security Area Population Projections," Alice H. Wade (Office of the Actuary, Social Security Administration), *Social Security Bulletin* 51, No. 2, February, 1988, p. 17.

★ 656 ★

Life Expectancy at Birth by Sex and Race, 1960-2010

[In years.]

Year	Total			White			Black and other			Black		
	Total	Male	Female	Total	Male	Female	Total	Male	Female	Total	Male	Female
1960	69.7	66.6	73.1	70.6	67.4	74.1	63.6	61.1	66.3	(NA)	(NA)	(NA)
1970	70.8	67.1	74.7	71.7	68.0	75.6	65.3	61.3	69.4	64.1	60.0	68.3
1975	72.6	68.8	76.6	73.4	69.5	77.3	68.0	63.7	72.4	66.8	62.4	71.3
1976	72.9	69.1	76.8	73.6	69.9	77.5	68.4	64.2	72.7	67.2	62.9	71.6
1977	73.3	69.5	77.2	74.0	70.2	77.9	68.9	64.7	73.2	67.7	63.4	72.0
1978	73.5	69.6	77.3	74.1	70.4	78.0	69.3	65.0	73.5	68.1	63.7	72.4
1979	73.9	70.0	77.8	74.6	70.8	78.4	69.8	65.4	74.1	68.5	64.0	72.9
1980	73.7	70.0	77.4	74.4	70.7	78.1	69.5	65.3	73.6	68.1	63.8	72.5
1981	74.2	70.4	77.8	74.8	71.1	78.4	70.3	66.1	74.4	68.9	64.5	73.2
1982	74.5	70.9	78.1	75.1	71.5	78.7	71.0	66.8	75.0	69.4	65.1	73.7
1983	74.6	71.0	78.1	75.2	71.7	78.7	71.1	67.2	74.9	69.6	65.4	73.6
1984	74.7	71.2	78.2	75.3	71.8	78.7	71.3	67.4	75.0	69.7	65.6	73.7
1985	74.7	71.2	78.2	75.3	71.9	78.7	71.2	67.2	75.0	69.5	65.3	73.5
1986	74.8	71.3	78.3	75.4	72.0	78.8	71.2	67.2	75.1	69.4	65.2	73.5
1987	75.0	71.5	78.4	75.6	72.2	78.9	71.3	67.3	75.2	69.4	65.2	73.6
1988	74.9	71.5	78.3	75.6	72.3	78.9	71.2	67.1	75.1	69.2	64.9	73.4
1989, prel.	75.2	71.8	78.5	75.9	72.6	79.1	71.7	67.5	75.7	69.7	65.2	74.0
Projections[1]												
1990	75.6	72.1	79.0	76.2	72.7	79.6	(NA)	(NA)	(NA)	71.4	67.7	75.0
1995	76.3	72.8	79.7	76.8	73.4	80.2	(NA)	(NA)	(NA)	72.4	68.8	76.0
2000	77.0	73.5	80.4	77.5	74.0	80.9	(NA)	(NA)	(NA)	73.5	69.9	77.1
2005	77.6	74.2	81.0	78.1	74.6	81.5	(NA)	(NA)	(NA)	74.6	71.0	78.1
2010	77.9	74.4	81.3	78.3	74.9	81.7	(NA)	(NA)	(NA)	75.0	71.4	78.5

Source: Statistical Abstract of the United States, 1991, p. 73. Primary source: Except as noted, U.S. National Center for Health Statistics, *Vital Statistics of the United States*, annual; and unpublished data. *Notes:* Beginning with 1970 excludes deaths of nonresidents of the United States. NA stands for not available. 1. Based on middle mortality assumptions, U.S. Bureau of the Census, *Current Population Reports*, series P-25, No. 1018.

★ 657 ★

Population Surviving to Exact Ages, 1990-2065

[Numbers per 100,000 births]

Age	Date									
	1990	1995	2000	2010	2020	2030	2040	2050	2060	2065
0	100,000	100,000	100,000	100,000	100,000	100,000	100,000	100,000	100,000	100,000
1	99,120	99,253	99,366	99,544	99,672	99,764	99,830	99,878	99,912	99,926
5	98,985	99,143	99,276	99,483	99,631	99,737	99,812	99,866	99,904	99,919
10	98,890	99,062	99,208	99,434	99,596	99,712	99,794	99,853	99,895	99,911
15	98,791	98,977	99,134	99,380	99,556	99,682	99,773	99,837	99,883	99,901

[Continued]

★ 657 ★

Population Surviving to Exact Ages, 1990-2065
[Continued]

| Age | Date | | | | | | | | | |
	1990	1995	2000	2010	2020	2030	2040	2050	2060	2065
20	98,458	98,671	98,853	99,143	99,357	99,514	99,631	99,718	99,783	99,809
25	98,033	98,285	98,503	98,854	99,118	99,318	99,469	99,585	99,673	99,710
30	97,622	97,915	98,170	98,586	98,902	99,143	99,329	99,472	99,582	99,628
35	97,148	97,490	97,789	98,280	98,657	98,947	99,172	99,346	99,482	99,539
40	96,480	96,888	97,247	97,840	98,301	98,659	98,939	99,158	99,330	99,402
45	95,420	95,921	96,365	97,108	97,694	98,157	98,523	98,814	99,046	99,144
50	93,669	94,297	94,860	95,818	96,590	97,214	97,718	98,128	98,461	98,604
55	90,837	91,636	92,362	93,620	94,661	95,523	96,239	96,835	97,333	97,550
60	86,550	87,565	88,500	90,153	91,556	92,765	93,765	94,632	95,373	95,702
65	80,235	81,500	82,681	84,813	86,673	88,296	89,714	90,953	92,037	92,528
70	71,723	73,275	74,745	77,451	79,872	82,036	83,969	85,694	87,234	87,940
75	60,561	62,419	64,204	67,561	70,643	73,464	76,039	78,384	80,514	81,504
80	47,098	49,256	51,364	55,423	59,256	62,850	66,201	69,311	72,183	73,532
85	31,780	33,972	36,166	40,531	44,821	48,992	53,007	56,840	60,471	62,206
90	16,953	18,681	20,470	24,202	28,091	32,078	36,108	40,131	44,101	46,055
95	6,290	7,220	8,226	10,462	12,983	15,763	18,771	21,968	25,314	27,030
100	1,301	1,569	1,874	2,608	3,520	4,621	5,920	7,418	9,113	10,031
105	104	131	163	248	363	515	710	955	1,254	1,427
110	0	0	0	0	0	0	0	0	0	0

Source: "Modeling and Forecasting U.S. Mortality," Ronald D. Lee and Lawrence R. Carter, *Journal of the American Statistical Association* 87, No. 419, September, 1992, p. 667. Forecasts of the mortality index are based on a model fit to data from 1900-1989; for explanation, see original source.

★ 658 ★

Remaining Life Expectancy at Exact Ages, 1990-2065

Age	1990	1995	2000	2010	2020	2030	2040	2050	2060	2065
0	75.83	76.68	77.49	79.04	80.48	81.84	83.13	84.34	85.50	86.05
1	75.50	76.25	76.99	78.40	79.75	81.04	82.27	83.44	84.57	85.12
5	71.60	72.33	73.05	74.45	75.78	77.06	78.28	79.45	80.58	81.12
10	66.66	67.39	67.10	69.48	70.81	72.08	73.30	74.46	75.59	76.13
15	61.73	62.45	63.15	64.52	65.83	67.10	68.31	69.48	70.59	71.13
20	56.93	57.63	58.32	59.67	60.96	62.21	63.40	64.56	65.66	66.20
25	52.16	52.85	53.52	54.83	56.10	57.32	58.50	59.64	60.73	61.26
30	47.37	48.04	48.69	49.98	51.22	52.42	53.58	54.70	55.78	56.31
35	42.59	43.24	43.87	45.12	46.34	47.52	48.66	49.77	50.84	51.36
40	37.87	38.49	39.10	40.31	41.50	42.65	43.77	44.86	45.91	46.42
45	33.26	33.85	34.44	35.60	36.74	37.85	38.94	40.00	41.04	41.54
50	28.83	29.39	29.94	31.04	32.13	33.19	34.24	35.27	36.26	36.75
55	24.64	25.16	25.68	26.71	27.73	28.73	29.73	30.70	31.65	32.12
60	20.73	21.21	21.68	22.63	23.57	24.51	25.44	26.35	27.25	27.68
65	17.16	17.59	18.02	18.89	19.75	20.61	21.47	22.31	23.14	23.54

[Continued]

★ 658 ★

Remaining Life Expectancy at Exact Ages, 1990-2065
[Continued]

Age	1990	1995	2000	2010	2020	2030	2040	2050	2060	2065
70	13.88	14.27	14.65	15.43	16.21	16.99	17.75	18.52	19.26	19.63
75	10.96	11.30	11.63	12.31	12.99	13.66	14.33	15.00	15.65	15.98
80	8.36	8.63	8.90	9.44	9.98	10.53	11.08	11.62	12.16	12.42
85	6.18	6.37	6.57	6.97	7.37	7.78	8.18	8.59	9.00	9.20
90	4.46	4.59	4.72	4.99	5.27	5.54	5.82	6.10	6.38	6.52
95	3.10	3.18	3.27	3.43	3.60	3.77	3.93	4.10	4.26	4.34
100	1.91	1.98	2.04	2.16	2.27	2.37	2.46	2.55	2.64	2.68
105	.00	.00	.11	.31	.48	.63	.76	.88	.99	1.04
110	.00	.00	.00	.00	.00	.00	.00	.00	.00	.00

Source: "Modeling and Forecasting U.S. Mortality," Ronald D. Lee and Lawrence R. Carter, *Journal of the American Statistical Association* 87, No. 419, September, 1992, p. 667. Forecasts of the mortality index are based on a model fit to data from 1900-1989; for explanation, see original source.

Households and Families

★ 659 ★

Average Annual Percent Change of Population Aged 25-54 and Household Formation, 1950-2009

"Household formation generally follows population growth, concluded First Chicago bank in a 1992 demographic study. During the '90s, population growth will slow to an average of 1% a year from 2.2% in the 1980s, the bank concluded from 1990 census projections."

	Population growth aged 25-54	Household formation
1950-59	0.7	1.9
1960-69	0.6	1.8
1970-79	1.9	2.5
1980-89	2.2	1.6
1990-99	1.0[1]	1.2[1]
2000-09	0.0[1]	

Source: "Reflection of Times: Baby Boomers Take to Home Furnishings," *Discount Store News-The International Newspaper of Discount Retailing* 31, No. 10, May 18, 1990, p. 97. Primary source: First Chicago. *Note:* 1. Based on 1990 Bureau of the Census projections.

★ 660 ★

Changing Composition of U.S. Households, 1960-2000

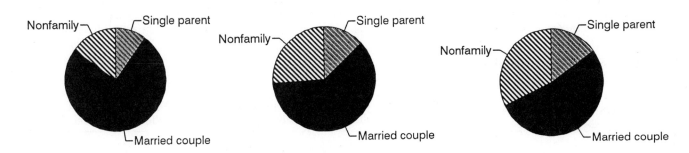

"In 1960, married couples (both with and without children) comprised 75 percent of all households. By 1980, this proportion dropped to 60 percent, and by 2000 married couples will represent just over half (53 percent) of all households. Meanwhile, the proportion of nonfamily households, that is, persons who live alone or with unrelated individuals, steadily increased. Whereas nonfamily households represented 15 percent of all household units in 1960, they will account for almost one-third of all households by 2000."

	1960	1980	2000
Married couple	75.0	61.0	53.0
Nonfamily	15.0	26.0	32.0
Single parent	10.0	13.0	15.0

Source: "Changing Composition of U.S. Households: 1960 to 2000," Population Reference Bureau, *America in the 21st Century: A Demographic Overview*, May, 1989, p. 7. Primary source: U.S. Bureau of the Census.

★ 661 ★

Households by Type, 1995-2000

As of July. Series A reflects the assumption that the recent moderation in marriage and divorce trends will continue but that historical changes spanning the last 25 years must be taken into consideration. Series A assumes a continuation of past trends in householder proportions but changes in recent years are given more weight. Series B reflects assumptions intermediate between series A and C, namely changes in marriage and divorce will slow considerably, but will not cease during the next 15 years. Series C reflects the assumption that the rapid change in marriage and divorce may have come to an end, and householder proportions will remain constant for the next 15 years.

[Numbers in thousands]

Year and series	Total	Family				Nonfamily		
		Total	Married couple	Male householder[1]	Female householder[1]	Total	Male householder	Female householder
1995								
Series A	102,785	68,219	52,178	3,276	12,765	34,565	16,102	18,463
Series B	100,308	69,787	54,863	2,940	11,984	30,520	13,666	16,854
Series C	98,180	71,294	57,410	2,667	11,217	26,887	11,490	15,396
2000								
Series A	110,217	70,024	52,263	3,845	13,916	40,193	19,471	20,722
Series B	105,933	72,277	56,294	3,282	12,701	33,656	15,452	18,204
Series C	102,440	74,449	60,080	2,855	11,515	27,991	11,985	16,006

Source: Statistical Abstract of the United States, 1991, p. 45. Primary source: U.S. Bureau of the Census, *Current Population Reports*, series P-25, No. 986. *Note:* 1. With no spouse present.

★ 662 ★

Projected Percent Change in Number of Households by Type, 1988-2000

"Households headed by men will experience fastest growth from 1988 to 2000."

	Percent
Nonfamily households headed by men	72.0
Nonfamily households headed by women	42.0
Single-parent families headed by men	42.0
Single-parent families headed by women	31.0
Married couple households	<1.0

Source: "Nine Forces Reshaping America," United Way Strategic Institute, The Futurist XXIV, No. 4, July-August, 1990, p. 15. Primary source: U.S. Bureau of the Census, 1989.

★ 663 ★

Total Household Projections by Age, 1990-2000

Number of family and nonfamily households by age of householder. These projections are based on an 'adjusted' 1990 census population base, trends in household headship rates by age from the Census Bureau's Current Population Survey, and a population projection series that assumes a continuation of current migration patterns and moderate levels of fertility and mortality.

[Households in thousands]

	1990	Percent	1995	Percent	2000	Percent	Percent change 1990-2000
Total households	91,951	100.0	98,265	100.0	103,828	100.0	13.0
Under 35	25,138	27.0	24,274	25.0	23,072	22.0	-8.0
35-54	35,059	38.0	40,921	41.0	45,441	44.0	30.0
55 and older	31,754	35.0	33,070	34.0	35,315	34.0	11.0
Family households	65,336	100.0	70,073	100.0	74,174	100.0	14.0
Under 35	17,370	27.0	16,807	24.0	15,905	21.0	-8.0
35-54	28,399	43.0	33,147	47.0	36,810	50.0	30.0
55 and older	19,567	30.0	20,119	29.0	21,459	29.0	10.0
Nonfamily households	26,615	100.0	28,192	100.0	29,654	100.0	11.0
Under 35	7,768	29.0	7,467	26.0	7,167	24.0	-8.0
35-54	6,660	25.0	7,774	28.0	8,631	29.0	30.0
55 and older	12,187	46.0	12,951	46.0	13,856	47.0	14.0

Source: "Middle-Aging Households," Thomas G. Exter, *American Demographics* 14, No. 7, July, 1992, p. 61. Primary source: TGE Demographics. Reprinted with permission (c) *American Demographics* (July, 1992). For subscription information, please call (800) 828-1133.

★ 664 ★

Age-Adjusted Marriage Rates by Alternative, 1990-2011

Includes the populations of Puerto Rico, Guam, American Samoa, the Virgin Islands, and U.S. citizens living abroad. The age-adjusted central marriage rate is decided by first determining "an expected number of marriages by applying the age-of-husband-age-of-wife-specific central marriage rates for that year to the square root of the product of the corresponding age groupings of unmarried males and unmarried females in the Marriage Registration Area as of July 1, 1982. The total age-adjusted central marriage rate is then obtained by dividing the expected number of marriages by the square root of the product of the number of unmarried males (aged 15 or older) and unmarried females (aged 15 or older) in the Marriage Registration Area as of July 1, 1982." Alternatives in the table below are "based on three different sets of assumptions about future net immigration, birth rates, and death rates.... Alternative I is designated as optimistic because among the three projections the assumptions selected produce the most favorable financial effect for the OASDI program. Conversely, the assumptions chosen for Alternative III, designated pessimistic, produce the most unfavorable financial effect."

[Per hundred thousand unmarried of each sex]

Calendar year	Alternative I	Alternative II	Alternative III
1990	5,706	6,106	6,497
1991	5,611	6,106	6,599
1992	5,517	6,106	6,702
1993	5,424	6,106	6,807
1994	5,333	6,106	6,913
1995	5,244	6,106	7,021
1996	5,156	6,106	7,131
1997	5,069	6,106	7,243
1998	4,984	6,106	7,356
1999	4,900	6,106	7,471
2000	4,818	6,106	7,588
2001	4,737	6,106	7,706
2002	4,658	6,106	7,827
2003	4,580	6,106	7,949
2004	4,503	6,106	8,074
2005	4,427	6,106	8,200
2006	4,353	6,106	8,328
2007	4,280	6,106	8,458
2008	4,208	6,106	8,591
2009	4,138	6,106	8,725
2010	4,068	6,106	8,861
2011	4,000	6,106	9,000

Source: "Social Security Area Population Projections," Alice H. Wade (Office of the Actuary, Social Security Administration), *Social Security Bulletin* 51, No. 2, February, 1988, p. 20.

★ 665 ★

Population by Marital Status and Age, 1987-2080

Includes the populations of Puerto Rico, Guam, American Samoa, the Virgin Islands, and U.S. citizens living abroad. The disunity ratio is defined as "the ratio of the number of divorced persons to the number of married and widowed persons." Alternatives in the table below are "based on three different sets of assumptions about future net immigration, birth rates, and death rates.... Alternative I is designated as optimistic because among the three projections the assumptions selected produce the most favorable financial effect for the OASDI program. Conversely, the assumptions chosen for Alternative III, designated pessimistic, produce the most unfavorable financial effect."

[Numbers in thousands]

Alternative and Calendar year	Marital status				Age				Disunity ratio
	Single	Married	Widowed	Divorced	Total	0-19	20-64	65 or older	
Alternative I									
1987	107,222	113,472	14,832	16,217	251,743	73,418	148,183	30,142	.126
1988	107,915	114,242	14,897	16,971	254,025	73,663	149,632	30,730	.131
1989	108,669	114,982	14,963	17,684	256,297	73,887	151,109	31,302	.136
1990	109,478	115,695	15,030	18,348	258,551	74,041	152,668	31,841	.140
1991	110,339	116,357	15,096	18,985	260,777	74,215	154,237	32,325	.144
1992	111,247	116,948	15,161	19,615	262,971	74,566	155,629	32,777	.148
1993	112,200	117,476	15,224	20,229	265,129	75,097	156,830	33,202	.152
1994	113,192	117,952	15,284	20,820	267,249	75,682	157,988	33,579	.156
1995	114,224	118,385	15,343	21,383	269,335	76,252	159,177	33,906	.160
1996	115,290	118,774	15,399	21,925	271,389	76,790	160,423	34,176	.163
1997	116,389	119,124	15,452	22,451	273,417	77,264	161,781	34,372	.167
1998	117,518	119,444	15,504	22,960	275,425	77,671	163,246	34,508	.170
1999	118,673	119,744	15,553	23,450	277,420	78,005	164,784	34,631	.173
2000	119,854	120,033	15,600	23,921	279,408	78,258	166,377	34,773	.176
2010	133,787	122,270	16,098	27,798	299,953	81,581	179,700	38,671	.201
2020	149,910	124,232	17,168	29,657	320,967	88,266	182,280	50,422	.210
2030	164,110	126,124	19,025	29,864	339,124	94,119	182,062	62,942	.206
2040	177,228	128,722	20,167	29,739	355,856	99,607	191,882	64,367	.200
2050	189,909	133,331	19,838	30,046	373,124	106,490	202,606	64,027	.196
2060	202,404	140,560	19,319	31,102	393,385	112,804	214,663	65,917	.195
2070	215,168	149,518	19,757	32,796	417,239	119,664	228,820	68,755	.194
2080	228,198	159,115	20,768	34,815	442,895	126,975	241,816	74,105	.194
Alternative II									
1987	107,113	113,519	14,823	16,184	251,639	73,374	148,121	30,144	.126
1988	107,550	114,424	14,869	16,865	253,707	73,518	149,446	30,743	.130
1989	107,979	115,369	14,915	17,490	255,753	73,616	150,800	31,337	.134
1990	108,402	116,350	14,962	18,055	257,769	73,619	152,239	31,911	.137
1991	108,819	117,335	15,008	18,584	259,745	73,616	153,691	32,438	.140
1992	109,230	118,297	15,053	19,097	261,677	73,767	154,965	32,945	.143
1993	109,636	119,237	15,096	19,590	263,559	74,074	156,051	33,434	.146
1994	110,038	120,161	15,139	20,053	265,391	74,413	157,094	33,884	.148
1995	110,435	121,075	15,180	20,485	267,175	74,715	158,169	34,290	.150
1996	110,827	121,974	15,220	20,891	268,912	74,963	159,302	34,647	.152
1997	111,209	122,862	15,259	21,278	270,608	75,125	160,548	34,935	.154
1998	111,578	123,746	15,298	21,646	272,267	75,200	161,902	35,166	.156
1999	111,930	124,634	15,336	21,993	273,894	75,177	163,331	35,386	.157
2000	112,265	125,534	15,375	22,320	275,493	75,053	164,814	35,626	.158

[Continued]

★ 665 ★

Population by Marital Status and Age, 1987-2080
[Continued]

Alternative and Calendar year	Marital status				Age				Disunity ratio
	Single	Married	Widowed	Divorced	Total	0-19	20-64	65 or older	
2010	115,211	134,802	15,894	24,772	290,681	73,488	176,764	40,429	.164
2020	118,611	141,870	17,193	26,025	303,698	74,816	175,784	53,099	.164
2030	121,066	144,822	19,607	26,381	311,875	75,442	169,712	66,722	.160
2040	122,313	145,635	21,681	26,377	316,005	75,404	171,551	` 69,051	.158
2050	123,286	146,023	22,139	26,328	317,776	76,327	172,285	69,163	.157
2060	124,161	147,385	21,752	26,487	319,785	76,678	172,726	70,381	.157
2070	125,155	149,480	21,771	26,857	323,264	77,143	174,975	71,146	.157
2080	126,217	151,535	22,014	27,275	327,041	77,781	175,776	73,484	.157
Alternative III									
1987	106,999	113,564	14,814	16,152	251,529	73,324	148,059	30,146	0.126
1988	107,168	114,594	14,841	16,762	253,365	73,349	149,260	30,755	.130
1989	107,253	115,733	14,868	17,302	255,156	73,293	150,491	31,372	.132
1990	107,260	116,967	14,895	17,772	256,894	73,106	151,810	31,978	.135
1991	107,195	118,257	14,920	18,197	258,570	72,880	153,141	32,548	.137
1992	107,066	119,568	14,945	18,599	260,178	72,775	154,297	33,106	.138
1993	106,877	120,895	14,969	18,973	261,714	72,795	155,264	33,655	.140
1994	106,634	122,241	14,993	19,311	263,178	72,818	156,189	34,171	.141
1995	106,340	123,604	15,016	19,611	264,572	72,775	157,145	34,651	.141
1996	105,996	124,979	15,040	19,882	265,897	72,650	158,161	35,086	.142
1997	105,599	126,365	15,063	20,129	267,157	72,412	159,288	35,457	.142
1998	105,146	127,770	15,088	20,353	268,358	72,059	160,525	35,774	.142
1999	104,634	129,201	15,114	20,553	269,501	71,582	161,836	36,083	.142
2000	104,060	130,663	15,141	20,730	270,593	70,977	163,202	36,415	.142
2010	95,627	146,366	15,585	21,621	279,198	63,283	173,665	42,250	.134
2020	87,791	156,588	16,868	22,101	283,348	58,497	168,433	56,419	.127
2030	81,448	158,215	19,441	22,352	281,455	54,026	155,251	72,179	.126
2040	74,810	154,660	22,107	22,106	273,683	49,324	147,630	76,729	.125
2050	68,686	148,067	23,219	21,404	261,376	45,671	137,170	78,534	.125
2060	63,232	140,698	22,813	20,554	247,298	42,127	125,578	79,592	.126
2070	58,466	133,317	22,118	19,692	233,593	38,870	116,953	77,769	.127
2080	54,315	125,669	21,315	18,773	220,072	36,051	108,177	75,844	.128

Source: "Social Security Area Population Projections," Alice H. Wade (Office of the Actuary, Social Security Administration), *Social Security Bulletin* 51, No. 2, February, 1988, p. 26-7.

★ 666 ★

Projection of Married-Parent Households by Age, 1990-2000

Based on married couples with children under age 18 and those without children under age 18. "Projections are based on an 'adjusted' 1990 census population base (modified to account for undernumeration), trends in household headship rates by age from the Census Bureau's Current Population Survey, and a population projection series that assumes a continuation of current immigration patterns and moderate levels of fertility and mortality."

[Numbers in thousands]

	1990	1995	2000	Percent growth 1990-95	Percent growth 1995-2000
Total married couples	51,726	55,536	58,877	7.4	6.0
Under age 35	12,761	12,356	11,649	-3.2	-5.7
35 to 54	22,550	26,335	29,283	16.8	11.2
55 and older	16,415	16,845	17,945	2.6	6.5
With children	24,931	26,945	27,982	8.1	3.8
Under age 35	9,045	8,789	8,249	-2.8	-6.1
35 to 54	14,712	16,968	18,404	15.3	8.5
55 and older	1,174	1,188	1,329	1.2	11.9
Without children	26,795	28,591	30,895	6.7	8.1
Under age 35	3,716	3,567	3,400	-4.0	-4.7
35 to 54	7,838	9,367	10,879	19.5	16.1
55 and older	15,241	15,657	16,616	2.7	6.1

Source: "Married in the 1990s," Thomas G. Exter, *American Demographics* 14, No. 8, August, 1992, p. 63. Primary source: TGE Demographics, Inc. Reprinted with permission (c) *American Demographics* (August, 1992). For subscription information, please call (800) 828-1133.

★ 667 ★

Projection of Single Population by Age and Sex of Householder, 1990-2000

"Projections are based on 'adjusted' 1990 census population base, trends in household headship rates by age from the Census Bureau's Current Population Survey, and a population projection series that assumes a continuation of current immigration patterns and moderate levels of fertility and mortality."

[Households in thousands]

	1990	1995	2000	Percent change 1990-2000
Total living alone	22,399	23,899	25,282	12.9
Under age 35	5,097	4,907	4,683	-8.1
35 to 54	5,558	6,497	7,231	30.1
55 and older	11,744	12,495	13,368	13.8
Women living alone	13,500	14,477	15,422	14.2
Under age 35	2,079	1,997	1,911	-8.1
35 to 54	2,559	3,008	3,383	32.2
55 and older	8,862	9,472	10,128	14.3
Men living alone	8,899	9,422	9,860	10.8
Under age 35	3,018	2,910	2,772	-8.2
35 to 54	2,999	3,489	3,848	28.3
55 and older	2,882	3,023	3,240	12.4

Source: "Home Alone in 2000," by Thomas G. Exter, *American Demographics* 14, No. 9, September, 1992, p. 67. Primary source: TGE Demographics, Inc. Reprinted with permission (c) *American Demographics* (September, 1992). For subscription information, please call (800) 828-1133.

★ 668 ★

Total Marriages and Divorces by Alternative, 1990-2080

Includes the populations of Puerto Rico, Guam, American Samoa, the Virgin Islands, and U.S. citizens living abroad. Alternatives in the table below are "based on three different sets of assumptions about future net immigration, birth rates, and death rates.... Alternative I is designated as optimistic because among the three projections the assumptions selected produce the most favorable financial effect for the OASDI program. Conversely, the assumptions chosen for Alternative III, designated pessimistic, produce the most unfavorable financial effect."

[Numbers in thousands]

Alternative and calendar year	Marriages	Divorces
Alternative I		
1990	2,568	1,250
1991	2,546	1,255
1992	2,521	1,257
1993	2,495	1,252
1994	2,470	1,242
1995	2,444	1,231
1996	2,421	1,223
1997	2,402	1,215
1998	2,387	1,204
1999	2,374	1,193
2000	2,364	1,181
2005	2,324	1,131
2010	2,275	1,088
2015	2,345	1,057
2020	2,411	1,050
2025	2,478	1,060
2030	2,568	1,081
2035	2,663	1,112
2040	2,743	1,146
2045	2,814	1,179
2050	2,890	1,212
2055	2,979	1,248
2060	3,076	1,286
2065	3,170	1,327
2070	3,260	1,367
2075	3,351	1,407
2080	3,447	1,449
Alternative II		
1990	2,698	1,258
1991	2,701	1,268
1992	2,700	1,277
1993	2,696	1,278
1994	2,691	1,275
1995	2,686	1,270
1996	2,683	1,270
1997	2,683	1,268
1998	2,688	1,266

[Continued]

★ 668 ★

Total Marriages and Divorces by Alternative, 1990-2080
[Continued]

Alternative and calendar year	Marriages	Divorces
1999	2,696	1,262
2000	2,707	1,258
2005	2,772	1,251
2010	2,811	1,253
2015	2,804	1,253
2020	2,777	1,249
2025	2,768	1,245
2030	2,788	1,246
2035	2,813	1,253
2040	2,820	1,259
2045	2,816	1,262
2050	2,815	1,264
2055	2,826	1,268
2060	2,843	1,273
2065	2,855	1,279
2070	2,862	1,285
2075	2,867	1,289
2080	2,876	1,294
Alternative III		
1990	2,820	1,267
1991	2,847	1,282
1992	2,868	1,295
1993	2,885	1,302
1994	2,899	1,305
1995	2,912	1,307
1996	2,926	1,313
1997	2,944	1,319
1998	2,966	1,323
1999	2,992	1,326
2000	3,021	1,330
2005	3,172	1,361
2010	3,254	1,402
2015	3,077	1,417
2020	2,901	1,390
2025	2,773	1,349
2030	2,678	1,306
2035	2,590	1,263
2040	2,492	1,219
2045	2,386	1,174
2050	2,285	1,129
2055	2,197	1,087
2060	2,118	1,047
2065	2,040	1,010
2070	1,961	973

[Continued]

★ 668 ★

Total Marriages and Divorces by Alternative, 1990-2080
[Continued]

Alternative and calendar year	Marriages	Divorces
2075	1,884	937
2080	1,813	903

Source: "Social Security Area Population Projections," Alice H. Wade (Office of the Actuary, Social Security Administration), *Social Security Bulletin* 51, No. 2, February, 1988, p. 24.

★ 669 ★

Dependency Rates as Compared to Those of Other Major Industrial Countries, 1980-2025

"What is particularly important about (future) trends ... is that the increase in the share of the elderly is principally at the expense of the share of the working-age population. Thus, the elderly dependency rate is expected to increase sharply, from an average of 24 percent by 2010 (19 percent in 1980) to more than 31 percent by 2025. Even the youth dependency rate will increase in most countries, albeit by a small amount."

[Numbers in percent]

Country and dependency rate	1980	2000	2010	2025
Canada				
Elderly dependency rate[1]	15.0	16.0	20.0	30.0
Youth dependency rate[2]	35.0	31.0	29.0	30.0
Ratio of age group 75 and over to age group 65 and over	40.0	41.0	41.0	40.0
France				
Elderly dependency rate[1]	24.0	24.0	23.0	25.0
Youth dependency rate[2]	35.0	33.0	31.0	32.0
Ratio of age group 75 and over to age group 65 and over	42.0	43.0	50.0	37.0
Federal Republic of Germany				
Elderly dependency rate[1]	25.0	28.0	32.0	37.0
Youth dependency rate[2]	27.0	27.0	23.0	24.0
Ratio of age group 75 and over to age group 65 and over	40.0	42.0	41.0	44.0
Italy				
Elderly dependency rate[1]	22.0	25.0	26.0	30.0
Youth dependency rate[2]	35.0	30.0	28.0	28.0
Ratio of age group 75 and over to age group 65 and over	36.0	42.0	45.0	47.0
Japan				
Elderly dependency rate[1]	14.0	23.0	29.0	35.0
Youth dependency rate[2]	36.0	27.0	30.0	30.0
Ratio of age group 75 and over to age group 65 and over	35.0	37.0	42.0	52.0

[Continued]

★ 669 ★

Dependency Rates as Compared to Those of Other Major Industrial Countries, 1980-2025
[Continued]

Country and dependency rate	1980	2000	2010	2025
United Kingdom				
Elderly dependency rate[1]	23.0	23.0	24.0	30.0
Youth dependency rate[2]	32.0	31.0	29.0	30.0
Ratio of age group 75 and over to age group 65 and over	40.0	46.0	43.0	58.0
United States				
Elderly dependency rate[1]	18.0	20.0	22.0	30.0
Youth dependency rate[2]	34.0	31.0	30.0	30.0
Ratio of age group 75 and over to age group 65 and over	42.0	52.0	50.0	43.0

Source: "Population Dynamics in the Seven Major Industrial Countries," *Aging and Social Expenditure in the Major Industrial Countries, 1980-2025,* Peter S. Heller et al, International Monetary Fund, Washington, D.C., September, 1986, p. 26. Projections are based on middle demographic data from census and public pension sources used by the countries concerned. *Notes:* Magnitudes estimated from published chart. 1. Ratio of population aged 65 and over to population aged 15-64 (in percent). 2. Ratio of population aged under 15 to population aged 15-64 (in percent).

★ 670 ★

Projection of the Preschool Population by Age, 1990-2000

"If the current birth boom continues through 1992, the number of preschoolers could peak at 20.2 million in 1994. This is almost as high as the number of preschoolers in 1960 (20.3 million), when the original baby boom was peaking. And it is fully 12 percent higher than the Census Bureau's earlier middle series projection."

[Numbers in thousands]

Year	Under one	One	Two	Three	Four	Total under five
1990	4,003	3,868	3,746	3,668	3,645	18,930
1991	4,159	3,978	3,843	3,719	3,641	19,339
1992	4,180	4,132	3,950	3,815	3,691	19,768
1993	4,095	4,153	4,103	3,921	3,785	20,058
1994	4,009	4,068	4,124	4,073	3,891	20,165
1995	3,924	3,984	4,040	4,093	4,040	20,080
1996	3,916	3,899	3,957	4,010	4,060	19,842
1997	3,913	3,891	3,873	3,928	3,978	19,583
1998	3,915	3,889	3,865	3,845	3,897	19,410
1999	3,923	3,891	3,862	3,837	3,815	19,328
2000	3,937	3,898	3,864	3,834	3,807	19,341

Source: "And Baby Makes 20 Million," Thomas Exter, *American Demographics* 13, No. 7, July, 1991, p. 55.

★ 671 ★

Trends in the Social and Economic Status of Children

[We can] expect to see the following overall trends in the socioeconomic status of children:

- Over the next 30 years, the number of children living in poverty is expected to increase 37 percent, to over 20 million.

- The number of children not living with both parents is expected to increase 30 percent, to over 21 million.

- The number of children living with poorly educated mothers will grow by 56 percent, to over 21 million.

Source: "Demographic Changes and Higher Education," Charles G. Treadwell, *The Education Digest* 57, No. 6, February, 1992, p. 34.

★ 672 ★

Aged Dependency Ratios at Selected Retirement Ages by Alternative, 1987-2080

Includes the populations of Puerto Rico, Guam, American Samoa, the Virgin Islands, and U.S. citizens living abroad. The aged dependency ratio calculated at a selected age is defined as "the ratio of the number of persons in the population as of July 1 who are as old or older than the selected age to the number of persons in the population as of July 1 who are between age 19 and the selected age." Alternatives in the table below are "based on three different sets of assumptions about future net immigration, birth rates, and death rates.... Alternative I is designated as optimistic because among the three projections the assumptions selected produce the most favorable financial effect for the OASDI program. Conversely, the assumptions chosen for Alternative III, designated pessimistic, produce the most unfavorable financial effect."

Alternative and calendar year	Age			
	62	65	67	70
Alternative I				
1987	.260	.203	.170	.129
1988	.261	.205	.172	.130
1989	.262	.207	.174	.131
1990	.263	.209	.176	.133
1991	.263	.210	.177	.134
1992	.263	.211	.179	.136
1993	.263	.212	.180	.138
1994	.263	.213	.181	.139
1995	.262	.213	.182	.141
1996	.261	.213	.183	.142

[Continued]

★ 672 ★

Aged Dependency Ratios at Selected Retirement Ages by Alternative, 1987-2080

[Continued]

Alternative and calendar year	Age			
	62	65	67	70
1997	.260	.212	.183	.143
1998	.259	.211	.183	.143
1999	.258	.210	.182	.144
2000	.257	.209	.181	.144
2010	.285	.215	.180	.137
2020	.369	.277	.227	.167
2030	.430	.346	.293	.220
2040	.409	.335	.293	.234
2050	.393	.316	.271	.213
2060	.380	.307	.264	.207
2070	.374	.300	.258	.204
2080	.382	.306	.262	.205
Alternative II				
1987	.260	.204	.170	.129
1988	.261	.206	.173	.130
1989	.263	.208	.175	.132
1990	.264	.210	.177	.134
1991	.265	.211	.179	.136
1992	.266	.213	.181	.138
1993	.266	.214	.183	.140
1994	.266	.216	.184	.142
1995	.266	.217	.186	.144
1996	.266	.217	.187	.145
1997	.266	.218	.188	.147
1998	.265	.217	.188	.148
1999	.265	.217	.188	.149
2000	.265	.216	.188	.149
2010	.301	.229	.192	.148
2020	.400	.302	.249	.185
2030	.487	.393	.334	.254
2040	.488	.403	.354	.285
2050	.497	.401	.346	.275
2060	.498	.407	.354	.282
2070	.498	.407	.354	.285
2080	.513	.418	.363	.290
Alternative III				
1987	.260	.204	.170	.129
1988	.262	.206	.173	.131
1989	.264	.208	.175	.132
1990	.265	.211	.178	.134
1991	.266	.213	.180	.137
1992	.268	.215	.183	.139
1993	.269	.217	.185	.142
1994	.270	.219	.187	.144

[Continued]

★ 672 ★

Aged Dependency Ratios at Selected Retirement Ages by Alternative, 1987-2080
[Continued]

Alternative and calendar year	Age			
	62	65	67	70
1995	.270	.221	.189	.147
1996	.271	.222	.191	.149
1997	.271	.223	.193	.151
1998	.272	.223	.194	.153
1999	.272	.223	.194	.154
2000	.273	.223	.194	.155
2010	.318	.243	.205	.159
2020	.441	.335	.277	.208
2030	.573	.465	.397	.304
2040	.628	.520	.459	.373
2050	.707	.573	.496	.397
2060	.765	.634	.555	.449
2070	.800	.665	.587	.484
2080	.843	.701	.618	.508

Source: "Social Security Area Population Projections," Alice H. Wade (Office of the Actuary, Social Security Administration), *Social Security Bulletin* 51, No. 2, February, 1988, pp. 28-9.

★ 673 ★

Retirement Age at Selected Aged Dependency Ratios by Alternative, 1987-2080

Includes the populations of Puerto Rico, Guam, American Samoa, the Virgin Islands, and U.S. citizens living abroad. The aged dependency ratio for a selected age is defined as "the ratio of the number of persons in the population as of July 1 who are as old or older than the selected age to the number of persons in the population as of July 1 who are between age 19 and the selected age." Alternatives in the table below are "based on three different sets of assumptions about future net immigration, birth rates, and death rates.... Alternative I is designated as optimistic because among the three projections the assumptions selected produce the most favorable financial effect for the OASDI program. Conversely, the assumptions chosen for Alternative III, designated pessimistic, produce the most unfavorable financial effect."

Alternative and calendar year	Dependency ratio		
	0.20	0.25	0.30
Alternative I			
1987	65	62	60
1988	65	63	60
1989	65	63	60
1990	66	63	60
1991	66	63	60
1992	66	63	60

[Continued]

★ 673 ★

Retirement Age at Selected Aged Dependency Ratios by Alternative, 1987-2080

[Continued]

Alternative and calendar year	Dependency ratio		
	0.20	0.25	0.30
1993	66	63	60
1994	66	63	60
1995	66	63	60
1996	66	63	60
1997	66	63	60
1998	66	63	60
1999	66	62	60
2000	66	62	60
2010	66	63	61
2020	68	66	64
2030	71	69	67
2040	72	69	67
2050	71	68	66
2060	70	68	65
2070	70	67	65
2080	70	68	65
Alternative II			
1987	65	63	60
1988	65	63	60
1989	65	63	60
1990	66	63	60
1991	66	63	60
1992	66	63	60
1993	66	63	60
1994	66	63	60
1995	66	63	60
1996	66	63	60
1997	66	63	60
1998	66	63	60
1999	66	63	60
2000	66	63	60
2010	67	64	62
2020	69	67	65
2030	72	70	68
2040	74	72	69
2050	74	71	69
2060	74	72	69
2070	75	72	69
2080	75	72	70
Alternative III			
1987	65	63	60
1988	65	63	60
1989	65	63	60
1990	66	63	60

[Continued]

★ 673 ★

Retirement Age at Selected Aged Dependency Ratios by Alternative, 1987-2080

[Continued]

Alternative and calendar year	Dependency ratio		
	0.20	0.25	0.30
1991	66	63	60
1992	66	63	60
1993	66	63	60
1994	66	63	60
1995	66	63	60
1996	66	63	60
1997	67	63	60
1998	67	63	60
1999	67	63	61
2000	67	63	61
2010	67	65	63
2020	70	68	66
2030	74	72	70
2040	78	75	73
2050	79	76	74
2060	80	77	75
2070	81	79	77
2080	82	80	77

Source: "Social Security Area Population Projections," Alice H. Wade (Office of the Actuary, Social Security Administration), *Social Security Bulletin* 51, No. 2, February, 1988, pp. 29-30.

★ 674 ★

Projections of Pet Populations, 1990-2000

Projections of dog and cat populations at the national level, in millions. Based on the 3 series of projections for the United States human population size, as presented by the U.S. Bureau of the Census. Method 1 is based on housing projections obtained from the U.S. Census of Housing for the years 1950-1985. Method 2 is based on 3 series of projections for the United States human population size, as presented by the U.S. Bureau of the Census.

	Method	Population by year		
		1990	1995	2000
Middle series				
Dogs	1	55.87	80.81	88.27
	2	55.70	80.55	88.18
Cats	1	58.34	83.56	89.10
	2	58.38	83.28	89.00
Low series				
Dogs	2	54.83	58.75	83.25
Cats	2	57.47	61.41	65.95

[Continued]

★ 674 ★

Projections of Pet Populations, 1990-2000
[Continued]

	Method	Population by year		
		1990	1995	2000
High series				
Dogs	2	58.70	82.55	89.54
Cats	2	59.42	85.37	72.50

Source: "Projections of Pet Populations from Census Demographic Data," by R. Nassar and J. Mosier, *Journal of the American Veterinary Medical Association* 198, No. 7, April 1, 1991, p. 1158.

★ 675 ★

Projections of Pet Populations by Region, 1990-2000

Projections of national dog and cat populations.

[Numbers in millions]

Region	Population by year		
	1990	1995	2000
Dogs			
Northeast	9.65	10.36	11.21
South	21.48	24.06	27.04
Midwest	13.48	14.27	15.22
West	12.42	14.11	16.02
Cats			
Northeast	11.65	12.50	13.53
South	20.78	23.27	26.16
Midwest	12.53	13.26	14.15
West	14.51	18.48	18.71

Source: "Projections of Pet Populations from Census Demographic Data," R. Nassar and J. Mosier, *Journal of the American Veterinary Medical Association* 198, No. 7, April 1, 1991, p. 1158.

Chapter 12

RECREATION

Facilities: Funding and Utilization

★ 676 ★

Acreage of Land for Public Recreation, 1965-2000

[Numbers in thousands of acres]

Region	Total	Class						Number of
		I	II	III	IV	V	VI	Golf courses[1]
United States								
1965	338,619	728	26,858	255,459	8,415	46,641	519	10.5
1980	340,623	759	27,435	256,816	8,451	46,641	520	16.8
2000	343,278	800	28,201	258,615	8,499	46,641	522	26.0
Northeast								
1965	6,392	64	396	5,536	180	198	18	3.1
1980	6,452	66	404	5,584	181	198	18	4.8
2000	6,531	70	416	5,647	182	198	18	9.7
North Central								
1965	36,889	110	5,468	29,585	401	1,304	21	4.1
1980	37,267	114	5,586	29,840	402	1,304	21	6.3
2000	37,769	121	5,742	30,177	405	1,304	21	13.1
South								
1965	34,091	212	6,078	25,079	793	1,863	66	1.6
1980	34,450	221	6,208	25,295	796	1,863	66	2.6
2000	34,926	233	6,382	25,581	801	1,863	67	5.6
West								
1965	261,247	343	14,916	195,258	7,041	43,276	414	1.7
1980	262,454	357	15,237	196,097	7,072	43,276	415	3.1
2000	264,052	377	15,662	197,210	7,112	43,276	416	8.6

Source: "Public Recreation Lands by Type and Census Region," Charles J. Cicchetti, *Forecasting Recreation in the United States: An Economic Review of Methods and Applications to Plan for the Required Environmental Resources,* Lexington, Mass.: Lexington Books/D.C. Heath and Co., 1973, p. 109. Public recreation acreage by the Bureau of Outdoor Recreation land classification, 1965, and hypothetical acreage for 1980 and 2000 based on extension of present regional distribution. Findings assume that index of growth in amusement and private commercial recreation increases by a factor of 1.25 from 1965 to 1980 and a factor of 1.73 from 1965 to 2000. Designated classification of recreational acreage by the Bureau of Outdoor Recreation includes: Class I, high-density recreation acreage; Class II, general outdoor recreation acreage; Class III, natural environment acreage; Class IV, outstanding natural areas acreage; Class V, primitive areas acreage; and Class VI, historic and cultural areas acreage. *Note:* 1. In thousands.

★ 677 ★

Acreage of Land, Wetlands, and Water for Public Recreation, 1965-2000

[Numbers in thousands of acres]

Region	Total	Land	Wetlands	Water	Number of swimming pools
United States					
1965	346,169	322,452	11,330	12,387	34.3
1980	348,172	324,413	11,330	12,429	57.7
2000	350,828	327,012	11,330	12,486	127.1
Northeast					
1965	10,052	9,484	174	394	6.6
1980	10,112	9,543	174	395	10.4
2000	10,191	9,621	174	396	20.9
North Central					
1965	38,835	30,925	4,580	3,330	6.0
1980	39,213	31,295	4,580	3,338	12.8
2000	39,715	31,785	4,580	3,350	22.8
South					
1965	34,859	28,225	2,957	3,677	9.9
1980	35,218	28,575	2,957	3,686	16.7
2000	35,694	29,040	2,957	3,697	35.9
West					
1965	262,423	253,818	3,619	4,986	11.8
1980	263,629	255,000	3,619	5,010	21.2
2000	265,228	256,566	3,619	5,043	50.9

Source: "Public Recreation Lands and Water by Census Region," Charles J. Cicchetti, *Forecasting Recreation in the United States: An Economic Review of Methods and Applications to Plan for the Required Environmental Resources*, Lexington, Mass.: Lexington Books/D.C. Heath and Co., 1973, p. 108. Public recreation of land, wetlands, and water, 1965, and hypothetical acreage for 1980 and 2000 based on extension of present regional distribution.

★ 678 ★

National Forest System Funding in 1987 and 2040

[Numbers in percent]

	1987	Strategy 1 for the year 2040	Strategy 2 for the year 2040	Strategy 3 for the year 2040	Strategy 4 for the year 2040	Strategy 5 for the year 2040
Support	39.0	41.0	37.0	37.0	37.0	40.0
Timber	44.0	42.0	37.0	37.0	36.0	29.0
Recreation	8.0	8.0	15.0	14.0	14.0	15.0
Wildlife	3.0	4.0	5.0	5.0	8.0	10.0
Minerals	1.0	2.0	2.0	2.0	2.0	2.0

[Continued]

★ 678 ★

National Forest System Funding in 1987 and 2040
[Continued]

	1987	Strategy 1 for the year 2040	Strategy 2 for the year 2040	Strategy 3 for the year 2040	Strategy 4 for the year 2040	Strategy 5 for the year 2040
Range	2.0	2.0	2.0	2.0	2.0	2.0
Water	2.0	2.0	2.0	2.0	2.0	2.0

Source: "National Forest System Funding in 1987 and 2040," U.S. Congress, Office of Technology Assessment, *Forest Service Planning: Setting Strategic Direction under the Forest and Rangeland Renewable Resources Planning Act of 1974,* July, 1990, p. 92. Primary source: U.S. Department of Agriculture, Forest Service, *Draft 1990 RPA Program* June, 1989. All five strategies are shown to require an increase in funds. Under strategy 1—continuation of the current budget—the budget would increase by nearly 3 percent. Strategies 2 through 5 propose substantial increases in funding—more than 50 percent for Strategies 2 and 4, more than 60 percent for Strategy 3, and more than 40 percent for Strategy 5.

Participation

★ 679 ★

Marine Recreational Fishing, 1985-2025
[Numbers in thousands]

Coastal area	Forecast of participation Behavioral method			
	1985	1990	2000	2025
Northeast region				
Maine and New Hampshire	162	165	196	244
Massachusetts	541	566	611	647
Connecticut and Rhode Island	420	433	472	516
New York	1,020	1,072	1,117	1,118
New Jersey	719	753	797	836
Delaware and Maryland	559	572	593	618
Virginia[1]	562	600	630	656
Regional total	3,984	4,161	4,416	4,635
Southeast region				
North Carolina[1]	609	630	691	722
South Carolina and Georgia	650	708	774	853
Florida	1,584	1,684	1,825	1,924
Alabama, Mississippi, and Louisiana	586	635	673	715
Texas	1,086	1,200	1,326	1,418
Regional total	4,514	4,856	5,289	5,631
Southwest region				
California and Hawaii	2,188	2,362	2,579	2,672

[Continued]

★ 679 ★

Marine Recreational Fishing, 1985-2025
[Continued]

Coastal area	Forecast of participation Behavioral method			
	1985	1990	2000	2025
Northwest region				
Oregon and Washington	868	897	955	1,021
Total	11,555	12,276	13,239	13,959

Source: "Forecasts of In-State Participation in Marine Recreational Fishing," Steven F. Edwards, *Transactions of the American Fisheries Society* 118, No. 5, September, 1989, p. 569. All participants at least 16 years old. Participation in 1985 was forecast by the behavioral method (model 3, described on page 566 of Edwards's paper). 1985 data determined by a different method are not included. *Notes:* Based upon the U.S. Fish and Wildlife Service reports *1980 National Survey of Fishing, Hunting, and Wildlife-associated Recreation*, 1982 and *1985 National Survey of Fishing, Hunting, and Wildlife-Associated Recreation*, 1988. 1. Participation in Virginia and North Carolina was prorated for the two states according to the relative size of each state's population.

★ 680 ★

Number of Participants in Various Recreational Activities, 1985-2030

Substantial increases in participation are expected in all of the recreational activities studied for this report.

[Index: 1977 = 100]

Type of activity	Year		
	1985	2000	2030
All land-based			
High	114	144	247
Medium	107	122	163
Low	103	109	121
Camping (developed)			
High	124	130	369
Medium	116	150	245
Low	111	133	181
Camping (dispersed)			
High	119	161	311
Medium	110	133	205
Low	107	121	155
Nature study			
High	114	147	247
Medium	106	121	155
Low	102	107	113
Hiking			
High	115	149	270
Medium	106	117	159
Low	101	102	109

[Continued]

★ 680 ★

Number of Participants in Various Recreational Activities, 1985-2030

[Continued]

Type of activity	Year		
	1985	2000	2030
Horseback riding			
High	116	152	293
Medium	106	118	181
Low	102	103	124
Driving off-road vehicles			
High	111	134	201
Medium	105	118	148
Low	104	115	126
Picnicking			
High	112	140	230
Medium	107	124	162
Low	103	114	127
Sightseeing			
High	113	143	242
Medium	107	123	163
Low	103	111	123
Pleasure walking			
High	111	136	215
Medium	105	116	143
Low	102	105	109
Driving for pleasure			
High	111	136	215
Medium	106	119	149
Low	103	110	118
All flat water and stream-based			
High	119	165	336
Medium	111	135	218
Low	105	116	152
Canoeing			
High	125	183	403
Medium	113	141	249
Low	106	118	166
Sailing			
High	136	223	546
Medium	127	185	367
Low	118	156	263
Water skiing			
High	117	157	320
Medium	106	118	185
Low	100	96	112
Other boating			
High	120	165	330
Medium	112	137	220
Low	106	119	155

[Continued]

★ 680 ★

Number of Participants in Various Recreational Activities, 1985-2030

[Continued]

Type of activity	Year		
	1985	2000	2030
Swimming outdoors			
High	115	160	287
Medium	109	127	190
Low	104	111	136
Snow and ice-based			
High	124	180	389
Medium	114	144	250
Low	103	124	178
Downhill skiing			
High	138	228	558
Medium	125	179	352
Low	116	147	238
Snowmobiling			
High	117	151	277
Medium	106	120	181
Low	105	114	141
Cross-country skiing			
High	133	211	479
Medium	120	161	280
Low	112	134	190
Ice skating			
High	123	177	382
Medium	114	144	250
Low	109	125	179
Sledding			
High	120	166	347
Medium	111	133	227
Low	106	116	162

Source: "Indexed Projections of the Number of Participants in Various Activities in the Contiguous United States," John G. Ho and H. Fred Kaiser, *Projections of Future Forest Recreation Use*, Washington, D.C.: U.S. Department of Agriculture Forest Service, 1983, p. 6. The high, medium, and low scenarios are based on U.S. Census Bureau Series I, II, and III projections, and can be interpreted as high, medium and low projections of recreation participation.

★ 681 ★

Visits to National Parks, 1989-2015

"Right now the 354 units of the National Park System receive a total of 287.6 million recreation visits per year. At the current rate of population growth, it is expected that recreation visits to the parks will reach at least a third of a billion by the year 2015, a jump of 16 percent."

Source: "National Parks: Year 2000," William Penn Mott, Jr., *National Parks* 63, Nos. 1-2, January-February, 1989, p. 18.

Chapter 13

SCIENCE, ENERGY, AND TECHNOLOGY

Electric Power

★ 682 ★

Comparisons of Electricity Price Projections, 2000

The Reference Case combines an assumption of an annual economic growth rate of 2.1 percent and an intermediate world oil price path rising from $22 per barrel to $34 per barrel by 2010. No new legislation or regulations are incorporated in this case. The High Oil Price Case combines a high world oil price path that reaches $45 per barrel by 2010 and an average annual economic growth rate of 2.1 percent. This case also assumes a strong commitment to energy conservation, resulting in a lower rate of annual growth in electricity sales than the Reference Case. The High Economic Growth Case assumes a rate of economic growth of 2.8 percent per year, combined with a low world oil price path that reaches $23 per barrel by 2010.

[Numbers in 1990 cents per kilowatt hour]

	EIA			GRI	DRI	AGA	NERC (1999)	NCA
	High oil price	Reference Case	High economic growth					
Electricity prices								
Residential	8.2	8.1	8.1	7.1	7.6	7.6	NA	NA
Commercial/other	7.4	7.4	7.4	6.5	7.0	7.0	NA	NA
Industrial	5.2	5.2	5.3	4.8	5.2	4.8	NA	NA
Average	6.9	6.9	6.8	6.1	6.6	6.5	NA	NA
Components of price								
Capital[1]	2.5	2.5	2.4	2.7	2.7	NA	NA	NA
Fuel	2.3	2.3	2.4	2.0	2.3	NA	NA	NA
Operations and Maintenance	2.1	2.1	2.0	1.5	1.6	NA	NA	NA
Total	6.9	6.9	6.8	6.1	6.6	NA	NA	NA

Source: "Outlook for U.S. Electric Power through 2010," *Annual Outlook for U.S. Electric Power 1991: Projections through 2010,* Washington, D.C., p. 28. Primary source: U.S. Department of Energy, Energy Information Administration, 1991; AEO 1991 Forecasting System; Gas Research Institute, *Baseline Projection Data Book, 1991*; DRI/McGraw-Hill, *Energy Review,* Fall 1990; American Gas Association, Total Energy Resources Analysis Demand/Marketplace Model, 14 December, 1990; North American Electric Reliability Council, *1990 Electricity Supply and Demand for 1990-1999,* November, 1990; National Coal Association, *Coal, Energy for the Next Decade and Beyond: Forecasts for U.S. Coal, 1990-2000,* February, 1989. NA = not available. *Note:* 1. The capital component in the GRI projection includes net interchange.

★ 683 ★

Comparisons of Electric Power Projections: 2010 - I

The Reference Case combines an assumption of an annual economic growth rate of 2.1 percent and an intermediate world oil price path rising from $22 per barrel to $34 per barrel by 2010. No new legislation or regulations are incorporated in this case. The High Oil Price Case combines a high world oil price path that reaches $45 per barrel by 2010 and an average annual economic growth rate of 2.1 percent. This case also assumes a strong commitment to energy conservation, resulting in a lower rate of annual growth in electricity sales than the Reference Case. The High Economic Growth Case assumes a rate of economic growth of 2.8 percent per year, combined with a low world oil price path that reaches $23 per barrel by 2010.

	EIA			GRI	DRI	AGA[1]	NERC[2] (1999)	NCA
	High Oil Price	Reference Case	High Economic Growth					
Sales (billion kWh)								
Residential	1,012	1,068	1,093	1,095	1,090	1,178	NA	NA
Commercial/other	998	1,050	1,058	1,013	998	1,044	NA	NA
Industrial	1,151	1,164	1,275	1,169	1,041	1,151	NA	NA
Total	3,162	3,282	3,426	3,276	3,129	3,373	3,476[2]	NA
Generation (billion kWh)								
Coal[3]	1,724	1,731	1,745	1,753	1,769	1,799	1,803	1,788
Oil and Gas	529	625	745	619	532	289	454	611
Nuclear	592	594	595	636	640	625	642	632
Hydroelectric/Other	322	322	322	329	345	309	292	262
Nonutility Generation[4] (sales to grid)	204	223	243	232	109	649	219	159
Total Domestic Generation	3,370	3,495	3,650	3,570	3,395	3,670	3,409	3,451
Net Imports	55	55	55	45	38	NA	67	71
Total Net Energy for Load	3,425	3,550	3,704	3,615	3,433	NA	3,476	3,522
Fuel Inputs (trillion Btu)								
Coal	18,169	18,250	18,429	18,299	17,479	17,141	18,454	NA
Oil	1,648	2,079	2,659	2,904	1,940	2,207	1,576	NA
Gas	4,868	5,627	6,471	4,083	4,629	7,043	3,336	NA
Nuclear	6,454	6,473	6,482	7,083	6,873	6,754	NA	NA
Hydro	3,270	3,270	3,270	3,298	3,680	3,715	NA	NA
Other	1,737	1,738	1,736	1,333	240	2,076	NA	NA
Total	36,146	37,437	39,047	36,999	34,841	38,937	NA	NA
Capacity (gigawatts)	Summer[5]	Summer[5]	Summer[5]	Nameplate[6]	Nameplate[6]	Nameplate[6]	Summer[5]	Summer[5]
Coal	303	303	303	335	350	461	309	309
Oil and Gas	203	208	224	264	261	221	217	196
Nuclear	105	105	105	104	105	114	104	102
Hydroelectric/Other[7]	102	102	102	97	96	91	99	93
Nonutility Generators[8]	57	61	66	92	59	120	33	39
Total	770	779	800	891	871	1,006	761	740

Source: "Outlook for U.S. Electric Power through 2010," *Annual Outlook for U.S. Electric Power 1991: Projections through 2010*, Washington, D.C., p. 25. Primary source: U.S. Department of Energy, Energy Information Administration, 1991; AEO 1991 Forecasting System; Gas Research Institute, *Baseline Projection Data Book, 1991*; DRI/McGraw-Hill, *Energy Review*, Fall, 1990; American Gas Association, Total Energy Resources Analysis Demand/Marketplace Model, 14 December, 1990; North American Electric Reliability Council, *1990 Electricity Supply and Demand for 1990-1999*, November, 1990; National Coal Association, *Coal, Energy for the Next Decade and Beyond: Forecasts for U.S. Coal, 1990-2000*, February, 1989. *Notes:* NA = not available. 1. AGA does not break down generation and capacity into the fuel types depicted here. EIA has aggregated the AGA projections of generation and capacity for comparison purposes. 2. The NERC projection in the sales column is actually net energy for load. Net energy for load minus transmission and distribution losses is equal to sales. 3. To provide a basis for comparison between NCA and EIA, NCA projects electric utilities to consume 872 million tons of coal in 2000. EIA projects that 861 million tons of coal will be consumed. 4. Electricity that is sold to the grid. Excludes electricity generated for own use except for AGA. 5. Net Summer Capability: The steady hourly output which generating equipment is expected to supply to system load exclusive of auxiliary power as demonstrate by tests at the time of summer peak demand. 6. Installed Nameplate Capacity: The full-load continuous rating of a generator, prime mover, or other electrical equipment under specified conditions as designated by the manufacturer. Installed nameplate capacity is usually indicated on a nameplate attached physically to the equipment and does not include auxiliary units. Nameplate capacity is generally accepted to be approximately 5 percent greater than summer capacity. 7. Generation is net energy used for pumped storage. 8. Nonutility capacity for NCA and NERC includes only that capacity that produces electricity for the grid. NERC projections included only that capacity that has been contracted and that NERC members believe will be secured by contract. All forecasters, except GRI, include capacity for the grid and own use. GRI does not include commercial cogeneration capacity for own use. Totals may not equal the sum of components because of rounding.

★ 684 ★

Comparisons of Electric Power Projections: 2010 - II

The Reference Case combines an assumption of an annual economic growth rate of 2.1 percent and an intermediate world oil price path rising from $22 per barrel to $34 per barrel by 2010. No new legislation or regulations are incorporated in this case. The High Oil Price Case combines a high world oil price path that reaches $45 per barrel by 2010 and an average annual economic growth rate of 2.1 percent. This case also assumes a strong commitment to energy conservation, resulting in a lower rate of annual growth in electricity sales than the Reference Case. The High Economic Growth Case assumes a rate of economic growth of 2.8 percent per year, combined with a low world oil price path that reaches $23 per barrel by 2010.

	EIA			GRI	DRI	AGA[1]	NERC[2] (1999)	NCA
	High Oil Price	Reference Case	High Economic Growth					
Sales (billion kWh)								
Residential	1,060	1,179	1,233	1,256	1,192	1,340		
Commercial/other	1,180	1,318	1,337	1,249	1,110	1,186		
Industrial	1,462	1,489	1,751	1,387	1,125	1,295		
Total	3,702	3,985	4,321	3,892	3,563	3,821		
Generation (billion kWh)								
Coal	1,972	2,194	2,355	2,008	2,095	2,142		
Oil and Gas	681	736	842	750	664	312		
Nuclear	623	611	654	630	647	528		
Hydroelectric/Other	333	333	332	334	358	323		
Nonutility Generation[2] (sales to grid)	318	358	408	547	112	824		
Total Domestic Generation	3,927	4,232	4,591	4,269	3,876	4,128		
Net Imports	68	68	68	57	44	NA		
Total Net Energy for Load	3,996	4,300	4,660	4,326	3,920	NA		
Fuel Inputs (trillion Btu)								
Coal	20,717	22,933	24,639	22,918	20,793	20,367		
Oil	1,813	1,733	2,860	4,071	2,163	2,426		
Gas	6,093	6,561	6,406	4,803	5,803	8,232		
Nuclear	6,7982	6,667	7,139	7,019	6,950	5,705		
Hydro	3,270	3,270	3,270	3,298	3,869	3,915		
Other	2,756	2,750	2,746	1,786	240	2,899		
Total	41,441	43,914	47,060	43,895	39,818	43,544		
Capacity (gigawatts)	Summer[3]	Summer[3]	Summer[3]	Nameplate[4]	Nameplate[4]	Nameplate[4]	Summer[5]	Summer[5]
Coal	336	374	400	364	397	550		
Oil and Gas	228	252	285	287	274	242		
Nuclear	104	101	110	101	102	113		
Hydroelectric/Other[5]	103	103	103	98	96	93		
Nonutility Generators[6]	81	89	100	168	61	153		
Total	853	918	999	1,018	929	1,152		

Source: "Outlook for U.S. Electric Power through 2010," *Annual Outlook for U.S. Electric Power 1991: Projections through 2010*, Washington, D.C., p. 26. Primary source: U.S. Department of Energy, Energy Information Administration, 1991; AEO 1991 Forecasting System; Gas Research Institute, *Baseline Projection Data Book, 1991;* DRI/McGraw-Hill, *Energy Review*, Fall, 1990; American Gas Association, Total Energy Resources Analysis Demand/Marketplace Model, 14 December, 1990; North American Electric Reliability Council, *1990 Electricity Supply and Demand for 1990-1999*, November, 1990; National Coal Association, *Coal, Energy for the Next Decade and Beyond: Forecasts for U.S. Coal, 1990-2000*, February, 1989. Totals may not equal the sum of components because of rounding. *Notes:* NA = not available. 1. AGA does not break down generation and capacity into the fuel types depicted here. EIA has aggregated the AGA projections of generation and capacity for comparison purposes. 2. Electricity that is sold to the grid. Excludes electricity generated for own use except for AGA. 3. Net Summer Capacity: The steady hourly output which generating equipment is expected to supply to system load exclusive of auxiliary power as demonstrated by tests at the time of summer peak demand. 4. Installed Nameplate Capacity: The full-load continuous rating of a generator, prime mover, or other electrical equipment under specified conditions as designated by the manufacturer. Installed nameplate capacity is usually indicated on a nameplate attached physically to the equipment and does not include auxiliary units. Nameplate capacity is generally accepted to be approximately 5 percent greater than summer capability. 5. Generation is net energy used for pumped storage. 6. Includes all capacity for sale to the grid and own use, except GRI. GRI does not include commercial cogeneration capacity for own use.

★ 685 ★

Components of Electricity Price, 1989-2010

The Reference Case combines an assumption of an annual economic growth rate of 2.1 percent and an intermediate world oil price path rising from $22 per barrel to $34 per barrel by 2010. No new legislation or regulations are incorporated in this case.

	1989	1990	2000	2010	Annual growth rate 1989-2000 (percent)	Annual growth rate 2000-2010 (percent)
Sales (billion kWh)	2,647	2,707	3,282	3,985	2.0	2.0
Revenue requirements[1] (billion 1990 dollars)						
Fuel	48.4	47.6	76.1	115.6	4.2	4.3
Operating and maintenance	56.6	57.7	68.3	82.1	1.7	1.9
Capital						
Depreciation	21.4	21.8	21.2	21.0	-0.1	-0.1
Taxes	18.3	18.8	22.7	27.8	2.0	2.0
Return on ratebase	41.8	42.0	36.5	41.3	-1.2	1.2
Ratebase[2]	376.7	378.3	340.2	403.8	-0.9	1.7
Rate of return[3] (percent)	11.1	11.1	10.7	10.2	-0.3	-0.5
Total capital	81.4	82.6	80.4	90.1	-0.1	1.1
Total revenue requirements	186.3	187.9	224.8	287.7	1.7	2.5
Component of price[4] (1990 cents per kWh)						
Fuel	1.83	1.76	2.32	2.91	2.2	2.3
Operating and maintenance	2.14	2.13	2.08	2.06	-0.3	-0.1
Capital						
Depreciation	0.81	0.80	0.65	0.53	-2.0	-2.0
Taxes	0.69	0.69	0.69	0.70	0.0	0.1
Return on ratebase	1.58	1.55	1.11	1.04	-3.1	-0.7
Total capital	3.09	3.05	2.45	2.25	-2.1	-0.8
Total component of price	7.06	6.94	6.85	7.22	-0.2	0.5

Source: "Outlook for U.S. Electric Power through 2010," Annual Outlook for U.S. Electric Power 1991: Projections through 2010, Washington, D.C., p. 20. Primary source: U.S. Department of Energy, Energy Information Administration, 1991; AEO 1991 Forecasting System. *Notes:* 1. Revenue requirements are the expenses that ratemaking commissions allow regulated utilities to recover from ratepayers. 2. The ratebase is the total value of capital assets, net of accumulated depreciation, on which utilities are allowed to earn a return ratemaking commissions. 3. The return to investors on all classes of securities. 4. The component of price equals the revenue requirements divided by total sales to identify the impact of a given component (fuel, operating and maintenance, or capital related) on the price of electricity on a per kilowatt-hour basis. Totals may not equal sum of components because of rounding.

★ 686 ★

Data for U.S. Electric Power, 1989-2010

The Reference Case combines an assumption of an annual economic growth rate of 2.1 percent and an intermediate world oil price path rising from $22 per barrel to $34 per barrel by 2010. No new legislation or regulations are incorporated in this case. The High Oil Price Case combines a high world oil price path that reaches $45 per barrel by 2010 and an average annual economic growth rate of 2.1 percent. This case also assumes a strong commitment to energy conservation, resulting in a lower rate of annual growth in electricity sales than the Reference Case. The High Economic Growth Case assumes a rate of economic growth of 2.8 percent per year, combined with a low world oil price path that reaches $23 per barrel by 2010.

Selected values	1989	1990	Projections					
			2000			2010		
			High oil price	Reference	High economic growth	High oil price	Reference	High economic growth
Electricity sales (billion kilowatthours)								
Industrial	926	938	1,151	1,164	1,275	1,462	1,489	1,751
Residential	906	922	1,012	1,068	1,093	1,060	1,179	1,233
Commercial/other[1]	816	846	998	1,050	1,058	1,180	1,318	1,337
Total sales	2,647	2,707	3,162	3,282	3,426	3,702	3,985	4,321
Generation for own use	95	104	105	110	122	127	131	149
Total electricity demand	2,742	2,810	3,267	3,392	3,548	3,829	4,117	4,470
T&D[2] losses and unaccounted								
(billion kilowatthours)	238	218	263	268	278	294	314	339
Net energy for load (billion kilowatthours)	2,885	2,924	3,425	3,550	3,704	3,996	4,300	4,660
Net electricity imports	11	2	55	55	55	68	68	68
Purchases from nonutilities	90	115	204	223	243	318	358	408
Generation by utilities	2,784	2,807	3,167	3,272	3,406	3,609	3,874	4,184
Generation by fuel type (billion kilowatthours)								
Net utility generation								
Coal	1,554	1,558	1,724	1,731	1,745	1,972	2,194	2,355
Natural gas	267	264	377	432	500	515	576	580
Oil	158	117	152	193	245	167	160	262
Nuclear	529	577	592	594	594	623	611	654
Renewables/other[3]	276	291	322	322	322	333	333	332
Total	2,784	2,807	3,167	3,272	3,406	3,609	3,874	4,184
Nonutility generation[4]								
Coal	33	34	43	43	47	90	118	149
Natural gas	78	93	109	133	161	123	138	174
Oil	3	3	4	4	4	5	5	6
Renewables/other[3]	71	89	153	153	153	228	228	228
Total	185	219	309	334	365	446	489	556
Total net generation	2,970	3,026	3,476	3,605	3,771	4,055	4,363	4,740
End-use sectoral prices								
(1990 cents per kilowatt-hour)								
Residential	8.2	8.1	8.2	8.1	8.1	8.8	8.7	8.7
Commercial/other	7.8	7.7	7.4	7.4	7.4	7.6	7.7	7.7
Industrial	5.2	5.1	5.2	5.2	5.3	5.6	5.7	5.7
Components of electricity price[5]								
(1990 cents per Kilowatt-hour)								
Capital	3.1	3.1	2.5	2.5	2.4	2.1	2.3	2.3
Fuel	1.8	1.8	2.3	2.3	2.4	3.0	2.9	2.9

[Continued]

★ 686 ★

Data for U.S. Electric Power, 1989-2010
[Continued]

Selected values	1989	1990	Projections					
			2000			2010		
			High oil price	Reference	High economic growth	High oil price	Reference	High economic growth
Operating and maintenance	2.1	2.1	2.1	2.1	2.0	2.1	2.1	2.0
Total average electricity price	7.0	6.9	6.9	6.9	6.8	7.2	7.2	7.2

Source: "Outlook for U.S. Electric Power through 2010," *Annual Outlook for U.S. Electric Power 1991: Projections through 2010,* Washington, D.C., p. 13. Primary source: U.S. Department of Energy, Energy Information Administration, *Electric Power Monthly.* Notes: 1. Other includes street lighting and the transportation sector. 2. Transmission and distribution. 3. Includes conventional hydroelectric, pumpedstorage hydroelectric, geothermal, wood, wind, waste, and solar. 4. Nonutilities consist of cogenerators, small power producers, and independent power producers. 5. Projected prices are from model simulations and represent average revenue per kilowatt-hour of demand over all customer classes.

★ 687 ★

Electricity Demand by Region, 1990-2010
[Numbers of kilowatthours in billions]

Federal region	1990	1995	2000	2005	2010
New England	86.8	83.0	89.6	93.0	97.3
NY/NJ	182.4	169.4	179.7	198.9	205.4
Mid-Atlantic	267.0	280.0	304.3	333.8	367.4
South Atlantic	578.7	629.5	692.1	763.3	839.0
Midwest	509.6	538.8	582.2	642.4	706.4
Southwest	357.0	392.1	434.8	476.2	500.7
Central	132.4	145.7	157.9	172.6	188.0
North Central	83.5	90.6	98.9	109.3	121.3
West	234.9	263.6	288.8	308.2	334.5
Northwest	147.0	157.7	172.5	191.7	211.4
Total	2,579.5	2,750.6	3,001.0	3,289.4	3,571.6

Source: "Electricity Demand Used by NCM by Federal Region for the Reference, High Oil Price, and Low Oil Price Cases, 1990-2010," *Assumptions for the Annual Energy Outlook 1992,* January, 1992, p. 65. Primary source: U.S. Department of Energy, Energy Information Administration, Office of Integrated Analysis and forecasting. NCM = National Coal Model. Totals may not equal sum of components due to rounding.

★ 688 ★

Energy Consumption and End-Use Electricity Consumption Data, 1989-2010

The Reference Case combines an assumption of an annual economic growth rate of 2.1 percent and an intermediate world oil price path rising from $22 per barrel to $34 per barrel by 2010. No new legislation or regulations are incorporated in this case. The High Oil Price Case combines a high world oil price path that reaches $45 per barrel by 2010 and an average annual economic growth rate of 2.1 percent. This case also assumes a strong commitment to energy conservation, resulting in a lower rate of annual growth in electricity sales than the Reference Case. The High Economic Growth Case assumes a rate of economic growth of 2.8 percent per year, combined with a low world oil price path that reaches $23 per barrel by 2010.

[Numbers in quadrillion BTUs]

Sector	1989	1990	Projections					
			2000			2010		
			High oil price	Reference	High economic growth	High oil price	Reference	High economic growth
Total U.S. Primary Energy Consumption	81.3	81.5	92.8	95.6	100.3	101.3	106.9	116.8
Energy consumption for electricity generation								
Electric utilities	29.3	29.6	35.4	36.5	38.0	40.6	42.9	45.9
Nonutilities	1.5	1.6	2.6	2.7	2.9	4.1	4.4	5.0
Total	30.8	31.2	37.9	39.2	40.9	44.6	47.4	50.8
End-use energy consumption								
Residential	9.7	9.3	10.3	11.0	11.1	10.4	11.7	12.0
Commercial/other[1]	29.0	28.7	30.7	31.7	33.8	33.8	36.0	40.4
Industrial[2]	22.4	23.1	27.2	27.6	29.2	29.2	29.9	33.4
Total	61.1	61.2	68.2	70.3	74.1	73.4	77.5	85.7
End-use electricity consumption by sector								
Residential	3.1	3.1	3.5	3.6	3.7	3.6	4.0	4.2
Commercial/other[1]	2.8	2.9	3.4	3.6	3.6	4.0	4.5	4.6
Industrial	3.5	3.5	4.3	4.4	4.8	5.4	5.5	6.5
Total	9.4	9.6	11.2	11.6	12.1	13.1	14.1	15.3

Source: "Outlook for U.S. Electric Power through 2010," *Annual Outlook for U.S. Electric Power 1991: Projections through 2010,* Washington, D.C., p. 11. Primary source: U.S. Department of Energy, Energy Information Administration, Office of Coal, Nuclear, Electric and Alternate Fuels, AEO 1991 Forecasting System, Reference Case, *Monthly Energy Review,* April 1991. *Notes:* Totals may not equal sum of components because of rounding. 1. Other includes street lighting and the transportation sector. 2. Industrial energy consumption includes energy consumed to produce electricity for own use.

★ 689 ★

Independent Power Production Market by Ownership, 1989 and 2000

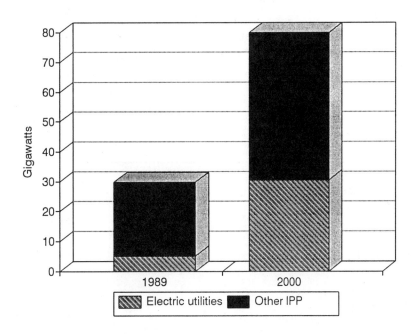

"Diversifying utilities are ... focusing on the independent power, or nonutility, generation business. The appeal is simple. It will be the best place to maintain or gain power generation market share in the 1990s. Approximately 40 utilities have already invested in the IPP business, and more are considering it. By the year 2000, the IPP business will nearly triple its current share of the power generation market and grow nearly 10 percent per year—15 times as fast as regulated utility production capacity is expected to grow."

[Values in gigawatts]

	Independent Power Production (Gigawatts)	Electric Utilites' Share (Percent)
1989	30	17.0
2000	80	38.0

Source: "Utility Diversification—It Takes More Than Money," Francis J. Andrews, *Electric Perspectives* 15, No. 5, September/October, 1991, p. 24.

Employment of Scientists and Engineers

★ 690 ★

Civilian Employment of Scientists, Engineers, and Technicians (SET) by Field, 1986 and 2000

Field	Number employed, 1986	Projected percentage increase in employment, 2000
Total, SET fields	4,245,600	36
Total scientists*	1,131,600	45
Computer specialists	331,000	76
Life	140,000	21
Mathematical	48,000	29
Physical	180,000	13
Social	432,600	36
Total engineers	1,371,000	32
Aeronautical/astronautical	53,000	11
Chemical	52,000	15
Civil	199,000	25
Electrical/electronics	401,000	48
Industrial	117,000	30
Mechanical	233,000	33
Other	316,000	24
Total technicians	1,743,000	36
Computer programmers	479,000	70
Draftsmen	348,000	2
Electrical/electronics	313,000	46
Other engineering	376,000	26
Physical, mathematical, and life sciences	227,000	15

Source: *Women in Science and Engineering: Increasing Their Numbers in the 1990's,* Committee on Women in Science and Engineering, Office of Scientific and Engineering Personnel National Research Council, National Academy Press, Washington, DC, 1991, p. 8. Primary source: U.S. Department of Labor, Bureau of Labor Statistics. *Note:* * indicates figure includes 97,300 environmental scientists.

Energy Use and Fuel Supply and Consumption

★ 691 ★

Baseline Energy Use and Supply by Quadrillion Btu, 1989-2015

[Numbers in quadrillion Btus]

	1989	2015
Demand		
Residential		
Natural gas	5.0	4.2
Electricity[1]	3.1	4.0
Oil	1.8	1.1
Coal	0.1	0.1
Renewables	0.9	1.5
Total	10.9	10.9
Commercial		
Natural gas	2.7	3.4
Electricity[1]	2.7	5.2
Oil	0.7	0.9
Coal	ne	0.1
Total	6.1	9.6
Transportation		
Oil	21.6	27.5
Natural gas	0.6	0.7
Electricity[1]	ne	ne
Total	22.2	28.2
Industrial		
Natural gas	8.3	7.7
Oil (fuel)	3.8	5.0
Oil (nonfuel)	4.4	5.7
Electricity[1]	3.2	5.3
Renewables	1.9	3.5
Coal	2.9	4.6
Total	24.5	31.8
Total Demand[1]	63.6	80.5
Electricity[2]		
Coal	16.0	29.1
Nuclear	5.7	3.8
Gas	2.9	6.3
Oil	1.7	1.6
Renewables	3.0	5.7
Total	29.2	46.4
Supply		
Oil	34.0	41.8
Domestic	(18.3)	(12.0)
Imported	(17.0)	(27.8)
Exported	(1.8)	(0.0)

[Continued]

★ 691 ★

Baseline Energy Use and Supply by Quadrillion Btu, 1989-2015

[Continued]

	1989	2015
Synthetic	(ne)	(2.0)
Gas	19.5	22.3
Domestic	(17.5)	(16.5)
Imported	(1.4)	(5.8)
Synthetic	(ne)	(ne)
Coal	18.9	38.8[3]
Produced	(21.2)	(40.7)
Exported	(2.7)	(4.0)
Synfuel feed	(ne)	(2.9)
Nuclear	5.7	3.8
Renewable	5.8	10.7
Total	83.9	112.4

Source: *Energy Technology Choices: Shaping Our Future*, U.S. Congress, Office of Technology Assessment, Washington, D.C., July, 1991, p. 113. Primary source: U.S. Energy Information Administration, *Annual Energy Review 1989*; Office of Technology Assessment, 1991. *Notes:* ne = negligible. 1. Does not include conversion losses at power plants, which make up about two-thirds of the total consumed there. 2. All fuels used for power, with hydroelectric and other nonthermal power plants artificially rated at average thermal efficiency. 3. A total of 40.1 quads of coal are mined, 2.9 quads of which are converted into 2 quads of synthetic fuel, which are included under oil.

★ 692 ★

Comparison of Commercial Energy-Use Forecasts, 1985-2010

Forecast	Primary energy use (quadrillion Btu)			
	1985	1990	2000	2010
Lawrence Berkeley Laboratory (1987)[1]	11.6	13.3	15.8	18.5
U.S. Department of Energy (1985)[2]	-	13.3	16.1	18.0
U.S. Energy Information Administration (1987)[3]	11.6	12.8	15.4	-
Data Resources Inc. (1986)[4]	11.5	12.8	14.6	17.4
Gas Research Institute (1985)[5]	-	12.2	14.0	16.7
American Gas Association (1986)[6]	12.7	13.3	15.6	-
Oak Ridge National Laboratory[7]	10.8	13.1	16.0	18.8
National Energy Strategy[8]	-	13.8	(17.6)	21.3

Source: *Energy Technology Choices: Shaping Our Future*, U.S. Congress, Office of Technology Assessment, Washington, D.C., July, 1991, p. 29. Primary source: Brookhaven National Laboratory, "Analysis and Technology Transfer Annual Report—1986," August, 1987, and references cited in *Notes* below. *Notes:* 1. Pacific Northwest Laboratory Commercial Energy Use Model. 2. Office of Planning, Policy, and Analysis, U.S. Department of Energy, "National Energy Plan Projections to the Year 2010," 1985. 3. U.S. Energy Information Administration, "Annual Energy Outlook 1987," March, 1988. 4. Data Resources, Inc., "Energy Review," Summer, 1986. 5. Gas Research Institute, "1987 GRI Baseline Projection of U.S. Energy Supply and Demand to 2010," December, 1987 (not including renewable energy sources). 6. American Gas Association, "AGA-TERA Base Case 1986-I," January, 1986. 7. Oak Ridge National Laboratory, "Energy Efficiency: Haw Far Can We Go?", January, 1990, p. 7. 8. National Energy Strategy, First Edition 1991/1992, February, 1991.

★ 693 ★

Comparison of Residential Energy-Use Forecast, 1985-2010

Forecast	Primary energy use (quadrillion Btu)			
	1985	1990	2000	2010
Lawrence Berkeley Laboratory (1987)[1]	15.5	17.0	18.0	19.9
U.S. Department of Energy (1985)[2]	-	17.8	19.8	21.3
U.S. Energy Information Administration (1987)[3]	15.2	16.9	18.6	-
Data Resources, Inc.[4]	15.0	16.8	17.9	18.7
Gas Research Institute (1985)[5]	-	16.9	17.8	18.7
American Gas Association (1986)[6]	14.3	13.8	14.8	-
Oak Ridge National Laboratory[7]	16.0	17.2	18.4	20.4
National Energy Strategy[8]	-	18.2	(20.8)	23.3

Source: Energy Technology Choices: Shaping Our Future, U.S. Congress, Office of Technology Assessment, Washington, D.C., July, 1991, p. 29. Primary source: Brookhaven National Laboratory, "Analysis and Technology Transfer Annual Report—1986," August, 1987, and references cited in *Notes* below. *Notes:* 1. Computer run provided by Jim McMahon, Lawrence Berkeley Laboratory, November, 1987. 2. Office of Planning, Policy, and Analysis, U.S. Department of Energy, "National Energy Plan Projections to the Year 2010," 1985. 3. U.S. Energy Information Administration, "Annual Energy Outlook 1987," March, 1988. 4. Data Resources, Inc., "Energy Review," Summer, 1986. 5. Gas Research Institute, "1987 GRI Baseline Projection of U.S. Energy Supply and Demand to 2010," December, 1987. 6. American Gas Association, "AGA-TERA Base Case 1986-I," January, 1986. 7. Oak Ridge National Laboratory, "Energy Efficiency: How Far Can We Go?", January, 1990, p. 7. 8. National Energy Strategy, First Edition 1991/1992, February, 1991.

★ 694 ★

Cumulative Energy Impacts of the National Appliance Energy Conservation Amendments of 1988: 1990-2015

Department of Energy region	Base case		Savings		Electricity (%)	Savings All fuels (%)
	Electricity (TWh)	All fuels (quads)	Electricity (TWh)	All fuels (quads)		
New England	1,261	18.1	13	0.1	1.0	0.7
New York/New Jersey	1,833	28.6	27	0.3	1.5	1.0
Mid Atlantic	3,464	30.9	69	0.2	2.0	0.8
South Atlantic	9,112	21.8	320	0.1	3.5	0.4
Midwest	5,234	63.1	110	0.5	2.1	0.8
Southwest	4,022	23.1	135	0.2	3.4	0.8
Central	1,584	14.3	38	0.1	2.4	0.7
North Central	1,312	13.3	20	0.1	1.5	0.7
West	3,423	26.9	61	0.3	1.8	1.1
Northwest	2,087	5.8	29	(0.0)	1.4	(0.3)
Total	33,332	245.8	822	1.9	2.5	0.8

Source: Energy Technology Choices: Shaping Our Future, U.S. Congress/Office of Technology Assessment, Washington, DC, July, 1991, p. 56. Primary source: Lawrence Berkeley Laboratory, "The Regional and Economic Impacts of the National Appliance Energy Conservation Act of 1987," Berkeley, CA, June, 1988., National Appliance Energy Conservation Amendments.

★ 695 ★

Energy Plant Sulfur Dioxide Emission Allowance Costs by Region, 1995-2010

"Under the CAA Amendments, generating units are allocated permits, or allowances, to emit a specified amount of SO_2 [sulfur dioxide] in a given year. Most, but not all, generating units are affected units (i.e., subject to the requirements of the CAA Amendments). Therefore, EIA assumes that unaffected generating units will continue to emit at historical levels. When emissions for unaffected units are combined with an estimate of allowances for affected units, an emission limit is established. This limit ranges from approximately 14 million short tons of SO_2 in 1995 decreasing to almost 9 million short tons in 2010. No allowances are distributed for NO_x emissions. Instead, the intent of the CAA Amendments is that a 2-million-short-ton reduction in NO_x [nitrogen oxides] emissions be achieved by 2000. To do this, EIA assumes that all units will be retrofitted with low NO_x burners at a cost of approximately $4 per kilowatt. Estimates of allowance banking and the costs of retrofitting units with flue gas desulfurization equipment (scrubbers) are also input into the NCM. EIA assumes that slightly more than 1 million tons of allowances will be banked (saved for later use) between 1995 and 1999. The use of the banked allowances is assumed to be distributed evenly over the period 2000 through 2009. The regional cost of retrofitting units with scrubbers ranges from $190 to $418 (1990 dollars) per kilowatt, with the national average at $264 (1990 dollars) per kilowatt. Almost 143 gigawatts of existing capacity can be retrofitted with scrubbers. Using these inputs, the NCM determines the amount of capacity that will be retrofitted with scrubbers, the amount of low sulfur coal and oil that will be consumed and the amount of emission trading that will occur. The fuel shares by sulfur content are then input into the EMM [Electricity Market Module]. In addition, the revenues and costs of trading allowances and the scrubber and low NO_x burner retrofit costs are input to the NUFS [National Utility Financial Statement] model, which determines electricity prices."

[Numbers in million 1990 dollars]

Federal region	1995	2000	2005	2010
New England	0	20	41	-32
New York/New Jersey	0	13	47	-26
Mid Atlantic	0	295	317	267
South Atlantic	0	7	11	35
Midwest	0	-11	-23	144
Southwest	0	-165	-195	-217
Central	0	-7	-15	31
North Central	0	-98	-109	-113
West	0	-53	-66	-80
Northwest	0	-2	-8	-8
Total United States	0	0	0	0

Source: "Costs from Trading Allowances," *Assumptions for the Annual Energy Outlook 1992*, January, 1992, p. 85. Primary source: U.S. Department of Energy, Energy Information Administration, Office of Integrated Analysis and Forecasting, National Coal Model (NCM). A positive number indicates that the region is a net purchaser of allowances; negative cost indicates that the region is a net seller of allowances.

★ 696 ★

Fossil Fuel Consumption and Prices, 1989-2010

The Reference Case combines an assumption of an annual economic growth rate of 2.1 percent and an intermediate world oil price path rising from $22 per barrel to $34 per barrel by 2010. No new legislation or regulations are incorporated in this case. The High Oil Price Case combines a high world oil price path that reaches $45 per barrel by 2010 and an average annual economic growth rate of 2.1 percent. This case also assumes a strong commitment to energy conservation, resulting in a lower rate of annual growth in electricity sales than the Reference Case. The High Economic Growth Case assumes a rate of economic growth of 2.8 percent per year, combined with a low world oil price path that reaches $23 per barrel by 2010.

			Projections					
			2000			2010		
Sector	1989	1990	High oil price	Reference	High economic growth	High oil price	Reference	High economic growth
Utility fossil fuel consumption (quadrillion Btu)								
Coal	16.0	16.2	17.9	17.9	18.1	20.4	22.6	24.3
Natural gas	2.9	2.9	4.2	4.8	5.5	5.3	5.7	5.4
Oil	1.7	1.3	1.6	2.1	2.6	1.8	1.7	2.8
Nonutility fossil fuel consumption (quadrillion Btu)								
Coal	0.2	0.2	0.3	0.3	0.3	0.7	1.0	1.3
Natural gas	0.5	0.6	0.7	0.8	1.0	0.8	0.9	1.0
Oil	—[1]	—[1]	—[1]	—[1]	—[1]	—[1]	—[1]	—[1]
Delivered price of fossil fuels to electric utilities (1990 dollars per million Btu)								
Coal	1.5	1.5	1.8	1.8	1.8	2.0	2.1	2.2
Natural gas	2.4	2.4	2.9	3.2	3.7	5.2	5.5	5.6
Residual fuel oil	3.0	3.3	5.4	4.6	3.9	7.8	5.9	4.6
Distillate fuel oil	4.4	5.4	6.3	5.3	4.9	9.0	6.9	6.1
Delivered price of fossil fuels to nonutilities[2] (1990 dollars per million Btu)								
Coal	1.6	1.6	1.9	1.9	1.9	2.2	2.2	2.3
Natural gas	3.0	2.9	3.5	3.8	4.3	5.8	6.2	6.3
Residual fuel oil	2.6	3.0	5.0	4.2	3.4	7.3	5.4	4.1
Distillate fuel oil	4.7	5.6	6.6	5.6	5.1	9.3	7.2	6.4

Source: "Outlook for U.S. Electric Power through 2010," *Annual Outlook for U.S. Electric Power 1991: Projections through 2010*, Washington, D.C., p. 18. Primary source: U.S. Department of Energy, Energy Information Administration, *Monthly Energy Review*, April, 1991; AEO 1991 Forecasting System. *Notes:* 1. Less than 0.05 quadrillion Btu. 2. Listed prices are industrial sector prices.

★ 697 ★

New Car Fuel Efficiency Estimates and Base Prices, 1990-2010

	1990	1995	2000	2005	2010
Average new car mpg	28.1	29.2	31.8	34.3	36.5
Average new light truck mpg	20.8	21.6	23.4	25.0	26.4
Base gasoline price (1990 dollars per gallon)	1.17	1.22	1.28	1.45	1.54

Source: "Initial New Car Fuel Efficiency Estimates and Base Prices," *Assumptions for the Annual Energy Outlook 1992*, January, 1992, p. 25. Primary source: U.S. Department of Energy, Energy Information Administration, Office of Integrated Analysis and Forecasting, Energy and Environmental Analysis Incorporated.

★ 698 ★

Plant Retirements for Fossil-Fueled Plants, 1991-2010

"Between 1991 and 2010, retirements from fossil-fueled (coal steam, gas steam, gas/oil steam, combined cycle, gas turbine, oil turbine, and gas/oil turbine) plants are expected to total 43.3 gigawatts; 11.4 gigawatts have been reported by utilities and EIA assumes that an additional 31.9 gigawatts will be retired over the forecast period. Because utilities are only required to report planned retirements for the next 10 years, many planned retirements after 2000 may be as yet unreported. EIA assumes that fossil steam plants with no scheduled retirement date will be retired after 45 years of age if their nameplate capacity is under 100 megawatts. Small fossil-fuel plants were retired after 45 years of service because historical evidence shows that similar plants which have been retired have averaged between 38 and 42 years of age at retirement. Most plants which have already retired were built in the 1940's. Plants built in the 1950's and 1960's are expected to operate slightly longer."

[Numbers in gigawatts]

Plant type	1991-1995	1996-2000	2001-2005	2006-2010	Total
Steam					
Coal	4.4	5.8	3.2	2.8	16.1
Gas	0.5	1.1	1.0	0.4	3.0
Oil	2.3	1.8	1.5	0.6	6.2
Gas/oil	3.4	4.5	4.6	2.7	15.2
Combined cycle	0	0	0	0	0
Combustion turbine	0.3	0.3	1.4	0.2	2.1
Nuclear	0	0.2	0	3.8	3.9
Hydro/other	0	0	0	0	0.1
Total	10.9	13.5	11.7	10.5	46.6

Source: "Electric Power Supply Assumptions," *Assumptions for the Annual Energy Outlook 1992*, January, 1992, p. 78. Primary source: U.S. Department of Energy, Energy Information Administration (EIA), Office of Integrated Analysis and Forecasting, Form EIA-860, "Annual Electric Generator Report." *Notes:* The data shown include those announced retirements reported by utilities and other retirements expected by Energy Information Administration. Retirements scheduled in December are treated as retiring on January 1 of the following year. Totals may not equal sum of components because of rounding.

★ 699 ★

Effect of Technology on Fuel Economy Standards, 1995 and 2001

"Through the use of available technology, automakers will help keep carbon dioxide emissions constant through the end of the century, according to David Greene, a researcher at the Center for Transportation Analysis. If automakers make no significant changes to their cars, the average fuel economy of this country's car fleet would increase 24 percent to 33.5 mpg between 1987 and 2001 just because older, less fuel efficient cars will be scrapped. If maximum use of current technologies is made, fuel efficiency could increase 46 percent to 39.4 mpg in 2001. Similar gains would be made with light trucks."

	1995		2001	
	Existing technology level	Maximum technology	Existing technology level	Maximum technology
Autos	29.30 mpg	31.53 mpg	33.50 mpg	39.40 mpg
Light trucks	22.45 mpg	23.07 mpg	24.95 mpg	27.00 mpg

Source: "Curry Questions Data Supporting Boost in CAFE," Jack Keebler and Diana T. Kurylko, *Automotive News*, No. 5338, 7 May, 1990, p. 4. The Center for Transportation Analysis, Oak Ridge National Laboratory, Oak Ridge, Tennessee.

Natural Gas

★ 700 ★

Comparison of Natural Gas Supply, Consumption, and Prices, 2010

Supply, consumption, and prices	Annual Outlook for Oil and Gas 1991	Gas Research Institute	Data Resources, Inc.	Wharton Econometric Forecasting Associates	American Gas Association
Supply (trillion cubic feet)					
Production					
Lower 48/South Alaska	18.16	17.71	18.00	15.55	20.82[1]
Alaska North Slope	0.92	1.16	1.26	1.00	1.15[1]
Supplemental Supplies	0.23	0.28[2]	0.14	NA	0.05
Net imports	3.09	2.69	3.34	2.99	2.41
Total supply[3]	22.40	21.84[4]	22.74	19.59	24.43
Consumption (trillion cubic feet)					
Residential	4.55	4.44	4.67	4.64	5.23
Commercial	2.89	3.69	3.17	3.15	3.66
Industrial	6.79	7.66[5]	7.69	6.29	8.05

[Continued]

★ 700 ★

Comparison of Natural Gas Supply, Consumption, and Prices, 2010
[Continued]

Supply, consumption, and prices	Annual Outlook for Oil and Gas 1991	Gas Research Institute	Data Resources, Inc.	Wharton Econometric Forecasting Associates	American Gas Association
Lease and plant fuel	1.15	1.27	0.96	0.70	1.04
Pipeline fuel	0.75	0.74	0.71	0.62	0.58
Electric utility	5.54	4.66	5.28	4.21	4.70
Transportation[6]	0.06	0.16	NA	NA	1.14
Total consumption	21.73	22.62	22.47	19.62	24.40
Price (1990 dollars per thousand cubic feet)					
Average wellhead price	5.04	5.55	5.43	4.86	3.48
Average price by sector					
Residential	9.17	9.31	9.56	8.94	7.79
Commercial	8.29	8.34	8.63	8.60	6.80
Industrial	6.35	6.57	6.75	5.94	4.99
Electric utility	5.65	6.11	6.20	5.07	4.13
Transportation[6]	9.23	NA	NA	NA	NA
Average price to all sectors	7.09	7.39	7.48	6.96	5.75

Source: Annual Outlook for Oil and Gas 1991, U.S. Department of Energy, Energy Information Administration (EIA), Office of Oil and Gas, Washington, D.C., June 1991, p. 84. Primary source: *Energy Review*, Winter 1990-91; Wharton Econometric Forecasting Associates, *Energy Analysis Quarterly*, Winter, 1991; Gas Research Institute, *1991 GRI Baseline Projection of U.S. Energy Supply and Demand to 2010*; American Gas Association, 1991 *TERA Base Case Analysis*, 14 December, 1990. Totals may not equal sum of components due to rounding. NA = Not available. *Notes:* 1. The number listed as Alaska North Slope includes South Alaska. 2. Sum of "Other Gas" and High Btu Coal Gas. 3. Excludes net storage withdrawals and unaccounted for. 4. Does not include Lease and Plant Fuel. 5. Includes raw materials reported separately by GRI. 6. Compressed natural gas used in motor vehicles.

★ 701 ★

Natural Gas Imports and Exports, Reference Case, 1989-2010

The Reference Case assumes an annual economic growth rate of 2.1 percent combined with a mid-level path for world oil price reaching $34.20 per barrel in 2010. For fuels other than petroleum and natural gas, the Reference Case assumes no changes to current laws and regulations.

[Numbers in trillion cubic feet]

Imports and exports	1989	1990	1995	2000	2005	2010
Imports						
Pipeline	1.34	1.47	2.03	2.06	2.28	2.35
Canada	1.34	1.47	2.03	2.03	2.03	1.85
Mexico	0.00	0.00	0.00	0.04	0.25	0.50
Liquefied natural gas	0.04	0.04	0.34	0.57	0.75	0.82
Total imports	1.38	1.51	2.37	2.63	3.02	3.16

[Continued]

★ 701 ★

Natural Gas Imports and Exports, Reference Case, 1989-2010

[Continued]

Imports and exports	1989	1990	1995	2000	2005	2010
Exports						
Pipeline	0.06	0.05	0.03	0.03	0.03	0.03
Liquefied natural gas	0.05	0.05	0.05	0.05	0.05	0.05
Total exports	0.11	0.10	0.08	0.08	0.08	0.08
Total net imports	1.27	1.41	2.29	2.56	2.95	3.09

Source: Annual Outlook for Oil and Gas 1991, U.S. Department of Energy, Energy Information Administration, Office of Oil and Gas, Washington, D.C., June, 1991, p. 38. Primary source: *Natural Gas Monthly*, March, 1991. *Note:* Totals may not equal sum of components due to rounding.

★ 702 ★

Natural Gas Supply, Consumption, and Prices, 1989-2010

The four cases present results which vary because of differences for world oil prices and domestic economic growth. In the Reference Case, the assumed annual economic growth rate of 2.1 percent is combined with a mid-level path for world oil price reaching $34.20 per barrel in 2010. The High Oil Price Case uses the high oil price path. The assumed oil price path in the Low Oil Price and High Economic Growth Case reaches a value in 2010 that is approximately one-third lower than in the Reference Case. The High Oil Price Case assumed a world oil price that is almost a third higher than the 2010 world oil price in the Reference Case. Each of the cases incorporates existing oil and gas regulations and legislation, including the Clean Air Act (CAA) Amendments of 1990. For fuels other than petroleum and natural gas, the Reference Case assumes no changes to current laws and regulations.

Supply, consumption, and prices	1989	1990	2010			
			Reference	High economic growth	Low oil price	High oil price
Supply (trillion cubic feet)						
Dry gas production	17.25	17.51	19.08	19.23	17.88	18.68
Supplemental supplies	0.11	0.11	.023	.040	0.35	0.15
Net imports	1.28	1.41	3.09	3.09	3.09	2.68
Consumption (trillion cubic feet)						
Residential	4.78	4.41	4.55	4.60	4.53	3.91
Commercial	2.72	2.67	2.89	2.85	2.88	2.75
Industrial	6.82	7.18	6.79	7.42	6.78	7.08
Lease & plant fuel	1.07	1.22	1.15	1.16	1.09	1.13
Pipeline fuel	0.63	0.59	0.75	0.77	0.70	0.72
Electric utilities	2.79	2.78	5.54	5.19	4.69	5.16
Transportation[1]	(s)	(s)	0.06	0.02	0.02	0.10
Total consumption	18.80	18.83	21.73	22.02	20.68	20.84
Price (1990 dollars per thousand cubic feet)						
Average wellhead price	1.76	1.72	5.04	5.21	4.68	4.73

[Continued]

★ 702 ★

Natural Gas Supply, Consumption, and Prices, 1989-2010
[Continued]

Supply, consumption, and prices	1989	1990	2010			
			Reference	High economic growth	Low oil price	High oil price
Average delivered price						
Residential	5.87	5.77	9.17	9.33	8.80	8.86
Commercial	4.93	4.83	8.29	8.45	7.92	7.98
Industrial	3.09	2.92	6.35	6.52	5.99	6.02
Electric utilities	2.52	2.34	5.65	5.82	5.32	5.33
Transportation[1]	-	-	9.23	9.40	8.86	8.91

Source: Annual Outlook for Oil and Gas 1991, U.S. Department of Energy, Energy Information Administration (EIA), Office of Oil and Gas, Washington, D.C., June, 1991, p. xi. Primary source: *Natural Gas Monthly*, March, 1991. (s) = Less than 10 billion cubic feet. Totals may not equal sum of components due to rounding. *Note:* 1. Compressed natural gas used in motor vehicles.

New Technologies and Construction

★ 703 ★

New Nuclear Plant Construction Schedule, 2000-2015

Data assumes improved public acceptance of nuclear reactors and improved nuclear technology.

Year	Plants started in year	Total new starts	Operating capacity (MWe)
2000	2	4	0
2001	4	8	1,200
2002	8	16	1,200
2003	12	28	1,200
2004	16	44	1,200
2005	20	64	2,400
2006	22	86	4,800
2007	24	110	9,600
2008	26	136	16,800
2009	28	164	26,400
2010	30	194	38,400
2011	32	226	51,600
2012	34	260	66,000
2013	36	296	81,600

[Continued]

★ 703 ★

New Nuclear Plant Construction Schedule, 2000-2015
[Continued]

Year	Plants started in year	Total new starts	Operating capacity (MWe)
2014	38	334	98,400
2015	40	374	116,400

Source: Energy Technology Choices: Shaping Our Future, U.S. Congress, Office of Technology Assessment, Washington, D.C., July, 1991, p. 128. Primary source: Office of Technology Assessment, 1991.

★ 704 ★

Undersea Telephone Cable Systems, 1970-1996

Table shows cables put into service since 1970 and the number of simultaneous calls each can handle.

In service	Cable	Type	Capacity	Status
Transpacific				
1974	TPC-2	Analog	845	Active
1989	TPC-3	Digital	40,000	Active
Nov. 1992	TPC-4	Digital	80,000	Under construction
1996	TPC-5	Digital	320,000	Planned
Not yet set	APCN	Digital	160,000	Planned
Transatlantic				
1970	TAT-5	Analog	1,690	Due to retire
1976	TAT-6	Analog	8,400	Active
1983	TAT-7	Analog	8,400	Active
1988	TAT-8	Digital	40,000	Active
1992	TAT-9	Digital	80,000	Active
1992	TAT-10	Digital	80,000	Active
Aug. 1993	TAT-11	Digital	80,000	Under construction
Late 1994	Columbus 2	Digital	80,000	Planned
1996	TAT-12	Digital	700,000	Planned

Source: "2nd Asia Link Considered by A.T.&T.," Anthony Ramirez, *New York Times*, November 3, 1992, p. D3. Primary source: American Telephone & Telegraph.

Crude Oil and Petroleum Supply and Consumption

★ 705 ★

Crude Oil Production Excluding the 48 Contiguous United States, 1995-2010

[Barrels per day in thousands]

Source/World oil price path	1995	2000	2005	2010
Alaska				
High	1,391	1,024	975	1,175
Mid-level	1,332	933	692	779
Low	1,252	833	549	426
Offshore				
High	1,046	1,018	1,087	1,106
Mid-level	987	924	1,002	1,030
Low	899	773	818	848
Enhanced Oil Recovery				
High	692	775	814	845
Mid-level	657	591	686	772
Low	657	497	330	291

Source: "Exogenous Crude Oil Production Projections," *Assumptions for the Annual Energy Outlook 1992*, January, 1992, p. 38. Primary source: U.S. Department of Energy, Energy Information Administration, Office of Integrated Analysis and Forecasting, "Technical Notes for the *Annual Energy Outlook 1992*: Documentation for the Alaskan Oil Projection," Washington, D.C., November, 1991; "Technical Notes for the Annual Energy Outlook 1992: Documentation for the Outer Continental Shelf Oil Production Forecast Condensate Projection," Washington, D.C., November, 1991; "Technical Notes for the Annual Energy Outlook 1991: Documentation for Projections of Crude Oil by Enhanced Oil Recovery (EOR) Methods," Washington, D.C., February, 1991. *Note:* Data is given for projected low, mid-level, and high oil price scenarios.

★ 706 ★

Production of Crude Oil and Natural Gas, Reference Case, 1989-2010

The Reference Case assumes an economic growth rate of 2.1 percent is combined with a mid-level path for world oil price reaching $34.20 per barrel in 2010. For fuels other than petroleum and natural gas, the Reference Case assumes no changes to current laws and regulations.

Production	1989	1990	1995	2000	2005	2010
Crude oil (million barrels per day)						
Lower 48 onshore						
Conventional	4.12	3.98	3.85	3.05	2.57	2.23
Enhanced oil recovery	0.63	0.66	0.75	0.62	0.64	0.71
Lower 48 offshore	0.99	0.89	0.87	0.78	0.71	0.70
Lower 48 subtotal	5.74	5.53	5.47	4.45	3.92	3.64
Alaska	1.87	1.77	1.32	0.90	0.67	0.78
Total crude oil	7.61	7.30	6.79	5.36	4.59	4.42
Natural gas (trillion cubic feet)						
Lower 48 onshore						
Nonassociated						
Conventional	8.50	8.79	9.47	11.14	11.33	9.53
Unconventional	1.25	1.26	1.87	2.57	3.45	4.35
Associated-dissolved	2.14	2.06	2.00	1.58	1.34	1.19
Lower 48 offshore	4.98	5.02	4.43	3.86	3.22	2.65
Lower 48 subtotal	16.87	17.13	17.76	19.15	19.36	17.71
Alaska	0.37	0.38	0.46	0.47	0.46	1.37
Total natural gas	17.25	17.51	18.22	19.62	19.82	19.08

Source: Annual Outlook for Oil and Gas 1991, U.S. Department of Energy, Energy Information Administration (EIA), Office of Oil and Gas, Washington, D.C., June, 1991, p. 20. Primary source: *Petroleum Supply Annual 1989*; *Crude Oil, Natural Gas, and Natural Gas Liquids Reserves 1989*; *Petroleum Supply Monthly*, February, 1991; *Natural Gas Monthly*, March, 1991. Totals may not equal sum of components due to rounding.

★ 707 ★

Comparison of Petroleum Supply and Consumption Projections, 2010

[Numbers in million barrels per day]

Supply and Consumption	AOOG91	GRI	DRI	WEFA
Supply				
Domestic production				
Lower 48 crude oil	3.64	5.72	4.13	3.70
Alaska crude oil	0.78	0.59	0.59	0.70
Natural gas liquids	1.62	1.56	1.60	1.54
Other/processing gain	1.11	0.84	0.91	0.84

[Continued]

★ 707 ★

Comparison of Petroleum Supply and Consumption Projections, 2010
[Continued]

Supply and Consumption	AOOG91	GRI	DRI	WEFA
Total production	7.15	8.71	7.23	6.78
Net imports				
Crude oil	9.21	8.37	9.72	10.92
Refined products	3.77	6.16	4.15	2.28
Total net imports	12.98	14.53	3.86	13.19
Total supply	20.12	23.24	21.09	19.97
Consumption				
Motor gasoline	8.08	8.23	8.66	7.70
Jet fuel	2.22	2.06	1.96	2.34
Distillate fuel	3.87	4.73	4.21	4.04
Residual fuel	1.47	3.34	1.69	2.14
Other products	4.62	4.87	4.72	3.76
Total consumption	20.27	23.24	21.25	19.97

Source: Annual Outlook for Oil and Gas 1991, U.S. Department of Energy, Energy Information Administration (EIA), Office of Oil and Gas, Washington, D.C., June, 1991, p. 82. Primary source: *Energy Review*, Winter 1990-91; Wharton Econometric Forecasting Associates, *Energy Analysis Quarterly*, Winter, 1991; Gas Research Institute, *1991 GRI Baseline Projection of U.S. Energy Supply and Demand to 2010*; American Gas Association, *1991 TERA Base Case Analysis*, December 14, 1990.

★ 708 ★

Oil Use in the Transportation Sector, 1990-2030

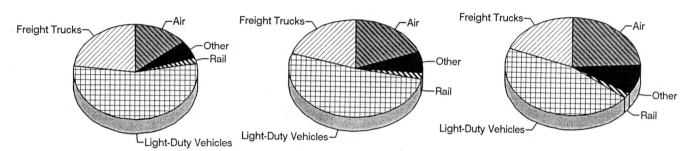

1990   2010   2030

[Numbers in percent]

	1990	2010	2030
Light-duty vehicles	55.0	51.0	45.0
Air	14.0	19.0	24.0
Freight trucks	23.0	20.0	19.0
Rail	2.0	2.0	2.0
Other	6.0	7.0	10.0

Source: "Oil Use in the Transportation Sector (by Mode)," *National Energy Strategy: Powerful Ideas for America*, Office of Scientific and Technical Information, Washington, D.C., February, 1991, p. 65.

★ 709 ★

Petroleum Consumption by End-Use Sector, Reference Case, 1989-2010

The Reference Case assumes an annual economic growth rate of 2.1 percent combined with a mid-level path for world oil price reaching $34.20 per barrel in 2010. For fuels other than petroleum and natural gas, the reference Case assumes no changes to current laws and regulations.

[Numbers in million barrels per day]

Sector	1989	1990	1995	2000	2005	2010
Residential and commercial	1.41	1.33	1.25	1.11	0.99	0.89
Industrial[1]	4.32	4.25	4.46	4.85	5.19	5.51
Transportation	10.86	10.79	10.98	11.67	12.44	13.13
Electric utilities[2]	0.74	0.55	0.65	0.90	0.86	0.74
Total consumption	17.33	16.92	17.34	18.53	19.49	20.27

Source: Annual Outlook for Oil and Gas 1991, U.S. Department of Energy, Energy Information Administration (EIA), Office of Oil and Gas, Washington, D.C., June, 1991, p. 31. Primary source: *State Energy Data Report: Consumption Estimates 1960-1988, Petroleum Supply Annual 1989*; *Petroleum Supply Monthly*, February, 1991. *Notes:* 1. Includes consumption by cogenerators. 2. Includes consumption by independent power producers.

★ 710 ★

Petroleum Product Prices, 1989-2010

The four cases present results which vary because of differences in assumptions for world oil prices and domestic economic growth. In the Reference Case, the assumed annual economic growth rate of 2.1 percent is combined with a mid-level path for world oil price reaching $34.20 per barrel in 2010. The High Oil Price Case uses the high oil price path. The assumed oil price path in the Low Oil Price and High Economic Growth Case reaches a value in 2010 that is approximately one-third lower than in the Reference Case. The High Oil Price Case assumed a world oil price that is almost a third higher than the 2010 world oil price in the Reference Case. Each of the cases incorporates existing oil and gas regulations and legislation, including the Clean Air Act (CAA) Amendments of 1990. For fuels other than petroleum and natural gas, the Reference Case assumes no changes to current laws and regulations.

[Numbers in 1990 dollars per gallon except where noted]

Average prices to all users	1989	1990	2010 High economic growth	2010 Low oil price	2010 Reference	2010 High oil price
Selected petroleum products						
Motor gasoline[1]	1.07	1.16	1.42	1.42	1.53	1.84
Distillate fuel[2]	0.92	1.06	1.24	1.23	1.35	1.65
Jet fuel[3]	0.61	0.77	0.89	0.89	1.00	1.29
Liquefied petroleum gas	0.64	0.74	0.71	0.72	0.81	1.03
Residual fuel (dollars per barrel)	17.07	18.97	27.54	27.83	34.97	46.47

[Continued]

★ 710 ★

Petroleum Product Prices, 1989-2010
[Continued]

Average prices to all users	1989	1990	2010			
			High economic growth	Low oil price	Reference	High oil price
Average all petroleum products[4] (dollars per barrel)	35.58	40.55	47.42	47.36	53.18	65.05

Source: Annual Outlook for Oil and Gas 1991, U.S. Department of Energy, Energy Information Administration (EIA), Office of Oil and Gas, Washington, D.C., June, 1991, p. 30. Primary source: *Petroleum Marketing Annual 1989, State Energy Price and Expenditure Report 1988. Notes:* 1. Average price for all grades. Includes Federal and State taxes and excludes county and local taxes. 2. Includes Federal and State taxes on diesel fuel and excludes county and local taxes. 3. Kerosene-type jet fuel. 4. Includes average price for Petrochemical feedstocks and Miscellaneous Petroleum Products not listed.

★ 711 ★

Petroleum Production, Imports, and Consumption, 1989-2010

The four cases present results which vary because of differences in assumptions for world oil prices and domestic economic growth. In the Reference Case, the assumed annual economic growth rate of 2.1 percent is combined with a mid-level path for world oil price reaching $34.20 per barrel in 2010. The High Oil Price Case uses the high oil price path. The assumed oil price path in the Low Oil Price and High Economic Growth Case reaches a value in 2010 that is approximately one-third lower than in the Reference Case. The High Oil Price Case assumed a world oil price that is almost a third higher than the 2010 world oil price in the Reference Case. Each of the cases incorporates existing oil and gas regulations and legislation, including the Clean Air Act (CAA) Amendments of 1990. For fuels other than petroleum and natural gas, the Reference Case assumes no changes to current laws and regulations.

[Numbers in million barrels per day]

Production, imports and consumption	1989	1990	2010			
			Reference	High economic growth	Low oil price	High oil price
Production						
Crude oil production[1]	7.61	7.30	4.42	3.37	3.36	5.18
Alaska	1.87	1.77	0.78	0.42	0.42	1.17
Lower 48 States	5.74	5.53	3.64	2.95	2.94	4.00
Other[2]	2.27	2.29	2.73	2.81	2.56	2.70
Total production	9.88	9.59	7.15	6.19	5.92	7.89
Net imports (including SPR[3])	7.20	7.09	12.98	17.67	15.79	10.84
Consumption						
Residential and commercial	1.41	1.33	0.89	.94	0.92	0.75
Industrial	4.32	4.25	5.51	6.47	5.91	5.01
Transportation	10.86	10.79	13.13	15.34	13.69	12.32

[Continued]

★ 711 ★

Petroleum Production, Imports, and Consumption, 1989-2010
[Continued]

Production, imports and consumption	1989	1990	2010			
			Reference	High economic growth	Low oil price	High oil price
Electric utilities	0.74	0.55	0.74	1.23	1.32	0.78
Total consumption	17.33	16.92	20.27	23.98	21.84	18.87

Source: Annual Outlook for Oil and Gas 1991, U.S. Department of Energy, Energy Information Administration (EIA), Office of Oil and Gas, Washington, D.C., June, 1991, p. x. Primary source: *Petroleum Supply Annual 1989*; *State Energy Data Report: Consumption Estimates 1960-1988*; *Petroleum Supply Monthly*, February, 1991; *Monthly Energy Review*, March, 1991; AEO 1991 Forecasting System. *Notes:* Totals may not equal sum of components due to rounding. 1. Includes lease condensate. 2. Includes natural gas plant liquids, processing gain, other hydrocarbons, alcohols, and synthetic crude oil. 3. SPR = Strategic Petroleum Reserve.

★ 712 ★

Petroleum Products Supplied, Reference Case, 1989-2010

The Reference Case assumes an annual economic growth rate of 2.1 percent combined with a mid-level path for world oil price reaching $34.20 per barrel in 2010. For fuels other than petroleum and natural gas, the Reference Case assumes no changes to current laws and regulations. Products supplied is an approximation of consumption and is calculated by adding refinery production, natural gas liquids production, supply of other liquids, imports, and stock withdrawals, and subtracting stock additions, refinery inputs, and exports.

[Numbers in million barrels per day]

Product	1989	1990	1995	2000	2005	2010
Motor gasoline[1]	7.33	7.21	7.22	7.50	7.83	8.08
Distillate fuel	3.16	3.02	3.25	3.49	3.70	3.87
Residual fuel	1.37	1.23	1.29	1.53	1.53	1.47
Jet fuel[2]	1.49	1.49	1.61	1.82	2.01	2.22
Liquefied petroleum gases	1.67	1.55	1.70	1.83	1.96	2.08
Petrochemical feedstocks	0.46	0.53	0.52	0.61	0.68	0.75
Other[3]	1.85	1.89	1.75	1.75	1.79	1.80
Total products supplied	17.33	16.92	17.34	18.53	19.49	20.27

Source: Annual Outlook for Oil and Gas 1991, U.S. Department of Energy, Energy Information Administration (EIA), Office of Oil and Gas, Washington, D.C., June, 1991, p. 29. Primary source: *Petroleum Supply Annual 1989*; *Petroleum Supply Monthly*, February, 1991. *Notes:* Totals may not equal sum of parts because of rounding. 1. Includes ethanol blended into gasoline. 2. Includes naphtha and kerosene type. 3. Includes aviation gasoline, special naphthas, pentanes plus, unfinished oils, motor gasoline blending components, aviation gasoline blending components, crude oil, kerosene, lubricants, waxes, petroleum coke, asphalt and road oil, still gas, and miscellaneous products.

★ 713 ★

Petroleum Supply Balance, Reference Case, 1989-2010

The Reference Case assumes an annual economic growth rate of 2.1 percent combined with a mid-level path for world oil price reaching $34.20 per barrel in 2010. For fuels other than petroleum and natural gas, the Reference Case assumes no changes to current laws and regulations.

[Numbers in million barrels per day]

Source	1989	1990	1995	2000	2005	2010
Production						
Crude oil[1]	7.61	7.30	6.79	5.36	4.59	4.42
Natural gas plant liquids	1.55	1.55	1.55	1.67	1.68	1.62
Other domestic[2]	0.06	0.07	0.19	0.27	0.35	0.48
Processing gain[3]	0.66	0.67	0.64	0.66	0.64	0.63
Imports (including SPR[4])						
Crude oil	5.84	5.88	6.35	8.62	9.25	9.29
Refined products	2.22	2.08	2.51	2.67	3.68	4.56
Exports						
Crude oil	0.14	0.12	0.10	0.08	0.07	0.08
Refined products	0.72	0.75	0.66	0.71	0.75	0.79
Net imports (including SPR)	7.20	7.09	8.10	10.51	12.11	12.98
Total primary supply[5]	17.14	16.58	17.19	18.38	19.34	20.12
Unaccounted for crude oil	0.20	0.34	0.15	0.15	0.15	0.15
Total product supplied	17.33	16.92	17.34	18.53	19.49	20.27

Source: Annual Outlook for Oil and Gas 1991, U.S. Department of Energy, Energy Information Administration (EIA), Office of Oil and Gas, Washington, D.C., June, 1991, p. 26. Primary source: *Petroleum Supply Annual 1989*; *Petroleum Supply Monthly*, February, 1991. *Notes:* 1. Includes lease condensate. 2. Includes other hydrocarbons, alcohols, and synthetic crude oil. 3. Represents volumetric gain in refinery distillation and cracking processes. 4. SPR = Strategic Petroleum Reserve. 5. Includes Primary Stock Changes not shown.

Renewable Energy Resources

★ 714 ★

Projected Energy From Renewable Sources, 1989 and 2000

"Under current energy trends and without premium price adjustments, the use or renewable energy is expected to increase from 8 percent of total energy use today to 9 percent in 2000, 11 percent in 2010, and 15 percent in 2030. If federal research, development, and demonstration funding should increase, however, use of renewables would also increase to 10 percent in 2000, 18 percent in 2010, and 28 percent in 2030."

[Values in megawatts]

Resource	1989	2000
Biomass	5,154	10,000
Geothermal	2,657	6,000
Photovoltaics	30	1,000
Solar thermal	202	1,000
Wind	1,500	6,000
Non-hydro total	9,543	24,000
Hydro	70,800	80,000
Pumped hydro	17,100	25,000
Hydro total	87,900	105,000
Total renewable electric capacity	97,443	129,000

Source: The 1992 Information Please Environmental Almanac, World Resources Institute, Houghton, 1992, p. 83. Primary source: Public Citizen, 1989.

★ 715 ★

Projections of Electric Capability for Renewable Technologies, 1990-2010

[Numbers in gigawatts]

Renewables	1990[2]		1995		2000		2005		2010	
	Utility	Nonutility	Utility	Nonutility	Utility	Nonutility	Utility	Nonutility	Utility	Nonutility
Conventional hydro	73.6	2.1	74.9	3.5	74.9	3.6	74.9	3.6	74.9	3.8
Pumped storage	17.3	0.0	18.7	0.0	20.3	1.5	20.3	1.5	20.3	1.5
Wind	0.0	2.0	0.0	2.6	0.0	3.5	0.0	4.3	0.0	5.2
Solar thermal	0.0	0.4	0.1	1.2	0.1	1.2	0.1	1.3	0.1	1.6
Geothermal	1.6	1.0	1.8	1.4	2.7	2.6	3.8	4.0	4.1	4.3
Photovoltaic	0.0	0.0	0.0	0.1	0.1	0.0	0.0	0.0	0.0	0.0
Wood	0.3	5.0	0.3	5.7	0.4	6.0	0.4	6.2	0.5	6.4

[Continued]

★ 715 ★

Projections of Electric Capability for Renewable Technologies, 1990-2010

[Continued]

Renewables	1990[2]		1995		2000		2005		2010	
	Utility	Nonutility	Utility	Nonutility	Utility	Nonutility	Utility	Nonutility	Utility	Nonutility
Municipal solid waste	0.4	2.0	0.5	4.7	0.8	7.0	1.0	9.7	1.2	11.7
Total[1]	93.2	12.4	96.1	19.0	99.0	25.3	100.5	30.5	101.1	34.3

Source: "Projections of Utility and Nonutility Electric Capability for Renewable Technologies," *Assumptions for the Annual Energy Outlook 1992*, January, 1992, p. 75. Primary source: U.S. Department of Energy, Energy Information Administration, Office of Integrated Analysis and Forecasting. *Notes:* 1. Total may not equal sum of components because of rounding. 2. The 1990 numbers are estimated.

★ 716 ★

Average Annual Capacity Factors for Renewable Technologies, 1995-2010

"The capacity factors for renewable technologies ... are based on historical performance. For geothermal, wind, and solar thermal technologies, the capacity factors are assumed to improve over time with technological advancement from ongoing research and development."

[Numbers in percent]

Technology	1995	2000	2005	2010
Hydroelectric	46	45	45	45
Geothermal	66	73	80	81
Municipal solid waste	69	69	70	70
Biomass/other solid waste	60	66	68	72
Solar thermal	23	28	28	28
Solar photovoltaic	11	11	11	11
Wind	17	23	25	25

Source: "Average Annual Capacity Factors for Renewable Technologies," *Assumption for the Annual Energy Outlook 1992*, January, 1992, p. 74. Primary source: U.S. Department of Energy, Energy Information Administration, Office of Integrated Analysis and Forecasting.

Chapter 14

TRANSPORTATION

Air and Waterborne Freight

★ 717 ★

Domestic Air Freight Ton-Miles, Energy Use, and Energy Intensity, 1970-2010

TMT = Ton-miles traveled. Within the ANL-9ON model, a constant share of ton-miles is allocated between all-cargo aircraft and the cargo hold (belly) of passenger aircraft. "Belly" freight is assigned an energy intensity of zero, since the fuel is already counted in the fuel consumed by passenger aircraft. "Historically, all-cargo aircraft have accounted for about 30% of air freight ton-miles. This share is expected to grow somewhat as airport congestion restricts carriers' ability to haul cargo in the lower holds of passenger aircraft (e.g., by banning unloading during daytime hours) and lower-cost 'minihubs' offer attractive alternatives. Thus the baseline scenario assumes the all-cargo share grows from 30% to 38% by 2010.... Since all-cargo aircraft may carry an increasing share of air freight, total energy intensity is projected to improve by only 17% (compared with an overall improvement of 33% for both passenger and cargo aircraft). Total ton-miles (i.e., belly plus all-cargo freight) grow by 136% between 1985 and 2010. Although somewhat less than historical growth in air freight traffic, this growth rate (3.5%/ yr) exceeds growth in both economic output and total ton-miles, resulting in an increase in air freight mode share."

Year	TMT[1] (10^9)	Energy use (10^15 Btu)		Energy intensity (Btu/TMT)	
		Total	All-cargo	Total[2]	All-cargo
1970	3.01	NA[3]	NA	NA	26,821
1975	3.47	NA	NA	NA	21,530
1980	4.53	NA	NA	NA	23,750[4]
1985	6.16	0.061	0.040	9903	21,670
1990	7.75	0.074	0.047	9548	18,809
1995	8.93	0.082	0.049	9183	16,255
2000	10.42	0.092	0.053	8829	14,037
2010	14.54	0.119	0.064	8184	11,618
Average annual percentage change					
1970-1985	4.89	NA	NA	NA	-1.41
1985-2010	3.50	2.71	1.9	-0.76	-2.46

Source: U.S. Department of Energy, *Forecast of Transportation Energy Demand through the Year 2010*, M.M. Mintz and A.D. Vyas, Center for Transportation Research, Energy Systems Division, Argonne National Laboratory, November, 1990 (rev. April, 1991), p. 53. *Notes:* 1. Total includes belly freight. 2. Weighted average of all - cargo and belly freight. Belly freight assigned a value of zero since fuel is already included in passenger totals. 3. NA = data not available. 4. 1979.

★ 718 ★

Domestic Waterborne Freight Ton-Miles, Energy Use, and Energy Intensity, 1970-2010

TMT = Ton-miles traveled. Domestic waterborne commerce is defined as shipping on the Great Lakes, in U.S. coastal waters, and on inland waterways. Domestic shipping is heavily concentrated in seven bulk commodities: agricultural products, metallic ores, nonmetallic ores, coal, crude oil, chemicals, and petroleum products. "Were it not for Alaskan oil development, domestic marine ton-miles, energy intensity, and energy consumption would have been nearly flat in the past. [As shown in the table], ANL-9ON forecasts a return to this pattern. Both ton-miles and energy use fluctuate with the changing fortunes of major marine-using industrial sectors. For the most part, growth in agricultural products, coal, ores, and chemicals is balanced against a steady decline in crude oil traffic. The latter is also responsible for near stable energy intensity. As coastal tankers come to comprise a declining share of domestic marine traffic, the resulting increase in energy intensity is more or less offset by technical and operational improvements..."

Year	TMT (10^9)	Energy use $(10^{15}$ Btu)	Energy intensity (Btu/TMT)
1970	596.0	0.325	545
1975	566.0	0.311	549
1980	922.0	0.330	358
1985	893.3	0.329	368
1990	911.1	0.337	370
1995	898.5	0.334	372
2000	912.0	0.340	373
2010	998.7	0.376	377
Average annual percentage change			
1970-1985	2.73	0.08	-2.58
1985-2010	0.45	0.54	0.10

Source: U.S. Department of Energy, *Forecast of Transportation Energy Demand through the Year 2000*, M.M. Mintz and A.D. Vyas, Center for Transportation Research, Energy Systems Division, Argonne National Laboratory, November, 1990 (rev. April, 1991), p. 50. Primary source: For projections, ANL-9ON (forecast developed by the Center for Transportation Research at Argonne National Laboratory [ANL], under contract to the Office of Transportation Technologies, Office of the Secretary for Conservation and Renewable Energy, U.S. Department of Energy) and the Energy Information Administration (EIA) of the U.S. Department of Energy.

Aviation

★ 719 ★

Active Pilots by Type of Certificate, 1985-2001

Detail may not add to total because of independent rounding.

[Numbers in thousands]

As of January 1	Students	Private	Commercial	Airline transport	Helicopter	Glider	Lighter-than-air	Total	Instrument rated[1]
Historical									
1985	150.1	320.1	155.9	79.2	7.5	8.4	1.2	722.4	256.6
1986	146.7	311.1	151.6	82.7	8.1	8.2	1.1	709.5	258.6
1987	150.3	305.7	147.8	87.2	8.6	8.4	1.1	709.1	262.4
1988	146.0	300.9	143.6	91.3	8.7	7.9	1.2	699.7	266.1
1989E	136.9	299.8	143.0	97.0	8.6	7.6	1.1	704.8	273.8
Forecast									
1990	139.6	300.7	145.0	101.5	8.7	7.7	1.1	704.3	278.7
1991	142.0	302.8	146.5	104.7	9.0	8.3	1.2	714.5	280.7
1992	144.1	303.7	148.0	108.6	9.1	8.4	1.2	723.1	284.9
1993	145.9	304.3	149.4	112.6	9.2	8.5	1.2	731.1	289.2
1994	147.3	304.9	150.9	116.7	9.4	8.6	1.3	739.1	293.5
1995	148.4	305.8	152.4	121.0	9.5	8.7	1.4	747.2	297.0
1996	149.1	306.8	154.0	124.4	9.6	8.8	1.5	754.2	300.6
1997	149.7	307.7	155.5	127.8	9.7	8.9	1.6	760.9	304.2
1998	150.2	308.6	157.1	131.3	9.8	9.0	1.7	767.7	307.9
1999	150.7	309.5	158.6	133.9	9.9	9.1	1.8	773.5	310.4
2000	151.2	310.5	160.2	136.6	10.0	9.2	1.9	779.6	312.0
2001	151.7	311.4	161.8	139.3	10.1	9.3	2.0	785.6	313.6

Source: U.S. Department of Transportation, Federal Aviation Administration, *FAA Aviation Forecasts, Fiscal Years 1990-2001*, March, 1990, p. 198, Table 20. Primary source: For historical data: FAA Statistical Handbook of Aviation. *Notes:* 1. Instrument rated pilots should not be added to other categories in deriving total.

★ 720 ★

Airborne Hours of Commercial Air Carriers by Type of Aircraft, 1989 and 2001

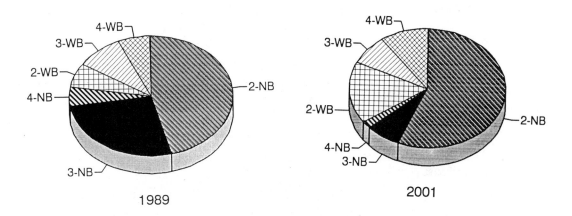

1989   2001

Types of aircraft are distinguished on the pie chart and in the table by the number of engines on the craft (2, 3, or 4) and its wide-bodied (WB) or narrow-bodied (NB) design. "For the period 1996-2001, FAA aviation forecasts are based on consensus growth rates of key economic variables provided by Data Resources, Inc., Evans Economics, Inc., and the WEFA Group. These projections are combined with projections of aviation variables and professional judgment on the probabilities and consequences of events that affect aviation. The combination is used as input to the econometric models from which the forecasts are generated. By the year 2001, the number of airborne hours [of commercial air carriers] is forecast to increase to 13.4 million, an average annual increase of 2.4 percent." A large part of the growth in airborne hours (43.2 percent) projected for 1989 through 2001 is expected to occur at the beginning of this period, between 1990 and 1992, reflecting the large numbers of smaller aircraft scheduled to be delivered to U.S. airlines during this period. A continued growth in "hubbing activity" (the concentrating of aviation activity by commercial airlines at selected large and medium-sized hub airports) will contribute to the increase in total number of airborne hours projected through the year 2001.

[Numbers in percent]

	1989	2001
2 NB	46.1	55.9
3 NB	26.5	7.1
4 NB	5.3	1.9
2 WB	6.5	17.0
3 WB	9.3	8.0
4 WB	6.3	10.1

Source: U.S. Department of Transportation, Federal Aviation Administration, *FAA Aviation Forecasts, Fiscal Years 1990-2001*, March, 1990, p. 68, bottom.

★ 721 ★

Airports Expected to Exceed 20,000 Hours of Annual Delays by Region in 1997

"On the basis of the federal government's estimates of demand and supply, delays can only be expected to worsen at many airports in the years ahead. The FAA projects that the number of operations (arrivals and departures) by major commercial domestic carriers will increase by one-third between 1988 and 2000.... At present 21 airports experience more than 20,000 hours of annual flight delays. The FAA estimates that even if planned improvements to primary airports are made, 33 primary airports will exceed 20,000 hours of delay in 1997.... [It] appears that most of the future demand will occur in the commercial segment of the industry at commercial airports. Some increased General Aviation [GA] business will also occur at commercial airports but will account for a small share of total operations."

Area	Airport
Northeast	Boston Logan New York City: Kennedy, LaGuardia, Newark Pittsburgh Philadelphia
South	Washington: National, Dulles Charlotte Nashville Memphis Atlanta Orlando Miami Dallas-Fort Worth Houston: Hobby and Houston Intercontinental
Midwest	Cleveland Columbus Cincinnati Detroit Chicago O'Hare St. Louis Minneapolis
West	Salt Lake City Las Vegas Phoenix Seattle-Tacoma San Francisco San Jose Los Angeles: Los Angeles International and Ontario Honolulu

Source: Transportation Research Board, National Research Council, *Winds of Change: Domestic Air Transport Since Deregulation*, Washington, D.C., 1991, p. 217. Primary source: U.S. Department of Transportation, Federal Aviation Administration, *FAA Aviation Forecasts Fiscal Years 1989-2000*, Report FAA-APO-89-1; U.S. Department of Transportation, Federal Aviation Administration, FAA Aviation Forecasts Fiscal Years 1990-2001, Report FAA-APO-90-1.

★ 722 ★

Alternative Scenarios for Revenue Passenger Miles as Variously Projected by the FAA and the Port Authority of New York and New Jersey, 1985-2050

The econometric models created by the FAA and the Port Authority both required assumptions for gross national product (GNP) and domestic airline yield (average fare). The FAA model assigned a higher weight to GNP, while the Port Authority model was weighted more heavily in favor of yield.

[Numbers in billions]

Year	Gross national product					
	Base Port Authority	FAA	High Port Authority	FAA	Low Port Authority	FAA
Constant yield						
1985	273.0	265.8	273.0	265.8	273.0	265.8
2000	403.3	463.6	430.3	463.6	417.1	446.2
2010	544.3	617.2	549.8	624.7	511.3	573.9
2020	667.3	783.0	688.3	810.7	594.7	688.4
2030	792.4	952.8	843.6	1,019.3	655.8	775.0
2040	912.7	1,116.2	1,034.7	1,273.8	686.6	821.5
2050	1,018.6	1,261.7	1,269.6	1,584.3	681.5	821.5
Low yield						
1985	273.0	265.8	273.0	265.8	273.0	265.8
2000	452.5	470.3	452.5	470.3	438.7	452.9
2010	594.3	627.7	600.3	635.1	558.2	584.4
2020	757.3	797.3	781.2	824.9	675.0	702.7
2030	936.1	970.6	996.6	1,037.0	774.8	792.8
2040	1,124.0	1,137.4	1,274.1	1,295.1	845.5	843.0
2050	1,309.5	1,286.5	1,632.2	1,609.1	876.1	846.3
High yield						
1985	273.0	265.8	273.0	265.8	273.0	265.8
2000	410.0	457.9	410.0	457.9	397.5	440.5
2010	501.6	608.0	506.8	615.5	471.2	564.7
2020	595.4	770.3	614.1	798.0	530.6	675.7
2030	685.1	936.6	729.4	1,003.1	567.0	758.8
2040	765.3	1,095.8	867.5	1,253.5	575.7	801.4
2050	828.9	1,237.0	1,033.1	1,559.5	554.6	796.8

Source: Transportation Research Board, National Research Council, *Future Development of the U.S. Airport Network: Preliminary Report and Recommended Study Plan*, Washington, D.C., 1988, Appendix A, p. 35, Table A-1.

★ 723 ★

Baseline Air Carrier Forecast Assumptions: Total System Operations

Forecasts were generated by the FAA Office of Aviation Policy and Plans. The RSPA is a division of the U.S. Department of Transportation. It is responsible for the collection of air carrier traffic and financial data on form 41, formerly collected by the Civil Aeronautics Board.

Fiscal year	Average seats per aircraft (seats)	Average passenger trip length (miles)	Revenue per passenger mile		Average jet fuel price	
			current $ (cents)	1982-84 $ (cents)	current $ (cents)	1982-84 $ (cents)
Historical[1]						
1985	166.9	881.6	11.77	11.04	81.5	76.5
1986	167.4	874.8	11.02	10.09	64.6	59.2
1987	166.6	894.8	10.93	9.82	52.0	46.2
1988	168.4	927.8	11.81	10.21	56.2	48.6
1989E	168.7	948.4	12.43	10.26	56.4	46.5
Forecast						
1990	171	960	12.31	9.77	58.2	46.2
1991	173	967	12.60	9.60	59.1	45.1
1992	175	974	13.00	9.54	61.6	45.2
1993	176	980	13.47	9.52	64.1	45.3
1994	179	989	13.98	9.57	66.1	45.2
1995	181	996	14.56	9.66	68.5	45.5
1996	184	1,002	15.23	9.58	73.2	46.1
1997	187	1,008	15.93	9.51	78.5	46.9
1998	190	1,014	16.69	9.45	83.9	47.5
1999	194	1,020	17.49	9.39	89.7	48.1
2000	198	1,025	18.33	9.33	95.9	48.8
2001	202	1,030	19.21	9.28	102.8	49.7

Source: U.S. Department of Transportation, Federal Aviation Administration, *FAA Aviation Forecasts, 1990-2001,* March, 1990, p. 182, Table 4. *Note:* 1. Source for historical data: The Research and Special Programs Administration (RSPA), Fo

★ 724 ★

Baseline Air Carrier Forecast Assumptions: Domestic Operations, 1985-2001

Forecasts were generated by the FAA Office of Aviation Policy and Plans. The RSPA is a division of the U.S. Department of Transportation. It is responsible for the collection of air carrier traffic and financial data on Form 41, formerly collected by the Civil Aeronautics Board.

Fiscal year	Average seats per aircraft (seats)	Average passenger trip length (miles)	Revenue per passenger mile		Average jet fuel price	
			Current $ (cents)	1982-84 $ (cents)	Current $ (cents)	1982-84 $ (cents)
Historical[1]						
1985	152.3	758.6	12.36	11.59	80.7	75.7
1986	153.0	764.1	11.33	10.38	63.5	58.2
1987	152.5	775.4	11.20	10.07	50.8	45.7
1988	153.0	785.9	12.23	10.57	55.1	47.6
1989E	151.9	790.2	13.05	10.77	55.4	45.7
Forecast						
1990	154	792	12.95	10.27	57.2	45.3
1991	155	794	13.30	10.14	58.1	44.3
1992	156	796	13.75	10.09	60.5	44.4
1993	157	798	14.26	10.08	63.0	44.5
1994	159	801	14.86	10.17	64.9	44.4
1995	161	804	15.50	10.29	67.3	44.6
1996	163	807	16.26	10.23	71.9	45.3
1997	166	810	17.05	10.18	77.1	46.0
1998	169	813	17.91	10.14	82.4	46.7
1999	172	816	18.80	10.09	88.0	47.3
2000	176	819	19.74	10.05	92.4	48.0
2001	180	822	20.73	10.01	101.0	48.8

Source: U.S. Department of Transportation, Federal Aviation Administration, *FAA Aviation Forecasts, 1990-2001,* March, 1990, p. 183, Table 5. *Note:* 1. Source for historical data: The Research and Special Programs Administration (RSPA), Form 41.

★ 725 ★

Baseline Air Carrier Forecast Assumptions: International Operations, 1985-2001

Forecasts were generated by the FAA Office of Aviation Policy and Plans. The RSPA is a division of the U.S. Department of Transportation. It is responsible for the collection of air carrier traffic and financial data on Form 41, formerly collected by the Civil Aeronautics Board.

Fiscal year	Average seats per aircraft (seats)	Average passenger trip length (miles)	Revenue per passenger mile		Average jet fuel price	
			Current $ (cents)	1982-84 $ (cents)	Current $ (cents)	1982-84 $ (cents)
Historical[1]						
1985	292.2	2,636.2	9.38	8.80	84.9	79.6
1986	291.8	2,605.7	9.63	8.82	69.1	63.1
1987	283.0	2,583.9	9.76	8.78	56.9	51.2
1988	278.9	2,644.2	10.31	8.91	60.2	52.0
1989E	275.8	2,735.1	10.36	8.55	59.9	49.4
Forecast						
1990	276	2,766	10.35	8.21	61.8	49.0
1991	278	2,786	10.50	8.00	62.8	47.8
1992	279	2,807	10.80	7.93	65.4	48.0
1993	280	2,822	11.19	7.91	68.0	48.1
1994	283	2,844	11.55	7.91	70.2	48.0
1995	285	2,859	11.99	7.95	72.7	48.2
1996	288	2,877	12.45	7.84	77.7	48.9
1997	290	2,891	12.95	7.73	83.3	49.7
1998	293	2,904	13.49	7.64	89.1	50.4
1999	295	2,916	14.07	7.55	95.2	51.1
2000	298	2,923	14.68	7.47	101.8	51.8
2001	300	2,934	15.31	7.39	109.2	52.7

Source: U.S. Department of Transportation, Federal Aviation Administration, *FAA Aviation Forecasts, 1990-2001,* March, 1990, p. 184, Table 6. *Note:* 1. Source for historical data: The Research and Special Programs Administration (RSPA), Form 41.

★ 726 ★

Makeup of the Commercial Air Carrier Fleet by Type of Aircraft, 1989 and 2001

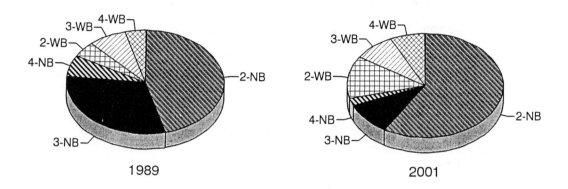

1989   2001

Types of aircraft are distinguished on the pie chart and in the table by number of engines on the craft (2, 3, or 4) and its wide-bodied (WB) or narrow-bodied (NB) design. "For the period 1996-2001, FAA aviation forecasts are based on consensus growth rates of key economic variables provided by Data Resources, Inc., Evans Economics, Inc., and the WEFA Group. These projections are combined with projections of aviation variables and professional judgment on the probabilities and consequences of events that affect aviation. The combination is used as input to the econometric models from which the forecasts are generated."

[Numbers in precent]

	1989	2001
2 NB	45.6	58.8
3 NB	30.8	9.9
4 NB	6.6	2.2
2 WB	4.8	13.4
3 WB	7.8	8.5
4 WB	4.4	7.3

Source: U.S. Department of Transportation, Federal Aviation Administration, *FAA Aviation Forecasts, Fiscal Years 1990-2001*, March, 1990, p. 67, bottom.

★ 727 ★

Commercial Air Carriers: Scheduled International Passenger Traffic, 1985-2001

Forecasts were generated by the FAA Office of Aviation Policy and Plans. The RSPA is a division of the U.S. Department of Transportation. It is responsible for the collection of air carrier traffic and financial data on Form 41, formerly collected by the Civil Aeronautics Board.

| Fiscal year | Revenue passenger enplanements (MIL) | | | | Revenue passenger miles (BIL) | | | |
| | | Latin | | | | Latin | | |
	Atlantic	America	Pacific	Total	Atlantic	America	Pacific	Total
Historical[1]								
1985	11.4	7.9	5.0	24.3	36.1	9.7	18.6	64.4
1986	10.5	8.5	5.4	24.4	32.6	11.1	20.3	64.0
1987	12.4	10.4	6.6	29.4	38.5	13.0	24.5	76.0
1988	14.6	11.5	8.2	34.3	46.1	14.2	30.2	90.5
1989E	15.0	11.8	10.0	36.8	49.1	14.7	36.8	100.6
Forecast								
1990	15.7	12.5	11.8	40.0	51.5	15.6	43.3	110.4
1991	16.4	13.2	13.3	42.9	54.2	16.4	48.7	119.3
1992	17.2	13.7	14.7	45.6	57.1	17.0	54.1	128.2
1993	18.0	14.3	15.9	48.2	59.8	17.7	58.4	135.9
1994	18.9	15.0	17.8	51.7	62.8	18.6	65.4	146.8
1995	19.6	15.7	19.4	54.7	65.3	19.5	71.6	156.4
1996	20.5	16.2	20.9	57.6	68.3	20.2	77.2	165.7
1997	21.3	16.8	22.3	60.4	71.3	21.0	82.5	174.8
1998	22.3	17.5	23.9	63.7	74.5	21.9	88.2	184.6
1999	23.3	18.1	25.4	66.8	77.9	22.8	93.9	194.6
2000	24.2	19.0	26.8	70.0	81.3	23.9	99.3	204.5
2001	25.3	19.6	28.2	73.1	84.9	24.8	104.8	214.5

Source: U.S. Department of Transportation, Federal Aviation Administration, *FAA Aviation Forecasts, 1990-2001*, March, 1990, p. 187, Table 9. *Note:* 1. Source for historical data: The Research and Special Programs Administration (RSPA), Form 41.

★ 728 ★

Commercial Air Carriers: Scheduled Passenger Traffic, 1985-2001

Forecasts were generated by the FAA Office of Aviation Policy and Plans. The RSPA is a division of the U.S. Department of Transportation. It is responsible for the collection of air carrier traffic and financial data on Form 41, formerly collected by the Civil Aeronautics Board. San Juan and Virgin Islands traffic is reported as domestic, beginning January 1, 1981.

Fiscal year	Revenue passenger enplanements Millions			Revenue passenger miles Billions		
	Domestic	International	Total	Domestic	International	Total
Historical[1]						
1985	350.4	24.6	375.0	265.8	64.8	330.6
1986	385.2	24.6	409.8	294.4	64.1	358.5
1987	415.5	29.4	444.9	322.1	76.0	398.1
1988	414.2	34.3	448.5	325.5	90.5	416.0
1989E	415.6	36.8	452.4	328.4	100.6	429.0
Forecast						
1990	430.6	40.0	470.6	341.0	110.4	451.4
1991	451.0	42.9	493.9	358.1	119.3	477.4
1992	471.0	45.6	516.6	374.9	128.2	503.1
1993	488.6	48.2	536.8	389.9	135.9	525.8
1994	508.2	51.7	559.9	407.1	146.8	553.9
1995	529.6	54.7	584.3	425.8	156.8	582.2
1996	552.4	57.6	610.0	445.8	165.7	611.5
1997	575.2	60.4	635.6	465.9	174.8	640.7
1998	598.2	63.7	661.9	486.3	184.6	670.9
1999	621.7	66.8	688.5	507.3	194.6	701.9
2000	645.3	70.0	715.3	528.5	204.5	733.0
2001	670.4	73.1	743.5	551.1	214.5	765.6

Source: U.S. Department of Transportation, Federal Aviation Administration, *FAA Aviation Forecasts, 1990-2001*, March, 1990, p. 186, Table 8. *Note:* 1. Source for historical data: The Research and Special Programs Administration (RSPA), Form 41.

★ 729 ★

Cost of Off-Airport Access Needs to the Year 2000

The ground access system has been studied at various airports on a case-by-case basis, but there is no national standard for the performance of these systems, nor is there a current national data base on the subject. An analysis of May 1989 by AASHTO's Aviation Needs Task Force estimated that off-airport access needs through the year 2000 are $11.4 billion. The distribution of these needs was projected to be 82.5% for hub airports, 9.5% for other commercial service airports and 8.0% for reliever and general aviation airports. "The estimate was derived from a survey of States and is believed to be very conservative because most States included only a portion of their airports, concentrated on near-term and committed projects, and did not include the access needs of new airports."

[Numbers in millions of dollars]

Category	Million $
Land acquisition	636
Highway	
Upgrade	2,644
Rehabilitation	1,355
New	3,929
Other	258
Public transit	
Rail	1,204
Satellite terminals	902
Bus/limo/taxi	258
Water	167
Total	11,353

Source: U.S. Department of Transportation, Federal Aviation Administration, *National Plan of Integrated Airport Systems (NPIAS), 1990-1999*, 1991, p. 17, Table 4-4. Primary source: American Association of State Highway and Transportation Officials (AASHTO), Aviation Needs Task Force, May, 1989.

★ 730 ★

Estimates of Total Capital Requirements for Airports, 1990-2015

Only those noise mitigation expenses eligible for Federal funding assistance under current law (1990) have been included in the estimates. The NPIAS data have been updated using the information in the FAA's NPI data base as of September 11, 1989. "These estimates are for funding requirements from all public sources, not just Federal. [They] are based on an analysis of funding requirements for the period through 1999, as reflected in the FAA's NPIAS data as of February 6, 1990. The NPIAS includes airport development plans that have been approved at appropriate local and State planning levels. The estimates for long-term capital requirements for airports were developed by extrapolating the average annual estimated over the first five years of the NPIAS (1990 through 1994). While the NPIAS covers a period of 10 years, through 1999, planning is incomplete for the period beyond 1994. This is especially true for general aviation and reliever airport requirements, which are often not known more than five years in advance."

[Numbers in billions of 1989 dollars]

Time period	Period	Average per year
1990-94		
AIP eligible NPIAs	$23.3	$4.7
Non-AIP Eligible	5.0	1.0
Total 1990-1994	28.3	5.7
1995-2000	34.2	5.7
2001-2015	85.5	5.7
Total 1990-2015	$148.0	$5.7

Source: U.S. Department of Transportation, *National Transportation Strategic Planning Study*, March, 1990, Table 11-5. Primary source: National Plan of Integrated Airport Systems (NPIAS), as of February 6, 1990.

★ 731 ★

National Airspace System Plan to Increase Airway Capacity through Upgrading of the Air Traffic Control System, 1993-2004

"The FAA's most ambitious response to the increased demand experienced since deregulation is its plan to replace and upgrade the ATC [Air Traffic Control] system. The National Airspace System Plan (NAS Plan) was originally promulgated in 1981 as a 10-year, $12 billion program to replace outmoded technology-literally to replace vacuum-tube electronics and in some cases surplus World war II radars with state-of-the-art, solid-state systems. During the past decade the NAS Plan has evolved into an ongoing multiyear capital improvement program currently estimated to cost $27 billion and with completion of all the elements in the current program not expected until 2005.... The program, as currently structured, would substantially upgrade the computers, radars, weather sensors, information systems, and communication links between ATC and aircraft that make up the ATC system.... The various components are now not expected to be fully in place until between 1993 and 2004. If the system works out as anticipated, the FAA projects a roughly 30 percent gain in airspace capacity."

Source: Transportation Research Board, National Research Council, *Winds of Change: domestic Air Transport since Deregulation*, Washington, D.C., 1991, pp. 297-98.

★ 732 ★

National Summary of Air Carrier Aircraft Operations by Region, 1985-2003

This table provides summaries and regional comparisons from 1985 through 2003 for all air carrier aircraft operations for all airports published in the Terminal Area Forecasts report (a total of 866 airports). Of this total, 399 airports had FAA air traffic control towers in FY 1989. In addition, there are 25 airports with FAA contract towers. Historical operations at FAA towered airports are derived from FAA air traffic activity reports.

[Numbers in thousands[1]]

Fiscal year	Alaska	Central	Eastern	Great Lakes	New England	Northwest Mountain	Southern	Southwest	Western Pacific
Historical									
1985	186	582	1,859	1,993	372	897	2,391	1,353	1,815
1986	178	593	2,022	2,166	383	953	2,614	1,436	2,072
1987	181	578	2,146	2,160	402	969	2,843	1,540	2,335
1988	171	573	2,163	1,938	402	982	2,845	1,530	2,305
1989	170	605	2,101	2,039	398	960	2,706	1,549	2,320
Forecast									
1990	169	532	2,129	2,064	409	952	2,846	1,590	2,377
1991	173	524	2,173	2,070	413	985	2,980	1,669	2,503
1992	177	550	2,248	2,143	427	1,025	3,039	1,753	2,652
1993	180	576	2,322	2,213	441	1,065	3,170	1,835	2,801
1994	184	602	2,393	2,284	454	1,111	3,302	1,917	2,952

[Continued]

★ 732 ★

National Summary of Air Carrier Aircraft Operations by Region, 1985-2003
[Continued]

Fiscal year	Alaska	Central	Eastern	Great Lakes	New England	Northwest Mountain	Southern	Southwest	Western Pacific
1995	188	628	2,465	2,359	468	1,155	3,435	1,986	3,107
1996	192	653	2,530	2,424	481	1,189	3,545	2,041	3,235
1997	196	675	2,594	2,489	495	1,224	3,650	2,094	3,347
1998	199	697	2,658	2,555	507	1,259	3,756	2,148	3,458
1999	203	720	2,719	2,618	519	1,294	3,861	2,201	3,570
2000	207	742	2,781	2,682	530	1,328	4,000	2,254	3,684
2001	210	762	2,824	2,736	539	1,359	4,080	2,305	3,802
2002	214	782	2,867	2,791	546	1,389	4,166	2,355	3,923
2003	218	802	2,910	2,845	554	1,420	4,266	2,404	4,042

Source: U.S. Department of Transportation, Federal Aviation Administration, *Terminal Area Forecasts, FY 1991-2005*, July, 1991, p. 15, Table 4. Includes air carrier operations at tower and nontower airports. *Note:* 1. Regional totals may not add to national total because of rounding.

★ 733 ★

National Summary of Air Carrier Passenger Enplanements by Region, 1985-2003

"Growth factors were applied to the base year (FY 1989) data at individual airports to project annual activity through FY 2005. Measures of aviation activity obtained from *FAA Aviation Forecasts: Fiscal Years 1990-2001*, March, 1990, were used as control factors and to determine growth forecasts from major hub reports, as well as facility-specific information provided by the nine major FAA regions.... Enplanements are based on data submitted to the Research and Special Progress Administration (RSPA) by the U.S. scheduled and nonscheduled commercial air carriers on Form 298-C reports. These data are supplemented by an FAA survey of air taxi operators, by reports of foreign flag traffic from the U.S. Immigration and Naturalization Service, and by State aviation commissions' and airport managers' reports.... Historical operations at FAA towered airports are derived from FAA air traffic activity reports."

Fiscal year	Alaska	Central	Eastern	Great Lakes	New England	Northwest Mountain	Southern	Southwest	Western Pacific
				Enplanements in thousands					
Historical									
1985	2,308	15,914	71,496	52,694	12,947	30,499	72,066	48,903	71,607
1986	2,093	16,987	76,026	59,214	14,241	34,991	78,697	49,782	80,524
1987	1,956	17,651	78,703	64,931	15,563	35,544	89,494	52,307	88,827
1988	2,126	17,327	79,594	66,509	16,023	34,415	93,024	53,564	90,982
1989	2,326	16,880	75,842	66,955	15,638	32,645	91,484	56,352	94,685
Forecast									
1990	2,329	15,945	75,792	67,544	15,848	32,523	95,903	56,573	96,096
1991	2,481	16,019	77,845	67,845	16,191	34,055	100,426	60,381	102,074
1992	2,634	17,516	82,545	71,658	17,266	35,813	107,085	64,766	108,889
1993	2,786	18,749	86,701	75,389	18,346	37,600	113,793	69,110	115,690
1994	2,938	19,983	90,858	79,126	19,427	39,938	120,561	73,392	122,491

[Continued]

★ 733 ★

National Summary of Air Carrier Passenger Enplanements by Region, 1985-2003
[Continued]

Fiscal year	Alaska	Central	Eastern	Great Lakes	New England	Northwest Mountain	Southern	Southwest	Western Pacific
1995	3,090	21,440	95,040	82,961	20,514	42,500	127,240	77,217	129,464
1996	3,218	22,593	99,069	86,662	21,263	44,331	132,728	80,511	135,856
1997	3,346	23,746	103,108	90,370	22,017	46,159	138,262	83,830	142,355
1998	3,473	24,899	107,155	94,082	22,772	47,988	143,818	87,175	148,661
1999	3,600	26,052	110,959	97,797	23,430	49,817	149,351	90,546	155,077
2000	3,727	27,206	114,778	101,515	24,091	51,646	154,844	93,947	161,504
2001	3,855	28,227	117,996	104,441	24,819	53,724	160,163	97,055	168,453
2002	3,982	29,249	121,228	107,367	25,546	55,801	165,482	100,163	175,407
2003	4,109	30,270	124,469	110,295	26,274	57,879	170,807	103,270	182,359

Source: U.S. Department of Transportation, Federal Aviation Administration, *Terminal Area Forecasts, FY 1991-2005,* July, 1991, p. 14, Table 3. *Note:* 1. Includes U.S. domestic and international air carriers plus data for foreign flag, interstate, and supplemental air carriers. Excludes commuter and air taxi enplanements.

★ 734 ★

National Summary of Total Aircraft Operations at Airports with FAA Towers by Region, 1985-2003

Of the 866 airports published in the Terminal Area Forecasts report, 399 airports had FAA air traffic control towers in FY 1989. In addition, there are 25 airports with FAA contract towers. "Growth factors were applied to the base year (FY 1989) data at individual airports to project annual activity levels through [FY 2003]. Measures of aviation activity obtained from *FAA Aviation Forecasts: Fiscal Years 1990-2001,* March, 1990, were used as control factors and to determine growth rates for some airports. Preliminary projections were modified using forecasts from major hub reports ... as well as facility-specific information provided by the nine FAA regions. The data for individual airports were eventually added...." Other sources, such as the Official Airline Guide as well as traffic reports of the Airport Operators' Council International, provided data and background information used in forecasting the type of operations and the level of activity at specific airports. Historical operations at FAA towered airports are derived from FAA air traffic activity reports.

[Numbers in millions]

	Alaska	Central	Eastern	Great Lakes	New England	Northwest Mountain	Southern	Southwest	Western-Pacific
Historical									
1985	1.1	2.4	8.2	8.9	3.4	4.8	10.3	6.8	12.6
1986	1.1	2.4	8.3	9.2	3.4	4.9	10.7	6.7	12.8
1987	1.1	2.5	8.5	9.7	3.6	5.1	11.2	6.5	13.4
1988	1.0	2.5	8.4	9.7	3.6	5.2	11.4	6.6	13.3
1989	1.0	2.5	8.3	9.9	3.4	5.2	11.3	6.6	13.6
Forecast									
1990[1]	1.1	2.5	8.4	9.9	3.4	5.5	11.9	6.8	14.3
1991	1.1	2.5	8.6	10.2	3.4	5.7	12.1	7.2	14.6
1992	1.1	2.6	8.9	10.4	3.5	5.8	12.6	7.6	15.0

[Continued]

★ 734 ★

National Summary of Total Aircraft Operations at Airports with FAA Towers by Region, 1985-2003

[Continued]

	Alaska	Central	Eastern	Great Lakes	New England	Northwest Mountain	Southern	Southwest	Western-Pacific
1993	1.1	2.7	9.2	10.7	3.6	6.0	13.0	7.9	15.4
1994	1.2	2.9	9.4	11.0	3.7	6.1	13.4	8.3	15.9
1995	1.2	3.0	9.7	11.2	3.8	6.3	13.8	8.6	16.3
1996	1.3	3.1	9.9	11.5	3.9	6.4	14.2	9.0	16.6
1997	1.3	3.2	10.1	11.7	4.0	6.6	14.6	9.3	16.9
1998	1.3	3.3	10.4	12.0	4.1	6.7	15.0	9.6	17.2
1999	1.4	3.4	10.6	12.2	4.2	6.9	15.4	10.0	17.5
2000	1.4	3.5	10.8	12.5	4.3	7.0	15.8	10.3	17.8
2001	1.4	3.6	11.0	12.7	4.4	7.2	16.1	10.6	18.1
2002	1.5	3.7	11.2	13.0	4.5	7.3	16.5	10.9	18.4
2003	1.5	3.8	11.4	13.2	4.6	7.4	16.8	11.2	18.8

Source: U.S. Department of Transportation, Federal Aviation Administration, *Terminal Area Forecasts, FY 1991-2005*, July 1991, p. 17, Table 6.
Note: 1. Preliminary, not forecast, data.

★ 735 ★

Numbers of Air Travelers by Age Group, 1985 and 2050

For the year 2050 two differing scenarios were used: 1) one which assumed no future change in the percentage of each age group that now travels by air 2) one in which a gradual rise was assumed in the percentage of each age group traveling by air, amounting to a one-third increase overall by the year 2050. Within each scenario, three variations in travel frequency were used: the present average of 2.9 round trips per air traveler per year and increases to 4 and 5 per year.

	Age group								
	18-21	22-29	30-39	40-49	50-64	65 and over	All adults	Under 18[1]	Total
1985 Survey data									
Number (millions)	15.1	34.9	39.2	26.4	32.8	29.3	177.7	63.2	240.9
Air travelers (millions)	4.4	11.5	12.7	9.0	9.8	6.4	53.8	12.6	66.4
Percent	29	33	35	34	30	22	30	20	28
2050 Projections									
Number (millions)	14.6	30.0	39.1	37.7	55.8	67.4	244.6	64.8	309.4
Air travelers, no increase[2] (millions)	4.2	9.9	13.7	12.8	16.7	14.8	72.1	13.0	85.1
Percent	29	33	35	34	30	22	30	20	28

[Continued]

★ 735 ★

Numbers of Air Travelers by Age Group, 1985 and 2050
[Continued]

	Age group								
	18-21	22-29	30-39	40-49	50-64	65 and over	All adults	Under 18[1]	Total
Air travelers, increase[2] (millions)	5.1	12.0	17.6	17.0	22.3	23.6	97.6	16.2	113.8
Percent	35	40	45	45	40	35	40	25	37

Source: Transportation Research Board, National Research Council, *Future Development of the U.S. Airport Network: Preliminary Report and Recommended Study Plan*, Washington, D.C., 1988, Appendix A, p. 37, Table A-2. Primary source: *1986 Air Travel Survey*, The Gallup Organization, Inc., Princeton, N.J., 1986; U.S. Department of Commerce, Bureau of the Census, *Projections of the Population of the United States by Age, Sex, and Race: 1983 to 2080*, Current Population Reports and Estimates Projections Series P-25, No. 952. *Notes*: 1. Estimated. 2. No increase assumes that for each age group the percentage who now travel by air at least once per year does not change through 2050. Increase assumes that the proportion of air travelers in each age group will gradually rise to the percentage indicated.

★ 736 ★

Passenger Enplanements at Large Hub Airports, 1988-2005 - I

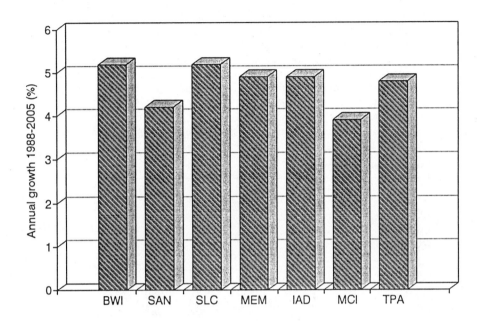

BWI= Baltimore, SAN = San Diego, SLC = Salt Lake City, MEM = Memphis, IAD = Washington Dulles, MCI = Kansas City, TPA = Tampa. A hub is defined here as a City or a Metropolitan Statistical Area requiring aviation services. Such a hub may include more than one airport. Hubs are ranked in size according to the community's percentage of the total enplaned passengers by scheduled air carriers in the 50 United States, the District of Columbia, and other U.S. areas designated by the FAA. An airport is classified as a large hub if it serves at least 1 percent of the enplaned passengers within these areas during a given calendar year. Fiscal year 1988 was used as the base for forecasts of enplanements for fiscal years 1995, 2000, and 2005.

[Annual growth in percent]

	Percent
BWI	5.2
SAN	4.2
SLC	5.2
MEM	4.9
IAD	4.9
MCI	3.9
TPA	4.8

Source: U.S. Department of Transportation, Federal Aviation Administration, *FAA Aviation Forecasts, Fiscal Years 1990-2001*, March, 1990, p. 140, lower right. Primary source: *FAA Terminal Area Forecasts FY 1990-2005.*

★ 737 ★

Passenger Enplanements at Large Hub Airports, 1988-2005 - II

BOS = Boston, LGA = N.Y. La Guardia, EWR = Neward, HNL = Honolulu, STL = St. Louis, DTW = Detroit, PHX = Phoenix, PIT = Pittsburgh. A hub is defined here as a City or a Metropolitan Statistical Area requiring aviation services. Such a hub may include more than one airport. Hubs are ranked in size according to the community's percentage of the total enplaned passengers by scheduled air carriers in the 50 United States, the District of Columbia, and other U.S. areas designated by the FAA. An airport is classified as a large hub if it serves at least 1 percent of the enplaned passengers within these areas during a given calendar year. Fiscal year 1988 was used as the base for forecasts of enplanements for fiscal years 1995, 2000, and 2005.

[Annual growth in percent]

	Percent
BOS	2.8
LGA	2.1
EWR	4.3
HNL	2.4
STL	3.7
DTW	4.2
PHX	5.5
PIT	4.9

Source: U.S. Department of Transportation, Federal Aviation Administration, *FAA Aviation Forecasts, Fiscal Years 1990-2001*, March, 1990, p. 140, upper left. Primary source: *FAA Terminal Area Forecasts FY 1990-2005.*

★ 738 ★

Passenger Enplanements at Large Hub Airports, 1988-2005 - III

ORD = Chicago O'Hare, ATL = Atlanta, DFW = Dallas/Fort Worth, LAX = Los Angeles International, JFK = New York Kennedy, DEN = Denver, SFO = San Francisco, MIA = Miami. A hub is defined here as a City or a Metropolitan Statistical Area requiring aviation services. Such a hub may include more than one airport. Hubs are ranked in size according to the community's percentage of the total enplaned passengers by scheduled air carriers in the 50 United States, the District of Columbia, and other U.S. areas designated by the FAA. An airport is classified as a large hub if it serves at least 1 percent of the enplaned passengers within these areas during a given calendar year. Fiscal year 1988 was used as the base for forecasts of enplanements for fiscal years 1995, 2000, and 2005.

[Annual growth in percent]

	Percent
ORD	2.9
ATL	2.2
DFW	3.4
LAX	1.2
JFK	2.6
DEN	5.6
SFO	1.8
MIA	2.1

Source: U.S. Department of Transportation, Federal Aviation Administration, *FAA Aviation Forecasts, Fiscal Years 1990-2001,* March, 1990, p. 140, upper left. Primary source: *FAA Terminal Area Forecasts FY 1990-2005.*

★ 739 ★

Passenger Enplanements at Large Hub Airports, 1988-2005 - IV

MSP = Minneapolis, IAH = Houston Intercontinental, MCO = Orlando, DCA = Washington National, PHL = Philadelphia, SEA = Seattle, LAS = Las Vegas, CLT = Charlotte. A hub is defined here as a City or a Metropolitan Statistical Area requiring aviation services. Such a hub may include more than one airport. Hubs are ranked in size according to the community's percentage of the total enplaned passengers by scheduled air carriers in the 50 United States, the District of Columbia, and other U.S. areas designated by the FAA. An airport is classified as a large hub if it serves at least 1 percent of the enplaned passengers within these areas during a given calendar year. Fiscal year 1988 was used as the base for forecasts of enplanements for fiscal years 1995, 2000, and 2005.

[Annual growth in percent]

	Percent
MSP	4.6
IAH	4.1
MCO	4.6
DCA	1
PHL	4.5
SEA	2.9
LAS	5.6
CLT	3.7

Source: U.S. Department of Transportation, Federal Aviation Administration, *FAA Aviation Forecasts, Fiscal Years 1990-2001*, March, 1990, p. 140, lower left. Primary source: *FAA Terminal Area Forecasts FY 1990-2005.*

★ 740 ★

Regional/Commuter Airlines: Growth in Scheduled Passenger Enplanements, 1981-2001

For the purpose of this forecast, regional/commuter airlines are defined as those air carriers that provide regularly scheduled passenger service and whose fleets are composed largely of aircraft having 60 seats or fewer. The data for each fiscal year represent the total scheduled passenger enplanements within the 48 contiguous states, Hawaii, Puerto Rico and the Virgin Islands. Alaska, U.S. territories, and other foreign territories are excluded from the data base.

[Numbers of passengers in millions]

1980	14.0
1981	15.0
1982	17.0
1983	20.0
1984	22.0
1985	23.0
1986	25.0
1987	27.0
1988	30.0
1989	32.1
1990	34.9
1991	37.5
1992	40.0
1993	42.0
1994	45.0
1995	49.0
1996	52.0
1997	56.0
1998	60.0
1999	63.0
2000	66.0
2001	71.2

Source: U.S. Department of Transportation, Federal Aviation Administration, *FAA Aviation Forecasts, Fiscal Year 1990-2001*, p. 83, bottom. Magnitudes estimated from published chart.

★ 741 ★

Regional/Commuter Airlines: Growth in Scheduled Revenue Passenger Miles, 1980-2001

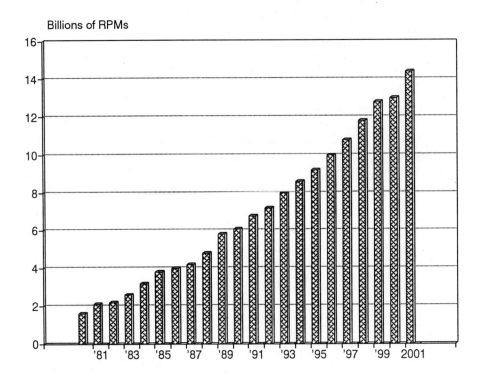

Billions of RPMs

For the purpose of this forecast, regional/commuter airlines are defined as those air carriers that provide regularly scheduled passenger service and whose fleets are composed largely of aircraft having 60 seats or fewer.

[Numbers in billions of revenue passenger miles (RPMs)]

1980	1.6
1981	2.1
1982	2.2
1983	2.6
1984	3.2
1985	3.8
1986	4.0
1987	4.2
1988	4.8
1989	5.8
1990	6.1
1991	6.8
1992	7.2
1993	8.0
1994	8.6
1995	9.2

[Continued]

★ 741 ★

Regional/Commuter Airlines: Growth in Scheduled Revenue Passenger Miles, 1980-2001

[Continued]

1996	10.0
1997	10.8
1998	11.8
1999	12.8
2000	13.0
2001	14.4

Source: U.S. Department of Transportation, Federal Aviation Administration, *FAA Aviation Forecasts: Fiscal Years 1990-2001*, March, 1990, p. 83, top. Magnitudes estimated from published chart.

★ 742 ★

Special Hub Forecasts: Atlanta, 1987-2005

In 1978 the FAA began an effort to forecast changes at individual hub airports over the long term. The Atlanta hub was one of five metropolitan hubs studied during 1988.

"There are 22 public-use airports in the Atlanta hub. Of these, three airports have FAA-operated air traffic control towers. Located 10 miles southwest of the downtown area, Atlanta Hartsfield International Airport is the hub's only air carrier airport. Hartsfield and the other public use airports provide takeoff and landing services to general aviation and military aircraft in the Atlanta area." Atlanta is served by both domestic and international carriers, including Delta Air Lines, which utilizes Hartsfield as the center of its hub and spoke network.

"Total passenger enplanements in the Atlanta hub are projected at approximately 34.2 million in the year 2005. This number is 45 percent higher than the 23.6 million passengers recorded in 1987. Commercial aircraft operations in the hub are expected to reach 946,300 by the year 2005, about 22 percent more than the 774,100 operations handled in 1987."

Source: U.S. Department of Transportation, Federal Aviation Administration, *FAA Aviation Forecasts, Fiscal Years 1990-2005*, March, 1990, p. 145.

★ 743 ★

Special Hub Forecasts: Cincinnati, 1987-2005

In 1978 the FAA began an effort to forecast changes at individual hub airports over the long term. The Cincinnati hub was one of five metropolitan hubs studied during 1988.

"There are 12 public-use airports in the Cincinnati hub. Of these, two (Greater Cincinnati International and Luken Field) are FAA air route traffic control tower airports." Total passenger enplanements in the Cincinnati hub are projected to reach 12.6 million in the year 2005, and increase of 215 percent from 1988 to 2005. Commercial aircraft activity in the hub is expected to reach 559,600 operations by 2005, approximately 124 percent more than the operations handled during 1987.

Source: U.S. Department of Transportation, Federal Aviation Administration, *FAA Aviation Forecasts, Fiscal Years 1990-2005*, March, 1990, p. 145.

★ 744 ★

Special Hub Forecasts: Dayton, Ohio, 1987-2005

In 1978 the FAA began an effort to forecast changes at individual hub airports over the long term. The Dayton hub was one of five metropolitan hubs studied during 1988.

"There are 19 public-use airports in the Dayton Metropolitan Statistical Area. Of these, only the James M. Cox Dayton International Airport has an FAA-operated air traffic control tower....

"Total passenger enplanements in the Dayton hub are projected to reach 5.1 million in 2005. This represents an increase of 113 percent over the 2.4 million passengers enplaned in 1988. Commercial aircraft operations are forecast to reach 282,100 by 2005, representing a 62 percent increase over the 173,800 commercial aircraft operations that occurred in 1988."

Source: U.S. Department of Transportation, Federal Aviation Administration, *FAA Aviation Forecasts, Fiscal Years 1990-2005*, March, 1990, p. 150.

★ 745 ★

Special Hub Forecasts: Nashville, 1987-2005

In 1978 the FAA began an effort to forecast changes at individual hub airports over the long term. The Nashville hub was one of five metropolitan hubs studied during 1988.

There are 12 public use airports in the Nashville Metropolitan Statistical Area, of which only the Nashville Airport has an FAA-operated air traffic control tower. The airport provides international, domestic, and commuter air carrier services to the greater Nashville area. American Airlines uses Nashville International as part of its hub and spoke route system.

"Total passenger enplanements in the Nashville hub are projected to reach 8.6 million in 2005. This represents an increase of 153 percent over the 3.4 million passengers enplaned in 1988. Commercial aircraft operations are forecast to reach 288,800 by 2005, representing a 78 percent increase over the 162,300 commercial aircraft operations that occurred in 1988."

Source: U.S. Department of Transportation, Federal Aviation Administration, *FAA Aviation Forecasts, Fiscal Years 1990-2005*, March, 1990, pp. 150-51.

★ 746 ★

Special Hub Forecasts: Raleigh/Durham, 1987-2005

In 1978 the FAA began an effort to forecast changes at individual hub airports over the long term. The Raleigh/Durham hub was one of five metropolitan hubs studied during 1988.

There are eight public use airports in the Raleigh/Durham Metropolitan Statistical Area, including Raleigh/Durham International Airport, the only one of the eight with an FAA-operated control tower. International, domestic, and commuter air carrier services are provided at Raleigh/Durham International, and American Airlines uses the airport as one of its hubs.

"Total passenger enplanements in the Raleigh/Durham hub are projected to reach 12.2 million in 2005. This represents an increase of 408 percent over the 2.4 million passengers enplaned in 1987. Commercial aircraft operations are forecast to reach 439,800 by 2005, representing a 287 percent increase over the 113,500 commercial aircraft operations that occurred in 1987."

Source: U.S. Department of Transportation, Federal Aviation Administration, *FAA Aviation Forecasts, Fiscal Years 1990-2005*, March, 1990, p. 155.

★ 747 ★

Summary of Aircraft Operations at Hub Airports, 1988-2005

Air Traffic Hubs are defined as Cities and Metropolitan Statistical Areas requiring aviation services. Such hubs may include more than one airport. Hub airports are classed as large, medium, or small according to the community's percentage of the total enplaned passengers by scheduled air carriers in the 50 United States, the District of Columbia, and other U.S. areas designated by the Federal Aviation Administration. Large hubs are airports that serve 1.00 percent of more of the enplaned passengers during a given calendar year. Medium hubs serve 0.25 to 0.999 percent of the enplaned passengers while small hubs serve 0.05 to 0.249 percent. In fiscal year 1988, the FAA defined 31 large hub airports, 39 medium, and 64 small hub airports. Aircraft operations at both the medium and small hubs are expected to grow faster than for the large hubs during the period between 1988 and 2005.

[Numbers in millions]

	1988	1995	2005	Average annual percent change	
				1988-1995	1995-2205
Large hubs	12.4	15.0	17.7	2.8%	1.7%
Medium hubs	8.5	11.0	13.9	3.8	2.4
Small hubs	8.8	11.1	14.1	3.4	2.4

Source: U.S. Department of Transportation, Federal Aviation Administration, *FAA Aviation Forecasts, Fiscal Years 1990-2001*, March, 1990, p. 144, bottom.

★ 748 ★

Summary of Passenger Enplanements at Hub Airports, 1988-2005

Air Traffic Hubs are defined as Cities and Metropolitan Statistical Areas requiring aviation services. Such hubs may include more than one airport. Hub airports are classed as large, medium, or small according to the community's percentage of the total enplaned passengers by scheduled air carriers in the 50 United States, the District of Columbia, and other U.S. areas designated by the Federal Aviation Administration. Large hubs are airports that serve 1.00 percent or more of the enplaned passengers during a given calendar year. Medium hubs serve 0.25 to 0.999 percent of the enplaned passengers while small hubs serve 0.05 to 0.249 percent. "In fiscal year 1988, there were 31 large hub airports, 39 medium hub airports, and 64 small hub airports.... The large hub airports accounted for ... 69.8 percent of approximately 493.8 million air carrier/commuter/air taxi passengers enplaned nationally. The medium hub airports enplaned ... 18.9 percent and the small hubs 7.3 percent of the total."

[Numbers in millions]

	1988	1995	2005	Average annual percent change	
				1988-1995	1995-2005
Large hubs	344.6	464.0	616.8	4.3	2.9
Medium hubs	91.5	144.8	215.0	6.8	4.0
Small hubs	36.0	50.2	72.5	4.9	3.7

Source: U.S. Department of Transportation, Federal Aviation Administration, *FAA Aviation Forecasts, Fiscal Years 1990-2001*, March, 1990, p. 144, top.

★ 749 ★

Total Aircraft Operations at Large Hub Airports, 1988-2005[1]

Aircraft operations are defined here as the airborne movement of aircraft in controlled or noncontrolled airport terminal areas, and counts at en route fixes or other points where counts can be made. Total operations are made up of local and itinerant operations. By the year 2005, growth in total aircraft operations at Dallas/Fort Worth is expected to make it the busiest airport in the United States. Atlanta is expected to move up to second busiest by 2005, Denver is forecast to become third in the nation, while Chicago O'Hare (ranked the busiest airport in 1988) is expected to be displaced to fourth busiest in the nation. "The increases in aviation activity at these and other airports will come from growth in developments. These developments may include the addition of new airline gates and the restructuring of airline fleets and, in the case of Denver, the construction of a new air carrier airport."

[Numbers in thousands]

Airport	FY 1988	FY 1995	FY 2000	FY 2005
Chicago O'Hare	796	813	827	842
Atlanta[2]	783	883	932	962
Dallas/Ft. Worth	664	924	1031	1145
Los Angeles	632	657	666	702
New York Kennedy	329	359	377	396
Denver	511	748	816	867
San Francisco	461	486	494	523
Miami	358	440	490	540
Boston	445	475	521	568
New York LaGuardia	363	382	382	382
Newark	377	427	445	464
Honolulu	367	461	484	512
St. Louis	429	468	503	538
Detroit	380	485	514	543
Phoenix	455	551	599	647
Pittsburgh	387	487	573	664
Minneapolis	380	466	527	589
Houston Intercont'l	297	363	408	454
Orlando	290	429	527	626
Washington National	328	366	385	401
Philadelphia	416	496	564	643
Seattle-Tacoma	311	356	384	405
Las Vegas	373	490	533	561
Charlotte	405	496	540	585
Baltimore	304	370	425	479
San Diego	206	240	266	290
Salt Lake City	289	413	474	536
Memphis	359	457	505	552

[Continued]

★ 749 ★

Total Aircraft Operations at Large Hub Airports, 1988-2005

[Continued]

Airport	FY 1988	FY 1995	FY 2000	FY 2005
Washington Dulles	241	408	452	490
Kansas City	226	288	341	395
Tampa	245	303	335	366

Source: U.S. Department of Transportation, Federal Aviation Administration, *FAA Aviation Forecasts, Fiscal Years 1990-2001*, March, 1990, pp. 141. Primary source: *FAA Terminal Area Forecasts FY 1990-2005*. *Notes:* 1. Includes total itinerant and local operations performed by commercial air carriers, air taxis, military, and general aviation. 2. Forecasts as shown in individual hub forecast reports (or as adjusted).

★ 750 ★

Total Aircraft Operations at Large Hub Airports, 1988-2005 - I

BWI = Baltimore, SAN = San Diego, SLC = Salt Lake City, MEM = Memphis, IAD = Washington Dulles, MCI = Kansas City, TPA = Tampa. Aircraft operations are defined here as the airborne movement of aircraft in controlled or noncontrolled airport terminal areas, and counts at en route fixes or other points where counts can be made. Total operations are made up of local and itinerant operations.

[Annual growth in percentages]

BWI	2.7
SAN	2.0
SLC	3.7
MEM	2.6
IAD	4.3
MCI	3.3
TPA	2.4

Source: U.S. Department of Transportation, Federal Aviation Administration, *FAA Aviation Forecasts, Fiscal Years 1990-2001*, March, 1990, p. 142, lower right. Primary source: *FAA Terminal Area Forecasts FY 1990-2005*.

★ 751 ★

Total Aircraft Operations at Large Hub Airports, 1988-2005 - II

BOS = Boston, LGA = N.Y. La Guardia, EWR = Newark, HNL = Honolulu, STL = St. Louis, DTW = Detroit, PHX = Phoenix, PIT = Pittsburgh.

[Annual growth in percentages]

BOS	1.5
LGA	0.3
EWR	1.2
HNL	2.0
STL	1.3
DTW	2.1
PHX	2.1
PIT	3.2

Source: U.S. Department of Transportation, Federal Aviation Administration, *FAA Aviation Forecasts, Fiscal Years 1990-2001*, March, 1990, p. 142, upper right. Primary source: *FAA Terminal Area Forecasts FY 1990-2005*.

★ 752 ★

Total Aircraft Operations at Large Hub Airports, 1988-2005 - III

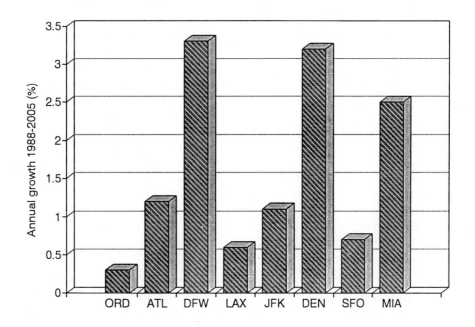

ORD = Chicago O'Hare, ATL = Atlanta, DFW = Dallas/Fort Worth, LAX = Los Angeles International, JFK = N.Y. Kennedy, DEN = Denver, SFO = San Francisco, MIA = Miami.

[Annual growth in percentages]

ORD	0.3
ATL	1.2
DFW	3.3
LAX	0.6
JFK	1.1
DEN	3.2
SFO	0.7
MIA	2.6

Source: U.S. Department of Transportation, Federal Aviation Administration, *FAA Aviation Forecasts, Fiscal Years 1990-2001*, March, 1990, p. 142, upper left. Primary source: *FAA Terminal Area Forecasts FY 1990-2005.*

★ 753 ★

Total Aircraft Operations at Large Hub Airports, 1988-2005 - IV

MSP = Minneapolis, IAH = Houston Intercontinental, MCO = Orlando, DCA = Washington National, PHL = Philadelphia, SEA = Seattle, LAS = Las Vegas, CLT = Charlotte. Aircraft operations are defined here as the airborne movement of aircraft in controlled or noncontrolled airport terminal areas, and counts at en route fixes or other points where counts can be made. Total operations are made up of local and itinerant operations.

[Annual growth in percentages]

MSP	2.6
IAH	2.5
MCO	4.6
DCA	1.2
PHL	2.6
SEA	1.5
LAS	2.4
CLT	2.2

Source: U.S. Department of Transportation, Federal Aviation Administration, *FAA Aviation Forecasts, Fiscal Years 1990-2001*, March, 1990, p. 142, lower left. Primary source: *FAA Terminal Area Forecasts FY 1990-2005*.

★ 754 ★

Total Passenger Enplanements at Large Hub Airports, 1988-2005[1]

A hub is defined here as a City or a Metropolitan Statistical Area requiring aviation services. Such a hub may include more than one airport. Hubs are ranked in size according to the community's percentage of the total enplaned passengers by scheduled air carriers in the 50 United States, the District of Columbia, and other U.S. areas designated by the FAA. An airport is classified as a large hub if it serves at least 1 percent of the enplaned passengers within these areas during a given calendar year. In fiscal year 1988 the 31 airports classified as large hubs accounted for 69.8 percent of the air carrier, commuter, and air taxi passenger enplanements nationally. Fiscal year 1988 was used as the base for 1995, 2000, and 2005. The FAA forecasts that the rankings of the six busiest airports will change somewhat, relative to each other, by the year 2005. It is projected that both Dallas/Fort Worth and Denver will have surpassed Atlanta in total enplaned passengers by the year 2005.

[Numbers in thousands]

Airport	FY 1988	FY 1995	FY 2000	FY 2005
Chicago O'Hare	28,850	38,635	42,301	46,660
Atlanta[2]	23,537	27,884	31,270	34,174
Dallas/Ft. Worth	23,029	29,676	35,073	40,829
Los Angeles	22,179	23,641	25,808	27,307
New York Kennedy	19,415	23,484	26,742	30,000
Denver	15,015	27,419	33,197	38,060
San Francisco	14,683	17,250	18,584	19,917
Miami	14,316	15,728	18,079	20,432
Boston	11,802	14,469	16,584	18,978
New York LaGuardia	11,790	13,949	15,382	16,809
Newark	11,580	16,567	20,616	23,558
Honolulu	11,081	13,629	15,148	16,435
St. Louis	10,139	13,671	16,192	18,896
Detroit	10,044	14,493	17,284	20,074
Phoenix	9,559	15,147	19,406	23,663
Pittsburgh	8,971	14,566	17,313	20,138
Minneapolis	8,939	13,577	16,447	19,309
Houston	8,142	11,667	14,173	15,991
Orlando	8,122	12,732	19,349	17,411
Washington National	7,888	8,888	9,116	9,345
Philadelphia	7,789	11,598	13,930	16,389
Seattle	7,659	10,374	11,379	12,386
Las Vegas	7,658	12,289	15,967	19,369
Charlotte	7,613	10,019	12,029	14,039
Baltimore	5,363	8,147	10,414	12,680
San Diego	5,328	7,506	9,012	10,799
Salt Lake City	4,977	8,106	9,895	11,686

[Continued]

★ 754 ★

Total Passenger Enplanements at Large Hub Airports, 1988-2005
[Continued]

Airport	FY 1988	FY 1995	FY 2000	FY 2005
Memphis	4,947	7,803	9,481	11,159
Washington Dulles	4,771	7,647	9,238	10,830
Kansas City	4,726	6,488	7,747	9,005
Tampa	4,719	6,961	8,704	10,449

Source: U.S. Department of Transportation, Federal Aviation Administration, *FAA Aviation Forecasts, Fiscal Years 1990-2001,* March, 1990, p. 139. Primary source: *FAA Terminal Area Forecasts FY 1990-2005. Notes:* 1. Includes U.S. certified route air carriers, foreign flag carriers, supplementals, air commuters and air taxis. 2. Forecasts as shown in individual hub forecast reports (or as adjusted).

Comparative Transportation Modes

★ 755 ★

Intercity Personal Transportation by Mode of Transport, 1900-2050

	1900	1950	2000	2050
Railroad	90	18		
Air		15	35	80
Automobile		72	66	25

Source: "Introduction," *Transportation for the Future,* David F. Batten and Roland Thord, eds., Berlin, 1989, p. 4, Figure 1.3. Primary source: A.E. Anderson, et al., *Future Transport in Sweden,* Ministry of Communication, Dsk 1987:16, Stockholm, 1987 (in Swedish).

★ 756 ★

Transportation Activity by Mode, 1970-2010

VMT = vehicle miles traveled. RPM = revenue passenger miles. TMT = ton-miles traveled. Making no efficiency assumptions, the forecast projects slow and steady moderation in travel growth, particularly for passenger modes. Relatively slow population growth, the aging of the "baby boomers" and other population segments, and only modest increases in personal income are expected to depress growth in personal travel demand. With increasing traffic congestion, telecommunications is projected to substitute for a growing share of local trips. Current modes of transportation will continue to be in use through the decade 2000-2010 for long distance trips. In the absence of the "extraordinary" events that have been responsible for much of their recent performance, however, growth in these long-distance modes will slow to more moderate levels. "Extraordinary" events include airline, rail, and motor carrier deregulation; the near total shift to diesel engines in class 8 trucks; the development of the Alaskan oil fields, which rapidly boosted coastal tanker traffic; and tighter regulations on the fuel economy, emissions, and safety of cars than of light trucks. The sole "extraordinary" event included in the baseline scenario is the growth in coal use which has been forecast by the National Energy Policy Plan. It is assumed here that all incremental coal production will come from sources west of the Mississippi. This will result in a disproportionate increase in rail ton-miles traveled, because of the relatively longer lengths of haul required, even if much of the increased coal freight is shipped to waterborne modes of transport.

[Numbers in vehicle-miles of travel for highway modes and ton-miles or passenger revenue-miles of travel for nonhighway modes]

Year	Highway modes				Nonhighway modes		
	Auto (10^9VMT)	Light truck (10^9 VMT)	Heavy truck (10^9 VMT)	Total (10^9 VMT)	Air[1] (10^9 RPM)	Rail (10^9 TMT)	Marine[1] (10^9 TMT)
1970	907	123	67	1110	109	771	596
1975	1023	201	87	1328	137	759	566
1980	1105	291	115	1527	204	932	922
1985	1260	373	131	1774	278	898	893
1990	1447	453	153	2094	344	1075	911
1995	1546	517	167	2270	410	1252	899
2000	1657	570	186	2444	487	1490	912
2010	1895	659	237	2795	669	2069	999
Average annual percentage change							
1970-1985	2.22	7.68	4.57	3.18	6.44	1.02	2.77
1990-2010	1.36	1.89	2.21	1.45	3.38	3.33	0.46

Source: U.S. Department of Energy, *Forecast of Transportation Energy Demand through the Year 2010*, M.M. Mintz and A.D. Vyas, Center for Transportation Research, Energy Systems Division, Argonne National Laboratory, November, 1990 (rev. April, 1991), Table 4.4. Primary source: 1970-85 from *Highway Statistics*, U.S. Department of Transportation, Federal Highway Administration (various years); *National Transportation Statistics*, U.S. Department of Transportation, Research and Special Projects Administration (various years); S. Davis, et. al., *Transportation Energy Data Book: Edition 10*, Oak Ridge National Laboratory, ORNL-6565, September, 1989; *Annual Energy Review 1989*, U.S. Department of Energy, Energy Information Administration Report DOE/EIA-0384 (89), May 1990. For projections, ANL-9ON (forecast developed by the Center for Transportation Research at Argonne National Laboratory [ANL], under contract to the Office of Transportation Technologies, Office of the Secretary for Conservation and Renewable Energy, U.S. Department of Energy) and the Energy Information Administration (EIA) of the U.S. Department of Energy. *Note:* 1. Domestic operations of U.S. flag carriers.

★ 757 ★

Transportation Energy Use by Mode, 1970-2010

The ANL-9ON forecast projects that energy efficiency improvements will fail to keep pace with increases in travel demand. For this reason, commercial transportation modes-especially rail and heavy-duty trucking-are expected to experience the fastest growth in energy use; automobiles, on the other hand, will experience the slowest growth as older, less fuel-efficient vehicles will continue to be retired from use. Because of these divergent trends in fuel use by personal and commercial transportation, commercial modes are projected to surpass personal modes shortly after the year 2000, when they will begin to account for the majority of transportation energy use.

[Energy use in 10^{15} Btu]

Year	Highway modes			Nonhighway modes				Total
	Auto	Lt. truck	Hvy. truck	Air[1]	Rail[2]	Marine[3]	Other[4]	
1970	8.526	1.540	1.611	1.307	0.575	0.753	0.993	15.305
1975	9.611	2.240	1.908	1.274	0.596	0.851	0.849	17.329
1980	9.037	2.951	2.564	1.528	0.645	1.677	0.915	19.317
1985	8.673	3.630	3.085	1.881	0.501	1.311	0.781	19.862
1990	9.066	3.988	3.654	2.298	0.529	0.956	0.690	21.182
1995	9.365	4.337	3.927	2.544	0.604	1.020	0.737	22.533
2000	9.713	4.630	4.166	2.765	0.704	1.101	0.748	23.828
2010	9.586	4.871	5.103	2.988	0.950	1.304	0.712	25.513
Average annual percentage change								
1970-1985	0.11	5.88	4.43	2.46	-0.91	3.77	-1.59	1.68
1990-2010	0.28	1.01	1.68	1.32	2.97	1.56	0.16	0.93

Source: U.S. Department of Energy, *Forecast of Transportation Energy Demand through the Year 2010,* M.M. Mintz and A.D. Vyas, Center for Transportation Research, Energy Systems Division, Argonne National Laboratory, November, 1990 (rev. April, 1991), Table 4.1. Primary source: For projections, ANL-9ON (forecast developed by the Center for Transportation Research at Argonne National Laboratory [ANL], under contract to the Office of Transportation Technologies, Office of the Secretary for conservation and Renewable Energy, U.S. Department of Energy) and the Energy Information Administration (EIA) of the U.S. Department of Energy. *Notes:* 1. Passenger, freight, and general aviation. Includes U.S. fuel purchased by foreign flag carriers. 2. Freight only. 3. Domestic freight and U.S. fuel purchases for international shipping. 4. Pipeline, transit and rail passengers.

Fuel

★ 758 ★

Changes in Transportation Fuel Prices, 1985-2010

As crude oil prices rise toward $37 per barrel in 2010, prices of petroleum products such as gasoline, diesel fuel, and jet fuel will also increase, providing incentives for fuel economy improvements. In real terms, gasoline prices are projected to grow by 50 percent between 1989 and 2010, while diesel and jet fuels are also expected to show substantial increases.

[Numbers in 1989 dollars per gallon]

Year	Gasoline	Diesel	Jet fuel
1985	1.32	1.20	0.94
1990	1.05	0.96	0.54
2000	1.32	1.24	0.88
2010	1.51	1.49	1.16

Source: U.S. Department of Transportation, *National Transportation Strategic Planning Study*, March, 1990, p. 3-9, Table 3-8. Primary source: Projected figures communicated by John Pearson, U.S. Department of Energy.

★ 759 ★

Fuel Efficiency of Air and Road Vehicular Travel, 1985-2010

New car fuel efficiency doubled between 1973 and 1988 and light truck fuel economy has also increased. For automobiles, most of the improvement in efficiency during the last decade is due to vehicle technology, such as front wheel drive, fuel injection, advanced transmissions, better aerodynamics and electronic engine control, rather than to reduced passenger car weights, which have largely stabilized since 1980. Current generation aircraft deliver 55 to 70 seat miles per gallon (SMPG). According to the Department of Transportation, advanced technologies in engine design, aerodynamics, computer controls, and use of lightweight materials could deliver 130 to 150 SMPG early in the 21st century.

[Numbers in miles per gallon and billions of miles]

| Year | New car MPG | New light truck MPG | Cars and light trucks | | Commercial air revenue passenger miles (billions) |
			Fleet avg. road MPG	Total vehicle miles (billions)	
1985	27.0	20.4	17.0	1,452	415
1990	28.6	20.6	18.7	1,553	543
2000	32.8	22.4	21.0	1,834	776
2010	36.9	23.9	23.11	2,241	1,101

Source: U.S. Department of Transportation, *National Transportation Strategic Planning Study*, March, 1990, p. 3-8, Table 3-7. Primary source: Projected figures communicated by John Pearson, U.S. Department of Energy.

★ 760 ★

Fuel Use: All Transportation Modes, 1985-2010

Highway transportation accounts for over 70 percent of all the energy used in the transportation sector. Projections by the Department of Energy assume slow but steady growth in motor gasoline consumption as expected increases in travel exceed anticipated gains in efficiency. Demand for diesel fuel is expected to rise steadily, as a continued steady increase in truck miles of over 2 percent last year is expected to offset a projected 36 percent improvement in truck freight fuel efficiency. Use of jet fuel is projected to grow slowly but steadily, with air traffic levels expected to rise by 3.6 percent annually, 1.6 percent faster than aircraft efficiency improvements.

[Numbers in quadrillion Btus]

Year	Gasoline	Diesel	Jet fuel	Fuel, lubes, etc.	Total petroleum fuels	Total alcohol fuels	Natural gas
1985	12.8	3.2	2.5	1.2	19.6	-	0.5
1990	13.9	3.8	3.1	1.0	21.7	-	0.6
2000	14.5	4.4	3.5	1.2	23.7	0.007	0.6
2010	15.8	5.2	4.1	1.4	26.4	0.014	0.6

Source: U.S. Department of Transportation, *National Transportation Strategic Planning Study*, March, 1990, p. 3-8, Table 3-6. Primary source: Projected use communicated by John Pearson, U.S. Department of Energy.

★ 761 ★

Total Energy Consumed by the Transportation Sector by Mode and Fuel Type, 1985-2010

This table on energy consumption is part of the documentation for a forecast developed by the Center for Transportation Research at Argonne National Laboratory under contract to the Office of Transportation Technologies under the Assistant Secretary for Conservation and Renewable Energy of the U.S. Department of Energy. The current forecast carries the acronym ANL-9ON and is meant to serve as a baseline against which trends can be analyzed and existing and proposed energy conservation programs can be evaluated.

[Numbers in 10^{15} Btu]

Item	Energy consumption (10^{15} Btu), by Year					Change, 1985-2010
	1985	1990	1995	2000	2010	(%/yr)
By mode						
Autos						
Personal	7.396	7.825	8.045	8.265	8.085	0.36
Fleet	1.286	1.242	1.320	1.448	1.501	0.62
Total	8.682	9.066	9.365	9.713	9.586	0.40
Light trucks						
Personal	1.921	2.223	2.544	2.743	2.718	1.40
Commercial	1.670	1.765	1.793	1.887	2.153	1.02
Total	3.591	3.988	4.337	4.630	4.871	1.23

[Continued]

★ 761 ★

Total Energy Consumed by the Transportation Sector by Mode and Fuel Type, 1985-2010
[Continued]

Item	Energy consumption (10^{15} Btu), by Year					Change, 1985-2010
	1985	1990	1995	2000	2010	(%/yr)
Heavy-duty hwy. vehicles						
Trucks	3.066	3.485	3.751	3.982	4.913	1.90
Buses	0.161	0.169	0.176	0.184	0.190	0.67
Total	3.227	3.654	3.927	4.166	5.103	1.85
All hwy. modes	15.500	16.708	17.628	18.510	19.560	0.93
Rail freight	0.446	0.529	0.604	0.704	0.950	3.07
Marine freight	1.015	0.956	1.020	1.101	1.304	1.01
Air	2.539	2.979	3.225	3.446	3.669	1.48
Pipeline	0.657	0.676	0.722	0.733	0.696	0.23
Other	0.014	0.014	0.015	0.015	0.016	0.50
All nonhwy. modes	4.671	5.154	5.586	5.999	6.635	1.41
Total	20.170	21.863	23.214	24.509	26.194	1.05
By fuel type						
Gasoline	12.892	13.603	14.228	14.804	14.851	0.57
Diesel	3.249	3.835	4.202	4.611	5.881	2.40
Jet fuel	2.539	2.979	3.225	3.446	3.669	1.48
Residual oil	0.819	0.755	0.821	0.900	1.082	1.12
Natural gas	0.504	0.525	0.579	0.596	0.571	0.50
Other	0.167	0.166	0.158	0.152	0.142	-0.65
Total	20.170	21.863	23.213	24.509	26.196	1.05

Source: U.S. Department of Energy, *Forecast of Transportation Energy Demand through the Year 2010*, M.M. Mintz and A.D. Vyas, Center for Transportation Research, Energy Systems Division, Argonne National Laboratory, November, 1990 9rev. April, 1991), Table S.3.

★ 762 ★

Total Jet Fuel and Aviation Gasoline Fuel Consumption by Civil Aviation Aircraft, 1985-2001

"The FAA's forecasting process is a continuous and interactive one that involves the FAA Forecast Branch, other FAA Offices and Services, other Government agencies, and aviation industry groups. In addition, the process uses various economic and aviation data bases, econometric models and equations, and other analytical techniques.... [An] intermediate step in the FAA aviation forecast process is the public dissemination of the forecast results, solicitation of industry comments, and critique of the forecasts. The main avenue used for this purpose is the 'FAA Aviation Forecast Conference' held annually in February or March. The 500 to 600 participants at the conference generally include airline executives, aircraft and engine manufacturers, consumer groups and other industry representatives, and the news media."

[Numbers in millions of gallons]

Fiscal year	Jet fuel					Aviation gasoline			Total fuel consumed
	U.S. air carriers			General aviation	Total	Air carrier	General aviation	Total	
	Domestic	Int'l	Total						
Historical									
1985	9,906	2,387	12,293	702	12,995	5	437	442	13,437
1986	10,733	2,525	13,258	738	13,996	5	411	416	14,412
1987	11,487	2,765	14,252	662	14,914	4	395	399	15,313
1988	11,902	3,192	15,094	654	15,748	4	394	398	16,146
1989E	12,087	3,537	15,624	712	16,336	3	374	377	16,713
Forecast									
1990	12,652	3,872	16,524	746	17,270	3	371	374	17,644
1991	13,065	4,131	17,196	790	17,986	2	369	371	18,357
1992	13,413	4,346	17,759	838	18,597	2	370	372	18,969
1993	13,776	4,538	18,314	863	19,177	2	373	375	19,552
1994	14,082	4,816	18,898	911	19,809	2	374	376	20,185
1995	14,358	4,999	19,357	955	20,312	2	377	379	20,691
1996	14,642	5,147	19,789	1,007	20,796	2	378	380	21,176
1997	14,855	5,279	20,134	1,052	21,186	2	380	382	21,568
1998	15,035	5,412	20,447	1,089	21,536	2	381	383	21,919
1999	15,221	5,528	20,749	1,126	21,875	2	382	384	22,259
2000	15,328	5,637	20,965	1,170	22,135	2	386	388	22,523
2001	15,442	5,734	21,176	1,199	22,375	2	387	389	22,764

Source: U.S. Department of Transportation, Federal Aviation Administration, *FAA Aviation Forecasts, 1990-2001*, March, 1990, p. 191, Table 13. Primary source: Air carrier jet fuel, the Research and Special Programs Administration (RSPA), Form 41. All others, FAA Aviation Policy and Plans Office (APO) estimates.

★ 763 ★

World Oil Price, 1970-2010

OPEC oil production is projected to increase sharply between 1988 and 2010. "As a result, oil prices are expected to rise through the early 1990's as the OPEC share of world oil trade increases.... By the late 1990's or early in the next century, the DOE projects that OPEC output will approach 85 percent of capacity, causing sharp price increases. In the absence of conservation and efficiency measures, world oil prices could more than double in real terms from $17 per barrel in 1989 to $37 per barrel in 2010."

[Numbers in 1989 dollars per barrel]

Year	World oil prices
1970	9.04
1980	50.71
1990	16.80
2000	27.80
2010	36.90

Source: U.S. Department of Transportation, *National Transportation Strategic Planning Study*, March, 1990, p. 3-7, Table 3-4. Primary source: Projected prices provided by U.S. Department of Energy, Office of Policy, Planning and Analysis, *Long Range Energy Projections to 2010*, Washington, D.C., 1988, pp. 2-10.

Transportation Infrastructure

★ 764 ★

Capital Investment Requirements by All Units of Government for the Existing Highway and Bridge Systems, 1987-2005

"Poor highway conditions can increase per-mile costs of highway usage by up to 30 percent and travel time by up to 20 percent when compared to costs for roads with good to excellent conditions.... In general, the FHWA estimates [for capital investment requirements] are lower than those published elsewhere, since they refer only to capital requirements on existing nonlocal roads. By way of comparison, other published capital needs estimate range from $40 to $100 billion per year. These higher estimates include local road needs, significant new construction ... and the use of different minimum conditions and design criteria. All estimates include capital costs...." The table summarizes two possible investment options: 1) the cost to maintain current overall highway conditions 2) the cost to remove all highway deficiencies, where practicable, by construction. These options are based on the FHWA's analysis of State-reported Highway Performance and Monitoring System data. All capital requirements refer to existing nonlocal roads only; new highway and bridge construction and needs on the local road system are not included. Noncapital program requirements are also omitted.

[Numbers in billions of 1987 dollars]

Functional system	Cost to maintain 1985 overall conditions[1]		Constrained[2] Full needs	
VMT growth rate (percent)	2.0	3.0	2.0	3.0
Rural				
Interstate	34.8[1]	42.5[1]	34.8	42.5
Other principal arterials	18.8	23.6	42.5	51.5
Minor arterials	20.5	22.9	48.3	53.9
Major collectors	33.2	34.6	86.1	90.1
Minor collectors	15.1	16.1	51.0	54.5
Subtotal	122.4	139.7	262.7	292.5
Urban				
Interstate	53.8[1]	73.8[1]	53.8	73.8
Other freeways and expressways	28.0	34.1	28.0	33.8
Other principal arterials	90.1	103.6	89.9	103.6
Minor arterials	60.7	71.3	82.1	97.2
Collectors	28.1	31.4	49.0	54.7
Subtotal	260.7	314.2	302.8	363.1
Total highway	383.1[1]	453.9[1]	565.5	655.6
(average annual)	20.2	23.9	29.9	34.5
Total bridge[3]	92.9	92.9	92.9	92.9
(average annual)	4.9	4.9	4.9	4.9

[Continued]

★ 764 ★

Capital Investment Requirements by All Units of Government for the Existing Highway and Bridge Systems, 1987-2005
[Continued]

Functional system	Cost to maintain 1985 overall conditions[1]		Constrained[2] Full needs	
Total highway and bridge (average annual)	476.0[1] 25.1[1]	546.8[1] 28.8[1]	658.4 34.7	748.5 39.4

Source: U.S. Department of Transportation, *National Transportation Strategic Planning Study*, March, 1990, p. 10-26, Table 10-6. Primary source: The Federal Highway Administration (FHWA), "America's Challenge for Highway Transportation in the 21st Century," (report), November, 1988. *Notes:* 1. At this level of investment, overall conditions cannot be maintained on the Interstate System within existing rights-of-way. A shortfall of between 11,000 and 15,000 lane-miles of new capacity, or their equivalent, would be the result. Options to address this shortfall include new construction, systems operation improvements, toll facilities, peak-hour demand management, and transit. 2. This investment strategy assumes that capacity improvement will be made only where rights-of-way are currently available. This would result in system performance improvements on the lower functional systems, but performance deterioration on the higher systems, especially in highly congested urban areas where rights-of-way are at a premium. 3. Bridge needs are based on a 2.34 percent average annual growth in travel. These estimates could change under alternative travel scenarios or investment strategies. The investment strategies under each scenario represent the full cost of eliminating all backlog and accruing deficiencies.

★ 765 ★

Highway and Related Expenditures Authorized by the Intermodal Surface Transportation Efficiency Act of 1992, 1992-1997

The figures include some estimates. The Intermodal Surface Transportation Efficiency Act of 1992, signed into law on December 18, 1991, has been calculated by the Federal Highway Administration to authorize $155.4 billion for highway and mass transit construction along with safety research, over the period 1992-97. Besides improving America's transportation systems, the funds authorized by the law are expected to have an immediate effect in creating new jobs within the engineering and construction arenas, according to Deputy Federal Highway Administrator Eugene R. McCormick. The program will also provide a "six-year stable foundation for the future," which will allow state governments to plan which projects will be funded and completed.

[Numbers in millions of dollars]

Program	Authorization in dollars (millions)						
	1992	1993	1994	1995	1996	1997	Total
Title I total (highways)	18,700	20,489	20,479	20,406	20,397	20,398	120,869
Total II total (highway safety)	295	297	300	303	219	219	1,633
Title III total (mass transit)	3,639	5,235	5,125	5,125	5,125	7,250	31,499
Title IV total (motor carrier safety)	121	77	81	83	85	90	537
Title VI total (research)	119	138	143	140	145	150	836
Total	22,874	26,236	26,128	26,057	25,971	28,107	155,374

Source: "Transportation Funds Begin to Flow," Tom Ichniowski and Rob McManamy, *Engineering News* 228, No. 1, January 6, 1992, p. 9. Primary source: Federal Highway Administration.

★ 766 ★

U.S. Army Corps of Engineers Expenditures for Inland Waterway Infrastructure, 1977-2020

"Locks and dams that comprise the inland waterway are aging at a much faster rate than replacement or other modernization actions can keep pace. The system includes some original projects well over 100 years old.... Through intensive maintenance, however, many older projects operate effectively at relatively low levels of traffic well beyond their design lives. While the majority of lock replacements recommended are to provide greater capacity, some replacements are required because of age and/or deteriorated structural condition. Because waterway traffic is largely random, it resembles highway use rather than railroads. There is a potential for much more intensive use of locks by scheduling traffic.... The reality of geography is that there are few opportunities for major new projects to expand the waterways system. There is a need to develop and improve system tributaries, side channels, and harbors."

[Numbers in millions of dollars]

Time period and waterway improvement	Actual or estimated expenditures[1]	Expenditures in constant 1988 dollars[1]
1977-88 total	4,030	5,209
1989-95 trust fund projects	1,755	1,682
1989-95 other projects	881	787
1989-95 rehabilitation	111	92
1989-95 total	2,747	2,561
1995-2020 scheduled projects	1,009	558
1995-2020 unscheduled projects	620	401
1995-2020 prospective improvements	4,572	2,152
1995-2020 total	6,201	3,111

Source: U.S. Department of Transportation, *National Transportation Strategic Planning Study*, March, 1990, p. 14-21, Table 14-12. Primary source: U.S. Army Corps of Engineers, *Waterborne Commerce of the United States*, Washington, D.C., 1988. *Notes:* 1. 1989-95 inflation rates vary with project components. 1995-2020 inflation is a uniform 5.5 percent annually. 1977-88 converted to 1988 dollars with GNP deflator.

Marine and Rail Transport

★ 767 ★

Numbers and Types of Ocean-Going U.S.-Flag Merchant Marine Ships in 2000

In this fleet forecast the Maritime Administration has assumed no changes in current government policies and programs. The forecast encompasses self-propelled, deep-sea, ocean-going vessels designed to carry general cargo, including vessels engaged in foreign and domestic trade.

[Tonnage in thousands; vessels limited to 1,000 gross tons and over]

Ship type	Number of ships			Total dwt
	Foreign/ domestic trade	On charter to MSC	Total	
Dry cargo				
Breakbulk/Cont-BB	-	6	6	92
Container ships	47	-	47	1,744
Container bulk	5	-	5	273
Container Ro/Ro	7	2	9	233
Car carriers	6	-	6	98
Ro/Ro	6	2	8	122
Ro/Ro (MPS)	-	13	13	322
Barge transports	-	5	5	198
Container/passenger	-	-	0	0
Flo-Flo	-	1	1	51
Subtotal	71	29	100	3,134
Tankers				
Petroleum				
Under 100,000 dwt coated	32	23	55	2,137
Under 100,000 dwt uncoated	2	-	2	97
Over 100,000 dwt	22	-	22	4,760
Subtotal	56	23	79	6,994
Special product				
LNG/LPG	12	-	12	865
Chemical/others	1	-	1	50
Subtotal	13	-	13	915
Bulk	22	-	22	1,061
Passenger	3	-	3	21
Total	165	52	217	12,124

Source: U.S. Department of Transportation, *National Transportation Strategic Planning Study*, March, 1990, p. 14-22. Primary source: U.S. Maritime Administration, *Third Report of the Commission on Merchant Marine and Defense*, Appendix B-1, Washington, D.C., 1988.

★ 768 ★

Future Prospects for the Passenger Railroad System

"Factors outside the control of the transportation sector, most notably the strength of the economy, will affect the extent of personal and business travel and particularly the ability of U.S. and foreign travelers to afford the luxury of long-distance train travel. In addition, characteristics of the competing transportation modes, such as congestion and the prices of gasoline and airplane tickets, will affect future passenger train travel. However, in general, the near-term prospects for growth in the passenger railroad business in the United States are expected to be modest. Amtrak is projecting growth in ridership of 2 to 5 percent annually, assuming that high-speed rail technology will not be introduced. If the financial obstacles to such developments are overcome, much more dramatic increases in railroad ridership could result. Even without installation of higher-speed track or equipment, however, much of Amtrak's expected growth in ridership will depend upon the railroad's ability to overcome the equipment limitations that currently are limiting ridership on its more popular routes.

"In the longer-term, high-speed, or magnetically levitated rail service is likely to be developed in a number of corridors. The speed and other characteristics of those operations are projected to make the new services competitive with at least short-distance air travel, potentially diverting passengers from airlines between cities in the 100-to-500 mile range, or between major international airports and travelers' origin and destination points. They may also offer advantages over plane or automobile travel in terms of fuel efficiency, environmental effects, and safety."

Source: U.S. Department of Transportation, *National Transportation Strategic Planning Study*, March, 1990, pp. 13-24 to 13-25.

★ 769 ★

Rail Freight Ton-Miles, Fuel Consumption, and Fuel Efficiency, 1985-2010

TMT = ton-miles traveled. "Because railroads account for less than 2.3% of the fuel consumed by the transportation sector, few forecasters project rail activity or energy use. Thus, the ANL forecast is compared to only one other effort, that of the Department of Energy's Energy Information Administration (EIA).... EIA expects considerably less growth in rail ton-miles and fuel use, and constant rail fuel efficiency. The EIA's ton-mile forecast is lower because that study expects relatively less growth in coal use, particularly from sources west of the Mississippi. In 1985, coal transport accounted for 9.2% of rail ton-miles. Because western sources have relatively longer lengths of haul, increases in western coal production result in disproportionate increases in rail ton-miles."

	Value, by year						Growth, 1985-
	1985	1990	1995	2000	2005	2010	2010 (%/yr)
TMT (10^9)							
ANL	898	1075	1252	1490	1756	2069	3.39
EIA	868[1]	917	993	1044	1107	1187	1.43
Fuel (10^{15} Btu)							
ANL	0.446	0.529	0.604	0.704	0.818	0.950	3.07
EIA	0.441[1]	0.465	0.504	0.530	0.562	0.603	1.43
Efficiency (Btu/TMT)							
ANL	497	492	482	472	466	459	-0.32
EIA	508[1]	507	508	508	508	508	0

Source: U.S. Department of Energy, *Forecast of Transportation Energy Demand through the Year 2010*, M.M. Mintz and A.D. Vyas, Center for Transportation Research, Energy Systems Division, Argonne National Laboratory, November, 1990 (rev. April, 1991), Table 3.9. Primary source: *Annual Energy Outlook*, U.S. Department of Energy, Energy Information Administration, Report DOE/EIA-0383 (90), January, 1990; ANL-9ON (forecast developed by the Center for Transportation Research at Argonne National Laboratory (ANL), under contract to the Office of Transportation Technologies, Office of the Secretary for Conservation and Renewable Energy, U.S. Department of Energy) and the Energy Information Administration (EIA) of the U.S. Department of Energy. *Note:* 1. 1988.

★ 770 ★

State Estimates of Railroad-Related Improvement Needs, 1988-2020

"Since major rail maintenance work historically has occurred in waves, most recently in the 1940's and the late 1970's, another substantial replacement cycle may occur in the next decade.... Critical to the railroads' success in maintaining their system is their ability to generate sufficient capital to underwrite the significant investments required." The table summarizes the results of a survey of 1988 by the National Conference of State Railway Officials requesting state transportation agencies to estimate the costs of railroad improvements needed in the period 1990 to 2020 and that may not be covered by private funding. "The response produced a figure of over $11 billion over the next 30-year period, representing $347 million annually. This includes 25 percent for rail rehabilitation, 51 percent for rail-highway grade crossing improvements, 16 percent for highway access improvements, and acquisition of abandoned rail lines, primarily associated with Class I railroad network. This is only a fraction of the $4.4 billion that the Class I freight railroads alone spend each year on railroad track maintenance and rehabilitation."

[Numbers in millions of 1987 dollars]

Activity	Total cost
Rail rehabilitation	1,894.1
Access-related rail needs	
At-grade rail crossings	2,027.5
Grade separated crossings	3,764.0
Rural highway access to rail	1,675.4
Urban highway access to rail	138.9
Rail/truck transfer facilities	129.1
Subtotal	7,734.9
Acquire rail rights-of-way	823.4
Total	8,558.3
Annual average	347.0

Source: U.S. Department of Transportation, *National Transportation Strategic Planning Study,* March, 1990, p. 13-18, Table 13-8. Primary source: American Association of State Highway and Transportation Officials, *Modal Interlink for Air, Water, and Rail-* Appendix 3 to the Bottom Line, Washington, D.C., 1988, p. 78.

Road Vehicles

★ 771 ★

Annual Retail Truck Sales in Thousands of Units, 1990-1996

Light-duty trucks include vans, pickup trucks, and sport-utility vehicles and are divided into three classes: class 1 (up to 6,000 lbs. or 2.7 metric tons [MT] of allowable gross vehicle weight), class 2 (6,001-10,000 lbs. or 4.5 MT) and class 3 (10,001 to 14,000 lbs. or 6.3 MT). The remaining truck classes are used only for commercial purposes, and their sales closely track overall economic trends. The medium-weight group comprises classes four through seven (14,001-33,000 lbs., or 6.31-14.85 MT of gross vehicle weight). Class eight trucks are those weighing 33,000 lbs. (14.85 MT) or over. "Overall, class 1 and 2 truck sales will advance modestly for the next several years. Numerous new product offerings, coupled with increased availability of established popular models, will generate more competition in the compact passenger van market. The increased competition comes at a time when this market may be peaking. The new four-door sport-utility vehicles are expected to gain market share at the expense of two-door sport-utility vehicles, minivans, and traditional station wagons. [Sport utility vehicles refer to the new entrants into the light truck market which aim to combine passenger car comfort and sports car performance with truck-like styling and carrying capacity.] Because of their novelty and increasing popularity, sales of sport utility vehicles could increase far more than anticipated growth of other personal vehicles."

[Numbers in thousands of units]

Year	Class			
	Light 1-3	Medium 4-7	Heavy 8	Total 1-8
1990	4,558	156	121	4,835
1991[1]	4,200	125	100	4,425
1992[2]	4,600	135	100	4,835
1993[2]	4,900	129	121	5,150
1994[2]	5,000	140	120	5,260
1995[2]	5,100	150	120	5,370
1996[2]	5,100	163	117	5,380

Source: U.S. Department of Commerce, *U.S. Industrial Outlook '92: Business Forecasts for 350 Industries,* January, 1992, p. 36-9, Table 5. Primary source: Motor Vehicle Association of the United States; *Ward's Automotive Reports. Notes:* 1. Estimate. 2. Forecast for 1992-96 by U.S. Department of Commerce, Office of Automotive Industry Affairs.

★ 772 ★

Automobile Sales in the United States as Compared to Global Sales by Region, 1990-2010

EC = European Community, EFTA = European Free Trade Association, CIS = Commonwealth of Independent States, MDC = More developed countries, LDC = Less developed countries.

[Numbers in thousands]

Region	1990	1995	2000	2005	2010
Total EC	12,088	13,569	14,375	14,948	15,233
Total EFTA	1,086	1,247	1,293	1,313	1,305
Total West Europe	13,174	14,816	15,668	16,261	16,538
Australia/New Zealand	566	624	672	724	781
Canada	886	1,180	1,240	1,287	1,320
Japan	5,103	5,200	5,465	5,673	5,889
United States	9,300	9,850	10,352	10,747	11,156
Total Pan-Pacific	15,855	16,854	17,729	18,431	19,146
Total MDC	29,029	31,670	33,397	34,692	35,684
East Europe	1,570	1,866	2,288	2,742	3,230
CIS	1,364	1,565	1,904	2,316	2,956
Total East Europe	2,934	3,431	4,192	5,058	6,186
Total Africa	401	456	536	642	781
Total Americas	1,308	1,619	2,053	2,615	3,391
Total Asia	1,981	2,749	4,001	5,155	6,566
Others	147	166	190	220	264
Total LDC	6,771	8,421	10,972	13,690	17,188
Global total	35,800	40,091	44,369	48,382	52,872

Source: "The Recovery Inches Upward... But at a Snail's Pace," *Ward's Auto World* 28, No. 8, August, 1992, p. 24. Primary source: Pemberton Associates, World Vehicle Forecast and Strategies.

★ 773 ★

Characteristics of the Personal Vehicle Fleet, 1985-2010

"The TEEMS [Transportation Energy and Emissions Modeling System] component that forecasts personal vehicle use is driven by demographic, economic, and technological changes.... The composition of the stock of household vehicles was estimated by type and size using a vehicle stock allocation model. Only two vehicle types—automobiles and light trucks—[have been considered]. Within each type, several vehicles—characterized by size, fuel, and technology—may be defined. The size classification is based on interior volume and/or seating capacity."

Vehicle type and size (seats)	1985			2000			2010		
	Curb weight (lb.)	Engine power (hp)	Fuel economy (mpg)	Curb weight (lb.)	Engine power (hp)	Fuel economy (mpg)	Curb weight (lb.)	Engine power (hp)	Fuel economy (mpg)
Automobile									
Small (2-4)	2205	75	22.7	1906	63	25.8	1645	54	29.3
Compact (4)	2674	90	19.2	2312	77	22.6	1988	66	25.7
Midsize (5)	3178	108	16.8	2747	93	19.8	2363	80	22.6
Large (6)	3874	135	14.6	3349	116	17.2	2880	100	19.6

[Continued]

★ 773 ★

Characteristics of the Personal Vehicle Fleet, 1985-2010

[Continued]

Vehicle type and size (seats)	1985			2000			2010		
	Curb weight (lb.)	Engine power (hp)	Fuel economy (mpg)	Curb weight (lb.)	Engine power (hp)	Fuel economy (mpg)	Curb weight (lb.)	Engine power (hp)	Fuel economy (mpg)
Light truck									
Compact	3496	90	17.2	3121	84	19.5	2778	77	21.5
Std. truck	4158	130	13.1	3712	119	14.8	3304	107	16.4
Minivan/sm.									
utility (7-8)	4126	101	16.7	3604	101	19.0	3208	92	21.1
Std. van/utility (11-15)	4926	140	12.4	4398	127	14.0	3914	115	15.5

Source: U.S. Department of Energy, *Forecast of Transportation Energy Demand through the Year 2010*, M.M. Mintz and A.D. Vyas, Center for Transportation Research, Energy Systems Division, Argonne National Laboratory, November, 1990 (rev. April, 1991), Table 2.1. *Note:* Average values applicable to all vehicles on the road.

★ 774 ★

Initial New Car Fuel Efficiency Estimates and Base Prices, 1990-2010

"Energy consumption in [the sector of light-duty vehicle travel] is the product of two ... estimates—new car fuel efficiency and the level of light-duty vehicle travel. Assumed new car (and new light truck) fuel efficiency is itself estimated in two parts: an initial Corporate Average Fuel Economy (CAFE) estimate is forecast to 2010 that is based on assumed technological improvements associated with a Reference Case gasoline price path. These estimates are provided by Energy and Environmental Analysis Incorporated. Their forecasting methodology takes into account the net savings consumers can realize if specific fuel efficiency-improving technologies are introduced.... [It] has been assumed that automobile characteristics (size and performance) remain unchanged over the forecast. Higher gasoline prices increase the forecast fuel efficiency because they increase gasoline expenditures without affecting the cost of available fuel efficiency-improving technologies."

	1990	1995	2000	2005	2010
Average new car MPG	28.1	29.2	31.8	34.3	36.5
Average new light truck MPG	20.8	21.6	23.4	25.0	26.4
Base gasoline price (1990 dollars per gallon)	1.17	1.22	1.28	1.45	1.54

Source: U.S. Department of Energy, Energy Information Administration, Office of Integrated Analysis and Forecasting, *Assumptions for the Annual Energy Outlook 1992*, January, 1992, p. 25, Table 14. Primary source: Energy and Environmental Analysis Incorporated, except light truck MPG in 2010, which was calculated by Energy Information Administration by the extrapolation of 1990 to 2005 estimate.

★ 775 ★

Local Travel by Private Vehicle, Age Group, Number of Vehicles, and Vehicle-Miles Driven, 1980-2020

Numbers of licensed drivers, vehicles, and vehicle-miles were derived by applying age-and sex-specific rates of licensing and travel mileage (based on the 1969, 1977, and 1983 Nationwide Personal Transportation Studies) to national projections of the population by age and sex. Author Ira S. Lowry is responsible for projecting licensing rates, vehicles per licensed driver, and annual miles per driver to 1990 and beyond. Estimates of annual miles per driver are based on direct estimates by survey respondents; extrapolation from individual trip reports yields substantially smaller annual totals. "The journey to work no doubt remains the most important regular trip made by household members, but it is by no means the only trip. Americans go home to wash and change clothes before going somewhere else. And when they go out again—to a friend's house, a fast-food outlet, a movie, or a shopping mall—they go by car.... Because the population is aging and the elderly make fewer and shorter trips even when they keep their automobiles, mileage per driver and per vehicle should drop slightly [after the year 2000]. The total number of miles traveled in private vehicles will increase much less rapidly in the future than it has in the recent past, and will level off just after the year 2020. The good news, then, is that the demographic and life-style pressure for capacity expansion is decreasing nationally.... The bad news, to most of those who worry about urban problems, is that the plans must deal with the reality of nearly universal ownership of personal—not family—automobiles and a dispersed pattern of travel. One judges that more is to be gained from synchronizing traffic lights on suburban arterials than from building fixed-rail mass transit systems for commuters to the central business district."

Year	Millions of persons						Vehicles per driver	Millions of vehicles	Annual miles per driver	Billions of vehicle miles
	All ages	Under 16 years	16-19 years	20-64 years	65+ years	Licensed drivers				
1980	227	55	17	129	26	141	0.96	135	10,191	1,434
1990	250	58	14	146	32	162	0.98	159	10,318	1,676
2000	268	60	15	158	35	176	1.00	176	10,300	1,814
2010	283	57	15	171	39	191	1.00	191	10,115	1,933
2020	297	59	14	172	51	199	1.00	199	9,906	1,975
					Percent change					
1980-90	10.2	4.5	-19.9	13.9	24.1	15.4	2.1	17.8	1.2	16.9
1990-00	7.3	3.3	9.9	8.0	10.2	8.4	2.0	10.6	-0.2	8.2
2000-10	5.7	-4.2	2.1	8.4	12.2	8.5	0.0	8.5	-1.8	6.6
2010-20	4.7	2.8	-6.8	0.3	31.2	4.3	0.0	4.3	-2.1	2.1

Source: "Planning for Urban Sprawl," Ira S. Lowry, *A Look Ahead: Year 2020 (Proceedings of the Conference on Long-Range Trends and Requirements for the Nation's Highway and Public Transit System)*, Special Report 220, Transportation Research Board, National Research Council, Washington, D.C., 1988, p. 307, Table 15. Primary source: Ira S. Lowry, *Personal Travel in the U.S.*, 21, Vol. 1, p. 4-2, Table 4-1, Table E-10; 1980 U.S. Census, Series PC80-1-B1 (23, Table 43); Current Population Reports 952 (24).

★ 776 ★

Prospects for Sales of Automobiles by American Automakers, 1991-1995

"Data supplied by the Motor Vehicle Manufacturers' Association (MVMA) indicate that the average age of the passenger car fleet in the United States has increased from 5.5 years in 1970 to 7.8 years in 1990. During the same period, the number of cars 12 or more years old has increased from 4.9 million units (6.2 percent of the car population) to 25 million (20.3 percent). These vehicles, despite their much greater initial quality, must now be at the very edge of their economically useful lives and are prime candidates for replacement over the next several years, particularly if the overall economic climate remains favorable.

"[Fuel] economy and safety legislation could increase vehicle production costs, which could have a negative effect upon retail prices. Operating costs are likely to become more burdensome. All these factors could restrain future sales. California will require that 10-to-20 percent of new car sales in 1994-96 have ultra-low emissions, and that by 1998 2 percent must be zero-emission vehicles. Other states are poised to implement similar requirements, which led the Big Three to join with the U.S. Department of Energy and Electric Power Research Institute in March 1991 to develop battery technology for electric vehicles.

"The Big Three are gearing up now to increase their U.S. exports and to reinforce their local operations in Mexico, where they already enjoy a 55 percent share of the market. Mexico has 85 million citizens and an automobile population of less than 6.5 million cars, but is poised for explosive growth. [If the North American Free Trade Area (NAFTA) pact is ratified by all parties], Mexican auto sales could easily exceed the 30 percent annual growth rate the country has experienced since 1988. New car sales will probably total 625,000 units in 1991, and could reach a level of 1.5 million units annually by 1995."

Source: U.S. Department of Commerce, *U.S. Industrial Outlook '92: Business Forecasts for 350 Industries,* January, 1992, pp. 36-7 and 36-8.

★ 777 ★

Road Vehicles, Fuel Economy, and Miles Traveled, 1985-2010

This table on road travel is part of the documentation for a forecast developed by the Center for Transportation Research at Argonne National Laboratory under contract to the Office of Transportation Technologies under the Assistant Secretary for Conservation and Renewable Energy of the U.S. Department of Energy. The current forecast carries the acronym ANL-9ON and is meant to serve as a baseline against which trends can be analyzed and existing and proposed energy conservation programs can be evaluated.

Item	Value, by year					Change 1985-2010
	1985	1990	1995	2000	2010	(%/yr)
Vehicles (10⁶)						
Autos						
Personal	122.3	140.4	150.6	161.5	184.7	1.66
Fleet	8.9	9.2	9.9	10.8	13.0	1.52
Total	131.2	149.6	160.6	172.3	197.7	1.66
Light trucks						
Personal	23.5	29.6	35.4	39.6	44.6	2.59
Commercial	12.0	13.6	14.7	16.2	19.6	1.96
Total	35.6	43.2	50.2	55.8	64.2	2.39
Heavy trucks	5.3	6.1	6.6	7.3	9.2	2.21
Fuel economy (mpg)						
Autos	18.2	20.0	20.7	21.3	24.7	1.24
Light trucks	13.0	14.2	14.9	15.4	17.0	1.08
Personal	13.6	15.0	15.4	15.8	17.7	1.05
Commercial	12.2	13.3	14.3	15.0	16.0	1.09
Heavy trucks	5.8	5.9	6.1	6.4	6.6	0.52
Medium	8.0	8.1	8.2	8.3	8.4	0.21
Lt.-heavy	6.9	7.0	7.2	7.3	7.4	0.31
Heavy-heavy	5.4	5.6	5.7	6.1	6.3	0.60
All trucks	10.6	11.6	12.2	12.7	13.6	1.00
Vehicle-miles traveled (10⁹)						
Autos	1262.5	1446.5	1546.4	1656.9	1894.7	1.64
Light trucks						
Personal	209.3	266.0	312.9	345.4	384.9	2.47
Comml. gasoline	157.9	180.3	196.4	215.4	258.9	2.00
Comml. diesel	4.7	6.5	7.7	9.3	14.9	4.73
Total	371.8	452.8	517.0	570.1	658.6	2.31
Heavy duty vehicles						
Gas trucks	39.3	37.2	36.7	35.9	37.2	-0.22
Diesel trucks	91.9	115.6	130.5	150.3	199.7	3.15
Buses	6.3	6.7	7.0	7.4	7.7	0.81
Total	137.5	159.4	174.1	1932.6	244.6	2.33
Total, all vehicles	1771.8	2058.7	2237.5	4159.6	2797.9	1.84

Source: U.S. Department of Energy, *Forecast of Transportation Energy Demand through the Year 2010*, M.M. Mintz and A.D. Vyas, Center for Transportation Research, Energy Systems Division, Argonne National Laboratory, November, 1990 (rev. April, 1991), Table S.4.

Road Vehicles: New Technologies

★ 778 ★

The Electric Car, 1982-2010

"The arrival of fusion will mean abundant, inexpensive electricity and will turn the entire world to an electric economy. Oil will no longer be needed. The electric car will appear, not the tiny experimental electric car we sometimes see today that never moves faster than 40 miles an hour and whose batteries have to be recharged every 50 miles but a normal-sized electric car whose batteries or fuel cells require recharging every 250 miles. That's acceptable. After all, we fill up our gas tanks every 250 miles so why should we object to recharging our batteries every 250 miles at the same gas stations we now use to get our gasoline? The arrival of electric cars could even mean electrified highways where the cars attach themselves to an electrified rail by the side of the highway the way subway trains operate. That way, cars could run on highways for an indefinite time without having to recharge their batteries. Hooked up to an electrified rail, a motorist wouldn't even have to stay behind the wheel of an electric car on the highway. All the cars on the highway would be moving at the same speed, keeping the same distance between them. We think France will be the first country to try out this scheme. Not only does France have the longest experience with an electrified railroad network, it is also turning rapidly to an all-nuclear, all-electric economy. While we are forecasting an electric economy that produces electric cars, we are not forecasting an end to the internal combustion engine. There will always be cars that run on gasoline, though they will cost twice what electric cars cost. By the year 2010, oil will no longer be the world's main source of energy. The price of oil and its availability will determine when electric cars make a widescale appearance. If the price of oil levels off or comes down before it begins to run out, the electric car will be postponed. As soon as oil begins to disappear and the price runs up again, the electric car will be here to stay."

Source: "Energy Sources for Tomorrow," *Encounters with the Future: A Forecast of Life into the 21st Century,* Marvin Cetron and Thomas O'Toole, McGraw-Hill Book, Co., New York, 1982, p. 100.

★ 779 ★

The Role of Advanced Electrical Features in Automobiles of the Future, 1992-2000

The University of Michigan's biennial Delphi study is based on multiple polls of automobile industry experts and presents a consensus of their opinions concerning developments to be expected in the industry in the future. Its forecasts concern only vehicles produced in North America.

"One of the key projections of the Delphi VI participants [issued in 1991] is continued strong growth in the application of electronic transmission control. The median response [to the Delphi survey] predict[ed] a 25 percent installation rate in 1995 cars, 60 percent in 2000 and 90 percent in 2005.... Another big winner, predict[ed] the panel, will be anti-lock brake systems (ABS), but it won't happen as quickly as panels in the past had predicted. In 1987 Delphi IV predicted half the vehicles would have ABS by 1995. Delphi V, in 1989, predicted a 30 percent ABS installation rate by 1995. Delphi VI projects a 25 percent installation rate in that year. By 2000, according to the panel, installation rates will reach 75 percent.... Dramatic gains are forecast for air bags for both passengers and drivers. By 2000 some 98 percent of the vehicles produced will have driver-side air bags. Eighty percent will have driver-side and passenger-side air bags, making air bags virtually a standard feature."

"Many advanced convenience features will not become widespread very soon, according to the panel. These include voice-activated controls, CRT touch screens, in-car personal computers and facsimile machines. All are expected to reach installation rates of only 3 percent or less by 2000."

Source: "Automotive Electronics: More Oracular Predictions from the Delphi," Michael G. Sheldrick, *Electronic News* 38, No. 1909, April 27, 1992, p. 20.

SUBJECT INDEX

The Subject Index holds nearly 3,000 terms referring to topics, organizations, and issues contained in *Statistical Forecasts of the U.S.* Each term is followed by one or more page numbers, marked by the letter "p." The table numbers follow in brackets and are marked with a star. For access to *SFUS* by year of forecast, please use the Index of Forecasts by Year, which immediately follows.

Subject Index

Subject Index

INDEX OF FORECASTS BY YEAR

The Index of Forecasts by Year holds more than 800 references arranged by year and major topic. Each reference is followed by one or more page numbers, marked by the letter "p." The table or entry numbers that follow in brackets are marked with a star. For access to *Statistical Forecasts of the U.S.* by subject, please consult the Subject Index.